MR. GREWGIOUS EXPERIENCES A NEW SENSATION.

THE

MYSTERY OF EDWIN DROOD,

MASTER HUMPHREY'S CLOCK,

AND

SKETCHES BY "BOZ."

BY

CHARLES DICKENS.

PHILADELPHIA:

PORTER & COATES,

822 CHESTNUT STREET.

SHERMAN & CO.,
Printers, Phila.

CONTENTS.

THE MYSTERY OF EDWIN DROOD.

MASTER HUMPHREY'S CLOCK, AND OTHER PIECES.

SKETCHES BY BOZ.

HOLIDAY ROMANCE.

IN FOUR PARTS.

GEORGE SILVERMAN'S EXPLANATION.

THE MYSTERY OF EDWIN DROOD.

CHAPTER I.

THE DAWN.

AN ancient English Cathedral Tower? How can the ancient English Cathedral tower be here! The well-known massive gray square tower of its old Cathedral? How can that be here! There is no spike of rusty iron in the air, between the eye and it, from any point of the real prospect. What is the spike that intervenes, and who has set it up? Maybe, it is set up by the Sultan's orders for the impaling of a horde of Turkish robbers, one by one. It is so, for cymbals clash, and the Sultan goes by to his palace in long procession. Ten thousand scimitars flash in the sunlight, and thrice ten thousand dancing-girls strew flowers. Then follow white elephants caparisoned in countless gorgeous colors, and infinite in number and attendants. Still, the Cathedral tower rises in the background, where it cannot be, and still no writhing figure is on the grim spike. Stay! Is the spike so low a thing as the rusty spike on the top of a post of an old bedstead that has tumbled all awry? Some vague period of drowsy laughter must be devoted to the consideration of this possibility.

Shaking from head to foot, the man whose scattered consciousness has thus fantastically pieced itself together at length rises, supports his trembling frame upon his arms, and looks around. He is in the meanest and closest of small rooms. Through the ragged window-curtain, the light of early day steals in from a miserable court. He lies, dressed, across a large unseemly bed, upon a bedstead that has indeed given way under the weight upon it. Lying, also dressed and also across the bed, not longwise, are a Chinaman, a Lascar, and a haggard woman. The two first are in a sleep or stupor; the last is blowing at a kind of pipe to kindle it. And as she blows, and, shading it with her lean hand, concentrates its red spark of light, it serves in the dim morning as a lamp to show him what he sees of her.

"Another?" says this woman, in a querulous, rattling whisper. "Have another?"

He looks about him, with his hand to his forehead.

"Ye 've smoked as many as five since ye come in at midnight," the woman goes on, as she chronically complains. "Poor me, poor me, my head is so bad! Them two come in after ye. Ah, poor me, the business is slack, is slack! Few Chinamen about the docks, and fewer Lascars, and no ships coming in, these say! Here 's another ready for ye, deary. Ye 'll remember, like a good soul, won't ye, that the market price is dreffle high just now? More nor three shillings and sixpence for a thimbleful! And ye 'll remember that nobody but me (and Jack Chinaman t' other side the court; but he can't do it as well as me) has the true secret of mixing it? Ye 'll pay up according, deary, won't ye?

She blows at the pipe as she speaks, and, occasionally bubbling at it, inhales much of its contents.

"O me, O me, my lungs is weak, my lungs is bad! It 's nearly ready for ye, deary. Ah, poor me, poor me, my poor hand shakes like to drop off! I see ye coming-to, and I ses to my poor self, 'I 'll have another ready for him, and he 'll bear in mind the market price of opium, and pay according.' O my poor head! I makes my pipes of old penny ink-bottles, ye see deary — this is one — and I fits in a mouthpiece, this way, and I takes my mixter out of this thimble with this little horn spoon; and so I fills, deary. Ah, my poor nerves! I got Heavens-hard drunk for sixteen year afore I took to this; but this don't hurt me, not to speak of. And it takes away the hunger as well as wittles, deary."

She hands him the nearly emptied pipe, and sinks back, turning over on her face.

He rises unsteadily from the bed, lays the pipe upon the hearthstone, draws back the ragged curtain, and looks with repugnance at his three companions. He notices that the woman has opium-smoked herself into a strange likeness of the Chinaman. His form of cheek, eye, and temple, and his color, are repeated in her. Said Chinaman convulsively wrestles with one of his many Gods, or Devils, perhaps, and snarls horribly. The Lascar laughs and dribbles at the mouth. The hostess is still.

"What visions can *she* have?" the waking man muses, as he turns her face towards him, and stands looking down at it. "Visions of many butchers' shops, and public-houses, and much credit? Of an increase of hideous customers, and this horrible bedstead set upright again, and this horrible court swept clean? What can she rise to, under any quantity of opium, higher than that! — Eh?"

He bends down his ear, to listen to her mutterings.

"Unintelligible!"

As he watches the spasmodic shoots and darts that break out of her face and limbs, like fitful lightning out of a dark sky, some contagion in them seizes upon him: insomuch that he has to withdraw himself to a lean arm-chair by the hearth, — placed there, perhaps, for such emergencies, — and to sit in it, holding tight, until he has got the better of this unclean spirit of imitation.

Then he comes back, pounces on the Chinaman, and, seizing him with both hands by the throat, turns him violently on the bed. The Chinaman clutches the aggressive hands, resists, gasps, and protests.

"What do you say?"

A watchful pause.

"Unintelligible!"

Slowly loosening his grasp as he listens to the incoherent jargon with an attentive frown, he turns to the Lascar and fairly drags him forth upon the floor. As he falls, the Lascar starts into a half-risen attitude, glares with his eyes, lashes about him fiercely with his arms, and draws a phantom knife. It then becomes apparent that the woman has taken possession of his knife, for safety's sake; for, she too starting up, and restraining and expostulating with him, the knife is visible in her dress, not in his, when they drowsily drop back, side by side.

There has been chattering and clattering enough between them, but to no purpose. When any distinct word has been flung into the air, it has had no sense or sequence. Wherefore "unintelligible!" is again the comment of the watcher, made with some reassured nodding of his head, and a gloomy smile. He then lays certain silver money on the table, finds his hat, gropes his way down the broken stairs, gives a good morning to some rat-ridden doorkeeper, in bed in a black hutch beneath the stairs, and passes out.

That same afternoon, the massive gray square tower of an old Cathedral rises before the sight of a jaded traveller. The bells are going for daily vesper service, and he must needs attend it, one would say, from his haste to reach the open Cathedral door. The choir are getting on their sullied white robes, in a hurry, when he arrives among them, gets on his own robe, and falls into the procession filing in to service. Then the Sacristan locks the iron-barred gates that divide the sanctuary from the chancel, and all of the procession, having scuttled into their places, hide their faces; and then the intoned words, "WHEN THE WICKED MAN —" rise among groins of arches and beams of roof, awakening muttered thunder.

CHAPTER II.

A DEAN, AND A CHAPTER ALSO.

WHOSOEVER has observed that sedate and clerical bird, the rook, may perhaps have noticed that when he wings his way homeward towards nightfall, in a sedate and clerical company, two rooks will suddenly detach themselves from the rest, will retrace their flight for some distance, and will there poise and linger, — conveying to mere men the fancy that it is of some occult importance to the body politic that this artful couple should pretend to have renounced connection with it.

Similarly, service being over in the old Cathedral with the square tower, and the choir scuffling out again, and divers venerable persons of rook-like aspect dispersing, two of these latter retrace their steps, and walk together in the echoing Close.

Not only is the day waning, but the year. The low sun is fiery and yet cold behind the monastery ruin, and the Virginia creeper on the Cathedral wall has showered half its deep-red leaves down on the pavement. There has been rain this afternoon, and a wintry shudder goes among the little pools on the cracked, uneven flag-stones, and through the giant elm-trees as they shed a gust of tears. Their fallen leaves lie strewn thickly about. Some of these leaves, in a timid rush, seek sanctuary within the low arched Cathedral door; but two men, coming out, resist them, and cast them forth again with their feet; this done, one of the two locks the door with a goodly key, and the other flits away with a folio music-book.

"Mr. Jasper was that, Tope?"

"Yes, Mr. Dean."

"He has stayed late."

"Yes, Mr. Dean. I have stayed for him, your Reverence. He has been took a little poorly."

"Say 'taken, Tope' — to the Dean," the younger rook interposes in a low tone with this touch of correction, as who should say, "You may offer bad grammar to the laity, or the humbler clergy, not to the Dean."

Mr. Tope, Chief Verger and Showman, and accustomed to be high with excursion-parties, declines with a silent loftiness to perceive that any suggestion has been tendered to him.

"And when and how has Mr. Jasper been taken — for, as Mr. Crisparkle has remarked, it is better to say taken — taken —" repeats the Dean; "when and how has Mr. Jasper been taken —"

"Taken, sir," Tope deferentially murmurs.

"— Poorly, Tope?"

"Why, sir, Mr. Jasper was that breathed —"

"I would n't say 'That breathed,' Tope," Mr. Crisparkle interposes, with the same touch as before. "Not English — to the Dean."

"Breathed to that extent," the Dean (not unflattered by this indirect homage) condescendingly remarks, "would be preferable."

"Mr. Jasper's breathing was so remarkably short," thus discreetly does Mr. Tope work his way round the sunken rock, "when he came in, that it distressed him mightily to get his notes out: which was perhaps the cause of his having a kind of fit on him after a little. His memory grew DAZED." Mr. Tope, with his eyes on the Reverend Mr. Crisparkle, shoots this word out, as defying him to improve upon it: "and a dimness and giddiness crept over him as strange as ever I saw; though he did n't seem to mind it particularly, himself. However, a little time and a little water brought him out of his DAZE." Mr Tope repeats the word and its emphasis, with the air of saying, "As I *have* made a success, I 'll make it again."

"And Mr. Jasper has gone home quite himself, has he?" asked the Dean.

"Your Reverence, he has gone home quite himself. And I 'm glad to see he 's having his fire kindled up, for it 's chilly after the wet, and the Cathedral had both a damp feel and a damp touch this afternoon, and he was very shivery."

They all three looked towards an old stone gatehouse crossing the Close, with an arched thoroughfare passing beneath it. Through its latticed window, a fire shines out upon the fast-darkening scene, involving in shadow the pendant masses of ivy and creeper covering the building's front. As the deep Cathedral bell strikes the hour, a ripple of wind goes through these at their distance, like a ripple of the solemn sound that hums through tomb and tower, broken niche and defaced statue, in the pile close at hand.

"Is Mr. Jasper's nephew with him?" the Dean asks.

"No, sir," replies the Verger, "but expected. There 's his own solitary shadow betwixt his two windows — the one looking this way, and the one looking down into the High Street — drawing his own curtains now"

"Well, well," says the Dean, with a sprightly air of breaking up the little conference, "I hope Mr. Jasper's heart may not be too much set upon his nephew. Our affections, however laudable, in this transitory world, should never master us; we should guide them, guide them. I find I am not disagreeably reminded of my dinner, by hearing my dinner-bell. Perhaps, Mr. Crisparkle, you will, before going home, look in on Jasper?"

"Certainly, Mr. Dean. And tell him that you had the kindness to desire to know how he was?"

"Ay, do so, do so. Certainly. Wished to know how he was. By all means. Wished to know how he was."

With a pleasant air of patronage, the Dean as nearly cocks his quaint hat as a Dean in good spirits may, and directs his comely gaiters towards the ruddy dining-room of the snug old red-brick house, where he is at present "in residence" with Mrs. Dean and Miss Dean.

Mr. Crisparkle, Minor Canon, fair and rosy, and perpetually pitching himself headforemost into all the deep running water in the surrounding country; Mr. Crisparkle, Minor Canon, early riser, musical, classical, cheerful, kind, good-natured, social, contented, and boy-like; Mr. Crisparkle, Minor Canon and good man, lately "Coach" upon the chief Pagan high-roads, but since promoted by a patron (grateful for a well-taught son) to his present Christian beat; betakes himself to the gatehouse, on his way home to his early tea.

"Sorry to hear from Tope that you have not been well, Jasper."

"O, it was nothing, nothing!"

"You look a little worn."

"Do I? O, I don't think so. What is better, I don't feel so. Tope has made too much of it, I suspect. It 's his trade to make the most of everything appertaining to the Cathedral, you know."

"I may tell the Dean — I call expressly from the Dean — that you are all right again?"

The reply, with a slight smile, is, "Certainly; with my respects and thanks to the Dean."

"I 'm glad to hear that you expect young Drood."

"I expect the dear fellow every moment."

"Ah! He will do you more good than a doctor, Jasper."

"More good than a dozen doctors; for I love him dearly, and I don't love doctors, or doctors' stuff."

Mr. Jasper is a dark man of some six-and-twenty, with thick, lustrous, well-arranged black hair and whisker. He looks older than he is, as dark men often do. His voice is deep and good, his face and figure are good, his manner is a little sombre. His room is a little sombre, and may have had its influence in forming his manner. It is mostly in shadow. Even when the sun shines brilliantly, it seldom touches the grand piano in the recess, or the folio music-books on the stand or the bookshelves on the wall, or the unfinished picture of a blooming school-girl hanging over the chimney-piece; her flowing brown hair tied with a blue riband, and her beauty remarkable for a quite childish, almost babyish, touch of saucy discontent, comically conscious of itself. (There is not the least artistic merit in this picture, which is a mere daub; but it is clear that the painter has made it humorously — one might almost say, revengefully — like the original.)

"We shall miss you, Jasper, at the 'Alternate Musical Wednesdays' to-night; but no doubt you are best at home. Good night. God bless you! 'Tell me, shep-herds, te-e-ell me; tell me-e-e, have you seen (have you seen, have you seen, have you seen) my-y-y Flo-o-ora-a pass this way?'" Melodiously good Minor Canon the Reverend Septimus Crisparkle thus delivers himself, in musical rhythm, as he withdraws his amiable face from the doorway and conveys it down stairs.

Sounds of greeting and recognition pass between the Reverend Septimus and somebody else, at the stair-foot. Mr. Jasper listens, starts from his chair, and catches a young fellow in his arms, exclaiming, —

"My dear Edwin!"

"My dear Jack! So glad to see you!"

"Get off your great-coat, bright boy, and sit down here in your own corner. Your feet are not wet? Pull your boots off. Do pull your boots off."

"My dear Jack, I am as dry as a bone. Don't moddley-coddley, there 's a good fellow. I like anything better than being moddley-coddleyed."

With the check upon him of being unsympathetically restrained in a genial outburst of enthusiasm, Mr. Jasper stands still, and looks on intently at the young fellow, divesting himself of his outer coat, hat, gloves, and so forth. Once for all, a look of intentness and intensity — a look of hungry, exacting, watchful, and yet devoted affection — is always now and ever afterwards, on the Jasper face whenever the Jasper face is addressed in this direction. And whenever it is so addressed, it is never, on this occasion or on any other, dividedly addressed; it is always concentrated.

"Now I am right, and now I 'll take my corner, Jack. Any dinner, Jack?"

Mr Jasper opens a door at the upper end of the room, and discloses a small inner room pleasantly lighted and prepared, wherein a comely dame is in the act of setting dishes on table.

"What a jolly old Jack it is!" cries the young fellow, with a clap of his hands. "Look here, Jack; tell me; whose birthday is it?"

"Not yours, I know," Mr. Jasper answers, pausing to consider.

"Not mine, you know? No; not mine, *I* know! Pussy's!"

Fixed as the look the young fellow meets is, there is yet in it some strange power of suddenly including the sketch over the chimney-piece.

"Pussy's, Jack! We must drink Many happy returns to her. Come, uncle, take your dutiful and sharp-set nephew in to dinner."

As the boy (for he is little more) lays a hand on Jasper's shoulder, Jasper cordially and gayly lays a hand on *his* shoulder, and so Marseillaise-wise they go in to dinner."

"And Lord! Here 's Mrs. Tope!" cries the boy. "Lovelier than ever!"

"Never you mind me, Master Edwin," retorts the Verger's wife; "I can take care of myself."

"You can't. You 're much too handsome. Give me a kiss, because it 's Pussy's birthday."

"I 'd Pussy you, young man, if I was Pussy, as you call her," Mrs. Tope blushingly retorts, after being saluted. "Your uncle 's too much wrapped up in you, that 's where it is. He makes so much of you that it 's my opinion you think you 've only to call your Pussys by the dozen, to make 'em come."

"You forget, Mrs. Tope," Mr. Jasper interposes, taking his place at table with a genial smile, "and so do you, Ned, that Uncle and Nephew are words prohibited here by common consent and express agreement. For what we are going to receive His holy name be praised!"

"Done like the Dean! Witness, Edwin Drood! Please to carve, Jack, for I can't."

This sally ushers in the dinner. Little to the present purpose, or to any purpose, is said, while it is in course of being disposed of. At length the cloth is drawn, and a dish of walnuts and a decanter of rich-colored sherry are placed upon the table.

"I say! Tell me, Jack," the young fellow then flows on; "do you really and truly feel as if the mention of our relationship divided us at all? I don't."

"Uncles as a rule, Ned, are so much older than their nephews," is the reply, "that I have that feeling instinctively."

"As a rule? Ah, maybe! But what is a difference in age of half a dozen years or so; And some uncles, in large families, are even younger than their nephews. By George, I wish it was the case with us!"

"Why?"

"Because if it was, I 'd take the lead with you, Jack, and be as wise as Begone dull care that turned a young man gray, and begone dull care that turned an old man to clay. Halloa, Jack! Don't drink."

"Why not?"

"Asks why not, on Pussy's birthday, and no Happy Returns proposed! Pussy, Jack, and many of 'em! Happy returns, I mean."

Laying an affectionate and laughing touch on the boy's extended hand, as if it were at once his giddy head and his light heart, Mr. Jasper drinks the toast in silence

"Hip, hip, hip, and nine times nine, and one to finish with, and all that, understood. Hooray, hooray, hooray! And now, Jack, let 's have a little talk about Pussy. Two pairs of nut-crackers? Pass me one, and take the other." Crack. "How 's Pussy getting on, Jack?"

"With her music? Fairly."

"What a dreadfully conscientious fellow you are, Jack! But *I* know, Lord bless you! Inattentive, is n't she?"

"She can learn anything, if she will."

"*If* she will? Egad, that 's it. But if she won't?"

Crack. On Mr. Jasper's part.

"How 's she looking, Jack?"

Mr Jasper's concentrated face again includes the portrait as he returns, "Very like your sketch indeed."

"I *am* a little proud of it," says the young fellow, glancing up at the sketch with complacency, and then shutting one eye, and taking a corrected prospect of it over a level bridge of nut-cracker in the air: "Not badly hit off from memory. But I ought to have caught that expression pretty well, for I have seen it often enough."

Crack. On Edwin Drood's part.

Crack. On Mr. Jasper's part.

"In point of fact," the former resumes, after some silent dipping among his fragments of walnut with an air of pique, "I see it whenever I go to see Pussy. If I don't find it on her face, I leave it there. — You know I do, Miss Scornful Pert. Booh!" With a twirl of the nut-crackers at the portrait.

Crack. Crack. Crack. Slowly, on Mr. Jasper's part.

Crack. Sharply on the part of Edwin Drood.

Silence on both sides.

"Have you lost your tongue, Jack?"

"Have you found yours, Ned?"

"No, but really; — is n't it, you know, after all?"

Mr. Jasper lifts his dark eyebrows inquiringly.

"Is n't it unsatisfactory to be cut off from choice in such a matter? There, Jack! I tell you! If I could choose, I would choose Pussy from all the pretty girls in the world."

"But you have not got to choose."

"That 's what I complain of. My dead-and-gone father and Pussy's dead-and-gone father must needs marry us together by anticipation. Why the — Devil, I was going to say, if it had been respectful to their memory — could 'nt they leave us alone?"

"Tut, tut, dear boy," Mr. Jasper remonstrates, in a tone of gentle deprecation.

"Tut, tut? Yes, Jack, it 's all very well for *you*. *You* can take it easily. *Your* life is not laid down to scale, and lined and dotted out for you, like a surveyor's plan. *You* have no uncomfortable suspicion that you are forced upon anybody, nor has anybody an uncomfortable suspicion that she is forced upon you, or that you are forced upon her. *You* can choose for yourself. Life, for *you*, is a plum with the natural bloom on; it has n't been over-carefully wiped off for *you* — "

"Don't stop, dear fellow. Go on."

"Can I anyhow have hurt your feelings, Jack?"

"How can you have hurt my feelings?"

"Good Heaven, Jack, you look frightfully ill! There 's a strange film come over your eyes"

Mr. Jasper, with a forced smile, stretches out his right hand, as if at once to disarm apprehension and gain time to get better. After a while he says faintly, —

"I have been taking opium for a pain — an agony — that sometimes overcomes me. The effects of the medicine steal over me like a blight or a cloud, and pass.

You see them in the act of passing; they will be gone directly. Look away from me. They will go all the sooner."

With a scared face the younger man complies, by casting his eyes downward at the ashes on the hearth. Not relaxing his own gaze at the fire, but rather strengthening it with a fierce, firm grip upon his elbow-chair, the elder sits for a few moments rigid, and then, with thick drops standing on his forehead, and a sharp catch of his breath, becomes as he was before. On his so subsiding in his chair, his nephew gently and assiduously tends him while he quite recovers. When Jasper is restored, he lays a tender hand upon his nephew's shoulder, and, in a tone of voice less troubled than the purport of his words — indeed, with something of raillery or banter in it — thus addresses him: —

"There is said to be a hidden skeleton in every house; but you thought there was none in mine, dear Ned."

"Upon my life, Jack, I did think so. However, when I come to consider that even in Pussy's house — if she had one — and in mine — if I had one — "

"You were going to say (but that I interrupted you in spite of myself) what a quiet life mine is. No whirl and uproar around me, no distracting commerce or calculation, no risk, no change of place, myself devoted to the art I pursue, my business my pleasure."

"I really was going to say something of the kind, Jack; but you see, you, speaking of yourself, almost necessarily leave out much that I should have put in. For instance: I should have put in the foreground your being so much respected as Lay Precentor, or Lay Clerk, or whatever you call it of this Cathedral; your enjoying the reputation of having done such wonders with the choir; your choosing your society, and holding such an independent position in this queer old place; your gift of teaching (why, even Pussy, who don't like being taught, says there never was such a Master as you are!) and your connection."

"Yes; I saw what you were tending to. I hate it."

"Hate it, Jack?" (Much bewildered.)

"I hate it. The cramped monotony of my existence grinds me away by the grain. How does our service sound to you?"

"Beautiful! Quite celestial."

"It often sounds to me quite devilish. I am so weary of it. The echoes of my own voice among the arches seem to mock me with my daily drudging round. No wretched monk who droned his life away in that gloomy place, before me, can have been more tired of it than I am. He could take for relief (and did take) to carving demons out of the stalls and seats and desks. What shall I do? Must I take to carving them out of my heart?"

"I thought you had so exactly found your niche in life, Jack," Edwin Drood returns, astonished, bending forward in his chair to lay a sympathetic hand on Jasper's knee, and looking at him with an anxious face.

"I know you thought so. They all think so."

"Well; I suppose they do," says Edwin, meditating aloud. "Pussy thinks so."

"When did she tell you that?"

"The last time I was here. You remember when. Three months ago."

"How did she phrase it?"

"Oh! She only said that she had become your pupil, and that you were made for your vocation."

The younger man glances at the portrait. The elder sees it in him.

"Anyhow, my dear Ned," Jasper resumes, as he shakes his head with a grave cheerfulness, "I must subdue myself to my vocation, which is much the same thing outwardly. It's too late to find another now. This is a confidence between us."

"It shall be sacredly preserved, Jack."

"I have reposed it in you, because — "

"I feel it, I assure you. Because we are fast friends, and because you love and trust me, as I love and trust you. Both hands, Jack."

As each stands looking into the other's eyes, and as the uncle holds the nephew's hands, the uncle thus proceeds: —

"You know now, don't you, that even a poor monotonous chorister and grinder of music, in his niche, may be troubled with some stray sort of ambition, aspiration, restlessness, dissatisfaction, what shall we call it?"

"Yes, dear Jack."

"And you will remember?"

"My dear Jack, I only ask you, am I likely to forget what you have said with so much feeling?"

"Take it as a warning, then."

In the act of having his hands released, and of moving a step back, Edwin pauses for an instant to consider the application of these last words. The instant over, he says, sensibly touched, —

"I am afraid I am but a shallow, surface kind of fellow, Jack, and that my headpiece is none of the best. But I need n't say I am young; and perhaps I shall not grow worse as I grow older. At all events, I hope I have something impressible within me, which feels — deeply feels — the disinterestedness of your painfully laying your inner self bare, as a warning to me."

Mr. Jasper's steadiness of face and figure becomes so marvellous that his breathing seems to have stopped.

"I could n't fail to notice, Jack, that it cost you a great effort, and that you were very much moved, and very unlike your usual self. Of course I knew that you were extremely fond of me, but I really was not prepared for your, as I may say, sacrificing yourself to me, in that way."

Mr. Jasper, becoming a breathing man again without the smallest stage of transition between the two extreme states, lifts his shoulders, laughs, and waves his right arm.

"No; don't put the sentiment away, Jack; please don't; for I am very much in earnest. I have no doubt that that unhealthy state of mind which you have so powerfully described is attended with some real suffering, and is hard to bear. But let me reassure you, Jack, as to the chances of its overcoming Me. I don't think I am in the way of it. In some few months less than another year, you know, I shall carry Pussy off from school as Mrs. Edwin Drood I shall then go engineering into the East, and Pussy with me. And although we have our little tiffs now, arising out of a certain unavoidable flatness that attends our love-making, owing to its end being all settled beforehand, still, I have no doubt of our getting on capitally then, when it 's done and can't be helped. In short, Jack, to go back to the old song I was freely quoting at dinner (and who knows old songs better than you!), my wife shall dance and I will sing, so merrily pass the day. Of Pussy's being beautiful there cannot be a doubt; — and when you are good besides, Little Miss Impudence," once more apostrophizing the portrait, "I'll burn your comic likeness and paint your music-master another."

Mr. Jasper, with his hand to his chin, and with an expression of musing benevolence on his face, has attentively watched every animated look and gesture attending the delivery of these words. He remains in that attitude after they are spoken, as if in a kind of fascination attendant on his strong interest in the youthful spirit that he loves so well. Then, he says with a quiet smile, —

"You won't be warned, then?"

"No, Jack."

"You can't be warned, then?"

"No, Jack, not by you. Besides that I don't really consider myself in danger, I don't like your putting yourself in that position."

"Shall we go and walk in the churchyard?"

"By all means. You won't mind my slipping out of it for half a moment to the Nuns' House, and leaving a parcel there? Only gloves for Pussy; as many pairs of gloves as she is years old to-day. Rather poetical, Jack?"

Mr. Jasper, still in the same attitude, murmurs, "'Nothing half so sweet in life,' Ned!"

"Here 's the parcel in my great-coat pocket. They must be presented to-night, or the poetry is gone. It 's against regulations for me to call at night, but not to leave a packet. I am ready, Jack!"

Mr. Jasper dissolves his attitude, and they go out together.

CHAPTER III.

THE NUNS' HOUSE.

For sufficient reasons, which this narrative will itself unfold as it advances, a fictitious name must be bestowed upon the old Cathedral town. Let it stand in these pages as Cloisterham. It was once possibly known to the Druids by another name, and certainly to the Romans by another, and to the Saxons by another, and to the Normans by another; and a name more or less in the course of many centuries can be of little moment to its dusty chronicles.

An ancient city Cloisterham, and no meet dwelling-place for any one with hankerings after the noisy world. A monotonous, silent city, deriving an earthly flavor throughout, from its Cathedral cript, and so abounding in vestiges of monastic graves, that the Cloisterham children grow small salad in the dust of abbots and abbesses, and make dirt-pies of nuns and friars; while every ploughman in its outlying fields renders to once puissant Lord Treasurers, Archbishops, Bishops, and such-like, the attention which the Ogre in the story-book desired to render to his unbidden visitor, and grinds their bones to make his bread.

A drowsy city Cloisterham, whose inhabitants seem to suppose, with an inconsistency more strange than rare, that all its changes lie behind it, and that there are no more to come. A queer moral to derive from antiquity, yet older than any traceable antiquity. So silent are the streets of Cloisterham (though prone to echo on the smallest provocation), that of a summer-day the sunblinds of its shops scarce dare to flap in the south wind; while the sun-browned tramps who pass along and stare, quicken their limp a little, that they may the sooner get beyond the confines of its oppressive respectability. This is a feat not difficult of achievement, seeing that the streets of Cloisterham city are little more than one narrow street by which you get into it and get out of it: the rest being mostly disappointing yards with pumps in them and no thoroughfare,— exception made of the Cathedral close, and a paved Quaker settlement, in color and general conformation very like a Quakeress's bonnet, up in a shady corner.

In a word, a city of another and a bygone time is Cloisterham, with its hoarse Cathedral bell, its hoarse rooks hovering about the Cathedral tower, its hoarser and less distinct rooks in the stalls far beneath. Fragments of old wall, saint's chapel, chapter-house, convent, and monastery have got incongruously or obstructively built into many of its houses and gardens, much as kindred jumbled notions have become incorporated into many of its citizens' minds. All things in it are of the past. Even its single pawnbroker takes in no pledges, nor has he for a long time, but offers vainly an unredeemed stock for sale, of which the costlier articles are dim and pale old watches apparently in a slow perspiration, tarnished sugar-tongs with ineffectual legs, and odd volumes of dismal books. The most abundant and the most agreeable evidences of progressing life in Cloisterham are the evidences of vegetable life in its many gardens; even its drooping and despondent little theatre has its poor strip of garden, receiving the foul fiend, when he ducks from its stage into the infernal regions, among scarlet beans or oyster-shells, according to the season of the year.

In the midst of Cloisterham stands the Nuns' House; a venerable brick edifice whose present appellation is doubtless derived from the legend of its conventual uses. On the trim gate enclosing its old court-yard is a resplendent brass plate flashing forth the legend: "Seminary for Young Ladies. Miss Twinkleton." The house-front is so old and worn, and the brass plate is so shining and staring, that the general result has reminded imaginative strangers of a battered old beau with a large modern eye-glass stuck in his blind eye.

Whether the nuns of yore, being of a submissive rather than a stiff-necked generation, habitually bent their contemplative heads to avoid collision with the beams in the low ceilings of the many chambers of their House; whether they sat in its long low windows, telling their beads for their mortification instead of making necklaces of them for their adornment; whether they were ever walled up alive in odd angles and jutting gables of the building for having some ineradicable leaven of busy mother Nature in them which has kept the fermenting world alive ever since; — these may be matters of interest to its haunting ghosts (if any), but constitute no item in Miss Twinkleton's half-yearly accounts. They are neither of Miss Twinkleton's inclusive regulars, nor of her extras. The lady who undertakes the poetical department of the establishment at so much (or so little) a quarter, has no pieces in her list of recitals bearing on such unprofitable questions.

As, in some cases of drunkenness, and in others of animal magnetism, there are two states of consciousness which never clash, but each of which pursues its separate course as though it were continuous instead of broken (thus if I hide my watch when I am drunk, I must be drunk again before I can remember where), so Miss Twinkleton has two distinct and separate phases of being. Every night, the moment the young ladies have retired to rest, does Miss Twinkleton smarten up her curls a little, brighten up her eyes a little, and become a sprightlier Miss Twinkleton than the young ladies have ever seen. Every night, at the same hour, does Miss Twinkleton resume the topics of the previous night, comprehending the tenderer scandal of Cloisterham, of which she has no knowledge whatever by day, and references to a certain season at Tunbridge Wells (airily called by Miss Twinkleton in this state of her existence "The Wells"), notably the season wherein a certain finished gentleman (compassionately called by Miss Twinkleton in this state of her existence, "Foolish Mr. Porters") revealed a homage of the heart, whereof Miss Twinkleton, in her scholastic state of existence, is as ignorant as a granite pillar. Miss Twinkleton's companion in both states of existence, and equally adaptable to either, is one Mrs. Tisher, a deferential widow with a weak back, a chronic sigh, and a suppressed voice, who looks after the young ladies' wardrobes, and leads them to infer that she has seen better days. Perhaps this is the reason why it is an article of faith with the servants, handed down from race to race, that the departed Tisher was a hairdresser.

The pet pupil of the Nuns' House is Miss Rosa Bud, of course called Rosebud;

wonderfully pretty, wonderfully childish, wonderfully whimsical. An awkward interest (awkward because romantic) attaches to Miss Bud in the minds of the young ladies, on account of its being known to them that a husband has been chosen for her by will and bequest, and that her guardian is bound down to bestow her on that husband when he comes of age. Miss Twinkleton, in her seminarial state of existence, has combated the romantic aspect of this destiny by affecting to shake her head over it behind Miss Bud's dimpled shoulders, and to brood on the unhappy lot of that doomed little victim. But with no better effect — possibly some unfelt touch of foolish Mr. Porters has undermined the endeavor — than to evoke from the young ladies a unanimous bedchamber cry of "Oh! what a pretending old thing Miss Twinkleton is, my dear!"

The Nuns' House is never in such a state of flutter as when this allotted husband calls to see little Rosebud. (It is unanimously understood by the young ladies that he is lawfully entitled to this privilege, and that if Miss Twinkleton disputed it she would be instantly taken up and transported.) When his ring at the gate bell is expected, or takes place, every young lady who can, under any pretence, look out of window, looks out of window; while every young lady who is "practising" practises out of time; and the French class becomes so demoralized that the Mark goes round as briskly as the bottle at a convivial party in the last century.

On the afternoon of the day next after the dinner of two at the Gate House, the bell is rung with the usual fluttering results.

"Mr. Edwin Drood to see Miss Rosa."

This is the announcement of the parlor-maid in chief. Miss Twinkleton, with an exemplary air of melancholy on her, turns to the sacrifice, and says, "You may go down, my dear." Miss Bud goes down, followed by all eyes.

Mr. Edwin Drood is waiting in Miss Twinkleton's own parlor, — a dainty room, with nothing more directly scholastic in it than a terrestrial and a celestial globe. These expressive machines imply (to parents and guardians) that even when Miss Twinkleton retires into the bosom of privacy, duty may at any moment compel her to become a sort of Wandering Jewess, scouring the earth and soaring through the skies in search of knowledge for her pupils.

The last new maid, who has never seen the young gentleman Miss Rosa is engaged to, and who is making his acquaintance between the hinges of the open door, left open for the purpose, stumbles guiltily down the kitchen stairs, as a charming little apparition with its face concealed by a little silk apron thrown over its head, glides into the parlor.

"Oh! It *is* so ridiculous!" says the apparition, stopping and shrinking. "Don't, Eddy!"

"Don't what, Rosa?"

"Don't come any nearer, please. It *is* so absurd."

"What is absurd, Rosa?"

"The whole thing is. It *is* so absurd to be an engaged orphan; and it *is* so absurd to have the girls and the servants scuttling about after one, like mice in the wainscot; and it *is* so absurd to be called upon!"

The apparition appears to have a thumb in the corner of its mouth while making this complaint.

"You give me an affectionate reception, Pussy, I must say."

"Well, I will in a minute, Eddy, but I can't just yet. How are you?" (very shortly.)

"I am unable to reply that I am much the better for seeing you, Pussy, inasmuch as I see nothing of you."

This second remonstrance brings a dark, bright, pouting eye out from a corner of the apron; but it swiftly becomes invisible again, as the apparition exclaims, "Oh! Good Gracious, you have had half your hair cut off!"

"I should have done better to have had my head cut off, I think," says Edwin, rumpling the hair in question, with a fierce glance at the looking-glass, and giving an impatient stamp. "Shall I go?"

"No, you need n't go just yet, Eddy. The girls would all be asking questions why you went."

"Once for all, Rosa, will you uncover that ridiculous little head of yours and give me a welcome?"

The apron is pulled off the childish head, as its wearer replies, "You 're very welcome, Eddy. There! I 'm sure that 's nice. Shake hands. No, I can't kiss you, because I 've got an acidulated drop in my mouth."

"Are you at all glad to see me, Pussy?"

"O yes, I 'm dreadfully glad. — Go and sit down. — Miss Twinkleton."

It is the custom of that excellent lady, when these visits occur, to appear every three minutes, either in her own person or in that of Mrs. Tisher, and lay an offering on the shrine of Propriety by affecting to look for some desiderated article. On the present occasion, Miss Twinkleton, gracefully gliding in and out, says, in passing, "How do you do, Mr. Drood? Very glad indeed to have the pleasure. Pray excuse me. Tweezers. Thank you!"

"I got the gloves last evening, Eddy, and I like them very much. They are beauties."

"Well, that 's something," the affianced replies, half grumbling. "The smallest encouragement thankfully received. And how did you pass your birthday, Pussy?"

"Delightfully! Everybody gave me a present. And we had a feast. And we had a ball at night."

"A feast and a ball, eh? These occasions seem to go off tolerably well without me, Pussy."

"De-lightfully!" cries Rosa, in a quite spontaneous manner, and without the least pretence of reserve.

"Hah! And what was the feast?"

"Tarts, oranges, jellies, and shrimps."

"Any partners at the ball?"

"We danced with one another, of course, sir. But some of the girls made game to be their brothers. It *was* so droll!"

"Did anybody make game to be —"

"To be you? O dear, yes!" cries Rosa, laughing with great enjoyment. "That was the first thing done"

"I hope she did it pretty well," says Edwin, rather doubtfully.

"Oh! It was excellent! — I would n't dance with you, you know."

Edwin scarcely seems to see the force of this; begs to know if he may take the liberty to ask why?

"Because I was so tired of you," returns Rosa. But she quickly adds, and pleadingly, too, seeing displeasure in his face: "Dear Eddy, you were just as tired of me, you know."

"Did I say so, Rosa?"

"Say so! Do you ever say so? No, you only showed it. Oh, sne did it so well!" cries Rosa, in a sudden ecstasy with her counterfeit betrothed.

"It strikes me that she must be a devilish impudent girl," says Edwin Drood. "And so, Pussy, you have passed your last birthday in this old house."

"Ah, yes!" Rosa clasps her hands, looks down with a sigh, and shakes her head.

"You seem to be sorry, Rosa."

"I am sorry for the poor old place. Somehow, I feel as if it would miss me, when I am gone so far away, so young."

"Perhaps we had better stop short, Rosa!"

She looks up at him with a swift, bright look; next moment shakes her head, sighs, and looks down again.

"That is to say, is it, Pussy, that we are both resigned?"

She nods her head again, and after a short silence, quaintly bursts out with, "You know we must be married, and married from here, Eddy, or the poor girls will be so dreadfully disappointed!"

For the moment there is more of compassion, both for her and for himself, in her affianced husband s face, than there is of love. He checks the look, and asks, "Shall I take you out for a walk, Rosa dear?"

Rosa dear does not seem at all clear on this point, until her face, which has been comically reflective, brightens "O yes, Eddy; let us go for a walk! And I tell you what we 'll do. You shall pretend that you are engaged to somebody else, and I 'll pretend that I am not engaged to anybody, and then we sha' n't quarrel."

"Do you think that will prevent our falling out, Rosa?"

"I know it will. Hush! Pretend to look out of window — Mrs. Tisher!"

Through a fortuitous concourse of accidents, the matronly Tisher heaves in sight, says, in rustling through the room like the legendary ghost of a dowager in silken skirts, "I hope I see Mr. Drood well; though I need n't ask, if I may judge from his complexion? I trust I disturb no one; but there *was* a paper-knife — O, thank you, I am sure!" and disappears with her prize.

"One other thing you must do, Eddy, to oblige me," says Rosebud. "The moment we get into the street, you must put me outside, and keep close to the house yourself, — squeeze and graze yourself against it."

"By all means, Rosa, if you wish it. Might I ask why?"

"Oh! because I don't want the girls to see you."

"It 's a fine day: but would you like me to carry an umbrella up?"

"Don't be foolish, sir. You have n't got polished leather boots on," pouting, with one shoulder raised.

"Perhaps that might escape the notice of the girls, even if they did see me," remarks Edwin, looking down at his boots with a sudden distaste for them.

"Nothing escapes their notice, sir. And then I know what would happen. Some of them would begin reflecting on me by saying (for *they* are free) that they never will on any account engage themselves to lovers without polished leather boots. Hark! Miss Twinkleton. I 'll ask for leave."

That discreet lady being indeed heard without, inquiring of nobody in a blandly conversational tone as she advances, "Eh? Indeed! Are you quite sure you saw my mother-of-pearl button-holder on the work-table in my room?" is at once solicited for walking leave, and graciously accords it. And soon the young couple go out of the Nuns' House, taking all precautions against the discovery of the so vitally defective boots of Mr. Edwin Drood, — precautions, let us hope, effective for the peace of Mrs. Edwin Drood, that is to be.

"Which way shall we take, Rosa?"

Rosa replies, "I want to go to the Lumps-of-Delight shop."

"To the —"

"A Turkish sweetmeat, sir. My gracious me! don't you understand anything? Call yourself an Engineer, and not know *that?*"

"Why, how should I know it, Rosa?"

"Because I am very fond of them. But oh! I forgot what we are to pretend. No, you need n't know anything about them; never mind."

So he is gloomily borne off to the Lumps-of-Delight shop, where Rosa makes her purchase, and, after offering some to him (which he rather indignantly declines), begins to partake of it with great zest, previously taking off and rolling up a pair of little pink gloves, like rose-leaves, and occasionally putting her little pink fingers to her rosy lips, to cleanse them from the Dust of Delight that comes off the Lumps.

"Now, be a good-tempered Eddy, and pretend. And so you are engaged?"

"And so I am engaged."

"Is she nice?"

"Charming."

"Tall?"

"Immensely tall!" (Rosa being short.)

"Must be gawky, I should think," is Rosa's quiet commentary.

"I beg your pardon: not at all," contradiction rising in him. "What is termed a fine woman, a splendid woman."

"Big nose, no doubt," is the quiet commentary again.

"Not a little one, certainly," is the quick reply. (Rosa's being a little one.)

"Long pale nose, with a red knob in the middle. *I* know the sort of nose," says Rosa, with a satisfied nod, and tranquilly enjoying the Lumps.

"You *don't* know the sort of nose, Rosa," with some warmth; "because it 's nothing of the kind."

"Not a pale nose, Eddy?"

"No." Determined not to assent.

"A red nose? Oh! I don't like red noses. However, to be sure, she can always powder it."

"She would scorn to powder it," says Edwin, becoming heated.

"Would she? What a stupid thing she must be? Is she stupid in everything?"

"No. In nothing."

After a pause, in which the whimsically wicked face has not been unobservant of him, Rosa says, —

"And this most sensible of creatures likes the idea of being carried off to Egypt; does she, Eddy?"

"Yes. She takes a sensible interest in triumphs of engineering skill, especially when they are to change the whole condition of an undeveloped country."

"Lor!" says Rosa, shrugging her shoulders, with a little laugh of wonder.

"Do you object," Edwin inquires, with a majestic turn of his eyes downward upon the fairy figure, — "do you object, Rosa, to her feeling that interest?"

"Object? My dear Eddy! But really. Does n't she hate boilers and things?"

"I can answer for her not being so idiotic as to hate Boilers," he returns, with angry emphasis; "though I cannot answer for her views about Things, really not understanding what Things are meant."

"But don't she hate Arabs, and Turks, and Fellahs, and people?"

"Certainly not," very firmly.

"At least, she *must* hate the Pyramids? Come, Eddy?"

"Why should she be such a little — tall, I mean — Goose, as to hate the Pyramids, Rosa?"

"Ah! you should hear Miss Twinkleton," often nodding her head, and much enjoying the Lumps, "bore about them, and then you would n't ask. Tiresome old burying-grounds! Isises, and Ibises, and Cheopses, and Pharaohses: who cares about them? And then there was Belzoni or somebody, dragged out by the legs, half choked with bats and dust. All the girls say serve him right, and hope it hurt him, and wish he had been quite choked."

The two youthful figures, side by side, but not now arm in arm, wander discontentedly about the old Close; and each sometimes stops and slowly imprints a deeper footstep in the fallen leaves.

"Well!" says Edwin, after a lengthy silence. "According to custom. We can't get on, Rosa."

Rosa tosses her head, and says she don't want to get on.

"That 's a pretty sentiment, Rosa, considering."

"Considering what?"

"If I say what, you 'll go wrong again."

"*You* 'll go wrong, you mean, Eddy. Don't be ungenerous."

"Ungenerous! I like that!"

"Then I *don't* like that, and so I tell you plainly," Rosa pouts.

"Now, Rosa, I put it to you. Who disparaged my profession, my destination —"

"You are not going to be buried in the Pyramids, I hope?" she interrupts, arching her delicate eyebrows. "You never said you were. If you are, why have n't you mentioned it to me? I can't find out your plans by instinct."

"Now, Rosa, you know very well what I mean, my dear."

"Well, then, why did you begin with your detestable red-nosed giantesses? And she would, she would, she would, she would, she WOULD powder it!" cries Rosa, in a little burst of comical contradictory spleen.

"Somehow or other, I never can come right in these discussions," says Edwin, sighing and becoming resigned.

"How is it possible, sir, that you ever can come right when you 're always wrong? And as to Belzoni, I suppose he 's dead; — I 'm sure I hope he is — and how can his legs or his chokes concern you?"

"It is nearly time for your return, Rosa. We have not had a very happy walk, have we?"

"A happy walk? A detestably unhappy walk, sir. If I go up stairs the moment I get in and cry till I can't take my dancing lesson, you are responsible, mind!"

"Let us be friends, Rosa."

"Ah!" cries Rosa, shaking her head and bursting into real tears. "I wish we *could* be friends! It 's because we can't be friends, that we try one another so. I am a young little thing, Eddy, to have an old heartache; but I really, really have, sometimes. Don't be angry. I know you have one yourself, too often. We should both of us have done better, if What is to be had been left, What might have been. I am quite a serious little thing now, and not teasing you. Let each of us forbear, this one time, on our own account, and on the other's!"

Disarmed by this glimpse of a woman's nature in the spoilt child, though for an instant disposed to resent it as seeming to involve the enforced infliction of himself upon her, Edwin Drood stands watching her as she childishly cries and sobs, with both hands to the handkerchief at her eyes, and then — she becoming more composed, and indeed beginning in her young inconstancy to laugh at herself for having been so moved — leads her to a seat hard by under the elm-trees.

"One clear word of understanding, Pussy dear. I am not clever out of my own line, — now I come to think of it I don't know that I am particularly clever in it, — but I want to do right. There is not — there may be — I really don't see my way to what I want to say, but I must say it before we part, — there is not any other young —"

"O no, Eddy! It 's generous of you to ask me; but no, no, no!"

They have come very near to the Cathedral windows, and at this moment the organ and the choir sound out sublimely. As they sit listening to the solemn swell, the confidence of last night rises in young Edwin Drood's mind, and he thinks how unlike this music is to that discordance.

"I fancy I can distinguish Jack's voice," is his remark in a low tone in connection with the train of thought.

"Take me back at once, please," urges his Affianced, quickly laying her light hand upon his wrist. "They will all be coming out directly; let us get away. O, what a resounding chord! But don't let us stop to listen to it; let us get away!"

Her hurry is over, as soon as they have passed out of the Close. They go, arm in arm now, gravely and deliberately enough, along the old High Street, to the Nuns' House. At the gate, the street being within sight empty, Edwin bends down his face to Rosebud's.

She remonstrates, laughing, and is a childish school-girl again.

"Eddy, no! I 'm too sticky to be kissed. But give me your hand, and I 'll blow a kiss into that."

He does so. She breathes a light breath into it, and asks, retaining it and looking into it, —

"Now say, what do you see?"

"See, Rosa?"

"Why, I thought you Egyptian boys could look into a hand and see all sorts of phantoms? Can't you see a happy Future?"

For certain, neither of them sees a happy Present, as the gate opens and closes, and one goes in and the other goes away.

CHAPTER IV.

MR. SAPSEA.

ACCEPTING the Jackass as the type of self-sufficient stupidity and conceit, — a custom, perhaps, like some few other customs, more conventional than fair, — then the purest Jackass in Cloisterham is Mr. Thomas Sapsea, Auctioneer.

Mr. Sapsea "dresses at" the Dean; has been bowed to for the Dean, in mistake; has even been spoken to in the street as My Lord, under the impression that he was the Bishop come down unexpectedly, without his chaplain. Mr. Sapsea is very proud of this, and of his voice, and of his style. He has even (in selling landed property) tried the experiment of slightly intoning in his pulpit, to make himself more like what he takes to be the genuine ecclesiastical article. So, in ending a Sale by Public Auction, Mr. Sapsea finishes off with an air of bestowing a benediction on the assembled brokers, which leaves the real Dean — a modest and worthy gentleman — far behind.

Mr. Sapsea has many admirers; indeed, the proposition is carried by a large local majority, even including non-believers in his wisdom, that he is a credit to Cloisterham. He possesses the great qualities of being portentous and dull, and of having a roll in his speech, and another roll in his gait; not to mention a certain gravely flowing action with his hands, as if he were presently going to Confirm the individual with whom he holds discourse. Much nearer sixty years of age than fifty, with a flowing outline of stomach, and horizontal creases in his waistcoat; reputed to be rich; voting at elections in the strictly respectable interest; morally satisfied that nothing but he himself has grown since he was a baby; how can dunder-headed Mr. Sapsea be otherwise than a credit to Cloisterham, and society?

Mr. Sapsea's premises are in the High Street, over against the Nuns' House. They are of about the period of the Nuns' House, irregularly modernized here and there, as steadily deteriorating generations found, more and more, that they preferred air and light to Fever and the Plague. Over the doorway is a wooden effigy, about half life-size, representing Mr. Sapsea's father, in a curly wig and toga, in the act of selling. The chastity of the idea, and the natural appearance of the little finger, hammer, and pulpit, have been much admired.

Mr. Sapsea sits in his dull, ground-floor sitting-room, giving first on his paved back yard, and then on his railed-off garden. Mr. Sapsea has a bottle of port wine on a table before the fire, — the fire is an early luxury, but pleasant on a cool, chilly autumn evening, — and is characteristically attended by his portrait, his eight-day clock, and his weather-glass. Characteristically, because he would uphold himself against mankind, his weather-glass against weather, and his clock against time.

By Mr. Sapsea's side on the table are a writing-desk and writing materials. Glancing at a scrap of manuscript, Mr. Sapsea reads it to himself with a lofty air, and then, slowly pacing the room with his thumbs in the arm-holes of his waistcoat, repeats it from memory: so internally, though with much dignity, that the word "Ethelinda" is alone audible.

There are three clean wineglasses in a tray on the table. His serving-maid entering, and announcing "Mr. Jasper is come, sir," Mr. Sapsea waves "Admit him," and draws two wineglasses from the rank, as being claimed.

"Glad to see you, sir. I congratulate myself on having the honor of receiving you here for the first time." Mr. Sapsea does the honors of his house in this wise.

"You are very good. The honor is mine and the self-congratulation is mine."

"You are pleased to say so, sir. But I do assure you that it is a satisfaction to me to receive you in my humble home. And that is what I would not say to everybody." Ineffable loftiness on Mr. Sapsea's part accompanies these words, as leaving the sentence to be understood: "You will not easily believe that your society can be a satisfaction to a man like myself; nevertheless, it is."

"I have for some time desired to know you, Mr. Sapsea."

"And I, sir, have long known you by reputation as a man of taste. Let me fill your glass. I will give you, sir," says Mr. Sapsea, filling his own, —

"When the French come over,
May we meet them at Dover!"

This was a patriotic toast in Mr. Sapsea's infancy, and he is therefore fully convinced of its being appropriate to any subsequent era.

"You can scarcely be ignorant, Mr. Sapsea," observes Jasper, watching the auctioneer with a smile, as the latter stretches out his legs before the fire, "that you know the world."

"Well, sir," is the chuckling reply, "I think I know something of it, — something of it."

"Your reputation for that knowledge has always interested and surprised me, and made me wish to know you. For, Cloisterham is a little place. Cooped up in it myself, I know nothing beyond it, and feel it to be a very little place."

"If I have not gone to foreign countries, young man," Mr. Sapsea begins, and then stops, — "You will excuse my calling you young man, Mr. Jasper? You are much my junior."

"By all means."

"If I have not gone to foreign countries, young man, foreign countries have come to me. They have come to me in the way of business, and I have improved upon my opportunities. Put it that I take an inventory, or make a catalogue. I see a French clock. I never saw him before in my life, but I instantly lay my finger on him and say 'Paris!' I see some cups and saucers of Chinese make, equally strangers to me personally: I put my finger on them, then and there, and I say 'Pekin, Nankin, and Canton.' It is the same with Japan, with Egypt, and with bamboo and sandal-wood from the East Indies; I put my finger on them all. I have put my finger on the North Pole before now, and said, 'Spear of Esquimaux make, for half a pint of pale sherry!"

"Really? A very remarkable way, Mr. Sapsea, of acquiring a knowledge of men and things."

"I mention it, sir," Mr. Sapsea rejoins, with unspeakable complacency, "because, as I say, it don't do to boast of what you are; but show how you came to be it, and then you prove it."

"Most interesting. We were to speak of the late Mrs. Sapsea."

"We were, sir." Mr. Sapsea fills both glasses, and takes the decanter into safekeeping again. "Before I consult your opinion as a man of taste on this little trifle," — holding it up, — "which is *but* a trifle, and still has required some thought, sir, some little fever of the brow, I ought perhaps to describe the character of the late Mrs. Sapsea, now dead three quarters of a year."

Mr. Jasper, in the act of yawning behind his wineglass, puts down that screen and calls up a look of interest. It is a little impaired in its expressiveness by his having a shut-up gape still to dispose of, with watering eyes.

"Half a dozen years ago, or so," Mr. Sapsea proceeds, "when I had enlarged my mind up to — I will not say to what it now is, for that might seem to aim at too much, but up to the pitch of wanting another mind to be absorbed in it — I cast my eye about me for a nuptial partner. Because, as I say, it is not good for man to be alone."

Mr. Jasper appears to commit this original idea to memory.

"Miss Brobity at that time kept, I will not call it the rival establishment to the establishment at the Nuns' House opposite, but I will call it the other parallel establishment down town. The world did have it that she showed a passion for attending my sales, when they took place on half-holidays, or in vacation time. The world did put it about that she admired my style. The world did notice that, as time flowed by, my style became traceable in the dictation-exercises of Miss Brobity's pupils. Young man, a whisper even sprang up in obscure malignity, that one ignorant and besotted Churl (a parent) so committed himself as to object to it by name. But I do not believe this. For is it likely that any human creature in his right senses would so lay himself open to be pointed at, by what I call the finger of scorn?"

Mr. Jasper shakes his head. Not in the least likely. Mr. Sapsea, in a grandiloquent state of absence of mind, seems to refill his visitor's glass, which is full already, and does really refill his own, which is empty.

"Miss Brobity's Being, young man, was deeply imbued with homage to Mind. She revered Mind, when launched, or, as I say, precipitated, on an extensive knowledge of the world. When I made my proposal, she did me the honor to be so overshadowed with a species of Awe, as to be able to articulate only the two words, 'O Thou!' — meaning myself. Her limpid blue eyes were fixed upon me, her semi-transparent hands were clasped together, pallor overspread her aquiline features, and, though encouraged to proceed, she never did proceed a word further. I disposed of the parallel establishment, by private contract, and we became as nearly one as could be expected under the circumstances. But she never could, and she never did, find a phrase satisfactory to her perhaps-too-favorable estimate of my intellect. To the very last (feeble action of liver), she addressed me in the same unfinished terms."

Mr. Jasper has closed his eyes as the auctioneer has deepened his voice. He now abruptly opens them, and says, in unison with the deepened voice, "Ah!" — rather as if stopping himself on the extreme verge of adding — "men!"

"I have been since," says Mr. Sapsea, with his legs stretched out, and solemnly enjoying himself with the wine and the fire, "what you behold me; I have been since a solitary mourner; I have been since, as I say, wasting my evening conversation on the desert air. I will not say that I have reproached myself; but there have been times when I have asked myself the question, What if her husband had been nearer on a level with her? If she had not had to look up quite so high, what might the stimulating action have been upon the liver?"

Mr. Jasper says, with an appearance of having fallen into dreadfully low spirits, that he "supposes it was to be."

"We can only suppose so, sir," Mr. Sapsea coincides. "As I say, Man proposes, Heaven disposes. It may or may not be putting the same thought in another form; but that is the way I put it."

Mr. Jasper murmurs assent.

"And now, Mr. Jasper," resumes the auctioneer, producing his scrap of manuscript, "Mrs. Sapsea's monument having had full time to settle and dry, let me take your opinion, as a man of taste, on the inscription I have (as I before remarked, not without some little fever of the brow) drawn out for it. Take it in your own hand. The setting out of the lines requires to be followed with the eye, as well as the contents with the mind."

Mr. Jasper, complying, sees and reads as follows: —

ETHELINDA,
Reverential Wife of
MR. THOMAS SAPSEA,
AUCTIONEER, VALUER, ESTATE AGENT, &C.,
OF THIS CITY.
Whose Knowledge of the World,
Though somewhat extensive,
Never brought him acquainted with
A SPIRIT
More capable of
LOOKING UP TO HIM.
STRANGER, PAUSE
And ask thyself the Question,
CANST THOU DO LIKEWISE?
If Not,
WITH A BLUSH RETIRE.

Mr. Sapsea having risen and stationed himself with his back to the fire, for the purpose of observing the effect of these lines on the countenance of a man of taste, consequently has his face towards the door, when his serving-maid, again appearing, announces, "Durdles is come, sir!" He promptly draws forth and fills the third wineglass, as being now claimed, and replies, "Show Durdles in."

"Admirable!" quoth Mr. Jasper, handing back the paper.

"You approve, sir?"

"Impossible not to approve. Striking, characteristic, and complete."

The auctioneer inclines his head, as one accepting his due and giving a receipt, and invites the entering Durdles to take off that glass of wine (handing the same), for it will warm him.

Durdles is a stone-mason · chiefly in the gravestone, tomb, and monument way, and wholly of their color from head to foot. No man is better known in Cloisterham. He is the chartered libertine of the place. Fame trumpets him a wonderful workman, — which for aught that anybody knows, he may be (as he never works); and a wonderful sot, — which everybody knows he is. With the Cathedral crypt he is better acquainted than any living authority; it may even be than any dead one. It is said that the intimacy of this acquaintance began in his habitually resorting to that secret place, to lock out the Cloisterham boy-populace, and sleep off the fumes of liquor, he having ready access to the Cathedral, as contractor for rough repairs. Be this as it may, he does know much about it, and, in the demolition of impedimental fragments of wall, buttress, and pavement, has seen strange sights. He often speaks of himself in the third person; perhaps being a little misty as to his own identity when he narrates; perhaps impartially adopting the Cloisterham nomenclature in reference to a character of acknowledged distinction. Thus he will say, touching his strange sights, "Durdles come upon the old chap," in reference to a buried magnate of ancient time and high degree, "by striking right into the coffin with his pick. The old chap gave Durdles a look with his open eyes, as much as to say, 'Is your name Durdles? Why, my man, I 've been waiting for you a Devil of a time!' And then he turned to powder." With a two-foot rule always in his pocket, and a mason's hammer all but always in his hand, Durdles goes continually sounding and tapping all about and about the Cathedral; and whenever he says to Tope, "Tope, here 's another old 'un in here!" Tope announces it to the Dean as an established discovery.

In a suit of coarse flannel with horn buttons, a yellow neckerchief with draggled ends, an old hat more russet-colored than black, and laced boots of the hue of his stony calling, Durdles leads a hazy, gypsy sort of life, carrying his dinner about with him in a small bundle, and sitting on all manner of tombstones to dine. This dinner of Durdles's has become quite a Cloisterham institution; not only because of his never appearing in public without it, but because of its having been, on certain renowned occasions, taken into custody along with Durdles (as drunk and incapable), and exhibited before the Bench of Justices at the Town Hall. These occasions, however, have been few and far apart, Durdles being as seldom drunk as sober. For the rest, he is an old bachelor, and he lives in a little antiquated hole of a house that was never finished, supposed to be built, so far, of stones stolen from the city wall. To this abode there is an approach, ankle-deep in stone chips, resembling a petrified grove of tombstones, urns, draperies, and broken columns, in all stages of sculpture. Herein, two journeymen incessantly chip, while other two journeymen, who face each other, incessantly saw stone, dipping as regularly in and out of their sheltering sentry-boxes, as if they were mechanical figures emblematical of Time and Death.

To Durdles, when he has consumed his glass of port, Mr. Sapsea intrusts that precious effort of his Muse. Durdles unfeelingly takes out his two-foot rule, and measures the lines calmly, alloying them with stone-grit.

"This is for the monument, is it, Mr Sapsea?"

"The Inscription. Yes." Mr. Sapsea waits for its effect on a common mind.

"It 'll come in to a eighth of a inch," says Durdles. "Your servant, Mr. Jasper. Hope I see you well."

"How are you, Durdles?"

"I 've got a touch of the Tombatism on me, Mr. Jasper, but that I must expect."

"You mean the Rheumatism," says Sapsea, in a sharp tone. (He is nettled by having his composition so mechanically received.)

"No, I don't. I mean, Mr. Sapsea, the Tombatism. It 's another sort from Rheumatism. Mr. Jasper knows what Durdles means. You get among them Tombs afore it 's well light on a winter morning, and keep on, as the Catechism says, a walking in the same all the days of your life, and *you* 'll know what Durdles means."

"It is a bitter cold place," Mr. Jasper assents, with an antipathetic shiver.

"And if it 's bitter cold for you, up in the chancel, with a lot of live breath smoking out about you, what the bitterness is to Durdles, down in the crypt among the earthy damps there, and the dead breath of the old 'uns," returns that individual, "Durdles leaves you to judge. — Is this to be put in hand at once, Mr. Sapsea?"

Mr. Sapsea, with an Author's anxiety to rush into publication, replies that it cannot be out of hand too soon.

"You had better let me have the key, then," says Durdles.

Why, man, it is not to be put inside the monument!"

"Durdles knows where it 's to be put, Mr. Sapsea; no man better. Ask 'ere a man in Cloisterham whether Durdles knows his work."

Mr. Sapsea rises, takes a key from a drawer, unlocks an iron safe let into the wall, and takes from it another key.

"When Durdles puts a touch or a finish upon his work, no matter where, inside or outside, Durdles likes to look at his work all round, and see that his work is a doing him credit," Durdles explains, doggedly.

The key proffered him by the bereaved widower being a large one, he slips his two-foot rule into a side pocket of his flannel trousers made for it, and deliberately opens his flannel coat, and opens the mouth of a large breast-pocket within it before taking the key to place in that repository.

"Why, Durdles!" exclaims Jasper, looking on amused. "You are undermined with pockets!"

"And I carries weight in 'em too, Mr. Jasper. Feel those," producing two other large keys.

"Hand me Mr. Sapsea's likewise. Surely this is the heaviest of the three."

"You 'll find 'em much of a muchness, I expect," says Durdles. "They all belong to monuments. They all open Durdles's work. Durdles keeps the keys of his work mostly. Not that they 're much used."

"By the by," it comes into Jasper's mind to say, as he idly examines the keys, "I have been going to ask you, many a day, and have always forgotten. You know they sometimes call you Stony Durdles, don't you?"

"Cloisterham knows me as Durdles, Mr. Jasper."

"I am aware of that, of course. But the boys sometimes — "

"Oh! If you mind them young Imps of boys — " Durdles gruffly interrupts.

"I don't mind them any more than you do. But there was a discussion the other day among the Choir, whether Stony stood for Tony"; clinking one key against another.

("Take care of the wards, Mr. Jasper.")

"Or whether Stony stood for Stephen"; clinking with a change of keys.

("You can't make a pitch-pipe of 'em, Mr. Jasper.")

"Or whether the name comes from your trade. How stands the fact?"

Mr. Jasper weighs the three keys in his hand, lifts his head from his idly stooping attitude over the fire, and delivers the keys to Durdles with an ingenuous and friendly face.

But the stony one is a gruff one likewise, and that hazy state of his is always an uncertain state, highly conscious of its dignity, and prone to take offence. He drops his two keys back into his pocket one by one, and buttons them up; he takes his dinner-bundle from the chair-back on which he hung it when he came in; he distributes the weight he carries, by tying the third key up in it, as though he were an Ostrich, and liked to dine off cold iron: and he gets out of the room, deigning no word of answer.

Mr. Sapsea then proposes a hit at backgammon, which, seasoned with his own improving conversation, and terminating in a supper of cold roast beef and salad, beguiles the golden evening until pretty late. Mr. Sapsea's wisdom being, in its delivery to mortals, rather of the diffuse than the epigrammatic order, is by no means expended even then; but his visitor intimates that he will come back for more of the precious commodity on future occasions, and Mr. Sapsea lets him off for the present, to ponder on the instalment he carries away.

CHAPTER V.

MR. DURDLES AND FRIEND.

JOHN JASPER, on his way home through the Close, is brought to a standstill by the spectacle of Stony Durdles, dinner-bundle and all, leaning his back against the iron railing of the burial-ground enclosing it from the old cloister-arches; and a hideous small boy in rags flinging stones at him as a well-defined mark in the moonlight. Sometimes the stones hit him, and sometimes they miss him, but Durdles seems indifferent to either fortune. The hideous small boy, on the contrary, whenever he hits Durdles, blows a whistle of triumph through a jagged gap convenient for the purpose, in the front of his mouth, where half his teeth are wanting; and whenever he misses him, yelps out "Mulled agin!" and tries to atone for the failure by taking a more correct and vicious aim.

"What are you doing to the man?" demands Jasper, stepping out into the moonlight from the shade.

"Making a cock-shy of him," replies the hideous small boy.

"Give me those stones in your hand."

"Yes, I 'll give 'em you down your throat, if you come a ketching hold of me," says the small boy, shaking himself loose, and backing. "I 'll smash your eye, if you don't look out!"

"Baby-Devil that you are, what has the man done to you?"

"He won't go home."

"What is that to you?"

"He gives me a 'apenny to pelt him home if I ketches him out too late," says the boy. And then chants, like a little savage, half stumbling and half dancing among the rags and laces of his dilapidated boots.—

"Widdy widdy wen!
I — ket — ches — Im — out — ar — ter — ten,
Widdy widdy wy!
Then — E — don't — go — then — I — shy —
Widdy Widdy Wake-cock warning!"

—with a comprehensive sweep on the last word, and one more delivery at Durdles.

This would seem to be a poetical note of preparation, agreed upon as a caution to Durdles to stand clear if he can, or to betake himself homeward.

John Jasper invites the boy with a beck of his head to follow him (feeling it hopeless to drag him, or coax him) and crosses to the iron railing where the Stony (and stoned) One is profoundly meditating.

"Do you know this thing, this child?" asks Jasper, at a loss for a word that will define this thing.

"Deputy," says Durdles, with a nod.

"Is that its — his — name?"

"Deputy," assents Durdles.

"I 'm man-servant up at the Travellers' Twopenny in Gas Works Garding," this thing explains. "All us man-servants at Travellers Lodgings is named Deputy. When we 're chock full and the Travellers is all a-bed I come out for my 'elth." Then, withdrawing into the road, and taking aim, he resumes, —

"Widdy widdy wen!
I — ket — ches — Im — out — ar — ter — "

"Hold your hand," cries Jasper, "and don't throw while I stand so near him, or I 'll kill you! Come, Durdles; let me walk home with you to-night. Shall I carry your bundle?"

"Not on any account," replies Durdles, adjusting it. "Durdles was making his reflections here when you come up, sir, surrounded by his works, like a poplar Author. — Your own brother-in-law"; introducing a sarcophagus within the railing, white and cold in the moonlight. "Mrs. Sapsea"; introducing the monument of that devoted wife. "Late Incumbent"; introducing the Reverend Gentleman's broken column. "Departed Assessed Taxes"; introducing a vase and towel, standing on what might represent the cake of soap. "Former pastry-cook and muffin-maker, much respected"; introducing gravestone. "All safe and sound here, sir, and all Durdles's work! Of the common folk that is merely bundled up in turf and brambles, the less said, the better. A poor lot, soon forgot."

"This creature, Deputy, is behind us," says Jasper, looking back. "Is he to follow us?"

The relations between Durdles and Deputy are of a capricious kind; for, on Durdles's turning himself about with the slow gravity of beery soddenness, Deputy makes a pretty wide circuit into the road and stands on the defensive.

"You never cried Widdy Warning before you begun to-night," says Durdles, unexpectedly reminded of, or imagining, an injury.

"Yer lie, I did," says Deputy, in his only form of polite contradiction.

"Own brother, sir," observes Durdles, turning himself about again, and as unexpectedly forgetting his offence as he had recalled or conceived it; "own brother to Peter the Wild Boy! But I gave him an object in life."

"At which he takes aim?" Mr. Jasper suggests.

"That 's it, sir," returns Durdles, quite satisfied; "at which he takes aim. I took him in hand and gave him an object. What was he before? A destroyer. What work did he do? Nothing but destruction. What did he earn by it? Short terms in Cloisterham Jail. Not a person, not a piece of property, not a winder, not a horse, nor a dog, nor a cat, nor a bird, nor a fowl, nor a pig, but what he stoned for want of an enlightened object. I put that enlightened object before him, and now he can turn his honest halfpenny by the three penn'orth a week."

"I wonder he has no competitors."

"He has plenty, Mr. Jasper, but he stones 'em all away. Now, I don't know what this scheme of mine comes to," pursues Durdles, considering about it with the same sodden gravity; "I don't know what you may precisely call it. It ain't a sort of a — scheme of a — National Education?"

"I should say not," replies Jasper.

"*I* should say not," assents Durdles; "then we won't try to give it a name."

"He still keeps behind us," repeats Jasper, looking over his shoulder; "is he to follow us?"

"We can't help going round by the Travellers' Twopenny, if we go the short way, which is the back way," Durdles answers, "and we ll drop him there."

So they go on; Deputy, as a rear rank of one, taking open order, and invading the silence of the hour and place by stoning every wall, post, pillar, and other inanimate object, by the deserted way.

"Is there anything new down in the crypt, Durdles?" asks John Jasper.

"Anything old, I think you mean," growls Durdles. "It ain't a spot for novelty."

"Any new discovery on your part, I meant."

"There 's a old 'un under the seventh pillar on the left as you go down the broken steps of the little underground chapel as formerly was, I make him out (so fur as I 've made him out yet) to be one of them old 'uns with a crook. To judge from the size of the passages in the walls, and of the steps and doors, by which they come and went, them crooks must have been a good deal in the way of the old 'uns! Two on 'em meeting promiscuous must have hitched one another by the mitre, pretty often, I should say."

Without any endeavor to correct the literality of this opinion, Jasper surveys his companion — covered from head to foot with old mortar, lime, and stone grit — as though he, Jasper, were getting imbued with a romantic interest in his weird life.

"Yours is a curious existence."

Without furnishing the least clew to the question, whether he receives this as a compliment or as quite the reverse, Durdles gruffly answers, "Yours is another."

"Well! Inasmuch as my lot is cast in the same old earthy, chilly, never-changing place, Yes. But there is much more mystery and interest in your connection with the Cathedral than in mine. Indeed, I am beginning to have some idea of asking you to take me on as a sort of student, or free 'prentice, under you, and to let me go about with you sometimes, and see some of these odd nooks in which you pass your days."

The Stony One replies, in a general way, All right. Everybody knows where to find Durdles when he 's wanted. Which, if not strictly true, is approximately so, if taken to express that Durdles may always be found in a state of vagabondage somewhere.

"What I dwell upon most," says Jasper, pursuing his subject of romantic interest, "is the remarkable accuracy with which you would seem to find out where people are buried. — What is the matter? That buudle is in your way; let me hold it."

Durdles has stopped and backed a little (Deputy, attentive to all his movements, immediately skirmishing into the road), and was looking about for some ledge or corner to place his bundle on, when thus relieved of it.

"Just you give me my hammer out of that," says Durdles," "and I 'll show you."

Clink, clink. And his hammer is handed him.

"Now, lookee here. You pitch your note, don't you, Mr. Jasper?"

"Yes."

"So I sound for mine. I take my hammer, and I tap." (Here he strikes the pavement, and the attentive Deputy skirmishes at a rather wider range, as supposing that his head may be in requisition) "I tap, tap, tap. Solid! I go on tapping. Solid still! Tap again. Holloa! Hollow! Tap again, persevering. Solid in hollow! Tap, tap, tap, to try it better. Solid in hollow; and inside solid, hollow again! There you are! Old 'un crumbled away in stone coffin, in vault!"

"Astonishing!"

"I have even done this," says Durdles, drawing out his two-foot rule (Deputy meanwhile skirmishing nearer, as suspecting that Treasure may be about to be discovered, which may somehow lead to his own enrichment, and the delicious treat of the discoverers being hanged by the neck, on his evidence, until they are dead). "Say that hammer of mine 's a wall — my work. Two; four; and two is six," measuring on the pavement. "Six foot inside that wall is Mrs. Sapsea."

"Not really Mrs. Sapsea?"

"Say Mrs. Sapsea. Her wall 's thicker, but say Mrs. Sapsea. Durdles taps that wall represented by that hammer, and says, after good sounding, 'Something betwixt us?' Sure enough, some rubbish has been left in that same six-foot space by Durdles's men!"

Jasper opines that such accuracy "is a gift."

"I would n't have it at a gift," returns Durdles, by no means receiving the observation in good part. "I worked it out for myself. Durdles comes by *his* knowledge through grubbing deep for it, and having it up by the roots when it don't wan't to come. — Halloa, you Deputy!"

"Widdy!" is Deputy's shrill response, standing off again.

"Catch that ha'penny. And don't let me see any more of you to-night, after we come to the Travellers' Twopenny."

"Warning!" returns Deputy, having caught the halfpenny, and appearing by this mystic word to express his assent to the arrangement.

They have but to cross what was once the vineyard, belonging to what was once the Monastery, to come into the narrow back lane wherein stands the crazy wooden house of two low stories currently known as the Travellers' Twopenny, — a house all warped and distorted, like the morals of the travellers, with scant remains of a latice-work porch over the door, and also of a rustic fence before its stamped-out garden; by reason of the travellers being so bound to the premises by a tender sentiment (or so fond of having a fire by the roadside in the course of the day), that they can never be persuaded or threatened into departure, without violently possessing themselves of some wooden forget-me-not, and bearing it off.

The semblance of an inn is attempted to be given to this wretched place by fragments of conventional red curtaining in the windows, which rags are made muddily transparent in the night-season by feeble lights of rush or cotton dip burning dully in the close air of the inside. As Durdles and Jasper come near, they are addressed by an inscribed paper lantern over the door, setting forth the purport of the house. They are also addressed by some half-dozen other hideous small boys, — whether twopenny lodgers or followers or hangers-on of such, who knows! — who, as if attracted by some carrion-scent of Deputy in the air, start into the moonlight, as vultures might gather in the desert, and instantly fall to stoning him and one another.

"Stop, you young brutes," cries Jasper, angrily, "and let us go by!"

This remonstrance being received with yells and flying stones, according to a custom of late years comfortably established among the police regulations of our English communities, where Christians are stoned on all sides, as if the days of Saint Stephen were revived, Durdles remarks of the young savages, with some point, that "they have n't got an object," and leads the way down the lane.

At the corner of the lane, Jasper, hotly enraged, checks his companion and looks back. All is silent. Next moment, a stone coming rattling at his hat, and a distant yell of "Wake-Cock! Warning!" followed by a crow, as from some infernally hatched Chanticleer, apprising him under whose victorious fire he stands, he turns the corner into safety, and takes Durdles home: Durdles stumbling among the litter of his stony yard as if he were going to turn head foremost into one of the unfinished tombs.

John Jasper returns by another way to his gate house, and, entering softly with his key, finds his fire still burning. He takes from a locked press a peculiar-looking pipe, which he fills, — but not with tobacco, — and, having adjusted the contents of the bowl, very carefully, with a little instrument, ascends an inner staircase of only a few steps, leading to two rooms. One of these is his own sleeping-chamber, the other is his nephew's. There is a light in each.

His nephew lies asleep, calm and untroubled. John Jasper stands looking down upon him, his unlighted pipe in his hand, for some time, with a fixed and deep attention. Then, hushing his footsteps, he passes to his own room, lights his pipe, and delivers himself to the Spectres it invokes at midnight.

CHAPTER VI.

PHILANTHROPY IN MINOR CANON CORNER.

THE Reverend Septimus Crisparkle (Septimus, because six little brother Crisparkles before him went out, one by one, as they were born, like six weak little rushlights, as they were lighted) having broken the thin morning ice near Cloisterham Weir with his amiable head, much to the invigoration of his frame, was now assisting his circulation by boxing at a looking-glass with great science and prowess. A fresh and healthy portrait the looking-glass presented of the Reverend Septimus, feinting and dodging with the utmost artfulness, and hitting out from the shoulder with the utmost straightness, while his radiant features teemed with innocence, and soft-hearted benevolence beamed from his boxing-gloves.

It was scarcely breakfast-time yet, for Mrs. Crisparkle — mother, not wife, of the Reverend Septimus — was only just down, and waiting for the urn. Indeed, the Reverend Septimus left off at this very moment to take the pretty old lady's entering face between his boxing-gloves and kiss it. Having done so with tenderness, the Reverend Septimus turned to again, countering with his left, and putting in his right, in a tremendous manner.

"I say, every morning of my life, that you 'll do it at last, Sept," remarked the old lady, looking on; "and so you will."

"Do what, Ma dear?"

"Break the pier-glass, or burst a bloodvessel."

"Neither, please God, Ma dear. Here 's wind, Ma. Look at this!"

In a concluding round of great severity, the Reverend Septimus administered and escaped all sorts of punishment, and wound up by getting the old lady's cap into Chancery — such is the technical term used in scientific circles by the learned in the Noble Art — with a lightness of touch that hardly stirred the lightest lavender or cherry riband on it. Magnanimously releasing the defeated, just in time to get his gloves into a drawer, and feign to be looking out of window in a contemplative state of mind when a servant entered, the Reverend Septimus then gave place to the urn and other preparations for breakfast. These completed, and the two alone again, it was pleasant to see (or would have been, if there had been any one to see it, which there never was) the old lady standing to say the Lord's Prayer aloud, and her son, Minor Canon nevertheless, standing with head bent to hear it, he being within five years of forty: much as he had stood to hear the same words from the same lips when he was within five months of four.

What is prettier than an old lady — except a young lady — when her eyes are bright, when her figure is trim and compact, when her face is cheerful and calm, when her dress is as the dress of a china shepherdess: so dainty in its colors, so individually assorted to herself, so neatly moulded on her? Nothing is prettier, thought the good Minor Canon frequently, when taking his seat at table opposite his long-widowed mother. Her thought at such times may be condensed into the two words that oftenest did duty together in all her conversations: "My Sept!"

They were a good pair to sit breakfasting together in Minor Canon Corner, Cloisterham. For Minor Canon Corner was a quiet place in the shadow of the Cathedral, which the cawing of the rooks, the echoing footsteps of rare passers, the sound of the Cathedral bell, or the roll of the Cathedral organ, seemed to render more quiet than absolute silence. Swaggering fighting men had had their centuries of ramping and raving about Minor Canon Corner, and beaten serfs had had their centuries of drudging and dying there, and powerful monks had had their centuries of being sometimes useful and sometimes harmful there, and behold they were all gone out of Minor Canon Corner, and so much the better. Perhaps one of the highest uses of their ever having been there, was, that there might be left behind that blessed air of tranquillity which pervaded Minor Canon Corner, and that serenely romantic state of the mind — productive for the most part of pity and forbearance — which is engendered by a sorrowful story that is all told, or a pathetic play that is played out.

Red-brick walls harmoniously toned down in color by time, strong-rooted ivy, latticed windows, panelled rooms, big oaken beams in little places, and stone-walled gardens where annual fruit yet ripened upon monkish trees, were the principal surroundings of pretty old Mrs. Crisparkle and the Reverend Septimus as they sat at breakfast.

"And what, Ma dear," inquired the Minor Canon, giving proof of a wholesome and vigorous appetite, "does the letter say?"

The pretty old lady, after reading it, had just laid it down upon the breakfast-cloth. She handed it over to her son.

Now the old lady was exceedingly proud of her bright eyes being so clear that she could read writing without spectacles. Her son was also so proud of the circumstance, and so dutifully bent on her deriving the utmost possible gratification from it, that he had invented the pretence that he himself could *not* read writing without spectacles. Therefore he now assumed a pair, of grave and prodigious proportions, which not only seriously inconvenienced his nose and his breakfast, but seriously impeded his perusal of the letter. For he had the eyes of a microscope and a telescope combined, when they were unassisted.

"It's from Mr. Honeythunder, of course," said the old lady, folding her arms.

"Of course," assented her son. He then lamely read on: —

"Haven of Philanthropy, Chief Offices, London, Wednesday.

'Dear Madam, —

"'I write in the —' In the what's this? What does he write in?"

"In the chair," said the old lady.

The Reverend Septimus took off his spectacles, that he might see her face, as he exclaimed, —

"Why, what should he write in?"

"Bless me, bless me, Sept," returned the old lady, "you don't see the context! Give it back to me, my dear."

Glad to get his spectacles off (for they always made his eyes water), her son obeyed, murmuring that his sight for reading manuscript got worse and worse daily.

"'I write,'" his mother went on, reading very perspicuously and precisely, "'from the chair, to which I shall probably be confined for some hours.'"

Septimus looked at the row of chairs against the wall, with a half-protesting and half-appealing countenance.

"'We have,'" the old lady read on with a little extra emphasis, "'a meeting of our Convened Chief Composite Committee of Central and District Philanthropists, at our Head Haven as above; and it is their unanimous pleasure that I take the chair.'"

Septimus breathed more freely, and muttered, "Oh! If he comes to *that*, let him."

"'Not to lose a day's post, I take the opportunity of a long report being read, denouncing a public miscreant —'"

"It is a most extraordinary thing," interposed the gentle Minor Canon, laying down his knife and fork to rub his ear in a vexed manner, "that these Philanthropists are always denouncing somebody. And it is another most extraordinary thing that they are always so violently flush of miscreants!"

"'Denouncing a public miscreant!'" — the old lady resumed, "'to get our little affair of business off my mind. I have spoken with my two wards, Neville and Helena Landless, on the subject of their defective education, and they give in to the plan proposed; as I should have taken good care they did, whether they liked it or not.'"

"And it is another most extraordinary thing," remarked the Minor Canon in the same tone as before, "that these Philanthropists are so given to seizing their fellow-creatures by the scruff of the neck, and (as one may say) bumping them into the paths of peace. — I beg your pardon, Ma dear, for interrupting."

"'Therefore, dear Madam, you will please prepare your son, the Rev. Mr. Septimus, to expect Neville, as an inmate to be read with, on Monday next. On the same day Helena will accompany him to Cloisterham, to take up her quarters at the Nuns' House, the establishment recommended by yourself and son jointly. Please likewise to prepare for her reception and tuition there. The terms in both cases are understood to be exactly as stated to me in writing by yourself, when I opened a correspondence with you on this subject, after the honor of being introduced to you at your sister's house in town here. With compliments to the Rev. Mr. Septimus, I am, Dear Madam, Your affectionate brother (In Philanthropy),

"'LUKE HONEYTHUNDER.'"

"Well, Ma," said Septimus, after a little more rubbing of his ear, "we must try it. There can be no doubt that we have room for an inmate, and that I have time to bestow upon him, and inclination too. I must confess to feeling rather glad that he is not Mr. Honeythunder himself. Though that seems wretchedly prejudiced — does it not? — for I never saw him. Is he a large man, Ma?"

"I should call him a large man, my dear," the old lady replied, after some hesitation, "but that his voice is so much larger."

"Than himself?"

"Than anybody."

"Hah!" said Septimus. And finished his breakfast as if the flavor of the Superior Family Souchong, and also of the ham and toast and eggs, were a little on the wane.

Mrs. Crisparkle's sister, another piece of Dresden china, and matching her so neatly that they would have made a delightful pair of ornaments for the two ends of any capacious old-fashioned chimney-piece, and by right should never have been seen apart, was the childless wife of a clergyman holding Corporation preferment in London City. Mr. Honeythunder, in his public character of Professor of Philanthropy, had come to know Mrs. Crisparkle during the last rematching of the china ornaments (in other words, during her last annual visit to her sister), after a public occasion of a philanthropic nature, when certain devoted orphans of tender years had been glutted with plum buns, and plump bumptiousness. These were all the antecedents known in Minor Canon Corner of the coming pupils.

"I am sure you will agree with me, Ma," said Mr. Crisparkle, after thinking the matter over, "that the first thing to be done, is, to put these young people as much at their ease as possible. There is nothing disinterested in the notion, because we cannot be at our ease with them unless they are at their ease with us. Now Jasper's nephew is down here at present; and like takes to like, and youth takes to youth. He is a cordial young fellow, and we will have him to meet the brother and sister at dinner. That 's three. We can't think of asking him, without asking Jasper. That 's four. Add Miss Twinkleton and the fairy bride that is to be, and that 's six. Add our two selves, and that 's eight. Would eight at a friendly dinner at all put you out, Ma?"

"Nine would, Sept," returned the old lady, visibly nervous.

"My dear Ma, I particularize eight."

"The exact size of the table and the room, my dear."

So it was settled that way; and when Mr. Crisparkle called with his mother upon Miss Twinkleton, to arrange for the reception of Miss Helena Landless at the Nuns' House, the two other invitations having reference to that establishment were proffered and accepted. Miss Twinkleton did, indeed, glance at the globes, as regretting that they were not formed to be taken out into society; but became reconciled to leaving them behind. Instructions were then despatched to the Philanthropist for the departure and arrival, in good time for dinner, of Mr. Neville and Miss Helena; and stock for soup became fragrant in the air of Minor Canon Corner.

In those days there was no railway to Cloisterham, and Mr. Sapsea said there never would be. Mr. Sapsea said more; he said there never should be. And yet, marvellous to consider, it has come to pass, in these days, that Express Trains don't think Cloisterham worth stopping at, but yell and whirl through it on their larger errands, casting the dust off their wheels as a testimony against its insignificance. Some remote fragment of Main Line to somewhere else, there was, which was going to ruin the Money Market if it failed, and Church and State if it succeeded, and (of course) the Constitution, whether or no; but even that had already so unsettled Cloisterham traffic, that the traffic, deserting the high-road, came sneaking in from an unprecedented part of the country by a back stable-way, for many years labelled at the corner: "Beware of the Dog."

To this ignominious avenue of approach, Mr. Crisparkle repaired, awaiting the arrival of a short squat omnibus, with a disproportionate heap of luggage on the roof, — like a little Elephant with infinitely too much Castle, — which was then the daily service between Cloisterham and external mankind. As this vehicle lumbered up, Mr. Crisparkle could hardly see anything else of it for a large outside passenger seated on the box, with his elbows squared, and his hands on his knees, compressing the driver into a most uncomfortably small compass, and glowering about him with a strongly marked face.

"Is this Cloisterham?" demanded the passenger, in a tremendous voice.

"It is," replied the driver, rubbing himself as if he ached, after throwing the reins to the ostler. "And I never was so glad to see it."

"Tell your master to make his box-seat wider then," returned the passenger. "Your master is morally bound — and ought to be legally, under ruinous penalties — to provide for the comfort of his fellow-man."

The driver instituted, with the palms of his hands, a superficial perquisition into the state of his skeleton; which seemed to make him anxious.

"Have I sat upon you?" asked the passenger.

"You have," said the driver, as if he did n't like it at all.

"Take that card, my friend."

"I think I won't deprive you on it," returned the driver, casting his eyes over it with no great favor, without taking it. "What 's the good of it to me?"

"Be a Member of that Society," said the passenger.

"What shall I get by it?" asked the driver.

"Brotherhood," returned the passenger, in a ferocious voice.

"Thankee," said the driver, very deliberately, as he got down; "my mother was contented with myself, and so am I. I don't want no brothers."

"But you must have them," replied the passenger, also descending, "whether you like it or not. I am your brother"

"I say!" expostulated the driver, becoming more chafed in temper; "not too fur! The worm *will*, when — "

But here Mr. Crisparkle interposed, remonstrating aside, in a friendly voice, "Joe, Joe, Joe! Don't forget yourself, Joe, my good fellow!" and then, when Joe peaceably touched his hat, accosting the passenger with, "Mr. Honeythunder?"

"That is my name, sir."

"My name is Crisparkle."

"Reverend Mr. Septimus? Glad to see you, sir. Neville and Helena are inside. Having a little succumbed of late, under the pressure of my public labors, I thought I would take a mouthful of fresh air, and come down with them, and return at night So you are the Reverend Mr. Septimus, are you?" surveying him on the whole with disappointment, and twisting a double eye-glass by its riband, as if he were roasting it; but not otherwise using it. "Hah! I expected to see you older, sir."

"I hope you will," was the good-humored reply.

"Eh?" demanded Mr. Honeythunder.

"Only a poor little joke. Not worth repeating."

"Joke? Ay; I never see a joke," Mr. Honeythunder frowningly retorted. "A joke is wasted upon me, sir. Where are they? Helena and Neville, come here! Mr. Crisparkle has come down to meet you."

An unusually handsome lithe young fellow, and an unusually handsome lithe girl; much alike; both very dark, and very rich in color; she of almost the gypsy type; something untamed about them both; a certain air upon them of hunter and huntress; yet withal a certain air of being the objects of the chase, rather than the followers. Slender, supple, quick of eye and limb; half shy, half defiant; fierce of look; an indefinable kind of pause coming and going on their whole expression, both of face and form, which might be equally likened to the pause before a crouch, or a bound. The rough mental notes made in the first five minutes by Mr. Crisparkle would have read thus, *verbatim*.

He invited Mr. Honeythunder to dinner, with a troubled mind (for the discomfiture of the dear old china shepherdess lay heavy on it), and gave his arm to Helena Landless. Both she and her brother, as they walked all together through the ancient streets, took great delight in what he pointed out of the Cathedral and the Monastery-ruin, and wondered — so his notes ran on — much as if they were beautiful barbaric captives brought from some wild tropical dominion. Mr. Honeythunder walked in the middle of the road, shouldering the natives out of his way, and loudly developing a scheme he had, for making a raid on all the unemployed persons in the United Kingdom, laying them every one by the heels in jail, and forcing them, on the pain of prompt extermination, to become philanthropists.

Mrs. Crisparkle had need of her own share of philanthropy when she beheld this very large and very loud excrescence on the little party. Always something in the nature of a Boil upon the face of society, Mr. Honeythunder expanded into an inflammatory Wen in Minor Canon Corner. Though it was not literally true, as was facetiously charged against him by public unbelievers, that he called aloud to his fellow-creatures, "Curse your souls and bodies, come here and be blessed!" still his philanthropy was of that gunpowderous sort that the difference between it and animosity was hard to determine. You were to abolish military force, but you were first to bring all commanding officers who had done their duty, to trial by court-martial for that offence, and shoot them. You were to abolish war, but were to make converts by making war upon them, and charging them with loving war as the apple of their eye. You were to have no capital punishment, but were first to sweep off the face of the earth all legislators, jurists, and judges who were of the contrary opinion. You were to have universal concord, and were to get it by eliminating all the people who would n't or conscientiously could n't, be concordant. You were to love your brother as yourself, but after an indefinite interval of maligning him (very much as if you hated him), and calling him all manner of names. Above all things, you were to do nothing in private, or on your own account. You were to go to the offices of the Haven of Philanthropy, and put your name down as a Member and a Professing Philanthropist. Then you were to pay up your subscription, get your card of membership and your riband and medal, and were evermore to live upon a platform, and evermore to say what Mr. Honeythunder said, and what the Treasurer said, and what the sub-Treasurer said, and what the Committee said, and what the sub-Committee said, and what the Secretary said, and what the Vice-Secretary said. And this was usually said in the unanimously carried resolution under hand and seal, to the effect: "That this assembled Body of Professing Philanthropists views, with indignant scorn and contempt, not unmixed with utter detestation and loathing abhorrence," — in short, the baseness of all those who do not belong to it, and pledges itself to make as many obnoxious statements as possible about them, without being at all particular as to facts.

The dinner was a most doleful breakdown. The philanthropist deranged the symmetry of the table, sat himself in the way of the waiting, blocked up the thoroughfare, and drove Mr. Tope (who assisted the parlor-maid) to the verge of distraction by passing plates and dishes on, over his own head. Nobody could talk to anybody, because he held forth to everybody at once, as if the company had no individual existence, but were a Meeting. He impounded the Reverend Mr. Septimus, as an official personage to be addressed, or kind of human peg to hang his oratorical hat on, and fell into the exasperating habit, common among such orators, of impersonating him as a wicked and weak opponent. Thus, he would ask, "And will you, sir, now stultify yourself by telling me" — and so forth, when the innocent man had not opened his lips, nor meant to open them. Or he would say, "Now see, sir, to what a position you are reduced. I will leave you no escape. After exhausting all the resources of fraud and falsehood, during years upon years; after exhibiting a combination of dastardly meanness with ensanguined daring, such as the world has not often witnessed; you have now the hypocrisy to bend the knee before the most degraded of mankind, and to sue and whine and howl for mercy!" Whereat the unfortunate Minor Canon would look, in part indignant and in part perplexed: while his worthy mother sat bridling, with tears in her eyes, and the remainder of the party lapsed into a sort of gelatinous state, in which there was no flavor or solidity, and very little resistance.

But the gush of philanthropy that burst forth when the departure of Mr. Honeythunder began to impend must have been highly gratifying to the feelings of that distinguished man. His coffee was produced, by the special activity of Mr. Tope, a full hour before he wanted it. Mr. Crisparkle sat with his watch in his hand, for about the same period, lest he should overstay his time. The four young people were unanimous in believing that the Cathedral clock struck three quarters, when it actually struck but one. Miss Twinkleton estimated the distance to the omnibus at five-and-twenty minutes' walk, when it was really five. The affectionate kindness of the whole circle hustled him into his great-coat, and shoved him out into the moonlight, as if he were a fugitive traitor with whom they sympathized, and a troop of horse were at the back door Mr. Crisparkle and his new charge, who took him to the omnibus, were so fervent in their apprehensions of his catching cold, that they shut him up in it instantly and left him, with still half an hour to spare.

CHAPTER VII.

MORE CONFIDENCES THAN ONE.

"I KNOW very little of that gentleman, sir," said Neville to the Minor Canon as they turned back.

"You know very little of your guardian?" the Minor Canon repeated.

"Almost nothing."

"How came he —"

"To *be* my guardian? I'll tell you, sir. I suppose you know that we come (my sister and I) from Ceylon?"

"Indeed, no."

"I wonder at that. We lived with a stepfather there. Our mother died there, when we were little children. We have had a wretched existence. She made him our guardian, and he was a miserly wretch who grudged us food to eat, and clothes to wear. At his death, he passed us over to this man; for no better reason that I know of, than his being a friend or connection of his, whose name was always in print and catching his attention."

"That was lately, I suppose?"

"Quite lately, sir. This stepfather of ours was a cruel brute as well as a grinding one. It was well he died when he did, or I might have killed him."

Mr. Crisparkle stopped short in the moonlight and looked at his hopeful pupil in consternation.

"I surprise you, sir?" he said, with a quick change to a submissive manner.

"You shock me; unspeakably shock me."

The pupil hung his head for a little while, as they walked on, and then said, "You never saw him beat your sister. I have seen him beat mine, more than once or twice, and I never forgot it."

"Nothing," said Mr. Crisparkle, "not even a beloved and beautiful sister's tears under dastardly ill-usage," he became less severe, in spite of himself, as his indignation rose, "could justify those horrible expressions that you used."

"I am sorry I used them, and especially to you, sir. I beg to recall them. But permit me to set you right on one point. You spoke of my sister's tears. My sister would have let him tear her to pieces, before she would have let him believe that he could make her shed a tear."

Mr. Crisparkle reviewed those mental notes of his, and was neither at all surprised to hear it, nor at all disposed to question it.

"Perhaps you will think it strange, sir," — this was said in a hesitating voice, — "that I should so soon ask you to allow me to confide in you, and to have the kindness to hear a word or two from me in my defence?"

"Defence?" Mr. Crisparkle repeated. "You are not on your defence, Mr. Neville."

"I think I am, sir. At least I know I should be, if you were better acquainted with my character."

"Well, Mr. Neville," was the rejoinder. "What if you leave me to find it out?"

"Since it is your pleasure, sir," answered the young man, with a quick change in his manner to sullen disappointment, — "since it is your pleasure to check me in my impulse, I must submit."

There was that in the tone of this short speech which made the conscientious man to whom it was addressed uneasy. It hinted to him that he might, without meaning it, turn aside a trustfulness beneficial to a misshapen young mind and perhaps to his own power of directing and improving it. They were within sight of the lights in his windows, and he stopped.

"Let us turn back and take a turn or two up and down, Mr. Neville, or you may not have time to finish what you wish to say to me. You are hasty in thinking that I mean to check you. Quite the contrary. I invite your confidence."

"You have invited it, sir, without knowing it, ever since I came here. I say 'ever since,' as if I had been here a week! The truth is, we came here (my sister and I) to quarrel with you, and affront you, and break away again."

"Really?" said Mr. Crisparkle, at a dead loss for anything else to say.

"You see, we could not know what you were beforehand, sir; could we?"

"Clearly not," said Mr. Crisparkle.

"And having liked no one else with whom we have ever been brought into contact, we had made up our minds not to like you."

"Really?" said Mr. Crisparkle again.

"But we do like you, sir, and we see an unmistakable difference between your house and your reception of us, and anything else we have ever known. This, — and my happening to be alone with you, — and everything around us seeming so quiet and peaceful after Mr. Honeythunder's departure, — and Cloisterham being so old and grave and beautiful, with the moon shining on it, — these things inclined me to open my heart."

"I quite understand, Mr. Neville. And it is salutary to listen to such influences."

"In describing my own imperfections, sir, I must ask you not to suppose that I am describing my sister's. She has come out of the disadvantages of our miserable life as much better than I am as that Cathedral tower is higher than those chimneys."

Mr. Crisparkle in his own breast was not so sure of this.

"I have had, sir, from my earliest remembrance, to suppress a deadly and bitter hatred. This has made me secret and revengeful. I have been always tyrannically held down by the strong hand. This has driven me, in my weakness, to the resource of being false and mean. I have been stinted of education, liberty, money, dress, the very necessaries of life, the commonest pleasures of childhood, the commonest possessions of youth. This has caused me to be utterly wanting in I don't know what emotions, or remembrances, or good instincts, — I have not even a name for the thing, you see! — that you have had to work upon in other young men to whom you have been accustomed."

"This is evidently true. But this is not encouraging," thought Mr. Crisparkle as they turned again.

"And to finish with, sir: I have been brought up among abject and servile dependants, of an inferior race, and I may easily have contracted some affinity with them. Sometimes, I don't know but that it may be a drop of what is tigerish in their blood."

"As in the case of that remark just now," thought Mr. Crisparkle.

"In a last word of reference to my sister, sir (we are twin children), you ought to know, to her honor, that nothing in our misery ever subdued her, though it often cowed me. When we ran away from it (we ran away four times in six years, to be soon brought back and cruelly punished), the flight was always of her planning and leading. Each time she dressed as a boy, and showed the daring of a man. I take it we were seven years old when we first decamped; but I remember, when I lost the pocket-knife with which she was to have cut her hair short, how desperately she tried to tear it out, or bite it off. I have nothing further to say, sir, except that I hope you will bear with me and make allowance for me."

"Of that, Mr. Neville, you may be sure," returned the Minor Canon. "I don't preach more than I can help, and I will not repay your confidence with a sermon. But I entreat you to bear in mind, very seriously and steadily, that if I am to do you any good, it can only be with your own assistance; and that you can only render that, efficiently, by seeking aid from Heaven."

"I will try to do my part, sir."

"And, Mr. Neville, I will try to do mine. Here is my hand on it. May God bless our endeavors!"

They were now standing at his house-door, and a cheerful sound of voices and laughter was heard within.

"We will take one more turn before going in," said Mr. Crisparkle, "for I want to ask you a question. When you said you were in a changed mind concerning me, you spoke, not only for yourself, but for your sister too."

"Undoubtedly I did, sir."

"Excuse me, Mr. Neville, but I think you have had no opportunity of communicating with your sister since I met you. Mr. Honeythunder was very eloquent; but perhaps I may venture to say, without ill-nature, that he rather monopolized the occasion. May you not have answered for your sister without sufficient warrant?"

Neville shook his head with a proud smile.

"You don't know, sir, yet, what a complete understanding can exist between my sister and me, though no spoken word — perhaps hardly as much as a look — may have passed between us. She not only feels as I have described, but she very well knows that I am taking this opportunity of speaking to you, both for her and for myself."

Mr. Crisparkle looked in his face, with some incredulity; but his face expressed such absolute and firm conviction of the truth of what he said, that Mr. Crisparkle looked at the pavement, and mused, until they came to his door again.

"I will ask for one more turn, sir, this time," said the young man with a rather heightened color rising in his face. "But for Mr. Honeythunder's — I think you called it eloquence, sir ?" (somewhat slyly.)

"I — yes, I called it eloquence," said Mr. Crisparkle.

"But for Mr. Honeythunder's eloquence, I might have had no need to ask you what I am going to ask you. This Mr. Edwin Drood, sir : I think that 's the name ?"

"Quite correct," said Mr. Crisparkle. "D-r-double o-d."

"Does he — or did he — read with you, sir ?"

"Never, Mr. Neville. He comes here visiting his relation, Mr. Jasper."

"Is Miss Bud his relation too, sir ?"

("Now, why should he ask that, with sudden superciliousness!" thought Mr. Crisparkle.) Then he explained, aloud, what he knew of the little story of their betrothal.

"Oh! *That* 's it, is it?" said the young man. "I understand his air of proprietorship now!"

This was said so evidently to himself, or to anybody rather than Mr. Crisparkle, that the latter instinctively felt as if to notice it would be almost tantamount to noticing a passage in a letter which he had read by chance over the writer's shoulder. A moment afterwards they re-entered the house.

Mr. Jasper was seated at the piano as they came into his drawing-room, and was accompanying Miss Rosebud while she sang. It was a consequence of his playing the accompaniment without notes, and of her being a heedless little creature very apt to go wrong, that he followed her lips most attentively, with his eyes as well as hands; carefully and softly hinting the key-note from time to time. Standing with an arm drawn round her, but with a face far more intent on Mr. Jasper than on her singing, stood Helena, between whom and her brother an instantaneous recognition passed, in which Mr. Crisparkle saw, or thought he saw, the understanding that had been spoken of flash out. Mr. Neville then took his admiring station, leaning against the piano, opposite the singer; Mr. Crisparkle sat down by the china shepherdess; Edwin Drood gallantly furled and unfurled Miss Twinkleton's fan; and that lady passively claimed that sort of exhibitor's proprietorship in the accomplishment on view, which Mr. Tope, the Verger, daily claimed in the Cathedral service.

The song went on. It was a sorrowful strain of parting, and the fresh young voice was very plaintive and tender. As Jasper watched the pretty lips, and ever and again hinted the one note, as though it were a low whisper from himself, the voice became less steady, until all at once the singer broke into a burst of tears, and shrieked out, with her hands over her eyes, "I can't bear this! I am frightened! Take me away!"

With one swift turn of her lithe figure, Helena laid the little beauty on a sofa, as if she had never caught her up. Then, on one knee beside her, and with one hand upon her rosy mouth, while with the other she appealed to all the rest, Helena said to them, "It 's nothing; it 's all over; don't speak to her for one minute, and she is well!"

Jasper's hands had, in the same instant, lifted themselves from the keys, and were now poised above them, as though he waited to resume. In that attitude he yet sat quiet: not even looking round, when all the rest had changed their places and were reassuring one another.

"Pussy 's not used to an audience; that 's the fact," said Edwin Drood. "She got nervous, and could n't hold out. Besides, Jack, you are such a conscientious master, and require so much, that I believe you make her afraid of you. No wonder."

"No wonder," repeated Helena.

"There, Jack, you hear! You would be afraid of him, under similar circumstances, would n't you, Miss Landless?"

"Not under any circumstances," returned Helena.

Jasper brought down his hands, looked over his shoulder, and begged to thank Miss Landless for her vindication of his character. Then he fell to dumbly playing, without striking the notes, while his little pupil was taken to an open window for air, and was otherwise petted and restored. When she was brought back, his place was empty. "Jack's gone, Pussy," Edwin told her. "I am more than half afraid he did n't like to be charged with being the Monster who had frightened you." But she answered never a word, and shivered, as if they had made her a little too cold.

Miss Twinkleton now opining that indeed these were late hours, Mrs. Crisparkle, for finding ourselves outside the walls of the Nuns' House, and that we who undertook the formation of the future wives and mothers of England (the last words in a lower voice, as requiring to be communicated in confidence) were really bound (voice coming up again) to set a better example than one of rakish habits, wrappers were put in requisition, and the two young cavaliers volunteered to see the ladies home. It was soon done, and the gate of the Nuns' House closed upon them.

The boarders had retired, and only Mrs. Tisher in solitary vigil awaited the new pupil. Her bedroom being within Rosa's, very little introduction or explanation was necessary, before she was placed in charge of her new friend, and left for the night.

"This is a blessed relief, my dear," said Helena. "I have been dreading all day, that I should be brought to bay at this time."

"There are not many of us," returned Rosa, "and we are good-natured girls; at least the others are; I can answer for them."

"I can answer for you," laughed Helena, searching the lovely little face with her dark fiery eyes, and tenderly caressing the small figure. "You will be a friend to me, won't you?"

"I hope so. But the idea of my being a friend to you seems too absurd, though."

"Why?"

"Oh! I am such a mite of a thing, and you are so womanly and handsome. You seem to have resolution and power enough to crush me. I shrink into nothing by the side of your presence even."

"I am a neglected creature, my dear, unacquainted with all accomplishments, sensitively conscious that I have everything to learn, and deeply ashamed to own my ignorance."

"And yet you acknowledge everything to me!" said Rosa.

"My pretty one, can I help it? There is a fascination in you."

"Oh! Is there, though?" pouted Rosa, half in jest and half in earnest. "What a pity Master Eddy does n't feel it more!"

Of course her relations towards that young gentleman had been already imparted, in Minor Canon Corner.

"Why, surely he must love you with all his heart!" cried Helena, with an earnestness that threatened to blaze into ferocity if he did n't.

"Eh? O, well, I suppose he does," said Rosa, pouting again; "I am sure I have no right to say he does n't. Perhaps it's my fault. Perhaps I am not as nice to him as I ought to be. I don't think I am. But it *is* so ridiculous!"

Helena's eyes demanded what was.

"*We* are," said Rosa, answering as if she had spoken. "We are such a ridiculous couple. And we are always quarrelling."

"Why?"

"Because we both know we are ridiculous, my dear!" Rosa gave that answer as if it were the most conclusive answer in the world.

Helena's masterful look was intent upon her face for a few moments, and then she impulsively put out both her hands and said, —

"You will be my friend and help me?"

"Indeed, my dear, I will," replied Rosa, in a tone of affectionate childishness that went straight and true to her heart; "I will be as good a friend as such a mite of a thing can be to such a noble creature as you. And be a friend to me, please; for I don't understand myself; and I want a friend who can understand me, very much indeed."

Helena Landless kissed her, and, retaining both her hands, said, —

"Who is Mr. Jasper?"

Rosa turned aside her head in answering, "Eddy's uncle, and my music-master."

"You do not love him?"

"Ugh!" She put her hands up to her face, and shook with fear or horror.

"You know that he loves you?"

"O, don't, don't, don't!" cried Rosa, dropping on her knees, and clinging to her new resource. "Don't tell me of it! He terrifies me. He haunts my thoughts, like a dreadful ghost. I feel that I am never safe from him. I feel as if he could pass in through the wall when he is spoken of." She actually did look round, as if she dreaded to see him standing in the shadow behind her.

"Try to tell me more about it, darling."

"Yes, I will, I will. Because you are so strong. But hold me the while, and stay with me afterwards."

"My child! You speak as if he had threatened you in some dark way."

"He has never spoken to me about — that. Never."

"What has he done?"

"He has made a slave of me with his looks. He has forced me to understand him, without his saying a word; and he has forced me to keep silence, without his uttering a threat. When I play, he never moves his eyes from my hands. When I sing, he never moves his eyes from my lips. When he corrects me, and strikes a note, or a chord, or plays a passage, he himself is in the sounds, whispering that he pursues me as a lover, and commanding me to keep his secret. I avoid his eyes, but he forces me to see them without looking at them. Even when a glaze comes over them (which is sometimes the case), and he seems to wander away into a frightful sort of dream, in which he threatens most, he obliges me to know it, and to know that he is sitting close at my side, more terrible to me then than ever."

"What is this imagined threatening, pretty one? What is threatened?"

"I don't know. I have never even dared to think or wonder what it is."

"And was this all, to-night?"

"This was all; except that to-night when he watched my lips so closely as I was singing, besides feeling terrified, I felt ashamed and passionately hurt. It was as if he kissed me, and I could n't bear it, but cried out. You must never breathe this to any one. Eddy is devoted to him. But you said to-night that you would not be afraid of him, under any circumstances, and that gives me — who am so much afraid of him — courage to tell only you. Hold me! Stay with me! I am too frightened to be left by myself."

The lustrous gypsy-face drooped over the clinging arms and bosom, and the wild black hair fell down protectingly over the childish form. There was a slumbering gleam of fire in the intense dark eyes, though they were then softened with compassion and admiration. Let whomsoever it most concerned look well to it.

CHAPTER VIII.

DAGGERS DRAWN.

THE two young men, having seen the damsels, their charges, enter the courtyard of the Nuns' House, and finding themselves coldly stared at by the brazen door-plate, as if the battered old beau with the glass in his eye were insolent, look at one another, look along the perspective of the moonlit street, and slowly walk away together.

"Do you stay here long, Mr. Drood?" says Neville.

"Not this time," is the careless answer. "I leave for London again to-morrow. But I shall be here, off and on, until next Midsummer; then I shall take my leave of Cloisterham, and England too; for many a long day, I expect."

"Are you going abroad?"

"Going to wake up Egypt a little," is the condescending answer.

"Are you reading?"

"Reading!" repeats Edwin Drood, with a touch of contempt. "No. Doing, working, engineering. My small patrimony was left a part of the capital of the Firm I am with, by my father, a former partner; and I am a charge upon the Firm until I come of age; and then I step into my modest share in the concern. Jack — you met him at dinner — is, until then, my guardian and trustee."

"I heard from Mr. Crisparkle of your other good fortune."

"What do you mean by my other good fortune?"

Neville has made his remark in a watchfully advancing, and yet furtive and shy manner, very expressive of that peculiar air already noticed, of being at once hunter and hunted. Edwin has made his retort with an abruptness not at all polite. They stop and interchange a rather heated look.

"I hope," says Neville, "there is no offence, Mr. Drood, in my innocently referring to your betrothal?"

"By George!" cries Edwin, leading on again at a somewhat quicker pace. "Everybody in this chattering old Cloisterham refers to it. I wonder no public-house has been set up, with my portrait for the sign of the Betrothed's Head. Or Pussy's portrait. One or the other."

"I am not accountable for Mr. Crisparkle's mentioning the matter to me, quite openly," Neville begins.

"No; that 's true; you are not," Edwin Drood assents.

"But," resumes Neville, "I am accountable for mentioning it to you. And I did so, on the supposition that you could not fail to be highly proud of it."

Now, there are these two curious touches of human nature working the secret springs of this dialogue. Neville Landless is already enough impressed by little Rosebud to feel indignant that Edwin Drood (far below her) should hold his prize so lightly. Edwin Drood is already enough impressed by Helena, to feel indignant that Helena's brother (far below her) should dispose of him so coolly, and put him out of the way so entirely.

However, the last remark had better be answered. So, says Edwin, —

"I don't know, Mr. Neville" (adopting that mode of address from Mr. Crisparkle), "that what people are proudest of they usually talk most about; I don't know either, that what they are proudest of they most like other people to talk about. But I live a busy life, and I speak under correction by you readers, who ought to know everything, and I dare say do."

By this time they have both become savage: Mr. Neville out in the open;

Edwin Drood under the transparent cover of a popular tune, and a stop now and then to pretend to admire picturesque effects in the moonlight before him.

"It does not seem to me very civil in you," remarks Neville, at length, "to reflect upon a stranger who comes here, not having had your advantages, to try to make up for lost time. But, to be sure, *I* was not brought up in 'busy life,' and my ideas of civility were formed among Heathens."

"Perhaps the best civility, whatever kind of people we are brought up among," retorts Edwin Drood, "is to mind our own business. If you will set me that example, I promise to follow it."

"Do you know that you take a great deal too much upon yourself," is the angry rejoinder; "and that in the part of the world I come from, you would be called to account for it?"

"By whom, for instance?" asks Edwin Drood, coming to a halt, and surveying the other with a look of disdain.

But here a startling right hand is laid on Edwin's shoulder, and Jasper stands between them. For it would seem that he, too, had strolled round by the Nuns' House, and has come up behind them on the shadowy side of the road.

"Ned, Ned, Ned!" he says. "We must have no more of this. I don't like this. I have overheard high words between you two. Remember, my dear boy, you are almost in the position of host to-night. You belong, as it were, to the place, and in a manner represent it towards a stranger. Mr Neville is a stranger, and you should respect the obligations of hospitality. And, Mr. Neville," laying his left hand on the inner shoulder of that young gentleman, and thus walking on between them, hand to shoulder on either side, "you will pardon me; but I appeal to you to govern your temper too. Now, what is amiss? But why ask! Let there be nothing amiss, and the question is superfluous. We are all three on a good understanding, are we not?"

After a silent struggle between the two young men who shall speak last, Edwin Drood strikes in with, "So far as I am concerned, Jack, there is no anger in me."

"Nor in me," says Neville Landless, though not so freely, or perhaps so carelessly. "But if Mr. Drood knew all that lies behind me, far away from here, he might know better how it is that sharp-edged words have sharp edges to wound me."

"Perhaps," says Jasper, in a smoothing manner, "we had better not qualify our good understanding. We had better not say anything having the appearance of a remonstrance or condition; it might not seem generous. Frankly and freely, you see there is no anger in Ned. Frankly and freely, there is no anger in you, Mr. Neville?"

"None at all, Mr. Jasper." Still, not quite so frankly or so freely; or, be it said once again, not quite so carelessly perhaps.

"All over then! Now, my bachelor gatehouse is a few yards from here, and the heater is on the fire, and the wine and glasses are on the table, and it is not a stone's throw from Minor Canon Corner. Ned, you are up and away to-morrow. We will carry Mr. Neville in with us, to take a stirrup-cup."

"With all my heart, Jack."

"And with all mine, Mr. Jasper." Neville feels it impossible to say less, but would rather not go. He has an impression upon him that he has lost hold of his temper; feels that Edwin Drood's coolness, so far from being infectious, makes him red-hot.

Mr. Jasper, still walking in the centre, hand to shoulder on either side, beautifully turns the Refrain of a drinking-song, and they all go up to his rooms. There, the first object visible, when he adds the light of a lamp to that of the fire, is the portrait over the chimney-piece. It is not an object calculated to improve the understanding between the two young men, as rather awkwardly reviving the subject of their difference. Accordingly they both glance at it consciously, but say nothing. Jasper, however (who would appear from his conduct to have gained but an imperfect clew to the cause of their late high words), directly calls attention to it.

"You recognize that picture, Mr. Neville?" shading the lamp to throw the light upon it.

"I recognize it, but it is far from flattering the original."

"O, you are hard upon it! It was done by Ned, who made me a present of it."

"I am sorry for that, Mr. Drood." Neville apologizes, with a real intention to apologize; "if I had known I was in the artist's presence —"

"O, a joke, sir, a mere joke," Edwin cuts in, with a provoking yawn. "A little humoring of Pussy's points! I 'm going to paint her gravely, one of these days, if she 's good."

The air of leisurely patronage and indifference with which this is said, as the speaker throws himself back in a chair and clasps his hands at the back of his head, as a rest for it, is very exasperating to the excitable and excited Neville. Jasper looks observantly from the one to the other, slightly smiles, and turns his back to mix a jug of mulled wine at the fire. It seems to require much mixing and compounding.

"I suppose, Mr. Neville," says Edwin, quick to resent the indignant protest against himself in the face of young Landless, which is fully as visible as the portrait, or the fire, or the lamp, — "I suppose that if you painted the picture of your lady-love —"

"I can't paint," is the hasty interruption.

"That 's your misfortune, and not your fault. You would if you could. But if you could, I suppose you would make her (no matter what she was in reality) Juno, Minerva, Diana, and Venus, all in one. Eh?"

"I have no lady-love, and I can't say."

"If I were to try my hand," says Edwin, with a boyish boastfulness getting up in him, "on a portrait of Miss Landless, — in earnest, mind you; in earnest, — you should see what I could do!"

"My sister's consent to sit for it being first got, I suppose? As it never will be got, I am afraid I shall never see what you can do. I must bear the loss."

Jasper turns round from the fire, fills a large goblet glass for Neville, fills a large goblet glass for Edwin, and hands each his own; then fills for himself, saying, —

"Come, Mr. Neville, we are to drink to my Nephew, Ned. As it is his foot that is in the stirrup — metaphorically — our stirrup-cup is to be devoted to him. Ned, my dearest fellow, my love!"

Jasper sets the example of nearly emptying his glass, and Neville follows it. Edwin Drood says, "Thank you both very much," and follows the double example.

"Look at him!" cries Jasper, stretching out his hand admiringly and tenderly, though rallyingly too. "See where he lounges so easily, Mr. Neville! The world is all before him where to choose. A life of stirring work and interest, a life of change and excitement, a life of domestic ease and love! Look at him!"

Edwin Drood's face has become quickly and remarkably flushed by the wine; so has the face of Neville Landless. Edwin still sits thrown back in his chair, making that rest of clasped hands for his head.

"See how little he heeds it all!" Jasper proceeds in a bantering vein. "It is hardly worth his while to pluck the golden fruit that hangs ripe on the tree for him. And yet consider the contrast, Mr. Neville. You and I have no prospect of stirring work and interest, or of change and excitement, or of domestic ease and love. You and I have no prospect (unless you are more fortunate than I am, which may easily be) but the tedious, unchanging round of this dull place."

"Upon my soul, Jack," says Edwin, complacently, "I feel quite apologetic for having my way smoothed as you describe. But you know what I know, Jack, and it may not be so very easy as it seems, after all. May it, Pussy?" To the portrait, with a snap of his thumb and finger. "We have got to hit it off yet; have n't we, Pussy? You know what I mean, Jack."

His speech has become thick and indistinct. Jasper, quiet and self-possessed, looks to Neville, as expecting his answer or comment. When Neville speaks, *his* speech is also thick and indistinct.

"It might have been better for Mr. Drood to have known some hardships," he says, defiantly.

"Pray," retorts Edwin, turning merely his eyes in that direction, — "pray why might it have been better for Mr. Drood to have known some hardships?"

"Ay," Jasper assents with an air of interest; "let us know why?"

"Because they might have made him more sensible," says Neville, "of good fortune, that is not by any means necessarily the result of his own merits."

Mr. Jasper quickly looks to his nephew for his rejoinder.

"Have *you* known hardships, may I ask?" says Edwin Drood, sitting upright.

Mr. Jasper quickly looks to the other for his retort.

"I have."

"And what have they made *you* sensible of?"

Mr. Jasper's play of eyes between the two holds good throughout the dialogue, to the end.

"I have told you once before to-night."

"You have done nothing of the sort."

"I tell you I have. That you take a great deal too much upon yourself."

"You added something else to that, if I remember?"

"Yes, I did say something else."

"Say it again."

"I said that in the part of the world I come from you would be called to account for it."

"Only there?" cries Edwin Drood, with a contemptuous laugh. "A long way off, I believe? Yes; I see! That part of the world is at a safe distance."

"Say here, then," rejoins the other, rising in a fury. "Say anywhere! Your vanity is intolerable, your conceit is beyond endurance, you talk as if you were some rare and precious prize, instead of a common boaster. You are a common fellow, and a common boaster."

"Pooh, pooh," says Edwin Drood, equally furious, but more collected; "how should you know? You may know a black common fellow, or a black common boaster, when you see him (and no doubt you have a large acquaintance that way); but you are no judge of white men."

This insulting allusion to his dark skin infuriates Neville to that violent degree that he flings the dregs of his wine at Edwin Drood, and is in the act of flinging the goblet after it, when his arm is caught in the nick of time by Jasper.

"Ned, my dear fellow!" he cries in a loud voice; "I entreat you, I command you, to be still!" There has been a rush of all the three, and a clattering of glasses and overturning of chairs. "Mr. Neville, for shame! Give this glass to me. Open your hand, sir. I WILL have it!"

But Neville throws him off, and pauses for an instant, in a raging passion, with the goblet yet in his uplifted hand. Then, he dashes it down under the grate, with such force that the broken splinters fly out again in a shower; and he leaves the house.

When he first emerges into the night air, nothing around him is still or steady; nothing around him shows like what it is; he only knows that he stands with a bare head in the midst of a blood-red whirl, waiting to be struggled with, and to struggle to the death.

But, nothing happening, and the moon looking down upon him as if he were dead after a fit of wrath, he holds his steam-hammer beating head and heart, and staggers away. Then he becomes half conscious of having heard himself bolted and barred out, like a dangerous animal; and thinks what shall he do?

Some wildly passionate ideas of the river dissolve under the spell of the moonlight on the Cathedral and the graves, and the remembrance of his sister, and the thought of what he owes to the good man who has but that very day won his confidence and given him his pledge. He repairs to Minor Canon Corner, and knocks softly at the door.

It is Mr. Crisparkle's custom to sit up last of the early household, very softly touching his piano and practising his favorite parts in concerted vocal music. The south wind that goes where it lists, by way of Minor Canon Corner on a still night, is not more subdued than Mr. Crisparkle at such times, regardful of the slumbers of the China shepherdess.

His knock is immediately answered by Mr. Crisparkle himself. When he opens the door, candle in hand, his cheerful face falls, and disappointed amazement is in it.

"Mr. Neville! In this disorder! Where have you been?"

"I have been to Mr. Jasper's, sir. With his nephew."

"Come in."

The Minor Canon props him by the elbow with a strong hand (in a strictly scientific manner, worthy of his morning trainings), and turns him into his own little book-room, and shuts the door.

"I have begun ill, sir. I have begun dreadfully ill."

"Too true. You are not sober, Mr. Neville."

"I am afraid I am not, sir, though I can satisfy you at another time that I have had very little indeed to drink, and that it overcame me in the strangest and most sudden manner."

"Mr. Neville, Mr. Neville," says the Minor Canon, shaking his head with a sorrowful smile, "I have heard that said before."

"I think — my mind is much confused, but I think — it is equally true of Mr. Jasper's nephew, sir."

"Very likely," is the dry rejoinder.

"We quarrelled, sir. He insulted me most grossly. He had heated that tigerish blood I told you of to-day, before then."

"Mr. Neville," rejoins the Minor Canon, mildly, but firmly, "I request you not to speak to me with that clenched right hand. Unclench it, if you please."

"He goaded me, sir," pursues the young man, instantly obeying, "beyond my power of endurance. I cannot say whether or no he meant it at first, but he did it. He certainly meant it at last. In short, sir," with an irrepressible outburst, "in the passion into which he lashed me, I would have cut him down if I could, and I tried to do it."

"You have clenched that hand again," is Mr. Crisparkle's quiet commentary.

"I beg your pardon, sir."

"You know your room, for I showed it to you before dinner; but I will accompany you to it once more. Your arm, if you please. Softly, for the house is all abed."

Scooping his hand into the same scientific elbow-rest as before, and backing it up with the inert strength of his arm, as skilfully as a Police Expert, and with an apparent repose quite unattainable by novices, Mr. Crisparkle conducts his pupil to the pleasant and orderly old room prepared for him. Arrived there, the young man throws himself into a chair, and, flinging his arms upon his reading-table, rests his head upon them with an air of wretched self-reproach.

The gentle Minor Canon has had it in his thoughts to leave the room, without a word. But, looking round at the door, and seeing this dejected figure, he turns back to it, touches it with a mild hand, and says, "Good night!" A sob is his only acknowledgment. He might have had many a worse; perhaps could have had few better.

Another soft knock at the outer door attracts his attention as he goes down stairs. He opens it to Mr. Jasper, holding in his hand the pupil's hat.

"We have had an awful scene with him," says Jasper, in a low voice.

"Has it been so bad as that?"

"Murderous!"

Mr. Crisparkle remonstrates, "No, no, no. Do not use such strong words."

"He might have laid my dear boy dead at my feet. It is no fault of his that he did not. But that I was, through the mercy of God, swift and strong with him, he would have cut him down on my hearth."

The phrase smites home.

"Ah!" thinks Mr. Crisparkle. "His own words!"

"Seeing what I have seen to-night, and hearing what I have heard," adds Jasper, with great earnestness, "I shall never know peace of mind when there is danger of those two coming together with no one else to interfere. It was horrible. There is something of the tiger in his dark blood."

"Ah!" thinks Mr. Crisparkle. "So he said."

"You, my dear sir," pursues Jasper, taking his hand, "even you have accepted a dangerous charge"

"You need have no fear for me, Jasper," returns Mr. Crisparkle, with a quiet smile. "I have none for myself."

"I have none for myself," returns Jasper, with an emphasis on the last pronoun, "because I am not, nor am I in the way of being, the object of his hostility. But you may be, and my dear boy has been. Good night!"

Mr. Crisparkle goes in, with the hat that has so easily, so almost imperceptibly, acquired the right to be hung up in his hall, hangs it up, and goes thoughtfully to bed.

CHAPTER IX.

BIRDS IN THE BUSH.

ROSA, having no relation that she knew of in the world, had, from the seventh year of her age, known no home but the Nuns' House, and no mother but Miss Twinkleton. Her remembrance of her own mother was of a pretty little creature like herself (not much older than herself, it seemed to her), who had been brought home in her father's arms, drowned. The fatal accident had happened at a party of pleasure. Every fold and color in the pretty summer dress, and even the long wet hair, with scattered petals of ruined flowers still clinging to it, as the dead young figure in its sad, sad beauty lay upon the bed, were fixed indelibly in Rosa's recollection. So were the wild despair and the subsequent bowed-down grief of her poor young father, who died broken-hearted on the first anniversary of that hard day.

The betrothal of Rosa grew out of the soothing of his year of mental distress by his fast friend and old college companion, Drood: who likewise had been left a widower in his youth. But he, too, went the silent road into which all earthly pilgrimages merge, some sooner and some later; and thus the young couple had come to be as they were.

The atmosphere of pity surrounding the little orphan girl when she first came to Cloisterham had never cleared away. It had taken brighter hues as she grew older, happier, prettier; now it had been golden, now roseate, and now azure; but it had always adorned her with some soft light of its own. The general desire to console and caress her had caused her to be treated in the beginning as a child much younger than her years; the same desire had caused her to be still petted when she was a child no longer. Who should be her favorite? who should anticipate this or that small present, or do her this or that small service? who should take her home for the holidays? who should write to her the oftenest when they were separated? and whom she would most rejoice to see again when they were reunited; — even these gentle rivalries were not without their slight dashes of bitterness in the Nuns' House. Well for the poor nuns in their day, if they hid no harder strife under their veils and rosaries.

Thus Rosa had grown to be an amiable, giddy, wilful, winning little creature; spoilt, in the sense of counting upon kindness from all around her; but not in the sense of repaying it with indifference. Possessing an exhaustless well of affection in her nature, its sparkling waters had freshened and brightened the Nuns' House for years, and yet its depths had never yet been moved: what might betide when that came to pass; what developing changes might fall upon the heedless head and light heart then, remained to be seen.

By what means the news that there had been a quarrel between the two young men over-night, involving even some kind of onslaught by Mr. Neville upon Edwin Drood, got into Miss Twinkleton's establishment before breakfast, it is impossible to say. Whether it was brought in by the birds of the air, or came blowing in with the very air itself, when the casement windows were set open; whether the baker brought it kneaded into the bread, or the milkman delivered it as part of the adulteration of his milk; or the housemaids, beating the dust out of their mats against the gateposts, received it in exchange deposited on the mats by the town atmosphere; certain it is that the news permeated every gable of the old building before Miss Twinkleton was down, and that Miss Twinkleton herself received it through Mrs. Tisher, while yet in the act of dressing; or (as she might have expressed the phrase to a parent or guardian of a mythological turn) of sacrificing to the Graces.

Miss Landless's brother had thrown a bottle at Mr. Edwin Drood.

Miss Landless's brother had thrown a knife at Mr. Edwin Drood.

A knife became suggestive of a fork, and Miss Landless's brother had thrown a fork at Mr. Edwin Drood.

As in the governing precedent of Peter Piper, alleged to have picked the peck of pickled pepper, it was held physically desirable to have evidence of the existence of the peck of pickled pepper which Peter Piper was alleged to have picked; so, in this case, it was held psychologically important to know, Why Miss Landless's brother threw a bottle, knife, or fork — or bottle, knife, *and* fork — for the cook had been given to understand it was all three — at Mr. Edwin Drood?

Well, then. Miss Landless's brother had said he admired Miss Bud. Mr. Edwin Drood had said to Miss Landless's brother that he had no business to admire Miss Bud. Miss Landless's brother had then "up'd" (this was the cook's exact information) with the bottle, knife, fork, and decanter (the decanter now coolly flying at everybody's head, without the least introduction), and thrown them all at Mr. Edwin Drood.

Poor little Rosa put a forefinger into each of her ears when these rumors began to circulate, and retired into a corner, beseeching not to be told any more; but Miss Landless, begging permission of Miss Twinkleton to go and speak with her brother, and pretty plainly showing that she would take it if it were not given, struck out the more definite course of going to Mr. Crisparkle's for accurate intelligence.

When she came back (being first closeted with Miss Twinkleton, in order that anything objectionable in her tidings might be retained by that discreet filter), she imparted to Rosa only what had taken place; dwelling with a flushed cheek on the provocation her brother had received, but almost limiting it to that last gross affront as crowning "some other words between them," and, out of consideration for her new friend, passing lightly over the fact that the other words had originated in her lover's taking things in general so very easily. To Rosa direct, she brought a petition from her brother that she would forgive him; and, having delivered it with sisterly earnestness, made an end of the subject.

It was reserved for Miss Twinkleton to tone down the public mind of the Nuns' House. That lady, therefore, entering in a stately manner what plebeians might have called the school-room, but what, in the patrician language of the head of the Nuns' House, was euphuistically, not to say roundaboutedly, denominated "the apartment allotted to study," and saying with a forensic air, "Ladies!" all rose Mrs. Tisher at the same time grouped herself behind her chief, as representing Queen Elizabeth's first historical female friend at Tilbury Fort. Miss Twinkleton then proceeded to remark that Rumor, Ladies, had been represented by the Bard of Avon,—needless were it to mention the immortal SHAKESPEARE, also called the Swan of his native river, not improbably with some reference to the ancient superstition that that bird of graceful plumage (Miss Jennings will please stand upright) sang sweetly on the approach of death, for which we have no ornithological authority,—Rumor, Ladies, had been represented by that bard—hem!—

"who drew
The celebrated Jew,"

as painted full of tongues. Rumor in Cloisterham (Miss Ferdinand will honor me with her attention) was no exception to the great limner's portrait of Rumor elsewhere. A slight *fracas* between two young gentlemen occurring last night within a hundred miles of these peaceful walls (Miss Ferdinand, being apparently incorrigible, will have the kindness to write out this evening, in the original language, the first four fables of our vivacious neighbor, Monsieur La Fontaine) had been very grossly exaggerated by Rumor's voice. In the first alarm and anxiety arising from our sympathy with a sweet young friend, not wholly to be dissociated from one of the gladiators in the bloodless arena in question (the impropriety of Miss Reynolds's appearing to stab herself in the band with a pin, is far too obvious, and too glaringly unladylike, to be pointed out), we descended from our maiden elevation to discuss this uncongenial and this unfit theme. Responsible inquiries having assured us that it was but one of those "airy nothings" pointed at by the Poet (whose name and date of birth Miss Giggles will supply within half an hour), we would now discard the subject, and concentrate our minds upon the grateful labors of the day.

But the subject so survived all day, nevertheless, that Miss Ferdinand got into new trouble by surreptitiously clapping on a paper mustache at dinner-time, and going through the motions of aiming a water-bottle at Miss Giggles, who drew a table-spoon in defence.

Now, Rosa thought of this unlucky quarrel a great deal, and thought of it with an uncomfortable feeling that she was involved in it, as cause, or consequence, or what not, through being in a false position altogether as to her marriage engagement. Never free from such uneasiness when she was with her affianced husband, it was not likely that she would be free from it when they were apart. To-day, too, she was cast in upon herself, and deprived of the relief of talking freely with her new friend, because the quarrel had been with Helena's brother, and Helena undisguisedly avoided the subject as a delicate and difficult one to herself. At this critical time, of all times, Rosa's guardian was announced as having come to see her.

Mr. Grewgious had been well selected for his trust, as a man of incorruptible integrity, but certainly for no other appropriate quality discernible on the surface. He was an arid, sandy man, who, if he had been put into a grinding-mill, looked as if he would have ground immediately into high-dried snuff. He had a scanty flat crop of hair, in color and consistency like some very mangy yellow fur tippet; it was so unlike hair, that it must have been a wig, but for the stupendous improbability of anybody's voluntarily sporting such a head. The little play of feature that his face presented was cut deep into it, in a few hard curves that made it more like work; and he had certain notches in his forehead, which looked as though Nature had been about to touch them into sensibility or refinement, when she had impatiently thrown away the chisel, and said, "I really cannot be worried to finish off this man; let him go as he is."

With too great length of throat at his upper end, and too much ankle-bone and heel at his lower; with an awkward and hesitating manner; with a shambling walk, and with what is called a near sight, — which perhaps prevented his observing how much white cotton stocking he displayed to the public eye, in contrast with his black suit. — Mr. Grewgious still had some strange capacity in him of making on the whole an agreeable impression.

Mr. Grewgious was discovered by his ward, much discomfited by being in Miss Twinkleton's company in Miss Twinkleton's own sacred room. Dim forebodings of being examined in something, and not coming well out of it, seemed to oppress the poor gentleman when found in these circumstances.

"My dear, how do you do? I am glad to see you. My dear, how much improved you are. Permit me to hand you a chair, my dear."

"Miss Twinkleton rose at her little writing-table, saying, with general sweetness, as to the polite Universe, "Will you permit me to retire?"

"By no means, madam, on my account. I beg that you will not move."

"I must entreat permission to *move*," returned Miss Twinkleton, repeating the word with a charming grace; "but I will not withdraw, since you are so obliging. If I wheel my desk to this corner window, shall I be in the way?"

"Madam! In the way!"

"You are very kind. Rosa, my dear, you will be under no restraint, I am sure."

Here Mr. Grewgious, left by the fire with Rosa, said again, "My dear, how do you do? I am glad to see you, my dear." And having waited for her to sit down, sat down himself.

"My visits," says Mr. Grewgious, "are, like those of the angels, — not that I compare myself to an angel."

"No, sir," said Rosa.

"Not by any means," assented Mr. Grewgious. "I merely refer to my visits, which are few and far between. The angels are, we know very well, up stairs."

Miss Twinkleton looked round with a kind of stiff stare.

"I refer, my dear," said Mr. Grewgious, laying his hand on Rosa's, as the possibility thrilled through his frame of his otherwise seeming to take the awful liberty of calling Miss Twinkleton my dear, — "I refer to the other young ladies."

Miss Twinkleton resumed her writing.

Mr. Grewgious, with a sense of not having managed his opening point quite as neatly as he might have desired, smoothed his head from back to front as if he had just dived, and were pressing the water out, — this smoothing action, however superfluous, was habitual with him, — and took a pocket-book from his coat-pocket, and a stump of black-lead pencil from his waistcoat-pocket.

"I made," he said, turning the leaves, — "I made a guiding memorandum or so, — as I usually do, for I have no conversational powers whatever, — to which I will, with your permission, my dear, refer. 'Well and happy.' Truly. You are well and happy, my dear? You look so."

"Yes, indeed, sir," answered Rosa.

"For which," said Mr. Grewgious, with a bend of his head towards the corner window, "our warmest acknowledgments are due, and I am sure are rendered, to the maternal kindness and the constant care and consideration of the lady whom I have now the honor to see before me."

This point, again, made but a lame departure from Mr. Grewgious, and never got to its destination; for Miss Twinkleton, feeling that the courtesies required her to be by this time quite outside the conversation, was biting the end of her pen, and looking upward, as waiting for the descent of an idea from any member of the Celestial Nine who might have one to spare.

Mr. Grewgious smoothed his smooth head again, and then made another reference to his pocket-book; lining out "well and happy" as disposed of.

"'Pounds, shillings, and pence' is my next note. A dry subject for a young lady, but an important subject too. Life is pounds, shillings, and pence. Death is —" A sudden recollection of the death of her two parents seemed to stop him, and he said in a softer tone, and evidently inserting the negative as an afterthought, "Death is *not* pounds, shillings, and pence."

His voice was as hard and dry as himself, and Fancy might have ground it straight, like himself, into high-dried snuff. And yet, through the very limited means of expression that he possessed, he seemed to express kindness. If Nature had but finished him off, kindness might have been recognizable in his face at this moment. But if the notches in his forehead would n't fuse together, and if his face would work and could n't play, what could he do, poor man!

"'Pounds, shillings, and pence.' You find your allowance always sufficient for your wants, my dear?"

Rosa wanted for nothing, and therefore it was ample.

"And you are not in debt?"

Rosa laughed at the idea of being in debt. It seemed, to her inexperience, a comical vagary of the imagination. Mr. Grewgious stretched his near sight to be sure that this was her view of the case. "Ah!" he said, as comment, with a furtive glance towards Miss Twinkleton, and lining out "pounds, shillings, and pence," "I spoke of having got among the angels! So I did!"

Rosa felt what his next memorandum would prove to be, and was blushing and folding a crease in her dress with one embarrassed hand long before he found it.

"'Marriage.' Hem!" Mr. Grewgious carried his smoothing hand down over his eyes and nose, and even chin, before drawing his chair a little nearer, and speaking a little more confidentially: "I now touch, my dear, upon the point that is the direct cause of my troubling you with the present visit. Otherwise, being a particularly Angular man, I should not have intruded here. I am the last man to intrude into a sphere for which I am so entirely unfitted. I feel, on these premises, as if I was a bear — with the cramp — in a youthful Cotillon."

His ungainliness gave him enough of the air of his simile to set Rosa off laughing heartily.

"It strikes you in the same light," said Mr. Grewgious, with perfect calmness. "Just so. To return to my memorandum. Mr. Edwin has been to and fro here, as was arranged. You have mentioned that, in your quarterly letters to me. And you like him, and he likes you."

"I *like* him very much, sir," rejoined Rosa.

"So I said, my dear," returned her guardian, for whose ear the timid emphasis was much too fine. "Good And you correspond."

"We write to one another," said Rosa, pouting, as she recalled their epistolary differences.

"Such is the meaning that I attach to the word 'correspond' in this application, my dear," said Mr. Grewgious. "Good. All goes well, time works on, and at this next Christmas-time it will become necessary, as a matter of form, to give the exemplary lady in the corner window, to whom we are so much indebted, business notice of your departure in the ensuing half-year. Your relations with her are far more than business relations, no doubt; but a residue of business remains in them, and business is business ever. I am a particularly Angular man," proceeded Mr. Grewgious, as if it suddenly occurred to him to mention it, "and I am not used to give anything away. If, for these two reasons, some competent Proxy would give *you* away, I should take it very kindly."

Rosa intimated, with her eyes on the ground, that she thought a substitute might be found, if required.

"Surely, surely," said Mr. Grewgious. "For instance, the gentleman who teaches Dancing here, — he would know how to do it with graceful propriety. He would advance and retire in a manner satisfactory to the feelings of the officiating clergyman, and of yourself, and the bridegroom, and all parties concerned. I am — I am a particularly Angular man," said Mr. Grewgious, as if he had made up his mind to screw it out at last, "and should only blunder."

Rosa sat still and silent. Perhaps her mind had not got quite so far as the ceremony yet, but was lagging on the way there.

"Memorandum, 'Will.' Now, my dear," said Mr. Grewgious, referring to his notes, disposing of "marriage" with his pencil, and taking a paper from his pocket, "although I have before possessed you with the contents of your father's will, I think it right at this time to leave a certified copy of it in your hands. And although Mr. Edwin is also aware of its contents, I think it right at this time likewise to place a certified copy of it in Mr. Jasper's hands — "

"Not in his own?" asked Rosa, looking up quickly. "Cannot the copy go to Eddy himself?"

"Why, yes, my dear, if you particularly wish it; but I spoke of Mr. Jasper as being his trustee."

"I do particularly wish it, if you please," said Rosa, hurriedly and earnestly; "I don't like Mr. Jasper to come between us, in any way."

"It is natural, I suppose," said Mr. Grewgious, "that your young husband should be all in all. Yes. You observe that I say, I suppose. The fact is, I am a particularly Unnatural man, and I don't know from my own knowledge."

Rosa looked at him with some wonder.

"I mean," he explained, "that young ways were never my ways. I was the only offspring of parents far advanced in life, and I half believe I was born advanced in life myself. No personality is intended towards the name you will so soon change, when I remark that while the general growth of people seem to have come into existence buds, I seem to have come into existence a chip. I was a chip — and a very dry one — when I first became aware of myself. Respecting the other certified copy, your wish shall be complied with. Respecting your inheritance, I think you know all. It is an annuity of two hundred and fifty pounds. The savings upon that annuity, and some other items to your credit, all duly carried to account, with vouchers, will place you in possession of a lump-sum of money, rather exceeding Seventeen Hundred Pounds. I am empowered to advance the cost of your preparations for your marriage out of that fund. All is told."

"Will you please tell me," said Rosa, taking the paper with a prettily knitted brow, but not opening it, "whether I am right in what I am going to say? I can understand what you tell me so very much better than what I read in law-writings. My poor papa and Eddy's father made their agreement together, as very dear and firm and fast friends, in order that we too might be very dear and firm and fast friends after them?"

"Just so."

"For the lasting good of both of us, and the lasting happiness of both of us?"

"Just so."

"That we might be to one another even much more than they had been to one another?"

"Just so."

"It was not bound upon Eddy, and it was not bound upon me, by any forfeit, in case —"

"Don't be agitated, my dear. In the case that it brings tears into your affectionate eyes even to picture to yourself, — in the case of your not marrying one another, — no, no forfeiture on either side. You would then have been my ward until you were of age. No worse would have befallen you. Bad enough, perhaps!"

"And Eddy?"

"He would have come into his partnership derived from his father, and into its arrears to his credit (if any), on attaining his majority, just as now."

Rosa, with her perplexed face and knitted brow, bit the corner of her attested copy, as she sat with her head on one side, looking abstractedly on the floor, and smoothing it with her foot.

"In short," said Mr. Grewgious, "this betrothal is a wish, a sentiment, a friendly project, tenderly expressed on both sides. That it was strongly felt, and that there was a lively hope that it would prosper, there can be no doubt. When you were both children, you began to be accustomed to it, and it *has* prospered. But circumstances alter cases; and I made this visit to-day partly, indeed principally, to discharge myself of the duty of telling you, my dear, that two young people can only be betrothed in marriage (except as a matter of convenience, and therefore mockery and misery) of their own free will, their own attachment, and their own assurance (it may or may not prove a mistaken one, but we must take our chance of that) that they are suited to each other and will make each other happy. Is it to be supposed, for example, that if either of your fathers were living now, and had any mistrust on that subject, his mind would not be changed by the change of circumstances involved in the change of your years? Untenable, unreasonable, inconclusive, and preposterous!"

Mr. Grewgious said all this as if he were reading it aloud; or, still more, as if he were repeating a lesson. So expressionless of any approach to spontaneity were his face and manner.

"I have now, my dear," he added, blurring out "Will" with his pencil, "discharged myself of what is doubtless a formal duty in this case, but still a duty in such a case. Memorandum: 'Wishes.' My dear, is there any wish of yours that I can further?"

Rosa shook her head, with an almost plaintive air of hesitation in want of help.

"Is there any instruction that I can take from you with reference to your affairs?"

"I—I should like to settle them with Eddy first, if you please," said Rosa, plaiting the crease in her dress.

"Surely. Surely," returned Mr. Grewgious. "You two should be of one mind in all things. Is the young gentleman expected shortly?"

"He has gone away only this morning. He will be back at Christmas."

"Nothing could happen better. You will, on his return at Christmas, arrange all matters of detail with him; you will then communicate with me, and I will discharge myself (as a mere business acquittance) of my business responsibilities towards the accomplished lady in the corner window. They will accrue at that season." Blurring pencil once again. "Memorandum: 'Leave.' Yes. I will now, my dear, take my leave."

"Could I," said Rosa, rising, as he jerked out of his chair in his ungainly way,—"could I ask you most kindly to come to me at Christmas, if I had anything particular to say to you?"

"Why, certainly, certainly," he rejoined, apparently—if such a word can be used of one who had no apparent lights or shadows about him—complimented by the question. "As a particularly Angular man, I do not fit smoothly into the social circle, and consequently I have no other engagement at Christmas-time than to partake, on the twenty-fifth, of a boiled turkey and celery sauce with a—with a particularly Angular clerk I have the good fortune to possess, whose father, being a Norfolk farmer, sends him up (the turkey up), as a present to me, from the neighborhood of Norwich. I should be quite proud of your wishing to see me, my dear. As a professional Receiver of rents, so very few people *do* wish to see me, that the novelty would be bracing."

For his ready acquiescence, the grateful Rosa put her hands upon his shoulders, stood on tiptoe, and instantly kissed him.

"Lord bless me!" cried Mr. Grewgious. "Thank you, my dear. The honor is almost equal to the pleasure. Miss Twinkleton, madam, I have had a most satisfactory conversation with my ward, and I will now release you from the encumbrance of my presence."

"Nay, sir," rejoined Miss Twinkleton, rising with a gracious condescension, "say not encumbrance. Not so, by any means. I cannot permit you to say so."

"Thank you, madam. I have read in the newspapers," said Mr. Grewgious, stammering a little, "that when a distinguished visitor (not that I am one: far from it) goes to a school (not that this is one: far from it), he asks for a holiday, or some sort of grace. It being now the afternoon in the—College—of which you are the eminent head, the young ladies might gain nothing, except in name, by having the rest of the day allowed them. But if there is any young lady at all under a cloud, might I solicit—"

"Ah, Mr. Grewgious, Mr. Grewgious!" cried Miss Twinkleton, with a chastely rallying forefinger. "O you gentlemen, you gentlemen! Fie for shame, that you are so hard upon us poor maligned disciplinarians of our sex, for your sakes! But as Miss Ferdinand is at present weighed down by an incubus,"—Miss Twinkleton might have said a pen-and-ink-ubus of writing out Monsieur La Fontaine,—"go to her, Rosa, my dear, and tell her the penalty is remitted, in deference to the intercession of your guardian, Mr. Grewgious."

Miss Twinkleton here achieved a courtesy, suggestive of marvels happening to her respected legs, and which she came out of nobly, three yards behind her starting-point.

As he held it incumbent upon him to call on Mr. Jasper before leaving Cloisterham, Mr. Grewgious went to the Gate House, and climbed its postern stair. But Mr. Jasper's door being closed, and presenting on a slip of paper the word "Cathedral," the fact of its being service-time was borne into the mind of Mr. Grewgious. So he descended the stair again, and, crossing the Close, paused at the great western folding-door of the Cathedral, which stood open on the fine and bright, though short-lived, afternoon, for the airing of the place.

"Dear me," said Mr. Grewgious, peeping in, "it 's like looking down the throat of Old Time."

Old Time heaved a mouldy sigh from tomb and arch and vault; and gloomy shadows began to deepen in corners; and damps began to rise from green patches of stone; and jewels, cast upon the pavement of the nave from stained glass by the declining sun, began to perish. Within the grill-gate of the chancel, up the steps surmounted loomingly by the fast-darkening organ, white robes could be dimly seen, and one feeble voice, rising and falling in a cracked monotonous mutter, could at intervals be faintly heard. In the free outer air, the river, the green pastures, and the brown arable lands, the teeming hills and dales, were reddened by the sunset: while the distant little windows in windmills and farm homesteads, shone, patches of bright beaten gold. In the Cathedral, all became gray, murky, and sepulchral, and the cracked monotonous mutter went on like a dying voice, until the organ and the choir burst forth, and drowned it in a sea of music. Then the sea fell, and the dying voice made another feeble effort, and then the sea rose high, and beat its life out, and lashed the roof, and surged among the arches, and pierced the heights of the great tower; and then the sea was dry, and all was still.

Mr. Grewgious had by that time walked to the chancel-steps, where he met the living waters coming out.

"Nothing is the matter?" Thus Jasper accosted him, rather quickly. "You have not been sent for?"

"Not at all, not at all. I came down of my own accord. I have been to my pretty ward's, and am now homeward bound again."

"You found her thriving?"

"Blooming indeed. Most blooming. I merely came to tell her, seriously, what a betrothal by deceased parents is."

"And what is it — according to your judgment?"

Mr. Grewgious noticed the whiteness of the lips that asked the question, and put it down to the chilling account of the Cathedral.

"I merely came to tell her that it could not be considered binding, against any such reason for its dissolution as a want of affection, or want of disposition to carry it into effect, on the side of either party."

"May I ask, had you any especial reason for telling her that?"

Mr. Grewgious answered somewhat sharply, "The especial reason of doing my duty, sir. Simply that." Then he added, "Come, Mr. Jasper; I know your affection for your nephew, and that you are quick to feel on his behalf. I assure you that this implies not the least doubt of, or disrespect to, your nephew."

"You could not," returned Jasper, with a friendly pressure of his arm, as they walked on side by side, "speak more handsomely."

Mr. Grewgious pulled off his hat to smooth his head, and, having smoothed it, nodded it contentedly, and put his hat on again.

"I will wager," said Jasper, smiling, — his lips were still so white that he was conscious of it, and bit and moistened them while speaking, — "I will wager that she hinted no wish to be released from Ned."

"And you will win your wager, if you do," retorted Mr. Grewgious. "We should allow some margin for little maidenly delicacies in a young motherless creature, under such circumstances, I suppose; it is not in my line; what do you think?"

"There can be no doubt of it."

"I am glad you say so. Because," proceeded Mr. Grewgious, who had all this time very knowingly felt his way round to action on his remembrance of what she had said of Jasper himself, — "because she seems to have some little delicate instinct that all preliminary arrangements had best be made between Mr. Edwin Drood and herself, don't you see? She don't want us, don't you know?"

Jasper touched himself on the breast, and said, somewhat indistinctly, "You mean me."

Mr. Grewgious touched himself on the breast, and said, "I mean us. Therefore, let them have their little discussions and councils together, when Mr. Edwin Drood comes back here at Christmas, and then you and I will step in, and put the final touches to the business."

"So you settled with her that you would come back at Christmas?" observed Jasper. "I see! Mr. Grewgious, as you quite fairly said just now, there is such an exceptional attachment between my nephew and me, that I am more sensitive for the dear, fortunate, happy, happy fellow than for myself. But it is only right that the young lady should be considered, as you have pointed out, and that I should accept my cue from you. I accept it. I understand that at Christmas they will complete their preparations for May, and that their marriage will be put in final train by themselves, and that nothing will remain for us but to put ourselves in train also, and have everything ready for our formal release from our trusts on Edwin's birthday."

"That is my understanding," assented Mr. Grewgious, as they shook hands to part. "God bless them both!"

"God save them both!" cried Jasper.

"I said, bless them," remarked the former, looking back over his shoulder.

"I said, save them," returned the latter. "Is there any difference?"

CHAPTER X.

SMOOTHING THE WAY.

It has been often enough remarked that women have a curious power of divining the characters of men, which would seem to be innate and instinctive; seeing that it is arrived at through no patient process of reasoning, that it can give no satisfactory or sufficient account of itself, and that it pronounces in the most confident manner even against accumulated observation on the part of the other sex. But it has not been quite so often remarked that this power (fallible, like every other human attribute) is for the most part absolutely incapable of self-revision; and that when it has delivered an adverse opinion which by all human lights is subsequently proved to have failed, it is undistinguishable from prejudice, in respect of its determination not to be corrected. Nay, the very possibility of contradiction or disproof, however remote, communicates to this feminine judgment from the first, in nine cases out of ten, the weakness attendant on the testimony of an interested witness; so personally and strongly does the fair diviner connect herself with her divination.

"Now, don't you think, Ma dear," said the Minor Canon to his mother one day as she sat at her knitting in his little bookroom, "that you are rather hard on Mr. Neville?"

"No, I do *not*, Sept," returned the old lady.

"Let us discuss it, Ma."

"I have no objection to discuss it, Sept. I trust, my dear, I am always open to discussion." There was a vibration in the old lady's cap, as though she internally added, "And I should like to see the discussion that would change *my* mind!"

"Very good, Ma," said her conciliatory son. "There is nothing like being open to discussion."

"I hope not, my dear," returned the old lady, evidently shut to it.

"Well! Mr. Neville, on that unfortunate occasion, commits himself under provocation."

"And under mulled wine," added the old lady.

"I must admit the wine. Though I believe the two young men were much alike in that regard."

"I don't!" said the old lady.

"Why not, Ma?"

"Because I *don't*," said the old lady. "Still, I am quite open to discussion."

"But, my dear Ma, I cannot see how we are to discuss, if you take that line."

"Blame Mr. Neville for it, Sept, and not me," said the old lady with stately severity.

"My dear Ma! Why Mr. Neville?"

"Because," said Mrs. Crisparkle, retiring on first principles, "he came home intoxicated, and did great discredit to this house, and showed great disrespect to this family."

"That is not to be denied, Ma. He was then, and he is now, very sorry for it."

"But for Mr. Jasper's well-bred consideration in coming up to me next day, after service, in the Nave itself, with his gown still on, and expressing his hope that I had not been greatly alarmed or had my rest violently broken, I believe I might never have heard of that disgraceful transaction," said the old lady.

"To be candid, Ma, I think I should have kept it from you if I could, though I had not decidedly made up my mind. I was following Jasper out to confer with him on the subject, and to consider the expediency of his and my jointly hushing the thing up on all accounts, when I found him speaking to you. Then it was too late."

"Too late, indeed, Sept. He was still as pale as gentlemanly ashes at what had taken place in his rooms over night."

"If I *had* kept it from you, Ma, you may be sure it would have been for your peace and quiet, and for the good of the young men, and in my best discharge of my duty according to my lights."

The old lady immediately walked across the room and kissed him, saying, "Of course, my dear Sept, I am sure of that."

"However, it became the town-talk," said Mr. Crisparkle, rubbing his ear, as his mother resumed her seat and her knitting, "and passed out of my power."

"And I said then, Sept," returned the old lady, "that I thought ill of Mr. Neville. And I say now, that I think ill of Mr. Neville. And I said then, and I say now, that I hope Mr. Neville may come to good, but I don't believe he will." Here the cap vibrated again, considerably.

"I am sorry to hear you say so, Ma — "

"I am sorry to say so, my dear," interposed the old lady, knitting on firmly, "but I can't help it."

"— For," pursued the Minor Canon, "it is undeniable that Mr. Neville is exceedingly industrious and attentive, and that he improves apace, and that he has — I hope I may say — an attachment to me."

"There is no merit in the last article, my dear," said the old lady, quickly, "and if he says there is, I think the worse of him for the boast."

"But, my dear Ma, he never said there was."

"Perhaps not," returned the old lady; "still, I don't see that it greatly signifies."

There was no impatience in the pleasant look with which Mr. Crisparkle contemplated the pretty old piece of china as it knitted; but there was, certainly, a humorous sense of its not being a piece of china to argue with very closely.

"Besides, Sept. Ask yourself what he would be without his sister. You know what an influence she has over him; you know what a capacity she has; you know that whatever he reads with you, he reads with her. Give her her fair share of your praise, and how much do you leave for him?"

At these words Mr. Crisparkle fell into a little revery, in which he thought of several things. He thought of the times he had seen the brother and sister together in deep converse over one of his own old college books; now, in the rimy mornings, when he made those sharpening pilgrimages to Cloisterham Weir; now, in the sombre evenings, when he faced the wind at sunset, having climbed his favorite outlook, a beetling fragment of monastery ruin; and the two studious figures passed below him along the margin of the river, in which the town fires and lights already shone, making the landscape bleaker. He thought how the consciousness had stolen upon him that, in teaching one, he was teaching two; and how he had almost insensibly adapted his explanations to both minds, — that with which his own was daily in contact, and that which he only approached through it. He thought of the gossip that had reached him from the Nuns' House, to the effect that Helena, whom he had mistrusted as so proud and fierce, submitted herself to the fairy-bride (as he called her), and learnt from her what she knew. He thought of the picturesque alliance between those two, externally so very different. He thought — perhaps most of all — could it be that these things were yet but so many weeks old, and had become an integral part of his life?

As, whenever the Reverend Septimus fell a-musing, his good mother took it to be an infallible sign that he "wanted support," the blooming old lady made all haste to the dining-room closet, to produce from it the support embodied in a glass of Constantia and a home-made biscuit. It was a most wonderful closet, worthy of Cloisterham and of Minor Canon Corner. Above it, a portrait of Handel in a flowing wig beamed down at the spectator, with a knowing air of being up to the contents of the closet, and a musical air of intending to combine all its harmonies in one delicious fugue. No common closet with a vulgar door on hinges, openable all at once, and leaving nothing to be disclosed by degrees, this rare closet had a lock in mid-air, where two perpendicular slides met; the one falling down, and the other pushing up. The upper slide, on being pulled down (leaving the lower a double mystery), revealed deep shelves of pickle-jars, jam-pots, tin canisters, spice-boxes, and agreeably outlandish vessels of blue and white, the luscious lodgings of preserved tamarinds and ginger. Every benevolent inhabitant of this retreat had his name inscribed upon his stomach. The pickles, in a uniform of rich brown double-breasted buttoned coat, and yellow or sombre drab continuations, announced their portly forms, in printed capitals, as Walnut, Gherkin, Onion, Cabbage, Cauliflower, Mixed, and other members of that noble family. The jams, as being of a less masculine temperament, and as wearing curl-papers, announced themselves in feminine caligraphy, like a soft whisper, to be Raspberry, Gooseberry, Apricot, Plum, Damson, Apple, and Peach. The scene closing on these charmers, and the lower slide ascending, oranges were revealed, attended by a mighty japanned sugar-box, to temper their acerbity if unripe. Home-made biscuits waited at the Court of these Powers, accompanied by a goodly fragment of plum-cake, and various slender ladies' fingers, to be dipped into sweet wine and kissed. Lowest of all, a compact leaden vault enshrined the sweet wine and a stock of cordials: whence issued whispers of Seville Orange, Lemon, Almond, and Caraway-seed. There was a crowning air upon this closet of closets, of having been for ages hummed through by the Cathedral bell and organ, until those venerable bees had made sublimated honey of everything in store; and it was always observed that every dipper among the shelves (deep, as has been noticed, and swallowing up head, shoulders, and elbows) came forth again mellow-faced, and seeming to have undergone a saccharine transfiguration.

The Reverend Septimus yielded himself up quite as willing a victim to a nauseous medicinal herb-closet, also presided over by the china shepherdess, as to this glorious cupboard. To what amazing infusions of gentian, peppermint, gilliflower, sage, parsley, thyme, rue, rosemary, and dandelion, did his courageous stomach submit itself! In what wonderful wrappers enclosing layers of dried leaves, would he swathe his rosy and contented face, if his mother suspected him of a toothache! What botanical blotches would he cheerfully stick upon his cheek or forehead, if the dear old lady convicted him of an imperceptible pimple there! Into this herbaceous penitentiary, situated on an upper staircase-landing, — a low and narrow whitewashed cell, where bunches of dried leaves hung from rusty hooks in the ceiling, and were spread out upon shelves, in company with portentous bottles, — would the Reverend Septimus submissively be led, like the highly popular lamb who has so long and unresistingly been led to the slaughter, and there would he, unlike that lamb, bore nobody but himself. Not even doing that much, so that the old lady were busy and pleased, he would quietly swallow what was given him, merely taking a corrective dip of hands and face into the great bowl of dried rose-leaves, and into the other great bowl of dried lavender, and then would go out, as confident in the sweetening powers of Cloisterham Weir and a wholesome mind, as Lady Macbeth was hopeless of those of all the seas that roll.

In the present instance the good Minor Canon took his glass of Constantia with an excellent grace, and, so supported to his mother's satisfaction, applied himself to the remaining duties of the day. In their orderly and punctual progress they brought round Vesper Service and twilight. The Cathedral, being very cold, he set off for a brisk trot after service; the trot to end in a charge at his favorite fragment of ruin, which was to be carried by storm, without a pause for breath.

He carried it in a masterly manner, and, not breathed even then, stood looking down upon the river. The river at Cloisterham is sufficiently near the sea to throw up oftentimes a quantity of sea-weed. An unusual quantity had come in with the last tide, and this, and the confusion of the water, and the restless dipping and flapping of the noisy gulls, and an angry light out seaward beyond the brown-sailed barges that were turning black, foreshadowed a stormy night. In his mind he was contrasting the wild and noisy sea with the quiet harbor of Minor Canon Corner, when Helena and Neville Landless passed below him. He had had the two together in his thoughts all day, and at once climbed down to speak to them together. The footing was rough in an uncertain light for any tread save that of a good climber; but the Minor Canon was as good a climber as most men, and stood beside them before many good climbers would have been half-way down.

"A wild evening, Miss Landless! Do you not find your usual walk with your brother too exposed and cold for the time of year? Or at all events, when the sun is down, and the weather is driving in from the sea?"

Helena thought not. It was their favorite walk. It was very retired.

"It is very retired," assented Mr. Crisparkle, laying hold of his opportunity straightway, and walking on with them. "It is a place of all others where one can speak without interruption, as I wish to do. Mr. Neville, I believe you tell your sister everything that passes between us?"

"Everything, sir."

"Consequently," said Mr. Crisparkle, "your sister is aware that I have repeatedly urged you to make some kind of apology for that unfortunate occurrence which befell, on the night of your arrival here."

In saying it he looked to her, and not to him; therefore it was she, and not he, who replied, —

"Yes."

"I call it unfortunate, Miss Helena," resumed Mr. Crisparkle, "forasmuch as it certainly has engendered a prejudice against Neville. There is a notion about that he is a dangerously passionate fellow, of an uncontrollable and furious temper; he is really avoided as such."

"I have no doubt he is, poor fellow," said Helena, with a look of proud compassion at her brother, expressing a deep sense of his being ungenerously treated. "I should be quite sure of it, from your saying so; but what you tell me is confirmed by suppressed hints and references that I meet with every day."

"Now," Mr. Crisparkle again resumed, in a tone of mild though firm persuasion, "is not this to be regretted, and ought it not to be amended? These are early days of Neville's in Cloisterham, and I have no fear of his not outliving such a prejudice, and proving himself to have been misunderstood. But how much wiser to take action at once than to trust to uncertain time! Besides, apart from its being politic, it is right. For there can be no question that Neville was wrong."

"He was provoked," Helena submitted.

"He was the assailant," Mr. Crisparkle submitted.

They walked on in silence, until Helena raised her eyes to the Minor Canon's face, and said, almost reproachfully, "O Mr. Crisparkle, would you have Neville throw himself at young Drood's feet, or at Mr. Jasper's, who maligns him every day! In your heart you cannot mean it. From your heart you could not do it, if his case were yours."

"I have represented to Mr. Crisparkle, Helena," said Neville, with a glance of deference towards his tutor, "that if I could do it from my heart I would. But I cannot, and I revolt from the pretence. You forget, however, that to put the case to Mr. Crisparkle as his own, is to suppose Mr. Crisparkle to have done what I did."

"I ask his pardon," said Helena.

"You see," remarked Mr. Crisparkle, again laying hold of his opportunity, though with a moderate and delicate touch, "you both instinctively acknowledge that Neville did wrong! Then why stop short, and not otherwise acknowledge it?"

"Is there no difference," asked Helena, with a little faltering in her manner, "between submission to a generous spirit, and submission to a base or trivial one?"

Before the worthy Minor Canon was quite ready with his argument in reference to this nice distinction, Neville struck in, —

"Help me to clear myself with Mr. Crisparkle, Helena. Help me to convince him that I cannot be the first to make concessions without mockery and falsehood. My nature must be changed before I can do so, and it is not changed I am sensible of inexpressible affront, and deliberate aggravation of inexpressible affront, and I am angry. The plain truth is, I am still as angry when I recall that night as I was that night."

"Neville," hinted the Minor Canon, with a steady countenance, "you have repeated that former action of your hands, which I so much dislike."

"I am sorry for it, sir, but it was involuntary. I confessed that I was still as angry."

"And I confess," said Mr. Crisparkle, "that I hoped for better things."

"I am sorry to disappoint you, sir, but it would be far worse to deceive you, and I should deceive you grossly if I pretended that you had softened me in this respect. The time may come when your powerful influence will do even that with the difficult pupil whose antecedents you know; but it has not come yet. Is this so, and in spite of my struggles against myself, Helena?"

She, whose dark eyes were watching the effect of what he said on Mr. Crisparkle's face, replied — to Mr Crisparkle, not to him, "It is so." After a short pause, she answered the slightest look of inquiry conceivable, in her brother's eyes, with as slight an affirmative bend of her own head; and he went on: —

"I have never yet had the courage to say to you, sir, what in full openness I ought to have said when you first talked with me on this subject. It is not easy to say, and I have been withheld by a fear of its seeming ridiculous, which is very strong upon me down to this last moment, and might, but for my sister, prevent my being quite open with you even now. — I admire Miss Bud, sir, so very much, that I cannot bear her being treated with conceit or indifference; and even if I did not feel that I had an injury against young Drood on my own account, I should feel that I had an injury against him on hers."

Mr. Crisparkle, in utter amazement, looked at Helena for corroboration, and met in her expressive face full corroboration, and a plea for advice.

"The young lady of whom you speak is, as you know, Mr. Neville, shortly to be married," said Mr. Crisparkle, gravely; "therefore your admiration, if it be of that special nature which you seem to indicate, is outrageously misplaced. Moreover, it is monstrous that you should take upon yourself to be the young lady's champion against her chosen husband. Besides, you have seen them only once. The young lady has become your sister's friend; and I wonder that your sister, even on her behalf, has not checked you in this irrational and culpable fancy."

"She has tried, sir, but uselessly. Husband or no husband, that fellow is incapable of the feeling with which I am inspired towards the beautiful young creature whom he treats like a doll. I say he is as incapable of it as he is unworthy of her. I say she is sacrificed in being bestowed upon him. I say that I love her, and despise and hate him!" This with a face so flushed, and a gesture so violent, that his sister crossed to his side and caught his arm, remonstrating, "Neville, Neville!"

Thus recalled to himself, he quickly became sensible of having lost the guard he had set upon his passionate tendency, and covered his face with his hand, as one repentant and wretched.

Mr. Crisparkle, watching him attentively, and at the same time meditating how to proceed, walked on for some paces in silence. Then he spoke: —

"Mr. Neville, Mr. Neville, I am sorely grieved to see in you more traces of a character as sullen, angry, and wild, as the night now closing in. They are of too serious an aspect to leave me the resource of treating the infatuation you have disclosed as undeserving serious consideration. I give it very serious consideration, and I speak to you accordingly. This feud between you and young Drood must not go on. I cannot permit it to go on any longer, knowing what I now know from you, and you living under my roof. Whatever prejudiced and unauthorized constructions your blind and envious wrath may put upon his character, it is a frank, good-natured character. I know I can trust to it for that. Now, pray observe what I am about to say. On reflection, and on your sister's representation, I am willing to admit that, in making peace with young Drood, you have a right to be met half-way. I will engage that you shall be, and even that young Drood shall make the first advance. This condition fulfilled, you will pledge me the honor of a Christian gentleman that the quarrel is forever at an end on your side. What may be in your heart when you give him your hand, can only be known to the Searcher of all hearts; but it will never go well with you if there be any treachery there. So far, as to that; next as to what I must again speak of as your infatuation. I understand it to have been confided to me, and to be known to no other person save your sister and yourself. Do I understand aright?"

Helena answered in a low voice, "It is only known to us three who are here together."

"It is not at all known to the young lady, your friend?"

"On my soul, no!"

"I require you, then, to give me your similar and solemn pledge, Mr. Neville, that it shall remain the secret it is, and that you will take no other action whatsoever upon it than endeavoring (and that most earnestly) to erase it from your mind. I will not tell you that it will soon pass; I will not tell you that it is the fancy of the moment; I will not tell you that such caprices have their rise and fall among the young and ardent every hour; I will leave you undisturbed in the belief that it has few parallels or none, that it will abide with you a long time, and that it will be very difficult to conquer. So much the more weight shall I attach to the pledge I require from you, when it is unreservedly given."

The young man twice or thrice essayed to speak, but failed.

"Let me leave you with your sister, whom it is time you took home," said Mr. Crisparkle. "You will find me alone in my room by and by."

"Pray do not leave us yet," Helena implored him. "Another minute."

"I should not," said Neville, pressing his hand upon his face, "have needed so much as another minute, if you had been less patient with me, Mr. Crisparkle, less considerate of me, and less unpretendingly good and true. O, if in my childhood I had known such a guide!"

"Follow your guide now, Neville," murmured Helena, "and follow him to Heaven!"

There was that in her tone which broke the good Minor Canon's voice, or it would have repudiated her exaltation of him. As it was, he laid a finger on his lips, and looked towards her brother.

"To say that I give both pledges, Mr. Crisparkle, out of my innermost heart, and to say that there is no treachery in it, is to say nothing!" Thus Neville, greatly moved. "I beg your forgiveness for my miserable lapse into a burst of passion."

"Not mine, Neville, not mine. You know with whom forgiveness lies as the highest attribute conceivable. Miss Helena, you and your brother are twin children. You came into this world with the same dispositions, and you passed your younger days together surrounded by the same adverse circumstances. What you have overcome in yourself, can you not overcome in him? You see the rock that lies in his course. Who but you can keep him clear of it?"

"Who but you, sir?" replied Helena. "What is my influence, or my weak wisdom, compared with yours!"

"You have the wisdom of Love," returned the Minor Canon, "and it was the highest wisdom ever known upon this earth, remember. As to mine — but the less said of that commonplace commodity the better. Good night!"

She took the hand he offered her, and gratefully and almost reverently raised it to her lips.

"Tut!" said the Minor Canon, softly, "I am much overpaid!" And turned away.

Retracing his steps towards the Cathedral Close, he tried, as he went along in the dark, to think out the best means of bringing to pass what he had promised to effect, and what must somehow be done. "I shall probably be asked to marry them," he reflected, "and I would they were married and gone! But this presses first." He debated principally, whether he should write to young Drood, or whether he should speak to Jasper. The consciousness of being popular with the whole Cathedral establishment inclined him to the latter course, and the well-timed sight of the lighted Gate House decided him to take it. "I will strike while the iron is hot," he said, "and see him now."

Jasper was lying asleep on a couch before the fire, when, having ascended the postern-stair, and received no answer to his knock at the door, Mr. Crisparkle gently turned the handle and looked in. Long afterwards he had cause to remember how Jasper sprang from the couch in a delirious state between sleeping and waking, crying out, "What is the matter? Who did it?"

"It is only I, Jasper. I am sorry to have disturbed you."

The glare of his eyes settled down into a look of recognition, and he moved a chair or two, to make a way to the fireside.

"I was dreaming at a great rate, and am glad to be disturbed from an indigestive after-dinner sleep. Not to mention that you are always welcome."

"Thank you. I am not confident," returned Mr. Crisparkle, as he sat himself down in the easy-chair placed for him, "that my subject will at first sight be quite as welcome as myself; but I am a minister of peace, and I pursue my subject in the interests of peace. In a word, Jasper, I want to establish peace between these two young fellows."

A very perplexed expression took hold of Mr. Jasper's face; a very perplexing expression too, for Mr. Crisparkle could make nothing of it.

"How?" was Jasper's inquiry, in a low and slow voice, after a silence.

"For the 'How' I come to you. I want to ask you to do me the great favor and service of interposing with your nephew (I have already interposed with Mr. Neville), and getting him to write you a short note, in his lively way, saying that he is willing to shake hands. I know what a good-natured fellow he is, and what influence you have with him. And without in the least defending Mr. Neville, we must all admit that he was bitterly stung."

Jasper turned that perplexed face towards the fire. Mr. Crisparkle, continuing to observe it, found it even more perplexing than before, inasmuch as it seemed to denote (which could hardly be) some close internal calculation.

"I know that you are not prepossessed in Mr. Neville's favor," the Minor Canon was going on, when Jasper stopped him: —

"You have cause to say so. I am not, indeed."

"Undoubtedly, and I admit his lamentable violence of temper, though I hope he and I will get the better of it between us. But I have exacted a very solemn promise from him as to his future demeanor towards your nephew, if you do kindly interpose; and I am sure he will keep it."

"You are always responsible and trustworthy, Mr. Crisparkle. Do you really feel sure that you can answer for him so confidently?"

"I do."

The perplexed and perplexing look vanished.

"Then you relieve my mind of a great dread and a heavy weight," said Jasper; "I will do it."

Mr. Crisparkle, delighted by the swiftness and completeness of his success, acknowledged it in the handsomest terms.

"I will do it," repeated Jasper, "for the comfort of having your guaranty against my vague and unfounded fears. You will laugh, — but do you keep a Diary?"

"A line for a day; not more."

"A line for a day would be quite as much as my uneventful life would need, Heaven knows," said Jasper, taking a book from a desk; "but that my Diary is, in fact, a Diary of Ned's life too. You will laugh at this entry; you will guess when it was made: —

"'Past midnight. — After what I have just now seen, I have a morbid dread upon me of some horrible consequences resulting to my dear boy, that I cannot reason with or in any way contend against. All my efforts are vain. The demoniacal passion of this Neville Landless, his strength in his fury, and his savage rage for the destruction of its object, appall me. So profound is the impression, that twice since have I gone into my dear boy's room, to assure myself of his sleeping safely, and not lying dead in his blood.'

"Here is another entry next morning: —

"'Ned up and away. Light-hearted and unsuspicious as ever. He laughed when I cautioned him, and said he was as good a man as Neville Landless any day. I told him that might be, but he was not as bad a man. He continued to make light of it, but I travelled with him as far as I could, and left him most unwillingly. I am unable to shake off these dark intangible presentiments of evil, — if feelings founded upon startling facts are to be so called.'

"Again and again," said Jasper, in conclusion, twirling the leaves of the book before putting it by, "I have relapsed into these moods, as other entries show. But I have now your assurance at my back, and shall put it in my book, and make it an antidote to my black humors."

"Such an antidote, I hope," returned Mr. Crisparkle, "as will induce you before long to consign the black humors to the flames. I ought to be the last to find any fault with you this evening, when you have met my wishes so freely; but I must say, Jasper, that your devotion to your nephew has made you exaggerative here."

"You are my witness," said Jasper, shrugging his shoulders, "what my state of mind honestly was, that night, before I sat down to write, and in what words I expressed it. You remember objecting to a word I used, as being too strong? It was a stronger word than any in my Diary."

"Well, well. Try the antidote," rejoined Mr. Crisparkle, "and may it give you a brighter and better view of the case! We will discuss it no more, now. I have to thank you for myself, and I thank you sincerely."

"You shall find," said Jasper, as they shook hands, "that I will not do the thing you wish me to do by halves. I will take care that Ned, giving way at all, shall give way thoroughly."

On the third day after this conversation, he called on Mr. Crisparkle with the following letter: —

"MY DEAR JACK,

"I am touched by your account of your interview with Mr. Crisparkle, whom I much respect and esteem. At once I openly say that I forgot myself on that occasion quite as much as Mr. Landless did, and that I wish that bygone to be a bygone, and all to be right again.

"Look here, dear old boy. Ask Mr. Landless to dinner on Christmas Eve (the better the day the better the deed), and let there be only we three, and let us shake hands all round there and then, and say no more about it.

"My dear Jack,

"Ever your most affectionate,

"EDWIN DROOD.

"P. S. — Love to Miss Pussy at the next music lesson."

"You expect Mr. Neville, then?" said Mr. Crisparkle.

"I count upon his coming," said Mr. Jasper.

CHAPTER XI.

A PICTURE AND A RING.

BEHIND the most ancient part of Holborn, London, where certain gabled houses some centuries of age still stand looking on the public way, as if disconsolately looking for the Old Bourne that has long run dry, is a little nook composed of two irregular quadrangles, called Staple Inn. It is one of those nooks, the turning into which out of the clashing street imparts to the relieved pedestrian the sensation of having put cotton in his ears and velvet soles on his boots. It is one of those nooks where a few smoky sparrows twitter in smoky trees, as though they called to one another, "Let us play at country," and where a few feet of garden mould and a few yards of gravel enable them to do that refreshing violence to their tiny understandings. Moreover, it is one of those nooks which are legal nooks; and it contains a little Hall, with a little lantern in its roof; to what obstructive purposes devoted, and at whose expense, this history knoweth not.

In the days when Cloisterham took offence at the existence of a railroad afar off, as menacing that sensitive constitution, the property of us Britons; the odd fortune of which sacred institutions it is to be in exactly equal degrees croaked about, trembled for, and boasted of, whatever happens to anything, anywhere in the world; in those days no neighboring architecture of lofty proportions had arisen to overshadow Staple Inn. The westering sun bestowed bright glances on it, and the southwest wind blew into it unimpeded.

Neither wind nor sun, however, favored Staple Inn, one December afternoon towards six o'clock, when it was filled with fog, and candles shed murky and blurred rays through the windows of all its then-occupied sets of chambers; notably, from a set of chambers in a corner house in the little inner quadrangle, presenting in black and white over its ugly portal the mysterious inscription: —

P
J T
1747.

In which set of chambers, never having troubled his head about the inscription, unless to bethink himself at odd times on glancing up at it, that haply it might mean Perhaps John Thomas, or Perhaps Joe Tyler, sat Mr. Grewgious writing by his fire.

Who could have told, by looking at Mr. Grewgious, whether he had ever known ambition or disappointment? He had been bred to the Bar, and had laid himself out for chamber practice; to draw deeds; "convey the wise it call," as Pistol says. But Conveyancing and he had made such a very indifferent marriage of it that they had separated by consent, —if there can be said to be separation where there has never been coming together.

No. Coy Conveyancing would not come to Mr. Grewgious. She was wooed, not won, and they went their several ways. But an Arbitration being blown towards him by some unaccountable wind, and he gaining great credit in it as one indefatigable in seeking out right and doing right, a pretty fat Receivership was next blown into his pocket by a wind more traceable to its source. So, by chance, he had found his niche. Receiver and Agent now, to two rich estates, and deputing their legal business, in an amount worth having, to a firm of solicitors on the floor below, he had snuffed out his ambition (supposing him to have ever lighted it) and had settled down with his snuffers for the rest of his life under the dry vine and fig-tree of P. J. T., who planted in seventeen-forty-seven.

Many accounts and account-books, many files of correspondence, and several strong boxes, garnished Mr. Grewgious's room. They can scarcely be represented as having lumbered it, so conscientious and precise was their orderly arrangement. The apprehension of dying suddenly, and leaving one fact or one figure with any incompleteness or obscurity attaching to it, would have stretched Mr. Grewgious stone dead any day. The largest fidelity to a trust was the life-blood of the man. There are sorts of life-blood that course more quickly, more gayly, more attractively; but there is no better sort in circulation.

There was no luxury in his room. Even its comforts were limited to its being dry and warm, and having a snug though faded fireside. What may be called its private life was confined to the hearth, and an easy-chair, and an old-fashioned occasional round table that was brought out upon the rug after business hours, from a corner where it elsewise remained turned up like a shining mahogany shield. Behind it, when standing thus on the defensive, was a closet, usually containing something good to drink. An outer room was the clerk's room; Mr. Grewgious's sleeping-room was across the common stair; and he held some not empty cellarage at the bottom of the common stair. Three hundred days in the year, at least, he crossed over to the hotel in Furnival's Inn for his dinner, and after dinner crossed back again, to make the most of these simplicities until it should become broad business day once more, with P. J. T., date seventeen-forty-seven.

As Mr. Grewgious sat and wrote by his fire that afternoon, so did the clerk of Mr. Grewgious sit and write by *his* fire. A pale, puffy-faced, dark-haired person of thirty, with big dark eyes that wholly wanted lustre, and a dissatisfied doughy complexion, that seemed to ask to be sent to the baker's, this attendant was a mysterious being, possessed of some strange power over Mr. Grewgious. As though he had been called into existence, like a fabulous Familiar, by a magic spell which had failed when required to dismiss him, he stuck tight to Mr. Grewgious's stool, although Mr. Grewgious's comfort and convenience would manifestly have been advanced by dispossessing him. A gloomy person with tangled locks, and a general air of having been reared under the shadow of that baleful tree of Java which has given shelter to more lies than the whole botanical kingdom, Mr. Grewgious, nevertheless, treated him with unaccountable consideration.

"Now, Bazzard," said Mr. Grewgious, on the entrance of his clerk, looking up from his papers as he arranged them for the night, "what is in the wind besides fog?"

"Mr. Drood," said Bazzard.

"What of him?"

"Has called," said Bazzard.

"You might have shown him in."

"I am doing it," said Bazzard.

The visitor came in accordingly.

"Dear me!" said Mr. Grewgious, looking round his pair of office candles. "I thought you had called and merely left your name, and gone. How do you do, Mr. Edwin? Dear me, you 're choking!"

"It 's this fog," returned Edwin, "and it makes my eyes smart like cayenne pepper."

"Is it really so bad as that? Pray undo your wrappers. It 's fortunate I have so good a fire; but Mr. Bazzard has taken care of me."

"No, I have n't," said Mr. Bazzard at the door.

"Ah! Then it follows that I must have taken care of myself without observing it," said Mr. Grewgious. "Pray be seated in my chair. No. I beg! Coming out of such an atmosphere, in *my* chair."

Edwin took the easy-chair in the corner; and the fog he had brought in with him, and the fog he took off with his great-coat and neck-shawl was speedily licked up by the eager fire.

"I look," said Edwin, smiling, "as if I had come to stop."

"— By the by," cried Mr. Grewgious, "excuse my interrupting you; do stop. The fog may clear in an hour or two. We can have dinner in from just across Holborn. You had better take your cayenne pepper here than outside; pray stop and dine."

"You are very kind," said Edwin, glancing about him, as though attracted by the notion of a new and relishing sort of gypsy-party.

"Not at all," said Mr. Grewgious; "*you* are very kind to join issue with a bachelor in chambers, and take pot-luck. And I 'll ask," said Mr. Grewgious, dropping his voice, and speaking with a twinkling eye, as if inspired with a bright thought, — "I 'll ask Bazzard. He might n't like it else. Bazzard!"

Bazzard reappeared.

"Dine presently with Mr. Drood and me."

"If I am ordered to dine, of course I will, sir," was the gloomy answer.

"Save the man!" cried Mr. Grewgious. "You 're not ordered; you 're invited."

"Thank you, sir," said Bazzard; "in that case I don't care if do."

"That 's arranged. And perhaps you would n't mind," said Mr. Grewgious, "stepping over to the hotel in Furnival's, and asking them to send in materials for laying the cloth. For dinner we 'll have a tureen of the hottest and strongest soup available, and we 'll have the best made-dish that can be recommended, and we 'll have a joint (such as a haunch of mutton), and we 'll have a goose or a turkey, or any little stuffed thing of that sort that may happen to be in the bill of fare, — in short, we 'll have whatever there is on hand."

These liberal directions Mr. Grewgious issued with his usual air of reading an inventory, or repeating a lesson, or doing anything else by rote. Bazzard, after drawing out the round table, withdrew to execute them.

"I was a little delicate, you see," said Mr. Grewgious in a lower tone, after his clerk's departure, "about employing him in the foraging or commissariat department. Because he might n't like it."

"He seems to have his own way, sir," remarked Edwin.

"His own way?" returned Mr. Grewgious. "O dear, no! Poor fellow, you quite mistake him. If he had his own way, he would n't be here."

"I wonder where he would be!" Edwin thought. But he only thought it, because Mr. Grewgious came and stood himself with his back to the other corner of the fire, and his shoulder-blades against the chimney-piece, and collected his skirts for easy conversation.

"I take it, without having the gift of prophecy, that you have done me the favor of looking in to mention that you are going down yonder — where I can tell you, you are expected — and to offer to execute any little commission from me to my charming ward, and perhaps to sharpen me up a bit in any proceedings? Eh, Mr. Edwin?"

"I called, sir, before going down, as an act of attention."

"Of attention!" said Mr. Grewgious. "Ah! of course, not of impatience?"

"Impatience, sir?"

Mr. Grewgious had meant to be arch, — not that he in the remotest degree expressed that meaning, — and had brought himself into scarcely supportable proximity with the fire, as if to burn the fullest effect of his archness into himself, as other subtle impressions are burnt into hard metals. But his archness suddenly flying before the composed face and manner of his visitor, and only the fire remaining, he started and rubbed himself.

"I have lately been down yonder," said Mr. Grewgious, rearranging his skirts; "and that was what I referred to when I said I could tell you, you are expected."

"Indeed, sir! Yes, I knew that Pussy was looking out for me."

"Do you keep a cat down there?" asked Mr. Grewgious.

Edwin colored a little as he explained, "I call Rosa Pussy."

"O, really," said Mr. Grewgious, smoothing down his head, "that 's very affable."

Edwin glanced at his face, uncertain whether or no he seriously objected to the appellation. But Edwin might as well have glanced at the face of a clock

"A pet name, sir," he explained again.

"Umps," said Mr. Grewgious, with a nod. But with such an extraordinary compromise between an unqualified assent and a qualified dissent that his visitor was much disconcerted.

"Did PRosa —" Edwin began, by way of recovering himself.

"PRosa?" repeated Mr. Grewgious.

"I was going to say Pussy, and changed my mind; — did she tell you anything about the Landlesses?"

"No," said Mr. Grewgious. "What is the Landlesses? An estate? A villa? A farm?"

"A brother and sister. The sister is at the Nuns' House, and has become a great friend of P —"

"PRosa's," Mr. Grewgious struck in, with a fixed face.

"She is a strikingly handsome girl, sir, and I thought she might have been described to you, or presented to you, perhaps?"

"Neither," said Mr. Grewgious. "But here is Bazzard."

Bazzard returned, accompanied by two waiters, — an immovable waiter and a flying waiter; and the three brought in with them as much fog as gave a new roar to the fire. The flying waiter, who had brought everything on his shoulders, laid the cloth with amazing rapidity and dexterity; while the immovable waiter, who had brought nothing, found fault with him. The flying waiter then highly polished all the glasses he had brought, and the immovable waiter looked through them. The flying waiter then flew across Holborn for the soup and flew back again, and then took another flight for the made-dish and flew back again, and then took another flight for the joint and poultry and flew back again, and between whiles took supplementary flights for a great variety of articles as it was discovered from time to time that the immovable waiter had forgotten them all. But let the flying waiter cleave the air as he might, he was always reproached on his return by the immovable waiter for bringing fog with him and being out of breath. At the conclusion of the repast, by which time the flying waiter was severely blown, the immovable waiter gathered up the tablecloth under his arm with a grand air, and having sternly (not to say with indignation) looked on at the flying waiter while he set clean glasses round, directed a valedictory glance towards Mr. Grewgious, conveying, "Let it be clearly understood between us that the reward is mine, and that Nil is the claim of this slave," and pushed the flying waiter before him out of the room.

It was like a highly finished miniature painting representing My Lords of the Circumlocutional Department, Commandership-in-Chief of any sort, Government. It was quite an edifying little picture to be hung on the line in the National Gallery.

As the fog had been the proximate cause of this sumptuous repast, so the fog served for its general sauce. To hear the out-door clerks sneezing, wheezing, and beating their feet on the gravel was a zest far surpassing Doctor Kitchener's. To bid, with a shiver, the unfortunate flying waiter shut the door before he had opened it, was a condiment of a profounder flavor than Harvey. And here let it be noticed parenthetically that the leg of this young man in its application to the door evinced the finest sense of touch; always preceding himself and tray (with something of an angling air about it) by some seconds, and always lingering after he and the tray had disappeared, like Macbeth's leg when accompanying him off the stage with reluctance to the assassination of Duncan.

The host had gone below to the cellar, and had brought up bottles of ruby, straw-colored, and golden drinks, which had ripened long ago in lands where no fogs are, and had since lain slumbering in the shade. Sparkling and tingling after so long a nap, they pushed at their corks to help the corkscrew (like prisoners helping rioters to force their gates), and danced out gayly. If P. J. T. in seventeen-forty-seven, or in any other year of his period, drank such wines, then, for a certainty, P. J. T. was Pretty Jolly Too.

Externally, Mr. Grewgious showed no signs of being mellowed by these glowing vintages. Instead of his drinking them, they might have been poured over him in his high-dried snuff form, and run to waste, for any lights and shades they caused to flicker over his face. Neither was his manner influenced. But, in his wooden way, he had observant eyes for Edwin; and when, at the end of dinner, he motioned Edwin back to his own easy-chair in the fireside corner, and Edwin luxuriously sank into it after very brief remonstrance, Mr. Grewgious, as he turned his seat round towards the fire too, and smoothed his head and face, might have been seen looking at his visitor between his smoothing fingers.

"Bazzard!" said Mr. Grewgious, suddenly turning to him.

"I follow you, sir," returned Bazzard, who had done his work of consuming meat and drink, in a workmanlike manner, though mostly in speechlessness.

"I drink to you, Bazzard; Mr. Edwin, success to Mr. Bazzard!"

"Success to Mr. Bazzard!" echoed Edwin, with a totally unfounded appearance of enthusiasm, and with the unspoken addition, "What in, I wonder!"

"And May!" pursued Mr. Grewgious, — "I am not at liberty to be definite — May! — my conversational powers are so very limited that I know I shall not come well out of this — May! — it ought to be put imaginatively, but I have no imagination — May! — the thorn of anxiety is as nearly the mark as I am likely to get — May it come out at last!"

Mr. Bazzard, with a frowning smile at the fire, put a hand into his tangled locks, as if the thorn of anxiety were there; then into his waistcoat, as if it were there; then into his pockets, as if it were there. In all these movements he was closely followed by the eyes of Edwin, as if that young gentleman expected to see the thorn in action. It was not produced, however, and Mr. Bazzard merely said, "I follow you, sir, and I thank you."

"I am going," said Mr. Grewgious, jingling his glass on the table with one hand and bending aside under cover of the other to whisper to Edwin, "to drink to my ward. But I put Bazzard first. He might n't like it else."

This was said with a mysterious wink; or what would have been a wink if, in Mr. Grewgious's hands, it could have been quick enough. So Edwin winked responsively without the least idea what he meant by doing so.

"And now," said Mr. Grewgious, "I devote a bumper to the fair and fascinating Miss Rosa. Bazzard, the fair and fascinating Miss Rosa!"

"I follow you, sir," said Bazzard, "and I pledge you!"

"And so do I!" said Edwin.

"Lord bless me!" cried Mr. Grewgious, breaking the blank silence which of course ensued, though why these pauses *should* come upon us when we have performed any small social rite not directly inducive of self-examination or mental despondency who can tell! "I am a particularly Angular man, and yet I fancy (if I may use the word, not having a morsel of fancy) that I could draw a picture of a true lover's state of mind to-night."

"Let us follow you, sir," said Bazzard, "and have the picture."

"Mr. Edwin will correct it where it 's wrong," resumed Mr. Grewgious, "and will throw in a few touches from the life. I dare say it is wrong in many particulars, and wants many touches from the life, for I was born a Chip, and have neither soft sympathies nor soft experiences. Well! I hazard the guess that the true lover's mind is completely permeated by the beloved object of his affections. I hazard the guess that her dear name is precious to him, cannot be heard or repeated without emotion, and is preserved sacred. If he has any distinguishing appellation of fondness for her, it is reserved for her and is not for common ears. A name that it would be a privilege to call her by, being alone with her own bright self, it would be a liberty, a coldness, an insensibility, almost a breach of good faith, to flaunt elsewhere."

It was wonderful to see Mr. Grewgious sitting bolt upright, with his hands on his knees, continuously chopping this discourse out of himself, much as a charity-boy with a very good memory might get his catechism said, and evincing no correspondent emotion whatever, unless in a certain occasional little tingling perceptible at the end of his nose.

"My picture," Mr. Grewgious proceeded, "goes on to represent (under correction from you, Mr. Edwin) the true lover as ever impatient to be in the presence or vicinity of the beloved object of his affections. as caring very little for his ease in any other society, and as constantly seeking that. If I was to say seeking that as a bird seeks its nest, I should make an ass of myself, because that would trench upon what I understand to be poetry; and I am so far from trenching upon poetry at any time, that I never to my knowledge got within ten thousand miles of it. And I am besides totally unacquainted with the habits of birds, except the birds of Staple Inn, who seek their nests on ledges and in gutter-pipes and chimney-pots, not constructed for them by the beneficent hand of Nature. I beg, therefore, to be understood as foregoing the bird's-nest. But my picture does represent the true lover as having no existence separable from that of the beloved object of his affections, and as living at once a doubled life and a halved life. And if I do not clearly express what I mean by that, it is either for the reason that having no conversational powers, I cannot express what I mean, or that, having no meaning, I do not mean what I fail to express. Which, to the best of my belief, is not the case."

Edwin had turned red and turned white as certain points of this picture came into the light. He now sat looking at the fire and bit his lip.

"The speculations of an Angular man," resumed Mr. Grewgious, still sitting and speaking exactly as before, "are probably erroneous on so globular a topic. But I figure to myself (subject as before to Mr. Edwin's correction) that there can be no coolness, no lassitude, no doubt, no indifference, no half-fire and half-smoke state of mind in a real lover. Pray am I at all near the mark in my picture?"

As abrupt in his conclusion as in his commencement and progress, he jerked this inquiry at Edwin, and stopped when one might have supposed him in the middle of his oration.

"I should say, sir," stammered Edwin, "as you refer the question to me —"

"Yes," said Mr. Grewgious, "I refer it to you as an authority."

"I should say then, sir," Edwin went on, embarrassed, "that the picture you have drawn is generally correct; but I submit that perhaps you may be rather hard upon the unlucky lover."

"Likely so," assented Mr. Grewgious, — "likely so. I am a hard man in the grain."

"He may not show," said Edwin, "all he feels; or he may not — "

There he stopped so long to find the rest of his sentence that Mr. Grewgious rendered his difficulty a thousand times the greater by unexpectedly striking in with, —

"No, to be sure; he *may* not!"

After that they all sat silent; the silence of Mr. Bazzard being occasioned by slumber.

"His responsibility is very great though," said Mr. Grewgious, at length, with his eyes on the fire.

Edwin nodded assent, with *his* eyes on the fire.

"And let him be sure that he trifles with no one," said Mr. Grewgious; "neither with himself, nor with any other."

Edwin bit his lip again, and still sat looking at the fire.

"He must not make a plaything of a treasure. Woe betide him if he does! Let him take that well to heart," said Mr. Grewgious.

Though he said these things in short sentences, much as the supposititious charity-boy just now referred to might have repeated a verse or two from the Book of Proverbs, there was something dreamy (for so literal a man) in the way in which he now shook his right forefinger at the live coals in the grate, and again fell silent.

But not for long. As he sat upright and stiff in his chair, he suddenly rapped his knees, like the carved image of some queer Joss or other coming out of its revery, and said, "We must finish this bottle, Mr. Edwin. Let me help you. I 'll help Bazzard, too, though he *is* asleep. He might n't like it else."

He helped them both, and helped himself, and drained his glass, and stood it bottom upward on the table, as though he had just caught a bluebottle in it.

"And now, Mr. Edwin," he proceeded, wiping his mouth and hands upon his handkerchief, "to a little piece of business. You received from me, the other day, a certified copy of Miss Rosa's father's will. You knew its contents before, but you received it from me as a matter of business. I should have sent it to Mr. Jasper, but for Miss Rosa's wishing it to come straight to you, in preference. You received it?"

"Quite safely, sir."

"You should have acknowledged its receipt," said Mr. Grewgious, "business being business all the world over. However, you did not."

"I meant to have acknowledged it when I first came in this evening, sir."

"Not a business-like acknowledgment," returned Mr Grewgious; "however, let that pass. Now, in that document you have observed a few words of kindly allusion to its being left to me to discharge a little trust, confided to me in conversation, at such time as I in my discretion may think best."

"Yes, sir."

"Mr. Edwin, it came into my mind just now, when I was looking at the fire, that I could, in my discretion, acquit myself of that trust at no better time than the present. Favor me with your attention half a minute."

He took a bunch of keys from his pocket, singled out by the candle-light the key he wanted, and then, with a candle in his hand, went to a bureau or escritoire, unlocked it, touched the spring of a little secret drawer, and took from it an ordinary ring-case made for a single ring. With this in his hand he returned to his chair. As he held it up for the young man to see, his hand trembled.

"Mr. Edwin, this rose of diamonds and rubies, delicately set in gold, was a ring belonging to Miss Rosa's mother. It was removed from her dead hand, in my presence, with such distracted grief as I hope it may never be my lot to contemplate again. Hard man as I am, I am not hard enough for that. See how bright these stones shine!" opening the case. "And yet the eyes that were so much brighter, and that so often looked upon them with a light and a proud heart, have been ashes among ashes, and dust among dust, some years! If I had any imagination (which it is needless to say I have not), I might imagine that the lasting beauty of these stones was almost cruel."

He closed the case again as he spoke.

"This ring was given to the young lady who was drowned so early in her beautiful and happy career, by her husband, when they first plighted their faith to one another. It was he who removed it from her unconscious hand, and it was he who, when his death drew very near, placed it in mine. The trust in which I received it, was, that, you and Miss Rosa growing to manhood and womanhood, and your betrothal prospering and coming to maturity, I should give it to you to place upon her finger. Failing those desired results, it was to remain in my possession."

Some trouble was in the young man's face, and some indecision was in the action of his hand, as Mr. Grewgious, looking steadfastly at him, gave him the ring."

"Your placing it on her finger," said Mr. Grewgious, "will be the solemn seal upon your strict fidelity to the living and the dead. You are going to her to make the last irrevocable preparations for your marriage. Take it with you."

The young man took the little case and placed it in his breast.

"If anything should be amiss, if anything should be even slightly wrong between you, if you should have any secret consciousness, that you are committing yourself to this step for no higher reason than because you have long been accustomed to look forward to it; then," said Mr. Grewgious, "I charge you once more, by the living and by the dead, to bring that ring back to me!"

Here Bazzard awoke himself by his own snoring; and, as is usual in such cases, sat apoplectically staring at vacancy, as defying vacancy to accuse him of having been asleep.

"Bazzard!" said Mr. Grewgious, harder than ever.

"I follow you, sir," said Bazzard, "and I have been following you."

"In discharge of a trust, I have handed Mr. Edwin Drood a ring of diamonds and rubies. You see?"

Edwin reproduced the little case and opened it ; and Bazzard looked into it.

"I follow you both, sir," returned Bazzard, "and I witness the transaction."

Evidently anxious to get away and be alone, Edwin Drood now resumed his outer clothing, muttering something about time and appointments. The fog was reported no clearer (by the flying waiter, who alighted from a speculative flight in the coffee interest), but he went out into it; and Bazzard, after his manner, "followed" him.

Mr. Grewgious, left alone, walked softly and slowly to and fro for an hour and more. He was restless to-night, and seemed dispirited.

"I hope I have done right," he said. "The appeal to him seemed necessary. It was hard to lose the ring, and yet it must have gone from me very soon."

He closed the empty little drawer with a sigh, and shut and locked the escritoire, and came back to the solitary fireside.

"Her ring," he went on. "Will it come back to me? My mind hangs about her ring very uneasily to-night. But that is explainable. I have had it so long, and I have prized it so much! I wonder — "

He was in a wondering mood as well as a restless ; for though he checked himself at that point, and took another walk, he resumed his wondering when he sat down again.

"I wonder (for the ten thousandth time, and what a weak fool I, for what can it signify now!) whether he confided the charge of their orphan child to me because he knew — Good God, how like her mother she has become!

"I wonder whether he ever so much as suspected that some one doted on her at a hopeless, speechless distance when he struck in and won her! I wonder whether it ever crept into his mind who that unfortunate some one was!

"I wonder whether I shall sleep to-night! At all events I will shut out the world with the bedclothes, and try."

Mr. Grewgious crossed the staircase to his raw and foggy bedroom, and was soon ready for bed. Dimly catching sight of his face in the misty looking-glass, he held his candle to it for a moment.

"A likely some one, *you*, to come into anybody's thoughts in such an aspect!" he exclaimed. "There, there! there! Get to bed, poor man, and cease to jabber!"

With that he extinguished his light, pulled up the bedclothes around him, and with another sigh shut out the world. And yet there are such unexplored romantic nooks in the unlikeliest men, that even old tinderous and touchwoody P. J. T. Possibly Jabbered Thus, at some odd times, in or about seventeen-forty-seven.

CHAPTER XII.

A NIGHT WITH DURDLES.

WHEN Mr. Sapsea has nothing better to do towards evening, and finds the contemplation of his own profundity becoming a little monotonous in spite of the vastness of the subject, he often takes an airing in the Cathedral Close and thereabout. He likes to pass the churchyard with a swelling air of proprietorship, and to encourage in his breast a sort of benignant-landlord feeling in that he has been bountiful towards that meritorious tenant, Mrs. Sapsea, and has publicly given her a prize. He likes to see a stray face or two looking in through the railings and perhaps reading his inscription. Should he meet a stranger coming from the churchyard with a quick step, he is morally convinced that the stranger is "with a blush retiring," as monumentally directed.

Mr. Sapsea's importance has received enhancement, for he has become Mayor of Cloisterham. Without mayors and many of them, it cannot be disputed that the whole framework of society -- Mr. Sapsea is confident that he invented that forcible figure — would fall to pieces. Mayors have been knighted for "going up" with addresses: explosive machines intrepidly discharging shot and shell into the English Grammar. Mr. Sapsea may "go up" with an address. Rise, Sir Thomas Sapsea! Of such is the salt of the earth.

Mr. Sapsea has improved the acquaintance of Mr. Jasper since their first meeting to partake of port, epitaph, backgammon, beef, and salad. Mr. Sapsea has been received at the Gate House with kindred hospitality; and on that occasion Mr. Jasper seated himself at the piano, and sang to him, tickling his ears — figuratively, long enough to present a considerable area for tickling. What Mr. Sapsea likes in that young man is, that he is always ready to profit by the wisdom of his elders, and that he is sound, sir, at the core. In proof of which he sang to Mr. Sapsea that evening no kickshaw ditties, favorites with national enemies, but gave him the genuine George the Third home-brewed, exhorting him (as "my brave boys") to reduce to a smashed condition all other islands but this island, and all continents, peninsulas, isthmuses, promontories, and other geographical forms of land soever, besides sweeping the seas in all directions. In short, he rendered it pretty clear that Providence made a distinct mistake in originating so small a nation of hearts of oak, and so many other verminous peoples.

Mr. Sapsea, walking slowly this moist evening near the churchyard with his hands behind him on the lookout for a blushing and retiring stranger, turns a corner and comes instead into the goodly presence of the Dean conversing with the Verger and Mr. Jasper. Mr Sapsea makes his obeisance, and is instantly stricken far more ecclesiastical than any Archbishop of York or Canterbury.

"You are evidently going to write a book about us, Mr. Jasper," quoth the Dean; "to write a book about us. Well! We are very ancient, and we ought to make a good book. We are not so richly endowed in possessions as in age; but perhaps you will put *that* in your book, among other things, and call attention to our wrongs."

Mr. Tope, as in duty bound, is greatly entertained by this.

"I really have no intention at all, sir," replies Jasper, "of turning author or archæologist. It is but a whim of mine. And even for my whim, Mr. Sapsea here is more accountable than I am."

"How so, Mr. Mayor?" says the Dean, with a nod of good-natured recognition of his Fetch. "How is that, Mr. Mayor?"

"I am not aware," Mr. Sapsea remarks, looking about him for information, "to what the Very Reverend the Dean does me the honor of referring." And then falls to studying his original in minute points of detail.

"Durdles," Mr. Tope hints.

"Ay!" the Dean echoes; "Durdles, Durdles!"

"The truth is, sir," explains Jasper, "that my curiosity in the man was first really stimulated by Mr. Sapsea. Mr. Sapsea's knowledge of mankind, and power of drawing out whatever is recluse or odd around him, first led to my bestowing a second thought upon the man: though of course I had met him constantly about. You would not be surprised by this, Mr. Dean, if you had seen Mr. Sapsea deal with him in his own parlor, as I did."

"Oh!" cries Sapsea, picking up the ball thrown to him with ineffable complacency and pomposity; "yes, yes. The Very Reverend the Dean refers to that?

Yes. I happened to bring Durdles and Mr. Jasper together. I regard Durdles as a Character."

"A character, Mr. Sapsea, that with a few skilful touches you turn inside out," says Jasper.

"Nay, not quite that," returns the lumbering auctioneer. "I may have a little influence over him, perhaps; and a little insight into his character, perhaps. The Very Reverend the Dean will please to bear in mind that I have seen the world." Here Mr. Sapsea gets a little behind the Dean, to inspect his coat-buttons.

"Well!" says the Dean, looking about him to see what has become of his copyist: "I hope, Mr. Mayor, you will use your study and knowledge of Durdles to the good purpose of exhorting him not to break our worthy and respected Choir-Master's neck; we cannot afford it; his head and voice are much too valuable to us."

Mr. Tope is again highly entertained, and, having fallen into respectful convulsions of laughter, subsides into a deferential murmur, importing that surely any gentleman would deem it a pleasure and an honor to have his neck broken in return for such a compliment from such a source.

"I will take it upon myself, sir," observes Sapsea, loftily, "to answer for Mr. Jasper's neck. I will tell Durdles to be careful of it. He will mind what *I* say. How is it at present endangered?" he inquires, looking about him with magnificent patronage.

"Only by my making a moonlight expedition with Durdles among the tombs, vaults, towers, and ruins," returns Jasper. "You remember suggesting when you brought us together, that, as a lover of the picturesque, it might be worth my while?"

"*I* remember!" replies the auctioneer. And the solemn idiot really believes that he does remember.

"Profiting by your hint," pursues Jasper, "I have had some day-rambles with the extraordinary old fellow, and we are to make a moonlight hole-and-corner exploration to-night."

"And here he is," says the Dean.

Durdles, with his dinner-bundle in his hand, is indeed beheld slouching towards them. Slouching nearer, and perceiving the Dean, he pulls off his hat, and is slouching away with it under his arm, when Mr. Sapsea stops him.

"Mind you take care of my friend," is the injunction Mr. Sapsea lays upon him

"What friend o' yourn is dead?" asks Durdles. "No orders has come in for any friend o' yourn."

"I mean my live friend, there."

"Oh! Him?" says Durdles. "He can take care of himself, can Mister Jarsper."

"But do you take care of him too," says Sapsea.

Whom Durdles (there being command in his tone) surlily surveys from head to foot.

"With submission to his Reverence the Dean, if you 'll mind what concerns you, Mr. Sapsea, Durdles he 'll mind what concerns him."

"You 're out of temper," says Mr. Sapsea, winking to the company to observe how smoothly he will manage him. "My friend concerns me, and Mr. Jasper is my friend. And you are my friend."

"Don't you get into a bad habit of boasting," retorts Durdles with a grave, cautionary nod. "It 'll grow upon you."

"You are out of temper," says Sapsea again, reddening, but again winking to the company.

"I own to it," returns Durdles; "I don't like liberties."

Mr. Sapsea winks a third wink to the company, as who should say, "I think you will agree with me that I have settled *his* business"; and stalks out of the controversy.

Durdles then gives the Dean a good evening, and adding, as he puts his hat on, "You 'll find me at home, Mister Jarsper, as agreed, when you want me; I 'm a going home to clean myself," soon slouches out of sight. This going home to clean himself is one of the man's incomprehensible compromises with inexorable facts; he, and his hat, and his boots, and his clothes, never showing any trace of cleaning, but being uniformly in one condition of dust and grit.

The lamplighter now dotting the quiet Close with specks of light, and running at a great rate up and down his little ladder with that object, — his little ladder under the sacred shadow of whose inconvenience generations had grown up, and which all Cloisterham would have stood aghast at the idea of abolishing, — the Dean withdraws to his dinner, Mr. Tope to his tea, and Mr. Jasper to his piano. There, with no light but that of the fire, he sits chanting choir music in a low and beautiful voice for two or three hours; in short, until it has been for some time dark, and the moon is about to rise.

Then he closes his piano softly, softly changes his coat for a pea-jacket with a goodly wicker-cased bottle in its largest pocket, and, putting on a low-crowned, flap-brimmed hat, goes softly out. Why does he move so softly to-night? No outward reason is apparent for it. Can there be any sympathetic reason crouching darkly within him?

Repairing to Durdles's unfinished house, or hole in the city wall, and seeing a light within it, he softly picks his course among the gravestones, monuments, and stony lumber of the yard, already touched here and there, sidewise, by the rising moon. The two journeymen have left their two great saws sticking in their blocks of stone; and two skeleton journeymen out of the Dance of Death might be grinning in the shadow of their sheltering sentry-boxes about to slash away at cutting out the gravestones of the next two people destined to die in Cloisterham. Likely enough the two think little of that now, being alive, and perhaps merry. Curious to make a guess at the two, — or say at one of the two!

"Ho! Durdles!"

The light moves, and he appears with it at the door. He would seem to have been "cleaning himself" with the aid of a bottle, jug, and tumbler; for no other cleansing instruments are visible in the bare brick room with rafters overhead and no plastered ceiling, into which he shows his visitor.

"Are you ready?"

"I am ready, Mister Jarsper. Let the old uns come out if they dare when we go among their tombs. My spirits is ready for 'em."

"Do you mean animal spirits, or ardent?"

"The one 's the t' other," answers Durdles, "and I mean 'em both."

He takes a lantern from a hook, puts a match or two in his pocket wherewith to light it, should there be need, and they go out together, dinner-bundle and all.

Surely an unaccountable sort of expedition! That Durdles himself, who is always prowling among old graves and ruins like a Ghoul, — that he should be stealing forth to climb and dive and wander without an object, is nothing extraordinary; but that the Choir-Master or any one else should hold it worth his while to be with him, and to study moonlight effects in such company, is another affair. Surely an unaccountable sort of expedition therefore!

"'Ware that there mound by the yard-gate, Mister Jarsper."

"I see it. What is it?"

"Lime."

Mr. Jasper stops, and waits for him to come up, for he lags behind. "What you call quicklime?"

"Ay!" says Durdles; "quick enough to eat your boots. With a little handy stirring, quick enough to eat your bones."

They go on, presently passing the red windows of the Travellers' Twopenny and emerging into the clear moonlight of the Monks' Vineyard. This crossed, they come to Minor Canon Corner, of which the greater part lies in shadow until the moon shall rise higher in the sky.

The sound of a closing house-door strikes their ears, and two men come out. These are Mr. Crisparkle and Neville. Jasper, with a strange and sudden smile upon his face, lays the palm of his hand upon the breast of Durdles, stopping him where he stands.

At that end of Minor Canon Corner the shadow is profound in the existing state of the light: at that end, too, there is a piece of old dwarf wall, breast high, the only remaining boundary of what was once a garden, but is now the thoroughfare. Jasper and Durdles would have turned this wall in another instant, but, stopping so short, stand behind it.

"Those two are only sauntering," Jasper whispers; "they will go out into the moonlight soon. Let us keep quiet here, or they will detain us, or want to join us, or what not."

Durdles nods assent, and falls to munching some fragments from his bundle. Jasper folds his arms upon the top of the wall, and, with his chin resting on them, watches. He takes no note whatever of the Minor Canon, but watches Neville, as though his eye were at the trigger of a loaded rifle and he had covered him, and were going to fire. A sense of destructive power is so expressed in his face, that even Durdles pauses in his munching, and looks at him, with an unmunched something in his cheek.

Meanwhile Mr. Crisparkle and Neville walk to and fro, quietly talking together. What they say cannot be heard consecutively, but Mr. Jasper has already distinguished his own name more than once.

"This is the first day of the week," Mr. Crisparkle can be distinctly heard to observe as they turn back, "and the last day of the week is Christmas Eve."

"You may be certain of me, sir."

The echoes were favorable at those points, but as the two approach the sound of their talking becomes confused again. The word "confidence," shattered by the echoes, but still capable of being pieced together, is uttered by Mr. Crisparkle. As they draw still nearer, this fragment of a reply is heard: "Not deserved yet, but shall be, sir." As they turn away again Jasper again hears his own name in connection with the words from Mr. Crisparkle, "Remember that I said I answered for you confidently." Then the sound of their talk becomes confused again; they halting for a little while, and some earnest action on the part of Neville succeeding. When they move once more, Mr. Crisparkle is seen to look up at the sky, and to point before him. They then slowly disappear, passing out into the moonlight at the opposite end of the Corner.

It is not until they are gone that Mr. Jasper moves. But then he turns to Durdles, and bursts into a fit of laughter. Durdles, who still has that suspended something in his cheek, and who sees nothing to laugh at, stares at him until Mr. Jasper lays his face down on his arms to have his laugh out. Then Durdles bolts the something, as if desperately resigning himself to indigestion.

Among those secluded nooks there is very little stir or movement after dark. There is little enough in the high-tide of the day, but there is next to none at night. Besides that the cheerfully frequented High Street lies nearly parallel to the spot (the old Cathedral rising between the two), and is the natural channel in which the Cloisterham traffic flows a certain awful hush pervades the ancient pile, the cloisters, and the churchyard, after dark, which not many people care to encounter Ask the first hundred citizens of Cloisterham, met at random in the streets at noon, if they believed in Ghosts, they would tell you no; but put them to choose at night between these eyry Precincts and the thoroughfare of shops, and you would find that ninety-nine declared for the longer round and the more frequented way. The cause of this is not to be found in any local superstition that attaches to the Precincts, — albeit a mysterious lady, with a child in her arms and a rope dangling from her neck, has been seen flitting about there by sundry witnesses as intangible as herself, — but it is to be sought in the innate shrinking of dust with the breath of life in it from dust out of which the breath of life has passed; also, in the widely diffused, and almost as widely unacknowledged, reflection: "If the dead do, under any circumstances, become visible to the living, these are such likely surroundings for the purpose that I, the living, will get out of them as soon as I can."

Hence, when Mr. Jasper and Durdles pause to glance around them, before descending into the crypt by a small side door, of which the latter has a key, the whole expanse of moonlight in their view is utterly deserted. One might fancy that the tide of life was stemmed by Mr. Jasper's own Gate House. The murmur of the tide is heard beyond; but no wave passes the archway, over which his lamp burns red behind his curtain, as if the building were a lighthouse.

They enter, locking themselves in, descend the rugged steps, and are down in the crypt. The lantern is not wanted, for the moonlight strikes in at the groined windows, bare of glass, the broken frames for which cast patterns on the ground. The heavy pillars which support the roof engender masses of black shade, but between them there are lanes of light. Up and down these lanes they walk, Durdles discoursing of the "old uns" he yet counts on disinterring, and slapping a wall, in which he considers "a whole family on 'em" to be stoned and earthed up, just as if he were a familar friend of the family. The taciturnity of Durdles is for the time overcome by Mr. Jasper's wicker bottle, which circulates freely; — in the sense, that is to say, that its contents enter freely into Mr. Durdles's circulation, while Mr. Jasper only rinses his mouth once, and casts forth the rinsing.

They are to ascend the great Tower. On the steps by which they rise to the Cathedral, Durdles pauses for new store of breath. The steps are very dark, but out of the darkness they can see the lanes of light they have traversed. Durdles seats himself upon a step. Mr. Jasper seats himself upon another. The odor from the wicker bottle (which has somehow passed into Durdles's keeping) soon intimates that the cork has been taken out; but this is not ascertainable through the sense of sight, since neither can descry the other. And yet, in talking, they turn to one another, as though their faces could commune together.

"This is good stuff, Mr. Jarsper!"

"It is very good stuff, I hope. I bought it on purpose."

"They don't show, you see, the old uns don't, Mister Jarsper!"

"It would be a more confused world than it is, if they could"

"Well, it *would* lead towards a mixing of things," Durdles acquiesces; pausing on the remark, as if the idea of ghosts had not previously presented itself to him in a merely inconvenient light, domestically, or chronologically. "But do you think there may be Ghosts of other things, though not of men and women?"

"What things? Flower-beds and watering-pots? Horses and harness?"

"No. Sounds."

"What sounds?"

"Cries."

"What cries do you mean? Chairs to mend?"

"No. I mean screeches. Now, I 'll tell you, Mister Jarsper. Wait a bit till I put the bottle right." Here the cork is evidently taken out again, and replaced again. "There! *Now* it 's right! This time last year, only a few days later, I happened to have been doing what was correct by the season, in the way of giving it the welcome it had a right to expect, when them town-boys set on me at their worst. At length I gave 'em the slip and turned in here. And here I fell asleep. And what woke me? The ghost of a cry. The ghost of one terrific shriek, which shriek was followed by the ghost of the howl of a dog, a long, dismal, woful howl, such as a dog gives when a person 's dead. That was *my* last Christmas Eve."

"What do you mean?" is the very abrupt, and, one might say, fierce retort.

"I mean that I made inquiries everywhere about, and that no living ears but mine heard either that cry or that howl. So I say they was both ghosts; though why they came to me, I 've never made out."

"I thought you were another kind of man," says Jasper, scornfully.

"So I thought myself," answers Durdles, with his usual composure; "and yet I was picked out for it."

Jasper had risen suddenly, when he asked him what he meant, and he now says, "Come, we shall freeze here; lead the way."

Durdles complies, not over-steadily; opens the door at the top of the steps with the key he has already used; and so emerges on the Cathedral level, in a passage at the side of the chancel. Here, the moonlight is so very bright again that the colors of the nearest stained-glass window are thrown upon their faces. The appearance of the unconscious Durdles, holding the door open for his companion to follow, as if from the grave, is ghastly enough, with a purple band across his face, and a yellow splash upon his brow; but he bears the close scrutiny of his companion in an insensible way, although it is prolonged while the latter fumbles among his pockets for a key confided to him that will open an iron gate so to enable them to pass to the staircase of the great tower.

"That and the bottle are enough for you to carry," he says, giving it to Durdles, "hand your bundle to me; I am younger and longer-winded than you." Durdles hesitates for a moment between bundle and bottle; but gives the preference to the bottle as being by far the better company, and consigns the dry-weight to his fellow-explorer.

Then they go up the winding staircase of the great tower, toilsomely, turning and turning, and lowering their heads to avoid the stairs above, or the rough stone pivot around which they twist. Durdles has lighted his lantern, by drawing from the cold hard wall a spark of that mysterious fire which lurks in everything, and, guided by this speck, they clamber up among the cobwebs and the dust. Their way lies through strange places. Twice or thrice they emerge into level, low-arched galleries, whence they can look down into the moonlit nave; and where Durdles, waving his lantern, shows the dim angels' heads upon the corbels of the roof, seeming to watch their progress. Anon, they turn into narrower and steeper staircases, and the night air begins to blow upon them, and the chirp of some startled jackdaw or frightened rook precedes the heavy beating of wings in a confined space, and the beating down of dust and straws upon their heads. At last, leaving their light behind a stair, — for it blows fresh up here, — they look down on Cloisterham, fair to see in the moonlight; its ruined habitations and sanctuaries of the dead, at the tower's base; its moss-softened, red-tiled roofs and red-brick houses of the living, clustered beyond; its river winding down from the mist on the horizon, as though that were its source, and already heaving with a restless knowledge of its approach towards the sea.

Once again, an unaccountable expedition this! Jasper (always moving softly, with no visible reason) contemplates the scene, and especially that stillest part of it which the Cathedral overshadows. But he contemplates Durdles quite as curiously, and Durdles is by times conscious of his watchful eyes.

Only by times, because Durdles is growing drowsy. As aeronauts lighten the load they carry, when they wish to rise, similarly Durdles has lightened the wicker bottle in coming up. Snatches of sleep surprise him on his legs, and stop him in his talk. A mild fit of calenture seizes him, in which he deems that the ground, so far below, is on a level with the tower, and would as lief walk off the tower into the air as not. Such is his state when they begin to come down. And as aeronauts make themselves heavier when they wish to descend, similarly Durdles charges himself with more liquid from the wicker bottle, that he may come down the better.

The iron gate attained and locked, — but not before Durdles has tumbled twice, and cut an eyebrow open once, — they descend into the crypt again, with the intent of issuing forth as they entered. But, while returning among those lanes of light, Durdles becomes so very uncertain, both of foot and speech, that he half drops, half throws himself down, by one of the heavy pillars, scarcely less heavy than itself, and indistinctly appeals to his companion for forty winks of a second each.

"If you will have it so, or must have it so," replies Jasper, "I 'll not leave you here. Take them while I walk to and fro."

Durdles is asleep at once; and in his sleep he dreams a dream.

It is not much of a dream, considering the vast extent of the domains of dreamland, and their wonderful productions; it is only remarkable for being unusually restless, and unusually real. He dreams of lying there, asleep, and yet counting his companion's footsteps as he walks to and fro. He dreams that the footsteps die away into distance of time and of space, and that something touches him, and that something falls from his hand. Then something clinks and gropes about, and he dreams that he is alone for so long a time, that the lanes of light take new directions as the moon advances in her course. From succeeding unconsciousness, he passes into a dream of slow uneasiness from cold, and painfully awakes to a perception of the lanes of light — really changed, much as he had dreamed — and Jasper walking among them, beating his hands and feet.

"Holloa!" Durdles cries out, unmeaningly alarmed.

"Awake at last?" says Jasper, coming up to him. "Do you know that your forties have stretched into thousands?"

"No."

"They have though."

"What's the time?"

"Hark! The bells are going in the tower!"

They strike four quarters, and then the great bell strikes.

"Two!" cries Durdles, scrambling up; "why did n't you try to wake me, Mister Jarsper?"

"I did. I might as well have tried to wake the dead; — your own family of dead, up in the corner there."

"Did you touch me?"

"Touch you? Yes. Shook you."

As Durdles recalls that touching something in his dream, he looks down on the pavement, and sees the key of the crypt door lying close to where he himself lay.

"I dropped you, did I?" he says, picking it up, and recalling that part of his dream. As he gathers himself again into an upright position, or into a position as nearly upright as he ever maintains, he is again conscious of being watched by his companion.

"Well?" says Jasper, smiling. "Are you quite ready? Pray don't hurry."

"Let me get my bundle right, Mister Jarsper, and I 'm with you."

As he ties it afresh, he is once more conscious that he is very narrowly observed.

"What do you suspect me of, Mister Jarsper?" he asks, with drunken displeasure. "Let them as has any suspicions of Durdles name 'em."

"I 've no suspicions of you, my good Mr. Durdles; but I have suspicions that my bottle was filled with something stiffer than either of us supposed. And I also have suspicions," Jasper adds, taking it from the pavement and turning it bottom upward, "that it 's empty."

Durdles condescends to laugh at this. Continuing to chuckle when his laugh is over, as though remonstrant with himself on his drinking powers, he rolls to the door and unlocks it. They both pass out, and Durdles relocks it, and pockets his key.

"A thousand thanks for a curious and interesting night," says Jasper, giving him his hand; "you can make your own way home?"

"I should think so!" answered Durdles. "If you was to offer Durdles the affront to show him his way home, he would n't go home.

Durdles would n't go home till morning,
And *then* Durdles would n't go home,

Durdles would n't." This, with the utmost defiance.

"Good night, then."

"Good night, Mister Jarsper."

Each is turning his own way, when a sharp whistle rends the silence, and the jargon is yelped out: —

"Widdy widdy wen!
I — ket — ches — Im — out — ar — ter — ten.
Widdy widdy wy!
Then — E — don't — go — then — I — shy —
Widdy Widdy Wake-cock warning!"

Instantly afterwards, a rapid fire of stones rattles at the Cathedral wall, and the hideous small boy is beheld opposite, dancing in the moonlight.

"What! Is that baby-devil on the watch!" cries Jasper, in a fury, so quickly roused, and so violent, that he seems an older devil himself. "I shall shed the blood of that Impish wretch! I know I shall do it!" Regardless of the fire, though it hits him more than once, he rushes at Deputy, collars him, and tries to bring him across. But Deputy is not to be so easily brought across. With a diabolical insight into the strongest part of his position, he is no sooner taken by the throat than he curls up his legs, forces his assailant to hang him, as it were, and gurgles in his throat, and screws his body, and twists, as already undergoing the first agonies of strangulation. There is nothing for it but to drop him. He instantly gets himself together, backs over to Durdles, and cries to his assailant, gnashing the great gap in front of his mouth with rage and malice: —

"I 'll blind yer, s'elp me! I 'll stone yer eyes out, s'elp me! If I don't have yer eyesight, bellows me!" at the same time dodging behind Durdles, and snarling at Jasper, now from this side of him and now from that: prepared, if pounced upon, to dart away in all manner of curvilinear directions, and, if run down after all, to grovel in the dust, and cry, "Now, hit me when I 'm down! Do it!"

"Don't hurt the boy, Mister Jarsper," urges Durdles, shielding him. "Recollect yourself."

"He followed us to-night, when we first came here!"

"Yer lie, I did n't!" replies Deputy, in his one form of polite contradiction.

"He has been prowling near us ever since!"

"Yer lie, I have n't!" returns Deputy. "I 'd only jist come out for my 'elth when I see you two a coming out of the Kinfreederel. If—

I — ket — ches — Im — out — ar — ter — ten"

(with the usual rhythm and dance, though dodging behind Durdles), "it ain't *my* fault, is it?"

"Take him home, then," retorts Jasper, ferociously, though with a strong check upon himself, "and let my eyes be rid of the sight of you!"

Deputy, with another sharp whistle, at once expressing his relief, and his commencement of a milder stoning of Mr. Durdles, begins stoning that respectable gentleman home, as if he were a reluctant ox. Mr. Jasper goes to his Gate House, brooding. And thus, as everything comes to an end, the unaccountable expedition comes to an end — for the time.

CHAPTER XIII.

BOTH AT THEIR BEST.

Miss Twinkleton's establishment was about to undergo a serene hush. The Christmas recess was at hand. What had once, and at no remote period, been called, even by the erudite Miss Twinkleton herself, "the half," but what was now called, as being more elegant, and more strictly collegiate, "the term," would expire to-morrow. A noticeable relaxation of discipline had for some few days pervaded the Nuns' House. Club suppers had occurred in the bedrooms, and a dressed tongue had been carved with a pair of scissors, and handed round with the curling-tongs. Portions of marmalade had likewise been distributed on a service of plates constructed of curl-paper; and cowslip wine had been quaffed from the small squat measuring-glass in which little Rickitts (a junior of weakly constitution) took her steel drops daily. The housemaids had been bribed with various fragments of riband, and sundry pairs of shoes more or less down at heel, to make no mention of crumbs in the beds; the airiest costumes had been worn on these festive occasions; and the daring Miss Ferdinand had even surprised the company with a sprightly solo on the comb-and-curl-paper, until suffocated in her own pillow by two flowing-haired executioners.

Nor were these the only tokens of dispersal. Boxes appeared in the bedrooms (where they were capital at other times), and a surprising amount of packing took place, out of all proportion to the amount packed. Largess, in the form of odds and ends of cold cream and pomatum, and also of hairpins, was freely distributed among the attendants. On charges of inviolable secrecy, confidences were interchanged respecting golden youth of England expected to call, "at home," on the first opportunity. Miss Giggles (deficient in sentiment) did indeed profess that she, for her part, acknowledged such homage by making faces at the golden youth; but this young lady was outvoted by an immense majority

On the last night before a recess, it was always expressly made a point of honor that nobody should go to sleep, and that Ghosts should be encouraged by all possible means. This compact invariably broke down, and all the young ladies went to sleep very soon and got up very early.

The concluding ceremony came off at twelve o'clock on the day of departure; when Miss Twinkleton, supported by Mrs. Tisher, held a Drawing-Room in her own apartment (the globes already covered with brown holland), where glasses of white wine, and plates of cut pound-cake were discovered on the table. Miss Twinkleton then said, Ladies, another revolving year had brought us round to that festive period at which the first feelings of our nature bounded in our — Miss Twinkleton was annually going to add "bosoms," but annually stopped on the brink of that expression, and substituted "hearts." Hearts; our hearts. Hem! Again a revolving year, ladies, had brought us to a pause in our studies, — let us hope our greatly advanced studies, — and, like the mariner in his bark, the warrior in his tent, the captive in his dungeon, and the traveller in his various conveyances, we yearned for home. Did we say, on such an occasion, in the opening words of Mr. Addison's impressive tragedy —

"The dawn is overcast, the morning lowers,
And heavily in clouds brings on the day,
The great, th' important day — "?

Not so. From horizon to zenith all was *couleur de rose*, for all was redolent of our relations and friends. Might *we* find *them* prospering as *we* expected; might *they* find *us* prospering as *they* expected! Ladies, we would now, with our love to one another, wish one another good by, and happiness, until we meet again. And when the time should come for our resumption of those pursuits which (here a general depression set in all round), pursuits which, pursuits which; — then let us ever remember what was said by the Spartan General, in words too trite for repetition, at the battle it were superfluous to specify.

The handmaidens of the establishment, in their best caps, then handed the trays, and the young ladies sipped and crumbled, and the bespoken coaches began to choke the street. Then, leave-taking was not long about, and Miss Twinkleton, in saluting each young lady's cheek, confided to her an exceedingly neat letter, addressed to her next friend at law, "with Miss Twinkleton's best compliments" in the corner. This missive she handed with an air as if it had not the least connection with the bill, but were something in the nature of a delicate and joyful surprise.

So many times had Rosa seen such dispersals, and so very little did she know of any other Home, that she was contented to remain where she was, and was even better contented than ever before, having her latest friend with her. And yet her latest friendship had a blank place in it of which she could not fail to be sensible. Helena Landless, having been a party to her brother's revelation about Rosa, and having entered into that compact of silence with Mr. Crisparkle, shrank from any allusion to Edwin Drood's name. Why she so avoided it was mysterious to Rosa, but she perfectly perceived the fact. But for the fact, she might have relieved her own little perplexed heart of some of its doubts and hesitations, by taking Helena into her confidence. As it was, she had no such vent: she could only ponder on her own difficulties, and wonder more and more why this avoidance of Edwin's name should last, now that she knew — for so much Helena had told her — that a good understanding was to be re-established between the two young men when Edwin came down.

It would have made a pretty picture, so many pretty girls kissing Rosa in the cold porch of the Nuns' House, and that sunny little creature peeping out of it (unconscious of sly faces carved on spout and gable peeping at her), and waving farewells to the departing coaches, as if she represented the spirit of rosy youth abiding in the place to keep it bright and warm in its desertion. The hoarse

High Street became musical with the cry, in various silvery voices, "Good by, Rosebud, Darling!" and the effigy of Mr. Sapsea's father over the opposite doorway seemed to say to mankind, "Gentlemen, favor me with your attention to this charming little last lot left behind, and bid with a spirit worthy of the occasion!" Then the staid street, so unwontedly sparkling, youthful, and fresh for a few rippling moments, ran dry, and Cloisterham was itself again.

If Rosebud in her bower now waited Edwin Drood's coming with an uneasy heart, Edwin for his part was uneasy too. With far less force of purpose in his composition than the childish beauty, crowned by acclamation fairy queen of Miss Twinkleton's establishment, he had a conscience, and Mr. Grewgious had pricked it. That gentleman's steady convictions of what was right and what was wrong in such a case as his were neither to be frowned aside nor laughed aside. They would not be moved. But for the dinner in Staple Inn, and but for the ring he carried in the breast-pocket of his coat, he would have drifted into their wedding-day without another pause for real thought, loosely trusting that all would go well, left alone. But that serious putting him on his truth to the living and the dead had brought him to a check. He must either give the ring to Rosa, or he must take it back Once put into this narrowed way of action, it was curious that he began to consider Rosa's claims upon him more unselfishly than he had ever considered them before, and began to be less sure of himself than he had ever been in all his easy-going days.

"I will be guided by what she says, and by how we get on," was his decision, walking from the Gate House to the Nuns' House. "Whatever comes of it, I will bear his words in mind, and try to be true to the living and the dead."

Rosa was dressed for walking. She expected him. It was a bright frosty day, and Miss Twinkleton had already graciously sanctioned fresh air. Thus they got out together before it became necessary for either Miss Twinkleton, or the Deputy High Priest, Mrs. Tisher, to lay even so much as one of those usual offerings on the shrine of Propriety.

"My dear Eddy," said Rosa, when they had turned out of the High Street, and had got among the quiet walks in the neighborhood of the Cathedral and the river, "I want to say something very serious to you. I have been thinking about it for a long long time."

"I want to be serious with you too, Rosa, dear. I mean to be serious and earnest."

"Thank you, Eddy. And you will not think me unkind because I begin, will you? You will not think I speak for myself only because I speak first? That would not be generous, would it? And I know you are generous!"

He said, "I hope I am not ungenerous to you, Rosa." He called her Pussy no more. Never again.

"And there is no fear," pursued Rosa, "of our quarrelling, is there? Because, Eddy," clasping her hand on his arm, "we have so much reason to be very lenient to each other!"

"We will be, Rosa."

"That's a dear good boy! Eddy, let us be courageous. Let us change to brother and sister from this day forth."

"Never be husband and wife?"

"Never!"

Neither spoke again for a little while. But after that pause he said, with some effort, —

"Of course I know that this has been in both our minds, Rosa, and of course I am in honor bound to confess freely that it does not originate with you."

"No, nor with you, dear," she returned, with pathetic earnestness. "It has sprung up between us. You are not truly happy in our engagement; I am not truly happy in it. O, I am so sorry, so sorry!" And there she broke into tears.

"I am deeply sorry too, Rosa. Deeply sorry for you."

"And I for you, poor boy! And I for you!"

This pure young feeling, this gentle and forbearing feeling of each towards the other, brought with it its reward in a softening light that seemed to shine on their position. The relations between them did not look wilful, or capricious, or a failure, in such a light: they became elevated into something more self-denying, honorable, affectionate, and true.

"If we knew yesterday," said Rosa, as she dried her eyes, "and we did know yesterday, and on many, many yesterdays, that we were far from right together in those relations which were not of our own choosing, what better could we do to-day than change them? It is natural that we should be sorry, and you see how sorry we both are; but how much better to be sorry now than then!"

"When, Rosa?"

"When it would be too late. And then we should be angry, besides."

Another silence fell upon them.

"And you know," said Rosa, innocently, "you could n't like me then; and you can always like me now, for I shall not be a drag upon you, or a worry to you. And I can always like you now, and your sister will not tease or trifle with you. I often did when I was not your sister, and I beg your pardon for it."

"Don't let us come to that, Rosa; or I shall want more pardoning than I like to think of."

"No, indeed, Eddy; you are too hard, my generous boy, upon yourself. Let us sit down, brother, on these ruins, and let me tell you how it was with us. I think I know, for I have considered about it very much since you were here last time. You liked me, did n't you? You thought I was a nice little thing?"

"Everybody thinks that, Rosa."

"Do they?" She knitted her brow musingly for a moment, and then flashed out with the bright little induction: "Well; but say they do. Surely it was not enough that you should think of me only as other people did; now, was it?"

The point was not to be got over. It was not enough.

"And that is just what I mean; that is just how it was with us," said Rosa. "You liked me very well, and you had grown used to me, and had grown used to the idea of our being married. You accepted the situation as an inevitable kind of thing, did n't you? It was to be, you thought, and why discuss or dispute it."

It was new and strange to him to have himself presented to himself so clearly, in a glass of her holding up. He had always patronized her, in his superiority to her share of woman's wit. Was that but another instance of something radically amiss in the terms on which they had been gliding towards a life long bondage?

"All this that I say of you is true of me as well, Eddy. Unless it was, I might not be bold enough to say it. Only, the difference between us was, that by little and little there crept into my mind a habit of thinking about it, instead of dismissing it. My life is not so busy as yours, you see, and I have not so many things to think of. So I thought about it very much, and I cried about it very much too (though that was not your fault, poor boy); when all at once my guardian came down to prepare for my leaving the Nuns' House. I tried to hint to him that I was not quite settled in my mind, but I hesitated and failed, and he did n't understand me. But he is a good, good man. And he put before me so kindly, and yet so strongly, how seriously we ought to consider, in our circumstances, that I resolved to speak to you the next moment we were alone and grave. And if I seemed to come to it easily just now, because I came to it all at once, don't think it was so really, Eddy, for O, it was very, very hard, and O, I am very, very sorry!"

Her full heart broke into tears again. He put his arm about her waist, and they walked by the river-side together.

"Your guardian has spoken to me too, Rosa dear. I saw him before I left London." His right hand was in his breast, seeking the ring; but he checked it as he thought, "If I am to take it back, why should I tell her of it?"

"And that made you more serious about it, did n't it, Eddy? And if I had not spoken to you, as I have, you would have spoken to me? I hope you can tell me so? I don't like it to be *all* my doing, though it *is* so much better for us."

"Yes, I should have spoken; I should have put everything before you; I came intending to do it. But I never could have spoken to you as you have spoken to me, Rosa."

"Don't say you mean so coldly or unkindly, Eddy, please, if you can help it."

"I mean so sensibly and delicately, so wisely and affectionately."

"That 's my dear brother!" She kissed his hand in a little rapture. "The dear girls will be dreadfully disappointed," added Rosa, laughing, with the dew-drops glistening in her bright eyes. "They have looked forward to it so, poor pets!"

"Ah! But I fear it will be a worse disappointment to Jack," said Edwin Drood, with a start. "I never thought of Jack!"

Her swift and intent look at him as he said the words could no more be recalled than a flash of lightning can. But it appeared as though she would have instantly recalled it, if she could; for she looked down, confused, and breathed quickly.

"You don't doubt it 's being a blow to Jack, Rosa?"

She merely replied, and that evasively and hurriedly, Why should she? She had not thought about it. He seemed, to her, to have so little to do with it.

"My dear child! Can you suppose that any one so wrapped up in another — Mrs. Tope's expression: not mine — as Jack is in me, could fail to be struck all of a heap by such a sudden and complete change in my life? I say sudden, because it will be sudden to *him*, you know."

She nodded twice or thrice, and her lips parted as if she would have assented. But she uttered no sound, and her breathing was no slower.

"How shall I tell Jack!" said Edwin, ruminating. If he had been less occupied with the thought, he must have seen her singular emotion. "I never thought of Jack. It must be broken to him, before the town-crier knows it. I dine with the dear fellow to-morrow and next day, — Christmas Eve and Christmas Day, — but it would never do to spoil his feast days. He always worries about me, and molley-coddles in the merest trifles. The news is sure to overset him. How on earth shall this be broken to Jack!"

"He must be told, I suppose?" said Rosa.

"My dear Rosa! Who ought to be in our confidence, if not Jack?"

"My guardian promised to come down, if I should write and ask him. I am going to do so. Would you like to leave it to him?"

"A bright idea!" cried Edwin. "The other trustee. Nothing more natural. He comes down, he goes to Jack, he relates what we have agreed upon, and he states our case better than we could. He has already spoken feelingly to you, he has already spoken feelingly to me, and he 'll put the whole thing feelingly to Jack. That 's it! I am not a coward, Rosa, but to tell you a secret, I am a little afraid of Jack."

"No, no! You are not afraid of him?" cried Rosa, turning white and clasping her hands.

"Why, Sister Rosa, Sister Rosa, what do you see from the turret?" said Edwin, rallying her. "My dear girl!"

"You frightened me."

"Most unintentionally, but I am as sorry as if I had meant to do it. Could you possibly suppose for a moment, from any loose way of speaking of mine, that I was literally afraid of the dear fond fellow? What I mean is, that he is subject to a kind of paroxysm or fit, — I saw him in it once, — and I don't know but that so great a surprise, coming upon him direct from me, whom he is so wrapped up in, might bring it on perhaps. Which — and this is the secret I was going to tell you — is another reason for your guardian's making the communication. He is so steady, precise, and exact, that he will talk Jack's thoughts into shape in no time; whereas with me Jack is always impulsive and hurried, and, I may say, almost womanish."

Rosa seemed convinced. Perhaps from her own very different point of view of "Jack," she felt comforted and protected by the interposition of Mr. Grewgious between herself and him.

And now, Edwin Drood's right hand closed again upon the ring in its little case, and again was checked by the consideration: "It is certain, now, that I am to give it back to him, then why should I tell her of it?" That pretty sympathetic nature which could be so sorry for him in the blight of their childish hopes of happiness together, and could so quietly find itself alone in a new world to weave fresh wreaths of such flowers as it might prove to bear, the old world's flowers being withered, would be grieved by those sorrowful jewels; and to what purpose? Why should it be? They were but a sign of broken joys and baseless projects; in their very beauty, they were (as the unlikeliest of men had said) almost a cruel satire on the loves, hopes, plans, of humanity, which are able to forecast nothing, and are so much brittle dust. Let them be. He would restore them to her guardian when he came down; he in his turn would restore them to the cabinet from which he had unwillingly taken them; and there, like old letters or old vows, or records of old aspirations come to nothing, they would be disregarded, until, being valuable, they were sold into circulation again, to repeat their former round.

Let them be. Let them lie unspoken of, in his breast. However distinctly or indistinctly he entertained these thoughts, he arrived at the conclusion, Let them be. Among the mighty store of wonderful chains that are forever forging, day and night, in the vast iron-works of time and circumstance, there was one chain forged in the moment of that small conclusion, riveted to the foundations of heaven and earth, and gifted with invincible force to hold and drag.

They walked on by the river. They began to speak of their separate plans. He would quicken his departure from England, and she would remain where she was, at least as long as Helena remained. The poor dear girls should have their disappointment broken to them gently, and, as the first preliminary, Miss Twinkleton should be confided in by Rosa, even in advance of the reappearance of Mr. Grewgious. It should be made clear in all quarters that she and Edwin were the best of friends. There had never been so serene an understanding between them since they were first affianced. And yet there was one reservation on each side; on hers, that she intended through her guardian to withdraw herself immediately from the tuition of her music-master; on his, that he did already entertain some wandering speculations whether it might ever come to pass that he would know more of Miss Landless.

The bright frosty day declined as they walked and spoke together. The sun dipped in the river far behind them, and the old city lay red before them, as their walk drew to a close. The moaning water cast its sea-weed duskily at their feet, when they turned to leave its margin; and the rooks hovered above them with hoarse cries, darker splashes in the darkening air.

"I will prepare Jack for my flitting soon," said Edwin, in a low voice, "and I will but see your guardian when he comes, and then go before they speak together. It will be better done without my being by. Don't you think so?"

"Yes."

"We know we have done right, Rosa?"

"Yes."

"We know we are better so, even now?"

"And shall be far, far better so by and by."

Still, there was that lingering tenderness in their hearts towards the old positions they were relinquishing, that they prolonged their parting. When they came among the elm-trees by the Cathedral, where they had last sat together, they stopped, as by consent, and Rosa raised her face to his, as she had never raised it in the old days, — for they were old already.

"God bless you, dear! Good by!"

"God bless you, dear! Good by!"

They kissed each other, fervently.

"Now, please take me home, Eddy, and let me be by myself."

"Don't look round, Rosa," he cautioned her, as he drew her arm through his, and led her away. "Did n't you see Jack?"

"No! Where?"

"Under the trees. He saw us, as we took leave of each other. Poor fellow! he little thinks we have parted. This will be a blow to him, I am much afraid!"

She hurried on, without resting, and hurried on until they had passed under the Gate House into the street; once there, she asked, —

"Has he followed us? You can look without seeming to. Is he behind?"

"No. Yes! he is! He has just passed out under the gateway. The dear sympathetic old fellow likes to keep us in sight. I am afraid he will be bitterly disappointed!"

She pulled hurriedly at the pendant handle of the hoarse old bell, and the gate soon opened. Before going in, she gave him one last wide wondering look, as if she would have asked him with imploring emphasis, "Oh! don't you understand?" And out of that look he vanished from her view.

CHAPTER XIV.

WHEN SHALL THESE THREE MEET AGAIN?

CHRISTMAS Eve in Cloisterham. A few strange faces in the streets; a few other faces, half strange and half familiar, once the faces of Cloisterham children, now the faces of men and women who come back from the outer world at long intervals to find the city wonderfully shrunken in size, as if it had not washed by any means well in the mean while. To these, the striking of the Cathedral clock, and the cawing of the rooks from the Cathedral tower, are like voices of their nursery time. To such as these, it has happened in their dying hours afar off, that they have imagined their chamber floor to be strewn with the autumnal leaves fallen from the elm-trees in the Close; so have the rustling sounds and fresh scents of their earliest impressions revived, when the circle of their lives was very nearly traced, and the beginning and the end were drawing close together.

Seasonable tokens are about. Red berries shine here and there in the lattices of Minor Canon Corner; Mr. and Mrs. Tope are daintily sticking sprigs of holly into the carvings and sconces of the Cathedral stalls, as if they were sticking them into the coat-buttonholes of the Dean and Chapter. Lavish profusion is in the shops: particularly in the articles of currants, raisins, spices, candied peel, and moist sugar. An unusual air of gallantry and dissipation is abroad; evinced in an immense bunch of mistletoe hanging in the green-grocer's shop doorway, and a poor little Twelfth Cake, culminating in the figure of a Harlequin, — such a very poor little Twelfth Cake, that one would rather call it a Twenty-Fourth Cake, or a Forty-Eighth Cake, — to be raffled for at the pastrycook's, terms one shilling per member. Public amusements are not wanting. The Wax-Work which made so deep an impression on the reflective mind of the Emperor of China is to be seen by particular desire during Christmas Week only, on the premises of the bankrupt livery-stable keeper up the lane; and a new grand comic Christmas pantomime is to be produced at the Theatre; the latter heralded by the portrait of Signor Jacksonini the clown, saying, "How do you do to-morrow," quite as large as life, and almost as miserably. In short, Cloisterham is up and doing; though from this description the High School and Miss Twinkleton's are to be excluded. From the former establishment the scholars have gone home, every one of them in love with one of Miss Twinkleton's young ladies (who knows nothing about it); and only the handmaidens flutter occasionally in the windows of the latter. It is noticed, by the by, that these damsels become, within the limits of decorum, more skittish when thus intrusted with the concrete representation of their sex, than when dividing the representation with Miss Twinkleton's young ladies.

Three are to meet at the Gate House to-night. How does each one of the three get through the day?

Neville Landless, though absolved from his books for the time by Mr. Crisparkle, — whose fresh nature is by no means insensible to the charms of a holiday, — reads and writes in his quiet room, with a concentrated air, until it is two hours past noon. He then sets himself to clearing his table, to arranging his books, and to tearing up and burning his stray papers. He makes a clean sweep of all untidy accumulations, puts all his drawers in order, and leaves no note or scrap of paper undestroyed, save such memoranda as bear directly on his studies. This done, he turns to his wardrobe, selects a few articles of ordinary wear, — among them, change of stout shoes and socks for walking, — and packs these in a knapsack. This knapsack is new, and he bought it in the High Street yesterday He also purchased, at the same time and at the same place, a heavy walking-stick: strong in the handle for the grip of the hand, and iron shod. He tries this, swings it, poises it, and lays it by, with the knapsack, on a window-seat. By this time his arrangements are complete.

He dresses for going out, and is in the act of going — indeed, has left his room, and has met the Minor Canon on the staircase, coming out of his bedroom upon the same story — when he turns back again for his walking-stick, thinking he will carry it now. Mr. Crisparkle, who has paused on the staircase, sees it in his hand on his immediately reappearing, takes it from him, and asks him with a smile how he chooses a stick.

"Really I don't know that I understand the subject," he answers. "I chose it for its weight."

"Much too heavy, Neville; *much* too heavy."

"To rest upon in a long walk, sir?"

"Rest upon?" repeats Mr. Crisparkle, throwing himself into pedestrian form. "You don't rest upon it; you merely balance with it."

"I shall know better, with practice, sir. I have not lived in a walking country, you know."

"True," says Mr. Crisparkle. "Get into a little training, and we will have a few score miles together. I should leave you nowhere now. Do you come back before dinner?"

"I think not, as we dine early."

Mr. Crisparkle gives him a bright nod and a cheerful good by, expressing (not without intention) absolute confidence and ease.

Neville repairs to the Nuns' House, and requests that Miss Landless may be informed that her brother is there, by appointment. He waits at the gate, not even crossing the threshold; for he is on his parole not to put himself in Rosa's way.

His sister is at least as mindful of the obligation they have taken on themselves, as he can be, and loses not a moment in joining him. They meet affectionately, avoid lingering there, and walk towards the upper inland country

"I am not going to tread upon forbidden ground, Helena," says Neville, when they have walked some distance and are turning; "you will understand in another moment that I cannot help referring to — what shall I say — my infatuation."

"Had you not better avoid it, Neville? You know that I can hear nothing."

"You can hear, my dear, what Mr. Crisparkle has heard, and heard with approval"

"Yes; I can hear so much."

"Well, it is this. I am not only unsettled and unhappy myself, but I am conscious of unsettling and interfering with other people. How do I know that, but for my unfortunate presence, you, and — and — the rest of that former party, our engaging guardian excepted, might be dining cheerfully in Minor Canon Corner to-morrow? Indeed it probably would be so. I can see too well that I am not high in the old lady's opinion and it is easy to understand what an irksome clog I must be upon the hospitalities of her orderly house, — especially at this time of year, — when I must be kept asunder from this person, and there is such a reason for my not being brought into contact with that person, and an unfavorable reputation has preceded me with such another person, and so on. I have put this very gently to Mr. Crisparkle, for you know his self-denying ways; but still I have put it. What I have laid much greater stress upon at the same time, is, that I am engaged in a miserable struggle with myself, and that a little change and absence may enable me to come through it the better. So, the weather being bright and hard, I am going on a walking expedition, and intend taking myself out of everybody's way (my own included, I hope) to-morrow morning."

"When to come back?"

"In a fortnight."

"And going quite alone?"

"I am much better without company, even if there were any one but you to bear me company, my dear Helena."

"Mr. Crisparkle entirely agrees, you say?"

"Entirely. I am not sure but that at first he was inclined to think it rather a moody scheme, and one that might do a brooding mind harm. But we took a moonlight walk, last Monday night, to talk it over at leisure, and I represented the case to him as it really is. I showed him that I do want to conquer myself, and that, this evening well got over, it is surely better that I should be away from here just now than here. I could hardly help meeting certain people walking together here, and that could do no good, and is certainly not the way to forget. A fortnight hence, that chance will probably be over, for the time; and when it again arises for the last time, why, I can again go away. Further, I really do feel hopeful of bracing exercise and wholesome fatigue. You know that Mr. Crisparkle allows such things their full weight in the preservation of his own sound mind in his own sound body, and that his just spirit is not likely to maintain one set of natural laws for himself and another for me. He yielded to my view of the matter, when convinced that I was honestly in earnest, and so, with his full consent, I start to-morrow morning. Early enough to be not only out of the streets, but out of hearing of the bells, when the good people go to church."

Helena thinks it over, and thinks well of it. Mr. Crisparkle doing so, she would do so; but she does originally, out of her own mind, think well of it as a healthy project, denoting a sincere endeavor, and an active attempt, at self-correction. She is inclined to pity him, poor fellow, for going away solitary on the great Christmas festival; but she feels it much more to the purpose to encourage him. And she does encourage him.

He will write to her?

He will write to her every alternate day, and tell her all his adventures.

Does he send clothes on, in advance of him?

"My dear Helena, no. Travel like a pilgrim, with wallet and staff. My wallet — or my knapsack — is packed, and ready for strapping on; and here is my staff."

He hands it to her; she makes the same remark as Mr. Crisparkle, that it is very heavy; and gives it back to him, asking what wood it is? Iron-wood.

Up to this point he has been extremely cheerful. Perhaps the having to carry his case with her, and therefore to present it in its brightest aspect, has roused his spirits. Perhaps the having done so with success is followed by a revulsion. As the day closes in, and the city lights begin to spring up before them, he grows depressed.

"I wish I were not going to this dinner, Helena."

"Dear Neville, is it worth while to care much about it? Think how soon it will be over."

"How soon it will be over," he repeats, gloomily. "Yes. But I don't like it."

There may be a moment's awkwardness, she cheeringly represents to him, but it can only last a moment. He is quite sure of himself.

"I wish I felt as sure of everything else as I feel of myself," he answers her.

"How strangely you speak, dear! What do you mean?"

"Helena, I don't know, I only know that I don't like it. What a strange dead weight there is in the air!"

She calls his attention to those copperous clouds beyond the river, and says that the wind is rising. He scarcely speaks again until he takes leave of her at the gate of the Nuns' House. She does not immediately enter when they have parted, but remains looking after him along the street. Twice he passes the Gate House, reluctant to enter. A length, the Cathedral clock chiming one quarter, with a rapid turn he hurries in.

And so *he* goes up the postern stair.

Edwin Drood passes a solitary day. Something of deeper moment than he had thought has gone out of his life; and in the silence of his own chamber he wept for it last night. Though the image of Miss Landless still hovers in the background of his mind, the pretty little affectionate creature, so much firmer and wiser than he had supposed, occupies its stronghold. It is with some misgiving of his own unworthiness that he thinks of her, and of what they might have been to one another, if he had been more in earnest some time ago; if he had set a higher value on her; if, instead of accepting his fortune in life as an inheritance of course, he had studied the right way to its apppreciation and enhancement. And still, for all this, and though there is a sharp heartache in all this, the vanity and caprice of youth sustain that handsome figure of Miss Landless in the background of his mind.

That was a curious look of Rosa's when they parted at the gate. Did it mean that she saw below the surface of his thoughts, and down into their twilight depths? Scarcely that, for it was a look of astonished and keen inquiry. He decides that he cannot understand it, though it was remarkably expressive.

As he only waits for Mr. Grewgious now, and will depart immediately after having seen him, he takes a sauntering leave of the ancient city and its neighborhood. He recalls the time when Rosa and he walked here or there, mere children, full of the dignity of being engaged. Poor children! he thinks, with a pitying sadness.

Finding that his watch has stopped, he turns into the jeweller's shop to have it wound and set. The jeweller is knowing on the subject of a bracelet, which he begs leave to submit, in a general and quite aimless way. It would suit (he considers) a young bride to perfection; especially if of a rather diminutive style of beauty. Finding the bracelet but coldly looked at, the jeweller invites attention to a tray of rings for gentlemen; here is a style of ring now, he remarks; a very chaste signet; which gentlemen are much given to purchasing when changing their condition. A ring of a very responsible appearance. With the date of their wedding-day engraved inside, several gentlemen have preferred it to any other kind of memento.

The rings are as coldly viewed as the bracelet. Edwin tells the tempter that he wears no jewelry but his watch and chain, which were his father's, and his shirt-pin.

"That I was aware of," is the jeweller's reply, "for Mr. Jasper dropped in for a watch-glass the other day, and, in fact, I showed these articles to him, remarking that if he *should* wish to make a present to a gentleman relative, on any particular occasion — But he said with a smile that he had an inventory in his mind of all the jewelry his gentleman relative ever wore; namely, his watch and chain and his shirt-pin." Still (the jeweller considers) that might not apply to all times, though applying to the present time. "Twenty minutes past two, Mr. Drood, I set your watch at. Let me recommend you not to let it run down, sir."

Edwin takes his watch, puts it on, and goes out, thinking, "Dear old Jack! If I were to make an extra crease in my neckcloth, he would think it worth noticing!"

He strolls about and about, to pass the time until the dinner hour. It somehow happens that Cloisterham seems reproachful to him to-day; has fault to find with him, as if he had not used it well; but is far more pensive with him than angry. His wonted carelessness is replaced by a wistful looking at and dwelling upon, all the old landmarks. He will soon be far away, and may never see them again, he thinks. Poor youth! Poor youth!

As dusk draws on, he paces the Monks' Vineyard. He has walked to and fro, full half an hour by the Cathedral chimes, and it has closed in dark, before he becomes quite aware of a woman crouching on the ground near a wicket gate in a corner. The gate commands a cross by-path, little used in the gloaming; and the figure must have been there all the time, though he has but gradually and lately made it out.

He strikes into that path, and walks up to the wicket. By the light of a lamp near it, he sees that the woman is of a haggard appearance, and that her weazen chin is resting on her hands, and that her eyes are staring — with an unwinking, blind sort of steadfastness — before her.

Always kindly, but moved to be unusually kind this evening, and having bestowed kind words on most of the children and aged people he has met, he at once bends down, and speaks to this woman.

"Are you ill?"

"No, deary," she answers, without looking at him, and with no departure from her strange blind stare.

"Are you blind?"

"No, deary."

"Are you lost, homeless, faint? What is the matter, that you stay here in the cold so long, without moving?"

By slow and stiff efforts, she appears to contract her vision until it can rest upon him; and then a curious film passes over her, and she begins to shake.

He straightens himself, recoils a step, and looks down at her in a dread amazement; for he seems to know her.

"Good Heaven!" he thinks, next moment. "Like Jack that night!"

As he looks down at her, she looks up at him and whimpers, "My lungs is weakly; my lungs is dreffle bad. Poor me, poor me, my cough is rattling dry!" And coughs in confirmation horribly.

"Where do you come from?"

"Come from London, deary." (Her cough still rending her.)

"Where are you going to?"

"Back to London, deary. I came here, looking for a needle in a haystack, and I ain't found it. Look 'ee, deary; give me three and sixpence, and don't you be afeard for me. I 'll get back to London then, and trouble no one. I 'm in a business. Ah me! It 's slack, it 's slack, and times is very bad! — but I can make a shift to live by it."

"Do you eat opium?"

"Smokes it," she replies with difficulty, still racked by her cough. "Give me three and sixpence, and I 'll lay it out well, and get back. If you don't give me three and sixpence, don't give me a brass farden. And if you do give me three and sixpence, deary, I 'll tell you something."

He counts the money from his pocket, and puts it in her hand. She instantly clutches it tight, and rises to her feet with a croaking laugh of satisfaction.

"Bless ye! Harkee, dear genl'mn. What 's your Chris'en name?"

"Edwin."

"Edwin, Edwin, Edwin," she repeats, trailing off into a drowsy repetition of the word, and then asks suddenly, "Is the short of that name, Eddy?"

"It is sometimes called so," he replies, with the color starting to his face.

"Don't sweethearts call it so?" she asks, pondering.

"How should I know?"

"Have n't you a sweetheart, upon your soul?"

"None."

She is moving away with another "Bless ye, and thank 'ee, deary!' when he adds, "You were to tell me something; you may as well do so."

"So I was, so I was. Well, then. Whisper. You be thankful that your name ain't Ned."

He looks at her, quite steadily, as he asks, "Why?"

"Because it 's a bad name to have just now."

"How a bad name?"

"A threatened name. A dangerous name."

"The proverb says that threatened men live long," he tells her lightly.

"Then Ned — so threatened is he, wherever he may be while I am a talking to you, deary — should live to all eternity!" replies the woman.

She has leaned forward, to say it in his ear, with her forefinger shaking before his eyes, and now huddles herself together, and with another "Bless ye, and thank'ee!" goes away in the direction of the Travellers' Lodging House.

This is not an inspiriting close to a dull day. Alone, in a sequestered place, surrounded by vestiges of old time and decay, it rather has a tendency to call a shudder into being. He makes for the better-lighted streets, and resolves as he walks on to say nothing of this to-night, but to mention it to Jack (who alone calls him Ned), as an odd coincidence, to-morrow; of course only as a coincidence, and not as anything better worth remembering.

Still it holds to him, as many things much better worth remembering never did. He has another mile or so to linger out before the dinner-hour; and, when he walks over the bridge and by the river, the woman's words are in the rising wind, in the angry sky, in the troubled water, in the flickering lights. There is some solemn echo of them, even in the Cathedral chime, which strikes a sudden surprise to his heart as he turns in under the archway of the Gate House.

And so *he* goes up the postern stair.

John Jasper passes a more agreeable and cheerful day than either of his guests. Having no music-lessons to give in the holiday season, his time is his own, but for the Cathedral services. He is early among the shopkeepers, ordering little table luxuries that his nephew likes. His nephew will not be with him long, he tells his provision-dealers, and so must be petted and made much of. While out on his hospitable preparations, he looks in on Mr Sapsea, and mentions that dear Ned, and that inflammable young spark of Mr. Crisparkle's, are to dine at the Gate House to-day, and make up their difference. Mr. Sapsea is by no means friendly towards the inflammable young spark. He says that his complexion is "Un-English." And when Mr. Sapsea has once declared anything to be Un-English, he considers that thing everlastingly sunk in the bottomless pit.

John Jasper is truly sorry to hear Mr. Sapsea speak thus, for he knows right well that Mr. Sapsea never speaks without a meaning, and that he has a subtle trick of being right. Mr. Sapsea (by a very remarkable coincidence) is of exactly that opinion.

Mr. Jasper is in beautiful voice this day. In the pathetic supplication to have his heart inclined to keep this law, he quite astonishes his fellows by his melodious power. He has never sung difficult music with such skill and harmony as in this day's Anthem. His nervous temperament is occasionally prone to take difficult music a little too quickly; to-day, his time is perfect.

These results are probably attained through a grand composure of the spirits. The mere mechanism of his throat is a little tender, for he wears, both with his singing-robe and with his ordinary dress, a large black scarf of strong close-woven silk, slung loosely round his neck. But his composure is so noticeable, that Mr. Crisparkle speaks of it as they come out from Vespers.

"I must thank you, Jasper, for the pleasure with which I have heard you to-day. Beautiful! Delightful! You could not have so outdone yourself, I hope, without being wonderfully well."

"I *am* wonderfully well."

"Nothing unequal," says the Minor Canon, with a smooth motion of his hand: "nothing unsteady, nothing forced, nothing avoided; all thoroughly done in a masterly manner, with perfect self-command."

"Thank you. I hope so, if it is not too much to say."

"One would think, Jasper, you had been trying a new medicine for that occasional indisposition of yours."

"No, really? That 's well observed; for I have."

"Then stick to it, my good fellow," says Mr. Crisparkle, clapping him on the shoulder with friendly encouragement, — "stick to it."

"I will."

"I congratulate you," Mr. Crisparkle pursues, as they come out of the Cathedral, "on all accounts."

"Thank you again. I will walk round to the Corner with you, if you don't object; I have plenty of time before my company come; and I want to say a word to you, which I think you will not be displeased to hear."

"What is it?"

"Well. We were speaking, the other evening, of my black humors."

Mr. Crisparkle's face falls, and he shakes his head deploringly.

"I said, you know, that I should make you an antidote to those black humors; and you said you hoped I would consign them to the flames."

"And I still hope so, Jasper."

"With the best reason in the world! I mean to burn this year's Diary at the year's end."

"Because you — ?" Mr. Crisparkle brightens greatly as he thus begins.

"You anticipate me. Because I feel that I have been out of sorts, gloomy, bilious, brain-oppressed, whatever it may be. You said I had been exaggerative. So I have."

Mr. Crisparkle's brightened face brightens still more.

"I could n't see it then, because I *was* out of sorts; but I am in a healthier state now, and I acknowledge it with genuine pleasure. I made a great deal of a very little; that 's the fact."

"It does me good," cries Mr. Crisparkle, "to hear you say it!"

"A man leading a monotonous life," Jasper proceeds, "and getting his nerves, or his stomach, out of order, dwells upon an idea until it loses its proportions. That was my case with the idea in question. So I shall burn the evidence of my case, when the book is full, and begin the next volume with a clearer vision."

"This is better," says Mr. Crisparkle, stopping at the steps of his own door to shake hands, "than I could have hoped!"

"Why, naturally," returns Jasper. "You had but little reason to hope that I should become more like yourself. You are always training yourself to be, mind and body, as clear as crystal, and you always are, and never change; whereas, I am a muddy, solitary, moping weed. However, I have got over that mope. Shall I wait, while you ask if Mr. Neville has left for my place? If not, he and I may walk round together."

"I think," says Mr. Crisparkle, opening the entrance door with his key, "that he left some time ago; at least I know he left, and I think he has not come back. But I 'll inquire. You won't come in?"

"My company wait," says Jasper, with a smile.

The Minor Canon disappears, and in a few moments returns. As he thought, Mr. Neville has not come back; indeed, as he remembers now, Mr. Neville said he would probably go straight to the Gate House.

"Bad manners in a host!" says Jasper. "My company will be there before me! What will you bet that I don't find my company embracing?"

"I will bet — or I would, if I ever did bet," returns Mr. Crisparkle, "that your company will have a gay entertainer this evening."

Jasper nods, and laughs Good Night!

He retraces his steps to the Cathedral door, and turns down past it to the Gate House. He sings, in a low voice and with delicate expression, as he walks along. It still seems as if a false note were not within his power to-night, and as if nothing could hurry or retard him. Arriving thus, under the arched entrance of his dwelling, he pauses for an instant in the shelter to pull off that great black scarf, and hang it in a loop upon his arm. For that brief time, his face is knitted and stern. But it immediately clears, as he resumes his singing, and his way.

And so *he* goes up the postern stair.

The red light burns steadily all the evening in the lighthouse on the margin of the tide of busy life. Softened sounds and hum of traffic pass it and flow on irregularly into the lonely Precincts; but very little else goes by, save violent rushes of wind. It comes on to blow a boisterous gale.

The Precincts are never particularly well lighted; but the strong blasts of wind blowing out many of the lamps (in some instances shattering the frames too, and bringing the glass rattling to the ground), they are unusually dark to-night. The darkness is augmented and confused by flying dust from the earth, dry twigs from the trees, and great ragged fragments from the rooks' nests up in the tower. The trees themselves so toss and creak, as this tangible part of the darkness madly whirls about, that they seem in peril of being torn out of the earth; while ever and again a crack, and a rushing fall, denote that some large branch has yielded to the storm.

No such power of wind has blown for many a winter night. Chimneys topple in the streets, and people hold to posts and corners, and to one another, to keep themselves upon their feet. The violent rushes abate not, but increase in frequency and fury until at midnight, when the streets are empty, the storm goes thundering along them, rattling at all the latches, and tearing at all the shutters, as if warning the people to get up and fly with it, rather than have the roofs brought down upon their brains.

Still, the red light burns steadily. Nothing is steady but the red light.

All through the night the wind blows, and abates not. But early in the morning when there is barely enough light in the east to dim the stars, it begins to lull. From that time, with occasional wild charges, like a wounded monster dying, it drops and sinks; and at full daylight it is dead.

It is then seen that the hands of the Cathedral clock are torn off; that lead from the roof has been stripped away, rolled up, and blown into the Close; and that some stones have been displaced upon the summit of the great tower. Christmas morning though it be, it is necessary to send up workmen, to ascertain the extent of the damage done. These, led by Durdles, go aloft; while Mr. Tope and a crowd of early idlers gather down in Minor Canon Corner, shading their eyes and watching for their appearance up there.

This cluster is suddenly broken and put aside by the hands of Mr. Jasper; all the gazing eyes are brought down to the earth by his loudly inquiring of Mr. Crisparkle, at an open window,—

"Where is my nephew?"

"He has not been here. Is he not with you?"

"No. He went down to the river last night with Mr. Neville, to look at the storm, and has not been back. Call Mr. Neville!"

"He left this morning, early."

"Left this morning, early? Let me in, let me in!"

There is no more looking up at the tower, now. All the assembled eyes are turned on Mr. Jasper, white, half dressed, panting, and clinging to the rail before the Minor Canon's house.

CHAPTER XV

IMPEACHED.

NEVILLE LANDLESS had started so early and walked at so good a pace, that when the church bells began to ring in Cloisterham for morning service, he was eight miles away. As he wanted his breakfast by that time, having set forth on a crust of bread, he stopped at the next roadside tavern to refresh.

Visitors in want of breakfast — unless they were horses or cattle, for which class of guests there was preparation enough in the way of water-trough and hay — were so unusual at the sign of The Tilted Wagon, that it took a long time to get the wagon into the track of tea and toast and bacon. Neville, in the interval, sitting in a sanded parlor, wondering in how long a time after he had gone the sneezy fire of damp fagots would begin to make somebody else warm.

Indeed, The Tilted Wagon, as a cool establishment on the top of a hill, where the ground before the door was puddled with damp hoofs and trodden straw; where a scolding landlady slapped a moist baby (with one red sock on and one wanting) in the bar; where the cheese was cast aground upon a shelf, in company with a mouldy tablecloth and a green-handled knife, in a sort of cast-iron canoe; where the pale faced bread shed tears of crumb over its shipwreck in another canoe; where the family linen, half washed and half dried, led a public life of lying about; where everything to drink was drunk out of mugs, and everything else was suggestive of a rhyme to mugs, — The Tilted Wagon, all these things considered, hardly kept its painted promise of providing good entertainment for Man and Beast. However, Man, in the present case, was not critical, but took what entertainment he could get, and went on again after a longer rest than he needed.

He stopped at some quarter of a mile from the house, hesitating whether to pursue the road, or to follow a cart-track between two high hedgerows, which led across the slope of a breezy heath, and evidently struck into the road again by and by. He decided in favor of this latter track, and pursued it with some toil; the rise being steep, and the way worn into deep ruts.

He was laboring along, when he became aware of some other pedestrians behind him. As they were coming up at a faster pace than his, he stood aside, against one of the high banks, to let them pass. But their manner was very curious. Only four of them passed. Other four slackened speed, and loitered as intending to follow him when he should go on. The remainder of the party (half a dozen perhaps) turned, and went back at a great rate.

He looked at the four behind him, and he looked at the four before him. They all returned his look. He resumed his way. The four in advance went on, constantly looking back; the four in the rear came closing up.

When they all ranged out from the narrow track upon the open slope of the heath, and this order was maintained, let him diverge as he would to either side, there was no longer room to doubt that he was beset by these fellows. He stopped, as a last test, and they all stopped.

"Why do you attend upon me in this way?" he asked the whole body. "Are you a pack of thieves?"

"Don't answer him," said one of the number; he did not see which. "Better be quiet."

"Better be quiet?" repeated Neville. "Who said so?"

Nobody replied.

"It's good advice, whichever of you skulkers gave it," he went on angrily. "I will not submit to be penned in between four men there, and four men there. I wish to pass, and I mean to pass, those four in front."

They were all standing still, himself included.

"If eight men, or four men, or two men, set upon one," he proceeded, growing more enraged, "the one has no chance but to set his mark upon some of them. And by the Lord I 'll do it, if I am interrupted any further!"

Shouldering his heavy stick, and quickening his pace, he shot on to pass the four ahead. The largest and strongest man of the number changed swiftly to the side on which he came up, and dexterously closed with him and went down with him; but not before the heavy stick had descended smartly.

"Let him be!" said this man in a suppressed voice, as they struggled together on the grass. "Fair play! His is the build of a girl to mine, and he 's got a weight strapped to his back besides. Let him alone. I 'll manage him."

After a little rolling about, in a close scuffle, which caused the faces of both to be besmeared with blood, the man took his knee from Neville's chest, and rose, saying, "There! Now take him arm in arm, any two of you!"

It was immediately done.

"As to our being a pack of thieves, Mr. Landless," said the man, as he spat out some blood, and wiped more from his face, "you know better than that, at midday. We would n't have touched you, if you had n't forced us. We 're going to take you round to the high-road, anyhow, and you 'll find help enough against thieves there, if you want it. Wipe his face, somebody; see how it 's a trickling down him!"

When his face was cleansed, Neville recognized in the speaker, Joe, driver of the Cloisterham omnibus, whom he had seen but once, and that on the day of his arrival.

"And what I recommend you for the present, is, don't talk, Mr. Landless. You 'll find a friend waiting for you, at the high-road, — gone ahead by the other way when we split into two parties, — and you had much better say nothing till you come up with him. Bring that stick along, somebody else, and let 's be moving!"

Utterly bewildered, Neville stared around him and said not a word. Walking between his two conductors, who held his arms in theirs, he went on, as in a dream, until they came again into the high-road, and into the midst of a little group of people. The men who had turned back were among the group, and its central figures were Mr. Jasper and Mr. Crisparkle. Neville's conductors took him up to the Minor Canon, and there released him, as an act of deference to that gentleman.

"What is all this, sir? What is the matter? I feel as if I had lost my senses!" cried Neville, the group closing in around him.

"Where is my nephew?" asked Mr. Jasper, wildly.

"Where is your nephew?" repeated Neville. "Why do you ask me?"

"I ask you," retorted Jasper, "because you were the last person in his company, and he is not to be found."

"Not to be found!" cried Neville, aghast.

"Stay, stay," said Mr. Crisparkle. "Permit me, Jasper. Mr. Neville, you are confounded; collect your thoughts; it is of great importance that you should collect your thoughts; attend to me."

"I will try, sir, but I seem mad."

"You left Mr. Jasper's last night, with Edwin Drood?"

"Yes."

"At what hour?"

"Was it at twelve o'clock?" asked Neville, with his hand to his confused head, and appealing to Jasper.

"Quite right," said Mr. Crisparkle; "the hour Mr Jasper has already named to me. You went down to the river together?"

"Undoubtedly. To see the action of the wind there."

"What followed? How long did you stay there?"

"About ten minutes; I should say not more. We then walked together to your house, and he took leave of me at the door."

"Did he say that he was going down to the river again?"

"No. He said that he was going straight back."

The bystanders looked at one another, and at Mr. Crisparkle. To whom, Mr. Jasper, who had been intensely watching Neville, said, in a low, distinct, suspicious voice, "What are those stains upon his dress?"

All eyes were turned towards the blood upon his clothes.

"And here are the same stains upon this stick!" said Jasper, taking it from the hand of the man who held it. "I know the stick to be his, and he carried it last night. What does this mean?"

"In the name of God, say what it means, Neville!" urged Mr. Crisparkle.

"That man and I," said Neville, pointing out his late adversary, "had a struggle for the stick just now, and you may see the same marks on him, sir. What was I to suppose, when I found myself molested by eight people? Could I dream of the true reason when they would give me none at all?"

They admitted that they had thought it discreet to be silent, and that the struggle had taken place. And yet the very men who had seen it looked darkly at the smears which the bright cold air had already dried.

"We must return, Neville," said Mr. Crisparkle; "of course you will be glad to come back to clear yourself?"

"Of course, sir."

"Mr. Landless will walk at my side," the Minor Canon continued, looking around him. "Come, Neville!"

They set forth on the walk back; and the others, with one exception, straggled after them at various distances Jasper walked on the other side of Neville, and never quitted that position. He was silent, while Mr. Crisparkle more than once repeated his former questions, and while Neville repeated his former answers; also, while they both hazarded some explanatory conjectures. He was obstinately silent, because Mr. Crisparkle's manner directly appealed to him to take some part in the discussion, and no appeal would move his fixed face. When they drew near to the city, and it was suggested by the Minor Canon that they might do well in calling on the Mayor at once, he assented with a stern nod; but he spake no word until they stood in Mr. Sapsea's parlor.

Mr. Sapsea being informed by Mr. Crisparkle of the circumstances under which they desired to make a voluntary statement before him, Mr. Jasper broke silence by declaring that he placed his whole reliance, humanly speaking, on Mr. Sapsea's penetration. There was no conceivable reason why his nephew should have suddenly absconded, unless Mr. Sapsea could suggest one, and then he would defer. There was no intelligible likelihood of his having returned to the river, and been accidentally drowned in the dark, unless it should appear likely to Mr. Sapsea, and then again he would defer. He washed his hands as clean as he could of all horrible suspicions, unless it should appear to Mr. Sapsea that some such were inseparable from his last companion before his disappearance (not on good terms with previously), and then, once more, he would defer. His own state of mind, he being distracted with doubts, and laboring under dismal apprehensions, was not to be safely trusted; but Mr. Sapsea's was.

Mr. Sapsea expressed his opinion that the case had a dark look; in short (and here his eyes rested full on Neville's countenance), an Un-English complexion.

Having made this grand point, he wandered into a denser haze and maze of nonsense than even a mayor might have been expected to disport himself in, and came out of it with the brilliant discovery that to take the life of a fellow-creature was to take something that did n't belong to you. He wavered whether or no he should at once issue his warrant for the committal of Neville Landless to jail, under circumstances of grave suspicion; and he might have gone so far as to do it but for the indignant protest of the Minor Canon, who undertook for the young man's remaining in his own house, and being produced by his own hands, whenever demanded. Mr. Jasper then understood Mr. Sapsea to suggest that the river should be dragged, that its banks should be rigidly examined, that particulars of the disappearance should be sent to all outlying places and to London, and that placards and advertisements should be widely circulated imploring Edwin Drood, if for any unknown reason he had withdrawn himself from his uncle's home and society, to take pity on that loving kinsman's sore bereavement and distress, and somehow inform him that he was yet alive. Mr. Sapsea was perfectly understood, for this was exactly his meaning (though he had said nothing about it); and measures were taken towards all these ends immediately.

It would be difficult to determine which was the more oppressed with horror and amazement, Neville Landless or John Jasper. But that Jasper's position forced him to be active, while Neville's forced him to be passive, there would have been nothing to choose between them. Each was bowed down and broken.

With the earliest light of the next morning, men were at work upon the river, and other men — most of whom volunteered for the service — were examining the banks. All the livelong day the search went on; upon the river, with barge and pole, and drag and net; upon the muddy and rushy shore, with jack-boot, hatchet, spade, rope, dogs, and all imaginable appliances. Even at night the river was specked with lanterns, and lurid with fires; far-off creeks, into which the tide washed as it changed, had their knots of watchers, listening to the lapping of the stream, and looking out for any burden it might bear; remote shingly causeways near the sea, and lonely points off which there was a race of water, had their unwonted flaring cressets and rough-coated figures when the next day dawned; but no trace of Edwin Drood revisited the light of the sun.

All that day, again, the search went on. Now, in barge and boat; and now ashore among the osiers, or tramping amidst mud and stakes and jagged stones in low-lying places, where solitary watermarks and signals of strange shapes showed like spectres, John Jasper worked and toiled. But to no purpose; for still no trace of Edwin Drood revisited the light of the sun.

Setting his watches for that night again, so that vigilant eyes should be kept on every change of tide, he went home exhausted. Unkempt and disordered, bedaubed with mud that had dried upon him, and with much of his clothing torn to rags, he had but just dropped into his easy-chair, when Mr. Grewgious stood before him. "This is strange news," said Mr. Grewgious.

"Strange and fearful news."

Jasper had merely lifted up his heavy eyes to say it, and now dropped them again, as he drooped, worn out, over one side of his easy-chair.

Mr. Grewgious smoothed his head and face, and stood looking at the fire.

"How is your ward?" asked Jasper, after a time, in a faint, fatigued voice.

"Poor little thing! You may imagine her condition."

"Have you seen his sister?" inquired Jasper, as before.

"Whose?"

The curtness of the counter-question, and the cool, slow manner in which, as he put it, Mr. Grewgious moved his eyes from the fire to his companion's face, might at any other time have been exasperating. In his depression and exhaustion, Jasper merely opened his eyes to say, "The suspected young man's."

"Do you suspect him?" asked Mr. Grewgious.

"I don't know what to think. I cannot make up my mind."

"Nor I," said Mr. Grewgious. "But as you spoke of him as the suspected young man, I thought you *had* made up your mind. — I have just left Miss Landless."

"What is *her* state?"

"Defiance of all suspicion, and unbounded faith in her brother."

"Poor thing!"

"However," pursued Mr. Grewgious, "it is not of her that I came to speak. It is of my ward. I have a communication to make that will surprise you. At least it has surprised me."

Jasper, with a groaning sigh, turned wearily in his chair.

"Shall I put it off till to-morrow?" said Mr. Grewgious. "Mind! I warn you, that I think it will surprise you!"

More attention and concentration came into John Jasper's eyes as they caught sight of Mr. Grewgious smoothing his head again, and again looking at the fire; but now, with a compressed and determined mouth.

"What is it?" demanded Jasper, becoming upright in his chair.

"To be sure," said Mr. Grewgious, provokingly slowly and internally, as he kept his eyes on the fire, "I might have known it sooner; she gave me the opening; but I am such an exceedingly Angular man that it never occurred to me; I took all for granted."

"What is it?" demanded Jasper, once more.

Mr. Grewgious, alternately opening and shutting the palms of his hands as he warmed them at the fire, and looking fixedly at him sideways, and never changing either his action or his look in all that followed, went on to reply.

"This young couple, the lost youth and Miss Rosa, my ward, though so long betrothed, and so long recognizing their betrothal, and so near being married —"

Mr. Grewgious saw a staring white face and two quivering white lips, in the easy-chair, and saw two muddy hands gripping its sides. But for the hands, he might have thought he had never seen the face.

"— This young couple came gradually to the discovery (made on both sides pretty equally, I think) that they would be happier and better, both in their present and their future lives, as affectionate friends, or say rather as brother and sister, than as husband and wife."

Mr. Grewgious saw a lead-colored face in the easy-chair, and on its surface dreadful starting drops or bubbles, as if of steel.

"This young couple formed at length the healthy resolution of interchanging their discoveries, openly, sensibly, and tenderly. They met for that purpose. After some innocent and generous talk, they agreed to dissolve their existing, and their intended, relations, for ever and ever."

Mr. Grewgious saw a ghastly figure rise, open-mouthed, from the easy-chair, and lift its outspread hands towards its head.

"One of this young couple, and that one your nephew, fearful, however, that in the tenderness of your affection for him you would be bitterly disappointed by so wide a departure from his projected life, forbore to tell you the secret, for a few days, and left it to be disclosed by me, when I should come down to speak to you, and he would be gone. I speak to you, and he IS gone."

Mr. Grewgious saw the ghastly figure throw back its head, clutch its hair with its hands, and turn with a writhing action from him.

"I have now said all I have to say, except that this young couple parted, firmly, though not without tears and sorrow, on the evening when you last saw them together."

Mr. Grewgious heard a terrible shriek, and saw no ghastly figure, sitting or standing; saw nothing but a heap of torn and miry clothes upon the floor.

Not changing his action even then, he opened and shut the palms of his hands as he warmed them, and looked down at it.

CHAPTER XVI.

DEVOTED.

WHEN John Jasper recovered from his fit or swoon, he found himself being tended by Mr. and Mrs. Tope, whom his visitor had summoned for the purpose. His visitor, wooden of aspect, sat stiffly in a chair, with his hands upon his knees, watching his recovery.

"There! You 've come to, nicely now, sir," said the tearful Mrs. Tope; "you were thoroughly worn out, and no wonder!"

"A man," said Mr. Grewgious, with his usual air of repeating a lesson, "cannot have his rest broken, and his mind cruelly tormented, and his body overtaxed by fatigue, without being thoroughly worn out."

"I fear I have alarmed you?" Jasper apologized faintly, when he was helped into his easy-chair.

"Not at all, I thank you," answered Mr. Grewgious.

"You are too considerate."

"Not at all, I thank you," answered Mr. Grewgious again.

"You must take some wine, sir," said Mrs. Tope, "and the jelly that I had ready for you, and that you would n't put your lips to at noon, though I warned you what would come of it, you know, and you not breakfasted; and you must have a wing of the roast fowl that has been put back twenty times if it 's been put back once. It shall all be on table in five minutes, and this good gentleman belike will stop and see you take it."

This good gentleman replied with a snort, which might mean yes, or no or anything, or nothing, and which Mrs. Tope would have found highly mystifying, but that her attention was divided by the service of the table.

"You will take something with me?" said Jasper, as the cloth was laid.

"I could n't get a morsel down my throat, I thank you," answered Mr. Grewgious.

Jasper both ate and drank almost voraciously. Combined with the hurry in his mode of doing it, was an evident indifference to the taste of what he took, suggesting that he ate and drank to fortify himself against any other failure of the spirits, far more than to gratify his palate. Mr. Grewgious in the mean time sat upright, with no expression in his face, and a hard kind of imperturbably polite protest all over him: as though he would have said, in reply to some invitation to discourse, "I could n't originate the faintest approach to an observation on any subject whatever, I thank you"

"Do you know," said Jasper, when he had pushed away his plate and glass, and had sat meditating for a few minutes, — "do you know that I find some crumbs of comfort in the communication with which you have so much amazed me?"

"*Do* you?" returned Mr. Grewgious; pretty plainly adding the unspoken clause, "I don't, I thank you!"

"After recovering from the shock of a piece of news of my dear boy, so entirely unexpected, and so destructive of all the castles I had built for him; and after having had time to think of it; yes."

"I shall be glad to pick up your crumbs," said Mr. Grewgious, dryly.

"Is there not, or is there, — if I deceive myself, tell me so, and shorten my pain, — is there not, or is there, hope that, finding himself in this new position, and becoming sensitively alive to the awkward burden of explanation, in this quarter, and that, and the other, with which it would load him, he avoided the awkwardness, and took to flight?"

"Such a thing might be," said Mr. Grewgious, pondering.

"Such a thing has been. I have read of cases in which people, rather than face a seven days' wonder, and have to account for themselves to the idle and importunate, have taken themselves away, and been long unheard of."

"I believe such things have happened," said Mr. Grewgious, pondering still.

"When I had, and could have, no suspicion," pursued Jasper, eagerly following the new track, "that the dear lost boy had withheld anything from me, — most of all, such a leading matter as this, — what gleam of light was there for me in the whole black sky? When I supposed that his intended wife was here, and his marriage close at hand, how could I entertain the possibility of his voluntarily leaving this place, in a manner that would be so unaccountable, capricious, and cruel? But now that I know what you have told me, is there no little chink through which day pierces? Supposing him to have disappeared of his own act, is not his disappearance more accountable and less cruel? The fact of his having just parted from your ward is in itself a sort of reason for his going away. It does not make his mysterious departure the less cruel to me, it is true; but it relieves it of cruelty to her."

Mr. Grewgious could not but assent to this.

"And even as to me," continued Jasper, still pursuing the new track, with ardor, and, as he did so, brightening with hope, "he knew that you were coming to me; he knew that you were intrusted to tell me what you have told me; if your doing so has awakened a new train of thought in my perplexed mind, it reasonably follows that, from the same premises, he might have foreseen the inferences that I should draw. Grant that he did foresee them; and even the cruelty to me — and who am I! — John Jasper, Music Master! — vanishes."

Once more, Mr. Grewgious could not but assent to this.

"I have had my distrusts, and terrible distrusts they have been," said Jasper; "but your disclosure, overpowering as it was at first, — showing me that my own dear boy had had a great disappointing reservation from me, who so fondly loved him, — kindles hope within me. You do not extinguish it when I state it, but admit it to be a reasonable hope. I begin to believe it possible" — here he clasped his hands — "that he may have disappeared from among us of his own accord, and that he may yet be alive and well!"

Mr. Crisparkle came in at the moment, to whom Mr. Jasper repeated, —

"I begin to believe it possible that he may have disappeared of his own accord, and may yet be alive and well!"

Mr. Crisparkle, taking a seat, and inquiring "Why so?" Mr. Jasper repeated the arguments he had just set forth. If they had been less plausible than they were, the good Minor Canon's mind would have been in a state of preparation to receive them, as exculpatory of his unfortunate pupil. But he, too, did really attach great importance to the lost young man's having been, so immediately before his disappearance, placed in a new and embarrassing relation towards every one acquainted with his projects and affairs; and the fact seemed to him to present the question in a new light.

"I stated to Mr. Sapsea, when we waited on him," said Jasper, as he really had done, "that there was no quarrel or difference between the two young men at their last meeting. We all know that their first meeting was, unfortunately, very far from amicable; but all went smoothly and quietly when they were last together at my house. My dear boy was not in his usual spirits; he was depressed, — I noticed that, — and I am bound henceforth to dwell upon the circumstance the more, now that I know there was a special reason for his being depressed, — a reason, moreover, which may possibly have induced him to absent himself."

"I pray to Heaven it may turn out so!" exclaimed Mr. Crisparkle.

"*I* pray to Heaven it may turn out so!" repeated Jasper. "You know — and Mr. Grewgious should now know likewise — that I took a great prepossession against Mr. Neville Landless, arising out of his furious conduct on that first occasion. You know that I came to you, extremely apprehensive, on my dear boy's behalf, of his mad violence. You know that I even entered in my Diary, and showed the entry to you, that I had dark forebodings against him. Mr. Grewgious ought to be possessed of the whole case. He shall not, through any suppression of mine, be informed of a part of it, and kept in ignorance of another part of it. I wish him to be good enough to understand that the communication he has made to me has hopefully influenced my mind, in spite of its having been, before this mysterious occurrence took place, profoundly impressed against young Landless."

This fairness troubled the Minor Canon much. He felt that he was not as open in his own dealing. He charged against himself reproachfully that he had suppressed, so far, the two points of a second strong outbreak of temper against Edwin Drood on the part of Neville, and of the passion of jealousy having, to his own certain knowledge, flamed up in Neville's breast against him. He was convinced of Neville's innocence of any part in the ugly disappearance, and yet so many little circumstances combined so wofully against him, that he dreaded to add two more to their cumulative weight. He was among the truest of men; but he had been balancing in his mind, much to its distress, whether his volunteering to tell these two fragments of truth, at this time, would not be tantamount to a piecing together of falsehood in the place of truth.

However, here was a model before him. He hesitated no longer. Addressing Mr. Grewgious, as one placed in authority by the revelation he had brought to bear on the mystery (and surpassingly Angular Mr. Grewgious became when he found himself in that unexpected position), Mr. Crisparkle bore his testimony to Mr. Jasper's strict sense of justice, and, expressing his absolute confidence in the complete clearance of his pupil from the least taint of suspicion, sooner or later, avowed that his confidence in that young gentleman had been formed, in spite of his confidential knowledge that his temper was of the hottest and fiercest, and that it was directly incensed against Mr. Jasper's nephew, by the circumstance of his romantically supposing himself to be enamored of the same young lady. The sanguine reaction manifest in Mr. Jasper was proof even against this unlooked-for declaration. It turned him paler; but he repeated that he would cling to the hope he had derived from Mr. Grewgious; and that if no trace of his dear boy were found, leading to the dreadful inference that he had been made away with, he would cherish unto the last stretch of possibility, the idea, that he might have absconded of his own wild will.

Now, it fell out that Mr. Crisparkle, going away from this conference still very uneasy in his mind, and very much troubled on behalf of the young man whom he held as a kind of prisoner in his own house, took a memorable night walk.

He walked to Cloisterham Weir.

He often did so, and consequently there was nothing remarkable in his footsteps tending that way. But the preoccupation of his mind so hindered him from planning any walk, or taking heed of the objects he passed, that his first consciousness of being near the Weir was derived from the sound of the falling water close at hand

"How did I come here!" was his first thought, as he stopped.

"Why did I come here!" was his second

Then he stood intently listening to the water. A familiar passage in his reading, about airy tongues that syllable men's names, rose so unbidden to his ear, that he put it from him with his hand, as if it were tangible.

It was starlight. The Weir was full two miles above the spot to which the young men had repaired to watch the storm. No search had been made up here, for the tide had been running strongly down at that time of the night of Christmas Eve, and the likeliest places for the discovery of a body, if a fatal accident had happened under such circumstances, all lay — both when the tide ebbed, and when it flowed again — between that spot and the sea. The water came over the Weir, with its usual sound on a cold starlight night, and little could be seen of it; yet Mr. Crisparkle had a strange idea that something unusual hung about the place.

He reasoned with himself: What was it? where was it? Put it to the proof. Which sense did it address?

No sense reported anything unusual there. He listened again, and his sense of hearing again checked the water coming over the Weir, with its usual sound on a cold starlight night.

Knowing very well that the mystery with which his mind was occupied might of itself give the place this haunted air, he strained those hawk's eyes of his for the correction of his sight. He got closer to the Weir, and peered at its well-known posts and timbers. Nothing in the least unusual was remotely shadowed forth. But he resolved that he would come back early in the morning.

The Weir ran through his broken sleep all night, and he was back again at sunrise. It was a bright frosty morning. The whole composition before him, when he stood where he had stood last night, was clearly discernible in its minutest details. He had surveyed it closely for some minutes, and was about to withdraw his eyes, when they were attracted keenly to one spot.

He turned his back upon the Weir, and looked far away at the sky, and at the earth, and then looked again at that one spot. It caught his sight again immedidiately, and he concentrated his vision upon it. He could not lose it now, though it was but such a speck in the landscape. It fascinated his sight. His hands began plucking off his coat. For it struck him that at that spot — a corner of the Weir — something glistened, which did not move and come over with the glistening water-drops, but remained stationary.

He assured himself of this, he threw off his clothes, he plunged into the icy water, and swam for the spot. Climbing the timbers, he took from them, caught among their interstices by its chain, a gold watch, bearing engraved upon its back, E D.

He brought the watch to the bank, swam to the Weir again, climbed it, and dived off. He knew every hole and corner of all the depths, and dived and dived and dived, until he could bear the cold no more. His notion was that he would find the body; but he only found a shirt-pin sticking in some mud and ooze.

With these discoveries he returned to Cloisterham, and, taking Neville Landless with him, went straight to the Mayor Mr. Jasper was sent for, the watch and shirt-pin were identified, Neville was detained, and the wildest frenzy and fatuity of evil report arose against him. He was of that vindictive and violent nature, that but for his poor sister, who alone had influence over him, and out of whose sight he was never to be trusted, he would be in the daily commission of murder. Before coming to England he had caused to be whipped to death sundry "Natives," — nomadic persons, encamping now in Asia, now in Africa, now in the West Indies, and now at the North Pole, — vaguely supposed in Cloisterham to be always black, always of great virtue, always calling themselves Me, and everybody else Massa or Missie (according to sex), and always reading tracts of the obscurest meaning, in broken English, but always understanding them in the purest mother tongue. He had nearly brought Mrs. Crisparkle's gray hairs with sorrow to the grave. (Those original expressions were Mr. Sapsea's.) He had repeatedly said he would have Mr. Crisparkle's life. He had repeatedly said he would have everybody's life, and become in effect the last man. He had been brought down to Cloisterham, from London, by an eminent Philanthropist, and why? Because that Philanthropist had expressly declared, "I owe it to my fellow-creatures that he should be, in the words of BENTHAM, where he is the cause of the greatest danger to the smallest number."

These dropping shots from the blunderbusses of blunderheadedness might not have hit him in a vital place. But he had to stand against a train and well-directed fire of arms of precision too. He had notoriously threatened the lost young man, and had, according to the showing of his own faithful friend and tutor, who strove so hard for him, a cause of bitter animosity (created by himself, and stated by himself) against that ill-starred fellow. He had armed himself with an offensive weapon for the fatal night, and he had gone off early in the morning, after making preparations for departure. He had been found with traces of blood on him; truly, they might have been wholly caused as he represented, but they might not, also. On a search-warrant being issued for the examination of his room, clothes, and so forth, it was discovered that he had destroyed all his papers, and rearranged all his possessions, on the very afternoon of the disappearance. The watch found at the Weir was challenged by the jeweller as one he had wound and set for Edwin Drood, at twenty minutes past two on that same afternoon; and it had run down, before being cast into the water; and it was the jeweller's positive opinion that it had never been rewound. This would justify the hypothesis that the watch was taken from him not long after he left Mr. Jasper's house at midnight, in company with the last person seen with him, and that it had been thrown away after being retained some hours. Why thrown away? If he had been murdered, and so artfully disfigured, or concealed, or both, as that the murderer hoped identification to be impossible, except from something that he wore, assuredly the murderer would seek to remove from the body the most lasting, the best known, and the most easily recognizable things upon it. Those things would be the watch and shirt-pin. As to his opportunities of casting them into the river; if he were the object of these suspicions, they were easy. For he had been seen by many persons, wandering about on that side of the city — indeed on all sides of it — in a miserable and seemingly half-distracted manner. As to the choice of the spot, obviously such criminating evidence had better take its chance of being found anywhere, rather than upon himself or in his possession. Concerning the reconciliatory nature of the appointed meeting between the two young men, very little could be made of that, in young Landless's favor; for it distinctly appeared that the meeting originated, not with him, but with Mr. Crisparkle, and that it was urged on by Mr. Crisparkle; and who could say how unwillingly, or in what ill-conditioned mood, his enforced pupil had gone to it? The more his case was looked into, the weaker it became in every point. Even the broad suggestion that the lost young man had absconded was rendered additionally improbable on the showing of the young lady from whom he had so lately parted; for, what did she say, with great earnestness and sorrow, when interrogated? That he had, expressly and enthusiastically, planned with her, that he would await the arrival of her guardian, Mr. Grewgious. And yet, be it observed, he disappeared before that gentleman appeared.

On the suspicions thus urged and supported, Neville was detained and re-detained, and the search was pressed on every hand, and Jasper labored night and day. But nothing more was found. No discovery being made which proved the lost man to be dead, it at length became necessary to release the person suspected of having made away with him. Neville was set at large. Then a consequence ensued which Mr. Crisparkle had too well foreseen. Neville must leave the place, for the place shunned him and cast him out. Even had it not been so, the dear old china shepherdess would have worried herself to death with fears for her son, and with general trepidation occasioned by their having such an inmate. Even had that not been so, the authority to which the Minor Canon deferred officially would have settled the point.

"Mr. Crisparkle," quoth the Dean, "human justice may err, but it must act according to its lights. The days of taking sanctuary are past. This young man must not take sanctuary with us."

"You mean that he must leave my house, sir?"

"Mr. Crisparkle," returned the prudent Dean, "I claim no authority in your house. I merely confer with you, on the painful necessity you find yourself under, of depriving this young man of the great advantages of your counsel and instruction."

"It is very lamentable, sir," Mr. Crisparkle represented.

"Very much so," the Dean assented.

"And if it be a necessity," Mr. Crisparkle faltered.

"As you unfortunately find it to be — " returned the Dean.

Mr. Crisparkle bowed submissively. "It is hard to prejudge his case, sir, but I am sensible that — "

"Just so. Perfectly. As you say, Mr. Crisparkle," interposed the Dean, nodding his head smoothly, "there is nothing else to be done. No doubt, no doubt. There is no alternative, as your good sense has discovered."

"I am entirely satisfied of his perfect innocence, sir, nevertheless."

"We-e-ell!" said the Dean, in a more confidential tone, and slightly glancing around him, "I would not say so, generally. Not generally. Enough of suspicion attaches to him to — no, I think I would not say so, generally."

Mr. Crisparkle bowed again.

"It does not become us, perhaps," pursued the Dean, "to be partisans. Not partisans. We clergy keep our hearts warm and our heads cool, and we hold a judicious middle course."

"I hope you do not object, sir, to my having stated in public, emphatically, that he will reappear here, whenever any new suspicion may be awakened, or any new circumstance may come to light in this extraordinary matter?"

"Not at all," returned the Dean. "And yet, do you know, I don't think," with a very nice and neat emphasis on those two words, "I *don't think* I would state it, emphatically. State it? Ye-e-es! But emphatically? No-o-o. I *think* not. In point of fact, Mr. Crisparkle, keeping our hearts warm and our heads cool, we need do nothing emphatically."

So Minor Canon Row knew Neville Landless no more, and he went whithersoever he would, or could, with a blight upon his name and fame.

It was not until then that John Jasper silently resumed his place in the choir. Haggard and red-eyed, his hopes plainly had deserted him, his sanguine mood was gone, and all his worst misgivings had come back. A day or two afterwards, while unrobing, he took his Diary from a pocket of his coat, turned the leaves, and with an impressive look, and without one spoken word, handed this entry to Mr Crisparkle to read : —

" My dear boy is murdered. The discovery of the watch and shirt-pin convinces me that he was murdered that night, and that his jewelry was taken from him to prevent identification by its means. All the delusive hopes I had founded on his separation from his betrothed wife, I give to the winds. They perish before this fatal discovery. I now swear, and record the oath on this page, That I nevermore will discuss this mystery with any human creature, until I hold the clew to it in my hand. That I never will relax in my secrecy or in my search. That I will fasten the crime of the murder of my dear dead boy upon the murderer. And That I devote myself to his destruction."

CHAPTER XVII.

PHILANTHROPY, PROFESSIONAL AND UNPROFESSIONAL.

FULL half a year had come and gone, and Mr. Crisparkle sat in a waiting-room in the London chief offices of the Haven of Philanthropy, until he could have audience of Mr. Honeythunder.

In his college-days of athletic exercises, Mr. Crisparkle had known professors of the Noble Art of fisticuffs, and had attended two or three of their gloved gatherings. He had now an opportunity of observing that as to the phrenological formation of the backs of their heads, the Professing Philanthropists were uncommonly like the Pugilists. In the development of all those organs which constitute, or attend, a propensity to " pitch into " your fellow-creatures, the Philanthropists were remarkably favored. There were several Professors passing in and out, with exactly the aggressive air upon them of being ready for a turn-up with any Novice who might happen to be on hand, that Mr. Crisparkle well remembered in the circles of the Fancy. Preparations were in progress for a moral little Mill somewhere on the rural circuit, and other Professors were backing this or that Heavy-Weight as good for such or such speech-making hits, so very much after the manner of the sporting publicans that the intended Resolutions might have been Rounds. In an official manager of these displays much celebrated for his platform tactics, Mr. Crisparkle recognized (in a suit of black) the counterpart of a deceased benefactor of his species, an eminent public character, once known to fame as Frosty-faced Fogo, who in days of yore superintended the formation of the magic circle with the ropes and stakes. There were only three conditions of resemblance wanting between these Professors and those. Firstly, the Philanthropists were in very bad training: much too fleshy, and presenting, both in face and figure, a superabundance of what is known to Pugilistic Experts as Suet Pudding. Secondly, the Philanthropists had not the good temper of the Pugilists, and used worse language. Thirdly, their fighting code stood in great need of revision, as empowering them not only to bore their man to the ropes, but to bore him to the confines of distraction ; alsc to hit him when he was down, hit him anywhere and anyhow, kick him, stamp upon him, gouge him, and maul him behind his back without mercy. In these last particulars the Professors of the Noble Art were much nobler than the Professors of Philanthropy.

Mr. Crisparkle was so completely lost in musing on these similarities and dissimilarities, at the same time watching the crowd which came and went by, always, as it seemed, on errands of antagonistically snatching something from somebody, and never giving anything to anybody: that his name was called before he heard it. On his at length responding, he was shown by a miserably shabby and underpaid stipendiary Philanthropist (who could hardly have done worse if he had taken service with a declared enemy of the human race) to Mr. Honeythunder's room.

"Sir," said Mr. Honeythunder in his tremendous voice, like a schoolmaster issuing orders to a boy of whom he had a bad opinion, "sit down."

Mr. Crisparkle seated himself.

Mr. Honeythunder, having signed the remaining few score of a few thousand circulars, calling upon a corresponding number of families without means to come forward, stump up instantly, and be Philanthropists, or go to the Devil, another shabby stipendiary Philanthropist (highly disinterested, if in earnest) gathered these into a basket and walked off with them.

"Now, Mr. Crisparkle," said Mr. Honeythunder, turning his chair half round towards him when they were alone, and squaring his arms with his hands on his knees, and his brows knitted as if he added, I am going to make short work of *you*, — "now, Mr Crisparkle, we entertain different views, you and I, sir, of the sanctity of human life."

"Do we?" returned the Minor Canon.

"We do, sir."

"Might I ask you," said the Minor Canon, "what are your views on that subject?"

"That human life is a thing to be held sacred, sir."

"Might I ask you," pursued the Minor Canon as before, "what you suppose to be my views on that subject?"

"By George, sir!" returned the Philanthropist, squaring his arms still more, as he frowned on Mr. Crisparkle: "they are best known to yourself."

"Readily admitted. But you began by saying that we took different views, you know. Therefore (or you could not say so) you must have set up some views as mine. Pray, what views *have* you set up as mine?"

"Here is a man — and a young man," said Mr. Honeythunder as if that made the matter infinitely worse, and he could have easily borne the loss of an old one: "swept off the face of the earth by a deed of violence. What do you call that?"

"Murder," said the Minor Canon.

"What do you call the doer of that deed, sir?"

"A murderer," said the Minor Canon.

"I am glad to hear you admit so much, sir," retorted Mr Honeythunder, in his most offensive manner; "and I candidly tell you that I did n't expect it." Here he lowered heavily at Mr. Crisparkle again.

"Be so good as to explain what you mean by those very unjustifiable expressions."

"I don't sit here, sir," returned the Philanthropist, raising his voice to a roar, "to be browbeaten."

"As the only other person present, no one can possibly know that better than I do," returned the Minor Canon very quietly. "But I interrupt your explanation."

"Murder!" proceeded Mr. Honeythunder, in a kind of boisterous revery, with his platform folding of his arms, and his platform nod of abhorrent reflection after each short sentiment of a word. "Bloodshed! Abel! Cain! I hold no terms with Cain. I repudiate with a shudder the red hand when it is offered me."

Instead of instantly leaping into his chair and cheering himself hoarse, as the Brotherhood in public meeting assembled would infallibly have done on this cue, Mr. Crisparkle merely reversed the quiet crossing of his legs, and said mildly, "Don't let me interrupt your explanation — when you begin it."

"The Commandments say no murder. NO murder, sir!" proceeded Mr. Honeythunder, platformally pausing as if he took Mr. Crisparkle to task for having distinctly asserted that they said, You may do a little murder and then leave off.

"And they also say, you shall bear no false witness," observed Mr. Crisparkle.

"Enough!" bellowed Mr. Honeythunder, with a solemnity and severity that would have brought the house down at a meeting, "E—e—nough! My late wards being now of age, and I being released from a trust which I cannot contemplate without a thrill of horror, there are the accounts which you have undertaken to accept on their behalf, and there is a statement of the balance which you have undertaken to receive, and which you cannot receive too soon. And let me tell you, sir, I wish, that as a man and a Minor Canon, you were better employed," with a nod. "Better employed," with another nod. "Bet—ter em—ployed!" with another, and the three nods added up.

Mr. Crisparkle rose, a little heated in the face, but with perfect command of himself.

"Mr. Honeythunder," he said, taking up the papers referred to, "my being better or worse employed than I am at present is a matter of taste and opinion. You might think me better employed in enrolling myself a member of your Society."

"Ay, indeed, sir!" retorted Mr. Honeythunder, shaking his head in a threatening manner. "It would have been better for you if you had done that long ago!"

"I think otherwise."

"Or," said Mr. Honeythunder, shaking his head again, "I might think one of your profession better employed in devoting himself to the discovery and punishment of guilt than in leaving that duty to be undertaken by a layman."

"I may regard my profession from a point of view which teaches me that its first duty is towards those who are in necessity and tribulation, who are desolate and oppressed," said Mr Crisparkle. "However, as I have quite clearly satisfied myself that it is no part of my profession to make professions, I say no more of that. But I owe it to Mr. Neville, and to Mr. Neville's sister (and in a much lower degree to myself), to say to you that I *know* I was in the full possession and understanding of Mr. Neville's mind and heart at the time of this occurrence; and that, without in the least coloring or concealing what was to be deplored in him and required to be corrected, I feel certain that his tale is true. Feeling that certainty, I befriend him. As long as that certainty shall last, I will befriend him. And if any consideration could shake me in this resolve, I should be so ashamed of myself for my meanness that no man's good opinion, — no, nor no woman's, — so gained, could compensate me for the loss of my own."

Good fellow! Manly fellow! And he was so modest, too. There was no more self-assertion in the Minor Canon than in the school-boy who had stood in the breezy playing-fields keeping a wicket. He was simply and stanchly true to his duty alike in the large case and in the small. So all true souls ever are. So every true soul ever was, ever is, and ever will be. There is nothing little to the really great in spirit.

"Then who do you make out did the deed?" asked Mr. Honeythunder, turning on him abruptly.

"Heaven forbid," said Mr. Crisparkle, "that in my desire to clear one man I should lightly criminate another! I accuse no one."

"Tcha!" ejaculated Mr. Honeythunder with great disgust; for this was by no means the principle on which the Philanthropic Brotherhood usually proceeded. "And, sir, you are not a disinterested witness, we must bear in mind."

"How am I an interested one?" inquired Mr. Crisparkle, smiling innocently, at a loss to imagine.

"There was a certain stipend, sir, paid to you for your pupil, which may have warped your judgment a bit," said Mr. Honeythunder, coarsely.

"Perhaps I expect to retain it still?" Mr. Crisparkle returned, enlightened; "do you mean that too?"

"Well, sir," returned the professional Philanthropist, getting up, and thrusting his hands down into his trousers' pockets, "I don't go about measuring people for caps. If people find I have any about me that fit 'em, they can put 'em on and wear 'em, if they like. That 's their lookout, not mine."

Mr. Crisparkle eyed him with a just indignation, and took him to task thus:—

"Mr. Honeythunder, I hoped when I came in here that I might be under no necessity of commenting on the introduction of platform manners or platform manœuvres among the decent forbearances of private life. But you have given me such a specimen of both, that I should be a fit subject for both if I remained silent respecting them. They are detestable."

"They don't suit *you*, I dare say, sir."

"They are," repeated Mr. Crisparkle, without noticing the interruption, "detestable. They violate equally the justice that should belong to Christians, and the restraints that should belong to gentlemen. You assume a great crime to have been committed by one whom I, acquainted with the attendant circumstances, and having numerous reasons on my side, devoutly believe to be innocent of it. Because I differ from you on that vital point, what is your platform resource? Instantly to turn upon me, charging that I have no sense of the enormity of the crime itself, but am its aider and abettor! So, another time—taking me as representing your opponent in other cases—you set up a platform credulity: a moved and seconded and carried unanimously profession of faith in some ridiculous delusion or mischievous imposition. I decline to believe it, and you fall back upon your platform resource of proclaiming that I believe nothing; that because I will not bow down to a false God of your making, I deny the true God! Another time, you make the platform discovery that War is a calamity, and you propose to abolish it by a string of twisted resolutions tossed into the air like the tail of a kite. I do not admit the discovery to be yours in the least, and I have not a grain of faith in your remedy. Again, your platform resource of representing me as revelling in the horrors of a battle-field like a fiend incarnate! Another time, in another of your undiscriminating platform rushes, you would punish the sober for the drunken. I claim consideration for the comfort, convenience, and refreshment of the sober; and you presently make platform proclamation that I have a depraved desire to turn Heaven's creatures into swine and wild beasts! In all such cases your movers, and your seconders, and your supporters—your regular Professors of all degrees—run amuck like so many mad Malays; habitually attributing the lowest and basest motives with the utmost recklessness (let me call your attention to a recent instance in yourself for which you should blush), and quoting figures which you know to be as wilfully one-sided as a statement of any complicated account that should be all Creditor side and no Debtor, or all Debtor side and no Creditor. Therefore it is, Mr. Honeythunder, that I consider the platform a sufficiently bad example and a sufficiently bad school, even in public life; but hold that, carried into private life, it becomes an unendurable nuisance."

"These are strong words, sir!" exclaimed the Philanthropist.

"I hope so," said Mr. Crisparkle. "Good morning."

He walked out of the Haven at a great rate, but soon fell into his regular brisk pace, and soon had a smile upon his face as he went along, wondering what the china shepherdess would have said if she had seen him pounding Mr. Honeythunder in the late little lively affair. For Mr. Crisparkle had just enough of harmless vanity to hope that he had hit hard, and to glow with the belief that he had trimmed the Philanthropic jacket pretty handsomely.

He took himself to Staple Inn, but not to P. J. T. and Mr. Grewgious. Full many a creaking stair he climbed before he reached some attic rooms in a corner, turned the latch of their unbolted door, and stood beside the table of Neville Landless.

An air of retreat and solitude hung about the rooms and about their inhabitant. He was much worn, and so were they. Their sloping ceilings, cumbrous rusty locks and grates, and heavy wooden bins and beams, slowly mouldering withal, had a prisonous look, and he had the haggard face of a prisoner. Yet the sunlight shone in at the ugly garret window which had a penthouse to itself thrust out among the tiles; and on the cracked and smoke-blackened parapet beyond, some of the deluded sparrows of the place rheumatically hopped, like little feathered cripples who had left their crutches in their nests; and there was a play of living leaves at hand that changed the air, and made an imperfect sort of music in it that would have been melody in the country.

The rooms were sparely furnished, but with good store of books. Everything expressed the abode of a poor student. That Mr. Crisparkle had been either chooser, lender, or donor of the books, or that he combined the three characters, might have been easily seen in the friendly beam of his eyes upon them as he entered.

"How goes it, Neville?"

"I am in good heart, Mr. Crisparkle, and working away."

"I wish your eyes were not quite so large and not quite so bright," said the Minor Canon, slowly releasing the hand he had taken in his.

"They brighten at the sight of you," returned Neville. "If you were to fall away from me, they would soon be dull enough."

"Rally, rally!" urged the other, in a stimulating tone. "Fight for it, Neville!"

"If I were dying, I feel as if a word from you would rally me; if my pulse had stopped, I feel as if your touch would make it beat again," said Neville. "But I *have* rallied, and am doing famously."

Mr. Crisparkle turned him with his face a little more towards the light.

"I want to see a ruddier touch here, Neville," he said, indicating his own healthy cheek by way of pattern; "I want more sun to shine upon you."

Neville drooped suddenly as he replied in a lowered voice, "I am not hardy enough for that yet. I may become so, but I cannot bear it yet. If you had gone through those Cloisterham streets as I did; if you had seen, as I did, those averted eyes, and the better sort of people silently giving me too much room to pass, that I might not touch them or come near them, you would n't think it quite unreasonable that I cannot go about in the daylight."

"My poor fellow!" said the Minor Canon, in a tone so purely sympathetic that the young man caught his hand: "I never said it was unreasonable: never thought so. But I should like you to do it."

"And that would give me the strongest motive to do it. But I cannot yet. I cannot persuade myself that the eyes of even the stream of strangers I pass in this vast city look at me without suspicion. I feel marked and tainted, even when I go out — as I do only — at night. But the darkness covers me then, and I take courage from it."

Mr. Crisparkle laid a hand upon his shoulder, and stood looking down at him.

"If I could have changed my name," said Neville, "I would have done so. But as you wisely pointed out to me, I can't do that, for it would look like guilt. If I could have gone to some distant place, I might have found relief in that, but the thing is not to be thought of, for the same reason. Hiding and escaping would be the construction in either case. It seems a little hard to be so tied to a stake, and innocent; but I don't complain."

"And you must expect no miracle to help you, Neville," said Mr. Crisparkle, compassionately.

"No, sir, I know that. The ordinary fulness of time and circumstance is all I have to trust to."

"It will right you at last, Neville."

"So I believe, and I hope I may live to know it."

But perceiving that the despondent mood into which he was falling cast a shadow on the Minor Canon, and (it may be) feeling that the broad hand upon his shoulder was not then quite as steady as its own natural strength had rendered it when it first touched him just now, he brightened and said,—

"Excellent circumstances for study anyhow! and you know, Mr. Crisparkle, what need I have of study in all ways. Not to mention that you have advised me to study for the difficult profession of the law, specially, and that of course I am guiding myself by the advice of such a friend and helper. Such a good friend and helper!"

He took the fortifying hand from his shoulder, and kissed it. Mr. Crisparkle beamed at the books, but not so brightly as when he had entered.

"I gather from your silence on the subject that my late guardian is adverse, Mr. Crisparkle?"

The Minor Canon answered, "Your late guardian is a — a most unreasonable person, and it signifies nothing to any reasonable person whether he is *ad*verse or *per*verse, or the *re*verse."

"Well for me that I have enough with economy to live upon," sighed Neville, half wearily and half cheerily, "while I wait to be learned and wait to be righted! Else I might have proved the proverb that while the grass grows the steed starves!"

He opened some books as he said it, and was soon immersed in their interleaved and annotated passages, while Mr. Crisparkle sat beside him, expounding, correcting, and advising. The Minor Canon's cathedral duties made these visits of his difficult to accomplish, and only to be compassed at intervals of many weeks. But they were as serviceable as they were precious to Neville Landless.

When they had got through such studies as they had in hand, they stood leaning on the window-sill, and looking down upon the patch of garden. "Next week," said Mr. Crisparkle, "you will cease to be alone, and will have a devoted companion."

"And yet," returned Neville, "this seems an uncongenial place to bring my sister to!"

"I don't think so," said the Minor Canon. "There is duty to be done here; and there are womanly feeling, sense, and courage wanted here."

"I meant," explained Neville, "that the surroundings are so dull and unwomanly, and that Helena can have no suitable friend or society here."

"You have only to remember," said Mr. Crisparkle, "that you are here yourself, and that she has to draw you into the sunlight."

They were silent for a little while, and then Mr. Crisparkle began anew.

"When we first spoke together, Neville, you told me that your sister had risen out of the disadvantages of your past lives as superior to you as the tower of Cloisterham Cathedral is higher than the chimneys of Minor Canon Corner. Do you remember that?"

"Right well!"

"I was inclined to think it at the time an enthusiastic flight. No matter what I think it now. What I would emphasize is, that under the head of Pride your sister is a great and opportune example to you."

"Under *all* heads that are included in the composition of a fine character, she is."

"Say so; but take this one. Your sister has learnt how to govern what is proud in her nature. She can dominate it even when it is wounded through her sympathy with you. No doubt she has suffered deeply in those same streets where you suffered deeply. No doubt her life is darkened by the cloud that darkens yours. But bending her pride into a grand composure that is not haughty or aggressive, but is sustained confidence in you and in the truth, she has won her way through those streets until she passes along them as high in the general respect as any one who treads them. Every day and hour of her life since Edwin Drood's disappearance, she has faced malignity and folly — for you — as only a brave nature well directed can. So it will be with her to the end. Another and weaker kind of pride might sink broken-hearted, but never such a pride as hers: which knows no shrinking, and can get no mastery over her."

The pale cheek beside him flushed under the comparison and the hint implied in it. "I will do all I can to imitate her," said Neville.

"Do so, and be a truly brave man as she is a truly brave woman," answered Mr. Crisparkle, stoutly. "It is growing dark. Will you go my way with me, when it is quite dark? Mind! It is not I who wait for darkness."

Neville replied that he would accompany him directly. But Mr. Crisparkle said he had a moment's call to make on Mr. Grewgious as an act of courtesy, and would run across to that gentleman's chambers, and rejoin Neville on his own doorstep if he would come down there to meet him.

Mr. Grewgious, bolt upright as usual, sat taking his wine in the dusk at his open window; his wineglass and decanter on the round table at his elbow; himself and his legs on the window-seat; only one hinge in his whole body, like a bootjack.

"How do you do, reverend sir?" said Mr. Grewgious, with abundant offers of hospitality which were as cordially declined as made. "And how is your charge getting on over the way in the set that I had the pleasure of recommending to you as vacant and eligible?"

Mr. Crisparkle replied suitably.

"I am glad you approve of them," said Mr. Grewgious, "because I entertain a sort of fancy for having him under my eye."

As Mr. Grewgious had to turn his eye up considerably, before he could see the chambers, the phrase was to be taken figuratively and not literally.

"And how did you leave Mr. Jasper, reverend sir?" said Mr. Grewgious.

Mr. Crisparkle had left him pretty well.

"And where did you leave Mr. Jasper, reverend sir?"

Mr. Crisparkle had left him at Cloisterham.

"And when did you leave Mr. Jasper, reverend sir?"

That morning.

"Umps!" said Mr. Grewgious. "He did n't say he was coming, perhaps?"

"Coming where?"

"Anywhere, for instance?" said Mr. Grewgious.

"No"

"Because here he is," said Mr. Grewgious, who had asked all these questions with his preoccupied glance directed out at window. "And he don't look agreeable; does he?"

Mr. Crisparkle was craning towards the window, when Mr. Grewgious added,—

"If you will kindly step round here behind me in the gloom of the room, and will cast your eye at the second floor landing window, in yonder house, I think you will hardly fail to see a slinking individual in whom I recognize our local friend."

"You are right!" cried Mr. Crisparkle.

"Umps!" said Mr. Grewgious. Then he added, turning his face so abruptly that his head nearly came into collision with Mr Crisparkle's: "What should you say that our local friend was up to?"

The last passage he had been shown in the Diary returned on Mr. Crisparkle's mind with the force of a strong recoil, and he asked Mr. Grewgious if he thought it possible that Neville was to be harassed by the keeping of a watch upon him?

"A watch," repeated Mr. Grewgious, musingly. "Ay!"

"Which would not only of itself haunt and torture his life," said Mr. Crisparkle, warmly, "but would expose him to the torment of a perpetually reviving suspicion, whatever he might do, or wherever he might go?"

"Ay!" said Mr. Grewgious, musingly still. "Do I see him waiting for you?"

"No doubt you do."

"Then *would* you have the goodness to excuse my getting up to see you out, and to go out to join him, and to go the way that you were going, and to take no notice of our local friend?" said Mr. Grewgious. "I entertain a sort of fancy for having *him* under my eye to-night, do you know?"

Mr. Crisparkle, with a significant nod, complied, and, rejoining Neville, went away with him. They dined together, and parted at the yet unfinished and undeveloped railway station: Mr. Crisparkle to get home; Neville to walk the streets, cross the bridges, make a wide round of the city in the friendly darkness, and tire himself out.

It was midnight when he returned from his solitary expedition, and climbed his staircase. The night was hot, and the windows of the staircase were all wide open. Coming to the top, it gave him a passing chill of surprise (there being no rooms but his up there) to find a stranger sitting on the window-sill, more after the manner of a venturesome glazier than an amateur ordinarily careful of his neck; in fact, so much more outside the window than inside, as to suggest the thought that he must have come up by the waterspout instead of the stairs.

The stranger said nothing until Neville put his key in his door; then, seeming to make sure of his identity from the action, he spoke:—

"I beg your pardon," he said, coming from the window with a frank and smiling air, and a prepossessing address: "the beans."

Neville was quite at a loss.

"Runners," said the visitor. "Scarlet. Next door at the back."

"Oh!" returned Neville. "And the mignonette and wallflower?

"The same," said the visitor.

"Pray walk in."

"Thank you."

Neville lighted his candles, and the visitor sat down. A handsome gentleman, with a young face, but an older figure in its robustness and its breadth of shoulder; say a man of eight-and-twenty, or, at the utmost, thirty: so extremely sunburnt that the contrast between his brown visage and the white forehead shaded out of doors by his hat, and the glimpses of white throat below the neckerchief, would have been almost ludicrous but for his broad temples, bright blue eyes, clustering brown hair, and laughing teeth.

"I have noticed," said he; "—my name is Tartar."

Neville inclined his head.

"I have noticed (excuse me) that you shut yourself up a good deal, and that you seem to like my garden aloft here. If you would like a little more of it, I could throw out a few lines and stays between my windows and yours, which the runners would take to directly. And I have some boxes, both of mignonette and wallflower, that I could shove on along the gutter (with a boat-hook I have by me) to your windows, and draw back again when they wanted watering or gardening, and shove on again when they were ship-shape, so that they would cause you no trouble. I could n't take this liberty without asking your permission, so I venture to ask it. Tartar, corresponding set, next door."

"You are very kind."

"Not at all. I ought to apologize for looking in so late. But having noticed (excuse me) that you generally walk out at night, I thought I should inconvenience you least by awaiting your return. I am always afraid of inconveniencing busy men, being an idle man."

"I should not have thought so, from your appearance."

"No? I take it as a compliment. In fact, I was bred in the Royal Navy, and was First Lieutenant when I quitted it. But an uncle, disappointed in the service, leaving me his property on condition that I left the Navy, I accepted the fortune and resigned my commission."

"Lately, I presume?"

"Well, I had had twelve or fifteen years of knocking about first. I came here some nine months before you; I had had one crop before you came. I chose this place because, having served last in a little Corvette, I knew I should feel more at home where I had a constant opportunity of knocking my head against the ceiling. Besides, it would never do for a man who had been aboard ship from his boyhood to turn luxurious all at once. Besides, again: having been accustomed to a very short allowance of land all my life, I thought I 'd feel my way to the command of a landed estate by beginning in boxes."

Whimsically as this was said, there was a touch of merry earnestness in it that made it doubly whimsical.

"However," said the Lieutenant, "I have talked quite enough about myself. It is not my way I hope; it has merely been to present myself to you naturally. If you will allow me to take the liberty I have described, it will be a charity, for it will give me something more to do. And you are not to suppose that it will entail any interruption or intrusion on you, for that is far from my intention"

Neville replied that he was greatly obliged, and that he thankfully accepted the kind proposal.

"I am very glad to take your windows in tow," said the Lieutenant. "From what I have seen of you when I have been gardening at mine, and you have been looking on, I have thought you (excuse me) rather too studious and delicate! May I ask, is your health at all affected?"

"I have undergone some mental distress," said Neville, confused, "which has stood me in the stead of illness."

"Pardon me," said Mr. Tartar.

With the greatest delicacy he shifted his ground to the windows again, and asked if he could look at one of them. On Neville's opening it, he immediately sprang out, as if he were going aloft with a whole watch in an emergency, and were setting a bright example.

"For Heaven's sake!" cried Neville, "don't do that! Where are you going, Mr. Tartar? You 'll be dashed to pieces!"

"All well!" said the Lieutenant, coolly looking about him on the housetop. "All taut and trim here. Those lines and stays shall be rigged before you turn out in the morning. May I take this short cut home and say, Good night?"

"Mr. Tartar!" urged Neville. "Pray! It makes me giddy to see you!"

But Mr. Tartar, with a wave of his hand and the deftness of a cat, had already dipped through his scuttle of scarlet runners without breaking a leaf, and "gone below."

Mr. Grewgious, his bedroom window-blind held aside with his hand, happened at that moment to have Neville's chambers under his eye for the last time that night. Fortunately his eye was on the front of the house and not the back, or this remarkable appearance and disappearance might have broken his rest, as a phenomenon. But Mr. Grewgious seeing nothing there, not even a light in the windows, his gaze wandered from the windows to the stars, as if he would have read in them something that was hidden from him. Many of us would if we could; but none of us so much as know our letters in the stars yet — or seem likely to do it in this state of existence — and few languages can be read until their alphabets are mastered.

CHAPTER XVIII.

A SETTLER IN CLOISTERHAM.

At about this time a stranger appeared in Cloisterham, a white-haired personage with black eyebrows. Being buttoned up in a tightish blue surtout, with a buff waistcoat and gray trousers, he had something of a military air; but he announced himself at the Crozier (the orthodox hotel, where he put up with a portmanteau) as an idle dog who lived upon his means; and he further announced that he had a mind to take a lodging in the picturesque old city for a month or two, with a view of settling down there altogether. Both announcements were made in the coffee room of the Crozier, to all whom it might, or might not, concern, by the stranger as he stood with his back to the empty fireplace, waiting for his fried sole, veal cutlet, and pint of sherry. And the waiter (business being chronically slack at the Crozier) represented all whom it might or might not concern, and absorbed the whole of the information.

This gentleman's white head was unusually large, and his shock of white hair was unusually thick and ample. "I suppose, waiter," he said, shaking his shock of hair, as a Newfoundland dog might shake his before sitting down to dinner, "that a fair lodging for a single buffer might be found in these parts, eh?"

The waiter had no doubt of it.

"Something old," said the gentleman. "Take my hat down for a moment from that peg, will you? No, I don't want it; look into it. What do you see written there?"

The waiter read, "Datchery."

"Now you know my name," said the gentleman, — "Dick Datchery. Hang it up again. I was saying something old is what I should prefer, something odd and out of the way; something venerable, architectural, and inconvenient."

"We have a good choice of inconvenient lodgings in the town, sir, I think," replied the waiter, with modest confidence in its resources that way; "indeed, I have no doubt that we could suit you that far, however particular you might be. But a architectural lodging!" That seemed to trouble the waiter's head, and he shook it.

"Anything Cathedraly now," Mr. Datchery suggested.

"Mr. Tope," said the waiter, brightening, as he rubbed his chin with his hand, "would be the likeliest party to inform in that line."

"Who is Mr. Tope?" inquired Dick Datchery.

The waiter explained that he was the Verger, and that Mrs. Tope had indeed once upon a time let lodgings herself, — or offered to let them; but that, as nobody had ever taken them, Mrs. Tope's window-bill, long a Cloisterham Institution, had disappeared; probably had tumbled down one day, and never been put up again.

"I'll call on Mrs. Tope," said Mr. Datchery, "after dinner."

So when he had done his dinner, he was duly directed to the spot, and sallied out for it. But the Crozier being an hotel of a most retiring disposition, and the waiter's directions being fatally precise, he soon became bewildered, and went boggling about and about the Cathedral Tower, whenever he could catch a glimpse of it, with a general impression on his mind that Mrs. Tope's was somewhere very near it, and that, like the children in the game of hot boiled beans and very good butter, he was warm in his search when he saw the Tower, and cold when he did n't see it.

He was getting very cold indeed when he came upon a fragment of burial-ground in which an unhappy sheep was grazing. Unhappy, because a hideous small boy was stoning it through the railings, and had already lamed it in one leg, and was much excited by the benevolent sportsman-like purpose of breaking its other three legs, and bringing it down.

"'It 'im ag'in!" cried the boy, as the poor creature leaped, "and made a dint in his wool!"

"Let him be!" said Mr. Datchery. "Don't you see you have lamed him?"

"Yer lie," returned the sportsman. "'E went and lamed 'isself. I see 'im do it, and I giv' 'im a shy as a Widdy-warning to 'im not to go a bruisin' 'is master's mutton any more."

"Come here."

"I won't; I'll come when yer can ketch me."

"Stay there then, and show me which is Mr. Tope's."

"'Ow can I stay here and show you which is Topeseses, when Topeseses is t' other side the Kinfreederal, and over the crossings, and round ever so many corners? Stoo-pid! Ya-a-ah!"

"Show me where it is, and I'll give you something."

"Come on, then!"

This brisk dialogue concluded, the boy led the way, and by and by stopped at some distance from an arched passage, pointing.

"Lookie yonder. You see that there winder and door?"

"That's Tope's?"

"Yer lie: it ain't. That's Jarsper's."

"Indeed?" said Mr. Datchery, with a second look of some interest.

"Yes, and I ain't a-goin' no nearer 'IM, I tell yer."

"Why not?"

"'Cos I ain't a-going to be lifted off my legs and 'ave my braces bust and be choked; not if I knows it, and not by 'Im. Wait till I set a jolly good flint a flyin' at the back o' 'is jolly old 'ed some day! Now look t' other side the harch; not the side where Jarsper's door is; t' other side."

"I see."

"A little way in, o' that side, there's a low door, down two steps. That's Topeseses with 'is name on a hoval plate."

"Good. See here," said Mr. Datchery, producing a shilling. "You owe me half of this."

"Yer lie; I don't owe yer nothing; I never seen yer."

"I tell you you owe me half of this, because I have no sixpence in my pocket. So the next time you meet me you shall do something else for me, to pay me."

"All right, give us 'old."

"What is your name, and where do you live?"

"Deputy. Travellers' Twopenny, 'cross the green."

The boy instantly darted off with the shilling, lest Mr. Datchery should repent, but stopped at a safe distance, on the happy chance of his being uneasy in his mind about it, to goad him with a demon dance expressive of its irrevocability.

Mr. Datchery, taking off his hat to give that shock of white hair of his another shake, seemed quite resigned, and betook himself whither he had been directed.

Mr. Tope's official dwelling, communicating by an upper stair with Mr. Jasper's (hence Mrs. Tope's attendance on that gentleman), was of very modest proportions, and partook of the character of a cool dungeon. Its ancient walls were massive, and its rooms rather seemed to have been dug out of them than to have been designed beforehand with any reference to them. The main door opened at once on a chamber of no describable shape, with a groined roof, which, in its turn, opened on another chamber of no describable shape, with another groined roof. Their windows small and in the thickness of the walls, these two chambers, close as to their atmosphere and swarthy as to their illumination by natural light, were the apartments which Mrs. Tope had so long offered to an unappreciative city. Mr. Datchery, however, was more appreciative. He found that if he sat with the main door open he would enjoy the passing society of all comers to and fro by the gateway, and would have light enough. He found that if Mr. and Mrs. Tope, living overhead, used for their own egress and ingress a little side stair that came plump into the Precincts by a door opening outward, to the surprise and inconvenience of a limited public of pedestrians in a narrow way, he would be alone, as in a separate residence. He found the rent moderate, and everything as quaintly inconvenient as he could desire. He agreed, therefore, to take the lodging then and there, and money down, possession to be had next evening on condition that reference was permitted him to Mr. Jasper as occupying the Gate House, of which, on the other side of the gateway, the Verger's hole in the wall was an appanage or subsidiary part.

The poor dear gentleman was very solitary and very sad, Mrs. Tope said, but she had no doubt he would "speak for her." Perhaps Mr. Datchery had heard something of what had occurred there last winter?

Mr. Datchery had as confused a knowledge of the event in question, on trying to recall it, as he well could have. He begged Mrs. Tope's pardon when she found it incumbent on her to correct him in every detail of his summary of the facts, but pleaded that he was merely a single buffer getting through life upon his means as idly as he could, and that so many people were so constantly making away with so many other people, as to render it difficult for a buffer of an easy temper to preserve the circumstances of the several cases unmixed in his mind.

Mr. Jasper proving willing to speak for Mrs. Tope, Mr. Datchery, who had sent up his card, was invited to ascend the postern staircase. The Mayor was there, Mrs. Tope said; but he was not to be regarded in the light of company, as he and Mr. Jasper were great friends.

"I beg pardon," said Mr. Datchery, making a leg with his hat under his arm, as he addressed himself equally to both gentlemen; "a selfish precaution on my part and not personally interesting to anybody but myself. But as a buffer living on his means, and having an idea of doing it in this lovely place in peace and quiet, for remaining span of life, beg to ask if the Tope family are quite respectable?"

Mr. Jasper could answer for that without the slightest hesitation.

"That is enough, sir," said Mr. Datchery.

"My friend, the Mayor," added Mr. Jasper, presenting Mr. Datchery with a courtly motion of his hand towards that potentate, "whose recommendation is actually much more important to a stranger than that of an obscure person like myself, will testify in their behalf, I am sure."

"The Worshipful the Mayor," said Mr. Datchery, with a low bow, "places me under an infinite obligation."

"Very good people, sir, Mr. and Mrs. Tope," said Mr. Sapsea, with condescension. "Very good opinions. Very well behaved. Very respectful. Much approved by the Dean and Chapter."

"The Worshipful the Mayor gives them a character," said Mr. Datchery, "of which they may indeed be proud. I would ask his Honor (if I might be permitted) whether there are not many objects of great interest in the city which is under his beneficent sway?"

"We are, sir," returned Mr. Sapsea, "an ancient city, and an ecclesiastical city. We are a constitutional city, as it becomes such a city to be, and we uphold and maintain our glorious privileges."

"His Honor," said Mr. Datchery, bowing, "inspires me with a desire to know more of the city, and confirms me in my inclination to end my days in the city."

"Retired from the Army, sir?" suggested Mr. Sapsea.

"His Honor the Mayor does me too much credit," returned Mr. Datchery.

"Navy, sir?" suggested Mr. Sapsea.

"Again," repeated Mr. Datchery, "His Honor the Mayor does me too much credit."

"Diplomacy is a fine profession," said Mr. Sapsea, as a general remark.

"There, I confess, His Honor the Mayor is too many for me," said Mr Datchery, with an ingenuous smile and bow; "even a diplomatic bird must fall to such a gun."

Now, this was very soothing. Here was a gentleman of a great—not to say a grand—address, accustomed to rank and dignity, really setting a fine example how to behave to a Mayor. There was something in that third-person style of being spoken to, that Mr. Sapsea found particularly recognizant of his merits and position.

"But I crave pardon," said Mr. Datchery. "His Honor the Mayor will bear with me, if for a moment I have been deluded into occupying his time, and have forgotten the humble claims upon my own, of my hotel, the Crozier."

"Not at all, sir," said Mr. Sapsea. "I am returning home, and if you would like to take the exterior of our Cathedral in your way, I shall be glad to point it out."

"His Honor the Mayor," said Mr. Datchery, "is more than kind and gracious."

As Mr. Datchery, when he had made his acknowledgments to Mr. Jasper, could not be induced to go out of the room before the Worshipful, the Worshipful led the way down stairs, Mr. Datchery following with his hat under his arm, and his shock of white hair streaming in the evening breeze.

"Might I ask His Honor," said Mr. Datchery, "whether that gentleman we have just left is the gentleman of whom I have heard in the neighborhood as being much afflicted by the loss of a nephew, and concentrating his life on avenging the loss?"

"That is the gentleman. John Jasper, sir."

"Would His Honor allow me to inquire whether there are strong suspicions of any one?"

"More than suspicions, sir," returned Mr. Sapsea, "all but certainties."

"Only think now!" cried Mr. Datchery.

"But proof, sir, proof, must be built up, stone by stone," said the Mayor.

"As I say, the end crowns the work. It is not enough that Justice should be morally certain; she must be immorally certain — legally, that is"

"His Honor," said Mr. Datchery, "reminds me of the nature of the law. Immoral! How true!"

"As I say, sir," pompously went on the Mayor, "the arm of the law is a strong arm, and a long arm. That is the way *I* put it. A strong arm and a long arm."

"How forcible! — And yet, again, how true!" murmured Mr. Datchery.

"And without betraying what I call the secrets of the prison-house," said Mr. Sapsea; "the secrets of the prison-house is the term I used on the bench."

"And what other term than His Honor's would express it!" said Mr. Datchery.

"Without, I say, betraying them, I predict to you, knowing the iron will of the gentleman we have just left (I take the bold step of calling it iron, on account of its strength), that in this case the long arm will reach, and the strong arm will strike. This is our Cathedral, sir. The best judges are pleased to admire it, and the best among our townsmen own to being a little vain of it."

All this time Mr. Datchery had walked with his hat under his arm, and his white hair streaming. He had an odd momentary appearance upon him of having forgotten his hat, when Mr. Sapsea now touched it; and he clapped his hand up to his head as if with some vague expectation of finding another hat upon it.

"Pray be covered, sir," entreated Mr. Sapsea; magnificently implying, "I shall not mind it, I assure you."

"His Honor is very good, but I do it for coolness," said Mr. Datchery.

Then Mr. Datchery admired the Cathedral, and Mr. Sapsea pointed it out as if he himself had invented and built it; there were a few details indeed of which he did not approve, but those he glossed over, as if the workmen had made mistakes in his absence. The Cathedral disposed of, he led the way by the churchyard, and stopped to extol the beauty of the evening — by chance — in the immediate vicinity of Mrs. Sapsea's epitaph.

"And by the by," said Mr. Sapsea, appearing to descend from an elevation to remember it all of a sudden, like Apollo shooting down from Olympus to pick up his forgotten lyre, "*that* is one of our small lions. The partiality of our people has made it so, and strangers have been seen taking a copy of it now and then. I am not a judge of it myself, for it is a little work of my own. But it was troublesome to turn, sir; I may say, difficult to turn with elegance."

Mr. Datchery became so ecstatic over Mr. Sapsea's composition that, in spite of his intention to end his days in Cloisterham, and therefore his probably having in reserve many opportunities of copying it, he would have transcribed it into his pocket-book on the spot, but for the slouching towards them of its material producer and perpetuator, Durdles, whom Mr. Sapsea hailed, not sorry to show him a bright example of behavior to superiors.

"Ah, Durdles! This is the mason, sir; one of our Cloisterham worthies; everybody here knows Durdles. Mr. Datchery, Durdles; a gentleman who is going to settle here."

"I would n't do it if I was him," growled Durdles. "We 're a heavy lot."

"You surely don't speak for yourself, Mr. Durdles," returned Mr. Datchery, "any more than for His Honor."

"Who 's His Honor?" demanded Durdles.

"His Honor the Mayor."

"I never was brought afore him," said Durdles, with anything but the look of a loyal subject of the mayoralty, "and it'll be time enough for me to Honor him when I am. Until which, and when, and where:—

'Mister Sapsea is his name,
England is his nation,
Cloisterham's his dwelling-place,
Aukshneer's his occupation.'"

Here, Deputy (preceded by a flying oyster-shell) appeared upon the scene, and requested to have the sum of threepence instantly "chucked" to him by Mr. Durdles, whom he had been vainly seeking up and down, as lawful wages overdue. While that gentleman, with his bundle under his arm, slowly found and counted out the money, Mr. Sapsea informed the new settler of Durdles's habits, pursuits, abode, and reputation. "I suppose a curious stranger might come to see you, and your works, Mr. Durdles, at any odd time?" said Mr. Datchery upon that.

"Any gentleman is welcome to come and see me any evening if he brings liquor for two with him," returned Durdles, with a penny between his teeth and certain half-pence in his hands. "Or if he likes to make it twice two, he'll be doubly welcome."

"I shall come. Master Deputy, what do you owe me?"

"A job."

"Mind you pay me honestly with the job of showing me Mr. Durdles's house when I want to go there."

Deputy, with a piercing broadside of whistle through the whole gap in his mouth, as a receipt in full for all arrears, vanished.

The Worshipful and the Worshipper then passed on together until they parted, with many ceremonies, at the Worshipful's door; even then, the Worshipper carried his hat under his arm, and gave his streaming white hair to the breeze.

Said Mr. Datchery to himself that night, as he looked at his white hair in the gas-lighted looking-glass over the coffee-room chimney-piece at the Crozier, and shook it out: "For a single buffer, of an easy temper, living idly on his means, I have had a rather busy afternoon!"

CHAPTER XIX.

SHADOW ON THE SUNDIAL.

Again Miss Twinkleton has delivered her valedictory address, with the accompaniments of white wine and pound cake, and again the young ladies have departed to their several homes. Helena Landless has left the Nuns' House to attend her brother's fortunes, and pretty Rosa is alone.

Cloisterham is so bright and sunny in these summer days that the Cathedral and the monastery-ruin show as if their strong walls were transparent A soft glow seems to shine from within them rather than upon them from without, such is their mellowness as they look forth on the hot corn-fields and the smoking roads that distantly wind among them. The Cloisterham gardens blush with ripening fruit. Time was when travel-stained pilgrims rode in clattering parties through the city's welcome shades; time is when wayfarers, leading a gypsy life between haymaking time and harvest, and looking as if they were just made of the dust of the earth, so very dusty are they, lounge about on cool doorsteps, trying to mend their unmendable shoes, or giving them to the city kennels as a hopeless job, and seeking others in the bundles that they carry, along with their yet unused sickles swathed in bands of straw. At all the more public pumps there is much cooling of bare feet, together with much bubbling and gurgling of drinking with hand to spout on the part of these Bedouins; the Cloisterham police meanwhile looking askant from their beats with suspicion, and manifest impatience that the intruders should depart from within the civic bounds, and once more fry themselves on the simmering high-roads.

On the afternoon of such a day, when the last Cathedral service is done, and when that side of the High Street on which the Nuns' House stands is in grateful shade, save where its quaint old garden opens to the west between the boughs of trees, a servant informs Rosa, to her terror, that Mr. Jasper desires to see her.

If he had chosen his time for finding her at a disadvantage, he could have done no better. Perhaps he has chosen it. Helena Landless is gone, Mrs Tisher is absent on leave, Miss Twinkleton (in her amateur state of existence) has contributed herself and a veal-pie to a picnic.

"O, why, why, why did you say I was at home!" cries Rosa, helplessly.

The maid replies that Mr. Jasper never asked the question. That he said he knew she was at home, and begged she might be told that he asked to see her.

"What shall I do? what shall I do?" thinks Rosa, clasping her hands.

Possessed by a kind of desperation, she adds in the next breath that she will come to Mr. Jasper in the garden. She shudders at the thought of being shut up with him in the house; but many of its windows command the garden, and she can be seen as well as heard there, and can shriek in the free air and run away. Such is the wild idea that flutters through her mind.

She has never seen him since the fatal night, except when she was questioned before the Mayor, and then he was present in gloomy watchfulness, as representing his lost nephew and burning to avenge him. She hangs her garden-hat on her arm, and goes out. The moment she sees him from the porch, leaning on the sundial, the old horrible feeling of being compelled by him asserts its hold upon her. She feels that she would even then go back, but that he draws her feet towards him. She cannot resist, and sits down, with her head bent, on the garden-seat beside the sundial. She cannot look up at him for abhorrence, but she has perceived that he is dressed in deep mourning. So is she. It was not so at first; but the lost has long been given up, and mourned for, as dead.

He would begin by touching her hand. She feels the intention, and draws her hand back. His eyes are then fixed upon her, she knows, though her own see nothing but the grass.

"I have been waiting," he begins, "for some time, to be summoned back to my duty near you."

After several times forming her lips, which she knows he is closely watching, into the shape of some other hesitating reply, and then into none, she answers, "Duty, sir?"

"The duty of teaching you, serving you as your faithful music-master."

"I have left off that study."

"Not left off, I think. Discontinued. I was told by your guardian that you discontinued it under the shock that we have all felt so acutely. When will you resume?"

"Never, sir."

"Never? You could have done no more if you had loved my dear boy."

"I did love him!" cries Rosa, with a flash of anger.

"Yes; but not quite—not quite in the right way, shall I say! Not in the intended and expected way. Much as my dear boy was, unhappily, too self-conscious and self-satisfied (I'll draw no parallel between him and you in that respect)

JASPER'S SACRIFICES.

to love as he should have loved, or as any one in his place would have loved; must have loved!"

She sits in the same still attitude, but shrinking a little more.

"Then, to be told that you discontinued your study with me, was to be politely told that you abandoned it altogether?" he suggested.

"Yes," says Rosa, with sudden spirit. "The politeness was my guardian's, not mine. I told him that I was resolved to leave off, and that I was determined to stand by my resolution."

"And you still are?"

"I still am, sir. And I beg not to be questioned any more about it. At all events, I will not answer any more; I have that in my power."

She is so conscious of his looking at her with a gloating admiration of the touch of anger on her, and the fire and animation it brings with it, that even as her spirit rises, it falls again, and she struggles with a sense of shame, affront, and fear, much as she did that night at the piano.

"I will not question you any more, since you object to it so much; I will confess."

"I do not wish to hear you, sir," cries Rosa, rising.

This time he does touch her with his outstretched hand. In shrinking from it, she shrinks into her seat again.

"We must sometimes act in opposition to our wishes," he tells her in a low voice. "You must do so now, or do more harm to others than you can ever set right."

"What harm?"

"Presently, presently. You question *me*, you see, and surely that 's not fair when you forbid me to question you. Nevertheless, I will answer the question presently. Dearest Rosa! Charming Rosa!"

She starts up again.

This time he does not touch her. But his face looks so wicked and menacing, as he stands leaning against the sundial, — setting, as it were, his black mark upon the very face of day, — that her flight is arrested by horror as she looks at him.

"I do not forget how many windows command a view of us," he says, glancing towards them. "I will not touch you again, I will come no nearer to you than I am. Sit down, and there will be no mighty wonder in your music-master's leaning idly against a pedestal and speaking with you, remembering all that has happened and our shares in it. Sit down, my beloved."

She would have gone once more, — was all but gone, — and once more his face darkly threatening what would follow if she went, has stopped her. Looking at him with the expression of the instant frozen on her face, she sits down on the seat again.

"Rosa, even when my dear boy was affianced to you, I loved you madly; even when I thought his happiness in having you for his wife was certain, I loved you madly; even when I strove to make him more ardently devoted to you, I loved you madly; even when he gave me the picture of your lovely face so carelessly traduced by him, which I feigned to hang always in my sight for his sake, but worshipped in torment for years, I loved you madly. In the distasteful work of the day, in the wakeful misery of the night, girded by sordid realities, or wandering through Paradises and Hells of visions into which I rushed, carrying your image in my arms, I loved you madly."

If anything could make his words more hideous to her than they are in themselves, it would be the contrast between the violence of his look and delivery, and the composure of his assumed attitude.

"I endured it all in silence. So long as you were his, or so long as I supposed you to be his, I hid my secret loyally. Did I not?"

This lie, so gross, while the mere words in which it is told are so true, is more than Rosa can endure. She answers, with kindling indignation, "You were as false throughout, sir, as you are now. You were false to him, daily and hourly. You know that you made my life unhappy by your pursuit of me. You know that you made me afraid to open his generous eyes, and that you forced me, for his own trusting, good, good sake, to keep the truth from him, that you were a bad, bad man!"

His preservation of his easy attitude rendering his working features and his convulsive hands absolutely diabolical, he returns, with a fierce extreme of admiration: —

"How beautiful you are! You are more beautiful in anger than in repose. I don't ask you for your love; give me yourself and your hatred; give me yourself and that pretty rage; give me yourself and that enchanting scorn; it will be enough for me."

Impatient tears rise to the eyes of the trembling little beauty, and her face flames; but as she again rises to leave him in indignation, and seek protection within the house, he stretches out his hand towards the porch, as though he invited her to enter it.

"I told you, you rare charmer, you sweet witch, that you must stay and hear me, or do more harm than can ever be undone. You asked me what harm. Stay, and I will tell you. Go, and I will do it!"

Again Rosa quails before his threatening face, though innocent of its meaning, and she remains. Her panting breathing comes and goes as if it would choke her; but with a repressive hand upon her bosom, she remains.

"I have made my confession that my love is mad. It is so mad that, had the ties between me and my dear lost boy been one silken thread less strong, I might have swept even him from your side when you favored him."

A film comes over the eyes she raises for an instant, as though he had turned her faint.

"Even him," he repeats. "Yes, even him! Rosa, you see me and you hear me. Judge for yourself whether any other admirer shall love you and live, whose life is in my hand."

"What do you mean, sir?"

"I mean to show you how mad my love is. It was hawked through the late inquiries by Mr. Crisparkle that young Landless had confessed to him that he was a rival of my lost boy. That is an inexpiable offence in my eyes. The same Mr. Crisparkle knows under my hand that I have devoted myself to the murderer's discovery and destruction, be he whom he might, and that I determined to discuss the mystery with no one until I should hold the clew in which to entangle the murderer as in a net. I have since worked patiently to wind and wind it round him; and it is slowly winding as I speak."

"Your belief, if you believe in the criminality of Mr. Landless, is not Mr. Crisparkle's belief, and he is a good man," Rosa retorts

"My belief is my own; and I reserve it, worshipped of my soul! Circumstances may accumulate so strongly *even against an innocent man*, that, directed, sharpened, and pointed, they may slay him. One wanting link discovered by perseverance against a guilty man proves his guilt, however slight its evidence before, and he dies. Young Landless stands in deadly peril either way."

"If you really suppose," Rosa pleads with him, turning paler, "that I favor Mr. Landless, or that Mr. Landless has ever in any way addressed himself to me, you are wrong."

He puts that from him with a slighting action of his hand and a curled lip.

"I was going to show you how madly I love you. More madly now than ever, for I am willing to renounce the second object that has arisen in my life to divide it with you; and henceforth to have no object in existence but you only. Miss Landless has become your bosom friend. You care for her peace of mind?"

"I love her dearly."

"You care for her good name?"

"I have said, sir, I love her dearly."

"I am unconsciously," he observes, with a smile, as he folds his hands upon the sundial and leans his chin upon them, so that his talk would seem from the windows (faces occasionally come and go there) to be of the airiest and playfullest, — "I am unconsciously giving offence by questioning again. I will simply make statements, therefore, and not put questions. You do care for your bosom friend's good name, and you do care for her peace of mind. Then remove the shadow of the gallows from her, dear one!"

"You dare propose to me to — "

"Darling, I dare propose to you. Stop there. If it be bad to idolize you, I am the worst of men; if it be good, I am the best. My love for you is above all other love, and my truth to you is above all other truth. Let me have hope and favor, and I am a forsworn man for your sake."

Rosa puts her hands to her temples, and, pushing back her hair, looks wildly and abhorrently at him, as though she were trying to piece together what it is his deep purpose to present to her only in fragments.

"Reckon up nothing at this moment, angel, but the sacrifices that I lay at those dear feet, which I could fall down among the vilest ashes and kiss, and put upon my head as a poor savage might. There is my fidelity to my dear boy after death. Tread upon it!"

With an action of his hands, as though he cast down something precious.

"There is the inexpiable offence against my adoration of you. Spurn it!"

With a similar action.

"There are my labors in the cause of a just vengeance for six toiling months. Crush them!"

With another repetition of the action.

"There is my past and my present wasted life. There is the desolation of my heart and my soul. There is my peace; there is my despair. Stamp them into the dust, so that you take me, were it even mortally hating me!"

The frightful vehemence of the man, now reaching its full height, so additionally terrifies her as to break the spell that has held her to the spot. She swiftly moves towards the porch; but in an instant he is at her side, and speaking in her ear.

"Rosa, I am self-repressed again. I am walking calmly beside you to the house. I shall wait for some encouragement and hope. I shall not strike too soon. Give me a sign that you attend to me."

She slightly and constrainedly moves her hand.

"Not a word of this to any one, or it will bring down the blow, as certainly as night follows day. Another sign that you attend to me."

She moves her hand once more.

"I love you, love you, love you If you were to cast me off now — but you will not — you would never be rid of me. No one should come between us. I would pursue you to the death."

The handmaid coming out to open the gate for him, he quietly pulls off his hat as a parting salute, and goes away with no greater show of agitation than is visible in the effigy of Mr. Sapsea's father opposite. Rosa faints in going up stairs, and is carefully carried to her room, and laid down on her bed. A thunder-storm is coming on, the maids say, and the hot and stifling air has overset the pretty dear; no wonder; they have felt their own knees all of a tremble all day long.

CHAPTER XX.

A FLIGHT.

ROSA no sooner came to herself than the whole of the late interview was before her. It even seemed as if it had pursued her into her insensibility, and she had not had a moment's unconsciousness of it. What to do, she was at a frightened loss to know: the only one clear thought in her mind was, that she must fly from this terrible man.

But where could she take refuge, and how could she go? She had never breathed her dread of him to any one but Helena. If she went to Helena, and told her what had passed, that very act might bring down the irreparable mischief that he threatened he had the power, and that she knew he had the will, to do. The more fearful he appeared to her excited memory and imagination, the more alarming her responsibility appeared: seeing that a slight mistake on her part, either in action or delay, might let his malevolence loose on Helena's brother.

Rosa's mind throughout the last six months had been stormily confused. A half-formed, wholly unexpressed suspicion tossed in it, now heaving itself up, and now sinking into the deep; now gaining palpability, and now losing it. His self-absorption in his nephew when he was alive, and his unceasing pursuit of the inquiry how he came by his death, if he were dead were themes so rife in the place, that no one appeared able to suspect the possibility of foul play at his hands. She had asked herself the question, "Am I so wicked in my thoughts as to conceive a wickedness that others cannot imagine?" Then she had considered, Did the suspicion come of her previous recoiling from him before the fact? And if so, was not that a proof of its baselessness? Then she had reflected, "What motive could he have, according to my accusation?" She was ashamed to answer in her mind, "The motive of gaining *me!*" And covered her face as if the lightest shadow of the idea of founding murder on such an idle vanity were a crime almost as great.

She ran over in her mind again all that he had said by the sundial in the garden. He had persisted in treating the disappearance as murder, consistently with his whole public course since the finding of the watch and shirt-pin. If he were afraid of the crime being traced out, would he not rather encourage the idea of a voluntary disappearance? He had even declared that if the ties between him and his nephew had been less strong, he might have swept "even him" away from her side. Was that like his having really done so? He had spoken of laying his six months' labors in the cause of a just vengeance at her feet. Would he have done that, with that violence of passion, if they were a pretence? Would he have ranged them with his desolate heart and soul, his wasted life, his peace, and his despair? The very first sacrifice that he represented himself as making for her was his fidelity to his dear boy after death. Surely these facts were strong against a fancy that scarcely dared to hint itself. And yet he was so terrible a man! In short, the poor girl (for what could she know of the criminal intellect, which its own professed students perpetually misread, because they persist in trying to reconcile it with the average intellect of average men, instead of identifying it as a horrible wonder apart), could get by no road to any other conclusion than that he *was* a terrible man, and must be fled from.

She had been Helena's stay and comfort during the whole time. She had constantly assured her of her full belief in her brother's innocence, and of her sympathy with him in his misery. But she had never seen him since the disappearance, nor had Helena ever spoken one word of his avowal to Mr. Crisparkle in regard of Rosa, though as a part of the interest of the case it was well known far and wide. He was Helena's unfortunate brother, to her, and nothing more. The assurance she had given her odious suitor was strictly true, though it would have been better (she considered now) if she could have restrained herself from so giving it. Afraid of him as the bright and delicate little creature was, her spirit swelled at the thought of his knowing it from her own lips.

But where was she to go? Anywhere beyond his reach, was no reply to the question. Somewhere must be thought of. She determined to go to her guardian, and to go immediately. The feeling she had imparted to Helena on the night of their first confidence was so strong upon her — the feeling of not being safe from him, and of the solid walls of the old convent being powerless to keep out his ghostly following of her — that no reasoning of her own could calm her terrors. The fascination of repulsion had been upon her so long, and now culminated so darkly, that she felt as if he had power to bind her by a spell. Glancing out at window, even now, as she rose to dress, the sight of the sundial, on which he had leaned when he declared himself, turned her cold, and made her shrink from it, as though he had invested it with some awful quality from his own nature.

She wrote a hurried note to Miss Twinkleton, saying that she had sudden reason for wishing to see her guardian promptly, and had gone to him; also, entreating the good lady not to be uneasy, for all was well with her. She hurried a few quite useless articles into a very little bag, left the note in a conspicuous place, and went out, softly closing the gate after her.

It was the first time she had ever been even in Cloisterham High Street alone. But knowing all its ways and windings very well, she hurried straight to the corner from which the omnibus departed. It was at that very moment going off.

"Stop and take me, if you please, Joe. I am obliged to go to London."

In less than another minute she was on her road to the railway, under Joe's protection. Joe waited on her when she got there, put her safely into the railway carriage, and handed in the very little bag after her, as though it were some enormous trunk, hundred weights heavy, which she must on no account endeavor to lift.

"Can you go round when you get back, and tell Miss Twinkleton that you saw me safely off, Joe?"

"It shall be done, Miss."

"With my love, please, Joe."

"Yes, Miss, — and I would n't mind having it myself!" But Joe did not articulate the last clause; only thought it.

Now that she was whirling away for London in real earnest, Rosa was at leisure to resume the thoughts which her personal hurry had checked. The indignant thought that his declaration of love soiled her; that she could only be cleansed from the stain of its impurity by appealing to the honest and true; supported her for a time against her fears, and confirmed her in her hasty resolution. But as the evening grew darker and darker, and the great city impended nearer and nearer, the doubts usual in such cases began to arise. Whether this was not a wild proceeding after all; how Mr. Grewgious might regard it; whether she should find him at the journey's end; how she would act if he were absent; what might become of her, alone, in a place so strange and crowded; how if she had but waited and taken counsel first; whether, if she could now go back, she would not do it thankfully: a multitude of such uneasy speculations disturbed her, more and more as they accumulated. At length the train came into London over the housetops; and down below lay the gritty streets with their yet unneeded lamps aglow, on a hot light summer night.

"Hiram Grewgious, Esquire, Staple Inn, London." This was all Rosa knew of her destination; but it was enough to send her rattling away again in a cab, through deserts of gritty streets, where many people crowded at the corners of courts and byways to get some air, and where many other people walked with a miserably monotonous noise of shuffling feet on hot paving-stones, and where all the people and all their surroundings were so gritty and so shabby.

There was music playing here and there, but it did not enliven the case. No barrel-organ mended the matter, and no big drum beat dull care away. Like the chapel bells that were also going here and there, they only seemed to evoke echoes from brick surfaces, and dust from everything. As to the flat wind instruments, they seemed to have cracked their hearts and souls in pining for the country.

Her jingling conveyance stopped at last at a fast-closed gateway which appeared to belong to somebody who had gone to bed very early, and was much afraid of house-breakers; Rosa, discharging her conveyance, timidly knocked at this gateway, and was let in, very little bag and all, by a watchman.

"Does Mr. Grewgious live here?"

"Mr. Grewgious lives there, Miss," said the watchman, pointing farther in.

So Rosa went farther in, and when the clocks were striking ten, stood on P. J. T.'s doorsteps, wondering what P. J. T. had done with his street door.

Guided by the painted name of Mr. Grewgious, she went up stairs and softly tapped and tapped several times. But no one answering, and Mr. Grewgious's door-handle yielding to her touch, she went in, and saw her guardian sitting on a window-seat at an open window, with a shaded lamp placed far from him on a table in a corner.

Rosa drew nearer to him in the twilight of the room. He saw her, and he said in an undertone, "Good Heaven!"

Rosa fell upon his neck, with tears, and then he said, returning her embrace,—

"My child, my child! I thought you were your mother!"

"But what, what, what," he added, soothingly, "has happened? My dear, what has brought you here? Who has brought you here?"

"No one. I came alone."

"Lord bless me!" ejaculated Mr. Grewgious. "Came alone! Why did n't you write to me to come and fetch you?"

"I had no time. I took a sudden resolution. Poor, poor Eddy!"

"Ah, poor fellow, poor fellow!"

"His uncle has made love to me. I cannot bear it," said Rosa, at once with a burst of tears, and a stamp of her little foot; "I shudder with horror of him, and I have come to you to protect me and all of us from him, if you will?"

"I will!" cried Mr. Grewgious, with a sudden rush of amazing energy. "Damn him!

"Confound his politics,
Frustrate his knavish tricks!
On Thee his hopes to fix?
Damn him again!"

After this most extraordinary outburst, Mr. Grewgious, quite beside himself, plunged about the room, to all appearance undecided whether he was in a fit of loyal enthusiasm, or combative denunciation.

He stopped and said, wiping his face, "I beg your pardon, my dear, but you will be glad to know I feel better. Tell me no more just now, or I might do it again. You must be refreshed and cheered. What did you take last? Was it breakfast, lunch, dinner, tea, or supper? And what will you take next? Shall it be breakfast, lunch, dinner, tea, or supper?"

The respectful tenderness with which, on one knee before her, he helped her to remove her hat, and disentangle her pretty hair from it, was quite a chivalrous sight. Yet who, knowing him only on the surface, would have expected chivalry — and of the true sort, too: not the spurious — from Mr. Grewgious?

"Your rest too must be provided for," he went on, "and you shall have the prettiest chamber in Furnival's. Your toilet must be provided for, and you shall have everything that an unlimited head-chambermaid — by which expression I mean a head-chambermaid not limited as to outlay — can procure. Is that a bag?" He looked hard at it; sooth to say, it required hard looking at to be seen at all in a dimly lighted room: "and is it your property, my dear?"

"Yes, sir. I brought it with me."

"It is not an extensive bag," said Mr. Grewgious, candidly, "though admirably calculated to contain a day's provision for a canary-bird. Perhaps you brought a canary-bird?"

Rosa smiled, and shook her head.

"If you had he should have been made welcome," said Mr. Grewgious, "and I think he would have been pleased to be hung upon a nail outside and pit himself against our Staple sparrows; whose execution must be admitted to be not quite equal to their intention. Which is the case with so many of us! You did n't say what meal, my dear. Have a nice jumble of all meals."

Rosa thanked him, but said she could only take a cup of tea. Mr. Grewgious, after several times running out, and in again, to mention such supplementary items as marmalade, eggs, water-cresses, salted fish, and frizzled ham, ran across to Furnival's without his hat, to give his various directions. And soon afterwards they were realized in practice, and the board was spread.

"Lord bless my soul!" cried Mr. Grewgious, putting the lamp upon it, and taking his seat opposite Rosa, "what a new sensation for a poor old Angular bachelor, to be sure!"

Rosa's expressive little eyebrows asked him what he meant?

"The sensation of having a sweet young presence in the place that whitewashes it, paints it, papers it, decorates it with gilding, and makes it Glorious," said Mr. Grewgious. "Ah me! Ah me!"

As there was something mournful in his sigh, Rosa, in touching him with his teacup, ventured to touch him with her small hand too.

"Thank you, my dear," said Mr. Grewgious. "Ahem! Let 's talk."

"Do you always live here, sir?" asked Rosa.

"Yes, my dear."

"And always alone?"

"Always alone; except that I have daily company in a gentleman by the name of Bazzard; my clerk."

"*He* does n't live here?"

"No, he goes his ways after office hours. In fact, he is off duty here, altogether, just at present; and a Firm down stairs with which I have business relation lend me a substitute. But it would be extremely difficult to replace Mr. Bazzard."

"He must be very fond of you," said Rosa.

"He bears up against it with commendable fortitude if he is," returned Mr.

Grewgious, after considering the matter. "But I doubt if he is. Not particularly so. You see, he is discontented, poor fellow."

"Why is n't he contented?" was the natural inquiry.

"Misplaced," said Mr. Grewgious, with great mystery.

Rosa's eyebrows resumed their inquisitive and perplexed expression.

"So misplaced," Mr. Grewgious went on, "that I feel constantly apologetic towards him. And he feels (though he does n't mention it) that I have reason to be."

Mr. Grewgious had by this time grown so very mysterious, that Rosa did not know how to go on. While she was thinking about it, Mr. Grewgious suddenly jerked out of himself for the second time: —

"Let 's talk. We were speaking of Mr. Bazzard. It 's a secret, and moreover it is Mr. Bazzard's secret; but the sweet presence at my table makes me so unusually expansive, that I feel I must impart it in inviolable confidence. What do you think Mr Bazzard has done?"

"O dear!" cried Rosa, drawing her chair a little nearer, and her mind reverting to Jasper, "nothing dreadful, I hope?"

"He has written a play," said Mr. Grewgious, in a solemn whisper. "A tragedy."

Rosa seemed much relieved.

"And nobody," pursued Mr. Grewgious, in the same tone, "will hear, on any account whatever, of bringing it out."

Rosa looked reflective, and nodded her head slowly; as who should say, "Such things are, and why are they!"

"Now, you know," said Mr. Grewgious, "*I* could n't write a play."

"Not a bad one, sir?" asked Rosa, innocently, with her eyebrows again in action.

"No. If I was under sentence of decapitation, and was about to be instantly decapitated, and an express arrived with a pardon for the condemned convict Grewgious if he wrote a play, I should be under the necessity of resuming the block and begging the executioner to proceed to extremities, — meaning," said Mr. Grewgious, passing his hand under his chin, "the singular number, and this extremity."

Rosa appeared to consider what she would do if the awkward supposititious case were hers.

"Consequently," said Mr. Grewgious, "Mr. Bazzard would have a sense of my inferiority to himself under any circumstances; but when I am his master, you know, the case is greatly aggravated."

Mr. Grewgious shook his head seriously, as if he felt the offence to be a little too much, though of his own committing.

"How came you to be his master, sir?" asked Rosa.

"A question that naturally follows," said Mr. Grewgious. "Let 's talk. Mr. Bazzard's father, being a Norfolk farmer, would have furiously laid about him with a flail, a pitchfork, and every agricultural implement available for assaulting purposes, on the slightest hint of his son's having written a play. So the son, bringing to me the father's rent (which I receive), imparted his secret, and pointed out that he was determined to pursue his genius, and that it would put him in peril of starvation, and that he was not formed for it."

"For pursuing his genius, sir?"

"No, my dear," said Mr. Grewgious, "for starvation. It was impossible to deny the position that Mr. Bazzard was not formed to be starved, and Mr. Bazzard then pointed out that it was desirable that I should stand between him and a fate so perfectly unsuited to his formation In that way Mr. Bazzard became my clerk, and he feels it very much."

"I am glad he is grateful," said Rosa.

"I did n't quite mean that, my dear. I mean that he feels the degradation. There are some other geniuses that Mr. Bazzard has become acquainted with, who have also written tragedies, which likewise nobody will on any account whatever hear of bringing out, and these choice spirits dedicate their plays to one another in a highly panegyrical manner. Mr. Bazzard has been the subject of one of these dedications. Now, you know, *I* never had a play dedicated to *me!*"

Rosa looked at him as if she would have liked him to be the recipient of a thousand dedications.

"Which again, naturally, rubs against the grain of Mr. Bazzard," said Mr. Grewgious. "He is very short with me sometimes, and then I feel that he is meditating, 'This blockhead is my master! A fellow who could n't write a tragedy on pain of death, and who will never have one dedicated to him with the most complimentary congratulations on the high position he has taken in the eyes of posterity!' Very trying, very trying. However, in giving him directions, I reflect beforehand, 'Perhaps he may not like this,' or 'He might take it ill if I asked that,' and so we get on very well. Indeed, better than I could have expected."

"Is the tragedy named, sir?" asked Rosa.

"Strictly between ourselves," answered Mr. Grewgious, "it has a dreadfully appropriate name. It is called The Thorn of Anxiety. But Mr. Bazzard hopes — and I hope — that it will come out at last."

It was not hard to divine that Mr. Grewgious had related the Bazzard history thus fully, at least quite as much for the recreation of his ward's mind from the subject that had driven her there, as for the gratification of his own tendency to be social and communicative. "And now, my dear," he said at this point, "if you are not too tired to tell me more of what passed to-day, — but only if you feel quite able, — I should be glad to hear it. I may digest it the better, if I sleep on it to-night."

Rosa, composed now, gave him a faithful account of the interview. Mr. Grewgious often smoothed his head while it was in progress, and begged to be told a second time those parts which bore on Helena and Neville. When Rosa had finished, he sat, grave, silent, and meditative, for a while.

"Clearly narrated," was his only remark at last, "and I hope, clearly put away here," smoothing his head again. "See, my dear," taking her to the open window, "where they live! The dark windows over yonder."

"I may go to Helena to-morrow?" asked Rosa.

"I should like to sleep on that question to-night," he answered, doubtfully. "But let me take you to your own rest, for you must need it."

With that, Mr. Grewgious helped her to get her hat on again, and hung upon his arm the very little bag that was of no earthly use, and led her by the hand (with a certain stately awkwardness, as if he were going to walk a minuet) across Holborn, and into Furnival's Inn. At the hotel door, he confided her to the Unlimited head-chambermaid, and said that while she went up to see her room, he would remain below, in case she should wish it exchanged for another, or should find that there was anything she wanted.

Rosa's room was airy, clean, comfortable, almost gay. The Unlimited had laid in everything omitted from the very little bag (that is to say, everything she could possibly need), and Rosa tripped down the great many stairs again, to thank her guardian for his thoughtful and affectionate care of her.

"Not at all, my dear," said Mr. Grewgious, infinitely gratified; "it is I who thank you for your charming confidence and for your charming company. Your breakfast will be provided for you in a neat, compact, and graceful little sitting-room (appropriate to your figure), and I will come to you at ten o'clock in the morning. I hope you don't feel very strange indeed, in this strange place."

"O no, I feel so safe!"

"Yes, you may be sure that the stairs are fire-proof," said Mr. Grewgious, "and that any outbreak of the devouring element would be perceived and suppressed by the watchmen."

"I did not mean that," Rosa replied. "I mean, I feel so safe from him."

"There is a stout gate of iron bars to keep him out," said Mr. Grewgious, smiling, "and Furnival's is fire-proof and specially watched and lighted, and *I* live over the way!" In the stoutness of his knight-errantry, he seemed to think the last-named protection all-sufficient. In the same spirit, he said to the gate-porter as he went out, "If some one staying in the hotel should wish to send across the road to me in the night, a crown will be ready for the messenger." In the same spirit, he walked up and down outside the iron gate for the best part of an hour, with some solicitude; occasionally looking in between the bars, as if he had laid a dove in a high roost in a cage of lions, and had it on his mind that she might tumble out.

CHAPTER XXI.

A RECOGNITION.

NOTHING occurred in the night to flutter the tired dove, and the dove arose refreshed. With Mr. Grewgious, when the clock struck ten in the morning, came Mr. Crisparkle, who had come at one plunge out of the river at Cloisterham.

"Miss Twinkleton was so uneasy, Miss Rosa," he explained to her, "and came round to Ma and me with your note, in such a state of wonder, that to quiet her, I volunteered on this service by the very first train to be caught in the morning. I wished at the time that you had come to me; but now I think it best that you did *as* you did, and came to your guardian."

"I did think of you," Rosa told him; "but Minor Canon Corner was so near him—"

"I understand. It was quite natural"

"I have told Mr. Crisparkle," said Mr. Grewgious, "all that you told me last night, my dear. Of course I should have written it to him immediately; but his coming was most opportune. And it was particularly kind of him to come, for he had but just gone."

"Have you settled," asked Rosa, appealing to them both, "what is to be done for Helena and her brother?"

"Why really," said Mr. Crisparkle, "I am in great perplexity. If even Mr. Grewgious, whose head is much longer than mine, and who is a whole night's cogitation in advance of me, is undecided, what must I be!"

The Unlimited here put her head in at the door,—after having rapped, and been authorized to present herself,—announcing that a gentleman wished for a word with another gentleman named Crisparkle, if any such gentleman were there. If no such gentleman were there, he begged pardon for being mistaken.

"Such a gentleman is here," said Mr. Crisparkle, "but is engaged just now."

"Is it a dark gentleman?" interposed Rosa, retreating on her guardian.

"No, Miss, more of a brown gentleman."

"You are sure not with black hair?" asked Rosa, taking courage.

"Quite sure of that, Miss. Brown hair and blue eyes."

"Perhaps," hinted Mr. Grewgious, with habitual caution, "it might be well to see him, reverend sir, if you don't object. When one is in a difficulty or at a loss, one never knows in what direction a way out may chance to open. It is a business principle of mine, in such a case, not to close up any direction, but to keep an eye on every direction that may present itself. I could relate an anecdote in point, but that it would be premature."

"If Miss Rosa will allow me then? Let the gentleman come in," said Mr. Crisparkle.

The gentleman came in; apologized, with a frank but modest grace, for not finding Mr. Crisparkle alone; turned to Mr. Crisparkle, and smilingly asked the unexpected question, "Who am I?"

"You are the gentleman I saw smoking under the trees in Staple Inn a few minutes ago."

"True. There I saw you. Who else am I?"

Mr. Crisparkle concentrated his attention on a handsome face, much sunburnt; and the ghost of some departed boy seemed to rise gradually and dimly in the room.

The gentleman saw a struggling recollection lighten up the Minor Canon's features, and, smiling again, said, "What will you have for breakfast this morning? You are out of jam."

"Wait a moment!" cried Mr. Crisparkle, raising his right hand. "Give me another instant! Tartar!"

The two shook hands with the greatest heartiness, and then went the wonderful length — for Englishmen — of laying their hands, each on the other's shoulders, and looking joyfully each into the other's face.

"My old fag!" said Mr. Crisparkle.

"My old master!" said Mr. Tartar.

"You saved me from drowning!" said Mr. Crisparkle.

"After which you took to swimming, you know!" said Mr. Tartar.

"God bless my soul!" said Mr. Crisparkle.

"Amen!" said Mr. Tartar.

And then they fell to shaking hands most heartily again.

"Imagine," exclaimed Mr. Crisparkle, with glistening eyes, — "Miss Rosa Bud and Mr. Grewgious, imagine Mr. Tartar, when he was the smallest of juniors, diving for me, catching me, a big heavy senior, by the hair of the head, and striking out for the shore with me like a water-giant!"

"Imagine my not letting him sink, as I was his fag!" said Mr. Tartar. "But the truth being that he was my best protector and friend, and did me more good than all the masters put together, an irrational impulse seized me to pick him up or go down with him."

"Hem! Permit me, sir, to have the honor," said Mr. Grewgious, advancing with extended hand, "for an honor I truly esteem it. I am proud to make your acquaintance. I hope you did n't take cold. I hope you were not inconvenienced by swallowing too much water. How have you been since?"

It was by no means apparent that Mr. Grewgious knew what he said, though it was very apparent that he meant to say something highly friendly and appreciative.

If Heaven, Rosa thought, had but sent such courage and skill to her poor mother's aid! And he to have been so slight and young then!

"I don't wish to be complimented upon it, I thank you, but I think I have an idea," Mr. Grewgious announced, after taking a jog-trot or two across the room, so unexpected and unaccountable that they had all stared at him, doubtful whether he was choking or had the cramp. "I *think* I have an idea. I believe I have.

had the pleasure of seeing Mr. Tartar's name as tenant of the top set in the house next the top set in the corner?"

"Yes, sir," returned Mr. Tartar. "You are right so far."

"I am right so far," said Mr. Grewgious. "Tick that off," which he did, with his right thumb on his left. "Might you happen to know the name of your neighbor in the top set on the other side of the party-wall?" coming very close to Mr. Tartar, to lose nothing of his face, in his shortness of sight.

"Landless."

"Tick that off," said Mr. Grewgious, taking another trot and then coming back. "No personal knowledge, I suppose, sir?"

"Slight, but some."

"Tick that off," said Mr. Grewgious, taking another trot and again coming back. "Nature of knowledge, Mr. Tartar?"

"I thought he seemed to be a young fellow in a poor way, and I asked his leave — only within a day or so — to share my flowers up there with him; that is to say, to extend my flower-garden to his windows."

"Would you have the kindness to take seats?" said Mr. Grewgious. "I *have* an idea."

They complied; Mr. Tartar more the less readily for being all abroad; and Mr. Grewgious, seated in the centre, with his hands upon his knees, thus stated his idea with his usual manner of having got the statement by heart.

"I cannot as yet make up my mind whether it is prudent to hold open communication under present circumstances, and on the part of the fair member of the present company, with Mr. Neville or Miss Helena. I have reason to know that a local friend of ours (on whom I beg to bestow a passing but a hearty malediction, with the kind permission of my reverend friend) sneaks to and fro, and dodges up and down. When not doing so himself, he may have some informant skulking about, in the person of a watchman, porter, or such-like hanger-on of Staple. On the other hand, Miss Rosa very naturally wishes to see her friend Miss Helena, and it would seem important that at least Miss Helena (if not her brother too, through her) should privately know from Miss Rosa's lips what has occurred and what has been threatened. Am I agreed with generally in the views I take?"

"I entirely coincide with them," said Mr. Crisparkle, who had been very attentive.

"As I have no doubt I should," added Mr. Tartar, smiling, "if I understood them."

"Fair and softly, sir," said Mr. Grewgious; "we shall fully confide in you directly, if you will favor us with your permission. Now, if our local friend should have any informant on the spot, it is tolerably clear that such informant can only be set to watch the chambers in the occupation of Mr. Neville. He reporting to our local friend, who comes and goes there, our local friend would supply for himself, from his own previous knowledge, the identity of the parties. Nobody can be set to watch all Staple, or to concern himself with comers and goers to other sets of chambers, unless, indeed, mine."

"I begin to understand to what you tend," said Mr. Crisparkle, "and highly approve of your caution."

"I need n't repeat that I know nothing yet of the why and wherefore," said Mr. Tartar; "but I also understood to what you tend, so let me say at once that my chambers are freely at your disposal."

"There!" cried Mr. Grewgious, smoothing his head triumphantly. "Now we have all got the idea. You have it, my dear?"

"I think I have," said Rosa, blushing a little as Mr. Tartar looked quickly towards her.

"You see, you go over to Staple with Mr. Crisparkle and Mr. Tartar," said Mr. Grewgious; "I going in and out and out and in, alone, in my usual way; you go up with those gentlemen to Mr. Tartar's rooms; you look into Mr. Tartar's flower-garden; you wait for Miss Helena's appearance there, or you signify to Miss Helena that you are close by; and you communicate with her freely, and no spy can be the wiser."

"I am very much afraid I shall be —"

"Be what, my dear?" asked Mr. Grewgious, as she hesitated. "Not frightened?"

"No, not that," said Rosa, shyly; "in Mr. Tartar's way. We seem to be appropriating Mr. Tartar's residence so very coolly."

"I protest to you," returned that gentleman, "that I shall think the better of it forevermore if your voice sounds in it only once."

Rosa, not quite knowing what to say about that, cast down her eyes, and, turning to Mr. Grewgious, dutifully asked if she should put her hat on. Mr. Grewgious being of opinion that she could not do better, she withdrew for the purpose. Mr. Crisparkle took the opportunity of giving Mr. Tartar a summary of the distresses of Neville and his sister. The opportunity was quite long enough, as the hat happened to require a little extra fitting on.

Mr. Tartar gave his arm to Rosa, and Mr. Crisparkle walked, detached, in front.

"Poor, poor Eddy!" thought Rosa, as they went along.

Mr. Tartar waved his right hand as he bent his head down over Rosa, talking in an animated way.

"It was not so powerful or so sun-browned when it saved Mr Crisparkle," thought Rosa, glancing at it; "but it must have been very steady and determined even then."

Mr. Tartar told her he had been a sailor, roving everywhere for years and years.

"When are you going to sea again?" asked Rosa.

"Never!"

Rosa wondered what the girls would say if they could see her crossing the wide street on the sailor's arm. And she fancied that the passers-by must think her very little and very helpless contrasted with the strong figure that could have caught her up and carried her out of any danger, miles and miles without resting.

She was thinking further that his far-seeing blue eyes looked as if they had been used to watch danger afar off, and to watch it without flinching, drawing nearer and nearer, when, happening to raise her own eyes, she found that he seemed to be thinking something about *them*.

This a little confused Rosebud, and may account for her never afterwards quite knowing how she ascended (with his help) to his garden in the air, and seemed to get into a marvellous country that came into sudden bloom like the country on the summit of the magic beanstalk. May it flourish forever!

CHAPTER XXII.

A GRITTY STATE OF THINGS COMES ON.

MR. TARTAR'S chambers were the neatest, the cleanest, and the best-ordered chambers ever seen under the sun, moon, and stars. The floors were scrubbed to that extent that you might have supposed the London blacks emancipated forever and gone out of the land for good. Every inch of brass work in Mr. Tartar's possession was polished and burnished till it shone like a brazen mirror. No speck, nor spot, nor spatter soiled the purity of any of Mr. Tartar's household gods, large, small, or middle-sized. His sitting-room was like the admiral's cabin; his bath-room was like a dairy; his sleeping-chamber, fitted all about with lockers and drawers, was like a seedsman's shop; and his nicely balanced cot just stirred in the midst as if it breathed. Everything belonging to Mr. Tartar had quarters of its own assigned to it; his maps and charts had their quarters; his books had theirs; his brushes had theirs; his boots had theirs; his clothes had theirs; his case-bottles had theirs; his telescopes and other instruments had theirs. Everything was readily accessible. Shelf, bracket, locker, hook, and drawer were equally within reach, and were equally contrived with a view to avoiding waste of room, and providing some snug inches of stowage for something that would have exactly fitted nowhere else. His gleaming little service of plate was so arranged upon his sideboard as that a slack salt-spoon would have instantly betrayed itself; his toilet implements were so arranged upon his dressing-table as that a toothpick of slovenly deportment could have been reported at a glance. So with the curiosities he had brought home from various voyages. Stuffed, dried, repolished, or otherwise preserved, according to their kind; birds, fishes, reptiles, arms, articles of dress, shells, sea-weeds, grasses, or memorials of coral reef; each was displayed in its especial place, and each could have been displayed in no better place. Paint and varnish seemed to be kept somewhere out of sight, in constant readiness to obliterate stray finger-marks wherever any might become perceptible in Mr. Tartar's chambers. No man-of-war was ever kept more spick and span from careless touch. On this bright summer day a neat awning was rigged over Mr. Tartar's flower-garden as only a sailor could rig it; and there was a sea-going air upon the whole effect, so delightfully complete that the flower-garden might have appertained to stern-windows afloat, and the whole concern might have bowled away gallantly with all on board, if Mr. Tartar had only clapped to his lips the speaking-trumpet that was slung in a corner, and given hoarse orders to have the anchor up, look alive there, men, and get all sail upon her!

Mr. Tartar, doing the honors of this gallant craft, was of a piece with the rest. When a man rides an amiable hobby that shies at nothing and kicks nobody, it is only agreeable to find him riding it with a humorous sense of the droll side of the creature. When the man is a cordial and an earnest man by nature, and withal is perfectly fresh and genuine, it may be doubted whether he is ever seen to greater advantage than at such a time. So Rosa would have naturally thought (even if she had n't been conducted over ship with all the homage due to the First Lady of the Admiralty, or First Fairy of the Sea), that it was charming to see and hear Mr. Tartar half laughing at, and half rejoicing in his various contrivances. So Rosa would have naturally thought, anyhow, that the sunburnt sailor showed to great advantage when, the inspection finished, he delicately withdrew out of his Admiral's Cabin, beseeching her to consider herself its Queen, and waving her free of his flower-garden with the hand that had had Mr. Crisparkle's life in it.

"Helena! Helena Landless! Are you there?"

"Who speaks to me? Not Rosa?" Then a second handsome face appearing.

"Yes, my darling!"

"Why, how did you come here, dearest?"

"I — I don't quite know," said Rosa with a blush; "unless I am dreaming!"

Why with a blush? For their two faces were alone with the other flowers. Are blushes among the fruits of the country of the magic beanstalk?

"*I* am not dreaming," said Helena, smiling. "I should take more for granted if I were. How do we come together — or so near together — so very unexpectedly?"

Unexpectedly indeed, among the dingy gables and chimney-pots of P. J. T.'s connection, and the flowers that had sprung from the salt sea But Rosa, waking, told in a hurry how they came to be together, and all the why and wherefore of that matter.

"And Mr. Crisparkle is here," said Rosa, in rapid conclusion; "and could you believe it? Long ago, he saved his life!"

"I could believe any such thing of Mr. Crisparkle," returned Helena, with a mantling face.

(More blushes in the Beanstalk country!)

"Yes, but it was n't Mr. Crisparkle," said Rosa, quickly putting in the correction.

"I don't understand, love."

"It was very nice of Mr. Crisparkle to be saved," said Rosa, "and he could n't have shown his high opinion of Mr. Tartar more expressively. But it was Mr. Tartar who saved him."

Helena's dark eyes looked very earnestly at the bright face among the leaves, and she asked, in a slower and more thoughtful tone, —

"Is Mr. Tartar with you now, dear?"

"No; because he has given up his rooms to me — to us, I mean. It *is* such a beautiful place!"

"Is it?"

"It is like the inside of the most exquisite ship that ever sailed. It is like — it is like — "

"Like a dream?" suggested Helena.

Rosa answered with a little nod, and smelled the flowers.

Helena resumed, after a short pause of silence, during which she seemed (or it was Rosa's fancy) to compassionate somebody: "My poor Neville is reading in his own room, the sun being so very bright on this side just now. I think he had better not know that you are so near."

"O, I think so, too!" cried Rosa, very readily.

"I suppose," pursued Helena, doubtfully, "that he must know by and by all you have told me; but I am not sure. Ask Mr. Crisparkle's advice, my darling. Ask him whether I may tell Neville as much or as little of what you have told me as I think best."

Rosa subsided into her state-cabin, and propounded the question. The Minor Canon was for the free exercise of Helena's judgment.

"I thank him very much," said Helena, when Rosa emerged again with her report. "Ask him whether it would be best to wait until any more maligning and pursuing of Neville on the part of this wretch shall disclose itself, or to try to anticipate it; I mean, so far as to find out whether any such goes on darkly about us?"

The Minor Canon found this point so difficult to give a confident opinion on, that, after two or three attempts and failures, he suggested a reference to Mr.

Grewgious. Helena acquiescing, he betook himself (with a most unsuccessful assumption of lounging indifference) across the quadrangle to P. J. T.'s, and stated it. Mr. Grewgious held decidedly to the general principle that if you could steal a march upon a brigand or a wild beast, you had better do it; and he also held decidedly to the special case that John Jasper was a brigand and a wild beast in combination.

Thus advised, Mr. Crisparkle came back again and reported to Rosa, who in her turn reported to Helena. She, now steadily pursuing her train of thought at her window, considered thereupon.

"We may count on Mr. Tartar's readiness to help us, Rosa?" she inquired.

O yes! Rosa shyly thought so. O yes, Rosa shyly believed she could almost answer for it. But should she ask Mr. Crisparkle? "I think your authority on the point as good as his, my dear," said Helena, sedately, "and you need n't disappear again for that." Odd of Helena!

"You see, Neville," Helena pursued after more reflection, "knows no one else here: he has not so much as exchanged a word with any one else here. If Mr. Tartar would call to see him openly and often; if he would spare a minute for the purpose, frequently; if he would even do so, almost daily; something might come of it."

"Something might come of it, dear?" repeated Rosa, surveying her friend's beauty with a highly perplexed face. "Something might?"

"If Neville's movements are really watched, and if the purpose really is to isolate him from all friends and acquaintance and wear his daily life out, grain by grain (which would seem to be the threat to you), does it not appear likely," said Helena, "that his enemy would in some way communicate with Mr. Tartar to warn him off from Neville? In which case we might not only know the fact, but might know from Mr. Tartar what the terms of the communication were."

"I see!" cried Rosa. And immediately darted into her state-cabin again.

Presently her pretty face reappeared, with a greatly heightened color, and she said that she had told Mr. Crisparkle, and that Mr. Crisparkle had fetched in Mr. Tartar, and that Mr. Tartar — "who is waiting now in case you want him," added Rosa, with a half-look back, and in not a little confusion, between the inside of the state-cabin and out — had declared his readiness to act as she had suggested, and to enter on his task that very day.

"I thank him from my heart," said Helena. "Pray tell him so."

Again not a little confused between the Flower-Garden and the Cabin, Rosa dipped in with her message, and dipped out again with more assurances from Mr. Tartar, and stood wavering in a divided state between Helena and him, which proved that confusion is not always necessarily awkward, but may sometimes present a very pleasant appearance.

"And now, darling," said Helena, "we will be mindful of the caution that has restricted us to this interview for the present, and will part. I hear Neville moving too. Are you going back?"

"To Miss Twinkleton's?" asked Rosa.

"Yes."

"O, I could never go there any more; I could n't, indeed, after that dreadful interview!" said Rosa.

"Then where *are* you going, pretty one?"

"Now I come to think of it, I don't know," said Rosa. "I have settled nothing at all yet but my guardian will take care of me. Don't be uneasy, dear. I shall be sure to be somewhere."

(It did seem likely.)

"And I shall hear of my Rosebud from Mr. Tartar?" inquired Helena.

"Yes, I suppose so; from —" Rosa looked back again in a flutter, instead of supplying the name. "But tell me one thing before we part, dearest Helena. Tell me that you are sure, sure, sure, I could n't help it."

"Help it, love?"

"Help making him malicious and revengeful. I could n't hold any terms with him, could I?"

"You know how I love you, darling," answered Helena, with indignation, "but I would sooner see you dead at his wicked feet."

"That 's a great comfort to me! And you will tell your poor brother so, won't you? And you will give him my remembrance and my sympathy? And you will ask him not to hate me?"

With a mournful shake of the head, as if that would be quite a superfluous entreaty, Helena lovingly kissed her two hands to her friend, and her friend's two hands were kissed to her, and then she saw a third hand (a brown one) appear among the flowers and leaves, and help her friend out of sight.

The reflection that Mr. Tartar produced in the Admiral's Cabin by merely touching the spring knob in a locker and the handle of a drawer, was a dazzling enchanted repast. Wonderful macaroons, glittening liqueurs, magically preserved tropical spices, and jellies of celestial tropical fruits, displayed themselves profusely at an instant's notice. But Mr. Tartar could not make time stand still; and time, with his hard-hearted fleetness, strode on so fast that Rosa was obliged to come down from the Beanstalk country to earth, and her guardian's chambers.

"And now, my dear," said Mr. Grewgious, "what is to be done next? To put the same thought in another form; what is to be done with you?"

Rosa could only look apologetically sensible of being very much in her own way, and in everybody else's. Some passing idea of living, fire-proof, up a good many stairs in Furnival's Inn for the rest of her life was the only thing in the nature of a plan that occurred to her.

"It has come into my thoughts," said Mr. Grewgious, "that as the respected lady, Miss Twinkleton, occasionally repairs to London in the recess, with the view of extending her connection, and being available for interviews with metropolitan parents, if any, — whether, until we have time in which to turn ourselves round, we might invite Miss Twinkleton to come and stay with you for a month?"

"Stay where, sir?"

"Whether," explained Mr. Grewgious, "we might take a furnished lodging in town for a month, and invite Miss Twinkleton to assume the charge of you in it for that period?"

"And afterwards?" hinted Rosa.

"And afterwards," said Mr. Grewgious, "we should be no worse off than we are now."

"I think that might smooth the way," assented Rosa.

"Then let us," said Mr. Grewgious, rising, "go and look for a furnished lodging. Nothing could be more acceptable to me than the sweet presence of last evening for all the remaining evenings of my existence; but these are not fit surroundings for a young lady. Let us set out in quest of adventures, and look for a furnished lodging. In the mean time, Mr. Crisparkle here, about to return home immediately, will, no doubt, kindly see Miss Twinkleton and invite that lady to co-operate in our plan."

Mr. Crisparkle, willingly accepting the commission, took his departure; Mr. Grewgious and his ward set forth on their expedition

As Mr. Grewgious's idea of looking at a furnished lodging was to get on the opposite side of the street to a house with a suitable bill in the window, and stare at it; and then work his way tortuously to the back of the house, and stare at that; and then not go in, but make similar trials of another house, with the same result, their progress was but slow. At length he bethought himself of a widowed cousin, divers times removed, of Mr. Bazzard's, who had once solicited his influence in the lodger world, and who lived in Southampton Street, Bloomsbury Square. This lady's name, stated in uncompromising capitals of considerable size on a brass door-plate, and yet not lucidly as to sex or condition, was BILLICKIN.

Personal faintness and an overpowering personal candor were the distinguishing features of Mrs. Billickin's organization. She came languishing out of her own exclusive back parlor, with the air of having been expressly brought to for the purpose from an accumulation of several swoons.

"I hope I see you well, sir," said Mrs. Billickin, recognizing her visitor with a bend.

"Thank you, quite well. And you, ma'am?" returned Mr. Grewgious.

"I am as well" said Mrs. Billickin, becoming aspirational with excess of faintness, "as I hever ham"

"My ward and an elderly lady," said Mr. Grewgious, "wish to find a genteel lodging for a month or so. Have you any apartments available, ma'am?"

"Mr. Grewgious," returned Mrs. Billickin, "I will not deceive you, far from it. I *have* apartments available."

This, with the air of adding, "Convey me to the stake, if you will, but while I live, I will be candid."

"And now, what apartments, ma'am?" asked Mr. Grewgious, cosily. To tame a certain severity apparent on the part of Mrs. Billickin.

"There is this sitting-room, — which call it what you will, it is the front parlor, Miss," said Mrs. Billickin, impressing Rosa into the conversation; "the back parlor being what I cling to and never part with; and there is two bedrooms at the top of the 'ouse with gas laid on. I do not tell you that your bedroom floors is firm, for firm they are not. The gas-fitter himself allowed that to make a firm job, he must go right under your jistes, and it were not worth the outlay as a yearly tenant so to do: The piping is carried above your jistes, and it is best that it should be made known to you."

Mr. Grewgious and Rosa exchanged looks of some dismay, though they had not the least idea what latent horrors this carriage of the piping might involve. Mrs. Billickin put her hand to her heart, as having eased it of a load.

"Well! The roof is all right, no doubt," said Mr. Grewgious, plucking up a little.

"Mr. Grewgious," returned Mrs. Billickin, "if I was to tell you, sir, that to have nothink above you is to have a floor above you, I should put a deception upon you which I will not do. No, sir. Your slates WILL rattle loose at that elewation in windy weather, do your utmost, best or worst! I defy you, sir, be you what you may, to keep your slates tight, try how you can." Here Mrs. Billickin, having been warm with Mr. Grewgious, cooled a little, not to abuse the moral power she held over him. "Consequent," proceeded Mrs. Billickin, more mildly, but still firmly in her incorruptible candor, — "consequent it would be worse than of no use for me to trapse and travel up to the top of the 'ouse with you, and for you to say, 'Mrs. Billickin, what stain do I notice in the ceiling, for a stain I do consider it?' and for me to answer, 'I do not understand you, sir.' No, sir; I will not be so underhand. I *do* understand you before you p'int it out. It is the wet, sir. It do come in, and it do not come in. You may lay dry there half your lifetime, but the time will come, and it is best that you should know it, when a dripping sop would be no name for you."

Mr. Grewgious looked much disgraced by being prefigured in this pickle.

"Have you any other apartments, ma'am?" he asked.

"Mr Grewgious," returned Mrs. Billickin, with much solemnity, "I have. You ask me have I, and my open and my honest answer air, I have. The first and second floors is wacant, and sweet rooms."

"Come, come! There 's nothing against *them*," said Mr. Grewgious, comforting himself.

"Mr. Grewgious," replied Mrs. Billickin, "pardon me, there is the stairs. Unless your mind is prepared for the stairs, it will lead to inevitable disappointment. You cannot, miss," said Mrs. Billickin, addressing Rosa, reproachfully, "place a first floor, and far less a second, on the level footing of a parlor. No, you cannot do it, Miss, it is beyond your power, and wherefore try?"

Mrs. Billickin put it very feelingly, as if Rosa had shown a headstrong determination to hold the untenable position.

"Can we see these rooms, ma'am?" inquired her guardian.

"Mr. Grewgious," returned Mrs. Billickin, "you can. I will not disguise it from you, sir, you can."

Mrs Billickin then sent into her back parlor for her shawl (it being a state fiction dating from immemorial antiquity, that she could never go anywhere without being wrapped up), and having been enrolled by her attendant, led the way. She made various genteel pauses on the stairs for breath, and clutched at her heart in the drawing-room as if it had very nearly got loose, and she had caught it in the act of taking wing.

"And the second floor?" said Mr. Grewgious, on finding the first satisfactory.

"Mr. Grewgious," replied Mrs. Billickin, turning upon him with ceremony, as if the time had now come when a distinct understanding on a difficult point must be arrived at, and a solemn confidence established, "the second floor is over this."

"Can we see that too, ma'am?"

"Yes, sir," returned Mrs. Billickin, "it is open as the day."

That also proving satisfactory, Mr. Grewgious retired into a window with Rosa for a few words of consultation, and then, asking for pen and ink, sketched out a line or two of agreement. In the mean time Mrs. Billickin took a seat, and delivered a kind of Index to, or Abstract of, the general question.

"Five-and-forty shillings per week by the month certain at the time of year," said Mrs. Billickin, "is only reasonable to both parties. It is not Bond Street nor yet St. James's Palace; but it is not pretended that it is. Neither is it attempted to be denied — for why should it? — that the Arching leads to a Mews. Mewses must exist. Respecting attendance; two is kep' at liberal wages Words *has* arisen as to tradesmen, but dirty shoes on fresh hearth-stoning was attributable, and no wish for a commission on your orders. Coals is either *by* the fire, or *per* the scuttle." She emphasized the prepositions as marking a subtle but immense difference. "Dogs is not viewed with favior. Besides litter, they gets stole, and sharing suspicions is apt to creep in, and unpleasantness takes place."

By this time Mr. Grewgious had his agreement-lines and his earnest-money ready. "I have signed it for the ladies, ma'am," he said, "and you 'll have the goodness to sign it for yourself, Christian and Surname, there, if you please."

"Mr. Grewgious," said Mrs. Billickin, in a new burst of candor, "no, sir. You must excuse the Christian name."

Mr. Grewgious stared at her.

"The door-plate is used as a protection," said Mrs. Billickin, "and acts as such, and go from it I will not."

Mr. Grewgious stared at Rosa.

"No, Mr. Grewgious, you must excuse me. So long as this 'ouse is known indefinite as Billickin's, and so long as it is a doubt with the riff-raff where Billickin may be hidin', near the street door or down the airy, and what his weight and size, so long I feel safe. But commit myself to a solitary female statement, no, Miss! Nor would you for a moment wish," said Mrs. Billickin, with a strong sense of injury, "to take that advantage of your sex, if you was not brought to it by inconsiderate example."

Rosa, reddening as if she had made some most disgraceful attempt to overreach the good lady, besought Mr Grewgious to rest content with any signature. And accordingly, in a baronical way, the sign-manual BILLICKIN got appended to the document.

Details were then settled for taking possession on the next day but one, when Miss Twinkleton might be reasonably expected; and Rosa went back to Furnival's Inn on her guardian's arm.

Behold Mr. Tartar walking up and down Furnival's Inn, checking himself when he saw them coming, and advancing towards them!

"It occurred to me," hinted Mr Tartar, "that we might go up the river, the weather being so delicious and the tide serving. I have a boat of my own at the Temple Stairs."

"I have not been up the river for this many a day," said Mr. Grewgious, tempted.

"I was never up the river," added Rosa.

Within half an hour they were setting this matter right by going up the river. The tide was running with them, the afternoon was charming. Mr. Tartar's boat was perfect. Mr. Tartar and Lobley (Mr Tartar's man) pulled a pair of oars. Mr. Tartar had a yacht, it seemed, lying somewhere down by Greenhithe; and Mr. Tartar's man had charge of this yacht, and was detached upon his present service. He was a jolly favored man, with tawny hair and whiskers, and a big red face. He was the dead image of the sun in old woodcuts, his hair and whiskers answering for rays all round him. Resplendent in the bow of the boat, he was a shining sight, with a man-of-war's man's shirt on — or off, according to opinion — and his arms and breast tattooed all sorts of patterns. Lobley seemed to take it easily, and so did Mr Tartar; yet their oars bent as they pulled, and the boat bounded under them. Mr Tartar talked as if he were doing nothing, to Rosa, who was really doing nothing, and to Mr Grewgious, who was doing this much that he steered all wrong; but what did that matter when a turn of Mr. Tartar's skilful wrist, or a mere grin of Mr. Lobley's over the bow, put all to rights! The tide bore them on in the gayest and most sparkling manner, until they stopped to dine in some everlastingly green garden, needing no matter-of-fact identification here; and then the tide obligingly turned, — being devoted to that party alone for that day; and as they floated idly among some osier beds, Rosa tried what she could do in the rowing way, and came off splendidly, being much assisted; and Mr Grewgious tried what he could do, and came off on his back, doubled up with an oar under his chin, being not assisted at all. Then there was an interval of rest under boughs (such rest!) what time Mr Lobley mopped, and, arranging cushions, stretchers, and the like, danced the tight rope the whole length of the boat like a man to whom shoes were a superstition and stockings slavery; and then came the sweet return among delicious odors of limes in bloom, and musical ripplings; and all too soon the great black city cast its shadow on the waters, and its dark bridges spanned them as death spans life, and the everlastingly green garden seemed to be left for everlasting, unregainable and far away.

"Cannot people get through life without gritty stages, I wonder!" Rosa thought next day, when the town was very gritty again, and everything had a strange and an uncomfortable appearance of seeming to wait for something that would n't come? No She began to think that now the Cloisterham school days had glided past and gone, the gritty stages would begin to set in at intervals and make themselves wearily known!

Yet what did Rosa expect? Did she expect Miss Twinkleton? Miss Twinkleton duly came. Forth from her back parlor issued the Billickin to receive Miss Twinkleton, and War was in the Billickin's eye from that fell moment.

Miss Twinkleton brought a quantity of luggage with her, having all Rosa's as well as her own. The Billickin took it ill that Miss Twinkleton's mind, being sorely disturbed by this luggage, failed to take in her personal identity with that clearness of perception which was due to its demands. Stateliness mounted her gloomy throne upon the Billickin's brow in consequence. And when Miss Twinkleton, in agitation, taking stock of her trunks and packages, of which she had seventeen, particularly counted in the Billickin herself as number eleven, the B. found it necessary to repudiate

"Things cannot too soon be put upon the footing," said she, with a candor so demonstrative as to be almost obtrusive, "that the person of the 'ouse is not a box nor yet a bundle, nor a carpet-bag. No, I am 'ily obleeged to you, Miss Twinkleton, nor yet a beggar."

This last disclaimer had reference to Miss Twinkleton's distractedly pressing two and sixpence on her instead of the cabman.

Thus cast off, Miss Twinkleton wildly inquired, "which gentleman" was to be paid? There being two gentlemen in that position (Miss Twinkleton having arrived with two cabs), each gentleman, on being paid, held forth his two and sixpence on the flat of his open hand, and with a speechless stare and a dropped jaw displayed his wrong to heaven and earth. Terrified by this alarming spectacle, Miss Twinkleton placed another shilling in each hand, at the same time appealing to the law in flurried accents and recounting her luggage, this time with the two gentlemen in, who caused the total to come out complicated. Meanwhile the two gentlemen, each looking very hard at the last shilling grumblingly, as if it might become eighteenpence if he kept his eyes on it, descended the door-steps, ascended their carriages, and drove away, leaving Miss Twinkleton on a bonnet-box in tears.

The Billickin beheld this manifestation of weakness without sympathy, and gave directions for "a young man to be got in" to wrestle with the luggage. When that gladiator had disappeared from the arena, peace ensued, and the new lodgers dined.

But the Billickin had somehow come to the knowledge that Miss Twinkleton kept a school The leap from that knowledge to the inference that Miss Twinkleton set herself to teach *her* something was easy. "But you don't do it," soliloquized the Billickin; "*I* am not your pupil, whatever she," meaning Rosa, "may be, poor thing!"

Miss Twinkleton, on the other hand, having changed her dress and recovered her spirits, was animated by a bland desire to improve the occasion in all ways, and to be as serene a model as possible. In a happy compromise between her two states of existence she had already become, with her work-basket before her, the equably vivacious companion with a slight judicious flavoring of information, when the Billickin announced herself.

"I will not hide from you, ladies," said the B., enveloped in the shawl of state, "for it is not my character to hide, neither my motives, nor my actions, that I take the liberty to look in upon you to express a 'ope that your dinner was to your liking. Though not Professed but Plain, still her wages should be a sufficient object to her to stimulate to soar above mere roast and biled."

"We dined very well indeed," said Rosa, "thank you."

"Accustomed," said Miss Twinkleton, with a gracious air, which to the jealous ears of the Billickin seemed to add "My good woman," — "accustomed to a liberal and nutritious, yet plain and salutary diet, we have found no reason to bemoan our absence from the ancient city and the methodical household in which the quiet routine of our lot has been hitherto cast."

"I did think it well to mention to my cook," observed the Billickin, with a gush of candor, "which I 'ope you will agree with, Miss Twinkleton, was a right precaution, that the young lady being used to what we should consider here but poor diet, had better be brought forward by degrees. For, a rush from scanty feeding to generous feeding, and from what you may call messing to what you call method, do require a power of constitution, which is not often found in youth, particular when undermined by boarding-school?"

It will be seen that the Billickin now openly pitted herself against Miss Twinkleton, as one whom she had fully ascertained to be her natural enemy.

"Your remarks," returned Miss Twinkleton, from a remote moral eminence, "are well meant, I have no doubt; but you will permit me to observe that they develop a mistaken view of the subject, which can only be imputed to your extreme want of accurate information."

"My information," retorted the Billickin, throwing in an extra syllable for the sake of emphasis at once polite and powerful, — "my information, Miss Twinkleton, were my own experience, which I believe is usually considered to be good guidance. But whether so or not, I was put in youth to a very genteel boarding-school, the mistress being no less a lady than yourself, of about your own age or it may be some years younger, and a poorness of blood flowed from the table which has run through my life."

"Very likely," said Miss Twinkleton, still from her distant eminence; "and very much to be deplored. — Rosa, my dear, how are you getting on with your work?"

"Miss Twinkleton," resumed the Billickin, in a courtly manner, "before retiring on the Int, as a lady should, I wish to ask of yourself as a lady, whether I am to consider that my words is doubted?"

"I am not aware on what ground you cherish such a supposition," began Miss Twinkleton, when the Billickin neatly stopped her.

"Do not, if you please, put suppositions betwixt my lips, where none such have been imparted by myself. Your flow of words is great, Miss Twinkleton, and no doubt is expected from you by your pupils, and no doubt is considered worth the money. *No* doubt, I am sure. But not paying for flows of words, and not asking to be favored with them here, I wish to repeat my question."

"If you refer to the poverty of your circulation," began Miss Twinkleton, when again the Billickin neatly stopped her.

"I have used no such expressions."

"If you refer then to the poorness of your blood."

"Brought upon me," stipulated the Billickin, expressly, "at a boarding-school."

"Then," resumed Miss Twinkleton, "all I can say is, that I am bound to believe on your asseveration that it is very poor indeed. I cannot forbear adding, that if that unfortunate circumstance influences your conversation, it is much to be lamented, and it is eminently desirable that your blood were richer. Rosa, my dear, how are you getting on with your work?"

"Hem! Before retiring, Miss," proclaimed the Billickin to Rosa, loftily cancelling Miss Twinkleton, "I should wish it to be understood between yourself and me that my transactions in future is with you alone. I know no elderly lady here, Miss, none older than yourself."

"A highly desirable arrangement, Rosa, my dear," observed Miss Twinkleton.

"It is not, Miss," said the Billickin, with a sarcastic smile, "that I possess the Mill I have heard of, in which old single ladies could be ground up young (what a gift it would be to some of us!) but that I limit myself to you totally."

"When I have any desire to communicate a request to the person of the house, Rosa, my dear," observed Miss Twinkleton, with majestic cheerfulness, "I will make it known to you, and you will kindly undertake, I am sure, that it is conveyed to the proper quarter."

"Good evening, Miss," said the Billickin, at once affectionately and distantly. "Being alone in my eyes, I wish you good evening with best wishes, and do not find myself drove, I am truly 'appy to say, into expressing my contempt for any indiwidual, unfortunately for yourself, belonging to you."

The Billickin gracefully withdrew with this parting speech, and from that time Rosa occupied the restless position of shuttlecock between these two battledores. Nothing could be done without a smart match being played out. Thus, on the daily arising question of dinner, Miss Twinkleton would say, the three being present together: —

"Perhaps, my love, you will consult with the person of the house whether she can procure us a lamb's fry; or, failing that, a roast fowl."

On which the Billickin would retort (Rosa not having spoken a word), "If you was better accustomed to butcher's meat, Miss, you would not entertain the idea of a lamb's fry. Firstly, because lambs has long been sheep, and secondly, because there is such things as killing-days, and there is not. As to roast fowls, Miss, why you must be quite surfeited with roast fowls, letting alone your buying, when you market for yourself, the agedest of poultry with the scaliest of legs, quite as if you was accustomed to picking 'em out for cheapness. Try a little inwention, Miss. Use yourself to 'ousekeeping a bit. Come now, think of somethink else."

To this encouragement, offered with the indulgent toleration of a wise and liberal expert, Miss Twinkleton would rejoin, reddening, —

"Or, my dear, you might propose to the person of the house a duck."

"Well, Miss!" the Billickin would exclaim (still no word being spoken by Rosa), "you do surprise me when you speak of ducks! Not to mention that they are getting out of season and very dear, it really strikes to my heart to see you have a duck, for the breast, which is the only delicate cuts in a duck, always goes in a direction which I cannot imagine where, and your own plate comes down so miserably skin-and-bony! Try again, Miss. Think more of yourself and less of others. A dish of sweetbreads now, or a bit of mutton. Somethink at which you can get your equal chance."

Occasionally the game would wax very brisk indeed, and would be kept up with a smartness rendering such an encounter as this quite tame. But the Billickin almost invariably made by far the higher score, and would come in with side hits of the most unexpected and extraordinary description, when she seemed without a chance.

All this did not improve the gritty state of things in London, or the air that London had acquired in Rosa's eyes of waiting for something that never came. Tired of working and conversing with Miss Twinkleton, she suggested working and reading; to which Miss Twinkleton readily assented, as an admirable reader, of tried powers. But Rosa soon made the discovery that Miss Twinkleton did n't read fairly. She cut the love scenes, interpolated passages in praise of female celibacy, and was guilty of other glaring pious frauds. As an instance in point, take the glowing passage: "'Ever dearest and best adored' said Edward, clasping the dear head to his breast, and drawing the silken hair through his caressing fingers, from which he suffered it to fall like golden rain ; 'ever dearest and best adored, let us fly from the unsympathetic world and the sterile coldness of the stony-hearted, to the rich warm Paradise of Trust and Love.'" Miss Twinkleton's fraudulent version tamely ran thus : "'Ever engaged to me, with the consent of our parents on both sides, and the approbation of the silver-haired rector of the district,' said Edward, respectfully raising to his lips the taper fingers so skilful in embroidery, tambour, crochet, and other truly feminine arts ; 'let me call on thy papa ere to-morrow's dawn has sunk into the west, and propose a suburban establishment, lowly it may be, but within our means, where he will be always welcome as an evening guest, and where every arrangement shall invest economy and constant interchange of scholastic acquirements with the attributes of the ministering angel to domestic bliss.'"

As the days crept on and nothing happened, the neighbors began to say that the pretty girl at Billickin's, who looked so wistfully and so much out of the gritty windows of the drawing-room, seemed to be losing her spirits. The pretty girl might have lost them but for the accident of lighting on some books of voyages and sea-adventure. As a compensation against their romance, Miss Twinkleton, reading aloud, made the most of all the latitudes and longitudes, bearings, winds, currents, offsets, and other statistics (which she felt to be none the less improving because they expressed nothing whatever to her) ; while Rosa, listening intently, made the most of what was nearest to her heart. So they both did better than before.

CHAPTER XXIII.

THE DAWN AGAIN.

ALTHOUGH Mr. Crisparkle and John Jasper met daily under the Cathedral roof, nothing at any time passed between them bearing reference to Edwin Drood after the time, more than half a year gone by, when Jasper mutely showed the Minor Canon the conclusion and the resolution entered in his Diary. It is not likely that they ever met, though so often, without the thoughts of each reverting to the subject. It is not likely that they ever met, though so often, without a sensation on the part of each that the other was a perplexing secret to him. Jasper as the denouncer and pursuer of Neville Landless, and Mr. Crisparkle as his consistent advocate and protector, must at least have stood sufficiently in opposition to have speculated with keen interest on the steadiness and next direction of the other's designs. But neither ever broached the theme.

False pretence not being in the Minor Canon's nature, he doubtless displayed openly that he would at any time have revived the subject, and even desired to discuss it. The determined reticence of Jasper, however, was not to be so approached. Impassive, moody, solitary, resolute, so concentrated on one idea, and on its attendant fixed purpose, that he would share it with no fellow-creature, he lived apart from human life. Constantly exercising an Art which brought him into mechanical harmony with others, and which could not have been pursued unless he and they had been in the nicest mechanical relations and unison, it is curious to consider that the spirit of the man was in moral accordance or interchange with nothing around him. This indeed he had confided to his lost nephew before the occasion for his present inflexibility arose.

That he must know of Rosa's abrupt departure, and that he must divine its cause was not to be doubted. Did he suppose that he had terrified her into silence, or did he suppose that she had imparted to any one — to Mr. Crisparkle himself, for instance — the particulars of his last interview with her? Mr. Crisparkle could not determine this in his mind. He could not but admit, however, as a just man, that it was not, of itself, a crime to fall in love with Rosa, any more than it was a crime to offer to set love above revenge.

The dreadful suspicion of Jasper which Rosa was so shocked to have received into her imagination appeared to have no harbor in Mr. Crisparkle's. If it ever haunted Helena's thoughts, or Neville's, neither gave it one spoken word of utterance. Mr. Grewgious took no pains to conceal his implacable dislike of Jasper, yet he never referred it, however distantly, to such a source. But he was a reticent as well as an eccentric man; and he made no mention of a certain evening when he warmed his hands at the Gate House fire, and looked steadily down upon a certain heap of torn and miry clothes upon the floor.

Drowsy Cloisterham, whenever it awoke to a passing reconsideration of a story above six months old and dismissed by the bench of magistrates, was pretty equally divided in opinion whether John Jasper's beloved nephew had been killed by his treacherously passionate rival, or in an open struggle; or had, for his own purposes, spirited himself away. It then lifted up its head to notice that the bereaved Jasper was still ever devoted to discovery and revenge; and then dozed off again. This was the condition of matters, all round, at the period to which the present history has now attained.

The Cathedral doors have closed for the night, and the Choir Master, on a short leave of absence for two or three services, sets his face towards London. He travels thither by the means by which Rosa travelled, and arrives, as Rosa arrived, on a hot, dusty evening.

His travelling baggage is easily carried in his hand, and he repairs with it, on foot, to a hybrid hotel in a little square behind Aldersgate Street, near the General Post-Office. It is hotel, boarding-house, or lodging-house, at its visitor's option. It announces itself in the new Railway Advertisers, as a novel enterprise timidly beginning to spring up. It bashfully, almost apologetically, gives the traveller to understand that it does not expect him, on the good old constitutional hotel plan, to order a pint of sweet blacking for his drinking, and throw it away; but insinuates that he may have his boots blacked instead of his stomach, and maybe also have bed, breakfast, attendance, and a porter up all night, for a certain fixed charge. From these and similar premises many true Britons in the lowest spirits deduce that the times are levelling times, except in the article of high-roads, of which there will shortly be not one in England.

He eats without appetite, and soon goes forth again. Eastward and still eastward through the stale streets he takes his way, until he reaches his destination; a miserable court, specially miserable among many such.

He ascends a broken staircase, opens a door, looks into a dark, stifling room, and says, "Are you alone here?"

"Alone, deary; worse luck for me and better for you," replies a croaking voice. "Come in, come in, whoever you be: I can't see you till I light a match, yet I seem to know the sound of your speaking. I am acquainted with you, ain't I?"

"Light your match, and try."

"So I will, deary, so I will; but my hand that shakes, as I can't lay it on the match all in a moment. And I cough so, that, put my matches where I may, I never find 'em there. They jump and start, as I cough and cough, like live things. Are you off a voyage, deary?"

"No."

"Not sea-fearing?"

"No."

"Well, there's land customers and there's water customers. I'm a mother to both. Different from Jack Chinaman, t'other side the court. He ain't a father to neither. It ain't in him. And he ain't got the true secret of mixing, though he charges as much as me that has, and more if he can get it. Here's a match, and now where's the candle? If my cough takes me, I shall cough out twenty matches afore I gets a light."

But she finds the candle, and lights it before the cough comes on. It seizes her in the moment of success, and she sits down rocking herself to and fro, and gasping at intervals. "O, my lungs is awful bad, my lungs is wore away to cabbage-nets!" until the fit is over. During its continuance she has had no power of sight, or any other power not absorbed in the struggle; but as it leaves her, she begins to strain her eyes, and as soon as she is able to articulate, she cries, staring, —

"Why, it's you!"

"Are you so surprised to see me?"

"I thought I never should have seen you again, deary. I thought you was dead and gone to Heaven."

"Why?"

"I did n't suppose you could have kept away, alive, so long, from the poor old soul with the real receipt for mixing it. And you are in mourning too! Why did n't you come and have a pipe or two of comfort? Did they leave you money, perhaps, and so you did n't want comfort?"

"No!"

"Who was they as died, deary?"

"A relative."

"Died of what, lovey?"

"Probably, Death."

"We are short to-night!" cries the woman, with a propitiatory laugh. "Short and snappish we are! But we're out of sorts for want of a smoke. We've got the all-overs, have n't us, deary? But this is the place to cure 'em in; this is the place where the all-overs is smoked off!"

"You may make ready then," replies the visitor, "as soon as you like."

He divests himself of his shoes, loosens his cravat, and lies across the foot of the squalid bed, with his head resting on his left hand.

"Now you begin to look like yourself," says the woman, approvingly. "Now I begin to know my old customer indeed! Been trying to mix for yourself this long time, poppet?"

"I have been taking it now and then in my own way."

"Never take it your own way. It ain't good for trade, and it ain't good for you. Where's my ink-bottle, and where's my thimble, and where's my little spoon? He's going to take it in a artful form now, my deary dear!"

Entering on her process, and beginning to bubble and blow at the faint spark enclosed in the hollow of her hands, she speaks from time to time in a tone of snuffling satisfaction, without leaving off. When he speaks, he does so without looking at her, and as if his thoughts were already roaming away by anticipation.

"I've got a pretty many smokes ready for you, first and last, have n't I, chuckey?"

"A good many."

"When you first come, you was quite new to it; warn't ye?"

"Yes, I was easily disposed of, then."

"But you got on in the world, and was able by and by to take your pipe with the best of 'em, warn't ye?"

"Ay. And the worst."

"It 's just ready for you. What a sweet singer you was when you first come! Used to drop your head, and sing yourself off, like a bird! It 's ready for you now, deary."

He takes it from her with great care, and puts the mouthpiece to his lips. She seats herself beside him, ready to refill the pipe. After inhaling a few whiffs in silence, he doubtingly accosts her with, —

"Is it as potent as it used to be?"

"What do you speak of, deary?"

"What should I speak of, but what I have in my mouth?"

"It 's just the same. Always the identical same."

"It does n't taste so. And it 's slower."

"You 've got more used to it, you see."

"That may be the cause, certainly. Look here." He stops, becomes dreamy, and seems to forget that he has invited her attention. She bends over him, and speaks in his ear.

"I 'm attending to you. Says you just now, look here. Says I now, I am attending to ye. We was talking just before of your being used to it."

"I know all that. I was only thinking. Look here. Suppose you had something in your mind; something you were going to do."

"Yes, deary; something I was going to do?"

"But had not quite determined to do."

"Yes, deary."

"Might or might not do, you understand."

"Yes." With the point of a needle she stirs the contents of the bowl.

"Should you do it in your fancy when you were lying here doing this?"

She nods her head. "Over and over again."

"Just like me! I did it over and over again. I have done it hundreds of thousands of times in this room."

"It 's to be hoped it was pleasant to do, deary."

"It *was* pleasant to do!"

He says this with a savage air, and a spring or start at her. Quite unmoved, she retouches and replenishes the contents of the bowl with her little spatula. Seeing her intent upon the occupation, he sinks into his former attitude.

"It was a journey, a difficult and dangerous journey. That was the subject in my mind. A hazardous and perilous journey, over abysses where a slip would be destruction. Look down, look down! You see what lies at the bottom there?"

He has darted forward to say it, and to point at the ground, as though at some imaginary object far beneath. The woman looks at him as his spasmodic face approaches close to hers, and not at his pointing. She seems to know what the influence of her perfect quietude will be; if so, she has not miscalculated it, for he subsides again.

"Well; I have told you, I did it, here, hundreds of thousands of times. What do I say? I did it millions and billions of times. I did it so often and through such vast expanses of time that when it was really done, it seemed not worth the doing, it was done so soon."

"That 's the journey you have been away upon?" she quietly remarks.

He glares at her as he smokes; and then, his eyes becoming filmy, answers: "That 's the journey."

Silence ensues. His eyes are sometimes closed and sometimes open. The woman sits beside him, very attentive to the pipe, which is all the while at his lips.

"I 'll warrant," she observes, when he has been looking fixedly at her for some consecutive moments, with a singular appearance in his eyes of seeming to see her a long way off, instead of so near him, — "I 'll warrant you made the journey in a many ways when you made it so often?"

"No, always in one way."

"Always in the same way?"

"Ay."

"In the way in which it was really made at last?"

"Ay"

"And always took the same pleasure in harping on it?"

"Ay"

For the time he appears unequal to any other reply than this lazy monosyllabic assent. Probably to assure herself that it is not the assent of a mere automaton, she reverses the form of her next sentence.

"Did you never get tired of it, deary, and try to call up something else for a change?"

He struggles into a sitting posture, and retorts upon her: "What do you mean? What did I want? What did I come for?"

She gently lays him back again, and, before returning him the instrument he has dropped, revives the fire in it with her own breath; then says to him coaxingly, —

"Sure, sure, sure! Yes, yes, yes! Now I go along with you. You was too quick for me. I see now. You come o' purpose to take the journey. Why, I might have known it, through its standing by you so."

He answers first with a laugh, and then with a passionate setting of his teeth: "Yes, I came on purpose. When I could not bear my life I came to get the relief, and I got it. It WAS one! It WAS one!" This repetition with extraordinary vehemence, and the snarl of a wolf.

She observes him very cautiously, as though mentally feeling her way to her next remark. It is: "There was a fellow-traveller, deary."

"Ha ha ha!" He breaks into a ringing laugh, or rather yell.

"To think," he cries, "how often fellow-traveller, and yet not know it! To think how many times he went the journey, and never saw the road!"

The woman kneels upon the floor, with her arms crossed on the coverlet of the bed, close by him, and her chin upon them. In this crouching attitude she watches him. The pipe is falling from his mouth. She puts it back, and, laying her hand upon his chest, moves him slightly from side to side. Upon that he speaks, as if she had spoken.

"Yes! I always made the journey first, before the changes of colors and the great landscapes and glittering processions began. They could n't begin till it was off my mind. I had no room till then for anything else."

Once more he lapses into silence. Once more she lays her hand upon his chest, and moves him slightly to and fro, as a cat might stimulate a half-slain mouse. Once more he speaks, as if she had spoken.

"What? I told you so. When it comes to be real at last, it is so short that it seems unreal for the first time. Hark!"

"Yes, deary. I 'm listening."

"Time and place are both at hand."

He is on his feet speaking in a whisper, and as if in the dark.

"Time, place, and fellow-traveller," she suggests, adopting his tone, and holding him softly by the arm.

"How could the time be at hand unless the fellow-traveller was? Hush! The journey 's made. It 's over."

"So soon?"

"That's what I said to you. So soon. Wait a little. This is a vision. I shall sleep it off. It has been too short and easy. I must have a better vision than this; this is the poorest of all. No struggle, no consciousness of peril, no entreaty, — and yet I never saw *that* before" With a start.

"Saw what, deary?"

"Look at it! Look what a poor, mean, miserable thing it is! *That* must be real. It's over!"

He has accompanied this incoherence with some wild, unmeaning gestures; but they trail off into the progressive inaction of stupor, and he lies a log upon the bed.

The woman, however, is still inquisitive. With a repetition of her cat-like action, she slightly stirs his body again, and listens; stirs again, and listens; whispers to it, and listens. Finding it past all rousing for the time, she slowly gets upon her feet, with an air of disappointment, and flicks the face with the back of her hand in turning from it.

But she goes no farther away from it than the chair upon the hearth. She sits in it, with an elbow on one of its arms, and her chin upon her hand, intent upon him. "I heard ye say once," she croaks under her breath, — "I heard ye say once, when I was lying where you're lying, and you were making your speculations upon me, 'Unintelligible!' I heard you say so, of two more than me. But don't ye be too sure always; don't ye be too sure, beauty!"

Unwinking, cat-like, and intent, she presently adds: "Not so potent as it once was? Ah! Perhaps not at first You may be more right there. Practice makes perfect. I may have learned the secret how to make ye talk, deary."

He talks no more, whether or no. Twitching in an ugly way from time to time, both as to his face and limbs, he lies heavy and silent. The wretched candle burns down; the woman takes its expiring end between her fingers, lights another at it, crams the guttering, frying morsel deep into the candlestick, and rams it home with the new candle, as if she were loading some ill-savored and unseemly weapon of witchcraft; the new candle, in its turn, burns down; and still he lies insensible. At length, what remains of the last candle is blown out, and daylight looks into the room.

It has not looked very long, when he sits up, chilled and shaking, slowly recovers consciousness of where he is, and makes himself ready to depart. The woman receives what he pays her with a grateful "Bless ye, bless ye, deary!" and seems, tired out, to begin making herself ready for sleep as he leaves the room.

But seeming may be false or true. It is false in this case, for, the moment the stairs have ceased to creak under his tread, she glides after him, muttering emphatically, "I'll not miss ye twice!"

There is no egress from the court but by its entrance. With a weird peep from the doorway she watches for his looking back. He does not look back before disappearing, with a wavering step. She follows him, peeps from the court, sees him still faltering on without looking back, and holds him in view.

He repairs to the back of Aldersgate Street, where a door immediately opens to his knocking. She crouches in another doorway, watching that one, and easily comprehending that he puts up temporarily at that house. Her patience is unexhausted by hours. For sustenance she can, and does, buy bread within a hundred yards, and milk as it is carried past her.

He comes forth again at noon, having changed his dress, but carrying nothing in his hand, and having nothing carried for him. He is not going back into the country, therefore, just yet. She follows him a little way, hesitates, instantaneously turns confidently, and goes straight into the house he has quitted.

"Is the gentleman from Cloisterham in-doors?"

"Just gone out"

"Unlucky. When does the gentleman return to Cloisterham?"

"At six this evening."

"Bless ye and thank ye. May the Lord prosper a business where a civil question, even from a poor soul, is so civilly answered!"

"I 'll not miss ye twice!" repeats the poor soul in the street, and not so civilly. "I lost ye last where that omnibus you got into nigh your journey's end plied betwixt the station and the place. I was n't so much as certain that you even went right on to the place. Now I know ye did. My gentleman from Cloisterham, I 'll be there before ye and bide your coming. I 've sworn my oath that I 'll not miss ye twice!"

Accordingly, that same evening the poor soul stands in Cloisterham, High Street, looking at the many quaint gables of the Nuns' House, and getting through the time as she best can until nine o'clock; at which hour she has reason to suppose that the arriving omnibus passengers may have some interest for her. The friendly darkness, at that hour, renders it easy for her to ascertain whether this be so or not; and it is so, for the passenger not to be missed twice arrives among the rest.

"Now, let me see what becomes of you. Go on!"

An observation addressed to the air. And yet it might be addressed to the passenger, so compliantly does he go on along the High Street until he comes to an arched gateway, at which he unexpectedly vanishes. The poor soul quickens her pace; is swift, and close upon him entering under the gateway; but only sees a postern staircase on one side of it, and on the other side an ancient vaulted room, in which a large-headed, gray-haired gentleman is writing, under the odd circumstances of sitting open to the thoroughfare and eying all who pass, as if he were toll-taker of the gateway: though the way is free.

"Halloa!" he cries in a low voice, seeing her brought to a stand-still: "who are you looking for?"

"There was a gentleman passed in here this minute, sir."

"Of course there was. What do you want with him?"

"Where do he live, deary?"

"Live? Up the staircase."

"Bless ye! Whisper. What 's his name, deary?"

"Surname Jasper, Christian name John. Mr. John Jasper."

"Has he a calling, good gentleman?"

"Calling? Yes. Sings in the choir."

"In the spire?"

"Choir."

"What 's that?"

Mr. Datchery rises from his papers, and comes to his doorstep. "Do you know what a cathedral is?" he asks jocosely.

The woman nods.

"What is it?"

She looks puzzled, casting about in her mind to find a definition, when it occurs to her that it is easier to point out the substantial object itself, massive against the dark blue sky and the early stars.

"That 's the answer. Go in there at seven to-morrow morning, and you may see Mr. John Jasper, and hear him too."

"Thank ye! Thank ye!"

The burst of triumph in which she thanks him does not escape the notice of the single buffer of an easy temper living idly on his means. He glances at her;

clasps his hands behind him, as the wont of such buffers is; and lounges along the echoing precincts at her side.

"Or," he suggests, with a backward hitch of his head, "you can go up at once to Mr. Jasper's rooms there."

The woman eyes him with a cunning smile, and shakes her head.

"Oh! You don't want to speak to him?"

She repeats her dumb reply, and forms with her lips a soundless "No."

"You can admire him at a distance three times a day, whenever you like. It 's a long way to come for that, though."

The woman looks up quickly. If Mr. Datchery thinks she is to be so induced to declare where she comes from, he is of a much easier temper than she is. But she acquits him of such an artful thought, as he lounges along, like the chartered bore of the city, with his uncovered gray hair blowing about, and his purposeless hands rattling the loose money in the pockets of his trousers.

The chink of the money has an attraction for her greedy ears. "Would n't you help me to pay for my travellers' lodging, dear gentleman, and to pay my way along? I am a poor soul, I am indeed, and troubled with a grievous cough."

"You know the travellers' lodging, I perceive, and are making directly for it," is Mr. Datchery's bland comment, still rattling his loose money. "Been here often, my good woman?"

"Once in all my life."

"Ay, ay?"

They have arrived at the entrance to the Monks' Vineyard. An appropriate remembrance, presenting an exemplary model for imitation, is revived in the woman's mind by the sight of the place. She stops at the gate, and says energetically,—

"By this token, though you may n't believe it, That a young gentleman gave me three and sixpence as I was coughing my breath away on this very grass. I asked him for three and sixpence, and he gave it me."

"Was n't it a little cool to name your sum?" hints Mr. Datchery, still rattling. Is n't it customary to leave the amount open? Might n't it have had the appearance, to the young gentleman, only the appearance, that he was rather dictated to?"

"Look 'ee here, deary," she replies, in a confidential and persuasive tone, "I wanted the money to lay it out on a medicine as does me good, and as I deal in. I told the young gentleman so, and he gave it me, and I laid it out honest to the last brass farden. I want to lay out the same sum in the same way now; and if you 'll give it me, I 'll lay it out honest to the last brass farden again, upon my soul!"

"What 's the medicine?"

"I 'll be honest with you beforehand, as well as after. It 's opium."

Mr. Datchery, with a sudden change of countenance, gives her a sudden look.

"It 's opium, deary. Neither more nor less. And it 's like a human creetur so far, that you always hear what can be said against it, but seldom what can be said in its praise."

Mr. Datchery begins very slowly to count out the sum demanded of him. Greedily watching his hands, she continues to hold forth on the great example set him.

"It was last Christmas Eve, just arter dark, the once that I was here afore, when the young gentleman gave me the three and six."

Mr. Datchery stops in his counting, finds he has counted wrong, shakes his money together, and begins again.

"And the young gentleman's name," she adds, "was Edwin."

Mr. Datchery drops some money, stoops to pick it up, and reddens with the exertion as he asks,—

"How do you know the young gentleman's name?"

"I asked him for it, and he told it me. I only asked him the two questions, what was his Chris'en name, and whether he'd a sweetheart? And he answered, Edwin, and he had n't."

Mr. Datchery pauses with the selected coins in his hand, rather as if he were falling into a brown study of their value, and could n't bear to part with them. The woman looks at him distrustfully, and with her anger brewing for the event of his thinking better of the gift; but he bestows it on her as if he were abstracting his mind from the sacrifice, and with many servile thanks she goes her way.

John Jasper's lamp is kindled, and his Lighthouse is shining when Mr. Datchery returns alone towards it. As mariners on a dangerous voyage, approaching an iron-bound coast, may look along the beams of the warning light to the haven lying beyond it that may never be reached, so Mr. Datchery's wistful gaze is directed to this beacon, and beyond.

His object in now revisiting his lodging is merely to put on the hat which seems so superfluous an article in his wardrobe. It is half past ten by the Cathedral clock, when he walks out into the Precincts again; he lingers and looks about him, as though, the enchanted hour when Mr. Durdles may be stoned home having struck, he had some expectation of seeing the Imp who is appointed to the mission of stoning him.

In effect, that Power of Evil is abroad. Having nothing living to stone at the moment, he is discovered by Mr. Datchery in the unholy office of stoning the dead, through the railings of the churchyard. The Imp finds this a relishing and piquing pursuit: firstly, because their resting-place is announced to be sacred; and secondly, because the tall headstones are sufficiently like themselves, on their beat in the dark, to justify the delicious fancy that they are hurt when hit.

Mr. Datchery hails him with: "Halloa, Winks!"

He acknowledges the hail with: "Halloa, Dick!" Their acquaintance seemingly having been established on a familiar footing.

"But I say," he remonstrates, "don't yer go a making my name public. I never means to plead to no name, mind yer. When they says to me in the Lock-up, a going to put me down in the book, 'What's your name?' I says to them, 'Find out.' Likeways when they says, 'What's your religion?' I says, 'Find out.'"

Which, it may be observed in passing, it would be immensely difficult for the State, however statistical, to do.

"Asides which," adds the boy, "there ain't no family of Winkses."

"I think there must be."

"Yer lie, there ain't. The travellers give me the name on account of my getting no settled sleep and being knocked up all night; whereby I gets one eye roused open afore I've shut the other. That's what Winks means. Deputy's the nighest name to indict me by: but yer would n't catch me pleading to that, neither."

"Deputy be it always then. We two are good friends; eh, Deputy?"

"Jolly good."

"I forgave you the debt you owed me when we first became acquainted, and many of my sixpences have come your way since; eh, Deputy?"

"Ah! And what's more, yer ain't no friend o' Jarsper's. What did he go a histing me off my legs for?"

"What indeed! But never mind him now. A shilling of mine is going your way to-night, Deputy. You have just taken in a lodger I have been speaking to; an infirm woman with a cough."

"Puffer," assents Deputy, with a shrewd leer of recognition, and smoking an imaginary pipe, with his head very much on one side, and his eyes very much out of their places: "Hopeum Puffer."

"What is her name?"

"'Er Royal Highness the Princess Puffer."

"She has some other name than that; where does she live?"

"Up in London. Among the Jacks."

"The sailors?"

"I said so; Jacks. And Chayner men. And hother Knifers."

"I should like to know, through you, exactly where she lives."

"All right. Give us 'old."

A shilling passes; and, in that spirit of confidence which should pervade all business transactions between principals of honor, this piece of business is considered done

"But here 's a lark!" cries Deputy. "Where did yer think 'Er Royal Highness is a goin' to, to-morrow morning? Blest if she ain't a goin' to the KIN-FREE-DER-EL!" He greatly prolongs the word in his ecstasy, and smites his leg, and doubles himself up in a fit of shrill laughter.

"How do you know that, Deputy?"

"Cos she told me so just now. She said she must he hup and hout o' purpose. She ses, 'Deputy, I must 'ave a early wash, and make myself as swell as I can, for I 'm a goin' to take a turn at the KIN-FREE-DER-EL!'" He separates the syllables with his former zest, and, not finding his sense of the ludicrous sufficiently relieved by stamping about on the pavement, breaks into a slow and stately dance, perhaps supposed to be performed by the Dean.

Mr. Datchery receives the communication with a well-satisfied though a pondering face, and breaks up the conference. Returning to his quaint lodging, and sitting long over the supper of bread and cheese and salad and ale which Mrs. Tope has left prepared for him, he still sits when his supper is finished. At length he rises, throws open the door of a corner cupboard, and refers to a few uncouth chalked strokes on its inner side.

"I like," says Mr. Datchery, "the old tavern way of keeping scores. Illegible, except to the scorer. The scorer not committed, the scored debited with what is against him. Hum; ha! A very small score this; a very poor score!"

He sighs over the contemplation of its poverty, takes a bit of chalk from one of the cupboard shelves, and pauses with it in his hand, uncertain what addition to make to the account.

"I think a moderate stroke," he concludes, "is all I am justified in scoring up"; so, suits the action to the word, closes the cupboard, and goes to bed.

A brilliant morning shines on the old city. Its antiquities and ruins are surpassingly beautiful, with the lusty ivy gleaming in the sun, and the rich trees waving in the balmy air. Changes of glorious light from moving boughs, songs of birds, scents from gardens, woods, and fields, — or, rather, from one great garden of the whole cultivated island in its yielding time, — penetrate into the Cathedral, subdue its earthy odor, and preach the Resurrection and the Life. The cold stone tombs of centuries ago grow warm; and flecks of brightness dart into the sternest marble corners of the building, fluttering their light wings.

Comes Mr. Tope with his large keys, and yawningly unlocks and sets open. Come Mrs. Tope and attendant sweeping sprites Come, in due time, organist and bellows-boy, peeping down from the red curtains in the loft, fearlessly flapping dust from books up at that remote elevation, and whisking it from stops and pedals. Come sundry rooks, from various quarters of the sky, back to the great tower; who may be presumed to enjoy vibration, and to know that bell and organ are going to give it them. Come a very small and straggling congregation indeed: chiefly from Minor Canon Corner and the Precincts. Come Mr. Crisparkle, fresh and bright; and his ministering brethren, not quite so fresh and bright. Come the Choir in a hurry (always in a hurry, and struggling into their nightgowns at the last moment, like children shirking bed), and comes John Jasper leading their line. Last of all comes Mr. Datchery into a stall, one of a choice empty collection very much at his service, and glancing about him for Her Royal Highness the Princess Puffer.

The service is pretty well advanced before Mr. Datchery can discern Her Royal Highness. But by that time he has made her out, in the shade. She is behind a pillar, carefully withdrawn from the Choir Master's view, but regards him with the closest attention. All unconscious of her presence, he chants and sings. She grins when he is most musically fervid, and — yes, Mr. Datchery sees her do it! — shakes her fist at him behind the pillar's friendly shelter.

Mr. Datchery looks again to convince himself. Yes, again! As ugly and withered as one of the fantastic carvings on the under brackets of the stall seats, as malignant as the Evil One, as hard as the big brass eagle holding the sacred books upon his wings (and, according to the sculptor's representation of his ferocious attributes, not at all converted by them), she hugs herself in her lean arms, and then shakes both fists at the leader of the Choir.

And at that moment, outside the grated door of the Choir, having eluded the vigilance of Mr. Tope by shifty resources in which he is an adept, Deputy peeps, sharp-eyed, through the bars, and stares astounded from the threatener to the threatened.

The service comes to an end, and the servitors disperse to breakfast. Mr. Datchery accosts his last new acquaintance outside, when the Choir (as much in a hurry to get their bedgowns off, as they were but now to get them on) have scuffled away.

"Well, mistress. Good morning. You have seen him?"

"*I*'ve seen him, deary; *I*'ve seen him!"

"And you know him?"

"Know him! Better far than all the Reverend Parsons put together know him."

Mrs. Tope's care has spread a very neat, clean breakfast ready for her lodger. Before sitting down to it, he opens his corner-cupboard door; takes his bit of chalk from its shelf; adds one thick line to the score, extending from the top of the cupboard door to the bottom; and then falls to with an appetite.

* * * * *

MASTER HUMPHREY'S CLOCK

AND

OTHER PIECES.

PREFACE TO MASTER HUMPHREY'S CLOCK.

WHEN the author commenced this Work, he proposed to himself three objects.

First. To establish a periodical, which should enable him to present, under one general head, and not as separate and distinct publications, certain fictions which he had it in contemplation to write.

Secondly. To produce these Tales in weekly numbers; hoping that to shorten the intervals of communication between himself and his readers, would be to knit more closely the pleasant relations they had held for Forty Months.

Thirdly. In the execution of this weekly task, to have as much regard as its exigencies would permit, to each story as a whole, and to the possibility of its publication at some distant day, apart from the machinery in which it had its origin.

The characters of Master Humphrey and his three friends, and the little fancy of the clock, were the result of these considerations. When he sought to interest his readers in those who talked, and read, and listened, he revived Mr. Pickwick and his humble friends, not with any intention of reopening an exhausted and abandoned mine, but to connect them, in the thoughts of those whose favorites they had been, with the tranquil enjoyments of Master Humphrey.

It was never the author's intention to make the Members of Master Humphrey's Clock active agents in the stories they are supposed to relate. Having brought himself, in the commencement of his undertaking, to feel an interest in these quiet creatures, and to imagine them in their old chamber of meeting, eager listeners to all he had to tell, the author hoped — as authors will — to succeed in awakening some of his own emotions in the bosoms of his readers. Imagining Master Humphrey in his chimney-corner, resuming night after night the narrative — say, of the Old Curiosity Shop — picturing to himself the various sensations of his hearers — thinking how Jack Redburn might incline to poor Kit, and perhaps lean too favorably even towards the lighter vices of Mr. Richard Swiveller — how the deaf gentleman would have his favorite, and Mr. Miles his — and how all these gentle spirits would trace some faint reflection of their past lives in the varying current of the tale — he has insensibly fallen into the belief that they are present to his readers as they are to him, and has forgotten that, like one whose vision is disordered, he may be conjuring up bright figures where there is nothing but empty space.

The short papers which are to be found at the beginning of this volume were indispensable to the form of publication and the limited extent of each number, as no story of lengthened interest could be begun until "The Clock" was wound up and fairly going.

The author would fain hope that there are not many who would disturb Master Humphrey and his friends in their seclusion; who would have them forego their present enjoyments to exchange those confidences with each other, the absence of which is the foundation of their mutual trust. For when their occupation is gone, when their tales are ended, and but their personal histories remain, the chimney-corner will be growing cold, and the clock will be about to stop forever.

One other word in his own person, and he returns to the more grateful task of speaking for those imaginary people whose little world lies within these pages.

It may be some consolation to the well-disposed ladies or gentlemen who, in the interval between the conclusion of his last work and the commencement of this, originated a report that he had gone raving mad, to know that it spread as rapidly as could be desired, and was made the subject of considerable dispute; not as regarded the fact, for that was as thoroughly established as the duel between Sir Peter Teazle and Charles Surface in the "School for Scandal"; but with reference to the unfortunate lunatic's place of confinement, — one party insisting positively on Bedlam, another inclining favorably towards St. Luke's, and a third swearing strongly by the asylum at Hanwell; while each backed its case by circumstantial evidence of the same excellent nature as that brought to bear by Sir Benjamin Backbite on the pistol-shot which struck against the little bronze bust of Shakespeare over the fireplace, grazed out of the window at a right angle, and wounded the postman, who was coming to the door with a double letter from Northamptonshire.

It will be a great affliction to these ladies and gentlemen to learn — and he is so unwilling to give pain, that he would not whisper the circumstance on any account, did he not feel in a manner bound to do so, in gratitude to those among his friends who were at the trouble of being angry with the absurdity — that their invention made the author's home unusually merry, and gave rise to an extraordinary number of jests, of which he will only add, in the words of the good Vicar of Wakefield, "I cannot say whether we had more wit among us than usual; but I am sure we had more laughing."

MASTER HUMPHREY'S CLOCK.

I.

MASTER HUMPHREY, FROM HIS CLOCK-SIDE IN THE CHIMNEY-CORNER.

THE reader must not expect to know where I live. At present, it is true, my abode may be a question of little or no import to anybody, but if I should carry my readers with me, as I hope to do, and there should spring up, between them and me, feelings of homely affection and regard attaching something of interest to matters ever so slightly connected with my fortunes or my speculations, even my place of residence might one day have a kind of charm for them. Bearing this possible contingency in mind, I wish them to understand in the outset, that they must never expect to know it.

I am not a churlish old man. Friendless I can never be, for all mankind are my kindred, and I am on ill terms with no one member of my great family. But for many years I have led a lonely, solitary life; — what wound I sought to heal, what sorrow to forget, originally, matters not now; it is sufficient that retirement has become a habit with me, and that I am unwilling to break the spell which for so long a time has shed its quiet influence upon my home and heart.

I live in a venerable suburb of London, in an old house, which in bygone days was a famous resort for merry roysterers and peerless ladies, long since departed. It is a silent, shady place, with a paved court-yard so full of echoes that sometimes I am tempted to believe that faint responses to the noises of old times linger there yet, and that these ghosts of sound haunt my footsteps as I pace it up and down. I am the more confirmed in this belief, because, of late years, the echoes that attend my walks have been less loud and marked than they were wont to be; and it is pleasanter to imagine in them the rustling of silk brocade, and the light step of some lovely girl, than to recognize in their altered note the failing tread of an old man.

Those who like to read of brilliant rooms and gorgeous furniture would derive but little pleasure from a minute description of my simple dwelling. It is dear to me for the same reason that they would hold it in slight regard. Its worm-eaten doors, and low ceilings crossed by clumsy beams; its walls of wainscot, dark stairs, and gaping closets; its small chambers, communicating with each other by winding passages or narrow steps; its many nooks, scarce larger than its corner-cupboards; its very dust and dulness, all are dear to me. The moth and spider are my constant tenants, for in my house the one basks in his long sleep, and the other plies his busy loom, secure and undisturbed. I have a pleasure in thinking on a summer's day, how many butterflies have sprung for the first time into light and sunshine from some dark corner of these old walls.

When I first came to live here, which was many years ago, the neighbors were curious to know who I was, and whence I came, and why I lived so much alone. As time went on, and they still remained unsatisfied on these points, I became the centre of a popular ferment, extending for half a mile round, and in one direction for a full mile. Various rumors were circulated to my prejudice. I was a spy, an infidel, a conjurer, a kidnapper of children, a refugee, a priest, a monster. Mothers caught up their infants and ran into their houses as I passed; men eyed me spitefully, and muttered threats and curses. I was the object of suspicion and distrust; ay, of downright hatred, too.

But when in course of time they found I did no harm, but, on the contrary, inclined towards them despite their unjust usage, they began to relent. I found my footsteps no longer dogged, as they had often been before, and observed that the women and children no longer retreated, but would stand and gaze at me as I passed their doors. I took this for a good omen, and waited patiently for better times. By degrees I began to make friends among these humble folks, and though they were yet shy of speaking, would give them "good day," and so pass on. In a little time, those whom I had thus accosted, would make a point of coming to their doors and windows at the usual hour, and nod or courtesy to me; children, too, came timidly within my reach, and ran away quite scared when I patted their heads and bade them be good at school. These little people soon grew more familiar. From exchanging mere words of course with my older neighbors, I gradually became their friend and adviser, the depositary of their cares and sorrows, and sometimes, it may be, the reliever, in my small way, of their distresses. And now I never walk abroad, but pleasant recognitions and smiling faces wait on Master Humphrey.

It was a whim of mine, perhaps as a whet to the curiosity of my neighbors, and a kind of retaliation upon them for their suspicions, — it was, I say, a whim of mine, when I first took up my abode in this place, to acknowledge no other name than Humphrey. With my detractors I was Ugly Humphrey. When I began to convert them into friends, I was Mr. Humphrey, and Old Mr. Humphrey. At length I settled down into plain Master Humphrey, which was understood to be the title most pleasant to my ear; and so completely a matter of course has it become, that sometimes when I am taking my morning walk in my little courtyard, I overhear my barber — who has a profound respect for me, and would not, I am sure, abridge my honors for the world — holding forth on the other side of the wall, touching the state of "Master Humphrey's" health, and communicating to some friend the substance of the conversation that he and Master Humphrey have had together in the course of the shaving which he has just concluded.

That I may not make acquaintance with my readers under false pretences, or give them cause to complain hereafter, that I have withheld any matter which it was essential for them to have learnt at first, I wish them to know — and I smile sorrowfully to think that the time has been when the confession would have given me pain — that I am a misshapen, deformed old man.

I have never been made a misanthrope by this cause. I have never been stung by any insult, nor wounded by any jest upon my crooked figure. As a child I was melancholy and timid, but that was because the gentle consideration paid to my misfortune sunk deep into my spirit and made me sad, even in those early days. I was but a very young creature when my poor mother died, and yet I remember that often when I hung around her neck, and oftener still when I played about the room before her, she would catch me to her bosom, and bursting into tears, would soothe me with every term of fondness and affection. God knows I was a happy child at those times, — happy to nestle in her breast, — happy to weep when she did, — happy in not knowing why.

These occasions are so strongly impressed upon my memory, that they seem to have occupied whole years. I had numbered very, very few when they ceased forever, but before then their meaning had been revealed to me.

I do not know whether all children are imbued with a quick perception of childish grace and beauty, and a strong love for it, but I was. I had no thought that I remember, either that I possessed it myself or that I lacked it, but I admired it with an intensity that I cannot describe. A little knot of playmates,— they must have been beautiful, for I see them now — were clustered one day round my mother's knee in eager admiration of some picture representing a group of infant angels, which she held in her hand. Whose the picture was, whether it was familiar to me or otherwise, or how all the children came to be there, I forget; I have some dim thought it was my birthday, but the beginning of my recollection is that we were all together in a garden, and it was summer weather, — I am sure of that, for one of the little girls had roses in her sash. There were many lovely angels in this picture, and I remember the fancy coming upon me to point out which of them represented each child there, and that when I had gone through my companions, I stopped and hesitated, wondering which was most like me. I remember the children looking at each other, and my turning red and hot, and their crowding round to kiss me, saying that they loved me all the same; and then, and when the old sorrow came into my dear mother's mild and tender look, the truth broke upon me for the first time, and I knew, while watching my awkward and ungainly sports, how keenly she had felt for her poor crippled boy.

I used frequently to dream of it afterwards, and now my heart aches for that child as if I had never been he, when I think how often he awoke from some fairy change to his own old form, and sobbed himself to sleep again.

Well, well — all these sorrows are past. My glancing at them may not be without its use, for it may help in some measure to explain why I have all my life been attached to the inanimate objects that people my chamber, and how I have come to look upon them rather in the light of old and constant friends, than as mere chairs and tables which a little money could replace at will.

Chief and first among all these is my Clock, — my old, cheerful, companionable Clock. How can I ever convey to others an idea of the comfort and consolation that this old clock has been for years to me!

It is associated with my earliest recollections. It stood upon the staircase at home (I call it home still mechanically), nigh sixty years ago. I like it for that, but it is not on that account, nor because it is a quaint old thing in a huge oaken case curiously and richly carved, that I prize it as I do. I incline to it as if it were alive, and could understand and give me back the love I bear it.

And what other thing that has not life could cheer me as it does; what other thing that has not life (I will not say how few things that have) could have proved the same patient, true, untiring friend! How often have I sat in the long winter evenings feeling such society in its cricket-voice, that raising my eyes from my book and looking gratefully towards it, the face reddened by the glow of the shining fire has seemed to relax from its staid expression and to regard me kindly; how often in the summer twilight, when my thoughts have wandered back to a melancholy past, have its regular whisperings recalled them to the calm and peaceful present; how often in the dead tranquillity of night has its bell broken the oppressive silence, and seemed to give me assurance that the old clock was still a faithful watcher at my chamber door! My easy-chair, my desk, my ancient furniture, my very books, I can scarcely bring myself to love even these last, like my old clock!

It stands in a snug corner, midway between the fireside and a low arched door leading to my bedroom. Its fame is diffused so extensively throughout the neighborhood, that I have often the satisfaction of hearing the publican, or the baker, and sometimes even the parish-clerk, petitioning my housekeeper (of whom I shall have much to say by and by) to inform him the exact time by Master Humphrey's Clock. My barber, to whom I have referred, would sooner believe it than the sun. Nor are these its only distinctions. It has acquired, I am happy to say, another, inseparably connecting it not only with my enjoyments and reflections, but with those of other men; as I shall now relate.

I lived alone here for a long time without any friend or acquaintance. In the course of my wanderings by night and day, at all hours and seasons, in city streets and quiet country parts, I came to be familiar with certain faces, and to take it to heart as quite a heavy disappointment if they failed to present themselves each at its accustomed spot. But these were the only friends I knew, and beyond them I had none.

It happened, however, when I had gone on thus for a long time, that I formed an acquaintance with a deaf gentleman, which ripened into intimacy and close companionship. To this hour, I am ignorant of his name. It is his humor to conceal it, or he has a reason and purpose for so doing. In either case I feel that he has a right to require a return of the trust he has reposed, and as he has never sought to discover my secret, I have never sought to penetrate his. There may have been something in this tacit confidence in each other, flattering and pleasant to us both, and it may have imparted in the beginning an additional zest, perhaps, to our friendship Be this as it may, we have grown to be like brothers, and still I only know him as the deaf gentleman.

I have said that retirement has become a habit with me. When I add that the deaf gentleman and I have two friends, I communicate nothing which is inconsistent with that declaration. I spend many hours of every day in solitude and study, have no friends or change of friends, but these, only see them at stated periods, and am supposed to be of a retired spirit by the very nature and object of our association.

We are men of secluded habits, with something of a cloud upon our early fortunes, whose enthusiasm, nevertheless, has not cooled with age, whose spirit of romance is not yet quenched, who are content to ramble through the world in a pleasant dream, rather than ever waken again to its harsh realities. We are alchemists who would extract the essence of perpetual youth from dust and ashes, tempt coy Truth in many light and airy forms from the bottom of her well, and discover one crumb of comfort or one grain of good in the commonest and least regarded matter that passes through our crucible. Spirits of past times, creatures of imagination, and people of to-day, are alike the objects of our seeking, and, unlike the objects of search with most philosophers, we can insure their coming at our command.

The dear gentleman and I first began to beguile our days with these fancies, and our nights in communicating them to each other. We are now four. But in my room there are six old chairs, and we have decided that the two empty seats shall always be placed at our table when we meet, to remind us that we may yet increase our company by that number, if we should find two men to our mind. When one among us dies his chair will always be set in its usual place, but never occupied again; and I have caused my will to be so drawn out, that when we are all dead the house shall be shut up, and the vacant chairs still left in their accustomed places. It is pleasant to think that even then our shades may, perhaps, assemble together as of yore we did, and join in ghostly converse.

One night in every week, as the clock strikes ten, we meet. At the second stroke of two, I am alone.

And now shall I tell how that my old servant, besides giving us note of time, and ticking cheerful encouragement of our proceedings, lends its name to our society, which for its punctuality and my love, is christened "Master Humphrey's Clock"? Now shall I tell, how that in the bottom of the old dark closet, where the steady pendulum throbs and beats with healthy action, though the pulse of him who made it stood still long ago, and never moved again, there are piles of dusty papers constantly placed there by our hands, that we may link our enjoyments with my old friend, and draw means to beguile time from the heart of time itself? Shall I, or can I, tell with what a secret pride I open this repository when we meet at night, and still find new store of pleasure in my dear old Clock!

Friend and companion of my solitude! mine is not a selfish love; I would not keep your merits to myself, but disperse something of pleasant association with your image through the whole wide world; I would have men couple with your name cheerful and healthy thoughts; I would have them believe that you keep true and honest time; and how it would gladden me to know that they recognized some hearty English work in Master Humphrey's Clock!

THE CLOCK-CASE.

It is my intention constantly to address my readers from the chimney-corner, and I would fain hope that such accounts as I shall give them of our histories and proceedings, our quiet speculations or more busy adventures, will never be unwelcome. Lest, however, I should grow prolix in the outset by lingering too long upon our little association, confounding the enthusiasm with which I regard this chief happiness of my life with that minor degree of interest which those to whom I address myself may be supposed to feel for it, I have deemed it expedient to break off as they have seen.

But, still clinging to my old friend, and naturally desirous that all its merits should be known, I am tempted to open (somewhat irregularly and against our laws, I must admit) the clock-case. The first roll of paper on which I lay my hand is in the writing of the deaf gentleman. I shall have to speak of him in my next paper, and how can I better approach that welcome task than by prefacing it with a production of his own pen, consigned to the safe keeping of my honest clock by his own hands?

The manuscript runs thus: —

INTRODUCTION TO THE GIANT CHRONICLES.

Once upon a time, that is to say, in this our time, — the exact year, month, and day are of no matter, — there dwelt in the city of London a substantial citizen, who united in his single person the dignities of wholesale fruiterer, alderman, common-councilman, and member of the worshipful company of Patten-makers: who had superadded to these extraordinary distinctions the important post and title of Sheriff, and who at length, and to crown all, stood next in rotation for the high and honorable office of Lord Mayor.

He was a very substantial citizen indeed. His face was like the full moon in a fog, with two little holes punched out for his eyes, a very ripe pear stuck on for his nose, and a wide gash to serve for a mouth. The girth of his waistcoat was hung up and lettered in his tailor's shop as an extraordinary curiosity. He breathed like a heavy snorer, and his voice in speaking came thickly forth, as if it were oppressed and stifled by feather-beds. He trod the ground like an elephant, and eat and drank like — like nothing but an alderman, as he was.

This worthy citizen had risen to his great eminence from small beginnings. He had once been a very lean, weazen little boy, never dreaming of carrying such a weight of flesh upon his bones or of money in his pockets, and glad enough to take his dinner at a baker's door, and his tea at a pump. But he had long ago forgotten all this, as it was proper that a wholesale fruiterer, alderman, common-councilman, member of the worshipful company of Patten-makers, past sheriff, and above all, a Lord Mayor that was to be, should; and he never forgot it more completely in all his life than on the eighth of November in the year of his election to the great golden civic chair which was the day before his grand dinner at Guildhall.

It happened that as he sat that evening all alone in his counting-house, looking over the bill of fare for next day, and checking off the fat capons in fifties and the turtle-soup by the hundred quarts for his private amusement, — it happened that as he sat alone occupied in these pleasant calculations, a strange man came in and asked him how he did, adding, "If I am half as much changed as you, sir, you have no recollection of me, I am sure."

The strange man was not over and above well dressed, and was very far from being fat or rich-looking in any sense of the word, yet he spoke with a kind of modest confidence, and assumed an easy, gentlemanly sort of an air, to which nobody but a rich man can lawfully presume. Besides this, he interrupted the good citizen just as he had reckoned three hundred and seventy-two fat capons and was carrying them over to the next column, and as if that were not aggravation enough, the learned recorder for the city of London had only ten minutes previously gone out at that very same door, and had turned round and said, "Good night, my lord." Yes, he had said, "my lord," — he, a man of birth and education, of the Honorable Society of the Middle Temple, Barrister at Law, — he who had an uncle in the House of Commons, and an aunt almost but not quite in the House of Lords (for she had married a feeble peer, and made him vote as she liked), — he, this man, this learned recorder, had said, "my lord." "I 'll not wait till to-morrow to give you your title, my Lord Mayor," says he, with a bow and a smile; "you are Lord Mayor *de facto*, if not *de jure*. Good night, my lord!"

The Lord Mayor elect thought of this, and turning to the stranger, and sternly bidding him "go out of his private counting-house," brought forward the three hundred and seventy-two fat capons, and went on with his account.

"Do you remember," said the other, stepping forward, — "*do* you remember little Joe Toddyhigh?"

The port wine fled for a moment from the fruiterer's nose as he muttered, "Joe Toddyhigh! What about Joe Toddyhigh?"

"*I* am Joe Toddyhigh," cried the visitor. "Look at me, look hard at me — harder, harder. You know me now? you know little Joe again? What a happiness to us both, to meet the very night before your grandeur! Oh! give me your hand, Jack — both hands — both, for the sake of old times."

"You pinch me, sir. You 're a hurting of me," said the Lord Mayor elect pettishly. "Don't — suppose anybody should come — Mr. Toddyhigh, sir."

"Mr Toddyhigh!" repeated the other ruefully.

"Oh! don't bother," said the Lord Mayor elect, scratching his head. "Dear me! Why, I thought you was dead. What a fellow you are!"

Indeed, it was a pretty state of things, and worthy the tone of vexation and disappointment in which the Lord Mayor spoke. Joe Toddyhigh had been a poor boy with him at Hull, and had oftentimes divided his last penny and parted his last crust to relieve his wants; for though Joe was a destitute child in those times, he was as faithful and affectionate in his friendship as ever man of might could be. They parted one day to seek their fortunes in different directions. Joe went to sea, and the now wealthy citizen begged his way to London. They separated with many tears, like foolish fellows as they were, and agreed to remain fast friends, and if they lived, soon to communicate again.

When he was an errand-boy, and even in the early days of his apprenticeship, the citizen had many a time trudged to the Post-office to ask if there were any letter from poor little Joe, and had gone home again with tears in his eyes, when he found no news of his only friend. The world is a wide place, and it was a long time before the letter came; when it did, the writer was forgotten. It turned from white to yellow from lying in the Post-office with nobody to claim it, and in course of time was torn up with five hundred others, and sold for waste-paper. And now at last, and when it might least have been expected, here was this Joe Toddyhigh turning up and claiming acquaintance with a great public character, who on the morrow would be cracking jokes with the Prime Minister of England, and who had only, at any time during the next twelve months, to say the word, and he could shut up Temple Bar, and make it no thoroughfare for the king himself!

"I am sure I don't know what to say, Mr Toddyhigh," said the Lord Mayor elect; "I really don't. It 's very inconvenient. I 'd sooner have given twenty pound — it 's very inconvenient, really."

A thought had come into his mind that perhaps his old friend might say something passionate which would give him an excuse for being angry himself. No such thing. Joe looked at him steadily, but very mildly, and did not open his lips.

"Of course I shall pay you what I owe you," said the Lord Mayor elect, fidgeting in his chair. "You lent me — I think it was a shilling or some small coin — when we parted company, and that of course I shall pay, with good interest. I can pay my way with any man, and always have done. If you look into the Mansion House the day after to-morrow — some time after dusk — and ask for my private clerk, you 'll find he has a draft for you. I have n't got time to say anything more just now, unless" — he hesitated, for, coupled with a strong desire to glitter for once in all his glory in the eyes of his former companion, was a distrust of his appearance, which might be more shabby than he could tell by that feeble light — "unless you 'd like to come to the dinner to-morrow. I don't mind your having this ticket, if you like to take it. A great many people would give their ears for it, I can tell you."

His old friend took the card without speaking a word, and instantly departed. His sunburnt face and gray hair were present to the citizen's mind for a moment; but by the time he reached three hundred and eighty-one fat capons, he had quite forgotten him.

Joe Toddyhigh had never been in the capital of Europe before, and he wandered up and down the streets that night amazed at the number of churches and other public buildings, the splendor of the shops, the riches that were heaped up on every side, the glare of light in which they were displayed, and the concourse of people who hurried to and fro, indifferent, apparently, to all the wonders that surrounded them. But in all the long streets and broad squares, there were none but strangers; it was quite a relief to turn down a by-way and hear his own footsteps on the pavement. He went home to his inn; thought that London was a dreary, desolate place, and felt disposed to doubt the existence of one true-hearted man in the whole worshipful company of Patten-makers. Finally, he went to bed, and dreamed that he and the Lord Mayor elect were boys again.

He went next day to the dinner, and when, in a burst of light and music, and in the midst of splendid decorations and surrounded by brilliant company, his former friend appeared at the head of the Hall, and was hailed with shouts and cheering, he cheered and shouted with the best, and for the moment could have cried. The next moment he cursed his weakness in behalf of a man so changed and selfish, and quite hated a jolly-looking old gentleman opposite for declaring himself in the pride of his heart a Patten-maker.

As the banquet proceeded, he took more and more to heart the rich citizen's unkindness: and that, not from any envy, but because he felt that a man of his state and fortune could all the better afford to recognize an old friend, even if he were poor and obscure. The more he thought of this, the more lonely and sad he felt. When the company dispersed and adjourned to the ball-room, he paced the hall and passages alone ruminating in a very melancholy condition upon the disappointment he had experienced.

It chanced, while he was lounging about in this moody state, that he stumbled upon a flight of stairs, dark, steep, and narrow, which he ascended without any thought about the matter, and so came into a little music-gallery, empty and deserted. From this elevated post, which commanded the whole hall, he amused himself in looking down upon the attendants who were clearing away the fragments of the feast very lazily, and drinking out of all the bottles and glasses with most commendable perseverance.

His attention gradually relaxed, and he fell fast asleep.

When he awoke, he thought there must be something the matter with his eyes; but, rubbing them a little, he soon found that the moonlight was really streaming through the east window, that the lamps were all extinguished, and that he was alone. He listened, but no distant murmur in the echoing passages, not even the shutting of a door, broke the deep silence; he groped his way down the stairs, and found that the door at the bottom was locked on the other side. He began now to comprehend that he must have slept a long time, that he had been overlooked, and was shut up there for the night.

His first sensation, perhaps, was not altogether a comfortable one, for it was a dark, chilly, earthy-smelling place, and something too large, for a man so situated, to feel at home in. However, when the momentary consternation of his surprise was over, he made light of the accident, and resolved to feel his way up the stairs again, and make himself as comfortable as he could in the gallery until morning. As he turned to execute this purpose, he heard the clocks strike three.

Any such invasion of a dead stillness as the striking of distant clocks, causes it to appear the more intense and insupportable when the sound has ceased. He listened with strained attention in the hope that some clock, lagging behind its fellows, had yet to strike,—looking all the time into the profound darkness before him until it seemed to weave itself into a black tissue, patterned with a hundred reflections of his own eyes. But the bells had all pealed out their warning for that once, and the gust of wind that moaned through the place seemed cold and heavy with their iron breath.

The time and circumstances were favorable to reflection. He tried to keep his thoughts to the current, unpleasant though it was, in which they had moved all day, and to think with what a romantic feeling he had looked forward to shaking his old friend by the hand before he died, and what a wide and cruel difference there was between the meeting they had had, and that which he had so often and so long anticipated. Still, he was disordered by waking to such sudden loneliness, and could not prevent his mind from running upon odd tales of people of undoubted courage, who, being shut up by night in vaults or churches, or other dismal places, had scaled great heights to get out, and fled from silence as they had never done from danger. This brought to his mind the moonlight through the window, and bethinking himself of it, he groped his way back up the crooked stairs,—but very stealthily, as though he were fearful of being overheard.

He was very much astonished when he approached the gallery again, to see a light in the building: still more so, on advancing hastily and looking round, to observe no visible source from which it could proceed. But how much greater yet was his astonishment at the spectacle which this light revealed.

The statues of the two giants, Gog and Magog, each above fourteen feet in height, those which succeeded to still older and more barbarous figures after the Great Fire of London, and which stand in the Guildhall to this day, were endowed with life and motion. These guardian genii of the City had quitted their pedestals, and reclined in easy attitudes in the great stained-glass window. Between them was an ancient cask, which seemed to be full of wine; for the younger Giant, clapping his huge hand upon it, and throwing up his mighty leg, burst into an exulting laugh, which reverberated through the hall like thunder.

Joe Toddyhigh instinctively stooped down, and, more dead than alive, felt his hair stand on end, his knees knock together, and a cold damp break out upon his forehead. But even at that minute curiosity prevailed over every other feeling, and somewhat reassured by the good-humor of the Giants and their apparent unconsciousness of his presence, he crouched in a corner of the gallery, in as small a space as he could, and peeping between the rails, observed them closely.

It was then that the elder Giant, who had a flowing gray beard, raised his thoughtful eyes to his companion's face, and in a grave and solemn voice addressed him thus: —

FIRST NIGHT OF THE GIANT CHRONICLES.

Turning towards his companion, the elder Giant uttered these words in a grave, majestic tone: —

"Magog, does boisterous mirth beseem the Giant Warder of this ancient city? Is this becoming demeanor for a watchful spirit over whose bodiless head so many years have rolled, so many changes swept like empty air,— in whose impalpable nostrils the scent of blood and crime, pestilence, cruelty and horror, has been familiar as breath to mortals, — in whose sight Time has gathered in the harvest of centuries, and garnered so many crops of human pride, affections, hopes, and sorrows? Bethink you of our compact. The night wanes; feasting, revelry, and music have encroached upon our usual hours of solitude, and morning will be here apace. Ere we are stricken mute again, bethink you of our compact."

Pronouncing these latter words with more of impatience than quite accorded with his apparent age and gravity, the Giant raised a long pole (which he still bears in his hand) and tapped his brother Giant rather smartly on the head; indeed, the blow was so smartly administered, that the latter quickly withdrew his lips from the cask to which they had been applied, and catching up his shield and halberd assumed an attitude of defence. His irritation was but momentary, for he laid these weapons aside as hastily as he had assumed them, and said as he did so: —

"You know, Gog, old friend, that when we animate these shapes which the Londoners of old assigned (and not unworthily) to the guardian genii of their city, we are susceptible of some of the sensations which belong to human kind. Thus when I taste wine, I feel blows; when I relish the one, I disrelish the other. Therefore, Gog, the more especially as your arm is none of the lightest, keep your good staff by your side, else we may chance to differ. Peace be between us."

"Amen!" said the other, leaning his staff in the window-corner. "Why did you laugh just now?"

"To think," replied the Giant Magog, laying his hand upon the cask, "of him who owned this wine, and kept it in a cellar hoarded from the light of day, for thirty years, — 'till it should be fit to drink,' quoth he. He was two score and ten years old when he buried it beneath his house, and yet never thought that he might be scarcely 'fit to drink' when the wine became so. I wonder it never occurred to him to make himself unfit to be eaten. There is very little of him left by this time."

"The night is waning," said Gog mournfully.

"I know it," replied his companion, "and I see you are impatient. But look. Through the eastern window — placed opposite to us, that the first beams of the rising sun may every morning gild our giant faces — the moon-rays fall upon the pavement in a stream of light that to my fancy sinks through the cold stone and gushes into the old crypt below. The night is scarcely past its noon, and our great charge is sleeping heavily."

They ceased to speak, and looked upward at the moon. The sight of their large, black, rolling eyes filled Joe Toddyhigh with such horror that he could scarcely draw his breath. Still they took no note of him, and appeared to believe themselves quite alone.

"Our compact," said Magog after a pause, "is, if I understand it, that, instead of watching here in silence through the dreary nights, we entertain each other with stories of our past experience; with tales of the past, the present, and the future; with legends of London and her sturdy citizens from the old simple times. That every night at midnight, when St. Paul's bell tolls out one and we may move and speak, we thus discourse, nor leave such themes till the first gray gleam of day shall strike us dumb. Is that our bargain, brother?"

"Yes," said the Giant Gog, "that is the league between us who guard this city, by day in spirit, and by night in body also; and never on ancient holidays have its conduits run wine more merrily than we will pour forth our legendary lore. We are old chroniclers from this time hence. The crumbled walls encircle us once more, the postern gates are closed, the drawbridge is up, and pent in its narrow den beneath, the water foams and struggles with the sunken starlings. Jerkins and quarter-staves are in the streets again, the nightly watch is set, the rebel, sad and lonely in his Tower dungeon, tries to sleep and weeps for home and children. Aloft upon the gates and walls are noble heads glaring fiercely down upon the dreaming city, and vexing the hungry dogs that scent them in the air, and tear the ground beneath with dismal howlings. The axe, the block, the rack, in their dark chambers give signs of recent use. The Thames, floating past long lines of cheerful windows whence comes a burst of music and a stream of light, bears sullenly to the Palace wall the last red stain brought on the tide from Traitor's Gate. But your pardon, brother. The night wears, and I am talking idly."

The other Giant appeared to be entirely of this opinion, for during the foregoing rhapsody of his fellow-sentinel he had been scratching his head with an air of comical uneasiness, or rather with an air that would have been very comical if he had been a dwarf or an ordinary-sized man. He winked, too, and though it could not be doubted for a moment that he winked to himself, still, he certainly cocked his enormous eye towards the gallery where the listener was concealed. Nor was this all, for he gaped; and when he gaped, Joe was horribly reminded of the popular prejudice on the subject of giants, and of their fabled power of smelling out Englishmen, however closely concealed.

His alarm was such that he nearly swooned, and it was some little time before his power of sight or hearing was restored. When he recovered he found that the elder Giant was pressing the younger to commence the Chronicles, and that the latter was endeavoring to excuse himself, on the ground that the night was far spent and it would be better to wait until the next. Well assured by this that he was certainly about to begin directly, the listener collected his faculties by a great effort, and distinctly heard Magog express himself to the following effect: —

In the sixteenth century and in the reign of Queen Elizabeth of glorious memory (albeit her golden days are sadly rusted with blood), there lived in the city of London a bold young 'prentice who loved his master's daughter. There were no doubt within the walls a great many prentices in this condition, but I speak of only one, and his name was Hugh Graham.

This Hugh was apprenticed to an honest Bowyer who dwelt in the ward of Cheype and was rumored to possess great wealth. Rumor was quite as infallible in those days as at the present time, but it happened then as now to be sometimes right by accident. It stumbled upon the truth when it gave the old Bowyer a mint of money. His trade had been a profitable one in the time of King Henry the Eighth, who encouraged English archery to the utmost, and he had been prudent and discreet. Thus it came to pass that Mistress Alice, his only daughter, was the richest heiress in all his wealthy ward Young Hugh had often maintained with staff and cudgel that she was the handsomest. To do him justice, I believe she was.

If he could have gained the heart of pretty Mistress Alice by knocking this conviction into stubborn people's heads, Hugh would have had no cause to fear. But though the Bowyer's daughter smiled in secret to hear of his doughty deeds for her sake, and though her little waiting-woman reported all her smiles (and many more) to Hugh, and though he was at a vast expense in kisses and small coin to recompense her fidelity, he made no progress in his love. He durst not whisper it to Mistress Alice save on sure encouragement, and that she never gave him. A glance of her dark eye as she sat at the door on a summer's evening after prayer-time, while he and the neighboring 'prentices exercised themselves in the street with blunted sword and buckler, would fire Hugh's blood so that none could stand before him; but then she glanced at others quite as kindly as on him, and where was the use of cracking crowns if Mistress Alice smiled upon the cracked as well as on the cracker?

Still Hugh went on, and loved her more and more. He thought of her all day, and dreamed of her all night long. He treasured up her every word and gesture, and had a palpitation of the heart whenever he heard her footstep on the stairs or her voice in an adjoining room. To him, the old Bowyer's house was haunted by an angel; there was enchantment in the air and space in which she moved. It would have been no miracle to Hugh if flowers had sprung from the rush-strewn floors beneath the tread of lovely Mistress Alice.

Never did 'prentice long to distinguish himself in the eyes of his lady-love so ardently as Hugh. Sometimes he pictured to himself the house taking fire by night, and he, when all drew back in fear, rushing through flame and smoke and bearing her from the ruins in his arms. At other times he thought of a rising of fierce rebels, an attack upon the city, a strong assault upon the Bowyer's house in particular, and he falling on the threshold pierced with numberless wounds in defence of Mistress Alice. If he could only enact some prodigy of valor, do some wonderful deed, and let her know that she had inspired it, he thought he could die contented.

Sometimes the Bowyer and his daughter would go out to supper with a worthy citizen at the fashionable hour of six o'clock, and on such occasions Hugh, wearing his blue 'prentice cloak as gallantly as 'prentice might, would attend with a lantern and his trusty club to escort them home. These were the brightest moments of his life. To hold the light while Mistress Alice picked her steps, to touch her hand as he helped her over broken ways, to have her leaning on his arm, — it sometimes even came to that, — this was happiness indeed!

When the nights were fair, Hugh followed in the rear, his eyes riveted on the graceful figure of the Bowyer's daughter as she and the old man moved on before him. So they threaded the narrow winding streets of the city, now passing beneath the overhanging gables of old wooden houses whence creaking signs projected into the street, and now emerging from some dark and frowning gateway into the clear moonlight. At such times, or when the shouts of straggling brawlers met her ear, the Bowyer's daughter would look timidly back at Hugh beseeching him to draw nearer; and then how he grasped his club and longed to do battle with a dozen rufflers, for the love of Mistress Alice!

The old Bowyer was in the habit of lending money on interest to the gallants of the Court, and thus it happened that many a richly dressed gentleman dismounted at his door. More waving plumes and gallant steeds, indeed, were seen at the Bowyer's house, and more embroidered silks and velvets sparkled in his dark shop and darker private closet, than at any merchant's in the city. In those times no less than in the present it would seem that the richest-looking cavaliers often wanted money the most.

Of these glittering clients there was one who always came alone. He was always nobly mounted, and having no attendant gave his horse in charge to Hugh while he and the Bowyer were closeted within. Once as he sprung into the saddle Mistress Alice was seated at an upper window, and before she could withdraw he had doffed his jewelled cap and kissed his hand. Hugh watched him caracoling down the street, and burnt with indignation. But how much deeper was the glow that reddened in his cheeks when, raising his eyes to the casement, he saw that Alice watched the stranger too!

He came again and often, each time arrayed more gayly than before, and still the little casement showed him Mistress Alice. At length one heavy day, she fled from home. It had cost her a hard struggle, for all her old father's gifts were strewn about her chamber as if she had parted from them one by one, and knew that the time must come when these tokens of his love would wring her heart, — yet she was gone.

She left a letter commending her poor father to the care of Hugh, and wishing he might be happier than he could ever have been with her, for he deserved the love of a better and a purer heart than she had to bestow. The old man's forgiveness (she said) she had no power to ask, but she prayed God to bless him, — and so ended with a blot upon the paper where her tears had fallen.

At first the old man's wrath was kindled, and he carried his wrong to the Queen's throne itself; but there was no redress he learnt at Court, for his daughter had been conveyed abroad. This afterwards appeared to be the truth, as there came from France, after an interval of several years, a letter in her hand. It was written in trembling characters, and almost illegible. Little could be made out save that she often thought of home and her old dear pleasant room, — and that she had dreamt her father was dead and had not blessed her, — and that her heart was breaking.

The poor old Bowyer lingered on, never suffering Hugh to quit his sight, for he knew now that he had loved his daughter, and that was the only link that bound him to earth. It broke at length and he died, bequeathing his old 'prentice his trade and all his wealth, and solemnly charging him with his last breath to revenge his child if ever he who had worked her misery crossed his path in life again.

From the time of Alice's flight, the tilting-ground, the fields, the fencing-school, the summer-evening sports, knew Hugh no more. His spirit was dead within him. He rose to great eminence and repute among the citizens, but was seldom seen to smile, and never mingled in their revelries or rejoicings. Brave, humane, and generous, he was beloved by all He was pitied too by those who knew his story, and these were so many that when he walked along the streets alone at dusk, even the rude common people doffed their caps and mingled a rough air of sympathy with their respect.

One night in May — it was her birthnight and twenty years since she had left her home — Hugh Graham sat in the room she had hallowed in his boyish days. He was now a gray-haired man, though still in the prime of life. Old thoughts had borne him company for many hours, and the chamber had gradually grown quite dark, when he was roused by a low knocking at the outer door.

He hastened down, and opening it, saw by the light of a lamp which he had seized upon the way, a female figure crouching in the portal. It hurried swiftly past him and glided up the stairs. He looked for pursuers. There were none in sight. No, not one.

He was inclined to think it a vision of his own brain, when suddenly a vague suspicion of the truth flashed upon his mind. He barred the door and hastened wildly back. Yes, there she was, — there, in the chamber he had quitted, — there in her old innocent happy home, so changed that none but he could trace one gleam of what she had been, — there upon her knees, — with her hands clasped in agony and shame before her burning face.

"My God, my God!" she cried, "now strike me dead! Though I have brought death and shame and sorrow on this roof, oh, let me die at home in mercy!"

There was no tear upon her face then, but she trembled and glanced round the chamber. Everything was in its old place. Her bed looked as if she had risen from it but that morning. The sight of these familiar objects, marking the dear remembrance in which she had been held, and the blight she had brought upon herself, was more than the woman's better nature that had carried her there could bear. She wept and fell upon the ground.

A rumor was spread about, in a few days' time, that the Bowyer's cruel daughter had come home, and that Master Graham had given her lodging in his house. It was rumored too that he had resigned her fortune, in order that she might bestow it in acts of charity; and that he had vowed to guard her in her solitude, but that they were never to see each other more. These rumors greatly incensed all virtuous wives and daughters in the ward, especially when they appeared to receive some corroboration from the circumstance of Master Graham taking up his abode in another tenement hard by. The estimation in which he was held, however, forbade any questioning on the subject; and as the Bowyer's house was close shut up, and nobody came forth when public shows and festivities were in progress, or to flaunt in the public walks, or to buy new fashions at the mercers' booths, all the well-conducted females agreed among themselves that there could be no woman there.

These reports had scarcely died away when the wonder of every good citizen, male and female, was utterly absorbed and swallowed up by a Royal Proclamation, in which her Majesty, strongly censuring the practice of wearing long Spanish rapiers of preposterous length (as being a bullying and swaggering custom, tending to bloodshed and public disorder), commanded that on a particular day therein named, certain grave citizens should repair to the city gates, and there, in public, break all rapiers worn or carried by persons claiming admission, that exceeded, though it were only by a quarter of an inch, three standard feet in length.

Royal Proclamations usually take their course, let the public wonder never so much. On the appointed day two citizens of high repute took up their stations at each of the gates, attended by a party of the city guard: the main body to enforce the Queen's will, and take custody of all such rebels (if any) as might have the temerity to dispute it; and a few to bear the standard measures and instruments for reducing all unlawful sword-blades to the prescribed dimensions. In pursuance of these arrangements, Master Graham and another were posted at Lud Gate, on the hill before Saint Paul's.

A pretty numerous company were gathered together at this spot, for, besides the officers in attendance to enforce the proclamation, there was a motley crowd of lookers-on of various degrees, who raised from time to time such shouts and cries as the circumstances called forth. A spruce young courtier was the first who approached; he unsheathed a weapon of burnished steel that shone and glistened in the sun, and handed it with the newest air to the officer, who, finding it exactly three feet long, returned it with a bow. Thereupon the gallant raised his hat and crying "God save the Queen," passed on amidst the plaudits of the mob. Then came another — a better courtier still — who wore a blade but two feet long, whereat the people laughed, much to the disparagement of his honor's dignity. Then came a third, a sturdy old officer of the army, girded with a rapier at least a foot and a half beyond her Majesty's pleasure; at him they raised a great shout and most of the spectators (but especially those who were armorers or cutlers) laughed very heartily at the breakage which would ensue. But they were disappointed, for the old campaigner, coolly unbuckling his sword and bidding his servant carry it home again, passed through unarmed, to the great indignation of all the beholders. They relieved themselves in some degree by hooting a tall blustering fellow with a prodigious weapon, who stopped short on coming in sight of the preparations, and after a little consideration turned back again; but all this time no rapier had been broken although it was high noon, and all cavaliers of any quality or appearance were taking their way towards St. Paul's churchyard.

During these proceedings Master Graham had stood apart, strictly confining himself to the duty imposed upon him, and taking little heed of anything beyond. He stepped forward now as a richly dressed gentleman on foot, followed by a single attendant, was seen advancing up the hill.

As this person drew nearer, the crowd stopped their clamor, and bent forward with eager looks. Master Graham standing alone in the gateway, and the stranger coming slowly towards him, they seemed, as it were, set face to face. The nobleman (for he looked one) had a haughty and disdainful air, which bespoke the slight estimation in which he held the citizen. The citizen on the other hand preserved the resolute bearing of one who was not to be frowned down or daunted, and who cared very little for any nobility but that of worth and manhood. It was perhaps some consciousness on the part of each, of these feelings in the other, that infused a more stern expression into their regards as they came closer together.

"Your rapier, worthy sir!"

At the instant that he pronounced these words Graham started, and falling back some paces, laid his hand upon the dagger in his belt.

"You are the man whose horse I used to hold before the Bowyer's door? You are that man? Speak!"

"Out, you 'prentice hound!" said the other.

"You are he! I know you well now!" cried Graham. "Let no man step between us two, or I shall be his murderer." With that he drew his dagger and rushed in upon him.

The stranger had drawn his weapon from the scabbard ready for the scrutiny, before a word was spoken. He made a thrust at his assailant, but the dagger which Graham clutched in his left hand being the dirk in use at that time for parrying such blows, promptly turned the point aside They closed. The dagger fell rattling upon the ground, and Graham wresting his adversary's sword from his grasp, plunged it through his heart As he drew it out it snapped in two, leaving a fragment in the dead man's body.

All this passed so swiftly that the bystanders looked on without an effort to interfere , but the man was no sooner down than an uproar broke forth which rent the air. The attendant rushing through the gate proclaimed that his master, a nobleman, had been set upon and slain by a citizen ; the word quickly spread from mouth to mouth , Saint Paul's Cathedral, and every book shop, ordinary, and smoking-house in the churchyard poured out its stream of cavaliers and their followers, who, mingling together in a dense tumultuous body, struggled, sword in hand, towards the spot.

With equal impetuosity, and stimulating each other by loud cries and shouts, the citizens and common people took up the quarrel on their side, and encircling Master Graham a hundred deep, forced him from the gate. In vain he waved the broken sword above his head, crying that he would die on London's threshold for their sacred homes. They bore him on, and ever keeping him in the midst so that no man could attack him, fought their way into the city.

The clash of swords and roar of voices, the dust and heat and pressure, the trampling under foot of men, the distracted looks and shrieks of women at the windows above as they recognized their relatives or lovers in the crowd, the rapid tolling of alarm bells, the furious rage and passion of the scene, were fearful. Those who, being on the outskirts of each crowd, could use their weapons with effect, fought desperately, while those behind, maddened with baffled rage, struck at each other over the heads of those before them, and crushed their own fellows. Wherever the broken sword was seen above the people's heads, towards that spot the cavaliers made a new rush. Every one of these charges was marked by sudden gaps in the throng where men were trodden down, but as fast as they were made, the tide swept over them, and still the multitude pressed on again, a confused mass of swords, clubs, staves, broken plumes, fragments of rich cloaks and doublets and angry bleeding faces, all mixed up together in inextricable disorder.

The design of the people was to force Master Graham to take refuge in his dwelling, and to defend it until the authorities could interfere or they could gain time for parley. But either from ignorance or in the confusion of the moment they stopped at his old house, which was closely shut. Some time was lost in beating the doors open and passing him to the front. About a score of the boldest of the other party threw themselves into the torrent while this was being done, and reaching the door at the same moment with himself cut him off from his defenders.

" I never will turn in such a righteous cause, so help me Heaven! " cried Graham, in a voice that at last made itself heard, and confronting them as he spoke. " Least of all will I turn upon this threshold which owes its desolation to such men as ye. I give no quarter, and I will have none! Strike ! "

For a moment they stood at bay. At that moment a shot from an unseen hand, apparently fired by some person who had gained access to one of the opposite houses, struck Graham in the brain, and he fell dead. A low wail was heard in the air, — many people in the concourse cried that they had seen a spirit glide across the little casement window of the Bowyer's house —

A dead silence succeeded. After a short time some of the flushed and heated throng lay down their arms and softly carried the body within doors. Others fell off or slunk away in knots of two or three, others whispered together in groups, and before a numerous guard which then rode up could muster in the street, it was nearly empty.

Those who carried Master Graham to the bed up stairs were shocked to see a woman lying beneath the window with her hands clasped together After trying to recover her in vain, they laid her near the citizen, who still retained, tightly grasped in his right hand, the first and last sword that was broken that day at Lud Gate.

The Giant uttered these concluding words with sudden precipitation, and on the instant the strange light which had filled the hall faded away. Joe Toddyhigh glanced involuntarily at the eastern window and saw the first pale gleam of morning. He turned his head again towards the other window in which the Giants had been seated. It was empty. The cask of wine was gone, and he could dimly make out that the two great figures stood mute and motionless upon their pedestals.

After rubbing his eyes and wondering for full half an hour, during which time he observed morning come creeping on apace, he yielded to the drowsiness which overpowered him and fell into a refreshing slumber. When he awoke it was broad day; the building was open, and workmen were busily engaged in removing the vestiges of last night's feast.

Stealing gently down the little stairs and assuming the air of some early lounger who had dropped in from the street, he walked up to the foot of each pedestal in turn, and attentively examined the figure it supported. There could be no doubt about the features of either; he recollected the exact expression they had worn at different passages of their conversation, and recognized in every line and lineament the Giants of the night. Assured that it was no vision, but that he had heard and seen with his own proper senses, he walked forth, determining at all hazards to conceal himself in the Guildhall again that evening. He further resolved to sleep all day, so that he might be very wakeful and vigilant, and above all that he might take notice of the figures at the precise moment of their becoming animated and subsiding into their old state, which he greatly reproached himself for not having done already.

CORRESPONDENCE.

TO MASTER HUMPHREY.

"SIR, — Before you proceed any further in your account of your friends and what you say and do when you meet together, excuse me if I proffer my claim to be elected to one of the vacant chairs in that old room of yours. Don't reject me without full consideration, for if you do you 'll be sorry for it afterwards, — you will, upon my life.

"I enclose my card, sir, in this letter. I never was ashamed of my name, and I never shall be. I am considered a devilish gentlemanly fellow, and I act up to the character. If you want a reference, ask any of the men at our club. Ask any fellow who goes there to write his letters, what sort of conversation mine is. Ask him if he thinks I have the sort of voice that will suit your deaf friend and make him hear, if he can hear anything at all. Ask the servants what they think of me. There 's not a rascal among 'em, sir, but will tremble to hear my name. That reminds me, — don't you say too much about that housekeeper of yours; it 's a low subject, damned low.

"I tell you what, sir. If you vote me into one of those empty chairs, you 'll have among you a man with a fund of gentlemanly information that 'll rather astonish you. I can let you into a few anecdotes about some fine women of title, that are quite high life, sir, — the tiptop sort of thing. I know the name of every man who has been out on an affair of honor within the last five-and-twenty years; I know the private particulars of every cross and squabble that has taken place upon the turf, at the gaming-table or elsewhere, during the whole of that time. I have been called the gentlemanly chronicle. You may consider yourself a lucky dog; upon my soul you may congratulate yourself, though I say so.

"It 's an uncommon good notion that of yours, not letting anybody know where you live. I have tried it, but there has always been an anxiety respecting me which has found me out. Your deaf friend is a cunning fellow to keep his name so close I have tried that too, but have always failed. I shall be proud to make his acquaintance, — tell him so, with my compliments.

"You must have been a queer fellow when you were a child, confounded queer. It 's odd all that about the picture in your first paper, — prosy, but told in a devilish gentlemanly sort of way. In places like that, I could come in with great effect with a touch of life — Don't you feel that?

"I am anxiously waiting for your next paper to know whether your friends live upon the premises, and at your expense, which I take it for granted is the case. If I am right in this impression, I know a charming fellow (an excellent companion and most delightful company) who will be proud to join you. Some years ago he seconded a great many prize-fighters, and once fought an amateur match himself; since then, he has driven several mails, broken at different periods all the lamps on the right-hand side of Oxford Street, and six times carried away every bell-handle in Bloomsbury Square, besides turning off the gas in various thoroughfares. In point of gentlemanliness he is unrivalled, and I should say that next to myself he is of all men the best suited to your purpose.

"Expecting your reply,

"I am,

"&c., &c."

Master Humphrey informs this gentleman that his application, both as it concerns himself and his friend, is rejected.

MASTER HUMPHREY'S CLOCK.

II.

MASTER HUMPHREY FROM HIS CLOCK-SIDE IN THE CHIMNEY-CORNER.

MY old companion tells me it is midnight The fire glows brightly, crackling with a sharp and cheerful sound, as if it loved to burn. The merry cricket on the hearth (my constant visitor), this ruddy blaze, my clock, and I, seem to share the world among us, and to be the only things awake. The wind, high and boisterous but now, has died away and hoarsely mutters in its sleep. I love all times and seasons each in its turn, and am apt perhaps to think the present one the best; but past or coming, I always love this peaceful time of night, when long-buried thoughts, favored by the gloom and silence, steal from their graves, and haunt the scenes of faded happiness and hope.

The popular faith in ghosts has a remarkable affinity with the whole current of our thoughts at such an hour as this, and seems to be their necessary and natural consequence. For who can wonder that man should feel a vague belief in tales of disembodied spirits wandering through those places which they once dearly affected, when he himself, scarcely less separated from his old world than they, is forever lingering upon past emotions and bygone times, and hovering, the ghost of his former self, about the places and people that warmed his heart of old? It is thus that at this quiet hour I haunt the house where I was born, the rooms I used to tread, the scenes of my infancy, my boyhood, and my youth; it is thus that I prowl around my buried treasure (though not of gold or silver) and mourn my loss; it is thus that I revisit the ashes of extinguished fires, and take my silent stand at old bedsides. If my spirit should ever glide back to this chamber when my body is mingled with the dust, it will but follow the course it often took in the old man's lifetime, and add but one more change to the subjects of its contemplation.

In all my idle speculations I am greatly assisted by various legends connected with my venerable house, which are current in the neighborhood, and are so numerous that there is scarce a cupboard or corner that has not some dismal story of its own. When I first entertained thoughts of becoming its tenant I was assured that it was haunted from roof to cellar, and I believe the bad opinion in which my neighbors once held me had its rise in my not being torn to pieces, or at least distracted with terror, on the night I took possession: in either of which cases I should doubtless have arrived by a short cut at the very summit of popularity.

But traditions and rumors all taken into account, who so abets me in every fancy and chimes with my every thought, as my dear deaf friend; and how often have I cause to bless the day that brought us two together! Of all days in the year I rejoice to think that it should have been Christmas Day, with which from childhood we associate something friendly, hearty, and sincere.

I had walked out to cheer myself with the happiness of others, and, in the little tokens of festivity and rejoicing, of which the streets and houses present so many upon that day, had lost some hours. Now I stopped to look at a merry party hurrying through the snow on foot to their place of meeting, and now turned back to see a whole coachful of children safely deposited at the welcome house At one time, I admired how carefully the workingman carried the baby in its gaudy hat and feathers, and how his wife, trudging patiently on behind, forgot even her care of her gay clothes, in exchanging greetings with the child as it crowed and laughed over the father's shoulder ; at another, I pleased myself with some passing scene of gallantry or courtship, and was glad to believe that for a season half the world of poverty was gay.

As the day closed in, I still rambled through the streets, feeling a companionship in the bright fires that cast their warm reflection on the windows as I passed, and losing all sense of my own loneliness in imagining the sociality and kind-fellowship that everywhere prevailed. At length I happened to stop before a Tavern, and encountering a Bill of Fare in the window, it all at once brought it into my head to wonder what kind of people dined alone in Taverns upon Christmas Day.

Solitary men are accustomed, I suppose, unconsciously to look upon solitude as their own peculiar property. I had sat alone in my room on many, many anniversaries of this great holiday, and had never regarded it but as one of universal assemblage and rejoicing. I had excepted, and with an aching heart, a crowd of prisoners and beggars, but *these* were not the men for whom the Tavern doors were open. Had they any customers or was it a mere form? — a form no doubt.

Trying to feel quite sure of this, I walked away, but before I had gone many paces, I stopped and looked back. There was a provoking air of business in the lamp above the door which I could not overcome. I began to be afraid there might be many customers, — young men perhaps struggling with the world, utter strangers in this great place, whose friends lived at a long distance off, and whose means were too slender to enable them to make the journey. The supposition gave rise to so many distressing little pictures, that, in preference to carrying them home with me, I determined to encounter the realities. So I turned, and walked in.

I was at once glad and sorry to find that there was only one person in the dining-room ; glad to know that there were not more, and sorry that he should be there by himself. He did not look so old as I, but like me he was advanced in life, and his hair was nearly white. Though I made more noise in entering and seating myself than was quite necessary, with the view of attracting his attention and saluting him in the good old form of that time of year, he did not raise his head but sat with it resting on his hand, musing over his half-finished meal

I called for something which would give me an excuse for remaining in the room (I had dined early, as my housekeeper was engaged at night to partake of some friend's good cheer), and sat where I could observe without intruding on him. After a time he looked up. He was aware that somebody had entered, but could see very little of me as I sat in the shade and he in the light. He was sad and thoughtful, and I forbore to trouble him by speaking.

Let me believe that it was something better than curiosity which riveted my attention and impelled me strongly towards this gentleman. I never saw so patient and kind a face. He should have been surrounded by friends and yet here he sat dejected and alone when all men had their friends about them. As often as he roused himself from his revery he would fall into it again, and it was plain that whatever were the subject of his thoughts they were of a melancholy kind, and would not be controlled.

He was not used to solitude. I was sure of that, for I know by myself that if he had been, his manner would have been different, and he would have taken some slight interest in the arrival of another. I could not fail to mark that he had no appetite; that he tried to eat in vain; that time after time the plate was pushed away, and he relapsed into his former posture.

His mind was wandering among old Christmas Days, I thought. Many of them sprung up together, not with a long gap between each, but in unbroken succession like days of the week. It was a great change to find himself for the first time (I quite settled that it *was* the first) in an empty silent room with no soul to care for. I could not help following him in imagination through crowds of pleasant faces, and then coming back to that dull place with its bough of mistletoe sickening in the gas, and sprigs of holly parched up already by a Simoom of roast and boiled. The very waiter had gone home, and his representative, a poor, lean, hungry man, was keeping Christmas in his jacket.

I grew still more interested in my friend. His dinner done, a decanter of wine was placed before him. It remained untouched for a long time, but at length with a quivering hand he filled a glass and raised it to his lips. Some tender wish to which he had been accustomed to give utterance on that day, or some beloved name that he had been used to pledge, trembled upon them at the moment. He put it down very hastily, — took it up once more, — again put it down, — pressed his hand upon his face — yes — and tears stole down his cheeks, I am certain

Without pausing to consider whether I did right or wrong, I stepped across the room, and sitting down beside him laid my hand gently on his arm.

"My friend," I said, "forgive me if I beseech you to take comfort and consolation from the lips of an old man. I will not preach to you what I have not practised, indeed. Whatever be your grief, be of a good heart, — be of a good heart, pray!"

"I see that you speak earnestly," he replied, "and kindly I am very sure, but — "

I nodded my head to show that I understood what he would say, for I had already gathered from a certain fixed expression in his face, and from the attention with which he watched me while I spoke, that his sense of hearing was destroyed. "There should be a freemasonry between us," said I, pointing from himself to me to explain my meaning; "if not in our gray hairs, at least in our misfortunes. You see that I am but a poor cripple."

I never felt so happy under my affliction since the trying moment of my first becoming conscious of it, as when he took my hand in his with a smile that has lighted my path in life from that day, and we sat down side by side.

This was the beginning of my friendship with the deaf gentleman, and when was ever the slight and easy service of a kind word in season, repaid by such attachment and devotion as he has shown to me!

He produced a little set of tablets and a pencil to facilitate our conversation, on that our first acquaintance, and I well remember how awkward and constrained I was in writing down my share of the dialogue, and how easily he guessed my meaning before I had written half of what I had to say. He told me in a faltering voice that he had not been accustomed to be alone on that day, — that it had always been a little festival with him, — and seeing that I glanced at his dress in the expectation that he wore mourning he added hastily that it was not that; if it had been, he thought he could have borne it better. From that time to the present we have never touched upon this theme. Upon every return of the same day we have been together; and although we make it our annual custom to drink to each other hand in hand after dinner, and to recall with affectionate garrulity every circumstance of our first meeting, we always avoid this one as if by mutual consent

Meantime we have gone on strengthening in our friendship and regard, and forming an attachment which, I trust and believe, will only be interrupted by death, to be renewed in another existence. I scarcely know how we communicate as we do, but he has long since ceased to be deaf to me. He is frequently the companion of my walks, and even in crowded streets replies to my slightest look or gesture as though he could read my thoughts. From the vast number of objects which pass in rapid succession before our eyes, we frequently select the same for some particular notice or remark; and when one of these little coincidences occurs, I cannot describe the pleasure which animates my friend, or the beaming countenance he will preserve for half an hour afterwards at least.

He is a great thinker from living so much within himself, and having a lively imagination, has a facility of conceiving and enlarging upon odd ideas, which renders him invaluable to our little body, and greatly astonishes our two friends. His powers in this respect are much assisted by a large pipe, which he assures us once belonged to a German Student. Be this as it may, it has undoubtedly a very ancient and mysterious appearance, and is of such capacity that it takes three hours and a half to smoke it out. I have reason to believe that my barber, who is the chief authority of a knot of gossips who congregate every evening at a small tobacconist's hard by, has related anecdotes of this pipe and the grim figures that are carved upon its bowl at which all the smokers in the neighborhood have stood aghast; and I know that my housekeeper, while she holds it in high veneration, has a superstitious feeling connected with it which would render her exceedingly unwilling to be left alone in its company after dark.

Whatever sorrow my deaf friend has known, and whatever grief may linger in some secret corner of his heart, he is now a cheerful, placid, happy creature. Misfortune can never have fallen upon such a man but for some good purpose; and when I see its traces in his gentle nature and his earnest feeling, I am the less disposed to murmur at such trials as I may have undergone myself. With regard to the pipe, I have a theory of my own; I cannot help thinking that it is in some manner connected with the event that brought us together, for I remember that it was a long time before he even talked about it; that when he did, he grew reserved and melancholy; and that it was a long time yet before he brought it forth. I have no curiosity, however, upon this subject, for I know that it promotes his tranquillity and comfort, and I need no other inducement to regard it with my utmost favor.

Such is the deaf gentleman. I can call up his figure now, clad in sober gray, and seated in the chimney-corner. As he puffs out the smoke from his favorite pipe, he casts a look on me brimful of cordiality and friendship, and says all manner of kind and genial things in a cheerful smile; then he raises his eyes to my clock which is just about to strike, and glancing from it to me and back again, seems to divide his heart between us. For myself, it is not too much to say that I would gladly part with one of my poor limbs, could he but hear the old clock's voice.

Of our two friends the first has been all his life one of that easy, wayward, truant class whom the world is accustomed to designate as nobody's enemies but their own. Bred to a profession for which he never qualified himself, and reared in the expectation of a fortune he has never inherited, he has undergone every vicissitude of which such an existence is capable. He and his younger brother, both orphans from their childhood, were educated by a wealthy relative who taught them to expect an equal division of his property; but too indolent to court, and too honest to flatter, the elder gradually lost ground in the affections of a capricious old man, and the younger, who did not fail to improve his opportunity, now triumphs in the possession of enormous wealth His triumph is to hoard it in solitary wretchedness. and probably to feel with the expenditure of every shilling a greater pang than the loss of his whole inheritance ever cost his brother.

Jack Redburn — he was Jack Redburn at the first little school he went to, where every other child was mastered and surnamed, and he has been Jack Redburn all his life, or he would perhaps have been a richer man by this time — has been an inmate of my house these eight years past. He is my librarian, secretary, steward, and first minister; director of all my affairs and inspector-general of my household. He is something of a musician, something of an author, something of an actor, something of a painter, very much of a carpenter, and an extraordinary gardener; having had all his life a wonderful aptitude for learning everything that was of no use to him. He is remarkably fond of children, and is the best and kindest nurse in sickness that ever drew the breath of life. He has mixed with every grade of society and known the utmost distress, but there never was a less selfish, a more tender-hearted, a more enthusiastic, or a more guileless man; and I dare say if few have done less good, fewer still have done less harm in the world than he. By what chance Nature forms such whimsical jumbles I don't know, but I do know that she sends them among us very often, and that the king of the whole race is Jack Redburn.

I should be puzzled to say how old he is. His health is none of the best, and he wears a quantity of iron-gray hair which shades his face and gives it rather a worn appearance; but we consider him quite a young fellow notwithstanding, and if a youthful spirit surviving the roughest contact with the world confers upon its possessor any title to be considered young, then he is a mere child. The only interruptions to his careless cheerfulness are on a wet Sunday, when he is apt to be unusually religious and solemn, and sometimes of an evening when he has been blowing a very slow tune on the flute. On these last-named occasions he is apt to incline towards the mysterious or the terrible. As a specimen of his powers in this mood, I refer my readers to the extract from the clock-case which follows this paper: he brought it to me not long ago at midnight, and informed me that the main incident had been suggested by a dream of the night before.

His apartments are two cheerful rooms looking towards the garden, and one of his great delights is to arrange and rearrange the furniture in these chambers and put it in every possible variety of position. During the whole time he has been here, I do not think he has slept for two nights running with the head of his bed in the same place, and every time he moves it is to be the last. My housekeeper was at first wellnigh distracted by these frequent changes, but she has become quite reconciled to them by degrees, and has so fallen in with his humor that they often consult together with great gravity upon the next final alteration. Whatever his arrangements are, however, they are always a pattern of neatness, and every one of the manifold articles connected with his manifold occupations is to be found in its own particular place. Until within the last two or three years he was subject to an occasional fit (which usually came upon him in very fine weather), under the influence of which he would dress himself with peculiar care, and going out under pretence of taking a walk, disappear for several days together. At length after the interval between each outbreak of this disorder had gradually grown longer and longer, it wholly disappeared, and now he seldom stirs abroad except to stroll out a little way on a summer's evening. Whether he yet mistrusts his own constancy in this respect, and is therefore afraid to wear a coat, I know not; but we seldom see him in any other upper garment than an old spectral-looking dressing-gown with very disproportionate pockets, full of a miscellaneous collection of odd matters which he picks up wherever he can lay his hands upon them.

Everything that is a favorite with our friend is a favorite with us, and thus it happens that the fourth among us is Mr. Owen Miles, a most worthy gentleman who had treated Jack with great kindness before my deaf friend and I encountered him by an accident, to which I may refer on some future occasion. Mr. Miles was once a very rich merchant, but receiving a severe shock in the death of his wife, he retired from business and devoted himself to a quiet, unostentatious life. He is an excellent man of thoroughly sterling character: not of quick apprehension, and not without some amusing prejudices, which I shall leave to their own development. He holds us all in profound veneration, but Jack Redburn he esteems as a kind of pleasant wonder, that he may venture to approach familiarly. He believes, not only that no man ever lived who could do so many things as Jack, but that no man ever lived who could do anything so well; and he never calls my attention to any of his ingenious proceedings but he whispers in my ear, nudging me at the same time with his elbow, "If he had only made it his trade, sir, — if he had only made it his trade!"

They are inseparable companions; one would almost suppose that although Mr. Miles never by any chance does anything in the way of assistance, Jack could do nothing without him. Whether he is reading, writing, painting, carpentering, gardening, flute-playing, or what not, there is Mr. Miles beside him, buttoned up to the chin in his blue coat, and looking on with a face of incredulous delight, as though he could not credit the testimony of his own senses, and had a misgiving that no man could be so clever but in a dream.

These are my friends; I have now introduced myself and them.

THE CLOCK-CASE.

A CONFESSION FOUND IN A PRISON IN THE TIME OF CHARLES THE SECOND.

I HELD a lieutenant's commission in His Majesty's army, and served abroad in the campaigns of 1677 and 1678. The treaty of Nimeguen being concluded, I returned home, and retiring from the service withdrew to a small estate lying a few miles east of London, which I had recently acquired in right of my wife.

This is the last night I have to live, and I will set down the naked truth without disguise. I was never a brave man, and had always been from my childhood of a secret, sullen, distrustful nature. I speak of myself as if I had passed from the world, for while I write this my grave is digging and my name is written in the black book of death.

Soon after my return to England, my only brother was seized with mortal illness. This circumstance gave me slight or no pain, for since we had been men we had associated but very little together. He was open-hearted and generous, handsomer than I, more accomplished, and generally beloved. Those who sought my acquaintance abroad or at home, because they were friends of his, seldom attached themselves to me long, and would usually say in our first conversation that they were surprised to find two brothers so unlike in their manners and appearance. It was my habit to lead them on to this avowal, for I knew what comparisons they must draw between us; and having a rankling envy in my heart, I sought to justify it to myself.

We had married two sisters. This additional tie between us, as it may appear to some, only estranged us the more. His wife knew me well. I never struggled with any secret jealousy or gall when she was present, but that woman knew it as well as I did I never raised my eyes at such times but I found hers fixed upon me; I never bent them on the ground or looked another way, but I felt that she overlooked me always. It was an inexpressible relief to me when we quarrelled, and a greater relief still when I heard abroad that she was dead. It seems to me now as if some strange and terrible foreshadowing of what has happened since must have hung over us then. I was afraid of her; she haunted me; her fixed and steady look comes back upon me now, like the memory of a dark dream, and makes my blood run cold.

She died shortly after giving birth to a child, — a boy. When my brother knew that all hope of his own recovery was passed, he called my wife to his bedside and confided this orphan, a child of four years old, to her protection. He bequeathed to him all the property he had, and willed that in case of his child's death it should pass to my wife, as the only acknowledgment he could make her for her care and love. He exchanged a few brotherly words with me, deploring our long separation, and being exhausted fell into a slumber from which he never awoke.

We had no children, and as there had been a strong affection between the sisters, and my wife had almost supplied the place of a mother to this boy, she loved him as if he had been her own. The child was ardently attached to her; but he was his mother's image in face and spirit, and always mistrusted me.

I can scarcely fix the date when the feeling first came upon me, but I soon began to be uneasy when this child was by. I never roused myself from some moody train of thought but I marked him looking at me: not with mere childish wonder, but with something of the purpose and meaning that I had so often noted in his mother. It was no effort of my fancy, founded on close resemblance of feature and expression. I never could look the boy down. He feared me, but seemed by some instinct to despise me while he did so; and even when he drew back beneath my gaze, — as he would when we were alone, to get nearer to the door, — he would keep his bright eyes upon me still.

Perhaps I hide the truth from myself, but I do not think that when this began, I meditated to do him any wrong. I may have thought how serviceable his inheritance would be to us, and may have wished him dead, but I believe I had no thought of compassing his death. Neither did the idea come upon me at once, but by very slow degrees, presenting itself at first in dim shapes at a very great distance, as men may think of an earthquake or the last day, — then drawing nearer and nearer and losing something of its horror and improbability, — then coming to be part and parcel, nay, nearly the whole sum and substance of my daily thoughts, and resolving itself into a question of means and safety; not of doing or abstaining from the deed.

While this was going on within me, I never could bear that the child should see me looking at him, and yet I was under a fascination which made it a kind of business with me to contemplate his slight and fragile figure and think how easily it might be done. Sometimes I would steal up stairs and watch him as he slept, but usually I hovered in the garden near the window of the room in which he learnt his little tasks; and there, as he sat upon a low seat beside my wife, I would peer at him for hours together from behind a tree: starting like the guilty wretch I was at every rustling of a leaf, and still gliding back to look and start again.

Hard by our cottage, but quite out of sight, and (if there were any wind astir) of hearing too, was a deep sheet of water. I spent days in shaping with my pocket-knife a rough model of a boat, which I finished at last and dropped in the child's way. Then I withdrew to a secret place which he must pass if he stole away alone to swim this bauble, and lurked there for his coming. He came neither that day nor the next, though I waited from noon till nightfall. I was sure that I had him in my net, for I had heard him prattling of the toy and knew that in his infant pleasure he kept it by his side in bed. I felt no weariness or fatigue, but waited patiently, and on the third day he passed me, running joyously along, with his silken hair streaming in the wind, and he singing, — God have mercy upon me! — singing a merry ballad, — who could hardly lisp the words.

I stole down after him, creeping under certain shrubs which grow in that place, and none but devils know with what terror I, a strong, full-grown man, tracked the footsteps of that baby as he approached the water's brink I was close upon him, had sunk upon my knee and raised my hand to thrust him in, when he saw my shadow in the stream and turned him round.

His mother's ghost was looking from his eyes. The sun burst forth from behind a cloud: it shone in the bright sky, the glistening earth, the clear water, the sparkling drops of rain upon the leaves. There were eyes in everything. The whole great universe of light was there to see the murder done. I know not what he said; he came of bold and manly blood, and, child as he was, he did not crouch or fawn upon me. I heard him cry that he would try to love me, — not that he did, — and then I saw him running back towards the house. The next I saw was my own sword naked in my hand, and he lying at my feet stark dead, — dabbled here and there with blood, but otherwise no different from what I had seen him in his sleep, — in the same attitude too, with his cheek resting upon his little hand.

I took him in my arms and laid him — very gently now that he was dead — in a thicket. My wife was from home that day and would not return until the next. Our bedroom window, the only sleeping-room on that side of the house, was but a few feet from the ground, and I resolved to descend from it at night and bury him in the garden. I had no thought that I had failed in my design, no thought that the water would be dragged and nothing found, that the money must now lie waste since I must encourage the idea that the child was lost or stolen. All my thoughts were bound up and knotted together, in the one absorbing necessity of hiding what I had done.

How I felt when they came to tell me that the child was missing, when I ordered scouts in all directions, when I gasped and trembled at every one's approach, no tongue can tell or mind of man conceive. I buried him that night. When I parted the boughs and looked into the dark thicket, there was a glow-worm shining like the visible spirit of God upon the murdered child. I glanced down into his grave when I had placed him there, and still it gleamed upon his breast; an eye of fire looking up to Heaven in supplication to the stars that watched me at my work.

I had to meet my wife, and break the news, and give her hope that the child would soon be found. All this I did — with some appearance, I suppose, of being sincere, for I was the object of no suspicion. This done I sat at the bedroom window all day long, and watched the spot where the dreadful secret lay.

It was in a piece of ground which had been dug up to be newly turfed, and which I had chosen on that account, as the traces of my spade were less likely to attract attention. The men who laid down the grass must have thought me mad. I called to them continually to expedite their work, ran out and worked beside them, trod down the earth with my feet, and hurried them with frantic eagerness. They had finished their task before night, and then I thought myself comparatively safe.

I slept — not as men do who awake refreshed and cheerful, but I did sleep, passing from vague and shadowy dreams of being hunted down, to visions of the plot of grass, through which now a hand and now a foot and now the head itself was starting out. At this point I always woke and stole to the window, to make sure that it was not really so. That done I crept to bed again, and thus I spent the night in fits and starts, getting up and lying down full twenty times, and dreaming the same dream over and over again — which was far worse than lying awake, for every dream had a whole night's suffering of its own. Once I thought the child was alive and that I had never tried to kill him. To wake from that dream was the most dreadful agony of all.

The next day I sat at the window again, never once taking my eyes from the place, which, although it was covered by the grass, was as plain to me — its shape, its size, its depth, its jagged sides, and all — as if it had been open to the light of day. When a servant walked across it, I felt as if he must sink in; when he had passed, I looked to see that his feet had not worn the edges. If a bird lighted there, I was in terror lest by some tremendous interposition it should be instrumental in the discovery; if a breath of air sighed across it, to me it whispered murder. There was not a sight or a sound, — how ordinary, mean, or unimportant soever, — but was fraught with fear. And in this state of ceaseless watching I spent three days.

On the fourth, there came to the gate one who had served with me abroad, accompanied by a brother officer of his whom I had never seen. I felt that I could not bear to be out of sight of the place. It was a summer evening, and I bade my people take a table and a flask of wine into the garden Then I sat down *with my chair upon the grave*, and being assured that nobody could disturb it now, without my knowledge, tried to drink and talk.

They hoped that my wife was well, — that she was not obliged to keep her chamber, — that they had not frightened her away. What could I do but tell them with a faltering tongue about the child? The officer whom I did not know was a down-looking man, and kept his eyes upon the ground while I was speaking. Even that terrified me! I could not divest myself of the idea that he saw something there which caused him to suspect the truth. I asked him hurriedly if he supposed that — and stopped. "That the child has been murdered?" said he, looking mildly at me. "O no! what could a man gain by murdering a poor child?" *I* could have told him what a man gained by such a deed, no one better, but I held my peace and shivered as with an ague.

Mistaking my emotion they were endeavoring to cheer me with the hope that the boy would certainly be found — great cheer that was for me — when we heard a low deep howl, and presently there sprung over the wall two great dogs, who, bounding into the garden, repeated the baying sound we had heard before.

"Bloodhounds!" cried my visitors

What need to tell me that! I had never seen one of that kind in all my life, but I knew what they were and for what purpose they had come. I grasped the elbows of my chair, and neither spoke nor moved.

"They are of the genuine breed," said the man whom I had known abroad, "and being out for exercise have no doubt escaped from their keeper."

Both he and his friend turned to look at the dogs, who with their noses to the ground moved restlessly about, running to and fro, and up and down, and across, and round in circles, careering about like wild things, and all this time taking no notice of us, but ever and again repeating the yell we had heard already, then dropping their noses to the ground again and tracking earnestly here and there. They now began to snuff the earth more eagerly than they had done yet, and although they were still very restless, no longer beat about in such wide circuits, but kept near to one spot, and constantly diminished the distance between themselves and me.

At last they came up close to the great chair on which I sat, and raising their frightful howl once more, tried to tear away the wooden rails that kept them from the ground beneath. I saw how I looked, in the faces of the two who were with me.

"They scent some prey," said they, both together.

"They scent no prey!" cried I.

"In Heaven's name, move," said the one I knew, very earnestly, "or you will be torn to pieces."

"Let them tear me from limb to limb, I'll never leave this place!" cried I. "Are dogs to hurry men to shameful deaths? Hew them down, cut them in pieces."

"There is some foul mystery here!" said the officer whom I did not know, drawing his sword. "In King Charles's name, assist me to secure this man"

They both set upon me and forced me away, though I fought and bit and caught at them like a madman. After a struggle they got me quietly between them, and then, my God! I saw the angry dogs tearing at the earth and throwing it up into the air like water.

What more have I to tell? That I fell upon my knees and with chattering teeth confessed the truth and prayed to be forgiven. That I have since denied and now confess to it again. That I have been tried for the crime, found guilty, and sentenced. That I have not the courage to anticipate my doom or to bear up manfully against it. That I have no compassion, no consolation, no hope, no friend. That my wife has happily lost for the time those faculties which would enable her to know my misery or hers. That I am alone in this stone dungeon with my evil spirit, and that I die to-morrow! *

* * * * *

CORRESPONDENCE.

Master Humphrey has been favored with the following letter, written on strongly scented paper, and sealed in light blue wax with the representation of two very plump doves, interchanging beaks. It does not commence with any of the usual forms of address, but begins as is here set forth.

Bath, *Wednesday Night.*

Heavens! into what an indiscretion do I suffer myself to be betrayed! To address these faltering lines to a total stranger, and that stranger one of a conflicting sex! — and yet I am precipitated into the abyss, and have no power of self-snatchation (forgive me if I coin that phrase) from the yawning gulf before me.

Yes, I am writing to a man, but let me not think of that, for madness is in the thought. You will understand my feelings? O yes! I am sure you will! and you will respect them too, and not despise them, — will you?

Let me be calm. That portrait, — smiling as once he smiled on me; that cane, — dangling as I have seen it dangle from his hand I know not how oft; those legs

* Old Curiosity Shop begins here.

that have glided through my nightly dreams and never stopped to speak; the perfectly gentlemanly, though false original, — can I be mistaken? O no, no.

Let me be calmer yet; I would be calm as coffins. You have published a letter from one whose likeness is engraved, but whose name (and wherefore?) is suppressed. Shall *I* breathe that name! Is it — but why ask when my heart tells me too truly that it is!

I would not upbraid him with his treachery, I would not remind him of those times when he plighted the most eloquent of vows, and procured from me a small pecuniary accommodation; and yet I would see him — see him did I say — *him* — alas! such is woman's nature. For as the poet beautifully says — but you will already have anticipated the sentiment. Is it not sweet? O yes!

It was in this city (hallowed by the recollection) that I met him first, and assuredly if mortal happiness be recorded anywhere, then those rubbers with their three-and-sixpenny points are scored on tablets of celestial brass. He always held an honor, — generally two. On that eventful night, we stood at eight. He raised his eyes (luminous in their seductive sweetness) to my agitated face. "*Can* you?" said he, with peculiar meaning. I felt the gentle pressure of his foot on mine; our corns throbbed in unison. "*Can* you?" he said again, and every lineament of his expressive countenance added the words "resist me?" I murmured "No," and fainted.

They said when I recovered, it was the weather. *I* said it was the nutmeg in the negus. How little did they suspect the truth! How little did they guess the deep mysterious meaning of that inquiry! He called next morning on his knees: I do not mean to say that he actually came in that position to the house door, but that he went down upon those joints directly the servant had retired. He brought some verses in his hat which he said were original, but which I have since found were Milton's. Likewise a little bottle labelled laudanum: also a pistol and a swordstick. He drew the latter, uncorked the former, and clicked the trigger of the pocket fire-arm. He had come, he said, to conquer or to die. He did not die. He wrested from me an avowal of my love, and let off the pistol out of a back window previous to partaking of a slight repast.

Faithless, inconstant man! How many ages seem to have elapsed since his unaccountable and perfidious disappearance! Could I still forgive him both that and the borrowed lucre that he promised to pay next week! Could I spurn him from my feet if he approached in penitence, and with a matrimonial object! Would the blandishing enchanter still weave his spells around me, or should I burst them all and turn away in coldness! I dare not trust my weakness with the thought.

My brain is in a whirl again. You know his address, his occupations, his mode of life, — are acquainted, perhaps, with his inmost thoughts. You are a humane and philanthropic character; reveal all you know, — all; but especially the street and number of his lodgings. The post is departing, the bellman rings, — pray heaven it be not the knell of love and hope to

BELINDA.

P. S. Pardon the wanderings of a bad pen and a distracted mind. Address to the Post-office. The bellman, rendered impatient by delay, is ringing dreadfully in the passage.

P. P. S. I open this to say that the bellman is gone, and that you must not expect it till the next post; so don't be surprised when you don't get it.

Master Humphrey does not feel himself at liberty to furnish his fair correspondent with the address of the gentleman in question, but he publishes her letter as a public appeal to his faith and gallantry.

MASTER HUMPHREY'S CLOCK.

III.

MASTER HUMPHREY'S VISITOR.

WHEN I am in a thoughtful mood, I often succeed in diverting the current of some mournful reflections, by conjuring up a number of fanciful associations with the objects that surround me, and dwelling upon the scenes and characters they suggest.

I have been led by this habit to assign to every room in my house, and every old staring portrait on its walls, a separate interest of its own. Thus, I am persuaded that a stately dame, terrible to behold in her rigid modesty, who hangs above the chimney-piece of my bedroom, is the former lady of the mansion. In the court-yard below is a stone face of surpassing ugliness, which I have somehow — in a kind of jealousy, I am afraid — associated with her husband. Above my study is a little room with ivy peeping through the lattice, from which I bring their daughter, a lovely girl of eighteen or nineteen years of age, and dutiful in all respects save one, that one being her devoted attachment to a young gentleman on the stairs, whose grandmother (degraded to a disused laundry in the garden) piques herself upon an old family quarrel, and is the implacable enemy of their love With such materials as these, I work out many a little drama, whose chief merit is, that I can bring it to a happy end at will; I have so many of them on hand, that if on my return home one of these evenings I were to find some bluff old wight of two centuries ago comfortably seated in my easy-chair, and a love-lorn damsel vainly appealing to his heart and leaning her white arm upon my clock itself, I verily believe I should only express my surprise that they had kept me waiting so long, and never honored me with a call before.

I was, in such a mood as this, sitting in my garden yesterday morning under the shade of a favorite tree revelling in all the bloom and brightness about me, and feeling every sense of hope and enjoyment quickened by this most beautiful season of spring, when my meditations were interrupted by the unexpected appearance of my barber at the end of the walk, who I immediately saw was coming towards me with a hasty step that betokened something remarkable.

My barber is at all times a very brisk, bustling, active little man, — for he is, as it were, chubby all over, without being stout or unwieldy, — but yesterday his alacrity was so very uncommon that it quite took me by surprise. For could I fail to observe when he came up to me, that his gray eyes were twinkling in a most extraordinary manner, that his little red nose was in an unusual glow, that every line in his round, bright face was twisted and curved into an expression of pleased surprise, and that his whole countenance was radiant with glee? I was still more surprised to see my housekeeper, who usually preserves a very staid air, and stands somewhat upon her dignity, peeping round the hedge at the bottom of the walk, and exchanging nods and smiles with the barber, who twice or thrice looked over his shoulder for that purpose I could conceive no announcement to which these appearances could be the prelude, unless it were that they had married each other that morning.

I was, consequently, a little disappointed when it only came out that there was a gentleman in the house who wished to speak with me.

"And who is it?" said I.

The barber, with his face screwed up still tighter than before, replied that the gentleman would not send his name, but wished to see me. I pondered for a moment, wondering who this visitor might be, and I remarked that he embraced the opportunity of exchanging another nod with the housekeeper, who still lingered in the distance.

"Well!" said I, "bid the gentleman come here."

This seemed to be the consummation of the barber's hopes, for he turned sharp round, and actually ran away.

Now, my sight is not very good at a distance, and therefore when the gentleman first appeared in the walk, I was not quite clear whether he was a stranger to me or otherwise. He was an elderly gentleman, but came tripping along in the pleasantest manner conceivable, avoiding the garden-roller and the borders of the beds with inimitable dexterity, picking his way among the flower-pots, and smiling with unspeakable good-humor. Before he was half-way up the walk he began to salute me; then I thought I knew him; but when he came towards me with his hat in his hand, the sun shining on his bald head, his bland face, his bright spectacles, his fawn-colored tights, and his black gaiters, — then, my heart warmed towards him and I felt quite certain that it was Mr. Pickwick.

"My dear sir," said that gentleman as I rose to receive him, "pray be seated. Pray sit down. Now, do not stand on my account. I must insist upon it, really." With these words Mr. Pickwick gently pressed me down into my seat, and taking my hand in his, shook it again and again with a warmth of manner perfectly irresistible. I endeavored to express in my welcome something of that heartiness and pleasure which the sight of him awakened, and made him sit down beside me. All this time he kept alternately releasing my hand and grasping it again, and surveying me through his spectacles with such a beaming countenance as I never beheld.

"You knew me directly!" said Mr. Pickwick. "What a pleasure it is to think that you knew me directly!"

I remarked that I had read his adventures very often, and his features were quite familiar to me from the published portraits. As I thought it a good opportunity of adverting to the circumstance, I condoled with him upon the various libels on his character which had found their way into print. Mr. Pickwick shook his head, and for a moment looked very indignant, but smiling again directly, added that no doubt I was acquainted with Cervantes's introduction to the second part of Don Quixote, and that it fully expressed his sentiments on the subject.

"But now," said Mr. Pickwick, "don't you wonder how I found you out?"

"I shall never wonder, and, with your good leave, never know," said I, smiling in my turn. "It is enough for me that you give me this gratification. I have not the least desire that you should tell me by what means I have obtained it."

"You are very kind," returned Mr. Pickwick, shaking me by the hand again; "you are so exactly what I expected! But for what particular purpose do you think I have sought you, my dear sir? Now, what *do* you think I have come for?"

Mr. Pickwick put this question as though he were persuaded that it was morally impossible that I could by any means divine the deep purpose of his visit, and that it must be hidden from all human ken. Therefore, although I was rejoiced to think that I had anticipated his drift, I feigned to be quite ignorant of it, and after a brief consideration shook my head despairingly.

"What should you say," said Mr Pickwick, laying the forefinger of his left hand upon my coat-sleeve, and looking at me with his head thrown back, and a little on one side, — "what should you say if I confessed that after reading your account of yourself and your little society, I had come here, a humble candidate for one of those empty chairs?"

"I should say," I returned, "that I know of only one circumstance which could still further endear that little society to me, and that would be the associating with it my old friend, — for you must let me call you so, — my old friend, Mr. Pickwick."

As I made him this answer every feature of Mr. Pickwick's face fused itself into one all-pervading expression of delight. After shaking me heartily by both hands at once, he patted me gently on the back, and then — I well understood why — colored up to the eyes, and hoped with great earnestness of manner that he had not hurt me.

If he had I would have been content that he should have repeated the offence a hundred times rather than suppose so; but as he had not, I had no difficulty in changing the subject by making an inquiry which had been upon my lips twenty times already.

"You have not told me," said I, "anything about Sam Weller."

"Oh! Sam," replied Mr. Pickwick, "is the same as ever. The same true, faithful fellow that he ever was. What should I tell you about Sam my dear sir, except that he is more indispensable to my happiness and comfort every day of my life?"

"And Mr. Weller senior?" said I.

"Old Mr. Weller," returned Mr. Pickwick, "is in no respect more altered than Sam, unless it be that he is a little more opinionated than he was formerly, and perhaps at times more talkative. He spends a good deal of his time now in our neighborhood, and has so constituted himself a part of my body-guard, that when I ask permission for Sam to have a seat in your kitchen on clock nights (supposing your three friends think me worthy to fill one of the chairs), I am afraid I must often include Mr. Weller too."

I very readily pledged myself to give both Sam and his father a free admission to my house at all hours and seasons; and this point settled, we fell into a lengthy conversation which was carried on with as little reserve on both sides as if we had been intimate friends from our youth, and which conveyed to me the comfortable assurance that Mr. Pickwick's buoyancy of spirit, and indeed all his old cheerful characteristics, were wholly unimpaired. As he had spoken of the consent of my friends as being yet in abeyance, I repeatedly assured him that his proposal was certain to receive their most joyful sanction, and several times entreated that he would give me leave to introduce him to Jack Redburn and Mr. Miles (who were near at hand) without further ceremony.

To this proposal, however, Mr. Pickwick's delicacy would by no means allow him to accede, for he urged that his eligibility must be formally discussed, and that, until this had been done, he could not think of obtruding himself further. The utmost I could obtain from him was a promise that he would attend upon our next night of meeting, that I might have the pleasure of presenting him immediately on his election.

Mr. Pickwick, having with many blushes placed in my hands a small roll of paper, which he termed his "qualification," put a great many questions to me touching my friends, and particularly Jack Redburn, whom he repeatedly termed "a fine fellow," and in whose favor I could see he was strongly predisposed. When I had satisfied him on these points, I took him up into my room that he might make acquaintance with the old chamber which is our place of meeting.

"And this," said Mr Pickwick, stopping short, "is the clock! Dear me! And this is really the old clock!"

I thought he would never have come away from it. After advancing towards it softly, and laying his hand upon it with as much respect and as many smiling looks as if it were alive, he set himself to consider it in every possible direction, now mounting on a chair to look at the top, now going down upon his knees to examine the bottom, now surveying the sides with his spectacles almost touching the case, and now trying to peep between it and the wall to get a slight view of the back. Then he would retire a pace or two and look up at the dial to see it go, and then draw near again and stand with his head on one side to hear it tick: never failing to glance towards me at intervals of a few seconds each, and nod his head with such complacent gratification as I am quite unable to describe. His admiration was not confined to the clock either, but extended itself to every article in the room, and really, when he had gone through them every one, and at last sat himself down in all the six chairs, one after another, to try how they felt, I never saw such a picture of good-humor and happiness as he presented, from the top of his shining head down to the very last button of his gaiters.

I should have been well pleased, and should have had the utmost enjoyment of his company, if he had remained with me all day, but my favorite, striking the hour, reminded him that he must take his leave. I could not forbear telling him once more how glad he had made me, and we shook hands all the way down stairs.

We had no sooner arrived in the Hall, than my housekeeper, gliding out of her little room (she had changed her gown and cap, I observed), greeted Mr. Pickwick with her best smile and courtesy; and the barber, feigning to be accidentally passing on his way out, made him a vast number of bows. When the housekeeper courtesied, Mr Pickwick bowed with the utmost politeness, and when he bowed, the housekeeper courtesied again; between the housekeeper and the barber, I should say that Mr. Pickwick faced about and bowed with undiminished affability, fifty times at least.

I saw him to the door; an omnibus was at the moment passing the corner of the lane, which Mr. Pickwick hailed and ran after with extraordinary nimbleness. When he had got about half-way he turned his head, and seeing that I was still looking after him and that I waved my hand, stopped, evidently irresolute whether to come back and shake hands again, or to go on. The man behind the omnibus shouted, and Mr. Pickwick ran a little way towards him: then he looked round at me and ran a little way back again. Then there was another shout, and he turned round once more and ran the other way. After several of these vibrations, the man settled the question by taking Mr. Pickwick by the arm, and putting him into the carriage; but his last action was to let down the window and wave his hat to me as it drove off.

I lost no time in opening the parcel he had left with me. The following were its contents: —

MR. PICKWICK'S TALE.

A good many years have passed away since old John Podgers lived in the town of Windsor, where he was born, and where, in course of time, he came to be comfortably and snugly buried. You may be sure that in the time of King James the First, Windsor was a very quaint, queer old town, and you may take it upon my authority that John Podgers was a very quaint, queer old fellow; consequently he and Windsor fitted each other to a nicety, and seldom parted company even for half a day.

John Podgers was broad, sturdy, Dutch-built, short, and a very hard eater, as men of his figure often are. Being a hard sleeper likewise, he divided his time pretty equally between these two recreations, always falling asleep when he had done eating, and always taking another turn at the trencher when he had done sleeping, by which means he grew more corpulent and more drowsy every day of his life. Indeed it used to be currently reported that when he sauntered up and down the sunny side of the street before dinner (as he never failed to do in fair weather), he enjoyed his soundest nap; but many people held this to be a fiction, as he had several times been seen to look after fat oxen on market-days, and had even been heard, by persons of good credit and reputation, to chuckle at the sight, and say to himself with great glee, "Live beef, live beef!" It was upon this evidence that the wisest people in Windsor (beginning with the local authorities of course) held that John Podgers was a man of strong sound sense, — not what is called smart, perhaps, and it might be of a rather lazy and apoplectic turn, but still a man of solid parts, and one who meant much more than he cared to show. This impression was confirmed by a very dignified way he had of shaking his head and imparting, at the same time, a pendulous motion to his double chin; in short he passed for one of those people who, being plunged into the Thames, would make no vain efforts to set it afire, but would straightway flop down to the bottom with a deal of gravity, and be highly respected in consequence by all good men.

Being well to do in the world, and a peaceful widower, — having a great appetite, which, as he could afford to gratify it, was a luxury and no inconvenience, and a power of going to sleep, which, as he had no occasion to keep awake, was a most enviable faculty, — you will readily suppose that John Podgers was a happy man. But appearances are often deceptive when they least seem so, and the truth is that, notwithstanding his extreme sleekness, he was rendered uneasy in his mind and exceedingly uncomfortable by a constant apprehension that beset him night and day.

You know very well that in those times there flourished divers evil old women who, under the name of Witches, spread great disorder through the land, and inflicted various dismal tortures upon Christian men; sticking pins and needles into them when they least expected it, and causing them to walk in the air with their feet upwards, to the great terror of their wives and families, who were naturally very much disconcerted when the master of the house unexpectedly came home, knocking at the door with his heels and combing his hair on the scraper. These were their commonest pranks, but they every day played a hundred others, of which none were less objectionable and many were much more so, being improper besides; the result was that vengeance was denounced against all old women, with whom even the king himself had no sympathy (as he certainly ought to have had), for with his own most Gracious hand he penned a most Gracious consignment of them to everlasting wrath, and devised most Gracious means for their confusion and slaughter, in virtue whereof scarcely a day passed but one witch at the least was most graciously hanged, drowned, or roasted in some part of his dominions. Still, the press teemed with strange and terrible news from the North or the South, or the East or the West, relative to witches and their unhappy victims in some corner of the country, and the Public's hair stood on end to that degree that it lifted its hat off its head, and made its face pale with terror.

You may believe that the little town of Windsor did not escape the general contagion. The inhabitants boiled a witch on the King's birthday and sent a bottle of the broth to court, with a dutiful address expressive of their loyalty. The King, being rather frightened by the present, piously bestowed it upon the Archbishop of Canterbury, and returned an answer to the address, wherein he gave them golden rules for discovering witches, and laid great stress upon certain protecting charms, and especially horseshoes. Immediately the townspeople went to work nailing up horseshoes over every door, and so many anxious parents apprenticed their children to farriers, to keep them out of harm's way, that it became quite a genteel trade and flourished exceedingly.

In the midst of all this bustle John Podgers ate and slept as usual, but shook his head a great deal oftener than was his custom, and was observed to look at the oxen less, and at the old women more He had a little shelf put up in his sitting-room, whereon was displayed, in a row which grew longer every week, all the witchcraft literature of the time; he grew learned in charms and exorcisms, hinted at certain questionable females on broomsticks whom he had seen from his chamber window, riding in the air at night, and was in constant terror of being bewitched. At length, from perpetually dwelling upon this one idea, which, being alone in his head, had it all its own way, the fear of witches became the single passion of his life. He, who up to that time had never known what it was to dream, began to have visions of witches whenever he fell asleep; waking, they were incessantly present to his imagination likewise; and, sleeping or waking, he had not a moment's peace. He began to set witch-traps in the highway, and was often seen lying in wait round the corner for hours together, to watch their effect. These engines were of simple construction, usually consisting of two straws disposed in the form of a cross, or a piece of a Bible cover with a pinch of salt upon it; but they were infallible, and if an old woman chanced to stumble over them (as not unfrequently happened, the chosen spot being a broken and stony place), John started from a doze, pounced out upon her, and hung round her neck till assistance arrived, when she was immediately carried away and drowned. By dint of constantly inveigling old ladies and disposing of them in this summary manner, he acquired the reputation of a great public character; and as he received no harm in these pursuits beyond a scratched face or so, he came, in course of time, to be considered witch-proof.

There was but one person who entertained the least doubt of John Podgers's gifts, and that person was his own nephew, a wild roving young fellow of twenty who had been brought up in his uncle's house and lived there still, — that is to say, when he was at home, which was not as often as it might have been. As he was an apt scholar, it was he who read aloud every fresh piece of strange and terrible intelligence that John Podgers bought; and this he always did of an evening in the little porch in front of the house, round which the neighbors would flock in crowds to hear the direful news, — for people like to be frightened, and when they can be frightened for nothing and at another man's expense, they like it all the better.

One fine midsummer evening, a group of persons were gathered in this place, listening intently to Will Marks (that was the nephew's name), as with his cap very much on one side, his arm coiled slyly round the waist of a pretty girl who sat beside him, and his face screwed into a comical expression intended to represent extreme gravity, he read — with Heaven knows how many embellishments of his own — a dismal account of a gentleman down in Northamptonshire under the influence of witchcraft and taken forcible possession of by the Devil, who was playing his very self with him. John Podgers, in a high sugar-loaf hat and short cloak, filled the opposite seat, and surveyed the auditory with a look of mingled pride and horror very edifying to see; while the hearers, with their heads thrust forward and their mouths open, listened and trembled, and hoped there was a great deal more to come. Sometimes Will stopped for an instant to look round upon his eager audience, and then, with a more comical expression of face than before and a settling of himself comfortably, which included a squeeze of the young lady before mentioned, he launched into some new wonder surpassing all the others.

The setting sun shed his last golden rays upon this little party who, absorbed in their present occupation, took no heed of the approach of night or the glory in which the day went down, when the sound of a horse, approaching at a good round trot, invading the silence of the hour, caused the reader to make a sudden stop and the listeners to raise their heads in wonder. Nor was their wonder diminished when a horseman dashed up to the porch, and abruptly checking his steed, inquired where one John Podgers dwelt.

"Here!" cried a dozen voices, while a dozen hands pointed out sturdy John, still basking in the terrors of the pamphlet.

The rider, giving his bridle to one of those who surrounded him, dismounted, and approached John, hat in hand, but with great haste.

"Whence come ye?" said John.

"From Kingston, master."

"And wherefore?"

"On most pressing business."

"Of what nature?"

"Witchcraft."

Witchcraft! Everybody looked aghast at the breathless messenger, and the breathless messenger looked equally aghast at everybody, — except Will Marks, who, finding himself unobserved, not only squeezed the young lady again, but kissed her twice. Surely he must have been bewitched himself, or he never could have done it, — and the young lady too, or she never would have let him.

"Witchcraft?" cried Will, drowning the sound of his last kiss, which was rather a loud one.

The messenger turned towards him, and with a frown, repeated the word more solemnly than before; then told his errand, which was, in brief, that the people of Kingston had been greatly terrified for some nights past by hideous revels, held by witches beneath the gibbet within a mile of the town, and related and deposed to by chance wayfarers who had passed within ear-shot of the spot; that the sound of their voices in their wild orgies had been plainly heard by many persons; that three old women labored under strong suspicion, and that precedents had been consulted and solemn council had, and it was found that to identify the hags some single person must watch upon the spot alone; that no single person had the courage to perform the task, and that he had been despatched express to solicit John Podgers to undertake it that very night, as being a man of great renown, who bore a charmed life, and was proof against unholy spells.

John received this communication with much composure, and said in a few words, that it would have afforded him inexpressible pleasure to do the Kingston people so slight a service, if it were not for his unfortunate propensity to fall asleep, which no man regretted more than himself upon the present occasion, but which quite settled the question. Nevertheless, he said, there *was* a gentleman present (and here he looked very hard at a tall farrier) who, having been engaged all his life in the manufacture of horseshoes, must be quite invulnerable to the power of witches, and who, he had no doubt, from his own reputation for bravery and good-nature, would readily accept the commission. The farrier politely thanked him for his good opinion, which it would always be his study to deserve, but added that, with regard to the present little matter, he could n't think of it on any account, as his departing on such an errand would certainly occasion the instant death of his wife, to whom, as they all knew, he was tenderly attached. Now, so far from this circumstance being notorious, everybody had suspected the reverse, as the farrier was in the habit of beating his lady rather more than tender husbands usually do; all the married men present, however, applauded his resolution with great vehemence, and one and all declared that they would stop at home and die if needful (which happily it was not) in defence of their lawful partners.

This burst of enthusiasm over, they began to look, as by one consent, toward Will Marks, who, with his cap more on one side than ever, sat watching the proceedings with extraordinary unconcern. He had never been heard openly to express his disbelief in witches, but had often cut such jokes at their expense as left it to be inferred; publicly stating on several occasions that he considered a broomstick an inconvenient charger, and one especially unsuited to the dignity of the female character, and indulging in other free remarks of the same tendency, to the great amusement of his wild companions.

As they looked at Will, they began to whisper and murmur among themselves, and at length one man cried, "Why don't you ask Will Marks?"

As this was what everybody had been thinking of, they all took up the word, and cried in concert, "Ah! why don't you ask Will?"

"*He* don't care," said the farrier.

"Not he," added another voice in the crowd.

"He don't believe in it, you know," sneered a little man with a yellow face and a taunting nose and chin, which he thrust out from under the arm of a long man before him.

"Besides," said a red-faced gentleman with a gruff voice, "he 's a single man."

"That 's the point!" said the farrier; and all the married men murmured, ah! that was it, and they only wished they were single themselves; they would show him what spirit was, very soon.

The messenger looked towards Will Marks beseechingly.

"It will be a wet night, friend, and my gray nag is tired after yesterday's work — "

Here there was a general titter.

"But," resumed Will, looking about him with a smile, "if nobody else puts in a better claim to go, for the credit of the town, I am your man, and I would be if I had to go afoot. In five minutes I shall be in the saddle, unless I am depriving any worthy gentleman here of the honor of the adventure, which I would n't do for the world."

But here arose a double difficulty, for not only did John Podgers combat the resolution with all the words he had, which were not many, but the young lady combated it too with all the tears she had, which were very many indeed. Will, however, being inflexible, parried his uncle's objections with a joke, and coaxed the young lady into a smile in three short whispers. As it was plain that he would go and set his mind upon it, John Podgers offered him a few first-rate charms out of his own pocket which he dutifully declined to accept, and the young lady gave him a kiss which he also returned

"You see what a rare thing it is to be married," said Will, "and how careful and considerate all these husbands are. There 's not a man among them but his heart is leaping to forestall me in this adventure, and yet a strong sense of duty keeps him back. The husbands in this one little town are a pattern to the world, and so must the wives be too, for that matter, or they could never boast half the influence they have?"

Waiting for no reply to this sarcasm, he snapped his fingers and withdrew into the house, and thence into the stable, while some busied themselves in refreshing the messenger, and others in baiting his steed. In less than the specified time, he returned by another way, with a good cloak hanging over his arm, a good sword girded by his side, and leading his good horse caparisoned for the journey.

"Now," said Will, leaping into the saddle at a bound, "up and away. Upon your mettle, friend, and push on. Good night!"

He kissed his hand to the girl, nodded to his drowsy uncle, waved his cap to the rest, — and off they flew pellmell, as if all the witches in England were in their horses' legs. They were out of sight in a minute.

The men who were left behind shook their heads doubtfully, stroked their chins, and shook their heads again. The farrier said that certainly Will Marks was a good horseman, nobody should ever say he denied that; but he was rash, very rash, and there was no telling what the end of it might be: what did he go for, that was what he wanted to know? He wished the young fellow no harm, but why did he go? Everybody echoed these words, and shook their heads again, having done which they wished John Podgers good night, and straggled home to bed.

The Kingston people were in their first sleep, when Will Marks and his conductor rode through the town and up to the door of a house where sundry grave functionaries were assembled, anxiously expecting the arrival of the renowned Podgers. They were a little disappointed to find a gay young man in his place, but they put the best face upon the matter, and gave him full instructions how he was to conceal himself behind the gibbet, and watch and listen to the witches, and how at a certain time he was to burst forth and cut and slash among them vigorously, so that the suspected parties might be found bleeding in their beds next day, and thoroughly confounded. They gave him a great quantity of wholesome advice besides, and — which was more to the purpose with Will — a good supper. All these things being done, and midnight nearly come, they sallied forth to show him the spot where he was to keep his dreary vigil.

The night was by this time dark and threatening. There was a rumbling of distant thunder, and a low sighing of wind among the trees, which was very dismal. The potentates of the town kept so uncommonly close to Will that they trod upon his toes, or stumbled against his ankles, or nearly tripped up his heels at every step he took, and, besides these annoyances, their teeth chattered so with fear that he seemed to be accompanied by a dirge of castanets.

At last they made a halt at the opening of a lonely, desolate space, and, pointing to a black object at some distance, asked Will if he saw that, yonder.

"Yes," he replied. "What then?"

Informing him abruptly that it was the gibbet where he was to watch, they wished him good night in an extremely friendly manner, and ran back as fast as their feet would carry them.

Will walked boldly to the gibbet, and, glancing upward when he came under it, saw — certainly with satisfaction — that it was empty, and that nothing dangled from the top but some iron chains, which swung mournfully to and fro as they were moved by the breeze. After a careful survey of every quarter, he determined to take his station with his face towards the town; both because that would place him with his back to the wind, and because if any trick or surprise were attempted, it would probably come from that direction in the first instance. Having taken these precautions, he wrapped his cloak about him so that it left the handle of his sword free, and ready to his hand, and leaning against the gallows-tree, with his cap not quite so much on one side as it had been before, took up his position for the night.

SECOND CHAPTER OF MR. PICKWICK'S TALE.

We left Will Marks leaning under the gibbet with his face towards the town, scanning the distance with a keen eye, which sought to pierce the darkness and catch the earliest glimpse of any person or persons that might approach towards him. But all was quiet, and save the howling of the wind as it swept across the heath in gusts, and the creaking of the chains that dangled above his head, there was no sound to break the sullen stillness of the night. After half an hour or so, this monotony became more disconcerting to Will than the most furious uproar would have been, and he heartily wished for some one antagonist with whom he might have a fair stand-up fight, if it were only to warm himself.

Truth to tell, it was a bitter wind, and seemed to blow to the very heart of a man whose blood, heated but now with rapid riding, was the more sensitive to the chilling blast. Will was a daring fellow, and cared not a jot for hard knocks or sharp blades; but he could not persuade himself to move or walk about, having just that vague expectation of a sudden assault which made it a comfortable thing to have something at his back, even though that something were a gallows-tree. He had no great faith in the superstitions of the age, still such of them as occurred to him did not serve to lighten the time, or to render his situation the more endurable. He remembered how witches were said to repair at that ghostly hour to churchyards and gibbets, and such like dismal spots, to pluck the bleeding mandrake or scrape the flesh from dead men's bones, as choice ingredients for their spells; how, stealing by night to lonely places, they dug graves with their finger-nails, or anointed themselves before riding in the air with a delicate pomatum made of the fat of infants newly boiled. These, and many other fabled practices of a no less agreeable nature, and all having some reference to the circumstances in which he was placed, passed and repassed in quick succession through the mind of Will Marks, and adding a shadowy dread to that distrust and watchfulness which his situation inspired, rendered it, upon the whole, sufficiently uncomfortable. As he had foreseen, too, the rain began to descend heavily, and driving before the wind in a thick mist, obscured even those few objects which the darkness of the night had before imperfectly revealed.

"Look!" shrieked a voice; "Great Heaven, it has fallen down and stands erect as if it lived!"

The speaker was close behind him; the voice was almost at his ear. Will threw off his cloak, drew his sword, and darting swiftly round, seized a woman by the wrist, who, recoiling from him with a dreadful shriek, fell struggling upon her knees. Another woman clad, like her whom he had grasped, in mourning garments, stood roofed to the spot on which they were, gazing upon his face with wild and glaring eyes that quite appalled him.

"Say," cried Will, when they had confronted each other thus for some time, "what are ye?"

"Say what are *you*," returned the woman, "who trouble even this obscene resting-place of the dead, and strip the gibbet of its honored burden? Where is the body?"

He looked in wonder and affright from the woman who questioned him to the other whose arm he clutched

"Where is the body?" repeated his questioner more firmly than before. "You wear no livery which marks you for the hireling of the government. You are no friend to us, or I should recognize you, for the friends of such as we are few in number. What are you then, and wherefore are you here?"

"I am no foe to the distressed and helpless," said Will. "Are ye among that number? ye should be by your looks."

"We are!" was the answer.

"It is ye who have been wailing and weeping here under cover of the night?" said Will.

"It is," replied the woman sternly; and pointing, as she spoke, towards her companion, "she mourns a husband and I a brother. Even the bloody law that wreaks its vengeance on the dead does not make that a crime, and if it did 't would be alike to us who are past its fear or favor"

Will glanced at the two females, and could barely discern that the one whom he addressed was much the elder, and that the other was young and of a slight figure. Both were deadly pale, their garments wet and worn, their hair dishevelled and streaming in the wind, themselves bowed down with grief and misery; their whole appearance most dejected, wretched, and forlorn. A sight so different from any he had expected to encounter touched him to the quick, and all idea of anything but their pitiable condition vanished before it.

"I am a rough, blunt yeoman," said Will. "Why I came here is told in a word: you have been overheard at a distance in the silence of the night, and I have undertaken a watch for hags or spirits. I came here expecting an adventure, and prepared to go through with any If there be aught that I can do to help or aid you, name it, and on the faith of a man who can be secret and trusty, I will stand by you to the death"

"How comes this gibbet to be empty?" asked the elder female.

"I swear to you," replied Will, "that I know as little as yourself. But this I know, that when I came here an hour ago or so, it was as it is now; and if, as I gather from your question, it was not so last night, sure I am that it has been secretly disturbed without the knowledge of the folks in yonder town. Bethink you, therefore, whether you have no friends in league with you or with him on whom the law has done its worst, by whom these sad remains have been removed for burial."

The women spoke together, and Will retired a pace or two while they conversed apart. He could hear them sob and moan, and saw that they wrung their hands in fruitless agony. He could make out little that they said, but between whiles he gathered enough to assure him that his suggestion was not very wide of the mark, and that they not only suspected by whom the body had been removed, but also whither it had been conveyed. When they had been in conversation a long time, they turned towards him once more. This time the younger female spoke.

"You have offered us your help?"

"I have."

"And given a pledge that you are still willing to redeem?"

"Yes So far as I may, keeping all plots and conspiracies at arm's length."

"Follow us, friend."

Will, whose self-possession was now quite restored, needed no second bidding, but with his drawn sword in his hand, and his cloak so muffled over his left arm as to serve for a kind of shield without offering any impediment to its free action, suffered them to lead the way. Through mud and mire, and wind and rain, they walked in silence a full mile. At length they turned into a dark lane, where, suddenly starting out from beneath some trees where he had taken shelter, a man appeared having in his charge three saddled horses. One of these (his own apparently), in obedience to a whisper from the women, he consigned to Will, who, seeing that they mounted, mounted also. Then without a word spoken, they rode on together, leaving the attendant behind.

They made no halt nor slackened their pace until they arrived near Putney At a large wooden house which stood apart from any other, they alighted, and giving their horses to one who was already waiting, passed in by a side door, and so up some narrow, creaking stairs into a small panelled chamber, where Will was left alone. He had not been here very long, when the door was softly opened, and there entered to him a cavalier whose face was concealed beneath a black mask.

Will stood upon his guard, and scrutinized this figure from head to foot. The form was that of a man pretty far advanced in life, but of a firm and stately carriage. His dress was of a rich and costly kind, but so soiled and disordered that it was scarcely to be recognized for one of those gorgeous suits which the expensive taste and fashion of the time prescribed for men of any rank or station. He was booted and spurred, and bore about him even as many tokens of the state of the roads as Will himself. All this he noted, while the eyes behind the mask regarded him with equal attention. This survey over, the cavalier broke silence.

"Thou 'rt young and bold, and wouldst be richer than thou art?"

"The two first I am,' returned Will. "The last I have scarcely thought of. But be it so. Say that I would be richer than I am; what then?"

"The way lies before thee now," replied the Mask.

"Show it me."

"First let me inform thee, that thou wert brought here to-night lest thou shouldst too soon have told thy tale to those who placed thee on the watch."

"I thought as much when I followed," said Will. "But I am no blab, not I."

"Good," returned the Mask. "Now listen. He who was to have executed the enterprise of burying that body, which, as thou hast suspected, was taken down to-night, has left us in our need."

Will nodded, and thought within himself that if the Mask were to attempt to play any tricks, the first eyelet-hole on the left-hand side of his doublet, counting from the buttons up the front, would be a very good place in which to pink him neatly.

"Thou art here, and the emergency is desperate. I propose his task to thee. Convey the body (now coffined in this house), by means that I shall show, to the church of Saint Dunstan in London to-morrow night, and thy service shall be richly paid. Thou 'rt about to ask whose corpse it is. Seek not to know. I warn thee, seek not to know. Felons hang in chains on every moor and heath. Believe, as others do, that this was one, and ask no further. The murders of state policy, its victims or avengers, had best remain unknown to such as thee."

"The mystery of this service," said Will, "bespeaks its danger. What is the reward?"

"One hundred golden unities," replied the cavalier. "The danger to one who cannot be recognized as the friend of a fallen cause is not great, but there is some hazard to be run Decide between that and the reward."

"What if I refuse?" said Will.

"Depart in peace, in God's name," returned the Mask in a melancholy tone, "and keep our secret: remembering that those who brought thee here were crushed and stricken women, and that those who bade thee go free could have had thy life with one word, and no man the wiser."

Men were readier to undertake desperate adventures in those times than they are now. In this case the temptation was great, and the punishment, even in case of detection, was not likely to be very severe, as Will came of a loyal stock, and his uncle was in good repute, and a passable tale to account for his possession of the body and his ignorance of the identity, might be easily devised. The cavalier explained that a covered cart had been prepared for the purpose; that the time of departure could be arranged so that he should reach London Bridge at dusk, and proceed through the City after the day had closed in; that people would be ready at his journey's end to place the coffin in a vault without a minute's delay; that officious inquirers in the streets would be easily repelled by the tale that he was carrying for interment the corpse of one who had died of the plague; and in short showed him every reason why he should succeed, and none why he should fail. After a time they were joined by another gentleman, masked like the first, who added new arguments to those which had been already urged; the wretched wife, too, added her tears and prayers to their calmer representations; and in the end, Will, moved by compassion and good-nature, by a love of the marvellous, by a mischievous anticipation of the terrors of the Kingston people when he should be missing next day, and finally, by the prospect of gain, took upon himself the task, and devoted all his energies to its successful execution.

The following night, when it was quite dark, the hollow echoes of old London Bridge responded to the rumbling of the cart which contained the ghastly load, the object of Will Marks's care. Sufficiently disguised to attract no attention by his garb, Will walked at the horse's head, as unconcerned as a man could be who was sensible that he had now arrived at the most dangerous part of his undertaking, but full of boldness and confidence.

It was now eight o'clock. After nine, none could walk the streets without danger of their lives, and even at this hour, robberies and murder were of no uncommon occurrence. The shops upon the bridge were all closed; the low wooden arches thrown across the way were like so many black pits, in every one of which ill-favored fellows lurked in knots of three or four; some standing upright against the wall, lying in wait; others skulking in gateways, and thrusting out their uncombed heads and scowling eyes; others crossing and recrossing, and constantly jostling both horse and man to provoke a quarrel; others stealing away and summoning their companions in a low whistle. Once, even in that short passage, there was the noise of scuffling and the clash of swords behind him, but Will, who knew the city and its ways, kept straight on and scarcely turned his head.

The streets being unpaved, the rain of the night before had converted them into a perfect quagmire, which the splashing water-spouts from the gables, and the filth and offal cast from the different houses, swelled in no small degree. These odious matters being left to putrefy in the close and heavy air, emitted an insupportable stench, to which every court and passage poured forth a contribution of its own. Many parts, even of the main streets, with their projecting stories tottering overhead and nearly shutting out the sky, were more like huge chimneys than open ways. At the corners of some of these, great bonfires were burning to prevent infection from the plague, of which it was rumored that some citizens had lately died; and few, who availing themselves of the light thus afforded paused for a moment to look around them, would have been disposed to doubt the existence of the disease, or wonder at its dreadful visitations.

But it was not in such scenes as these, or even in the deep and miry road, that Will Marks found the chief obstacles to his progress. There were kites and ravens feeding in the streets (the only scavengers the City kept), who, scenting what he carried, followed the cart or fluttered on its top, and croaked their knowledge of its burden and their ravenous appetite for prey. There were distant fires, where the poor wood and plaster tenements wasted fiercely, and whither crowds made their way, clamoring eagerly for plunder, beating down all who came within their reach, and yelling like devils let loose. There were single-handed men flying from bands of ruffians, who pursued them with naked weapons, and hunted them savagely; there were drunken, desperate robbers issuing from their dens and staggering through the open streets where no man dared molest them; there were vagabond servitors returning from the Bear Garden, where had been good sport that day, dragging after them their torn and bleeding dogs, or leaving them to die and rot upon the road. Nothing was abroad but cruelty, violence, and disorder.

Many were the interruptions which Will Marks encountered from these stragglers, and many the narrow escapes he made. Now some stout bully would take his seat upon the cart, insisting to be driven to his own home, and now two or three men would come down upon him together and demand that on peril of his life he showed them what he had inside. Then a party of the City Watch, upon their rounds, would draw across the road, and not satisfied with his tale, question him closely and revenge themselves by a little cuffing and hustling for maltreatment sustained at other hands that night. All these assailants had to be rebutted, some by fair words, some by foul, and some by blows. But Will Marks was not the man to be stopped or turned back now he had penetrated so far, and though he got on slowly, still he made his way down Fleet Street and reached the church at last.

As he had been forewarned, all was in readiness. Directly he stopped, the coffin was removed by four men who appeared so suddenly that they seemed to have started from the earth. A fifth mounted the cart, and scarcely allowing Will time to snatch from it a little bundle containing such of his own clothes as he had thrown off on assuming his disguise, drove briskly away. Will never saw cart or man again.

He followed the body into the church, and it was well he lost no time in doing so, for the door was immediately closed. There was no light in the building save that which came from a couple of torches borne by two men in cloaks who stood upon the brink of a vault. Each supported a female figure, and all observed a profound silence.

By this dim and solemn glare, which made Will feel as though light itself were dead, and its tomb the dreary arches that frowned above, they placed the coffin in the vault, with uncovered heads, and closed it up. One of the torch-bearers then turned to Will and stretched forth his hand, in which was a purse of gold. Something told him directly that those were the same eyes which he had seen beneath the mask.

"Take it," said the cavalier in a low voice, "and be happy. Though these have been hasty obsequies, and no priest has blessed the work, there will not be the less peace with thee hereafter, for having laid his bones beside those of his little children. Keep thy own counsel, for thy sake no less than ours, and God be with thee!"

"The blessing of a widowed mother on thy head, good friend!" cried the younger lady through her tears; "the blessing of one who has now no hope or rest but in this grave!"

Will stood with the purse in his hand, and involuntarily made a gesture as though he would return it, for though a thoughtless fellow he was of a frank and generous nature. But the two gentlemen, extinguishing their torches, cautioned him to be gone, as their common safety would be endangered by a longer delay; and at the same time their retreating footsteps sounded through the church. He turned, therefore, towards the point at which he had entered, and seeing by a faint gleam in the distance that the door was again partially open, groped his way towards it and so passed into the street.

Meantime the local authorities of Kingston had kept watch and ward all the previous night, fancying every now and then that dismal shrieks were borne towards them on the wind, and frequently winking to each other and drawing closer to the fire as they drank the health of the lonely sentinel, upon whom a clerical gentleman present was especially severe by reason of his levity and youthful folly. Two or three of the gravest in company, who were of a theological turn, propounded to him the question whether such a character was not but poorly armed for single combat with the devil, and whether he himself would not have been a stronger opponent; but the clerical gentleman, sharply reproving them for their presumption in discussing such questions, clearly showed that a fitter champion than Will could scarcely have been selected, not only for that being a child of Satan he was the less likely to be alarmed by the appearance of his own father, but because Satan himself would be at his ease in such company, and would not scruple to kick up his heels to an extent which it was quite certain he would never venture before clerical eyes, under whose influence (as was notorious) he became quite a tame and milk-and-water character.

But when next morning arrived, and with it no Will Marks, and when a strong party repairing to the spot, as a strong party ventured to do in broad day, found Will gone and the gibbet empty, matters grew serious indeed. The day passing away and no news arriving, and the night going on also without any intelligence, the thing grew more tremendous still; in short, the neighborhood worked itself up to such a comfortable pitch of mystery and horror that it is a great question whether the general feeling was not one of excessive disappointment, when, on the second morning, Will Marks returned.

However this may be, back Will came in a very cool and collected state, and appearing not to trouble himself much about anybody except old John Podgers, who having been sent for, was sitting in the Town Hall crying slowly and dozing between whiles. Having embraced his uncle and assured him of his safety, Will mounted on a table and told his story to the crowd.

And surely they would have been the most unreasonable crowd that ever assembled together, if they had been in the least respect disappointed with the tale he told them, for besides describing the Witches' Dance to the minutest motion of their legs, and performing it in character on the table, with the assistance of a broomstick, he related how they had carried off the body in a copper caldron, and so bewitched him that he lost his senses until he found himself lying under a hedge at least ten miles off, whence he had straightway returned as they then beheld. The story gained such universal applause that it soon afterwards brought down express from London the great witch-finder of the age, the Heaven-born Hopkins, who having examined Will closely on several points, pronounced it the most extraordinary and the best accredited witch story ever known, under which title it was published at the Three-Bibles on London Bridge, in small quarto, with a view of the caldron from an original drawing, and a portrait of the clerical gentleman as he sat by the fire.

On one point Will was particularly careful: and that was to describe for the witches he had seen, three impossible old females whose likenesses never were or will be. Thus he saved the lives of the suspected parties, and of all other old women who were dragged before him to be identified.

This circumstance occasioned John Podgers much grief and sorrow, until happening one day to cast his eyes upon his housekeeper, and observing her to be plainly afflicted with rheumatism, he procured her to be burnt as an undoubted witch. For this service to the state he was immediately knighted, and became from that time Sir John Podgers.

Will Marks never gained any clew to the mystery in which he had been an actor, nor did any inscription in the church, which he often visited afterwards, nor any of the limited inquiries that he dared to make, yield him the least assistance.

As he kept his own secret, he was compelled to spend the gold discreetly and sparingly. In the course of time he married the young lady of whom I have already told you, whose maiden name is not recorded, with whom he led a prosperous and happy life. Years and years after this adventure, it was his wont to tell her upon a stormy night that it was a great comfort to him to think those bones, to whomsoever they might have once belonged, were not bleaching in the troubled air, but were mouldering away with the dust of their own kith and kindred in a quiet grave.

FURTHER PARTICULARS OF MASTER HUMPHREY'S VISITOR.

Being very full of Mr. Pickwick's application, and highly pleased with the compliment he had paid me, it will be readily supposed that long before our next night of meeting I communicated it to my three friends, who unanimously voted his admission into our body. We all looked forward with some impatience to the occasion which would enroll him among us, but I am greatly mistaken if Jack Redburn and myself were not by many degrees the most impatient of the party.

At length the night came, and a few minutes after ten Mr. Pickwick's knock was heard at the street door. He was shown into a lower room, and I directly took my crooked stick and went to accompany him up stairs, in order that he might be presented with all honor and formality.

"Mr. Pickwick," said I on entering the room, "I am rejoiced to see you, — rejoiced to believe that this is but the opening of a long series of visits to this house, and but the beginning of a close and lasting friendship."

That gentleman made a suitable reply with a cordiality and frankness peculiarly his own, and glanced with a smile towards two persons behind the door, whom I had not at first observed, and whom I immediately recognized as Mr. Samuel Weller and his father.

It was a warm evening, but the elder Mr. Weller was attired, notwithstanding, in a most capacious great-coat, and his chin enveloped in a large speckled shawl, such as is usually worn by stage coachmen on active service. He looked very rosy and very stout, especially about the legs, which appeared to have been compressed into his top-boots with some difficulty. His broad-brimmed hat he held under his left arm, and with the forefinger of his right hand he touched his forehead a great many times in acknowledgment of my presence.

"I am very glad to see you in such good health, Mr. Weller," said I.

"Why, thankee, sir," returned Mr. Weller, "the axle an't broke yet. We keeps up a steady pace, — not too sewere but vith a moderate degree o' friction, — and the consekens is that ve 're still a runnin' and comes in to the time reg'lar. — My son Samivel, sir, as you may have read on in history," added Mr. Weller, introducing his first-born.

I received Sam very graciously, but before he could say a word his father struck in again.

"Samivel Veller, sir," said the old gentleman, "has con-ferred upon me the ancient title o' grandfather vich had long laid dormouse, and wos s'posed to be nearly hex-tinct in our family. Sammy, relate a anecdote o' vun o' them boys, — that 'ere little anecdote about young Tony sayin' as he *vould* smoke a pipe unbeknown to his mother."

"Be quiet, can't you?" said Sam; "I never see such a old magpie — never!"

"That 'ere Tony is the blessedest boy," said Mr. Weller, heedless of this rebuff, — "the blessedest boy as ever *I* see in *my* days! of all the charmin'est infants as ever I heerd tell on, includin' them as wos kivered over by the robin-redbreasts arter they 'd committed sooicide with blackberries, there never wos any like that 'ere little Tony. He 's alvays a playin' vith a quart pot, that boy is! To see him a settin' down on the doorstep pretending to drink out of it, and fetching a long breath artervards, and smoking a bit of fire-vood and sayin', 'Now I 'm grandfather,' — to see him a doin' that at two year old is better than any play as wos ever wrote. 'Now I 'm grandfather!' He would n't take a pint pot if you wos to make him a present on it, but he gets his quart, and then he says, 'Now I 'm grandfather!'"

Mr. Weller was so overpowered by this picture that he straightway fell into a most alarming fit of coughing, which must certainly have been attended with some fatal result but for the dexterity and promptitude of Sam, who, taking a firm grasp of the shawl just under his father's chin, shook him to and fro with great violence, at the same time administering some smart blows between his shoulders. By this curious mode of treatment Mr. Weller was finally recovered, but with a very crimson face, and in a state of great exhaustion.

"He 'll do now, Sam," said Mr. Pickwick, who had been in some alarm himself.

"He 'll do, sir!" cried Sam, looking reproachfully at his parent. "Yes, he *will* do one o' these days, — he 'll do for his-self and then he 'll wish he had n't. Did anybody ever see sich a inconsiderate old file, — laughing into conwulsions afore company, and stamping on the floor as if he 'd brought his own carpet vith him and wos under a wager to punch the pattern out in a given time? He 'll begin again in a minute. There, — he 's agoin' off, — I said he would!"

In fact, Mr. Weller, whose mind was still running upon his precocious grandson, was seen to shake his head from side to side, while a laugh, working like an earthquake, below the surface, produced various extraordinary appearances in his face, chest, and shoulders, — the more alarming because unaccompanied by any noise whatever. These emotions, however, gradually subsided, and after three or four short relapses he wiped his eyes with the cuff of his coat, and looked about him with tolerable composure.

"Afore the governor vith-draws," said Mr. Weller, "there is a pint, respecting vich Sammy has a qvestion to ask. Vile that qvestion is a perwadin' this here conwersation, p'raps the genl'men vill permit me to re-tire."

"Wot are you goin' away for?" demanded Sam, seizing his father by the coat-tail.

"I never see such a undootiful boy as you, Samivel," returned Mr. Weller. "Did n't you make a solemn promise, amountin' almost to a speeches o' wow, that you 'd put that ere qvestion on my account?"

"Well, I 'm agreeable to do it," said Sam, "but not if you go cuttin' away like that, as the bull turned round and mildly observed to the drover ven they wos a goadin' him into the butcher's door. The fact is, sir," said Sam, addressing me, "that he wants to know somethin' respectin' that 'ere lady as is housekeeper here."

"Ay. What is that?"

"Vy, sir," said Sam, grinning still more, "he wishes to know vether she —"

"In short," interposed old Mr. Weller, decisively, a perspiration breaking out upon his forehead, "vether that 'ere old creetur is or is not a widder."

Mr. Pickwick laughed heartily, and so did I, as I replied, decisively, that "my housekeeper was a spinster."

"There!" cried Sam, "now you 're satisfied. You hear she 's a spinster."

"A wot?" said his father with deep scorn.

"A spinster," replied Sam

Mr. Weller looked very hard at his son for a minute or two, and then said, —

"Never mind vether she makes jokes or not, that 's no matter. Wot I say is, is that 'ere female a widder, or is she not?"

"Wot do you mean by her making jokes?" demanded Sam, quite aghast at the obscurity of his parent's speech.

"Never you mind, Samivel," returned Mr. Weller, gravely; "puns may be wery good things or they may be wery bad 'uns, and a female may be none the better or she may be none the vurse for making of 'em; that 's got nothing to do vith widders."

"Wy now," said Sam, looking round, "would anybody believe as a man at his time o' life could be a running his head ag'in spinsters and punsters being the same thing?"

"There an't a straw's difference between 'em," said Mr. Weller. "Your father did n't drive a coach for so many years, not to be ekal to his own langvidge as far as *that* goes, Sammy."

Avoiding the question of etymology, upon which the old gentleman's mind was quite made up, he was several times assured that the housekeeper had never been married. He expressed great satisfaction on hearing this, and apologized for the question, remarking that he had been greatly terrified by a widow not long before, and that his natural timidity was increased in consequence.

"It wos on the rail," said Mr. Weller, with strong emphasis; "I wos a goin' down to Birmingham by the rail, and I wos locked up in a close carriage vith a living widder. Alone we wos; the widder and me wos alone; and I believe it wos only because we *wos* alone and there wos no clergyman in the conwayance, that that 'ere widder did n't marry me afore ve reached the half-way station. Ven I think how she began a screaming as we wos a goin' under them tunnels in the dark, — how she kept on a faintin' and ketchin' hold o' me, — and how I tried to bust open the door as was tight-locked and perwented all escape — Ah! It was a awful thing, most awful!"

Mr. Weller was so very much overcome by this retrospect that he was unable, until he had wiped his brow several times, to return any reply to the question whether he approved of railway communication, notwithstanding that it would appear from the answer which he ultimately gave, that he entertained strong opinions on the subject.

"I con-sider," said Mr. Weller, "that the rail is unconstitootional and an inwaser o' priwileges, and I should wery much like to know what that 'ere old Carter as once stood up for our liberties and wun 'em too, — I should like to know wot he vould say if he wos alive now, to Englishmen being locked up with widders, or with anybody again their wills. Wot a old Carter would have said, a old Coachman may say, and I as-sert that in that pint o' view alone, the rail is an inwaser. As to the comfort, vere 's the comfort o' sittin' in a harm-cheer lookin' at brick walls or heaps o' mud, never comin' to a public-house, never seein' a glass o' ale, never goin' through a pike, never meetin' a change o' no kind (horses or othervise), but alvays comin' to a place, ven you come to one at all, the wery picter o' the last, vith the same p'leesemen standing about, the same blessed old bell a ringin', the same unfort'nate people standing behind the bars, a waitin' to be let in; and everythin' the same except the name, vich is wrote up in the same sized letters as the last name, and vith the same colors. As to the *h*onor and dignity o' travellin', vere can that be vithout a coachman; and wot 's the rail to sich coachmen and guards as is sometimes forced to go by it, but a outrage and a insult? As to the pace, wot sort o' pace do you think I, Tony Veller, could have kept a coach goin' at, for five hundred thousand pound a mile, paid in adwance afore the coach was on the road? And as to the ingein, — a nasty, wheezin', creaking, gasping, puffin', bustin' monster, alvays out o' breath, vith a shiny green and gold back, like a unpleasant beetle in that 'ere gas magnifier, — as to the ingein as is alvays a pourin' out red-hot coals at night, and black smoke in the day, the sensiblest thing it does in my opinion, is, ven there 's somethin' in the vay and it sets up that 'ere frightful scream vich seems to say, 'Now here 's two hundred and forty passengers in the wery greatest extremity o' danger, and here 's their two hundred and forty screams in vun!'"

By this time I began to fear that my friends would be rendered impatient by my protracted absence. I therefore begged Mr. Pickwick to accompany me up stairs, and left the two Mr. Wellers in the care of the housekeeper; laying strict injunctions upon her to treat them with all possible hospitality.

MASTER HUMPHREY'S CLOCK.

IV.

THE CLOCK.

AS we were going up stairs, Mr. Pickwick put on his spectacles, which he had held in his hand hitherto ; arranged his neckerchief, smoothed down his waistcoat, and made many other little preparations of that kind which men are accustomed to be mindful of, when they are going among strangers for the first time, and are anxious to impress them pleasantly. Seeing that I smiled, he smiled too, and said that if it had occurred to him before he left home, he would certainly have presented himself in pumps and silk stockings.

"I would, indeed, my dear sir," he said, very seriously ; "I would have shown my respect for the society, by laying aside my gaiters."

"You may rest assured," said I, "that they would have regretted your doing so very much, for they are quite attached to them."

"No, really!" cried Mr. Pickwick, with manifest pleasure. "Do you think they care about my gaiters? Do you seriously think that they identify me at all with my gaiters?"

"I am sure they do," I replied.

"Well, now," said Mr. Pickwick, "that is one of the most charming and agreeable circumstances that could possibly have occurred to me!"

I should not have written down this short conversation, but that it developed a slight point in Mr. Pickwick's character, with which I was not previously acquainted. He has a secret pride in his legs. The manner in which he spoke, and the accompanying glance he bestowed upon his tights, convince me that Mr. Pickwick regards his legs with much innocent vanity.

"But here are our friends," said I, opening the door and taking his arm in mine; "let them speak for themselves. Gentlemen, I present to you Mr. Pickwick."

Mr. Pickwick and I must have been a good contrast just then. I, leaning quietly on my crutch-stick, with something of a care-worn, patient air; he, having hold of my arm, and bowing in every direction with the most elastic politeness, and an expression of face whose sprightly cheerfulness and good-humor knew no bounds. The difference between us must have been more striking yet as we advanced towards the table, and the amiable gentleman, adapting his jocund step to my poor tread, had his attention divided between treating my infirmities with the utmost consideration, and affecting to be wholly unconscious that I required any.

I made him personally known to each of my friends in turn. First, to the deaf gentleman, whom he regarded with much interest, and accosted with great frankness and cordiality. He had evidently some vague idea, at the moment, that my friend being deaf must be dumb also; for when the latter opened his lips to express the pleasure it afforded him to know a gentleman of whom he had heard so much, Mr. Pickwick was so extremely disconcerted that I was obliged to step in to his relief.

His meeting with Jack Redburn was quite a treat to see. Mr. Pickwick smiled, and shook hands, and looked at him through his spectacles, and under them, and over them, and nodded his head approvingly, and then nodded to me, as much as to say, "This is just the man; you were quite right"; and then turned to Jack and said a few hearty words, and then did and said everything over again with unimpaired vivacity. As to Jack himself, he was quite as much delighted with Mr. Pickwick, as Mr Pickwick could possibly be with him. Two people never can have met together since the world began, who exchanged a warmer or more enthusiastic greeting.

It was amusing to observe the difference between this encounter, and that which succeeded, between Mr. Pickwick and Mr. Miles. It was clear that the latter gentleman viewed our new member as a kind of rival in the affections of Jack Redburn, and besides this, he had more than once hinted to me, in secret, that although he had no doubt Mr. Pickwick was a very worthy man, still, he did consider that some of his exploits were unbecoming a gentleman of his years and gravity Over and above these grounds of distrust, it is one of his fixed opinions that the law never can by possibility do anything wrong; he therefore looks upon Mr. Pickwick as one who has justly suffered in purse and peace for a breach of his plighted faith to an unprotected female, and holds that he is called upon to regard him with some suspicion on that account. These causes led to a rather cold and formal reception; which Mr. Pickwick acknowledged with the same stateliness and intense politeness as was displayed on the other side. Indeed, he assumed an air of such majestic defiance that I was fearful he might break out into some solemn protest or declaration, and therefore inducted him into his chair without a moment's delay.

This piece of generalship was perfectly successful. The instant he took his seat, Mr. Pickwick surveyed us all with a most benevolent aspect, and was taken with a fit of smiling full five minutes long. His interest in our ceremonies was immense. They are not very numerous or complicated, and a description of them may be comprised in very few words. As our transactions have already been, and must necessarily continue to be, more or less anticipated by being presented in these pages at different times and under various forms, they do not require a detailed account.

Our first proceeding when we are assembled is to shake hands all round, and greet each other with cheerful and pleasant looks. Remembering that we assemble not only for the promotion of our happiness, but with the view of adding something to the common stock, an air of languor or indifference in any member of our body would be regarded by the others as a kind of treason. We have never had an offender in this respect; but if we had, there is no doubt that he would be taken to task pretty severely.

Our salutation over, the venerable piece of antiquity from which we take our name is wound up in silence. This ceremony is always performed by Master Humphrey himself (in treating of the club, I may be permitted to assume the historical style, and speak of myself in the third person), who mounts upon a chair for the purpose, armed with a large key. While it is in progress, Jack Redburn is required to keep at the farther end of the room under the guardianship of Mr. Miles, for he is known to entertain certain aspiring and unhallowed thoughts connected with the clock, and has even gone so far as to state that if he might take the works out for a day or two, he thinks he could improve them. We pardon him his presumption in consideration of his good intentions, and his keeping this respectful distance, which last penalty is insisted on, lest by secretly wounding the object of our regard in some tender part, in the ardor of his zeal for its improvement, he should fill us all with dismay and consternation.

This regulation afforded Mr. Pickwick the highest delight, and seemed, if possible, to exalt Jack in his good opinion.

The next ceremony is the opening of the clock-case (of which Master Humphrey has likewise the key), the taking from it as many papers as will furnish forth our evening's entertainment, and arranging in the recess such new contributions as have been provided since our last meeting. This is always done with peculiar solemnity. The deaf gentleman then fills and lights his pipe, and we once more take our seats round the table before mentioned, Master Humphrey acting as president, — if we can be said to have any president, where all are on the same social footing, — and our friend Jack as secretary. Our preliminaries being now concluded, we fall into any train of conversation that happens to suggest itself, or proceed immediately to one of our readings. In the latter case, the paper selected is consigned to Master Humphrey, who flattens it carefully on the table and makes dog's ears in the corner of every page, ready for turning over easily; Jack Redburn trims the lamp with a small machine of his own invention, which usually puts it out; Mr. Miles looks on with great approval notwithstanding; the deaf gentleman draws in his chair, so that he can follow the words on the paper or on Master Humphrey's lips as he pleases; and Master Humphrey himself, looking round with mighty gratification, and glancing up at his old clock, begins to read aloud.

Mr. Pickwick's face, while his tale was being read, would have attracted the attention of the dullest man alive. The complacent motion of his head and forefinger as he gently beat time and corrected the air with imaginary punctuation, the smile that mantled on his features at every jocose passage, and the sly look he stole around to observe its effect, the calm manner in which he shut his eyes and listened when there was some little piece of description, the changing expression with which he acted the dialogue to himself, his agony that the deaf gentleman should know what it was all about, and his extraordinary anxiety to correct the reader when he hesitated at a word in the manuscript, or substituted a wrong one, were alike worthy of remark. And when at last, endeavoring to communicate with the deaf gentleman by means of the finger alphabet, with which he constructed such words as are unknown to any civilized or savage language, he took up a slate and wrote in large text, one word in a line, the question, "How — do — you — like — it?" When he did this, and handing it over the table awaited the reply, with a countenance only brightened and improved by his great excitement, even Mr. Miles relaxed, and could not forbear looking at him for the moment with interest and favor.

"It has occurred to me," said the deaf gentleman, who had watched Mr. Pickwick and everybody else with silent satisfaction, — "it has occurred to me," said the deaf gentleman, taking his pipe from his lips, "that now is our time for filling our only empty chair."

As our conversation had naturally turned upon the vacant seat, we lent a willing ear to this remark, and looked at our friend inquiringly.

"I feel sure," said he, "that Mr. Pickwick must be acquainted with somebody who would be an acquisition to us; that he must know the man we want. Pray let us not lose any time, but set this question at rest. Is it so, Mr. Pickwick?"

The gentleman addressed was about to return a verbal reply, but remembering our friend's infirmity, he substituted for this kind of answer some fifty nods. Then taking up the slate and printing on it a gigantic "Yes," he handed it across the table, and rubbing his hands as he looked round upon our faces, protested that he and the deaf gentleman quite understood each other, already.

"The person I have in my mind," said Mr. Pickwick, "and whom I should not have presumed to mention to you until some time hence, but for the opportunity you have given me, is a very strange old man. His name is Bamber."

"Bamber!" said Jack. "I have certainly heard the name before."

"I have no doubt, then," returned Mr. Pickwick, "that you remember him in those adventures of mine (the Posthumous Papers of our old club, I mean), although he is only incidentally mentioned; and, if I remember right, appears but once."

"That 's it," said Jack. "Let me see. He is the person who has a grave interest in old mouldy chambers and the Inns of Court, and who relates some anecdotes having reference to his favorite theme, — and an odd ghost story, — is that the man?"

"The very same. Now," said Mr. Pickwick, lowering his voice to a mysterious and confidential tone, "he is a very extraordinary and remarkable person; living, and talking, and looking, like some strange spirit, whose delight is to haunt old buildings; and absorbed in that one subject which you have just mentioned, to an extent which is quite wonderful. When I retired into private life, I sought him out, and I do assure you that the more I see of him, the more strongly I am impressed with the strange and dreamy character of his mind."

"Where does he live?" I inquired.

"He lives," said Mr. Pickwick, "in one of those dull, lonely old places with which his thoughts and stories are all connected; quite alone, and often shut up close, for several weeks together. In this dusty solitude he broods upon the fancies he has so long indulged, and when he goes into the world, or anybody from the world without goes to see him, they are still present to his mind and still his favorite topic. I may say, I believe, that he has brought himself to entertain a regard for me, and an interest in my visits; feelings which I am certain he would extend to Master Humphrey's Clock if he were once tempted to join us. All I wish you to understand is, that he is a strange secluded visionary, in the world but not of it; and as unlike anybody here as he is unlike anybody elsewhere that I have ever met or known."

Mr. Miles received this account of our proposed companion with rather a wry face, and after murmuring that perhaps he was a little mad, inquired if he were rich.

"I never asked him," said Mr. Pickwick.

"You might know, sir, for all that," retorted Mr. Miles, sharply.

"Perhaps so, sir," said Mr. Pickwick, no less sharply than the other, "but I do not. Indeed," he added, relapsing into his usual mildness, "I have no means of judging He lives poorly, but that would seem to be in keeping with his character. I never heard him allude to his circumstances, and never fell into the society of any man who had the slightest acquaintance with them. I have really told you all I know about him, and it rests with you to say whether you wish to know more, or know quite enough already."

We were unanimously of opinion that we would seek to know more; and as a sort of compromise with Mr. Miles (who, although he said, "Yes, — O, certainly, — he should like to know more about the gentleman, — he had no right to put himself in opposition to the general wish," and so forth, shook his head doubtfully, and hemmed several times with peculiar gravity), it was arranged that Mr. Pickwick should carry me with him on an evening visit to the subject of our discussion, for which purpose an early appointment between that gentleman and myself was immediately agreed upon; it being understood that I was to act upon my own responsibility, and to invite him to join us or not, as I might think proper. This solemn question determined, we returned to the clock-case (where we have been forestalled by the reader), and between its contents, and the conversation they occasioned, the remainder of our time passed very quickly.

When we broke up, Mr. Pickwick took me aside to tell me that he had spent a most charming and delightful evening. Having made this communication with an air of the strictest secrecy, he took Jack Redburn into another corner to tell him the same, and then retired into another corner with the deaf gentleman and the slate, to repeat the assurance. It was amusing to observe the contest in his mind whether he should extend his confidence to Mr. Miles, or treat him with dignified reserve. Half a dozen times he stepped up behind him with a friendly air, and as often stepped back again without saying a word; at last, when he was close at that gentleman's ear and upon the very point of whispering something conciliating and agreeable, Mr. Miles happened suddenly to turn his head, upon which Mr. Pickwick skipped away, and said with some fierceness, "Good night, sir, — I was about to say good night, sir, — nothing more"; and so made a bow and left him.

"Now, Sam," said Mr. Pickwick when he had got down stairs.

"All right, sir," replied Mr. Weller. "Hold hard, sir. Right arm fust, — now the left, — now one strong conwulsion, and the great-coat 's on, sir."

Mr. Pickwick acted upon these directions, and being further assisted by Sam, who pulled at one side of the collar, and Mr. Weller, who pulled hard at the other, was speedily enrobed. Mr. Weller senior then produced a full-sized stable lantern, which he had carefully deposited in a remote corner, on his arrival, and inquired whether Mr. Pickwick would have "the lamps alight."

"I think not to-night," said Mr. Pickwick.

"Then if this here lady vill per-mit," rejoined Mr. Weller, "we 'll leave it here, ready for next journey. This here lantern, mum," said Mr. Weller, handing it to the housekeeper, "vunce belonged to the celebrated Bill Blinder as is now at grass, as all on us vill be in our turns. Bill, mum, wos the hostler as had charge o' them two vell-known piebald leaders that run in the Bristol fast coach, and vould never go to no other tune but a sutherly vind and a cloudy sky, which wos consekvently played incessant, by the guard, wenever they wos on duty. He wos took wery bad one arternoon, arter having been off his feed, and wery shaky on his legs for some veeks; and he says to his mate, 'Matey,' he says, 'I think I 'm a-goin' the wrong side o' the post, and that my foot 's wery near the bucket. Don't say I an't,' he says, 'for I know I am, and don't let me be interrupted,' he says, 'for I 've saved a little money, and I 'm a-goin' into the stable to make my last vill and testymint.' 'I 'll take care as nobody interrupts,' says his mate, 'but you on'y hold up your head, and shake your ears a bit, and you 're good for twenty years to come.' Bill Blinder makes him no answer, but he goes avay into the stable, and there he soon artervards lays himself down a'tween the two piebalds, and dies, — prevously a-writin' outside the corn-chest, 'This is the last vill and testymint of Villiam Blinder.' They wos nat'rally wery much amazed at this, and arter looking among the litter, and up in the loft, and vere not, they opens the corn-chest, and finds that he 'd been and chalked his vill inside the lid; so the lid wos obligated to be took off the hinges, and sent up to Doctor Commons to be proved, and under that ere wery instrument this here lantern was passed to 'Tony Veller, vich circumstarnce, mum, gives it a wally in my eyes, and makes me rek-vest, if you vill be so kind, as to take partickler care on it."

The housekeeper graciously promised to keep the object of Mr. Weller's regard in the safest possible custody, and Mr. Pickwick, with a laughing face, took his leave. The body-guard followed, side by side: old Mr. Weller buttoned and wrapped up from his boots to his chin; and Sam with his hands in his pockets and his hat half off his head, remonstrating with his father, as he went, on his extreme loquacity.

I was not a little surprised, on turning to go up stairs, to encounter the barber in the passage at that late hour; for his attendance is usually confined to some half-hour in the morning. But Jack Redburn, who finds out (by instinct, I think) everything that happens in the house, informed me with great glee, that a society in imitation of our own had been that night formed in the kitchen, under the title of "Mr. Weller's Watch," of which the barber was a member; and that he could pledge himself to find means of making me acquainted with the whole of its future proceedings, which I begged him, both on my own account and that of my readers, by no means to neglect doing.*

*   *   *   *   *

* Old Curiosity Shop is continued here to the end of No. IV.

MASTER HUMPHREY'S CLOCK.

V.

MR. WELLER'S WATCH.

IT seems that the housekeeper and the two Mr. Wellers were no sooner left together on the occasion of their first becoming acquainted, than the housekeeper called to her assistance Mr. Slithers, the barber, who had been lurking in the kitchen in expectation of her summons; and with many smiles and much sweetness introduced him as one who would assist her in the responsible office of entertaining her distinguished visitors.

"Indeed," said she, "without Mr. Slithers I should have been placed in quite an awkward situation."

"There is no call for any hock'erdness, mum," said Mr. Weller, with the utmost politeness; "no call wotsumever. A lady," added the old gentleman, looking about him with the air of one who establishes an incontrovertible position, — "a lady can't be hock'erd. Natur' has otherwise purwided."

The housekeeper inclined her head and smiled yet more sweetly. The barber, who had been fluttering about Mr. Weller and Sam in a state of great anxiety to improve their acquaintance, rubbed his hands and cried, "Hear, hear! Very true, sir"; whereupon Sam turned about and steadily regarded him for some seconds in silence.

"I never knew," said Sam, fixing his eyes in a ruminative manner upon the blushing barber, — "I never knew but vun o' your trade, but *he* wos worth a dozen, and wos indeed dewoted to his callin'!"

"Was he in the easy shaving way, sir," inquired Mr. Slithers; "or in the cutting and curling line?"

"Both," replied Sam; "easy shavin' was his natur', and cuttin' and curlin' was his pride and glory. His whole delight wos in his trade. He spent all his money in bears, and run in debt for 'em besides, and there they wos a growling avay down in the front cellar all day long, and ineffectooally gnashing their teeth, vile the grease o' their relations and friends wos being re-tailed in gallipots in the shop above, and the first-floor winder wos ornamented vith their heads; not to speak o' the dreadful aggrawation it must have been to 'em to see a man alvays a walkin' up and down the pavement outside, vith the portrait of a bear in his last agonies, and underneath in large letters, 'Another fine animal wos slaughtered yesterday at Jinkinson's!' Hows'ever, there they wos, and there Jinkinson wos till he wos took wery ill with some inn'ard disorder, lost the use of his legs, and wos confined to his bed vere he laid a wery long time, but sich wos his pride in his profession even then, that wenever he wos worse than usual the doctor used to go down stairs and say, 'Jinkinson's wery low this mornin'; we must give the bears a stir'; and as sure as ever they stirred 'em up a bit and made 'em roar, Jinkinson opens his eyes if he wos ever so bad, calls out, 'There's the bears!' and rewives agin."

"Astonishing!" cried the barber.

"Not a bit," said Sam, "human natur' neat as imported. Vun day the doctor happenin' to say, 'I shall look in as usual to-morrow mornin',' Jinkinson catches hold of his hand and says, 'Doctor,' he says, 'will you grant me one favor?' 'I will, Jinkinson,' says the doctor. 'Then, doctor,' says Jinkinson, 'vill you come unshaved, and let me shave you?' 'I will,' says the doctor. 'God bless you,' says Jinkinson. Next day the doctor came, and arter he'd been shaved all skilful and reg'lar, he says, 'Jinkinson,' he says, 'it's wery plain this does you good. Now,' he says, 'I've got a coachman as has got a beard that it 'ud warm your heart to work on, and though the footman,' he says, 'has n't got much of a beard, still he's a trying it on vith a pair o' viskers to that extent that razors is Christian charity. If they take it in turns to mind the carriage wen it's a waitin' below,' he says, 'wot's to hinder you from operatin' on both of 'em ev'ry day as well as upon me? you v'e got six children,' he says, 'wot's to hinder you from shavin' all their heads and keepin' 'em shaved? you've got two assistants in the shop down stairs, wot's to hinder you from cuttin' and curlin' them as often as you like? Do this,' he says, 'and you're a man agin.' Jinkinson squeedged the doctor's hand and begun that wery day; he kept his tools upon the bed, and wenever he felt his-self gettin' worse, he turned to at vun o' the children who wos a runnin' about the house vith heads like clean Dutch cheeses, and shaved him ag'in. Vun day the lawyer come to make his vill; all the time he wos a takin' it down, Jinkinson was secretly a clippin' avay at his hair vith a large pair of scissors. 'Wot's that 'ere snippin' noise?' says the lawyer every now and then; 'it's like a man havin' his hair cut.' 'It *is* wery like a man havin' his hair cut,' says poor Jinkinson, hidin' the scissors, and lookin' quite innocent. By the time the lawyer found it out, he was wery nearly bald. Jinkinson wos kept alive in this vay for a long time, but at last vun day he has in all the children vun arter another, shaves each on 'em wery clean, and gives him vun kiss on the crown o' his head; then he has in the two assistants, and arter cuttin' and curlin' of 'em in the first style of elegance, says he should like to hear the woice o' the greasiest bear, vich rekvest is immedetly complied with; then he says that he feels wery happy in his mind and vishes to be left alone; and then he dies, prevously cuttin' his own hair and makin' one flat curl in the wery middle of his forehead."

This anecdote produced an extraordinary effect, not only upon Mr. Slithers, but upon the housekeeper also, who evinced so much anxiety to please and be pleased, that Mr. Weller, with a manner betokening some alarm, conveyed a whispered inquiry to his son whether he had gone "too fur."

"Wot do you mean by too fur?" demanded Sam.

"In that 'ere little compliment respectin' the want of hock'erdness in ladies, Sammy," replied his father.

"You don't think she's fallen in love with you in consekens o' that, do you?" said Sam.

"More unlikelier things have come to pass, my boy," replied Mr. Weller in a hoarse whisper; "I'm always afeerd of inadwertent captiwation, Sammy. If I know'd how to make myself ugly or unpleasant, I'd do it, Samivel, raything than live in this here state of perpetival terror!"

Mr. Weller had, at that time, no further opportunity of dwelling upon the apprehensions which beset his mind, for the immediate occasion of his fears proceeded to lead the way down stairs, apologizing as they went for conducting him into the kitchen, which apartment, however, she was induced to proffer for his accommodation in preference to her own little room, the rather as it afforded greater facilities for smoking, and was immediately adjoining the ale-cellar. The preparations which were already made sufficiently proved that these were not mere words of course, for on the deal table were a sturdy ale jug and glasses, flanked with clean pipes and a plentiful supply of tobacco for the old gentleman and his son, while on a dresser hard by was goodly store of cold meat and other eatables. At sight of these arrangements Mr. Weller was at first distracted between his love of joviality and his doubts whether they were not to be considered as so many evidences of captivation having already taken place; but he soon yielded to his natural impulse, and took his seat at the table with a very jolly countenance.

"As to imbibin' any o' this here flagrant veed, mum, in the presence of a lady," said Mr. Weller, taking up a pipe and laying it down again, "it could n't be. Samivel, total abstinence, if *you* please."

"But I like it of all things," said the housekeeper.

"No," rejoined Mr. Weller, shaking his head, — "no."

"Upon my word I do," said the housekeeper. "Mr. Slithers knows I do."

Mr. Weller coughed, and notwithstanding the barber's confirmation of the statement, said "No" again, but more feebly than before. The housekeeper lighted a piece of paper, and insisted on applying it to the bowl of the pipe with her own fair hands; Mr. Weller resisted; the housekeeper cried that her fingers would be burnt; Mr. Weller gave way. The pipe was ignited, Mr. Weller drew a long puff of smoke, and detecting himself in the very act of smiling on the housekeeper, put a sudden constraint upon his countenance and looked sternly at the candle, with a determination not to captivate, himself, or encourage thoughts of captivation in others. From this iron frame of mind he was roused by the voice of his son.

"I don't think," said Sam, who was smoking with great composure and enjoyment, "that if the lady wos agreeable it 'ud be wery far out 'o the vay for us four to make up a club of our own like the governors does up stairs, and let him," Sam pointed with the stem of his pipe towards his parent, "be the president."

The housekeeper affably declared that it was the very thing she had been thinking of. The barber said the same. Mr. Weller said nothing, but he laid down his pipe as if in a fit of inspiration, and performed the following manœuvres.

Unbuttoning the three lower buttons of his waistcoat, and pausing for a moment to enjoy the easy flow of breath consequent upon this process, he laid violent hands upon his watch-chain and slowly and with extreme difficulty drew from his fob an immense double-cased silver watch, which brought the lining of the pocket with it, and was not to be disentangled but by great exertions and an amazing redness of face. Having fairly got it out at last, he detached the outer case and wound it up with a key of corresponding magnitude; then put the case on again, and having applied the watch to his ear to ascertain that it was still going, gave it some half-dozen hard knocks on the table to improve its performance.

"That," said Mr. Weller, laying it on the table with its face upwards, "is the title and emblem o' this here society. Sammy, reach them two stools this vay for the wacant cheers. Ladies and gen'lmen, Mr. Weller's Watch is vound up and now a goin'. Order!"

By way of enforcing this proclamation, Mr. Weller, using the watch after the manner of a president's hammer, and remarking with great pride that nothing hurt it, and that falls and concussions of all kinds materially enhanced the excellence of the works and assisted the regulator, knocked the table a great many times, and declared the association formally constituted.

"And don't let 's have no grinnin' at the cheer, Samivel," said Mr. Weller to his son, "or I shall be committin' you to the cellar, and then p'r'aps we may get into wot the 'Merrikins call a fix, and the English a qvestion o' privileges."

Having uttered this friendly caution, the president settled himself in his chair with great dignity, and requested that Mr. Samuel would relate an anecdote.

"I 've told one," said Sam.

"Wery good, sir; tell another," returned the chair.

"We wos a talking jist now, sir," said Sam, turning to Slithers, "about barbers. Pursuing that 'ere fruitful theme, sir, I 'll tell you in a wery few words a romantic little story about another barber as p'r'aps you may never have heerd."

"Samivel!" said Mr. Weller, again bringing his watch and the table into smart collision, "address your observations to the cheer, sir, and not to priwate indiwiduals!"

"And if I might rise to order," said the barber, in a soft voice, and looking round him with a conciliatory smile as he leant over the table, with the knuckles of his left hand resting upon it, — "if I *might* rise to order, I would suggest that 'barbers' is not exactly the kind of language which is agreeable and soothing to our feelings. You, sir, will correct me if I 'm wrong, but I believe there *is* such a word in the dictionary as hair-dressers."

"Well, but suppose he was n't a hair-dresser," suggested Sam.

"Wy then, sir, be parliamentary, and call him vun all the more," returned his father. "In the same vay as ev'ry gen'lman in another place is a *h*onorable, ev'ry barber in this place is a hair-dresser. Ven you read the speeches in the papers, and see as vun gen'lman says of another, 'the *h*onorable member, if he vill allow me to call him so,' you vill understand, sir, that that means, 'if he vill allow me to keep up that 'ere pleasant and uniwersal fiction?'"

It is a common remark, confirmed by history and experience, that great men rise with the circumstances in which they are placed. Mr Weller came out so strong in his capacity of chairman, that Sam was for some time prevented from speaking by a grin of surprise, which held his faculties enchained, and at last subsided in a long whistle of a single note. Nay, the old gentleman appeared even to have astonished himself, and that to no small extent, as was demonstrated by the vast amount of chuckling in which he indulged, after the utterance of these lucid remarks.

"Here 's the story," said Sam. "Vunce upon a time there wos a young hair-dresser as opened a wery smart little shop vith four wax dummies in the winder, two gen'lmen and two ladies, — the gen'lmen vith blue dots for their beards, wery large viskers, ou-dacious heads of hair, uncommon clear eyes, and nostrils of amazin' pinkness, — the ladies vith their heads o' one side, their right forefingers on their lips, and their forms deweloped beautiful, in vich last respect they had the adwantage over the gen'lmen, as was n't allowed but wery little shoulder, and terminated rayther abrupt, in fancy drapery. He had also a many hair-brushes and tooth-brushes bottled up in the winder, neat glass cases on the counter, a floor-clothed cuttin'-room up stairs, and a weighin'-macheen in the shop right opposite the door; but the great attraction and ornament wos the dummies, which this here young hair-dresser wos constantly a runnin' out in the road to look at, and constantly a runnin' in agin to touch up and polish; in short, he wos so proud on 'em that ven Sunday come, he wos always wretched and mis'rable to think they wos behind the shutters, and looked anxiously for Monday on that account. Vun o' these dummies wos a fav'rite vith him beyond the others, and ven any of his acquaintance asked him wy he did n't get married, — as the young ladies he know'd, in partickler, often did, — he used to say, 'Never! I never vill enter into the bonds of vedlock,' he says, 'until I meet vith a young 'ooman as realizes my idea o' that 'ere fairest dummy vith the light hair. Then and not till then,' he says, 'I vill approach the altar!' All the young ladies he know'd as had got dark hair told him this wos wery sinful and that he wos wurshippin' a idle, but them as wos at all near the same shade as the dummy colored up wery much, and wos observed to think him a wery nice young man."

"Samivel," said Mr. Weller, gravely; "a member o' this assosiashun bein' one o' that 'ere tender sex which is now immedetly referred to, I have to rekvest that you vill make no reflexions."

"I ain't a makin' any, am I?" inquired Sam.

"Order, sir!' rejoined Mr. Weller, with severe dignity; then, sinking the chairman in the father, he added in his usual tone of voice, "Samivel, drive on!"

Sam interchanged a smile with the housekeeper, and proceeded: —

"The young hair-dresser had n't been in the habit o' makin' this awowal above six months, ven he en-countered a young lady as wos the wery picter o' the fairest dummy. 'Now,' he says, 'it 's all up. I am a slave!' The young lady wos not only the picter o' the fairest dummy, but she wos wery romantic, as the young hair-dresser wos, too, and he says, 'Oh!' he says, 'here 's a community o' feelin', here 's a flow o' soul!' he says, 'here 's a interchange o' sentiment!' The young lady did n't say much, o' course, but she expressed herself agreeable, and shortly artervards vent to see him vith a mutual friend. The hair-dresser rushes out to meet her, but d'rectly she sees the dummies she changes color and falls a tremblin' wiolently. 'Look up, my love,' says the hair-dresser, 'behold your imige in my winder, but not correcter than in my art!' 'My imige!' she says. 'Yourn!' replies the hair-dresser. 'But whose imige is *that!*' she says, a pinting at vun o' the gen'lmen. 'No vun's, my love,' he says, 'it is but a idea.' 'A idea!' she cries; 'it is a portrait, I feel it is a portrait, and that 'ere noble face must be in the millingtary!' 'Wot do I hear!' says he, a crumplin' his curls. 'Villiam Gibbs,' she says, quite firm, 'never renoo the subject. I respect you as a friend,' she says, 'but my affections is set upon that manly brow.' 'This,' says the hair-dresser, 'is a reg'lar blight, and in it I perceive the hand of Fate. Farevell!' Vith these vords he rushes into the shop, breaks the dummy's nose vith a blow of his curlin'-irons, melts him down at the parlor fire, and never smiles arterverds."

"The young lady, Mr. Weller?" said the housekeeper.

"Why, ma'am," said Sam, "finding that Fate had a spite agin her, and everybody she come into contact vith, she never smiled neither, but read a deal o' poetry and pined avay, — by rayther slow degrees, for she an't dead yet. It took a deal o' poetry to kill the hair-dresser, and some people say arter all, that it was more the gin and water as caused him to be run over, p'r'aps it wos a little o' both, and came o' mixing the two."

The barber declared that Mr. Weller had related one of the most interesting stories that had ever come within his knowledge, in which opinion the housekeeper entirely concurred.

"Are you a married man, sir?" inquired Sam.

The barber replied that he had not that honor.

"I s'pose you mean to be?" said Sam.

"Well," replied the barber, rubbing his hands smirkingly, "I don't know, I don't think it 's very likely."

"That 's a bad sign," said Sam; "if you 'd said you meant to be vun o' these days, I should ha' looked upon you as bein' safe. You 're in a wery precarious state."

"I am not conscious of any danger, at all events," returned the barber.

"No more wos I, sir," said the elder Mr. Weller, interposing; "those vere my symptoms, exactly. I 've been took that vay twice. Keep your vether eye open, my friend, or you 're gone."

There was something so very solemn about this admonition, both in its matter and manner, and also in the way in which Mr. Weller still kept his eye fixed upon the unsuspecting victim, that nobody cared to speak for some little time, and might not have cared to do so for some time longer, if the housekeeper had not happened to sigh, which called off the old gentleman's attention and gave rise to a gallant inquiry whether "there wos anythin' wery piercin' in that 'ere little heart."

"Dear me, Mr. Weller!" said the housekeeper, laughing.

"No, but is there anythin' as agitates it?" pursued the old gentleman. "Has it always been obderrate, always opposed to the happiness o' human creeturs? Eh? Has it?"

At this critical juncture for her blushes and confusion, the housekeeper discovered that more ale was wanted, and hastily withdrew into the cellar to draw the same, followed by the barber, who insisted on carrying the candle. Having looked after her with a very complacent expression of face, and after him with some disdain, Mr. Weller caused his glance to travel slowly round the kitchen until at length it rested on his son.

"Sammy," said Mr. Weller, "I mistrust that barber."

"Wot for?" returned Sam, "wot 's he got to do with you? You 're a nice man, you are, arter pretendin' all kinds o' terror, to go a payin' compliments and talkin' about hearts and piercers."

The imputation of gallantry appeared to afford Mr. Weller the utmost delight, for he replied in a voice choked by suppressed laughter, and with the tears in his eyes, —

"Wos I a talkin' about hearts and piercers, — wos I though, Sammy, eh?"

"Wos you? of course you wos."

"She don't know no better, Sammy; there an't no harm in it, — no danger, Sammy; she 's only a punster. She seemed pleased, though, did n't she? O' course, she wos pleased, it 's nat'ral she should be, wery nat'ral."

"He 's wain of it!" exclaimed Sam, joining in his father's mirth. "He 's actually wain!"

"Hush!" replied Mr. Weller, composing his features, "they 're a comin' back, — the little heart 's a comin' back. But mark these wurds o' mine once more, and remember 'em ven your father says he said 'em. Samivel, I mistrust that 'ere deceitful barber." *

* * * *

* Old Curiosity Shop is continued to the end of the number.

MASTER HUMPHREY'S CLOCK.

VI.

MASTER HUMPHREY FROM HIS CLOCK-SIDE IN THE CHIMNEY-CORNER.

TWO or three evenings after the institution of Mr. Weller's Watch, I thought I heard, as I walked in the garden, the voice of Mr. Weller himself at no great distance; and stopping once or twice to listen more attentively, I found that the sounds proceeded from my housekeeper's little sitting-room, which is at the back of the house. I took no further notice of the circumstance at that time, but it formed the subject of a conversation between me and my friend Jack Redburn next morning, when I found that I had not been deceived in my impression. Jack furnished me with the following particulars, and as he appeared to take extraordinary pleasure in relating them, I have begged him in future to jot down any such domestic scenes or occurrences that may please his humor, in order that they may be told in his own way. I must confess that, as Mr. Pickwick and he are constantly together, I have been influenced, in making this request, by a secret desire to know something of their proceedings.

On the evening in question, the housekeeper's room was arranged with particular care, and the housekeeper herself was very smartly dressed. The preparations, however, were not confined to mere showy demonstrations, as tea was prepared for three persons, with a small display of preserves and jams and sweet cakes, which heralded some uncommon occasion. Miss Benton (my housekeeper bears that name) was in a state of great expectation, too, frequently going to the front door and looking anxiously down the lane, and more than once observing to the servant-girl that she expected company, and hoped no accident had happened to delay them.

A modest ring at the bell at length allayed her fears, and Miss Benton, hurrying into her own room and shutting herself up in order that she might preserve that appearance of being taken by surprise which is so essential to the polite reception of visitors, awaited their coming with a smiling countenance.

"Good ev'nin', mum," said the older Mr. Weller, looking in at the door after a prefatory tap. "I 'm afeerd we 've come in rayther arter the time, mum, but the young colt being full o' wice, has been a boltin' and shyin' and gettin' his leg over the traces to sich a extent that if he an't wery soon broke in, he 'll wex me into a broken heart, and then he 'll never be brought out no more except to learn his letters from the writin' on his grandfather's tombstone."

With these pathetic words, which were addressed to something outside the door about two feet six from the ground, Mr. Weller introduced a very small boy firmly set upon a couple of very sturdy legs, who looked as if nothing could ever knock him down. Besides having a very round face strongly resembling Mr. Weller's, and a stout little body of exactly his build, this young gentleman, standing with his little legs very wide apart as if the top-boots were familiar to them, actually winked upon the housekeeper with his infant eye, in imitation of his grandfather.

"There 's a naughty boy, mum," said Mr. Weller, bursting with delight; "there 's a immoral Tony. Wos there ever a little chap o' four year and eight months old as vinked his eye at a strange lady afore?"

As little affected by this observation as by the former appeal to his feelings, Master Weller elevated in the air a small model of a coach whip which he carried in his hand, and addressing the housekeeper with a shrill "ya — hip!" inquired if she was "going down the road"; at which happy adaptation of a lesson he had been taught from infancy, Mr. Weller could restrain his feelings no longer, but gave him twopence on the spot.

"It 's in wain to deny it, mum," said Mr. Weller, "this here is a boy arter his grandfather's own heart, and beats out all the boys as ever wos or will be. Though at the same time, mum," added Mr. Weller, trying to look gravely down upon his favorite, "it was wery wrong on him to want to — over all the posts as we come along, and wery cruel on him to force poor grandfather to lift him cross-legged over every vun of 'em. He would n't pass vun single blessed post, mum, and at the top o' the lane there 's seven-and-forty on 'em all in a row, and wery close together"

Here Mr. Weller, whose feelings were in a perpetual conflict between pride in his grandson's achievements, and a sense of his own responsibility and the importance of impressing him with moral truths, burst into a fit of laughter, and suddenly checking himself, remarked in a severe tone that little boys as made their grandfathers put 'em over posts never went to heaven at any price.

By this time the housekeeper had made tea, and little Tony, placed on a chair beside her, with his eyes nearly on a level with the top of the table, was provided with various delicacies which yielded him extreme contentment. The housekeeper (who seemed rather afraid of the child, notwithstanding her caresses) then patted him on the head and declared that he was the finest boy she had ever seen.

"Wy, mum," said Mr. Weller, "I don't think you 'll see a many sich, and that 's the truth. But if my son Samivel vould give me my vay, mum, and only dispense vith his — *might* I wenter to say the vurd?"

"What word, Mr. Weller?" said the housekeeper, blushing slightly.

"Petticuts, mum," returned that gentleman, laying his hand upon the garments of his grandson. "If my son Samivel, mum, vould only dis-pense vith these here, you 'd see such a alteration in his appearance, as the imagination can't depicter."

"But what would you have the child wear instead, Mr. Weller?" said the housekeeper.

"I 've offered my son Samivel, mum, agen and agen," returned the old gentleman, "to purwide him at my own cost vith a suit o' clothes as 'ud be the makin' on him, and form his mind in infancy for those pursuits as I hope the family o' the Vellers vill alvays dewote themselves to. Tony, my boy, tell the lady wot them clothes are, as grandfather says, father ought to let you vear."

"A little white hat and a little sprig weskut and little knee cords and little top boots and a little green coat with little bright buttons and a little welwet collar," replied Tony, with great readiness and no stops.

"That 's the cos-toom, mum," said Mr. Weller, looking proudly at the housekeeper "Once make sich a model on him as that, and you 'd say he *wos* a angel!"

Perhaps the housekeeper thought that in such a guise young Tony would look more like the angel at Islington than anything else of that name, or perhaps she was disconcerted to find her previously conceived ideas disturbed, as angels are not commonly represented in top-boots and sprig waistcoats. She coughed, doubtfully, but said nothing.

"How many brothers and sisters have you, my dear?" she asked, after a short silence.

"One brother and no sister at all," replied Tony. "Sam his name is, and so 's my father's. Do you know my father?"

"O yes, I know him," said the housekeeper, graciously.

"Is my father fond of you?" pursued Tony.

"I hope so," rejoined the smiling housekeeper.

Tony considered a moment, and then said, "Is my grandfather fond of you?"

This would seem a very easy question to answer, but instead of replying to it, the housekeeper smiled in great confusion, and said that really children did ask such extraordinary questions that it was the most difficult thing in the world to talk to them. Mr. Weller took upon himself to reply that he was very fond of the lady; but the housekeeper entreating that he would not put such things into the child's head, Mr. Weller shook his own while she looked another way, and seemed to be troubled with a misgiving that captivation was in progress. It was, perhaps, on this account that he changed the subject precipitately.

"It 's wery wrong in little boys to make game o' their grandfathers, an't it, mum?" said Mr. Weller, shaking his head waggishly, until Tony looked at him, when he counterfeited the deepest dejection and sorrow.

"O, very sad!" assented the housekeeper. "But I hope no little boys do that?"

"There is vun young Turk, mum," said Mr. Weller, "as havin' seen his grandfather a little overcome vith drink on the occasion of a friend's birthday, goes a reelin' and staggerin' about the house, and makin' believe that he 's the old gen'l'm'n."

"O, quite shocking!" cried the housekeeper.

"Yes, mum," said Mr. Weller, "and prevously to so doin', this here young traitor that I 'm a speakin' of, pinches his little nose to make it red, and then he gives a hiccup and says, 'I 'm all right,' he says, 'give us another song!' Ha, ha! 'Give us another song,' he says. Ha, ha, ha!"

In his excessive delight, Mr. Weller was quite unmindful of his moral responsibility, until little Tony kicked up his legs, and laughing immoderately, cried, "That was me, that was"; whereupon the grandfather, by a great effort, became extremely solemn.

"No, Tony, not you," said Mr. Weller. "I hope it war n't you, Tony. It must ha' been that 'ere naughty little chap as comes sometimes out o' the empty watch-box round the corner, — that same little chap as wos found standing on the table afore the looking-glass, pretending to shave himself vith a oyster-knife."

"He did n't hurt himself, I hope?" observed the housekeeper.

"Not he, mum," said Mr. Weller, proudly; "bless your heart, you might trust that 'ere boy vith a steam-engine a'most, he 's such a knowin' young —" But suddenly recollecting himself and observing that Tony perfectly understood and appreciated the compliment, the old gentleman groaned and observed that "it wos all wery shockin' — wery."

"O, he 's a bad 'un," said Mr. Weller, "is that 'ere watch-box boy, makin' such a noise and litter in the back yard, he does, waterin' wooden horses and feedin' of 'em vith grass, and perpetivally spillin' his little brother out of a veelbarrow and frightenin' his mother out of her wits, at the wery moment wen she 's expectin' to increase his stock of happiness vith another playfeller, — O, he 's a bad 'un! He 's even gone so far as to put on a pair o' paper spectacles as he got his father to make for him, and walk up and down the garden vith his hands behind him in imitation of Mr. Pickwick, — but Tony don't do sich things, O no!"

"O no!" echoed Tony.

"He knows better, he does," said Mr. Weller. "He knows that if he wos to come sich games as these nobody would n't love him, and that his grandfather in partickler could n't abear the sight on him; for vich reasons Tony 's always good."

"Always good," echoed Tony; and his grandfather immediately took him on his knee and kissed him, at the same time, with many nods and winks, slyly pointing at the child's head with his thumb, in order that the housekeeper, otherwise deceived by the admirable manner in which he (Mr. Weller) had sustained his character, might not suppose that any other young gentleman was referred to, and might clearly understand that the boy of the watch-box was but an imaginary creation, and a fetch of Tony himself, invented for his improvement and reformation.

Not confining himself to a mere verbal description of his grandson's abilities, Mr. Weller, when tea was finished, incited him by various gifts of pence and halfpence to smoke imaginary pipes, drink visionary beer from real pots, imitate his grandfather without reserve, and in particular to go through the drunken scene, which threw the old gentleman into ecstasies and filled the housekeeper with wonder. Nor was Mr. Weller's pride satisfied with even this display, for when he took his leave he carried the child, like some rare and astonishing curiosity, first to the barber's house and afterwards to the tobacconist's, at each of which places he repeated his performances with the utmost effect to applauding and delighted audiences. It was half past nine o'clock when Mr. Weller was last seen carrying him home upon his shoulder, and it has been whispered abroad that at that time the infant Tony was rather intoxicated.*

[Master Humphrey is revived thus at the close of The Old Curiosity Shop, merely to introduce Barnaby Rudge.]

I was musing the other evening upon the characters and incidents with which I had been so long engaged; wondering how I could ever have looked forward with pleasure to the completion of my tale, and reproaching myself for having done so, as if it were a kind of cruelty to those companions of my solitude whom I had now dismissed, and could never again recall; when my clock struck ten. Punctual to the hour, my friends appeared.

On our last night of meeting, we had finished the story which the reader has just concluded. Our conversation took the same current as the meditations which the entrance of my friends had interrupted, and The Old Curiosity Shop was the staple of our discourse.

I may confide to the reader now, that in connection with this little history I had something upon my mind; something to communicate which I had all along with difficulty repressed; something I had deemed it, during the progress of the story, necessary to its interest to disguise, and which, now that it was over, I wished, and was yet reluctant to disclose.

* Old Curiosity Shop is continued from here to the end without interruption.

To conceal anything from those to whom I am attached, is not in my nature. I can never close my lips where I have opened my heart. This temper, and the consciousness of having done some violence to it in my narrative, laid me under a restraint which I should have had great difficulty in overcoming, but for a timely remark from Mr. Miles, who, as I hinted in a former paper, is a gentleman of business habits, and of great exactness and propriety in all his transactions.

"I could have wished," my friend objected, "that we had been made acquainted with the single gentleman's name. I don't like his withholding his name. It made me look upon him at first with suspicion, and caused me to doubt his moral character, I assure you. I am fully satisfied by this time of his being a worthy creature, but in this respect he certainly would not appear to have acted at all like a man of business."

"My friends," said I, drawing to the table, at which they were by this time seated in their usual chairs, "do you remember that this story bore another title besides that one we have so often heard of late?"

Mr. Miles had his pocket-book out in an instant, and referring to an entry therein, rejoined, "Certainly. Personal Adventures of Master Humphrey. Here it is. I made a note of it at the time."

I was about to resume what I had to tell them, when the same Mr. Miles again interrupted me, observing that the narrative originated in a personal adventure of my own, and that was no doubt the reason for its being thus designated.

This led me to the point at once.

"You will one and all forgive me," I returned, "if, for the greater convenience of the story, and for its better introduction, that adventure was fictitious. I had my share, indeed, — no light or trivial one, — in the pages we have read, but it was not the share I feigned to have at first. The younger brother, the single gentleman, the nameless actor in this little drama, stands before you now."

It was easy to see they had not expected this disclosure.

"Yes," I pursued. "I can look back upon my part in it with a calm, half-smiling pity for myself as for some other man. But I am he, indeed; and now the chief sorrows of my life are yours."

I need not say what true gratification I derived from the sympathy and kindness with which this acknowledgment was received; nor how often it had risen to my lips before; nor how difficult I had found it — how impossible, when I came to those passages which touched me most, and most nearly concerned me — to sustain the character I had assumed. It is enough to say that I replaced in the clock-case the record of so many trials, — sorrowfully, it is true, but with a softened sorrow which was almost pleasure; and felt that in living through the past again, and communicating to others the lesson it had helped to teach me, I had been a happier man.

We lingered so long over the leaves from which I had read, that as I consigned them to their former resting-place, the hand of my trusty clock pointed to twelve, and there came towards us upon the wind the voice of the deep and distant bell of St. Paul's as it struck the hour of midnight.

"This," said I, returning with a manuscript I had taken, at the moment, from the same repository, "to be opened to such music, should be a tale where London's face by night is darkly seen, and where some deed of such a time as this is dimly shadowed out. Which of us here has seen the working of that great machine whose voice has just now ceased?"

Mr. Pickwick had, of course, and so had Mr. Miles. Jack and my deaf friend were in the minority.

I had seen it but a few days before, and could not help telling them of the fancy I had had about it.

I paid my fee of twopence upon entering, to one of the money-changers who sit within the Temple; and falling, after a few turns up and down, into the quiet train of thought which such a place awakens, paced the echoing stones like some old monk whose present world lay all within its walls. As I looked afar up into the lofty dome, I could not help wondering what were his reflections whose genius reared that mighty pile, when, the last small wedge of timber fixed, the last nail driven into its home for many centuries, the clang of hammers, and the hum of busy voices gone, and the Great Silence whole years of noise had helped to make, reigning undisturbed around, he mused as I did now, upon his work, and lost himself amid its vast extent. I could not quite determine whether the contemplation of it would impress him with a sense of greatness or of insignificance; but when I remembered how long a time it had taken to erect, in how short a space it might be traversed even to its remotest parts, for how brief a term he, or any of those who cared to bear his name, would live to see it or know of its existence, I imagined him far more melancholy than proud, and looking with regret upon his labor done. With these thoughts in my mind, I began to ascend, almost unconsciously, the flight of steps leading to the several wonders of the building, and found myself before a barrier where another money-taker sat, who demanded which among them I would choose to see. There were the stone-gallery, he said, and the whispering gallery, the geometrical staircase, the room of models, the clock, — the clock being quite in my way, I stopped him there, and chose that sight from all the rest.

I groped my way into the Turret which it occupies, and saw before me, in a kind of loft, what seemed to be a great, old, oaken press with folding doors. These being thrown back by the attendant (who was sleeping when I came upon him, and looked a drowsy fellow, as though his close companionship with Time had made him quite indifferent to it), disclosed a complicated crowd of wheels and chains in iron and brass, — great, sturdy, rattling engines, — suggestive of breaking a finger put in here or there, and grinding the bone to powder, — and these were the Clock! Its very pulse, if I may use the word, was like no other clock. It did not mark the flight of every moment with a gentle second stroke, as though it would check old Time, and have him stay his pace in pity, but measured it with one sledge-hammer beat, as if its business were to crush the seconds as they came trooping on, and remorselessly to clear a path before the Day of Judgment.

I sat down opposite to it, and hearing its regular and never-changing voice, that one deep constant note, uppermost amongst all the noise and clatter in the streets below, — marking that, let that tumult rise or fall, go on or stop — let it be night or noon, to-morrow or to-day, this year or next, — it still performed its functions with the same dull constancy, and regulated the progress of the life around, the fancy came upon me that this was London's Heart, and that when it should cease to beat, the City would be no more.

It is night. Calm and unmoved amidst the scenes that darkness favors, the great heart of London throbs in its Giant breast. Wealth and beggary, vice and virtue, guilt and innocence, repletion and the direst hunger, all treading on each other and crowding together, are gathered round it. Draw but a little circle above the clustering house-tops, and you shall have within its space everything, with its opposite extreme and contradiction, close beside. Where yonder feeble light is shining, a man is but this moment dead. The taper at a few yards' distance is seen by eyes that have this instant opened on the world. There are two houses separated by but an inch or two of wall. In one, there are quiet minds at rest; in the other, a waking conscience that one might think would trouble the very air. In that close corner where the roofs shrink down and cower together as if to hide their secrets from the handsome street hard by, there are such dark crimes, such miseries and horrors, as could be hardly told in whispers. In the handsome street, there are folks asleep who have dwelt there all their lives, and have no more knowledge of these things than if they had never been, or were transacted at the remotest limits of the world, — who, if they were hinted at, would shake their heads, look wise, and frown, and say they were impossible and out of Nature, — as if all great towns were not. Does not this Heart of London, that nothing moves, nor stops, nor quickens, — that goes on the same let what will be done, — does it not express the city's character well!

The day begins to break, and soon there is the hum and noise of life. Those who have spent the night on doorsteps and cold stones crawl off to beg; they who have slept in beds come forth to their occupation, too, and business is astir. The fog of sleep rolls slowly off, and London shines awake. The streets are filled with carriages, and people gayly clad. The jails are full, too, to the throat, nor have the workhouses or hospitals much room to spare. The courts of law are crowded. Taverns have their regular frequenters by this time, and every mart of traffic has its throng. Each of these places is a world, and has its own inhabitants; each is distinct from, and almost unconscious of the existence of any other. There are some few people well to do, who remember to have heard it said, that numbers of men and women — thousands, they think it was — get up in London every day, unknowing where to lay their heads at night; and that there are quarters of the town where misery and famine always are. They don't believe it quite, — there may be some truth in it, but it is exaggerated, of course. So, each of these thousand worlds goes on, intent upon itself, until night comes again, — first with its lights and pleasures, and its cheerful streets; then with its guilt and darkness.

Heart of London, there is a moral in thy every stroke! as I look on at thy indomitable working, which neither death, nor press of life, nor grief, nor gladness out of doors will influence one jot, I seem to hear a voice within thee which sinks into my heart, bidding me, as I elbow my way among the crowd, have some thought for the meanest wretch that passes, and, being a man, to turn away with scorn and pride from none that bear the human shape.

I am by no means sure that I might not have been tempted to enlarge upon the subject, had not the papers that lay before me on the table been a silent reproach for even this digression. I took them up again when I had got thus far, and seriously prepared to read.

The handwriting was strange to me, for the manuscript had been fairly copied. As it is against our rules, in such a case, to inquire into the authorship until the reading is concluded, I could only glance at the different faces round me, in search of some expression which should betray the writer. Whoever he might be, he was prepared for this, and gave no sign for my enlightenment.

I had the papers in my hand, when my deaf friend interposed with a suggestion.

"It has occurred to me," he said, "bearing in mind your sequel to the tale we have finished, that if such of us as have anything to relate of our own lives could interweave it with our contribution to the Clock, it would be well to do so. This need be no restraint upon us, either as to time, or place, or incident, since any real passage of this kind may be surrounded by fictitious circumstances, and represented by fictitious characters. What if we make this an article of agreement among ourselves?"

The proposition was cordially received, but the difficulty appeared to be that here was a long story written before we had thought of it.

"Unless," said I, "it should have happened that the writer of this tale — which is not impossible, for men are apt to do so when they write — has actually mingled with it something of his own endurance and experience."

Nobody spoke, but I thought I detected in one quarter that this was really the case.

"If I have no assurance to the contrary," I added, therefore, "I shall take it for granted that he has done so, and that even these papers come within our new agreement. Everybody being mute, we hold that understanding, if you please "

And here I was about to begin again, when Jack informed us softly, that during the progress of our last narrative, Mr. Weller's Watch had adjourned its sittings from the kitchen, and regularly met outside our door, where he had no doubt that august body would be found at the present moment. As this was for the convenience of listening to our stories, he submitted that they might be suffered to come in, and hear them more pleasantly.

To this we one and all yielded a ready assent, and the party being discovered, as Jack had supposed, and invited to walk in, entered (though not without great confusion at having been detected), and were accommodated with chairs at a little distance.

Then, the lamp being trimmed, the fire well stirred and burning brightly, the hearth clean swept, the curtains closely drawn, the clock wound up, we entered on our new story, — BARNABY RUDGE.

* * * *

[This is, as indicated, the last appearance of Master Humphrey's Clock. It forms the conclusion of Barnaby Rudge.]

It is again midnight. My fire burns cheerfully; the room is filled with my old friend's sober voice; and I am left to muse upon the story we have just now finished.

It makes me smile, at such a time as this, to think if there were any one to see me sitting in my easy-chair, my gray head hanging down, my eyes bent thoughtfully upon the glowing embers, and my crutch — emblem of my helplessness — lying upon the hearth at my feet, how solitary I should seem. Yet though I am the sole tenant of this chimney-corner, though I am childless and old, I have no sense of loneliness at this hour; but am the centre of a silent group whose company I love.

Thus, even age and weakness have their consolations. If I were a younger man, if I were more active, more strongly bound and tied to life, these visionary friends would shun me, or I should desire to fly from them. Being what I am, I can court their society, and delight in it; and pass whole hours in picturing to myself the shadows that perchance flock every night into this chamber, and in imagining with pleasure what kind of interest they have in the frail, feeble mortal, who is its sole inhabitant.

All the friends I have ever lost I find again among these visitors. I love to fancy their spirits hovering about me, feeling still some earthly kindness for their old companion, and watching his decay. "He is weaker, he declines apace, he draws nearer and nearer to us, and will soon be conscious of our existence." What is there to alarm me in this? It is encouragement and hope.

These thoughts have never crowded on me half so fast as they have done to-night. Faces I had long forgotten have become familiar to me once again; traits I had endeavored to recall for years, have come before me in an instant; nothing is changed but me: and even I can be my former self at will.

Raising my eyes but now to the face of my old clock, I remember, quite involuntarily, the veneration, not unmixed with a sort of childish awe, with which I used to sit and watch it as it ticked unheeded in a dark staircase corner. I recollect looking more grave and steady when I met its dusty face, as if, having that strange kind of life within it, and being free from all excess of vulgar appetite, and warning all the house by night and day, it were a sage. How often have I listened to it as it told the beads of time, and wondered at its constancy! How often watched it slowly pointing round the dial, and, while I panted for the eagerly expected hour to come, admired, despite myself, its steadiness of purpose and lofty freedom from all human strife, impatience, and desire!

I thought it cruel once. It was very hard of heart, to my mind, I remember. It was an old servant, even then; and I felt as though it ought to show some sorrow; as though it wanted sympathy with us in our distress, and were a dull, heartless, mercenary creature. Ah! how soon I learnt to know that in its ceaseless going on, and in its being checked or stayed by nothing, lay its greatest kindness, and the only balm for grief and wounded peace of mind!

To-night, to-night, when this tranquillity and calm are on my spirits, and memory presents so many shifting scenes before me, I take my quiet stand at will by many a fire that has been long extinguished, and mingle with the cheerful group that cluster round it. If I could be sorrowful in such a mood, I should grow sad to think what a poor blot I was upon their youth and beauty once, and now how few remain to put me to the blush; I should grow sad to think that such among them as I sometimes meet with in my daily walks are scarcely less infirm than I; that time has brought us to a level; and that all distinctions fade and vanish as we take our trembling steps towards the grave.

But memory was given us for better purposes than this, and mine is not a torment, but a source of pleasure. To muse upon the gayety and youth I have known, suggests to me glad scenes of harmless mirth that may be passing now. From contemplating them apart, I soon become an actor in these little dramas; and humoring my fancy, lose myself among the beings it invokes.

When my fire is bright and high, and a warm blush mantles in the walls and ceiling of this ancient room; when my clock makes cheerful music, like one of those chirping insects who delight in the warm hearth, and are sometimes, by a good superstition, looked upon as the harbingers of fortune and plenty to that household in whose mercies they put their humble trust; when everything is in a ruddy, genial glow, and there are voices in the crackling flame, and smiles in its flashing light; other smiles and other voices congregate around me, invading, with their pleasant harmony, the silence of the time.

For then a knot of youthful creatures gather round my fireside, and the room re-echoes to their merry voices. My solitary chair no longer holds its ample place before the fire, but is wheeled into a smaller corner, to leave more room for the broad circle formed about the cheerful hearth. I have sons, and daughters, and grandchildren; and we are assembled on some occasion of rejoicing common to us all. It is a birthday, perhaps, or perhaps it may be Christmas-time; but be it what it may, there is rare holiday among us; we are full of glee.

In the chimney-corner, opposite myself, sits one who has grown old beside me. She is changed, of course; much changed; and yet I recognize the girl even in that gray hair and wrinkled brow. Glancing from the laughing child who half hides in her ample skirts, and half peeps out, — and from her to the little matron of twelve years old, who sits so womanly and so demure at no great distance from me, — and from her again, to a fair girl in the full bloom of early womanhood, the centre of the group, who has glanced more than once towards the opening door, and by whom the children, whispering and tittering among themselves, *will* leave a vacant chair, although she bids them not, — I see her image thrice repeated, and feel how long it is before one form and set of features wholly pass away, if ever, from among the living. While I am dwelling upon this, and tracing out the gradual change from infancy to youth, from youth to perfect growth, from that to age; and thinking, with an old man's pride, that she is comely yet; I feel a slight, thin hand upon my arm, and, looking down, see seated at my feet a crippled boy, — a gentle, patient child, — whose aspect I know well. He rests upon a little crutch, — I know it too, — and leaning on it as he climbs my footstool, whispers in my ear, "I am hardly one of these, dear grandfather, although I love them dearly. They are very kind to me, but you will be kinder still, I know."

I have my hand upon his neck, and stoop to kiss him, when my clock strikes, my chair is in its old spot, and I am alone.

What if I be? What if this fireside be tenantless, save for the presence of one weak old man! From my house-top I can look upon a hundred homes, in every one of which these social companions are matters of reality. In my daily walks I pass a thousand men whose cares are all forgotten, whose labors are made light, whose dull routine of work from day to day is cheered and brightened by their glimpses of domestic joy at home. Amid the struggles of this struggling town what cheerful sacrifices are made; what toil endured with readiness; what patience shown and fortitude displayed for the mere sake of home and its affections! Let me thank Heaven that I can people my fireside with shadows such as these; with shadows of bright objects that exist in crowds about me; and let me say, "I am alone no more."

I never was less so — I write it with a grateful heart — than I am to-night. Recollections of the past and visions of the present come to bear me company; the meanest man to whom I have ever given alms appears to add his mite of peace and comfort to my stock; and whenever the fire within me shall grow cold, to light my path upon this earth no more, I pray that it may be at such an hour as this, and when I love the world as well as I do now.

THE DEAF GENTLEMAN FROM HIS OWN APARTMENT.

Our dear friend laid down his pen at the end of the foregoing paragraph, to take it up no more. I little thought ever to employ mine upon so sorrowful a task as that which he has left me, and to which I now devote it.

As he did not appear among us at his usual hour next morning, we knocked gently at his door. No answer being given, it was softly opened; and then, to our surprise, we saw him seated before the ashes of his fire, with a little table I was accustomed to set at his elbow when I left him for the night, at a short distance from him, as though he had pushed it away with the idea of rising and retiring to his bed. His crutch and footstool lay at his feet as usual, and he was dressed in his chamber-gown, which he had put on before I left him. He was reclining in his chair, in his accustomed posture, with his face towards the fire, and seemed absorbed in meditation, — indeed, at first, we almost hoped he was.

Going up to him, we found him dead. I have often, very often, seen him sleeping, and always peacefully, but I never saw him look so calm and tranquil. His face wore a serene, benign expression, which had impressed me very strongly when we last shook hands; not that he had ever any other look, God knows; but there was something in this so very spiritual, so strangely and indefinably allied to youth, although his head was gray and venerable, that it was new even in him. It came upon me all at once when on some slight pretence he called me back upon the previous night to take me by the hand again, and once more say, "God bless you."

A bell-rope hung within his reach, but he had not moved towards it, nor had he stirred, we all agreed, except, as I have said, to push away his table, which he could have done, and no doubt did, with a very slight motion of his hand. He had relapsed for a moment into his late train of meditation, and, with a thoughtful smile upon his face, had died.

I had long known it to be his wish that whenever this event should come to pass we might be all assembled in the house. I therefore lost no time in sending for Mr. Pickwick and for Mr. Miles, both of whom arrived before the messenger's return.

It is not my purpose to dilate upon the sorrow and affectionate emotions of which I was at once the witness and the sharer. But I may say, of the humbler mourners, that his faithful housekeeper was fairly heart-broken; that the poor barber would not be comforted; and that I shall respect the homely truth and warmth of heart of Mr. Weller and his son to the last moment of my life.

"And the sweet old creetur, sir," said the elder Mr. Weller to me in the afternoon, "has bolted. Him as had no wice, and was so free from temper that a infant might ha' drove him, has been took at last with that 'ere unawoidable fit o' staggers as we all must come to, and gone off his feed forever! I see him," said the old gentleman, with a moisture in his eye, which could not be mistaken, — "I see him gettin', every journey, more and more groggy; I says to Samivel, 'My boy! the Grey 's a goin' at the knees'; and now my predilictions is fatally werified, and him as I could never do enough to serve or show my likin' for, is up the great uniwersal spout o' natur'."

I was not the less sensible of the old man's attachment because he expressed it in his peculiar manner. Indeed, I can truly assert of both him and his son, that notwithstanding the extraordinary dialogues they held together, and the strange commentaries and corrections with which each of them illustrated the other's speech, I do not think it possible to exceed the sincerity of their regret; and that I am sure their thoughtfulness and anxiety in anticipating the discharge of many little offices of sympathy, would have done honor to the most delicate-minded persons.

Our friend had frequently told us that his will would be found in a box in the Clock-case, the key of which was in his writing-desk. As he had told us also that he desired it to be opened immediately after his death, whenever that should happen, we met together that night for the fulfilment of his request.

We found it where he had told us, wrapped in a sealed paper, and with it a codicil of recent date, in which he named Mr. Miles and Mr. Pickwick his executors, — as having no need of any greater benefit from his estate, than a generous token (which he bequeathed to them) of his friendship and remembrance.

After pointing out the spot in which he wished his ashes to repose, he gave to "his dear old friends," Jack Redburn and myself, his house, his books, his furniture, — in short, all that his house contained; and with this legacy more ample means of maintaining it in its present state than we, with our habits and at our terms of life, can ever exhaust. Besides these gifts, he left to us, in trust, an annual sum of no insignificant amount, to be distributed in charity among his accustomed pensioners — they are a long list — and such other claimants on his bounty as might, from time to time. present themselves. And as true charity not only covers a multitude of sins, but includes a multitude of virtues, such as forgiveness, liberal construction, gentleness and mercy to the faults of others, and the remembrance of our own imperfections and advantages, he bade us not inquire too closely into the venial errors of the poor, but finding that they *were* poor, first to relieve and then endeavor — at an advantage — to reclaim them.

To the housekeeper he left an annuity, sufficient for her comfortable maintenance and support through life. For the barber, who had attended him many years, he made a similar provision. And I may make two remarks in this place: first, that I think this pair are very likely to club their means together and make a match of it; and secondly, that I think my friend had this result in his mind, for I have heard him say, more than once, that he could not concur with the generality of mankind in censuring equal marriages made in later life, since there were many cases in which such unions could not fail to be a wise and rational source of happiness to both parties.

The elder Mr. Weller is so far from viewing this prospect with any feelings of jealousy, that he appears to be very much relieved by its contemplation; and his son, if I am not mistaken, participates in this feeling. We are all of opinion, however, that the old gentleman's danger, even at its crisis, was very slight, and that he merely labored under one of those transitory weaknesses to which persons of his temperament are now and then liable, and which become less and less alarming at every return, until they wholly subside. I have no doubt he will remain a jolly old widower for the rest of his life, as he has already inquired of me, with much gravity, whether a writ of habeas corpus would enable him to settle his property upon Tony beyond the possibility of recall; and has, in my presence, conjured his son, with tears in his eyes, that in the event of his ever becoming amorous again, he will put him in a strait-waistcoat until the fit is passed, and distinctly inform the lady that his property is "made over."

Although I have very little doubt that Sam would dutifully comply with these injunctions in a case of extreme necessity, and that he would do so with perfect composure and coolness, I do not apprehend things will ever come to that pass, as the old gentleman seems perfectly happy in the society of his son, his pretty daughter-in-law, and his grandchildren, and has solemnly announced his determination to "take arter the old 'un in all respects"; from which I infer that it is his intention to regulate his conduct by the model of Mr. Pickwick, who will certainly set him the example of a single life.

I have diverged for a moment from the subject with which I set out, for I know that my friend was interested in these little matters, and I have a natural tendency to linger upon any topic that occupied his thoughts or gave him pleasure and amusement. His remaining wishes are very briefly told. He desired that we would make him the frequent subject of our conversation; at the same time, that we would never speak of him with an air of gloom or restraint, but frankly, and as one whom we still loved and hoped to meet again. He trusted that the old house would wear no aspect of mourning, but that it would be lively and cheerful; and that we would not remove or cover up his picture, which hangs in our dining-room, but make it our companion as he had been. His own room, our place of meeting, remains, at his desire, in its accustomed state; our seats are placed about the table as of old; his easy-chair, his desk, his crutch, his footstool, hold their accustomed places, and the clock stands in its familiar corner. We go into the chamber at stated times to see that all is as it should be, and to take care that the light and air are not shut out, for on that point he expressed a strong solicitude. But it was his fancy that the apartment should not be inhabited; that it should be religiously preserved in this condition, and that the voice of his old companion should be heard no more.

My own history may be summed up in very few words; and even those I should have spared the reader but for my friend's allusion to me some time since. I have no deeper sorrow than the loss of a child, — an only daughter, who is living, and who fled from her father's house but a few weeks before our friend and I first met. I had never spoken of this even to him, because I have always loved her, and I could not bear to tell him of her error until I could tell him also of her sorrow and regret. Happily I was enabled to do so some time ago. And it will not be long, with Heaven's leave, before she is restored to me; before I find in her and her husband the support of my declining years.

For my pipe, it is an old relic of home, a thing of no great worth, a poor trifle, but sacred to me for her sake.

Thus, since the death of our venerable friend, Jack Redburn and I have been the sole tenants of the old house; and, day by day, have lounged together in his favorite walks. Mindful of his injunctions, we have long been able to speak of him with ease and cheerfulness, and to remember him as he would be remembered. From certain allusions which Jack has dropped, to his having been deserted and cast off in early life, I am inclined to believe that some passages of his youth may possibly be shadowed out in the history of Mr. Chester and his son, but seeing that he avoids the subject, I have not pursued it.

My task is done. The chamber in which we have whiled away so many hours, not, I hope, without some pleasure and some profit, is deserted; our happy hour of meeting strikes no more; the chimney-corner has grown cold; and MASTER HUMPHREY'S CLOCK has stopped forever.

FULL REPORT

OF THE FIRST MEETING OF THE MUDFOG ASSOCIATION FOR THE ADVANCEMENT OF EVERYTHING.

WE have made the most unparalleled and extraordinary exertions to place before our readers a complete and accurate account of the proceedings at the late grand meeting of the Mudfog Association, holden in the town of Mudfog ; it affords us great happiness to lay the result before them, in the shape of various communications received from our able, talented, and graphic correspondent, expressly sent down for the purpose, who has immortalized us, himself, Mudfog, and the association, all at one and the same time. We have been, indeed, for some days unable to determine who will transmit the greatest name to posterity, — ourselves, who sent our correspondent down ; our correspondent, who wrote an account of the matter ; or the association, who gave our correspondent something to write about. We rather incline to the opinion that we are the greatest man of the party, inasmuch as the notion of an exclusive and authentic report originated with us ; this may be prejudice : it may arise from a prepossession on our part in our own favor. Be it so. We have no doubt that every gentleman concerned in this mighty assemblage is troubled with the same complaint in a greater or less degree ; and it is a consolation to us to know that we have at least this feeling in common with the great scientific stars, the brilliant and extraordinary luminaries, whose speculations we record.

We give our correspondent's letters in the order in which they reached us. Any attempt at amalgamating them into one beautiful whole would only destroy that glowing tone, that dash of wildness, and rich vein of picturesque interest, which pervade them throughout.

"MUDFOG, Monday night, seven o'clock.

"We are in a state of great excitement here. Nothing is spoken of, but the approaching meeting of the association. The inn-doors are thronged with waiters anxiously looking for the expected arrivals ; and the numerous bills which are wafered up in the windows of private houses, intimating that there are beds to let within, give the streets a very animated and cheerful appearance, the wafers being of a great variety of colors, and the monotony of printed inscriptions being relieved by every possible size and style of handwriting. It is confidently rumored that Professors Snore, Doze, and Wheezy have engaged three beds and a sitting-room at the Pig and Tinder-Box. I give you the rumor as it has reached me ; but I cannot, as yet, vouch for its accuracy. The moment I have been enabled to obtain any certain information upon this interesting point, you may depend upon receiving it."

"Half past seven.

"I have just returned from a personal interview with the landlord of the Pig and Tinder-box. He speaks confidently of the probability of Professors Snore, Doze, and Wheezy taking up their residence at his house during the sitting of the association, but denies that the beds have been yet engaged; in which representation he is confirmed by the chambermaid, — a girl of artless manners, and interesting appearance. The boots denies that it is at all likely that Professors Snore, Doze, and Wheezy will put up here; but I have reason to believe that this man has been suborned by the proprietor of the Original Pig, which is the opposition hotel. Amidst such conflicting testimony it is difficult to arrive at the real truth; but you may depend upon receiving authentic information upon this point the moment the fact is ascertained. The excitement still continues. A boy fell through the window of the pastrycook's shop at the corner of the high street about an hour ago, which has occasioned much confusion. The general impression is that it was an accident. Pray Heaven it may prove so!"

"Tuesday, noon.

"At an early hour this morning the bells of all the churches struck seven o'clock; the effect of which, in the present lively state of the town, was extremely singular. While I was at breakfast, a yellow gig, drawn by a dark gray horse, with a patch of white over his right eyelid, proceeded at a rapid pace in the direction of the Original Pig stables; it is currently reported that this gentleman has arrived here for the purpose of attending the association, and, from what I have heard, I consider it extremely probable, although nothing decisive is yet known regarding him. You may conceive the anxiety with which we are all looking forward to the arrival of the four o'clock coach this afternoon.

"Notwithstanding the excited state of the populace, no outrage has yet been committed, owing to the admirable discipline and discretion of the police, who are nowhere to be seen. A barrel-organ is playing opposite my window, and groups of people, offering fish and vegetables for sale, parade the streets. With these exceptions everything is quiet, and I trust will continue so."

"Five o'clock.

"It is now ascertained beyond all doubt that Professors Snore, Doze, and Wheezy will *not* repair to the Pig and Tinder-Box, but have actually engaged apartments at the Original Pig. This intelligence is *exclusive;* and I leave you and your readers to draw their own inferences from it. Why Professor Wheezy, of all people in the world, should repair to the Original Pig in preference to the Pig and Tinder-Box, it is not easy to conceive. The professor is a man who should be above all such petty feelings. Some people here openly impute treachery and a distinct breach of faith to Professors Snore and Doze; while others, again, are disposed to acquit them of any culpability in the transaction, and to insinuate that the blame rests solely with Professor Wheezy. I own that I incline to the latter opinion; and, although it gives me great pain to speak in terms of censure or disapprobation of a man of such transcendent genius and acquirements, still I am bound to say, that if my suspicions be well founded, and if all the reports which have reached my ears be true, I really do not well know what to make of the matter.

"Mr. Slug, so celebrated for his statistical researches, arrived this afternoon by the four o'clock stage. His complexion is a dark purple, and he has a habit of sighing constantly. He looked extremely well, and appeared in high health and spirits. Mr. Woodensconse also came down in the same conveyance. The distinguished gentleman was fast asleep on his arrival, and I am informed by the guard that he had been so, the whole way. He was, no doubt, preparing for his approaching fatigues; but what gigantic visions must those be that flit through the brain of such a man when his body is in a state of torpidity!

"The influx of visitors increases every moment. I am told (I know not how truly) that two post-chaises have arrived at the Original Pig within the last half-hour; and I myself observed a wheelbarrow, containing three carpet-bags and a bundle, entering the yard of the Pig and Tinder-Box no longer ago than five minutes since. The people are still quietly pursuing their ordinary occupations; but there is a wildness in their eyes, and an unwonted rigidity in the muscles of their countenances, which shows to the observant spectator that their expectations are strained to the very utmost pitch. I fear, unless some very extraordinary arrivals take place to-night, that consequences may arise from this popular ferment, which every man of sense and feeling would deplore."

"Twenty minutes past six.

"I have just heard that the boy who fell through the pastrycook's window last night has died of the fright. He was suddenly called upon to pay three and sixpence for the damage done, and his constitution, it seems, was not strong enough to bear up against the shock. The inquest, it is said, will be held to-morrow."

"Three quarters past seven.

"Professors Muff and Nogo have just driven up to the hotel door; they at once ordered dinner with great condescension. We are all very much delighted with the urbanity of their manners, and the ease with which they adapt themselves to the forms and ceremonies of ordinary life. Immediately on their arrival they sent for the head-waiter, and privately requested him to purchase a live dog, — as cheap a one as he could meet with, — and to send him up after dinner, with a pie-board, a knife and fork, and a clean plate. It is conjectured that some experiments will be tried upon the dog to-night; if any particulars should transpire I will forward them by express."

"Half past eight.

"The animal has been procured. He is a pug-dog, of rather intelligent appearance, in good condition, and with very short legs. He has been tied to a curtain-peg in a dark room, and is howling dreadfully."

"Ten minutes to nine.

"The dog has just been rung for. With an instinct which would appear almost the result of reason, the sagacious animal seized the waiter by the calf of the leg when he approached to take him, and made a desperate, though ineffectual resistance. I have not been able to procure admission to the apartment occupied by the scientific gentlemen; but, judging from the sounds which reached my ears when I stood upon the landing-place just now, outside the door, I should be disposed to say that the dog had retreated growling beneath some article of furniture, and was keeping the professors at bay. This conjecture is confirmed by the testimony of the ostler, who, after peeping through the keyhole, assures me that he distinctly saw Professor Nogo on his knees, holding forth a small bottle of prussic acid, to which the animal, who was crouched beneath an arm-chair, obstinately declined to smell. You cannot imagine the feverish state of irritation we are in, lest the interests of science should be sacrificed to the prejudices of a brute creature, who is not endowed with sufficient sense to foresee the incalculable benefits which the whole human race may derive from so very slight a concession on his part."

"Nine o'clock.

"The dog's tail and ears have been sent down stairs to be washed; from which circumstance we infer that the animal is no more. His forelegs have been delivered to the boots to be brushed, which strengthens the supposition."

"Half after ten.

"My feelings are so overpowered by what has taken place in the course of the last hour and a half, that I have scarcely strength to detail the rapid succession of events which have quite bewildered all those who are cognizant of their occurrence. It appears that the pug-dog mentioned in my last was surreptitiously obtained, — stolen, in fact, — by some person attached to the stable department, from an unmarried lady resident in this town. Frantic on discovering the loss of her favorite, the lady rushed distractedly into the street, calling in the most heart-rending and pathetic manner upon the passengers to restore her her Augustus, — for so the deceased was named, in affectionate remembrance of a former lover of his mistress, to whom he bore a striking personal resemblance, which renders the circumstance additionally affecting. I am not yet in a condition to inform you what circumstances induced the bereaved lady to direct her steps to the hotel which had witnessed the last struggles of her *protégé*. I can only state that she arrived there, at the very instant when his detached members were passing through the passage on a small tray. Her shrieks still reverberate in my ears! I grieve to say that the expressive features of Professor Muff were much scratched and lacerated by the injured lady; and that Professor Nogo, besides sustaining several severe bites, has lost some handfuls of hair from the same cause. It must be some consolation to these gentlemen to know that their ardent attachment to scientific pursuits has alone occasioned these unpleasant consequences; for which the sympathy of a grateful country will sufficiently reward them. The unfortunate lady remains at the Pig and Tinder-Box, and up to this time is reported in a very precarious state.

"I need scarcely tell you that this unlooked-for catastrophe has cast a damp and gloom upon us in the midst of our exhilaration; natural in any case, but greatly enhanced in this, by the amiable qualities of the deceased animal, who appears to have been much and deservedly respected by the whole of his acquaintance."

"Twelve o'clock.

"I take the last opportunity before sealing my parcel to inform you that the boy who fell through the pastrycook's window is not dead, as was universally believed, but alive and well. The report appears to have had its origin in his mysterious disappearance. He was found half an hour since on the premises of a sweet-stuff maker, where a raffle had been announced for a second-hand sealskin cap and a tambourine; and where — a sufficient number of members not having been obtained at first — he had patiently waited until the list was completed. This fortunate discovery has in some degree restored our gayety and cheerfulness. It is proposed to get up a subscription for him without delay.

"Everybody is nervously anxious to see what to-morrow will bring forth. If any one should arrive in the course of the night, I have left strict directions to be called immediately. I should have sat up, indeed, but the agitating events of this day have been too much for me.

"No news, yet, of either of the Professors Snore, Doze, or Wheezy. It is very strange!"

"Wednesday afternoon.

"All is now over; and upon one point, at least, I am at length enabled to set the minds of your readers at rest. The three professors arrived at ten minutes after two o'clock, and, instead of taking up their quarters at the Original Pig, as it was universally understood in the course of yesterday that they would assuredly have done, drove straight to the Pig and Tinder-Box, where they threw off the mask at once, and openly announced their intention of remaining. Professor Wheezy *may* reconcile this very extraordinary conduct with *his* notions of fair and equitable dealing, but I would recommend Professor Wheezy to be cautious how he presumes too far upon his well-earned reputation. How such a man as Professor Snore, or, which is still more extraordinary, such an individual as Professor Doze, can quietly allow himself to be mixed up with such proceedings as these, you will naturally inquire. Upon this head rumor is silent; I have my speculations, but forbear to give utterance to them just now."

"Four o'clock.

"The town is filling fast; eighteen pence has been offered for a bed and refused. Several gentlemen were under the necessity last night of sleeping in the brick-fields, and on the steps of doors, for which they were taken before the magistrates in a body this morning, and committed to prison as vagrants for various terms. One of these persons I understand to be a highly respectable tinker, of great practical skill, who had forwarded a paper to the president of Section D, Mechanical Science, on the construction of pipkins with copper bottoms and safety-valves, of which report speaks highly. The incarceration of this gentleman is greatly to be regretted, as his absence will preclude any discussion on the subject.

"The bills are being taken down in all directions, and lodgings are being secured on almost any terms. I have heard of fifteen shillings a week for two rooms, exclusive of coals and attendance, but I can scarcely believe it. The excitement is dreadful. I was informed this morning that the civil authorities, apprehensive of some outbreak of popular feeling, had commanded a recruiting sergeant and two corporals to be under arms; and that, with the view of not irritating the people unnnecessarily by their presence, they had been requested to take up their position before daybreak in a turnpike, distant about a quarter of a mile from the town. The vigor and promptness of these measures cannot be too highly extolled.

"Intelligence has just been brought me, that an elderly female, in a state of inebriety, has declared in the open street her intention to 'do' for Mr. Slug. Some statistical returns compiled by that gentleman, relative to the consumption of raw spirituous liquors in this place, are supposed to be the cause of the wretch's animosity. It is added, that this declaration was loudly cheered by a crowd of persons who had assembled on the spot; and that one man had the boldness to designate Mr. Slug aloud by the opprobious epithet of 'Stick-in-the mud!' It is earnestly to be hoped that now, when the moment has arrived for their interference, the magistrates will not shrink from the exercise of that power which is vested in them by the constitution of our common country."

"Half past ten.

"The disturbance, I am happy to inform you, has been completely quelled, and the ringleader taken into custody. She had a pail of cold water thrown over her, previous to being locked up, and expresses great contrition and uneasiness. We are all in a fever of anticipation about to-morrow; but now that we are within a few hours of the meeting of the association, and at last enjoy the proud consciousness of having its illustrious members amongst us, I trust and hope everything may go off peaceably. I shall send you a full report of to-morrow's proceedings by the night coach."

"Eleven o'clock.

"I open my letter to say that nothing whatever has occurred since I folded it up."

"Thursday.

"The sun rose this morning at the usual hour. I did not observe anything particular in the aspect of the glorious planet, except that he appeared to me (it might have been a delusion of my heightened fancy) to shine with more than common brilliancy, and to shed a refulgent lustre upon the town, such as I had never observed before. This is the more extraordinary, as the sky was perfectly cloudless, and the atmosphere peculiarly fine. At half past nine o'clock the general committee assembled, with the last year's president in the chair. The report of the council was read; and one passage, which stated that the council had corresponded with no less than three thousand five hundred and seventy-one persons (all of whom paid their own postage), on no fewer than seven thousand two hundred and forty-three topics, was received with a degree of enthusiasm which no effort could suppress. The various committees and sections having been appointed, and the mere formal business transacted, the great proceedings of the meeting commenced at eleven o'clock precisely. I had the happiness of occupying a most eligible position at that time, in

"SECTION A. — ZOÖLOGY AND BOTANY.
"GREAT ROOM, PIG AND TINDER-BOX.
"PRESIDENT — PROFESSOR SNORE. VICE-PRESIDENTS —
"PROFESSORS DOZE AND WHEEZY.

"The scene at this moment was particularly striking. The sun streamed through the windows of the apartments, and tinted the whole scene with its brilliant rays, bringing out in strong relief the noble visages of the professors and scientific gentlemen, who, some with bald heads, some with red heads, some with brown heads, some with gray heads, some with black heads, some with block heads, presented a *coup-d'œil* which no eye-witness will readily forget. In front of these gentlemen were papers and inkstands; and round the room, on elevated benches extending as far as the forms could reach, were assembled a brilliant concourse of those lovely and elegant women for which Mudfog is justly acknowledged to be without a rival in the whole world. The contrast between their fair faces and the dark coats and trousers of the scientific gentlemen I shall never cease to remember while Memory holds her seat.

"Time having been allowed for a slight confusion, occasioned by the falling down of the greater part of the platforms, to subside, the president called on one of the secretaries to read a communication entitled, 'Some remarks on the industrious fleas, with considerations on the importance of establishing infant schools among that numerous class of society; of directing their industry to useful and practical ends; and of applying the surplus fruits thereof, towards providing for them a comfortable and respectable maintenance in their old age.'

"The Author stated, that, having long turned his attention to the moral and social condition of these interesting animals, he had been induced to visit an exhibition in Regent Street, London, commonly known by the designation of 'The Industrious Fleas.' He had there seen many fleas, occupied certainly in various pursuits and avocations, but occupied, he was bound to add, in a manner which no man of well-regulated mind could fail to regard with sorrow and regret. One flea, reduced to the level of a beast of burden, was drawing about a miniature gig, containing a particularly small effigy of his Grace the Duke of Wellington; while another was staggering beneath the weight of a golden model of his great adversary Napoleon Bonaparte. Some, brought up as mountebanks and ballet-dancers, were performing a figure-dance (he regretted to observe that, of the fleas so employed, several were females); others were in training, in a small card-board box, for pedestrians, — mere sporting characters, — and two were actually engaged in the cold-blooded and barbarous occupation of duelling; a pursuit from which humanity recoiled with horror and disgust. He suggested that measures should be immediately taken to employ the labor of these fleas as part and parcel of the productive power of the country, which might easily be done by the establishment among them of infant schools and houses of industry, in which a system of virtuous education, based upon sound principles, should be observed, and moral precepts strictly inculcated. He proposed that every flea who presumed to exhibit, for hire, music or dancing, or any species of theatrical entertainment, without a license, should be considered a vagabond, and treated accordingly; in which respect he only placed him upon a level with the rest of mankind. He would further suggest that their labor should be placed under the control and regulation of the State, who should set apart from the profits a fund for the support of superannuated or disabled fleas, their widows and orphans. With this view, he proposed that liberal premiums should be offered for the three best designs for a general almshouse; from which — as insect architecture was well known to be in a very advanced and perfect state — we might possibly derive many valuable hints for the improvement of our metropolitan universities, national galleries, and other public edifices.

"The President wished to be informed how the ingenious gentleman proposed to open a communication with fleas generally, in the first instance, so that they might be thoroughly imbued with a sense of the advantages they must necessarily derive from changing their mode of life, and apply themselves to honest labor. This appeared to him the only difficulty.

"The Author submitted that this difficulty was easily overcome, or rather that there was no difficulty at all in the case. Obviously the course to be pursued, if her Majesty's government could be prevailed upon to take up the plan, would be to secure at a remunerative salary, the individual to whom he had alluded as presiding over the exhibition in Regent Street at the period of his visit. That gentleman would at once be able to put himself in communication with the mass of the fleas, and to instruct them in pursuance of some general plan of education, to be sanctioned by Parliament, until such time as the more intelligent among them were advanced enough to officiate as teachers to the rest.

"The President and several members of the section highly complimented the author of the paper last read, on his most ingenious and important treatise. It was determined that the subject should be recommended to the immediate consideration of the council.

"Mr. Wigsby produced a cauliflower somewhat larger than a chaise-umbrella, which had been raised by no other artificial means than the simple application of highly carbonated soda-water as manure. He explained that by scooping out the head, which would afford a new and delicious species of nourishment for the poor, a parachute, in principle something similar to that constructed by M. Garnerin, was at once obtained; the stalk of course being kept downwards. He added that he was perfectly willing to make a descent from a height of not less than three miles and a quarter; and had, in fact, already proposed the same to the proprietors of the Vauxhall Gardens, who, in the handsomest manner, at once consented to his wishes, and appointed an early day next summer for the undertaking; merely stipulating that the rim of the cauliflower should be previously broken in three or four places to insure the safety of the descent.

"The President congratulated the public on the *grand gala* in store for them, and warmly eulogized the proprietors of the establishment alluded to, for their love of science, and regard for the safety of human life, both of which did them the highest honor.

"A member wished to know how many thousand additional lamps the royal property would be illuminated with, on the night after the descent.

"Mr Wigsby replied that the point was not yet finally decided; but he believed it was proposed, over and above the ordinary illuminations, to exhibit in various devices eight millions and a half of additional lamps.

"The member expressed himself much gratified with this announcement.

"Mr. Blunderum delighted the section with a most interesting and valuable paper 'on the last moments of the learned pig,' which produced a very strong impression upon the assembly, the account being compiled from the personal recollections of his favorite attendant. The account stated in the most emphatic terms that the animal's name was not Toby, but Solomon; and distinctly proved that he could have no near relatives in the profession, as many designing persons had falsely stated, inasmuch as his father, mother, brothers and sisters, had all fallen victims to the butcher at different times. An uncle of his, indeed, had with very great labor been traced to a sty in Somers Town; but as he was in a very infirm state at the time, being afflicted with measles, and shortly afterwards disappeared, there appeared too much reason to conjecture that he had been converted into sausages. The disorder of the learned pig was originally a severe cold, which, being aggravated by excessive trough indulgence, finally settled upon the lungs, and terminated in a general decay of the constitution. A melancholy instance of a presentiment entertained by the animal of his approaching dissolution was recorded. After gratifying a numerous and fashionable company with his performances, in which no falling-off whatever, was visible, he fixed his eyes on the biographer, and, turning to the watch which lay on the floor, and on which he was accustomed to point out the hour, deliberately passed his snout twice round the dial. In precisely four-and-twenty hours from that time he had ceased to exist!

"Professor Wheezy inquired whether, previous to his demise, the animal had expressed, by signs or otherwise, any wishes regarding the disposal of his little property.

"Mr. Blunderum replied, that, when the biographer took up the pack of cards at the conclusion of the performance, the animal grunted several times in a significant manner, and nodded his head as he was accustomed to do when gratified. From these gestures it was understood that he wished the attendant to keep the cards, which he had ever since done. He had not expressed any wish relative to his watch, which had accordingly been pawned by the same individual.

"The President wished to know whether any member of the section had ever seen or conversed with the pig-faced lady, who was reported to have worn a black velvet mask, and to have taken her meals from a golden trough.

"After some hesitation a member replied that the pig-faced lady was his mother-in-law, and that he trusted the president would not violate the sanctity of private life.

"The President begged pardon. He had considered the pig-faced lady a public character. Would the honorable member object to state, with a view to the advancement of science, whether she was in any way connected with the learned pig?

"The member replied in the same low tone, that, as the question appeared to involve a suspicion that the learned pig might be his half-brother, he must decline answering it.

"SECTION B. — ANATOMY AND MEDICINE.

"COACH-HOUSE, PIG AND TINDER-BOX.

"PRESIDENT — DR. TOORELL. VICE-PRESIDENTS — PROFESSORS MUFF AND NOGO.

"Dr. Kutankumagen (of Moscow) read to the section a report of a case which had occurred within his own practice, strikingly illustrative of the power of medicine, as exemplified in his successful treatment of a virulent disorder. He had been called in to visit the patient on the 1st of April, 1837. He was then laboring under symptoms peculiarly alarming to any medical man. His frame was stout and muscular, his step firm and elastic, his cheeks plump and red, his voice loud, his appetite good, his pulse full and round. He was in the constant habit of eating three meals *per diem,* and of drinking at least one bottle of wine, and one glass of spirituous liquors diluted with water, in the course of the four-and-twenty hours. He laughed constantly, and in so hearty a manner that it was terrible to hear him. By dint of powerful medicine, low diet and bleeding, the symptoms in the course of three days perceptibly decreased. A rigid perseverance in the same course of treatment for only one week, accompanied with small doses of water-gruel, weak broth, and barley-water, led to their entire disappearance. In the course of a month he was sufficiently recovered to be carried down stairs by two nurses, and to enjoy an airing in a close carriage, supported by soft pillows. At the present moment he was restored so far as to walk about, with the slight assistance of a crutch and a boy. It would perhaps be gratifying to the section to learn that he ate little, drank little, slept little, and was never heard to laugh by any accident whatever.

"Dr. W. R. Fee, in complimenting the honorable member upon the triumphant cure he had effected, begged to ask whether the patient still bled freely?

"Dr. Kutankumagen replied in the affirmative.

"Dr. W. R. Fee. — And you found that he bled freely during the whole course of the disorder?

"Dr. Kutankumagen. — O dear, yes; most freely.

"Dr. Neeshawts supposed, that if the patient had not submitted to be bled with great readiness and perseverance, so extraordinary a cure could never, in fact, have been accomplished. Dr. Kutankumagen rejoined, certainly not.

"Mr. Knight Bell (M. R. C. S.) exhibited a wax preparation of the interior of a gentleman who in early life had inadvertently swallowed a door-key. It was a curious fact that a medical student of dissipated habits, being present at the *post-mortem* examination, found means to escape unobserved from the room, with that portion of the coats of the stomach upon which an exact model of the instrument was distinctly impressed, with which he hastened to a locksmith of doubtful character, who made a new key from the pattern so shown to him. With this key the medical student entered the house of the deceased gentleman, and committed a burglary to a large amount, for which he was subsequently tried and executed.

"The President wished to know what became of the original key after the lapse of years. Mr. Knight Bell replied that the gentleman was always much accustomed to punch, and it was supposed the acid had gradually devoured it.

"Dr. Neeshawts and several of the members were of opinion that the key must have lain very cold and heavy upon the gentleman's stomach.

"Mr. Knight Bell believed it did at first. It was worthy of remark, perhaps, that for some years the gentleman was troubled with nightmare, under the influence of which he always imagined himself a wine-cellar door.

"Professor Muff related a very extraordinary and convincing proof of the wonderful efficacy of the system of infinitesimal doses, which the section were doubtless aware was based upon the theory that the very minutest amount of any given drug, properly dispersed through the human frame, would be productive of precisely the same result as a very large dose administered in the usual manner. Thus, the fortieth part of a grain of calomel was supposed to be equal to a five-grain calomel pill, and so on in proportion throughout the whole range of medicine. He had tried the experiment in a curious manner upon a publican who had been brought into the hospital with a broken head, and was cured upon the infinitesimal system in the incredibly short space of three months. This man was a hard drinker. He (Professor Muff) had dispersed three drops of rum through a bucket of water, and requested the man to drink the whole. What was the result? Before he had drunk a quart, he was in a state of beastly intoxication; and five other men were made dead-drunk with the remainder.

"The President wished to know whether an infinitesimal dose of soda-water would have recovered them? Professor Muff replied that the twenty-fifth part of a tea-spoonful, properly administered to each patient, would have sobered him immediately. The President remarked that this was a most important discovery, and he hoped the Lord Mayor and Court of Aldermen would patronize it immediately.

"A member begged to be informed whether it would be possible to administer — say, the twentieth part of a grain of bread and cheese to all grown-up paupers, and the fortieth part to children, with the same satisfying effect as their present allowance.

"Professor Muff was willing to stake his professional reputation on the perfect adequacy of such a quantity of food to the support of human life, — in workhouses; the addition of the fifteenth part of a grain of pudding twice a week would render it a high diet.

"Professor Nogo called the attention of the section to a very extraordinary case of animal magnetism. A private watchman, being merely looked at by the operator from the opposite side of a wide street, was at once observed to be in a very drowsy and languid state. He was followed to his box, and being once slightly rubbed on the palms of the hands, fell into a sound sleep, in which he continued without intermission for ten hours.

"SECTION C. — STATISTICS.

"HAY-LOFT, ORIGINAL PIG.

"PRESIDENT — MR WOODENSCONSE. VICE-PRESIDENTS — MR. LEDBRAIN AND MR. TIMBERED.

"Mr. Slug stated to the section the result of some calculations he had made with great difficulty and labor, regarding the state of infant education among the middle classes of London. He found that, within a circle of three miles from the Elephant and Castle, the following were the names and numbers of children's books principally in circulation: —

"Jack the Giant-killer	7,943
Ditto and Bean-stalk	8,621
Ditto and Eleven Brothers	2,845
Ditto and Jill	1,998
Total	21,407

"He found that the proportion of Robinson Crusoes to Philip Quarles was as four and a half to one; and that the preponderance of Valentine and Orsons over Goody Two Shoeses was as three and an eighth of the former to half a one of the latter; a comparison of Seven Champions with Simple Simons gave the same result. The ignorance that prevailed was lamentable. One child, on being asked whether he would rather be Saint George of England or a respectable tallow-chandler, instantly replied, 'Taint George of Ingling.' Another, a little boy of eight years old, was found to be firmly impressed with a belief in the existence of dragons, and openly stated that it was his intention when he grew up, to rush forth sword in hand for the deliverance of captive princesses, and the promiscuous slaughter of giants. Not one child among the number interrogated had ever heard of Mungo Park, — some inquiring whether he was at all connected with the black man that swept the crossing; and others whether he was in any way related to the Regent's Park. They had not the slightest conception of the commonest principles of mathematics, and considered Sindbad the Sailor the most enterprising voyager that the world had ever produced.

"A member strongly deprecating the use of all the other books mentioned, suggested that Jack and Jill might perhaps be exempted from the general censure, inasmuch as the hero and heroine, in the very outset of the tale, were depicted as going *up* a hill to fetch a pail of water, which was a laborious and useful occupation, — supposing the family linen was being washed, for instance.

"Mr. Slug feared that the moral effect of this passage was more than counterbalanced by another in a subsequent part of the poem, in which very gross allusion was made to the mode in which the heroine was personally chastised by her mother

"'For laughing at Jack's disaster';

besides, the whole work had this one great fault, *it was not true.*

"The President complimented the honorable member on the excellent distinction he had drawn. Several other members, too, dwelt upon the immense and urgent necessity of storing the minds of children with nothing but facts and figures; which process the President very forcibly remarked, had made them (the section) the men they were.

"Mr. Slug then stated some curious calculations respecting the dogs'-meat barrows of London. He found that the total number of small carts and barrows engaged in dispensing provisions to the cats and dogs of the metropolis was one thousand seven hundred and forty-three. The average number of skewers delivered daily with the provender by each dogs'-meat cart or barrow was thirty-six. Now, multiplying the number of skewers so delivered, by the number of barrows, a total of sixty-two thousand seven hundred and forty-eight skewers daily would be obtained. Allowing that, of these sixty-two thousand seven hundred and forty-eight skewers, the odd two thousand seven hundred and forty-eight were accidentally devoured with the meat, by the most voracious of the animals supplied, it followed that sixty thousand skewers per day, or the enormous number of twenty-one millions nine hundred thousand skewers annually, were wasted in the kennels and dust-holes of London; which, if collected and warehoused, would in ten years' time afford a mass of timber more than sufficient for the construction of a first-rate vessel of war for the use of her Majesty's navy, to be called 'The Royal Skewer,' and to become under that name the terror of all the enemies of this island.

"Mr. X. Ledbrain read a very ingenious communication, from which it appeared that the total number of legs belonging to the manufacturing population of one great town in Yorkshire was, in round numbers, forty thousand, while the total number of chair and stool legs in their houses was only thirty thousand, which, upon the very favorable average of three legs to a seat, yielded only ten thousand seats in all. From this calculation it would appear — not taking wooden or cork legs into the account, but allowing two legs to every person — that ten thousand individuals (one half of the whole population) were either destitute of any rest for their legs at all, or passed the whole of their leisure time in sitting upon boxes.

"SECTION D. — MECHANICAL SCIENCE.

"COACH-HOUSE, ORIGINAL PIG

"PRESIDENT — MR. CARTER. VICE-PRESIDENTS — MR. TRUCK AND MR. WAGHORN.

"Professor Queerspeck exhibited an elegant model of a portable railway, neatly mounted in a green case, for the waistcoat pocket. By attaching this beautiful instrument to his boots, any bank or public-office clerk could transport himself from his place of residence to his place of business, at the easy rate of sixty-five miles an hour, which, to gentlemen of sedentary pursuits, would be an incalculable advantage.

"The President was desirous of knowing whether it was necessary to have a level surface on which the gentleman was to run.

"Professor Queerspeck explained that City gentlemen would run in trains, being handcuffed together to prevent confusion or unpleasantness. For instance, trains would start every morning at eight, nine, and ten o'clock, from Camden Town, Islington, Camberwell, Hackney, and various other places in which City gentlemen are accustomed to reside. It would be necessary to have a level, but he had provided for this difficulty by proposing that the best line that the circumstances would admit of should be taken through the sewers which undermine the streets of the metropolis, and which, well lighted by jets from the gas-pipes which run immediately above them, would form a pleasant and commodious arcade, especially in winter-time, when the inconvenient custom of carrying umbrellas, now general, could be wholly dispensed with. In reply to another question, Professor Queerspeck stated that no substitute for the purposes to which these arcades were at present devoted had yet occurred to him, but that he hoped no fanciful objection on this head would be allowed to interfere with so great an undertaking.

"Mr. Jobba produced a forcing-machine on a novel plan, for bringing joint-stock railway shares prematurely to a premium. The instrument was in the form of an elegant gilt weather-glass of most dazzling appearance, and was worked behind, by strings, after the manner of a pantomime trick, the strings being always pulled by the directors of the company to which the machine belonged. The quicksilver was so ingeniously placed, that when the acting directors held shares in their pockets, figures denoting very small expenses and very large returns appeared upon the glass; but the moment the directors parted with these pieces of paper, the estimate of needful expenditure suddenly increased itself to an immense extent, while the statements of certain profits became reduced in the same proportion. Mr. Jobba stated that the machine had been in constant requisition for some months past, and he had never once known it to fail.

"A member expressed his opinion that it was extremely neat and pretty. He wished to know whether it was not liable to accidental derangement? Mr. Jobba said that the whole machine was undoubtedly liable to be blown up, but that was the only objection to it.

"Professor Nogo arrived from the anatomical section to exhibit a model of a safety fire-escape, which could be fixed at any time, in less than half an hour, and by means of which, the youngest or most infirm persons (successfully resisting the progress of the flames until it was quite ready) could be preserved if they merely balanced themselves for a few minutes on the sill of their bedroom window, and got into the escape without falling into the street. The Professor stated that the number of boys who had been rescued in the daytime by this machine from houses which were not on fire was almost incredible. Not a conflagration had occurred in the whole of London for many months past to which the escape had not been carried on the very next day, and put in action before a concourse of persons.

"The President inquired whether there was not some difficulty in ascertaining which was the top of the machine, and which the bottom, in cases of pressing emergency?

"Professor Nogo explained that of course it could not be expected to act quite as well when there was a fire as when there was not a fire; but in the former case he thought it would be of equal service whether the top were up or down."

With the last section, our correspondent concludes his most able and faithful report, which will never cease to reflect credit upon him for his scientific attainments, and upon us for our enterprising spirit. It is needless to take a review of the subjects which have been discussed; of the mode in which they have been examined; of the great truths which they have elicited. They are now before the world, and we leave them to read, to consider, and to profit.

The place of meeting for next year has undergone discussion, and has at length been decided; regard being had to, and evidence being taken upon, the goodness of its wines, the supply of its markets, the hospitality of its inhabitants, and the quality of its hotels. We hope at this next meeting our correspondent may again be present, and that we may be once more the means of placing his communications before the world. Until that period we have been prevailed upon to allow this number of our Miscellany to be retailed to the public, or wholesaled to the trade, without any advance upon our usual price.

We have only to add, that the committees are now broken up, and that Mudfog is once again restored to its accustomed tranquillity, — that Professors and Members have had balls, and *soirées*, and suppers, and great mutual complimentations, and have at length dispersed to their several homes, — whither all good wishes and joys attend them, until next year!

FULL REPORT

OF THE SECOND MEETING OF THE MUDFOG ASSOCIATION FOR THE ADVANCEMENT OF EVERYTHING.

In October last. we did ourselves the immortal credit of recording, at an enormous expense, and by dint of exertions unparalleled in the history of periodical publications, the proceedings of the Mudfog Association for the Advancement of Everything, which in that month held its first great half-yearly meeting, to the wonder and delight of the whole empire. We announced, at the conclusion of that extraordinary and most remarkable Report, that when the Second Meeting of the Society should take place, we should be found again at our post renewing our gigantic and spirited endeavors, and once more making the world ring with the accuracy, authenticity, immeasurable superiority, and intense remarkability of our account of its proceedings. In redemption of this pledge, we caused to be despatched, per steam, to Oldcastle, at which place this second meeting of the Society was held on the 20th instant, the same superhumanly endowed gentleman who furnished the former report, and who — gifted by nature with transcendent abilities, and furnished by us with a body of assistants scarcely inferior to himself — has forwarded a series of letters, which for faithfulness of description, power of language, fervor of thought, happiness of expression, and importance of subject-matter, have no equal in the epistolary literature of any age or country. We give this gentleman's correspondence entire, and in the order in which it reached our office.

"SALOON OF STEAMER, Thursday night, half past eight.

"When I left New Burlington Street this evening in the hackney cabriolet, number four thousand two hundred and eighty-five, I experienced sensations as novel as they were oppressive. A sense of importance of the task I had undertaken; a consciousness that I was leaving London, and stranger still, going somewhere else; a feeling of loneliness, and a sensation of jolting, quite bewildered my thoughts, and for a time rendered me even insensible to the presence of my carpet-bag and hat-box. I shall ever feel grateful to the driver of a Blackwall omnibus, who, by thrusting the pole of his vehicle through the small door of the cabriolet, awakened me from a tumult of imaginings that are wholly indescribable. But of such materials is our imperfect nature composed!

"I am happy to say that I am the first passenger on board, and shall thus be enabled to give you an account of all that happens in the order of its occurrence. The chimney is smoking a good deal, and so are the crew; and the captain, I am informed, is very drunk in a little house upon the deck, something like a black turnpike. I should infer, from all I hear, that he has got the steam up.

"You will readily guess with what feelings I have just made the discovery that my berth is in the same closet with those engaged by Professor Woodensconce, Mr. Slug, and Professor Grime. Professor Woodensconce has taken the shelf above me, and Mr. Slug and Professor Grime, the two shelves opposite. Their luggage has already arrived. On Mr. Slug's bed is a long tin tube of about three inches in diameter, carefully closed at both ends. What can this contain? Some powerful instrument of a new construction doubtless."

"Ten minutes past nine.

"Nobody has yet arrived, nor has anything fresh come in my way except several joints of beef and mutton, from which I conclude that a good plain, dinner has been provided for to-morrow. There is a singular smell below, which gave me some uneasiness at first; but as the steward says it is always there, and never goes away, I am quite comfortable again. I learn from this man that the different sections will be distributed at the Black Boy and Stomach-Ache, and the Boot-Jack and Countenance. If this intelligence be true, and I have no reason to doubt it, your readers will draw such conclusions as their different opinions may suggest.

"I write down these remarks as they occur to me, or as the facts come to my knowledge, in order that my first impressions may lose nothing of their original vividness. I shall despatch them in small packets as opportunities arise."

"Half past nine.

"Some dark object has just appeared upon the wharf. I think it is a travelling carriage."

"A quarter to ten.

"No, it is n't."

"Half past ten.

"The passengers are pouring in every instant. Four omnibuses full have just arrived upon the wharf, and all is bustle and activity. The noise and confusion are very great. Cloths are laid in the cabins, and the steward is placing blue plates full of knobs of cheese at equal distances down the centre of the tables. He drops a great many knobs; but, being used to it, picks them up again with great dexterity, and, after wiping them on his sleeve, throws them back into the plates. He is a young man of exceedingly prepossessing appearance, — either dirty or a mulatto, but I think the former.

"An interesting old gentleman who came to the wharf in an omnibus has just quarrelled violently with the porters, and is staggering towards the vessel with a large trunk in his arms. I trust and hope that he may reach it in safety; but the board he has to cross is narrow and slippery. Was that a splash? Gracious powers!

"I have just returned from the deck. The trunk is standing upon the extreme brink of the wharf, but the old gentleman is nowhere to be seen. The watchman is not sure whether he went down or not, but promises to drag for him the first thing to-morrow morning. May his humane efforts prove successful!

"Professor Nogo has this moment arrived with his nightcap on under his hat. He has ordered a glass of cold brandy-and-water, with a hard biscuit and a basin, and has gone straight to bed. What can this mean?

"The three other scientific gentlemen to whom I have already alluded have come on board, and have all tried their beds, with the exception of Professor Woodensconce, who sleeps in one of the top ones, and can't get into it. Mr. Slug, who sleeps in the other top one, is unable to get out of his, and is to have his supper handed up by a boy. I have had the honor to introduce myself to these gentlemen, and we have amicably arranged the order in which we shall retire to rest; which it is necessary to agree upon, because, although the cabin is very comfortable, there is not room for more than one gentleman to be out of bed at a time, and even he must take his boots off in the passage.

"As I anticipated, the knobs of cheese were provided for the passengers' supper, and are now in course of consumption. Your readers will be surprised to hear that Professor Woodensconce has abstained from cheese for eight years, although he takes butter in considerable quantities. Professor Grime, having lost several teeth, is unable, I observe, to eat his crusts without previously soaking them in his bottled porter. How interesting are these peculiarities!"

"Half past eleven.

"Professors Woodensconce and Grime, with a degree of good humor that delights us all, have just arranged to toss for a bottle of mulled port. There has been some discussion whether the payment should be decided by the first toss or the best out of three. Eventually the latter course has been determined on. Deeply do I wish that both gentlemen could win; but that being impossible, I own that my personal aspirations (I speak as an individual, and do not compromise either you or your readers by this expression of feeling) are with Professor Woodensconce. I have backed that gentleman to the amount of eighteen pence."

"Twenty minutes to twelve.

"Professor Grime has inadvertently tossed his half-crown out of one of the cabin-windows, and it has been arranged the steward shall toss for him. Bets are offered on any side to any amount, but there are no takers.

"Professor Woodensconce has just called 'woman'; but the coin having lodged in a beam is a long time coming down again. The interest and suspense of this one moment are beyond anything that can be imagined."

"Twelve o'clock.

"The mulled port is smoking on the table before me, and Professor Grime has won. Tossing is a game of chance; but on every ground, whether of public or private character, intellectual endowments, or scientific attainments, I cannot help expressing my opinion that Professor Woodensconce *ought* to have come off victorious. There is an exultation about Professor Grime incompatible, I fear, with greatness."

"A quarter past twelve.

"Professor Grime continues to exult, and to boast of his victory in no very measured terms, observing that he always does win, and that he knew it would be a 'head' beforehand, with many other remarks of a similar nature. Surely this gentleman is not so lost to every feeling of decency and propriety as not to feel and know the superiority of Professor Woodensconce. Is Professor Grime insane? or does he wish to be reminded in plain language of his true position in society, and the precise level of his acquirements and abilities? Professor Grime will do well to look to this."

"One o'clock.

"I am writing in bed. The small cabin is illuminated by the feeble light of a flickering lamp suspended from the ceiling; Professor Grime is lying on the opposite shelf, on the broad of his back, with his mouth wide open. The scene is indescribably solemn. The ripple of the tide, the noise of the sailors' feet overhead, the gruff voices on the river, the dogs on the shore, the snoring of the passengers, and a constant creaking of every plank in the vessel, are the only sounds that meet the ear. With these exceptions, all is profound silence.

"My curiosity has been within the last moment very much excited. Mr. Slug, who lies above Professor Grime, has cautiously withdrawn the curtains of his berth, and after looking anxiously out, as if to satisfy himself that his companions are asleep, has taken up the tin tube of which I have before spoken, and is regarding it with great interest. What rare mechanical combinations can be obtained in that mysterious case? It is evidently a profound secret to all."

"A quarter past one.

"The behavior of Mr. Slug grows more and more mysterious. He has unscrewed the top of the tube, and now renews his observation upon his companions; evidently to make sure that he is wholly unobserved. He is clearly on the eve of some great experiment. Pray Heaven that it be not a dangerous one; but the interests of science must be promoted, and I am prepared for the worst."

"Five minutes later.

"He has produced a large pair of scissors, and drawn a roll of some substance, not unlike parchment in appearance, from the tin case. The experiment is about to begin. I must strain my eyes to the utmost, in the attempt to follow its minutest operation."

"Twenty minutes before two.

"I have at length been enabled to ascertain that the tin tube contains a few yards of some celebrated plaster recommended, — as I discover on regarding the label attentively through my eye-glass, — as a preservative against sea-sickness. Mr. Slug has cut it up into small portions, and is now sticking it over himself in every direction."

"Three o'clock.

"Precisely a quarter of an hour ago we weighed anchor, and the machinery was suddenly put in motion with a noise so appalling, that Professor Woodensconce, who had ascended to his berth by means of a platform of carpet-bags arranged by himself on geometrical principles, darted from his shelf head-foremost, and gaining his feet with all the rapidity of extreme terror, ran wildly into the ladies' cabin, under the impression that we were sinking, and uttering loud cries for aid. I am assured that the scene which ensued baffles all description. There were one hundred and forty-seven ladies in their respective berths at the time.

"Mr. Slug has remarked, as an additional instance of the extreme ingenuity of the steam-engine as applied to purposes of navigation, that, in whatever part of the vessel a passenger's berth may be situated, the machinery always appears to be exactly under his pillow. He intends stating this very beautiful, though simple discovery to the association."

"Half past three.

"We are still in smooth water; that is to say, in as smooth water as a steam-vessel ever can be, for, as Professor Woodensconce, who has just woke up, learnedly remarks, another great point of ingenuity about a steamer is that it always carries a little storm with it. You can scarcely conceive how exciting the jerking pulsation of the ship becomes. It is a matter of positive difficulty to get to sleep."

"Friday afternoon, six o'clock.

"I regret to inform you that Mr. Slug's plaster has proved of no avail. He is in great agony, but has applied several large additional pieces, notwithstanding. How affecting is this extreme devotion to science and pursuit of knowledge under the most trying circumstances!

"We were extremely happy this morning, and the breakfast was one of the most animated description. Nothing unpleasant occurred until noon, with the exception of Dr. Foxey's brown silk umbrella and white hat becoming entangled in the machinery while he was explaining to a knot of ladies the construction of the steam-engine. I fear the gravy-soup for lunch was injudicious. We lost a great many passengers almost immediately afterwards."

"Half past six.

"I am again in bed. Anything so heart-rending as Mr. Slug's sufferings it has never yet been my lot to witness."

"Seven o'clock.

"A messenger has just come down for a clean pocket-handkerchief from Professor Woodensconce's bag, that unfortunate gentleman being quite unable to leave the deck, and imploring constantly to be thrown overboard. From this man I understand that Professor Nogo, though in a state of utter exhaustion, clings feebly to the hard biscuit and cold brandy-and-water, under the impression that they will yet restore him. Such is the triumph of mind over matter.

"Professor Grime is in bed, to all appearance quite well; but he *will* eat, and it is disagreeable to see him. Has this gentleman no sympathy with the sufferings of his fellow-creatures? If he has, on what principle can he call for mutton-chops, — and smile?"

"Black Boy and Stomach-Ache, Oldcastle, Saturday noon.

"You will be happy to learn that I have at length arrived here in safety. The town is excessively crowded, and all the private lodgings and hotels are filled with *savans* of both sexes. The tremendous assemblages of intellect that one encounters in every street is in the last degree overwhelming.

"Notwithstanding the throng of people here, I have been fortunate enough to meet with very comfortable accommodation on very reasonable terms, having secured a sofa in the first-floor passage at one guinea per night, which includes permission to take my meals in the bar, on condition that I walk about the streets at all other times, to make room for other gentlemen similarly situated. I have been over the outhouses intended to be devoted to the reception of the various sections, both here and at the Boot-Jack and Countenance, and am much delighted with the arrangements. Nothing can exceed the fresh appearance of the sawdust with which the floors are sprinkled. The forms are of unplaned deal, and the general effect, as you can well imagine, is extremely beautiful."

"Half past nine.

"The number and rapidity of the arrivals are quite bewildering. Within the last ten minutes a stage-coach has driven up to the door, filled, inside and out, with distinguished characters, comprising Mr. Muddlebrains, Mr. Drawley, Professor Muff, Mr. X. Misty, Mr. X. X. Misty, Mr. Purblind, Professor Rummun, The Honorable and Reverend Mr. Long Ears, Professor John Ketch, Sir William Joltered, Dr. Buffer, Mr. Smith, of London, Mr. Brown, of Edenburg, Sir Hookham Snivey, and Professor Pumpkinskull. The last ten named gentlemen were wet through, and looked extremely intelligent."

"Sunday, two o'clock, P. M.

"The Honorable and Reverend Mr. Long Ears, accompanied by Sir William Joltered, walked and drove this morning. They accomplished the former feat in boots, and the latter in a hired fly. This has naturally given rise to much discussion.

"I have just learned that an interview has taken place at the Boot-Jack and Countenance between Sowster, the active and intelligent beadle of this place, and Professor Pumpkinskull, who, as your readers are doubtless aware, is an influential member of the council. I forbear to communicate any of the rumors to which this very extraordinary proceeding has given rise until I have seen Sowster, and endeavor to ascertain the truth from him."

"Half past six.

"I engaged a donkey-chaise shortly after writing the above, and proceeded at a brisk trot in the direction of Sowster's residence, passing through a beautiful expanse of country, with red brick buildings on either side, and stopping in the market-place to observe the spot where Mr. Kwakley's hat was blown off yesterday. It is an uneven piece of paving, but has certainly no appearance which would lead one to suppose that any such event had recently occurred there. From this point I proceeded — passing the gas-works and tallow-melter's — to a lane which had been pointed out to me as the beadle's place of residence; and before I had driven a dozen yards farther, I had the good fortune to meet Sowster himself advancing towards me.

"Sowster is a fat man, with a more enlarged development of that peculiar conformation of countenance which is vulgarly termed a double chin than I remember to have ever seen before. He has also a very red nose, which he attributes to a habit of early rising, — so red, indeed, that but for this explanation I should have supposed it to proceed from occasional inebriety. He informed me that he did not feel himself at liberty to relate what had passed between himself and Professor Pumpkinskull, but had no objection to state that it was connected with a matter of police regulation, and added with peculiar significance, 'Never wos sitch times!'

"You will easily believe that this intelligence gave me considerable surprise, not wholly unmixed with anxiety, and that I lost no time in waiting on Professor Pumpkinskull, and stating the object of my visit. After a few moments' reflection, the Professor, who, I am bound to say, behaved with the utmost politeness, openly avowed (I marked the passage in italics) *that he had requested Sowster to attend on the Monday morning at the Boot-Jack and Countenance, to keep off the boys; and that he had further desired that the under-beadle might be stationed, with the same object, at the Black Boy and Stomach-Ache!*

"Now I leave this unconstitutional proceeding to your comments and the consideration of your readers. I have yet to learn that a beadle, without the precincts of a church, churchyard, or workhouse, and acting otherwise than under the express orders of churchwardens and overseers in council assembled, to enforce the law against people who come upon the parish, and other offenders, has any lawful authority whatever over the rising youth of this country. I have yet to learn that a beadle can be called out by any civilian to exercise a domination and despotism over the boys of Britain. I have yet to learn that a beadle will be permitted by the commissioners of poor-law regulation, to wear out the soles and heels of his boots in illegal interference with the liberties of people not proved poor, or otherwise criminal. I have yet to learn that a beadle has power to stop up the Queen's highway at his will and pleasure, or that the whole width of the street is not free and open to any man, boy, or woman in existence, up to the very walls of the houses, — ay, be they Black Boys and Stomach-Aches, or Boot-Jacks and Countenances, I care not."

"Nine o'clock.

"I have procured a local artist to make a faithful sketch of the tyrant Sowster, which, as he has acquired this infamous celebrity, you will no doubt wish to have engraved, for the purpose of presenting a copy with every copy of your next number. The under-beadle has consented to write his life, but it is to be strictly anonymous.

"The likeness is of course from the life, and complete in every respect. Even if I had been totally ignorant of the man's real character, and it had been placed before me without remark, I should have shuddered involuntarily. There is an intense malignity of expression in the features, and a baleful ferocity of purpose in the ruffian's eye, which appalls and sickens. His whole air is rampant with cruelty, nor is the stomach less characteristic of his demoniac propensities.

"Monday.

"The great day has at length arrived. I have neither eyes, nor ears, nor pens, nor ink, nor paper, for anything but the wonderful proceedings that have astounded my senses. Let me collect my energies and proceed to the account.

"SECTION A. — ZOÖLOGY AND BOTANY.
"FRONT PARLOR, BLACK BOY AND STOMACH-ACHE.
"PRESIDENT — SIR WILLIAM JOLTERED. VICE-PRESIDENTS — MR. MUDDLEBRAINS AND MR. DRAWLEY.

"Mr. X. X. Misty communicated some remarks on the disappearance of dancing bears from the streets of London, with observations on the exhibition of monkeys as connected with barrel-organs. The writer had observed with feelings of the utmost pain and regret, that some years ago a sudden and unaccountable change in the public taste took place with reference to itinerant bears, who, being discountenanced by the populace, gradually fell off one by one from the streets of the metropolis, until not one remained to create a taste for natural history in the breasts of the poor and uninstructed. One bear, indeed, — a brown and ragged animal, — had lingered about the haunts of his former triumphs, with a worn and dejected visage and feeble limbs, and had essayed to wield his quarter-staff for the amusement of the multitude; but hunger and an utter want of any due recompense for his abilities, had at length driven him from the field, and it was only too probable that he had fallen a sacrifice to the rising taste for grease. He regretted to add that a similar and no less lamentable change had taken place with reference to monkeys. Those delightful animals had formerly been almost as plentiful as the organs on the tops of which they were accustomed to sit; the proportion in the year 1829, it appeared by the parliamentary return, being as one monkey to three organs. Owing however to an altered taste in musical instruments and the substitution in a great measure of narrow boxes of music for organs, which left the monkeys nothing to sit upon, this source of public amusement was wholly dried up. Considering it a matter of the deepest importance in connection with national education, that the people should not lose such opportunities of making themselves acquainted with the manners and customs of two most interesting species of animals, the author submitted that some measures should be immediately taken for the restoration of those pleasing and truly intellectual amusements.

"The President inquired by what means the honorable member proposed to attain this most desirable end?

"The Author submitted that it could be most fully and satisfactorily accomplished, if her Majesty's government would cause to be brought over to England, and maintained at the public expense, and for the public amusement, such a number of bears as would enable every quarter of the town to be visited, — say at least by three bears a week. No difficulty whatever need be experienced in providing a fitting place for the reception of those animals, as a commodious bear-garden could be erected in the immediate neighborhood of both houses of Parliament; obviously the most proper and eligible spot for such an establishment.

"Professor Mull doubted very much whether any correct ideas of natural history were propagated by the means to which the honorable member had so ably adverted. On the contrary, he believed that they had been the means of diffusing very incorrect and imperfect notions on the subject. He spoke from personal observations and personal experience, when he said that many children of great abilities had been induced to believe, from what they had observed in the streets, at and before the period to which the honorable gentleman had referred, that all monkeys were born in red coats and spangles, and that their hats and features also came by nature. He wished to know distinctly whether the honorable gentleman attributed the want of encouragement the bears had met with to the decline of public taste in that respect, or to a want of ability on the part of the bears themselves?

"Mr. X. X. Misty replied that he could not bring himself to believe but there must be a great deal of floating talent among the bears and monkeys erally; which, in the absence of any proper encouragement, was disperse other directions.

"Professor Pumpkinskull wished to take that opportunity of calling the attention of the section to a most important and serious point. The author of the treatise just read had alluded to the prevalent taste for bears' grease as a means of promoting the growth of hair, which undoubtedly was diffused to a very great and, as it appeared to him, very alarming extent. No gentleman attending that section could fail to be aware of the fact that the youth of the present age evinced, by their behavior in the streets and all places of public resort, a considerable lack of that gallantry and gentlemanly feeling which, in more ignorant times, had been thought becoming. He wished to know whether it were possible that a constant outward application of bears' grease by the young gentlemen about town, had imperceptibly infused into those unhappy persons something of the nature and quality of the bear? He shuddered as he threw out the remark; but if this theory, on inquiry, should prove to be well founded, it would at once explain a great deal of unpleasant eccentricity of behavior, which, without some such discovery, was wholly unaccountable.

"The President highly complimented the learned gentleman on his most valuable suggestion, which produced the greatest effect upon the assembly; and remarked that only a week previous he had seen some young gentlemen at a theatre eying a box of ladies with a fierce intensity, which nothing but the influence of some brutish appetite could possibly explain. It was dreadful to reflect that our youth were so rapidly verging into a generation of bears.

"After a scene of scientific enthusiasm it was resolved that this important question should be immediately submitted to the consideration of the council.

"The President wished to know whether any gentleman could inform the section what had become of the dancing-dogs?

"A member replied, after some hesitation, that on the day after three glee-singers had been committed to prison as criminals by a late most zealous police-magistrate of the metropolis, the dogs had abandoned their professional duties, and dispersed themselves in different quarters of the town to gain a livelihood by less dangerous means. He was given to understand that since that period they had supported themselves by lying in wait for and robbing blind men's poodles.

"Mr. Flummery exhibited a twig, claiming to be a veritable branch of that noble tree known to naturalists as the Shakespeare, which has taken root in every land and climate, and gathered under the shade of its broad green boughs the great family of mankind. The learned gentleman remarked that the twig had been undoubtedly called by other names in its time; but that it had been pointed out to him by an old lady in Warwickshire, where the great tree had grown, as a shoot of the genuine Shakespeare, by which name he begged to introduce it to his countrymen.

"The President wished to know what botanical definition the honorable gentleman could afford of the curiosity?

"Mr. Flummery expressed his opinion that it was a DECIDED PLANT.

"SECTION B. — DISPLAY OF MODELS AND MECHANICAL SCIENCE.

"LARGE ROOM, BOOT-JACK AND COUNTENANCE.

"PRESIDENT — MR. MALLET. VICE-PRESIDENTS — MESSRS. LEAVER AND SCROO.

"Mr. Crinkles exhibited a most beautiful and delicate machine, of a little larger size than an ordinary snuff-box, manufactured entirely by himself, and composed exclusively of steel; by the aid of which more pockets were picked in one hour than by the present slow and tedious process in four-and-twenty. The inventor remarked that it had been put into active operation in Fleet Street, the Strand, and other thoroughfares, and had never been once known to fail.

"After some slight delay, occasioned by the various members of the section buttoning their pockets.

"The President narrowly inspected the invention, and declared that he had never seen a machine of more beautiful or exquisite construction. Would the inventor be good enough to inform the section whether he had taken any and what means for bringing it into general operation?

"Mr. Crinkles stated that after encountering some preliminary difficulties, he had succeeded in putting himself in communication with Mr. Fogle Hunter, and other gentlemen connected with the swell mob, who had awarded the invention the very highest and most unqualified approbation. He regretted to say, however, that those distinguished practitioners, in common with a gentleman of the name of Gimlet-eyed Tommy, and other members of a secondary grade of the profession whom he has understood to represent, entertained an insuperable objection to its being brought into general use, on the ground that it would have the inevitable effect of almost entirely superseding manual labor, and throwing a great number of highly deserving persons out of employment.

"The President hoped that no such fanciful objections would be allowed to stand in the way of such a great public improvement.

"Mr. Crinkles hoped so too; but he feared that if the gentlemen of the swell mob persevered in their objection, nothing could be done.

"Professor Grimes suggested that surely in that case her Majesty's government might be prevailed upon to take it up.

"Mr. Crinkles said that if the objection were found to be insuperable, he should apply to Parliament, who he thought could not fail to recognize the utility of the invention.

"The President observed that up to his time Parliament had certainly got on very well without it; but as they did their business on a very large scale, he had no doubt they would gladly adopt the improvement. His only fear was that the machine might be worn out by constant working.

"Mr. Coppernose called the attention of the section to a proposition of great magnitude and interest, illustrated by a vast number of models, and stated with much clearness and perspicuity in a treatise entitled 'Practical Suggestions on the necessity of providing some harmless and wholesome relaxation for the young noblemen of England.' His proposition was that a space of ground of not less than ten miles in length and four in breadth should be purchased by a new company, to be incorporated by act of Parliament, and enclosed by a brick wall of not less than twelve feet in height. He proposed that it should be laid out with highway roads, turnpikes, bridges, miniature villages, and every object that could conduce to the comfort and glory of Four-in-hand Clubs, so that they might be fairly presumed to require no drive beyond it. This delightful retreat would be fitted up with most commodious and extensive stables for the convenience of such of the nobility and gentry as had a taste for ostlering, and with houses of entertainment furnished in the most expensive and handsome style. It would be further provided with whole streets of door-knockers and bell-handles of extra size, so constructed that they could be easily wrenched off at night, and regularly screwed on again by attendants provided for the purpose, every day. There would also be gas-lamps of real glass, which could be broken at a comparatively small expense per dozen, and a broad and handsome foot-pavement for gentlemen to drive their cabriolets upon when they were humorously disposed, — for the full enjoyment of which feat, live pedestrians would be procured from the workhouse at a very small charge per head. The place being enclosed and carefully screened from the intrusion of the public, there would be no objections to gentlemen laying aside any article of their costume that was considered to interfere with a pleasant frolic, or, indeed, to their walking about without any costume at all, if they liked that better. In short, every facility of enjoyment would be afforded that the most gentlemanly person could possibly desire. But as even these advantages would be incomplete, unless there were some means provided of enabling the nobility and gentry to display their prowess when they sallied forth after dinner, and as some inconvenience might be experienced in the event of their being reduced to the necessity of pummelling each other, the inventor had turned his attention to the construction of an entirely new police-force, composed exclusively of automaton figures, which, with the assistance of the ingenious Signor Gagliardi, of Windmill Street in the Haymarket, he had succeeded in making with such nicety, that a policeman, cab-driver, or old woman, made upon the principle of the models exhibited, would walk about until knocked down like any real man; nay more, if set upon and beaten by six or eight noblemen or gentlemen, after it was down, the figure would utter divers groans mingled with entreaties for mercy; thus rendering the illusion complete, and the enjoyment perfect. But the invention did not stop even here, for station-houses would be built, containing good beds for noblemen and gentlemen during the night, and in the morning they would repair to a commodious police-office where a pantomimic investigation would take place before automaton magistrates, — quite equal to life, — who would fine them so many counters, with which they would be previously provided for the purpose. This office would be furnished with an inclined plane for the convenience of any nobleman or gentleman who might wish to bring in his horse as a witness, and the prisoners would be at perfect liberty, as they were now, to interrupt the complainants as much as they pleased, and to make any remarks that they thought proper. The charge for those amusements would amount to very little more than they already cost, and the inventor submitted that the public would be much benefited and comforted by the proposed arrangement.

"Professor Nogo wished to be informed what amount of automaton police-force it was proposed to raise in the first instance.

"Mr. Coppernose replied that it was proposed to begin with seven divisions of police of a score each, lettered from A to G inclusive. It was proposed that not more than half the number should be placed on active duty, and that the remainder should be kept on shelves in the police-office, ready to be called out at a moment's notice.

"The President, awarding the utmost merit to the ingenious gentleman who had originated the idea, doubted whether the automaton police would quite answer the purpose. He feared that noblemen and gentlemen would perhaps require the excitement of threshing living subjects.

"Mr. Coppernose submitted, that as the usual odds in such cases were ten noblemen or gentlemen to one policeman or cab-driver, it could make very little difference, in point of excitement, whether the policeman or cab-driver were a man or a block. The great advantage would be that a policeman's limb might be knocked off, and yet he would be in a condition to do duty next day. He might even give his evidence next morning with his head in his hand, and give it equally well.

"Professor Muff. — Will you allow me to ask you, sir, of what materials it is intended that the magistrates' heads shall be composed ?

"Mr. Coppernose. — The magistrates will have wooden heads of course, and they will be made of the toughest and thickest materials that can possibly be obtained.

"Professor Muff. — I am quite satisfied. This is a great invention.

"Professor Nogo. — I see but one objection to it. It appears to me that the magistrates ought to talk.

"Mr. Coppernose no sooner heard this suggestion than he touched a small spring in each of the two models of magistrates which were placed upon the table ; one of the figures immediately began to exclaim with great volubility, that he was sorry to see gentlemen in such a situation, and the other to express a fear that the policeman was intoxicated.

"The section as with one accord declared with a shout of applause, that the invention was complete ; and the President, much excited, retired with Mr. Coppernose, to lay it before the council. On his return, —

"Mr. Tickle displayed his newly invented spectacles, which enabled the wearer to discern in very bright colors objects at a great distance, and rendered him wholly blind to those immediately before him. It was, he said, a most valuable and useful invention, based strictly upon the principle of the human eye.

"The President required some information upon this point. He had yet to learn that the human eye was remarkable for the peculiarities of which the honorable gentleman had spoken.

"Mr. Tickle was rather astonished to hear this, when the President could not fail to be aware that a large number of most excellent persons and great statesmen could see with the naked eye most marvellous horrors on West India plantations, while they could discern nothing whatever in the interior of Manchester cotton-mills. He must know, too, with what quickness of perception most people could discover their neighbor's faults, and how very blind they were to their own. If the President differed from the great majority of men in this respect, his eye was a defective one, and it was to assist his vision that these glasses were made.

"Mr. Blank exhibited a model of a fashionable annual, composed of copper-plates, gold leaf, and silk boards, and worked entirely by milk and water.

"Mr. Prosee, after examining the machine, declared it to be so ingeniously composed, that he was wholly unable to discover how it went on at all.

"Mr. Blank. — Nobody can, and that is the beauty of it.

"SECTION C. — ANATOMY AND MEDICINE.
"BAR-ROOM, BLACK BOY AND STOMACH-ACHE.
"PRESIDENT — DR. SOEMUP. VICE-PRESIDENTS — MESSRS. PESSELL AND MORTAIR.

"Dr. Grummidge stated to the section a most interesting case of monomania, and described the course of treatment he had pursued with perfect success. The patient was a married lady in the middle rank of life, who, having seen another lady at an evening party in a full suit of pearls, was suddenly seized with a desire to possess a similar equipment, although her husband's finances were by no means equal to the necessary outlay. Finding her wish ungratified, she fell sick, and the symptoms soon became so alarming, that he, Dr. Grummidge, was called in. At this period the prominent tokens of the disorder were sullenness, a total indisposition to perform domestic duties, great peevishness, and extreme languor, except when pearls were mentioned, at which times the pulse quickened, the eyes grew brighter, the pupils dilated, and the patient, after various incoherent exclamations, burst into a passion of tears and exclaimed that nobody cared for her, and that she wished herself dead. Finding that the patient's appetite was affected in the presence of company, he began by ordering a total abstinence from all stimulants, and forbidding any sustenance but weak gruel; he then took twenty ounces of blood, applied a blister under each ear, one upon the chest, and another on the back; having done which, and administered five grains of calomel, he left the patient to her repose. The next day she was somewhat low, but decidedly better; and all appearances of irritation were removed. The next day she improved still further, and on the next again. On the fourth there was some appearance of a return of the old symptoms, which no sooner developed themselves than he administered another dose of calomel, and left strict orders, that unless a decidedly favorable change occurred within two hours, the patient's head should be immediately shaved to the very last curl. From that moment she began to mend, and in less than four-and-twenty hours was perfectly restored; she did not now betray the least emotion at the sight or mention of pearls or any other ornaments. She was cheerful and good humored, and a most beneficial change had been effected in her whole temperament and condition.

"Mr. Pipkin, M. R. C. S., read a short but most interesting communication in which he sought to prove the complete belief of Sir William Courtenay, otherwise Thom, recently shot at Canterbury in the Homœopathic system. The section would bear in mind that one of the Homœopathic doctrines was, that infinitesimal doses of any medicine which would occasion the disease under which the patient labored, supposing him to be in a healthy state, would cure it. Now it was a remarkable circumstance, — proved in the evidence, — that the diseased Thom employed a woman to follow him about all day with a pail of water, assuring her that one drop, a purely homœopathic remedy, the section would observe, placed upon his tongue after death, would restore him. What was the obvious inference? That Thom, who was marching and countermarching in osier beds, and other swampy places, was impressed with a presentiment that he should be drowned; in which case, had his instructions been complied with, he could not fail to have been brought to life again instantly by his own prescriptions. As it was, if this woman, or any other person, had administered an infinitesimal dose of lead and gunpowder, immediately after he fell, he would have recovered forthwith. But unhappily, the woman concerned did not possess the power of reasoning by analogy, or carrying out a principle, and thus the unfortunate gentleman had been sacrificed to the ignorance of the peasantry.

"SECTION D. — STATISTICS.
"OUT-HOUSE, BLACK BOY AND STOMACH-ACHE.
"PRESIDENT — MR. SLUG. VICE-PRESIDENTS — MESSRS. NOAKES AND STYLES.

"Mr. Kwakley stated the result of some most ingenious statistical inquiries relative to the difference between the value of the qualification of several members of Parliament, as published to the world, and its real nature and amount. After reminding the section that every member of Parliament for a town or borough was supposed to possess a clear freehold estate of three hundred pounds per annum, the honorable gentleman excited great amusement and laughter by stating the exact amount of freehold property possessed by a column of legislators, in which he had included himself. It appeared from this table that the amount of such income possessed by each was o pounds, o shillings, and o pence, yielding an average of the same. (Great laughter.) It was pretty well known that there were accommodating gentlemen in the habit of furnishing new members with temporary qualifications, to the ownership of which they swore solemnly, of course, as a mere matter of form. He argued from these *data* that it was wholly unnecessary for members of Parliament to possess any property at all, especially as, when they had none, the public could get them so much cheaper.

"SUPPLEMENTARY SECTION E. — UMBUGOLOGY AND DITCH-WATERISTICS.
"PRESIDENT — MR. GRUB. VICE-PRESIDENTS — MESSRS. DULL AND DUMMY.

"A paper was read by the secretary, descriptive of a bay pony with one eye, which had been seen by the author standing in a butcher's cart at the corner of Newgate Market. The communication described the author of the paper as having in the prosecution of a mercantile pursuit, betaken himself one Saturday morning last summer from Somers Town to Cheapside; in the course of which expedition he had beheld the extraordinary appearance above described. The pony had one distinct eye, and it had been pointed out to him by his friend Captain Blunderbore of the Horse Marines, who assisted the author in his search, that whenever he winked this eye he whisked his tail, possibly to drive the flies off, but that he always winked and whisked at the same time. The animal was lean, spavined, and tottering; and the author proposed to constitute it of the family of *Fitfordogsmeataurious*. It certainly did occur to him that there was no case on record of a pony with one clearly defined and distinct organ of vision, winking and whisking at the same moment.

"Mr. Q. J. Snuffletoffle had heard of a pony winking his eye, and likewise of a pony whisking his tail, but whether they were two ponies or the same pony he could not undertake positively to say. At all events he was acquainted with no authenticated instance of a simultaneous winking and whisking, and he really could not but doubt the existence of such a marvellous pony in opposition to all those natural laws by which ponies were governed. Referring however to the mere question of his one organ of vision, might he suggest the possibility of this pony having been literally half asleep at the time he was seen, and having closed only one eye?

"The President observed that whether the pony was half asleep or fast asleep, there could be no doubt that the association was awake, and therefore that they had better get the business over and go to dinner. He had certainly never seen anything analogous to this pony; but he was not prepared to doubt its existence, for he had seen many queerer ponies in his time, though he did not pretend to have seen any more remarkable donkeys than the other gentlemen around him.

"Professor John Ketch was then called upon to exhibit the skull of the late Mr. Greenacre, which he produced from a blue bag, remarking, on being invited to make any observations that occurred to him, 'that he 'd' pound it as that 'ere 'spectable section had never seed a more gamerer cove nor he vos.'

"A most animated discussion upon this interesting relic ensued; and some difference of opinion arising respecting the real character of the deceased gentleman, Mr. Blubb delivered a lecture upon the cranium before him, clearly showing that Mr. Greenacre possessed the organ of destructiveness to a most unusual extent, with a most remarkable development of the organ of carveativeness. Sir Hookham Snivey was proceeding to combat this opinion, when Professor Ketch suddenly interrupted the proceedings by exclaiming, with great excitement of manner, 'Walker!'

"The President begged to call the learned gentleman to order.

"Professor Ketch. — 'Order be blowed! you 've got the wrong 'un, I tell you. It ain't no 'ed at all; it 's a coker-nut as my brother-in-law has been acarvin' to hornament his new baked 'tatur-stall vots a-coming down here vile the 'sociation 's in the town. Hand over, vill you?'

"With these words Professor Ketch hastily repossessed himself of the cocoanut, and drew forth the skull, in mistake for which he had exhibited it. A most interesting conversation ensued; but, as there appeared some doubt ultimately whether the skull was Mr. Greenacre's, or a hospital patient's, or a pauper's, or a man's, or a woman's, or a monkey's, no particular result was attained.

"I cannot," says our talented correspondent in conclusion, — "I cannot close my account of these gigantic researches, and sublime and noble triumphs, without repeating a *bon-mot* of Professor Woodensconce's, which shows how the greatest minds may occasionally unbend, when truth can be presented to listening ears, clothed in an attractive and playful form. I was standing by, when, after a week of feasting and feeding, that learned gentleman, accompanied by the whole body of wonderful men, entered the hall yesterday, where a sumptuous dinner was prepared; where the richest wines sparkled on the board, and fat bucks — propitiatory sacrifices to learning — sent forth their savory odors. 'Ah!' said Professor Woodensconce, rubbing his hands, 'this is what we meet for; this is what inspires us; this is what keeps us together, and beckons us onward; this is the *spread* of science, and a glorious spread it is!'"

SKETCHES BY BOZ

ILLUSTRATIVE OF

EVERY-DAY LIFE AND EVERY-DAY PEOPLE.

PREFACE.

THE whole of these Sketches were written and published, one by one, when I was a very young man. They were collected and re-published while I was still a very young man, and sent into the world with all their imperfections (a good many) on their heads.

They comprise my first attempts at authorship—with the exception of certain tragedies achieved at the mature age of eight or ten, and represented with great applause to overflowing nurseries. I am conscious of their often being extremely crude and ill-considered, and bearing obvious marks of haste and inexperience; particularly in that section of the present volume which is comprised under the general head of Tales.

But as this collection is not originated now, and was very leniently and favourably received when it was first made, I have not felt it right either to remodel or expunge, beyond a few words and phrases here and there.

THE BEADLE.

SKETCHES BY BOZ.

OUR PARISH.

CHAPTER I.

THE BEADLE. THE PARISH ENGINE. THE SCHOOLMASTER.

How much is conveyed in those two short words—"The Parish!" And with how many tales of distress and misery, of broken fortune and ruined hopes, too often of unrelieved wretchedness and successful knavery, are they associated! A poor man, with small earnings, and a large family, just manages to live on from hand to mouth, and to procure food from day to day; he has barely sufficient to satisfy the present cravings of nature, and can take no heed of the future. His taxes are in arrear, quarter-day passes by, another quarter-day arrives: he can procure no more quarter for himself, and is summoned by—the parish. His goods are distrained, his children are crying with cold and hunger, and the very bed on which his sick wife is lying, is dragged from beneath her. What can he do? To whom is he to apply for relief? To private charity? To benevolent individuals? Certainly not—there is his parish. There are the parish vestry, the parish infirmary, the parish surgeon, the parish officers, the parish beadle. Excellent institutions, and gentle, kind-hearted men. The woman dies—she is buried by the parish. The children have no protector—they are taken care of by the parish. The man first neglects, and afterwards cannot obtain, work—he is relieved by the parish; and when distress and drunkenness have done their work upon him, he is maintained, a harmless babbling idiot, in the parish asylum.

The parish beadle is one of the most, perhaps *the* most, important member of the local administration. He is not so well off as the churchwardens, certainly, nor is he so learned as the vestry-clerk, nor does he order things quite so much his own way as either of them. But his power is very great, notwithstanding; and the dignity of his office is never impaired by the absence of efforts on his part to maintain it. The beadle of our parish is a splendid fellow. It is quite delightful to hear him, as he explains the state of the existing poor laws to the deaf old women in the board-room passage on business nights; and to hear what he said to the senior churchwarden, and what the senior churchwarden said to him; and what "we" (the beadle and the other gentlemen) came to the determination of doing.

A miserable-looking woman is called into the board-room, and represents a case of extreme destitution, affecting herself—a widow, with six small children. "Where do you live?" inquires one of the overseers. "I rents a two-pair back, gentlemen, at Mrs Brown's, Number 3, Little King William's-alley, which has lived there this fifteen year, and knows me to be very hard-working and industrious, and when my poor husband was alive, gentlemen, as died in the hospital"—"Well, well," interrupts the overseer, taking a note of the address, "I'll send Simmons, the beadle, to-morrow morning, to ascertain whether your story is correct; and if so, I suppose you must have an order into the House—Simmons, go to this woman's the first thing to-morrow morning, will you?" Simmons bows assent, and ushers the woman out. Her previous admiration of "the board" (who all sit behind great books, and with their hats on) fades into nothing before her respect for her lace-trimmed conductor; and her account of what has passed inside, increases—if that be possible—the marks of respect, shown by the assembled crowd, to that solemn functionary. As to taking out a summons, it's quite a hopeless case if Simmons attends it, on behalf of the parish. He knows all the titles of the Lord Mayor by heart; states the case without a single stammer: and it is even reported that on one occasion he ventured to make a joke, which the Lord Mayor's head footman (who happened to be present) afterwards told an intimate friend, confidentially, was almost equal to one of Mr. Hobler's.

See him again on Sunday in his state-coat and cocked-hat, with a large-headed staff for show in his left hand, and a small cane for use in his right. How pompously he marshals the children into their places! and how demurely the little urchins look at him askance as he surveys them when they are all seated, with a glare of the eye peculiar to beadles! The churchwardens and overseers being duly installed in their curtained pews, he seats himself on a mahogany bracket, erected expressly for him at the top of the aisle, and divides his attention between his prayer-book and the boys. Suddenly, just at the commencement of the communion service, when the whole congregation is hushed into a profound silence, broken only by the voice of the officiating clergyman, a penny is heard to ring on the stone floor of the aisle with astounding clearness. Observe the generalship of the beadle. His involuntary look of horror is instantly changed into one of perfect indifference, as if he were the only person present who had not heard the noise. The artifice succeeds. After putting forth his right leg now and then, as a feeler, the victim who dropped the money ventures to make one or two distinct dives after it; and the beadle, gliding softly round, salutes his little round head, when it again appears above the seat, with divers double knocks, administered with the cane before noticed, to the intense delight of three young men in an adjacent pew, who cough violently at intervals until the conclusion of the sermon.

Such are a few traits of the importance and gravity of a parish-beadle—a gravity which has never been disturbed in any case that has come under our observation, except when the services of that particularly useful machine, a parish fire-engine, are required: then indeed all is bustle. Two little boys run to the beadle as fast as their legs will carry them, and report from their own personal observation that some neighbouring chimney is on fire; the engine is hastily got out, and a plentiful supply of boys being obtained, and harnessed to it with ropes, away they rattle over the pavement, the beadle, running—we do not exaggerate—running at the side, until they arrive at some house, smelling strongly of soot, at the door of which the beadle knocks with considerable gravity for half-an-hour. No attention being paid to these manual applications, and the turn-cock having turned on the water, the engine turns off amidst the shouts of the boys; it pulls up once more at the workhouse, and the beadle "pulls up" the unfortunate householder next day, for the amount of his legal reward. We never saw a parish engine at a regular fire but once. It came up in gallant style—three miles and a half an hour, at least; there was a capital supply of water, and it was first on the spot. Bang went the pumps—the people cheered—the beadle perspired profusely; but it was unfortunately discovered, just as they were going to put the fire out, that nobody understood the process by which the engine was filled with water; and that eighteen boys, and a man, had exhausted themselves in pumping for twenty minutes, without producing the slightest effect!

The personages next in importance to the beadle, are the master of the workhouse and the parish schoolmaster. The vestry-clerk, as everybody knows, is a short, pudgy little man, in black, with a thick gold watch-chain of considerable length, terminating in two large seals and a key. He is an attorney, and generally in a bustle; at no time more so, than when he is hurrying to some parochial meeting, with his gloves crumpled up in one hand, and a large red book under the other arm. As to the churchwardens and overseers, we exclude them altogether, because all we know of them is, that they are usually respectable tradesmen, who wear hats with brims inclined to flatness, and who occasionally testify in gilt letters on a blue ground, in some conspicuous part of the church, to the important fact of a gallery having been enlarged and beautified, or an organ rebuilt.

The master of the workhouse is not, in our parish—nor is he usually in any other—one of that class of men the better part of whose existence has passed away, and who drag out the remainder in some inferior situation, with just enough thought of the past, to feel degraded by, and discontented with, the present. We are unable to guess precisely to our own satisfaction what station the man can have occupied before; we should think he had been an inferior sort of attorney's clerk, or else the master of a national school—whatever he was, it is clear his present position is a change for the better. His income is small certainly, as the rusty black coat and threadbare velvet collar demonstrate: but then he lives free of house-rent, has a limited allowance of coals and candles, and an almost unlimited allowance of authority in his petty kingdom. He is a tall, thin, bony man; always wears shoes and black cotton stockings with his surtout; and eyes you, as you pass his parlour-window, as if he wished you were a pauper, just to give you a specimen of his power. He is an admirable specimen of a small tyrant: morose, brutish, and ill-tempered; bullying to his inferiors, cringing to his superiors, and jealous of the influence and authority of the beadle.

Our schoolmaster is just the very reverse of this amiable official. He has been one of those men one occasionally hears of, on whom misfortune seems to have set her mark; nothing he ever did, or was concerned in, appears to have prospered. A rich old relation who had brought him up, and openly announced his intention of providing for him, left him 10,000*l.* in his will, and revoked the bequest in a codicil. Thus unexpectedly reduced to the necessity of providing for himself, he procured a situation in a public office. The young clerks below him, died off as if there were a plague among them; but the old fellows over his head, for the reversion of whose places he was anxiously waiting, lived on and on, as if they were immortal. He speculated and lost. He speculated again and won—but never got his money. His talents were great; his disposition, easy, generous and liberal. His friends profited by the one, and abused the other. Loss succeeded loss; misfortune crowded on misfortune; each successive day brought him nearer the verge of hopeless penury, and the quondam friends who had been warmest in their professions, grew strangely cold and indifferent. He had children whom he loved, and a wife on whom he doted. The former turned their backs on him; the latter died broken-hearted. He went with the stream—it had ever been his failing, and he had not courage sufficient to bear up against so many shocks—he had never cared for himself, and the only being who had cared for him, in his poverty and distress, was spared to him no longer. It was at this period that he applied for parochial relief. Some kind-hearted man who had known him in happier times, chanced to be churchwarden that year, and through his interest he was appointed to his present situation.

He is an old man now. Of the many who once crowded round him in all the hollow friendship of boon-companionship, some have died, some have fallen like himself, some have prospered—all have forgotten him. Time and misfortune have mercifully been permitted to impair his memory, and use has habituated him to his present condition. Meek, uncomplaining, and zealous in the discharge of his duties, he has been allowed to hold his situation long beyond the usual period · and he will no doubt continue to hold it, until infirmity renders him incapable, or death releases him. As the grey-headed old man feebly paces up and down the sunny side of the little court-yard between school hours, it would be difficult, indeed, for the most intimate of his former friends to recognise their once gay and happy associate, in the person of the Pauper Schoolmaster.

CHAPTER II.

THE CURATE. THE OLD LADY. THE HALF-PAY CAPTAIN.

WE commenced our last chapter with the beadle of our parish, because we are deeply sensible of the importance and dignity of his office. We will begin the present, with the clergyman. Our curate is a young gentleman of such prepossessing appearance, and fascinating manners, that within one month after his first appearance in the parish, half the young-lady inhabitants were melancholy with religion, and the other half, desponding with love. Never were so many young ladies seen in our parish-church on Sunday before; and never had the little round angels' faces on Mr. Tomkins's monument in the side aisle, beheld such devotion on earth as they all exhibited. He was about five-and-twenty when he first came to astonish the parishioners. He parted his hair on the centre of his forehead in the form of a Norman arch, wore a brilliant of the first water on the fourth finger of his left hand (which he always applied to his left cheek when he read prayers), and had a deep sepulchral voice of unusual solemnity. Innumerable were the calls made by prudent mammas on our new curate, and innumerable the invitations with which he was assailed, and which, to do him justice, he readily accepted. If his manner in the pulpit had created an impression in his favour, the sensation was increased tenfold, by his appearance in private circles. Pews in the immediate vicinity of the pulpit or reading-desk rose in value; sittings in the centre aisle were at a premium: an inch of room in the front row of the gallery could not be procured for love or money; and some people even went so far as to assert, that the three Miss Browns, who had an obscure family pew just behind the churchwardens', were detected, one Sunday, in the free seats by the communion-table, actually lying in wait for the curate as he passed to the vestry! He began to preach extempore sermons, and even grave papas caught the infection. He got out of bed at half-past twelve o'clock one winter's night, to half-baptise a washerwoman's child in a slop-basin, and the gratitude of the parishioners knew no bounds—the very churchwardens grew generous, and insisted on the parish defraying the expense of the watch-box on wheels, which the new curate had ordered for himself, to perform the funeral service in, in wet weather. He sent three pints of gruel and a quarter of a pound of tea to a poor woman who had been brought to bed of four small children, all at once—the parish were charmed. He got up a subscription for her—the woman's fortune was made. He spoke for one hour and twenty-five minutes, at an anti-slavery meeting at the Goat and Boots—the enthusiasm was at its height. A proposal was set on foot for presenting the curate with a piece of plate, as a mark of esteem for his valuable services rendered to the parish. The list of subscriptions was filled up in no time; the contest was, not who should escape the contribution, but who should be the foremost to subscribe. A splendid silver inkstand was made, and engraved with an appropriate inscription; the curate was invited to a public breakfast, at the before-mentioned Goat and Boots; the inkstand was presented in a neat speech by Mr. Gubbins, the ex-churchwarden, and acknowledged by the curate in terms which drew tears into the eyes of all present—the very waiters were melted.

One would have supposed that, by this time, the theme of universal admiration was lifted to the very pinnacle of popularity. No such thing. The curate began to cough; four fits of coughing one morning between the Litany and the Epistle, and five in the afternoon service. Here was a discovery—the curate was consumptive. How interestingly melancholy! If the young ladies were energetic before, their sympathy and solicitude now knew no bounds. Such a man as the curate—such a dear—such a perfect love—to be consumptive! It was too much. Anonymous presents of black-currant jam, and lozenges, elastic waistcoats, bosom friends, and warm stockings, poured in upon the curate until he was as completely fitted out, with winter clothing, as if he were on the verge of an expedition to the North Pole: verbal bulletins of the state of his health were circulated throughout the parish half-a-dozen times a day; and the curate was in the very zenith of his popularity.

About this period, a change came over the spirit of the parish. A very quiet, respectable, dozing old gentleman, who had officiated in our chapel-of-ease for twelve years previously, died one fine morning, without having given any notice whatever of his intention. This circumstance gave rise to counter-sensation the first; and the arrival of his successor occasioned counter-sensation the second. He was a pale, thin, cadaverous man, with large black eyes, and long straggling black hair: his dress was slovenly in the extreme, his manner ungainly, his doctrines startling; in short, he was in every respect the antipodes of the curate. Crowds of our female parishioners flocked to hear him; at first, because he was *so* odd-looking, then because his face was *so* expressive, then because he preached *so* well; and at last, because they really thought that, after all, there was something about him which it was quite impossible to describe. As to the curate, he was all very well; but certainly, after all, there was no denying that—that—in short, the curate wasn't a novelty, and the other clergyman was. The inconstancy of public opinion is proverbial: the congregation migrated one by one. The curate coughed till he was black in the face—it was in vain. He respired with difficulty—it was equally ineffectual in awakening sympathy. Seats are once again to be had in any part of our parish-church, and the chapel-of-ease is going to be enlarged, as it is crowded to suffocation every Sunday!

The best known and most respected among our parishioners, is an old lady, who resided in our parish long before our name was registered in the list of baptisms. Our parish is a suburban one, and the old lady lives in a neat row of houses in the most airy and pleasant part of it. The house is her own; and it, and everything about it, except the old lady herself, who looks a little older than she did ten years ago, is in just the same state as when the old gentleman was living. The little front parlour, which is the old lady's ordinary sitting-room, is a perfect picture of quiet neatness; the carpet is covered with brown Holland, the glass and picture-frames are carefully enveloped in yellow muslin; the table-covers are never taken off, except when the leaves are turpentined and bees'-waxed, an operation which is regularly commenced every other morning at half-past nine o'clock—and the little nicnacs are always arranged in precisely the same manner. The greater part of these are presents from little girls whose parents live in the same row; but some of them, such as the two old-fashioned watches (which never keep the same time, one being always a quarter of an hour too slow, and the other a quarter of an hour too fast), the little picture of the Princess Charlotte and Prince Leopold as they appeared in the Royal Box at Drury Lane Theatre, and others of the same class, have been in the old lady's possession for many years. Here the old lady sits with her spectacles on, busily engaged in needlework—near the window in summer time; and if she sees you coming up the steps, and you happen to be a favourite, she trots out to open the street-door for you before you knock, and as you must be fatigued after that hot walk, insists on your swallowing two glasses of sherry before you exert yourself by talking. If you call in the evening you will find her cheerful, but rather more serious than usual, with an open Bible on the table, before her, of which "Sarah," who is just as neat and methodical as her mistress, regularly reads two or three chapters in the parlour aloud.

The old lady sees scarcely any company, except the little girls before noticed, each of whom has always a regular fixed day for a periodical tea-drinking with her, to which the child looks forward as the greatest treat of its existence. She seldom visits at a greater distance than the next door but one on either side; and when she drinks tea here, Sarah runs out first and knocks a double-knock, to prevent the possibility of her "Missis's" catching cold by having to wait at the door. She is very scrupulous in returning these little invitations, and when she asks Mr. and Mrs. So-and-so, to meet Mr. and Mrs. Sombody-else, Sarah and she dust the urn, and the best china tea-service, and the Pope Joan board; and the visitors are received in the drawing-room in great state. She has but few relations, and they are scattered about in different parts of the country, and she seldom sees them. She has a son in India, whom she always describes to you as a fine, handsome fellow—so like the profile of his poor dear father over the sideboard, but the old lady adds, with a mournful shake of the head, that he has always been one of her greatest trials; and that indeed he once almost broke her heart; but it pleased God to enable her to get the better of it, and she would prefer your never mentioning the subject to her again. She has a great number of pensioners: and on Saturday, after she comes back from market, there is a regular levee of old men and women in the passage, waiting for their weekly gratuity. Her name always heads the list of any benevolent subscriptions, and hers are always the most liberal donations to the Winter Coal and Soup Distribution Society. She subscribed twenty pounds towards the erection of an organ in our parish church, and was so overcome the first Sunday the children sang to it, that she was obliged to be carried out by the pew-opener. Her entrance into church on Sunday is always the signal for a little bustle in the side aisle, occasioned by a general rise among the poor people, who bow and curtsy until the pew-opener has ushered the old lady into her accustomed seat, dropped a respectful curtsy, and shut the door: and the same ceremony is repeated on her leaving church, when she walks home with the family next door but one, and talks about the sermon all the way, invariably opening the conversation by asking the youngest boy where the text was.

Thus, with the annual variation of a trip to some quiet place on the sea-coast, passes the old lady's life. It has rolled on in the same unvarying and benevolent course for many years now, and must at no distant period be brought to its final close. She looks forward to its termination, with calmness and without apprehension. She has everything to hope and nothing to fear.

A very different personage, but one who has rendered himself very conspicuous in our parish, is one of the old lady's next-door neighbours. He is an old naval officer on half-pay, and his bluff and unceremonious behaviour disturbs the old lady's domestic economy, not a little. In the first place, he *will* smoke cigars in the front court, and when he wants something to drink with them—which is by no means an uncommon circumstance—he lifts up the old lady's knocker with his walking-stick, and demands to have a glass of table ale, handed over the rails. In addition to this cool proceeding, he is a bit of a Jack of all trades, or to use his own words, "a regular Robinson Crusoe;" and nothing delights him better than to experimentalise on the old lady's property. One morning he got up early, and planted three or four roots of full-grown marigolds in every bed of her front garden, to the inconceivable astonishment of the old lady, who actually thought when she got up and looked out of the window, that it was some strange eruption which had come out in the night. Another time he took to pieces the eight-day clock on the front landing, under pretence of cleaning the works, which he put together again, by some undiscovered process, in so wonderful a manner, that the large hand has done nothing but trip up the little one ever since. Then he took to breeding silk-worms, which he *would* bring in two or three times a day, in little paper boxes, to show the old lady, generally dropping a worm or two at every visit. The consequence was, that one morning a very stout silk-worm was discovered in the act of walking up-stairs—probably with the view of inquiring after his friends, for, on further inspection, it appeared that some of his companions had already found their way to every room in the house. The old lady went to the seaside in despair, and during her absence he completely effaced the name from her brass door-plate, in his attempts to polish it with aqua-fortis.

But all this is nothing to his seditious conduct in public life. He attends every vestry meeting that is held; always opposes the constituted authorities of the parish, denounces the profligacy of the churchwardens, contests legal points against the vestry-clerk, *will* make the tax-gatherer call for his money till he won't call any longer, and then he sends it: finds fault with the sermon every Sunday, says that the organist ought to be ashamed of himself, offers to back himself for any amount to sing the psalms better than all the children put together, male and female; and, in short, conducts himself in the most turbulent and uproarious manner. The worst of it is, that having a high regard for the old lady, he wants to make her a convert to his views, and therefore walks into her little parlour with his newspaper in his hand, and talks violent politics by the hour. He is a charitable, open-hearted old fellow at bottom, after all; so, although he puts the old lady a little out occasionally, they agree very well in the main, and she laughs as much at each feat of his handiwork when it is all over, as anybody else.

CHAPTER III.

THE FOUR SISTERS.

THE row of houses in which the old lady and her troublesome neighbour reside, comprises, beyond all doubt, a greater number of characters within its circumscribed limits, than all the rest of the parish put together. As we cannot, consistently with our present plan, however, extend the number of our parochial sketches beyond six, it will be better perhaps, to select the most peculiar, and to introduce them at once without further preface.

The four Miss Willises, then, settled in our parish thirteen years ago. It is a melancholy reflection that the old adage, "time and tide wait for no man," applies with equal force to the fairer portion of the creation; and willingly would we conceal the fact, that even thirteen years ago the Miss Willises were far from juvenile. Our duty as faithful parochial chroniclers, however, is paramount to every other consideration, and we are bound to state, that thirteen years since, the authorities in matrimonial cases, considered the youngest Miss Willis in a very precarious state, while the eldest sister was positively given over, as being far beyond all human hope. Well, the Miss Willises took a lease of the house; it was fresh painted and papered from top to bottom: the paint inside was all wainscoted, the marble all cleaned, the old grates taken down, and register-stoves, you could see to dress by, put up; four trees were planted in the back garden, several small baskets of gravel sprinkled over the front one, vans of elegant furniture arrived, spring blinds were fitted to the windows, carpenters who had been employed in the various preparations, alterations, and repairs, made confidential statements to the different maid-servants in the row, relative to the magnificent scale on which the Miss Willises were commencing; the maid-servants told their "Missises," the Missises told their friends, and vague rumours were circulated throughout the parish, that No. 25, in Gordon-place, had been taken by four maiden ladies of immense property.

At last, the Miss Willises moved in; and then the "calling" began. The house was the perfection of neatness—so were the four Miss Willises. Every thing was formal, stiff, and cold—so were the four Miss Willises. Not a single chair of the whole set was ever seen out of its place—not a single Miss Willis of the whole four was ever seen out of hers. There they always sat, in the same places, doing precisely the same things at the same hour. The eldest Miss Willis used to knit, the second to draw, the two others to play duets on the piano. They seemed to have no separate existence, but to have made up their minds just to winter through life together. They were three long graces in drapery, with the addition, like a school-dinner, of another long grace afterwards—the three fates with another sister—the Siamese twins multiplied by two. The eldest Miss Willis grew bilious—the four Miss Willises grew bilious immediately. The eldest Miss Willis grew ill-tempered and religious—the four Miss Willises were ill-tempered and religious directly. Whatever the eldest did, the others did, and whatever any body else did, they all disapproved of; and thus they vegetated—living in Polar harmony among themselves, and, as they sometimes went out, or saw company "in a quiet-way" at home, occasionally iceing the neighbours. Three years passed over in this way, when an unlooked for and extraordinary phenomenon occurred. The Miss Willises showed symptoms of summer, the frost gradually broke up; a complete thaw took place. Was it possible? one of the four Miss Willises was going to be married!

Now, where on earth the husband came from, by what feelings the poor man could have been actuated, or by what process of reasoning the four Miss Willises succeeded in persuading themselves that it was possible for a man to marry one of them, without marrying them all, are questions too profound for us to resolve: certain it is, however, that the visits of Mr. Robinson (a gentleman in a public office, with a good salary and a little property of his own, beside) were received—that the four Miss Willises were courted in due form by the said Mr. Robinson—that the neighbours were perfectly frantic in their anxiety to discover which of the four Miss Willises was the fortunate fair, and that the difficulty they experienced in solving the problem was not at all lessened by the announcement of the eldest Miss Willis,—"*We* are going to marry Mr. Robinson."

It was very extraordinary. They were so completely identified, the one with the other, that the curiosity of the whole row—even of the old lady herself—was roused almost beyond endurance. The subject was discussed at every little card-table and tea-drinking. The old gentleman of silkworm notoriety did not hesitate to express his decided opinion that Mr. Robinson was of Eastern descent, and contemplated marrying the whole family at once; and the row, generally, shook their heads with considerable gravity, and declared the business to be very mysterious. They hoped it might all end well;—it certainly had a very singular appearance, but still it would be uncharitable to express any opinion without good grounds to go upon, and certainly the Miss Willises were *quite* old enough to judge for themselves, and to be sure people ought to know their own business best, and so forth.

At last, one fine morning, at a quarter before eight o'clock, A.M., two glass-coaches drove up to the Miss Willises' door, at which Mr. Robinson had arrived in a cab ten minutes before, dressed in a light-blue coat and double-milled kersey pantaloons, white neckerchief, pumps, and dress-gloves, his manner denoting, as appeared from the evidence of the housemaid at No. 23, who was sweeping the door-steps at the time, a considerable degree of nervous excitement. It was also hastily reported on the same testimony, that the cook who opened the door, wore a large white bow of unusual dimensions, in a much smarter head-dress than the regulation cap to which the Miss Willises invariably restricted the somewhat excursive tastes of female servants in general.

The intelligence spread rapidly from house to house. It was quite clear that the eventful morning had at length arrived; the whole row stationed themselves behind their first and second-floor blinds, and waited the result in breathless expectation.

At last the Miss Willises' door opened; the door of the first glass-coach did the same. Two gentlemen, and a pair of ladies to correspond—friends of the family, no doubt; up went the steps, bang went the door, off went the first glass-coach, and up came the second.

The street door opened again; the excitement of the whole row increased—Mr. Robinson and the eldest Miss Willis. "I thought so," said the lady at No. 19; "I always said it was *Miss* Willis!"—"Well, I never!" ejaculated the young lady at No. 18 to the young lady at No. 17—"Did you ever, dear!" responded the young lady at No. 17 to the young lady at No. 18. "It's too ridiculous!" exclaimed a spinster of an *un*certain age, at No. 16, joining in the conversation. But who shall portray the astonishment of Gordon-place, when Mr. Robinson handed in *all* the Miss Willises, one after the other, and then squeezed himself into an acute angle of the glass-coach, which forthwith proceeded at a brisk pace, after the other glass-coach, which other glass-coach had itself proceeded, at a brisk pace, in the direction of the parish church! Who shall depict the perplexity of the clergyman, when *all* the Miss Willises knelt down at the communion table, and repeated the responses incidental to the marriage service in an audible voice—or who shall describe the confusion which prevailed, when—even after the difficulties thus occasioned had been adjusted—*all* the Miss Willises went into hysterics at the conclusion of the ceremony, until the sacred edifice resounded with their united wailings!

As the four sisters and Mr. Robinson continued to occupy the same house after this memorable occasion, and as the married sister, whoever she was, never appeared in public without the other three, we are not quite clear that the neighbours ever would have discovered the real Mrs. Robinson, but for a circumstance of the most gratifying description, which *will* happen occasionally in the best regulated families. Three quarter-days elapsed, and the row, on whom a new light appeared to have been bursting for some time, began to speak with a sort of implied confidence on the subject, and to wonder how Mrs. Robinson—the youngest Miss Willis that was—got on; and servants might be seen running up the steps, about nine or ten o'clock every morning, with "Missis's compliments, and wishes to know how Mrs. Robinson finds herself this morning?". And the answer always was, "Mrs. Robinson's compliments, and she's in very good spirits, and doesn't find herself any worse." The piano was heard no longer, the knitting-needles were laid aside, drawing was neglected, and mantua-making and millinery, on the smallest scale imaginable, appeared to have become the favourite amusement of the whole family. The parlour wasn't quite as tidy as it used to be, and if you called in the morning, you would see lying on a table, with an old newspaper carelessly thrown over them, two or three particularly small caps, rather larger than if they had been made for a moderate-sized doll, with a small piece of lace, in the shape of a horse-shoe, let in behind: or perhaps a white robe, not very large in circumference, but very much out of proportion in point of length, with a little tucker round the top, and a frill round the bottom; and once when we called, we saw a long white roller, with a kind of blue margin down each side, the probable use of which, we were at a loss to conjecture. Then we fancied that Mr. Dawson, the surgeon, &c., who displays a large lamp with a different colour in every pane of glass, at the corner of the row, began to be knocked up at night oftener than he used to be; and once we were very much alarmed by hearing a hackney-coach stop at Mrs. Robinson's door, at half-past two o'clock in the morning, out of which there emerged a fat old woman, in a cloak and nightcap, with a bundle in one hand, and a pair of pattens in the other, who looked as if she had been suddenly knocked up out of bed for some very special purpose.

When we got up in the morning we saw that the knocker was tied up in an old white kid glove; and we, in our innocence (we were in a state of bachelorship then), wondered what on earth it all meant, until we heard the eldest Miss Willis, *in propriâ personâ*, say, with great dignity, in answer to the next inquiry, "*My* compliments, and Mrs. Robinson's doing as well as can be expected, and the little girl thrives wonderfully." And then, in common with the rest of the row, our curiosity was satisfied, and we began to wonder it had never occurred to us what the matter was, before.

CHAPTER IV.

THE ELECTION FOR BEADLE.

A GREAT event has recently occurred in our parish. A contest of paramount interest has just terminated; a parochial convulsion has taken place. It has been succeeded by a glorious triumph, which the country—or at least the parish—it is all the same—will long remember. We have had an election; an election for beadle. The supporters of the old beadle system have been defeated in their stronghold, and the advocates of the great new beadle principles have achieved a proud victory.

Our parish, which, like all other parishes, is a little world of its own, has long been divided into two parties, whose contentions, slumbering for a while, have never failed to burst forth with unabated vigour, on any occasion on which they could by possibility be renewed. Watching-rates, lighting-rates, paving-rates, sewer's-rates, church-rates, poor's-rates—all sorts of rates, have been in their turns the subjects of a grand struggle; and as to questions of patronage, the asperity and determination with which they have been contested is scarcely credible.

The leader of the official party—the steady advocate of the churchwardens, and the unflinching supporter of the overseers—is an old gentleman who lives in our row. He owns some half a dozen houses in it, and always walks on the opposite side of the way, so that he may be able to take in a view of the whole of his property at once. He is a tall, thin, bony man, with an interrogative nose, and little restless perking eyes, which appear to have been given him for the sole purpose of peeping into other people's affairs with. He is deeply impressed with the importance of our parish business, and prides himself, not a little, on his style of addressing the parishioners in vestry assembled. His views are rather confined than extensive; his principles more narrow than liberal. He has been heard to declaim very loudly in favour of the liberty of the press, and advocates the repeal of the stamp duty on newspapers, because the daily journals who now have a monopoly of the public, never give *verbatim* reports of vestry meetings. He would not appear egotistical for the world, but at the same time he must say, that there *are* speeches—that celebrated speech of his own, on the emoluments of the sexton, and the duties of the office, for instance—which might be communicated to the public, greatly to their improvement and advantage.

His great opponent in public life is Captain Purday, the old naval officer on half-pay, to whom we have already introduced our readers. The captain being a determined opponent of the constituted authorities, whoever they may chance to be, and our other friend being their steady supporter, with an equal disregard of their individual merits, it will readily be supposed, that occasions for their coming into direct collision are neither few nor far between. They divided the vestry fourteen times on a motion for heating the church with warm water instead of coals: and made speeches about liberty and expenditure, and prodigality and hot water, which threw the whole parish into a state of excitement. Then the captain, when he was on the visiting committee, and his opponent overseer, brought forward certain distinct and specific charges relative to the management of the workhouse, boldly expressed his total want of confidence in the existing authorities, and moved for "a copy of the recipe by which the paupers' soup was prepared, together with any documents relating thereto." This the overseer steadily resisted; he fortified himself by precedent, appealed to the established usage, and declined to produce the papers, on the ground of the injury that would be done to the public service, if documents of a strictly private nature, passing between the master of the workhouse and the cook, were to be thus dragged to light on the motion of any individual member of the vestry. The motion was lost by a majority of two; and then the captain, who never allows himself to be defeated, moved for a committee of inquiry into the whole subject. The affair grew serious: the question was discussed at meeting after meeting, and vestry after vestry; speeches were made, attacks repudiated, personal defiances exchanged, explanations received, and the greatest excitement prevailed, until at last, just as the question was going to be finally decided, the vestry found that somehow or other, they had become entangled in a point of form, from which it was impossible to escape with propriety. So, the motion was dropped, and everybody looked extremely important, and seemed quite satisfied with the meritorious nature of the whole proceeding.

This was the state of affairs in our parish a week or two since, when Simmons, the beadle, suddenly died. The lamented deceased had over-exerted himself, a day or two previously, in conveying an aged female, highly intoxicated, to the strong room of the workhouse. The excitement thus occasioned, added to a severe cold, which this indefatigable officer had caught in his capacity of directu of the parish engine, by inadvertently playing over himself instead of a fire, proved too much for a constitution already enfeebled by age; and the intelligence was conveyed to the Board one evening that Simmons had died, and left his respects.

The breath was scarcely out of the body of the deceased functionary, when the field was filled with competitors for the vacant office, each of whom rested his claims to public support, entirely on the number and extent of his family, as if the office of beadle were originally instituted as an encouragement for the propagation of the human species. "Bung for Beadle. Five small children!"—"Hopkins for Beadle. Seven small children!!"—"Timkins for Beadle. Nine small children!!!" Such were the placards in large black letters on a white ground, which were plentifully pasted on the walls, and posted in the windows of the principal shops. Timkins's success was considered certain: several mothers of families half promised their votes, and the nine small children would have run over the course, but for the production of another placard, announcing the appearance of a still more meritorious candidate. "Spruggins for Beadle. Ten small children (two of them twins), and a wife!!!" There was no resisting this; ten small children would have been almost irresistible in themselves, without the twins, but the touching parenthesis about that interesting production of nature, and the still more touching allusion to Mrs. Spruggins, must ensure success. Spruggins was the favourite at once, and the appearance of his lady, as she went about to solicit votes (which encouraged confident hopes of a still further addition to the house of Spruggins at no remote period), increased the general prepossession in his favour. The other candidates, Bung alone excepted, resigned in despair. The day of election was fixed; and the canvass proceeded with briskness and perseverance on both sides.

The members of the vestry could not be supposed to escape the contagious excitement inseparable from the oc sion. The majority of the lady inhabitants of the parish declared at once for Sp uggins; and the *quondam* overseer took the same side, on the ground that men with large families always had been elected to the office, and that although he must admit, that, in other respects, Spruggins was the least qualified candidate of the two, still it was an old practice, and he saw no reason why an old practice should be departed from. This was enough for the captain. He immediately sided with Bung, canvassed for him personally in all directions, wrote squibs on Spruggins, and got his butcher to skewer them up on conspicuous joints in his shop-front; frightened his neighbour, the old lady, into a palpitation of the heart, by his awful denunciations of Spruggins's party; and bounced in and out, and up and down, and backwards and forwards, until all the sober inhabitants of the parish thought it inevitable that he must die of a brain fever, long before the election began.

The day of election arrived. It was no longer an individual struggle, but a party contest between the ins and outs. The question was, whether the withering influence of the overseers, the domination of the churchwardens, and the blighting despotism of the vestry-clerk, should be allowed to render the election of beadle a form—a nullity: whether they should impose a vestry-elected beadle on the parish, to do their bidding and forward their views, or whether the parishioners, fearlessly asserting their undoubted rights, should elect an independent beadle of their own.

The nomination was fixed to take place in the vestry, but so great was the throng of anxious spectators, that it was found necessary to adjourn to the church, where the ceremony commenced with due solemnity. The appearance of the churchwardens and overseers, and the ex-churchwardens and ex-overseers, with Spruggins in the rear, excited general attention. Spruggins was a little thin man, in rusty black, with a long pale face, and a countenance expressive of care and fatigue, which might either be attributed to the extent of his family or the anxiety of his feelings. His opponent appeared in a cast-off coat of the captain's—a blue coat with bright buttons: white trousers, and that description of shoes familiarly known by the appellation of "high-lows." There was a serenity in the open countenance of Bung—a kind of moral dignity in his confident air—an "I wish you may get it" sort of expression in his eye—which infused animation into his supporters, and evidently dispirited his opponents.

The ex-churchwarden rose to propose Thomas Spruggins for beadle. He had known him long. He had had his eye upon him closely for years; he had watched him with twofold vigilance for months. (A parishioner here suggested that this might be termed "taking a double sight," but the observation was drowned in loud cries of "Order!") He would repeat that he had had his eye upon him for years, and this he would say, that a more well-conducted, a more well-behaved, a more sober, a more quiet man, with a more well-regulated mind, he had never met with. A man with a larger family he had never known (cheers). The parish required a man who could be depended on ("Hear!" from the Spruggins side, answered by ironical cheers from the Bung party). Such a man he now proposed ("No," "Yes"). He would not allude to individuals (the ex-churchwarden continued, in the celebrated negative style adopted by great speakers). He would not advert to a gentleman who had once held a high rank in the service of his majesty; he would not say, that that gentleman was no gentleman; he would not assert, that that man was no man; he would not say, that he was a turbulent parishioner; he would not say, that he had grossly misbehaved himself, not only on this, but on all former occasions; he would not say, that he was one of those discontented and treasonable spirits, who carried confusion and disorder wherever they went; he would not say, that he harboured in his heart envy, and hatred, and malice, and all uncharitableness. No! He wished to have everything comfortable and pleasant, and therefore, he would say—nothing about him (cheers).

The captain replied in a similar parliamentary style. He would not say, he was astonished at the speech they had just heard; he would not say, he was disgusted (cheers). He would not retort the epithets which had been hurled against him (renewed cheering); he would not allude to men once in office, but now happily out of it, who had mismanaged the workhouse, ground the paupers, diluted the beer, slack-baked the bread, boned the meat, heightened the work, and lowered the soup (tremendous cheers). He would not ask what such men deserved (a voice, "Nothing a-day, and find themselves!"). He would not say, that one burst of general indignation should drive them from the parish they polluted with their presence ("Give it him!"). He would not allude to the unfortunate man who had been proposed—he would not say, as the vestry's tool, but as Beadle. He would not advert to that individual's family; he would not say, that nine children, twins, and a wife, were very bad examples for pauper imitation (loud cheers). He would not advert in detail to the qualifications of Bung. The man stood before him, and he would not say in his presence, what he might be disposed to say of him, if he were absent. (Here Mr. Bung telegraphed to a friend near him, under cover of his hat, by contracting his left eye, and applying his right thumb to the tip of his nose). It had been objected to Bung that he had only five children ("Hear, hear!" from the opposition). Well; he had yet to learn that the legislature had affixed any precise amount of infantine qualification to the office of beadle; but taking it for granted that an extensive family were a great requisite, he entreated them to look to facts, and compare *data*, about which there could be no mistake. Bung was 35 years of age. Spruggins

—of whom he wished to speak with all possible respect—was 50. Was it not more than possible—was it not very probable—that by the time Bung attained the latter age, he might see around him a family, even exceeding in number and extent, that to which Spruggins at present laid claim (deafening cheers and waving of handkerchiefs)? The captain concluded, amidst loud applause, by calling upon the parishioners to sound the tocsin, rush to the poll, free themselves from dictation, or be slaves for ever.

On the following day the polling began, and we never have had such a bustle in our parish since we got up our famous anti-slavery petition, which was such an important one, that the House of Commons ordered it to be printed, on the motion of the member for the district. The captain engaged two hackney-coaches and a cab for Bung's people—the cab for the drunken voters, and the two coaches for the old ladies, the greater portion of whom, owing to the captain's impetuosity, were driven up to the poll and home again, before they recovered from their flurry sufficiently to know, with any degree of clearness, what they had been doing. The opposite party wholly neglected these precautions, and the consequence was, that a great many ladies who were walking leisurely up to the church—for it was a very hot day—to vote for Spruggins, were artfully decoyed into the coaches, and voted for Bung. The captain's arguments, too, had produced considerable effect: the attempted influence of the vestry produced a greater. A threat of exclusive dealing was clearly established against the vestry-clerk—a case of heartless and profligate atrocity. It appeared that the delinquent had been in the habit of purchasing six penn'orth of muffins, weekly, from an old woman who rents a small house in the parish, and resides among the original settlers; on her last weekly visit, a message was conveyed to her through the medium of the cook, couched in mysterious terms, but indicating with sufficient clearness, that the vestry-clerk's appetite for muffins, in future, depended entirely on her vote on the beadleship. This was sufficient: the stream had been turning previously, and the impulse thus administered directed its final course. The Bung party ordered one shilling's-worth of muffins weekly for the remainder of the old woman's natural life; the parishioners were loud in their exclamations; and the fate of Spruggins was sealed.

It was in vain that the twins were exhibited in dresses of the same pattern, and night-caps to match, at the church door: the boy in Mrs. Spruggins's right arm, and the girl in her left—even Mrs. Spruggins herself failed to be an object of sympathy any longer. The majority attained by Bung on the gross poll was four hundred and twenty-eight, and the cause of the parishioners triumphed.

CHAPTER V.

THE BROKER'S MAN.

THE excitement of the late election has subsided, and our parish being once again restored to a state of comparative tranquillity, we are enabled to devote our attention to those parishioners who take little share in our party contests or in the turmoil and bustle of public life. And we feel sincere pleasure in acknowledging here, that in collecting materials for this task we have been greatly assisted by Mr. Bung himself, who has imposed on us a debt of obligation which we fear we can never repay. The life of this gentleman has been one of a very chequered description: he has undergone transitions—not from grave to gay, for he never was grave—not from lively to severe, for severity forms no part of his disposition;

his fluctuations have been between poverty in the extreme, and poverty modified, or, to use his own emphatic language, "between nothing to eat and just half enough." He is not, as he forcibly remarks, "one of those fortunate men who, if they were to dive under one side of a barge stark-naked, would come up on the other with a new suit of clothes on, and a ticket for soup in the waistcoat-pocket:" neither is he one of those, whose spirit has been broken beyond redemption by misfortune and want. He is just one of the careless, good-for-nothing, happy fellows, who float, cork-like, on the surface, for the world to play at hockey with: knocked here, and there, and everywhere: now to the right, then to the left, again up in the air, and anon to the bottom, but always re-appearing and bounding with the stream buoyantly and merrily along. Some few months before he was prevailed upon to stand a contested election for the office of beadle, necessity attached him to the service of a broker; and on the opportunities he here acquired of ascertaining the condition of most of the poorer inhabitants of the parish, his patron, the captain, first grounded his claims to public support. Chance threw the man in our way a short time since. We were, in the first instance, attracted by his prepossessing impudence at the election; we were not surprised, on further acquaintance, to find him a shrewd knowing fellow, with no inconsiderable power of observation; and, after conversing with him a little, were somewhat struck (as we dare say our readers have frequently been in other cases) with the power some men seem to have, not only of sympathising with, but to all appearance of understanding feelings to which they themselves are entire strangers. We had been expressing to the new functionary our surprise that he should ever have served in the capacity to which we have just adverted, when we gradually led him into one or two professional anecdotes. As we are induced to think, on reflection, that they will tell better in nearly his own words, than with any attempted embellishments of ours, we will at once entitle them

MR. BUNG'S NARRATIVE.

"It's very true, as you say, sir," Mr. Bung commenced, "that a broker's man's is not a life to be envied; and in course you know as well as I do, though you don't say it, that people hate and scout 'em because they're the ministers of wretchedness, like, to poor people. But what could I do, sir? The thing was no worse because I did it, instead of somebody else; and if putting me in possession of a house would put me in possession of three and sixpence a day, and levying a distress on another man's goods would relieve my distress and that of my family, it can't be expected but what I'd take the job and go through with it. I never liked it, God knows; I always looked out for something else, and the moment I got other work to do, I left it. If there is anything wrong in being the agent in such matters—not the principal, mind you—I'm sure the business, to a beginner like I was, at all events, carries its own punishment along with it. I wished again and again that the people would only blow me up, or pitch into me—that I wouldn't have minded, it's all in my way; but it's the being shut up by yourself in one room for five days, without so much as an old newspaper to look at, or anything to see out o' the winder but the roofs and chimneys at the back of the house, or anything to listen to, but the ticking, perhaps, of an old Dutch clock, the sobbing of the missis, now and then, the low talking of friends in the next room, who speak in whispers, lest 'the man' should overhear them, or perhaps the occasional opening of the door, as a child peeps in to look at you, and then runs half-frightened away—It's all this, that makes you feel sneaking somehow, and ashamed of yourself; and then, if it's winter time, they just give you fire enough to make you think you'd like more, and bring in your grub as if they wished it 'ud choke you—as I dare say they do, for the matter of that, most heartily. If they're very civil, they make you up a bed in the room at night, and if they don't, your master sends one in for you; but there you are, without being washed or shaved all the time, shunned by everybody, and spoken to by no one, unless some one comes in at dinner time, and asks you whether you want any more, in a tone as much as to say, 'I hope you don't,' or, in the evening, to inquire whether you wouldn't rather have a candle, after you've been sitting in the dark half the night. When I was left in this way, I used to sit, think, think, thinking, till I felt as lonesome as a kitten in a wash-house copper with the lid on; but I believe the old brokers' men who are regularly trained to it, never think at all. I have heard some on 'em say, indeed, that they don't know how!

"I put in a good many distresses in my time (continued Mr. Bung), and in course I wasn't long in finding, that some people are not as much to be pitied as others are, and that people with good incomes who get into difficulties, which they keep patching up day after day, and week after week, get so used to these sort of things in time, that at last they come scarcely to feel them at all. I remember the very first place I was put in possession of, was a gentleman's house in this parish here, that everybody would suppose couldn't help having money if he tried. I went with old Fixem, my old master, 'bout half arter eight in the morning; rang the area-bell; servant in livery opened the door: 'Governor at home?'—'Yes, he is,' says the man; 'but he's breakfasting just now.' 'Never mind,' says Fixem, 'just you tell him there's a gentleman here, as wants to speak to him partickler.' So the servant he opens his eyes, and stares about him all ways—looking for the gentleman, as it struck me, for I don't think anybody but a man as was stone-blind would mistake Fixem for one; and as for me, I was as seedy as a cheap cowcumber. Hows'ever, he turns round, and goes to the breakfast-parlour, which was a little snug sort of room at the end of the passage, and Fixem (as we always did in that profession), without waiting to be announced, walks in arter him, and before the servant could get out, 'Please, sir, here's a man as wants to speak to you,' looks in at the door as familiar and pleasant as may be. 'Who the devil are you, and how dare you walk into a gentleman's house without leave?' says the master, as fierce as a bull in fits. 'My name,' says Fixem, winking to the master to send the servant away, and putting the warrant into his hands folded up like a note, 'My name 's Smith,' says he, 'and I called from Johnson's about that business of Thompson's'—'Oh,' says the other, quite down on him directly, 'How *is* Thompson?' says he; 'Pray sit down, Mr. Smith: John, leave the room.' Out went the servant; and the gentleman and Fixem looked at one another till they couldn't look any longer, and then they varied the amusements by looking at me, who had been standing on the mat all this time. 'Hundred and fifty pounds, I see,' said the gentleman at last. 'Hundred and fifty pound,' said Fixem, 'besides cost of levy, sheriff's poundage, and all other incidental expenses.'—'Um,' says the gentleman, 'I shan't be able to settle this before to-morrow afternoon.'—'Very sorry; but I shall be obliged to leave my man here till then,' replies Fixem, pretending to look very miserable over it. 'That's very unfort'nate,' says the gentleman, 'for I have got a large party here to-night, and I'm ruined if those fellows of mine get an inkling of the matter—just step here, Mr. Smith,' says he, after a short pause. So Fixem walks with him up to the window, and after a good deal of whispering, and a little chinking of suverins, and looking at me, he comes back and says, 'Bung, you're a handy fellow, and very honest I know. This gentleman wants an assistant to clean the plate and wait at table to-day, and if you're not particularly engaged,' says old Fixem, grinning like mad, and shoving a couple of suverins into my hand, 'he'll be very glad to avail himself of your services.' Well, I laughed;

and the gentleman laughed, and we all laughed; and I went home and cleaned myself, leaving Fixem there, and when I went back, Fixem went away, and I polished up the plate, and waited at table, and gammoned the servants, and nobody had the least idea I was in possession, though it very nearly came out after all; for one of the last gentlemen who remained, came down stairs into the hall where I was sitting pretty late at night, and putting half-a-crown into my hand, says, 'Here, my man,' says he, 'run and get me a coach, will you?' I thought it was a do, to get me out of the house, and was just going to say so, sulkily enough, when the gentleman (who was up to everything) came running down stairs, as if he was in great anxiety. 'Bung,' says he, pretending to be in a consuming passion. 'Sir,' says I. 'Why the devil an't you looking after that plate?'—'I was just going to send him for a coach for me,' says the other gentleman. 'And I was just a-going to say,' says I—'Anybody else, my dear fellow,' interrupts the master of the house, pushing me down the passage to get out of the way—'anybody else; but I have put this man in possession of all the plate and valuables, and I cannot allow him on any consideration whatever, to leave the house. Bung, you scoundrel, go and count those forks in the breakfast-parlour instantly.' You may be sure I went laughing pretty hearty when I found it was all right. The money was paid next day, with the addition of something else for myself, and that was the best job that I (and I suspect old Fixem too) ever got in that line.

"But this is the bright side of the picture, sir, after all," resumed Mr. Bung, laying aside the knowing look, and flash air, with which he had repeated the previous anecdote—"and I'm sorry to say, it's the side one sees very, very seldom, in comparison with the dark one. The civility which money will purchase, is rarely extended to those who have none; and there's a consolation even in being able to patch up one difficulty, to make way for another, to which very poor people are strangers. I was once put into a house down George's-yard—that little dirty court at the back of the gas-works; and I never shall forget the misery of them people, dear me! It was a distress for half a year's rent—two pound ten I think. There was only two rooms in the house, and as there was no passage, the lodgers up stairs always went through the room of the people of the house, as they passed in and out; and every time they did so—which, on the average, was about four times every quarter of an hour—they blowed up quite frightful: for their things had been seized too, and included in the inventory. There was a little piece of enclosed dust in front of the house, with a cinder-path leading up to the door, and an open rain-water butt on one side. A dirty striped curtain, on a very slack string, hung in the window, and a little triangular bit of broken looking-glass rested on the sill inside. I suppose it was meant for the people's use, but their appearance was so wretched, and so miserable, that I'm certain they never could have plucked up courage to look themselves in the face a second time, if they survived the fright of doing so once. There was two or three chairs, that might have been worth, in their best days, from eightpence to a shilling a-piece; a small deal table, an old corner cupboard with nothing in it, and one of those bedsteads which turn up half way, and leave the bottom legs sticking out for you to knock your head against, or hang your hat upon; no bed, no bedding. There was an old sack, by way of rug, before the fire-place, and four or five children were grovelling about, among the sand on the floor. The execution was only put in, to get 'em out of the house, for there was nothing to take to pay the expenses; and here I stopped for three days, though that was a mere form too: for, in course, I knew, and we all knew, they could never pay the money. In one of the chairs, by the side of the place where the fire ought to have been, was an old 'ooman—the ugliest and dirtiest I ever see—who sat rocking herself backwards and forwards, backwards and forwards, without once stopping, except for an instant now and then, to clasp together the withered hands which, with these exceptions, she kept constantly rubbing upon her knees, just raising and depressing her fingers convulsively, in time to the rocking of the chair. On the other side sat the mother with an infant in her arms, which cried till it cried itself to sleep, and when it 'woke, cried till it cried itself off again. The old 'ooman's voice I never heard: she seemed completely stupified; and as to the mother's, it would have been better if she had been so too, for misery had changed her to a devil. If you had heard how she cursed the little naked children as was rolling on the floor, and seen how savagely she struck the infant when it cried with hunger, you'd have shuddered as much as I did. There they remained all the time: the children ate a morsel of bread once or twice, and I gave 'em best part of the dinners my missis brought me, but the woman ate nothing; they never even laid on the bedstead, nor was the room swept or cleaned all the time. The neighbours were all too poor themselves to take any notice of 'em, but from what I could make out from the abuse of the woman up stairs, it seemed the husband had been transported a few weeks before. When the time was up, the landlord and old Fixem too, got rather frightened about the family, and so they made a stir about it, and had 'em taken to the workhouse. They sent the sick couch for the old 'ooman, and Simmons took the children away at night. The old 'ooman went into the infirmary, and very soon died. The children are all in the house to this day, and very comfortable they are in comparison. As to the mother, there was no taming her at all. She had been a quiet, hard-working woman, I believe, but her misery had actually drove her wild; so after she had been sent to the house of correction half-a-dozen times, for throwing inkstands at the overseers, blaspheming the churchwardens, and smashing everybody as come near her, she burst a blood-vessel one mornin', and died too; and a happy release it was, both for herself and the old paupers, male and female, which she used to tip over in all directions, as if they were so many skittles, and she the ball.

"Now this was bad enough," resumed Mr. Bung, taking a half-step towards the door, as if to intimate that he had nearly concluded. "This was bad enough, but there was a sort of quiet misery—if you understand what I mean by that, sir—about a lady at one house I was put into, as touched me a good deal more. It doesn't matter where it was exactly: indeed, I'd rather not say, but it was the same sort o' job. I went with Fixem in the usual way—there was a year's rent in arrear; a very small servant-girl opened the door, and three or four fine-looking little children was in the front parlour we were shown into, which was very clean, but very scantily furnished, much like the children themselves. 'Bung,' says Fixem to me, in a low voice, when we were left alone for a minute, 'I know something about this here family, and my opinion is, it's no go.' 'Do you think they can't settle?' says I, quite anxiously; for I liked the looks of them children. Fixem shook his head, and was just about to reply, when the door opened, and in came a lady, as white as ever I see any one in my days, except about the eyes, which were red with crying. She walked in, as firm as I could have done; shut the door carefully after her, and sat herself down with a face as composed as if it was made of stone. 'What is the matter, gentlemen?' says she, in a surprisin' steady voice. '*Is* this an execution?' 'It is, mum,' says Fixem. The lady looked at him as steady as ever: she didn't seem to have understood him. 'It is, mum,' says Fixem again; 'this is my warrant of distress, mum,' says he, handing it over as polite as if it was a newspaper which had been bespoke arter the next gentleman.

"The lady's lip trembled as she took the printed paper. She cast her eye over it, and old Fixem began to explain the form, but I saw she wasn't reading it, plain enough, poor thing. 'Oh, my God!' says she, suddenly a-bursting out crying, letting the warrant fall, and hiding her face in her hands. 'Oh, my God! what will become of us!' The noise she made, brought in a young lady of about nineteen or twenty, who, I suppose, had been a-listening at the door, and who had got a little boy in her arms: she sat him down in the lady's lap, without speaking, and she hugged the poor little fellow to her bosom, and cried over him, till even old Fixem put on his blue spectacles to hide the two tears, that was a-trickling down, one on each side of his dirty face. 'Now, dear ma,' says the young lady, 'you know how much you have borne. For all our sakes—for pa's sake,' says she, 'don't give way to this!'—'No, no, I won't!' says the lady, gathering herself up, hastily, and drying her eyes; 'I am very foolish, but I'm better now—much better.' And then she roused herself up, went with us into every room while we took the inventory, opened all the drawers of her own accord, sorted the children's little clothes to make the work easier; and, except doing everything in a strange sort of hurry, seemed as calm and composed as if nothing had happened. When we came down stairs again, she hesitated a minute or two, and at last says, 'Gentlemen,' says she, 'I am afraid I have done wrong, and perhaps it may bring you into trouble. I secreted just now,' she says, 'the only trinket I have left in the world—here it is.' So she lays down on the table a little miniature mounted in gold. 'It's a miniature,' she says, 'of my poor dear father! I little thought once, that I should ever thank God for depriving me of the original, but I do, and have done for years back, most fervently. Take it away, sir,' she says, 'it's a face that never turned from me in sickness or distress, and I can hardly bear to turn from it now, when, God knows, I suffer both in no ordinary degree.' I couldn't say nothing, but I raised my head from the inventory which I was filling up, and looked at Fixem; the old fellow nodded to me significantly, so I ran my pen through the '*Mini*' I had just written, and left the miniature on the table.

"Well, sir, to make short of a long story, I was left in possession, and in possession I remained; and though I was an ignorant man, and the master of the house a clever one, I saw what he never did, but what he would give worlds now (if he had 'em) to have seen in time. I saw, sir, that his wife was wasting away, beneath cares of which she never complained, and griefs she never told. I saw that she was dying before his eyes; I knew that one exertion from him might have saved her, but he never made it. I don't blame him: I don't think he *could* rouse himself. She had so long anticipated all his wishes, and acted for him, that he was a lost man when left to himself. I used to think when I caught sight of her, in the clothes she used to wear, which looked shabby even upon her, and would have been scarcely decent on any one else, that if I was a gentleman it would wring my very heart to see the woman that was a smart and merry girl when I courted her, so altered through her love for me. Bitter cold and damp weather it was, yet, though her dress was thin, and her shoes none of the best, during the whole three days, from morning to night, she was out of doors running about to try and raise the money. The money *was* raised and the execution was paid out. The whole family crowded into the room where I was, when the money arrived. The father was quite happy as the inconvenience was removed—I dare say he didn't know how; the children looked merry and cheerful again; the eldest girl was bustling about, making preparations for the first comfortable meal they had had since the distress was put in; and the mother looked pleased to see them all so. But if ever I saw death in a woman's face, I saw it in hers that night.

"I was right, sir," continued Mr. Bung, hurriedly passing his coat-sleeve over his face; "the family grew more prosperous, and good fortune arrived. But it was too late. Those children are motherless now, and their father would give up all he has since gained—house, home, goods, money: all that he has, or ever can have, to restore the wife he has lost."

CHAPTER VI.

THE LADIES' SOCIETIES.

OUR Parish is very prolific in ladies' charitable institutions. In winter, when wet feet are common, and colds not scarce, we have the ladies' soup distribution society, the ladies' coal distribution society, and the ladies' blanket distribution society; in summer, when stone fruits flourish and stomach aches prevail, we have the ladies' dispensary, and the ladies' sick visitation committee; and all the year round we have the ladies' child's examination society, the ladies' bible and prayer-book circulation society, and the ladies' childbed-linen monthly loan society. The two latter are decidedly the most important; whether they are productive of more benefit than the rest, it is not for us to say, but we can take upon ourselves to affirm, with the utmost solemnity, that they create a greater stir and more bustle, than all the others put together.

We should be disposed to affirm, on the first blush of the matter, that the bible and prayer-book society is not so popular as the childbed-linen society; the bible and prayer-book society has, however, considerably increased in importance within the last year or two, having derived some adventitious aid from the factious opposition of the child's examination society; which factious opposition originated in manner following:—When the young curate was popular, and all the unmarried ladies in the parish took a serious turn, the charity children all at once became objects of peculiar and especial interest. The three Miss Browns (enthusiastic admirers of the curate) taught, and exercised, and examined, and re-examined the unfortunate children, until the boys grew pale, and the girls consumptive with study and fatigue. The three Miss Browns stood it out very well, because they relieved each other; but the children, having no relief at all, exhibited decided symptoms of weariness and care. The unthinking part of the parishioners laughed at all this, but the more reflective portion of the inhabitants abstained from expressing any opinion on the subject until that of the curate had been clearly ascertained.

The opportunity was not long wanting. The curate preached a charity sermon on behalf of the charity school, and in the charity sermon aforesaid, expatiated in glowing terms on the praiseworthy and indefatigable exertions of certain estimable individuals. Sobs were heard to issue from the three Miss Browns' pew; the pew-opener of the division was seen to hurry down the centre aisle to the vestry door, and to return immediately, bearing a glass of water in her hand. A low moaning ensued; two more pew-openers rushed to the spot, and the three Miss Browns, each supported by a pew-opener, were led out of the church, and led in again after the lapse of five minutes with white pocket-handkerchiefs to their eyes, as if they had been attending a funeral in the churchyard adjoining. If any doubt had for a moment existed, as to whom the allusion was intended to apply, it was at once removed. The wish to enlighten the charity children became universal, and the three Miss Browns were unanimously besought to divide the school into classes, and to assign each class to the superintendence of two young ladies.

A little learning is a dangerous thing, but a little patronage is more so; the three Miss Browns appointed all the old maids, and carefully excluded the young ones. Maiden aunts triumphed, mammas were reduced to the lowest depths of despair, and there is no telling in what act of violence the general indignation against the three Miss Browns might have vented itself, had not a perfectly providential occurrence changed the tide of public feeling. Mrs Johnson Parker, the mother of seven extremely fine girls—all unmarried—hastily reported to several other mammas of several other unmarried families, that five old men, six old women, and children innumerable, in the free seats near her pew, were in the habit of coming to church every Sunday, without either bible or prayer-book. Was this to be borne in a civilised country? Could such things be tolerated in a Christian land? Never! A ladies' bible and prayer-book distribution society was instantly formed: president, Mrs. Johnson Parker; treasurers, auditors, and secretary, the Misses Johnson Parker: subscriptions were entered into, books were bought, all the free-seat people provided therewith, and when the first lesson was given out, on the first Sunday succeeding these events, there was such a dropping of books, and rustling of leaves, that it was morally impossible to hear one word of the service for five minutes afterwards.

The three Miss Browns, and their party, saw the approaching danger, and endeavoured to avert it by ridicule and sarcasm. Neither the old men nor the old women could read their books, now they had got them, said the three Miss Browns. Never mind; they could learn, replied Mrs. Johnson Parker. The children couldn't read either, suggested the three Miss Browns. No matter; they could be taught, retorted Mrs. Johnson Parker. A balance of parties took place. The Miss Browns publicly examined—popular feeling inclined to the child's examination society. The Miss Johnson Parkers publicly distributed—a reaction took place in favour of the prayer-book distribution. A feather would have turned the scale, and a feather did turn it. A missionary returned from the West Indies; he was to be presented to the Dissenters' Missionary Society on his marriage with a wealthy widow. Overtures were made to the Dissenters by the Johnson Parkers. Their object was the same, and why not have a joint meeting of the two societies? The proposition was accepted. The meeting was duly heralded by public announcement, and the room was crowded to suffocation. The Missionary appeared on the platform; he was hailed with enthusiasm. He repeated a dialogue he had heard between two negroes, behind a hedge, on the subject of distribution societies; the approbation was tumultuous. He gave an imitation of the two negroes in broken English; the roof was rent with applause. From that period we date (with one trifling exception) a daily increase in the popularity of the distribution society, and an increase of popularity, which the feeble and impotent opposition of the examination party, has only tended to augment.

Now, the great points about the childbed-linen monthly loan society are, that it is less dependent on the fluctuations of public opinion then either the distribution or the child's examination; and that, come what may, there is never any lack of objects on which to exercise its benevolence. Our parish is a very populous one, and, if anything, contributes, we should be disposed to say, rather more than its due share to the aggregate amount of births in the metropolis and its environs. The consequence is, that the monthly loan society flourishes, and invests its members with a most enviable amount of bustling patronage. The society (whose only notion of dividing time, would appear to be its allotment into months) holds monthly tea-drinkings, at which the monthly report is received, a secretary elected for the month ensuing, and such of the monthly boxes as may not happen to be out on loan for the month, carefully examined.

We were never present at one of these meetings, from all of which it is scarcely necessary to say, gentlemen are carefully excluded; but Mr. Bung has been called before the board once or twice, and we have his authority for stating, that its proceedings are conducted with great order and regularity: not more than four members being allowed to speak at one time on any pretence whatever. The regular committee is composed exclusively of married ladies, but a vast number of young unmarried ladies of from eighteen to twenty-five years of age, respectively, are admitted as honorary members, partly because they are very useful in replenishing the boxes, and visiting the confined; partly because it is highly desirable that they should be initiated, at an early period, into the more serious and matronly duties of after-life; and partly, because prudent mammas have not unfrequently been known to turn this circumstance to wonderfully good account in matrimonial speculations.

In addition to the loan of the monthly boxes (which are always painted blue, with the name of the society in large white letters on the lid), the society dispense occasional grants of beef-tea, and a composition of warm beer, spice, eggs, and sugar, commonly known by the name of "caudle," to its patients. And here again the services of the honorary members are called into requisition, and most cheerfully conceded. Deputations of twos or threes are sent out to visit the patients, and on these occasions there is such a tasting of caudle and beef-tea, such a stirring about of little messes in tiny saucepans on the hob, such a dressing and undressing of infants, such a tying, and folding, and pinning; such a nursing and warming of little legs and feet before the fire, such a delightful confusion of talking and cooking, bustle, importance, and officiousness, as never can be enjoyed in its full extent but on similar occasions.

In rivalry of these two institutions, and as a last expiring effort to acquire parochial popularity, the child's examination people determined, the other day, on having a grand public examination of the pupils; and the large school-room of the national seminary was, by and with the consent of the parish authorities, devoted to the purpose. Invitation circulars were forwarded to all the principal parishioners, including, of course, the heads of the other two societies, for whose especial behoof and edification the display was intended; and a large audience was confidently anticipated on the occasion. The floor was carefully scrubbed the day before, under the immediate superintendence of the three Miss Browns; forms were placed across the room for the accommodation of the visitors, specimens in writing were carefully selected, and as carefully patched and touched up, until they astonished the children who had written them, rather more than the company who read them; sums in compound addition were rehearsed and re-rehearsed until all the children had the totals by heart; and the preparations altogether were on the most laborious and most comprehensive scale. The morning arrived: the children were yellow-soaped and flannelled, and towelled, till their faces shone again; every pupil's hair was carefully combed into his or her eyes, as the case might be; the girls were adorned with snow-white tippets, and caps bound round the head by a single purple ribbon: the necks of the elder boys were fixed into collars of startling dimensions.

The doors were thrown open, and the Misses Brown and Co. were discovered in plain white muslin dresses, and caps of the same—the child's examination uniform. The room filled: the greetings of the company were loud and cordial. The distributionists trembled, for their popularity was at stake. The eldest boy fell forward, and delivered a propitiatory address from behind his collar. It was from the pen of Mr. Henry Brown; the applause was universal, and the Johnson Parkers were aghast. The examination proceeded with success, and terminated in triumph. The child's examination society gained a momentary victory, and the Johnson Parkers retreated in despair.

A secret council of the distributionists was held that night, with Mrs. Johnson Parker in the chair, to consider of the best means of recovering the ground they had lost in the favour of the parish. What could be done? Another meeting! Alas! who was to attend it? The Missionary would not do twice; and the slaves were emancipated. A bold step must be taken. The parish must be astonished in some way or other; but no one was able to suggest what the step should be.

At length, a very old lady was heard to mumble, in indistinct tones, "Exeter Hall." A sudden light broke in upon the meeting. It was unanimously resolved, that a deputation of old ladies should wait upon a celebrated orator, imploring his assistance, and the favour of a speech; and the deputation should also wait on two or three other imbecile old women, not resident in the parish, and entreat their attendance. The application was successful, the meeting was held; the orator (an Irishman) came. He talked of green isles—other shores—vast Atlantic—bosom of the deep—Christian charity—blood and extermination—mercy in hearts—arms in hands—altars and homes—household gods. He wiped his eyes, he blew his nose, and he quoted Latin. The effect was tremendous—the Latin was a decided hit. Nobody knew exactly what it was about, but everybody knew it must be affecting, because even the orator was overcome. The popularity of the distribution society among the ladies of our parish is unprecedented; and the child's examination is going fast to decay.

CHAPTER VII.

OUR NEXT-DOOR NEIGHBOUR.

We are very fond of speculating as we walk through a street, on the character and pursuits of the people who inhabit it; and nothing so materially assists us in these speculations as the appearance of the house doors. The various expressions of the human countenance afford a beautiful and interesting study; but there is something in the physiognomy of street-door knockers, almost as characteristic, and nearly as infallible. Whenever we visit a man for the first time, we contemplate the features of his knocker with the greatest curiosity, for we well know, that between the man and his knocker, there will inevitably be a greater or less degree of resemblance and sympathy.

For instance, there is one description of knocker that used to be common enough, but which is fast passing away—a large round one, with the jolly face of a convivial lion smiling blandly at you, as you twist the sides of your hair into a curl, or pull up your shirt-collar while you are waiting for the door to be opened; we never saw that knocker on the door of a churlish man—so far as our experience is concerned, it invariably bespoke hospitality and another bottle.

No man ever saw this knocker on the door of a small attorney or bill-broker; they always patronise the other lion; a heavy ferocious-looking fellow, with a countenance expressive of savage stupidity—a sort of grand master among the knockers, and a great favourite with the selfish and brutal.

Then there is a little pert Egyptian knocker, with a long thin face, a pinched up nose, and a very sharp chin; he is most in vogue with your government-office people, in light drabs and starched cravats; little spare priggish men, who are perfectly satisfied with their own opinions, and consider themselves of paramount importance.

We were greatly troubled a few years ago, by the innovation of a new kind of knocker, without any face at all, composed of a wreath, depending from a hand or small truncheon. A little trouble and attention, however, enabled us to overcome this difficulty, and to reconcile the new system to our favourite theory. You will invariably find this knocker on the doors of cold and formal people, who always ask you why you *don't* come, and never say *do*.

Everybody knows the brass knocker is common to suburban villas, and extensive boarding-schools; and having noticed this genus we have recapitulated all the most prominent and strongly-defined species.

Some phrenologists affirm, that the agitation of a man's brain by different passions, produces corresponding developments in the form of his skull. Do not let us be understood as pushing our theory to the full length of asserting, that any alteration in a man's disposition would produce a visible effect on the feature of his knocker. Our position merely is, that in such a case, the magnetism which must exist between a man and his knocker, would induce the man to remove, and seek some knocker more congenial to his altered feelings. If you ever find a man changing his habitation without any reasonable pretext, depend upon it, that, although he may not be aware of the fact himself, it is because he and his knocker are at variance. This is a new theory, but we venture to launch it, nevertheless, as being quite as ingenious and infallible as many thousands of the learned speculations which are daily broached for public good and private fortune-making.

Entertaining these feelings on the subject of knockers, it will be readily imagined with what consternation we viewed the entire removal of the knocker from the door of the next house to the one we lived in, some time ago, and the substitution of a bell. This was a calamity we had never anticipated. The bare idea of anybody being able to exist without a knocker, appeared so wild and visionary, that it had never for one instant entered our imagination.

We sauntered moodily from the spot, and bent our steps towards Eaton-square, then just building. What was our astonishment and indignation to find that bells were fast becoming the rule, and knockers the exception! Our theory trembled beneath the shock. We hastened home; and fancying we foresaw in the swift progress of events, its entire abolition, resolved from that day forward to vent our speculations on our next-door neighbours in person. The house adjoining ours on the left hand was uninhabited, and we had, therefore, plenty of leisure to observe our next-door neighbours on the other side.

The house without the knocker was in the occupation of a city clerk, and there was a neatly-written bill in the parlour window intimating that lodgings for a single gentleman were to be let within.

It was a neat, dull little house, on the shady side of the way, with new, narrow floorcloth in the passage, and new, narrow stair-carpets up to the first floor. The paper was new, and the paint was new, and the furniture was new; and all three, paper, paint, and furniture, bespoke the limited means of the tenant. There was a little red and black carpet in the drawing-room, with a border of flooring all the way round; a few stained chairs and a pembroke table. A pink shell was displayed on each of the little sideboards, which, with the addition of a tea-tray and caddy, a few more shells on the mantelpiece, and three peacock's feathers tastefully arranged above them, completed the decorative furniture of the apartment.

This was the room destined for the reception of the single gentleman during the day, and a little back room on the same floor was assigned as his sleeping apartment by night.

The bill had not been long in the window, when a stout, good-humoured looking gentleman, of about five-and-thirty, appeared as a candidate for the tenancy. Terms were soon arranged, for the bill was taken down immediately after his first visit. In a day or two the single gentleman came in, and shortly afterwards his real character came out.

First of all, he displayed a most extraordinary partiality for sitting up till three or four o'clock in the morning, drinking whiskey-and-water, and smoking cigars; then he invited friends home, who used to come at ten o'clock, and begin to get happy about the small hours, when they evinced their perfect contentment by singing songs with half-a-dozen verses of two lines each, and a chorus of ten, which chorus used to be shouted forth by the whole strength of the company, in the most enthusiastic and vociferous manner, to the great annoyance of the neighbours, and the special discomfort of another single gentleman overhead.

Now, this was bad enough, occurring as it did three times a week on the average, but this was not all; for when the company *did* go away, instead of walking quietly down the street, as anybody else's company would have done, they amused themselves by making alarming and frightful noises, and counterfeiting the shrieks of females in distress; and one night, a red-faced gentleman in a white hat knocked in the most urgent manner at the door of the powdered-headed old gentleman at No. 3, and when the powdered-headed old gentleman, who thought one of his married daughters must have been taken ill prematurely, had groped down stairs, and after a great deal of unbolting and key-turning, opened the street door, the red-faced man in the white hat said he hoped he'd excuse his giving him so much trouble, but he'd feel obliged if he'd favour him with a glass of cold spring water, and the loan of a shilling for a cab to take him home, on which the old gentleman slammed the door and went up-stairs, and threw the contents of his water jug out of window—very straight, only it went over the wrong man; and the whole street was involved in confusion.

A joke's a joke; and even practical jests are very capital in their way, if you can only get the other party to see the fun of them; but the population of our street were so dull of apprehension, as to be quite lost to a sense of the drollery of this proceeding: and the consequence was, that our next-door neighbour was obliged to tell the single gentleman, that unless he gave up entertaining his friends at home, he really must be compelled to part with him. The single gentleman received the remonstrance with great good-humour, and promised from that time forward, to spend his evenings at a coffee-house—a determination which afforded general and unmixed satisfaction.

The next night passed off very well, everybody being delighted with the change; but on the next, the noises were renewed with greater spirit than ever. The single gentleman's friends being unable to see him in his own house every alternate night, had come to the determination of seeing him home every night; and what with the discordant greetings of the friends at parting, and the noise created by the single gentleman in his passage up-stairs, and his subsequent struggles to get his boots off, the evil was not to be borne. So, our next-door neighbour gave the single gentleman, who was a very good lodger in other respects, notice to quit; and the single gentleman went away, and entertained his friends in other lodgings.

The next applicant for the vacant first floor, was of a very different character from the troublesome single gentleman who had just quitted it. He was a tall, thin, young gentleman, with a profusion of brown hair, reddish whiskers, and very slightly developed mustaches. He wore a braided surtout, with frogs behind, light grey trousers, and wash-leather gloves, and had altogether rather a military appearance. So unlike the roystering single gentleman. Such insinuating manners, and such a delightful address! So seriously disposed, too! When he first came to look at the lodgings, he inquired most particularly whether he was sure to be able to get a seat in the parish church; and when he had agreed to take them, he requested to have a list of the different local charities, as he intended to subscribe his mite to the most deserving among them.

Our next-door neighbour was now perfectly happy. He had got a lodger at last, of just his own way of thinking—a serious, well-disposed man, who abhorred gaiety, and loved retirement. He took down the bill with a light heart, and pictured in imagination a long series of quiet Sundays, on which he and his lodger would exchange mutual civilities and Sunday papers.

The serious man arrived, and his luggage was to arrive from the country next morning. He borrowed a clean shirt, and a prayer-book, from our next-door neighbour, and retired to rest at an early hour, requesting that he might be called punctually at ten o'clock next morning—not before, as he was much fatigued.

He *was* called, and did not answer: he was called again, but there was no reply. Our next-door neighbour became alarmed, and burst the door open. The serious man had left the house mysteriously; carrying with him the shirt, the prayer-book, a teaspoon, and the bedclothes.

Whether this occurrence, coupled with the irregularities of his former lodger, gave our next-door neighbour an aversion to single gentlemen, we know not; we only know that the next bill which made its appearance in the parlour window intimated generally, that there were furnished apartments to let on the first floor. The bill was soon removed. The new lodgers at first attracted our curiosity, and afterwards excited our interest.

They were a young lad of eighteen or nineteen, and his mother, a lady of about fifty, or it might be less. The mother wore a widow's weeds, and the boy was also clothed in deep mourning. They were poor—very poor; for their only means of support arose from the pittance the boy earned, by copying writings, and translating for booksellers.

They had removed from some country place and settled in London; partly because it afforded better chances of employment for the boy, and partly, perhaps, with the natural desire to leave a place where they had been in better circumstances, and where their poverty was known. They were proud under their reverses, and above revealing their wants and privations to strangers. How bitter those privations were, and how hard the boy worked to remove them, no one ever knew but themselves. Night after night, two, three, four hours after midnight, could we hear the occasional raking up of the scanty fire, or the hollow and half-stifled cough, which indicated his being still at work; and day after day, could we see more plainly that nature had set that unearthly light in his plaintive face, which is the beacon of her worst disease.

Actuated, we hope, by a higher feeling than mere curiosity, we contrived to establish, first an acquaintance, and then a close intimacy, with the poor strangers. Our worst fears were realised; the boy was sinking fast. Through a part of the winter, and the whole of the following spring and summer, his labours were unceasingly prolonged: and the mother attempted to procure needlework, embroidery—anything for bread.

A few shillings now and then, were all she could earn. The boy worked steadily on; dying by minutes, but never once giving utterance to complaint or murmur.

One beautiful autumn evening we went to pay our customary visit to the invalid. His little remaining strength had been decreasing rapidly for two or three days preceding, and he was lying on the sofa at the open window, gazing at the setting sun. His mother had been reading the Bible to him, for she closed the book as we entered, and advanced to meet us.

"I was telling William," she said, "that we must manage to take him into the country somewhere, so that he may get quite well. He is not ill, you know, but he is not very strong, and has exerted himself too much lately." Poor thing! The tears that streamed through her fingers, as she turned aside, as if to adjust her close widow's cap, too plainly showed how fruitless was the attempt to deceive herself.

We sat down by the head of the sofa, but said nothing, for we saw the breath of life was passing gently but rapidly from the young form before us. At every respiration, his heart beat more slowly.

The boy placed one hand in ours, grasped his mother's arm with the other, drew her hastily towards him, and fervently kissed her cheek. There was a pause. He sunk back upon his pillow, and looked long and earnestly in his mother's face.

"William, William!" murmured the mother, after a long interval, "don't look at me so—speak to me, dear!"

The boy smiled languidly, but an instant afterwards his features resolved into the same cold, solemn gaze.

"William, dear William! rouse yourself; don't look at me so, love—pray don't! Oh, my God! what shall I do!" cried the widow, clasping her hands in agony—"my dear boy! he is dying!"

The boy raised himself by a violent effort, and folded his hands together—"Mother! dear, dear mother, bury me in the open fields—anywhere but in these dreadful streets. I should like to be where you can see my grave, but not in these close crowded streets; they have killed me; kiss me again, mother; put your arm round my neck—"

He fell back, and a strange expression stole upon his features; not of pain or suffering, but an indescribable fixing of every line and muscle.

The boy was dead.

SCENES.

CHAPTER I.

THE STREETS—MORNING.

THE appearance presented by the streets of London an hour before sunrise, on a summer's morning, is most striking even to the few whose unfortunate pursuits of pleasure, or scarcely less unfortunate pursuits of business, cause them to be well acquainted with the scene. There is an air of cold, solitary desolation about the noiseless streets which we are accustomed to see thronged at other times by a busy, eager crowd, and over the quiet, closely-shut buildings, which throughout the day are swarming with life and bustle, that is very impressive.

The last drunken man, who shall find his way home before sunlight, has just staggered heavily along, roaring out the burden of the drinking song of the previous night: the last houseless vagrant whom penury and police have left in the streets, has coiled up his chilly limbs in some paved corner, to dream of food and warmth. The drunken, the dissipated, and the wretched have disappeared; the more sober and orderly part of the population have not yet awakened to the labours of the day, and the stillness of death is over the streets; its very hue seems to be imparted to them, cold and lifeless as they look in the grey, sombre light of day-break. The coach-stands in the larger thoroughfares are deserted: the night-houses are closed; and the chosen promenades of profligate misery are empty.

An occasional policeman may alone be seen at the street corners, listlessly gazing on the deserted prospect before him; and now and then a rakish-looking cat runs stealthily across the road and descends his own area with as much caution and slyness—bounding first on the water-butt, then on the dust-hole, and then alighting on the flag-stones—as if he were conscious that his character depended on his gallantry of the preceding night escaping public observation. A partially opened bedroom-window here and there, bespeaks the heat of the weather, and the uneasy slumbers of its occupant; and the dim scanty flicker of the rushlight, through the window-blind, denotes the chamber of watching or sickness. With these few exceptions, the streets present no signs of life, nor the houses of habitation.

An hour wears away; the spires of the churches and roofs of the principal buildings are faintly tinged with the light of the rising sun; and the streets, by almost imperceptible degrees, begin to resume their bustle and animation. Market-carts roll slowly along: the sleepy-waggoner impatiently urging on his tired horses, or vainly endeavouring to awaken the boy, who, luxuriously stretched on the top of the fruit-baskets, forgets, in happy oblivion, his long-cherished curiosity to behold the wonders of London.

Rough, sleepy-looking animals of strange appearance, something between ostlers and hackney-coachmen, begin to take down the shutters of early public-houses; and little deal tables, with the ordinary preparations for a street breakfast, make their appearance at the customary stations. Numbers of men and women (principally the latter), carrying upon their heads heavy baskets of fruit, toil down the park side of Piccadilly, on their way to Covent Garden, and, following each other in rapid succession, form a long straggling line from thence to the turn of the road at Knightsbridge.

Here and there, a bricklayer's labourer, with the day's dinner tied up in a handkerchief, walks briskly to his work, and occasionally a little knot of three or four schoolboys on a stolen bathing expedition rattle merrily over the pavement, their boisterous mirth contrasting forcibly with the demeanour of the little sweep, who, having knocked and rung till his arm aches, and being interdicted by a merciful legislature from endangering his lungs by calling out, sits patiently down on the door-step, until the housemaid may happen to awake.

Covent Garden market, and the avenues leading to it, are thronged with carts of all sorts, sizes, and descriptions, from the heavy lumbering waggon, with its four stout horses, to the jingling costermonger's cart, with its consumptive donkey. The pavement is already strewed with decayed cabbage-leaves, broken hay-bands, and all the indescribable litter of a vegetable market; men are shouting, carts backing, horses neighing, boys fighting, basket-women talking, piemen expatiating on the excellence of their pastry, and donkeys braying. These and a hundred other sounds form a compound discordant enough to a Londoner's ears, and remarkably disagreeable to those of country gentlemen who are sleeping at the Hummums for the first time.

Another hour passes away, and the day begins in good earnest. The servant of all work, who, under the plea of sleeping very soundly, has utterly disregarded "Missis's" ringing for half an hour previously, is warned by Master (whom Missis has sent up in his drapery to the landing-place for that purpose), that it's half-past six, whereupon she awakes all of a sudden, with well-feigned astonishment, and goes down stairs very sulkily, wishing, while she strikes a light, that the principle of spontaneous combustion would extend itself to coals and kitchen range. When the fire is lighted, she opens the street-door to take in the milk, when, by the most singular coincidence in the world, she discovers that the servant next door has just taken in her milk too, and that Mr. Todd's young man over the way, is, by an equally extraordinary chance, taking down his master's shutters. The inevitable consequence is, that she just steps, milk-jug in hand, as far as next door, just to say "good morning," to Betsy Clark, and that Mr. Todd's young man just steps over the way to say "good morning" to both of 'em; and as the aforesaid Mr. Todd's young man is almost as good-looking and fascinating as the baker himself, the conversation quickly becomes very interesting, and probably would become more so, if Betsy Clark's Missis, who always will be a-followin' her about, didn't give an angry tap at her bedroom window, on which Mr. Todd's young man tries to whistle coolly, as he goes back to his shop much faster than he came from it; and the two girls run back to their respective places, and shut their street doors with surprising softness, each of them poking their heads out of the front parlour-window, a minute afterwards, however, ostensibly with the view of looking at the mail which just then passes by, but really for the purpose of catching another glimpse of Mr. Todd's young man, who being fond of mails, but more of females, takes a short look at the mails, and a long look at the girls, much to the satisfaction of all parties concerned.

The mail itself goes on to the coach-office in due course, and the passengers who are going out by the early coach, stare with astonishment at the passengers who are coming in by the early coach, who look blue and dismal, and are evidently under the influence of that odd feeling produced by travelling, which makes the events of yesterday morning seem as if they had happened at least six months ago, and induces people to wonder with considerable gravity whether the friends and relations they took leave of a fortnight before, have altered much since they have left them. The coach-office is all alive, and the coaches which are just going out, are surrounded by the usual crowd of Jews and nondescripts, who seem to consider, Heaven knows why, that it is quite impossible any man can mount a coach without requiring at least sixpennyworth of oranges, a penknife, a pocket-book, a last year's annual, a pencil-case, a piece of sponge, and a small series of caricatures.

Half an hour more, and the sun darts his bright rays cheerfully down the still half-empty streets, and shines with sufficient force to rouse the dismal laziness of the apprentice, who pauses every other minute from his task of sweeping out the shop and watering the pavement in front of it, to tell another apprentice similarly employed, how hot it will be to-day, or to stand with his right hand shading his eyes, and his left resting on the broom, gazing at the "Wonder," or the "Tally-ho," or the "Nimrod," or some other fast coach, till it is out of sight, when he re-enters the shop, envying the passengers on the outside of the fast coach, and thinking of the old red brick house "down in the country," where he went to school: the miseries of the milk and water, and thick bread and scrapings, fading into nothing before the pleasant recollection of the green field the boys used to play in, and the green pond he was caned for presuming to fall into, and other schoolboy associations.

Cabs, with trunks and band-boxes between the drivers' legs and outside the apron, rattle briskly up and down the streets on their way to the coach-offices or steam-packet wharfs; and the cab-drivers and hackney-coachmen who are on the stand polish up the ornamental part of their dingy vehicles—the former wondering how people can prefer "them wild beast cariwans of homnibuses, to a riglar cab with a fast trotter," and the latter admiring how people can trust their necks into one of "them crazy cabs, when they can have a 'spectable 'ackney cotche with a pair of 'orses as von't run away with no vun;" a consolation unquestionably founded on fact, seeing that a hackney-coach horse never was known to run at all, "except," as the smart cabman in front of the rank observes, "except one, and *he* run back'ards."

The shops are now completely opened, and apprentices and shopmen are busily engaged in cleaning and decking the windows for the day. The bakers' shops in town are filled with servants and children waiting for the drawing of the first batch of rolls—an operation which was performed a full hour ago in the suburbs; for the early clerk population of Somers and Camden towns, Islington, and Pentonville, are fast pouring into the city, or directing their steps towards Chancery-lane and the Inns of Court. Middle-aged men, whose salaries have by no means increased in the same proportion as their families, plod steadily along, apparently with no object in view but the counting-house; knowing by sight almost everybody they meet or overtake, for they have seen them every morning (Sundays excepted) during the last twenty years, but speaking to no one. If they do happen to overtake a personal acquaintance, they just exchange a hurried salutation, and keep walking on either by his side, or in front of him, as his rate of walking may chance to be. As to stopping to shake hands, or to take the friend's arm, they seem to think that as it is not included in their salary, they have no right to do it. Small office lads in large hats, who are made men before they are boys, hurry along in pairs, with their first coat carefully brushed, and the white trousers of last Sunday plentifully besmeared with dust and ink. It evidently requires a considerable mental struggle to avoid investing part of the day's dinner-money in the purchase of the stale tarts so temptingly exposed in dusty tins at the pastry-cooks' doors; but a consciousness of their own importance and the receipt of seven shillings a-week, with the prospect of an early rise to eight, comes to their aid, and they accordingly put their hats a little more on one side, and look under the bonnets of all the milliners' and staymakers' apprentices they meet—poor girls!—the hardest worked, the worst paid, and too often, the worst used class of the community.

Eleven o'clock, and a new set of people fill the streets. The goods in the shop-windows are invitingly arranged; the shopmen in their white neckerchiefs and spruce coats, look as if they couldn't clean a window if their lives depended on it; the carts have disappeared from Covent Garden; the waggoners have returned, and the costermongers repaired to their ordinary "beats" in the suburbs; clerks are at their offices, and gigs, cabs, omnibuses, and saddle-horses, are conveying their masters to the same destination. The streets are thronged with a vast concourse of people, gay and shabby, rich and poor, idle and industrious; and we come to the heat, bustle, and activity of NOON.

CHAPTER II.

THE STREETS—NIGHT.

BUT the streets of London, to be beheld in the very height of their glory, should be seen on a dark, dull, murky winter's night, when there is just enough damp gently stealing down to make the pavement greasy, without cleansing it of any of its impurities; and when the heavy lazy mist, which hangs over every object, makes the gas-lamps look brighter, and the brilliantly-lighted shops more splendid, from the contrast they present to the darkness around. All the people who are at home on such a night as this, seem disposed to make themselves as snug and comfortable as possible; and the passengers in the streets have excellent reason to envy the fortunate individuals who are seated by their own firesides.

In the larger and better kind of streets, dining parlour curtains are closely drawn, kitchen fires blaze brightly up, and savoury steams of hot dinners salute the nostrils of the hungry wayfarer, as he plods wearily by the area railings. In the suburbs, the muffin boy rings his way down the little street, much more slowly than he is wont to do; for Mrs. Macklin, of No. 4, has no sooner opened her little street-door, and screamed out "Muffins!" with all her might, than Mrs. Walker, at No. 5, puts her head out of the parlour-window, and screams "Muffins!" too; and Mrs. Walker has scarcely got the words out of her lips, than Mrs. Peplow, over the way, lets loose Master Peplow, who darts down the street, with a velocity which nothing but buttered muffins in perspective could possibly inspire, and drags the boy back by main force, whereupon Mrs. Macklin and Mrs. Walker, just to save the boy trouble, and to say a few neighbourly words to Mrs. Peplow at the same time, run over the way and buy their muffins at Mrs. Peplow's door, when it appears from the voluntary statement of Mrs. Walker, that her "kittle 's jist a-biling, and the cups and sarsers ready laid," and that, as it was such a wretched night out o' doors, she'd made up her mind to have a nice hot comfortable cup o' tea—a determination at which, by the most singular coincidence, the other two ladies had simultaneously arrived.

After a little conversation about the wretchedness of the weather and the merits of tea, with a digression relative to the viciousness of boys as a rule, and the amiability of Master Peplow as an exception, Mrs. Walker sees her husband coming down the street; and as he must want his tea, poor man, after his dirty walk from the Docks, she instantly runs across, muffins in hand, and Mrs. Macklin does the same, and after a few words to Mrs. Walker, they all pop into their little houses, and slam their little street doors, which are not opened again for the remainder of the evening, except to the nine o'clock "beer," who comes round with a lantern in front of his tray, and says, as he lends Mrs. Walker "Yesterday's 'Tiser," that he's blessed if he can hardly hold the pot, much less feel the paper, for it's one of the bitterest nights he ever felt, 'cept the night when the man was frozen to death in the Brick-field.

After a little prophetic conversation with the policeman at the street-corner, touching a probable change in the weather, and the setting-in of a hard frost, the nine o'clock beer returns to his master's house, and employs himself for the remainder of the evening, in assiduously stirring the tap-room fire, and deferentially taking part in the conversation of the worthies assembled round it.

The streets in the vicinity of the Marsh-gate and Victoria Theatre present an appearance of dirt and discomfort on such a night, which the groups who lounge about them in no degree tend to diminish. Even the little block-tin temple sacred to baked potatoes, surmounted by a splendid design in variegated lamps, looks less gay than usual; and as to the kidney-pie stand, its glory has quite departed. The candle in the transparent lamp, manufactured of oil-paper, embellished with "characters," has been blown out fifty times, so the kidney-pie merchant, tired with running backwards and forwards to the next wine-vaults, to get a light, has given up the idea of illumination in despair, and the only signs of his "whereabout," are the bright sparks, of which a long irregular train is whirled down the street every time he opens his portable oven to hand a hot kidney-pie to a customer.

Flat fish, oyster, and fruit venders linger hopelessly in the kennel, in vain endeavouring to attract customers; and the ragged boys who usually disport themselves about the streets, stand crouched in little knots in some projecting doorway, or under the canvas blind of a cheesemonger's, where great flaring gas-lights, unshaded by any glass, display huge piles of bright red, and pale yellow cheeses, mingled with little fivepenny dabs of dingy bacon, various tubs of weekly Dorset, and cloudy rolls of "best fresh."

Here they amuse themselves with theatrical converse, arising out of their last half-price visit to the Victoria gallery, admire the terrific combat, which is nightly encored, and expatiate on the inimitable manner in which Bill Thompson can "come the double monkey," or go through the mysterious involutions of a sailor's hornpipe.

It is nearly eleven o'clock, and the cold thin rain which has been drizzling so long, is beginning to pour down in good earnest; the baked-potato man has departed—the kidney-pie man has just walked away with his warehouse on his arm—the cheesemonger has drawn in his blind, and the boys have dispersed. The constant clicking of pattens on the slippy and uneven pavement, and the rustling of umbrellas, as the wind blows against the shop windows, bear testimony to the inclemency of the night; and the policeman, with his oilskin cape buttoned closely round him, seems as he holds his hat on his head, and turns round to avoid the gust of wind and rain which drives against him at the street-corner, to be very far from congratulating himself on the prospect before him.

The little chandler's shop with the cracked bell behind the door, whose melancholy tinkling has been regulated by the demand for quarterns of sugar and half-ounces of coffee, is shutting up. The crowds which have been passing to and fro during the whole day, are rapidly dwindling away; and the noise of shouting and quarrelling which issues from the public-houses, is almost the only sound that breaks the melancholy stillness of the night.

There was another, but it has ceased. That wretched woman with the infant in her arms, round whose meagre form the remnant of her own scanty shawl is carefully wrapped, has been attempting to sing some popular ballad, in the hope of wringing a few pence from the compassionate passer-by. A brutal laugh at her weak voice is all she has gained. The tears fall thick and fast down her own pale face; the child is cold and hungry, and its low half-stifled wailing adds to the misery of its wretched mother, as she moans aloud, and sinks despairingly down, on a cold damp door-step.

Singing! How few of those who pass such a miserable creature as this, think of the anguish of heart, the sinking of soul and spirit, which the very effort of singing produces. Bitter mockery! Disease, neglect, and starvation, faintly articulating the words of the joyous ditty, that has enlivened your hours of feasting and merriment, God knows how often! It is no subject of jeering. The weak tremulous voice tells a fearful tale of want and famishing; and the feeble singer of this roaring song may turn away, only to die of cold and hunger.

One o'clock! Parties returning from the different theatres foot it through the muddy streets; cabs, hackney-coaches, carriages, and theatre omnibuses, roll swiftly by; watermen with dim dirty lanterns in their hands, and large brass plates upon their breasts, who have been shouting and rushing about for the last two hours, retire to their watering-houses, to solace themselves with the creature comforts of pipes and purl; the half-price pit and box frequenters of the theatres throng to the different houses of refreshment; and chops, kidneys, rabbits, oysters, stout, cigars, and "goes" innumerable, are served up amidst a noise and confusion of smoking, running, knife-clattering, and waiter-chattering, perfectly indescribable.

The more musical portion of the play-going community betake themselves to some harmonic meeting. As a matter of curiosity let us follow them thither for a few moments.

In a lofty room of spacious dimensions, are seated some eighty or a hundred guests knocking little pewter measures on the tables, and hammering away, with the handles of their knives, as if they were so many trunk-makers. They are applauding a glee, which has just been executed by the three "professional gentlemen" at the top of the centre table, one of whom is in the chair—the little pompous man with the bald head just emerging from the collar of his green coat. The others are seated on either side of him—the stout man with the small voice, and the thin-faced dark man in black. The little man in the chair is a most amusing personage,—*such* condescending grandeur, and *such* a voice!

"Bass!" as the young gentleman near us with the blue stock forcibly remarks to his companion, "bass! I b'lieve you; he can go down lower than any man: so low sometimes that you can't hear him." And so he does. To hear him growling away, gradually lower and lower down, till he can't get back again, is the most delightful thing in the world, and it is quite impossible to witness unmoved the impressive solemnity with which he pours forth his soul in "My 'art's in the 'ighlands," or "The brave old Hoak." The stout man is also addicted to sentimentality, and warbles "Fly, fly from the world, my Bessy, with me," or some such song, with lady-like sweetness, and in the most seductive tones imaginable.

"Pray give your orders, gen'l'm'n—pray give your orders,"—says the pale-faced man with the red head; and demands for "goes" of gin and "goes" of brandy, and pints of stout, and cigars of peculiar mildness, are vociferously made from all parts of the room. The "professional gentlemen" are in the very height of their glory, and bestow condescending nods, or even a word or two of recognition, on the better-known frequenters of the room, in the most bland and patronising manner possible.

That little round-faced man, with the small brown surtout, white stockings and shoes, is in the comic line; the mixed air of self-denial, and mental consciousness of his own powers, with which he acknowledges the call of the chair, is particularly gratifying. "Gen'l'men," says the little pompous man, accompanying the word with a knock of the president's hammer on the table—"Gen'l'men, allow me to claim your attention—our friend, Mr. Smuggins, will oblige."—"Bravo!" shout the company; and Smuggins, after a considerable quantity of coughing by way of symphony, and a most facetious sniff or two, which afford general delight, sings a comic song, with a fal-de-ral—tol-de-rol chorus at the end of every verse, much longer than the verse itself. It is received with unbounded applause, and after some aspiring genius has volunteered a recitation, and failed dismally therein, the little pompous man gives another knock, and says "Gen'l'men, we will attempt a glee, if you please." This announcement calls forth tumultuous applause, and the more energetic spirits express the unqualified approbation it affords them, by knocking one or two stout glasses off their legs—a humorous dance; but one which frequently occasions some slight altercation when the form of paying the damage is proposed to be gone through by the waiter.

Scenes like these are continued until three or four o'clock in the morning; and even when they close, fresh ones open to the inquisitive novice. But as a description of all of them, however slight, would require a volume, the contents of which, however instructive, would be by no means pleasing, we make our bow, and drop the curtain.

CHAPTER III.

SHOPS AND THEIR TENANTS.

WHAT inexhaustible food for speculation, do the streets of London afford! We never were able to agree with Sterne in pitying the man who could travel from Dan to Beersheba, and say that all was barren; we have not the slightest commiseration for the man who can take up his hat and stick, and walk from Covent-garden to St. Paul's Churchyard, and back into the bargain, without deriving some amusement—we had almost said instruction—from his perambulation. And yet there are such beings: we meet them every day. Large black stocks and light waistcoats, jet canes and discontented countenances, are the characteristics of the race; other people brush quickly by you, steadily plodding on to business, or cheerfully running after pleasure. These men linger listlessly past, looking as happy and animated as a policeman on duty. Nothing seems to make an impression on their minds: nothing short of being knocked down by a porter, or run over by a cab, will disturb their equanimity. You will meet them on a fine day in any of the leading thoroughfares: peep through the window of a west-end cigar shop in the evening, if you can manage to get a glimpse between the blue curtains which intercept the vulgar gaze, and you see them in their only enjoyment of existence. There they are lounging about, on round tubs and pipe boxes, in all the dignity of whiskers, and gilt watch-guards; whispering soft nothings to the young lady in amber, with the large ear-rings, who, as she sits behind the counter in a blaze of adoration and gas-light, is the admiration of all the female servants in the neighbourhood, and the envy of every milliner's apprentice within two miles round.

One of our principal amusements is to watch the gradual progress—the rise or fall—of particular shops. We have formed an intimate acquaintance with several, in different parts of town, and are perfectly acquainted with their whole history. We could name off-hand, twenty at least, which we are quite sure have paid no taxes for the last six years. They are never inhabited for more than two months consecutively, and, we verily believe, have witnessed every retail trade in the directory.

There is one, whose history is a sample of the rest, in whose fate we have taken especial interest, having had the pleasure of knowing it ever since it has been a shop. It is on the Surrey side of the water—a little distance beyond the Marsh-gate. It was originally a substantial, good-looking private house enough; the landlord got into difficulties, the house got into Chancery, the tenant went away, and the house went to ruin. At this period our acquaintance with it commenced; the paint was all worn off; the windows were broken, the area was green with neglect and the overflowings of the water-butt; the butt itself was without a lid, and the street-door was the very picture of misery. The chief pastime of the children in the vicinity had been to assemble in a body on the steps, and to take it in turn to knock loud double knocks at the door, to the great satisfaction of the neighbours generally, and especially of the nervous old lady next door but one. Numerous complaints were made, and several small basins of water discharged over the offenders, but without effect. In this state of things, the marine-store dealer at the corner of the street, in the most obliging manner took the knocker off, and sold it: and the unfortunate house looked more wretched than ever.

We deserted our friend for a few weeks. What was our surprise, on our return, to find no trace of its existence! In its place was a handsome shop, fast approaching to a state of completion, and on the shutters were large bills, informing the public that it would shortly be opened with "an extensive stock of linen drapery and haberdashery." It opened in due course; there was the name of the proprietor "and Co." in gilt letters, almost too dazzling to look at. Such ribbons and shawls! and two such elegant young men behind the counter, each in a clean collar and white neckcloth, like the lover in a farce. As to the proprietor, he did nothing but walk up and down the shop, and hand seats to the ladies, and hold important conversations with the handsomest of the young men, who was shrewdly suspected by the neighbours to be the "Co." We saw all this with sorrow; we felt a fatal presentiment that the shop was doomed—and so it was. Its decay was slow, but sure. Tickets gradually appeared in the windows; then rolls of flannel, with labels on them, were stuck outside the door; then a bill was pasted on the street-door, intimating that the first floor was to let *un*furnished; then one of the young men disappeared altogether, and the other took to a black neckerchief, and the proprietor took to drinking. The shop became dirty, broken panes of glass remained unmended, and the stock disappeared piecemeal. At last the company's man came to cut off the water, and then the linen-draper cut off himself, leaving the landlord his compliments and the key.

The next occupant was a fancy stationer. The shop was more modestly painted than before, still it was neat; but somehow we always thought, as we passed, that it looked like a poor and struggling concern. We wished the man well, but we trembled for his success. He was a widower evidently, and had employment elsewhere, for he passed us every morning on his road to the city. The business was carried on by his eldest daughter. Poor girl! she needed no assistance. We occasionally caught a glimpse of two or three children, in mourning like herself, as they sat in the little parlour behind the shop; and we never passed at night without seeing the eldest girl at work, either for them, or in making some elegant little trifle for sale. We often thought, as her pale face looked more sad and pensive in the dim candle-light, that if those thoughtless females who interfere with the miserable market of poor creatures such as these, knew but one half of the misery they suffer, and the bitter privations they endure, in their honourable attempts to earn a scanty subsistence, they would, perhaps, resign even opportunities for the gratification of vanity, and an immodest love of self-display, rather than drive them to a last dreadful resource, which it would shock the delicate feelings of these *charitable* ladies to hear named.

But we are forgetting the shop. Well, we continued to watch it, and every day showed too clearly the increasing poverty of its inmates. The children were clean, it is true, but their clothes were threadbare and shabby; no tenant had been procured for the upper part of the house, from the letting of which, a portion of the means of paying the rent was to have been derived, and a slow, wasting consumption prevented the eldest girl from continuing her exertions. Quarter-day arrived. The landlord had suffered from the extravagance of his last tenant, and he had no compassion for the struggles of his successor; he put in an execution. As we passed one morning, the broker's men were removing the little furniture there was in the house, and a newly-posted bill informed us it was again "To Let." What became of the last tenant we never could learn; we believe the girl is past all suffering, and beyond all sorrow. God help her! We hope she is.

We were somewhat curious to ascertain what would be the next stage—for that the place had no chance of succeeding now, was perfectly clear. The bill was soon taken down, and some alterations were being made in the interior of the shop. We were in a fever of expectation; we exhausted conjecture—we imagined all possible trades, none of which were perfectly reconcileable with our idea of the gradual decay of the tenement. It opened, and we wondered why we had not guessed at the real state of the case before. The shop—not a large one at the best of times—had been converted into two: one was a bonnet-shape maker's, the other was opened by a tobacconist, who also dealt in walking-sticks and Sunday newspapers; the two were separated by a thin partition, covered with tawdry striped paper.

The tobacconist remained in possession longer than any tenant within our recollection. He was a red-faced, impudent, good-for-nothing dog, evidently accustomed to take things as they came, and to make the best of a bad job. He sold as many cigars as he could, and smoked the rest. He occupied the shop as long as he could make peace with the landlord, and when he could no longer live in quiet, he very coolly locked the door, and bolted himself. From this period, the two little dens have undergone innumerable changes. The tobacconist was succeeded by a theatrical hair-dresser, who ornamented the window with a great variety of "characters," and terrific combats. The bonnet-shape maker gave place to a green-grocer, and the histrionic barber was succeeded, in his turn, by a tailor. So numerous have been the changes, that we have of late done little more than mark the peculiar but certain indications of a house being poorly inhabited. It has been progressing by almost imperceptible degrees. The occupiers of the shops have gradually given up room after room, until they have only reserved the little parlour for themselves. First there appeared a brass plate on the private door, with "Ladies' School" legibly engraved thereon; shortly afterwards we observed a second brass plate, then a bell, and then another bell.

When we paused in front of our old friend, and observed these signs of poverty, which are not to be mistaken, we thought as we turned away, that the house had attained its lowest pitch of degradation. We were wrong. When we last passed it, a "dairy" was established in the area, and a party of melancholy-looking fowls were amusing themselves by running in at the front door, and out at the back one.

CHAPTER IV.

SCOTLAND-YARD.

SCOTLAND-YARD is a small—a very small—tract of land, bounded on one side by the river Thames, on the other by the gardens of Northumberland House: abutting at one end on the bottom of Northumberland-street, at the other on the back of Whitehall-place. When this territory was first accidentally discovered by a country gentleman who lost his way in the Strand, some years ago, the original settlers were found to be a tailor, a publican, two eating-house keepers, and a fruit-pie maker; and it was also found to contain a race of strong and bulky men, who repaired to the wharfs in Scotland-yard regularly every morning, about five or six o'clock, to fill heavy waggons with coal, with which they proceeded to distant places up the country, and supplied the inhabitants with fuel. When they had emptied their waggons, they again returned for a fresh supply; and this trade was continued throughout the year.

As the settlers derived their subsistence from ministering to the wants of these primitive traders, the articles exposed for sale, and the places where they were sold, bore strong outward marks of being expressly adapted to their tastes and wishes. The tailor displayed in his window a Lilliputian pair of leather gaiters, and a diminutive round frock, while each doorpost was appropriately garnished with a model of a coal-sack. The two eating-house keepers exhibited joints of a magnitude, and puddings of a solidity, which coalheavers alone could appreciate; and the fruit-pie maker displayed on his well-scrubbed window-board large white compositions of flour and dripping, ornamented with pink stains, giving rich promise of the fruit within, which made their huge mouths water, as they lingered past.

But the choicest spot in all Scotland-yard was the old public-house in the corner. Here, in a dark wainscoted-room of ancient appearance, cheered by the glow of a mighty fire, and decorated with an enormous clock, whereof the face was white, and the figures black, sat the lusty coalheavers, quaffing large draughts of Barclay's best, and puffing forth volumes of smoke, which wreathed heavily above their heads, and involved the room in a thick dark cloud. From this apartment might their voices be heard on a winter's night, penetrating to the very bank of the river, as they shouted out some sturdy chorus, or roared forth the burden of a popular song; dwelling upon the last few words with a strength and length of emphasis which made the very roof tremble above them.

Here, too, would they tell old legends of what the Thames was in ancient times, when the Patent Shot Manufactory wasn't built, and Waterloo-bridge had never been thought of; and then they would shake their heads with portentous looks, to the deep edification of the rising generation of heavers, who crowded round them, and wondered where all this would end; whereat the tailor would take his pipe solemnly from his mouth, and say, how that he hoped it might end well, but he very much doubted whether it would or not, and couldn't rightly tell what to make of it—a mysterious expression of opinion, delivered with a semi-prophetic air, which never failed to elicit the fullest concurrence of the assembled company; and so they would go on drinking and wondering till ten o'clock came, and with it the tailor's wife to fetch him home, when the little party broke up, to meet again in the same room, and say and do precisely the same things, on the following evening at the same hour.

About this time the barges that came up the river began to bring vague rumours to Scotland-yard of somebody in the city having been heard to say, that the Lord Mayor had threatened in so many words to pull down the old London-bridge, and build up a new one. At first these rumours were disregarded as idle tales, wholly destitute of foundation, for nobody in Scotland-yard doubted that if the Lord Mayor contemplated any such dark design, he would just be clapped up in the Tower for a week or two, and then killed off for high treason.

By degrees, however, the reports grew stronger, and more frequent, and at last a barge, laden with numerous chaldrons of the best Wallsend, brought up the positive intelligence that several of the arches of the old bridge were stopped, and that preparations were actually in progress for constructing the new one. What an excitement was visible in the old tap-room on that memorable night! Each man looked into his neighbour's face, pale with alarm and astonishment, and read therein an echo of the sentiments which filled his own breast. The oldest heaver present proved to demonstration, that the moment the piers were removed, all the water in the Thames would run clean off, and leave a dry gully in its place. What was to become of the coal-barges—of the trade of Scotland-yard—of the very existence of its population? The tailor shook his head more sagely than usual, and grimly pointing to a knife on the table, bid them wait and see what happened. He said nothing—not he; but if the Lord Mayor didn't fall a victim to popular indignation, why he would be rather astonished; that was all.

They did wait; barge after barge arrived, and still no tidings of the assassination of the Lord Mayor. The first stone was laid: it was done by a Duke—the King's brother. Years passed away, and the bridge was opened by the King himself. In course of time, the piers were removed; and when the people in Scotland-yard got up next morning in the confident expectation of being able to step over to Pedlar's Acre without wetting the soles of their shoes, they found to their unspeakable astonishment that the water was just where it used to be.

A result so different from that which they had anticipated from this first improvement, produced its full effect upon the inhabitants of Scotland-yard. One of the eating-house keepers began to court public opinion, and to look for customers among a new class of people. He covered his little dining-tables with white cloths, and got a painter's apprentice to inscribe something about hot joints from twelve to two, in one of the little panes of his shop-window. Improvement began to march with rapid strides to the very threshold of Scotland-yard. A new market sprung up at Hungerford, and the Police Commissioners established their office in Whitehall-place. The traffic in Scotland-yard increased; fresh Members were added to the House of Commons, the Metropolitan Representatives found it a near cut, and many other foot passengers followed their example.

We marked the advance of civilisation, and beheld it with a sigh. The eating-house keeper who manfully resisted the innovation of table-cloths, was losing ground every day, as his opponent gained it, and a deadly feud sprung up between them. The genteel one no longer took his evening's pint in Scotland-yard, but drank gin and water at a "parlour" in Parliament-street. The fruit-pie maker still continued to visit the old room, but he took to smoking cigars, and began to call himself a pastrycook, and to read the papers. The old heavers still assembled round the ancient fireplace, but their talk was mournful: and the loud song and the joyous shout were heard no more.

And what is Scotland-yard now? How have its old customs changed; and how has the ancient simplicity of its inhabitants faded away! The old tottering public-house is converted into a spacious and lofty "wine-vaults;" gold leaf has been used in the construction of the letters which emblazon its exterior, and the poet's art has been called into requisition, to intimate that if you drink a certain description of ale, you must hold fast by the rail. The tailor exhibits in his window the pattern of a foreign-looking brown surtout, with silk buttons, a fur collar, and fur cuffs. He wears a stripe down the outside of each leg of his trousers: and we have detected his assistants (for he has assistants now) in the act of sitting on the shop-board in the same uniform.

At the other end of the little row of houses a boot-maker has established himself in a brick box, with the additional innovation of a first floor; and here he exposes for sale, boots—real Wellington boots—an article which a few years ago, none of the original inhabitants had ever seen or heard of. It was but the other day, that a dress-maker opened another little box in the middle of the row; and, when we thought that the spirit of change could produce no alteration beyond that, a jeweller appeared, and not content with exposing gilt rings and copper bracelets out of number, put up an announcement, which still sticks in his window, that "ladies' ears may be pierced within." The dress-maker employs a young lady who wears pockets in her apron; and the tailor informs the public that gentlemen may have their own materials made up.

Amidst all this change, and restlessness, and innovation, there remains but one old man, who seems to mourn the downfall of this ancient place. He holds no converse with human kind, but, seated on a wooden bench at the angle of the wall which fronts the crossing from Whitehall-place, watches in silence the gambols of his sleek and well-fed dogs. He is the presiding genius of Scotland-yard. Years and years have rolled over his head; but, in fine weather or in foul, hot or cold, wet or dry, hail, rain, or snow, he is still in his accustomed spot. Misery and want are depicted in his countenance; his form is bent by age, his head is grey with length of trial, but there he sits from day to day, brooding over the past; and thither he will continue to drag his feeble limbs, until his eyes have closed upon Scotland-yard, and upon the world together.

A few years hence, and the antiquary of another generation looking into some mouldy record of the strife and passions that agitated the world in these times, may glance his eye over the pages we have just filled: and not all his knowledge of the history of the past, not all his black-letter lore, or his skill in book-collecting, not all the dry studies of a long life, or the dusty volumes that have cost him a fortune, may help him to the whereabouts, either of Scotland-yard, or of any one of the landmarks we have mentioned in describing it.

CHAPTER V

SEVEN DIALS.

We have always been of opinion that if Tom King and the Frenchman had not immortalised Seven Dials, Seven Dials would have immortalised itself. Seven Dials! the region of song and poetry—first effusions, and last dying speeches: hallowed by the names of Catnach and of Pitts—names that will entwine themselves with costermongers, and barrel-organs, when penny magazines shall have superseded penny yards of song, and capital punishment be unknown!

Look at the construction of the place. The gordian knot was all very well in its way: so was the maze of Hampton Court: so is the maze at the Beulah Spa: so were the ties of stiff white neckcloths, when the difficulty of getting one on, was only to be equalled by the apparent impossibility of ever getting it off again. But what involutions can compare with those of Seven Dials? Where is there such another maze of streets, courts, lanes, and alleys? Where such a pure mixture of

Englishmen and Irishmen, as in this complicated part of London? We boldly aver that we doubt the veracity of the legend to which we have adverted. We *can* suppose a man rash enough to inquire at random—at a house with lodgers too—for a Mr. Thompson, with all but the certainty before his eyes, of finding at least two or three Thompsons in any house of moderate dimensions; but a Frenchman—a Frenchman in Seven Dials! Pooh! He was an Irishman. Tom King's education had been neglected in his infancy, and as he couldn't understand half the man said, he took it for granted he was talking French.

The stranger who finds himself in "The Dials" for the first time, and stands Belzoni-like, at the entrance of seven obscure passages, uncertain which to take, will see enough around him to keep his curiosity and attention awake for no inconsiderable time. From the irregular square into which he has plunged, the streets and courts dart in all directions, until they are lost in the unwholesome vapour which hangs over the house-tops, and renders the dirty perspective uncertain and confined; and lounging at every corner, as if they came there to take a few gasps of such fresh air as has found its way so far, but is too much exhausted already, to be enabled to force itself into the narrow alleys around, are groups of people, whose appearance and dwellings would fill any mind but a regular Londoner's with astonishment.

On one side, a little crowd has collected round a couple of ladies, who having imbibed the contents of various "three-outs" of gin and bitters in the course of the morning, have at length differed on some point of domestic arrangement, and are on the eve of settling the quarrel satisfactorily, by an appeal to blows, greatly to the interest of other ladies who live in the same house, and tenements adjoining, and who are all partisans on one side or other.

"Vy don't you pitch into her, Sarah?" exclaims one half-dressed matron, by way of encouragement. "Vy don't you? if *my* 'usband had treated her with a drain last night, unbeknown to me, I'd tear her precious eyes out—a wixen!"

"What's the matter, ma'am?" inquires another old woman, who has just bustled up to the spot.

"Matter!" replies the first speaker, talking *at* the obnoxious combatant, "matter! Here's poor dear Mrs. Sulliwin, as has five blessed children of her own, can't go out a charing for one arternoon, but what hussies must be a comin', and 'ticing avay her oun' 'usband, as she's been married to twelve year come next Easter Monday, for I see the certificate ven I vas a drinkin' a cup o' tea vith her, only the werry last blessed Ven'sday as ever was sent. I 'appen'd to say promiscuously, 'Mrs. Sulliwin,' says I——"

"What do you mean by hussies?" interrupts a champion of the other party, who has evinced a strong inclination throughout to get up a branch fight on her own account ("Hooroar," ejaculates a pot-boy in parenthesis, "put the kye-bosk on her, Mary!"), "What do you mean by hussies?" reiterates the champion.

"Niver mind," replies the opposition expressively, "niver mind; *you* go home, and, ven you're quite sober, mend your stockings."

This somewhat personal allusion, not only to the lady's habits of intemperance, but also to the state of her wardrobe, rouses her utmost ire, and she accordingly complies with the urgent request of the bystanders to "pitch in," with considerable alacrity. The scuffle became general, and terminates, in minor play-bill phraseology, with "arrival of the policemen, interior of the station-house, and impressive *dénouement*."

In addition to the numerous groups who are idling about the gin-shops and squabbling in the centre of the road, every post in the open space has its occupant, who leans against it for hours, with listless perseverance. It is odd enough that one class of men in London appear to have no enjoyment beyond leaning against posts. We never saw a regular bricklayer's labourer take any other recreation, fighting excepted. Pass through St. Giles's in the evening of a week-day, there they are in their fustian dresses, spotted with brick-dust and whitewash, leaning against posts. Walk through Seven Dials on Sunday morning: there they are again, drab or light corduroy trousers, Blucher boots, blue coats, and great yellow waistcoats, leaning against posts. The idea of a man dressing himself in his best clothes, to lean against a post all day!

The peculiar character of these streets, and the close resemblance each one bears to its neighbour, by no means tends to decrease the bewilderment in which the unexperienced wayfarer through "the Dials" finds himself involved. He traverses streets of dirty, straggling houses, with now and then an unexpected court composed of buildings as ill-proportioned and deformed as the half-naked children that wallow in the kennels. Here and there, a little dark chandler's shop, with a cracked bell hung up behind the door to announce the entrance of a customer, or betray the presence of some young gentleman in whom a passion for shop tills has developed itself at an early age: others, as if for support, against some handsome lofty building, which usurps the place of a low dingy public-house; long rows of broken and patched windows expose plants that may have flourished when "the Dials" were built, in vessels as dirty as "the Dials" themselves; and shops for the purchase of rags, bones, old iron, and kitchen-stuff, vie in cleanliness with the bird-fanciers and rabbit-dealers, which one might fancy so many arks, but for the irresistible conviction that no bird in its proper senses, who was permitted to leave one of them, would ever come back again. Brokers' shops, which would seem to have been established by humane individuals, as refuges for destitute bugs, interspersed with announcements of day-schools, penny theatres, petition-writers, mangles, and music for balls or routs, complete the "still life" of the subject; and dirty men, filthy women, squalid children, fluttering shuttlecocks, noisy battledores, reeking pipes, bad fruit, more than doubtful oysters, attenuated cats, depressed dogs, and anatomical fowls, are its cheerful accompaniments.

If the external appearance of the houses, or a glance at their inhabitants, present but few attractions, a closer acquaintance with either is little calculated to alter one's first impression. Every room has its separate tenant, and every tenant is, by the same mysterious dispensation which causes a country curate to "increase and multiply" most marvellously, generally the head of a numerous family.

The man in the shop, perhaps, is in the baked "jemmy" line, or the fire-wood and hearth-stone line, or any other line which requires a floating capital of eighteen-pence or thereabouts: and he and his family live in the shop, and the small back parlour behind it. Then there is an Irish labourer and *his* family in the back kitchen, and a jobbing man—carpet-beater and so forth—with *his* family in the front one. In the front one-pair, there's another man with another wife and family, and in the back one-pair, there's "a young 'oman as takes in tambour-work, and dresses quite genteel," who talks a good deal about "my friend," and can't "a-bear anything low." The second floor front, and the rest of the lodgers, are just a second edition of the people below, except a shabby-genteel man in the back attic, who has his half-pint of coffee every morning from the coffee-shop next door but one, which boasts a little front den called a coffee-room, with a fire-place, over which is an inscription, politely requesting that, "to prevent mistakes," customers will "please to pay on delivery." The shabby-genteel man is an object of some mystery, but as he leads a life of seclusion, and never was known to buy anything beyond an occasional pen, except half-pints of coffee, penny loaves, and ha'porths of ink, his fellow-lodgers very naturally suppose him to be an author; and rumours are current in the Dials, that he writes poems for Mr. Warren.

Now anybody who passed through the Dials on a hot summer's evening, and saw the different women of the house gossiping on the steps, would he apt to think that all was harmony among them, and that a more primitive set of people than the native Diallers could not be imagined. Alas! the man in the shop illtreats his family; the carpet-beater extends his professional pursuits to his wife; the one-pair front has an undying feud with the two-pair front, in consequence of the two-pair front persisting in dancing over his (the one-pair front's) head, when he and his family have retired for the night; the two-pair back *will* interfere with the front kitchen's children; the Irishman comes home drunk every other night, and attacks everybody; and the one-pair back screams at everything. Animosities spring up between floor and floor; the very cellar asserts his equality. Mrs. A. "smacks" Mrs. B.'s child, for "making faces." Mrs. B. forthwith throws cold water over Mrs. B.'s child for "calling names." The husbands are embroiled—the quarrel becomes general—an assault is the consequence, and a police-officer the result.

CHAPTER VI.

MEDITATIONS IN MONMOUTH-STREET.

We have always entertained a particular attachment towards Monmouth-street, as the only true and real emporium for second-hand wearing apparel. Monmouth-street is venerable from its antiquity, and respectable from its usefulness. Holywell-street we despise; the red-headed and red-whiskered Jews who forcibly haul you into their squalid houses, and thrust you into a suit of clothes, whether you will or not, we detest.

The inhabitants of Monmouth-street are a distinct class; a peaceable and retiring race, who immure themselves for the most part in deep cellars, or small back parlours, and who seldom come forth into the world, except in the dusk and coolness of the evening, when they may be seen seated, in chairs on the pavement, smoking their pipes, or watching the gambols of their engaging children as they revel in the gutter, a happy troop of infantine scavengers. Their countenances bear a thoughtful and a dirty cast, certain indications of their love of traffic; and their habitations are distinguished by that disregard of outward appearance and neglect of personal comfort, so common among people who are constantly immersed in profound speculations, and deeply engaged in sedentary pursuits.

We have hinted at the antiquity of our favourite spot. "A Monmouth-street laced coat" was a by-word a century ago; and still we find Monmouth-street the same. Pilot greatcoats with wooden buttons, have usurped the place of the ponderous laced coats with full skirts; embroidered waistcoats with large flaps, have yielded to double-breasted checks with roll-collars; and three-cornered hats of quaint appearance, have given place to the low crowns and broad brims of the coachman school; but it is the times that have changed, not Monmouth-street. Through every alteration and every change, Monmouth-street has still remained the burial-place of the fashions; and such, to judge from all present appearances, it will remain until there are no more fashions to bury.

We love to walk among these extensive groves of the illustrious dead, and to indulge in the speculations to which they give rise; now fitting a deceased coat, then a dead pair of trousers, and anon the mortal remains of a gaudy waistcoat, upon some being of our own conjuring up, and endeavouring, from the shape and fashion of the garment itself, to bring its former owner before our mind's eye. We have gone on speculating in this way, until whole rows of coats have started from their pegs, and buttoned up, of their own accord, round the waists of imaginary wearers; lines of trousers have jumped down to meet them; waistcoats have almost burst with anxiety to put themselves on; and half an acre of shoes have suddenly found feet to fit them, and gone stumping down the street with a noise which has fairly awakened us from our pleasant reverie, and driven us slowly away, with a bewildered stare, an object of astonishment to the good people of Monmouth-street, and of no slight suspicion to the policemen at the opposite street corner.

We were occupied in this manner the other day, endeavouring to fit a pair of lace-up half-boots on an ideal personage, for whom, to say the truth, they were full a couple of sizes too small, when our eyes happened to alight on a few suits of clothes ranged outside a shop-window, which it immediately struck us, must at different periods have all belonged to, and been worn by, the same individual, and had now, by one of those strange conjunctions of circumstances which will occur sometimes, come to be exposed together for sale in the same shop. The idea seemed a fantastic one, and we looked at the clothes again with a firm determination not to be easily led away. No, we were right; the more we looked, the more we were convinced of the accuracy of our previous impression. There was the man's whole life written as legibly on those clothes, as if we had his autobiography engrossed on parchment before us.

The first was a patched and much-soiled skeleton suit; one of those straight blue cloth cases in which small boys used to be confined, before belts and tunics had come in, and old notions had gone out: an ingenious contrivance for displaying the full symmetry of a boy's figure, by fastening him into a very tight jacket, with an ornamental row of buttons over each shoulder, and then buttoning his trousers over it, so as to give his legs the appearance of being hooked on, just under the armpits. This was the boy's dress. It had belonged to a town boy, we could see; there was a shortness about the legs and arms of the suit; and a bagging at the knees, peculiar to the rising youth of London streets. A small day-school he had been at, evidently. If it had been a regular boys' school they wouldn't have let him play on the floor so much, and rub his knees so white. He had an indulgent mother too, and plenty of halfpence, as the numerous smears of some sticky substance about the pockets, and just below the chin, which even the salesman's skill could not succeed in disguising, sufficiently betokened. They were decent people, but not overburdened with riches, or he would not have so far out-grown the suit when he passed into those corduroys with the round jacket; in which he went to a boys' school, however, and learnt to write—and in ink of pretty tolerable blackness, too, if the place where he used to wipe his pen might be taken as evidence.

A black suit and the jacket changed into a diminutive coat. His father had died, and the mother had got the boy a message-lad's place in some office. A long-worn suit that one; rusty and threadbare before it was laid aside, but clean and free from soil to the last. Poor woman! We could imagine her assumed cheerfulness over the scanty meal, and the refusal of her own small portion, that her hungry boy might have enough. Her constant anxiety for his welfare, her pride in his growth mingled sometimes with the thought, almost too acute to bear, that as he grew to be a man his old affection might cool, old kindnesses fade from his mind, and old promises be forgotten—the sharp pain that even then a careless word or a cold look would give her—all crowded on our thoughts as vividly as if the very scene were passing before us.

These things happen every hour, and we all know it; and yet we felt as much sorrow when we saw, or fancied we saw—it makes no difference which—the change that began to take place now, as if we had just conceived the bare possibility of such a thing for the first time. The next suit, smart but slovenly; meant to be gay, and yet not half so decent as the threadbare apparel; redolent of the idle lounge, and the blackguard companions, told us, we thought, that the widow's comfort had rapidly faded away. We could imagine that coat—imagine! we could see it; we *had* seen it a hundred times—sauntering in company with three or four other coats of the same cut, about some place of profligate resort at night.

We dressed, from the same shop-window in an instant, half a dozen boys of from fifteen to twenty; and putting cigars into their mouths, and their hands into their pockets, watched them as they sauntered down the street, and lingered at the corner, with the obscene jest, and the oft-repeated oath. We never lost sight of them, till they had cocked their hats a little more on one side, and swaggered into the public-house; and then we entered the desolate home, where the mother sat late in the night, alone; we watched her, as she paced the room in feverish anxiety, and every now and then opened the door, looked wistfully into the dark and empty street, and again returned, to be again and again disappointed. We beheld the look of patience with which she bore the brutish threat, nay, even the drunken blow; and we heard the agony of tears that gushed from her very heart, as she sank upon her knees in her solitary and wretched apartment.

A long period had elapsed, and a greater change had taken place, by the time of casting off the suit that hung above. It was that of a stout, broad-shouldered, sturdy-chested man; and we knew at once, as anybody would, who glanced at that broad-skirted green coat, with the large metal buttons, that its wearer seldom walked forth without a dog at his heels, and some idle ruffian, the very counterpart of himself, at his side. The vices of the boy had grown with the man, and we fancied his home then—if such a place deserve the name.

We saw the bare and miserable room, destitute of furniture, crowded with his wife and children, pale, hungry, and emaciated; the man cursing their lamentations, staggering to the tap-room, from whence he had just returned, followed by his wife and a sickly infant, clamouring for bread; and heard the street-wrangle and noisy recrimination that his striking her occasioned. And then imagination led us to some metropolitan workhouse, situated in the midst of crowded streets and alleys, filled with noxious vapours, and ringing with boisterous cries, where an old and feeble woman, imploring pardon for her son, lay dying in a close dark room, with no child to clasp her hand, and no pure air from heaven to fan her brow. A stranger closed the eyes that settled into a cold unmeaning glare, and strange ears received the words that murmured from the white and half-closed lips.

A coarse round frock, with a worn cotton neckerchief, and other articles of clothing of the commonest description, completed the history. A prison, and the sentence—banishment or the gallows. What would the man have given then, to be once again the contented humble drudge of his boyish years; to have restored to life, but for a week, a day, an hour, a minute, only for so long a time as would enable him to say one word of passionate regret to, and hear one sound of heartfelt forgiveness from, the cold and ghastly form that lay rotting in the pauper's grave! The children wild in the streets, the mother a destitute widow; both deeply tainted with the deep disgrace of the husband and father's name, and impelled by sheer necessity, down the precipice that had led him to a lingering death, possibly of many years' duration, thousands of miles away. We had no clue to the end of the tale; but it was easy to guess its termination.

We took a step or two further on, and by way of restoring the naturally cheerful tone of our thoughts, began fitting visionary feet and legs into a cellar-board full of boots and shoes, with a speed and accuracy that would have astonished the most expert artist in leather, living. There was one pair of boots in particular—a jolly, good-tempered, hearty-looking, pair of tops, that excited our warmest regard; and we had got a fine, red-faced, jovial fellow of a market-gardener into them, before we had made their acquaintance half a minute. They were just the very thing for him. There were his huge fat legs bulging over the tops, and fitting them too tight to admit of his tucking in the loops he had pulled them on by; and his knee-cords with an interval of stocking; and his blue apron tucked up round his waist; and his red neckerchief and blue coat, and a white hat stuck on one side of his head; and there he stood with a broad grin on his great red face, whistling away, as if any other idea but that of being happy and comfortable had never entered his brain.

This was the very man after our own heart; we knew all about him; we had seen him coming up to Covent-garden in his green chaise-cart, with the fat tubby little horse, half a thousand times; and even while we cast an affectionate look upon his boots, at that instant, the form of a coquettish servant-maid suddenly sprung into a pair of Denmark satin shoes that stood beside them, and we at once recognised the very girl who accepted his offer of a ride, just on this side the Hammersmith suspension-bridge, the very last Tuesday morning we rode into town from Richmond.

A very smart female, in a showy bonnet, stepped into a pair of grey cloth boots, with black fringe and binding, that were studiously pointing out their toes on the other side of the top-boots, and seemed very anxious to engage his attention, but we didn't observe that our friend the market-gardener appeared at all captivated with these blandishments; for beyond giving a knowing wink when they first began, as if to imply that he quite understood their end and object, he took no further notice of them. His indifference, however, was amply recompensed by the excessive gallantry of a very old gentleman with a silver-headed stick, who tottered into a pair of large list shoes, that were standing in one corner of the board, and indulged in a variety of gestures expressive of his admiration of the lady in the cloth boots, to the immeasurable amusement of a young fellow we put into a pair of long-quartered pumps, who we thought would have split the coat that slid down to meet him, with laughing.

We had been looking on at this little pantomime with great satisfaction for some time, when, to our unspeakable astonishment, we perceived that the whole of the characters, including a numerous *corps de ballet* of boots and shoes in the back-ground, into which we had been hastily thrusting as many feet as we could press into the service, were arranging themselves in order for dancing; and some music striking up at the moment, to it they went without delay. It was perfectly delightful to witness the agility of the market-gardener. Out went the boots, first on one side, then on the other, then cutting, then shuffling, then setting to the Denmark satins, then advancing, then retreating, then going round, and then repeating the whole of the evolutions again, without appearing to suffer in the least from the violence of the exercise.

Nor were the Denmark satins a bit behindhand, for they jumped and bounded about, in all directions; and though they were neither so regular, nor so true to the time as the cloth boots, still, as they seemed to do it from the heart, and to enjoy it more, we candidly confess that we preferred their style of dancing to the other. But the old gentleman in the list shoes was the most amusing object in the whole party; for, besides his grotesque attempts to appear youthful, and amorous, which were sufficiently entertaining in themselves, the young fellow in the pumps managed so artfully that every time the old gentleman advanced to salute the lady in the cloth boots, he trod with his whole weight on the old fellow's toes, which made him roar with anguish, and rendered all the others like to die of laughing.

We were in the full enjoyment of these festivities when we heard a shrill, and by no means musical voice, exclaim, "Hope you'll know me agin, imperence!" and on looking intently forward to see from whence the sound came, we found that it proceeded, not from the young lady in the cloth boots, as we had at first been inclined to suppose, but from a bulky lady of elderly appearance who was seated in a chair at the head of the cellar-steps, apparently for the purpose of superintending the sale of the articles arranged there.

A barrel-organ, which had been in full force close behind us, ceased playing; the people we had been fitting into the shoes and boots took to flight at the interruption; and as we were conscious that in the depth of our meditations we might have been rudely staring at the old lady for half an hour without knowing it, we took to flight too, and were soon immersed in the deepest obscurity of the adjacent "Dials."

CHAPTER VII.

HACKNEY-COACH STANDS.

We maintain that hackney-coaches, properly so called, belong solely to the metropolis. We may be told, that there are hackney-coach stands in Edinburgh; and not to go quite so far for a contradiction to our position, we may be reminded that Liverpool, Manchester, "and other large towns" (as the Parliamentary phrase goes), have *their* hackney-coach stands. We readily concede to these places, the possession of certain vehicles, which may look almost as dirty, and even go almost as slowly, as London hackney-coaches: but that they have the slightest claim to compete with the metropolis, either in point of stands, drivers, or cattle, we indignantly deny.

Take a regular, ponderous, rickety, London hackney-coach of the old school, and let any man have the boldness to assert, if he can, that he ever beheld any object on the face of the earth which at all resembles it, unless, indeed, it were another hackney-coach of the same date. We have recently observed on certain stands, and we say it with deep regret, rather dapper green chariots, and coaches of polished yellow, with four wheels of the same colour as the coach, whereas it is perfectly notorious to every one who has studied the subject, that every wheel ought to be of a different colour, and a different size. These are innovations, and, like other mis-called improvements, awful signs of the restlessness of the public mind, and the little respect paid to our time-honoured institutions. Why should hackney-coaches be clean? Our ancestors found them dirty, and left them so. Why should we, with a feverish wish to "keep moving," desire to roll along at the rate of six miles an hour, while they were content to rumble over the stones at four? These are solemn considerations. Hackney-coaches are part and parcel of the law of the land; they were settled by the Legislature; plated and numbered by the wisdom of Parliament.

Then why have they been swamped by cabs and omnibuses? Or why should people be allowed to ride quickly for eightpence a mile, after Parliament had come to the solemn decision that they should pay a shilling a mile for riding slowly? We pause for a reply;—and, having no chance of getting one, begin a fresh paragraph.

Our acquaintance with hackney-coach stands is of long standing. We are a walking book of fares, feeling ourselves, half-bound, as it were, to be always in the right on contested points. We know all the regular watermen within three miles of Covent-garden by sight, and should be almost tempted to believe that all the hackney-coach horses in that district knew us by sight too, if one-half of them were not blind. We take great interest in hackney-coaches, but we seldom drive, having a knack of turning ourselves over when we attempt to do so. We are as great friends to horses, hackney-coach and otherwise, as the renowned Mr. Martin, of costermonger notoriety, and yet we never ride. We keep no horse, but a clothes-horse; enjoy no saddle so much as a saddle of mutton; and, following our own inclinations, have never followed the hounds. Leaving these fleeter means of getting over the ground, or of depositing oneself upon it, to those who like them, by hackney-coach stands we take our stand.

There is a hackney-coach stand under the very window at which we are writing; there is only one coach on it now, but it is a fair specimen of the class of vehicles to which we have alluded—a great, lumbering, square concern of a dingy yellow colour (like a bilious brunette), with very small glasses, but very large frames; the panels are ornamented with a faded coat of arms, in shape something like a dissected bat, the axletree is red, and the majority of the wheels are green. The box is partially covered by an old great-coat, with a multiplicity of capes, and some extraordinary-looking clothes; and the straw, with which the canvas cushion is stuffed, is sticking up in several places, as if in rivalry of the hay, which is peeping through the chinks in the boot. The horses, with drooping heads, and each with a mane and tail as scanty and straggling as those of a worn-out rocking-horse, are standing patiently on some damp straw, occasionally wincing, and rattling the harness; and now and then, one of them lifts his mouth to the ear of his companion, as if he were saying, in a whisper, that he should like to assassinate the coachman. The coachman himself is in the watering-house; and the waterman, with his hands forced into his pockets as far as they can possibly go, is dancing the "double shuffle," in front of the pump, to keep his feet warm.

The servant-girl, with the pink ribbons, at No. 5, opposite, suddenly opens the street-door, and four small children forthwith rush out, and scream "Coach!" with all their might and main. The waterman darts from the pump, seizes the horses by their respective bridles, and drags them, and the coach too, round to the house, shouting all the time for the coachman at the very top, or rather very bottom of his voice, for it is a deep bass growl. A response is heard from the tap-room; the coachman, in his wooden-soled shoes, makes the street echo again as he runs across it; and then there is such a struggling, and backing, and grating of the kennel, to get the coach-door opposite the house-door, that the children are in perfect ecstasies of delight. What a commotion! The old lady, who has been stopping there for the last month, is going back to the country. Out comes box after box, and one side of the vehicle is filled with luggage in no time; the children get into everybody's way, and the youngest, who has upset himself in his attempts to carry an umbrella, is borne off wounded and kicking. The youngsters disappear, and a short pause ensues, during which the old lady is, no doubt, kissing them all round in the back parlour. She appears at last, followed by her married daughter, all the children, and both the servants, who, with the joint assistance of the coachman and waterman, manage to get her safely into the coach. A cloak is handed in, and a little basket, which we could almost swear contains a small black bottle, and a paper of sandwiches. Up go the steps, bang goes the door, "Golden-cross, Charing-cross, Tom," says the waterman; "Good-bye, grandma," cry the children, off jingles the coach at the rate of three miles an hour, and the mamma and children retire into the house, with the exception of one little villain, who runs up the street at the top of his speed, pursued by the servant; not ill-pleased to have such an opportunity of displaying her attractions. She brings him back, and, after casting two or three gracious glances across the way, which are either intended for us or the potboy (we are not quite certain which), shuts the door, and the hackney-coach stand is again at a standstill.

We have been frequently amused with the intense delight with which "a servant of all work," who is sent for a coach, deposits herself inside; and the unspeakable gratification which boys, who have been despatched on a similar errand, appear to derive from mounting the box. But we never recollect to have been more amused with a hackney-coach party, than one we saw early the other morning in Tottenham-court-road. It was a wedding-party, and emerged from one of the inferior streets near Fitzroy-square. There were the bride, with a thin white dress, and a great red face; and the bridesmaid, a little, dumpy, good-humoured young woman, dressed, of course, in the same appropriate costume; and the bridegroom and his chosen friend, in blue coats, yellow waistcoats, white trousers, and Berlin gloves to match. They stopped at the corner of the street, and called a coach with an air of indescribable dignity. The moment they were in, the bridesmaid threw a red shawl, which she had, no doubt, brought on purpose, negligently over the number on the door, evidently to delude pedestrians into the belief that the hackney-coach was a private carriage; and away they went, perfectly satisfied that the imposition was successful, and quite unconscious that there was a great staring number stuck up behind, on a plate as large as a schoolboy's slate. A shilling a mile!—the ride was worth five, at least, to them.

What an interesting book a hackney-coach might produce, if it could carry as much in its head as it does in its body! The autobiography of a broken-down hackney-coach, would surely be as amusing as the autobiography of a broken-down hackneyed dramatist; and it might tell as much of its travels *with* the pole, as others have of their expeditions *to* it. How many stories might be related of the different people it had conveyed on matters of business or profit—pleasure or pain! And how many melancholy tales of the same people at different periods! The country-girl—the showy, over-dressed woman—the drunken prostitute! The raw apprentice—the dissipated spendthrift—the thief!

Talk of cabs! Cabs are all very well in cases of expedition, when it's a matter of neck or nothing, life or death, your temporary home or your long one. But, besides a cab's lacking that gravity of deportment which so peculiarly distinguishes a hackney-coach, let it never be forgotten that a cab is a thing of yesterday, and that he never was anything better. A hackney-cab has always been a hackney-cab, from his first entry into life; whereas a hackney-coach is a remnant of past gentility, a victim to fashion, a hanger-on of an old English family, wearing their arms, and, in days of yore, escorted by men wearing their livery, stripped of his finery, and thrown upon the world, like a once-smart footman when he is no longer sufficiently juvenile for his office, progressing lower and lower in the scale of four-wheeled degradation, until at last it comes to—*a stand!*

CHAPTER VIII.

DOCTORS' COMMONS.

WALKING, without any definite object through St. Paul's Churchyard, a little while ago, we happened to turn down a street entitled "Paul's-chain," and keeping straight forward for a few hundred yards, found ourself, as a natural consequence, in Doctors' Commons. Now Doctors' Commons being familiar by name to everybody, as the place where they grant marriage-licenses to love-sick couples, and divorces to unfaithful ones; register the wills of people who have any property to leave, and punish hasty gentlemen who call ladies by unpleasant names, we no sooner discovered that we were really within its precincts, than we felt a laudable desire to become better acquainted therewith; and as the first object of our curiosity was the Court, whose decrees can even unloose the bonds of matrimony, we procured a direction to it; and bent our steps thither without delay.

Crossing a quiet and shady court-yard, paved with stone, and frowned upon by old red brick houses, on the doors of which were painted the names of sundry learned civilians, we paused before a small, green-baized, brass-headed-nailed door, which yielding to our gentle push, at once admitted us into an old quaint-looking apartment, with sunken windows, and black carved wainscoting, at the upper end of which, seated on a raised platform, of semicircular shape, were about a dozen solemn-looking gentlemen, in crimson gowns and wigs.

At a more elevated desk in the centre, sat a very fat and red-faced gentleman, in tortoise-shell spectacles, whose dignified appearance announced the judge; and round a long green-baized table below, something like a billiard-table without the cushions and pockets, were a number of very self-important-looking personages, in stiff neckcloths, and black gowns with white fur collars, whom we at once set down as proctors. At the lower end of the billiard-table was an individual in an arm-chair, and a wig, whom we afterwards discovered to be the registrar; and seated behind a little desk, near the door, were a respectable-looking man in black, of about twenty stone weight or thereabouts, and a fat-faced, smirking, civil-looking body, in a black gown, black kid gloves, knee shorts, and silks, with a shirt-frill in his bosom, curls on his head, and a silver staff in his hand, whom we had no difficulty in recognising as the officer of the Court. The latter, indeed, speedily set our mind at rest upon this point, for, advancing to our elbow, and opening a conversation forthwith, he had communicated to us, in less than five minutes, that he was the apparitor, and the other the court-keeper; that this was the Arches Court, and therefore the counsel wore red gowns, and the proctors fur collars; and that when the other Courts sat there, they didn't wear red gowns or fur collars either; with many other scraps of intelligence equally interesting. Besides these two officers, there was a little thin old man, with long grizzly hair, crouched in a remote corner, whose duty, our communicative friend informed us, was to ring a large hand-bell when the Court opened in the morning, and who, for ought his appearance betokened to the contrary, might have been similarly employed for the last two centuries at least.

The red-faced gentleman in the tortoise-shell spectacles had got all the talk to himself just then, and very well he was doing it, too, only he spoke very fast, but that was habit; and rather thick, but that was good living. So we had plenty of time to look about us. There was one individual who amused us mightily. This was one of the bewigged gentlemen in the red robes, who was straddling before the fire in the centre of the Court, in the attitude of the brazen Colossus, to the complete exclusion of everybody else. He had gathered up his robe behind, in much the same manner as a slovenly woman would her petticoats on a very dirty day, in order that he might feel the full warmth of the fire. His wig was put on all awry, with the tail straggling about his neck, his scanty grey trousers and short black gaiters, made in the worst possible style, imparted an additional inelegant appearance to his uncouth person; and his limp, badly-starched shirt-collar almost obscured his eyes. We shall never be able to claim any credit as a physiognomist again, for, after a careful scrutiny of this gentleman's countenance, we had come to the conclusion that it bespoke nothing but conceit and silliness, when our friend with the silver staff whispered in our ear that he was no other than a doctor of civil law, and heaven knows what besides. So of course we were mistaken, and he must be a very talented man. He conceals it so well though—perhaps with the merciful view of not astonishing ordinary people too much—that you would suppose him to be one of the stupidest dogs alive.

The gentleman in the spectacles having concluded his judgment, and a few minutes having been allowed to elapse, to afford time for the buzz in the Court to subside, the registrar called on the next cause, which was "the office of the Judge promoted by Bumple against Sludberry." A general movement was visible in the Court, at this announcement, and the obliging functionary with silver staff whispered us that "there would be some fun now, for this was a brawling case."

We were not rendered much the wiser by this piece of information, till we found by the opening speech of the counsel for the promoter, that, under a half-obsolete statute of one of the Edwards, the court was empowered to visit with the penalty of excommunication, any person who should be proved guilty of the crime of "brawling," or "smiting," in any church, or vestry adjoining thereto; and it appeared, by some eight-and-twenty affidavits, which were duly referred to, that on a certain night, at a certain vestry-meeting, in a certain parish particularly set forth, Thomas Sludberry, the party appeared against in that suit, had made use of, and applied to Michael Bumple, the promoter, the words "You be blowed;" and that, on the said Michael Bumple and others remonstrating with the said Thomas Sludberry, on the impropriety of his conduct, the said Thomas Sludberry repeated the aforesaid expression, "You be blowed;" and furthermore desired and requested to know, whether the said Michael Bumple "wanted anything for himself;" adding, "that if the said Michael Bumple did want anything for himself, he, the said Thomas Sludberry, was the man to give it him;" at the same time making use of other heinous and sinful expressions, all of which, Bumple submitted, came within the intent and meaning of the Act; and therefore he, for the soul's health and chastening of Sludberry, prayed for sentence of excommunication against him accordingly.

Upon these facts a long argument was entered into, on both sides, to the great edification of a number of persons interested in the parochial squabbles, who crowded the court; and when some very long and grave speeches had been made *pro* and *con*, the red-faced gentleman in the tortoise-shell spectacles took a review of the case, which occupied half an hour more, and then pronounced upon Sludberry the awful sentence of excommunication for a fortnight, and payment of the costs of the suit. Upon this, Sludberry, who was a little, red-faced, sly-looking, ginger-beer seller, addressed the court, and said, if they'd be good enough to take off the costs, and excommunicate him for the term of his natural life instead, it would be much more convenient to him, for he never went to church at all. To this appeal the gentleman in the spectacles made no other reply than a look of virtuous indignation; and Sludberry and his friends retired. As the man with the silver staff informed us that the court was on the point of rising, we retired too—pondering, as we walked away, upon the beautiful spirit of these ancient ecclesiastical laws, the kind and neighbourly feelings they are calculated to awaken, and the strong attachment to religious institutions which they cannot fail to engender.

We were so lost in these meditations, that we had turned into the street, and run up against a door-post, before we recollected where we were walking. On looking upwards to see what house we had stumbled upon, the words "Prerogative-Office," written in large characters, met our eye; and as we were in a sight-seeing humour and the place was a public one, we walked in.

The room into which we walked, was a long, busy-looking place, partitioned off, on either side, into a variety of little boxes, in which a few clerks were engaged in copying or examining deeds. Down the centre of the room were several desks nearly breast high, at each of which, three or four people were standing, poring over large volumes. As we knew that they were searching for wills, they attracted our attention at once.

It was curious to contrast the lazy indifference of the attorneys' clerks who were making a search for some legal purpose, with the air of earnestness and interest which distinguished the strangers to the place, who were looking up the will of some deceased relative; the former pausing every now and then with an impatient yawn, or raising their heads to look at the people who passed up and down the room; the latter stooping over the book, and running down column after column of names in the deepest abstraction.

There was one little dirty-faced man in a blue apron, who after a whole morning's search, extending some fifty years back, had just found the will to which he wished to refer, which one of the officials was reading to him in a low hurried voice from a thick vellum book with large clasps. It was perfectly evident that the more the clerk read, the less the man with the blue apron understood about the matter. When the volume was first brought down, he took off his hat, smoothed down his hair, smiled with great self-satisfaction, and looked up in the reader's face with the air of a man who had made up his mind to recollect every word he heard. The first two or three lines were intelligible enough; but then the technicalities began, and the little man began to look rather dubious. Then came a whole string of complicated trusts, and he was regularly at sea. As the reader proceeded, it was quite apparent that it was a hopeless case, and the little man, with his mouth open and his eyes fixed upon his face, looked on with an expression of bewilderment and perplexity irresistibly ludicrous.

A little further on, a hard-featured old man with a deeply-wrinkled face, was intently perusing a lengthy will with the aid of a pair of horn spectacles: occasionally pausing from his task, and slily noting down some brief memorandum of the bequests contained in it. Every wrinkle about his toothless mouth, and sharp keen eyes, told of avarice and cunning. His clothes were nearly threadbare, but it was easy to see that he wore them from choice and not from necessity; all his looks and gestures down to the very small pinches of snuff which he every now and then took from a little tin canister, told of wealth, and penury, and avarice.

As he leisurely closed the register, put up his spectacles, and folded his scraps of paper in a large leathern pocket-book, we thought what a nice hard bargain he was driving with some poverty-stricken legatee, who, tired of waiting year after year, until some life-interest should fall in, was selling his chance, just as it began to grow most valuable, for a twelfth part of its worth. It was a good speculation—a very safe one. The old man stowed his pocket-book carefully in the breast of his great-coat, and hobbled away with a leer of triumph. That will had made him ten years younger at the lowest computation.

Having commenced our observations, we should certainly have extended them to another dozen of people at least, had not a sudden shutting up and putting away of the worm-eaten old books, warned us that the time for closing the office had arrived; and thus deprived us of a pleasure, and spared our readers an infliction.

We naturally fell into a train of reflection as we walked homewards, upon the curious old records of likings and dislikings; of jealousies and revenges; of affection defying the power of death, and hatred pursued beyond the grave, which these depositories contain; silent but striking tokens, some of them, of excellence of heart, and nobleness of soul; melancholy examples, others, of the worst passions of human nature. How many men as they lay speechless and helpless on the bed of death, would have given worlds but for the strength and power to blot out the silent evidence of animosity and bitterness, which now stands registered against them in Doctors' Commons!

CHAPTER IX.

LONDON RECREATIONS.

THE wish of persons in the humbler classes of life, to ape the manners and customs of those whom fortune has placed above them, is often the subject of remark, and not unfrequently of complaint. The inclination may, and no doubt does, exist to a great extent, among the small gentility—the would-be aristocrats—of the middle classes. Tradesmen and clerks, with fashionable novel-reading families, and circulating-library-subscribing daughters, get up small assemblies in humble imitation of Almack's, and promenade the dingy "large room" of some second-rate hotel with as much complacency as the enviable few who are privileged to exhibit their magnificence in that exclusive haunt of fashion and foolery. Aspiring young ladies, who read flaming accounts of some "fancy fair in high life," suddenly grow desperately charitable; visions of admiration and matrimony float before their eyes; some wonderfully meritorious institution, which, by the strangest accident in the world, has never been heard of before, is discovered to be in a languishing condition: Thomson's great room, or Johnson's nursery-ground, is forthwith engaged, and the aforesaid young ladies, from mere charity, exhibit themselves for three days, from twelve to four, for the small charge of one shilling per head! With the exception of these classes of society, however, and a few weak and insignificant persons, we do not think the attempt at imitation to which we have alluded, prevails in any great degree. The different character of the recreations of different classes, has often afforded us amusement; and we have chosen it for the subject of our present sketch, in the hope that it may possess some amusement for our readers.

If the regular City man, who leaves Lloyd's at five o'clock, and drives home to Hackney, Clapton, Stamford-hill, or elsewhere, can be said to have any daily recreation beyond his dinner, it is his garden. He never does anything to it with his own hands; but he takes great pride in it notwithstanding; and if you are desirous of paying your addresses to the youngest daughter, be sure to be in raptures with every flower and shrub it contains. If your poverty of expression compel you to make any distinction between the two, we would certainly recommend your bestowing more admiration on his garden than his wine. He always takes a walk round it, before he starts for town in the morning, and is particularly anxious that the fish-pond should be kept specially neat. If you call on him on Sunday in summer-time, about an hour before dinner, you will find him sitting in an arm-chair, on the lawn behind the house, with a straw hat on, reading a Sunday paper. A short distance from him you will most likely observe a handsome paroquet in a large brass-wire cage; ten to one but the two eldest girls are loitering in one of the side walks accompanied by a couple of young gentlemen, who are holding parasols over them—of course only to keep the sun off—while the younger children, with the under nursery-maid, are strolling listlessly about, in the shade. Beyond these occasions, his delight in his garden appears to arise more from the consciousness of possession than actual enjoyment of it. When he drives you down to dinner on a week-day, he is rather fatigued with the occupations of the morning, and tolerably cross into the bargain; but when the cloth is removed, and he has drank three or four glasses of his favourite port, he orders the French windows of his dining-room (which of course look into the garden) to be opened, and throwing a silk handkerchief over his head, and leaning back in his arm-chair, descants at considerable length upon its beauty, and the cost of maintaining it. This is to impress you—who are a young friend of the family—with a due sense of the excellence of the garden, and the wealth of its owner; and when he has exhausted the subject, he goes to sleep.

There is another and a very different class of men, whose recreation is their garden. An individual of this class, resides some short distance from town—say in the Hampstead-road, or the Kilburn-road, or any other road where the houses are small and neat, and have little slips of back garden. He and his wife—who is as clean and compact a little body as himself—have occupied the same house ever since he retired from business twenty years ago. They have no family. They once had a son, who died at about five years old. The child's portrait hangs over the mantelpiece in the best sitting-room, and a little cart he used to draw about, is carefully preserved as a relic.

In fine weather the old gentleman is almost constantly in the garden; and when it is too wet to go into it, he will look out of the window at it, by the hour together. He has always something to do there, and you will see him digging, and sweeping, and cutting, and planting, with manifest delight. In spring time, there is no end to the sowing of seeds, and sticking little bits of wood over them, with labels, which look like epitaphs to their memory; and in the evening, when the sun has gone down, the perseverance with which he lugs a great watering-pot about is perfectly astonishing. The only other recreation he has, is the newspaper, which he peruses every day, from beginning to end, generally reading the most interesting pieces of intelligence to his wife, during breakfast. The old lady is very fond of flowers, as the hyacinth-glasses in the parlour-window, and geranium-pots in the little front court, testify. She takes great pride in the garden too: and when one of the four fruit-trees produces rather a larger gooseberry than usual, it is carefully preserved under a wine-glass on the sideboard, for the edification of visitors, who are duly informed that Mr. So-and-so planted the tree which produced it, with his own hands. On a summer's evening, when the large watering-pot has been filled and emptied some fourteen times, and the old couple have quite exhausted themselves by trotting about, you will see them sitting happily together in the little summer-house, enjoying the calm and peace of the twilight, and watching the shadows as they fall upon the garden, and gradually growing thicker and more sombre, obscure the tints of their gayest flowers—no bad emblem of the years that have silently rolled over their heads, deadening in their course the brightest hues of early hopes and feelings which have long since faded away. These are their only recreations, and they require no more. They have within themselves, the materials of comfort and content; and the only anxiety of each, is to die before the other.

This is no ideal sketch. There *used* to be many old people of this description; their numbers may have diminished, and may decrease still more. Whether the course female education has taken of late days—whether the pursuit of giddy frivolities, and empty nothings, has tended to unfit women for that quiet domestic life, in which they show far more beautifully than in the most crowded assembly, is a question we should feel little gratification in discussing: we hope not.

Let us turn now, to another portion of the London population, whose recreations present about as strong a contrast as can well be conceived—we mean the Sunday pleasurers; and let us beg our readers to imagine themselves stationed by our side in some well-known rural "Tea-gardens."

The heat is intense this afternoon, and the people, of whom there are additional parties arriving every moment, look as warm as the tables which have been recently painted, and have the appearance of being red-hot. What a dust and noise! Men and women—boys and girls—sweethearts and married people—babies in arms, and children in chaises—pipes and shrimps—cigars and periwinkles—tea and tobacco. Gentlemen, in alarming waistcoats, and steel watch-guards, promenading about, three abreast, with surprising dignity (or as the gentleman in the next box facetiously observes, "cutting it uncommon fat!")—ladies, with great, long, white pocket-handkerchiefs like small table-cloths, in their hands, chasing one another on the grass in the most playful and interesting manner, with the view of attracting the attention of the aforesaid gentlemen—husbands in perspective ordering bottles of ginger-beer for the objects of their affections, with a lavish disregard of expense; and the said objects washing down huge quantities of "shrimps" and "winkles," with an equal disregard of their own bodily health and subsequent comfort—boys, with great silk hats just balanced on the top of their heads, smoking cigars, and trying to look as if they liked them—gentlemen in pink shirts and blue waistcoats, occasionally upsetting either themselves, or somebody else, with their own canes.

Some of the finery of these people provokes a smile, but they are all clean, and happy, and disposed to be good-natured and sociable. Those two motherly-looking women in the smart pelisses, who are chatting so confidentially, inserting a "ma'am" at every fourth word, scraped an acquaintance about a quarter of an hour ago: it originated in admiration of the little boy who belongs to one of them—that diminutive specimen of mortality in the three-cornered pink satin hat with black feathers. The two men in the blue coats and drab trousers, who are walking up and down, smoking their pipes, are their husbands. The party in the opposite box are a pretty fair specimen of the generality of the visitors. These are the father and mother, and old grandmother: a young man and woman, and an individual addressed by the euphonious title of "Uncle Bill," who is evidently the wit of the party. They have some half-dozen children with them, but it is scarcely necessary to notice the fact, for that is a matter of course here. Every woman in "the gardens," who has been married for any length of time, must have had twins on two or three occasions; it is impossible to account for the extent of juvenile population in any other way.

Observe the inexpressible delight of the old grandmother, at Uncle Bill's splendid joke of "tea for four: bread-and-butter for forty;" and the loud explosion of mirth which follows his wafering a paper "pigtail" on the waiter's collar. The young man is evidently "keeping company" with Uncle Bill's niece: and Uncle Bill's hints—such as "Don't forget me at the dinner, you know," "I shall look out for the cake, Sally," "I'll be godfather to your first—wager it's a boy," and so forth, are equally embarrassing to the young people, and delightful to the elder ones. As to the old grandmother, she is in perfect ecstasies, and does nothing but laugh herself into fits of coughing, until they have finished the "gin-and-water warm with," of which Uncle Bill ordered "glasses round" after tea, "just to keep the night air out, and do it up comfortable and riglar arter sitch an as-tonishing hot day!"

It is getting dark, and the people begin to move. The field leading to town is quite full of them; the little hand-chaises are dragged wearily along, the children are tired, and amuse themselves and the company generally by crying, or resort to the much more pleasant expedient of going to sleep—the mothers begin to wish they were at home again—sweethearts grow more sentimental than ever, as the time for parting arrives—the gardens look mournful enough, by the light of the two lanterns which hang against the trees for the convenience of smokers—and the waiters who have been running about incessantly for the last six hours, think they feel a little tired, as they count their glasses and their gains.

CHAPTER X.

THE RIVER.

"ARE you fond of the water?" is a question very frequently asked, in hot summer weather, by amphibious-looking young men. "Very," is the general reply, "An't you?"—"Hardly ever off it," is the response, accompanied by sundry adjectives, expressive of the speaker's heartfelt admiration of that element. Now, with all respect for the opinion of society in general, and cutter clubs in particular, we humbly suggest that some of the most painful reminiscences in the mind of every individual who has occasionally disported himself on the Thames, must be connected with his aquatic recreations. Who ever heard of a successful water-party?—or to put the question in a still more intelligible form, who ever saw one? We have been on water excursions out of number, but we solemnly declare that we cannot call to mind one single occasion of the kind, which was not marked by more miseries than any one would suppose could be reasonably crowded into the space of some eight or nine hours. Something has always gone wrong. Either the cork of the salad-dressing has come out, or the most anxiously expected member of the party has not come out, or the most disagreeable man in company would come out, or a child or two have fallen into the water, or the gentleman who undertook to steer has endangered everybody's life all the way, or the gentlemen who volunteered to row have been "out of practice," and performed very alarming evolutions, putting their oars down into the water and not being able to get them up again, or taking terrific pulls without putting them in at all; in either case, pitching over on the backs of their heads with startling violence, and exhibiting the soles of their pumps to the "sitters" in the boat, in a very humiliating manner.

We grant that the banks of the Thames are very beautiful at Richmond and Twickenham, and other distant havens, often sought though seldom reached; but from the "Red-us" back to Blackfriars-bridge, the scene is wonderfully changed. The Penitentiary is a noble building, no doubt, and the sportive youths who "go in" at that particular part of the river, on a summer's evening, may be all very well in perspective; but when you are obliged to keep in shore coming home, and the young ladies will colour up, and look perseveringly the other way, while the married dittoes cough slightly, and stare very hard at the water, you feel awkward—especially if you happen to have been attempting the most distant approach to sentimentality, for an hour or two previously.

Although experience and suffering have produced in our minds the result we have just stated, we are by no means blind to a proper sense of the fun which a looker on may extract from the amateurs of boating What can be more amusing than Searle's yard on a fine Sunday morning? It's a Richmond tide, and some dozen boats are preparing for the reception of the parties who have engaged them. Two or three fellows in great rough trousers and Guernsey shirts, are getting them ready by easy stages; now coming down the yard with a pair of sculls and a cushion—then having a chat with the "jack," who, like all his tribe, seems to be wholly incapable of doing anything but lounging about—then going back again, and returning with a rudder-line and a stretcher—then solacing themselves with another chat—and then wondering, with their hands in their capacious pockets, "where them gentlemen's got to as ordered the six." One of these, the head man, with the legs of his trousers carefully tucked up at the bottom, to admit the water, we presume—for it is an element in which he is infinitely more at home than on land—is quite a character, and shares with the defunct oyster-swallower the celebrated name of "Dando." Watch him, as taking a few minutes' respite from his toils, he negligently seats himself on the edge of a boat, and fans his broad bushy chest with a cap scarcely half so furry. Look at his magnificent, though reddish whiskers, and mark the somewhat native humour with which he "chaffs" the boys and 'prentices, or cunningly gammons the gen'lm'n into the gift of a glass of gin, of which we verily believe he swallows in one day as much as any six ordinary men, without ever being one atom the worse for it.

But the party arrives, and Dando, relieved from his state of uncertainty, starts up into activity. They approach in full aquatic costume, with round blue jackets, striped shirts, and caps of all sizes and patterns, from the velvet skull-cap of French manufacture, to the easy head-dress familiar to the students of the old spelling-books, as having, on the authority of the portrait, formed part of the costume of the Reverend Mr. Dilworth.

This is the most amusing time to observe a regular Sunday water-party. There has evidently been up to this period no inconsiderable degree of boasting on everybody's part relative to his knowledge of navigation; the sight of the water rapidly cools their courage, and the air of self-denial with which each of them insists on somebody else's taking an oar, is perfectly delightful. At length, after a great deal of changing and fidgeting, consequent upon the election of a stroke-oar: the inability of one gentleman to pull on this side, of another to pull on that, and of a third to pull at all, the boat's crew are seated. "Shove her off!" cries the cockswain, who looks as easy and comfortable as if he were steering in the Bay of Biscay. The order is obeyed; the boat is immediately turned completely round, and proceeds towards Westminster-bridge, amidst such a splashing and struggling as never was seen before, except when the Royal George went down. "Back wa'ater, sir," shouts Dando, "Back wa'ater, you sir, aft;" upon which everybody thinking he must be the individual referred to, they all back water, and back comes the boat, stern first, to the spot whence it started. "Back water, you sir, aft; pull round, you sir, for'ad, can't you?" shouts Dando, in a frenzy of excitement. "Pull round, Tom, can't you?" re-echoes one of the party. "Tom an't for'ad," replies another. "Yes, he is," cries a third; and the unfortunate young man, at the imminent risk of breaking a blood-vessel, pulls and pulls, until the head of the boat fairly lies in the direction of Vauxhall-bridge. "That's right—now pull all on you!" shouts Dando again, adding, in an under tone, to somebody by him, "Blowed if hever I see sich a set of muffs!" and away jogs the boat in a zigzag direction, every one of the six oars dipping into the water at a different time; and the yard is once more clear, until the arrival of the next party.

A well-contested rowing-match on the Thames, is a very lively and interesting scene. The water is studded with boats of all sorts, kinds, and descriptions; places in the coal-barges at the different wharfs are let to crowds of spectators, beer and tobacco flow freely about; men, women, and children wait for the start in breathless expectation; cutters of six and eight oars glide gently up and down, waiting to accompany their *protégés* during the race; bands of music add to the animation, if not to the harmony of the scene; groups of watermen are assembled at the different stairs, discussing the merits of the respective candidates; and the prize wherry, which is rowed slowly about by a pair of sculls, is an object of general interest.

Two o'clock strikes, and everybody looks anxiously in the direction of the bridge through which the candidates for the prize will come—half-past two, and the general attention which has been preserved so long begins to flag, when suddenly a gun is heard, and a noise of distant hurra'ing along each bank of the river—every head is bent forward—the noise draws nearer and nearer—the boats which have been waiting at the bridge start briskly up the river, and a well-manned galley shoots through the arch, the sitters cheering on the boats behind them, which are not yet visible.

"Here they are," is the general cry—and through darts the first boat, the men in her, stripped to the skin, and exerting every muscle to preserve the advantage they have gained—four other boats follow close astern; there are not two boats' length between them—the shouting is tremendous, and the interest intense. "Go on, Pink"—"Give it her, Red"—"Sulliwin for ever"—"Bravo! George"—"Now, Tom, now—now—now—why don't your partner stretch out?"—"Two pots to a pint on Yellow," &c., &c. Every little public-house fires its gun, and hoists its flag; and the men who win the heat, come in, amidst a splashing and shouting, and banging and confusion, which no one can imagine who has not witnessed it, and of which any description would convey a very faint idea.

One of the most amusing places we know, is the steam-wharf of the London Bridge, or St. Katharine's Dock Company, on a Saturday morning in summer, when the Gravesend and Margate steamers are usually crowded to excess; and as we have just taken a glance at the river above bridge, we hope our readers will not object to accompany us on board a Gravesend packet.

Coaches are every moment setting down at the entrance to the wharf, and the stare of bewildered astonishment with which the "fares" resign themselves and their luggage into the hands of the porters, who seize all the packages at once as a matter of course, and run away with them, heaven knows where, is laughable in the extreme. A Margate boat lies alongside the wharf, the Gravesend boat (which starts first) lies alongside that again; and as a temporary communication is formed between the two, by means of a plank and hand-rail, the natural confusion of the scene is by no means diminished.

"Gravesend?" inquires a stout father of a stout family, who follow him, under the guidance of their mother, and a servant, at the no small risk of two or three of them being left behind in the confusion. "Gravesend?"

"Pass on, if you please, sir," replies the attendant—"other boat, sir."

Hereupon the stout father, being rather mystified, and the stout mother rather distracted by maternal anxiety, the whole party deposit themselves in the Margate boat, and after having congratulated himself on having secured very comfortable seats, the stout father sallies to the chimney to look for his luggage, which he has a faint recollection of having given some man, something, to take somewhere. No luggage, however, bearing the most remote resemblance to his own, in shape or form, is to be discovered; on which the stout father calls very loudly for an officer, to whom he states the case, in the presence of another father of another family—a little thin man—who entirely concurs with him (the stout father) in thinking that it's high time something was done with these steam companies, and that as the Corporation Bill failed to do it, something else must; for really people's property is not to be sacrificed in this way; and that if the luggage isn't restored without delay, he will take care it shall be put in the papers, for the public is not to be the victim of these great monopolies. To this, the officer, in his turn, replies, that that company, ever since it has been St. Kat'rine's Dock Company, has protected life and property; that if it had been the London Bridge Wharf Company, indeed, he shouldn't have wondered, seeing that the morality of that company (they being the opposition) can't be answered for, by no one; but as it is, he's convinced there must be some mistake, and he wouldn't mind making a solemn oath afore a magistrate that the gentleman'll find his luggage afore he gets to Margate.

Here the stout father, thinking he is making a capital point, replies, that as it happens, he is not going to Margate at all, and that "Passenger to Gravesend" was on the luggage, in letters of full two inches long; on which the officer rapidly explains the mistake, and the stout mother, and the stout children, and the servant, are hurried with all possible despatch on board the Gravesend boat, which they reached just in time to discover that their luggage is there, and that their comfortable seats are not. Then the bell, which is the signal for the Gravesend boat starting, begins to ring most furiously: and people keep time to the bell, by running in and out of our boat at a double-quick pace. The bell stops; the boat starts: people who have been taking leave of their friends on board, are carried away against their will; and people who have been taking leave of their friends on shore, find that they have performed a very needless ceremony, in consequence of their not being carried away at all. The regular passengers, who have season tickets, go below to breakfast; people who have purchased morning papers, compose themselves to read them; and people who have not been down the river before, think that both the shipping and the water, look a great deal better at a distance.

When we get down about as far as Blackwall, and begin to move at a quicker rate, the spirits of the passengers appear to rise in proportion. Old women who have brought large wicker hand-baskets with them, set seriously to work at the demolition of heavy sandwiches, and pass round a wine-glass, which is frequently replenished from a flat bottle like a stomach-warmer, with considerable glee: handing it first to the gentleman in the foraging-cap, who plays the harp—partly as an expression of satisfaction with his previous exertions, and partly to induce him to play "Dumbledumb-deary," for "Alick" to dance to; which being done, Alick, who is a damp earthy child in red worsted socks, takes certain small jumps upon the deck, to the unspeakable satisfaction of his family circle. Girls who have brought the first volume of some new novel in their reticule, become extremely plaintive, and expatiate to Mr. Brown, or young Mr. O'Brien, who has been looking over them, on the blueness of the sky, and brightness of the water; on which Mr. Brown or Mr. O'Brien, as the case may be, remarks in a low voice that he has been quite insensible of late to the beauties of nature—that his whole thoughts and wishes have centred in one object alone—whereupon the young lady looks up, and failing in her attempt to appear unconscious, looks down again; and turns over the next leaf with great difficulty, in order to afford opportunity for a lengthened pressure of the hand.

Telescopes, sandwiches, and glasses of brandy-and-water cold without, begin to be in great requisition; and bashful men who have been looking down the hatchway at the engine, find, to their great relief, a subject on which they can converse with one another—and a copious one too—Steam.

"Wonderful thing steam, sir." "Ah! (a deep-drawn sigh) it is indeed, sir." "Great power, sir." "Immense—immense!" "Great deal done by steam, sir," "Ah! (another sigh at the immensity of the subject, and a knowing shake of the head) you may say that, sir." "Still in its infancy, they say, sir." Novel remarks of this kind, are generally the commencement of a conversation which is prolonged until the conclusion of the trip, and, perhaps, lays the foundation of a speaking acquaintance between half-a-dozen gentlemen, who, having their families at Gravesend, take season-tickets for the boat, and dine on board regularly every afternoon.

CHAPTER XI.

ASTLEY'S.

We never see any very large, staring, black Roman capitals, in a book, or shop-window, or placarded on a wall, without their immediately recalling to our mind an indistinct and confused recollection of the time when we were first initiated in the mysteries of the alphabet. We almost fancy we see the pin's point following the letter, to impress its form more strongly on our bewildered imagination; and wince involuntarily, as we remember the hard knuckles with which the reverend old lady who instilled into our mind the first principles of education for ninepence per week, or ten and sixpence per quarter, was wont to poke our juvenile head occasionally, by way of adjusting the confusion of ideas in which we were generally involved. The same kind of feeling pursues us in many other instances, but there is no place which recalls so strongly our recollections of childhood as Astley's. It was not a "Royal Amphitheatre" in those days, nor had Ducrow arisen to shed the light of classic taste and portable gas over the sawdust of the circus; but the whole character of the place was the same, the pieces were the same, the clown's jokes were the same, the riding-masters were equally grand, the comic performers equally witty, the tragedians equally hoarse, and the "highly-trained chargers" equally spirited. Astley's has altered for the better—we have changed for the worse. Our histrionic taste is gone, and with shame we confess, that we are far more delighted and amused with the audience, than with the pageantry we once so highly appreciated.

We like to watch a regular Astley's party in the Easter or Midsummer holidays —pa and ma, and nine or ten children, varying from five foot six to two foot eleven: from fourteen years of age to four. We had just taken our seat in one of the boxes, in the centre of the house, the other night, when the next was occupied by just such a party as we should have attempted to describe, had we depicted our *beau idéal* of a group of Astley's visitors.

First of all, there came three little boys and a little girl, who, in pursuance of pa's directions, issued in a very audible voice from the box-door, occupied the front row; then two more little girls were ushered in by a young lady, evidently the governess. Then came three more little boys, dressed like the first, in blue jackets and trousers, with lay-down shirt-collars: then a child in a braided frock and high state of astonishment, with very large round eyes, opened to their utmost width, was lifted over the seats—a process which occasioned a considerable display of little pink legs—then came ma and pa, and then the eldest son, a boy of fourteen years old, who was evidently trying to look as if he did not belong to the family.

The first five minutes were occupied in taking the shawls off the little girls, and adjusting the bows which ornamented their hair; then it was providentially discovered that one of the little boys was seated behind a pillar and could not see, so the governess was stuck behind the pillar, and the boy lifted into her place. Then pa drilled the boys, and directed the stowing away of their pocket-handkerchiefs, and ma having first nodded and winked to the governess to pull the girls' frocks a little more off their shoulders, stood up to review the little troop—an inspection which appeared to terminate much to her own satisfaction, for she looked with a complacent air at pa, who was standing up at the further end of the seat. Pa returned the glance, and blew his nose very emphatically; and the poor governess peeped out from behind the pillar, and timidly tried to catch ma's eye, with a look expressive of her high admiration of the whole family. Then two of the little boys who had been discussing the point whether Astley's was more than twice as large as Drury Lane, agreed to refer it to "George" for his decision; at which "George," who was no other than the young gentleman before noticed, waxed indignant, and remonstrated in no very gentle terms on the gross impropriety of having his name repeated in so loud a voice at a public place, on which all the children laughed very heartily, and one of the little boys wound up by expressing his opinion, that "George began to think himself quite a man now," whereupon both pa and ma laughed too; and George (who carried a dress cane and was cultivating whiskers) muttered that "William always was encouraged in his impertinence;" and assumed a look of profound contempt, which lasted the whole evening.

The play began, and the interest of the little boys knew no bounds. Pa was clearly interested too, although he very unsuccessfully endeavoured to look as if he wasn't. As for ma, she was perfectly overcome by the drollery of the principal comedian, and laughed till every one of the immense bows on her ample cap trembled, at which the governess peeped out from behind the pillar again, and whenever she could catch ma's eye, put her handkerchief to her mouth, and appeared, as in duty bound, to be in convulsions of laughter also. Then when the man in the splendid armour vowed to rescue the lady or perish in the attempt, the little boys applauded vehemently, especially one little fellow who was apparently on a visit to the family, and had been carrying on a child's flirtation, the whole evening, with a small coquette of twelve years old, who looked like a model of her mamma on a reduced scale; and who, in common with the other little girls (who generally speaking have even more coquettishness about them than much older ones), looked very properly shocked, when the knight's squire kissed the princess's confidential chambermaid.

When the scenes in the circle commenced, the children were more delighted than ever; and the wish to see what was going forward, completely conquering pa's dignity, he stood up in the box, and applauded as loudly as any of them. Between each feat of horsemanship, the governess leant across to ma, and retailed the clever remarks of the children on that which had preceded: and ma, in the openness of her heart, offered the governess an acidulated drop, and the governess, gratified to be taken notice of, retired behind her pillar again with a brighter countenance: and the whole party seemed quite happy, except the exquisite in the back of the box, who, being too grand to take any interest in the children, and too insignificant to be taken notice of by anybody else, occupied himself, from time to time, in rubbing the place where the whiskers ought to be, and was completely alone in his glory.

We defy any one who has been to Astley's two or three times, and is consequently capable of appreciating the perseverance with which precisely the same jokes are repeated night after night, and season after season, not to be amused with one part of the performances at least—we mean the scenes in the circle. For ourself, we know that when the hoop, composed of jets of gas, is let down, the curtain drawn up for the convenience of the half-price on their ejectment from the ring, the orange-peel cleared away, and the sawdust shaken, with mathematical precision, into a complete circle, we feel as much enlivened as the youngest child present; and actually join in the laugh which follows the clown's shrill shout of "Here we are!" just for old acquaintance' sake. Nor can we quite divest ourself of our old feeling of reverence for the riding-master, who follows the clown with a long whip in his hand, and bows to the audience with graceful dignity. He is none of your second-rate riding masters in nankeen dressing-gowns, with brown frogs, but the regular gentleman-attendant on the principal riders, who always wears a military uniform with a table-cloth inside the breast of the coat, in which costume he forcibly reminds one of a fowl trussed for roasting. He is—but why should we attempt to describe that of which no description can convey an adequate idea? Everybody knows the man, and everybody remembers his polished boots, his graceful demeanour, stiff, as some misjudging persons have in their jealousy considered it, and the splendid head of black hair, parted high on the forehead, to impart to the countenance an appearance of deep thought and poetic melancholy. His soft and pleasing voice, too, is in perfect unison with his noble bearing, as he humours the clown by indulging in a little badinage; and the striking recollection of his own dignity, with which he exclaims, "Now, sir, if you please, inquire for Miss Woolford, sir," can never be forgotten. The graceful air, too, with which he introduces Miss Woolford into the arena, and, after assisting her to the saddle, follows her fairy courser round the circle, can never fail to create a deep impression in the bosom of every female servant present.

When Miss Woolford, and the horse, and the orchestra, all stop together to take breath, he urbanely takes part in some such dialogue as the following (commenced by the clown): "I say, sir!"—"Well, sir?" (it's always conducted in the politest manner.)—"Did you ever happen to hear I was in the army, sir?"—"No, sir."—"Oh, yes, sir—I can go through my exercise, sir."—"Indeed, sir!"—"Shall I do it now, sir?"—"If you please, sir; come, sir—make haste" (a cut with the long whip, and "Ha' done now—I don't like it," from the clown). Here the clown throws himself on the ground, and goes through a variety of gymnastic convulsions, doubling himself up, and untying himself again, and making himself look very like a man in the most hopeless extreme of human agony, to the vociferous delight of the gallery, until he is interrupted by a second cut from the long whip, and a request to see "what Miss Woolford 's stopping for?" On which, to the inexpressible mirth of the gallery, he exclaims, "Now, Miss Woolford, what can I come for to go, for to fetch, for to bring, for to carry, for to do, for you, ma'am?" On the lady's announcing with a sweet smile that she wants the two flags, they are with sundry grimaces, procured and handed up; the clown facetiously observing after the performance of the latter ceremony—"He, he, oh! I say, sir, Miss Woolford knows me; she smiled at me." Another cut from the whip, a burst from the orchestra, a start from the horse, and round goes Miss Woolford again on her graceful performance, to the delight of every member of the audience, young or old. The next pause affords an opportunity for similar witticisms, the only additional fun being that of the clown making ludicrous grimaces at the riding-master every time his back is turned; and finally quitting the circle by jumping over his head, having previously directed his attention another way.

Did any of our readers ever notice the class of people, who hang about the stage-doors of our minor theatres in the daytime. You will rarely pass one of these entrances without seeing a group of three or four men conversing on the pavement, with an indescribable public-house-parlour swagger, and a kind of conscious air, peculiar to people of this description. They always seem to think they are exhibiting; the lamps are ever before them. That young fellow in the faded brown coat, and very full light green trousers, pulls down the wristbands of his check shirt, as ostentatiously as if it were of the finest linen, and cocks the white hat of the summer-before-last as knowingly over his right eye, as if it were a purchase of yesterday. Look at the dirty white Berlin gloves, and the cheap silk-handkerchief stuck in the bosom of his threadbare coat. Is it possible to see him for an instant, and not come to the conclusion that he is the walking gentleman who wears a blue surtout, clean collar, and white trousers, for half an hour, and then shrinks into his worn-out scanty clothes; who has to boast night after night of his splendid fortune, with the painful consciousness of a pound a-week and his boots to find; to talk of his father's mansion in the country, with a dreary recollection of his own two-pair back, in the New Cut; and to be envied and flattered as the favoured lover of a rich heiress, remembering all the while that the ex-dancer at home is in the family way, and out of an engagement?

Next to him, perhaps, you will see a thin pale man, with a very long face, in a suit of shining black, thoughtfully knocking that part of his boot which once had a heel, with an ash stick. He is the man who does the heavy business, such as prosy fathers, virtuous servants, curates, landlords, and so forth.

By the way, talking of fathers, we should very much like to see some piece in which all the dramatis personæ were orphans. Fathers are invariably great nuisances on the stage, and always have to give the hero or heroine a long explanation of what was done before the curtain rose, usually commencing with "It is now nineteen years, my dear child, since your blessed mother (here the old villain's voice falters) confided you to my charge. You were then an infant," &c. &c. Or else they have to discover, all of a sudden, that somebody whom they have been in constant communication with, during three long acts, without the slightest suspicion, is their own child: in which case they exclaim, "Ah! what do I see? This bracelet! That smile! These documents! Those eyes! Can I believe my senses?—It must be!—Yes—it is, it is my child!"—"My father!" exclaims the child; and they fall into each other's arms, and look over each other's shoulders, and the audience give three rounds of applause.

To return from this digression, we were about to say, that these are the sort of people whom you see talking, and attitudinising, outside the stage-doors of our minor theatres. At Astley's they are always more numerous than at any other place. There is generally a groom or two, sitting on the window-sill, and two or three dirty shabby-genteel men in checked neckerchiefs, and sallow linen, lounging about, and carrying, perhaps, under one arm, a pair of stage shoes badly wrapped up in a piece of old newspaper. Some years ago we used to stand looking, open-mouthed, at these men, with a feeling of mysterious curiosity, the very recollection of which provokes a smile at the moment we are writing. We could not believe that the beings of light and elegance, in milk-white tunics, salmon-coloured legs, and blue scarfs, who flitted on sleek cream-coloured horses before our eyes at night, with all the aid of lights, music, and artificial flowers, could be the pale, dissipated-looking creatures we beheld by day.

We can hardly believe it now. Of the lower class of actors we have seen something, and it requires no great exercise of imagination to identify the walking gentleman with the "dirty swell," the comic singer with the public-house chairman, or the leading tragedian with drunkenness and distress; but these other men are mysterious beings, never seen out of the ring, never beheld but in the costume of gods and sylphs. With the exception of Ducrow, who can scarcely be classed among them, who ever knew a rider at Astley's, or saw him but on horseback? Can our friend in the military uniform, ever appear in threadbare attire, or descend to the comparatively un-wadded costume of every-day life? Impossible! We cannot—we will not—believe it.

CHAPTER XII.

GREENWICH FAIR.

If the Parks be "the lungs of London," we wonder what Greenwich Fair is—a periodical breaking out, we suppose, a sort of spring-rash: a three days' fever, which cools the blood for six months afterwards, and at the expiration of which London is restored to its old habits of plodding industry, as suddenly and completely as if nothing had ever happened to disturb them.

In our earlier days, we were a constant frequenter of Greenwich Fair, for years. We have proceeded to, and returned from it, in almost every description of vehicle. We cannot conscientiously deny the charge of having once made the passage in a spring-van, accompanied by thirteen gentlemen, fourteen ladies, an unlimited number of children, and a barrel of beer; and we have a vague recollection of having, in later days, found ourself the eighth outside, on the top of a hackney-coach, at something past four o'clock in the morning, with a rather confused idea of our own name, or place of residence. We have grown older since then, and quiet, and steady: liking nothing better than to spend our Easter, and all our other holidays, in some quiet nook, with people of whom we shall never tire; but we think we still remember something of Greenwich Fair, and of those who resort to it. At all events we will try.

The road to Greenwich during the whole of Easter Monday, is in a state of perpetual bustle and noise. Cabs, hackney-coaches, "shay" carts, coal-waggons, stages, omnibuses, sociables, gigs, donkey-chaises—all crammed with people (for the question never is, what the horse can draw, but what the vehicle will hold), roll along at their utmost speed; the dust flies in clouds, ginger-beer corks go off in volleys, the balcony of every public-house is crowded with people, smoking and drinking, half the private houses are turned into tea-shops, fiddles are in great request, every little fruit-shop displays its stall of gilt gingerbread and penny toys; turnpike men are in despair; horses won't go on, and wheels will come off; ladies in "carawans" scream with fright at every fresh concussion, and their admirers find it necessary to sit remarkably close to them, by way of encouragement; servants of all-work, who are not allowed to have followers, and have got a holiday for the day, make the most of their time with the faithful admirer who waits for a stolen interview at the corner of the street every night, when they go to fetch the beer—apprentices grow sentimental, and straw-bonnet makers kind. Everybody is anxious to get on, and actuated by the common wish to be at the fair, or in the park, as soon as possible.

Pedestrians linger in groups at the roadside, unable to resist the allurements of the stout proprietress of the "Jack-in-the-box, three shies a penny," or the more splendid offers of the man with three thimbles and a pea on a little round board, who astonishes the bewildered crowd with some such address as, "Here's the sort o' game to make you laugh seven years arter you're dead, and turn ev'ry air on your ed gray vith delight! Three thimbles and vun little pea—with a vun, two, three, and a two, three, vun: catch him who can, look on, keep your eyes open, and niver say die! niver mind the change, and the expense: all fair and above board: them as don't play can't vin, and luck attend the ryal sportsman! Bet any gen'lm'n any sum of money, from harf-a-crown up to a suverin, as he doesn't name the thimble as kivers the pea!" Here some greenhorn whispers his friend that he distinctly saw the pea roll under the middle thimble—an impression which is immediately confirmed by a gentleman in top-boots, who is standing by, and who, in a low tone, regrets his own inability to bet, in consequence of having unfortunately left his purse at home, but strongly urges the stranger not to neglect such a golden opportunity. The "plant" is successful, the bet is made, the stranger of course loses: and the gentleman with the thimbles consoles him, as he pockets the money, with an assurance that it's "all the fortin of war! this time I vin, next time you vin: niver mind the loss of two bob and a bender! Do it up in a small parcel, and break out in a fresh place. Here's the sort o' game," &c.—and the eloquent harangue, with such variations as the speaker's exuberant fancy suggests, is again repeated to the gaping crowd, reinforced by the accession of several new comers.

The chief place of resort in the daytime, after the public-houses, is the park, in which the principal amusement is to drag young ladies up the steep hill which leads to the observatory, and then drag them down again, at the very top of their speed, greatly to the derangement of their curls and bonnet-caps, and much to the edification of lookers-on from below. "Kiss in the Ring," and "Threading my Grandmother's Needle," too, are sports which receive their full share of patronage. Love-sick swains, under the influence of gin-and-water, and the tender passion, become violently affectionate: and the fair objects of their regard enhance the value of stolen kisses, by a vast deal of struggling, and holding down of heads, and cries of "Oh! Ha' done, then, George—Oh, do tickle him for me, Mary—Well, I never!" and similar Lucretian ejaculations. Little old men and women, with a small basket under one arm, and a wine-glass, without a foot, in the other hand, tender "a drop o' the right sort" to the different groups; and young ladies, who are persuaded to indulge in a drop of the aforesaid right sort, display a pleasing degree of reluctance to taste it, and cough afterwards with great propriety.

The old pensioners, who, for the moderate charge of a penny, exhibit the mast-house, the Thames and shipping, the place where the men used to hang in chains, and other interesting sights, through a telescope, are asked questions about objects within the range of the glass, which it would puzzle a Solomon to answer; and requested to find out particular houses in particular streets, which it would have been a task of some difficulty for Mr. Horner (not the young gentleman who ate mince-pies with his thumb, but the man of Colosseum notoriety) to discover. Here and there, where some three or four couple are sitting on the grass together, you will see a sun-burnt woman in a red cloak "telling fortunes" and prophesying husbands, which it requires no extraordinary observation to describe, for the originals are before her. Thereupon, the lady concerned laughs and blushes, and ultimately buries her face in an imitation cambric handkerchief, and the gentleman described looks extremely foolish, and squeezes her hand, and fees the gipsy liberally; and the gipsy goes away, perfectly satisfied herself, and leaving those behind her perfectly satisfied also: and the prophecy, like many other prophecies of greater importance, fulfils itself in time.

But it grows dark: the crowd has gradually dispersed, and only a few stragglers are left behind. The light in the direction of the church shows that the fair is illuminated; and the distant noise proves it to be filling fast. The spot, which half an hour ago was ringing with the shouts of boisterous mirth, is as calm and quiet as if nothing could ever disturb its serenity; the fine old trees, the majestic building at their feet, with the noble river beyond, glistening in the moonlight, appear in all their beauty, and under their most favourable aspect; the voices of the boys, singing their evening hymn, are borne gently on the air; and the humblest mechanic who has been lingering on the grass so pleasant to the feet that beat the same dull round from week to week in the paved streets of London, feels proud to think as he surveys the scene before him, that he belongs to the country which has selected such a spot as a retreat for its oldest and best defenders in the decline of their lives.

Five minutes' walking brings you to the fair; a scene calculated to awaken very different feelings. The entrance is occupied on either side by the vendors of gingerbread and toys: the stalls are gaily lighted up, the most attractive goods profusely disposed, and unbonneted young ladies, in their zeal for the interest of their employers, seize you by the coat, and use all the blandishments of "Do, dear"—"There's a love"—"Don't be cross, now," &c., to induce you to purchase half a pound of the real spice nuts, of which the majority of the regular fair-goers carry a pound or two as a present supply, tied up in a cotton pocket-handkerchief. Occasionally you pass a deal table, on which are exposed pen'orths of pickled salmon (fennel included), in little white saucers: oysters, with shells as large as cheese-plates, and divers specimens of a species of snail (*wilks*, we think they are called), floating in a somewhat bilious-looking green liquid. Cigars, too, are in great demand; gentlemen must smoke, of course, and here they are, two a penny, in a regular authentic cigar-box, with a lighted tallow candle in the centre.

Imagine yourself in an extremely dense crowd, which swings you to and fro, and in and out, and every way but the right one; add to this the screams of women, the shouts of boys, the clanging of gongs, the firing of pistols, the ringing of bells, the bellowings of speaking-trumpets, the squeaking of penny dittoes, the noise of a dozen bands, with three drums in each, all playing different tunes at the same time, the hallooing of showmen, and an occasional roar from the wild-beast shows; and you are in the very centre and heart of the fair.

This immense booth, with the large stage in front, so brightly illuminated with variegated lamps, and pots of burning fat, is "Richardson's," where you have a melo-drama (with three murders and a ghost), a pantomime, a comic song, an overture, and some incidental music, all done in five-and-twenty minutes.

The company are now promenading outside in all the dignity of wigs, spangles, red-ochre, and whitening. See with what a ferocious air the gentleman who personates the Mexican chief, paces up and down, and with what an eye of calm dignity the principal tragedian gazes on the crowd below, or converses confidentially with the harlequin! The four clowns, who are engaged in a mock broad-sword combat, may be all very well for the low-minded holiday-makers; but these are the people for the reflective portion of the community. They look so noble in those Roman dresses, with their yellow legs and arms, long black curly heads, bushy eyebrows, and scowl expressive of assassination, and vengeance, and everything else that is grand and solemn. Then, the ladies—were there ever such innocent and awful-looking beings; as they walk up and down the platform in twos and threes, with their arms round each other's waists, or leaning for support on one of those majestic men! Their spangled muslin dresses and blue satin shoes and sandals (a *leetle* the worse for wear) are the admiration of all beholders; and the playful manner in which they check the advances of the clown, is perfectly enchanting.

"Just a-going to begin! Pray come for'erd, come for'erd," exclaims the man in the countryman's dress, for the seventieth time: and people force their way up the steps in crowds. The band suddenly strikes up, the harlequin and columbine set the example, reels are formed in less than no time, the Roman heroes place their arms a-kimbo, and dance with considerable agility; and the leading tragic actress, and the gentleman who enacts the "swell" in the pantomime, foot it to perfection. "All in to begin," shouts the manager, when no more people can be induced to "come for'erd," and away rush the leading members of the company to do the dreadful in the first piece.

A change of performance takes place every day during the fair, but the story of the tragedy is always pretty much the same. There is a rightful heir, who loves a young lady, and is beloved by her; and a wrongful heir, who loves her too, and isn't beloved by her; and the wrongful heir gets hold of the rightful heir, and throws him into a dungeon, just to kill him off when convenient, for which purpose he hires a couple of assassins—a good one and a bad one—who, the moment they are left alone, get up a little murder on their own account, the good one killing the bad one, and the bad one wounding the good one. Then the rightful heir is discovered in prison, carefully holding a long chain in his hands, and seated despondingly in a large arm-chair; and the young lady comes in to two bars of soft music, and embraces the rightful heir; and then the wrongful heir comes in to two bars of quick music (technically called "a hurry"), and goes on in the most shocking manner, throwing the young lady about as if she was nobody, and calling the rightful heir "Ar-recreant—ar-wretch!" in a very loud voice, which answers the double purpose of displaying his passion, and preventing the sound being deadened by the sawdust. The interest becomes intense; the wrongful heir draws his sword, and rushes on the rightful heir; a blue smoke is seen, a gong is heard, and a tall white figure (who has been all this time, behind the arm-chair, covered over with a table-cloth), slowly rises to the tune of "Oft in the stilly night." This is no other than the ghost of the rightful heir's father, who was killed by the wrongful heir's father, at sight of which the wrongful heir becomes apoplectic, and is literally "struck all of a heap," the stage not being large enough to admit of his falling down at full length. Then the good assassin staggers in, and says he was hired in conjunction with the bad assassin, by the wrongful heir, to kill the rightful heir; and he's killed a good many people in his time, but he's very sorry for it, and won't do so any more—a promise which he immediately redeems, by dying off hand without any nonsense about it. Then the rightful heir throws down his chain; and then two men, a sailor, and a young woman (the tenantry of the rightful heir) come in, and the ghost makes dumb motions to them, which they, by supernatural interference understand—for no one else can; and the ghost (who can't do anything without blue fire) blesses the rightful heir and the young lady, by half suffocating them with smoke: and then a muffin-bell rings, and the curtain drops.

The exhibitions next in popularity to these itinerant theatres are the travelling menageries, or, to speak more intelligibly, the "Wild-beast shows," where a military band in beef-eater's costume, with leopard-skin caps, play incessantly; and where large highly-coloured representations of tigers tearing men's heads open, and a lion being burnt with red-hot irons to induce him to drop his victim, are hung up outside, by way of attracting visitors.

The principal officer at these places is generally a very tall, hoarse man, in a scarlet coat, with a cane in his hand, with which he occasionally raps the pictures we have just noticed, by way of illustrating his description—something in this way. "Here, here, here; the lion, the lion (tap), exactly as he is represented on the canvas outside (three taps): no waiting, remember; no deception. The fe-ro-cious lion (tap, tap) who bit off the gentleman's head last Cambervel vos a twelvemonth, and has killed on the awerage three keepers a-year ever since he arrived at matoority. No extra charge on this account recollect; the price of admission is only sixpence." This address never fails to produce a considerable sensation, and sixpences flow into the treasury with wonderful rapidity.

The dwarfs are also objects of great curiosity, and as a dwarf, a giantess, a living skeleton, a wild Indian, "a young lady of singular beauty, with perfectly white hair and pink eyes," and two or three other natural curiosities, are usually exhibited together for the small charge of a penny, they attract very numerous audiences. The best thing about a dwarf is, that he has always a little box, about two feet six inches high, into which, by long practice, he can just manage to get, by doubling himself up like a boot-jack; this box is painted outside like a six-roomed house, and as the crowd see him ring a bell, or fire a pistol out of the first-floor window, they verily believe that it is his ordinary town residence, divided like other mansions into drawing-rooms, dining-parlour, and bedchambers. Shut up in this case, the unfortunate little object is brought out to delight the throng by holding a facetious dialogue with the proprietor: in the course of which, the dwarf (who is always particularly drunk) pledges himself to sing a comic song inside, and pays various compliments to the ladies, which induce them to "come for'erd" with great alacrity. As a giant is not so easily moved, a pair of indescribables of most capacious dimensions, and a huge shoe, are usually brought out, into which two or three stout men get all at once, to the enthusiastic delight of the crowd, who are quite satisfied with the solemn assurance that these habiliments form part of the giant's everyday costume.

The grandest and most numerously-frequented booth in the whole fair, however, is "The Crown and Anchor"—a temporary ball-room—we forget how many hundred feet long, the price of admission to which is one shilling Immediately on your right hand as you enter, after paying your money, is a refreshment place, at which cold beef, roast and boiled, French rolls, stout, wine, tongue, ham, even fowls, if we recollect right, are displayed in tempting array. There is a raised orchestra, and the place is boarded all the way down, in patches, just wide enough for a country dance.

There is no master of the ceremonies in this artificial Eden—all is primitive, unreserved, and unstudied. The dust is blinding, the heat insupportable, the company somewhat noisy, and in the highest spirits possible: the ladies, in the height of their innocent animation, dancing in the gentlemen's hats, and the gentlemen promenading the "the gay and festive scene" in the ladies' bonnets, or with the more expensive ornaments of false noses, and low-crowned, tinder-box-looking hats: playing children's drums, and accompanied by ladies on the penny trumpet.

The noise of these various instruments, the orchestra, the shouting, the "scratchers," and the dancing, is perfectly bewildering. The dancing, itself, beggars description—every figure lasts about an hour, and the ladies bounce up and down the middle, with a degree of spirit which is quite indescribable. As to the gentlemen, they stamp their feet against the ground, every time "hands four round" begins, go down the middle and up again, with cigars in their mouths, and silk handkerchiefs in their hands, and whirl their partners round, nothing loth, scrambling and falling, and embracing, and knocking up against the other couples, until they are fairly tired out, and can move no longer. The same scene is repeated again and again (slightly varied by an occasional "row") until a late hour at night: and a great many clerks and 'prentices find themselves next morning with aching heads, empty pockets, damaged hats, and a very imperfect recollection of how it was they did *not* get home.

CHAPTER XIII.

PRIVATE THEATRES.

"RICHARD THE THIRD.—DUKE OF GLO'STER, 2*l.*; EARL OF RICHMOND, 1*l.*; DUKE OF BUCKINGHAM, 15*s.*; CATESBY, 12*s.*; TRESSEL, 10*s.* 6*d.*; LORD STANLEY, 5*s.*; LORD MAYOR OF LONDON, 2*s.* 6*d.*"

Such are the written placards wafered up in the gentlemen's dressing-room, the green-room (where there is any), at a private theatre; and such are the sums extracted from the shop-till, or overcharged in the office expenditure, by the donkeys who are prevailed upon to pay for permission to exhibit their lamentable ignorance and boobyism on the stage of a private theatre. This they do, in proportion to the scope afforded by the character for the display of their imbecility. For instance, the Duke of Glo'ster is well worth two pounds, because he has it all to himself; he must wear a real sword, and what is better still, he must draw it, several times in the course of the piece. The soliloquies alone are well worth fifteen shillings; then there is the stabbing King Henry—decidedly cheap at three-and-sixpence, that's eighteen-and-sixpence; bullying the coffin-bearers—say eighteen-pence, though it's worth much more—that's a pound. Then the love scene with Lady Ann, and the bustle of the fourth act can't be dear at ten shillings more—that's only one pound ten, including the "off with his head!"—which is sure to bring down the applause, and it is very easy to do—"Orf with his ed" (very quick and loud;—then slow and sneeringly)—"So much for Bu-u-u-uckingham!" Lay the emphasis on the "uck;" get yourself gradually into a corner, and work with your right hand, while you're saying it, as if you were feeling your way, and it's sure to do. The tent scene is confessedly worth half-a-sovereign, and so you have the fight in, gratis, and everybody knows what an effect may be produced by a good combat. One—two—three—four—over; then, one—two—three—four—under; then thrust; then dodge and slide about; then fall down on one knee; then fight upon it, and then get up again and stagger. You may keep on doing this, as long as it seems to take—say ten minutes—and then fall down (backwards, if you can manage it without hurting yourself), and die game: nothing like it for producing an effect. They always do it at Astley's and Sadlers' Wells, and if they don't know how to do this sort of thing, who in the world does? A small child, or a female in white, increases the interest of a combat materially—indeed, we are not aware that a regular legitimate terrific broadsword combat could be done without; but it would be rather difficult, and somewhat unusual, to introduce this effect in the last scene of Richard the Third, so the only thing to be done, is, just to make the best of a bad bargain, and be as long as possible fighting it out.

The principal patrons of private theatres are dirty boys, low copying-clerks in attorneys' offices, capacious-headed youths from city counting-houses, Jews whose business, as lenders of fancy dresses, is a sure passport to the amateur stage, shop-boys who now and then mistake their masters' money for their own; and a choice miscellany of idle vagabonds. The proprietor of a private theatre may be an ex-scene-painter, a low coffee-house-keeper, a disappointed eighth-rate actor, a retired smuggler, or uncertificated bankrupt. The theatre itself may be in Catherine-street, Strand, the purlieus of the city, the neighbourhood of Gray's-inn-lane, or the vicinity of Sadlers' Wells; or it may, perhaps, form the chief nuisance of some shabby street, on the Surrey side of Waterloo-bridge.

The lady performers pay nothing for their characters, and it is needless to add, are usually selected from one class of society; the audiences are necessarily of much the same character as the performers, who receive, in return for their contributions to the management, tickets to the amount of the money they pay.

All the minor theatres in London, especially the lowest, constitute the centre of a little stage-struck neighbourhood. Each of them has an audience exclusively its own; and at any you will see dropping into the pit at half-price, or swaggering into the back of a box, if the price of admission be a reduced one, divers boys of from fifteen to twenty-one years of age, who throw back their coat and turn up their wristbands, after the portraits of Count D'Orsay, hum tunes and whistle when the curtain is down, by way of persuading the people near them, that they are not at all anxious to have it up again, and speak familiarly of the inferior performers as Bill Such-a-one, and Ned So-and-so, or tell each other how a new piece called *The Unknown Bandit of the Invisible Cavern*, is in rehearsal; how Mister Palmer is to play *The Unknown Bandit;* how Charley Scarton is to take the part of an English sailor, and fight a broadsword combat with six unknown bandits, at one and the same time (one theatrical sailor is always equal to half a dozen men at least); how Mister Palmer and Charley Scarton are to go through a double hornpipe in fetters in the second act; how the interior of the invisible cavern is to occupy the whole extent of the stage; and other town-surprising theatrical announcements. These gentlemen are the amateurs—the *Richards, Shylocks, Beverleys,* and *Othellos*—the *Young Dorntons, Rovers, Captain Absolutes,* and *Charles Surfaces*—of a private theatre.

See them at the neighbouring public-house or the theatrical coffee-shop! They are the kings of the place, supposing no real performers to be present; and roll about, hats on one side, and arms a-kimbo, as if they had actually come into possession of eighteen shillings a-week, and a share of a ticket night. If one of them does but know an Astley's supernumerary he is a happy fellow. The mingled air of envy and admiration with which his companions will regard him, as he converses familiarly with some mouldy-looking man in a fancy neckerchief, whose partially corked eyebrows, and half-rouged face, testify to the fact of his having just left the stage or the circle, sufficiently shows in what high admiration these public characters are held.

With the double view of guarding against the discovery of friends or employers, and enhancing the interest of an assumed character, by attaching a high-sounding name to its representative, these geniuses assume fictitious names, which are not the least amusing part of the play-bill of a private theatre. Belville, Melville, Treville, Berkeley, Randolph, Byron, St. Clair, and so forth, are among the humblest; and the less imposing titles of Jenkins, Walker, Thomson, Barker, Solomons, &c., are completely laid aside. There is something imposing in this, and it is an excellent apology for shabbiness into the bargain. A shrunken, faded coat, a decayed hat, a patched and soiled pair of trousers—nay, even a very dirty shirt (and none of these appearances are very uncommon among the members of the *corps dramatique*), may be worn for the purpose of disguise, and to prevent the remotest chance of recognition. Then it prevents any troublesome inquiries or explanations about employment and pursuits; everybody is a gentleman at large, for the occasion, and there are none of those unpleasant and unnecessary distinctions to which even genius must occasionally succumb elsewhere. As to the ladies (God bless them), they are quite above any formal absurdities; the mere circumstance of your being behind the scenes is a sufficient introduction to their society—for of course they know that none but strictly respectable persons would be admitted into that close fellowship with them, which acting engenders. They place implicit reliance on the manager, no doubt; and as to the manager, he is all affability when he knows you well,—or, in other words, when he has pocketed your money once, and entertains confident hopes of doing so again.

A quarter before eight—there will be a full house to-night—six parties in the boxes, already; four little boys and a woman in the pit; and two fiddles and a flute in the orchestra, who have got through five overtures since seven o'clock (the hour fixed for the commencement of the performances), and have just begun the sixth. There will be plenty of it, though, when it does begin, for there is enough in the bill to last six hours at least.

That gentleman in the white hat and checked shirt, brown coat and brass buttons, lounging behind the stage-box on the O. P. side, is Mr. Horatio St. Julien, alias Jem Larkins. His line is genteel comedy—his father's, coal and potato. He *does* Alfred Highflier in the last piece, and very well he'll do it—at the price. The party of gentlemen in the opposite box, to whom he has just nodded, are friends and supporters of Mr. Beverley (otherwise Loggins), the *Macbeth* of the night. You observe their attempts to appear easy and gentlemanly, each member of the party, with his feet cocked upon the cushion in front of the box! They let them do these things here, upon the same humane principle which permits poor people's children to knock double knocks at the door of an empty house—because they can't do it anywhere else. The two stout men in the centre box, with an opera-glass ostentatiously placed before them, are friends of the proprietor—opulent country managers, as he confidentially informs every individual among the crew behind the curtain—opulent country managers looking out for recruits; a representation which Mr. Nathan, the dresser, who is in the manager's interest, and has just arrived with the costumes, offers to confirm upon oath if required—corroborative evidence, however, is quite unnecessary, for the gulls believe it at once.

The stout Jewess who has just entered, is the mother of the pale bony little girl, with the necklace of blue glass beads, sitting by her; she is being brought up to "the profession." Pantomime is to be her line, and she is coming out to-night, in a hornpipe after the tragedy. The short thin man beside Mr. St. Julien, whose white face is so deeply seared with the small-pox, and whose dirty shirt-front is inlaid with open-work, and embossed with coral studs like ladybirds, is the low comedian and comic singer of the establishment. The remainder of the audience—a tolerably numerous one by this time—are a motley group of dupes and blackguards.

The foot-lights have just made their appearance: the wicks of the six little oil lamps round the only tier of boxes, are being turned up, and the additional light thus afforded serves to show the presence of dirt, and absence of paint, which forms a prominent feature in the audience part of the house. As these preparations, however, announce the speedy commencement of the play, let us take a peep "behind," previous to the ringing-up.

The little narrow passages beneath the stage are neither especially clean nor too brilliantly lighted; and the absence of any flooring, together with the damp mildewy smell which pervades the place, does not conduce in any great degree to their comfortable appearance. Don't fall over this plate basket—it's one of the "properties"—the caldron for the witches' cave; and the three uncouth-looking figures, with broken clothes-props in their hands, who are drinking gin-and-water out of a pint pot, are the weird sisters. This miserable room, lighted by candles in sconces placed at lengthened intervals round the wall, is the dressing-room, common to the gentlemen performers, and the square hole in the ceiling is *the* trap-door of the stage above. You will observe that the ceiling is ornamented with the beams that support the boards, and tastefully hung with cobwebs.

The characters in the tragedy are all dressed and their own clothes are scattered in hurried confusion over the wooden dresser which surrounds the room. That snuff-shop-looking figure, in front of the glass, is *Banquo:* and the young lady with the liberal display of legs, who is kindly painting his face with a hare's foot, is dressed for *Fleance.* The large woman, who is consulting the stage directions in Cumberland's edition of *Macbeth*, is the *Lady Macbeth* of the night; she is always selected to play the part, because she is tall and stout, and *looks* a little like Mrs. Siddons—at a considerable distance. That stupid-looking milksop, with light hair and bow legs—a kind of man whom you can warrant town-made—is fresh caught; he plays *Malcolm* to-night, just to accustom himself to an audience. He will get on better by degrees; he will play *Othello* in a month, and in a month more, will very probably be apprehended on a charge of embezzlement. The black-eyed female with whom he is talking so earnestly, is dressed for the "gentlewoman." It is *her* first appearance, too—in that character. The boy of fourteen who is having his eyebrows smeared with soap and whitening, is *Duncan*, King of Scotland; and the two dirty men with the corked countenances, in very old green tunics, and dirty drab boots, are the "army."

"Look sharp below there, gents," exclaims the dresser, a red-headed and red-whiskered Jew, calling through the trap, "they're a-going to ring up. The flute says he'll be blowed if he plays any more, and they're getting precious noisy in front." A general rush immediately takes place to the half-dozen little steep steps leading to the stage, and the heterogeneous group are soon assembled at the side scenes, in breathless anxiety and motley confusion.

"Now," cries the manager, consulting the written list which hangs behind the first P.S. wing, "Scene 1, open country—lamps down—thunder and lightning—all ready, White?" [This is addressed to one of the army.] "All ready."—"Very well. Scene 2, front chamber. Is the front chamber down?"—"Yes."—"Very well."—"Jones" [to the other army who is up in the flies]. "Hallo!"—"Wind up the open country when we ring up."—"I'll take care."—"Scene 3, back perspective with practical bridge. Bridge ready, White? Got the tressels there?"—"All right."

"Very well. Clear the stage," cries the manager, hastily packing every member of the company into the little space there is between the wings and the wall, and one wing and another. "Places, places. Now then, Witches—Duncan—Malcolm—bleeding officer—where's the bleeding officer?"—"Here!" replies the officer, who has been rose-pinking for the character. "Get ready, then; now, White, ring the second music-bell." The actors who are to be discovered, are hastily arranged, and the actors who are not to be discovered place themselves, in their anxiety to peep at the house, just where the audience can see them. The bell rings, and the orchestra, in acknowledgment of the call, play three distinct chords. The bell rings—the tragedy (!) opens—and our description closes.

CHAPTER XIV.

VAUXHALL-GARDENS BY DAY.

There was a time when if a man ventured to wonder how Vauxhall-gardens would look by day, he was hailed with a shout of derision at the absurdity of the idea. Vauxhall by daylight! A porter-pot without porter, the House of Commons without the Speaker, a gas-lamp without the gas—pooh, nonsense, the thing was not to be thought of. It was rumoured, too, in those times, that Vauxhall-gardens by day, were the scene of secret and hidden experiments; that there, carvers were exercised in the mystic art of cutting a moderate-sized ham into slices thin enough to pave the whole of the grounds; that beneath the shade of the tall trees, studious men were constantly engaged in chemical experiments, with the view of discovering how much water a bowl of negus could possibly bear; and that in some retired nooks, appropriated to the study of ornithology, other sage and learned men were, by a process known only to themselves, incessantly employed in reducing fowls to a mere combination of skin and bone.

Vague rumours of this kind, together with many others of a similar nature, cast over Vauxhall-gardens an air of deep mystery; and as there is a great deal in the mysterious. there is no doubt that to a good many people, at all events, the pleasure they afforded was not a little enhanced by this very circumstance.

Of this class of people we confess to having made one. We loved to wander among these illuminated groves, thinking of the patient and laborious researches which had been carried on there during the day, and witnessing their results in the suppers which were served up beneath the light of lamps and to the sound of music at night. The temples and saloons and cosmoramas and fountains glittered and sparkled before our eyes; the beauty of the lady singers and the elegant deportment of the gentlemen, captivated our hearts; a few hundred thousand of additional lamps dazzled our senses; a bowl or two of punch bewildered our brains; and we were happy.

In an evil hour, the proprietors of Vauxhall-gardens took to opening them by day. We regretted this, as rudely and harshly disturbing that veil of mystery which had hung about the property for many years, and which none but the noonday sun, and the late Mr. Simpson, had ever penetrated. We shrunk from going; at this moment we scarcely know why. Perhaps a morbid consciousness of approaching disappointment—perhaps a fatal presentiment—perhaps the weather; whatever it was, we did *not* go until the second or third announcement of a race between two balloons tempted us, and we went.

We paid our shilling at the gate, and then we saw for the first time, that the entrance, if there had been any magic about it at all, was now decidedly disenchanted, being, in fact, nothing more nor less than a combination of very roughly-painted boards and sawdust. We glanced at the orchestra and supper-room as we hurried past—we just recognised them, and that was all. We bent our steps to the firework-ground; there, at least, we should not be disappointed. We reached it, and stood rooted to the spot with mortification and astonishment. *That* the Moorish tower—that wooden shed with a door in the centre, and daubs of crimson and yellow all round, like a gigantic watch-case! *That* the place where night after night we had beheld the undaunted Mr. Blackmore make his terrific ascent, surrounded by flames of fire, and peals of artillery, and where the white garments of Madame Somebody (we forget even her name now), who nobly devoted her life to the manufacture of fireworks, had so often been seen fluttering in the wind, as she called up a red, blue, or party-coloured light to illumine her temple! *That* the—— but at this moment the bell rung; the people scampered away, pell-mell, to the spot from whence the sound proceeded; and we, from the mere force of habit, found ourself running among the first, as if for very life.

It was for the concert in the orchestra. A small party of dismal men in cocked hats were "executing" the overture to *Tancredi*, and a numerous assemblage of ladies and gentlemen, with their families, had rushed from their half-emptied stout mugs in the supper boxes, and crowded to the spot. Intense was the low murmur of admiration when a particularly small gentleman, in a dress coat, led on a particularly tall lady in a blue sarcenet pelisse and bonnet of the same, ornamented with large white feathers, and forthwith commenced a plaintive duet.

We knew the small gentleman well; we had seen a lithographed semblance of him, on many a piece of music, with his mouth wide open as if in the act of singing; a wine-glass in his hand; and a table with two decanters and four pine-apples on it in the background. The tall lady, too, we had gazed on, lost in raptures of admiration, many and many a time—how different people *do* look by daylight, and without punch, to be sure! It was a beautiful duet: first the small gentleman asked a question, and then the tall lady answered it; then the small gentleman and the tall lady sang together most melodiously; then the small gentleman went through a little piece of vehemence by himself, and got very tenor indeed, in the excitement of his feelings, to which the tall lady responded in a similar manner; then the small gentleman had a shake or two, after which the tall lady had the same, and then they both merged imperceptibly into the original air: and the band wound themselves up to a pitch of fury, and the small gentleman handed the tall lady out, and the applause was rapturous.

The comic singer, however, was the especial favourite; we really thought that a gentleman, with his dinner in a pocket-handkerchief, who stood near us, would have fainted with excess of joy. A marvellously facetious gentleman that comic singer is; his distinguishing characteristics are, a wig approaching to the flaxen, and an aged countenance, and he bears the name of one of the English counties, if we recollect right. He sang a very good song about the seven ages, the first half hour of which afforded the assembly the purest delight; of the rest we can make no report, as we did not stay to hear any more.

We walked about, and met with a disappointment at every turn; our favourite views were mere patches of paint; the fountain that had sparkled so showily by lamp-light, presented very much the appearance of a water-pipe that had burst; all the ornaments were dingy, and all the walks gloomy. There was a spectral attempt at rope-dancing in the little open theatre. The sun shone upon the spangled dresses of the performers, and their evolutions were about as inspiriting and appropriate as a country-dance in a family vault. So we retraced our steps to the firework-ground, and mingled with the little crowd of people who were contemplating Mr. Green.

Some half-dozen men were restraining the impetuosity of one of the balloons, which was completely filled, and had the car already attached; and as rumours had gone abroad that a Lord was "going up," the crowd were more than usually anxious and talkative. There was one little man in faded black, with a dirty face and a rusty black neckerchief with a red border, tied in a narrow wisp round his neck, who entered into conversation with everybody, and had something to say upon every remark that was made within his hearing. He was standing with his arms folded, staring up at the balloon, and every now and then vented his feelings of reverence for the aëronaut, by saying, as he looked round to catch somebody's eye, "He's a rum 'un is Green; think o' this here being up'ards of his two hundredth ascent; ecod the man as is ekal to Green never had the toothache yet, nor won't have within this hundred year, and that's all about it. When you meets with real talent, and native, too, encourage it, that's what I say;" and when he had delivered himself to this effect, he would fold his arms with more determination than ever, and stare at the balloon with a sort of admiring defiance of any other man alive, beyond himself and Green, that impressed the crowd with the opinion that he was an oracle.

"Ah, you're very right, sir," said another gentleman, with his wife, and children, and mother, and wife's sister, and a host of female friends, in all the gentility of white pocket-handkerchiefs, frills, and spencers, "Mr. Green is a steady hand, sir, and there's no fear about him."

"Fear!" said the little man: "isn't it a lovely thing to see him and his wife a going up in one balloon, and his own son and *his* wife a jostling up against them in another, and all of them going twenty or thirty mile in three hours or so, and then coming back in pochayses? I don't know where this here science is to stop, mind you; that's what bothers me."

Here there was a considerable talking among the females in the spencers.

"What's the ladies a laughing at, sir?" inquired the little man, condescendingly.

"It's only my sister Mary," said one of the girls, "as says she hopes his lordship won't be frightened when he's in the car, and want to come out again."

"Make yourself easy about that there, my dear," replied the little man. "If he was so much as to move a inch without leave, Green would jist fetch him a crack over the head with the telescope, as would send him into the bottom of the basket in no time, and stun him till they come down again."

"Would he, though?" inquired the other man.

"Yes, would he," replied the little one, "and think nothing of it, neither, if he was the king himself. Green's presence of mind is wonderful."

Just at this moment all eyes were directed to the preparations which were being made for starting. The car was attached to the second balloon, the two were brought pretty close together, and a military band commenced playing, with a zeal and fervour which would render the most timid man in existence but too happy to accept any means of quitting that particular spot of earth on which they were stationed. Then Mr. Green, sen., and his noble companion entered one car, and Mr. Green, jun., and *his* companion the other; and then the balloons went up, and the aërial travellers stood up, and the crowd outside roared with delight, and the two gentlemen who had never ascended before, tried to wave their flags, as if they were not nervous, but held on very fast all the while; and the balloons were wafted gently away, our little friend solemnly protesting, long after they were reduced to mere specks in the air, that he could still distinguish the white hat of Mr. Green. The gardens disgorged their multitudes, boys ran up and down screaming "bal-loon;" and in all the crowded thoroughfares people rushed out of their shops into the middle of the road, and having stared up in the air at two little black objects till they almost dislocated their necks, walked slowly in again, perfectly satisfied.

The next day there was a grand account of the ascent in the morning papers, and the public were informed how it was the finest day but four in Mr. Green's remembrance; how they retained sight of the earth till they lost it behind the clouds; and how the reflection of the balloon on the undulating masses of vapour was gorgeously picturesque; together with a little science about the refraction of the sun's rays, and some mysterious hints respecting atmospheric heat and eddying currents of air.

There was also an interesting account how a man in a boat was distinctly heard by Mr. Green, jun., to exclaim, "My eye!" which Mr. Green, jun., attributed to his voice rising to the balloon, and the sound being thrown back from its surface into the car; and the whole concluded with a slight allusion to another ascent next Wednesday, all of which was very instructive and very amusing, as our readers will see if they look to the papers. If we have forgotten to mention the date, they have only to wait till next summer, and take the account of the first ascent, and it will answer the purpose equally well.

CHAPTER XV.

EARLY COACHES.

We have often wondered how many months' incessant travelling in a post-chaise it would take to kill a man; and wondering by analogy, we should very much like to know how many months of constant travelling in a succession of early coaches, an unfortunate mortal could endure. Breaking a man alive upon the wheel, would be nothing to breaking his rest, his peace, his heart—everything but his fast—upon four; and the punishment of Ixion (the only practical person, by-the-bye, who has discovered the secret of the perpetual motion) would sink into utter insignificance before the one we have suggested. If we had been a powerful churchman in those good times when blood was shed as freely as water, and men were mowed down like grass, in the sacred cause of religion, we would have lain by very quietly till we got hold of some especially obstinate miscreant, who positively refused to be converted to our faith, and then we would have booked him for an inside place in a small coach, which travelled day and night: and securing the remainder of the places for stout men with a slight tendency to coughing and spitting, we would have started him forth on his last travels: leaving him mercilessly to all the tortures which the waiters, landlords, coachmen, guards, boots, chambermaids, and other familiars on his line of road, might think proper to inflict.

Who has not experienced the miseries inevitably consequent upon a summons to undertake a hasty journey? You receive an intimation from your place of business—wherever that may be, or whatever you may be—that it will be necessary to leave town without delay. You and your family are forthwith thrown into a state of tremendous excitement; an express is immediately dispatched to the washerwoman's; everybody is in a bustle; and you, yourself, with a feeling of dignity which you cannot altogether conceal, sally forth to the booking-office to secure your place. Here a painful consciousness of your own unimportance first rushes on your mind—the people are as cool and collected as if nobody were going out of town, or as if a journey of a hundred odd miles were a mere nothing. You enter a mouldy-looking room, ornamented with large posting-bills; the greater part of the place enclosed behind a huge lumbering rough counter, and fitted up with recesses that look like the dens of the smaller animals in a travelling menagerie, without the bars. Some half-dozen people are "booking" brown-paper parcels, which one of the clerks flings into the aforesaid recesses with an air of recklessness which you, remembering the new carpet-bag you bought in the morning, feel considerably annoyed at; porters, looking like so many Atlases, keep rushing in and out, with large packages on their shoulders; and while you are waiting to make the necessary inquiries, you wonder what on earth the booking-office clerks can have been before they were booking-office clerks; one of them with his pen behind his ear, and his hands behind him, is standing in front of the fire, like a full-length portrait of Napoleon; the other with his hat half off his head, enters the passengers' names in the books with a coolness which is inexpressibly provoking; and the villain whistles—actually whistles—while a man asks him what the fare is outside, all the way to Holyhead!—in frosty weather, too! They are clearly an isolated race, evidently possessing no sympathies or feelings in common with the rest of mankind. Your turn comes at last, and having paid the fare, you tremblingly inquire—"What time will it be necessary for me to be here in the morning?"—"Six o'clock," replies the whistler, carelessly pitching the sovereign you have just parted with, into a wooden bowl on the desk. "Rather before than arter," adds the man with the semi-roasted unmentionables, with just as much ease and complacency as if the whole world got out of bed at five. You turn into the street, ruminating as you bend your steps homewards on the extent to which men become hardened in cruelty, by custom.

If there be one thing in existence more miserable than another, it most unquestionably is the being compelled to rise by candle-light. If you ever doubted the fact, you are painfully convinced of your error, on the morning of your departure. You left strict orders, overnight, to be called at half-past four, and you have done nothing all night but dose for five minutes at a time, and start up suddenly from a terrific dream of a large church-clock with the small hand running round, with astonishing rapidity, to every figure on the dial-plate. At last, completely exhausted, you fall gradually into a refreshing sleep—your thoughts grow confused—the stage-coaches, which have been "going off" before your eyes all night, become less and less distinct, until they go off altogether; one moment you are driving with all the skill and smartness of an experienced whip—the next you are exhibiting *à la* Ducrow, on the off-leader; anon you are closely muffled up, inside, and have just recognised in the person of the guard an old schoolfellow, whose funeral, even in your dream, you remember to have attended eighteen years ago. At last you fall into a state of complete oblivion, from which you are aroused, as if into a new state of existence, by a singular illusion. You are apprenticed to a trunk-maker; how, or why, or when, or wherefore, you don't take the trouble to inquire; but there you are, pasting the lining in the lid of a portmanteau. Confound that other apprentice in the back shop, how he is hammering!—rap, rap, rap—what an industrious fellow he must be! you have heard him at work for half an hour past, and he has been hammering incessantly the whole time. Rap, rap, rap, again—he's talking now—what's that he said? Five o'clock! You make a violent exertion, and start up in bed. The vision is at once dispelled; the trunk-maker's shop is your own bed-room, and the other apprentice your shivering servant, who has been vainly endeavouring to wake you for the last quarter of an hour, at the imminent risk of breaking either his own knuckles or the panels of the door.

You proceed to dress yourself, with all possible dispatch. The flaring flat candle with the long snuff, gives light enough to show that the things you want, are not where they ought to be, and you undergo a trifling delay in consequence of having carefully packed up one of your boots in your over-anxiety of the preceding night. You soon complete your toilet, however, for you are not particular on such an occasion, and you shaved yesterday evening; so mounting your Petersham great-coat, and green travelling shawl, and grasping your carpet-bag in your right hand, you walk lightly down stairs, lest you should awaken any of the family, and after pausing in the common sitting-room for one moment, just to have a cup of coffee (the said common sitting-room looking remarkably comfortable, with everything out of its place, and strewed with the crumbs of last night's supper), you undo the chain and bolts of the street-door, and find yourself fairly in the street.

A thaw, by all that is miserable! The frost is completely broken up. You look down the long perspective of Oxford-street, the gas-lights mournfully reflected on the wet pavement, and can discern no speck in the road to encourage the belief that there is a cab or a coach to be had—the very coachmen have gone home in despair. The cold sleet is drizzling down with that gentle regularity, which betokens a duration of four-and-twenty hours at least; the damp hangs upon the house-tops and lamp-posts, and clings to you like an invisible cloak. The water is "coming in" in every area, the pipes have burst, the water-butts are running over; the kennels seem to be doing matches against time, pump-handles descend of their own accord, horses in market-carts fall-down, and there's no one to help them up again, policemen look as if they had been carefully sprinkled with powdered glass; here and there a milk-woman trudges slowly along, with a bit of list round each foot to keep her from slipping; boys who "don't sleep in the house," and are not allowed much sleep out of it, can't wake their masters by thundering at the shop-door, and cry with the cold—the compound of ice, snow, and water on the pavement, is a couple of inches thick—nobody ventures to walk fast to keep himself warm, and nobody could succeed in keeping himself warm if he did.

It strikes a quarter past five as you trudge down Waterloo-place on your way to the Golden Cross, and you discover, for the first time, that you were called about an hour too early. You have not time to go back; there is no place open to go into, and you have, therefore, no resource but to go forward, which you do, feeling remarkably satisfied with yourself, and everything about you. You arrive at the office, and look wistfully up the yard for the Birmingham High-flier, which, for aught you can see, may have flown away altogether, for no preparations appear to be on foot for the departure of any vehicle in the shape of a coach. You wander into the booking-office, which with the gas-lights and blazing fire, looks quite comfortable by contrast—that is to say, if any place *can* look comfortable at half-past five on a winter's morning. There stands the identical book-keeper in the same position as if he had not moved since you saw him yesterday. As he informs you, that the coach is up the yard, and will be brought round in about a quarter of an hour, you leave your bag, and repair to "The Tap"—not with any absurd idea of warming yourself, because you feel such a result to be utterly hopeless, but for the purpose of procuring some hot brandy-and-water, which you do,—when the kettle boils! an event which occurs exactly two minutes and a half before the time fixed for the starting of the coach.

The first stroke of six, peals from St. Martin's church steeple, just as you take the first sip of the boiling liquid. You find yourself at the booking-office in two seconds, and the tap-waiter finds himself much comforted by your brandy-and-water, in about the same period. The coach is out; the horses are in, and the guard and two or three porters, are stowing the luggage away, and running up the steps of the booking-office, and down the steps of the booking-office, with breathless rapidity. The place, which a few minutes ago was so still and quiet, is now all bustle; the early vendors of the morning papers have arrived, and you are assailed on all sides with shouts of "*Times*, gen'lm'n, *Times*," "Here's *Chron—Chron—Chron*," "*Herald*, ma'am," "Highly interesting murder, gen'lm'n," "Curious case o' breach o' promise, ladies." The inside passengers are already in their dens, and the outsides, with the exception of yourself, are pacing up and down the pavement to keep themselves warm; they consist of two young men with very long hair, to which the sleet has communicated the appearance of crystallised rats' tails; one thin young woman cold and peevish, one old gentleman ditto ditto, and something in a cloak and cap, intended to represent a military officer; every member of the party, with a large stiff shawl over his chin, looking exactly as if he were playing a set of Pan's pipes.

"Take off the cloths, Bob," says the coachman, who now appears for the first time, in a rough blue great-coat, of which the buttons behind are so far apart, that you can't see them both at the same time. "Now, gen'lm'n," cries the guard, with the waybill in his hand. "Five minutes behind time already!" Up jump the passengers—the two young men smoking like lime-kilns, and the old gentleman grumbling audibly. The thin young woman is got upon the roof, by dint of a great deal of pulling, and pushing, and helping and trouble, and she repays it by expressing her solemn conviction that she will never be able to get down again.

"All right," sings out the guard at last, jumping up as the coach starts, and blowing his horn directly afterwards, in proof of the soundness of his wind. "Let 'em go, Harry, give 'em their heads," cries the coachman—and off we start as briskly as if the morning were "all right," as well as the coach: and looking forward as anxiously to the termination of our journey, as we fear our readers will have done, long since, to the conclusion of our paper.

CHAPTER XVI.

OMNIBUSES.

It is very generally allowed that public conveyances afford an extensive field for amusement and observation. Of all the public conveyances that have been constructed since the days of the Ark—we think that is the earliest on record—to the present time, commend us to an omnibus. A long stage is not to be despised, but there you have only six insides, and the chances are, that the same people go all the way with you—there is no change, no variety. Besides, after the first twelve hours or so, people get cross and sleepy, and when you have seen a man in his nightcap, you lose all respect for him; at least, that is the case with us. Then on smooth roads people frequently get prosy, and tell long stories, and even those who don't talk, may have very unpleasant predilections. We once travelled four hundred miles, inside a stage-coach, with a stout man, who had a glass of rum-and-water, warm, handed in at the window at every place where we changed horses. This was decidedly unpleasant. We have also travelled occasionally, with a small boy of a pale aspect, with light hair, and no perceptible neck, coming up to town from school under the protection of the guard, and directed to be left at the Cross Keys till called for. This is, perhaps, even worse than rum-and-water in a close atmosphere. Then there is the whole train of evils consequent on a change of the coachman; and the misery of the discovery—which the guard is sure to make the moment you begin to doze—that he wants a brown-paper parcel, which he distinctly remembers to have deposited under the seat on which you are reposing. A great deal of bustle and groping takes place, and when you are thoroughly awakened, and severely cramped, by holding your legs up by an almost supernatural exertion, while he is looking behind them, it suddenly occurs to him that he put it in the fore-boot. Bang goes the door; the parcel is immediately found; off starts the coach again; and the guard plays the key-bugle as loud as he can play it, as if in mockery of your wretchedness.

Now, you meet with none of these afflictions in an omnibus; sameness there can never be. The passengers change as often in the course of one journey as the figures in a kaleidoscope, and though not so glittering, are far more amusing. We believe there is no instance on record, of a man's having gone to sleep in one of these vehicles. As to long stories, would any man venture to tell a long story in an omnibus? and even if he did, where would be the harm? nobody could possibly hear what he was talking about. Again; children, though occasionally, are not often to be found in an omnibus; and even when they are, if the vehicle be full, as is generally the case, somebody sits upon them, and we are unconscious of their presence. Yes, after mature reflection, and considerable experience, we are decidedly of opinion, that of all known vehicles, from the glass-coach in which we were taken to be christened, to that sombre caravan in which we must one day make our last earthly journey, there is nothing like an omnibus.

We will back the machine in which we make our daily peregrination from the top of Oxford-street to the city, against any "buss" on the road, whether it be for the gaudiness of its exterior, the perfect simplicity of its interior, or the native coolness of its cad. This young gentleman is a singular instance of self-devotion; his somewhat intemperate zeal on behalf of his employers, is constantly getting him into trouble, and occasionally into the house of correction. He is no sooner emancipated, however, than he resumes the duties of his profession with unabated ardour. His principal distinction is his activity. His great boast is, "that he can chuck an old gen'lm'n into the buss, shut him in, and rattle off, afore he knows where it's a-going to"—a feat which he frequently performs, to the infinite amusement of every one but the old gentleman concerned, who, somehow or other, never can see the joke of the thing.

We are not aware that it has ever been precisely ascertained, how many passengers our omnibus will contain. The impression on the cad's mind, evidently is, that it is amply sufficient for the accommodation of any number of persons that can be enticed into it. "Any room?" cries a very hot pedestrian. "Plenty o' room, sir," replies the conductor, gradually opening the door, and not disclosing the real state of the case, until the wretched man is on the steps. "Where?" inquires the entrapped individual, with an attempt to back out again. "Either side, sir," rejoins the cad, shoving him in, and slamming the door. "All right, Bill." Retreat is impossible; the new-comer rolls about, till he falls down somewhere, and there he stops.

As we get into the city a little before ten, four or five of our party are regular passengers. We always take them up at the same places, and they generally occupy the same seats; they are always dressed in the same manner, and invariably discuss the same topics—the increasing rapidity of cabs, and the disregard of moral obligations evinced by omnibus men. There is a little testy old man, with a powdered head, who always sits on the right-hand side of the door as you enter, with his hands folded on the top of his umbrella. He is extremely impatient, and sits there for the purpose of keeping a sharp eye on the cad, with whom he generally holds a running dialogue. He is very officious in helping people in and out, and always volunteers to give the cad a poke with his umbrella, when any one wants to alight. He usually recommends ladies to have sixpence ready, to prevent delay; and if any body puts a window down, that he can reach, he immediately puts it up again.

"Now, what are you stopping for?" says the little man every morning, the moment there is the slightest indication of "pulling up" at the corner of Regent-street, when some such dialogue as the following takes place between him and the cad:

"What are you stopping for?"

Here the cad whistles, and affects not to hear the question.

"I say [a poke], what are you stopping for?"

"For passengers, sir. Ba—nk.—Ty."

"I know you're stopping for passengers; but you've no business to do so. *Why* are you stopping?"

"Vy, sir, that's a difficult question. I think it is because we perfer stopping here to going on."

"Now mind," exclaims the little old man, with great vehemence, "I'll pull you up to-morrow; I've often threatened to do it; now I will."

"Thankee, sir," replies the cad, touching his hat with a mock expression of gratitude;—"werry much obliged to you indeed, sir." Here the young men in the omnibus laugh very heartily, and the old gentleman gets very red in the face, and seems highly exasperated.

The stout gentleman in the white neckcloth, at the other end of the vehicle, looks very prophetic, and says that something must shortly be done with these fellows, or there's no saying where all this will end; and the shabby-genteel man with the green bag, expresses his entire concurrence in the opinion, as he has done regularly every morning for the last six months.

A second omnibus now comes up, and stops immediately behind us. Another old gentleman elevates his cane in the air, and runs with all his might towards our omnibus; we watch his progress with great interest; the door is opened to receive him, he suddenly disappears—he has been spirited away by the opposition. Hereupon the driver of the opposition taunts our people with his having "regularly done 'em out of that old swell," and the voice of the "old swell" is heard, vainly protesting against this unlawful detention. We rattle off, the other omnibus rattles after us, and every time we stop to take up a passenger, they stop to take him too; sometimes we get him; sometimes they get him· but whoever don't get him, say they ought to have had him, and the cads of the respective vehicles abuse one another accordingly.

As we arrive in the vicinity of Lincoln's-inn-fields, Bedford-row, and other legal haunts, we drop a great many of our original passengers, and take up fresh ones, who meet with a very sulky reception. It is rather remarkable, that the people already in an omnibus, always look at new-comers, as if they entertained some undefined idea that they have no business to come in at all. We are quite persuaded the little old man has some notion of this kind, and that he considers their entry as a sort of negative impertinence.

Conversation is now entirely dropped; each person gazes vacantly through the window in front of him, and everybody thinks that his opposite neighbour is staring at him. If one man gets out at Shoe-lane, and another at the corner of Farringdon-street, the little old gentleman grumbles, and suggests to the latter, that if he had got out at Shoe-lane too, he would have saved them the delay of another stoppage; whereupon the young men laugh again, and the old gentleman looks very solemn, and says nothing more till he gets to the Bank, when he trots off as fast as he can, leaving us to do the same, and to wish, as we walk away, that we could impart to others any portion of the amusement we have gained for ourselves.

CHAPTER XVII.

THE LAST CAB-DRIVER, AND THE FIRST OMNIBUS CAD.

Of all the cabriolet-drivers whom we have ever had the honour and gratification of knowing by sight—and our acquaintance in this way has been most extensive—there is one who made an impression on our mind which can never be effaced, and who awakened in our bosom a feeling of admiration and respect, which we entertain a fatal presentiment will never be called forth again by any human being. He was a man of most simple and prepossessing appearance. He was a brown-whiskered, white-hatted, no-coated cabman; his nose was generally red, and his bright blue eye not unfrequently stood out in bold relief against a black border of artificial workmanship; his boots were of the Wellington form, pulled up to meet his corduroy knee-smalls, or at least to approach as near them as their dimensions would admit of; and his neck was usually garnished with a bright yellow handkerchief. In summer he carried in his mouth a flower; in winter, a straw—slight, but to a contemplative mind, certain indications of a love of nature, and a taste for botany.

His cabriolet was gorgeously painted—a bright red; and wherever we went, City or West End, Paddington or Holloway, North, East, West, or South, there was the red cab, bumping up against the posts at the street corners, and turning in and out, among hackney-coaches, and drays, and carts, and waggons, and omnibuses, and contriving by some strange means or other, to get out of places which no other vehicle but the red cab could ever by any possibility have contrived to get into at all. Our fondness for that red cab was unbounded. How we should have liked to have seen it in the circle at Astley's! Our life upon it, that it should have performed such evolutions as would have put the whole company to shame—Indian chiefs, knights, Swiss peasants, and all.

Some people object to the exertion of getting into cabs, and others object to the difficulty of getting out of them; we think both these are objections which take their rise in perverse and ill-conditioned minds. The getting into a cab is a very pretty and graceful process, which, when well performed, is essentially melodramatic. First, there is the expressive pantomime of every one of the eighteen cabmen on the stand, the moment you raise your eyes from the ground. Then there is your own pantomime in reply—quite a little ballet. Four cabs immediately leave the stand, for your especial accommodation; and the evolutions of the animals who draw them, are beautiful in the extreme, as they grate the wheels of the cabs against the curb-stones, and sport playfully in the kennel. You single out a particular cab, and dart swiftly towards it. One bound, and you are on the first step; turn your body lightly round to the right, and you are on the second; bend gracefully beneath the reins, working round to the left at the same time, and you are in the cab. There is no difficulty in finding a seat: the apron knocks you comfortably into it at once, and off you go.

The getting out of a cab, is, perhaps, rather more complicated in its theory, and a shade more difficult in its execution. We have studied the subject a great deal, and we think the best way is, to throw yourself out, and trust to chance for alighting on your feet. If you make the driver alight first, and then throw yourself upon him, you will find that he breaks your fall materially. In the event of your contemplating an offer of eightpence, on no account make the tender, or show the money, until you are safely on the pavement. It is very bad policy attempting to save the fourpence. You are very much in the power of a cabman, and he considers it a kind of fee not to do you any wilful damage. Any instruction, however, in the art of getting out of a cab, is wholly unnecessary if you are going any distance, because the probability is, that you will be shot lightly out before you have completed the third mile.

We are not aware of any instance on record in which a cab-horse has performed three consecutive miles without going down once. What of that? It is all excitement. And in these days of derangement of the nervous system and universal lassitude, people are content to pay handsomely for excitement; where can it be procured at a cheaper rate?

But to return to the red cab; it was omnipresent. You had but to walk down Holborn, or Fleet-street, or any of the principal thoroughfares in which there is a great deal of traffic, and judge for yourself. You had hardly turned into the street, when you saw a trunk or two, lying on the ground: an uprooted post, a hat-box, a portmanteau, and a carpet-bag, strewed about in a very picturesque manner: a horse in a cab standing by, looking about him with great unconcern; and a crowd, shouting and screaming with delight, cooling their flushed faces against the glass windows of a chemist's shop.—"What's the matter here, can you tell me?"—"O'ny a cab, sir."—"Anybody hurt, do you know?"—"O'ny the fare, sir. I see him a turnin' the corner, and I ses to another gen'lm'n 'that's a reg'lar little oss that, and he's a comin' along rayther sweet, an't he?'—'He just is,' ses the other gen'lm'n, ven bump they cums agin the post, and out flies the fare like bricks." Need we say it was the red cab; or that the gentleman with the straw in his mouth, who emerged so coolly from the chemist's shop and philosophically climbing into the little dickey, started off at full gallop, was the red cab's licensed driver?

The ubiquity of this red cab, and the influence it exercised over the risible muscles of justice itself, was perfectly astonishing. You walked into the justice-room of the Mansion-house; the whole court resounded with merriment. The

Lord Mayor threw himself back in his chair, in a state of frantic delight at his own joke; every vein in Mr. Hobler's countenance was swollen with laughter, partly at the Lord Mayor's facetiousness, but more at his own; the constables and police-officers were (as in duty bound) in ecstasies at Mr. Hobler and the Lord Mayor combined; and the very paupers, glancing respectfully at the beadle's countenance, tried to smile, as even he relaxed. A tall, weazen-faced man, with an impediment in his speech, would be endeavouring to state a case of imposition against the red cab's driver; and the red cab's driver, and the Lord Mayor, and Mr. Hobler, would be having a little fun among themselves, to the inordinate delight of everybody but the complainant. In the end, justice would be so tickled with the red-cab-driver's native humour, that the fine would be mitigated, and he would go away full gallop, in the red cab, to impose on somebody else without loss of time.

The driver of the red cab, confident in the strength of his own moral principles, like many other philosophers, was wont to set the feelings and opinions of society at complete defiance. Generally speaking, perhaps, he would as soon carry a fare safely to his destination, as he would upset him—sooner, perhaps, because in that case he not only got the money, but had the additional amusement of running a longer heat against some smart rival. But society made war upon him in the shape of penalties, and he must make war upon society in his own way. This was the reasoning of the red-cab-driver. So, he bestowed a searching look upon the fare, as he put his hand in his waistcoat pocket, when he had gone half the mile, to get the money ready; and if he brought forth eightpence, out he went.

The last time we saw our friend was one wet evening in Tottenham-court-road, when he was engaged in a very warm and somewhat personal altercation with a loquacious little gentleman in a green coat. Poor fellow! there were great excuses to be made for him: he had not received above eighteenpence more than his fare, and consequently laboured under a great deal of very natural indignation. The dispute had attained a pretty considerable height, when at last the loquacious little gentleman, making a mental calculation of the distance, and finding that he had already paid more than he ought, avowed his unalterable determination to "pull up" the cabman in the morning.

"Now, just mark this, young man," said the little gentleman, "I'll pull you up to-morrow morning."

"No! will you though?" said our friend, with a sneer.

"I will," replied the little gentleman, "mark my words, that's all. If I live till to-morrow morning, you shall repent this."

There was a steadiness of purpose, and indignation of speech, about the little gentleman, as he took an angry pinch of snuff, after this last declaration, which made a visible impression on the mind of the red-cab-driver. He appeared to hesitate for an instant. It was only for an instant; his resolve was soon taken.

"You'll pull me up, will you?" said our friend.

"I will," rejoined the little gentleman, with even greater vehemence than before.

"Very well," said our friend, tucking up his shirt sleeves very calmly. "There'll be three veeks for that. Wery good; that'll bring me up to the middle o' next month. Three veeks more would carry me on to my birthday, and then I've got ten pound to draw. I may as well get board, lodgin', and washin', till then, out of the county, as pay for it myself; consequently here goes!"

So, without more ado, the red-cab-driver knocked the little gentleman down, and then called the police to take himself into custody, with all the civility in the world.

THE LAST CAB-DRIVER.

A story is nothing without the sequel; and therefore, we may state, that to our certain knowledge, the board, lodging, and washing, were all provided in due course. We happen to know the fact, for it came to our knowledge thus: We went over the House of Correction for the county of Middlesex shortly after, to witness the operation of the silent system; and looked on all the "wheels" with the greatest anxiety, in search of our long-lost friend. He was nowhere to be seen, however, and we began to think that the little gentleman in the green coat must have relented, when, as we were traversing the kitchen-garden, which lies in a sequestered part of the prison, we were startled by hearing a voice, which apparently proceeded from the wall, pouring forth its soul in the plaintive air of "All round my hat," which was then just beginning to form a recognised portion of our national music.

We started.—"What voice is that?" said we.

The Governor shook his head.

"Sad fellow," he replied, "very sad. He positively refused to work on the wheel; so, after many trials, I was compelled to order him into solitary confinement. He says he likes it very much though, and I am afraid he does, for he lies on his back on the floor, and sings comic songs all day!"

Shall we add, that our heart had not deceived us; and that the comic singer was no other than our eagerly-sought friend, the red-cab-driver?

We have never seen him since, but we have strong reason to suspect that this noble individual was a distant relative of a waterman of our acquaintance, who, on one occasion, when we were passing the coach-stand over which he presides, after standing very quietly to see a tall man struggle into a cab, ran up very briskly when it was all over (as his brethren invariably do), and, touching his hat, asked, as a matter of course, for "a copper for the waterman." Now, the fare was by no means a handsome man; and, waxing very indignant at the demand, he replied —"Money! What for? Coming up and looking at me, I suppose?"—"Vell, sir," rejoined the waterman, with a smile of immoveable complacency, "*That's* worth twopence."

This identical waterman afterwards attained a very prominent station in society; and as we know something of his life, and have often thought of telling what we *do* know, perhaps we shall never have a better opportunity than the present.

Mr. William Barker, then, for that was the gentleman's name, Mr. William Barker was born ——— but why need we relate where Mr. William Barker was born, or when? Why scrutinise the entries in parochial ledgers, or seek to penetrate the Lucinian mysteries of lying-in hospitals? Mr. William Barker *was* born, or he had never been. There is a son—there was a father. There is an effect—there was a cause. Surely this is sufficient information for the most Fatima-like curiosity; and, if it be not, we regret our inability to supply any further evidence on the point. Can there be a more satisfactory, or more strictly parliamentary course? Impossible.

We at once avow a similar inability to record at what precise period, or by what particular process, this gentleman's patronymic, of William Barker, became corrupted into "Bill Boorker." Mr. Barker acquired a high standing, and no inconsiderable reputation, among the members of that profession to which he more peculiarly devoted his energies; and to them he was generally known, either by the familiar appellation of "Bill Boorker," or the flattering designation of "Aggerawatin Bill," the latter being a playful and expressive *sobriquet*, illustrative of Mr. Barker's great talent in "aggerawatin" and rendering wild such subjects of her Majesty as are conveyed from place to place, through the instrumentality of omnibuses. Of the early life of Mr. Barker little is known, and even that little is involved in considerable doubt and obscurity. A want of application, a restlessness of purpose, a thirsting after porter, a love of all that is roving and cadger-like in nature, shared in common with many other great geniuses, appear to have been his leading characteristics. The busy hum of a parochial free-school, and the shady repose of a county gaol, were alike inefficacious in producing the slightest alteration in Mr. Barker's disposition. His feverish attachment to change and variety nothing could repress; his native daring no punishment could subdue.

If Mr. Barker can be fairly said to have had any weakness in his earlier years, it was an amiable one—love; love in its most comprehensive form—a love of ladies, liquids, and pocket-handkerchiefs. It was no selfish feeling; it was not confined to his own possessions, which but too many men regard with exclusive complacency. No; it was a nobler love—a general principle. It extended itself with equal force to the property of other people.

There is something very affecting in this. It is still more affecting to know, that such philanthropy is but imperfectly rewarded. Bow-street, Newgate, and Millbank, are a poor return for general benevolence, evincing itself in an irrepressible love for all created objects. Mr. Barker felt it so. After a lengthened interview with the highest legal authorities, he quitted his ungrateful country, with the consent, and at the expense, of its Government; proceeded to a distant shore; and there employed himself, like another Cincinnatus, in clearing and cultivating the soil—a peaceful pursuit, in which a term of seven years glided almost imperceptibly away.

Whether, at the expiration of the period we have just mentioned, the British Government required Mr. Barker's presence here, or did not require his residence abroad, we have no distinct means of ascertaining. We should be inclined, however, to favour the latter position, inasmuch as we do not find that he was advanced to any other public post on his return, than the post at the corner of the Haymarket, where he officiated as assistant-waterman to the hackney-coach-stand. Seated, in this capacity, on a couple of tubs near the curb-stone, with a brass plate and number suspended round his neck by a massive chain, and his ankles curiously enveloped in haybands, he is supposed to have made those observations on human nature which exercised so material an influence over all his proceedings in later life.

Mr. Barker had not officiated for many months in this capacity, when the appearance of the first omnibus caused the public mind to go in a new direction, and prevented a great many hackney-coaches from going in any direction at all. The genius of Mr. Barker at once perceived the whole extent of the injury that would be eventually inflicted on cab and coach stands, and, by consequence, on watermen also, by the progress of the system of which the first omnibus was a part. He saw, too, the necessity of adopting some more profitable profession; and his active mind at once perceived how much might be done in the way of enticing the youthful and unwary, and shoving the old and helpless, into the wrong buss, and carrying them off, until, reduced to despair, they ransomed themselves by the payment of sixpence a-head, or, to adopt his own figurative expression in all its native beauty, "till they was rig'larly done over, and forked out the stumpy."

An opportunity for realising his fondest anticipations, soon presented itself Rumours were rife on the hackney-coach-stands, that a buss was building, to run from Lisson-grove to the Bank, down Oxford-street and Holborn; and the rapid increase of busses on the Paddington-road, encouraged the idea. Mr. Barker secretly and cautiously inquired in the proper quarters. The report was correct; the "Royal William" was to make its first journey on the following Monday. It was a crack affair altogether. An enterprising young cabman, of established reputation as a dashing whip—for he had compromised with the parents of three scrunched children, and just "worked out" his fine, for knocking down an old lady—was the driver; and the spirited proprietor, knowing Mr. Barker's qualifications, appointed him to the vacant office of cad on the very first application. The buss began to run, and Mr. Barker entered into a new suit of clothes, and on a new sphere of action.

To recapitulate all the improvements introduced by this extraordinary man, into the omnibus system—gradually, indeed, but surely—would occupy a far greater space than we are enabled to devote to this imperfect memoir. To him is universally assigned the original suggestion of the practice which afterwards became so general—of the driver of a second buss keeping constantly behind the first one, and driving the pole of his vehicle either into the door of the other, every time it was opened, or through the body of any lady or gentleman who might make an attempt to get into it; a humorous and pleasant invention, exhibiting all that originality of idea, and fine bold flow of spirits, so conspicuous in every action of this great man.

Mr. Barker had opponents of course; what man in public life has not? But even his worst enemies cannot deny that he has taken more old ladies and gentlemen to Paddington who wanted to go to the Bank, and more old ladies and gentlemen to the Bank who wanted to go to Paddington, than any six men on the road and however much malevolent spirits may pretend to doubt the accuracy of the statement, they well know it to be an established fact, that he has forcibly conveyed a variety of ancient persons of either sex, to both places, who had not the slightest or most distant intention of going anywhere at all.

Mr. Barker was the identical cad who nobly distinguished himself, some time since, by keeping a tradesman on the step—the omnibus going at full speed all the time—till he had thrashed him to his entire satisfaction, and finally throwing him away, when he had quite done with him. Mr. Barker it *ought* to have been, who honestly indignant at being ignominiously ejected from a house of public entertainment, kicked the landlord in the knee, and thereby caused his death. We say it *ought* to have been Mr. Barker, because the action was not a common one, and could have emanated from no ordinary mind.

It has now become matter of history; it is recorded in the Newgate Calendar; and we wish we could attribute this piece of daring heroism to Mr. Barker. We regret being compelled to state that it was not performed by him. Would, for the family credit we could add, that it was achieved by his brother!

It was in the exercise of the nicer details of his profession, that Mr. Barker's knowledge of human nature was beautifully displayed. He could tell at a glance where a passenger wanted to go to, and would shout the name of the place accordingly, without the slightest reference to the real destination of the vehicle. He knew exactly the kind of old lady that would be too much flurried by the process of pushing in and pulling out of the caravan, to discover where she had been put down, until too late; had an intuitive perception of what was passing in a passenger's mind when he inwardly resolved to "pull that cad up to-morrow morning;" and never failed to make himself agreeable to female servants, whom he would place next the door, and talk to all the way.

Human judgment is never infallible, and it would occasionally happen that Mr. Barker experimentalised with the timidity or forbearance of the wrong person, in which case a summons to a Police-office, was, on more than one occasion, followed by a committal to prison. It was not in the power of trifles such as these, however, to subdue the freedom of his spirit. As soon as they passed away, he resumed the duties of his profession with unabated ardour.

We have spoken of Mr. Barker and of the red-cab-driver, in the past tense. Alas! Mr. Barker has again become an absentee; and the class of men to which they both belonged are fast disappearing. Improvement has peered beneath the aprons of our cabs, and penetrated to the very innermost recesses of our omnibuses. Dirt and fustian will vanish before cleanliness and livery. Slang will be forgotten when civility becomes general: and that enlightened, eloquent, sage, and profound body, the Magistracy of London, will be deprived of half their amusement, and half their occupation.

CHAPTER XVIII.

A PARLIAMENTARY SKETCH.

We hope our readers will not be alarmed at this rather ominous title. We assure them that we are not about to become political, neither have we the slightest intention of being more prosy than usual—if we can help it. It has occurred to us that a slight sketch of the general aspect of "the House," and the crowds that resort to it on the night of an important debate, would be productive of some amusement: and as we have made some few calls at the aforesaid house in our time— have visited it quite often enough for our purpose, and a great deal too often for our own personal peace and comfort—we have determined to attempt the description. Dismissing from our minds, therefore, all that feeling of awe, which vague ideas of breaches of privilege, Serjeant-at-Arms, heavy denunciations, and still heavier fees, are calculated to awaken, we enter at once into the building, and upon our subject.

Half-past four o'clock—and at five the mover of the Address will be "on his legs," as the newspapers announce sometimes by way of novelty, as if speakers were occasionally in the habit of standing on their heads. The members are pouring in, one after the other, in shoals. The few spectators who can obtain standing-room in the passages, scrutinise them as they pass, with the utmost interest, and the man who can identify a member occasionally, becomes a person of great importance. Every now and then you hear earnest whispers of "That's Sir John Thomson." "Which? him with the gilt order round his neck?" "No, no; that's one of the messengers—that other with the yellow gloves, is Sir John Thomson," "Here's Mr. Smith." "Lor!" "Yes, how d'ye do, sir?—(He is our new member)—How do you do, sir?" Mr. Smith stops: turns round with an air of enchanting urbanity (for the rumour of an intended dissolution has been very extensively circulated this morning); seizes both the hands of his gratified constituent, and, after greeting him with the most enthusiastic warmth, darts into the lobby with an extraordinary display of ardour in the public cause, leaving an immense impression in his favour on the mind of his "fellow-townsman."

The arrivals increase in number, and the heat and noise increase in very unpleasant proportion. The livery servants form a complete lane on either side of the passage, and you reduce yourself into the smallest possible space to avoid being turned out. You see that stout man with the hoarse voice, in the blue coat, queer crowned, broad-brimmed hat, white corduroy breeches, and great boots, who has been talking incessantly for half an hour past, and whose importance has occasioned no small quantity of mirth among the strangers. That is the great conservator of the peace of Westminster. You cannot fail to have remarked the grace with which he saluted the noble Lord who passed just now, or the excessive dignity of his air, as he expostulates with the crowd. He is rather out of temper now, in consequence of the very irreverent behaviour of those two young fellows behind him, who have done nothing but laugh all the time they have been here.

"Will they divide to-night, do you think, Mr. —— ?" timidly inquires a little thin man in the crowd, hoping to conciliate the man of office.

"How *can* you ask such questions, sir ?" replies the functionary, in an incredibly loud key, and pettishly grasping the thick stick he carries in his right hand. "Pray do not, sir. I beg of you ; pray do not, sir." The little man looks remarkably out of his element, and the uninitiated part of the throng are in positive convulsions of laughter.

Just at this moment some unfortunate individual appears, with a very smirking air, at the bottom of the long passage. He has managed to elude the vigilance of the special constable down stairs, and is evidently congratulating himself on having made his way so far.

"Go back, sir—you must *not* come here," shouts the hoarse one, with tremendous emphasis of voice and gesture, the moment the offender catches his eye.

The stranger pauses.

"Do you hear, sir—will you go back ?" continues the official dignitary, gently pushing the intruder some half-dozen yards.

"Come, don't push me," replies the stranger, turning angrily round.

"I will, sir."

"You won't, sir."

"Go out, sir."

"Take your hands off me, sir."

"Go out off the passage, sir."

"You're a Jack-in-office, sir."

"A what ?" ejaculates he of the boots.

"A Jack-in-office, sir, and a very insolent fellow," reiterates the stranger, now completely in a passion.

"Pray do not force me to put you out, sir," retorts the other—"pray do not—my instructions are to keep this passage clear—it's the Speaker's orders, sir."

"D—n the Speaker, sir !" shouts the intruder.

"Here, Wilson !—Collins !" gasps the officer, actually paralysed at this insulting expression, which in his mind is all but high treason; "take this man out—take him out, I say ! How dare you, sir ?" and down goes the unfortunate man five stairs at a time, turning round at every stoppage, to come back again, and denouncing bitter vengeance against the commander-in-chief, and all his supernumeraries.

"Make way, gentlemen,—pray make way for the Members, I beg of you !" shouts the zealous officer, turning back, and preceding a whole string of the liberal and independent.

You see this ferocious-looking gentleman, with a complexion almost as sallow as his linen, and whose large black moustache would give him the appearance of a figure in a hairdresser's window, if his countenance possessed the thought which is communicated to those waxen caricatures of the human face divine. He is a militia-officer, and the most amusing person in the House. Can anything be more exquisitely absurd than the burlesque grandeur of his air, as he strides up to the lobby, his eyes rolling like those of a Turk's head in a cheap Dutch clock ? He never appears without that bundle of dirty papers which he carries under his left arm, and which are generally supposed to be the miscellaneous estimates for 1804, or some equally important documents. He is very punctual in his attendance at the House, and his self-satisfied "He-ar-He-ar," is not unfrequently the signal for a general titter.

This is the gentleman who once actually sent a messenger up to the Strangers' gallery in the old House of Commons, to inquire the name of an individual who was using an eye glass, in order that he might complain to the Speaker that the person in question was quizzing him! On another occasion, he is reported to have repaired to Bellamy's kitchen—a refreshment-room, where persons who are not Members are admitted on sufferance, as it were—and perceiving two or three gentlemen at supper, who he was aware were not Members, and could not, in that place, very well resent his behaviour, he indulged in the pleasantry of sitting with his booted leg on the table at which they were supping! He is generally harmless, though, and always amusing.

By dint of patience, and some little interest with our friend the constable, we have contrived to make our way to the Lobby, and you can just manage to catch an occasional glimpse of the House, as the door is opened for the admission of Members It is tolerably full already, and little groups of Members are congregated together here, discussing the interesting topics of the day.

That smart-looking fellow in the black coat with velvet facings and cuffs, who wears his *D'Orsay* hat so rakishly, is "Honest Tom," a metropolitan representative; and the large man in the cloak with the white lining—not the man by the pillar; the other with the light hair hanging over his coat collar behind—is his colleague. The quiet gentlemanly-looking man in the blue surtout, gray trousers, white neckerchief, and gloves, whose closely-buttoned coat displays his manly figure and broad chest to great advantage, is a very well-known character. He has fought a great many battles in his time, and conquered like the heroes of old, with no other arms than those the gods gave him. The old hard-featured man who is standing near him, is really a good specimen of a class of men, now nearly extinct. He is a county Member, and has been from time whereof the memory of man is not to the contrary. Look at his loose, wide, brown coat, with capacious pockets on each side; the knee-breeches and boots, the immensely long waistcoat, and silver watch-chain dangling below it, the wide-brimmed brown hat, and the white handkerchief tied in a great bow, with straggling ends sticking out beyond his shirt-frill. It is a costume one seldom sees nowadays, and when the few who wear it have died off, it will be quite extinct. He can tell you long stories of Fox, Pitt, Sheridan, and Canning, and how much better the House was managed in those times, when they used to get up at eight or nine o'clock, except on regular field-days, of which everybody was apprised beforehand. He has a great contempt for all young Members of Parliament, and thinks it quite impossible that a man can say anything worth hearing, unless he has sat in the House for fifteen years at least, without saying anything at all. He is of opinion that "that young Macaulay" was a regular impostor; he allows, that Lord Stanley may do something one of these days, but "he's too young, sir—too young." He is an excellent authority on points of precedent, and when he grows talkative, after his wine, will tell you how Sir Somebody Something, when he was whipper-in for the Government, brought four men out of their beds to vote in the majority, three of whom died on their way home again; how the House once divided on the question, that fresh candles be now brought in; how the Speaker was once upon a time left in the chair by accident, at the conclusion of business, and was obliged to sit in the House by himself for three hours, till some Member could be knocked up and brought back again, to move the adjournment; and a great many other anecdotes of a similar description.

There he stands, leaning on his stick; looking at the throng of Exquisites around him with most profound contempt; and conjuring up, before his mind's eye, the scenes he beheld in the old House, in days gone by, when his own feelings were fresher and brighter, and when, as he imagines, wit, talent, and patriotism flourished more brightly too.

You are curious to know who that young man in the rough great-coat is, who has accosted every Member who has entered the House since we have been standing here. He is not a Member; he is only an "hereditary bondsman," or, in other words, an Irish correspondent of an Irish newspaper, who has just procured his forty-second frank from a Member whom he never saw in his life before. There he goes again—another! Bless the man, he has his hat and pockets full already.

We will try our fortune at the Strangers' gallery, though the nature of the debate encourages very little hope of success. What on earth are you about? Holding up your order as if it were a talisman at whose command the wicket would fly open? Nonsense. Just preserve the order for an autograph, if it be worth keeping at all, and make your appearance at the door with your thumb and fore-finger expressively inserted in your waistcoat-pocket. This tall stout man in black is the door-keeper. "Any room?" "Not an inch—two or three dozen gentlemen waiting down stairs on the chance of somebody's going out." Pull out your purse—"Are you *quite* sure there's no room?"—"I'll go and look," replies the door-keeper, with a wistful glance at your purse, "but I'm afraid there's not." He returns, and with real feeling assures you that it is morally impossible to get near the gallery. It is of no use waiting. When you are refused admission into the Strangers' gallery at the House of Commons, under such circumstances, you may return home thoroughly satisfied that the place must be remarkably full indeed.*

Retracing our steps through the long passage, descending the stairs, and crossing Palace-yard, we halt at a small temporary door-way adjoining the King's entrance to the House of Lords. The order of the serjeant-at-arms will admit you into the Reporters' gallery, from whence you can obtain a tolerably good view of the House. Take care of the stairs, they are none of the best; through this little wicket—there. As soon as your eyes become a little used to the mist of the place, and the glare of the chandeliers below you, you will see that some unimportant personage on the Ministerial side of the House (to your right hand) is speaking, amidst a hum of voices and confusion which would rival Babel, but for the circumstance of its being all in one language.

The "hear, hear," which occasioned that laugh, proceeded from our warlike friend with the moustache; he is sitting on the back seat against the wall, behind the Member who is speaking, looking as ferocious and intellectual as usual. Take one look around you, and retire! The body of the House and the side galleries are full of Members; some, with their legs on the back of the opposite seat; some, with theirs stretched out to their utmost length on the floor; some going out, others coming in; all talking, laughing, lounging, coughing, o-ing, questioning, or groaning; presenting a conglomeration of noise and confusion, to be met with in no other place in existence, not even excepting Smithfield on a market-day, or a cock-pit in its glory.

But let us not omit to notice Bellamy's kitchen, or, in other words, the refreshment-room, common to both Houses of Parliament, where Ministerialists and Oppositionists, Whigs and Tories, Radicals, Peers, and Destructives, strangers from the gallery, and the more favoured strangers from below the bar, are alike at liberty to resort; where divers honourable members prove their perfect independence by remaining during the whole of a heavy debate, solacing themselves with the creature comforts; and whence they are summoned by whippers-in, when the House is on the point of dividing; either to give their "conscientious votes" on questions of which they are conscientiously innocent of knowing anything whatever, or to find a vent for the playful exuberance of their wine-inspired fancies, in

* This paper was written before the practice of exhibiting Members of Parliament, like other curiosities, for the small charge of half-a-crown, was abolished.

boisterous shouts of "Divide," occasionally varied with a little howling, barking, crowing, or other ebullitions of senatorial pleasantry.

When you have ascended the narrow staircase which, in the present temporary House of Commons, leads to the place we are describing, you will probably observe a couple of rooms on your right hand, with tables spread for dining. Neither of these is the kitchen, although they are both devoted to the same purpose; the kitchen is further on to our left, up these half-dozen stairs. Before we ascend the staircase, however, we must request you to pause in front of this little bar-place with the sash-windows; and beg your particular attention to the steady honest-looking old fellow in black, who is its sole occupant. Nicholas (we do not mind mentioning the old fellow's name, for if Nicholas be not a public man, who is?—and public men's names are public property)—Nicholas is the butler of Bellamy's, and has held the same place, dressed exactly in the same manner, and said precisely the same things, ever since the oldest of its present visitors can remember. An excellent servant Nicholas is—an unrivalled compounder of salad-dressing—an admirable preparer of soda-water and lemon—a special mixer of cold grog and punch—and, above all, an unequalled judge of cheese. If the old man have such a thing as vanity in his composition, this is certainly his pride; and if it be possible to imagine that anything in this world could disturb his impenetrable calmness, we should say it would be the doubting his judgment on this important point.

We needn't tell you all this, however, for if you have an atom of observation, one glance at his sleek, knowing-looking head and face—his prim white neckerchief, with the wooden tie into which it has been regularly folded for twenty years past, merging by imperceptible degrees into a small-plaited shirt-frill—and his comfortable-looking form encased in a well-brushed suit of black—would give you a better idea of his real character than a column of our poor description could convey.

Nicholas is rather out of his element now; he cannot see the kitchen as he used to in the old House; there, one window of his glass-case opened into the room, and then, for the edification and behoof of more juvenile questioners, he would stand for an hour together, answering deferential questions about Sheridan, and Percival, and Castlereagh, and Heaven knows who beside, with manifest delight, always inserting a "Mister" before every commoner's name.

Nicholas, like all men of his age and standing, has a great idea of the degeneracy of the times. He seldom expresses any political opinions, but we managed to ascertain, just before the passing of the Reform Bill, that Nicholas was a thorough Reformer. What was our astonishment to discover shortly after the meeting of the first reformed Parliament, that he was a most inveterate and decided Tory! It was very odd: some men change their opinions from necessity, others from expediency, others from inspiration; but that Nicholas should undergo any change in any respect, was an event we had never contemplated, and should have considered impossible. His strong opinion against the clause which empowered the metropolitan districts to return Members to Parliament, too, was perfectly unaccountable.

We discovered the secret at last; the metropolitan Members always dined at home. The rascals! As for giving additional Members to Ireland, it was even worse—decidedly unconstitutional. Why, sir, an Irish Member would go up there, and eat more dinner than three English Members put together. He took no wine; drank table-beer by the half-gallon; and went home to Manchester-buildings, or Millbank-street, for his whiskey-and-water. And what was the consequence? Why the concern lost—actually lost, sir—by his patronage. A queer old fellow is Nicholas, and as completely a part of the building as the house itself. We wonder he ever left the old place, and fully expected to see in the papers, the morning after the fire, a pathetic account of an old gentleman in black, of decent appearance, who was seen at one of the upper windows when the flames were at their height, and declared his resolute intention of falling with the floor. He must have been got out by force. However, he was got out—here he is again, looking as he always does, as if he had been in a bandbox ever since the last session. There he is, at his old post every night, just as we have described him: and, as characters are scarce, and faithful servants scarcer, long may he be there, say we!

Now, when you have taken your seat in the kitchen, and duly noticed the large fire and roasting-jack at one end of the room—the little table for washing glasses and draining jugs at the other—the clock over the window opposite St. Margaret's Church—the deal tables and wax candles—the damask table-cloths and bare floor—the plate and china on the tables, and the gridiron on the fire; and a few other anomalies peculiar to the place—we will point out to your notice two or three of the people present, whose station or absurdities render them the most worthy of remark.

It is half-past twelve o'clock, and as the division is not expected for an hour or two, a few Members are lounging away the time here in preference to standing at the bar of the House, or sleeping in one of the side galleries. That singularly awkward and ungainly-looking man, in the brownish-white hat, with the straggling black trousers which reach about half-way down the leg of his boots, who is leaning against the meat-screen, apparently deluding himself into the belief that he is thinking about something, is a splendid sample of a Member of the House of Commons concentrating in his own person the wisdom of a constituency. Observe the wig, of a dark hue but indescribable colour, for if it be naturally brown, it has acquired a black tint by long service, and if it be naturally black, the same cause has imparted to it a tinge of rusty brown; and remark how very materially the great blinker-like spectacles assist the expression of that most intelligent face. Seriously speaking, did you ever see a countenance so expressive of the most hopeless extreme of heavy dulness, or behold a form so strangely put together? He is no great speaker: but when he *does* address the House, the effect is absolutely irresistible.

The small gentleman with the sharp nose, who has just saluted him, is a Member of Parliament, an ex-Alderman, and a sort of amateur fireman. He, and the celebrated fireman's dog, were observed to be remarkably active at the conflagration of the two Houses of Parliament—they both ran up and down, and in and out, getting under people's feet, and into everybody's way, fully impressed with the belief that they were doing a great deal of good, and barking tremendously. The dog went quietly back to his kennel with the engine, but the gentleman kept up such an incessant noise for some weeks after the occurrence, that he became a positive nuisance. As no more parliamentary fires have occurred, however, and as he has consequently had no more opportunities of writing to the newspapers to relate how, by way of preserving pictures he cut them out of their frames, and performed other great national services, he has gradually relapsed into his old state of calmness.

That female in black—not the one whom the Lord's-Day-Bill Baronet has just chucked under the chin; the shorter of the two—is "Jane:" the Hebe of Bellamy's. Jane is as great a character as Nicholas, in her way. Her leading features are a thorough contempt for the great majority of her visitors; her predominant quality, love of admiration, as you cannot fail to observe, if you mark the glee with which she listens to something the young Member near her mutters somewhat unintelligibly in her ear (for his speech is rather thick from some cause or other), and how playfully she digs the handle of a fork into the arm with which he detains her, by way of reply.

Jane is no bad hand at repartees, and showers them about, with a degree of liberality and total absence of reserve or constraint, which occasionally excites no small amazement in the minds of strangers. She cuts jokes with Nicholas, too, but looks up to him with a great deal of respect; the immoveable stolidity with which Nicholas receives the aforesaid jokes, and looks on, at certain pastoral friskings and rompings (Jane's only recreations, and they are very innocent too) which occasionally take place in the passage, is not the least amusing part of his character.

The two persons who are seated at the table in the corner, at the farther end of the room, have been constant guests here, for many years past; and one of them has feasted within these walls, many a time, with the most brilliant characters of a brilliant period. He has gone up to the other House since then; the greater part of his boon companions have shared Yorick's fate, and his visits to Bellamy's are comparatively few.

If he really be eating his supper now, at what hour can he possibly have dined! A second solid mass of rump-steak has disappeared, and he eat the first in four minutes and three quarters, by the clock over the window. Was there ever such a personification of Falstaff! Mark the air with which he gloats over that Stilton, as he removes the napkin which has been placed beneath his chin to catch the superfluous gravy of the steak, and with what gusto he imbibes the porter which has been fetched, expressly for him, in the pewter pot. Listen to the hoarse sound of that voice, kept down as it is by layers of solids, and deep draughts of rich wine, and tell us if you ever saw such a perfect picture of a regular *gourmand*; and whether he is not exactly the man whom you would pitch upon as having been the partner of Sheridan's parliamentary carouses, the volunteer driver of the hackney-coach that took him home, and the involuntary upsetter of the whole party?

What an amusing contrast between his voice and appearance, and that of the spare, squeaking old man, who sits at the same table, and who, elevating a little cracked bantam sort of voice to its highest pitch, invokes damnation upon his own eyes or somebody else's at the commencement of every sentence he utters. "The Captain," as they call him, is a very old frequenter of Bellamy's; much addicted to stopping "after the House is up" (an inexpiable crime in Jane's eyes), and a complete walking reservoir of spirits and water.

The old Peer—or rather, the old man—for his peerage is of comparatively recent date—has a huge tumbler of hot punch brought him; and the other damns and drinks, and drinks and damns, and smokes. Members arrive every moment in a great bustle to report that "The Chancellor of the Exchequer's up," and to get glasses of brandy-and-water to sustain them during the division; people who have ordered supper, countermand it, and prepare to go down stairs, when suddenly a bell is heard to ring with tremendous violence, and a cry of "Di-vi-sion!" is heard in the passage. This is enough; away rush the members pell-mell. The room is cleared in an instant; the noise rapidly dies away; you hear the creaking of the last boot on the last stair, and are left alone with the leviathan of rump-steaks.

CHAPTER XIX.

PUBLIC DINNERS.

ALL public dinners in London, from the Lord Mayor's annual banquet at Guildhall, to the Chimney-sweepers' anniversary at White Conduit House; from the Goldsmiths' to the Butchers', from the Sheriffs' to the Licensed Victuallers'; are amusing scenes. Of all entertainments of this description, however, we think the annual dinner of some public charity is the most amusing. At a Company's dinner, the people are nearly all alike—regular old stagers, who make it a matter of business, and a thing not to be laughed at. At a political dinner, everybody is disagreeable, and inclined to speechify--much the same thing, by-the-bye; but at a charity dinner you see people of all sorts, kinds, and descriptions. The wine may not be remarkably special, to be sure, and we have heard some hard-hearted monsters grumble at the collection; but we really think the amusement to be derived from the occasion, sufficient to counterbalance, even these disadvantages.

Let us suppose you are induced to attend a dinner of this description—"Indigent Orphans' Friends' Benevolent Institution," we think it is. The name of the charity is a line or two longer, but never mind the rest. You have a distinct recollection, however, that you purchased a ticket at the solicitation of some charitable friend: and you deposit yourself in a hackney-coach, the driver of which—no doubt that you may do the thing in style—turns a deaf ear to your earnest entreaties to be set down at the corner of Great Queen-street, and persists in carrying you to the very door of the Freemasons', round which a crowd of people are assembled to witness the entrance of the indigent orphans' friends. You hear great speculations as you pay the fare, on the possibility of your being the noble Lord who is announced to fill the chair on the occasion, and are highly gratified to hear it eventually decided that you are only a "wocalist."

The first thing that strikes you, on your entrance, is the astonishing importance of the committee. You observe a door on the first landing, carefully guarded by two waiters, in and out of which stout gentlemen with very red faces keep running, with a degree of speed highly unbecoming the gravity of persons of their years and corpulency. You pause, quite alarmed at the bustle, and thinking, in your innocence, that two or three people must have been carried out of the dining-room in fits, at least. You are immediately undeceived by the waiter—"Up stairs, if you please, sir; this is the committee-room." Up stairs you go, accordingly; wondering, as you mount, what the duties of the committee can be, and whether they ever do anything beyond confusing each other, and running over the waiters.

Having deposited your hat and cloak, and received a remarkably small scrap of pasteboard in exchange (which, as a matter of course, you lose, before you require it again), you enter the hall, down which there are three long tables for the less distinguished guests, with a cross table on a raised platform at the upper end for the reception of the very particular friends of the indigent orphans. Being fortunate enough to find a plate without anybody's card in it, you wisely seat yourself at once, and have a little leisure to look about you. Waiters, with wine-baskets in their hands, are placing decanters of sherry down the tables, at very respectable distances; melancholy-looking salt-cellars, and decayed vinegar-cruets, which might have belonged to the parents of the indigent orphans in their time, are scattered at distant intervals on the cloth; and the knives and forks look as if they had done duty at every public dinner in London since the accession of George the First. The musicians are scraping and grating and screwing tremendously—

playing no notes but notes of preparation; and several gentlemen are gliding along the sides of the tables, looking into plate after plate with frantic eagerness, the expression of their countenances growing more and more dismal as they meet with everybody's card but their own.

You turn round to take a look at the table behind you, and—not being in the habit of attending public dinners—are somewhat struck by the appearance of the party on which your eyes rest. One of its principal members appears to be a little man, with a long and rather inflamed face, and gray hair brushed bolt upright in front; he wears a wisp of black silk round his neck, without any stiffener, as an apology for a neckerchief, and is addressed by his companions by the familiar appellation of "Fitz," or some such monosyllable. Near him is a stout man in a white neckerchief and buff waistcoat, with shining dark hair, cut very short in front, and a great round healthy-looking face, on which he studiously preserves a half sentimental simper. Next him, again, is a large-headed man, with black hair and bushy whiskers; and opposite them are two or three others, one of whom is a little round-faced person, in a dress-stock and blue under-waistcoat. There is something peculiar in their air and manner, though you could hardly describe what it is; you cannot divest yourself of the idea that they have come for some other purpose than mere eating and drinking. You have no time to debate the matter, however, for the waiters (who have been arranged in lines down the room, placing the dishes on table) retire to the lower end; the dark man in the blue coat and bright buttons, who has the direction of the music, looks up to the gallery, and calls out "band" in a very loud voice; out burst the orchestra, up rise the visitors, in march fourteen stewards, each with a long wand in his hand, like the evil genius in a pantomime; then the chairman, then the titled visitors; they all make their way up the room, as fast as they can, bowing, and smiling, and smirking, and looking remarkably amiable. The applause ceases, grace is said, the clatter of plates and dishes begins; and every one appears highly gratified, either with the presence of the distinguished visitors, or the commencement of the anxiously-expected dinner.

As to the dinner itself—the mere dinner—it goes off much the same everywhere. Tureens of soup are emptied with awful rapidity—waiters take plates of turbot away, to get lobster-sauce, and bring back plates of lobster-sauce without turbot; people who can carve poultry, are great fools if they own it, and people who can't have no wish to learn. The knives and forks form a pleasing accompaniment to Auber's music, and Auber's music would form a pleasing accompaniment to the dinner, if you could hear anything besides the cymbals. The substantials disappear—moulds of jelly vanish like lightning—hearty eaters wipe their foreheads, and appear rather overcome by their recent exertions—people who have looked very cross hitherto, become remarkably bland, and ask you to take wine in the most friendly manner possible—old gentlemen direct your attention to the ladies' gallery, and take great pains to impress you with the fact that the charity is always peculiarly favoured in this respect—every one appears disposed to become talkative—and the hum of conversation is loud and general.

"Pray, silence, gentlemen, if you please, for *Non nobis!*" shouts the toast-master with stentorian lungs—a toast-master's shirt-front, waistcoat, and neckerchief, by-the-bye, always exhibit three distinct shades of cloudy-white.—"Pray, silence, gentlemen, for *Non nobis!*" The singers, whom you discover to be no other than the very party that excited your curiosity at first, after "pitching" their voices immediately begin *too-too*ing most dismally, on which the regular old stagers burst into occasional cries of—"Sh—Sh—waiters!—Silence, waiters—stand still, waiters—keep back, waiters," and other exorcisms, delivered in a tone of indignant remonstrance. The grace is soon concluded, and the company resume their seats. The uninitiated portion of the guests applaud *Non nobis* as vehemently as if it were a capital comic song, greatly to the scandal and indignation of the regular diners, who immediately attempt to quell this sacrilegious approbation, by cries of "Hush, hush!" whereupon the others, mistaking these sounds for hisses, applaud more tumultuously than before, and, by way of placing their approval beyond the possibilitv of doubt, shout "*Encore!*" most vociferously.

The moment the noise ceases, up starts the toast-master:—"Gentlemen, charge your glasses, if you please!" Decanters having been handed about, and glasses filled, the toast-master proceeds, in a regular ascending scale;—"Gentlemen—*air*—you—all charged? Pray—silence—gentlemen—for—the cha—i—r!" The chairman rises, and, after stating that he feels it quite unnecessary to preface the toast he is about to propose, with any observations whatever, wanders into a maze of sentences, and flounders about in the most extraordinary manner, presenting a lamentable spectacle of mystified humanity, until he arrives at the words, "constitutional sovereign of these realms," at which elderly gentlemen exclaim "Bravo!" and hammer the table tremendously with their knife-handles. "Under any circumstances, it would give him the greatest pride, it would give him the greatest pleasure—he might almost say, it would afford him satisfaction [cheers] to propose that toast. What must be his feelings, then, when he has the gratification of announcing, that he has received her Majesty's commands to apply to the Treasurer of her Majesty's Household, for her Majesty's annual donation of 25*l.* in aid of the funds of this charity!" This announcement (which has been regularly made by every chairman, since the first foundation of the charity, forty-two years ago) calls forth the most vociferous applause; the toast is drunk with a great deal of cheering and knocking; and "God save the Queen" is sung by the "professional gentlemen;" the unprofessional gentlemen joining in the chorus, and giving the national anthem an effect which the newspapers, with great justice, describe as "perfectly electrical."

The other "loyal and patriotic" toasts having been drunk with all due enthusiasm, a comic song having been well sung by the gentleman with the small neckerchief, and a sentimental one by the second of the party, we come to the most important toast of the evening—"Prosperity to the charity." Here again we are compelled to adopt newspaper phraseology, and to express our regret at being "precluded from giving even the substance of the noble lord's observations." Suffice it to say, that the speech, which is somewhat of the longest, is rapturously received; and the toast having been drunk, the stewards (looking more important than ever) leave the room, and presently return, heading a procession of indigent orphans, boys and girls, who walk round the room, curtseying, and bowing, and treading on each other's heels, and looking very much as if they would like a glass of wine apiece, to the high gratification of the company generally, and especially of the lady patronesses in the gallery. *Exeunt* children, and re-enter stewards, each with a blue plate in his hand. The band plays a lively air; the majority of the company put their hands in their pockets and look rather serious; and the noise of sovereigns, rattling on crockery, is heard from all parts of the room.

After a short interval, occupied in singing and toasting, the secretary puts on his spectacles, and proceeds to read the report and list of subscriptions, the latter being listened to with great attention. "Mr. Smith, one guinea—Mr. Tompkins, one guinea—Mr. Wilson, one guinea—Mr. Hickson, one guinea—Mr. Nixon, one guinea—Mr. Charles Nixon, one guinea—[hear, hear!]—Mr. James Nixon, one guinea—Mr. Thomas Nixon, one pound one [tremendous applause]. Lord Fitz Binkle, the chairman of the day, in addition to an annual donation of fifteen pounds—thirty guineas [prolonged knocking: several gentlemen knock the stems off their wine-glasses, in the vehemence of their approbation]. Lady Fitz Binkle, in addition to an annual donation of ten pound—twenty pound" [protracted knocking and shouts of "Bravo!"] The list being at length concluded, the chairman rises, and proposes the health of the secretary, than whom he knows no more zealous or estimable individual. The secretary, in returning thanks, observes that *he* knows no more excellent individual than the chairman—except the senior officer of the charity, whose health *he* begs to propose. The senior officer, in returning thanks, observes that *he* knows no more worthy man than the secretary—except Mr. Walker, the auditor, whose health *he* begs to propose. Mr. Walker, in returning thanks, discovers some other estimable individual, to whom alone the senior officer is inferior—and so they go on toasting and lauding and thanking: the only other toast of importance being "The Lady Patronesses now present!" on which all the gentlemen turn their faces towards the ladies' gallery, shouting tremendously; and little priggish men, who have imbibed more wine than usual, kiss their hands and exhibit distressing contortions of visage.

We have protracted our dinner to so great a length, that we have hardly time to add one word by way of grace. We can only entreat our readers not to imagine, because we have attempted to extract some amusement from a charity dinner, that we are at all disposed to underrate, either the excellence of the benevolent institutions with which London abounds, or the estimable motives of those who support them.

CHAPTER XX.

THE FIRST OF MAY.

"Now ladies, up in the sky-parlour: only once a year, if you please!"
YOUNG LADY WITH BRASS LADLE.

"Sweep–sweep–sw-e-ep!"
ILLEGAL WATCHWORD.

THE first of May! There is a merry freshness in the sound, calling to our minds a thousand thoughts of all that is pleasant in nature and beautiful in her most delightful form. What man is there, over whose mind a bright spring morning does not exercise a magic influence—carrying him back to the days of his childish sports, and conjuring up before him the old green field with its gently-waving trees, where the birds sang as he has never heard them since—where the butterfly fluttered far more gaily than he ever sees him now, in all his ramblings—where the sky seemed bluer, and the sun shone more brightly—where the air blew more freshly over greener grass, and sweeter-smelling flowers—where everything wore a richer and more brilliant hue than it is ever dressed in now! Such are the deep feelings of childhood, and such are the impressions which every lovely object stamps upon its heart! The hardy traveller wanders through the maze of thick and pathless woods, where the sun's rays never shone, and heaven's pure air never played; he stands on the brink of the roaring waterfall, and, giddy and bewildered, watches the foaming mass as it leaps from stone to stone, and from crag to crag; he lingers in the fertile plains of a land of perpetual sunshine, and revels in the luxury of their balmy breath. But what are the deep forests, or the thundering waters, or the richest landscapes that bounteous nature ever spread, to charm the eyes, and captivate the senses of man, compared with the recollection of the old scenes of his early youth? Magic scenes indeed; for the fancies of childhood dressed them in colours brighter than the rainbow, and almost as fleeting!

In former times, spring brought with it not only such associations as these, connected with the past, but sports and games for the present—merry dances round rustic pillars, adorned with emblems of the season, and reared in honour of its coming. Where are they now! Pillars we have, but they are no longer rustic ones; and as to dancers, they are used to rooms, and lights, and would not show well in the open air. Think of the immorality, too! What would your sabbath enthusiasts say, to an aristocratic ring encircling the Duke of York's column in Carlton-terrace—a grand *poussette* of the middle classes, round Alderman Waithman's monument in Fleet-street,—or a general hands-four-round of ten-pound householders, at the foot of the Obelisk in St. George's-fields? Alas! romance can make no head against the riot act; and pastoral simplicity is not understood by the police.

Well; many years ago we began to be a steady and matter-of-fact sort of people, and dancing in spring being beneath our dignity, we gave it up, and in course of time it descended to the sweeps—a fall certainly, because, though sweeps are very good fellows in their way, and moreover very useful in a civilised community, they are not exactly the sort of people to give the tone to the little elegances of society. The sweeps, however, got the dancing to themselves, and they kept it up, and handed it down. This was a severe blow to the romance of spring-time, but, it did not entirely destroy it, either; for a portion of it descended to the sweeps with the dancing, and rendered them objects of great interest. A mystery hung over the sweeps in those days. Legends were in existence of wealthy gentlemen who had lost children, and who, after many years of sorrow and suffering, had found them in the character of sweeps. Stories were related of a young boy who, having been stolen from his parents in his infancy, and devoted to the occupation of chimney-sweeping, was sent, in the course of his professional career, to sweep the chimney of his mother's bedroom; and how, being hot and tired when he came out of the chimney, he got into the bed he had so often slept in as an infant, and was discovered and recognised therein by his mother, who once every year of her life, thereafter, requested the pleasure of the company of every London sweep, at half-past one o'clock, to roast beef, plum-pudding, porter, and sixpence.

Such stories as these, and there were many such, threw an air of mystery round the sweeps, and produced for them some of those good effects which animals derive from the doctrine of the transmigration of souls. No one (except the masters) thought of ill-treating a sweep, because no one knew who he might be, or what nobleman's or gentleman's son he might turn out. Chimney-sweeping was, by many believers in the marvellous, considered as a sort of probationary term, at an earlier or later period of which, divers young noblemen were to come into possession of their rank and titles: and the profession was held by them in great respect accordingly.

We remember, in our young days, a little sweep about our own age, with curly hair and white teeth, whom we devoutly and sincerely believed to be the lost son and heir of some illustrious personage—an impression which was resolved into an unchangeable conviction on our infant mind, by the subject of our speculations informing us, one day, in reply to our question, propounded a few moments before his ascent to the summit of the kitchen chimney, "that he believed he'd been born in the vurkis, but he'd never know'd his father." We felt certain, from that time forth, that he would one day be owned by a lord; and we never heard the church-bells ring, or saw a flag hoisted in the neighbourhood, without thinking that the happy event had at last occurred, and that his long-lost parent had arrived in a coach and six, to take him home to Grosvenor-square. He never came, however; and, at the present moment, the young gentleman in question is settled down as a master sweep in the neighbourhood of Battle-bridge, his distinguishing characteristics being a decided antipathy to washing himself, and the possession of a pair of legs very inadequate to the support of his unwieldy and corpulent body.

The romance of spring having gone out before our time, we were fain to console ourselves as we best could with the uncertainty that enveloped the birth and parentage of its attendant dancers, the sweeps; and we *did* console ourselves with it, for many years. But, even this wretched source of comfort received a shock from which it has never recovered—a shock which has been in reality its death-blow. We could not disguise from ourselves the fact that whole families of sweeps were regularly born of sweeps, in the rural districts of Somers Town and Camden Town—that the eldest son succeeded to the father's business, that the other branches assisted him therein, and commenced on their own account; that their children again, were educated to the profession; and that about their identity there could be no mistake whatever. We could not be blind, we say, to this melancholy truth, but we could not bring ourselves to admit it, nevertheless, and we lived on for some years in a state of voluntary ignorance. We were roused from our pleasant slumber by certain dark insinuations thrown out by a friend of ours, to the effect that children in the lower ranks of life were beginning to *choose* chimney-sweeping as their particular walk; that applications had been made by various boys to the constituted authorities, to allow them to pursue the object of their ambition with the full concurrence and sanction of the law; that the affair, in short, was becoming one of mere legal contract. We turned a deaf ear to these rumours at first, but slowly and surely they stole upon us. Month after month, week after week, nay, day after day, at last, did we meet with accounts of similar applications. The veil was removed, all mystery was at an end, and chimney-sweeping had become a favourite and chosen pursuit. There is no longer any occasion to steal boys; for boys flock in crowds to bind themselves. The romance of the trade has fled, and the chimney-sweeper of the present day, is no more like unto him of thirty years ago, than is a Fleet-street pickpocket to a Spanish brigand, or Paul Pry to Caleb Williams.

This gradual decay and disuse of the practice of leading noble youths into captivity, and compelling them to ascend chimneys, was a severe blow, if we may so speak, to the romance of chimney-sweeping, and to the romance of spring at the same time. But even this was not all, for some few years ago the dancing on May-day began to decline; small sweeps were observed to congregate in twos or threes, unsupported by a "green," with no "My Lord" to act as master of the ceremonies, and no "My Lady" to preside over the exchequer. Even in companies where there was a "green" it was an absolute nothing—a mere sprout—and the instrumental accompaniments rarely extended beyond the shovels and a set of Pan-pipes, better known to the many, as a "mouth-organ."

These were signs of the times, portentous omens of a coming change; and what was the result which they shadowed forth? Why, the master sweeps, influenced by a restless spirit of innovation, actually interposed their authority, in opposition to the dancing, and substituted a dinner—an anniversary dinner at White Conduit House—where clean faces appeared in lieu of black ones smeared with rose pink; and knee cords and tops superseded nankeen drawers and rosetted shoes.

Gentlemen who were in the habit of riding shy horses; and steady-going people who have no vagrancy in their souls, lauded this alteration to the skies, and the conduct of the master sweeps was described as beyond the reach of praise. But how stands the real fact? Let any man deny, if he can, that when the cloth had been removed, fresh pots and pipes laid upon the table, and the customary loyal and patriotic toasts proposed, the celebrated Mr. Sluffen, of Adam-and-Eve-court, whose authority not the most malignant of our opponents can call in question, expressed himself in a manner following: "That now he'd cotcht the cheerman's hi, he vished he might be jolly vell blessed, if he worn't a goin' to have his innings, vich he vould say these here obserwashuns—that how some mischeevus coves as know'd nuffin about the consarn, had tried to sit people agin the mas'r swips, and take the shine out o' their bis'nes, and the bread out o' the traps o' their preshus kids, by a makin' o' this here remark, as chimblies could be as vell svept by 'sheenery as by boys; and that the makin' use o' boys for that there purpuss vos babareous; vereas, he 'ad been a chummy—he begged the cheerman's parding for usin' such a wulgar hexpression—more nor thirty year—he might say he'd been born in a chimbley—and he know'd uncommon vell as 'sheenery vos vus nor o' no use: and as to kerhewelty to the boys, everybody in the chimbley line know'd as vell as he did, that they liked the climbin' better nor nuffin as vos." From this day, we date the total fall of the last lingering remnant of May-day dancing, among the *élite* of the profession: and from this period we commence a new era in that portion of our spring associations which relates to the 1st of May.

We are aware that the unthinking part of the population will meet us here, with the assertion, that dancing on May-day still continues—that "greens" are annually seen to roll along the streets—that youths in the garb of clowns, precede them, giving vent to the ebullitions of their sportive fancies; and that lords and ladies follow in their wake.

Granted. We are ready to acknowledge that in outward show, these processions have greatly improved: we do not deny the introduction of solos on the drum; we will even go so far as to admit an occasional fantasia on the triangle, but here our admissions end. We positively deny that the sweeps have art or part in these proceedings. We distinctly charge the dustmen with throwing what they ought to clear away, into the eyes of the public. We accuse scavengers, brickmakers, and gentlemen who devote their energies to the costermongering line, with obtaining money once a-year, under false pretences. We cling with peculiar fondness to the custom of days gone by, and have shut out conviction as long as we could, but it has forced itself upon us; and we now proclaim to a deluded public, that the May-day dancers are *not* sweeps. The size of them, alone, is sufficient to repudiate the idea. It is a notorious fact that the widely-spread taste for register-stoves has materially increased the demand for small boys; whereas the men, who, under a fictitious character, dance about the streets on the first of May nowadays, would be a tight fit in a kitchen flue, to say nothing of the parlour. This is strong presumptive evidence, but we have positive proof—the evidence of our own senses. And here is our testimony.

Upon the morning of the second of the merry month of May, in the year of our Lord one thousand eight hundred and thirty-six, we went out for a stroll, with a kind of forlorn hope of seeing something or other which might induce us to believe that it was really spring, and not Christmas. After wandering as far as Copenhagen House, without meeting anything calculated to dispel our impression that there was a mistake in the almanacks, we turned back down Maiden-lane, with the intention of passing through the extensive colony lying between it and Battle-bridge, which is inhabited by proprietors of donkey-carts, boilers of horse-flesh, makers of tiles, and sifters of cinders; through which colony we should have passed, without stoppage or interruption, if a little crowd gathered round a shed had not attracted our attention, and induced us to pause.

When we say a "shed," we do not mean the conservatory sort of building, which, according to the old song, Love tenanted when he was a young man, but a wooden house with windows stuffed with rags and paper, and a small yard at the side, with one dust-cart, two baskets, a few shovels, and little heaps of cinders, and fragments of china and tiles, scattered about it. Before this inviting spot we paused; and the longer we looked, the more we wondered what exciting circumstance it could be, that induced the foremost members of the crowd to flatten their noses against the parlour window, in the vain hope of ca ching a glimpse of what was going on inside. After staring vacantly about us for some minutes, we appealed, touching the cause of this assemblage, to a gentleman in a suit of tarpauling, who was smoking his pipe on our right hand; but as the only answer we obtained was a playful inquiry whether our mother had disposed of her mangle, we determined to await the issue in silence.

Judge of our virtuous indignation, when the street-door of the shed opened, and a party emerged therefrom, clad in the costume and emulating the appearance, of May-day sweeps!

The first person who appeared was "my lord," habited in a blue coat and bright buttons, with gilt paper tacked over the seams, yellow knee-breeches, pink cotton stockings, and shoes; a cocked hat, ornamented with shreds of various-coloured paper, on his head, a *bouquet*, the size of a prize cauliflower in his button-hole, a long Belcher handkerchief in his right hand, and a thin cane in his left. A murmur of applause ran through the crowd (which was chiefly composed of his lordship's personal friends), when this graceful figure made his appearance, which swelled into a burst of applause as his fair partner in the dance bounded forth to join him. Her ladyship was attired in pink crape over bed-furniture, with a low body and short sleeves. The symmetry of her ankles was partially concealed by a very perceptible pair of frilled trousers; and the inconvenience which might have resulted from the circumstance of her white satin shoes being a few sizes too large, was obviated by their being firmly attached to her legs with strong tape sandals.

Her head was ornamented with a profusion of artificial flowers; and in her hand she bore a large brass ladle, wherein to receive what she figuratively denominated "the tin." The other characters were a young gentleman in girl's clothes and a widow's cap; two clowns who walked upon their hands in the mud, to the immeasurable delight of all the spectators; a man with a drum; another man with a flageolet; a dirty woman in a large shawl, with a box under her arm for the money,—and last, though not least, the "green," animated by no less a personage than our identical friend in the tarpauling suit.

The man hammered away at the drum, the flageolet squeaked, the shovels rattled, the "green" rolled about, pitching first on one side and then on the other; my lady threw her right foot over her left ankle, and her left foot over her right ankle, alternately; my lord ran a few paces forward, and butted at the "green," and then a few paces backward upon the toes of the crowd, and then went to the right, and then to the left, and then dodged my lady round the "green;" and finally drew her arm through his, and called upon the boys to shout, which they did lustily—for this was the dancing.

We passed the same group, accidentally, in the evening. We never saw a "green" so drunk, a lord so quarrelsome (no: not even in the house of peers after dinner), a pair of clowns so melancholy, a lady so muddy, or a party so miserable.

How has May-day decayed!

CHAPTER XXI.

BROKERS' AND MARINE-STORE SHOPS.

WHEN we affirm that brokers' shops are strange places, and that if an authentic history of their contents could be procured, it would furnish many a page of amusement, and many a melancholy tale, it is necessary to explain the class of shops to which we allude. Perhaps when we make use of the term "Brokers' Shop," the minds of our readers will at once picture large, handsome warehouses, exhibiting a long perspective of French-polished dining-tables, rosewood chiffoniers, and mahogany wash-hand-stands, with an occasional vista of a four-post bedstead and hangings, and an appropriate foreground of dining-room chairs. Perhaps they will imagine that we mean an humble class of second-hand furniture repositories. Their imagination will then naturally lead them to that street at the back of Long-acre, which is composed almost entirely of brokers' shops; where you walk through groves of deceitful, showy-looking furniture, and where the prospect is occasionally enlivened by a bright red, blue, and yellow hearth-rug, embellished with the pleasing device of a mail-coach at full-speed, or a strange animal, supposed to have been originally intended for a dog, with a mass of worsted-work in his mouth, which conjecture has likened to a basket of flowers.

This, by-the-bye, is a tempting article to young wives in the humbler ranks of life, who have a first-floor front to furnish—they are lost in admiration, and hardly know which to admire most. The dog is very beautiful, but they have a dog already on the best tea-tray, and two more on the mantel-piece. Then, there is something so genteel about that mail-coach; and the passengers outside (who are all hat) give it such an air of reality!

The goods here are adapted to the taste, or rather to the means, of cheap purchasers. There are some of the most beautiful *looking* Pembroke tables that were ever beheld: the wood as green as the trees in the Park, and the leaves almost as certain to fall off in the course of a year. There is also a most extensive assortment of tent and turn-up bedsteads, made of stained wood, and innumerable specimens of that base imposition on society—a sofa bedstead.

A turn-up bedstead is a blunt, honest piece of furniture; it may be slightly disguised with a sham drawer; and sometimes a mad attempt is even made to pass it off for a bookcase; ornament it as you will, however, the turn-up bedstead seems to defy disguise, and to insist on having it distinctly understood that he is a turn-up bedstead, and nothing else—that he is indispensably necessary, and that being so useful, he disdains to be ornamental.

How different is the demeanour of a sofa bedstead! Ashamed of its real use, it strives to appear an article of luxury and gentility—an attempt in which it miserably fails. It has neither the respectability of a sofa, nor the virtues of a bed; every man who keeps a sofa bedstead in his house, becomes a party to a wilful and designing fraud—we question whether you could insult him more, than by insinuating that you entertain the least suspicion of its real use.

To return from this digression, we beg to say, that neither of these classes of brokers' shops, forms the subject of this sketch. The shops to which we advert, are immeasurably inferior to those on whose outward appearance we have slightly touched. Our readers must often have observed in some by-street, in a poor neighbourhood, a small dirty shop, exposing for sale the most extraordinary and confused jumble of old, worn-out, wretched articles, that can well be imagined. Our wonder at their ever having been bought, is only to be equalled by our astonishment at the idea of their ever being sold again. On a board, at the side of the door, are placed about twenty books—all odd volumes; and as many wine-glasses—all different patterns; several locks, an old earthenware pan, full of rusty keys; two or three gaudy chimney-ornaments—cracked, of course; the remains of a lustre, without any drops; a round frame like a capital O, which has once held a mirror; a flute, complete with the exception of the middle joint; a pair of curling-irons; and a tinder-box. In front of the shop-window, are ranged some half-dozen high-backed chairs, with spinal complaints and wasted legs; a corner cupboard; two or three very dark mahogany tables with flaps like mathematical problems; some pickle-jars, some surgeons' ditto, with gilt labels and without stoppers; an unframed portrait of some lady who flourished about the beginning of the thirteenth century, by an artist who never flourished at all; an incalculable host of miscellanies of every description, including bottles and cabinets, rags and bones, fenders and street-door knockers, fire-irons, wearing apparel and bedding, a hall-lamp, and a room-door. Imagine, in addition to this incongruous mass, a black doll in a white frock, with two faces—one looking up the street, and the other looking down, swinging over the door; a board with the squeezed-up inscription "Dealer in marine stores," in lanky white letters, whose height is strangely out of proportion to their width; and you have before you precisely the kind of shop to which we wish to direct your attention.

Although the same heterogeneous mixture of things will be found at all these places, it is curious to observe how truly and accurately some of the minor articles which are exposed for sale—articles of wearing apparel, for instance—mark the character of the neighbourhood. Take Drury-lane and Covent-garden for example.

This is essentially a theatrical neighbourhood. There is not a potboy in the vicinity who is not, to a greater or less extent, a dramatic character. The errand-boys and chandler's-shop-keepers' sons, are all stage-struck: they "gets up" plays in back kitchens hired for the purpose, and will stand before a shop-window for hours, contemplating a great staring portrait of Mr. somebody or other, of the Royal Coburg Theatre, "as he appeared in the character of Tongo the Denounced." The consequence is, that there is not a marine-store shop in the neighbourhood, which does not exhibit for sale some faded articles of dramatic finery, such as three or four pairs of soiled buff boots with turn-over red tops, heretofore worn by a "fourth robber," or "fifth mob;" a pair of rusty broad-swords, a few gauntlets, and certain resplendent ornaments, which, if they were yellow instead of white, might be taken for insurance plates of the Sun Fire-office. There are several of these shops in the narrow streets and dirty courts, of which there are so many near the national theatres, and they all have tempting goods of this description, with the addition, perhaps, of a lady's pink dress covered with spangles; white wreaths, stage shoes, and a tiara like a tin lamp reflector. They have been purchased of some wretched supernumeraries, or sixth-rate actors, and are now offered for the benefit of the rising generation, who, on condition of making certain weekly payments, amounting in the whole to about ten times their value, may avail themselves of such desirable bargains.

Let us take a very different quarter, and apply it to the same test. Look at a marine-store dealer's, in that reservoir of dirt, drunkenness, and drabs: thieves, oysters, baked potatoes, and pickled salmon—Ratcliff-highway. Here, the wearing apparel is all nautical. Rough blue jackets, with mother-of-pearl buttons, oil-skin hats, coarse checked shirts, and large canvas trousers that look as if they were made for a pair of bodies instead of a pair of legs, are the staple commodities. Then, there are large bunches of cotton pocket-handkerchiefs, in colour and pattern unlike any, one ever saw before, with the exception of those on the backs of the three young ladies without bonnets who passed just now. The furniture is much the same as elsewhere, with the addition of one or two models of ships, and some old prints of naval engagements in still older frames. In the window, are a few compasses, a small tray containing silver watches in clumsy thick cases; and tobacco-boxes, the lid of each ornamented with a ship, or an anchor, or some such trophy. A sailor generally pawns or sells all he has before he has been long ashore, and if he does not, some favoured companion kindly saves him the trouble. In either case, it is an even chance that he afterwards unconsciously repurchases the same things at a higher price than he gave for them at first.

Again: pay a visit with a similar object, to a part of London, as unlike both of these as they are to each other. Cross over to the Surrey side, and look at such shops of this description as are to be found near the King's Bench prison, and in "the Rules." How different, and how strikingly illustrative of the decay of some of the unfortunate residents in this part of the metropolis! Imprisonment and neglect have done their work. There is contamination in the profligate denizens of a debtor's prison; old friends have fallen off; the recollection of former prosperity has passed away; and with it all thoughts for the past, all care for the future. First, watches and rings, then cloaks, coats, and all the more expensive articles of dress, have found their way to the pawnbroker's. That miserable resource has failed at last, and the sale of some trifling article at one of these shops, has been the only mode left of raising a shilling or two, to meet the urgent demands of the moment. Dressing-cases and writing-desks, too old to pawn but too good to keep; guns, fishing-rods, musical instruments, all in the same condition; have first been sold, and the sacrifice has been but slightly felt. But hunger must be allayed, and what has already become a habit, is easily resorted to, when an emergency arises. Light articles of clothing, first of the ruined man, then of his wife, at last of their children, even of the youngest, have been parted with, piecemeal. There they are, thrown carelessly together until a purchaser presents himself, old, and patched and repaired, it is true; but the make and materials tell of better days; and the older they are, the greater the misery and destitution of those whom they once adorned.

CHAPTER XXII.

GIN-SHOPS.

It is a remarkable circumstance, that different trades appear to partake of the disease to which elephants and dogs are especially liable, and to run stark, staring, raving mad, periodically. The great distinction between the animals and the trades, is, that the former run mad with a certain degree of propriety—they are very regular in their irregularities. We know the period at which the emergency will arise, and provide against it accordingly. If an elephant run mad, we are all ready for him—kill or cure—pills or bullets, calomel in conserve of roses, or lead in a musket-barrel. If a dog happen to look unpleasantly warm in the summer months, and to trot about the shady side of the streets with a quarter of a yard of tongue hanging out of his mouth, a thick leather muzzle, which has been previously prepared in compliance with the thoughtful injunctions of the Legislature, is instantly clapped over his head, by way of making him cooler, and he either looks remarkably unhappy for the next six weeks, or becomes legally insane, and goes mad, as it were, by act of Parliament. But these trades are as eccentric as comets; nay, worse, for no one can calculate on the recurrence of the strange appearances which betoken the disease. Moreover, the contagion is general, and the quickness with which it diffuses itself, almost incredible.

We will cite two or three cases in illustration of our meaning. Six or eight years ago, the epidemic began to display itself among the linen-drapers and haberdashers. The primary symptoms were an inordinate love of plate-glass, and a passion for gas-lights and gilding. The disease gradually progressed, and at last attained a fearful height. Quiet dusty old shops in different parts of town, were pulled down; spacious premises with stuccoed fronts and gold letters, were erected instead; floors, were covered with Turkey carpets; roofs, supported by massive pillars; doors, knocked into windows; a dozen squares of glass into one, one shopman into a dozen; and there is no knowing what would have been done, if it had not been fortunately discovered, just in time, that the Commissioners of Bankruptcy were as competent to decide such cases as the Commissioners of Lunacy, and that a little confinement and gentle examination did wonders. The disease abated. It died away. A year or two of comparative tranquillity ensued. Suddenly it burst out again amongst the chemists; the symptoms were the same, with the addition of a strong desire to stick the royal arms over the shop-door, and a great rage for mahogany, varnish, and expensive floor-cloth. Then, the hosiers were infected, and began to pull down their shop-fronts with frantic recklessness. The mania again died away, and the public began to congratulate themselves on its entire disappearance, when it burst forth with ten-fold violence among the publicans, and keepers of "wine vaults." From that moment it has spread among them with unprecedented rapidity, exhibiting a concatenation of all the previous symptoms; onward it has rushed to every part of town, knocking down all the old public-houses, and depositing splendid mansions, stone balustrades, rosewood fittings, immense lamps, and illuminated clocks, at the corner of every street.

The extensive scale on which these places are established, and the ostentatious manner in which the business of even the smallest among them is divided into branches, is amusing. A handsome plate of ground glass in one door directs you "To the Counting-house;" another to the "Bottle Department;" a third to the "Wholesale Department;" a fourth, to "The Wine Promenade;" and so forth, until we are in daily expectation of meeting with a "Brandy Bell," or a "Whiskey Entrance." Then, ingenuity is exhausted in devising attractive titles for the different descriptions of gin; and the dram-drinking portion of the community as they gaze upon the gigantic black and white announcements, which are only to be equalled in size by the figures beneath them, are left in a state of pleasing hesitation between "The Cream of the Valley," "The Out and Out," "The No Mistake," "The Good for Mixing," "The real Knock-me-down," "The celebrated Butter Gin," "The regular Flare-up," and a dozen other, equally inviting and wholesome *liqueurs*. Although places of this description are to be met with in every second street, they are invariably numerous and splendid in precise proportion to the dirt and poverty of the surrounding neighbourhood. The gin-shops in and near Drury-lane, Holborn, St. Giles's, Covent-garden, and Clare-market, are the handsomest in London. There is more of filth and squalid misery near those great thoroughfares than in any part of this mighty city.

We will endeavour to sketch the bar of a large gin-shop, and its ordinary customers, for the edification of such of our readers as may not have had opportunities of observing such scenes; and on the chance of finding one well suited to our purpose, we will make for Drury-lane, through the narrow streets and dirty courts which divide it from Oxford-street, and that classical spot adjoining the brewery at the bottom of Tottenham-court-road, best known to the initiated as the "Rookery."

The filthy and miserable appearance of this part of London can hardly be imagined by those (and there are many such) who have not witnessed it. Wretched houses with broken windows patched with rags and paper: every room let out to a different family, and in many instances to two or even three—fruit and "sweet-stuff" manufacturers in the cellars, barbers and red-herring vendors in the front parlours, cobblers in the back; a bird-fancier in the first floor, three families on the second, starvation in the attics, Irishmen in the passage, a "musician" in the front kitchen, and a charwoman and five hungry children in the back one—filth everywhere—a gutter before the houses and a drain behind—clothes drying and slops emptying, from the windows; girls of fourteen or fifteen, with matted hair, walking about barefoot, and in white great-coats, almost their only covering; boys of all ages, in coats of all sizes and no coats at all; men and women, in every variety of scanty and dirty apparel, lounging, scolding, drinking, smoking, squabbling, fighting, and swearing.

You turn the corner. What a change! All is light and brilliancy. The hum of many voices issues from that splendid gin-shop which forms the commencement of the two streets opposite; and the gay building with the fantastically ornamented parapet, the illuminated clock, the plate-glass windows surrounded by stucco rosettes, and its profusion of gas-lights in richly-gilt burners, is perfectly dazzling when contrasted with the darkness and dirt we have just left. The interior is even gayer than the exterior. A bar of French-polished mahogany, elegantly carved, extends the whole width of the place; and there are two side-aisles of great casks, painted green and gold, enclosed within a light brass rail, and bearing such inscriptions, as "Old Tom, 549;" "Young Tom, 360;" "Samson, 1421"—the figures agreeing, we presume, with "gallons," understand. Beyond the bar is a lofty and spacious saloon, full of the same enticing vessels, with a gallery running round it, equally well furnished. On the counter, in addition to the usual spirit apparatus, are two or three little baskets of cakes and biscuits, which are carefully secured at top with wicker-work, to prevent their contents being unlawfully abstracted. Behind it, are two showily-dressed damsels with large necklaces, dispensing the spirits and "compounds." They are assisted by the ostensible proprietor of the concern, a stout coarse fellow in a fur cap, put on very much on one side to give him a knowing air, and to display his sandy whiskers to the best advantage.

The two old washerwomen, who are seated on the little bench to the left of the bar, are rather overcome by the head-dresses and haughty demeanour of the young ladies who officiate. They receive their half-quartern of gin and peppermint, with considerable deference, prefacing a request for "one of them soft biscuits," with a "Jist be good enough, ma'am." They are quite astonished at the impudent air of the young fellow in a brown coat and bright buttons, who, ushering in his two companions, and walking up to the bar in as careless a manner as if he had been used to green and gold ornaments all his life, winks at one of the young ladies with singular coolness, and calls for a "kervorten and a three-out-glass," just as if the place were his own. "Gin for you, sir?" says the young lady when she has drawn it: carefully looking every way but the right one, to show that the wink had no effect upon her. "For me, Mary, my dear," replies the gentleman in brown. "My name an't Mary as it happens," says the young girl, rather relaxing as she delivers the change. "Well, if it an't, it ought to be," responds the irresistible one; "all the Marys as ever *I* see, was handsome gals." Here the young lady, not precisely remembering how blushes are managed in such cases, abruptly ends the flirtation by addressing the female in the faded feathers who has just entered, and who, after stating explicitly, to prevent any subsequent misunderstanding, that "this gentleman pays," calls for "a glass of port wine and a bit of sugar."

Those two old men who came in "just to have a drain," finished their third quartern a few seconds ago; they have made themselves crying drunk; and the fat comfortable-looking elderly women, who had "a glass of rum-srub" each, having chimed in with their complaints on the hardness of the times, one of the women has agreed to stand a glass round, jocularly observing that "grief never mended no broken bones, and as good people 's wery scarce, what I says is, make the most on 'em, and that's all about it!" a sentiment which appears to afford unlimited satisfaction to those who have nothing to pay.

It is growing late, and the throng of men, women, and children, who have been constantly going in and out, dwindles down to two or three occasional stragglers—cold, wretched-looking creatures, in the last stage of emaciation and disease. The knot of Irish labourers at the lower end of the place, who have been alternately shaking hands with, and threatening the life of each other, for the last hour, become furious in their disputes, and finding it impossible to silence one man, who is particularly anxious to adjust the difference, they resort to the expedient of knocking him down and jumping on him afterwards. The man in the fur cap, and the potboy rush out; a scene of riot and confusion ensues; half the Irishmen get shut out, and the other half get shut in; the potboy is knocked among the tubs in no time; the landlord hits everybody, and everybody hits the landlord; the barmaids scream; the police come in; the rest is a confused mixture of arms, legs, staves, torn coats, shouting, and struggling. Some of the party are borne off to the station-house, and the remainder slink home to beat their wives for complaining, and kick the children for daring to be hungry.

We have sketched this subject very slightly, not only because our limits compel us to do so, but because, if it were pursued farther, it would be painful and repulsive. Well-disposed gentlemen, and charitable ladies, would alike turn with coldness and disgust from a description of the drunken besotted men, and wretched broken-down miserable women, who form no inconsiderable portion of the frequenters of these haunts; forgetting, in the pleasant consciousness of their own rectitude, the poverty of the one, and the temptation of the other. Gin-drinking is a great vice in England, but wretchedness and dirt are a greater; and until you improve the homes of the poor, or persuade a half-famished wretch not to seek relief in the temporary oblivion of his own misery, with the pittance which, divided among his family, would furnish a morsel of bread for each, gin-shops will increase in number and splendour. If Temperance Societies would suggest an antidote against hunger, filth, and foul air, or could establish dispensaries for the gratuitous distribution of bottles of Lethe-water, gin-palaces would be numbered among the things that were.

CHAPTER XXIII.

THE PAWNBROKER'S SHOP.

Of the numerous receptacles for misery and distress with which the streets of London unhappily abound, there are, perhaps, none which present such striking scenes as the pawnbrokers' shops. The very nature and description of these places occasions their being but little known, except to the unfortunate beings whose profligacy or misfortune drives them to seek the temporary relief they offer. The subject may appear, at first sight, to be anything but an inviting one, but we venture on it nevertheless, in the hope that, as far as the limits of our present paper are concerned, it will present nothing to disgust even the most fastidious reader.

There are some pawnbrokers' shops of a very superior description. There are grades in pawning as in everything else, and distinctions must be observed even in poverty. The aristocratic Spanish cloak and the plebeian calico shirt, the silver fork and the flat iron, the muslin cravat and the Belcher neckerchief, would but ill assort together; so, the better sort of pawnbroker calls himself a silversmith, and decorates his shop with handsome trinkets and expensive jewellery, while the more humble money-lender boldly advertises his calling, and invites observation. It is with pawnbrokers' shops of the latter class, that we have to do. We have selected one for our purpose, and will endeavour to describe it.

The pawnbroker's shop is situated near Drury-lane, at the corner of a court, which affords a side entrance for the accommodation of such customers as may be desirous of avoiding the observation of the passers-by, or the chance of recognition in the public street. It is a low, dirty-looking, dusty shop, the door of which stands always doubtfully, a little way open: half inviting, half repelling the hesitating visitor, who, if he be as yet uninitiated, examines one of the old garnet brooches in the window for a minute or two with affected eagerness, as if he contemplated making a purchase; and then looking cautiously round to ascertain that no one watches him, hastily slinks in: the door closing of itself after him, to just its former width. The shop front and the window-frames bear evident marks of having been once painted; but, what the colour was originally, or at what date it was probably laid on, are at this remote period questions which may be asked, but cannot be answered. Tradition states that the transparency in the front door, which displays at night three red balls on a blue ground, once bore also, inscribed in graceful waves, the words "Money advanced on plate, jewels, wearing apparel, and every description of property," but a few illegible hieroglyphics are all that now remain to attest the fact. The plate and jewels would seem to have disappeared, together with the announcement, for the articles of stock, which are displayed in some profusion in the window, do not include any very valuable luxuries of either kind. A few old china cups; some modern vases, adorned with paltry paintings of three Spanish cavaliers playing three Spanish guitars; or a party of boors carousing: each boor with one leg painfully elevated in the air, by way of expressing his perfect freedom and gaiety; several sets of chessmen, two or three flutes, a few fiddles, a round-eyed portrait staring in astonishment from a very dark ground; some gaudily-bound prayer-books and testaments, two rows of silver watches quite as clumsy and almost as large as Ferguson's first; numerous old-fashioned table and tea spoons, displayed, fan-like, in half-dozens; strings of coral with great broad gilt snaps; cards of rings and brooches, fastened and labelled separately, like the insects in the British Museum; cheap silver penholders and snuff-boxes, with a masonic star, complete the jewellery department; while five or six beds in smeary clouded ticks, strings of blankets and sheets, silk and cotton handkerchiefs, and wearing apparel of every description, form the more useful, though even less ornamental, part, of the articles exposed for sale. An extensive collection of planes, chisels, saws, and other carpenters' tools, which have been pledged, and never redeemed, form the foreground of the picture; while the large frames full of ticketed bundles, which are dimly seen through the dirty casement up stairs—the squalid neighbourhood—the adjoining houses, straggling, shrunken, and rotten, with one or two filthy, unwholesome-looking heads, thrust out of every window, and old red pans and stunted plants exposed on the tottering parapets, to the manifest hazard of the heads of the passers-by—the noisy men loitering under the archway at the corner of the court, or about the gin-shop next door—and their wives patiently standing on the curb-stone, with large baskets of cheap vegetables slung round them for sale, are its immediate auxiliaries.

If the outside of the pawnbroker's shop, be calculated to attract the attention, or excite the interest, of the speculative pedestrian, its interior cannot fail to produce the same effect in an increased degree. The front door, which we have before noticed, opens into the common shop, which is the resort of all those customers whose habitual acquaintance with such scenes renders them indifferent to the observation of their companions in poverty. The side door opens into a small passage from which some half-dozen doors (which may be secured on the inside by bolts) open into a corresponding number of little dens, or closets, which face the counter. Here, the more timid or respectable portion of the crowd shroud themselves from the notice of the remainder, and patiently wait until the gentleman behind the counter, with the curly black hair, diamond ring, and double silver watch-guard, shall feel disposed to favour them with his notice—a consummation which depends considerably on the temper of the aforesaid gentleman for the time being.

At the present moment, this elegantly-attired individual is in the act of entering the duplicate he has just made out, in a thick book: a process from which he is diverted occasionally, by a conversation he is carrying on with another young man similarly employed at a little distance from him, whose allusions to "that last bottle of soda-water last night," and "how regularly round my hat he felt himself when the young 'ooman gave 'em in charge," would appear to refer to the consequences of some stolen joviality of the preceding evening. The customers generally, however, seem unable to participate in the amusement derivable from this source, for an old sallow-looking woman, who has been leaning with both arms on the counter with a small bundle before her, for half an hour previously, suddenly interrupts the conversation by addressing the jewelled shopman—"Now, Mr. Henry, do make haste, there's a good soul, for my two grandchildren 's locked up at home, and I'm afeer'd of the fire." The shopman slightly raises his head, with an air of deep abstraction, and resumes his entry with as much deliberation as if he were engraving. "You're in a hurry, Mrs. Tatham, this ev'nin', an't you?" is the only notice he deigns to take, after the lapse of five minutes or so. "Yes, I am indeed, Mr. Henry; now, do serve me next, there's a good creetur. I wouldn't worry you, only it's all along o' them botherin' children." "What have you got here?" inquires the shopman, unpinning the bundle—"old concern, I suppose—pair o' stays and a petticut. You must look up somethin' else, old 'ooman; I can't lend you anything more upon them; they're completely worn out by this time, if it's only by putting in, and taking out again, three times a week." "Oh! you're a rum un, you are," replies the old woman, laughing extremely, as in duty bound; "I wish I'd got the gift of the gab like you; see if I'd be up the spout so often then! No, no; it an't the petticut; it's a child's frock and a beautiful silkankecher, as belongs to my husband. He gave four shillin' for it, the werry same blessed day as he broke his arm."—"What do you want upon these?" inquires Mr. Henry, slightly glancing at the articles, which in all probability are old acquaintances. "What do you want upon these?"—"Eighteenpence."—"Lend you ninepence."—"Oh, make it a shillin'; there's a dear—do now?"—"Not another farden." —"Well, I suppose I must take it." The duplicate is made out, one ticket pinned on the parcel, the other given to the old woman; the parcel is flung carelessly down into a corner, and some other customer prefers his claim to be served without further delay.

The choice falls on an unshaven, dirty, sottish-looking fellow, whose tarnished paper-cap, stuck negligently over one eye, communicates an additionally repulsive expression to his very uninviting countenance. He was enjoying a little relaxation from his sedentary pursuits a quarter of an hour ago, in kicking his wife up the court. He has come to redeem some tools:—probably to complete a job with, on account of which he has already received some money, if his inflamed countenance and drunken stagger, may be taken as evidence of the fact. Having waited some little time, he makes his presence known by venting his ill-humour on a ragged urchin, who, being unable to bring his face on a level with the counter by any other process, has employed himself in climbing up, and then hooking himself on with his elbows—an uneasy perch, from which he has fallen at intervals, generally alighting on the toes of the person in his immediate vicinity. In the present case, the unfortunate little wretch has received a cuff which sends him reeling to the door; and the donor of the blow is immediately the object of general indignation.

"What do you strike the boy for, you brute?" exclaims a slipshod woman, with two flat irons in a little basket. "Do you think he's your wife, you willin?" "Go and hang yourself!" replies the gentleman addressed, with a drunken look of savage stupidity, aiming at the same time a blow at the woman which fortunately misses its object. "Go and hang yourself; and wait till I come and cut you down."—"Cut you down," rejoins the woman, "I wish I had the cutting of you up, you wagabond! (loud.) Oh! you precious wagabond! (rather louder.) Where's your wife, you willin? (louder still; women of this class are always sympathetic, and work themselves into a tremendous passion on the shortest notice.) Your poor dear wife as you uses worser nor a dog—strike a woman—you a man! (very shrill;) I wish I had you—I'd murder you, I would, if I died for it!"—"Now be civil," retorts the man fiercely. "Be civil, you wiper!" ejaculates the woman contemptuously. "An't it shocking?" she continues, turning round, and appealing to an old woman who is peeping out of one of the little closets we have before described, and who has not the slightest objection to join in the attack, possessing, as she does, the comfortable conviction that she is bolted in. "An't it shocking, ma'am? (Dreadful! says the old woman in a parenthesis, not exactly knowing what the question refers to.) He's got a wife, ma'am, as takes in mangling, and is as 'dustrious and hard-working a young 'ooman as can be, (very fast) as lives in the back parlour of our 'ous, which my husband and me lives in the front one (with great rapidity)—and we hears him a beaten' on her sometimes when he comes home drunk, the whole night through, and not only a beaten' her, but beaten' his own child too, to make her more miserable—ugh, you beast! and she, poor creater, won't swear the peace agin him, nor do nothin', because she likes the wretch arter all—worse luck!" Here, as the woman has completely run herself out of breath, the pawnbroker himself, who has just appeared behind the counter in a gray dressing-gown, embraces the favourable opportunity of putting in a word:—"Now I won't have none of this sort of thing on my premises!" he interposes with an air of authority. "Mrs. Mackin, keep yourself to yourself, or you don't get fourpence for a flat iron here; and Jinkins, you leave your ticket here till you're sober, and send your wife for them two planes, for I won't have you in my shop at no price; so make yourself scarce, before I make you scarcer."

This eloquent address produces anything but the effect desired; the women rail in concert; the man hits about him in all directions, and is in the act of establishing an indisputable claim to gratuitous lodgings for the night, when the entrance of his wife, a wretched worn-out woman, apparently in the last stage of consumption, whose face bears evident marks of recent ill-usage, and whose strength seems hardly equal to the burden—light enough, God knows!—of the thin, sickly child she carries in her arms, turns his cowardly rage in a safer direction. "Come home, dear," cries the miserable creature, in an imploring tone; "*do* come home, there's a good fellow, and go to bed."—"Go home yourself," rejoins the furious ruffian. "Do come home quietly," repeats the wife, bursting into tears. "Go home yourself," retorts the husband again, enforcing his argument by a blow which sends the poor creature flying out of the shop. Her "natural protector" follows her up the court, alternately venting his rage in accelerating her progress, and in knocking the little scanty blue bonnet of the unfortunate child over its still more scanty and faded-looking face.

In the last box, which is situated in the darkest and most obscure corner of the shop, considerably removed from either of the gas-lights, are a young delicate girl of about twenty, and an elderly female, evidently her mother from the resemblance between them, who stand at some distance back, as if to avoid the observation even of the shopman. It is not their first visit to a pawnbroker's shop, for they answer without a moment's hesitation the usual questions, put in a rather respectful manner, and in a much lower tone than usual, of "What name shall I say?—Your own property, of course?—Where do you live?—Housekeeper or lodger?" They bargain, too, for a higher loan than the shopman is at first inclined to offer, which a perfect stranger would be little disposed to do; and the elder female urges her daughter on, in scarcely audible whispers, to exert her utmost powers of persuasion to obtain an advance of the sum, and expatiate on the value of the articles they have brought to raise a present supply upon. They are a small gold chain and a "Forget me not" ring: the girl's property, for they are both too small for the mother; given her in better times; prized, perhaps, once, for the giver's sake, but parted with now without a struggle; for want has hardened the mother, and her example has hardened the girl, and the prospect of receiving money, coupled with a recollection of the misery they have both endured from the want of it—the coldness of old friends—the stern refusal of some, and the still more galling compassion of others—appears to have obliterated the consciousness of self-humiliation, which the idea of their present situation would once have aroused.

In the next box, is a young female, whose attire, miserably poor, but extremely gaudy, wretchedly cold but extravagantly fine, too plainly bespeaks her station. The rich satin gown with its faded trimmings, the worn-out thin shoes, and pink silk stockings, the summer bonnet in winter, and the sunken face, where a daub of rouge only serves as an index to the ravages of squandered health never to be regained, and lost happiness never to be restored, and where the practised smile is a wretched mockery of the misery of the heart, cannot be mistaken. There is something in the glimpse she has just caught of her young neighbour, and in the sight of the little trinkets she has offered in pawn, that seems to have awakened in this woman's mind some slumbering recollection, and to have changed, for an instant, her whole demeanour. Her first hasty impulse was to bend forward as if to scan more minutely the appearance of her half-concealed companions; her next, on seeing them involuntarily shrink from her, to retreat to the back of the box, cover her face with her hands, and burst into tears.

There are strange chords in the human heart, which will lie dormant through years of depravity and wickedness, but which will vibrate at last to some sli ht circumstance apparently trivial in itself, but connected by some undefined and indistinct association, with past days that can never be recalled, and with bitter recollections from which the most degraded creature in existence cannot escape.

There has been another spectator, in the person of a woman in the common shop; the lowest of the low; dirty, unbonneted, flaunting, and slovenly. Her curiosity was at first attracted by the little she could see of the group; then her attention. The half-intoxicated leer changed to an expression of something like interest, and a feeling similar to that we have described, appeared for a moment, and only a moment, to extend itself even to her bosom.

Who shall say how soon these women may change places? The last has but two more stages—the hospital and the grave. How many females situated as her two companions are, and as she may have been once, have terminated the same wretched course, in the same wretched manner. One is already tracing her footsteps with frightful rapidity. How soon may the other follow her example! How many have done the same!

CHAPTER XXIV.

CRIMINAL COURTS.

We shall never forget the mingled feelings of awe and respect with which we used to gaze on the exterior of Newgate in our schoolboy days. How dreadful its rough heavy walls, and low massive doors, appeared to us—the latter looking as if they were made for the express purpose of letting people in, and never letting them out again. Then the fetters over the debtors' door, which we used to think were a *bonâ fide* set of irons, just hung up there, for convenience sake, ready to be taken down at a moment's notice, and riveted on the limbs of some refractory felon! We were never tired of wondering how the hackney-coachmen on the opposite stand could cut jokes in the presence of such horrors, and drink pots of half-and-half so near the last drop.

Often have we strayed here, in sessions time, to catch a glimpse of the whipping-place, and that dark building on one side of the yard, in which is kept the gibbet with all its dreadful apparatus, and on the door of which we half expected to see a brass plate, with the inscription "Mr. Ketch;" for we never imagined that the distinguished functionary could by possibility live anywhere else! The days of these childish dreams have passed away, and with them many other boyish ideas of a gayer nature. But we still retain so much of our original feeling, that to this hour we never pass the building without something like a shudder.

What London pedestrian is there who has not, at some time or other, cast a hurried glance through the wicket at which prisoners are admitted into this gloomy mansion, and surveyed the few objects he could discern, with an indescribable feeling of curiosity? The thick door, plated with iron and mounted with spikes, just low enough to enable you to see, leaning over them, an ill-looking fellow, in a broad-brimmed hat, belcher handkerchief and top-boots: with a brown coat, something between a great-coat and a "sporting" jacket, on his back, and an immense key in his left hand. Perhaps you are lucky enough to pass, just as the gate is being opened; then, you see on the other side of the lodge, another gate, the image of its predecessor, and two or three more turnkeys, who look like multiplications of the first one, seated round a fire which just lights up the whitewashed apartment sufficiently to enable you to catch a hasty glimpse of these different objects. We have a great respect for Mrs. Fry, but she certainly ought to have written more romances than Mrs. Radcliffe.

We were walking leisurely down the Old Bailey, some time ago, when, as we passed this identical gate, it was opened by the officiating turnkey. We turned quickly round, as a matter of course, and saw two persons descending the steps. We could not help stopping and observing them.

They were an elderly woman, of decent appearance, though evidently poor, and a boy of about fourteen or fifteen. The woman was crying bitterly ; she carried a small bundle in her hand, and the boy followed at a short distance behind her. Their little history was obvious. The boy was her son, to whose early comfort she had perhaps sacrificed her own—for whose sake she had borne misery without repining, and poverty without a murmur—looking steadily forward to the time, when he who had so long witnessed her struggles for himself, might be enabled to make some exertions for their joint support. He had formed dissolute connexions ; idleness had led to crime ; and he had been committed to take his trial for some petty theft. He had been long in prison, and, after receiving some trifling additional punishment, had been ordered to be discharged that morning. It was his first offence, and his poor old mother, still hoping to reclaim him, had been waiting at the gate to implore him to return home.

We cannot forget the boy ; he descended the steps with a dogged look, shaking his head with an air of bravado and obstinate determination. They walked a few paces, and paused. The woman put her hand upon his shoulder in an agony of entreaty, and the boy sullenly raised his head as if in refusal. It was a brilliant morning, and every object looked fresh and happy in the broad, gay sunlight ; he gazed round him for a few moments, bewildered with the brightness of the scene, for it was long since he had beheld anything save the gloomy walls of a prison. Perhaps the wretchedness of his mother made some impression on the boy's heart ; perhaps some undefined recollection of the time when he was a happy child, and she his only friend, and best companion, crowded on him—he burst into tears ; and covering his face with one hand, and hurriedly placing the other in his mother's, walked away with her.

Curiosity has occasionally led us into both Courts at the Old Bailey. Nothing is so likely to strike the person who enters them for the first time, as the calm indifference with which the proceedings are conducted ; every trial seems a mere matter of business. There is a great deal of form, but no compassion ; considerable interest, but no sympathy. Take the Old Court for example. There sit the Judges, with whose great dignity everybody is acquainted, and of whom therefore we need say no more. Then, there is the Lord Mayor in the centre, looking as cool as a Lord Mayor *can* look, with an immense *bouquet* before him, and habited in all the splendour of his office. Then, there are the Sheriffs, who are almost as dignified as the Lord Mayor himself ; and the Barristers, who are quite dignified enough in their own opinion ; and the spectators, who having paid for their admission, look upon the whole scene as if it were got up especially for their amusement. Look upon the whole group in the body of the Court—some wholly engrossed in the morning papers, others carelessly conversing in low whispers, and others, again, quietly dozing away an hour—and you can scarcely believe that the result of the trial is a matter of life or death to one wretched being present. But turn your eyes to the dock ; watch the prisoner attentively for a few moments ; and the fact is before you, in all its painful reality. Mark how restlessly he has been engaged for the last ten minutes, in forming all sorts of fantastic figures with the herbs which are strewed upon the ledge before him ; observe the asby paleness of his face when a particular witness appears, and how he changes his position and wipes his clammy forehead, and feverish hands, when the case for the prosecution is closed, as if it were a relief to him to feel that the jury knew the worst.

The defence is concluded; the judge proceeds to sum up the evidence; and the prisoner watches the countenances of the jury, as a dying man, clinging to life to the very last, vainly looks in the face of his physician for a slight ray of hope. They turn round to consult; you can almost hear the man's heart beat, as he bites the stalk of rosemary, with a desperate effort to appear composed. They resume their places—a dead silence prevails as the foreman delivers in the verdict—"Guilty!" A shriek bursts from a female in the gallery; the prisoner casts one look at the quarter from whence the noise proceeded; and is immediately hurried from the dock by the gaoler. The clerk directs one of the officers of the court to "take the woman out," and fresh business is proceeded with, as if nothing had occurred.

No imaginary contrast to a case like this, could be as complete as that which is constantly presented in the New Court, the gravity of which is frequently disturbed in no small degree, by the cunning and pertinacity of juvenile offenders. A boy of thirteen is tried, say for picking the pocket of some subject of her Majesty, and the offence is about as clearly proved as an offence can be. He is called upon for his defence, and contents himself with a little declamation about the jurymen and his country—asserts that all the witnesses have committed perjury, and hints that the police force generally have entered into a conspiracy "again" him. However probable this statement may be, it fails to convince the Court, and some such scene as the following then takes place:

Court: Have you any witnesses to speak to your character, boy?

Boy: Yes, my Lord; fifteen gen'lm'n is a vaten outside, and vos a vaten all day yesterday, vich they told me the night afore my trial vos a comin' on.

Court: Inquire for these witnesses.

Here, a stout beadle runs out, and vociferates for the witnesses at the very top of his voice; for you hear his cry grow fainter and fainter as he descends the steps into the court-yard below. After an absence of five minutes, he returns, very warm and hoarse, and informs the Court of what it knew perfectly well before—namely, that there are no such witnesses in attendance. Hereupon, the boy sets up a most awful howling; screws the lower part of the palms of his hands into the corners of his eyes; and endeavours to look the picture of injured innocence. The jury at once find him "guilty," and his endeavours to squeeze out a tear or two are redoubled. The governor of the gaol then states, in reply to an inquiry from the bench, that the prisoner has been under his care twice before. This the urchin resolutely denies in some such terms as—"S'elp me, gen'lm'n, I never vos in trouble afore—indeed, my Lord, I never vos. It's all a howen to my having a twin brother, vich has wrongfully got into trouble, and vich is so exactly like me, that no vun ever knows the difference atween us."

This representation, like the defence, fails in producing the desired effect, and the boy is sentenced, perhaps, to seven years' transportation. Finding it impossible to excite compassion, he gives vent to his feelings in an imprecation bearing reference to the eyes of "old big vig!" and as he declines to take the trouble of walking from the dock, is forthwith carried out, congratulating himself on having succeeded in giving everybody as much trouble as possible.

CHAPTER XXV.

A VISIT TO NEWGATE.

"The force of habit" is a trite phrase in everybody's mouth; and it is not a little remarkable that those who use it most as applied to others, unconsciously afford in their own persons singular examples of the power which habit and custom exercise over the minds of men, and of the little reflection they are apt to bestow on subjects with which every day's experience has rendered them familiar. If Bedlam could be suddenly removed like another Aladdin's palace, and set down on the space now occupied by Newgate, scarcely one man out of a hundred, whose road to business every morning lies through Newgate-street, or the Old Bailey, would pass the building without bestowing a hasty glance on its small, grated windows, and a transient thought upon the condition of the unhappy beings immured in its dismal cells; and yet these same men, day by day, and hour by hour, pass and repass this gloomy depository of the guilt and misery of London, in one perpetual stream of life and bustle, utterly unmindful of the throng of wretched creatures pent up within it—nay, not even knowing, or if they do, not heeding, the fact, that as they pass one particular angle of the massive wall with a light laugh or a merry whistle, they stand within one yard of a fellow-creature, bound and helpless, whose hours are numbered, from whom the last feeble ray of hope has fled for ever, and whose miserable career will shortly terminate in a violent and shameful death. Contact with death even in its least terrible shape, is solemn and appalling. How much more awful is it to reflect on this near vicinity to the dying—to men in full health and vigour, in the flower of youth or the prime of life, with all their faculties and perceptions as acute and perfect as your own; but dying, nevertheless—dying as surely—with the hand of death imprinted upon them as indelibly—as if mortal disease had wasted their frames to shadows, and corruption had already begun!

It was with some such thoughts as these that we determined, not many weeks since, to visit the interior of Newgate—in an amateur capacity, of course: and, having carried our intention into effect, we proceed to lay its results before our readers, in the hope—founded more upon the nature of the subject, than on any presumptuous confidence in our own descriptive powers—that this paper may not be found wholly devoid of interest. We have only to premise, that we do not intend to fatigue the reader with any statistical accounts of the prison; they will be found at length in numerous reports of numerous committees, and a variety of authorities of equal weight. We took no notes, made no memoranda, measured none of the yards, ascertained the exact number of inches in no particular room: are unable even to report of how many apartments the gaol is composed.

We saw the prison, and saw the prisoners; and what we did see, and what we thought, we will tell at once in our own way.

Having delivered our credentials to the servant who answered our knock at the door of the governor's house, we were ushered into the "office;" a little room, on the right-hand side as you enter, with two windows looking into the Old Bailey: fitted up like an ordinary attorney's office, or merchant's counting-house, with the usual fixtures—a wainscoted partition, a shelf or two, a desk, a couple of stools, a pair of clerks, an almanack, a clock, and a few maps. After a little delay, occasioned by sending into the interior of the prison for the officer whose duty it was to conduct us, that functionary arrived; a respectable-looking man of about two or three and fifty, in a broad-brimmed hat, and full suit of black, who, but for his keys, would have looked quite as much like a clergyman as a turnkey. We were disappointed; he had not even top-boots on. Following our conductor by a door opposite to that at which we had entered, we arrived at a small room, without any other furniture than a little desk, with a book for visitors' autographs, and a shelf, on which were a few boxes for papers, and casts of the heads and faces of the two notorious murderers, Bishop and Williams; the former, in particular, exhibiting a style of head and set of features, which might have afforded sufficient moral grounds for his instant execution at any time, even had there been no other evidence against him. Leaving this room also, by an opposite door, we found ourself in the lodge which opens on the Old Bailey; one side of which is plentifully garnished with a choice collection of heavy sets of irons, including those worn by the redoubtable Jack Sheppard—genuine; and those *said* to have been graced by the sturdy limbs of the no less celebrated Dick Turpin—doubtful. From this lodge, a heavy oaken gate, bound with iron, studded with nails of the same material, and guarded by another turnkey, opens on a few steps, if we remember right, which terminate in a narrow and dismal stone passage, running parallel with the Old Bailey, and leading to the different yards, through a number of tortuous and intricate windings, guarded in their turn by huge gates and gratings, whose appearance is sufficient to dispel at once the slightest hope of escape that any new comer may have entertained; and the very recollection of which, on eventually traversing the place again, involves one in a maze of confusion.

It is necessary to explain here, that the buildings in the prison, or in other words the different wards—form a square, of which the four sides abut respectively on the Old Bailey, the old College of Physicians (now forming a part of Newgate-market), the Sessions-house, and Newgate-street. The intermediate space is divided into several paved yards, in which the prisoners take such air and exercise as can be had in such a place. These yards, with the exception of that in which prisoners under sentence of death are confined (of which we shall presently give a more detailed description), run parallel with Newgate-street, and consequently from the Old Bailey, as it were, to Newgate-market. The women's side is in the right wing of the prison nearest the Sessions-house. As we were introduced into this part of the building first, we will adopt the same order, and introduce our readers to it also.

Turning to the right, then, down the passage to which we just now adverted, omitting any mention of intervening gates—for if we noticed every gate that was unlocked for us to pass through, and locked again as soon as we had passed, we should require a gate at every comma—we came to a door composed of thick bars of wood, through which were discernible, passing to and fro in a narrow yard, some twenty women: the majority of whom, however, as soon as they were aware of the presence of strangers, retreated to their wards. One side of this yard is railed off at a considerable distance, and formed into a kind of iron cage, about five feet ten inches in height, roofed at the top, and defended in front by iron bars, from which the friends of the female prisoners communicate with them. In one corner of this singular-looking den, was a yellow, haggard, decrepit old woman, in a tattered gown that had once been black, and the remains of an old straw bonnet, with faded ribbon of the same hue, in earnest conversation with a young girl—a prisoner, of course—of about two-and-twenty. It is impossible to imagine a more poverty-stricken object, or a creature so borne down in soul and body, by excess of misery and destitution as the old woman. The girl was a good-looking robust female, with a profusion of hair streaming about in the wind—for she had no bonnet on—and a man's silk pocket-handkerchief loosely thrown over a most ample pair of shoulders. The old woman was talking in that low, stifled tone of voice which tells so forcibly of mental anguish; and every now and then burst into an irrepressible sharp, abrupt cry of grief, the most distressing sound that ears can hear. The girl was perfectly unmoved. Hardened beyond all hope of redemption, she listened doggedly to her mother's entreaties, whatever they were: and, beyond inquiring after "Jem," and eagerly catching at the few halfpence her miserable parent had brought her, took no more apparent interest in the conversation than the most unconcerned spectators. Heaven knows there were enough of them, in the persons of the other prisoners in the yard, who were no more concerned by what was passing before their eyes, and within their hearing, than if they were blind and deaf. Why should they be? Inside the prison, and out, such scenes were too familiar to them, to excite even a passing thought, unless of ridicule or contempt for feelings which they had long since forgotten.

A little farther on, a squalid-looking woman in a slovenly, thick-bordered cap, with her arms muffled in a large red shawl, the fringed ends of which straggled nearly to the bottom of a dirty white apron, was communicating some instructions to *her* visitor—her daughter evidently. The girl was thinly clad, and shaking with the cold. Some ordinary word of recognition passed between her and her mother when she appeared at the grating, but neither hope, condolence, regret, nor affection was expressed on either side. The mother whispered her instructions, and the girl received them with her pinched-up half-starved features twisted into an expression of careful cunning. It was some scheme for the woman's defence that she was disclosing, perhaps; and a sullen smile came over the girl's face for an instant, as if she were pleased: not so much at the probability of her mother's liberation, as at the chnnce of her "getting off" in spite of her prosecutors. The dialogue was soon concluded; and with the same careless indifference with which they had approached each other, the mother turned towards the inner end of the yard, and the girl to the gate at which she had entered.

The girl belonged to a class—unhappily but too extensive—the very existence of which, should make men's hearts bleed. Barely past her childhood, it required but a glance to discover that she was one of those children, born and bred in neglect and vice, who have never known what childhood is: who have never been taught to love and court a parent's smile, or to dread a parent's frown. The thousand nameless endearments of childhood, its gaiety and its innocence, are alike unknown to them. They have entered at once upon the stern realities and miseries of life, and to their better nature it is almost hopeless to appeal in aftertimes, by any of the references which will awaken, if it be only for a moment, some good feeling in ordinary bosoms, however corrupt they may have become. Talk to *them* of parental solicitude, the happy days of childhood, and the merry games of infancy! Tell them of hunger and the streets, beggary and stripes, the gin-shop, the station-house, and the pawnbroker's, and they will understand you.

Two or three women were standing at different parts of the grating, conversing with their friends, but a very large proportion of the prisoners appeared to have no friends at all, beyond such of their old companions as might happen to be within the walls. So, passing hastily down the yard, and pausing only for an instant to notice the little incidents we have just recorded, we were conducted up a clean and well-lighted flight of stone stairs to one of the wards. There are several in this part of the building, but a description of one is a description of the whole.

It was a spacious, bare, whitewashed apartment, lighted of course, by windows looking into the interior of the prison, but far more light and airy than one could reasonably expect to find in such a situation. There was a large fire with a deal table before it, round which ten or a dozen women were seated on wooden forms at dinner. Along both sides of the room ran a shelf; below it, at regular intervals, a row of large hooks were fixed in the wall, on each of which was hung the sleeping mat of a prisoner: her rug and blanket being folded up, and placed on the shelf above. At night, these mats are placed on the floor, each beneath the hook on which it hangs during the day; and the ward is thus made to answer the purposes both of a day-room and sleeping apartment. Over the fireplace, was a large sheet of pasteboard, on which were displayed a variety of texts from Scripture, which were also scattered about the room in scraps about the size and shape of the copy-slips which are used in schools. On the table was a sufficient provision of a kind of stewed beef and brown bread, in pewter dishes, which are kept perfectly bright, and displayed on shelves in great order and regularity when they are not in use.

The women rose hastily, on our entrance, and retired in a hurried manner to either side of the fireplace. They were all cleanly—many of them decently—attired, and there was nothing peculiar, either in their appearance or demeanour. One or two resumed the needlework which they had probably laid aside at the commencement of their meal; others gazed at the visitors with listless curiosity; and a few retired behind their companions to the very end of the room, as if desirous to avoid even the casual observation of the strangers. Some old Irish women, both in this and other wards, to whom the thing was no novelty, appeared perfectly indifferent to our presence, and remained standing close to the seats from which they had just risen; but the general feeling among the females seemed to be one of uneasiness during the period of our stay among them: which was very brief. Not a word was uttered during the time of our remaining, unless, indeed, by the wardswoman in reply to some question which we put to the turnkey who accompanied us. In every ward on the female side, a wardswoman is appointed to preserve order, and a similar regulation is adopted among the males. The wardsmen and wardswomen are all prisoners, selected for good conduct. They alone are allowed the privilege of sleeping on bedsteads; a small stump bedstead being placed in every ward for that purpose. On both sides of the gaol, is a small receiving-room, to which prisoners are conducted on their first reception, and whence they cannot be removed until they have been examined by the surgeon of the prison.*

Retracing our steps to the dismal passage in which we found ourselves at first (and which, by-the-bye, contains three or four dark cells for the accommodation of refractory prisoners), we were led through a narrow yard to the "school"—a portion of the prison set apart for boys under fourteen years of age. In a tolerable-sized room, in which were writing-materials and some copy-books, was the schoolmaster, with a couple of his pupils; the remainder having been fetched from an adjoining apartment, the whole were drawn up in line for our inspection. There were fourteen of them in all, some with shoes, some without; some in pinafores without jackets, others in jackets without pinafores, and one in scarce anything at all. The whole number, without an exception we believe, had been committed for trial on charges of pocket-picking; and fourteen such terrible little faces we never beheld.—There was not one redeeming feature among them—not a glance of honesty—not a wink expressive of anything but the gallows and the hulks, in the whole collection. As to anything like shame or contrition, that was entirely out of the question. They were evidently quite gratified at being thought worth the trouble of looking at; their idea appeared to be, that we had come to see Newgate as a grand affair, and that they were an indispensable part of the show; and every boy as he "fell in" to the line, actually seemed as pleased and important as if he had done something excessively meritorious in getting there at all. We

* The regulations of the prison relative to the confinement of prisoners during the day, their sleeping at night, their taking their meals, and other matters of gaol economy, have been all altered —greatly for the better—since this sketch was first published. Even the construction of the prison itself has been changed.

never looked upon a more disagreeable sight, because we never saw fourteen such hopeless creatures of neglect, before.

On either side of the school-yard is a yard for men, in one of which—that towards Newgate-street—prisoners of the more respectable class are confined. Of the other, we have little description to offer, as the different wards necessarily partake of the same character. They are provided, like the wards on the women's side, with mats and rugs, which are disposed of in the same manner during the day; the only very striking difference between their appearance and that of the wards inhabited by the females, is the utter absence of any employment. Huddled together on two opposite forms, by the fireside, sit twenty men perhaps; here, a boy in livery; there, a man in a rough great-coat and top-boots; farther on, a desperate-looking fellow in his shirt sleeves, with an old Scotch cap upon his shaggy head; near him again, a tall ruffian, in a smock-frock; next to him, a miserable being of distressed appearance, with his head resting on his hand;—all alike in one respect, all idle and listless. When they do leave the fire, sauntering moodily about, lounging in the window, or leaning against the wall, vacantly swinging their bodies to and fro. With the exception of a man reading an old newspaper, in two or three instances, this was the case in every ward we entered.

The only communication these men have with their friends, is through two close iron gratings, with an intermediate space of about a yard in width between the two, so that nothing can be handed across, nor can the prisoner have any communication by touch with the person who visits him. The married men have a separate grating, at which to see their wives, but its construction is the same.

The prison chapel is situated at the back of the governor's house: the latter having no windows looking into the interior of the prison. Whether the associations connected with the place—the knowledge that here a portion of the burial service is, on some dreadful occasions, performed over the quick and not upon the dead—cast over it a still more gloomy and sombre air than art has imparted to it, we know not, but its appearance is very striking. There is something in a silent and deserted place of worship, solemn and impressive at any time; and the very dissimilarity of this one from any we have been accustomed to, only enhances the impression. The meanness of its appointments—the bare and scanty pulpit, with the paltry painted pillars on either side—the women's gallery with its great heavy curtain—the men's with its unpainted benches and dingy front—the tottering little table at the altar, with the commandments on the wall above it, scarcely legible through lack of paint, and dust and damp—so unlike the velvet and gilding, the marble and wood, of a modern church—are strange and striking. There is one object, too, which rivets the attention and fascinates the gaze, and from which we may turn horror-stricken in vain, for the recollection of it will haunt us, waking and sleeping, for a long time afterwards. Immediately below the reading-desk, on the floor of the chapel, and forming the most conspicuous object in its little area, is *the condemned pew*; a huge black pen, in which the wretched people, who are singled out for death, are placed on the Sunday preceding their execution, in sight of all their fellow-prisoners, from many of whom they may have been separated but a week before, to hear prayers for their own souls, to join in the responses of their own burial service, and to listen to an address, warning their recent companions to take example by their fate, and urging themselves, while there is yet time—nearly four-and-twenty hours—to "turn, and flee from the wrath to come!" Imagine what have been the feelings of the men whom that fearful pew has enclosed, and of whom, between the gallows and the knife, no mortal remnant may now remain! Think of the hopeless clinging to life to the last, and the wild despair, far exceeding in anguish the felon's death itself, by which they have heard the certainty of their speedy transmission to another world, with all their crimes upon their heads, rung into their ears by the officiating clergyman!

At one time—and at no distant period either—the coffins of the men about to be executed, were placed in that pew, upon the seat by their side, during the whole service. It may seem incredible, but it is true. Let us hope that the increased spirit of civilisation and humanity which abolished this frightful and degrading custom, may extend itself to other usages equally barbarous; usages which have not even the plea of utility in their defence, as every year's experience has shown them to be more and more inefficacious.

Leaving the chapel, descending to the passage so frequently alluded to, and crossing the yard before noticed as being allotted to prisoners of a more respectable description than the generality of men confined here, the visitor arrives at a thick iron gate of great size and strength. Having been admitted through it by the turnkey on duty, he turns sharp round to the left, and pauses before another gate; and, having passed this last barrier, he stands in the most terrible part of this gloomy building—the condemned ward.

The press-yard, well known by name to newspaper readers, from its frequent mention in accounts of executions, is at the corner of the building, and next to the ordinary's house, in Newgate-street: running from Newgate-street, towards the centre of the prison, parallel with Newgate-market. It is a long, narrow court, of which a portion of the wall in Newgate-street forms one end, and the gate the other. At the upper end, on the left-hand—that is, adjoining the wall in Newgate-street—is a cistern of water, and at the bottom a double grating (of which the gate itself forms a part) similar to that before described. Through these grates the prisoners are allowed to see their friends; a turnkey always remaining in the vacant space between, during the whole interview. Immediately on the right as you enter, is a building containing the press-room, day-room, and cells; the yard is on every side surrounded by lofty walls guarded by *chevaux de frise;* and the whole is under the constant inspection of vigilant and experienced turnkeys.

In the first apartment into which we were conducted—which was at the top of a staircase, and immediately over the press-room—were five-and-twenty or thirty prisoners, all under sentence of death, awaiting the result of the recorder's report—men of all ages and appearances, from a hardened old offender with swarthy face and grizzly beard of three days' growth, to a handsome boy, not fourteen years old, and of singularly youthful appearance even for that age, who had been condemned for burglary. There was nothing remarkable in the appearance of these prisoners. One or two decently-dressed men were brooding with a dejected air over the fire; several little groups of two or three had been engaged in conversation at the upper end of the room, or in the windows; and the remainder were crowded round a young man seated at a table, who appeared to be engaged in teaching the younger ones to write. The room was large, airy, and clean. There was very little anxiety or mental suffering depicted in the countenance of any of the men;—they had all been sentenced to death, it is true, and the recorder's report had not yet been made; but, we question whether there was a man among them, notwithstanding, who did not *know* that although he had undergone the ceremony, it never was intended that his life should be sacrificed. On the table lay a Testament, but there were no tokens of its having been in recent use.

In the press-room below, were three men, the nature of whose offence rendered it necessary to separate them, even from their companions in guilt. It is a long, sombre room, with two windows sunk into the stone wall, and here the wretched men are pinioned on the morning of their execution, before moving towards the scaffold. The fate of one of these prisoners was uncertain; some mitigatory circumstances having come to light since his trial, which had been humanely represented in the proper quarter. The other two had nothing to expect from the mercy of the crown; their doom was sealed; no plea could be urged in extenuation of their crime, and they well knew that for them there was no hope in this world. "The two short ones," the turnkey whispered, "were dead men."

The man to whom we have alluded as entertaining some hopes of escape, was lounging, at the greatest distance he could place between himself and his companions, in the window nearest to the door. He was probably aware of our approach, and had assumed an air of courageous indifference; his face was purposely averted towards the window, and he stirred not an inch while we were present. The other two men were at the upper end of the room. One of them, who was imperfectly seen in the dim light, had his back towards us, and was stooping over the fire, with his right arm on the mantel-piece, and his head sunk upon it. The other, was leaning on the sill of the farthest window. The light fell full upon him, and communicated to his pale, haggard face, and disordered hair, an appearance which, at that distance, was ghastly. His cheek rested upon his hand; and, with his face a little raised, and his eyes wildly staring before him, he seemed to be unconsciously intent on counting the chinks in the opposite wall. We passed this room again afterwards. The first man was pacing up and down the court with a firm military step—he had been a soldier in the foot-guards—and a cloth cap jauntily thrown on one side of his head. He bowed respectfully to our conductor, and the salute was returned. The other two still remained in the positions we have described, and were as motionless as statues.*

A few paces up the yard, and forming a continuation of the building, in which are the two rooms we have just quitted, lie the condemned cells. The entrance is by a narrow and obscure staircase leading to a dark passage, in which a charcoal stove casts a lurid tint over the objects in its immediate vicinity, and diffuses something like warmth around. From the left-hand side of this passage, the massive door of every cell on the story opens; and from it alone can they be approached. There are three of these passages, and three of these ranges of cells, one above the other; but in size, furniture and appearance, they are all precisely alike. Prior to the recorder's report being made, all the prisoners under sentence of death are removed from the day-room at five o'clock in the afternoon, and locked up in these cells, where they are allowed a candle until ten o'clock; and here they remain until seven next morning. When the warrant for a prisoner's execution arrives, he is removed to the cells and confined in one of them until he leaves it for the scaffold. He is at liberty to walk in the yard; but, both in his walks and in his cell, he is constantly attended by a turnkey who never leaves him on any pretence.

We entered the first cell. It was a stone dungeon, eight feet long by six wide, with a bench at the upper end, under which were a common rug, a bible, and prayer-book. An iron candlestick was fixed into the wall at the side; and a small high window in the back admitted as much air and light as could struggle in between a double row of heavy, crossed iron bars. It contained no other furniture of any description.

Conceive the situation of a man, spending his last night on earth in this cell. Buoyed up with some vague and undefined hope of reprieve, he knew not why—indulging in some wild and visionary idea of escaping, he knew not how—hour after hour of the three preceding days allowed him for preparation, has fled with a speed which no man living would deem possible, for none but this dying man

* These two men were executed shortly afterwards. The other was respited during his Majesty's pleasure.

A VISIT TO NEWGATE.

can know. He has wearied his friends with entreaties, exhausted the attendants with importunities, neglected in his feverish restlessness the timely warnings of his spiritual consoler; and, now that the illusion is at last dispelled, now that eternity is before him and guilt behind, now that his fears of death amount almost to madness, and an overwhelming sense of his helpless, hopeless state rushes upon him, he is lost and stupified, and has neither thoughts to turn to, nor power to call upon, the Almighty Being, from whom alone he can seek mercy and forgiveness, and before whom his repentance can alone avail.

Hours have glided by, and still he sits upon the same stone bench with folded arms, heedless alike of the fast decreasing time before him, and the urgent entreaties of the good man at his side. The feeble light is wasting gradually, and the deathlike stillness of the street without, broken only by the rumbling of some passing vehicle which echoes mournfully through the empty yards, warns him that the night is waning fast away. The deep bell of St. Paul's strikes—one! He heard it; it has roused him. Seven hours left! He paces the narrow limits of his cell with rapid strides, cold drops of terror starting on his forehead, and every muscle of his frame quivering with agony. Seven hours! He suffers himself to be led to his seat, mechanically takes the bible which is placed in his hand, and tries to read and listen. No: his thoughts will wander. The book is torn and soiled by use—and like the book he read his lessons in, at school, just forty years ago! He has never bestowed a thought upon it, perhaps, since he left it as a child: and yet the place, the time, the room—nay, the very boys he played with, crowd as vividly before him as if they were scenes of yesterday; and some forgotten phrase, some childish word, rings in his ears like the echo of one uttered but a minute since. The voice of the clergyman recalls him to himself. He is reading from the sacred book its solemn promises of pardon for repentance, and its awful denunciation of obdurate men. He falls upon his knees and clasps his hands to pray. Hush! what sound was that? He starts upon his feet. It cannot be two yet. Hark! Two quarters have struck;—the third—the fourth. It is! Six hours left. Tell him not of repentance! Six hours' repentance for eight times six years of guilt and sin! He buries his face in his hands, and throws himself on the bench.

Worn with watching and excitement, he sleeps, and the same unsettled state of mind pursues him in his dreams. An insupportable load is taken from his breast; he is walking with his wife in a pleasant field, with the bright sky above them, and a fresh and boundless prospect on every side—how different from the stone walls of Newgate! She is looking—not as she did when he saw her for the last time in that dreadful place, but as she used when he loved her—long, long ago, before misery and ill-treatment had altered her looks, and vice had changed his nature, and she is leaning upon his arm, and looking up into his face with tenderness and affection—and he does *not* strike her now, nor rudely shake her from him. And oh! how glad he is to tell her all he had forgotten in that last hurried interview, and to fall on his knees before her and fervently beseech her pardon for all the unkindness and cruelty that wasted her form and broke her heart! The scene suddenly changes. He is on his trial again: there are the judge and jury, and prosecutors, and witnesses, just as they were before. How full the court is—what a sea of heads—with a gallows, too, and a scaffold—and how all those people stare at *him!* Verdict, "Guilty." No matter; he will escape.

The night is dark and cold, the gates have been left open, and in an instant he is in the street, flying from the scene of his imprisonment like the wind. The streets are cleared, the open fields are gained and the broad wide country lies before him. Onward he dashes in the midst of darkness, over hedge and ditch, through mud and pool, bounding from spot to spot with a speed and lightness, astonishing even to himself. At length he pauses; he must be safe from pursuit now; he will stretch himself on that bank and sleep till sunrise.

A period of unconsciousness succeeds. He wakes, cold and wretched. The dull grey light of morning is stealing into the cell, and falls upon the form of the attendant turnkey. Confused by his dreams, he starts from his uneasy bed in momentary uncertainty. It is but momentary. Every object in the narrow cell is too frightfully real to admit of doubt or mistake. He is the condemned felon again, guilty and despairing; and in two hours more will be dead.

CHARACTERS.

CHAPTER I.

THOUGHTS ABOUT PEOPLE.

It is strange with how little notice, good, bad, or indifferent, a man may live and die in London. He awakens no sympathy in the breast of any single person; his existence is a matter of interest to no one save himself; he cannot be said to be forgotten when he dies, for no one remembered him when he was alive. There is a numerous class of people in this great metropolis who seem not to possess a single friend, and whom nobody appears to care for. Urged by imperative necessity in the first instance, they have resorted to London in search of employment, and the means of subsistence. It is hard, we know, to break the ties which bind us to our homes and friends, and harder still to efface the thousand recollections of happy days and old times, which have been slumbering in our bosoms for years, and only rush upon the mind, to bring before it associations connected with the friends we have left, the scenes we have beheld too probably for the last time, and the hopes we once cherished, but may entertain no more. These men, however, happily for themselves, have long forgotten such thoughts. Old country friends have died or emigrated; former correspondents have become lost, like themselves, in the crowd and turmoil of some busy city; and they have gradually settled down into mere passive creatures of habit and endurance.

We were seated in the enclosure of St. James's Park the other day, when our attention was attracted by a man whom we immediately put down in our own mind as one of this class. He was a tall, thin, pale person, in a black coat, scanty gray trousers, little pinched-up gaiters, and brown beaver gloves. He had an umbrella in his hand—not for use, for the day was fine—but, evidently, because he always carried one to the office in the morning. He walked up and down before the little patch of grass on which the chairs are placed for hire, not as if he were doing it for pleasure or recreation, but as if it were a matter of compulsion, just as he would walk to the office every morning from the back settlements of Islington. It was Monday; he had escaped for four-and-twenty hours from the thraldom of the desk; and was walking here for exercise and amusement—perhaps for the first time in his life. We were inclined to think he had never had a holiday before, and that he did not know what to do with himself. Children were playing on the grass; groups of people were loitering about, chatting and laughing; but the man walked steadily up and down, unheeding and unheeded, his spare pale face looking as if it were incapable of bearing the expression of curiosity or interest.

There was something in the man's manner and appearance which told us, we fancied, his whole life, or rather his whole day, for a man of this sort has no variety of days. We thought we almost saw the dingy little back office into which he walks every morning, hanging his hat on the same peg, and placing his legs beneath the same desk: first, taking off that black coat which lasts the year through, and putting on the one which did duty last year, and which he keeps in his desk to save the other. There he sits till five o'clock, working on, all day, as regularly as the dial over the mantel-piece, whose loud ticking is as monotonous as his whole existence: only raising his head when some one enters the counting-house, or when, in the midst of some difficult calculation, he looks up to the ceiling as if there were inspiration in the dusty skylight with a green knot in the centre of every pane of glass. About five, or half-past, he slowly dismounts from his accustomed stool, and again changing his coat, proceeds to his usual dining-place, somewhere near Bucklersbury. The waiter recites the bill of fare in a rather confidential manner—for he is a regular customer—and after inquiring "What's in the best cut?" and "What was up last?" he orders a small plate of roast beef, with greens, and half-a-pint of porter. He has a small plate to-day, because greens are a penny more than potatoes, and he had "two breads" yesterday, with the additional enormity of "a cheese" the day before. This important point settled, he hangs up his hat—he took it off the moment he sat down—and bespeaks the paper after the next gentleman. If he can get it while he is at dinner, he eats with much greater zest; balancing it against the water-bottle, and eating a bit of beef, and reading a line or two, alternately. Exactly at five minutes before the hour is up, he produces a shilling, pays the reckoning, carefully deposits the change in his waistcoat-pocket (first deducting a penny for the waiter), and returns to the office, from which, if it is not foreign post night, he again sallies forth, in about half an hour. He then walks home, at his usual pace, to his little back room at Islington, where he has his tea; perhaps solacing himself during the meal with the conversation of his landlady's little boy, whom he occasionally rewards with a penny, for solving problems in simple addition. Sometimes, there is a letter or two to take up to his employer's, in Russell-square; and then, the wealthy man of business, hearing his voice, calls out from the dining-parlour,—"Come in, Mr. Smith:" and Mr. Smith, putting his hat at the feet of one of the hall chairs, walks timidly in, and being condescendingly desired to sit down, carefully tucks his legs under his chair, and sits at a considerable distance from the table while he drinks the glass of sherry which is poured out for him by the eldest boy, and after drinking which, he backs and slides out of the room, in a state of nervous agitation from which he does not perfectly recover, until he finds himself once more in the Islington-road. Poor, harmless creatures such men are; contented but not happy; broken-spirited and humbled, they may feel no pain, but they never know pleasure.

Compare these men with another class of beings who, like them, have neither friend nor companion, but whose position in society is the result of their own choice. These are generally old fellows with white heads and red faces, addicted to port wine and Hessian boots, who from some cause, real or imaginary—generally the former, the excellent reason being that they are rich, and their relations poor—grow suspicious of everybody, and do the misanthropical in chambers, taking great delight in thinking themselves unhappy, and making everybody they come near, miserable. You may see such men as these, anywhere; you will know them at coffee-houses by their discontented exclamations and the luxury of their dinners; at theatres, by their always sitting in the same place and looking with a jaundiced eye on all the young people near them; at church, by the pomposity with which they enter, and the loud tone in which they repeat the responses; at parties, by their getting cross at whist and hating music. An old fellow of this kind will have his chambers splendidly furnished, and collect books, plate, and pictures about him in profusion; not so much for his own gratification, as to be superior to those who have the desire, but not the means, to compete with him. He belongs to two or three clubs, and is envied, and flattered, and hated by the members of them all. Sometimes he will be appealed to by a poor relation—a married nephew perhaps—for some little assistance: and then he will declaim with honest indignation on the improvidence of young married people, the worthlessness of a wife, the insolence of having a family, the atrocity of getting into debt with a hundred and twenty-five pounds a-year, and other unpardonable crimes; winding up his exhortations with a complacent review of his own conduct, and a delicate allusion to parochial relief. He dies, some day after dinner, of apoplexy, having bequeathed his property to a Public Society, and the Institution erects a tablet to his memory, expressive of their admiration of his Christian conduct in this world, and their comfortable conviction of his happiness in the next.

But, next to our very particular friends, hackney-coachmen, cabmen and cads, whom we admire in proportion to the extent of their cool impudence and perfect self-possession, there is no class of people who amuse us more than London apprentices. They are no longer an organised body, bound down by solemn compact to terrify his majesty's subjects whenever it pleases them to take offence in their heads and staves in their hands, They are only bound, now, by indentures; and, as to their valour, it is easily restrained by the wholesome dread of the New Police, and a perspective view of a damp station-house, terminating in a police-office and a reprimand. They are still, however, a peculiar class, and not the less pleasant for being inoffensive. Can any one fail to have noticed them in the streets on Sunday? And were there ever such harmless efforts at the grand and magnificent as the young fellows display! We walked down the Strand, a Sunday or two ago, behind a little group; and they furnished food for our amusement the whole way. They had come out of some part of the city; it was between three and four o'clock in the afternoon; and they were on their way to the Park. There were four of them, all arm-in-arm, with white kid gloves like so many bridegrooms, light trousers of unprecedented patterns, and coats for which the English language has yet no name—a kind of cross between a great-coat and a surtout, with the collar of the one, the skirts of the other, and pockets peculiar to themselves.

Each of the gentlemen carried a thick stick, with a large tassel at the top, which he occasionally twirled gracefully round; and the whole four, by way of looking easy and unconcerned, were walking with a paralytic swagger irresistibly ludicrous. One of the party had a watch about the size and shape of a reasonable Ribstone pippin, jammed into his waistcoat-pocket, which he carefully compared with the clocks at St. Clement's and the New Church, the illuminated clock at Exeter 'Change, the clock of St. Martin's Church, and the clock of the Horse Guards. When they at last arrived in Saint James's Park, the member of the party who had the best made boots on, hired a second chair expressly for his feet, and flung himself on this two-pennyworth of sylvan luxury with an air which levelled all distinctions between Brookes's and Snooks's, Crockford's and Bagnigge Wells.

We may smile at such people, but they can never excite our anger. They are usually on the best terms with themselves, and it follows almost as a matter of course, in good humour with every one about them. Besides, they are always the faint reflection of higher lights; and, if they do display a little occasional foolery in their own proper persons, it is surely more tolerable than precocious puppyism in the Quadrant, whiskered dandyism in Regent-street and Pall-mall, or gallantry in its dotage anywhere.

CHAPTER II.

A CHRISTMAS DINNER.

CHRISTMAS time! That man must be a misanthrope indeed, in whose breast something like a jovial feeling is not roused—in whose mind some pleasant associations are not awakened—by the recurrence of Christmas. There are people who will tell you that Christmas is not to them what it used to be; that each succeeding Christmas has found some cherished hope, or happy prospect, of the year before, dimmed or passed away; that the present only serves to remind them of reduced circumstances and straitened incomes—of the feasts they once bestowed on hollow friends, and of the cold looks that meet them now, in adversity and misfortune. Never heed such dismal reminiscences. There are few men who have lived long enough in the world, who cannot call up such thoughts any day in the year. Then do not select the merriest of the three hundred and sixty-five, for your doleful recollections, but draw your chair nearer the blazing fire—fill the glass and send round the song—and if your room be smaller than it was a dozen years ago, or if your glass be filled with reeking punch, instead of sparkling wine, put a good face on the matter, and empty it off-hand, and fill another, and troll off the old ditty you used to sing, and thank God it's no worse. Look on the merry faces of your children (if you have any) as they sit round the fire. One little seat may be empty; one slight form that gladdened the father's heart, and roused the mother's pride to look upon, may not be there. Dwell not upon the past; think not that one short year ago, the fair child now resolving into dust, sat before you, with the bloom of health upon its cheek, and the gaiety of infancy in its joyous eye. Reflect upon your present blessings—of which every man has many—not on your past misfortunes, of which all men have some. Fill your glass again, with a merry face and contented heart. Our life on it, but your Christmas shall be merry, and your new year a happy one!

Who can be insensible to the outpourings of good feeling, and the honest interchange of affectionate attachment, which abound at this season of the year? A Christmas family-party! We know nothing in nature more delightful! There seems a magic in the very name of Christmas. Petty jealousies and discords are forgotten; social feelings are awakened, in bosoms to which they have long been strangers; father and son, or brother and sister, who have met and passed with averted gaze, or a look of cold recognition, for months before, proffer and return the cordial embrace, and bury their past animosities in their present happiness. Kindly hearts that have yearned towards each other, but have been withheld by false notions of pride and self-dignity, are again reunited, and all is kindness and benevolence! Would that Christmas lasted the whole year through (as it ought), and that the prejudices and passions which deform our better nature, were never called into action among those to whom they should ever be strangers!

The Christmas family-party that we mean, is not a mere assemblage of relations, got up at a week or two's notice, originating this year, having no family precedent in the last, and not likely to be repeated in the next. No. It is an annual gathering of all the accessible members of the family, young or old, rich or poor; and all the children look forward to it, for two months beforehand, in a fever of anticipation. Formerly, it was held at grandpapa's; but grandpapa getting old, and grandmamma getting old too, and rather infirm, they have given up house-keeping, and domesticated themselves with uncle George; so, the party always takes place at uncle George's house, but grandmamma sends in most of the good things, and grandpapa always *will* toddle down, all the way to Newgate-market, to buy the turkey, which he engages a porter to bring home behind him in triumph, always insisting on the man's being rewarded with a glass of spirits, over and above his hire, to drink "a merry Christmas and a happy new year" to aunt George. As to grandmamma, she is very secret and mysterious for two or three days beforehand, but not sufficiently so, to prevent rumours getting afloat that she has purchased a beautiful new cap with pink ribbons for each of the servants, together with sundry books, and pen-knives, and pencil-cases, for the younger branches; to say nothing of divers secret additions to the order originally given by aunt George at the pastry-cook's, such as another dozen of mince-pies for the dinner, and a large plum-cake for the children.

On Christmas-eve, grandmamma is always in excellent spirits, and after employing all the children, during the day, in stoning the plums, and all that, insists, regularly every year, on uncle George coming down into the kitchen, taking off his coat, and stirring the pudding for half an hour or so, which uncle George good-humouredly does, to the vociferous delight of the children and servants. The evening concludes with a glorious game of blind-man's-buff, in an early stage of which grandpapa takes great care to be caught, in order that he may have an opportunity of displaying his dexterity.

On the following morning, the old couple, with as many of the children as the pew will hold, go to church in great state: leaving aunt George at home dusting decanters and filling castors, and uncle George carrying bottles into the dining-parlour, and calling for corkscrews, and getting into everybody's way.

When the church-party return to lunch, grandpapa produces a small sprig of mistletoe from his pocket, and tempts the boys to kiss their little cousins under it—a proceeding which affords both the boys and the old gentleman unlimited satisfaction, but which rather outrages grandmamma's ideas of decorum, until grandpapa says, that when he was just thirteen years and three months old, *he* kissed grandmamma under a mistletoe too, on which the children clap their hands, and laugh very heartily, as do aunt George and uncle George; and grandmamma looks pleased, and says, with a benevolent smile, that grandpapa was an impudent young dog, on which the children laugh very heartily again, and grandpapa more heartily than any of them.

But all these diversions are nothing to the subsequent excitement when grandmamma in a high cap, and slate-coloured silk gown; and grandpapa with a beautifully plaited shirt-frill, and white neckerchief; seat themselves on one side of the drawing-room fire, with uncle George's children and little cousins innumerable, seated in the front, waiting the arrival of the expected visitors. Suddenly a hackney-coach is heard to stop, and uncle George, who has been looking out of the window, exclaims "Here's Jane!" on which the children rush to the door, and helter-skelter down stairs; and uncle Robert and aunt Jane, and the dear little baby, and the nurse, and the whole party, are ushered up stairs amidst tumultuous shouts of "Oh, my!" from the children, and frequently repeated warnings not to hurt baby from the nurse. And grandpapa takes the child, and grandmamma kisses her daughter, and the confusion of this first entry has scarcely subsided, when some other aunts and uncles with more cousins arrive, and the grown-up cousins flirt with each other, and so do the little cousins too, for that matter, and nothing is to be heard but a confused din of talking, laughing, and merriment.

A hesitating double knock at the street-door, heard during a momentary pause in the conversation, excites a general inquiry of "Who's that?" and two or three children, who have been standing at the window, announce in a low voice, that it's "poor aunt Margaret." Upon which, aunt George leaves the room to welcome the new comer; and grandmamma draws herself up, rather stiff and stately; for Margaret married a poor man without her consent, and poverty not being a sufficiently weighty punishment for her offence, has been discarded by her friends, and debarred the society of her dearest relatives. But Christmas has come round, and the unkind feelings that have struggled against better dispositions during the year, have melted away before its genial influence, like half-formed ice beneath the morning sun. It is not difficult in a moment of angry feeling for a parent to denounce a disobedient child; but, to banish her at a period of general goodwill and hilarity, from the hearth, round which she has sat on so many anniversaries of the same day, expanding by slow degrees from infancy to girlhood, and then bursting, almost imperceptibly, into a woman, is widely different. The air of conscious rectitude, and cold forgiveness, which the old lady has assumed, sits ill upon her; and when the poor girl is led in by her sister, pale in looks and broken in hope—not from poverty, for that she could bear, but from the consciousness of undeserved neglect, and unmerited unkindness—it is easy to see how much of it is assumed. A momentary pause succeeds; the girl breaks suddenly from her sister and throws herself, sobbing, on her mother's neck. The father steps hastily forward, and takes her husband's hand. Friends crowd round to offer their hearty congratulations, and happiness and harmony again prevail.

As to the dinner, it's perfectly delightful—nothing goes wrong, and everybody is in the very best of spirits, and disposed to please and be pleased. Grandpapa relates a circumstantial account of the purchase of the turkey, with a slight digression relative to the purchase of previous turkeys, on former Christmas-days, which grandmamma corroborates in the minutest particular. Uncle George tells stories, and carves poultry, and takes wine, and jokes with the children at the side-table, and winks at the cousins that are making love, or being made love to, and exhilarates everybody with his good humour and hospitality; and when, at last, a stout servant, staggers in with a gigantic pudding, with a sprig of holly in the top, there is such a laughing, and shouting, and clapping of little chubby hands, and kicking up of fat dumpy legs, as can only be equalled by the applause with which the astonishing feat of pouring lighted brandy into mince-pies, is received by the younger visitors. Then the dessert!—and the wine!—and the fun! Such beautiful speeches, and *such* songs, from aunt Margaret's husband, who turns out to be such a nice man, and *so* attentive to grandmamma! Even grandpapa not only sings his annual song with unprecedented vigour, but on being honoured with an unanimous *encore*, according to annual custom, actually comes out with a new one which nobody but grandmamma ever heard before; and a young scape-grace of a cousin, who has been in some disgrace with the old people, for certain heinous sins of omission and commission—neglecting to call, and persisting in drinking Burton Ale—astonishes everybody into convulsions of laughter by volunteering the most extraordinary comic songs that ever were heard. And thus the evening passes, in a strain of rational good-will and cheerfulness, doing more to awaken the sympathies of every member of the party in behalf of his neighbour, and to perpetuate their good feeling during the ensuing year, than half the homilies that have ever been written, by half the Divines that have ever lived.

CHAPTER III.

THE NEW YEAR.

NEXT to Christmas-day, the most pleasant annual epoch in existence is the advent of the New Year. There are a lachrymose set of people who usher in the New Year with watching and fasting, as if they were bound to attend as chief mourners at the obsequies of the old one. Now, we cannot but think it a great deal more complimentary, both to the old year that has rolled away, and to the New Year that is just beginning to dawn upon us, to see the old fellow out, and the new one in, with gaiety and glee.

There must have been some few occurrences in the past year to which we can look back, with a smile of cheerful recollection, if not with a feeling of heartfelt thankfulness. And we are bound by every rule of justice and equity to give the New Year credit for being a good one, until he proves himself unworthy the confidence we repose in him.

This is our view of the matter; and entertaining it, notwithstanding our respect for the old year, one of the few remaining moments of whose existence passes away with every word we write, here we are, seated by our fireside on this last night of the old year, one thousand eight hundred and thirty-six, penning this article with as jovial a face as if nothing extraordinary had happened, or was about to happen, to disturb our good humour.

Hackney-coaches and carriages keep rattling up the street and down the street in rapid succession, conveying, doubtless, smartly-dressed coachfuls to crowded parties; loud and repeated double knocks at the house with green blinds, opposite, announce to the whole neighbourhood that there's one large party in the street at all events; and we saw through the window, and through the fog too, till it grew so thick that we rung for candles, and drew our curtains, pastrycooks' men with green boxes on their heads, and rout-furniture-warehouse-carts, with cane seats and French lamps, hurrying to the numerous houses where an annual festival is held in honour of the occasion.

We can fancy one of these parties, we think, as well as if we were duly dress-coated and pumped, and had just been announced at the drawing-room door.

Take the house with the green blinds for instance. We know it is a quadrille party, because we saw some men taking up the front drawing-room carpet while we sat at breakfast this morning, and if further evidence be required, and we must tell the truth, we just now saw one of the young ladies "doing" another of the young ladies' hair, near one of the bed-room windows, in an unusual style of splendour, which nothing else but a quadrille party could possibly justify.

The master of the house with the green blinds is in a public office; we know the fact by the cut of his coat, the tie of his neckcloth, and the self-satisfaction of his gait—the very green blinds themselves have a Somerset House air about them.

Hark!—a cab! That's a junior clerk in the same office; a tidy sort of young man, with a tendency to cold and corns, who comes in a pair of boots with black cloth fronts, and brings his shoes in his coat-pocket, which shoes he is at this very moment putting on in the hall. Now he is announced by the man in the passage to another man in a blue coat, who is a disguised messenger from the office.

The man on the first landing precedes him to the drawing-room door. "Mr. Tupple!" shouts the messenger. "How *are* you, Tupple?" says the master of the house, advancing from the fire, before which he has been talking politics and airing himself. "My dear, this is Mr. Tupple (a courteous salute from the lady of the house); Tupple, my eldest daughter; Julia, my dear, Mr. Tupple; Tupple, my other daughters; my son, sir;" Tupple rubs his hands very hard, and smiles as if it were all capital fun, and keeps constantly bowing and turning himself round, till the whole family have been introduced, when he glides into a chair at the corner of the sofa, and opens a miscellaneous conversation with the young ladies upon the weather, and the theatres, and the old year, and the last new murder, and the balloon, and the ladies' sleeves, and the festivities of the season, and a great many other topics of small talk.

More double knocks! what an extensive party! what an incessant hum of conversation and general sipping of coffee! We see Tupple now, in our mind's eye, in the height of his glory. He has just handed that stout old lady's cup to the servant; and now, he dives among the crowd of young men by the door, to intercept the other servant, and secure the muffin-plate for the old lady's daughter, before he leaves the room; and now, as he passes the sofa on his way back, he bestows a glance of recognition and patronage upon the young ladies, as condescending and familiar as if he had known them from infancy.

Charming person Mr. Tupple—perfect ladies' man—such a delightful companion, too! Laugh!—nobody ever understood papa's jokes half so well as Mr. Tupple, who laughs himself into convulsions at every fresh burst of facetiousness. Most delightful partner! talks through the whole set! and although he does seem at first rather gay and frivolous, so romantic and with so *much* feeling! Quite a love. No great favourite with the young men, certainly, who sneer at, and affect to despise him; but everybody knows that's only envy, and they needn't give themselves the trouble to depreciate his merits at any rate, for Ma says he shall be asked to every future dinner-party, if it's only to talk to people between the courses, and distract their attention when there's any unexpected delay in the kitchen.

At supper, Mr. Tupple shows to still greater advantage than he has done throughout the evening, and when Pa requests every one to fill their glasses for the purpose of drinking happiness throughout the year, Mr. Tupple is *so* droll: insisting on all the young ladies having their glasses filled, notwithstanding their repeated assurances that they never can, by any possibility, think of emptying them: and subsequently begging permission to say a few words on the sentiment which has just been uttered by Pa—when he makes one of the most brilliant and poetical speeches that can possibly be imagined, about the old year and the new one. After the toast has been drunk, and when the ladies have retired, Mr. Tupple requests that every gentleman will do him the favour of filling his glass, for he has a toast to propose: on which all the gentlemen cry "Hear! hear!" and pass the decanters accordingly: and Mr. Tupple being informed by the master of the house that they are all charged, and waiting for his toast, rises, and begs to remind the gentlemen present, how much they have been delighted by the dazzling array of elegance and beauty which the drawing-room has exhibited that night, and how their senses have been charmed, and their hearts captivated, by the bewitching concentration of female loveliness which that very room has so recently displayed. (Loud cries of "Hear!") Much as he (Tupple) would be disposed to deplore the absence of the ladies, on other grounds, he cannot but derive some consolation from the reflection that the very circumstance of their not being present, enables him to propose a toast, which he would have otherwise been prevented from giving—that toast he begs to say is—"The Ladies!" (Great applause.) The Ladies! among whom the fascinating daughters of their excellent host, are alike conspicuous for their beauty, their accomplishments, and their elegance. He begs them to drain a bumper to "The Ladies, and a happy new year to them!" (Prolonged approbation; above which the noise of the ladies dancing the Spanish dance among themselves, overhead, is distinctly audible.)

The applause consequent on this toast, has scarcely subsided, when a young gentleman in a pink under-waistcoat, sitting towards the bottom of the table, is observed to grow very restless and fidgety, and to evince strong indications of some latent desire to give vent to his feelings in a speech, which the wary Tupple at once perceiving, determines to forestal by speaking himself. He, therefore, rises again, with an air of solemn importance, and trusts he may be permitted to propose another toast (unqualified approbation, and Mr. Tupple proceeds). He is sure they must all be deeply impressed with the hospitality—he may say the splendour—with which they have been that night received by their worthy host and hostess. (Unbounded applause.) Although this is the first occasion on which he has had the pleasure and delight of sitting at that board, he has known his friend Dobble long and intimately; he has been connected with him in business—he wishes everybody present knew Dobble as well as he does. (A cough from the host). He (Tupple) can lay his hand upon his (Tupple's) heart, and declare his confident belief that a better man, a better husband, a better father, a better brother, a better son, a better relation in any relation of life, than Dobble, never existed. (Loud cries of "Hear!") They have seen him to-night in the peaceful bosom of his family; they should see him in the morning, in the trying duties of his office. Calm in the perusal of the morning papers, uncompromising in the signature of his name, dignified in his replies to the inquiries of stranger applicants, deferential in his behaviour to his superiors, majestic in his deportment to the messengers. (Cheers). When he bears this merited testimony to the excellent qualities of his friend Dobble, what can he say in approaching such a subject as Mrs. Dobble? Is it requisite for him to expatiate on the qualities of that amiable woman? No; he will spare his friend Dobble's feelings; he will spare the feelings of his friend—if he will allow him to have the honour of calling him so—Mr. Dobble, junior. (Here Mr. Dobble, junior, who has been previously distending his mouth to a considerable width, by thrusting a particularly fine orange into that feature, suspends operations, and assumes a proper appearance of intense melancholy). He will simply say—and he is quite certain it is a sentiment in which all who hear him will readily concur—that his friend Dobble is as superior to any man he ever knew, as Mrs. Dobble is far beyond any woman he ever saw (except her daughters); and he will conclude by proposing their worthy "Host and Hostess, and may they live to enjoy many more new years!"

The toast is drunk with acclamation; Dobble returns thanks, and the whole party rejoin the ladies in the drawing-room. Young men who were too bashful to dance before supper, find tongues and partners; the musicians exhibit unequivocal symptoms of having drunk the new year in, while the company were out; and dancing is kept up, until far in the first morning of the new year.

We have scarcely written the last word of the previous sentence, when the first stroke of twelve, peals from the neighbouring churches. There certainly—we must confess it now—is something awful in the sound. Strictly speaking, it may not be more impressive now, than at any other time; for the hours steal as swiftly on, at other periods, and their flight is little heeded. But, we measure man's life by years, and it is a solemn knell that warns us we have passed another of the landmarks which stand between us and the grave. Disguise it as we may, the reflection will force itself on our minds, that when the next bell announces the arrival of a new year, we may be insensible alike of the timely warning we have so often neglected, and of all the warm feelings that glow within us now.

CHAPTER IV.

MISS EVANS AND THE EAGLE.

MR. SAMUEL WILKINS was a carpenter, a journeyman carpenter of small dimensions, decidedly below the middle size—bordering, perhaps, upon the dwarfish. His face was round and shining, and his hair carefully twisted into the outer corner of each eye, till it formed a variety of that description of semi-curls, usually known as "aggerawators." His earnings were all-sufficient for his wants, varying from eighteen shillings to one pound five, weekly—his manner undeniable—his sabbath waistcoats dazzling. No wonder that, with these qualifications, Samuel Wilkins found favour in the eyes of the other sex: many women have been captivated by far less substantial qualifications. But, Samuel was proof against their blandishments, until at length his eyes rested on those of a Being for whom, from that time forth, he felt fate had destined him. He came, and conquered—proposed, and was accepted—loved, and was beloved. Mr. Wilkins "kept company" with Jemima Evans.

Miss Evans (or Ivins, to adopt the pronunciation most in vogue with her circle of acquaintance) had adopted in early life the useful pursuit of shoe-binding, to which she had afterwards superadded the occupation of a straw-bonnet maker. Herself, her maternal parent, and two sisters, formed an harmonious quartett in the most secluded portion of Camden-town; and here it was that Mr. Wilkins presented himself, one Monday afternoon, in his best attire, with his face more shining and his waistcoat more bright than either had ever appeared before. The family were just going to tea, and were *so* glad to see him. It was quite a little feast; two ounces of seven-and-sixpenny green, and a quarter of a pound of the best fresh; and Mr. Wilkins had brought a pint of shrimps, neatly folded up in a clean belcher, to give a zest to the meal, and propitiate Mrs. Ivins. Jemima was "cleaning herself" up stairs; so Mr. Samuel Wilkins sat down and talked domestic economy with Mrs. Ivins, whilst the two youngest Miss Ivinses poked bits of lighted brown paper between the bars under the kettle, to make the water boil for tea.

"I wos a thinking," said Mr. Samuel Wilkins, during a pause in the conversation—"I wos a thinking of taking J'mima to the Eagle to-night."—"O my!" exclaimed Mrs. Ivins. "Lor! how nice!" said the youngest Miss Ivins. "Well, I declare!" added the youngest Miss Ivins but one. "Tell J'mima to put on her white muslin, Tilly," screamed Mrs. Ivins, with motherly anxiety; and down came J'mima herself soon afterwards in a white muslin gown carefully hooked and eyed, a little red shawl, plentifully pinned, a white straw bonnet trimmed with red ribbons, a small necklace, a large pair of bracelets, Denmark satin shoes, and open-worked stockings; white cotton gloves on her fingers, and a cambric pocket-handkerchief, carefully folded up, in her hand—all quite genteel and ladylike. And away went Miss J'mima Ivins and Mr. Samuel Wilkins, and a dress cane, with a gilt knob at the top, to the admiration and envy of the street in general, and to the high gratification of Mrs. Ivins, and the two youngest Miss Ivinses in particular. They had no sooner turned into the Pancras-road, than who should Miss J'mima Ivins stumble upon, by the most fortunate accident in the world, but a young lady as she knew, with *her* young man!—And it is so strange how things do turn out sometimes—they were actually going to the Eagle too. So Mr. Samuel Wilkins was introduced to Miss J'mima Ivins's friend's young man, and they all walked on together, talking, and laughing, and joking away like anything; and when they got as far as Pentonville, Miss Ivins's friend's young man *would* have the ladies go into the Crown, to taste some shrub, which, after a great blushing and giggling, and hiding of faces in elaborate pocket-handkerchiefs, they consented to do. Having tasted it once, they were easily prevailed upon to taste it again; and they sat out in the garden tasting shrub, and looking at the Busses alternately, till it was just the proper time to go to the Eagle; and then they resumed their journey, and walked very fast, for fear they should lose the beginning of the concert in the rotunda.

"How ev'nly!" said Miss J'mima Ivins, and Miss J'mima Ivins's friend, both at once, when they had passed the gate and were fairly inside the gardens. There were the walks, beautifully gravelled and planted—and the refreshment-boxes, painted and ornamented like so many snuff-boxes—and the variegated lamps shedding their rich light upon the company's heads—and the place for dancing ready chalked for the company's feet—and a Moorish band playing at one end of the gardens—and an opposition military band playing away at the other. Then, the waiters were rushing to and fro with glasses of negus, and glasses of brandy-and-water, and bottles of ale, and bottles of stout; and ginger-beer was going off in one place, and practical jokes were going on in another; and people were crowding to the door of the Rotunda; and in short the whole scene was, as Miss J'mima Ivins, inspired by the novelty, or the shrub, or both, observed—"one of dazzling excitement." As to the concert-room, never was anything half so splendid. There was an orchestra for the singers, all paint, gilding, and plate-glass; and such an organ! Miss J'mima Ivins's friend's young man whispered it had cost "four hundred pound," which Mr. Samuel Wilkins said was "not dear neither;" an opinion in which the ladies perfectly coincided. The audience were seated on elevated benches round the room, and crowded into every part of it; and everybody was eating and drinking as comfortably as possible. Just before the concert commenced, Mr. Samuel Wilkins ordered two glasses of rum-and-water "warm with—" and two slices of lemon, for himself and the other young man, together with "a pint o' sherry wine for the ladies, and some sweet carraway-seed biscuits;" and they would have been quite comfortable and happy, only a strange gentleman with large whiskers *would* stare at Miss J'mima Ivins, and another gentleman in a plaid waistcoat *would* wink at Miss J'mima Ivins's friend; on which Miss J'mima Ivins's friend's young man exhibited symptoms of boiling over, and began to mutter about "people's imperence," and "swells out o' luck;" and to intimate, in oblique terms, a vague intention of knocking somebody's head off; which he was only prevented from announcing more emphatically, by both Miss J'mima Ivins and her friend threatening to faint away on the spot if he said another word.

The concert commenced—overture on the organ. "How solemn!" exclaimed Miss J'mima Ivins, glancing, perhaps unconsciously, at the gentleman with the whiskers. Mr. Samuel Wilkins, who had been muttering apart for some time past, as if he were holding a confidential conversation with the gilt knob of the dress cane, breathed hard—breathing vengeance, perhaps,—but said nothing. "The soldier tired," Miss Somebody in white satin. "Ancore!" cried Miss J'mima Ivins's friend. "Ancore!" shouted the gentleman in the plaid waistcoat immediately, hammering the table with a stout-bottle. Miss J'mima Ivins's friend's young man eyed the man behind the waistcoat from head to foot, and cast a look of interrogative contempt towards Mr. Samuel Wilkins. Comic song, accompanied on the organ. Miss J'mima Ivins was convulsed with laughter—so was the man with the whiskers. Everything the ladies did, the plaid waistcoat and whiskers did, by way of expressing unity of sentiment and congeniality of soul; and Miss J'mima Ivins, and Miss J'mima Ivins's friend, grew lively and talkative, as Mr. Samuel Wilkins, and Miss J'mima Ivins's friend's young man, grew morose and surly in inverse proportion.

Now, if the matter had ended here, the little party might soon have recovered their former equanimity; but Mr. Samuel Wilkins and his friend began to throw looks of defiance upon the waistcoat and whiskers. And the waistcoat and whiskers, by way of intimating the slight degree in which they were affected by the looks aforesaid, bestowed glances of increased admiration upon Miss J'mima Ivins and friend. The concert and vaudeville concluded, they promenaded the gardens. The waistcoat and whiskers did the same; and made divers remarks complimentary to the ankles of Miss J'mima Ivins and friend, in an audible tone. At length, not satisfied with these numerous atrocities, they actually came up and asked Miss J'mima Ivins, and Miss J'mima Ivins's friend, to dance, without taking no more notice of Mr. Samuel Wilkins, and Miss J'mima Ivins's friend's young man, than if they was nobody!

"What do you mean by that, scoundrel?" exclaimed Mr. Samuel Wilkins, grasping the gilt-knobbed dress-cane firmly in his right hand. "What's the matter with *you*, you little humbug?" replied the whiskers. "How dare you insult me and my friend?" inquired the friend's young man. "You and your friend be hanged!" responded the waistcoat. "Take that," exclaimed Mr. Samuel Wilkins. The ferrule of the gilt-nobbed dress-cane was visible for an instant, and then the light of the variegated lamps shone brightly upon it as it whirled into the air, cane and all. "Give it him," said the waistcoat. "Horficer!" screamed the ladies. Miss J'mima Ivins's beau, and the friend's young man, lay gasping on the gravel, and the waistcoat and whiskers were seen no more.

Miss J'mima Ivins and friend being conscious that the affray was in no slight degree attributable to themselves, of course went into hysterics forthwith; declared themselves the most injured of women; exclaimed, in incoherent ravings, that they had been suspected—wrongfully suspected—oh! that they should ever have lived to see the day—and so forth; suffered a relapse every time they opened their eyes and saw their unfortunate little admirers; and were carried to their respective abodes in a hackney-coach, and a state of insensibility, compounded of shrub, sherry, and excitement.

CHAPTER V.

THE PARLOUR ORATOR.

WE had been lounging one evening, down Oxford-street, Holborn, Cheapside, Coleman-street, Finsbury-square, and so on, with the intention of returning westward, by Pentonville and the New-road, when we began to feel rather thirsty, and disposed to rest for five or ten minutes. So, we turned back towards an old, quiet, decent public-house, which we remembered to have passed but a moment before (it was not far from the City-road), for the purpose of solacing ourself with a glass of ale. The house was none of your stuccoed, French-polished, illuminated palaces, but a modest public-house of the old school, with a little old bar, and a little old landlord, who, with a wife and daughter of the same pattern, was comfortably seated in the bar aforesaid--a snug little room with a cheerful fire, protected by a large screen: from behind which the young lady emerged on our representing our inclination for a glass of ale.

"Won't you walk into the parlour, sir?" said the young lady, in seductive tones.

"You had better walk into the parlour, sir," said the little old landlord, throwing his chair back, and looking round one side of the screen, to survey our appearance.

"You had much better step into the parlour, sir," said the little old lady, popping out her head, on the other side of the screen.

We cast a slight glance around, as if to express our ignorance of the locality so much recommended. The little old landlord observed it; bustled out of the small door of the small bar; and forthwith ushered us into the parlour itself.

It was an ancient, dark-looking room, with oaken wainscoting, a sanded floor, and a high mantelpiece. The walls were ornamented with three or four old coloured prints in black frames, each print representing a naval engagement, with a couple of men-of-war banging away at each other most vigorously, while another vessel or two were blowing up in the distance, and the foreground presented a miscellaneous collection of broken masts and blue legs sticking up out of the water. Depending from the ceiling in the centre of the room, were a gas-light and bell-pull; on each side were three or four long narrow tables, behind which was a thickly-planted row of those slippery, shiny-looking wooden chairs, peculiar to hostelries of this description. The monotonous appearance of the sanded boards was relieved by an occasional spittoon; and a triangular pile of those useful articles adorned the two upper corners of the apartment.

At the furthest table, nearest the fire, with his face towards the door at the bottom of the room, sat a stoutish man of about forty, whose short, stiff, black hair curled closely round a broad high forehead, and a face to which something besides water and exercise had communicated a rather inflamed appearance. He was smoking a cigar, with his eyes fixed on the ceiling, and had that confident oracular air which marked him as the leading politician, general authority, and universal anecdote-relater, of the place. He had evidently just delivered himself of something very weighty; for the remainder of the company were puffing at their respective pipes and cigars in a kind of solemn abstraction, as if quite overwhelmed with the magnitude of the subject recently under discussion.

On his right hand sat an elderly gentleman with a white head, and broad-brimmed brown hat; on his left, a sharp-nosed, light-haired man in a brown surtout reaching nearly to his heels, who took a whiff at his pipe, and an admiring glance at the red-faced man, alternately.

"Very extraordinary!" said the light-haired man after a pause of five minutes. A murmur of assent ran through the company.

"Not at all extraordinary—not at all," said the red-faced man, awakening suddenly from his reverie, and turning upon the light-haired man, the moment he had spoken.

"Why should it be extraordinary?—why is it extraordinary?—prove it to be extraordinary!"

"Oh, if you come to that—" said the light-haired man, meekly.

"Come to that!" ejaculated the man with the red face; "but we *must* come to that. We stand, in these times, upon a calm elevation of intellectual attainment, and not in the dark recess of mental deprivation. Proof, is what I require—proof, and not assertions, in these stirring times. Every gen'lem'n that knows me, knows what was the nature and effect of my observations, when it was in the contemplation of the Old-street Suburban Representative Discovery Society, to recommend a candidate for that place in Cornwall there—I forget the name of it. 'Mr. Snobee,' said Mr. Wilson, 'is a fit and proper person to represent the borough in Parliament.' 'Prove it,' says I. 'He is a friend to Reform,' says Mr. Wilson. 'Prove it,' says I. 'The abolitionist of the national debt, the unflinching opponent of pensions, the uncompromising advocate of the negro, the reducer of sinecures and the duration of Parliaments; the extender of nothing but the suffrages of the people,' says Mr. Wilson. 'Prove it,' says I. 'His acts prove it,' says he. 'Prove *them*,' says I.

"And he could not prove them," said the red-faced man, looking round triumphantly; "and the borough didn't have him; and if you carried this principle to the full extent, you'd have no debt, no pensions, no sinecures, no negroes, no nothing. And then, standing upon an elevation of intellectual attainment, and having reached the summit of popular prosperity, you might bid defiance to the nations of the earth, and erect yourselves in the proud confidence of wisdom and superiority. This is my argument—this always has been my argument—and if I was a Member of the House of Commons to-morrow, I'd make 'em shake in their shoes with it." And the red-faced man, having struck the table very hard with his clenched fist, to add weight to the declaration, smoked away like a brewery.

"Well!" said the sharp-nosed man, in a very slow and soft voice, addressing the company in general, "I always do say, that of all the gentlemen I have the pleasure of meeting in this room, there is not one whose conversation I like to hear so much as Mr. Rogers's, or who is such improving company."

"Improving company!" said Mr. Rogers, for that, it seemed, was the name of the red-faced man, "You may say I am improving company, for I've improved you all to some purpose; though as to my conversation being as my friend Mr. Ellis here describes it, that is not for me to say anything about. You, gentlemen, are the best judges on that point; but this I will say, when I came into this parish, and first used this room, ten years ago, I don't believe there was one man in it, who knew he was a slave—and now you all know it, and writhe under it. Inscribe that upon my tomb, and I am satisfied."

"Why, as to inscribing it on your tomb," said a little greengrocer with a chubby face, "of course you can have anything chalked up, as you likes to pay for, so far as it relates to yourself and your affairs; but, when you come to talk about slaves, and that there abuse, you'd better keep it in the family, 'cos I for one don't like to be called them names, night after night."

"You *are* a slave," said the red-faced man, "and the most pitiable of all slaves."

"Werry hard if I am," interrupted the greengrocer, "for I got no good out of the twenty million that was paid for 'mancipation, anyhow."

"A willing slave," ejaculated the red-faced man, getting more red with eloquence, and contradiction—"resigning the dearest birthright of your children—neglecting the sacred call of Liberty—who, standing imploringly before you, appeals to the warmest feelings of your heart, and points to your helpless infants, but in vain."

"Prove it," said the greengrocer.

"Prove it!" sneered the man with the red-face. "What! bending beneath the yoke of an insolent and factious oligarchy; bowed down by the domination of cruel laws; groaning beneath tyranny and oppression on every hand, at every side, and in every corner. Prove it!—" The red-faced man abruptly broke off, sneered melo-dramatically, and buried his countenance and his indignation together, in a quart pot.

"Ah, to be sure, Mr. Rogers," said a stout broker in a large waistcoat, who had kept his eyes fixed on this luminary all the time he was speaking. "Ah, to be sure," said the broker with a sigh, "that's the point."

"Of course, of course," said divers members of the company, who understood almost as much about the matter as the broker himself.

"You had better let him alone, Tommy," said the broker, by way of advice to the little greengrocer, "he can tell what's o'clock by an eight-day, without looking at the minute hand, he can. Try it on, on some other suit; it won't do with him, Tommy."

"What is a man?" continued the red-faced specimen of the species, jerking his hat indignantly from its peg on the wall. "What is an Englishman? Is he to be trampled upon by every oppressor? Is he to be knocked down at everybody's bidding? What's freedom? Not a standing army. What's a standing army? Not freedom. What's general happiness? Not universal misery. Liberty ain't the window-tax, is it? The Lords ain't the Commons, are they?" And the red-faced man, gradually bursting into a radiating sentence, in which such adjectives as "dastardly," "oppressive," "violent," and "sanguinary," formed the most conspicuous words, knocked his hat indignantly over his eyes, left the room, and slammed the door after him.

"Wonderful man!" said he of the sharp nose.

"Splendid speaker!" added the broker.

"Great power!" said everybody but the greengrocer. And as they said it, the whole party shook their heads mysteriously, and one by one retired, leaving us alone in the old parlour.

If we had followed the established precedent in all such instances, we should have fallen into a fit of musing, without delay. The ancient appearance of the room—the old panelling of the wall—the chimney blackened with smoke and age—would have carried us back a hundred years at least, and we should have gone dreaming on, until the pewter-pot on the table, or the little beer-chiller on the fire, had started into life, and addressed to us a long story of days gone by. But, by some means or other, we were not in a romantic humour; and although we tried very hard to invest the furniture with vitality, it remained perfectly unmoved, obstinate, and sullen. Being thus reduced to the unpleasant necessity of musing about ordinary matters, our thoughts reverted to the red-faced man, and his oratorical display.

A numerous race are these red-faced men; there is not a parlour, or club-room, or benefit society, or humble party of any kind, without its red-faced man. Weak-pated dolts they are, and a great deal of mischief they do to their cause, however good. So, just to hold a pattern one up, to know the others by, we took his likeness at once, and put him in here. And that is the reason why we have written this paper.

CHAPTER VI.

THE HOSPITAL PATIENT.

In our rambles through the streets of London after evening has set in, we often pause beneath the windows of some public hospital, and picture to ourself the gloomy and mournful scenes that are passing within. The sudden moving of a taper as its feeble ray shoots from window to window, until its light gradually disappears, as if it were carried farther back into the room to the bedside of some suffering patient, is enough to awaken a whole crowd of reflections; the mere glimmering of the low-burning lamps, which, when all other habitations are wrapped in darkness and slumber, denote the chamber where so many forms are writhing with pain, or wasting with disease, is sufficient to check the most boisterous merriment.

Who can tell the anguish of those weary hours, when the only sound the sick man hears, is the disjointed wanderings of some feverish slumberer near him, the low moan of pain, or perhaps the muttered, long-forgotten prayer of a dying man? Who, but they who have felt it, can imagine the sense of loneliness and desolation which must be the portion of those who in the hour of dangerous illness are left to be tended by strangers; for what hands, be they ever so gentle, can wipe the clammy brow, or smooth the restless bed, like those of mother, wife, or child?

Impressed with these thoughts, we have turned away, through the nearly-deserted streets; and the sight of the few miserable creatures still hovering about them, has not tended to lessen the pain which such meditations awaken. The hospital is a refuge and resting-place for hundreds, who but for such institutions must die in the streets and doorways; but what can be the feelings of some outcasts when they are stretched on the bed of sickness with scarcely a hope of recovery? The wretched woman who lingers about the pavement, hours after midnight, and the miserable shadow of a man—the ghastly remnant that want and drunkenness have left—which crouches beneath a window-ledge, to sleep where there is some shelter from the rain, have little to bind them to life, but what have they to look back upon, in death? What are the unwonted comforts of a roof and a bed, to them, when the recollections of a whole life of debasement stalk before them; when repentance seems a mockery, and sorrow comes too late?

About a twelvemonth ago, as we were strolling through Covent-garden (we had been thinking about these things overnight), we were attracted by the very prepossessing appearance of a pickpocket, who having declined to take the trouble of walking to the Police-office, on the ground that he hadn't the slightest wish to go there at all, was being conveyed thither in a wheelbarrow, to the huge delight of a crowd.

Somehow, we never can resist joining a crowd, so we turned back with the mob, and entered the office, in company with our friend the pickpocket, a couple of policemen, and as many dirty-faced spectators as could squeeze their way in.

There was a powerful, ill-looking young fellow at the bar, who was undergoing an examination, on the very common charge of having, on the previous night, ill-treated a woman, with whom he lived in some court hard by. Several witnesses bore testimony to acts of the grossest brutality; and a certificate was read from the house-surgeon of a neighbouring hospital, describing the nature of the injuries the woman had received, and intimating that her recovery was extremely doubtful.

Some question appeared to have been raised about the identity of the prisoner; for when it was agreed that the two magistrates should visit the hospital at eight o'clock that evening, to take her deposition, it was settled that the man should be taken there also. He turned pale at this, and we saw him clench the bar very hard when the order was given. He was removed directly afterwards, and he spoke not a word.

We felt an irrepressible curiosity to witness this interview, although it is hard to tell why, at this instant, for we knew it must be a painful one. It was no very difficult matter for us to gain permission, and we obtained it.

The prisoner, and the officer who had him in custody, were already at the hospital when we reached it, and waiting the arrival of the magistrates in a small room below stairs. The man was handcuffed, and his hat was pulled forward over his eyes. It was easy to see, though, by the whiteness of his countenance, and the constant twitching of the muscles of his face, that he dreaded what was to come. After a short interval, the magistrates and clerk were bowed in by the house-surgeon and a couple of young men who smelt very strong of tabacco-smoke—they were introduced as "dressers"—and after one magistrate had complained bitterly of the cold, and the other of the absence of any news in the evening paper, it was announced that the patient was prepared; and we were conducted to the "casualty ward" in which she was lying.

The dim light which burnt in the spacious room, increased rather than diminished the ghastly appearance of the hapless creatures in the beds, which were ranged in two long rows on either side. In one bed, lay a child enveloped in bandages, with its body half-consumed by fire; in another, a female, rendered hideous by some dreadful accident, was wildly beating her clenched fists on the coverlet, in pain; on a third, there lay stretched a young girl, apparently in the heavy stupor often the immediate precursor of death: her face was stained with blood, and her breast and arms were bound up in folds of linen. Two or three of the beds were empty, and their recent occupants were sitting beside them, but with faces so wan, and eyes so bright and glassy, that it was fearful to meet their gaze. On every face was stamped the expression of anguish and suffering.

The object of the visit was lying at the upper end of the room. She was a fine young woman of about two or three and twenty. Her long black hair, which had been hastily cut from near the wounds on her head, streamed over the pillow in jagged and matted locks. Her face bore deep marks of the ill-usage she had received: her hand was pressed upon her side, as if her chief pain were there; her breathing was short and heavy; and it was plain to see that she was dying fast. She murmured a few words in reply to the magistrate's inquiry whether she was in great pain; and, having been raised on the pillow by the nurse, looked vacantly upon the strange countenances that surrounded her bed. The magistrate nodded to the officer, to bring the man forward. He did so, and stationed him at the bedside. The girl looked on with a wild and troubled expression of face; but her sight was dim, and she did not know him.

"Take off his hat," said the magistrate. The officer did as he was desired, and the man's features were disclosed.

The girl started up, with an energy quite preternatural; the fire gleamed in her heavy eyes, and the blood rushed to her pale and sunken cheeks. It was a convulsive effort. She fell back upon her pillow, and covering her scarred and bruised face with her hands, burst into tears. The man cast an anxious look towards her, but otherwise appeared wholly unmoved. After a brief pause the nature of the errand was explained, and the oath tendered.

"Oh, no, gentlemen," said the girl, raising herself once more, and folding her hands together; "no, gentlemen, for God's sake! I did it myself—it was nobody's fault—it was an accident. He didn't hurt me; he wouldn't for all the world. Jack, dear Jack, you know you wouldn't!"

Her sight was fast failing her, and her hand groped over the bedclothes in search of his. Brute as the man was, he was not prepared for this. He turned his face from the bed, and sobbed. The girl's colour changed, and her breathing grew more difficult. She was evidently dying.

"We respect the feelings which prompt you to this," said the gentleman who had spoken first, "but let me warn you, not to persist in what you know to be untrue, until it is too late. It cannot save him."

"Jack," murmured the girl, laying her hand upon his arm, "they shall not persuade me to swear your life away. He didn't do it, gentlemen. He never hurt me." She grasped his arm tightly, and added, in a broken whisper, "I hope God Almighty will forgive me all the wrong I have done, and the life I have led. God bless you, Jack. Some kind gentleman take my love to my poor old father. Five years ago, he said he wished I had died a child. Oh, I wish I had! I wish I had!"

The nurse bent over the girl for a few seconds, and then drew the sheet over her face. It covered a corpse.

CHAPTER VII.

THE MISPLACED ATTACHMENT OF MR. JOHN DOUNCE.

If we had to make a classification of society, there are a particular kind of men whom we should immediately set down under the head of "Old Boys;" and a column of most extensive dimensions the old boys would require. To what precise causes the rapid advance of old boy population is to be traced, we are unable to determine. It would be an interesting and curious speculation, but, as we have not sufficient space to devote to it here, we simply state the fact that the numbers of the old boys have been gradually augmenting within the last few years, and that they are at this moment alarmingly on the increase.

Upon a general review of the subject, and without considering it minutely in detail, we should be disposed to subdivide the old boys into two distinct classes—the gay old boys, and the steady old boys. The gay old boys, are paunchy old men in the disguise of young ones, who frequent the Quadrant and Regent-street in the day-time: the theatres (especially theatres under lady management) at night; and who assume all the foppishness and levity of boys, without the excuse of youth or inexperience. The steady old boys are certain stout old gentlemen of clean appearance, who are always to be seen in the same taverns, at the same hours every evening, smoking and drinking in the same company.

There was once a fine collection of old boys to be seen round the circular table at Offley's every night, between the hours of half-past eight and half-past eleven. We have lost sight of them for some time. There were, and may be still, for aught we know, two splendid specimens in full blossom at the Rainbow Tavern in Fleet-street, who always used to sit in the box nearest the fireplace, and smoked long cherry-stick pipes which went under the table, with the bowls resting on the floor. Grand old boys they were—fat, red-faced, white-headed old fellows—always there—one on one side the table, and the other opposite—puffing and drinking away in great state. Everybody knew them, and it was supposed by some people that they were both immortal.

Mr. John Dounce was an old boy of the latter class (we don't mean immortal, but steady), a retired glove and braces maker, a widower, resident with three daughters—all grown up, and all unmarried—in Cursitor-street, Chancery-lane. He was a short, round, large-faced, tubbish sort of man, with a broad-brimmed hat, and a square coat; and had that grave, but confident, kind of roll, peculiar to old boys in general. Regular as clockwork—breakfast at nine—dress and tittivate a little—down to the Sir Somebody's Head—a glass of ale and the paper—come back again, and take daughters out for a walk—dinner at three—glass of grog and pipe—nap—tea—little walk—Sir Somebody's Head again—capital house—delightful evenings. There were Mr. Harris, the law-stationer, and Mr. Jennings, the robe-maker (two jolly young fellows like himself), and Jones, the barrister's clerk—rum fellow that Jones—capital company—full of anecdote!—and there they sat every night till just ten minutes before twelve, drinking their brandy-and-water, and smoking their pipes, and telling stories, and enjoying themselves with a kind of solemn joviality particularly edifying.

Sometimes Jones would propose a half-price visit to Drury Lane or Covent Garden, to see two acts of a five-act play, and a new farce, perhaps, or a ballet, on which occasions the whole four of them went together; none of your hurrying and nonsense, but having their brandy-and-water first, comfortably, and ordering a steak and some oysters for their supper against they came back, and then walking coolly into the pit, when the "rush" had gone in, as all sensible people do, and did when Mr. Dounce was a young man, except when the celebrated Master Betty was at the height of his popularity, and then, sir,—then—Mr. Dounce perfectly well remembered getting a holiday from business; and going to the pit doors at eleven o'clock in the forenoon, and waiting there, till six in the afternoon, with some sandwiches in a pocket-handkerchief and some wine in a phial; and fainting after all, with the heat and fatigue before the play began; in which situation he was lifted out of the pit, into one of the dress boxes, sir, by five of the finest women of that day, sir, who compassionated his situation and administered restoratives, and sent a black servant, six foot high, in blue and silver livery, next morning with their compliments, and to know how he found himself, sir—by G—! Between the acts Mr. Dounce and Mr. Harris, and Mr. Jennings, used to stand up, and look round the house, and Jones—knowing fellow that Jones—knew everybody—pointed out the fashionable and celebrated Lady So-and-So in the boxes, at the mention of whose name Mr. Dounce, after brushing up his hair, and adjusting his neckerchief, would inspect the aforesaid Lady So-and-So through an immense glass, and remark, either, that she was a "fine woman—very fine woman, indeed," or that "there might be a little more of her,—eh, Jones?" just as the case might happen to be. When the dancing began, John Dounce and the other old boys were particularly anxious to see what was going forward on the stage, and Jones—wicked dog that Jones—whispered little critical remarks into the ears of John Dounce, which John Dounce retailed to Mr. Harris and Mr. Harris to Mr. Jennings; and then they all four laughed, until the tears ran down, out of their eyes.

When the curtain fell, they walked back together, two and two, to the steaks and oysters; and when they came to the second glass of brandy-and-water, Jones—hoaxing scamp, that Jones—used to recount how he had observed a lady in white feathers, in one of the pit boxes, gazing intently on Mr. Dounce all the evening, and how he had caught Mr. Dounce, whenever he thought no one was looking at him, bestowing ardent looks of intense devotion on the lady in return; on which Mr. Harris and Mr. Jennings used to laugh very heartily, and John Dounce more heartily than either of them, acknowledging, however, that the time *had* been when he *might* have done such things; upon which Mr. Jones used to poke him in the ribs, and tell him he had been a sad dog in his time, which John Dounce, with chuckles confessed. And after Mr. Harris and Mr. Jennings had preferred their claims to the character of having been sad dogs too, they separated harmoniously, and trotted home.

The decrees of Fate, and the means by which they are brought about, are mysterious and inscrutable. John Dounce had led this life for twenty years and upwards, without wish for change, or care for variety, when his whole social system was suddenly upset, and turned completely topsy-turvy—not by an earthquake, or some other dreadful convulsion of nature, as the reader would be inclined to suppose, but by the simple agency of an oyster; and thus it happened.

Mr. John Dounce was returning one night from the Sir Somebody's Head, to his residence in Cursitor-street—not tipsy, but rather excited, for it was Mr. Jennings's birthday, and they had had a brace of partridges for supper, and a brace of extra glasses afterwards, and Jones had been more than ordinarily amusing—when his eyes rested on a newly-opened oyster-shop, on a magnificent scale, with natives laid, one deep, in circular marble basins in the windows, together with little round barrels of oysters directed to Lords and Baronets, and Colonels and Captains, in every part of the habitable globe.

Behind the natives were the barrels, and behind the barrels was a young lady of about five-and-twenty, all in blue, and all alone—splendid creature, charming face and lovely figure! It is difficult to say whether Mr. John Dounce's red countenance, illuminated as it was by the flickering gas-light in the window before which he paused, excited the lady's risibility, or whether a natural exuberance of animal spirits proved too much for that staidness of demeanour which the forms of society rather dictatorially prescribe. But certain it is, that the lady smiled; then put her finger upon her lip, with a striking recollection of what was due to herself, and finally retired, in oyster-like bashfulness, to the very back of the counter. The sad-dog sort of feeling came strongly upon John Dounce: he lingered—the lady in blue made no sign. He coughed—still she came not. He entered the shop.

"Can you open me an oyster, my dear?" said Mr. John Dounce.

"Dare say I can, sir," replied the lady in blue, with playfulness. And Mr. John Dounce eat one oyster, and then looked at the young lady, and then eat another, and then squeezed the young lady's hand as she was opening the third, and so forth, until he had devoured a dozen of those at eightpence in less than no time.

"Can you open me half-a-dozen more, my dear?" inquired Mr. John Dounce.

"I'll see what I can do for you, sir," replied the young lady in blue, even more bewitchingly than before; and Mr. John Dounce eat half-a-dozen more of those at eightpence.

"You couldn't manage to get me a glass of brandy-and-water, my dear, I suppose?" said Mr. John Dounce, when he had finished the oysters: in a tone which clearly implied his supposition that she could.

"I'll see, sir," said the young lady: and away she ran out of the shop, and down the street, her long auburn ringlets shaking in the wind in the most enchanting manner; and back she came again, tripping over the coal-cellar lids like a whipping-top, with a tumbler of brandy-and-water, which Mr. John Dounce insisted on her taking a share of, as it was regular ladies' grog—hot, strong, sweet, and plenty of it.

So, the young lady sat down with Mr. John Dounce, in a little red box with a green curtain, and took a small sip of the brandy-and-water, and a small look at Mr. John Dounce, and then turned her head away, and went through various other serio-pantomimic fascinations, which forcibly reminded Mr. John Dounce of the first time he courted his first wife, and which made him feel more affectionate than ever; in pursuance of which affection, and actuated by which feeling, Mr. John Dounce sounded the young lady on her matrimonial engagements, when the young lady denied having formed any such engagements at all—she couldn't abear the men, they were such deceivers; thereupon Mr. John Dounce inquired whether this sweeping condemnation was meant to include other than very young men; on which the young lady blushed deeply—at least she turned away her head, and said Mr. John Dounce had made her blush, so of course she *did* blush—and Mr. John Dounce was a long time drinking the brandy-and-water; and, at last, John Dounce went home to bed, and dreamed of his first wife, and his second wife, and the young lady, and partridges, and oysters, and brandy-and-water, and disinterested attachments.

The next morning, John Dounce was rather feverish with the extra brandy-and-water of the previous night; and, partly in the hope of cooling himself with an oyster, and partly with the view of ascertaining whether he owed the young lady anything, or not, went back to the oyster-shop. If the young lady had appeared beautiful by night, she was perfectly irresistible by day; and, from this time forward, a change came over the spirit of John Dounce's dream. He bought shirt-pins; wore a ring on his third finger; read poetry; bribed a cheap miniature-painter to perpetrate a faint resemblance to a youthful face, with a curtain over his head, six large books in the background, and an open country in the distance (this he called his portrait); "went on" altogether in such an uproarious manner, that the three Miss Dounces went off on small pensions, he having made the tenement in Cursitor-street too warm to contain them; and in short, comported and demeaned himself in every respect like an unmitigated old Saracen, as he was.

As to his ancient friends, the other old boys, at the Sir Somebody's Head, he dropped off from them by gradual degrees; for, even when he did go there, Jones—vulgar fellow that Jones—persisted in asking "when it was to be?" and "whether he was to have any gloves?" together with other inquiries of an equally offensive nature: at which not only Harris laughed, but Jennings also; so, he cut the two, altogether, and attached himself solely to the blue young lady at the smart oyster-shop.

Now comes the moral of the story—for it has a moral after all. The last mentioned young lady, having derived sufficient profit and emolument from John Dounce's attachment, not only refused, when matters came to a crisis, to take him for better for worse, but expressly declared, to use her own forcible words, that she "wouldn't have him at no price;" and John Dounce, having lost his old friends, alienated his relations, and rendered himself ridiculous to everybody, made offers successively to a schoolmistress, a landlady, a feminine tobacconist, and a housekeeper; and, being directly rejected by each and every of them, was accepted by his cook, with whom he now lives, a henpecked husband, a melancholy monument of antiquated misery, and a living warning to all uxorious old boys.

CHAPTER VIII.

THE MISTAKEN MILLINER. A TALE OF AMBITION.

Miss Amelia Martin was pale, tallish, thin, and two-and-thirty—what ill-natured people would call plain, and police reports interesting. She was a milliner and dressmaker, living on her business and not above it. If you had been a young lady in service, and had wanted Miss Martin, as a great many young ladies in service did, you would just have stepped up, in the evening, to number forty-seven, Drummond-street, George-street, Euston-square, and after casting your eye on a brass door-plate, one foot ten by one and a half, ornamented with a great brass knob at each of the four corners, and bearing the inscription "Miss Martin; millinery and dressmaking, in all its branches;" you'd just have knocked two loud knocks at the street-door; and down would have come Miss Martin herself, in a merino gown of the newest fashion, black velvet bracelets on the genteelest principle, and other little elegancies of the most approved description.

If Miss Martin knew the young lady who called, or if the young lady who called had been recommended by any other young lady whom Miss Martin knew, Miss Martin would forthwith show her up-stairs into the two-pair front, and chat she would—*so* kind, and *so* comfortable—it really wasn't like a matter of business, she was so friendly; and, then Miss Martin, after contemplating the figure and general appearance of the young lady in service with great apparent admiration, would say how well she would look, to be sure, in a low dress with short sleeves: made very full in the skirts, with four tucks in the bottom; to which the young lady in service would reply in terms expressive of her entire concurrence in the notion, and of the virtuous indignation with which she reflected on the tyranny of "Missis," who wouldn't allow a young girl to wear a short sleeve of an arternoon—no, nor nothing smart, not even a pair of ear-rings; let alone hiding people's heads of hair under them frightful caps. At the termination of this complaint, Miss

Amelia Martin would distantly suggest certain dark suspicions that some people were jealous on account of their own daughters, and were obliged to keep their servants' charms under, for fear they should get married first, which was no uncommon circumstance—leastways she had known two or three young ladies in service, who had married a great deal better than their missises, and *they* were not very good-looking either; and then the young lady would inform Miss Martin, in confidence, that how one of their young ladies was engaged to a young man and was a-going to be married, and Missis was so proud about it there was no bearing of her; but how she needn't hold her head quite so high neither, for, after all, he was only a clerk. And, after expressing due contempt for clerks in general, and the engaged clerk in particular, and the highest opinion possible of themselves and each other, Miss Martin and the young lady in service would bid each other good night, in a friendly but perfectly genteel manner: and the one went back to her "place," and the other, to her room on the second-floor front.

There is no saying how long Miss Amelia Martin might have continued this course of life; how extensive a connection she might have established among young ladies in service; or what amount her demands upon their quarterly receipts might have ultimately attained, had not an unforeseen train of circumstances directed her thoughts to a sphere of action very different from dressmaking or millinery.

A friend of Miss Martin's who had long been keeping company with an ornamental painter and decorator's journeyman, at last consented (on being at last asked to do so) to name the day which would make the aforesaid journeyman a happy husband. It was a Monday that was appointed for the celebration of the nuptials, and Miss Amelia Martin was invited, among others, to honour the wedding-dinner with her presence. It was a charming party; Somers'-town the locality, and a front parlour the apartment. The ornamental painter and decorator's journeyman had taken a house—no lodgings nor vulgarity of that kind, but a house—four beautiful rooms, and a delightful little washhouse at the end of the passage—which was the most convenient thing in the world, for the bridesmaids could sit in the front parlour and receive the company, and then run into the little washhouse and see how the pudding and boiled pork were getting on in the copper, and then pop back into the parlour again, as snug and comfortable as possible. And such a parlour as it was! Beautiful Kidderminster carpet—six bran-new cane-bottomed stained chairs—three wine-glasses and a tumbler on each sideboard—farmer's girl and farmer's boy on the mantelpiece: girl tumbling over a stile, and boy spitting himself, on the handle of a pitchfork—long white dimity curtains in the window—and, in short, everything on the most genteel scale imaginable.

Then, the dinner. There was baked leg of mutton at the top, boiled leg of mutton at the bottom, pair of fowls and leg of pork in the middle; porter-pots at the corners; pepper, mustard, and vinegar in the centre; vegetables on the floor; and plum-pudding and apple-pie and tartlets without number: to say nothing of cheese, and celery, and water-cresses, and all that sort of thing. As to the company! Miss Amelia Martin herself declared, on a subsequent occasion, that, much as she had heard of the ornamental painter's journeyman's connexion, she never could have supposed it was half so genteel. There was his father, such a funny old gentleman—and his mother, such a dear old lady—and his sister, such a charming girl—and his brother, such a manly-looking young man—with such a eye! But even all these were as nothing when compared with his musical friends, Mr. and Mrs. Jennings Rodolph, from White Conduit, with whom the ornamental painter's journeyman had been fortunate enough to contract an intimacy while engaged in decorating the concert-room of that noble institution. To hear them sing separately, was divine, but when they went through the tragic duet of "Red

Ruffian, retire!" it was, as Miss Martin afterwards remarked, "thrilling." And why (as Mr. Jennings Rodolph observed) why were they not engaged at one of the patent theatres? If he was to be told that their voices were not powerful enough to fill the House, his only reply was, that he would back himself for any amount to fill Russell-square—a statement in which the company, after hearing the duet, expressed their full belief; so they all said it was shameful treatment; and both Mr. and Mrs. Jennings Rodolph said it was shameful too; and Mr. Jennings Rodolph looked very serious, and said he knew who his malignant opponents were, but they had better take care how far they went, for if they irritated him too much he had not quite made up his mind whether he wouldn't bring the subject before Parliament; and they all agreed that it "'ud serve 'em quite right, and it was very proper that such people should be made an example of." So Mr. Jennings Rodolph said he'd think of it.

When the conversation resumed its former tone, Mr. Jennings Rodolph claimed his right to call upon a lady, and the right being conceded, trusted Miss Martin would favour the company—a proposal which met with unanimous approbation, whereupon Miss Martin, after sundry hesitatings and coughings, with a preparatory choke or two, and an introductory declaration that she was frightened to death to attempt it before such great judges of the art, commenced a species of treble chirruping containing frequent allusions to some young gentleman of the name of Hen-e-ry, with an occasional reference to madness and broken hearts. Mr. Jennings Rodolph, frequently interrupted the progress of the song, by ejaculating "Beautiful!"—"Charming!"—"Brilliant!"—"Oh! splendid," &c.; and at its close the admiration of himself, and his lady, knew no bounds.

"Did you ever hear so sweet a voice, my dear?" inquired Mr. Jennings Rodolph of Mrs. Jennings Rodolph.

"Never; indeed I never did, love;" replied Mrs. Jennings Rodolph.

"Don't you think Miss Martin, with a little cultivation, would be very like Signora Marra Boni, my dear?" asked Mr. Jennings Rodolph.

"Just exactly the very thing that struck me, my love," answered Mrs. Jennings Rodolph.

And thus the time passed away; Mr. Jennings Rodolph played tunes on a walking-stick, and then went behind the parlour-door and gave his celebrated imitations of actors, edge-tools, and animals; Miss Martin sang several other songs with increased admiration every time; and even the funny old gentleman began singing. His song had properly seven verses, but as he couldn't recollect more than the first one he sang that over, seven times, apparently very much to his own personal gratification. And then all the company sang the national anthem with national independence—each for himself, without reference to the other—and finally separated: all declaring that they never had spent so pleasant an evening: and Miss Martin inwardly resolving to adopt the advice of Mr. Jennings Rodolph, and to "come out" without delay.

Now, "coming out," either in acting, or singing, or society, or facetiousness, or anything else, is all very well, and remarkably pleasant to the individual principally concerned, if he or she can but manage to come out with a burst, and being out, to keep out, and not go in again; but, it does unfortunately happen that both consummations are extremely difficult to accomplish, and that the difficulties, of getting out at all in the first instance, and if you surmount them, of keeping out in the second, are pretty much on a par, and no slight ones either—and so Miss Amelia Martin shortly discovered. It is a singular fact (there being ladies in the case) that Miss Amelia Martin's principal foible was vanity, and the leading characteristic of Mrs. Jennings Rodolph an attachment to dress. Dismal wailings were heard to issue from the second-floor front, of number forty-seven, Drummond-street, George-street, Euston-square; it was Miss Martin practising. Half-suppressed murmurs disturbed the calm dignity of the White Conduit orchestra at the commencement of the season. It was the appearance of Mrs. Jennings Rodolph in full dress, that occasioned them. Miss Martin studied incessantly—the practising was the consequence. Mrs. Jennings Rodolph taught gratuitously now and then—the dresses were the result.

Weeks passed away; the White Conduit season had begun, and progressed, and was more than half over. The dressmaking business had fallen off, from neglect; and its profits had dwindled away almost imperceptibly. A benefit-night approached; Mr. Jennings Rodolph yielded to the earnest solicitations of Miss Amelia Martin, and introduced her personally to the "comic gentleman" whose benefit it was. The comic gentleman was all smiles and blandness—he had composed a duet, expressly for the occasion, and Miss Martin should sing it with him. The night arrived; there was an immense room—ninety-seven sixpenn'orths of gin-and-water, thirty-two small glasses of brandy-and-water, five-and-twenty bottled ales, and forty-one neguses; and the ornamental painter's journeyman, with his wife and a select circle of acquaintance, were seated at one of the side-tables near the orchestra. The concert began. Song—sentimental—by a light-haired young gentleman in a blue coat, and bright basket buttons—[applause]. Another song, doubtful, by another gentleman in another blue coat and more bright basket buttons—[increased applause]. Duet, Mr. Jennings Rodolph, and Mrs. Jennings Rodolph, "Red Ruffian, retire!"—[great applause]. Solo, Miss Julia Montague (positively on this occasion only)—"I am a Friar"—[enthusiasm]. Original duet, comic—Mr. H. Taplin (the comic gentleman) and Miss Martin—"The Time of Day." "Brayvo!—Brayvo!" cried the ornamental painter's journeyman's party, as Miss Martin was gracefully led in by the comic gentleman. "Go to work, Harry," cried the comic gentleman's personal friends. "Tap—tap—tap," went the leader's bow on the music-desk. The symphony began, and was soon afterwards followed by a faint kind of ventriloquial chirping, proceeding apparently from the deepest recesses of the interior of Miss Amelia Martin. "Sing out"—shouted one gentleman in a white great-coat. "Don't be afraid to put the steam on, old gal," exclaimed another, "S—s—s—s—s—s—s"—went the five-and-twenty bottled ales. "Shame, shame!" remonstrated the ornamental painter's journeyman's party—"S—s—s—s" went the bottled ales again, accompanied by all the gins, and a majority of the brandies.

"Turn them geese out," cried the ornamental painter's journeyman's party, with great indignation.

"Sing out," whispered Mr. Jennings Rodolph.

"So I do," responded Miss Amelia Martin.

"Sing louder," said Mrs. Jennings Rodolph.

"I can't," replied Miss Amelia Martin.

"Off, off, off," cried the rest of the audience.

"Bray-vo!" shouted the painter's party. It wouldn't do—Miss Amelia Martin left the orchestra, with much less ceremony than she had entered it; and, as she couldn't sing out, never came out. The general good humour was not restored until Mr. Jennings Rodolph had become purple in the face, by imitating divers quadrupeds for half an hour, without being able to render himself audible; and, to this day, neither has Miss Amelia Martin's good humour been restored, nor the dresses made for and presented to Mrs. Jennings Rodolph, nor the vocal abilities which Mr. Jennings Rodolph once staked his professional reputation that Miss Martin possessed.

CHAPTER IX.

THE DANCING ACADEMY.

OF all the dancing academies that ever were established, there never was one more popular in its immediate vicinity than Signor Billsmethi's, of the "King's Theatre." It was not in Spring-gardens, or Newman-street, or Berners-street, or Gower-street, or Charlotte-street, or Percy-street, or any other of the numerous streets which have been devoted time out of mind to professional people, dispensaries, and boarding-houses; it was not in the West-end at all—it rather approximated to the eastern portion of London, being situated in the populous and improving neighbourhood of Gray's-inn-lane. It was not a dear dancing academy—four-and-sixpence a quarter is decidedly cheap upon the whole. It was *very* select, the number of pupils being strictly limited to seventy-five, and a quarter's payment in advance being rigidly exacted. There was public tuition and private tuition—an assembly-room and a parlour. Signor Billsmethi's family were always thrown in with the parlour, and included in parlour price; that is to say, a private pupil had Signor Billsmethi's parlour to dance *in*, and Signor Billsmethi's family to dance *with;* and when he had been sufficiently broken in in the parlour, he began to run in couples in the Assembly-room.

Such was the dancing academy of Signor Billsmethi, when Mr. Augustus Cooper, of Fetter-lane, first saw an unstamped advertisement walking leisurely down Holborn-hill, announcing to the world that Signor Billsmethi, of the King's Theatre, intended opening for the season with a Grand Ball.

Now, Mr. Augustus Cooper was in the oil and colour line—just of age, with a little money, a little business, and a little mother, who, having managed her husband and *his* business in his lifetime, took to managing her son and *his* business after his decease; and so, somehow or other, he had been cooped up in the little back parlour behind the shop on week-days, and in a little deal box without a lid (called by courtesy a pew) at Bethel Chapel, on Sundays, and had seen no more of the world than if he had been an infant all his days; whereas Young White, at the gas-fitter's over the way, three years younger than him, had been flaring away like winkin' —going to the theatre—supping at harmonic meetings—eating oysters by the barrel—drinking stout by the gallon—even stopping out all night, and coming home as cool in the morning as if nothing had happened. So Mr. Augustus Cooper made up his mind that he would not stand it any longer, and had that very morning expressed to his mother a firm determination to be "blowed," in the event of his not being instantly provided with a street-door key. And he was walking down Holborn-hill, thinking about all these things, and wondering how he could manage to get introduced into genteel society for the first time, when his eyes rested on Signor Billsmethi's announcement, which it immediately struck him was just the very thing he wanted; for he should not only be able to select a genteel circle of acquaintance at once, out of the five-and-seventy pupils at four-and-sixpence a quarter, but should qualify himself at the same time to go through a hornpipe in private society, with perfect ease to himself and great delight to his friends. So, he stopped the unstamped advertisement—an animated sandwich, composed of a boy between two boards—and having procured a very small card with the Signor's address indented thereon, walked straight at once to the Signor's house—and very fast he walked too, for fear the list should be filled up, and the five-and-seventy completed, before he got there. The Signor was at home, and, what was still more gratifying, he was an Englishman! Such a nice man—and so polite! The list was not full, but it was a most extraordinary circumstance that there was only just one vacancy, and even that one would have been filled up, that very morning, only Signor Billsmethi was dissatisfied with the reference, and, being very much afraid that the lady wasn't select, wouldn't take her.

"And very much delighted I am, Mr. Cooper," said Signor Billsmethi, "that I did *not* take her. I assure you, Mr. Cooper—I don't say it to flatter you, for I know you're above it—that I consider myself extremely fortunate in having a gentleman of your manners and appearance, sir."

"I am very glad of it too, sir," said Augustus Cooper.

"And I hope we shall be better acquainted, sir," said Signor Billsmethi.

"And I'm sure I hope we shall too, sir," responded Augustus Cooper. Just then, the door opened, and in came a young lady, with her hair curled in a crop all over her head, and her shoes tied in sandals all over her ankles.

"Don't run away, my dear," said Signor Billsmethi; for the young lady didn't know Mr. Cooper was there when she ran in, and was going to run out again in her modesty, all in confusion-like. "Don't run away, my dear," said Signor Billsmethi, "this is Mr. Cooper—Mr. Cooper, of Fetter-lane. Mr. Cooper, my daughter, sir—Miss Billsmethi, sir, who I hope will have the pleasure of dancing many a quadrille, minuet, gavotte, country-dance, fandango, double-hornpipe, and farinagholkajingo with you, sir. She dances them all, sir; and so shall you, sir, before you're a quarter older, sir."

And Signor Billsmethi slapped Mr. Augustus Cooper on the back, as if he had known him a dozen years,—so friendly;—and Mr. Cooper bowed to the young lady, and the young lady curtseyed to him, and Signor Billsmethi said they were as handsome a pair as ever he'd wish to see; upon which the young lady exclaimed, "Lor, pa!" and blushed as red as Mr. Cooper himself—you might have thought they were both standing under a red lamp at a chemist's shop; and before Mr. Cooper went away it was settled that he should join the family circle that very night—taking them just as they were—no ceremony nor nonsense of that kind—and learn his positions in order that he might lose no time, and be able to come out at the forthcoming ball.

Well; Mr. Augustus Cooper went away to one of the cheap shoemakers' shops in Holborn, where gentlemen's dress-pumps are seven and sixpence, and men's strong walking just nothing at all, and bought a pair of the regular seven-and-sixpenny, long-quartered, town mades, in which he astonished himself quite as much as his mother, and sallied forth to Signor Billsmethi's. There were four other private pupils in the parlour: two ladies and two gentlemen. Such nice people! Not a bit of pride about them. One of the ladies in particular, who was in training for a Columbine, was remarkably affable; and she and Miss Billsmethi took such an interest in Mr. Augustus Cooper, and joked, and smiled, and looked so bewitching, that he got quite at home, and learnt his steps in no time. After the practising was over, Signor Billsmethi, and Miss Billsmethi, and Master Billsmethi, and a young lady, and the two ladies, and the two gentlemen, danced a quadrille—none of your slipping and sliding about, but regular warm work, flying into corners, and diving among chairs, and shooting out at the door,—something like dancing! Signor Billsmethi in particular, notwithstanding his having a little fiddle to play all the time, was out on the landing every figure, and Master Billsmethi, when everybody else was breathless, danced a hornpipe, with a cane in his hand, and a cheese-plate on his head, to the unqualified admiration of the whole company. Then, Signor Billsmethi insisted as they were so happy, that they should all stay to supper, and proposed sending Master Billsmethi for the beer and spirits, whereupon the two gentlemen swore, "strike 'em wulgar if they'd stand that;" and were just going to quarrel whr should pay for it, when Mr. Augustus Cooper said he would, if they'd have the kindness to allow him—and they *had* the kindness to allow him; and Master Billsmethi brought the beer in a can, and the rum in a quart-pot. They had a regular night of it; and Miss Billsmethi squeezed Mr. Augustus Cooper's hand under the table; and Mr. Augustus Cooper returned the squeeze, and returned home too, at something to six o'clock in the morning, when he was put to bed by main force by the apprentice, after repeatedly expressing an uncontrollable desire to pitch his revered parent out of the second-floor window, and to throttle the apprentice with his own neck-handkerchief.

Weeks had worn on, and the seven-and-sixpenny town-mades had nearly worn out, when the night arrived for the grand dress-ball at which the whole of the five-and-seventy pupils were to meet together, for the first time that season, and to take out some portion of their respective four-and-sixpences in lamp-oil and fiddlers. Mr. Augustus Cooper had ordered a new coat for the occasion—a two-pound-tenner from Turnstile. It was his first appearance in public; and, after a grand Sicilian shawl-dance by fourteen young ladies in character, he was to open the quadrille department with Miss Billsmethi herself, with whom he had become quite intimate since his first introduction. It *was* a night! Everything was admirably arranged. The sandwich-boy took the hats and bonnets at the street-door; there was a turn-up bedstead in the back parlour, on which Miss Billsmethi made tea and coffee for such of the gentlemen as chose to pay for it, and such of the ladies as the gentlemen treated; red port-wine negus and lemonade were handed round at eighteen-pence a head; and in pursuance of a previous engagement with the public-house at the corner of the street, an extra potboy was laid on for the occasion. In short, nothing could exceed the arrangements, except the company. Such ladies! Such pink silk stockings! Such artificial flowers! Such a number of cabs! No sooner had one cab set down a couple of ladies, than another cab drove up and set down another couple of ladies, and they all knew: not only one another, but the majority of the gentlemen into the bargain, which made it all as pleasant and lively as could be. Signor Billsmethi, in black tights, with a large blue bow in his buttonhole, introduced the ladies to such of the gentlemen as were strangers: and the ladies talked away—and laughed they did—it was delightful to see them.

As to the shawl-dance, it was the most exciting thing that ever was beheld; there was such a whisking, and rustling, and fanning, and getting ladies into a tangle with artificial flowers, and then disentangling them again! And as to Mr. Augustus Cooper's share in the quadrille, he got through it admirably. He was missing from his partner, now and then, certainly, and discovered on such occasions to be either dancing with laudable perseverance in another set, or sliding about in perspective, without any definite object; but, generally speaking, they managed to shove him through the figure, until he turned up in the right place. Be this as it may, when he had finished, a great many ladies and gentlemen came up and complimented him very much, and said they had never seen a beginner do anything like it before; and Mr. Augustus Cooper was perfectly satisfied with himself, and everybody else into the bargain; and "stood" considerable quantities of spirits-and-water, negus, and compounds, for the use and behoof of two or three dozen very particular friends, selected from the select circle of five-and-seventy pupils.

Now, whether it was the strength of the compounds, or the beauty of the ladies, or what not, it did so happen that Mr. Augustus Cooper encouraged, rather than repelled, the very flattering attentions of a young lady in brown gauze over white calico who had appeared particularly struck with him from the first; and when the encouragements had been prolonged for some time, Miss Billsmethi betrayed her spite and jealousy thereat by calling the young lady in brown gauze a "creeter," which induced the young lady in brown gauze to retort, in certain sentences containing a taunt founded on the payment of four-and-sixpence a quarter, which reference Mr. Augustus Cooper, being then and there in a state of considerable bewilderment, expressed his entire concurrence in. Miss Billsmethi, thus renounced, forthwith began screaming in the loudest key of her voice, at the rate of fourteen screams a minute; and being unsuccessful, in an onslaught on the eyes and face, first of the lady in gauze and then of Mr. Augustus Cooper, called distractedly on the other three-and-seventy pupils to furnish her with oxalic acid for her own private drinking; and, the call not being honoured, made another rush at Mr. Cooper, and then had her stay-lace cut, and was carried off to bed. Mr. Augustus Cooper, not being remarkable for quickness of apprehension, was at a loss to understand what all this meant, until Signor Billsmethi explained it in a most satisfactory manner, by stating to the pupils, that Mr. Augustus Cooper had made and confirmed divers promises of marriage to his daughter on divers occasions, and had now basely deserted her; on which, the indignation of the pupils became universal; and as several chivalrous gentlemen inquired rather pressingly of Mr. Augustus Cooper, whether he required anything for his own use, or, in other words, whether he "wanted anything for himself," he deemed it prudent to make a precipitate retreat. And the upshot of the matter was, that a lawyer's letter came next day, and an action was commenced next week; and that Mr. Augustus Cooper, after walking twice to the Serpentine for the purpose of drowning himself, and coming twice back without doing it, made a confidante of his mother, who compromised the matter with twenty pounds from the till: which made twenty pounds four shillings and sixpence paid to Signor Billsmethi, exclusive of treats and pumps. And Mr. Augustus Cooper went back and lived with his mother, and there he lives to this day; and as he has lost his ambition for society, and never goes into the world, he will never see this account of himself, and will never be any the wiser.

CHAPTER X.

SHABBY-GENTEEL PEOPLE.

THERE are certain descriptions of people who, oddly enough, appear to appertain exclusively to the metropolis. You meet them, every day, in the streets of London, but no one ever encounters them elsewhere; they seem indigenous to the soil, and to belong as exclusively to London as its own smoke, or the dingy bricks and mortar. We could illustrate the remark by a variety of examples, but, in our present sketch, we will only advert to one class as a specimen—that class which is so aptly and expressively designated as "shabby-genteel."

Now, shabby people, God knows, may be found anywhere, and genteel people are not articles of greater scarcity out of London than in it; but this compound of the two—this shabby-gentility—is as purely local as the statue at Charing-cross, or the pump at Aldgate. It is worthy of remark, too, that only men are shabby-genteel; a woman is always either dirty and slovenly in the extreme, or neat and respectable, however poverty-stricken in appearance. A very poor man, "who has seen better days," as the phrase goes, is a strange compound of dirty-slovenliness and wretched attempts at faded smartness.

We will endeavour to explain our conception of the term which forms the title of this paper. If you meet a man, lounging up Drury-lane, or leaning with his back against a post in Long-acre, with his hands in the pockets of a pair of drab trousers plentifully besprinkled with grease-spots: the trousers made very full over the boots, and ornamented with two cords down the outside of each leg—wearing, also, what has been a brown coat with bright buttons, and a hat very much pinched up at the sides, cocked over his right eye—don't pity him. He is not shabby-genteel. The "harmonic meetings" at some fourth-rate public-house, or the purlieus of a private theatre, are his chosen haunts; he entertains a rooted antipathy to any kind of work, and is on familiar terms with several pantomime men at the large houses. But, if you see hurrying along a by-street, keeping as close as he can to the area-railings, a man of about forty or fifty, clad in an old rusty suit of threadbare black cloth which shines with constant wear as if it had been bees-waxed—the trousers tightly strapped down, partly for the look of the thing and partly to keep his old shoes from slipping off at the heels,—if you observe, too, that his yellowish-white neckerchief is carefully pinned up, to conceal the tattered garment underneath, and that his hands are encased in the remains of an old pair of beaver gloves, you may set him down as a shabby-genteel man. A glance at that depressed face, and timorous air of conscious poverty, will make your heart ache—always supposing that you are neither a philosopher nor a political economist.

We were once haunted by a shabby-genteel man; he was bodily present to our senses all day, and he was in our mind's eye all night. The man of whom Sir Walter Scott speaks in his Demonology, did not suffer half the persecution from his imaginary gentleman-usher in black velvet, that we sustained from our friend in quondam black cloth. He first attracted our notice, by sitting opposite to us in the reading-room at the British Museum; and what made the man more remarkable was, that he always had before him a couple of shabby-genteel books—two old dogs-eared folios, in mouldy worm-eaten covers, which had once been smart. He was in his chair, every morning, just as the clock struck ten; he was always the last to leave the room in the afternoon; and when he did, he quitted it with the air of a man who knew not where else to go, for warmth and quiet. There he used to sit all day, as close to the table as possible, in order to conceal the lack of buttons on his coat: with his old hat carefully deposited at his feet, where he evidently flattered himself it escaped observation.

About two o'clock, you would see him munching a French roll or a penny loaf; not taking it boldly out of his pocket at once, like a man who knew he was only making a lunch; but breaking off little bits in his pocket, and eating them by stealth. He knew too well it was his dinner.

When we first saw this poor object, we thought it quite impossible that his attire could ever become worse. We even went so far, as to speculate on the possibility of his shortly appearing in a decent second-hand suit. We knew nothing about the matter; he grew more and more shabby-genteel every day. The buttons dropped off his waistcoat, one by one; then, he buttoned his coat; and when one side of the coat was reduced to the same condition as the waistcoat, he buttoned it over on the other side. He looked somewhat better at the begining of the week than at the conclusion, because the neckerchief, though yellow, was not quite so dingy; and, in the midst of all this wretchedness, he never appeared without gloves and straps. He remained in this state for a week or two. At length, one of the buttons on the back of the coat fell off, and then the man himself disappeared, and we thought he was dead.

We were sitting at the same table about a week after his disappearance, and as our eyes rested on his vacant chair, we insensibly fell into a train of meditation on the subject of his retirement from public life. We were wondering whether he had hung himself, or thrown himself off a bridge—whether he really was dead or had only been arrested—when our conjectures were suddenly set at rest by the entry of the man himself. He had undergone some strange metamorphosis, and walked up the centre of the room with an air which showed he was fully conscious of the improvement in his appearance. It was very odd. His clothes were a fine, deep, glossy black; and yet they looked like the same suit; nay, there were the very darns with which old acquaintance had made us familiar. The hat, too—nobody could mistake the shape of that hat, with its high crown gradually increasing in circumference towards the top. Long service had imparted to it a reddish-brown tint; but, now, it was as black as the coat. The truth flashed suddenly upon us—they had been "revived." It is a deceitful liquid that black and blue reviver; we have watched its effects on many a shabby-genteel man. It betrays its victims into a temporary assumption of importance: possibly into the purchase of a new pair of gloves, or a cheap stock, or some other trifling article of dress. It elevates their spirits for a week, only to depress them, if possible, below their original level. It was so in this case; the transient dignity of the unhappy man decreased, in exact proportion as the "reviver" wore off. The knees of the unmentionables, and the elbows of the coat, and the seams generally, soon began to get alarmingly white. The hat was once more deposited under the table, and its owner crept into his seat as quietly as ever.

There was a week of incessant small rain and mist. At its expiration the "reviver" had entirely vanished, and the shabby-genteel man never afterwards attempted to effect any improvement in his outward appearance.

It would be difficult to name any particular part of town as the principal resort of shabby-genteel men. We have met a great many persons of this description in the neighbourhood of the inns of court. They may be met with, in Holborn, between eight and ten any morning; and whoever has the curiosity to enter the Insolvent Debtors' Court will observe, both among spectators and practitioners, a great variety of them. We never went on 'Change, by any chance, without seeing some shabby-genteel men, and we have often wondered what earthly business they can have there. They will sit there, for hours, leaning on great, dropsical, mildewed umbrellas, or eating Abernethy biscuits. Nobody speaks to them, nor they to any one. On consideration, we remember to have occasionally seen two shabby-genteel men conversing together on 'Change, but our experience assures us that this is an uncommon circumstance, occasioned by the offer of a pinch of snuff, or some such civility.

It would be a task of equal difficulty, either to assign any particular spot for the residence of these beings, or to endeavour to enumerate their general occupations. We were never engaged in business with more than one shabby-genteel man; and he was a drunken engraver, and lived in a damp back-parlour in a new row of houses at Camden-town, half street, half brick-field, somewhere near the canal. A shabby-genteel man may have no occupation, or he may be a corn agent, or a coal agent, or a wine merchant, or a collector of debts, or a broker's assistant, or a broken-down attorney. He may be a clerk of the lowest description, or a contributor to the press of the same grade. Whether our readers have noticed these men, in their walks, as often as we have, we know not; this we know—that the miserably poor man (no matter whether he owes his distresses to his own conduct, or that of others) who feels his poverty and vainly strives to conceal it, is one of the most pitiable objects in human nature. Such objects, with few exceptions, are shabby-genteel people.

CHAPTER XI.

MAKING A NIGHT OF IT.

DAMON and Pythias were undoubtedly very good fellows in their way: the former for his extreme readiness to put in special bail for a friend: and the latter for a certain trump-like punctuality in turning up just in the very nick of time, scarcely less remarkable. Many points in their character have, however, grown obsolete. Damons are rather hard to find, in these days of imprisonment for debt (except the sham ones, and they cost half-a-crown); and, as to the Pythiases, the few that have existed in these degenerate times, have had an unfortunate knack of making themselves scarce, at the very moment when their appearance would have been strictly classical. If the actions of these heroes, however, can find no parallel in modern times, their friendship can. We have Damon and Pythias on the one hand. We have Potter and Smithers on the other; and, lest the two last-mentioned names should never have reached the ears of our unenlightened readers, we can do no better than make them acquainted with the owners thereof.

Mr. Thomas Potter, then, was a clerk in the city, and Mr. Robert Smithers was a ditto in the same; their incomes were limited, but their friendship was unbounded. They lived in the same street, walked into town every morning at the same hour, dined at the same slap-bang every day, and revelled in each other's company every night. They were knit together by the closest ties of intimacy and friendship, or, as Mr. Thomas Potter touchingly observed, they were "thick-and-thin pals, and nothing but it." There was a spice of romance in Mr. Smithers's disposition, a ray of poetry, a gleam of misery, a sort of consciousness of he didn't exactly know what, coming across him he didn't precisely know why—which stood out in fine relief against the off-hand, dashing, amateur-pickpocket-sort-of-manner, which distinguished Mr. Potter in an eminent degree.

The peculiarity of their respective dispositions, extended itself to their individual costume. Mr. Smithers generally appeared in public in a surtout and shoes, with a narrow black neckerchief and a brown hat, very much turned up at the sides—peculiarities which Mr. Potter wholly eschewed, for it was his ambition to do something in the celebrated "kiddy" or stage-coach way, and he had even gone so far as to invest capital in the purchase of a rough blue coat with wooden buttons, made upon the fireman's principle, in which, with the addition of a low-crowned, flower-pot-saucer-shaped hat, he had created no inconsiderable sensation at the Albion in Little Russell-street, and divers other places of public and fashionable resort.

Mr. Potter and Mr. Smithers had mutually agreed that, on the receipt of their quarter's salary, they would jointly and in company "spend the evening"—an evident misnomer—the spending applying, as everybody knows, not to the evening itself but to all the money the individual may chance to be possessed of, on the occasion to which reference is made; and they had likewise agreed that, on the evening aforesaid, they would "make a night of it"—an expressive term, implying the borrowing of several hours from to-morrow morning, adding them to the night before, and manufacturing a compound night of the whole.

The quarter-day arrived at last—we say at last, because quarter-days are as eccentric as comets: moving wonderfully quick when you have a good deal to pay, and marvellously slow when you have a little to receive. Mr. Thomas Potter and Mr. Robert Smithers met by appointment to begin the evening with a dinner;

and a nice, snug, comfortable dinner they had, consisting of a little procession of four chops and four kidneys, following each other, supported on either side by a pot of the real draught stout, and attended by divers cushions of bread, ard wedges of cheese.

When the cloth was removed, Mr. Thomas Potter ordered the waiter to bring in, two goes of his best Scotch whiskey, with warm water and sugar, and a couple of his "very mildest" Havannahs, which the waiter did. Mr. Thomas Potter mixed his grog, and lighted his cigar; Mr. Robert Smithers did the same; and then, Mr. Thomas Potter jocularly proposed as the first toast, "the abolition of all offices whatever" (not sinecures, but counting-houses), which was immediately drunk by Mr. Robert Smithers, with enthusiastic applause. So they went on, talking politics, puffing cigars, and sipping whiskey-and-water, until the "goes" —most appropriately so called—were both gone, which Mr. Robert Smithers perceiving, immediately ordered in two more goes of the best Scotch whiskey, and two more of the very mildest Havannahs; and the goes kept coming in, and the mild Havannahs kept going out, until, what with the drinking, and lighting, and puffing, and the stale ashes on the table, and the tallow-grease on the cigars, Mr. Robert Smithers began to doubt the mildness of the Havannahs, and to feel very much as if he had been sitting in a hackney-coach with his back to the horses.

As to Mr. Thomas Potter, he *would* keep laughing out loud, and volunteering inarticulate declarations that he was "all right;" in proof of which, he feebly bespoke the evening paper after the next gentleman, but finding it a matter of some difficulty to discover any news in its columns, or to ascertain distinctly whether it had any columns at all, walked slowly out to look for the moon, and, after coming back quite pale with looking up at the sky so long, and attempting to express mirth at Mr. Robert Smithers having fallen asleep, by various galvanic chuckles, laid his head on his arm, and went to sleep also. When he awoke again, Mr. Robert Smithers awoke too, and they both very gravely agreed that it was extremely unwise to eat so many pickled walnuts with the chops, as it was a notorious fact that they always made people queer and sleepy; indeed, if it had not been for the whiskey and cigars, there was no knowing what harm they mightn't have done 'em. So they took some coffee, and after paying the bill,—twelve and twopence the dinner, and the odd tenpence for the waiter—thirteen shillings in all—started out on their expedition to manufacture a night.

It was just half-past eight, so they thought they couldn't do better than go at half-price to the slips at the City Theatre, which they did accordingly. Mr. Robert Smithers, who had become extremely poetical after the settlement of the bill, enlivening the walk by informing Mr. Thomas Potter in confidence that he felt an inward presentiment of approaching dissolution, and subsequently embellishing the theatre, by falling asleep, with his head and both arms gracefully drooping over the front of the boxes.

Such was the quiet demeanour of the unassuming Smithers, and such were the happy effects of Scotch whiskey and Havannahs on that interesting person! But Mr. Thomas Potter, whose great aim it was to be considered as a "knowing card," a "fast goer," and so forth, conducted himself in a very different manner, and commenced going very fast indeed—rather too fast at last, for the patience of the audience to keep pace with him. On his first entry, he contented himself by earnestly calling upon the gentlemen in the gallery to "flare up," accompanying the demand with another request, expressive of his wish that they would instantaneously "form a union," both which requisitions were responded to, in the manner most in vogue on such occasions.

"Give that dog a bone!" cried one gentleman in his shirt-sleeves.

"Where have you been a having half a pint of intermediate beer?" cried a second. "Tailor!" screamed a third. "Barber's clerk!" shouted a fourth. "Throw him O—VER!" roared a fifth; while numerous voices concurred in desiring Mr. Thomas Potter to "go home to his mother!" All these taunts Mr. Thomas Potter received with supreme contempt, cocking the low-crowned hat a little more on one side, whenever any reference was made to his personal appearance, and, standing up with his arms a-kimbo, expressing defiance melodramatically.

The overture—to which these various sounds had been an *ad libitum* accompaniment—concluded, the second piece began, and Mr. Thomas Potter, emboldened by impunity, proceeded to behave in a most unprecedented and outrageous manner. First of all, he imitated the shake of the principal female singer; then, groaned at the blue fire, then, affected to be frightened into convulsions of terror at the appearance of the ghost; and, lastly, not only made a running commentary, in an audible voice, upon the dialogue on the stage, but actually awoke Mr. Robert Smithers, who, hearing his companion making a noise, and having a very indistinct notion where he was, or what was required of him, immediately, by way of imitating a good example, set up the most unearthly, unremitting, and appalling howling that ever audience heard. It was too much. "Turn them out!" was the general cry. A noise, as of shuffling of feet, and men being knocked up with violence against wainscoting, was heard: a hurried dialogue of "Come out?"—"I won't!"—"You shall!"—"I shan't!"—"Give me your card, Sir?"—"You're a scoundrel, Sir!" and so forth, succeeded. A round of applause betokened the approbation of the audience, and Mr. Robert Smithers and Mr. Thomas Potter found themselves shot with astonishing swiftness into the road, without having had the trouble of once putting foot to ground during the whole progress of their rapid descent.

Mr. Robert Smithers, being constitutionally one of the slow-goers, and having had quite enough of fast-going, in the course of his recent expulsion, to last until the quarter-day then next ensuing at the very least, had no sooner emerged with his companion from the precincts of Milton-street, than he proceeded to indulge in circuitous references to the beauties of sleep, mingled with distant allusions to the propriety of returning to Islington, and testing the influence of their patent Bramahs over the street-door locks to which they respectively belonged. Mr. Thomas Potter, however, was valorous and peremptory. They had come out to make a night of it: and a night must be made. So Mr. Robert Smithers, who was three parts dull, and the other dismal, despairingly assented; and they went into a wine-vaults, to get materials for assisting them in making a night; where they found a good many young ladies, and various old gentlemen, and a plentiful sprinkling of hackney-coachmen and cab-drivers, all drinking and talking together; and Mr. Thomas Potter and Mr. Robert Smithers drank small glasses of brandy, and large glasses of soda, until they began to have a very confused idea, either of things in general, or of anything in particular; and, when they had done treating themselves they began to treat everybody else; and the rest of the entertainment was a confused mixture of heads and heels, black eyes and blue uniforms, mud and gas-lights, thick doors, and stone paving.

Then, as standard novelists expressively inform us—"all was a blank!" and in the morning the blank was filled up with the words "STATION-HOUSE," and the station-house was filled up with Mr. Thomas Potter, Mr. Robert Smithers, and the major part of their wine-vault companions of the preceding night, with a comparatively small portion of clothing of any kind. And it was disclosed at the Police-office, to the indignation of the Bench, and the astonishment of the spectators, how one Robert Smithers, aided and abetted by one Thomas Potter, had knocked down and beaten, in divers streets, at different times, five men, four boys, and three women; how the said Thomas Potter had feloniously obtained possession of five door-knockers, two bell-handles, and a bonnet; how Robert Smithers, his friend, had sworn, at least forty pounds' worth of oaths, at the rate of five shillings a piece; terrified whole streets full of Her Majesty's subjects with awful shrieks and alarms of fire; destroyed the uniforms of five policemen; and committed various other atrocities, too numerous to recapitulate. And the magistrate, after an appropriate reprimand, fined Mr. Thomas Potter and Mr. Robert Smithers five shillings each, for being, what the law vulgarly terms, drunk; and thirty-four pounds for seventeen assaults at forty shillings a-head, with liberty to speak to the prosecutors.

The prosecutors *were* spoken to, and Messrs. Potter and Smithers lived on credit, for a quarter, as best they might; and, although the prosecutors expressed their readiness to be assaulted twice a week, on the same terms, they have never since been detected in "making a night of it."

CHAPTER XII.

THE PRISONERS' VAN.

We were passing the corner of Bow-street, on our return from a lounging excursion the other afternoon, when a crowd, assembled round the door of the Police Office, attracted our attention. We turned up the street accordingly. There were thirty or forty people, standing on the pavement and half across the road; and a few stragglers were patiently stationed on the opposite side of the way—all evidently waiting in expectation of some arrival. We waited too, a few minutes, but nothing occurred; so, we turned round to an unshorn, sallow-looking cobbler, who was standing next us with his hands under the bib of his apron, and put the usual question of "What's the matter?" The cobbler eyed us from head to foot, with superlative contempt, and laconically replied "Nuffin."

Now, we were perfectly aware that if two men stop in the street to look at any given object, or even to gaze in the air, two hundred men will be assembled in no time; but, as we knew very well that no crowd of people could by possibility remain in a street for five minutes without getting up a little amusement among themselves, unless they had some absorbing object in view, the natural inquiry next in order was, "What are all these people waiting here for?"—"Her Majesty's carriage," replied the cobbler. This was still more extraordinary. We could not imagine what earthly business Her Majesty's carriage could have at the Public Office, Bow-street. We were beginning to ruminate on the possible causes of such an uncommon appearance, when a general exclamation from all the boys in the crowd of "Here's the wan!" caused us to raise our heads, and look up the street.

The covered vehicle, in which prisoners are conveyed from the police offices to the different prisons, was coming along at full speed. It then occurred to us, for the first time, that Her Majesty's carriage was merely another name for the prisoners' van, conferred upon it, not only by reason of the superior gentility of the term, but because the aforesaid van is maintained at Her Majesty's expense: having been originally started for the exclusive accommodation of ladies and gentlemen under the necessity of visiting the various houses of call known by the general denomination of "Her Majesty's Gaols."

The van drew up at the office door, and the people thronged round the steps, just leaving a little alley for the prisoners to pass through. Our friend the cobbler, and the other stragglers, crossed over, and we followed their example. The driver, and another man who had been seated by his side in front of the vehicle, dismounted, and were admitted into the office. The office-door was closed after them, and the crowd were on the tiptoe of expectation.

After a few minutes' delay, the door again opened, and the two first prisoners appeared. They were a couple of girls, of whom the elder could not be more than sixteen, and the younger of whom had certainly not attained her fourteenth year. That they were sisters, was evident, from the resemblance which still subsisted between them, though two additional years of depravity had fixed their brand upon the elder girl's features, as legibly as if a red-hot iron had seared them. They were both gaudily dressed, the younger one especially; and, although there was a strong similarity between them in both respects, which was rendered the more obvious by their being handcuffed together, it is impossible to conceive a greater contrast than the demeanour of the two presented. The younger girl was weeping bitterly—not for display, or in the hope of producing effect, but for very shame; her face was buried in her handkerchief; and her whole manner was but too expressive of bitter and unavailing sorrow.

"How long are you for, Emily?" screamed a red-faced woman in the crowd. "Six weeks and labour," replied the elder girl with a flaunting laugh; "and that's better than the stone jug anyhow; the mill's a deal better than the Sessions, and here's Bella a-going too for the first time. Hold up your head, you chicken," she continued, boisterously tearing the other girl's handkerchief away; "Hold up your head, and show 'em your face. I an't jealous, but I'm blessed if I an't game!"—"That's right, old gal," exclaimed a man in a paper cap, who, in common with the greater part of the crowd, had been inexpressibly delighted with this little incident.—"Right!" replied the girl; "ah, to be sure; what's the odds, eh?"—"Come! In with you," interrupted the driver. "Don't you be in a hurry, coachman," replied the girl, "and recollect I want to be set down in Cold Bath Fields—large house with a high garden-wall in front; you can't mistake it. Hallo. Bella, where are you going to—you'll pull my precious arm off?" This was addressed to the younger girl, who, in her anxiety to hide herself in the caravan, had ascended the steps first, and forgotten the strain upon the handcuff. "Come down, and let's show you the way." And after jerking the miserable girl down with a force which made her stagger on the pavement, she got into the vehicle, and was followed by her wretched companion.

These two girls had been thrown upon London streets, their vices and debauchery, by a sordid and rapacious mother. What the younger girl was, then, the elder had been once; and what the elder then was, the younger must soon become. A melancholy prospect, but how surely to be realised; a tragic drama, but how often acted! Turn to the prisons and police offices of London—nay, look into the very streets themselves. These things pass before our eyes, day after day, and hour after hour—they have become such matters of course, that they are utterly disregarded. The progress of these girls in crime will be as rapid as the flight of a pestilence, resembling it too in its baneful influence and wide-spreading infection. Step by step, how many wretched females, within the sphere of every man's observation, have become involved in a career of vice, frightful to contemplate; hopeless at its commencement, loathsome and repulsive in its course; friendless, forlorn, and unpitied, at its miserable conclusion!

There were other prisoners—boys of ten, as hardened in vice as men of fifty—

a houseless vagrant, going joyfully to prison as a place of food and shelter, handcuffed to a man whose prospects were ruined, character lost, and family rendered destitute, by his first offence. Our curiosity, however, was satisfied. The first group had left an impression on our mind we would gladly have avoided, and would willingly have effaced.

The crowd dispersed; the vehicle rolled away with its load of guilt and misfortune; and we saw no more of the Prisoners' Van.

TALES.

CHAPTER I.

THE BOARDING-HOUSE. CHAPTER I.

Mrs. Tibbs was, beyond all dispute, the most tidy, fidgety, thrifty little personage that ever inhaled the smoke of London; and the house of Mrs. Tibbs was, decidedly, the neatest in all Great Coram-street. The area and the area-steps, and the street-door and the street-door steps, and the brass handle, and the door-plate, and the knocker, and the fan-light, were all as clean and bright, as indefatigable white-washing, and hearth-stoning, and scrubbing and rubbing, could make them. The wonder was, that the brass door-plate, with the interesting inscription "Mrs. Tibbs," had never caught fire from constant friction, so perseveringly was it polished. There were meat-safe-looking blinds in the parlour-windows, blue and gold curtains in the drawing-room, and spring-roller blinds, as Mrs. Tibbs was wont in the pride of her heart to boast, "all the way up." The bell-lamp in the passage looked as clear as a soap-bubble; you could see yourself in all the tables, and French-polish yourself on any one of the chairs. The bannisters were bees-waxed; and the very stair-wires made your eyes wink, they were so glittering.

Mrs. Tibbs was somewhat short of stature, and Mr. Tibbs was by no means a large man. He had, moreover, very short legs, but, by way of indemnification, his face was peculiarly long. He was to his wife what the o is in 90—he was of some importance *with* her—he was nothing without her. Mrs. Tibbs was always talking. Mr. Tibbs rarely spoke; but, if it were at any time possible to put in a word, when he should have said nothing at all, he had that talent. Mrs. Tibbs detested long stories, and Mr. Tibbs had one, the conclusion of which had never been heard by his most intimate friends. It always began, "I recollect when I was in the volunteer corps, in eighteen hundred and six,"—but, as he spoke very slowly and softly, and his better half very quickly and loudly, he rarely got beyond the introductory sentence. He was a melancholy specimen of the story-teller. He was the wandering Jew of Joe Millerism.

Mr. Tibbs enjoyed a small independence from the pension-list—about 43*l.* 15*s.* 10*d.* a-year. His father, mother, and five interesting scions from the same stock, drew a like sum from the revenue of a grateful country, though for what particular service was never known. But, as this said independence was not quite sufficient to furnish two people with *all* the luxuries of this life, it had occurred to the busy little spouse of Tibbs, that the best thing she could do with a legacy of 700*l.*, would be to take and furnish a tolerable house—somewhere in that partially-explored tract of country which lies between the British Museum, and a remote village called Somers'-town—for the reception of boarders. Great Coram-street was the spot pitched upon. The house had been furnished accordingly; two female servants and a boy engaged; and an advertisement inserted in the morning papers, informing the public that "Six individuals would meet with all the comforts of a cheerful musical home in a select private family, residing within ten minutes' walk of"—everywhere. Answers out of number were received, with all sorts of initials; all the letters of the alphabet seemed to be seized with a sudden wish to go out boarding and lodging; voluminous was the correspondence between Mrs. Tibbs and the applicants; and most profound was the secresy observed. "E." didn't like this; "I." couldn't think of putting up with that; "I. O. U." didn't think the terms would suit him; and "G. R." had never slept in a French bed. The result, however, was, that three gentlemen became inmates of Mrs. Tibbs's house, on terms which were "agreeable to all parties." In went the advertisement again, and a lady with her two daughters, proposed to increase—not their families, but Mrs. Tibbs's.

"Charming woman, that Mrs. Maplesone!" said Mrs. Tibbs, as she and her spouse were sitting by the fire after breakfast; the gentlemen having gone out on their several avocations. "Charming woman, indeed!" repeated little Mrs. Tibbs, more by way of soliloquy than anything else, for she never thought of consulting her husband. "And the two daughters are delightful. We must have some fish to-day; they'll join us at dinner for the first time."

Mr. Tibbs placed the poker at right angles with the fire shovel, and essayed to speak, but recollected he had nothing to say.

"The young ladies," continued Mrs. T., "have kindly volunteered to bring their own piano."

Tibbs thought of the volunteer story, but did not venture it. A bright thought struck him—

"It's very likely—" said he.

"Pray don't lean your head against the paper," interrupted Mrs. Tibbs; "and don't put your feet on the steel fender; that's worse."

Tibbs took his head from the paper, and his feet from the fender, and proceeded. "It's very likely one of the young ladies may set her cap at young Mr. Simpson, and you know a marriage——"

"A what!" shrieked Mrs. Tibbs. Tibbs modestly repeated his former suggestion.

"I beg you won't mention such a thing," said Mrs. T. "A marriage, indeed!—to rob me of my boarders—no, not for the world."

Tibbs thought in his own mind that the event was by no means unlikely, but, as he never argued with his wife, he put a stop to the dialogue, by observing it was "time to go to business." He always went out at ten o'clock in the morning, and returned at five in the afternoon, with an exceedingly dirty face, and smelling mouldy. Nobody knew what he was, or where he went; but Mrs. Tibbs used to say with an air of great importance, that he was engaged in the City.

The Miss Maplesones and their accomplished parent arrived in the course of the afternoon in a hackney-coach, and accompanied by a most astonishing number of packages. Trunks, bonnet-boxes, muff-boxes and parasols, guitar-cases, and parcels of all imaginable shapes, done up in brown paper, and fastened with pins, filled the passage. Then, there was such a running up and down with the luggage, such scampering for warm water for the ladies to wash in, and such a bustle, and confusion, and heating of servants, and curling-irons, as had never been known in Great Coram-street before. Little Mrs. Tibbs was quite in her element, bustling about, talking incessantly, and distributing towels and soap, like a head nurse in a hospital. The house was not restored to its usual state of quiet repose, until the ladies were safely shut up in their respective bedrooms, engaged in the important occupation of dressing for dinner.

"Are these gals 'andsome?" inquired Mr. Simpson of Mr. Septimus Hicks, another of the boarders, as they were amusing themselves in the drawing-room, before dinner, by lolling on sofas, and contemplating their pumps.

"Don't know," replied Mr. Septimus Hicks, who was a tallish, white-faced young man, with spectacles, and a black ribbon round his neck instead of a neckerchief—a most interesting person; a poetical walker of the hospitals, and a "very talented young man." He was fond of "lugging" into conversation all sorts of quotations from Don Juan, without fettering himself by the propriety of their application; in which particular he was remarkably independent. The other, Mr. Simpson, was one of those young men, who are in society what walking gentlemen are on the stage, only infinitely worse skilled in his vocation than the most indifferent artist. He was as empty-headed as the great bell of St. Paul's; always dressed according to the caricatures published in the monthly fashions; and spelt Character with a K.

"I saw a devilish number of parcels in the passage when I came home," simpered Mr. Simpson.

"Materials for the toilet, no doubt," rejoined the Don Juan reader.

> ——— "Much linen, lace, and several pair
> Of stockings, slippers, brushes, combs, complete;
> With other articles of ladies' fair,
> To keep them beautiful, or leave them neat."

"Is that from Milton?" inquired Mr. Simpson.

"No—from Byron," returned Mr. Hicks, with a look of contempt. He was quite sure of his author, because he had never read any other. "Hush! Here come the gals," and they both commenced talking in a very loud key.

"Mrs. Maplesone and the Miss Maplesones, Mr. Hicks. Mr. Hicks—Mrs. Maplesone and the Miss Maplesones," said Mrs. Tibbs, with a very red face, for she had been superintending the cooking operations below stairs, and looked like a wax doll on a sunny day. "Mr. Simpson, I beg your pardon—Mr. Simpson—Mrs. Maplesone and the Miss Maplesones"—and *vice versâ*. The gentlemen immediately began to slide about with much politeness, and to look as if they wished their arms had been legs, so little did they know what to do with them. The ladies smiled, curtseyed, and glided into chairs, and dived for dropped pocket-handkerchiefs: the gentlemen leant against two of the curtain-pegs; Mrs. Tibbs went through an admirable bit of serious pantomime with a servant who had come up to ask some question about the fish-sauce; and then the two young ladies looked at each other; and everybody else appeared to discover something very attractive in the pattern of the fender.

"Julia my love," said Mrs. Maplesone to her youngest daughter, in a tone loud enough for the remainder of the company to hear—"Julia."

"Yes, Ma."

"Don't stoop."—This was said for the purpose of directing general attention to Miss Julia's figure, which was undeniable. Everybody looked at her, accordingly, and there was another pause.

"We had the most uncivil hackney-coachman to-day, you can imagine," said Mrs. Maplesone to Mrs. Tibbs, in a confidential tone.

"Dear me!" replied the hostess, with an air of great commiseration. She couldn't say more, for the servant again appeared at the door, and commenced telegraphing most earnestly to her "Missis."

"I think hackney-coachmen generally *are* uncivil," said Mr. Hicks in his most insinuating tone.

"Positively I think they are," replied Mrs. Maplesone, as if the idea had never struck her before.

"And cabmen, too," said Mr. Simpson. This remark was a failure, for no one intimated, by word or sign, the slightest knowledge of the manners and customs of cabmen.

"Robinson, what *do* you want?" said Mrs. Tibbs to the servant, who, by way of making her presence known to her mistress, had been giving sundry hems and sniffs outside the door during the preceding five minutes.

"Please, ma'am, master wants his clean things," replied the servant, taken off her guard. The two young men turned their faces to the window, and "went off" like a couple of bottles of ginger-beer; the ladies put their handkerchiefs to their mouths; and little Mrs. Tibbs bustled out of the room to give Tibbs his clean linen,—and the servant warning.

Mr. Calton, the remaining boarder, shortly afterwards made his appearance, and proved a surprising promoter of the conversation. Mr. Calton was a superannuated beau—an old boy. He used to say of himself that although his features were not regularly handsome, they were striking. They certainly were. It was impossible to look at his face without being reminded of a chubby street-door knocker, half-lion half-monkey; and the comparison might be extended to his whole character and conversation. He had stood still, while everything else had been moving. He never originated a conversation, or started an idea; but if any commonplace topic were broached, or, to pursue the comparison, if anybody *lifted him up*, he would hammer away with surprising rapidity. He had the tic-doloreux occasionally, and then he might be said to be muffled, because he did not make quite as much noise as at other times, when he would go on prosing, rat-tat-tat the same thing over and over again. He had never been married; but he was still on the look-out for a wife with money. He had a life interest worth about 300*l.* a year—he was exceedingly vain, and inordinately selfish. He had acquired the reputation of being the very pink of politeness, and he walked round the park, and up Regent-street, every day.

This respectable personage had made up his mind to render himself exceedingly agreeable to Mrs. Maplesone—indeed, the desire of being as amiable as possible extended itself to the whole party; Mrs. Tibbs having considered it an admirable little bit of management to represent to the gentlemen that she had *some* reason to believe the ladies were fortunes, and to hint to the ladies, that all the gentlemen were "eligible." A little flirtation, she thought, might keep her house full, without leading to any other result.

Mrs. Maplesone was an enterprising widow of about fifty: shrewd, scheming, and good-looking. She was amiably anxious on behalf of her daughters; in proof whereof she used to remark, that she would have no objection to marry again, if it would benefit her dear girls—she could have no other motive. The "dear girls" themselves were not at all insensible to the merits of "a good establishment." One of them was twenty-five; the other, three years younger. They had been at different watering-places, for four seasons; they had gambled at libraries, read books in balconies, sold at fancy fairs, danced at assemblies, talked sentiment—in short, they had done all that industrious girls could do—but, as yet, to no purpose.

"What a magnificent dresser Mr. Simpson is!" whispered Matilda Maplesone to her sister Julia.

"Splendid!" returned the youngest. The magnificent individual alluded to wore a maroon-coloured dress-coat, with a velvet collar and cuffs of the same tint—very like that which usually invests the form of the distinguished unknown who condescends to play the "swell" in the pantomime at "Richardson's Show."

"What whiskers!" said Miss Julia.

"Charming!" responded her sister; "and what hair!" His hair was like a wig, and distinguished by that insinuating wave which graces the shining locks of those *chef-d'œuvres* of art surmounting the waxen images in Bartellot's window in Regent-street; his whiskers meeting beneath his chin, seemed strings wherewith to tie it on, ere science had rendered them unnecessary by her patent invisible springs.

"Dinner 's on the table, ma'am, if you please," said the boy, who now appeared for the first time, in a revived black coat of his master's.

"Oh! Mr. Calton, will you lead Mrs. Maplesone?—Thank you." Mr. Simpson offered his arm to Miss Julia; Mr. Septimus Hicks escorted the lovely Matilda; and the procession proceeded to the dining-room. Mr. Tibbs was introduced, and Mr. Tibbs bobbed up and down to the three ladies like a figure in a Dutch clock, with a powerful spring in the middle of his body, and then dived rapidly into his seat at the bottom of the table, delighted to screen himself behind a soup-tureen, which he could just see over, and that was all. The boarders were seated, a lady and gentleman alternately, like the layers of bread and meat in a plate of sandwiches; and then Mrs. Tibbs directed James to take off the covers. Salmon, lobster-sauce, giblet-soup, and the usual accompaniments were *dis*-covered: potatoes like petrifactions, and bits of toasted bread, the shape and size of blank dice.

"Soup for Mrs. Maplesone, my dear," said the bustling Mrs. Tibbs. She always called her husband "my dear" before company. Tibbs, who had been eating his bread, and calculating how long it would be before he should get any fish, helped the soup in a hurry, made a small island on the tablecloth, and put his glass upon it, to hide it from his wife.

"Miss Julia, shall I assist you to some fish?"

"If you please—very little—oh! plenty, thank you" (a bit about the size of a walnut put upon the plate).

"Julia is a *very* little eater," said Mrs. Maplesone to Mr. Calton.

The knocker gave a single rap. He was busy eating the fish with his eyes: so he only ejaculated, "Ah!"

"My dear," said Mrs. Tibbs to her spouse after every one else had been helped, "What do *you* take?" The inquiry was accompanied with a look intimating that he mustn't say fish, because there was not much left. Tibbs thought the frown referred to the island on the tablecloth; he therefore coolly replied, "Why—I'll take a little—fish, I think."

"Did you say fish, my dear?" (another frown).

"Yes, dear," replied the villain, with an expression of acute hunger depicted in his countenance. The tears almost started to Mrs. Tibbs's eyes, as she helped her "wretch of a husband," as she inwardly called him, to the last eatable bit of salmon on the dish.

"James, take this to your master, and take away your master's knife." This was deliberate revenge, as Tibbs never could eat fish without one. He was, however, constrained to chase small particles of salmon round and round his plate with a piece of bread and a fork, the number of successful attempts being about one in seventeen.

"Take away, James," said Mrs Tibbs, as Tibbs swallowed the fourth mouthful—and away went the plates like lightning.

"I'll take a bit of bread, James," said the poor "master of the house," more hungry than ever.

"Never mind your master now, James," said Mrs. Tibbs, "see about the meat." This was conveyed in the tone in which ladies usually give admonitions to servants in company, that is to say, a low one; but which, like a stage whisper, from its peculiar emphasis, is most distinctly heard by everybody present.

A pause ensued, before the table was replenished—a sort of parenthesis in which Mr. Simpson, Mr. Calton, and Mr. Hicks, produced respectively a bottle of sauterne, bucellas, and sherry, and took wine with everybody—except Tibbs. No one ever thought of him.

Between the fish and an intimated sirloin, there was a prolonged interval.

Here was an opportunity for Mr. Hicks. He could not resist the singularly appropriate quotation—

"But beef is rare within these oxless isles;
Goats' flesh there is, no doubt, and kid, and mutton,
And when a holiday upon them smiles,
A joint upon their barbarous spits they put on."

"Very ungentlemanly behaviour," thought little Mrs. Tibbs, "to talk in that way."

"Ah," said Mr. Calton, filling his glass. "Tom Moore is my poet."

"And mine," said Mrs. Maplesone.

"And mine," said Miss Julia.

"And mine," added Mr. Simpson.

"Look at his compositions," resumed the knocker.

"To be sure," said Simpson, with confidence,

"Look at Don Juan," replied Mr. Septimus Hicks.

"Julia's letter," suggested Miss Matilda.

"Can anything be grander than the Fire Worshippers?" inquired Miss Julia.

"To be sure," said Simpson.

"Or Paradise and the Peri," said the old beau.

"Yes; or Paradise and the Peer," repeated Simpson, who thought he was getting through it capitally.

"It's all very well," replied Mr. Septimus Hicks, who, as we have before hinted, never had read anything but Don Juan. "Where will you find anything finer than the description of the siege, at the commencement of the seventh canto?"

"Talking of a siege," said Tibbs, with a mouthful of bread—"when I was in the volunteer corps, in eighteen hundred and six, our commanding officer was Sir Charles Rampart; and one day, when we were exercising on the ground on which the London University now stands, he says, says he, Tibbs (calling me from the ranks) Tibbs—"

"Tell your master, James," interrupted Mrs. Tibbs, in an awfully distinct tone, "tell your master if he *won't* carve those fowls, to send them to me." The discomfited volunteer instantly set to work, and carved the fowls almost as expeditiously as his wife operated on the haunch of mutton. Whether he ever finished the story is not known; but, if he did, nobody heard it.

As the ice was now broken, and the new inmates more at home, every member of the company felt more at ease. Tibbs himself most certainly did, because he went to sleep immediately after dinner. Mr. Hicks and the ladies discoursed most eloquently about poetry, and the theatres, and Lord Chesterfield's Letters; and Mr. Calton followed up what everybody said, with continuous double knocks. Mrs. Tibbs highly approved of every observation that fell from Mrs. Maplesone; and as Mr. Simpson sat with a smile upon his face and said "Yes," or "Certainly," at intervals of about four minutes each, he received full credit for understanding what was going forward. The gentlemen rejoined the ladies in the drawing-room very shortly after they had left the dining-parlour. Mrs. Maplesone and Mr. Calton played cribbage, and the "young people" amused themselves with music and conversation. The Miss Maplesones sang the most fascinating duets, and accompanied themselves on guitars, ornamented with bits of ethereal blue ribbon. Mr. Simpson put on a pink waistcoat, and said he was in raptures; and Mr. Hicks felt in the seventh heaven of poetry or the seventh canto of Don

Juan—it was the same thing to him. Mrs. Tibbs was quite charmed with the new comers; and Mr. Tibbs spent the evening in his usual way—he went to sleep, and woke up, and went to sleep again, and woke at supper-time.

* * * * * * *

We are not about to adopt the license of novel-writers, and to let "years roll on;" but we will take the liberty of requesting the reader to suppose that six months have elapsed, since the dinner we have described, and that Mrs. Tibbs's boarders have, during that period, sang, and danced, and gone to theatres and exhibitions, together, as ladies and gentlemen, wherever they board, often do. And we will beg them, the period we have mentioned having elapsed, to imagine farther, that Mr. Septimus Hicks received, in his own bedroom (a front attic), at an early hour one morning, a note from Mr. Calton, requesting the favour of seeing him, as soon as convenient to himself, in his (Calton's) dressing-room on the second floor back.

"Tell Mr. Calton I'll come down directly," said Mr. Septimus to the boy. "Stop—is Mr. Calton unwell?" inquired this excited walker of hospitals, as he put on a bed-furniture-looking dressing-gown.

"Not as I knows on, sir," replied the boy. "Please, sir, he looked rather rum, as it might be."

"Ah, that's no proof of his being ill," returned Hicks, unconsciously. "Very well: I'll be down directly." Down stairs ran the boy with the message, and down went the excited Hicks himself, almost as soon as the message was delivered. "Tap, tap." "Come in."—Door opens, and discovers Mr. Calton sitting in an easy chair. Mutual shakes of the hand exchanged, and Mr. Septimus Hicks motioned to a seat. A short pause. Mr. Hicks coughed, and Mr. Calton took a pinch of snuff. It was one of those interviews where neither party knows what to say. Mr. Septimus Hicks broke silence.

"I received a note—" he said, very tremulously, in a voice like a Punch with a cold.

"Yes," returned the other, "you did."

"Exactly."

"Yes."

Now, although this dialogue must have been satisfactory, both gentlemen felt there was something more important to be said; therefore they did as most men in such a situation would have done—they looked at the table with a determined aspect. The conversation had been opened, however, and Mr. Calton had made up his mind to continue it with a regular double knock. He always spoke very pompously.

"Hicks," said he, "I have sent for you, in consequence of certain arrangements which are pending in this house, connected with a marriage."

"With a marriage!" gasped Hicks, compared with whose expression of countenance, Hamlet's, when he sees his father's ghost, is pleasing and composed.

"With a marriage," returned the knocker. "I have sent for you to prove the great confidence I can repose in you."

"And will you betray me?" eagerly inquired Hicks, who in his alarm had even forgotten to quote.

"*I* betray *you!* Won't *you* betray *me?*"

"Never: no one shall know, to my dying day, that you had a hand in the business," responded the agitated Hicks, with an inflamed countenance, and his hair standing on end as if he were on the stool of an electrifying machine in full operation.

"People must know that, some time or other—within a year, I imagine," said Mr. Calton, with an air of great self-complacency. "We *may* have a family."

"*We!*—That won't affect you, surely?"

"The devil it won't!"

"No! how can it?" said the bewildered Hicks. Calton was too much inwrapped in the contemplation of his happiness to see the equivoque between Hicks and himself; and threw himself back in his chair. "Oh, Matilda!" sighed the antique beau, in a lack-a-daisical voice, and applying his right hand a little to the left of the fourth button of his waistcoat, counting from the bottom. "Oh, Matilda!"

"What Matilda?" inquired Hicks, starting up.

"Matilda Maplesone," responded the other, doing the same.

"I marry her to-morrow morning," said Hicks.

"It's false," rejoined his companion: "I marry her!"

"You marry her?"

"I marry her!"

"You marry Matilda Maplesone?"

"Matilda Maplesone."

"*Miss* Maplesone marry *you?*"

"Miss Maplesone! No: Mrs. Maplesone."

"Good Heaven!" said Hicks, falling into his chair: "You marry the mother, and I the daughter!"

"Most extraordinary circumstance!" replied Mr. Calton, "and rather inconvenient too; for the fact is, that owing to Matilda's wishing to keep her intention secret from her daughters until the ceremony had taken place, she doesn't like applying to any of her friends to give her away. I entertain an objection to making the affair known to my acquaintance just now; and the consequence is, that I sent to you to know whether you'd oblige me by acting as father."

"I should have been most happy, I assure you," said Hicks, in a tone of condolence; "but, you see, I shall be acting as bridegroom. One character is frequently a consequence of the other; but it is not usual to act in both at the same time. There's Simpson—I have no doubt he'll do it for you."

"I don't like to ask him," replied Calton, "he's such a donkey."

Mr. Septimus Hicks looked up at the ceiling, and down at the floor; at last an idea struck him. "Let the man of the house, Tibbs, be the father," he suggested; and then he quoted, as peculiarly applicable to Tibbs and the pair—

"Oh Powers of Heaven! what dark eyes meets she there?
'Tis—'tis her father's—fixed upon the pair."

"The idea has struck me already," said Mr. Calton: "but, you see, Matilda, for what reason I know not, is very anxious that Mrs. Tibbs should know nothing about it, till it's all over. It's a natural delicacy, after all, you know."

"He's the best-natured little man in existence, if you manage him properly," said Mr. Septimus Hicks. "Tell him not to mention it to his wife, and assure him she won't mind it, and he'll do it directly. My marriage is to be a secret one, on account of the mother and *my* father; therefore he must be enjoined to secrecy."

A small double knock, like a presumptuous single one, was that instant heard at the street-door. It was Tibbs; it could be no one else; for no one else occupied five minutes in rubbing his shoes. He had been out to pay the baker's bill.

"Mr. Tibbs," called Mr. Calton in a very bland tone, looking over the bannisters.

"Sir!" replied he of the dirty face.

"Will you have the kindness to step up stairs for a moment?"

"Certainly, sir," said Tibbs, delighted to be taken notice of. The bedroom-door was carefully closed, and Tibbs, having put his hat on the floor (as most timid men do), and been accommodated with a seat, looked as astounded as if he were suddenly summoned before the familiars of the Inquisition.

"A rather unpleasant occurrence, Mr. Tibbs," said Calton, in a very portentous manner, "obliges me to consult you, and to beg you will not communicaté what I am about to say, to your wife."

Tibbs acquiesced, wondering in his own mind what the deuce the other could have done, and imagining that at least he must have broken the best decanters.

Mr. Calton resumed; "I am placed, Mr. Tibbs, in rather an unpleasant situation."

Tibbs looked at Mr. Septimus Hicks, as if he thought Mr. H.'s being in the immediate vicinity of his fellow-boarder might constitute the unpleasantness of his situation; but as he did not exactly know what to say, he merely ejaculated the monosyllable "Lor!"

"Now," continued the knocker, "let me beg you will exhibit no manifestations of surprise, which may be overheard by the domestics, when I tell you—command your feelings of astonishment—that two inmates of this house intend to be married to-morrow morning." And he drew back his chair, several feet, to perceive the effect of the unlooked-for announcement.

If Tibbs had rushed from the room, staggered down stairs, and fainted in the passage—if he had instantaneously jumped out of the window into the mews behind the house, in an agony of surprise—his behaviour would have been much less inexplicable to Mr. Calton than it was, when he put his hands into his inexpressible-pockets, and said with a half-chuckle, "Just so."

"You are not surprised, Mr. Tibbs?" inquired Mr. Calton.

"Bless you, no, sir," returned Tibbs; "after all, it's very natural. When two young people get together, you know——"

"Certainly, certainly," said Calton, with an indescribable air of self-satisfaction.

"You don't think it's at all an out-of-the-way affair then?" asked Mr. Septimus Hicks, who had watched the countenance of Tibbs in mute astonishment.

"No, sir," replied Tibbs; "I was just the same at his age." He actually smiled when he said this.

"How devilish well I must carry my years!" thought the delighted old beau, knowing he was at least ten years older than Tibbs at that moment.

"Well, then, to come to the point at once," he continued, "I have to ask you whether you will object to act as father on the occasion?"

"Certainly not," replied Tibbs; still without evincing an atom of surprise.

"You will not?"

"Decidedly not," reiterated Tibbs, still as calm as a pot of porter with the head off.

Mr. Calton seized the hand of the petticoat-governed little man, and vowed eternal friendship from that hour. Hicks, who was all admiration and surprise, did the same.

"Now, confess," asked Mr. Calton of Tibbs, as he picked up his hat, "were you not a little surprised?"

"I b'lieve you!" replied that illustrious person, holding up one hand; "I b'lieve you! When I first heard of it."

"So sudden," said Septimus Hicks.

"So strange to ask *me*, you know," said Tibbs.

"So odd altogether!" said the superannuated love-maker; and then all three laughed.

"I say," said Tibbs, shutting the door which he had previously opened, and giving full vent to a hitherto corked-up giggle, "what bothers me is, what *will* his father say?"

Mr. Septimus Hicks looked at Mr. Calton.

"Yes; but the best of it is," said the latter, giggling in his turn, "I haven't got a father—he! he! he!"

"*You* haven't got a father. No; but *he* has," said Tibbs.

"*Who* has?" inquired Septimus Hicks.

"Why *him.*"

"Him, who? Do you know my secret? Do you mean me?"

"You! No; you know who I mean," returned Tibbs with a knowing wink.

"For Heaven's sake, whom *do* you mean?" inquired Mr. Calton, who, like Septimus Hicks, was all but out of his senses at the strange confusion.

"Why Mr. Simpson, of course," replied Tibbs; "who else could I mean?"

"I see it all," said the Byron-quoter; "Simpson marries Julia Maplesone to-morrow morning!"

"Undoubtedly," replied Tibbs, thoroughly satisfied, "of course he does."

It would require the pencil of Hogarth to illustrate—our feeble pen is inadequate to describe—the expression which the countenances of Mr. Calton and Mr. Septimus Hicks respectively assumed, at this unexpected announcement. Equally impossible is it to describe, although perhaps it is easier for our lady readers to imagine, what arts the three ladies could have used, so completely to entangle their separate partners. Whatever they were, however, they were successful. The mother was perfectly aware of the intended marriage of both daughters; and the young ladies were equally acquainted with the intention of their estimable parent. They agreed, however, that it would have a much better appearance if each feigned ignorance of the other's engagement; and it was equally desirable that all the marriages should take place on the same day, to prevent the discovery of one clandestine alliance, operating prejudicially on the others. Hence, the mystification of Mr. Calton and Mr. Septimus Hicks, and the pre-engagement of the unwary Tibbs.

On the following morning, Mr. Septimus Hicks was united to Miss Matilda Maplesone. Mr. Simpson also entered into a "holy alliance" with Miss Julia; Tibbs acting as father, "his first appearance in that character." Mr. Calton, not being quite so eager as the two young men, was rather struck by the double discovery; and as he had found some difficulty in getting any one to give the lady away, it occurred to him that the best mode of obviating the inconvenience would be not to take her at all. The lady, however, "appealed," as her counsel said on the trial of the cause, *Maplesone* v. *Calton*, for a breach of promise, "with a broken heart, to the outraged laws of her country." She recovered damages to the amount of 1,000*l*. which the unfortunate knocker was compelled to pay. Mr. Septimus Hicks having walked the hospitals, took it into his head to walk off altogether. His injured wife is at present residing with her mother at Boulogne. Mr. Simpson, having the misfortune to lose his wife six weeks after marriage (by her eloping with an officer during his temporary sojourn in the Fleet Prison, in consequence of his inability to discharge her little mantua-maker's bill), and being disinherited by his father, who died soon afterwards, was fortunate enough to obtain a permanent engagement at a fashionable haircutter's; hairdressing being a science to which he had frequently directed his attention. In this situation he had necessarily many opportunities of making himself acquainted with the habits, and style of thinking, of the exclusive portion of the nobility of this kingdom. To this fortunate circumstance are we indebted for the production of those brilliant efforts of genius, his fashionable novels, which so long as good taste, unsullied by exaggeration, cant, and quackery, continues to exist, cannot fail to instruct and amuse the thinking portion of the community.

It only remains to add, that this complication of disorders completely deprived poor Mrs. Tibbs of all her inmates, except the one whom she could have best spared—her husband. That wretched little man returned home, on the day of the wedding, in a state of partial intoxication; and, under the influence of wine, excitement, and despair, actually dared to brave the anger of his wife. Since that ill-fated hour he has constantly taken his meals in the kitchen, to which apartment, it is understood, his witticisms will be in future confined: a turn-up bedstead having been conveyed there by Mrs. Tibbs's order for his exclusive accommodation. It is possible that he will be enabled to finish, in that seclusion, his story of the volunteers.

The advertisement has again appeared in the morning papers. Results must be reserved for another chapter.

CHAPTER THE SECOND.

"WELL!" said little Mrs. Tibbs to herself, as she sat in the front parlour of the Coram-street mansion one morning, mending a piece of stair-carpet off the first landing;—"Things have not turned out so badly, either, and if I only get a favourable answer to the advertisement, we shall be full again."

Mrs. Tibbs resumed her occupation of making worsted lattice-work in the carpet, anxiously listening to the twopenny postman, who was hammering his way down the street, at the rate of a penny a knock. The house was as quiet as possible. There was only one low sound to be heard—it was the unhappy Tibbs cleaning the gentlemen's boots in the back kitchen, and accompanying himself with a buzzing noise, in wretched mockery of humming a tune.

The postman drew near the house. He paused—so did Mrs. Tibbs. A knock—a bustle—a letter—post-paid.

"T. I. presents compt. to I. T. and T. I. begs To say that i see the advertisement And she will Do Herself the pleasure of calling On you at 12 o'clock to-morrow morning.

"T. I. as To apologise to I. T. for the shortness Of the notice But i hope it will not unconvenience you.

"I remain yours Truly
"Wednesday evening."

Little Mrs. Tibbs perused the document, over and over again; and the more she read it, the more was she confused by the mixture of the first and third person; the substitution of the "I" for the "T. I.;" and the transition from the "I. T." to the "you." The writing looked like a skein of thread in a tangle, and the note was ingeniously folded into a perfect square, with the direction squeezed up into the right-hand corner, as if it were ashamed of itself. The back of the epistle was pleasingly ornamented with a large red wafer, which, with the addition of divers ink-stains, bore a marvellous resemblance to a black beetle trodden upon. One thing, however, was perfectly clear to the perplexed Mrs. Tibbs. Somebody was to call at twelve. The drawing-room was forthwith dusted for the third time that morning; three or four chairs were pulled out of their places, and a corresponding number of books carefully upset, in order that there might be a due absence of formality. Down went the piece of stair-carpet before noticed, and up ran Mrs. Tibbs "to make herself tidy."

The clock of New Saint Pancras Church struck twelve, and the Foundling, with laudable politeness, did the same ten minutes afterwards. Saint something else struck the quarter, and then there arrived a single lady with a double knock, in a pelisse the colour of the interior of a damson pie; a bonnet of the same, with a regular conservatory of artificial flowers; a white veil, and a green parasol, with a cobweb border.

The visitor (who was very fat and red-faced) was shown into the drawing-room; Mrs. Tibbs presented herself, and the negotiation commenced.

"I called in consequence of an advertisement," said the stranger, in a voice as if she had been playing a set of Pan's pipes for a fortnight without leaving off.

"Yes!" said Mrs. Tibbs, rubbing her hands very slowly, and looking the applicant full in the face—two things she always did on such occasions.

"Money isn't no object whatever to me," said the lady, "so much as living in a state of retirement and obtrusion."

Mrs. Tibbs, as a matter of course, acquiesced in such an exceedingly natural desire.

"I am constantly attended by a medical man," resumed the pelisse wearer; "I have been a shocking unitarian for some time—I, indeed, have had very little peace since the death of Mr. Bloss."

Mrs. Tibbs looked at the relict of the departed Bloss, and thought he must have had very little peace in his time. Of course she could not say so; so she looked very sympathising.

"I shall be a good deal of trouble to you," said Mrs. Bloss; "but, for that trouble I am willing to pay. I am going through a course of treatment which renders attention necessary. I have one mutton chop in bed at half-past eight, and another at ten, every morning."

Mrs. Tibbs, as in duty bound, expressed the pity she felt for anybody placed in such a distressing situation; and the carnivorous Mrs. Bloss proceeded to arrange the various preliminaries with wonderful despatch. "Now mind," said that lady, after terms were arranged; "I am to have the second-floor front, for my bedroom?"

"Yes, ma'am."

"And you'll find room for my little servant Agnes?"

"Oh! certainly."

"And I can have one of the cellars in the area for my bottled porter."

"With the greatest pleasure;—James shall get it ready for you by Saturday."

"And I'll join the company at the breakfast-table on Sunday morning," said Mrs. Bloss. "I shall get up on purpose."

"Very well," returned Mrs. Tibbs, in her most amiable tone; for satisfactory references had "been given and required," and it was quite certain that the new comer had plenty of money. "It's rather singular," continued Mrs. Tibbs, with what was meant for a most bewitching smile, "that we have a gentleman now with us, who is in a very delicate state of health—a Mr. Gobler.—His apartment is the back drawing-room."

"The next room?" inquired Mrs. Bloss.

"The next room," repeated the hostess.

"How very promiscuous!" ejaculated the widow.

"He hardly ever gets up," said Mrs. Tibbs in a whisper.

"Lor!" cried Mrs. Bloss, in an equally low tone.

"And when he is up," said Mrs. Tibbs, "we never can persuade him to go to bed again."

"Dear me!" said the astonished Mrs. Bloss, drawing her chair nearer Mrs. Tibbs. "What is his complaint?"

"Why, the fact is," replied Mrs. Tibbs, with a most communicative air, "he has no stomach whatever."

"No what?" inquired Mrs. Bloss, with a look of the most indescribable alarm.

"No stomach," repeated Mrs. Tibbs, with a shake of the head.

"Lord bless us! what an extraordinary case!" gasped Mrs. Bloss, as if she understood the communication in its literal sense, and was astonished at a gentleman without a stomach finding it necessary to board anywhere.

"When I say he has no stomach," explained the chatty little Mrs. Tibbs, "I mean that his digestion is so much impaired, and his interior so deranged, that his stomach is not of the least use to him;—in fact, it's an inconvenience."

"Never heard such a case in my life!" exclaimed Mrs. Bloss. "Why, he's worse than I am."

"Oh, yes!" replied Mrs. Tibbs;—"certainly." She said this with great confidence, for the damson pelisse suggested that Mrs. Bloss, at all events, was not suffering under Mr. Gobler's complaint.

"You have quite incited my curiosity," said Mrs. Bloss, as she rose to depart. "How I long to see him!"

"He generally comes down, once a week," replied Mrs. Tibbs; "I dare say you'll see him on Sunday." With this consolatory promise Mrs. Bloss was obliged to be contented. She accordingly walked slowly down the stairs, detailing her complaints all the way; and Mrs. Tibbs followed her, uttering an exclamation of compassion at every step. James (who looked very gritty, for he was cleaning the knives) fell up the kitchen-stairs, and opened the street-door; and, after mutual farewells, Mrs. Bloss slowly departed, down the shady side of the street.

It is almost superfluous to say, that the lady whom we have just shown out at the street-door (and whom the two female servants are now inspecting from the second-floor windows) was exceedingly vulgar, ignorant, and selfish. Her deceased better-half had been an eminent cork-cutter, in which capacity he had amassed a decent fortune. He had no relative but his nephew, and no friend but his cook. The former had the insolence one morning to ask for the loan of fifteen pounds; and, by way of retaliation, he married the latter next day; he made a will immediately afterwards, containing a burst of honest indignation against his nephew (who supported himself and two sisters on 100*l.* a-year), and a bequest of his whole property to his wife. He felt ill after breakfast, and died after dinner. There is a mantelpiece-looking tablet in a civic parish church, setting forth his virtues, and deploring his loss. He never dishonoured a bill, or gave away a halfpenny.

The relict and sole executrix of this noble-minded man was an odd mixture of shrewdness and simplicity, liberality and meanness. Bred up as she had been, she knew no mode of living so agreeable as a boarding-house; and having nothing to do, and nothing to wish for, she naturally imagined she must be very ill—an impression which was most assiduously promoted by her medical attendant, Dr. Wosky, and her handmaid Agnes: both of whom, doubtless for good reasons, encouraged all her extravagant notions.

Since the catastrophe recorded in the last chapter, Mrs. Tibbs had been very shy of young-lady boarders. Her present inmates were all lords of the creation, and she availed herself of the opportunity of their assemblage at the dinner-table, to announce the expected arrival of Mrs. Bloss. The gentlemen received the communication with stoical indifference, and Mrs. Tibbs devoted all her energies to prepare for the reception of the valetudinarian. The second-floor front was scrubbed, and washed, and flannelled, till the wet went through to the drawing-room ceiling. Clean white counterpanes, and curtains, and napkins, water-bottles as clear as crystal, blue jugs, and mahogany furniture, added to the splendour, and increased the comfort, of the apartment. The warming-pan was in constant requisition, and a fire lighted in the room every day. The chattels of Mrs. Bloss were forwarded by instalments. First, there came a large hamper of Guinness's stout, and an umbrella; then, a train of trunks; then, a pair of clogs and a bandbox; then, an easy chair with an air-cushion; then, a variety of suspicious-looking packages; and—"though last not least"—Mrs. Bloss and Agnes: the latter in a cherry-coloured merino dress, open-work stockings, and shoes with sandals: like a disguised Columbine.

The installation of the Duke of Wellington, as Chancellor of the University of Oxford, was nothing, in point of bustle and turmoil, to the installation of Mrs. Bloss in her new quarters. True, there was no bright doctor of civil law to deliver a classical address on the occasion; but there were several other old women present, who spoke quite as much to the purpose, and understood themselves equally well. The chop-eater was so fatigued with the process of removal that she declined leaving her room until the following morning; so a mutton-chop, pickle, a pill, a pint bottle of stout, and other medicines, were carried up stairs for her consumption.

"Why, what *do* you think, ma'am?" inquired the inquisitive Agnes of her mistress, after they had been in the house some three hours; "what *do* you think, ma'am? the lady of the house is married."

"Married!" said Mrs. Bloss, taking the pill and a draught of Guinness—"married! Unpossible!"

"She is indeed, ma'am," returned the Columbine; "and her husband, ma'am, lives—he—he—he—lives in the kitchen, ma'am."

"In the kitchen!"

"Yes, ma'am: and he—he—he—the housemaid says, he never goes into the parlour except on Sundays; and that Mrs. Tibbs makes him clean the gentlemen's boots; and that he cleans the windows, too, sometimes; and that one morning early, when he was in the front balcony cleaning the drawing-room windows, he called out to a gentleman on the opposite side of the way, who used to live here—'Ah! Mr. Calton, sir, how are you?'" Here the attendant laughed till Mrs. Bloss was in serious apprehension of her chuckling herself into a fit.

"Well, I never!" said Mrs. Bloss.

"Yes. And please, ma'am, the servants gives him gin-and-water sometimes; and then he cries, and says he hates his wife and the boarders, and wants to tickle them."

"Tickle the boarders!" exclaimed Mrs. Bloss, seriously alarmed.

"No, ma'am, not the boarders, the servants."

"Oh, is that all!" said Mrs. Bloss, quite satisfied.

"He wanted to kiss me as I came up the kitchen-stairs, just now," said Agnes, indignantly; "but I gave it him—a little wretch!"

This intelligence was but too true. A long course of snubbing and neglect; his days spent in the kitchen, and his nights in the turn-up bedstead, had completely broken the little spirit that the unfortunate volunteer had ever possessed. He had no one to whom he could detail his injuries but the servants, and they were almost of necessity his chosen confidants. It is no less strange than true, however, that the little weaknesses which he had incurred, most probably during his military career, seemed to increase as his comforts diminished. He was actually a sort of journeyman Giovanni of the basement story.

The next morning, being Sunday, breakfast was laid in the front parlour at ten o'clock. Nine was the usual time, but the family always breakfasted an hour later on sabbath. Tibbs enrobed himself in his Sunday costume—a black coat, and exceedingly short, thin trousers; with a very large white waistcoat, white stockings and cravat, and Blucher boots—and mounted to the parlour aforesaid. Nobody had come down, and he amused himself by drinking the contents of the milkpot with a teaspoon.

A pair of slippers were heard descending the stairs. Tibbs flew to a chair; and a stern-looking man, of about fifty, with very little hair on his head, and a Sunday paper in his hand, entered the room.

"Good morning, Mr. Evenson," said Tibbs, very humbly, with something between a nod and a bow.

"How do you do, Mr. Tibbs?" replied he of the slippers, as he sat himself down, and began to read his paper without saying another word.

"Is Mr. Wisbottle in town to-day, do you know, sir?" inquired Tibbs, just for the sake of saying something.

"I should think he was," replied the stern gentleman. "He was whistling 'The Light Guitar,' in the next room to mine, at five o'clock this morning."

"He's very fond of whistling," said Tibbs, with a slight smirk.

"Yes—I ain't,' was the laconic reply.

Mr. John Evenson was in the receipt of an independent income, arising chiefly from various houses he owned in the different suburbs. He was very morose and discontented. He was a thorough radical, and used to attend a great variety of public meetings, for the express purpose of finding fault with everything that was proposed. Mr. Wisbottle, on the other hand, was a high Tory. He was a clerk in the Woods and Forests Office, which he considered rather an aristocratic employment; he knew the peerage by heart, and could tell you, off-hand, where any illustrious personage lived. He had a good set of teeth, and a capital tailor. Mr. Evenson looked on all these qualifications with profound contempt; and the consequence was that the two were always disputing, much to the edification of the rest of the house. It should be added, that, in addition to his partiality for whistling, Mr. Wisbottle had a great idea of his singing powers. There were two other boarders, besides the gentleman in the back drawing-room—Mr. Alfred Tomkins and Mr. Frederick O'Bleary. Mr. Tomkins was a clerk in a wine-house; he was a connoisseur in paintings, and had a wonderful eye for the picturesque. Mr. O'Bleary was an Irishman, recently imported; he was in a perfectly wild state; and had come over to England to be an apothecary, a clerk in a government office, an actor, a reporter, or anything else that turned up—he was not particular. He was on familiar terms with two small Irish members, and got franks for everybody in the house. He felt convinced that his intrinsic merits must procure him a high destiny. He wore shepherd's-plaid inexpressibles, and used to look under all the ladies' bonnets as he walked along the streets. His manners and appearance reminded one of Orson.

"Here comes Mr. Wisbottle," said Tibbs; and Mr. Wisbottle forthwith appeared in blue slippers, and a shawl dressing-gown, whistling "*Di piacer.*"

"Good morning, sir," said Tibbs again. It was almost the only thing he ever said to anybody.

"How are you, Tibbs?" condescendingly replied the amateur; and he walked to the window, and whistled louder than ever.

"Pretty air, that!" said Evenson, with a snarl, and without taking his eyes off the paper.

"Glad you like it," replied Wisbottle, highly gratified.

"Don't you think it would sound better, if you whistled it a little louder?" inquired the mastiff.

"No; I don't think it would," rejoined the unconscious Wisbottle.

"I'll tell you what, Wisbottle," said Evenson, who had been bottling up his anger for some hours—"the next time you feel disposed to whistle 'The Light Guitar' at five o'clock in the morning, I'll trouble you to whistle it with your head out o' window. If you don't, I'll learn the triangle—I will, by—"

The entrance of Mrs. Tibbs (with the keys in a little basket) interrupted the threat, and prevented its conclusion.

Mrs. Tibbs apologised for being down rather late; the bell was rung; James brought up the urn, and received an unlimited order for dry toast and bacon. Tibbs sat down at the bottom of the table, and began eating water-cresses like a Nebuchadnezzar. Mr. O'Bleary appeared, and Mr. Alfred Tomkins. The compliments of the morning were exchanged, and the tea was made.

"God bless me!" exclaimed Tomkins, who had been looking out at the window. "Here—Wisbottle—pray come here—make haste."

Mr. Wisbottle started from the table, and every one looked up.

"Do you see," said the connoisseur, placing Wisbottle in the right position—"a little more this way: there—do you see how splendidly the light falls upon the left side of that broken chimney-pot at No. 48?"

"Dear me! I see," replied Wisbottle, in a tone of admiration.

"I never saw an object stand out so beautifully against the clear sky in my life," ejaculated Alfred. Everybody (except John Evenson) echoed the sentiment; for Mr. Tomkins had a great character for finding out beauties which no one else could discover—he certainly deserved it.

"I have frequently observed a chimney-pot in College-green, Dublin, which has a much better effect," said the patriotic O'Bleary, who never allowed Ireland to be outdone on any point.

The assertion was received with obvious incredulity, for Mr. Tomkins declared that no other chimney-pot in the United Kingdom, broken or unbroken, could be so beautiful as the one at No. 48.

The room-door was suddenly thrown open, and Agnes appeared leading in Mrs. Bloss, who was dressed in a geranium-coloured muslin gown, and displayed a gold watch of huge dimensions; a chain to match; and a splendid assortment of rings, with enormous stones. A general rush was made for a chair, and a regular introduction took place. Mr. John Evenson made a slight inclination of the head; Mr. Frederick O'Bleary, Mr. Alfred Tomkins, and Mr. Wisbottle, bowed like the mandarins in a grocer's shop; Tibbs rubbed hands, and went round in circles. He was observed to close one eye, and to assume a clock-work sort of expression with the other; this has been considered as a wink, and it has been reported that Agnes was its object. We repel the calumny, and challenge contradiction.

Mrs. Tibbs inquired after Mrs. Bloss's health in a low tone. Mrs. Bloss, with a supreme contempt for the memory of Lindley Murray, answered the various questions in a most satisfactory manner; and a pause ensued, during which the eatables disappeared with awful rapidity.

"You must have been very much pleased with the appearance of the ladies going to the Drawing-room the other day, Mr. O'Bleary?" said Mrs. Tibbs, hoping to start a topic.

"Yes," replied Orson, with a mouthful of toast.

"Never saw anything like it before, I suppose?" suggested Wisbottle.

"No—except the Lord Lieutenant's levees," replied O'Bleary.

"Are they at all equal to our drawing-rooms?"

"Oh, infinitely superior!"

"Gad! I don't know,'" said the aristocratic Wisbottle, "the Dowager Marchioness of Publiccash was most magnificently dressed, and so was the Baron Slappenbachenhausen."

"What was he presented on?" inquired Evenson.

"On his arrival in England."

"I thought so," growled the radical; "you never hear of these fellows being presented on their going away again. They know better than that."

"Unless somebody pervades them with an apintment," said Mrs. Bloss, joining in the conversation in a faint voice.

"Well," said Wisbottle, evading the point, "it's a splendid sight."

"And did it never occur to you," inquired the radical, who never would be quiet; "did it never occur to you, that you pay for these precious ornaments of society?"

"It certainly *has* occurred to me," said Wisbottle, who thought this answer was a poser; "it *has* occurred to me, and I am willing to pay for them."

"Well, and it has occurred to me too," replied John Evenson, "and I ain't willing to pay for 'em. Then why should I?—I say, why should I?" continued the politician, laying down the paper, and knocking his knuckles on the table. "There are two great principles—demand—"

"A cup of tea if you please, dear," interrupted Tibbs.

"And supply—"

"May I trouble you to hand this tea to Mr. Tibbs?" said Mrs. Tibbs, interrupting the argument, and unconsciously illustrating it.

The thread of the orator's discourse was broken. He drank his tea and resumed the paper.

"If it's very fine," said Mr. Alfred Tomkins, addressing the company in general, "I shall ride down to Richmond to-day, and come back by the steamer. There are some splendid effects of light and shade on the Thames; the contrast between the blueness of the sky and the yellow water is frequently exceedingly beautiful." Mr. Wisbottle hummed, "Flow on, thou shining river."

"We have some splendid steam-vessels in Ireland," said O'Bleary.

"Certainly," said Mrs. Bloss, delighted to find a subject broached in which she could take part.

"The accommodations are extraordinary," said O'Bleary.

"Extraordinary indeed," returned Mrs. Bloss. "When Mr. Bloss was alive, he was promiscuously obligated to go to Ireland on business. I went with him, and raly the manner in which the ladies and gentlemen were accommodated with berths, is not creditable."

Tibbs, who had been listening to the dialogue, looked aghast, and evinced a strong inclination to ask a question, but was checked by a look from his wife. Mr. Wisbottle laughed, and said Tomkins had made a pun; and Tomkins laughed too, and said he had not.

The remainder of the meal passed off as breakfasts usually do. Conversation flagged, and people played with their teaspoons. The gentlemen looked out at the window; walked about the room; and, when they got near the door, dropped off one by one. Tibbs retired to the back parlour by his wife's orders, to check the greengrocer's weekly account; and ultimately Mrs. Tibbs and Mrs. Bloss were left alone together.

"Oh dear!" said the latter, "I feel alarmingly faint; it's very singular." (It certainly was, for she had eaten four pounds of solids that morning.) "By-the-bye," said Mrs. Bloss, "I have not seen Mr. What's his name yet."

"Mr. Gobler?" suggested Mrs. Tibbs.

"Yes."

"Oh!" said Mrs. Tibbs, "he is a most mysterious person. He has his meals regularly sent up stairs, and sometimes don't leave his room for weeks together."

"I haven't seen or heard nothing of him," repeated Mrs. Bloss.

"I dare say you'll hear him to-night," replied Mrs. Tibbs; "he generally groans a good deal on Sunday evenings."

"I never felt such an interest in any one in my life," ejaculated Mrs. Bloss. A little double-knock interrupted the conversation; Dr. Wosky was announced, and duly shown in. He was a little man with a red face,—dressed of course in black, with a stiff white neckerchief. He had a very good practice, and plenty of money, which he had amassed by invariably humouring the worst fancies of all the females of all the families he had ever been introduced into. Mrs. Tibbs offered to retire, but was entreated to stay.

"Well, my dear ma'am, and how are we?" inquired Wosky, in a soothing tone.

"Very ill, doctor—very ill," said Mrs. Bloss, in a whisper.

"Ah! we must take care of ourselves;—we must, indeed," said the obsequious Wosky, as he felt the pulse of his interesting patient.

"How is our appetite?"

Mrs. Bloss shook her head.

"Our friend requires great care," said Wosky, appealing to Mrs. Tibbs, who of course assented. "I hope, however, with the blessing of Providence, that we shall be enabled to make her quite stout again." Mrs. Tibbs wondered in her own mind what the patient would be when she was made quite stout.

"We must take stimulants," said the cunning Wosky—"plenty of nourishment, and, above all, we must keep our nerves quiet; we positively must not give way to our sensibilities. We must take all we can get," concluded the doctor, as he pocketed his fee, "and we must keep quiet."

"Dear man!" exclaimed Mrs. Bloss, as the doctor stepped into his carriage.

"Charming creature indeed—quite a lady's man!" said Mrs. Tibbs, and Docto Wosky rattled away to make fresh gulls of delicate females, and pocket fresh fees.

As we had occasion, in a former paper, to describe a dinner at Mrs. Tibbs's; and as one meal went off very like another on all ordinary occasions; we will not fatigue our readers by entering into any other detailed account of the domestic economy of the establishment. We will therefore proceed to events, merely premising that the mysterious tenant of the back drawing-room was a lazy, selfish hypochondriac; always complaining and never ill. As his character in many respects closely assimilated to that of Mrs. Bloss, a very warm friendship soon sprung up between them. He was tall, thin, and pale; he always fancied he had a severe pain somewhere or other, and his face invariably wore a pinched, screwed-up expression; he looked, indeed, like a man who had got his feet in a tub of exceedingly hot water, against his will.

For two or three months after Mrs. Bloss's first appearance in Coram-street, John Evenson was observed to become, every day, more sarcastic and more ill-natured; and there was a degree of additional importance in his manner, which clearly showed that he fancied he had discovered something, which he only wanted a proper opportunity of divulging. He found it at last.

One evening, the different inmates of the house were assembled in the drawing-room engaged in their ordinary occupations. Mr. Gobler and Mrs. Bloss were sitting at a small card-table near the centre window, playing cribbage; Mr. Wisbottle was describing semicircles on the music-stool, turning over the leaves of a book on the piano, and humming most melodiously; Alfred Tomkins was sitting at the round table, with his elbows duly squared, making a pencil sketch of a head considerably larger than his own; O'Bleary was reading Horace, and trying to look as if he understood it; and John Evenson had drawn his chair close to Mrs. Tibbs's work-table, and was talking to her very earnestly in a low tone.

"I can assure you, Mrs. Tibbs," said the radical, laying his forefinger on the muslin she was at work on; "I can assure you, Mrs. Tibbs, that nothing but the interest I take in your welfare would induce me to make this communication. I repeat, I fear Wisbottle is endeavouring to gain the affections of that young woman, Agnes, and that he is in the habit of meeting her in the store-room on the first floor, over the leads. From my bedroom I distinctly heard voices there, last night. I opened my door immediately, and crept very softly on to the landing; there I saw Mr. Tibbs, who, it seems, had been disturbed also.—Bless me, Mrs. Tibbs, you change colour!"

"No, no—it's nothing," returned Mrs. T. in a hurried manner; "it's only the heat of the room."

"A flush!" ejaculated Mrs. Bloss from the card-table; "that's good for four."

"If I thought it was Mr. Wisbottle," said Mrs. Tibbs, after a pause, "he should leave this house instantly."

"Go!" said Mrs. Bloss again.

"And if I thought," continued the hostess with a most threatening air, "if I thought he was assisted by Mr. Tibbs"—

"One for his nob!" said Gobler.

"Oh," said Evenson, in a most soothing tone—he liked to make mischief—"I should hope Mr. Tibbs was not in any way implicated. He always appeared to me very harmless."

"I have generally found him so," sobbed poor little Mrs. Tibbs; crying like a watering-pot.

"Hush! hush! pray—Mrs. Tibbs—consider—we shall be observed—pray, don't!" said John Evenson, fearing his whole plan would be interrupted. "We will set the matter at rest with the utmost care, and I shall be most happy to assist you in doing so."

Mrs. Tibbs murmured her thanks.

"When you think every one has retired to rest to-night," said Evenson very pompously, "if you'll meet me without a light, just outside my bedroom-door, by the staircase-window, I think we can ascertain who the parties really are, and you will afterwards be enabled to proceed as you think proper."

Mrs. Tibbs was easily persuaded; her curiosity was excited, her jealousy was roused, and the arrangement was forthwith made. She resumed her work, and John Evenson walked up and down the room with his hands in his pockets, looking as if nothing had happened. The game of cribbage was over, and conversation began again.

"Well, Mr. O'Bleary," said the humming top, turning round on his pivot, and facing the company, "what did you think of Vauxhall the other night?"

"Oh, it's very fair," replied Orson, who had been enthusiastically delighted with the whole exhibition.

"Never saw anything like that Captain Ross's set-out—eh?"

"No," returned the patriot, with his usual reservation—"except in Dublin."

"I saw the Count de Canky and Captain Fitzthompson in the Gardens," said Wisbottle: "they appeared much delighted."

"Then it *must* be beautiful," snarled Evenson.

"I think the white bears is partickerlerly well done," suggested Mrs. Bloss. "In their shaggy white coats, they look just like Polar bears—don't you think they do, Mr. Evenson?"

"I think they look a great deal more like omnibus cads on all fours," replied the discontented one.

"Upon the whole, I should have liked our evening very well," gasped Gobler; "only I caught a desperate cold which increased my pain dreadfully! I was obliged to have several shower-baths, before I could leave my room."

"Capital things those shower-baths!" ejaculated Wisbottle.

"Excellent!" said Tomkins.

"Delightful!" chimed in O'Bleary. (He had once seen one, outside a tin-man's.)

"Disgusting machines!" rejoined Evenson, who extended his dislike to almost every created object, masculine, feminine, or neuter.

"Disgusting, Mr. Evenson!" said Gobler, in a tone of strong indignation.—"Disgusting! Look at their utility—consider how many lives they have saved by promoting perspiration."

"Promoting perspiration, indeed," growled John Evenson, stopping short in his walk across the large squares in the pattern of the carpet—"I was ass enough to be persuaded some time ago to have one in my bedroom. 'Gad, I was in it once, and it effectually cured *me*, for the mere sight of it threw me into a profuse perspiration for six months afterwards."

A titter followed this announcement, and before it had subsided James brought up "the tray," containing the remains of a leg of lamb which had made its *début* at dinner; bread; cheese; an atom of butter in a forest of parsley; one pickled walnut and the third of another; and so forth. The boy disappeared, and returned again with another tray, containing glasses and jugs of hot and cold water. The gentlemen brought in their spirit-bottles; the housemaid placed divers plated bed-room candlesticks under the card-table; and the servants retired for the night.

Chairs were drawn round the table, and the conversation proceeded in the customary manner. John Evenson, who never ate supper, lolled on the sofa, and amused himself by contradicting everybody. O'Bleary ate as much as he could conveniently carry, and Mrs. Tibbs felt a due degree of indignation thereat; Mr. Gobler and Mrs. Bloss conversed most affectionately on the subject of pill-taking, and other innocent amusements; and Tomkins and Wisbottle "got into an argument;" that is to say, they both talked very loudly and vehemently, each flattering himself that he had got some advantage about something, and neither of them having more than a very indistinct idea of what they were talking about. An hour or two passed away; and the boarders and the brass candlesticks retired in pairs to their respective bedrooms. John Evenson pulled off his boots, locked his door, and determined to sit up until Mr. Gobler had retired. He always sat in the drawing-room an hour after everybody else had left it, taking medicine, and groaning.

Great Coram-street was hushed into a state of profound repose: it was nearly two o'clock. A hackney-coach now and then rumbled slowly by; and occasionally some stray lawyer's clerk, on his way home to Somers'-town, struck his iron heel on the top of the coal-cellar with a noise resembling the click of a smoke-jack. A low, monotonous, gushing sound was heard, which added considerably to the romantic dreariness of the scene. It was the water "coming in" at number eleven.

"He must be asleep by this time," said John Evenson to himself, after waiting with exemplary patience for nearly an hour after Mr. Gobler had left the drawing-room. He listened for a few moments; the house was perfectly quiet; he extinguished his rushlight, and opened his bedroom-door. The staircase was so dark that it was impossible to see anything.

"S—s—s!" whispered the mischief-maker, making a noise like the first indication a catherine-wheel gives of the probability of its going off.

"Hush!" whispered somebody else.

"Is that you, Mrs. Tibbs?"

"Yes, sir."

"Where?"

"Here;" and the misty outline of Mrs. Tibbs appeared at the staircase window, like the ghost of Queen Anne in the tent scene in Richard.

"This way, Mrs. Tibbs," whispered the delighted busybody: "give me your hand—there! Whoever these people are, they are in the store-room now, for I have been looking down from my window, and I could see that they accidentally upset their candlestick, and are now in darkness. You have no shoes on, have you?"

"No," said little Mrs. Tibbs, who could hardly speak for trembling.

"Well; I have taken my boots off, so we can go down, close to the store-room-door, and listen over the banisters;" and down stairs they both crept accordingly, every board creaking like a patent mangle on a Saturday afternoon.

"It's Wisbottle and somebody, I'll swear," exclaimed the radical in an energetic whisper, when they had listened for a few moments.

"Hush—pray let's hear what they say!" exclaimed Mrs. Tibbs, the gratification of whose curiosity was now paramount to every other consideration.

"Ah! if I could but believe you," said a female voice coquettishly, "I'd be bound to settle my missis for life."

"What does she say?" inquired Mr. Evenson, who was not quite so well situated as his companion.

"She says she'll settle her missis's life," replied Mrs. Tibbs. "The wretch! They're plotting murder."

"I know you want money," continued the voice, which belonged to Agnes; "and if you'd secure me the five hundred pound, I warrant she should take fire soon enough."

"What's that?" inquired Evenson again. He could just hear enough to want to hear [illegible]e.

"I think she says she'll set the house on fire," replied the affrighted Mrs. Tibbs. "But thank God I'm insured in the Phœnix!"

"The moment I have secured your mistress, my dear," said a man's voice in a strong Irish brogue, "you may depend on having the money."

"Bless my soul, it's Mr. O'Bleary!" exclaimed Mrs. Tibbs, in a parenthesis.

"The villain!" said the indignant Mr. Evenson.

"The first thing to be done," continued the Hibernian, "is to poison Mr. Gobler's mind."

"Oh, certainly," returned Agnes.

"What's that?" inquired Evenson again, in an agony of curiosity and a whisper.

"He says she's to mind and poison Mr. Gobler," replied Mrs. Tibbs, aghast at this sacrifice of human life.

"And in regard of Mrs. Tibbs," continued O'Bleary.—Mrs. Tibbs shuddered.

"Hush!" exclaimed Agnes, in a tone of the greatest alarm, just as Mrs. Tibbs was on the extreme verge of a fainting fit. "Hush!"

"Hush!" exclaimed Evenson, at the same moment to Mrs. Tibbs.

"There's somebody coming *up* stairs," said Agnes to O'Bleary.

"There's somebody coming *down* stairs," whispered Evenson to Mrs. Tibbs.

"Go into the parlour, sir," said Agnes to her companion. "You will get there, before whoever it is, gets to the top of the kitchen stairs."

"The drawing-room, Mrs. Tibbs!" whispered the astonished Evenson to his equally astonished companion; and for the drawing-room they both made, plainly hearing the rustling of two persons, one coming down stairs, and one coming up.

"What can it be?" exclaimed Mrs. Tibbs. "It's like a dream. I wouldn't be found in this situation for the world!"

"Nor I," returned Evenson, who could never bear a joke at his own expense. "Hush! here they are at the door."

"What fun!" whispered one of the newcomers.—It was Wisbottle.

"Glorious!" replied his companion, in an equally low tone.—This was Alfred Tomkins. "Who would have thought it?"

"I told you so," said Wisbottle, in a most knowing whisper. "Lord bless you, he has paid her most extraordinary attention for the last two months. I saw 'em when I was sitting at the piano to-night."

"Well, do you know I didn't notice it?" interrupted Tomkins.

"Not notice it!" continued Wisbottle. "Bless you; I saw him whispering to her, and she crying; and then I'll swear I heard him say something about to-night when we were all in bed."

"They're talking of *us!*" exclaimed the agonised Mrs. Tibbs, as the painful suspicion, and a sense of their situation, flashed upon her mind.

"I know it—I know it," replied Evenson, with a melancholy consciousness that there was no mode of escape.

"What's to be done? we cannot both stop here!" ejaculated Mrs. Tibbs, in a state of partial derangement.

"I'll get up the chimney," replied Evenson, who really meant what he said.

"You can't," said Mrs. Tibbs, in despair. "You can't—it's a register stove."

"Hush!" repeated John Evenson.

"Hush—hush!" cried somebody down stairs.

"What a d—d hushing!" said Alfred Tomkins, who began to get rather bewildered.

"There they are!" exclaimed the sapient Wisbottle, as a rustling noise was heard in the store-room.

"Hark!" whispered both the young men.

"Hark!" repeated Mrs. Tibbs and Evenson.

"Let me alone, sir," said a female voice in the store-room.

"Oh, Hagnes!" cried another voice, which clearly belonged to Tibbs, for nobody else ever owned one like it. "Oh, Hagnes—lovely creature!"

"Be quiet, sir!" (A bounce.)

"Hag—"

"Be quiet, sir—I am ashamed of you. Think of your wife, Mr. Tibbs. Be quiet, sir!"

"My wife!" exclaimed the valorous Tibbs, who was clearly under the influence of gin-and-water, and a misplaced attachment; "I ate her! Oh, Hagnes! when I was in the volunteer corps, in eighteen hundred and—"

"I declare I'll scream. Be quiet, sir, will you?" (Another bounce and a scuffle.)

"What's that?" exclaimed Tibbs, with a start.

"What's what?" said Agnes, stopping short.

"Why, that!"

"Ah! you have done it nicely now, sir," sobbed the frightened Agnes, as a tapping was heard at Mrs. Tibbs's bedroom door, which would have beaten any dozen woodpeckers hollow.

"Mrs. Tibbs! Mrs. Tibbs!" called out Mrs. Bloss. "Mrs. Tibbs, pray get up." (Here the imitation of a woodpecker was resumed with tenfold violence.)

"Oh, dear—dear!" exclaimed the wretched partner of the depraved Tibbs. "She's knocking at my door. We must be discovered! What will they think?"

"Mrs. Tibbs! Mrs. Tibbs!" screamed the woodpecker again.

"What's the matter!" shouted Gobler, bursting out of the back drawing-room, like the dragon at Astley's.

"Oh, Mr. Gobler!" cried Mrs. Bloss, with a proper approximation to hysterics; "I think the house is on fire, or else there's thieves in it. I have heard the most dreadful noises!"

"The devil you have!" shouted Gobler again, bouncing back into his den, in happy imitation of the aforesaid dragon, and returning immediately with a lighted candle. "Why, what's this? Wisbottle! Tomkins! O'Bleary! Agnes! What the deuce! all up and dressed?"

"Astonishing!" said Mrs. Bloss, who had run down stairs, and taken Mr. Gobler's arm.

"Call Mrs. Tibbs directly, somebody," said Gobler, turning into the front drawing-room.—"What! Mrs. Tibbs and Mr. Evenson!!"

"Mrs. Tibbs and Mr. Evenson!" repeated everybody, as that unhappy pair were discovered: Mrs. Tibbs seated in an arm-chair by the fireplace, and Mr. Evenson standing by her side.

We must leave the scene that ensued to the reader's imagination. We could tell, how Mrs. Tibbs forthwith fainted away, and how it required the united strength of Mr. Wisbottle and Mr. Alfred Tomkins to hold her in her chair; how Mr. Evenson explained, and how his explanation was evidently disbelieved; how Agnes repelled the accusations of Mrs. Tibbs by proving that she was negotiating with Mr. O'Bleary to influence her mistress's affections in his behalf; and how Mr. Gobler threw a damp counterpane on the hopes of Mr. O'Bleary by avowing that he (Gobler) had already proposed to, and been accepted by, Mrs. Bloss; how Agnes was discharged from that lady's service; how Mr. O'Bleary discharged himself from Mrs. Tibbs's house, without going through the form of previously discharging his bill; and how that disappointed young gentleman rails against England and the English, and vows there is no virtue or fine feeling extant, "except in Ireland." We repeat that we *could* tell all this, but we love to exercise our self-denial, and we therefore prefer leaving it to be imagined.

The lady whom we have hitherto described as Mrs. Bloss, is no more. Mrs. Gobler exists: Mrs. Bloss has left us for ever. In a secluded retreat in Newington Butts, far, far removed from the noisy strife of that great boarding-house, the world, the enviable Gobler and his pleasing wife revel in retirement: happy in their complaints, their table, and their medicine; wafted through life by the grateful prayers of all the purveyors of animal food within three miles round.

We would willingly stop here, but we have a painful duty imposed upon us, which we must discharge. Mr. and Mrs. Tibbs have separated by mutual consent, Mrs. Tibbs receiving one moiety of 43*l.* 15*s.* 10*d.*, which we before stated to be the amount of her husband's annual income, and Mr. Tibbs the other. He is spending the evening of his days in retirement; and he is spending also, annually, that small but honourable independence. He resides among the original settlers at Walworth; and it has been stated, on unquestionable authority, that the conclusion of the volunteer story has been heard in a small tavern in that respectable neighbourhood.

The unfortunate Mrs. Tibbs has determined to dispose of the whole of her furniture by public auction, and to retire from a residence in which she has suffered so much. Mr. Robins has been applied to, to conduct the sale, and the transcendent abilities of the literary gentlemen connected with his establishment are now devoted to the task of drawing up the preliminary advertisement. It is to contain, among a variety of brilliant matter, seventy-eight words in large capitals, and six original quotations in inverted commas.

CHAPTER II.

MR. MINNS AND HIS COUSIN.

MR. AUGUSTUS MINNS was a bachelor, of about forty as he said—of about eight-and-forty as his friends said. He was always exceedingly clean, precise, and tidy; perhaps somewhat priggish, and the most retiring man in the world. He usually wore a brown frock-coat without a wrinkle, light inexplicables without a spot, a neat neckerchief with a remarkably neat tie, and boots without a fault; moreover, he always carried a brown silk umbrella with an ivory handle. He was a clerk in Somerset-house, or, as he said himself, he held "a responsible situation under Government." He had a good and increasing salary, in addition to some 10,000*l.* of his own (invested in the funds), and he occupied a first floor in Tavistock-street, Covent-garden, where he had resided for twenty years, having been in the habit of quarrelling with his landlord the whole time: regularly giving notice of his intention to quit on the first day of every quarter, and as regularly countermanding it on the second. There were two classes of created objects which he held in the deepest and most unmingled horror; these were dogs, and children. He was not unamiable, but he could, at any time, have viewed the execution of a dog, or the assassination of an infant, with the liveliest satisfaction. Their habits were at variance with his love of order; and his love of order was as powerful as his love of life. Mr. Augustus Minns had no relations, in or near London, with the exception of his cousin, Mr. Octavius Budden, to whose son, whom he had never seen (for he disliked the father) he had consented to become godfather by proxy. Mr. Budden having realised a moderate fortune by exercising the trade or calling of a corn-chandler, and having a great predilection for the country, had purchased a cottage in the vicinity of Stamford-hill, whither he retired with the wife of his bosom, and his only son, Master Alexander Augustus Budden. One evening, as Mr. and Mrs. B. were admiring their son, discussing his various merits, talking over his education, and disputing whether the classics should be made an essential part thereof, the lady pressed so strongly upon her husband the propriety of cultivating the friendship of Mr. Minns in behalf of their son, that Mr. Budden at last made up his mind, that it should not be his fault if he and his cousin were not in future more intimate.

"I'll break the ice, my love," said Mr. Budden, stirring up the sugar at the bottom of his glass of brandy-and-water, and casting a sidelong look at his spouse to see the effect of the announcement of his determination, "by asking Minns down to dine with us, on Sunday."

"Then, pray Budden write to your cousin at once," replied Mrs. Budden. "Who knows, if we could only get him down here, but he might take a fancy to our Alexander, and leave him his property?—Alick, my dear, take your legs off the rail of the chair!"

"Very true," said Mr. Budden, musing, "very true indeed, my love!"

On the following morning, as Mr. Minns was sitting at his breakfast-table, alternately biting his dry toast and casting a look upon the columns of his morning paper, which he always read from the title to the printer's name, he heard a loud knock at the street-door; which was shortly afterwards followed by the entrance of his servant, who put into his hand a particularly small card, on which was engraven in immense letters, "Mr. Octavius Budden, Amelia Cottage (Mrs. B.'s name was Amelia), Poplar-walk, Stamford-hill."

"Budden!" ejaculated Minns, "what can bring that vulgar man here!—say I'm asleep—say I'm out, and shall never be home again—anything to keep him down stairs."

"But please, sir, the gentleman's coming up," replied the servant, and the fact was made evident, by an appalling creaking of boots on the staircase accompanied by a pattering noise; the cause of which, Minns could not, for the life of him divine.

"Hem—show the gentleman in," said the unfortunate bachelor. Exit servant, and enter Octavius preceded by a large white dog, dressed in a suit of fleecy hosiery, with pink eyes, large ears, and no perceptible tail.

The cause of the pattering on the stairs was but too plain. Mr. Augustus Minns staggered beneath the shock of the dog's appearance.

"My dear fellow, how are you?" said Budden, as he entered.

He always spoke at the top of his voice, and always said the same thing half-a-dozen times.

"How are you, my hearty?"

"How do you do, Mr. Budden?—pray take a chair!" politely stammered the discomfited Minns.

"Thank you—thank you—well—how are you, eh?"

"Uncommonly well, thank you," said Minns, casting a diabolical look at the dog, who, with his hind legs on the floor, and his fore paws resting on the table, was dragging a bit of bread and butter out of a plate, preparatory to devouring it, with the buttered side next the carpet.

"Ah, you rogue!" said Budden to his dog; "you see, Minns, he's like me, always at home, eh, my boy?—Egad, I'm precious hot and hungry! I've walked all the way from Stamford-hill this morning."

"Have you breakfasted?" inquired Minns.

"Oh, no!—came to breakfast with you; so ring the bell, my dear fellow, will you? and let's have another cup and saucer, and the cold ham.—Make myself at home, you see!" continued Budden, dusting his boots with a table-napkin. "Ha!—ha!—ha!—'pon my life, I'm hungry."

Minns rang the bell, and tried to smile.

"I decidedly never was so hot in my life," continued Octavius, wiping his forehead; "well, but how are you, Minns? 'Pon my soul, you wear capitally!"

"D'ye think so?" said Minns; and he tried another smile.

"'Pon my life, I do!"

"Mrs. B. and—what's his name—quite well?"

"Alick—my son, you mean; never better—never better. But at such a place as we've got at Poplar-walk, you know, he couldn't be ill if he tried. When I first saw it, by Jove! it looked so knowing, with the front garden, and the green railings, and the brass knocker, and all that—I really thought it was a cut above me."

"Don't you think you'd like the ham better," interrupted Minns, "if you cut it the other way?" He saw, with feelings which it is impossible to describe, that his visitor was cutting or rather maiming the ham, in utter violation of all established rules.

"No, thank ye," returned Budden, with the most barbarous indifference to crime, "I prefer it this way, it eats short. But I say, Minns, when will you come down and see us? You will be delighted with the place; I know you will. Amelia and I were talking about you the other night, and Amelia said—another lump of sugar, please; thank ye—she said, don't you think you could contrive, my dear, to say to Mr. Minns, in a friendly way—come down, sir—damn the dog! he's spoiling your curtains, Minns—ha!—ha!—ha!" Minns leaped from his seat as though he had received the discharge from a galvanic battery.

"Come out, sir!—go out, hoo!" cried poor Augustus, keeping nevertheless, at a very respectful distance from the dog; having read of a case of hydrophobia in the paper of that morning. By dint of great exertion, much shouting, and a marvellous deal of poking under the tables with a stick and umbrella, the dog was at last dislodged, and placed on the landing outside the door, where he immediately commenced a most appalling howling; at the same time vehemently scratching the paint off the two nicely-varnished bottom panels, until they resembled the interior of a back-gammon-board.

"A good dog for the country that!" coolly observed Budden to the distracted Minns, "but he's not much used to confinement. But now, Minns, when will you come down? I'll take no denial, positively. Let's see, to-day's Thursday.—Will you come on Sunday? We dine at five, don't say no—do."

After a great deal of pressing, Mr. Augustus Minns, driven to despair, accepted the invitation, and promised to be at Poplar-walk on the ensuing Sunday, at a quarter before five to the minute.

"Now mind the direction," said Budden: "the coach goes from the Flower-pot, in Bishopsgate-street, every half hour. When the coach stops at the Swan, you'll see, immediately opposite you, a white house."

"Which is your house—I understand," said Minns, wishing to cut short the visit, and the story, at the same time.

"No, no, that's not mine; that's Grogus's, the great ironmonger's. I was going to say—you turn down by the side of the white house till you can't go another step further—mind that!—and then you turn to your right, by some stables—well; close to you, you'll see a wall with 'Beware of the Dog' written on it in large letters—(Minns shuddered)—go along by the side of that wall for about a quarter of a mile—and anybody will show you which is my place."

"Very well—thank ye—good bye."

"Be punctual."

"Certainly: good morning."

"I say, Minns, you've got a card."

"Yes, I have; thank ye." And Mr. Octavius Budden departed leaving his cousin looking forward to his visit on the following Sunday, with the feelings of a penniless poet to the weekly visit of his Scotch landlady.

Sunday arrived; the sky was bright and clear; crowds of people were hurrying along the streets, intent on their different schemes of pleasure for the day; everything and everybody looked cheerful and happy except Mr. Augustus Minns.

The day was fine, but the heat was considerable; when Mr. Minns had fagged up the shady side of Fleet-street, Cheapside, and Threadneedle-street, he had become pretty warm, tolerably dusty, and it was getting late into the bargain. By the most extraordinary good fortune, however, a coach was waiting at the Flower-pot, into which Mr. Augustus Minns got, on the solemn assurance of the cad that the vehicle would start in three minutes—that being the very utmost extremity of time it was allowed to wait by Act of Parliament. A quarter of an hour elapsed, and there were no signs of moving. Minns looked at his watch for the sixth time.

"Coachman, are you going or not?" bawled Mr. Minns, with his head and half his body out of the coach-window.

"Di—rectly, sir," said the coachman, with his hands in his pockets, looking as much unlike a man in a hurry as possible.

"Bill, take them cloths off." Five minutes more elapsed: at the end of which time the coachman mounted the box, from whence he looked down the street, and up the street, and hailed all the pedestrians for another five minutes.

"Coachman! if you don't go this moment, I shall get out," said Mr. Minns, rendered desperate by the lateness of the hour, and the impossibility of being in Poplar-walk at the appointed time.

"Going this minute, sir," was the reply;—and, accordingly, the machine trundled on for a couple of hundred yards, and then stopped again. Minns doubled himself up in a corner of the coach, and abandoned himself to his fate, as a child, a mother, a bandbox and a parasol, became his fellow passengers.

The child was an affectionate and an amiable infant; the little dear mistook Minns for his other parent, and screamed to embrace him.

"Be quiet, dear," said the mamma, restraining the impetuosity of the darling, whose little fat legs were kicking, and stamping, and twining themselves into the most complicated forms, in an ecstasy of impatience. "Be quiet, dear, that's not your papa."

"Thank Heaven I am not!" thought Minns, as the first gleam of pleasure he had experienced that morning shone like a meteor through his wretchedness.

Playfulness was agreeably mingled with affection in the disposition of the boy. When satisfied that Mr. Minns was not his parent, he endeavoured to attract his notice by scraping his drab trousers with his dirty shoes, poking his chest with his mamma's parasol, and other nameless endearments peculiar to infancy, with which he beguiled the tediousness of the ride, apparently very much to his own satisfaction.

When the unfortunate gentleman arrived at the Swan, he found to his great dismay, that it was a quarter past five. The white house, the stables, the "Beware of the Dog,"—every landmark was passed, with a rapidity not unusual to a gentleman of a certain age when too late for dinner. After the lapse of a few minutes, Mr. Minns found himself opposite a yellow brick house with a green door, brass knocker, and door-plate, green window-frames and ditto railings, with "a garden" in front, that is to say, a small loose bit of gravelled ground, with one round and two scalene triangular beds, containing a fir-tree, twenty or thirty bulbs, and an unlimited number of marigolds. The taste of Mr. and Mrs. Budden was further displayed by the appearance of a Cupid on each side of the door, perched upon a heap of large chalk flints, variegated with pink conch-shells. His knock at the door was answered by a stumpy boy, in drab livery, cotton stockings and high-lows, who, after hanging his hat on one of the dozen brass pegs which ornamented the passage, denominated by courtesy "The Hall," ushered him into a front drawing-room commanding a very extensive view of the backs of the neighbouring houses. The usual ceremony of introduction, and so forth, over, Mr. Minns took his seat: not a little agitated at finding that he was the last comer, and, somehow or other, the Lion of about a dozen people, sitting together in a small drawing-room, getting rid of that most tedious of all time, the time preceding dinner.

"Well, Brogson," said Budden, addressing an elderly gentleman in a black coat, drab knee-breeches, and long gaiters, who, under pretence of inspecting the prints in an Annual, had been engaged in satisfying himself on the subject of Mr. Minns's general appearance, by looking at him over the tops of the leaves—"Well, Brogson, what do Ministers mean to do? Will they go out, or what?"

"Oh—why—really, you know, I'm the last person in the world to ask for news. Your cousin, from his situation, is the most likely person to answer the question."

Mr. Minns assured the last speaker, that although he was in Somerset-house, he possessed no official communication relative to the projects of his Majesty's Ministers. But his remark was evidently received incredulously; and no further conjectures being hazarded on the subject, a long pause ensued, during which the company occupied themselves in coughing and blowing their noses, until the entrance of Mrs. Budden caused a general rise.

The ceremony of introduction being over, dinner was announced, and down stairs the party proceeded accordingly—Mr. Minns escorting Mrs. Budden as far as the drawing-room door, but being prevented, by the narrowness of the staircase, from extending his gallantry any farther. The dinner passed off as such dinners usually do. Ever and anon, amidst the clatter of knives and forks, and the hum of conversation, Mr. B.'s voice might be heard, asking a friend to take wine, and assuring him he was glad to see him; and a great deal of by-play took place between Mrs. B. and the servants, respecting the removal of the dishes, during which her countenance assumed all the variations of a weather-glass, from "stormy" to "set fair."

Upon the dessert and wine being placed on the table, the servant, in compliance with a significant look from Mrs. B., brought down "Master Alexander," habited in a sky-blue suit with silver buttons; and possessing hair of nearly the same colour as the metal. After sundry praises from his mother, and various admonitions as to his behaviour from his father, he was introduced to his godfather.

"Well, my little fellow—you are a fine boy, ain't you?" said Mr. Minns, as happy as a tomtit on birdlime.

"Yes."

"How old are you?"

"Eight, next We'nsday. How old are *you?*"

"Alexander," interrupted his mother, "how dare you ask Mr. Minns how old he is!"

"He asked me how old *I* was," said the precocious child, to whom Minns had from that moment internally resolved that he never would bequeath one shilling. As soon as the titter occasioned by the observation, had subsided, a little smirking man with red whiskers, sitting at the bottom of the table, who during the whole of dinner had been endeavouring to obtain a listener to some stories about Sheridan, called out, with a very patronising air, "Alick, what part of speech is *be*."

"A verb."

"That's a good boy," said Mrs. Budden, with all a mother's pride. "Now, you know what a verb is?"

"A verb is a word which signifies to be, to do, or to suffer; as, I am—I rule—I am ruled. Give me an apple, Ma."

"I'll give you an apple," replied the man with the red whiskers, who was an established friend of the family, or in other words was always invited by Mrs. Budden, whether Mr. Budden liked it or not, "if you'll tell me what is the meaning of *be*."

"Be?" said the prodigy, after a little hesitation—"an insect that gathers honey."

"No, dear," frowned Mrs. Budden; "B double E is the substantive."

"I don't think he knows much yet about *common* substantives," said the smirking gentleman, who thought this an admirable opportunity for letting off a joke. "It's clear he's not very well acquainted with *proper names*. He! he! he!"

"Gentlemen," called out Mr. Budden, from the end of the table, in a stentorian voice, and with a very important air, "will you have the goodness to charge your glasses? I have a toast to propose."

"Hear! hear!" cried the gentlemen, passing the decanters. After they had made the round of the table, Mr. Budden proceeded—"Gentlemen; there is an individual present—"

"Hear! hear!" said the little man with red whiskers.

"*Pray* be quiet, Jones," remonstrated Budden.

"I say, gentlemen, there is an individual present," resumed the host, "in whose society, I am sure we must take great delight—and—and—the conversation of that individual must have afforded to every one present, the utmost pleasure." ["Thank Heaven, he does not mean *me*!" thought Minns, conscious that his diffidence and exclusiveness had prevented his saying above a dozen words since he entered the house.] "Gentlemen, I am but a humble individual myself, and I perhaps ought to apologise for allowing any individual feelings of friendship and affection for the person I allude to, to induce me to venture to rise, to propose the health of that person—a person that, I am sure—that is to say, a person whose virtues must endear him to those who know him—and those who have not the pleasure of knowing him, cannot dislike him."

"Hear! hear!" said the company, in a tone of encouragement and approval.

"Gentlemen," continued Budden, "my cousin is a man who—who is a relation of my own." (Hear! hear!) Minns groaned audibly. "Who I am most happy to see here, and who, if he were not here, would certainly have deprived us of the great pleasure we all feel in seeing him. (Loud cries of hear!) Gentlemen, I feel that I have already trespassed on your attention for too long a time. With every feeling—of—with every sentiment of—of—"

"Gratification"—suggested the friend of the family.

"—Of gratification, I beg to propose the health of Mr. Minns."

"Standing, gentlemen!" shouted the indefatigable little man with the whiskers—"and with the honours. Take your time from me, if you please. Hip! hip! hip!—Za!—Hip! hip! hip!—Za!—Hip! hip!—Za—a—a!"

All eyes were now fixed on the subject of the toast, who by gulping down port wine at the imminent hazard of suffocation, endeavoured to conceal his confusion. After as long a pause as decency would admit, he rose, but, as the newspapers sometimes say in their reports, "we regret that we are quite unable to give even the substance of the honourable gentleman's observations." The words "present company—honour—present occasion," and "great happiness"—heard occasionally, and repeated at intervals, with a countenance expressive of the utmost confusion and misery, convinced the company that he was making an excellent speech; and, accordingly, on his resuming his seat, they cried "Bravo!" and manifested tumultuous applause. Jones, who had been long watching his opportunity, then darted up.

"Budden," said he "will you allow *me* to propose a toast?"

"Certainly," replied Budden, adding in an under tone to Minns right across the table. "Devilish sharp fellow that: you'll be very much pleased with his speech. He talks equally well on any subject." Minns bowed, and Mr. Jones proceeded:

"It has on several occasions, in various instances, under many circumstances, and in different companies, fallen to my lot to propose a toast to those by whom, at the time, I have had the honour to be surrounded. I have sometimes, I will cheerfully own—for why should I deny it?—felt the overwhelming nature of the task I have undertaken, and my own utter incapability to do justice to the subject. If such have been my feelings, however, on former occasions, what must they be now—now—under the extraordinary circumstances in which I am placed. (Hear! hear!) To describe my feelings accurately, would be impossible; but I cannot give you a better idea of them, gentlemen, than by referring to a circumstance which happens, oddly enough, to occur to my mind at the moment. On one occasion, when that truly great and illustrious man, Sheridan, was—"

Now, there is no knowing what new villainy in the form of a joke would have been heaped on the grave of that very ill-used man, Mr. Sheridan, if the boy in drab had not at that moment entered the room in a breathless state, to report that, as it was a very wet night, the nine o'clock stage had come round, to know whether there was anybody going to town, as, in that case, he (the nine o'clock) had room for one inside.

Mr. Minns started up; and, despite countless exclamations of surprise, and entreaties to stay, persisted in his determination to accept the vacant place. But, the brown silk umbrella was nowhere to be found; and as the coachman couldn't wait, he drove back to the Swan, leaving word for Mr. Minns to "run round" and catch him. However, as it did not occur to Mr. Minns for some ten minutes or so, that he had left the brown silk umbrella with the ivory handle in the other coach, coming down; and, moreover, as he was by no means remarkable for speed, it is no matter of surprise that when he accomplished the feat of "running round" to the Swan, the coach—the last coach—had gone without him.

It was somewhere about three o'clock in the morning, when Mr. Augustus Minns knocked feebly at the street-door of his lodgings in Tavistock-street, cold, wet, cross, and miserable. He made his will next morning, and his professional man informs us, in that strict confidence in which we inform the public, that neither the name of Mr. Octavius Budden, nor of Mrs. Amelia Budden, nor of Master Alexander Augustus Budden, appears therein.

CHAPTER III.

SENTIMENT.

THE Miss Crumptons, or to quote the authority of the inscription on the garden-gate of Minerva House, Hammersmith, "The Misses Crumpton," were two unusually tall, particularly thin, and exceedingly skinny personages: very upright, and very yellow. Miss Amelia Crumpton owned to thirty-eight, and Miss Maria Crumpton admitted she was forty; an admission which was rendered perfectly unnecessary by the self-evident fact of her being at least fifty. They dressed in the most interesting manner—like twins! and looked as happy and comfortable as a couple of marigolds run to seed. They were very precise, had the strictest possible ideas of propriety, wore false hair, and always smelt very strongly of lavender.

Minerva House, conducted under the auspices of the two sisters, was a "finishing establishment for young ladies," where some twenty girls of the ages of from thirteen to nineteen inclusive, acquired a smattering of everything, and a knowledge of nothing; instruction in French and Italian, dancing lessons twice a-week; and other necessaries of life. The house was a white one, a little removed from the road-side, with close palings in front. The bed-room windows were always left partly open, to afford a bird's-eye view of numerous little bedsteads with very white dimity furniture, and thereby impress the passer-by with a due sense of the luxuries of the establishment; and there was a front parlour hung round with highly varnished maps which nobody ever looked at, and filled with books which no one ever read, appropriated exclusively to the reception of parents, who, whenever they called, could not fail to be struck with the very deep appearance of the place.

"Amelia, my dear," said Miss Maria Crumpton, entering the school-room one morning, with her false hair in papers: as she occasionally did, in order to impress the young ladies with a conviction of its reality. "Amelia, my dear, here is a most gratifying note I have just received. You needn't mind reading it aloud."

Miss Amelia, thus advised, proceeded to read the following note with an air of great triumph:

"Cornelius Brook Dingwall, Esq., M.P., presents his compliments to Miss Crumpton, and will feel much obliged by Miss Crumpton's calling on him, if she conveniently can, to-morrow morning at one o'clock, as Cornelius Brook Dingwall, Esq., M.P., is anxious to see Miss Crumpton on the subject of placing Miss Brook Dingwall under her charge.

"Adelphi.

"Monday morning."

"A Member of Parliament's daughter!" ejaculated Amelia, in an ecstatic tone.

"A Member of Parliament's daughter!" repeated Miss Maria, with a smile of delight, which, of course, elicited a concurrent titter of pleasure from all the young ladies.

"It's exceedingly delightful!" said Miss Amelia; whereupon all the young ladies murmured their admiration again. Courtiers are but school-boys, and court-ladies school-girls.

So important an announcement, at once superseded the business of the day. A holiday was declared, in commemoration of the great event; the Miss Crumptons retired to their private apartment to talk it over; the smaller girls discussed the probable manners and customs of the daughter of a Member of Parliament; and the young ladies verging on eighteen wondered whether she was engaged, whether she was pretty, whether she wore much bustle, and many other *whethers* of equal importance.

The two Miss Crumptons proceeded to the Adelphi at the appointed time next day, dressed, of course, in their best style, and looking as amiable as they possibly could—which, by-the-bye, is not saying much for them. Having sent in their cards, through the medium of a red-hot looking footman in bright livery, they were ushered into the august presence of the profound Dingwall.

Cornelius Brook Dingwall, Esq., M.P., was very haughty, solemn, and portentous. He had, naturally, a somewhat spasmodic expression of countenance, which was not rendered the less remarkable by his wearing an extremely stiff cravat. He was wonderfully proud of the M.P. attached to his name, and never lost an opportunity of reminding people of his dignity. He had a great idea of his own abilities, which must have been a great comfort to him, as no one else had; and in diplomacy, on a small scale, in his own family arrangements, he considered himself unrivalled. He was a county magistrate, and discharged the duties of his station with all due justice and impartiality; frequently committing poachers, and occasionally committing himself. Miss Brook Dingwall was one of that numerous class of young ladies, who, like adverbs, may be known by their answering to a commonplace question, and doing nothing else.

On the present occasion, this talented individual was seated in a small library at a table covered with papers, doing nothing, but trying to look busy—playing at shop. Acts of Parliament, and letters directed to "Cornelius Brook Dingwall, Esq., M.P.," were ostentatiously scattered over the table; at a little distance from which, Mrs. Brook Dingwall was seated at work. One of those public nuisances, a spoiled child, was playing about the room, dressed after the most approved fashion—in a blue tunic with a black belt a quarter of a yard wide, fastened with an immense buckle—looking like a robber in a melodrama, seen through a diminishing glass.

After a little pleasantry from the sweet child, who amused himself by running away with Miss Maria Crumpton's chair as fast as it was placed for her, the visitors were seated, and Cornelius Brook Dingwall, Esq., opened the conversation.

He had sent for Miss Crumpton, he said, in consequence of the high character he had received of her establishment from his friend, Sir Alfred Muggs.

Miss Crumpton murmured her acknowledgments to him (Muggs), and Cornelius proceeded.

"One of my principal reasons, Miss Crumpton, for parting with my daughter, is, that she has lately acquired some sentimental ideas, which it is most desirable to eradicate from her young mind." (Here the little innocent before noticed, fell out of an arm-chair with an awful crash.)

"Naughty boy!" said his mamma, who appeared more surprised at his taking the liberty of falling down, than at anything else; "I'll ring the bell for James to take him away."

"Pray don't check him, my love," said the diplomatist, as soon as he could make himself heard amidst the unearthly howling consequent upon the threat and the tumble. "It all arises from his great flow of spirits." This last explanation was addressed to Miss Crumpton.

"Certainly, sir," replied the antique Maria: not exactly seeing, however, the connexion between a flow of animal spirits, and a fall from an arm-chair.

Silence was restored, and the M.P. resumed: "Now, I know nothing so likely to effect this object, Miss Crumpton, as her mixing constantly in the society of girls of her own age; and, as I know that in your establishment she will meet such as are not likely to contaminate her young mind, I propose to send her to you."

The youngest Miss Crumpton expressed the acknowledgments of the establishment generally. Maria was rendered speechless by bodily pain. The dear little fellow, having recovered his animal spirits, was standing upon her most tender foot, by way of getting his face (which looked like a capital O in a red lettered play-bill) on a level with the writing-table.

"Of course, Lavinia will be a parlour boarder," continued the enviable father; "and on one point I wish my directions to be strictly observed. The fact is, that some ridiculous love affair, with a person much her inferior in life, has been the cause of her present state of mind. Knowing that of course, under your care, she can have no opportunity of meeting this person, I do not object to—indeed, I should rather prefer—her mixing with such society as you see yourself."

This important statement was again interrupted by the high-spirited little creature, in the excess of his joyousness breaking a pane of glass, and nearly precipitating himself into an adjacent area. James was rung for; considerable confusion and screaming succeeded; two little blue legs were seen to kick violently in the air as the man left the room, and the child was gone.

"Mr. Brook Dingwall would like Miss Brook Dingwall to learn everything," said Mrs. Brook Dingwall, who hardly ever said anything at all.

"Certainly," said both the Miss Crumptons together.

"And as I trust the plan I have devised will be effectual in weaning my daughter from this absurd idea, Miss Crumpton," continued the legislator, "I hope you will have the goodness to comply, in all respects, with any request I may forward to you."

The promise was of course made; and after a lengthened discussion, conducted on behalf of the Dingwalls with the most becoming diplomatic gravity, and on that of the Crumptons with profound respect, it was finally arranged that Miss Lavinia should be forwarded to Hammersmith on the next day but one, on which occasion the half-yearly ball given at the establishment was to take place. It might divert the dear girl's mind. This, by the way, was another bit of diplomacy.

Miss Lavinia was introduced to her future governess, and both the Miss Crumptons pronounced her "a most charming girl;" an opinion which, by a singular coincidence, they always entertained of any new pupil.

Courtesies were exchanged, acknowledgments expressed, condescension exhibited, and the interview terminated.

Preparations, to make use of theatrical phraseology, "on a scale of magnitude never before attempted," were incessantly made at Minerva House to give every effect to the forthcoming ball. The largest room in the house was pleasingly ornamented with blue calico roses, plaid tulips, and other equally natural-looking artificial flowers, the work of the young ladies themselves. The carpet was taken up, the folding-doors were taken down, the furniture was taken out, and rout-seats were taken in. The linen-drapers of Hammersmith were astounded at the sudden demand for blue sarsenet ribbon, and long white gloves. Dozens of geraniums were purchased for bouquets, and a harp and two violins were bespoke from town, in addition to the grand piano already on the premises. The young ladies who were selected to show off on the occasion, and do credit to the establishment, practised incessantly, much to their own satisfaction, and greatly to the annoyance of the lame old gentleman over the way; and a constant correspondence was kept up, between the Misses Crumpton and the Hammersmith pastrycook.

The evening came; and then there was such a lacing of stays, and tying of sandals, and dressing of hair, as never can take place with a proper degree of bustle out of a boarding-school. The smaller girls managed to be in everybody's way, and were pushed about accordingly; and the elder ones dressed, and tied, and flattered, and envied, one another, as earnestly and sincerely as if they had actually *come out.*

"How do I look, dear?" inquired Miss Emily Smithers, the belle of the house, of Miss Caroline Wilson, who was her bosom friend, because she was the ugliest girl in Hammersmith, or out of it.

"Oh! charming, dear. How do I?"

"Delightful! you never looked so handsome," returned the belle, adjusting her own dress, and not bestowing a glance on her poor companion.

"I hope young Hilton will come early," said another young lady to Miss somebody else, in a fever of expectation.

"I'm sure he'd be highly flattered if he knew it," returned the other, who was practising *l'été.*

"Oh! he's so handsome," said the first.

"Such a charming person!" added a second.

"Such a *distingué* air!" said a third.

"Oh, what *do* you think?" said another girl, running into the room; "Miss Crumpton says her cousin's coming."

"What! Theodosius Butler?" said everybody in raptures.

"Is *he* handsome?" inquired a novice.

"No, not particularly handsome," was the general reply; "but, oh, so clever!"

Mr. Theodosius Butler was one of those immortal geniuses who are to be met with in almost every circle. They have, usually, very deep, monotonous voices. They always persuade themselves that they are wonderful persons, and that they ought to be very miserable, though they don't precisely know why. They are very conceited, and usually possess half an idea; but, with enthusiastic young ladies, and silly young gentlemen, they are very wonderful persons. The individual in question, Mr. Theodosius, had written a pamphlet containing some very weighty considerations on the expediency of doing something or other; and as every sentence contained a good many words of four syllables, his admirers took it for granted that he meant a good deal.

"Perhaps that's he," exclaimed several young ladies, as the first pull of the evening threatened destruction to the bell of the gate.

An awful pause ensued. Some boxes arrived and a young lady—Miss Brook Dingwall, in full ball costume, with an immense gold chain round her neck, and her dress looped up with a single rose; an ivory fan in her hand, and a most interesting expression of despair in her face.

The Miss Crumptons inquired after the family, with the most excruciating anxiety, and Miss Brook Dingwall was formally introduced to her future companions. The Miss Crumptons conversed with the young ladies in the most mellifluous tones, in order that Miss Brook Dingwall might be properly impressed with their amiable treatment.

Another pull at the bell. Mr. Dadson the writing-master, and his wife. The wife in green silk, with shoes and cap-trimmings to correspond: the writing-master in a white waistcoat, black knee-shorts, and ditto silk stockings, displaying a leg large enough for two writing-masters. The young ladies whispered one another, and the writing-master and his wife flattered the Miss Crumptons, who were dressed in amber, with long sashes, like dolls.

Repeated pulls at the bell, and arrivals too numerous to particularise: papas and mammas, and aunts and uncles, the owners and guardians of the different pupils; the singing-master, Signor Lobskini, in a black wig; the piano-forte player and the violins; the harp, in a state of intoxication; and some twenty young men, who stood near the door, and talked to one another, occasionally bursting into a giggle. A general hum of conversation. Coffee handed round, and plentifully partaken of by fat mammas, who looked like the stout people who come on in pantomimes for the sole purpose of being knocked down.

The popular Mr. Hilton was the next arrival; and he having, at the request of the Miss Crumptons, undertaken the office of Master of the Ceremonies, the quadrilles commenced with considerable spirit. The young men by the door gradually advanced into the middle of the room, and in time became sufficiently at ease to consent to be introduced to partners. The writing-master danced every set, springing about with the most fearful agility, and his wife played a rubber in the back-parlour—a little room with five book-shelves, dignified by the name of the study. Setting her down to whist was a half-yearly piece of generalship on the part of the Miss Crumptons; it was necessary to hide her somewhere, on account of her being a fright.

The interesting Lavinia Brook Dingwall was the only girl present, who appeared to take no interest in the proceedings of the evening. In vain was she solicited to dance; in vain was the universal homage paid to her as the daughter of a member of parliament. She was equally unmoved by the splendid tenor of the inimitable Lobskini, and the brilliant execution of Miss Lætitia Parsons, whose performance of "The Recollections of Ireland" was universally declared to be almost equal to that of Moscheles himself. Not even the announcement of the arrival of Mr. Theodosius Butler could induce her to leave the corner of the back drawing-room in which she was seated.

"Now, Theodosius," said Miss Maria Crumpton, after that enlightened pamphleteer had nearly run the gauntlet of the whole company, "I must introduce you to our new pupil."

Theodosius looked as if he cared for nothing earthly.

"She's the daughter of a member of parliament," said Maria.—Theodosius started.

"And her name is——?" he inquired.

"Miss Brook Dingwall."

"Great Heaven!" poetically exclaimed Theodosius, in a low tone.

Miss Crumpton commenced the introduction in due form. Miss Brook Dingwall languidly raised her head.

"Edward!" she exclaimed, with a half-shriek, on seeing the well-known nankeen legs.

Fortunately, as Miss Maria Crumpton possessed no remarkable share of penetration, and as it was one of the diplomatic arrangements that no attention was to be paid to Miss Lavinia's incoherent exclamations, she was perfectly unconscious of the mutual agitation of the parties; and therefore, seeing that the offer of his hand for the next quadrille was accepted, she left him by the side of Miss Brook Dingwall.

"Oh, Edward!" exclaimed that most romantic of all romantic young ladies, as the light of science seated himself beside her, "Oh, Edward, is it you?"

Mr. Theodosius assured the dear creature, in the most impassioned manner, that he was not conscious of being anybody but himself.

"Then why—why—this disguise? Oh! Edward M'Neville Walter, what have I not suffered on your account?"

"Lavinia, hear me," replied the hero, in his most poetic strain. "Do not condemn me unheard. If anything that emanates from the soul of such a wretch as I, can occupy a place in your recollection—if any being, so vile, deserve your notice—you may remember that I once published a pamphlet (and paid for its publication) entitled 'Considerations on the Policy of Removing the Duty on Bees'-wax.'"

"I do—I do!" sobbed Lavinia.

"That," continued the lover, "was a subject to which your father was devoted, heart and soul."

"He was—he was!" reiterated the sentimentalist.

"I knew it," continued Theodosius, tragically; "I knew it—I forwarded him a copy. He wished to know me. Could I disclose my real name? Never! No, I assumed that name which you have so often pronounced in tones of endearment. As M'Neville Walter, I devoted myself to the stirring cause; as M'Neville Walter I gained your heart; in the same character I was ejected from your house by your father's domestics; and in no character at all have I since been enabled to see you. We now meet again, and I proudly own that I am—Theodosius Butler."

The young lady appeared perfectly satisfied with this argumentative address, and bestowed a look of the most ardent affection on the immortal advocate of bees'-wax.

"May I hope," said he, "that the promise your father's violent behaviour interrupted, may be renewed?"

"Let us join this set," replied Lavinia, coquettishly—for girls of nineteen can coquette.

"No," ejaculated he of the nankeens; "I stir not from this spot, writhing under this torture of suspense. May I—may I—hope?"

"You may."

"The promise is renewed?"

"It is."

"I have your permission?"

"You have."

"To the fullest extent?"

"You know it," returned the blushing Lavinia. The contortions of the interesting Butler's visage expressed his raptures.

We could dilate upon the occurrences that ensued. How Mr. Theodosius and Miss Lavinia danced, and talked, and sighed for the remainder of the evening—how the Miss Crumptons were delighted thereat. How the writing-master continued to frisk about with one-horse power, and how his wife, from some unaccountable freak, left the whist-table in the little back-parlour, and persisted in displaying her green head-dress in the most conspicuous part of the drawing-room. How the supper consisted of small triangular sandwiches in trays, and a tart here and there by way of variety; and how the visitors consumed warm water disguised with lemon, and dotted with nutmeg, under the denomination of negus. These, and other matters of as much interest, however, we pass over, for the purpose of describing a scene of even more importance.

A fortnight after the date of the ball, Cornelius Brook Dingwall, Esq., M.P., was seated at the same library-table, and in the same room, as we have before described. He was alone, and his face bore an expression of deep thought and solemn gravity--he was drawing up "A Bill for the better observance of Easter Monday."

The footman tapped at the door—the legislator started from his reverie, and "Miss Crumpton" was announced. Permission was given for Miss Crumpton to enter the *sanctum;* Maria came sliding in, and having taken her seat with a due portion of affectation, the footman retired, and the governess was left alone with the M.P. Oh! how she longed for the presence of a third party! Even the facetious young gentleman would have been a relief.

Miss Crumpton began the duet. She hoped Mrs. Brook Dingwall and the handsome little boy were in good health.

They were. Mrs. Brook Dingwall and little Frederick were at Brighton.

"Much obliged to you, Miss Crumpton," said Cornelius, in his most dignified manner, "for your attention in calling this morning. I should have driven down to Hammersmith, to see Lavinia, but your account was so very satisfactory, and my duties in the House occupy me so much, that I determined to postpone it for a week. How has she gone on?"

"Very well indeed, sir," returned Maria, dreading to inform the father that she had gone off.

"Ah, I thought the plan on which I proceeded would be a match for her."

Here was a favourable opportunity to say that somebody else had been a match for her. But the unfortunate governess was unequal to the task.

"You have persevered strictly in the line of conduct I prescribed, Miss Crumpton?"

"Strictly, sir."

"You tell me in your note that her spirits gradually improved."

"Very much indeed, sir."

"To be sure. I was convinced they would."

"But I fear, sir," said Miss Crumpton, with visible emotion, "I fear the plan has not succeeded, quite so well as we could have wished."

"No!" exclaimed the prophet. "Bless me! Miss Crumpton, you look alarmed. What has happened?"

"Miss Brook Dingwall, sir——"

"Yes, ma'am?"

"Has gone, sir"—said Maria, exhibiting a strong inclination to faint.

"Gone!"

"Eloped, sir."

"Eloped!—Who with—when—where—how?" almost shrieked the agitated diplomatist.

The natural yellow of the unfortunate Maria's face changed to all the hues of the rainbow, as she laid a small packet on the member's table.

He hurriedly opened it. A letter from his daughter, and another from Theodosius. He glanced over their contents—"Ere this reaches you, far distant—appeal to feelings—love to distraction—bees'-wax—slavery," &c., &c. He dashed his hand to his forehead, and paced the room with fearfully long strides, to the great alarm of the precise Maria.

"Now mind; from this time forward," said Mr. Brook Dingwall, suddenly stopping at the table, and beating time upon it with his hand; "from this time forward, I never will, under any circumstances whatever, permit a man who writes pamphlets to enter any other room of this house but the kitchen.—I'll allow my daughter and her husband one hundred and fifty pounds a-year, and never see their faces again; and, damme! ma'am, I'll bring in a bill for the abolition of finishing-schools."

Some time has elapsed since this passionate declaration. Mr. and Mrs. Butler are at present rusticating in a small cottage at Ball's-pond, pleasantly situated in the immediate vicinity of a brick-field. They have no family. Mr. Theodosius looks very important, and writes incessantly; but, in consequence of a gross combination on the part of publishers, none of his productions appear in print. His young wife begins to think that ideal misery is preferable to real unhappiness; and that a marriage, contracted in haste, and repented at leisure, is the cause of more substantial wretchedness than she ever anticipated.

On cool reflection, Cornelius Brook Dingwall, Esq., M.P., was reluctantly compelled to admit that the untoward result of his admirable arrangements was attributable, not to the Miss Crumptons, but his own diplomacy. He however consoles himself, like some other small diplomatists, by satisfactorily proving that if his plans did not succeed, they ought to have done so. Minerva House is in *statu quo*, and "The Misses Crumpton" remain in the peaceable and undisturbed enjoyment of all the advantages resulting from their Finishing-School.

CHAPTER IV.

THE TUGGS'S AT RAMSGATE.

ONCE upon a time, there dwelt, in a narrow street on the Surrey side of the water, within three minutes' walk of old London Bridge, Mr. Joseph Tuggs—a little dark-faced man, with shiny hair, twinkling eyes, short legs, and a body of very considerable thickness, measuring from the centre button of his waistcoat in front, to the ornamental buttons of his coat behind. The figure of the amiable Mrs. Tuggs, if not perfectly symmetrical, was decidedly comfortable; and the form of her only daughter, the accomplished Miss Charlotte Tuggs, was fast ripening into that state of luxuriant plumpness which had enchanted the eyes, and captivated the heart, of Mr. Joseph Tuggs in his earlier days. Mr. Simon Tuggs, his only son, and Miss Charlotte Tuggs's only brother, was as differently formed in body, as he was differently constituted in mind, from the remainder of his family. There was that elongation in his thoughtful face, and that tendency to weakness in his interesting legs, which tell so forcibly of a great mind and romantic disposition. The slightest traits of character in such a being, possess no mean interest to speculative minds. He usually appeared in public, in capacious shoes with black cotton stockings; and was observed to be particularly attached to a black glazed stock, without tie or ornament of any description.

There is perhaps no profession, however useful; no pursuit, however meritorious; which can escape the petty attacks of vulgar minds. Mr. Joseph Tuggs was a grocer. It might be supposed that a grocer was beyond the breath of calumny; but no—the neighbours stigmatised him as a chandler; and the poisonous voice of envy distinctly asserted that he dispensed tea and coffee by the quartern, retailed sugar by the ounce, cheese by the slice, tobacco by the screw, and butter by the pat. These taunts, however, were lost upon the Tuggs's. Mr. Tuggs attended to the grocery department; Mrs. Tuggs to the cheesemongery; and Miss Tuggs to her education. Mr. Simon Tuggs kept his father's books, and his own counsel.

One fine spring afternoon, the latter gentleman was seated on a tub of weekly Dorset, behind the little red desk with a wooden rail, which ornamented a corner of the counter; when a stranger dismounted from a cab, and hastily entered the shop. He was habited in black cloth, and bore with him, a green umbrella, and a blue bag.

"Mr. Tuggs?" said the stranger, inquiringly.

"*My* name is Tuggs," replied Mr. Simon.

"It's the other Mr. Tuggs," said the stranger, looking towards the glass door which led into the parlour behind the shop, and on the inside of which, the round face of Mr. Tuggs, senior, was distinctly visible, peeping over the curtain.

Mr. Simon gracefully waved his pen, as if in intimation of his wish that his father would advance. Mr. Joseph Tuggs, with considerable celerity, removed his face from the curtain and placed it before the stranger.

"I come from the Temple," said the man with the bag.

"From the Temple!" said Mrs. Tuggs, flinging open the door of the little parlour and disclosing Miss Tuggs in perspective.

"From the Temple!" said Miss Tuggs and Mr. Simon Tuggs at the same moment.

"From the Temple!" said Mr. Joseph Tuggs, turning as pale as a Dutch cheese.

"From the Temple," repeated the man with the bag; "from Mr. Cower's, the solicitor's. Mr. Tuggs, I congratulate you, sir. Ladies, I wish you joy of your prosperity! We have been successful." And the man with the bag leisurely divested himself of his umbrella and glove, as a preliminary to shaking hands with Mr. Joseph Tuggs.

Now the words "we have been successful," had no sooner issued from the mouth of the man with the bag, than Mr. Simon Tuggs rose from the tub of weekly Dorset, opened his eyes very wide, gasped for breath, made figures of eight in the air with his pen, and finally fell into the arms of his anxious mother, and fainted away without the slightest ostensible cause or pretence.

"Water!" screamed Mrs. Tuggs.

"Look up, my son," exclaimed Mr. Tuggs.

"Simon! dear Simon!" shrieked Miss Tuggs.

"I'm better now," said Mr. Simon Tuggs. "What! successful!" And then, as corroborative evidence of his being better, he fainted away again, and was borne into the little parlour by the united efforts of the remainder of the family, and the man with the bag.

To a casual spectator, or to any one unacquainted with the position of the family, this fainting would have been unaccountable. To those who understood the mission of the man with the bag, and were moreover acquainted with the excitability of the nerves of Mr. Simon Tuggs, it was quite comprehensible. A long-pending law-suit respecting the validity of a will, had been unexpectedly decided; and Mr. Joseph Tuggs was the possessor of twenty thousand pounds.

A prolonged consultation took place, that night, in the little parlour—a consultation that was to settle the future destinies of the Tuggs's. The shop was shut up, at an unusually early hour; and many were the unavailing kicks bestowed upon the closed door by applicants for quarterns of sugar, or half-quarterns of bread, or penn'orths of pepper, which were to have been "left till Saturday," but which fortune had decreed were to be left alone altogether.

"We must certainly give up business," said Miss Tuggs.

"Oh, decidedly," said Mrs. Tuggs.

"Simon shall go to the bar," said Mr. Joseph Tuggs.

"And I shall always sign myself 'Cymon' in future," said his son.

"And I shall call myself Charlotta," said Miss Tuggs.

"And you must always call *me* 'Ma,' and father 'Pa,'" said Mrs. Tuggs.

"Yes, and Pa must leave off all his vulgar habits," interposed Miss Tuggs.

"I'll take care of all that," responded Mr. Joseph Tuggs, complacently. He was, at that very moment, eating pickled salmon with a pocket-knife.

"We mus leave town immediately," said Mr. Cymcn Tuggs.

Everybody concurred that this was an indispensable preliminary to being genteel The question then arose, Where should they go?

"Gravesend?" mildly suggested Mr. Joseph Tuggs. The idea was unanimously scouted. Gravesend was *low*.

"Margate?" insinuated Mrs. Tuggs. Worse and worse—nobody there, but tradespeople.

"Brighton?" Mr. Cymon Tuggs opposed an insurmountable objection. All the coaches had been upset, in turn, within the last three weeks; each coach had averaged two passengers killed, and six wounded; and, in every case, the newspapers had distinctly understood that "no blame whatever was attributable to the coachman."

"Ramsgate?" ejaculated Mr. Cymon, thoughtfully. To be sure; how stupid they must have been, not to have thought of that before! Ramsgate was just the place of all others.

Two months after this conversation, the City of London Ramsgate steamer was running gaily down the river. Her flag was flying, her band was playing, her passengers were conversing; everything about her seemed gay and lively.—No wonder—the Tuggs's were on board.

"Charming, ain't it?" said Mr. Joseph Tuggs, in a bottle-green great-coat, with a velvet collar of the same, and a blue travelling-cap with a gold band.

"Soul-inspiring," replied Mr. Cymon Tuggs—he was entered at the bar. "Soul-inspiring!"

"Delightful morning, sir!" said a stoutish, military-looking gentleman in a blue surtout buttoned up to his chin, and white trousers chained down to the soles of his boots.

Mr. Cymon Tuggs took upon himself the responsibility of answering the observation. "Heavenly!" he replied.

"You are an enthusiastic admirer of the beauties of Nature, sir?" said the military gentleman.

"I am, sir," replied Mr. Cymon Tuggs.

"Travelled much, sir?" inquired the military gentleman.

"Not much," replied Mr. Cymon Tuggs.

"You've been on the continent, of course?" inquired the military gentleman.

"Not exactly," replied Mr. Cymon Tuggs—in a qualified tone, as if he wished it to be implied that he had gone half-way and come back again.

"You of course intend your son to make the grand tour, sir?" said the military gentleman, addressing Mr. Joseph Tuggs.

As Mr. Joseph Tuggs did not precisely understand what the grand tour was, or how such an article was manufactured, he replied, "Of course." Just as he said the word, there came tripping up, from her seat at the stern of the vessel, a young lady in a puce-coloured silk cloak, and boots of the same; with long black ringlets, large black eyes, brief petticoats, and unexceptionable ankles.

"Walter, my dear," said the young lady to the military gentleman.

"Yes, Belinda, my love," responded the military gentleman to the black-eyed young lady.

"What have you left me alone so long for?" said the young lady. "I have been stared out of countenance by those rude young men."

"What! stared at?" exclaimed the military gentleman, with an emphasis which made Mr. Cymon Tuggs withdraw his eyes from the young lady's face with inconceivable rapidity. "Which young men—where?" and the military gentleman clenched his fist, and glared fearfully on the cigar-smokers around.

"Be calm, Walter, I entreat," said the young lady.

"I won't," said the military gentleman.

"Do, sir," interposed Mr. Cymon Tuggs. "They ain't worth your notice."

"No—no—they are not, indeed," urged the young lady.

"I *will* be calm," said the military gentleman. "You speak truly, sir. I thank you for a timely remonstrance, which may have spared me the guilt of manslaughter." Calming his wrath, the military gentleman wrung Mr. Cymon Tuggs by the hand.

"My sister, sir!" said Mr. Cymon Tuggs; seeing that the military gentleman was casting an admiring look towards Miss Charlotta.

"My wife, ma'am—Mrs. Captain Waters," said the military gentleman, presenting the black-eyed young lady.

"My mother, ma'am—Mrs. Tuggs," said Mr. Cymon. The military gentleman and his wife murmured enchanting courtesies; and the Tuggs's looked as unembarrassed as they could.

"Walter, my dear," said the black-eyed young lady, after they had sat chatting with the Tuggs's some half hour.

"Yes, my love," said the military gentleman.

"Don't you think this gentleman (with an inclination of the head towards Mr. Cymon Tuggs) is very much like the Marquis Carriwini?"

"Lord bless me, very!" said the military gentleman.

"It struck me, the moment I saw him," said the young lady, gazing intently, and with a melancholy air, on the scarlet countenance of Mr. Cymon Tuggs. Mr. Cymon Tuggs looked at everybody; and finding that everybody was looking at him, appeared to feel some temporary difficulty in disposing of his eyesight.

"So exactly the air of the marquis," said the military gentleman.

"Quite extraordinary!" sighed the military gentleman's lady.

"You don't know the marquis, sir?" inquired the military gentleman.

Mr. Cymon Tuggs stammered a negative.

"If you did," continued Captain Walter Waters, "you would feel how much reason you have to be proud of the resemblance—a most elegant man, with a most prepossessing appearance."

"He is—he is indeed!" exclaimed Belinda Waters energetically. As her eye caught that of Mr. Cymon Tuggs, she withdrew it from his features in bashful confusion.

All this was highly gratifying to the feelings of the Tuggs's; and when, in the course of farther conversation, it was discovered that Miss Charlotta Tuggs was the *fac simile* of a titled relative of Mrs. Belinda Waters, and that Mrs. Tuggs herself was the very picture of the Dowager Duchess of Dobbleton, their delight in the acquisition of so genteel and friendly an acquaintance, knew no bounds. Even the dignity of Captain Walter Waters relaxed, to that degree, that he suffered himself to be prevailed upon by Mr. Joseph Tuggs, to partake of cold pigeon-pie and sherry, on deck; and a most delightful conversation, aided by these agreeable stimulants, was prolonged, until they ran alongside Ramsgate Pier.

"Good by'e, dear!" said Mrs. Captain Waters to Miss Charlotta Tuggs, just before the bustle of landing commenced; "we shall see you on the sands in the morning; and, as we are sure to have found lodgings before then, I hope we shall be inseparables for many weeks to come."

"Oh! I hope so," said Miss Charlotta Tuggs, emphatically.

"Tickets, ladies and gen'lm'n," said the man on the paddle-box.

"Want a porter, sir?" inquired a dozen men in smock-frocks.

"Now, my dear!" said Captain Waters.

"Good by'e!" said Mrs. Captain Waters—"good by'e, Mr. Cymon!" and with a pressure of the hand which threw the amiable young man's nerves into a state of considerable derangement, Mrs. Captain Waters disappeared among the crowd. A pair of puce-coloured boots were seen ascending the steps, a white handkerchief fluttered, a black eye gleamed. The Waters's were gone, and Mr. Cymon Tuggs was alone in a heartless world.

Silently and abstractedly, did that too sensitive youth follow his revered parents, and a train of smock-frocks and wheelbarrows, along the pier, until the bustle of the scene around, recalled him to himself. The sun was shining brightly; the sea, dancing to its own music, rolled merrily in; crowds of people promenaded to and fro; young ladies tittered; old ladies talked; nurse-maids displayed their charms to the greatest possible advantage; and their little charges ran up and down, and to and fro, and in and out, under the feet, and between the legs, of the assembled concourse, in the most playful and exhilarating manner. There were old gentlemen, trying to make out objects through long telescopes; and young ones, making objects of themselves in open shirt-collars; ladies, carrying about portable chairs, and portable chairs carrying about invalids; parties, waiting on the pier for parties who had come by the steam-boat; and nothing was to be heard but talking, laughing, welcoming, and merriment.

"Fly, sir?" exclaimed a chorus of fourteen men and six boys, the moment Mr. Joseph Tuggs, at the head of his little party, set foot in the street.

"Here's the gen'lm'n at last!" said one, touching his hat with mock politeness. "Werry glad to see you, sir,—been a-waitin' for you these six weeks. Jump in, if you please, sir!"

"Nice light fly and a fast trotter, sir," said another: "fourteen mile a hour, and surroundin' objects rendered inwisible by ex-treme welocity!"

"Large fly for your luggage, sir," cried a third. "Werry large fly here, sir—reg'lar bluebottle!"

"Here's *your* fly, sir!" shouted another aspiring charioteer, mounting the box, and inducing an old grey horse to indulge in some imperfect reminiscences of a canter. "Look at him, sir!—temper of a lamb and haction of a steam-ingein!"

Resisting even the temptation of securing the services of so valuable a quadruped as the last named, Mr. Joseph Tuggs beckoned to the proprietor of a dingy conveyance of a greenish hue, lined with faded striped calico; and, the luggage and the family having been deposited therein, the animal in the shafts, after describing circles in the road for a quarter of an hour, at last consented to depart in quest of lodgings.

"How many beds have you got?" screamed Mrs. Tuggs out of the fly, to the woman who opened the door of the first house which displayed a bill intimating that apartments were to be let within.

"How many did you want, ma'am?" was, of course, the reply.

"Three."

"Will you step in, ma'am?" Down got Mrs. Tuggs. The family were delighted. Splendid view of the sea from the front windows—charming! A short pause. Back came Mrs. Tuggs again.—One parlour and a mattress.

"Why the devil didn't they say so at first?" inquired Mr. Joseph Tuggs, rather pettishly.

"Don't know," said Mrs. Tuggs.

"Wretches!" exclaimed the nervous Cymon. Another bill—another stoppage. Same question—same answer—similar result.

"What do they mean by this?" inquired Mr. Joseph Tuggs, thoroughly out of temper.

"Don't know," said the placid Mrs. Tuggs.

"Orvis the vay here, sir," said the driver, by way of accounting for the circumstance in a satisfactory manner; and off they went again, to make fresh inquiries, and encounter fresh disappointments.

It had grown dusk when the "fly"—the rate of whose progress greatly belied its name—after climbing up four or five perpendicular hills, stopped before the door of a dusty house, with a bay window, from which you could obtain a beautiful glimpse of the sea—if you thrust half of your body out of it, at the imminent peril of falling into the area. Mrs. Tuggs alighted. One ground-floor sitting-room, and three cells with beds in them up stairs. A double house. Family on the opposite side. Five children milk-and-watering in the parlour, and one little boy, expelled for bad behaviour, screaming on his back in the passage.

"What's the terms?" said Mrs. Tuggs. The mistress of the house was considering the expediency of putting on an extra guinea; so, she coughed slightly, and affected not to hear the question.

"What's the terms?" said Mrs. Tuggs, in a louder key.

"Five guineas a week, ma'am, *with* attendance," replied the lodging-house keeper. (Attendance means the privilege of ringing the bell as often as you like, for your own amusement.)

"Rather dear," said Mrs. Tubbs.

"Oh dear, no, ma'am!" replied the mistress of the house, with a benign smile of pity at the ignorance of manners and customs, which the observation betrayed. "Very cheap!"

Such an authority was indisputable. Mrs. Tuggs paid a week's rent in advance, and took the lodgings for a month. In an hour's time, the family were seated at tea in their new abode.

"Capital srimps!" said Mr. Joseph Tuggs.

Mr. Cymon eyed his father with a rebellious scowl, as he emphatically said "*Shrimps.*"

"Well then, shrimps," said Mr. Joseph Tuggs. "Srimps or shrimps, don't much matter."

There was pity, blended with malignity, in Mr. Cymon's eye, as he replied, "Don't matter, father! What would Captain Waters say, if he heard such vulgarity?"

"Or what would dear Mrs. Captain Waters say," added Charlotta, "if she saw mother—ma, I mean—eating them whole, heads and all!"

"It won't bear thinking of!" ejaculated Mr. Cymon, with a shudder. "How different," he thought, "from the Dowager Duchess of Dobbleton!"

"Very pretty woman, Mrs. Captain Waters, is she not, Cymon?" inquired Miss Charlotta.

A glow of nervous excitement passed over the countenance of Mr. Cymon Tuggs, as he replied, "An angel of beauty!"

"Hallo!" said Mr. Joseph Tuggs, "Hallo, Cymon, my boy, take care. Married lady, you know;" and he winked one of his twinkling eyes knowingly.

"Why," exclaimed Cymon, starting up with an ebullition of fury, as unexpected as alarming, "Why am I to be reminded of that blight of my happiness, and ruin of my hopes? Why am I to be taunted with the miseries which are heaped upon my head? Is it not enough to—to—to" and the orator paused; but whether for want of words, or lack of breath, was never distinctly ascertained.

There was an impressive solemnity in the tone of this address, and in the air with which the romantic Cymon, at its conclusion, rang the bell, and demanded a flat candlestick, which effectually forbade a reply. He stalked dramatically to ned, and the Tuggs's went to bed too, half an hour afterwards, in a state of considerable mystification and perplexity.

If the pier had presented a scene of life and bustle to the Tuggs's on their first landing at Ramsgate, it was far surpassed by the appearance of the sands on the morning after their arrival. It was a fine, bright, clear day, with a light breeze from the sea. There were the same ladies and gentlemen, the same children, the same nursemaids, the same telescopes, the same portable chairs. The ladies were employed in needlework, or watch-guard making, or knitting, or reading novels; the gentlemen were reading newspapers and magazines; the children were digging holes in the sand with wooden spades, and collecting water therein; the nursemaids, with their youngest charges in their arms, were running in after the waves, and then running back with the waves after them; and, now and then, a little sailing-boat either departed with a gay and talkative cargo of passengers, or returned with a very silent, and particularly uncomfortable-looking one.

"Well, I never!" exclaimed Mrs. Tuggs, as she and Mr. Joseph Tuggs, and Miss Charlotta Tuggs, and Mr. Cymon Tuggs, with their eight feet in a corresponding number of yellow shoes, seated themselves on four rush-bottomed chairs, which, being placed in a soft part of the sand, forthwith sunk down some two feet and a half—"Well, I never!"

Mr. Cymon, by an exertion of great personal strength, uprooted the chairs, and removed them further back.

"Why, I'm blessed if there ain't some ladies a-going in!" exclaimed Mr. Joseph Tuggs, with intense astonishment.

"Lor, pa!" exclaimed Miss Charlotta.

"There *is*, my dear," said Mr. Joseph Tuggs. And, sure enough, four young ladies, each furnished with a towel, tripped up the steps of a bathing-machine. In went the horse, floundering about in the water; round turned the machine; down sat the driver; and presently out burst the young ladies aforesaid, with four distinct splashes.

"Well, that's sing'ler, too!" ejaculated Mr. Joseph Tuggs, after an awkward pause. Mr. Cymon coughed slightly.

"Why, here's some gentlemen a-going in on this side," exclaimed Mrs. Tuggs, in a tone of horror.

Three machines—three horses—three flounderings—three turnings round—three splashes—three gentlemen, disporting themselves in the water like so many dolphins.

"Well, *that's* sing'ler!" said Mr. Joseph Tuggs again. Miss Charlotta coughed this time, and another pause ensued. It was agreeably broken.

"How d'ye do, dear? We have been looking for you, all the morning," said a voice to Miss Charlotta Tuggs. Mrs. Captain Waters was the owner of it.

"How d'ye do?" said Captain Walter Waters, all suavity; and a most cordial interchange of greetings ensued.

"Belinda, my love," said Captain Walter Waters, applying his glass to his eye, and looking in the direction of the sea.

"Yes, my dear," replied Mrs. Captain Waters.

"There's Harry Thompson!"

"Where?" said Belinda, applying her glass to her eye.

"Bathing."

"Lor, so it is! He don't see us, does he?"

"No, I don't think he does," replied the captain. "Bless my soul, how very singular!"

"What?" inquired Belinda.

"There's Mary Golding, too."

"Lor!—where?" (Up went the glass again.)

"There!" said the captain, pointing to one of the young ladies before noticed, who, in her bathing costume, looked as if she was enveloped in a patent Mackintosh, of scanty dimensions.

"So it is, I declare!" exclaimed Mrs. Captain Waters. "How very curious we should see them both!"

"Very," said the captain, with perfect coolness.

"It's the reg'lar thing here, you see," whispered Mr. Cymon Tuggs to his father.

"I see it is," whispered Mr. Joseph Tuggs in reply. "Queer, though—ain't it?" Mr. Cymon Tuggs nodded assent.

"What do you think of doing with yourself this morning?" inquired the captain. "Shall we lunch at Pegwell?"

"I should like that very much indeed," interposed Mrs. Tuggs. She had never heard of Pegwell; but the word "lunch" had reached her ears, and it sounded very agreeably.

"How shall we go?" inquired the captain; "it's too warm to walk."

"A shay?" suggested Mr. Joseph Tuggs.

"Chaise," whispered Mr. Cymon.

"I should think one would be enough," said Mr. Joseph Tuggs aloud, quite unconscious of the meaning of the correction. "However, two shays if you like."

"I should like a donkey *so* much," said Belinda.

"Oh, so should I!" echoed Charlotta Tuggs.

"Well, we can have a fly," suggested the captain, "and you can have a couple of donkeys."

A fresh difficulty arose. Mrs. Captain Waters declared it would be decidedly improper for two ladies to ride alone. The remedy was obvious. Perhaps young Mr. Tuggs would be gallant enough to accompany them.

Mr. Cymon Tuggs blushed, smiled, looked vacant, and faintly protested that he was no horseman. The objection was at once overruled. A fly was speedily found; and three donkeys—which the proprietor declared on his solemn asseveration to be "three parts blood, and the other corn"—were engaged in the service.

"Kim up!" shouted one of the two boys who followed behind, to propel the donkeys, when Belinda Waters and Charlotta Tuggs had been hoisted, and pushed, and pulled, into their respective saddles.

"Hi—hi—hi!" groaned the other boy behind Mr. Cymon Tuggs. Away went the donkey, with the stirrups jingling against the heels of Cymon's boots, and Cymon's boots nearly scraping the ground.

"Way—way! Wo—o—o—o—!" cried Mr. Cymon Tuggs as well as he could, in the midst of the jolting.

"Don't make it gallop!" screamed Mrs. Captain Waters, behind.

"My donkey *will* go into the public-house!" shrieked Miss Tuggs in the rear.

"Hi—hi—hi!" groaned both the boys together; and on went the donkeys as if nothing would ever stop them.

Everything has an end, however; even the galloping of donkeys will cease in time. The animal which Mr. Cymon Tuggs bestrode, feeling sundry uncomfortable tugs at the bit, the intent of which he could by no means divine, abruptly sidled against a brick wall, and expressed his uneasiness by grinding Mr. Cymon Tuggs's leg on the rough surface. Mrs. Captain Waters's donkey, apparently under the influence of some playfulness of spirit, rushed suddenly, head first, into a hedge, and declined to come out again: and the quadruped on which Miss Tuggs was mounted, expressed his delight at this humorous proceeding by firmly planting his fore-feet against the ground, and kicking up his hind-legs in a very agile, but somewhat alarming manner.

THE TUGGSES AT RAMSGATE.

This abrupt termination to the rapidity of the ride, naturally occasioned some confusion. Both the ladies indulged in vehement screaming for several minutes; and Mr. Cymon Tuggs, besides sustaining intense bodily pain, had the additional mental anguish of witnessing their distressing situation, without having the power to rescue them, by reason of his leg being firmly screwed in between the animal and the wall. The efforts of the boys, however, assisted by the ingenious expedient of twisting the tail of the most rebellious donkey, restored order in a much shorter time than could have reasonably been expected, and the little party jogged slowly on together.

"Now let 'em walk," said Mr. Cymon Tuggs. "It's cruel to overdrive 'em."

"Werry well, sir," replied the boy, with a grin at his companion, as if he understood Mr. Cymon to mean that the cruelty applied less to the animals than to their riders.

"What a lovely day, dear!" said Charlotta.

"Charming; enchanting, dear!" responded Mrs. Captain Waters. "What a beautiful prospect, Mr. Tuggs!"

Cymon looked full in Belinda's face, as he responded—"Beautiful, indeed!" The lady cast down her eyes, and suffered the animal she was riding to fall a little back. Cymon Tuggs instinctively did the same.

There was a brief silence, broken only by a sigh from Mr. Cymon Tuggs.

"Mr. Cymon," said the lady suddenly, in a low tone, "Mr. Cymon—I am another's."

Mr. Cymon expressed his perfect concurrence in a statement which it was impossible to controvert.

"If I had not been—" resumed Belinda; and there she stopped.

"What—what?" said Mr. Cymon earnestly. "Do not torture me. What would you say?"

"If I had not been"—continued Mrs. Captain Waters—"if, in earlier life, it had been my fate to have known, and been beloved by, a noble youth—a kindred soul—a congenial spirit—one capable of feeling and appreciating the sentiments which—"

"Heavens! what do I hear?" exclaimed Mr. Cymon Tuggs. "Is it possible! can I believe my—Come up!" (This last unsentimental parenthesis was addressed to the donkey, who with his head between his fore-legs, appeared to be examining the state of his shoes with great anxiety.)

"Hi—hi—hi," said the boys behind. "Come up," expostulated Cymon Tuggs again. "Hi—hi—hi," repeated the boys. And whether it was that the animal felt indignant at the tone of Mr. Tuggs's command, or felt alarmed by the noise of the deputy proprietor's boots running behind him; or whether he burned with a noble emulation to outstrip the other donkeys; certain it is that he no sooner heard the second series of "hi—hi's," than he started away, with a celerity of pace which jerked Mr. Cymon's hat off, instantaneously, and carried him to the Pegwell Bay hotel in no time, where he deposited his rider without giving him the trouble of dismounting, by sagaciously pitching him over his head, into the very doorway of the tavern.

Great was the confusion of Mr. Cymon Tuggs, when he was put, right end uppermost, by two waiters; considerable was the alarm of Mrs. Tuggs in behalf of her son; agonizing were the apprehensions of Mrs. Captain Waters on his account. It was speedily discovered, however, that he had not sustained much more injury than the donkey—he was grazed, and the animal was grazing—and then it *was* a delightful party to be sure! Mr. and Mrs. Tuggs, and the captain, had ordered lunch in the little garden behind:—small saucers of large shrimps, dabs of butter, crusty loaves, and bottled ale. The sky was without a cloud;

there were flower-pots and turf before them; the sea, from the foot of the cliff, stretching away as far as the eye could discern anything at all; vessels in the distance with sails as white, and as small, as nicely-got-up cambric handkerchiefs. The shrimps were delightful, the ale better, and the captain even more pleasant than either. Mrs. Captain Waters was in *such* spirits after lunch!—chasing, first the captain across the turf, and among the flower-pots; and then Mr. Cymon Tuggs; and then Miss Tuggs; and laughing, too, quite boisterously. But as the captain said, it didn't matter; who knew what they were, there? For all the people of the house knew, they might be common people. To which Mr. Joseph Tuggs responded, "To be sure." And then they went down the steep wooden steps a little further on, which led to the bottom of the cliff; and looked at the crabs, and the seaweed, and the eels, till it was more than fully time to go back to Ramsgate again. Finally, Mr. Cymon Tuggs ascended the steps last, and Mrs. Captain Waters last but one; and Mr. Cymon Tuggs discovered that the foot and ankle of Mrs. Captain Waters, were even more unexceptionable than he had at first supposed.

Taking a donkey towards his ordinary place of residence, is a very different thing, and a feat much more easily to be accomplished, than taking him from it. It requires a great deal of foresight and presence of mind in the one case, to anticipate the numerous flights of his discursive imagination; whereas, in the other, all you have to do, is, to hold on, and place a blind confidence in the animal. Mr. Cymon Tuggs adopted the latter expedient on his return; and his nerves were so little discomposed by the journey, that he distinctly understood they were all to meet again at the library in the evening.

The library was crowded. There were the same ladies, and the same gentlemen, who had been on the sands in the morning, and on the pier the day before. There were young ladies, in maroon-coloured gowns and black velvet bracelets, dispensing fancy articles in the shop, and presiding over games of chance in the concert-room. There were marriageable daughters, and marriage-making mammas, gaming and promenading, and turning over music, and flirting. There were some male beaux doing the sentimental in whispers, and others doing the ferocious in moustache. There were Mrs. Tuggs in amber, Miss Tuggs in sky-blue, Mrs. Captain Waters in pink. There was Captain Waters in a braided surtout; there was Mr. Cymon Tuggs in pumps and a gilt waistcoat; there was Mr. Joseph Tuggs in a blue coat, and a shirt-frill.

"Numbers three, eight, and eleven!" cried one of the young ladies in the maroon-coloured gowns.

"Numbers three, eight, and eleven!" echoed another young lady in the same uniform.

"Number three's gone," said the first young lady. "Numbers eight and eleven!"

"Numbers eight and eleven!" echoed the second young lady.

"Number eight's gone, Mary Ann," said the first young lady.

"Number eleven!" screamed the second.

"The numbers are all taken now, ladies, if you please," said the first. The representatives of numbers three, eight, and eleven, and the rest of the numbers, crowded round the table.

"Will you throw, ma'am?" said the presiding goddess, handing the dice-box to the eldest daughter of a stout lady, with four girls.

There was a profound silence among the lookers on.

"Throw, Jane, my dear," said the stout lady. An interesting display of bashfulness—a little blushing in a cambric handkerchief—a whispering to a younger sister.

"Amelia, my dear, throw for your sister," said the stout lady; and then she turned to a walking advertisement of Rowlands' Macassar Oil, who stood next her, and said, "Jane is so *very* modest and retiring; but I can't be angry with her for it. An artless and unsophisticated girl is *so* truly amiable, that I often wish Amelia was more like her sister!"

The gentleman with the whiskers whispered his admiring approval.

"Now, my dear!" said the stout lady. Miss Amelia threw—eight for her sister, ten for herself.

"Nice figure, Amelia," whispered the stout lady to a thin youth beside her.

"Beautiful!"

"And *such* a spirit! I am like you in that respect. I can *not* help admiring that life and vivacity. Ah! (a sigh) I wish I could make poor Jane a little more like my dear Amelia!"

The young gentleman cordially acquiesced in the sentiment; both he, and the individual first addressed, were perfectly contented.

"Who's this?" inquired Mr. Cymon Tuggs of Mrs. Captain Waters, as a short female, in a blue velvet hat and feathers, was led into the orchestra, by a fat man in black tights and cloudy Berlins.

"Mrs. Tippin, of the London theatres," replied Belinda, referring to the programme of the concert.

The talented Tippin having condescendingly acknowledged the clapping of hands, and shouts of "bravo!" which greeted her appearance, proceeded to sing the popular cavatina of "Bid me discourse," accompanied on the piano by Mr. Tippin; after which, Mr. Tippin sang a comic song, accompanied on the piano by Mrs. Tippin: the applause consequent upon which, was only to be exceeded by the enthusiastic approbation bestowed upon an air with variations on the guitar, by Miss Tippin, accompanied on the chin by Master Tippin.

Thus passed the evening; thus passed the days and evenings of the Tuggs's, and the Waters's, for six weeks. Sands in the morning—donkeys at noon—pier in the afternoon—library at night—and the same people everywhere.

On that very night six weeks, the moon was shining brightly over the calm sea, which dashed against the feet of the tall gaunt cliffs, with just enough noise to lull the old fish to sleep, without disturbing the young ones, when two figures were discernible—or would have been, if anybody had looked for them—seated on one of the wooden benches which are stationed near the verge of the western cliff. The moon had climbed higher into the heavens, by two hours' journeying, since those figures first sat down—and yet they had moved not. The crowd of loungers had thinned and dispersed; the noise of itinerant musicians had died away; light after light had appeared in the windows of the different houses in the distance; blockade-man after blockade-man had passed the spot, wending his way towards his solitary post; and yet those figures had remained stationary. Some portions of the two forms were in deep shadow, but the light of the moon fell strongly on a puce-coloured boot and a glazed stock. Mr. Cymon Tuggs and Mrs. Captain Waters were seated on that bench. They spoke not, but were silently gazing on the sea.

"Walter will return to-morrow," said Mrs. Captain Waters, mournfully breaking silence.

Mr. Cymon Tuggs sighed like a gust of wind through a forest of gooseberry bushes, as he replied, "Alas! he will."

"Oh, Cymon!" resumed Belinda, "the chaste delight, the calm happiness, of this one week of Platonic love, is too much for me!"

Cymon was about to suggest that it was too little for him, but he stopped himself, and murmured unintelligibly.

"And to think that even this gleam of happiness, innocent as it is," exclaimed Belinda, "is now to be lost for ever!"

"Oh, do not say for ever, Belinda," exclaimed the excitable Cymon, as two strongly-defined tears chased each other down his pale face—it was so long that there was plenty of room for a chase—"Do not say for ever!"

"I must," replied Belinda.

"Why?" urged Cymon, "oh why? Such Platonic acquaintance as ours is so harmless, that even your husband can never object to it."

"My husband!" exclaimed Belinda. "You little know him. Jealous and revengeful; ferocious in his revenge—a maniac in his jealousy! Would you be assassinated before my eyes?" Mr. Cymon Tuggs, in a voice broken by emotion, expressed his disinclination to undergo the process of assassination before the eyes of anybody.

"Then leave me," said Mrs. Captain Waters. "Leave me, this night, for ever. It is late: let us return."

Mr. Cymon Tuggs sadly offered the lady his arm, and escorted her to her lodgings. He paused at the door—he felt a Platonic pressure of his hand. "Good night," he said, hesitating.

"Good night," sobbed the lady. Mr. Cymon Tuggs paused again.

"Won't you walk in, sir?" said the servant. Mr. Tuggs hesitated. Oh, that hesitation! He *did* walk in.

"Good night!" said Mr. Cymon Tuggs again, when he reached the drawing-room.

"Good night!" replied Belinda; "and, if at any period of my life, I—Hush!" The lady paused and stared with a steady gaze of horror, on the ashy countenance of Mr. Cymon Tuggs. There was a double knock at the street-door.

"It is my husband!" said Belinda, as the captain's voice was heard below.

"And my family!" added Cymon Tuggs, as the voices of his relatives floated up the staircase.

"The curtain! The curtain!" gasped Mrs. Captain Waters, pointing to the window, before which some chintz hangings were closely drawn.

"But I have done nothing wrong," said the hesitating Cymon.

"The curtain!" reiterated the frantic lady: "you will be murdered." This last appeal to his feelings was irresistible. The dismayed Cymon concealed himself behind the curtain with pantomimic suddenness.

Enter the captain, Joseph Tuggs, Mrs. Tuggs, and Charlotta.

"My dear," said the captain, "Lieutenant Slaughter." Two iron-shod boots and one gruff voice were heard by Mr. Cymon to advance, and acknowledge the honour of the introduction. The sabre of the lieutenant rattled heavily upon the floor, as he seated himself at the table. Mr. Cymon's fears almost overcame his reason.

"The brandy, my dear!" said the captain. Here was a situation! They were going to make a night of it! And Mr. Cymon Tuggs was pent up behind the curtain and afraid to breathe!

"Slaughter," said the captain, "a cigar?"

Now, Mr. Cymon Tuggs never could smoke without feeling it indispensably necessary to retire, immediately, and never could smell smoke without a strong disposition to cough. The cigars were introduced; the captain was a professed smoker; so was the lieutenant; so was Joseph Tuggs. The apartment was small, the door was closed, the smoke powerful: it hung in heavy wreathes over the room, and at length found its way behind the curtain. Cymon Tuggs held his nose, his mouth, his breath. It was all of no use—out came the cough.

"Bless my soul!" said the captain, "I beg your pardon, Miss Tuggs. You dislike smoking?"

"Oh, no; I don't indeed," said Charlotta.

"It makes you cough."

"Oh dear no."

"You coughed just now."

"Me, Captain Waters! Lor! how can you say so?"

"Somebody coughed," said the captain.

"I certainly thought so," said Slaughter. No; everybody denied it.

"Fancy," said the captain.

"Must be," echoed Slaughter.

Cigars resumed—more smoke—another cough—smothered, but violent.

"Damned odd!" said the captain, staring about him.

"Sing'ler!" ejaculated the unconscious Mr. Joseph Tuggs.

Lieutenant Slaughter looked first at one person mysteriously, then at another: then, laid down his cigar, then approached the window on tiptoe, and pointed with his right thumb over his shoulder, in the direction of the curtain.

"Slaughter!" ejaculated the captain, rising from table, "what do you mean?"

The lieutenant, in reply, drew back the curtain and discovered Mr. Cymon Tuggs behind it: pallid with apprehension, and blue with wanting to cough.

"Aha!" exclaimed the captain, furiously, "What do I see? Slaughter, your sabre!"

"Cymon!" screamed the Tuggs's.

"Mercy!" said Belinda.

"Platonic!" gasped Cymon.

"Your sabre!" roared the captain: "Slaughter—unhand me—the villain's life!"

"Murder!" screamed the Tuggs's.

"Hold him fast, sir!" faintly articulated Cymon.

"Water!" exclaimed Joseph Tuggs—and Mr. Cymon Tuggs and all the ladies forthwith fainted away, and formed a tableau.

Most willingly would we conceal the disastrous termination of the six weeks' acquaintance. A troublesome form, and an arbitrary custom, however, prescribe that a story should have a conclusion, in addition to a commencement; we have therefore no alternative. Lieutenant Slaughter brought a message—the captain brought an action. Mr. Joseph Tuggs interposed—the lieutenant negociated. When Mr. Cymon Tuggs recovered from the nervous disorder into which misplaced affection, and exciting circumstances, had plunged him, he found that his family had lost their pleasant acquaintance; that his father was minus fifteen hundred pounds; and the captain plus the precise sum. The money was paid to hush the matter up, but it got abroad notwithstanding; and there are not wanting some who affirm that three designing impostors never found more easy dupes, than did Captain Waters, Mrs. Waters, and Lieutenant Slaughter, in the Tuggs's at Ramsgate.

CHAPTER V.

HORATIO SPARKINS.

"INDEED, my love, he paid Teresa very great attention on the last assembly night," said Mrs. Malderton, addressing her spouse, who, after the fatigues of the day in the City, was sitting with a silk handkerchief over his head, and his feet on the fender, drinking his port;—"very great attention; and I say again, every possible encouragement ought to be given him. He positively must be asked down here to dine."

"Who must?" inquired Mr. Malderton.

"Why, you know whom I mean, my dear—the young man with the black whiskers and the white cravat, who has just come out at our assembly, and whom all the girls are talking about. Young—— dear me! what's his name?—Marianne, what *is* his name?" continued Mrs. Malderton, addressing her youngest daughter, who was engaged in netting a purse, and looking sentimental.

"Mr. Horatio Sparkins, ma," replied Miss Marianne, with a sigh.

"Oh! yes, to be sure—Horatio Sparkins," said Mrs. Malderton. "Decidedly the most gentleman-like young man I ever saw. I am sure in the beautifully-made coat he wore the other night, he looked like—like——"

"Like Prince Leopold, ma—so noble, so full of sentiment!" suggested Marianne, in a tone of enthusiastic admiration.

"You should recollect, my dear," resumed Mrs. Malderton, "that Teresa is now eight-and-twenty; and that it really is very important that something should be done."

Miss Teresa Malderton was a very little girl, rather fat, with vermillion cheeks, but good-humoured, and still disengaged, although, to do her justice, the misfortune arose from no lack of perseverance on her part. In vain had she flirted for ten years; in vain had Mr. and Mrs. Malderton assiduously kept up an extensive acquaintance among the young eligible bachelors of Camberwell, and even of Wandsworth and Brixton; to say nothing of those who "dropped in" from town. Miss Malderton was as well known as the lion on the top of Northumberland House, and had an equal chance of "going off."

"I am quite sure you'd like him," continued Mrs. Malderton, "he is so gentlemanly!"

"So clever!" said Miss Marianne.

"And has such a flow of language!" added Miss Teresa.

"He has a great respect for you, my dear," said Mrs. Malderton to her husband. Mr. Malderton coughed, and looked at the fire.

"Yes, I'm sure he's very much attached to pa's society," said Miss Marianne.

"No doubt of it," echoed Miss Teresa.

"Indeed, he said as much to me in confidence," observed Mrs. Malderton.

"Well, well," returned Mr. Malderton, somewhat flattered; "if I see him at the assembly to-morrow, perhaps I'll ask him down. I hope he knows we live at Oak Lodge, Camberwell, my dear?"

"Of course—and that you keep a one-horse carriage."

"I'll see about it," said Mr. Malderton, composing himself for a nap; "I'll see about it."

Mr. Malderton was a man whose whole scope of ideas was limited to Lloyd's, the Exchange, the India House, and the Bank. A few successful speculations had raised him from a situation of obscurity and comparative poverty, to a state of affluence. As frequently happens in such cases, the ideas of himself and his family became elevated to an extraordinary pitch as their means increased; they affected fashion, taste, and many other fooleries, in imitation of their betters, and had a very decided and becoming horror of anything which could, by possibility, be considered *low*. He was hospitable from ostentation, illiberal from ignorance, and prejudiced from conceit. Egotism and the love of display induced him to keep an excellent table: convenience, and a love of good things of this life, ensured him plenty of guests. He liked to have clever men, or what he considered such, at his table, because it was a great thing to talk about; but he never could endure what he called "sharp fellows." Probably, he cherished this feeling out of compliment to his two sons, who gave their respected parent no uneasiness in that particular. The family were ambitious of forming acquaintances and connexions in some sphere of society superior to that in which they themselves moved; and one of the necessary consequences of this desire, added to their utter ignorance of the world beyond their own small circle, was, that any one who could lay claim to an acquaintance with people of rank and title, had a sure passport to the table at Oak Lodge, Camberwell.

The appearance of Mr. Horatio Sparkins at the assembly, had excited no small degree of surprise and curiosity among its regular frequenters. Who could he be? He was evidently reserved, and apparently melancholy. Was he a clergyman?—He danced too well. A barrister?—he said he was not called. He used very fine words, and talked a great deal. Could he be a distinguished foreigner, come to England for the purpose of describing the country, its manners and customs; and frequenting public balls and public dinners, with the view of becoming acquainted with high life, polished etiquette, and English refinement?—No, he had not a foreign accent. Was he a surgeon, a contributor to the magazines, a writer of fashionable novels, or an artist?—No; to each and all of these surmises, there existed some valid objection.—"Then," said everybody, "he must be *somebody*."—"I should think he must be," reasoned Mr. Malderton, within himself, "because he perceives our superiority, and pays us so much attention."

The night succeeding the conversation we have just recorded, was "assembly night." The double-fly was ordered to be at the door of Oak Lodge at nine o'clock precisely. The Miss Maldertons were dressed in sky-blue satin trimmed with artificial flowers; and Mrs. M. (who was a little fat woman), in ditto ditto, looked like her eldest daughter multiplied by two. Mr. Frederick Malderton, the eldest son, in full-dress costume, was the very *beau ideal* of a smart waiter; and Mr. Thomas Malderton, the youngest, with his white dress-stock, blue coat, bright buttons, and red watch-ribbon, strongly resembled the portrait of that interesting, but rash young gentleman, George Barnwell. Every member of the party had made up his or her mind to cultivate the acquaintance of Mr. Horatio Sparkins. Miss Teresa, of course, was to be as amiable and interesting as ladies of eight-and-twenty on the look-out for a husband, usually are. Mrs. Malderton would be all smiles and graces. Miss Marianne would request the favour of some verses for her album. Mr. Malderton would patronise the great unknown by asking him to dinner. Tom intended to ascertain the extent of his information on the interesting topics of snuff and cigars. Even Mr. Frederick Malderton himself, the family authority on all points of taste, dress, and fashionable arrangement; who had lodgings of his own in town; who had a free admission to Covent-garden theatre; who always dressed according to the fashions of the months; who went up the water twice a-week in the season; and who actually had an intimate friend who once knew a gentleman who formerly lived in the Albany,—even he had determined that Mr. Horatio Sparkins must be a devilish good fellow, and that he would do him the honour of challenging him to a game at billiards.

The first object that met the anxious eyes of the expectant family on their entrance into the ball-room, was the interesting Horatio, with his hair brushed off his forehead, and his eyes fixed on the ceiling, reclining in a contemplative attitude on one of the seats.

"There he is, my dear," whispered Mrs. Malderton to Mr. Malderton.

"How like Lord Byron!" murmured Miss Teresa.

"Or Montgomery!" whispered Miss Marianne.

"Or the portraits of Captain Cook!" suggested Tom.

"Tom—don't be an ass!" said his father, who checked him on all occasions, probably with a view to prevent his becoming "sharp"—which was very unnecessary

The elegant Sparkins attitudinised with admirable effect, until the family had crossed the room. He then started up, with the most natural appearance of surprise and delight; accosted Mrs. Malderton with the utmost cordiality; saluted the young ladies in the most enchanting manner; bowed to, and shook hands with, Mr. Malderton, with a degree of respect amounting almost to veneration; and returned the greetings of the two young men in a half-gratified, half-patronising manner, which fully convinced them that he must be an important, and, at the same time, condescending personage.

"Miss Malderton," said Horatio, after the ordinary salutations, and bowing very low, "may I be permitted to presume to hope that you will allow me to have the pleasure——"

"I don't *think* I am engaged," said Miss Teresa, with a dreadful affectation of indifference—"but, really—so many——"

Horatio looked handsomely miserable.

"I shall be most happy," simpered the interesting Teresa, at last. Horatio's countenance brightened up, like an old hat in a shower of rain.

"A very genteel young man, certainly!" said the gratified Mr. Malderton, as the obsequious Sparkins and his partner joined the quadrille which was just forming.

"He has a remarkably good address," said Mr. Frederick.

"Yes, he is a prime fellow," interposed Tom, who always managed to put his foot in it—"he talks just like an auctioneer."

"Tom!" said his father solemnly, "I think I desired you, before, not to be a fool." Tom looked as happy as a cock on a drizzly morning.

"How delightful!" said the interesting Horatio to his partner, as they promenaded the room at the conclusion of the set—"how delightful, how refreshing it is, to retire from the cloudy storms, the vicissitudes, and the troubles, of life, even if it be but for a few short fleeting moments: and to spend those moments, fading and evanescent though they be, in the delightful, the blessed society of one individual—whose frowns would be death, whose coldness would be madness, whose falsehood would be ruin, whose constancy would be bliss; the possession of whose affection would be the brightest and best reward that Heaven could bestow on man?"

"What feeling! what sentiment!" thought Miss Teresa, as she leaned more heavily on her companion's arm.

"But enough—enough!" resumed the elegant Sparkins, with a theatrical air. "What have I said? what have I—I—to do with sentiments like these! Miss Malderton—" here he stopped short—"may I hope to be permitted to offer the humble tribute of——"

"Really, Mr. Sparkins," returned the enraptured Teresa, blushing in the sweetest confusion, "I must refer you to papa. I never can, without his consent, venture to—"

"Surely he cannot object—"

"Oh, yes. Indeed, indeed, you know him not!" interrupted Miss Teresa, well knowing there was nothing to fear, but wishing to make the interview resemble a scene in some romantic novel.

"He cannot object to my offering you a glass of negus," returned the adorable Sparkins, with some surprise.

"Is that all?" thought the disappointed Teresa. "What a fuss about nothing!"

"It will give me the greatest pleasure, sir, to see you to dinner at Oak Lodge, Camberwell, on Sunday next at five o'clock, if you have no better engagement," said Mr. Malderton, at the conclusion of the evening, as he and his sons were standing in conversation with Mr. Horatio Sparkins.

Horatio bowed his acknowledgments, and accepted the flattering invitation.

"I must confess," continued the father, offering his snuff-box to his new acquaintance, "that I don't enjoy these assemblies half so much as the comfort—I had almost said the luxury—of Oak Lodge. They have no great charms for an elderly man."

"And after all, sir, what is man?" said the metaphysical Sparkins. "I say, what is man?"

"Ah! very true," said Mr. Malderton; "very true."

"We know that we live and breathe," continued Horatio; "that we have wants and wishes, desires and appetites—"

"Certainly," said Mr. Frederick Malderton, looking profound.

"I say, we know that we exist," repeated Horatio, raising his voice, "but there we stop; there, is an end to our knowledge; there, is the summit of our attainments; there, is the termination of our ends. What more do we know?"

"Nothing," replied Mr. Frederick—than whom no one was more capable of answering for himself in that particular. Tom was about to hazard something, but, fortunately for his reputation, he caught his father's angry eye, and slunk off like a puppy convicted of petty larceny.

"Upon my word," said Mr. Malderton the elder, as they were returning home in the fly, "that Mr. Sparkins is a wonderful young man. Such surprising knowledge! such extraordinary information! and such a splendid mode of expressing himself!"

"I think he must be somebody in disguise," said Miss Marianne. "How charmingly romantic!"

"He talks very loud and nicely," timidly observed Tom, "but I don't exactly understand what he means."

"I almost begin to despair of *your* understanding anything, Tom," said his father, who, of course, had been much enlightened by Mr. Horatio Sparkins's conversation.

"It strikes me, Tom," said Miss Teresa, "that you have made yourself very ridiculous this evening."

"No doubt of it," cried everybody—and the unfortunate Tom reduced himself into the least possible space. That night, Mr. and Mrs. Malderton had a long conversation respecting their daughter's prospects and future arrangements. Miss Teresa went to bed, considering whether, in the event of her marrying a title, she could conscientiously encourage the visits of her present associates, and dreamed, all night, of disguised noblemen, large routs, ostrich plumes, bridal favours, and Horatio Sparkins.

Various surmises were hazarded on the Sunday morning, as to the mode of conveyance which the anxiously-expected Horatio would adopt. Did he keep a gig?—was it possible he could come on horseback?—or would he patronize the stage? These, and other various conjectures of equal importance, engrossed the attention of Mrs. Malderton and her daughters during the whole morning after church.

"Upon my word, my dear, it 's a most annoying thing that that vulgar brother of yours should have invited himself to dine here to-day," said Mr. Malderton to his wife. "On account of Mr. Sparkins's coming down, I purposely abstained from asking any one but Flamwell. And then to think of your brother—a tradesman—it 's insufferable! I declare I wouldn't have him mention his shop, before our new guest—no, not for a thousand pounds! I wouldn't care if he had the good sense to conceal the disgrace he is to the family; but he 's so fond of his horrible business, that he *will* let people know what he is."

Mr. Jacob Barton, the individual alluded to, was a large grocer; so vulgar, and so lost to all sense of feeling, that he actually never scrupled to avow that he wasn't above his business: "he'd made his money by it, and he didn't care who know'd it."

"Ah! Flamwell, my dear fellow, how d'ye do?" said Mr. Malderton, as a little spoffish man, with green spectacles, entered the room. "You got my note?"

"Yes, I did; and here I am in consequence."

"You don't happen to know this Mr. Sparkins by name? You know everybody?"

Mr. Flamwell was one of those gentlemen of remarkably extensive information whom one occasionally meets in society, who pretend to know everybody, but in reality know nobody. At Malderton's, where any stories about great people were received with a greedy ear, he was an especial favourite; and, knowing the kind of people he had to deal with, he carried his passion of claiming acquaintance with everybody, to the most immoderate length. He had rather a singular way of telling his greatest lies in a parenthesis, and with an air of self-denial, as if he feared being thought egotistical.

"Why, no, I don't know him by that name," returned Flamwell, in a low tone, and with an air of immense importance. "I have no doubt I know him, though. Is he tall?"

"Middle sized," said Miss Teresa.

"With black hair?" inquired Flamwell, hazarding a bold guess.

"Yes," returned Miss Teresa, eagerly.

"Rather a snub nose?"

"No," said the disappointed Teresa, "he has a Roman nose."

"I said a Roman nose, didn't I?" inquired Flamwell. "He's an elegant young man?"

"Oh, certainly."

"With remarkably prepossessing manners?"

"Oh, yes!" said all the family together. "You must know him."

"Yes, I thought you knew him, if he was anybody," triumphantly exclaimed Mr. Malderton. "Who d'ye think he is?"

"Why, from your description," said Flamwell, ruminating, and sinking his voice, almost to a whisper, "he bears a strong resemblance to the Honourable Augustus Fitz-Edward Fitz-John Fitz-Osborne. He 's a very talented young man, and rather eccentric. It's extremely probable he may have changed his name for some temporary purpose."

Teresa's heart beat high. Could he be the Honourable Augustus Fitz-Edward Fitz-John Fitz-Osborne! What a name to be elegantly engraved upon two glazed cards, tied together with a piece of white satin ribbon! "The Honourable Mrs. Augustus Fitz-Edward Fitz-John Fitz-Osborne!" The thought was transport.

"It's five minutes to five," said Mr. Malderton, looking at his watch: "I hope he's not going to disappoint us."

"There he is!" exclaimed Miss Teresa, as a loud double-knock was heard at the door. Everybody endeavoured to look—as people when they particularly expect a visitor always do—as if they were perfectly unsuspicious of the approach of anybody.

The room-door opened—"Mr. Barton!" said the servant.

"Confound the man!" murmured Malderton. "Ah! my dear sir, how d'ye do! Any news?"

"Why no," returned the grocer, in his usual bluff manner. "No, none partickler. None that I am much aware of. How d'ye do, gals and boys? Mr. Flamwell, sir—glad to see you."

"Here's Mr. Sparkins!" said Tom, who had been looking out at the window, "on *such* a black horse!" There was Horatio, sure enough, on a large black horse, curvetting and prancing along, like an Astley's supernumerary. After a great deal of reining in, and pulling up, with the accompaniments of snorting, rearing, and kicking, the animal consented to stop at about a hundred yards from the gate, where Mr. Sparkins dismounted, and confided him to the care of Mr. Malderton's groom. The ceremony of introduction was gone through, in all due form. Mr. Flamwell looked from behind his green spectacles at Horatio with an air of mysterious importance; and the gallant Horatio looked unutterable things at Teresa.

"Is he the Honourable Mr. Augustus what's his name?" whispered Mrs. Malderton to Flamwell, as he was escorting her to the dining-room.

"Why, no—at least not exactly," returned that great authority—"not exactly."

"Who *is* he then?"

"Hush!" said Flamwell, nodding his head with a grave air, importing that he knew very well; but was prevented, by some grave reasons of state, from disclosing the important secret. It might be one of the ministers making himself acquainted with the views of the people.

"Mr. Sparkins," said the delighted Mrs. Malderton, "pray divide the ladies. John, put a chair for the gentleman between Miss Teresa and Miss Marianne." This was addressed to a man who, on ordinary occasions, acted as half-groom, half-gardener; but who, as it was important to make an impression on Mr. Sparkins, had been forced into a white neckerchief and shoes, and touched up, and brushed, to look like a second footman.

The dinner was excellent; Horatio was most attentive to Miss Teresa, and every one felt in high spirits, except Mr. Malderton, who, knowing the propensity of his brother-in-law, Mr. Barton, endured that sort of agony which the newspapers inform us is experienced by the surrounding neighbourhood when a pot-boy hangs himself in a hay-loft, and which is "much easier to be imagined than described."

"Have you seen your friend, Sir Thomas Noland, lately, Flamwell?" inquired Mr. Malderton, casting a sidelong look at Horatio, to see what effect the mention of so great a man had upon him.

"Why, no—not very lately. I saw Lord Gubbleton the day before yesterday."

"Ah! I hope his lordship is very well?" said Malderton, in a tone of the greatest interest. It is scarcely necessary to say that, until that moment, he had been quite innocent of the existence of such a person.

"Why, yes; he was very well—very well indeed. He's a devilish good fellow. I met him in the City, and had a long chat with him. Indeed, I'm rather intimate with him. I couldn't stop to talk to him as long as I could wish, though, because I was on my way to a banker's, a very rich man, and a member of Parliament, with whom I am also rather, indeed I may say very, intimate."

"I know whom you mean," returned the host, consequentially—in reality knowing as much about the matter as Flamwell himself. "He has a capital business."

This was touching on a dangerous topic.

"Talking of business," interposed Mr. Barton, from the centre of the table. "A gentleman whom you knew very well, Malderton, before you made that first lucky spec of yours, called at our shop the other day, and—"

"Barton, may I trouble you for a potato," interrupted the wretched master of the house, hoping to nip the story in the bud.

"Certainly," returned the grocer, quite insensible of his brother-in-law's object—"and he said in a very plain manner——"

"*Floury*, if you please," interrupted Malderton again; dreading the termination of the anecdote, and fearing a repetition of the word "shop."

"He said, says he," continued the culprit, after despatching the potato; "says he, how goes on your business? So I said, jokingly—you know my way—says I, I'm never above my business, and I hope my business will never be above me. Ha, ha!"

"Mr. Sparkins," said the host, vainly endeavouring to conceal his dismay, "a glass of wine?"

"With the utmost pleasure, sir."

"Happy to see you."

"Thank you."

"We were talking the other evening," resumed the host, addressing Horatio, partly with the view of displaying the conversational powers of his new acquaintance, and partly in the hope of drowning the grocer's stories—"we were talking the other night about the nature of man. Your argument struck me very forcibly."

"And me," said Mr. Frederick. Horatio made a graceful inclination of the head.

"Pray, what is your opinion of woman, Mr. Sparkins?" inquired Mrs. Malderton. The young ladies simpered.

"Man," replied Horatio, "man, whether he ranged the bright, gay, flowery, plains of a second Eden, or the more sterile, barren, and I may say, commonplace regions, to which we are compelled to accustom ourselves, in times such as these; man, under any circumstances, or in any place—whether he were bending beneath the withering blasts of the frigid zone, or scorching under the rays of a vertical sun—man, without woman, would be—alone."

"I am very happy to find you entertain such honourable opinions, Mr. Sparkins," said Mrs. Malderton.

"And I," added Miss Teresa. Horatio looked his delight, and the young lady blushed.

"Now, it's my opinion," said Mr. Barton——

"I know what you're going to say," interposed Malderton, determined not to give his relation another opportunity, "and I don't agree with you."

"What!" inquired the astonished grocer.

"I am sorry to differ from you, Barton," said the host, in as positive a manner as if he really were contradicting a position which the other had laid down, "but I cannot give my assent to what I consider a very monstrous proposition."

"But I meant to say—"

"You never can convince me," said Malderton, with an air of obstinate determination. "Never."

"And I," said Mr. Frederick, following up his father's attack, "cannot entirely agree in Mr. Sparkins's argument."

"What!" said Horatio, who became more metaphysical, and more argumentative, as he saw the female part of the family listening in wondering delight—"what! Is effect the consequence of cause? Is cause the precursor of effect?"

"That's the point," said Flamwell.

"To be sure," said Mr. Malderton.

"Because, if effect is the consequence of cause, and if cause does precede effect, I apprehend you are wrong," added Horatio.

"Decidedly," said the toad-eating Flamwell.

"At least, I apprehend that to be the just and logical deduction?" said Sparkins, in a tone of interrogation.

"No doubt of it," chimed in Flamwell again. "It settles the point."

"Well, perhaps it does," said Mr. Frederick; "I didn't see it before."

"I don't exactly see it now," thought the grocer; "but I suppose it's all right."

"How wonderfully clever he is!" whispered Mrs. Malderton to her daughters, as they retired to the drawing-room.

"Oh, he's quite a love!" said both the young ladies together; "he talks like an oracle. He must have seen a great deal of life."

The gentlemen being left to themselves, a pause ensued, during which everybody looked very grave, as if they were quite overcome by the profound nature of the previous discussion. Flamwell, who had made up his mind to find out who and what Mr. Horatio Sparkins really was, first broke silence.

"Excuse me, sir," said that distinguished personage, "I presume you have studied for the bar? I thought of entering once, myself—indeed, I'm rather intimate with some of the highest ornaments of that distinguished profession."

"N—no!" said Horatio, with a little hesitation; "not exactly."

"But you have been much among the silk gowns, or I mistake?" inquired Flamwell, deferentially.

"Nearly all my life," returned Sparkins.

The question was thus pretty well settled in the mind of Mr. Flamwell. He was a young gentleman "about to be called."

"I shouldn't like to be a barrister," said Tom, speaking for the first time, and looking round the table to find somebody who would notice the remark.

No one made any reply.

"I shouldn't like to wear a wig," said Tom, hazarding another observation.

"Tom, I beg you will not make yourself ridiculous," said his father. "Pray listen, and improve yourself by the conversation you hear, and don't be constantly making these absurd remarks.

"Very well, father," replied the unfortunate Tom, who had not spoken a word since he had asked for another slice of beef at a quarter-past five o'clock, P.M., and it was then eight.

"Well, Tom," observed his good-natured uncle, "never mind! *I* think with you. *I* shouldn't like to wear a wig. I'd rather wear an apron."

Mr. Malderton coughed violently. Mr Barton resumed—"For if a man's above his business—"

The cough returned with tenfold violence, and did not cease until the unfortunate cause of it, in his alarm, had quite forgotten what he intended to say.

"Mr. Sparkins," said Flamwell, returning to the charge, "do you happen to know Mr. Delafontaine, of Bedford-square?"

"I have exchanged cards with him; since which, indeed, I have had an opportunity of serving him considerably," replied Horatio, slightly colouring; no doubt, at having been betrayed into making the acknowledgment.

"You are very lucky, if you have had an opportunity of obliging that great man," observed Flamwell, with an air of profound respect.

"I don't know who he is," he whispered to Mr. Malderton, confidentially, as they followed Horatio up to the drawing-room. "It's quite clear, however, that he belongs to the law, and that he is somebody of great importance, and very highly connected.

"No doubt, no doubt," returned his companion.

The remainder of the evening passed away most delightfully. Mr. Malderton, relieved from his apprehensions by the circumstance of Mr. Barton's falling into a profound sleep, was as affable and gracious as possible. Miss Teresa played the "Fall of Paris," as Mr. Sparkins declared, in a most masterly manner, and both of them, assisted by Mr. Frederick, tried over glees and trios without number; they having made the pleasing discovery that their voices harmonised beautifully To be sure, they all sang the first part; and Horatio, in addition to the slight drawback of having no ear, was perfectly innocent of knowing a note of music, still, they passed the time very agreeably, and it was past twelve o'clock before Mr. Sparkins ordered the mourning-coach-looking steed to be brought out—an order which was only complied with, on the distinct understanding that he was to repeat his visit on the following Sunday.

"But, perhaps, Mr. Sparkins will form one of our party to-morrow evening?" suggested Mrs. M. "Mr. Malderton intends taking the girls to see the pantomine." Mr. Sparkins bowed, and promised to join the party in box 48, in the course of the evening.

"We will not tax you for the morning," said Miss Teresa, bewitchingly; "for ma is going to take us to all sorts of places, shopping. I know that gentlemen have a great horror of that employment." Mr. Sparkins bowed again, and declared that he should be delighted, but business of importance occupied him in the morning. Flamwell looked at Malderton significantly.—"It's term time!" he whispered.

At twelve o'clock on the following morning, the "fly" was at the door of Oak Lodge, to convey Mrs. Malderton and her daughters on their expedition for the day. They were to dine and dress for the play at a friend's house. First, driving thither with their band-boxes, they departed on their first errand to make some purchases at Messrs. Jones, Spruggins, and Smith's, of Tottenham-court-road; after which, they were to go to Redmayne's in Bond-street; thence, to innumerable places that no one ever heard of. The young ladies beguiled the tediousness of the ride by eulogising Mr. Horatio Sparkins, scolding their mamma for taking them so far to save a shilling, and wondering whether they should ever reach their destination. At length, the vehicle stopped before a dirty-looking ticketed linen-draper's shop, with goods of all kinds, and labels of all sorts and sizes, in the window. There were dropsical figures of seven with a little three farthings in the corner; "perfectly invisible to the naked eye;" three hundred and fifty thousand ladies' boas, *from* one shilling and a penny half-penny; real French kid shoes, at two and ninepence per pair; green parasols, at an equally cheap rate; and "every description of goods," as the proprietors said—and they must know best—"fifty per cent. under cost price."

"Lor! ma, what a place you have brought us to!" said Miss Teresa; "what *would* Mr. Sparkins say if he could see us!"

"Ah! what, indeed!" said Miss Marianne, horrified at the idea.

"Pray be seated, ladies. What is the first article?" inquired the obsequious master of the ceremonies of the establishment, who, in his large white neckcloth and formal tie, looked like a bad "portrait of a gentleman" in the Somerset-house exhibition.

"I want to see some silks," answered Mrs. Malderton.

"Directly, ma'am.—Mr. Smith! Where *is* Mr. Smith?"

"Here, sir," cried a voice at the back of the shop.

"Pray make haste, Mr. Smith," said the M.C. "You never are to be found when you're wanted, sir."

Mr. Smith, thus enjoined to use all possible despatch, leaped over the counter with great agility, and placed himself before the newly-arrived customers. Mrs. Malderton uttered a faint scream; Miss Teresa, who had been stooping down to talk to her sister, raised her head, and beheld—Horatio Sparkins!

"We will draw a veil," as novel writers say, over the scene that ensued. The mysterious, philosophical, romantic, metaphysical Sparkins—he who, to the interesting Teresa, seemed like the embodied idea of the young dukes and poetical exquisites in blue silk dressing-gowns, and ditto ditto slippers, of whom she had read and dreamed, but had never expected to behold, was suddenly converted into

Mr. Samuel Smith, the assistant at a "cheap shop;" the junior partner in a slippery firm of some three weeks' existence. The dignified evanishment of the hero of Oak Lodge, on this unexpected recognition, could only be equalled by that of a furtive dog with a considerable kettle at his tail. All the hopes of the Maldertons were destined at once to melt away, like the lemon ices at a Company's dinner; Almacks was still to them as distant as the North Pole; and Miss Teresa had as much chance of a husband as Captain Ross had of the north-west passage.

Years have elapsed since the occurrence of this dreadful morning. The daisies have thrice bloomed on Camberwell-green; the sparrows have thrice repeated their vernal chirps in Camberwell-grove; but the Miss Maldertons are still unmated. Miss Teresa's case is more desperate than ever; but Flamwell is yet in the zenith of his reputation; and the family have the same predilection for aristocratic personages, with an increased aversion to anything *low.*

CHAPTER VI.

THE BLACK VEIL.

ONE winter's evening, towards the close of the year 1800, or within a year or two of that time, a young medical practitioner, recently established in business, was seated by a cheerful fire in his little parlour, listening to the wind which was beating the rain in pattering drops against the window, or rumbling dismally in the chimney. The night was wet and cold; he had been walking through mud and water the whole day, and was now comfortably reposing in his dressing-gown and slippers, more than half asleep and less than half awake, revolving a thousand matters in his wandering imagination. First, he thought how hard the wind was blowing, and how the cold, sharp rain would be at that moment beating in his face, if he were not comfortably housed at home. Then, his mind reverted to his annual Christmas visit to his native place and dearest friends; he thought how glad they would all be to see him, and how happy it would make Rose if he could only tell her that he had found a patient at last, and hoped to have more, and to come down again, in a few months' time, and marry her, and take her home to gladden his lonely fireside, and stimulate him to fresh exertions. Then, he began to wonder when his first patient would appear, or whether he was destined, by a special dispensation of Providence, never to have any patients at all; and then, he thought about Rose again, and dropped to sleep and dreamed about her, till the tones of her sweet merry voice sounded in his ears, and her soft tiny hand rested on his shoulder.

There *was* a hand upon his shoulder, but it was neither soft nor tiny; its owner being a corpulent round-headed boy, who, in consideration of the sum of one shilling per week and his food, was let out by the parish to carry medicine and messages. As there was no demand for the medicine, however, and no necessity for the messages, he usually occupied his unemployed hours—averaging fourteen a day—in abstracting peppermint drops, taking animal nourishment, and going to sleep.

"A lady, sir—a lady!" whispered the boy, rousing his master with a shake.

"What lady?" cried our friend, starting up, not quite certain that his dream was an illusion, and half expecting that it might be Rose herself.—"What lady? Where?"

"*There*, sir!" replied the boy, pointing to the glass door leading into the surgery, with an expression of alarm which the very unusual apparition of a customer might have tended to excite.

The surgeon looked towards the door, and started himself, for an instant, on beholding the appearance of his unlooked-for visitor.

It was a singularly tall woman, dressed in deep mourning, and standing so close to the door that her face almost touched the glass. The upper part of her figure was carefully muffled in a black shawl, as if for the purpose of concealment; and her face was shrouded by a thick black veil. She stood perfectly erect, her figure was drawn up to its full height, and though the surgeon *felt* that the eyes beneath the veil were fixed on him, she stood perfectly motionless, and evinced, by no gesture whatever, the slightest consciousness of his having turned towards her.

"Do you wish to consult me?" he inquired, with some hesitation, holding open the door. It opened inwards, and therefore the action did not alter the position of the figure, which still remained motionless on the same spot.

She slightly inclined her head, in token of acquiescence.

"Pray walk in," said the surgeon.

The figure moved a step forward; and then, turning its head in the direction of the boy—to his infinite horror—appeared to hesitate.

"Leave the room, Tom," said the young man, addressing the boy, whose large round eyes had been extended to their utmost width during this brief interview. "Draw the curtain, and shut the door."

The boy drew a green curtain across the glass part of the door, retired into the surgery, closed the door after him, and immediately applied one of his large eyes to the keyhole on the other side.

The surgeon drew a chair to the fire, and motioned the visitor to a seat. The mysterious figure slowly moved towards it. As the blaze shone upon the black dress, the surgeon observed that the bottom of it was saturated with mud and rain.

"You are very wet," he said.

"I am," said the stranger, in a low deep voice.

"And you are ill?" added the surgeon, compassionately, for the tone was that of a person in pain.

"I am," was the reply—"very ill: not bodily, but mentally. It is not for myself, or on my own behalf," continued the stranger, "that I come to you. If I laboured under bodily disease, I should not be out, alone, at such an hour, or on such a night as this; and if I were afflicted with it, twenty-four hours hence, God knows how gladly I would lie down and pray to die. It is for another that I beseech your aid, sir. I may be mad to ask it for him—I think I am; but, night after night, through the long dreary hours of watching and weeping, the thought has been ever present to my mind; and though even *I* see the hopelessness of human assistance availing him, the bare thought of laying him in his grave without it makes my blood run cold!" And a shudder, such as the surgeon well knew art could not produce, trembled through the speaker's frame.

There was a desperate earnestness in this woman's manner, that went to the young man's heart. He was young in his profession, and had not yet witnessed enough of the miseries which are daily presented before the eyes of its members, to have grown comparatively callous to human suffering.

"If," he said, rising hastily, "the person of whom you speak, be in so hopeless a condition as you describe, not a moment is to be lost. I will go with you instantly. Why did you not obtain medical advice before?"

"Because it would have been useless before—because it is useless even now," replied the woman, clasping her hands passionately.

The surgeon gazed, for a moment, on the black veil, as if to ascertain the expression of the features beneath it; its thickness, however, rendered such a result impossible.

"You *are* ill," he said, gently, "although you do not know it. The fever which has enabled you to bear, without feeling it, the fatigue you have evidently undergone, is burning within you now. Put that to your lips," he continued, pouring out a glass of water—"compose yourself for a few moments, and then tell me, as calmly as you can, what the disease of the patient is, and how long he has been ill. When I know what it is necessary I should know, to render my visit serviceable to him, I am ready to accompany you."

The stranger lifted the glass of water to her mouth, without raising the veil; put it down again untasted; and burst into tears.

"I know," she said, sobbing aloud, "that what I say to you now, seems like the ravings of fever. I have been told so before, less kindly than by you. I am not a young woman; and they do say, that as life steals on towards its final close, the last short remnant, worthless as it may seem to all beside, is dearer to its possessor than all the years that have gone before, connected though they be with the recollection of old friends long since dead, and young ones—children perhaps—who have fallen off from, and forgotten one as completely as if they had died too. My natural term of life cannot be many years longer, and should be dear on that account; but I would lay it down without a sigh—with cheerfulness—with joy—if what I tell you now, were only false, or imaginary. To-morrow morning he of whom I speak will be, I *know*, though I would fain think otherwise, beyond the reach of human aid; and yet, to-night, though he is in deadly peril, you must not see, and could not serve, him."

"I am unwilling to increase your distress," said the surgeon, after a short pause, "by making any comment on what you have just said, or appearing desirous to investigate a subject you are so anxious to conceal; but there is an inconsistency in your statement which I cannot reconcile with probability. This person is dying to-night, and I cannot see him when my assistance might possibly avail; you apprehend it will be useless to-morrow, and yet you would have me see him then! If he be, indeed, as dear to you, as your words and manner would imply, why not try to save his life before delay and the progress of his disease render it impracticable?"

"God help me!" exclaimed the woman, weeping bitterly, "how can I hope strangers will believe what appears incredible, even to myself? You will *not* see him then, sir?" she added, rising suddenly.

"I did not say that I declined to see him," replied the surgeon; "but I warn you, that if you persist in this extraordinary procrastination, and the individual dies, a fearful responsibility rests with you."

"The responsibility will rest heavily somewhere," replied the stranger bitterly. "Whatever responsibility rests with me, I am content to bear, and ready to answer."

"As I incur none," continued the surgeon, "by acceding to your request, I will see him in the morning, if you leave me the address. At what hour can he be seen?"

"*Nine*," replied the stranger.

"You must excuse my pressing these inquiries," said the surgeon. "But is he in your charge now?"

"He is not," was the rejoinder.

"Then, if I gave you instructions for his treatment through the night, you could not assist him?"

The woman wept bitterly, as she replied, "I could not."

Finding that there was but little prospect of obtaining more information by prolonging the interview; and anxious to spare the woman's feelings, which, subdued at first by a violent effort, were now irrepressible and most painful to witness; the surgeon repeated his promise of calling in the morning at the appointed hour. His visitor, after giving him a direction to an obscure part of Walworth, left the house in the same mysterious manner in which she had entered it.

It will be readily believed that so extraordinary a visit produced a considerable impression on the mind of the young surgeon; and that he speculated a great deal and to very little purpose on the possible circumstances of the case. In common with the generality of people, he had often heard and read of singular instances, in which a presentiment of death, at a particular day, or even minute, had been entertained and realised. At one moment he was inclined to think that the present might be such a case; but, then, it occurred to him that all the anecdotes of the kind he had ever heard, were of persons who had been troubled with a foreboding of their own death. This woman, however, spoke of another person—a man; and it was impossible to suppose that a mere dream or delusion of fancy would induce her to speak of his approaching dissolution with such terrible certainty as she had spoken. It could not be that the man was to be murdered in the morning, and that the woman, originally a consenting party, and bound to secresy by an oath, had relented, and, though unable to prevent the commission of some outrage on the victim, had determined to prevent his death if possible, by the timely interposition of medical aid? The idea of such things happening within two miles of the metropolis appeared too wild and preposterous to be entertained beyond the instant. Then, his original impression that the woman's intellects were disordered, recurred; and, as it was the only mode of solving the difficulty with any degree of satisfaction, he obstinately made up his mind to believe that she was mad. Certain misgivings upon this point, however, stole upon his thoughts at the time, and presented themselves again and again through the long dull course of a sleepless night; during which, in spite of all his efforts to the contrary, he was unable to banish the black veil from his disturbed imagination.

The back part of Walworth, at its greatest distance from town, is a straggling miserable place enough, even in these days; but, five-and-thirty years ago, the greater portion of it was little better than a dreary waste, inhabited by a few scattered people of questionable character, whose poverty prevented their living in any better neighbourhood, or whose pursuits and mode of life rendered its solitude desirable. Very many of the houses which have since sprung up on all sides, were not built until some years afterwards; and the great majority even of those which were sprinkled about, at irregular intervals, were of the rudest and most miserable description.

The appearance of the place through which he walked in the morning, was not calculated to raise the spirits of the young surgeon, or to dispel any feeling of anxiety or depression which the singular kind of visit he was about to make, had awakened. Striking off from the high road, his way lay across a marshy common, through irregular lanes, with here and there a ruinous and dismantled cottage fast falling to pieces with decay and neglect. A stunted tree, or pool of stagnant water, roused into a sluggish action by the heavy rain of the preceding night, skirted the path occasionally; and, now and then, a miserable patch of garden-ground, with a few old boards knocked together for a summer-house, and old palings imperfectly mended with stakes pilfered from the neighbouring hedges, bore testimony, at once to the poverty of the inhabitants, and the little scruple they entertained in appropriating the property of other people to their own use. Occasionally, a filthy-looking woman would make her appearance from the door of a dirty house, to empty the contents of some cooking utensil into the gutter in front, or to scream after a little slip-shod girl, who had contrived to stagger a few yards from the door under the weight of a sallow infant almost as big as herself; but, scarcely anything was stirring around: and so much of the prospect as could be faintly traced through the cold damp mist which hung heavily over it, presented a lonely and dreary appearance perfectly in keeping with the objects we have described.

After plodding wearily through the mud and mire; making many inquiries for the place to which he had been directed; and receiving as many contradictory and unsatisfactory replies in return; the young man at length arrived before the house which had been pointed out to him as the object of his destination. It was a small low building, one story above the ground, with even a more desolate and unpromising exterior than any he had yet passed. An old yellow curtain was closely drawn across the window up stairs, and the parlour shutters were closed, but not fastened. The house was detached from any other, and, as it stood at an angle of a narrow lane, there was no other habitation in sight.

When we say that the surgeon hesitated, and walked a few paces beyond the house, before he could prevail upon himself to lift the knocker, we say nothing that need raise a smile upon the face of the boldest reader. The police of London were a very different body in that day; the isolated position of the suburbs, when the rage for building and the progress of improvement had not yet begun to connect them with the main body of the city and its environs, rendered many of them (and this in particular) a place of resort for the worst and most depraved characters. Even the streets in the gayest parts of London were imperfectly lighted, at that time; and such places as these, were left entirely to the mercy of the moon and stars. The chances of detecting desperate characters, or of tracing them to their haunts, were thus rendered very few, and their offences naturally increased in boldness, as the consciousness of comparative security became the more impressed upon them by daily experience. Added to these considerations, it must be remembered that the young man had spent some time in the public hospitals of the metropolis; and, although neither Burke nor Bishop had then gained a horrible notoriety, his own observation might have suggested to him how easily the atrocities to which the former has since given his name, might be committed. Be this as it may, whatever reflection made him hesitate, he *did* hesitate: but, being a young man of strong mind and great personal courage, it was only for an instant;—he stepped briskly back and knocked gently at the door.

A low whispering was audible, immediately afterwards, as if some person at the end of the passage were conversing stealthily with another on the landing above. It was succeeded by the noise of a pair of heavy boots upon the bare floor. The door-chain was softly unfastened; the door opened; and a tall, ill-favoured man, with black hair, and a face, as the surgeon often declared afterwards, as pale and haggard, as the countenance of any dead man he ever saw, presented himself.

"Walk in, sir," he said in a low tone.

The surgeon did so, and the man having secured the door again, by the chain, led the way to a small back parlour at the extremity of the passage.

"Am I in time?"

"Too soon," replied the man. The surgeon turned hastily round, with a gesture of astonishment not unmixed with alarm, which he found it impossible to repress.

"If you'll step in here, sir," said the man, who had evidently noticed the action—"if you'll step in here, sir, you won't be detained five minutes, I assure you."

The surgeon at once walked into the room. The man closed the door, and left him alone.

It was a little cold room, with no other furniture than two deal chairs, and a table of the same material. A handful of fire, unguarded by any fender, was burning in the grate, which brought out the damp if it served no more comfortable purpose, for the unwholesome moisture was stealing down the walls, in long slug-like tracks. The window, which was broken and patched in many places, looked into a small enclosed piece of ground, almost covered with water. Not a sound was to be heard, either within the house, or without. The young surgeon sat down by the fire-place, to await the result of his first professional visit.

He had not remained in this position, many minutes, when the noise of some approaching vehicle struck his ear. It stopped; the street-door was opened; a low talking succeeded, accompanied with a shuffling noise of footsteps, along the passage and on the stairs, as if two or three men were engaged in carrying some heavy body to the room above. The creaking of the stairs, a few seconds afterwards, announced that the new comers having completed their task, whatever it was, were leaving the house. The door was again closed, and the former silence was restored.

Another five minutes had elapsed, and the surgeon had resolved to explore the house, in search of some one to whom he might make his errand known, when the room-door opened, and his last night's visitor, dressed in exactly the same manner, with the veil lowered as before, motioned him to advance. The singular height of her form, coupled with the circumstance of her not speaking, caused the idea to pass across his brain for an instant, that it might be a man disguised in woman's attire. The hysteric sobs which issued from beneath the veil, and the convulsive attitude of grief of the whole figure, however, at once exposed the absurdity of the suspicion; and he hastily followed.

The woman led the way up stairs to the front room, and paused at the door, to let him enter first. It was scantily furnished with an old deal box, a few chairs, and a tent bedstead, without hangings or cross-rails, which was covered with a patchwork counterpane. The dim light admitted through the curtain which he had noticed from the outside, rendered the objects in the room so indistinct, and communicated to all of them so uniform a hue, that he did not, at first, perceive the object on which his eye at once rested when the woman rushed frantically past him, and flung herself on her knees by the bedside.

Stretched upon the bed, closely enveloped in a linen wrapper, and covered with blankets, lay a human form, stiff and motionless. The head and face, which were those of a man, were uncovered, save by a bandage which passed over the head and under the chin. The eyes were closed. The left arm lay heavily across the bed, and the woman held the passive hand.

The surgeon gently pushed the woman aside, and took the hand in his.

"My God!" he exclaimed, letting it fall involuntarily—"the man is dead!"

The woman started to her feet and beat her hands together. "Oh! don't say so, sir," she exclaimed, with a burst of passion, amounting almost to frenzy. "Oh! don't say so, sir! I can't bear it! Men have been brought to life, before, when unskilful people have given them up for lost; and men have died, who might have been restored, if proper means had been resorted to. Don't let him lie here, sir, without one effort to save him! This very moment life may be passing away. Do try, sir,—do, for Heaven's sake!"—And while speaking, she hurriedly chafed, first the forehead, and then the breast, of the senseless form before her; and then, wildly beat the cold hands, which, when she ceased to hold them, fell listlessly and heavily back on the coverlet.

"It is of no use, my good woman," said the surgeon, soothingly, as he withdrew his hand from the man's breast. "Stay—undraw that curtain!"

"Why?" said the woman, starting up.

"Undraw that curtain!" repeated the surgeon in an agitated tone.

"*I* darkened the room on purpose," said the woman, throwing herself before him as he rose to undraw it.--"Oh! sir, have pity on me! If it can be of no use, and he is really dead, do not expose that form to other eyes than mine!"

"This man died no natural or easy death," said the surgeon, "I *must* see the body!" With a motion so sudden, that the woman hardly knew that he had slipped from beside her, he tore open the curtain, admitted the full light of day, and returned to the bedside.

"There has been violence here," he said, pointing towards the body, and gazing intently on the face, from which the black veil was now, for the first time, removed. In the excitement of a minute before, the female had thrown off the bonnet and veil, and now stood with her eyes fixed upon him. Her features were those of a woman about fifty, who had once been handsome. Sorrow and weeping had left traces upon them which not time itself would ever have produced without their aid; her face was deadly pale; and there was a nervous contortion of the lip, and an unnatural fire in her eye, which showed too plainly that her bodily and mental powers had nearly sunk, beneath an accumulation of misery.

"There has been violence here," said the surgeon, preserving his searching glance.

"There has!" replied the woman.

"This man has been murdered."

"That I call God to witness he has," said the woman, passionately; "pitilessly, inhumanly murdered!"

"By whom?" said the surgeon, seizing the woman by the arm.

"Look at the butchers' marks, and then ask me!" she replied.

The surgeon turned his face towards the bed, and bent over the body which now lay full in the light of the window. The throat was swollen, and a livid mark encircled it. The truth flashed suddenly upon him.

"This is one of the men who were hanged this morning!" he exclaimed, turning away with a shudder.

"It is," replied the woman, with a cold, unmeaning stare.

"Who was he?" inquired the surgeon.

"*My son,*" rejoined the woman; and fell senseless at his feet.

It was true. A companion, equally guilty with himself, had been acquitted for want of evidence; and this man had been left for death, and executed. To recount the circumstances of the case, at this distant period, must be unnecessary, and might give pain to some persons still alive. The history was an every-day one. The mother was a widow without friends or money, and had denied herself necessaries to bestow them on her orphan boy. That boy, unmindfnl of her prayers, and forgetful of the sufferings she had endured for him—incessant anxiety of mind, and voluntary starvation of body—had plunged into a career of dissipation and crime. And this was the result; his own death by the hangman's hands, and his mother's shame, and incurable insanity.

For many years after this occurrence, and when profitable and arduous avocations would have led many men to forget that such a miserable being existed, the young surgeon was a daily visitor at the side of the harmless mad woman; not only soothing her by his presence and kindness, but alleviating the rigour of her condition by pecuniary donations for her comfort and support, bestowed with no sparing hand. In the transient gleam of recollection and consciousness which preceded her death, a prayer for his welfare and protection, as fervent as mortal ever breathed, rose from the lips of this poor friendless creature. That prayer flew to Heaven, and was heard. The blessings he was instrumental in conferring, have been repaid to him a thousand-fold; but, amid all the honours of rank and station which have since been heaped upon him, and which he has so well earned, he can have no reminiscence more gratifying to his heart than that connected with The Black Veil.

CHAPTER VII.

THE STEAM EXCURSION.

MR. PERCY NOAKES was a law student, inhabiting a set of chambers on the fourth floor, in one of those houses in Gray's-inn-square which command an extensive view of the gardens, and their usual adjuncts—flaunting nursery-maids, and town-made children, with parenthetical legs. Mr. Percy Noakes was what is generally termed—"a devilish good fellow." He had a large circle of acquaintance, and seldom dined at his own expense. He used to talk politics to papas, flatter the vanity of mamas, do the amiable to their daughters, make pleasure engagements with their sons, and romp with the younger branches. Like those paragons of perfection, advertising footmen out of place, he was always "willing to make himself generally useful." If any old lady, whose son was in India, gave a ball, Mr. Percy Noakes was master of the ceremonies; if any young lady made a stolen match, Mr. Percy Noakes gave her away; if a juvenile wife presented her husband with a blooming cherub, Mr. Percy Noakes was either godfather, or deputy-godfather; and if any member of a friend's family died, Mr. Percy Noakes was invariably to be seen in the second mourning coach, with a white handkerchief to his eyes, sobbing—to use his own appropriate and expressive description —"like winkin'!"

It may readily be imagined that these numerous avocations were rather calculated to interfere with Mr. Percy Noakes's professional studies. Mr. Percy Noakes was perfectly aware of the fact, and had, therefore, after mature reflection, made up his mind not to study at all—a laudable determination, to which he adhered in the most praiseworthy manner. His sitting-room presented a strange chaos of dress-gloves, boxing-gloves, caricatures, albums, invitation-cards, foils, cricket-bats, card-board drawings, paste, gum, and fifty other miscellaneous articles, heaped together in the strangest confusion. He was always making something for somebody, or planning some party of pleasure, which was his great *forte*. He invariably spoke with astonishing rapidity; was smart, spoffish, and eight-and-twenty.

"Splendid idea, 'pon my life!" soliloquised Mr. Percy Noakes, over his morning's coffee, as his mind reverted to a suggestion which had been thrown out on the previous night, by a lady at whose house he had spent the evening. "Glorious idea!—Mrs. Stubbs."

"Yes, sir," replied a dirty old woman with an inflamed countenance, emerging from the bed-room, with a barrel of dirt and cinders.—This was the laundress. "Did you call, sir?"

"Oh! Mrs. Stubbs, I'm going out. If that tailor should call again, you'd better say—you'd better say I'm out of town, and shan't be back for a fortnight; and if that bootmaker should come, tell him I've lost his address, or I'd have sent him that little amount. Mind he writes it down; and if Mr. Hardy should call—you know Mr. Hardy?"

"The funny gentleman, sir?"

"Ah! the funny gentleman. If Mr. Hardy should call, say I've gone to Mrs. Taunton's about that water-party."

"Yes, sir."

"And if any fellow calls, and says he's come about a steamer, tell him to be here at five o'clock this afternoon, Mrs. Stubbs."

"Very well, sir."

Mr Percy Noakes brushed his hat, whisked the crumbs off his inexplicables with a silk handkerchief, gave the ends of his hair a persuasive roll round his forefinger, and sallied forth for Mrs. Taunton's domicile in Great Marlborough-street, where she and her daughters occupied the upper part of a house. She was a good-looking widow of fifty, with the form of a giantess and the mind of a child. The pursuit of pleasure, and some means of killing time, were the sole end of her existence. She doted on her daughters, who were as frivolous as herself.

A general exclamation of satisfaction hailed the arrival of Mr. Percy Noakes, who went through the ordinary salutations, and threw himself into an easy chair near the ladies' work-table, with the ease of a regularly established friend of the family. Mrs. Taunton was busily engaged in planting immense bright bows on every part of a smart cap on which it was possible to stick one; Miss Emily Taunton was making a watch-guard; Miss Sophia was at the piano, practising a new song—poetry by the young officer, or the police-officer, or the custom-house officer, or some other interesting amateur.

"You good creature!" said Mrs. Taunton, addressing the gallant Percy. "You really are a good soul! You've come about the water-party, I know."

"I should rather suspect I had," replied Mr. Noakes, triumphantly. "Now, come here, girls, and I'll tell you all about it." Miss Emily and Miss Sophia advanced to the table.

"Now," continued Mr. Percy Noakes, "it seems to me that the best way will be, to have a committee of ten, to make all the arrangements, and manage the whole set-out. Then, I propose that the expenses shall be paid by these ten fellows jointly."

"Excellent, indeed!" said Mrs. Taunton, who highly approved of this part of the arrangements.

"Then, my plan is, that each of these ten fellows shall have the power of asking five people. There must be a meeting of the committee, at my chambers, to make all the arrangements, and these people shall be then named; every member of the committee shall have the power of black-balling any one who is proposed; and one black ball shall exclude that person. This will ensure our having a pleasant party, you know."

"What a manager you are!" interrupted Mrs. Taunton again.

"Charming!" said the lovely Emily.

"I never did!" ejaculated Sophia.

"Yes, I think it'll do," replied Mr. Percy Noakes, who was now quite in his element. "I think it'll do. Then you know we shall go down to the Nore, and back, and have a regular capital cold dinner laid out in the cabin before we start, so that everything may be ready without any confusion; and we shall have the lunch laid out, on deck, in those little tea-garden-looking concerns by the paddle-boxes—I don't know what you call 'em. Then, we shall hire a steamer expressly for our party, and a band, and have the deck chalked, and we shall be able to dance quadrilles all day; and then, whoever we know that's musical, you know, why they'll make themselves useful and agreeable; and—and—upon the whole, I really hope we shall have a glorious day, you know!"

The announcement of these arrangements was received with the utmost enthusiasm. Mrs. Taunton, Emily, and Sophia, were loud in their praises.

"Well, but tell me, Percy," said Mrs. Taunton, "who are the ten gentlemen to be?"

"Oh! I know plenty of fellows who'll be delighted with the scheme," replied Mr. Percy Noakes; "of course we shall have——"

"Mr. Hardy!" interrupted the servant, announcing a visitor. Miss Sophia and Miss Emily hastily assumed the most interesting attitudes that could be adopted on so short a notice.

"How are you?" said a stout gentleman of about forty, pausing at the door in the attitude of an awkward harlequin. This was Mr. Hardy, whom we have before described, on the authority of Mrs. Stubbs, as "the funny gentleman." He was an Astley-Cooperish Joe Miller—a practical joker, immensely popular with married ladies, and a general favourite with young men. He was always engaged in some pleasure excursion or other, and delighted in getting somebody into a scrape on such occasions. He could sing comic songs, imitate hackney-coachmen and fowls, play airs on his chin, and execute concertos on the Jews'-harp. He always eat and drank most immoderately, and was the bosom friend of Mr. Percy Noakes. He had a red face, a somewhat husky voice, and a tremendous laugh.

"How *are* you?" said this worthy, laughing, as if it were the finest joke in the world to make a morning call, and shaking hands with the ladies with as much vehemence as if their arms had been so many pump-handles.

"You're just the very man I wanted," said Mr. Percy Noakes, who proceeded to explain the cause of his being in requisition.

"Ha! ha! ha!" shouted Hardy, after hearing the statement, and receiving a detailed account of the proposed excursion. "Oh, capital! glorious! What a day it will be! what fun!—But, I say, when are you going to begin making the arrangements?"

"No time like the present—at once, if you please."

"Oh, charming!" cried the ladies. "Pray, do!"

Writing materials were laid before Mr. Percy Noakes, and the names of the different members of the committee were agreed on, after as much discussion between him and Mr. Hardy as if the fate of nations had depended on their appointment. It was then agreed that a meeting should take place at Mr. Percy Noakes's chambers on the ensuing Wednesday evening at eight o'clock, and the visitors departed.

Wednesday evening arrived; eight o'clock came, and eight members of the committee were punctual in their attendance. Mr. Loggins, the solicitor, of Boswell-court, sent an excuse, and Mr. Samuel Briggs, the ditto of Furnival's Inn, sent his brother: much to his (the brother's) satisfaction, and greatly to the discomfiture of Mr. Percy Noakes. Between the Briggses and the Tauntons there existed a degree of implacable hatred, quite unprecedented. The animosity between the Montagues and Capulets, was nothing to that which prevailed between these two illustrious houses. Mrs. Briggs was a widow, with three daughters and two sons; Mr. Samuel, the eldest, was an attorney, and Mr. Alexander, the youngest, was under articles to his brother. They resided in Portland-street, Oxford-street, and moved in the same orbit as the Tauntons—hence their mutual dislike. If the Miss Briggses appeared in smart bonnets, the Miss Tauntons eclipsed them with smarter. If Mrs. Taunton appeared in a cap of all the hues of the rainbow, Mrs. Briggs forthwith mounted a toque, with all the patterns of the kaleidoscope. If Miss Sophia Taunton learnt a new song, two of the Miss Briggses came out with a new duet. The Tauntons had once gained a temporary triumph with the assistance of a harp, but the Briggses brought three guitars into the field, and effectually routed the enemy. There was no end to the rivalry between them.

Now, as Mr. Samuel Briggs was a mere machine, a sort of self-acting legal walking-stick; and as the party was known to have originated, however remotely, with Mrs. Taunton, the female branches of the Briggs family had arranged that Mr Alexander should attend, instead of his brother; and as the said Mr. Alexander was deservedly celebrated for possessing all the pertinacity of a bankruptcy-court attorney, combined with the obstinacy of that useful animal which browses on the thistle, he required but little tuition. He was especially enjoined to make himself as disagreeable as possible; and, above all, to black-ball the Tauntons at every hazard.

The proceedings of the evening were opened by Mr. Percy Noakes. After successfully urging on the gentlemen present the propriety of their mixing some brandy-and-water, he briefly stated the object of the meeting, and concluded by observing that the first step must be the selection of a chairman, necessarily possessing some arbitrary—he trusted not unconstitutional—powers, to whom the personal direction of the whole of the arrangements (subject to the approval of the committee) should be confided. A pale young gentleman, in a green stock and spectacles of the same, a member of the honourable society of the Inner Temple, immediately rose for the purpose of proposing Mr. Percy Noakes. He had known him long, and this he would say, that a more honourable, a more excellent, or a better-hearted fellow, never existed.—(Hear, hear!) The young gentleman, who was a member of a debating society, took this opportunity of entering into an examination of the state of the English law, from the days of William the Conqueror down to the present period; he briefly adverted to the code established by the ancient Druids; slightly glanced at the principles laid down by the Athenian law-givers; and concluded with a most glowing eulogium on pic-nics and constitutional rights.

Mr. Alexander Briggs opposed the motion. He had the highest esteem for Mr. Percy Noakes as an individual, but he did consider that he ought not to be intrusted with these immense powers—(oh, oh!)—He believed that in the proposed capacity Mr. Percy Noakes would not act fairly, impartially, or honourably; but he begged it to be distinctly understood, that he said this, without the slightest personal disrespect. Mr. Hardy defended his honourable friend, in a voice rendered partially unintelligible by emotion and brandy-and-water. The proposition was put to the vote, and there appearing to be only one dissentient voice, Mr. Percy Noakes was declared duly elected, and took the chair accordingly.

The business of the meeting now proceeded with rapidity. The chairman delivered in his estimate of the probable expense of the excursion, and every one present subscribed his portion thereof. The question was put that "The Endeavour" be hired for the occasion; Mr. Alexander Briggs moved as an amendment, that the word "Fly" be substituted for the word "Endeavour;" but after some debate consented to withdraw his opposition. The important ceremony of balloting then commenced. A tea-caddy was placed on a table in a dark corner of the apartment, and every one was provided with two backgammon men, one black and one white.

The chairman with great solemnity then read the following list of the guests whom he proposed to introduce:—Mrs. Taunton and two daughters, Mr. Wizzle, Mr. Simson. The names were respectively balloted for, and Mrs. Taunton and her daughters were declared to be black-balled. Mr. Percy Noakes and Mr. Hardy exchanged glances.

"Is your list prepared, Mr. Briggs?" inquired the chairman.

"It is," replied Alexander, delivering in the following:—"Mrs. Briggs and three daughters, Mr. Samuel Briggs. The previous ceremony was repeated, and Mrs. Briggs and three daughters were declared to be black-balled. Mr. Alexander Briggs looked rather foolish, and the remainder of the company appeared somewhat overawed by the mysterious nature of the proceedings.

The balloting proceeded; but, one little circumstance which Mr. Percy Noakes had not originally foreseen, prevented the system from working quite as well as he had anticipated. Everybody was black-balled. Mr. Alexander Briggs, by way of retaliation, exercised his power of exclusion in every instance, and the result was, that after three hours had been consumed in hard balloting, the names of only three gentlemen were found to have been agreed to. In this dilemma what was to be done? either the whole plan must fall to the ground, or a compromise must be effected. The latter alternative was preferable; and Mr. Percy Noakes therefore proposed that the form of balloting should be dispensed with, and that every gentleman should merely be required to state whom he intended to bring. The proposal was acceded to; the Tauntons and the Briggses were reinstated; and the party was formed.

The next Wednesday was fixed for the eventful day, and it was unanimously resolved that every member of the committee should wear a piece of blue sarsenet ribbon round his left arm. It appeared from the statement of Mr. Percy Noakes, that the boat belonged to the General Steam Navigation Company, and was then lying off the Custom-house; and, as he proposed that the dinner and wines should be provided by an eminent city purveyor, it was arranged that Mr. Percy Noakes should be on board by seven o'clock to superintend the arrangements, and that the remaining members of the committee, together with the company generally, should be expected to join her by nine o'clock. More brandy-and-water was despatched; several speeches were made by the different law students present; thanks were voted to the chairman; and the meeting separated.

The weather had been beautiful up to this period, and beautiful it continued to be. Sunday passed over, and Mr. Percy Noakes became unusually fidgety—rushing, constantly, to and from the Steam Packet Wharf, to the astonishment of the clerks, and the great emolument of the Holborn cabmen. Tuesday arrived, and the anxiety of Mr. Percy Noakes knew no bounds. He was every instant running to the window, to look out for clouds; and Mr. Hardy astonished the whole square by practising a new comic song for the occasion, in the chairman's chambers.

Uneasy were the slumbers of Mr. Percy Noakes that night; he tossed and tumbled about, and had confused dreams of steamers starting off, and gigantic clocks with the hands pointing to a quarter-past nine, and the ugly face of Mr. Alexander Briggs looking over the boat's side, and grinning, as if in derision of his fruitless attempts to move. He made a violent effort to get on board, and awoke. The bright sun was shining cheerfully into the bed-room, and Mr. Percy Noakes started up for his watch, in the dreadful expectation of finding his worst dreams realised.

It was just five o'clock. He calculated the time—he should be a good half-hour dressing himself; and as it was a lovely morning, and the tide would be then running down, he would walk leisurely to Strand-lane, and have a boat to the Custom-house.

He dressed himself, took a hasty apology for a breakfast, and sallied forth. The streets looked as lonely and deserted as if they had been crowded, overnight, for the last time. Here and there, an early apprentice, with quenched-looking sleepy eyes, was taking down the shutters of a shop; and a policeman or milk-woman might occasionally be seen pacing slowly along; but the servants had not yet begun to clean the doors, or light the kitchen fires, and London looked the picture of desolation. At the corner of a by-street, near Temple-bar, was stationed a "street-breakfast." The coffee was boiling over a charcoal fire, and large slices of bread and butter were piled one upon the other, like deals in a timber-yard. The company were seated on a form, which, with a view both to security and comfort, was placed against a neighbouring wall. Two young men, whose uproarious mirth and disordered dress bespoke the conviviality of the preceding evening, were treating three "ladies" and an Irish labourer. A little sweep was standing at a short distance, casting a longing eye at the tempting delicacies; and a policeman was watching the group from the opposite side of the street. The wan looks, and gaudy finery of the thinly-clad women contrasted as strangely with the gay sun-light, as did their forced merriment with the boisterous hilarity of the two young men, who, now and then, varied their amusements by "bonneting" the proprietor of this itinerant coffee-house.

Mr. Percy Noakes walked briskly by, and when he turned down Strand-lane, and caught a glimpse of the glistening water, he thought he had never felt so important or so happy in his life.

"Boat, sir?" cried one of the three watermen who were mopping out their boats, and all whistling. "Boat, sir?"

"No," replied Mr. Percy Noakes, rather sharply; for the inquiry was not made in a manner at all suitable to his dignity.

"Would you prefer a wessel, sir?" inquired another, to the infinite delight of the "Jack-in-the-water."

Mr. Percy Noakes replied with a look of supreme contempt.

"Did you want to be put on board a steamer, sir?" inquired an old fireman-waterman, very confidentially. He was dressed in a faded red suit, just the colour of the cover of a very old Court-guide.

"Yes, make haste—the Endeavour—off the Custom-house."

"Endeavour!" cried the man who had convulsed the "Jack" before. "Vy, I see the Endeavour go up half an hour ago."

"So did I," said another; "and I should think she'd gone down by this time, for she's a precious sight too full of ladies and gen'lemen."

Mr. Percy Noakes affected to disregard these representations, and stepped into the boat, which the old man, by dint of scrambling, and shoving, and grating, had brought up to the causeway. "Shove her off!" cried Mr. Percy Noakes, and away the boat glided down the river; Mr. Percy Noakes seated on the recently mopped seat, and the watermen at the stairs offering to bet him any reasonable sum that he'd never reach the "Custum-us."

"Here she is, by Jove!" said the delighted Percy, as they ran alongside the Endeavour.

"Hold hard!" cried the steward over the side, and Mr. Percy Noakes jumped on board.

"Hope you will find everything as you wished, sir. She looks uncommon well this morning."

"She does, indeed," replied the manager, in a state of ecstasy which it is impossible to describe. The deck was scrubbed, and the seats were scrubbed, and there was a bench for the band, and a place for dancing, and a pile of camp-stools, and an awning; and then, Mr. Percy Noakes bustled down below, and there were the pastrycook's men, and the steward's wife, laying out the dinner on two tables the whole length of the cabin; and then Mr. Percy Noakes took off his coat and rushed backwards and forwards, doing nothing, but quite convinced he was assisting everybody; and the steward's wife laughed till she cried, and Mr. Percy Noakes panted with the violence of his exertions. And then the bell at London-bridge wharf rang; and a Margate boat was just starting; and a Gravesend boat was just starting, and people shouted, and porters ran down the steps with luggage that would crush any men but porters; and sloping boards, with bits of wood nailed on them were placed between the outside boat and the inside boat; and the passengers ran along them, and looked like so many fowls coming out of an area; and then, the bell ceased, and the boards were taken away, and the boats started, and the whole scene was one of the most delightful bustle and confusion.

The time wore on; half-past eight o'clock arrived; the pastrycook's men went ashore; the dinner was completely laid out; and Mr. Percy Noakes locked the principal cabin, and put the key in his pocket, in order that it might be suddenly disclosed, in all its magnificence, to the eyes of the astonished company. The band came on board, and so did the wine.

Ten minutes to nine, and the committee embarked in a body. There was Mr. Hardy, in a blue jacket and waistcoat, white trousers, silk stockings, and pumps—in full aquatic costume, with a straw hat on his head, and an immense telescope under his arm; and there was the young gentleman with the green spectacles, in nankeen inexplicables, with a ditto waistcoat and bright buttons, like the pictures of Paul—not the saint, but he of Virginia notoriety. The remainder of the committee, dressed in white hats, light jackets, waistcoats, and trousers, looked something between waiters and West India planters.

Nine o'clock struck, and the company arrived in shoals. Mr. Samuel Briggs, Mrs. Briggs, and the Misses Briggs, made their appearance in a smart private wherry. The three guitars, in their respective dark green cases, were carefully stowed away in the bottom of the boat, accompanied by two immense portfolios of music, which it would take at least a week's incessant playing to get through. The Tauntons arrived at the same moment with more music, and a lion—a gentleman with a bass voice and an incipient red moustache. The colours of the Taunton party were pink; those of the Briggses a light blue. The Tauntons had artificial flowers in their bonnets; here the Briggses gained a decided advantage—they wore feathers.

"How d'ye do, dear?" said the Misses Briggs to the Misses Taunton. (The word "dear" among girls is frequently synonymous with "wretch.")

"Quite well, thank you, dear," replied the Misses Taunton to the Misses Briggs; and then, there was such a kissing, and congratulating, and shaking of hands, as might have induced one to suppose that the two families were the best friends in the world, instead of each wishing the other overboard, as they most sincerely did.

Mr. Percy Noakes received the visitors, and bowed to the strange gentleman, as if he should like to know who he was. This was just what Mrs. Taunton wanted. Here was an opportunity to astonish the Briggses.

"Oh! I beg your pardon," said the general of the Taunton party, with a careless air.—"Captain Helves—Mr. Percy Noakes—Mrs. Briggs—Captain Helves."

Mr. Percy Noakes bowed very low; the gallant captain did the same with all due ferocity, and the Briggses were clearly overcome.

"Our friend, Mr. Wizzle, being unfortunately prevented from coming," resumed Mrs. Taunton, "I did myself the pleasure of bringing the captain, whose musical talents I knew would be a great acquisition."

"In the name of the committee I have to thank you for doing so, and to offer you welcome, sir," replied Percy. (Here the scraping was renewed.) "But pray be seated—won't you walk aft? Captain, will you conduct Miss Taunton?—Miss Briggs, will you allow me?"

"Where could they have picked up that military man?" inquired Mrs. Briggs of Miss Kate Briggs, as they followed the little party.

"I can't imagine," replied Miss Kate, bursting with vexation; for the very fierce air with which the gallant captain regarded the company, had impressed her with a high sense of his importance.

Boat after boat came alongside, and guest after guest arrived. The invites had been excellently arranged: Mr. Percy Noakes having considered it as important that the number of young men should exactly tally with that of the young ladies, as that the quantity of knives on board should be in precise proportion to the forks.

"Now, is every one on board?" inquired Mr. Percy Noakes. The committee (who, with their bits of blue ribbon, looked as if they were all going to be bled) bustled about to ascertain the fact, and reported that they might safely start.

"Go on!" cried the master of the boat from the top of one of the paddle-boxes.

"Go on!" echoed the boy, who was stationed over the hatchway to pass the directions down to the engineer; and away went the vessel with that agreeable noise which is peculiar to steamers, and which is composed of a mixture of creaking, gushing, clanging, and snorting.

"Hoi—oi—oi—oi—oi—oi—o—i—i—i!" shouted half-a-dozen voices from a boat, a quarter of a mile astern.

"Ease her!" cried the captain: "do these people belong to us, sir?"

"Noakes," exclaimed Hardy, who had been looking at every object, far and near, through the large telescope, "it's the Fleetwoods and the Wakefields—and two children with them, by Jove!"

"What a shame to bring children!" said everybody; "how very inconsiderate!"

"I say, it would be a good joke to pretend not to see 'em, wouldn't it?" suggested Hardy, to the immense delight of the company generally. A council of war was hastily held, and it was resolved that the new comers should be taken on board, on Mr. Hardy's solemnly pledging himself to tease the children during the whole of the day.

"Stop her!" cried the captain.

"Stop her!" repeated the boy; whizz went the steam, and all the young ladies, as in duty bound, screamed in concert. They were only appeased by the assurance of the martial Helves, that the escape of steam consequent on stopping a vessel was seldom attended with any great loss of human life.

Two men ran to the side; and after some shouting, and swearing, and angling for the wherry with a boat-hook, Mr. Fleetwood, and Mrs. Fleetwood, and Master Fleetwood, and Mr. Wakefield, and Mrs. Wakefield, and Miss Wakefield, were safely deposited on the deck. The girl was about six years old, the boy about four; the former was dressed in a white frock with a pink sash and dog's-eared-looking little spencer: a straw bonnet and green veil, six inches by three and a half; the latter, was attired for the occasion in a nankeen frock, between the bottom of which, and the top of his plaid socks, a considerable portion of two small mottled legs was discernible. He had a light blue cap with a gold band and tassel on his head, and a damp piece of gingerbread in his hand, with which he had slightly embossed his countenance.

The boat once more started off; the band played "Off she goes;" the major part of the company conversed cheerfully in groups; and the old gentlemen walked up and down the deck in pairs, as perseveringly and gravely as if they were doing a match against time for an immense stake. They ran briskly down the Pool; the gentlemen pointed out the Docks, the Thames Police-office, and other elegant public edifices; and the young ladies exhibited a proper display of horror at the appearance of the coal-whippers and ballast-heavers. Mr. Hardy told stories to the married ladies, at which they laughed very much in their pocket-handkerchiefs, and hit him on the knuckles with their fans, declaring him to be "a naughty man—a shocking creature"—and so forth; and Captain Helves gave slight descriptions of battles and duels, with a most bloodthirsty air, which made him the admiration of the women, and the envy of the men. Quadrilling commenced; Captain Helves danced one set with Miss Emily Taunton, and another set with Miss Sophia Taunton. Mrs. Taunton was in ecstasies. The victory appeared to be complete; but alas! the inconstancy of man! Having performed this necessary duty, he attached himself solely to Miss Julia Briggs, with whom he danced no less than three sets consecutively, and from whose side he evinced no intention of stirring for the remainder of the day.

Mr. Hardy, having played one or two very brilliant fantasias on the Jews'-harp, and having frequently repeated the exquisitely amusing joke of slily chalking a large cross on the back of some member of the committee, Mr. Percy Noakes expressed his hope that some of their musical friends would oblige the company by a display of their abilities.

"Perhaps," he said in a very insinuating manner, "Captain Helves will oblige us?" Mrs. Taunton's countenance lighted up, for the captain only sang duets, and couldn't sing them with anybody but one of her daughters.

"Really," said that warlike individual, "I should be very happy, but—"

"Oh! pray do," cried all the young ladies.

"Miss Sophia, have you any objection to join in a duet?"

"Oh! not the slightest," returned the young lady, in a tone which clearly showed she had the greatest possible objection.

"Shall I accompany you, dear?" inquired one of the Miss Briggses, with the bland intention of spoiling the effect.

"Very much obliged to you, Miss Briggs," sharply retorted Mrs. Taunton, who saw through the manœuvre; "my daughters always sing without accompaniments."

"And without voices," tittered Mrs. Briggs, in a low tone.

"Perhaps," said Mrs. Taunton, reddening, for she guessed the tenor of the observation, though she had not heard it clearly—"Perhaps it would be as well for some people, if their voices were not quite so audible as they are to other people."

"And, perhaps, if gentlemen who are kidnapped to pay attention to some persons' daughters, had not sufficient discernment to pay attention to other persons' daughters," returned Mrs. Briggs, "some persons would not be so ready to display that ill-temper which, thank God, distinguishes them from other persons."

"Persons!" ejaculated Mrs. Taunton.

"Persons," replied Mrs. Briggs.

"Insolence!"

"Creature!"

"Hush! hush!" interrupted Mr. Percy Noakes, who was one of the very few by whom this dialogue had been overheard. "Hush!—pray, silence for the duet."

After a great deal of preparatory crowing and humming, the captain began the following duet from the opera of "Paul and Virginia," in that grunting tone in which a man gets down, Heaven knows where, without the remotest chance of ever getting up again. This, in private circles, is frequently designated "a bass voice."

"See (sung the captain) from o—ce—an ri—sing
Bright flames the or—b of d—ay.
From yon gro—ove, the varied so—ongs—"

Here, the singer was interrupted by varied cries of the most dreadful description, proceeding from some grove in the immediate vicinity of the starboard paddle-box.

"My child!" screamed Mrs. Fleetwood. "My child! it is his voice — I know it."

Mr. Fleetwood, accompanied by several gentlemen, here rushed to the quarter from whence the noise proceeded, and an exclamation of horror burst from the company; the general impression being, that the little innocent had either got his head in the water, or his legs in the machinery.

"What is the matter?" shouted the agonised father, as he returned with the child in his arms.

"Oh! oh! oh!" screamed the small sufferer again.

"What is the matter, dear?" inquired the father once more—hastily stripping off the nankeen frock, for the purpose of ascertaining whether the child had one bone which was not smashed to pieces.

"Oh! oh!—I'm so frightened!"

"What at, dear?—what at?" said the mother, soothing the sweet infant.

"Oh! he's been making such dreadful faces at me," cried the boy, relapsing into convulsions at the bare recollection.

"He!—who?" cried everybody, crowding round him.

"Oh!—him!" replied the child, pointing at Hardy, who affected to be the most concerned of the whole group.

The real state of the case at once flashed upon the minds of all present, with the exception of the Fleetwoods and the Wakefields. The facetious Hardy, in fulfilment of his promise, had watched the child to a remote part of the vessel, and, suddenly appearing before him with the most awful contortions of visage, had produced his paroxysm of terror. Of course, he now observed that it was hardly necessary for him to deny the accusation; and the unfortunate little victim was accordingly led below, after receiving sundry thumps on the head from both his parents, for having the wickedness to tell a story.

This little interruption having been adjusted, the captain resumed, and Miss Emily chimed in, in due course. The duet was loudly applauded, and, certainly, the perfect independence of the parties deserved great commendation. Miss Emily sung her part, without the slightest reference to the captain; and the captain sang so loud, that he had not the slightest idea what was being done by his partner. After having gone through the last few eighteen or nineteen bars by himself, therefore, he acknowledged the plaudits of the circle with that air of self-denial which men usually assume when they think they have done something to astonish the company.

"Now," said Mr. Percy Noakes, who had just ascended from the fore-cabin, where he had been busily engaged in decanting the wine, "if the Misses Briggs will oblige us with something before dinner, I am sure we shall be very much delighted."

One of those hums of admiration followed the suggestion, which one frequently hears in society, when nobody has the most distant notion what he is expressing his approval of. The three Misses Briggs looked modestly at their mamma, and the mamma looked approvingly at her daughters, and Mrs. Taunton looked scornfully at all of them. The Misses Briggs asked for their guitars, and several gentlemen seriously damaged the cases in their anxiety to present them. Then, there was a very interesting production of three little keys for the aforesaid cases, and a melodramatic expression of horror at finding a string broken; and a vast deal of screwing and tightening, and winding, and tuning, during which Mrs. Briggs expatiated to those near her on the immense difficulty of playing a guitar, and hinted at the wondrous proficiency of her daughters in that mystic art. Mrs. Taunton whispered to a neighbour that it was "quite sickening!" and the Misses Taunton looked as if they knew how to play, but disdained to do it.

At length, the Misses Briggs began in real earnest. It was a new Spanish composition, for three voices and three guitars. The effect was electrical. All eyes were turned upon the captain, who was reported to have once passed through Spain with his regiment, and who must be well acquainted with the national music. He was in raptures. This was sufficient; the trio was encored; the applause was universal; and never had the Tauntons suffered such a complete defeat.

"Bravo! bravo!" ejaculated the captain;—"Bravo!"

"Pretty! isn't it, sir?" inquired Mr. Samuel Briggs, with the air of a self-satisfied showman. By-the-bye, these were the first words he had been heard to utter since he left Boswell-court the evening before.

"De—lightful!" returned the captain, with a flourish, and a military cough;—"de—lightful!"

"Sweet instrument?" said an old gentleman with a bald head, who had been trying all the morning to look through a telescope, inside the glass of which Mr. Hardy had fixed a large black wafer.

"Did you ever hear a Portuguese tamborine?" inquired that jocular individual.

"Did *you* ever hear a tom-tom, sir?" sternly inquired the captain, who lost no opportunity of showing off his travels, real or pretended.

"A what?" asked Hardy, rather taken aback.

"A tom-tom."

"Never!"

"Nor a gum-gum?"

"Never!"

"What *is* a gum-gum?" eagerly inquired several young ladies.

"When I was in the East Indies," replied the captain. (Here was a discovery—he had been in the East Indies!)—"when I was in the East Indies, I was once stopping a few thousand miles up the country, on a visit at the house of a very particular friend of mine, Ram Chowdar Doss Azuph Al Bowlar—a devilish pleasant fellow. As we were enjoying our hookahs, one evening, in the cool verandah in front of his villa, we were rather surprised by the sudden appearance of thirty-four of his Kit-ma-gars (for he had rather a large establishment there), accompanied by an equal number of Con-su-mars, approaching the house with a threatening aspect, and beating a tom-tom. The Ram started up——"

"Who?" inquired the bald gentleman, intensely interested.

"The Ram—Ram Chowdar—"

"Oh!" said the old gentleman, "I beg your pardon; pray go on."

"—Started up and drew a pistol. 'Helves,' said he, 'my boy,'—he always called me, my boy—'Helves,' said he, 'do you hear that tom-tom?' 'I do,' said I. His countenance, which before was pale, assumed a most frightful appearance; his whole visage was distorted, and his frame shaken by violent emotions. 'Do you see that gum-gum?' said he. 'No,' said I, staring about me. 'You don't?' said he. 'No, I'll be damned if I do,' said I; 'and what's more, I don't know what a gum-gum is,' said I. I really thought the Ram would have dropped. He drew me aside, and with an expression of agony I shall never forget, said in a low whisper——"

"Dinner's on the table, ladies," interrupted the steward's wife.

"Will you allow me?" said the captain, immediately suiting the action to the word, and escorting Miss Julia Briggs to the cabin, with as much ease as if he had finished the story.

"What an extraordinary circumstance!" ejaculated the same old gentleman, preserving his listening attitude.

"What a traveller!" said the young ladies.

"What a singular name!" exclaimed the gentlemen, rather confused by the coolness of the whole affair.

"I wish he had finished the story," said an old lady. "I wonder what a gum-gum really is?"

"By Jove!" exclaimed Hardy, who until now had been lost in utter amazement, "I don't know what it may be in India, but in England I think a gum-gum has very much the same meaning as a hum-bug."

"How illiberal! how envious!" cried everybody, as they made for the cabin, fully impressed with a belief in the captain's amazing adventures. Helves was the sole lion for the remainder of the day—impudence and the marvellous are pretty sure passports to any society.

The party had by this time reached their destination, and put about on their return home. The wind, which had been with them the whole day, was now directly in their teeth; the weather had become gradually more and more overcast; and the sky, water, and shore, were all of that dull, heavy, uniform lead-colour, which house-painters daub in the first instance over a street-door which is gradually approaching a state of convalescence. It had been "spitting" with rain for the last half-hour, and now began to pour in good earnest. The wind was freshening very fast, and the waterman at the wheel had unequivocally expressed his opinion that there would shortly be a squall. A slight emotion on the part of the vessel, now and then, seemed to suggest the possibility of its pitching to a very uncomfortable extent in the event of its blowing harder; and every timber began to creak, as if the boat were an overladen clothes-basket. Sea-sickness, however, is like a belief in ghosts—every one entertains some misgivings on the subject, but few will acknowledge any. The majority of the company, therefore, endeavoured to look peculiarly happy, feeling all the while especially miserable.

"Don't it rain?" inquired the old gentleman before noticed, when, by dint of squeezing and jamming, they were all seated at table.

"I think it does—a little," replied Mr. Percy Noakes, who could hardly hear himself speak, in consequence of the pattering on the deck.

"Don't it blow?" inquired some one else.

"No—I don't think it does," responded Hardy, sincerely wishing that he could persuade himself that it did not; for he sat near the door, and was almost blown off his seat.

"It'll soon clear up," said Mr. Percy Noakes, in a cheerful tone.

"Oh, certainly!" ejaculated the committee generally.

"No doubt of it!" said the remainder of the company, whose attention was now pretty well engrossed by the serious business of eating, carving, taking wine, and so forth.

The throbbing motion of the engine was but too perceptible. There was a large, substantial, cold boiled leg of mutton, at the bottom of the table, shaking like blanc-mange; a previously hearty sirloin of beef looked as if it had been suddenly seized with the palsy; and some tongues, which were placed on dishes rather too large for them, went through the most surprising evolutions; darting from side to side, and from end to end, like a fly in an inverted wine-glass. Then, the sweets shook and trembled, till it was quite impossible to help them, and people gave up the attempt in despair; and the pigeon-pies looked as if the birds, whose legs were stuck outside, were trying to get them in. The table vibrated and started like a feverish pulse, and the very legs were convulsed—everything was shaking and jarring. The beams in the roof of the cabin seemed as if they were put there for the sole purpose of giving people headaches, and several elderly gentlemen became ill-tempered in consequence. As fast as the steward put the fire-irons up, they *would* fall down again; and the more the ladies and gentlemen tried to sit comfortably on their seats, the more the seats seemed to slide away from the ladies and gentlemen. Several ominous demands were made for small glasses of brandy; the countenances of the company gradually underwent most extraordinary changes; one gentleman was observed suddenly to rush from table without the slightest ostensible reason, and dart up the steps with incredible swiftness: thereby greatly damaging both himself and the steward, who happened to be coming down at the same moment.

The cloth was removed; the dessert was laid on the table; and the glasses were filled. The motion of the boat increased; several members of the party began to feel rather vague and misty, and looked as if they had only just got up. The young gentleman with the spectacles, who had been in a fluctuating state for some time —at one moment bright, and at another dismal, like a revolving light on the sea-coast—rashly announced his wish to propose a toast. After several ineffectual attempts to preserve his perpendicular, the young gentleman, having managed to hook himself to the centre leg of the table with his left hand, proceeded as follows:

"Ladies and gentlemen. A gentleman is among us—I may say a stranger—(here some painful thought seemed to strike the orator; he paused, and looked extremely odd)—whose talents, whose travels, whose cheerfulness—"

"I beg your pardon, Edkins," hastily interrupted Mr. Percy Noakes,—"Hardy, what's the matter?"

"Nothing," replied the "funny gentleman," who had just life enough left to utter two consecutive syllables.

"Will you have some brandy?"

"No!" replied Hardy in a tone of great indignation, and looking as comfortable as Temple-bar in a Scotch mist; "what should I want brandy for?"

"Will you go on deck?"

"No, I will *not.*" This was said with a most determined air, and in a voice which might have been taken for an imitation of anything; it was quite as much like a guinea-pig as a bassoon.

"I beg your pardon, Edkins," said the courteous Percy; "I thought our friend was ill. Pray go on."

A pause.

"Pray go on."

"Mr. Edkins *is* gone," cried somebody.

"I beg your pardon, sir," said the steward, running up to Mr. Percy Noakes, "I beg your pardon, sir, but the gentleman as just went on deck—him with the green spectacles—is uncommon bad, to be sure; and the young man as played the wiolin says, that unless he has some brandy he can't answer for the consequences. He says he has a wife and two children, whose werry subsistence depends on his breaking a wessel, and he expects to do so every moment. The flageolet 's been wery ill, but he's better, only he's in a dreadful prusperation."

All disguise was now useless; the company staggered on deck; the gentlemen tried to see nothing but the clouds; and the ladies, muffled up in such shawls and cloaks as they had brought with them, lay about on the seats, and under the seats, in the most wretched condition. Never was such a blowing, and raining, and pitching, and tossing, endured by any pleasure party before. Several remonstrances were sent down below, on the subject of Master Fleetwood, but they were totally unheeded in consequence of the indisposition of his natural protectors. That interesting child screamed at the top of his voice, until he had no voice left to scream with; and then, Miss Wakefield began, and screamed for the remainder of the passage.

Mr. Hardy was observed, some hours afterwards, in an attitude which induced his friends to suppose that he was busily engaged in contemplating the beauties of the deep; they only regretted that his taste for the picturesque should lead him to remain so long in a position, very injurious at all times, but especially so, to an individual labouring under a tendency of blood to the head.

The party arrived off the Custom-house at about two o'clock on the Thursday morning dispirited and worn out. The Tauntons were too ill to quarrel with the Briggses, and the Briggses were too wretched to annoy the Tauntons. One of the guitar-cases was lost on its passage to a hackney-coach, and Mrs. Briggs has not scrupled to state that the Tauntons bribed a porter to throw it down an area. Mr. Alexander Briggs opposes vote by ballot—he says from personal experience of its inefficacy; and Mr. Samuel Briggs, whenever he is asked to express his sentiments on the point, says he has no opinion on that or any other subject.

Mr. Edkins—the young gentleman in the green spectacles—makes a speech on every occasion on which a speech can possibly be made: the eloquence of which can only be equalled by its length. In the event of his not being previously appointed to a judgeship, it is probable that he will practise as a barrister in the New Central Criminal Court.

Captain Helves continued his attention to Miss Julia Briggs, whom he might possibly have espoused, if it had not unfortunately happened that Mr. Samuel arrested him, in the way of business, pursuant to instructions received from Messrs. Scroggins and Payne, whose town-debts the gallant captain had condescended to collect, but whose accounts, with the indiscretion sometimes peculiar to military minds, he had omitted to keep with that dull accuracy which custom has rendered necessary. Mrs. Taunton complains that she has been much deceived in him. He introduced himself to the family on board a Gravesend steam-packet, and certainly, therefore, ought to have proved respectable.

Mr. Percy Noakes is as light-hearted and careless as ever.

CHAPTER VIII.

THE GREAT WINGLEBURY DUEL.

THE little town of Great Winglebury is exactly forty-two miles and three-quarters from Hyde Park corner. It has a long, straggling, quiet High-street, with a great black and white clock at a small red Town-hall, half-way up—a market-place—a cage—an assembly-room—a church—a bridge—a chapel—a theatre—a library—an inn—a pump—and a Post-office. Tradition tells of a "Little Winglebury," down some cross-road about two miles off; and, as a square mass of dirty paper, supposed to have been originally intended for a letter, with certain tremulous characters inscribed thereon, in which a lively imagination might trace a remote resemblance to the word "Little," was once stuck up to be owned in the sunny window of the Great Winglebury Post-office, from which it only disappeared when it fell to pieces with dust and extreme old age, there would appear to be some foundation for the legend. Common belief is inclined to bestow the name upon a little hole at the end of a muddy lane about a couple of miles long, colonised by one wheelwright, four paupers, and a beer-shop; but, even this authority, slight as it is, must be regarded with extreme suspicion, inasmuch as the inhabitants of the hole aforesaid, concur in opining that it never had any name at all, from the earliest ages down to the present day.

The Winglebury Arms, in the centre of the High-street, opposite the small building with the big clock, is the principal inn of Great Winglebury—the commercial-inn, posting-house, and excise-office; the "Blue" house at every election, and the Judges' house at every assizes. It is the head-quarters of the Gentlemen's Whist Club of Winglebury Blues (so called in opposition to the Gentlemen's Whist Club of Winglebury Buffs, held at the other house, a little further down): and whenever a juggler, or wax-work man, or concert-giver, takes Great Winglebury in his circuit, it is immediately placarded all over the town that Mr. So-and-so, "trusting to that liberal support which the inhabitants of Great Winglebury have long been so liberal in bestowing, has at a great expense engaged the elegant and commodious assembly-rooms, attached to the Winglebury Arms." The house is a large one, with a red brick and stone front; a pretty spacious hall, ornamented with evergreen plants, terminates in a perspective view of the bar, and a glass case, in which are displayed a choice variety of delicacies ready for dressing, to catch the eye of a new-comer the moment he enters, and excite his appetite to the highest possible pitch. Opposite doors lead to the "coffee" and "commercial" rooms; and a great wide, rambling staircase,—three stairs and a landing—four stairs and another landing—one step and another landing—half-a-dozen stairs and another landing—and so on—conducts to galleries of bedrooms, and labyrinths of sitting-rooms, denominated "private," where you may enjoy yourself, as privately as you can in any place where some bewildered being walks into your room every five minutes, by mistake, and then walks out again, to open all the doors along the gallery until he finds his own.

Such is the Winglebury Arms, at this day, and such was the Winglebury Arms some time since—no matter when—two or three minutes before the arrival of the London stage. Four horses with cloths on—change for a coach—were standing quietly at the corner of the yard surrounded by a listless group of post-boys in shiny hats and smock-frocks, engaged in discussing the merits of the cattle; half a dozen ragged boys were standing a little apart, listening with evident interest to the conversation of these worthies; and a few loungers were collected round the horse-trough, awaiting the arrival of the coach.

The day was hot and sunny, the town in the zenith of its dulness, and with the exception of these few idlers, not a living creature was to be seen. Suddenly, the loud notes of a key-bugle broke the monotonous stillness of the street; in came the coach, rattling over the uneven paving with a noise startling enough to stop even the large-faced clock itself. Down got the outsides, up went the windows in all directions, out came the waiters, up started the ostlers, and the loungers, and the post-boys, and the ragged boys, as if they were electrified—unstrapping, and unchaining, and unbuckling, and dragging willing horses out, and forcing reluctant horses in, and making a most exhilarating bustle. "Lady inside, here!" said the guard. "Please to alight, ma'am," said the waiter. "Private sitting-room?" interrogated the lady. "Certainly, ma'am," responded the chambermaid. "Nothing but these 'ere trunks, ma'am?" inquired the guard. "Nothing more," replied the lady. Up got the outsides again, and the guard, and the coachman; off came the cloths, with a jerk; "All right," was the cry; and away they went. The loungers lingered a minute or two in the road, watching the coach until it turned the corner, and then loitered away one by one. The street was clear again, and the town, by contrast, quieter than ever.

"Lady in number twenty-five," screamed the landlady.—"Thomas!"

"Yes, ma'am."

"Letter just been left for the gentleman in number nineteen. Boots at the Lion left it. No answer."

"Letter for you, sir," said Thomas, depositing the letter on number nineteen's table.

"For me?" said number nineteen, turning from the window, out of which he had been surveying the scene just described.

"Yes, sir,"—(waiters always speak in hints, and never utter complete sentences,)—"yes, sir,—Boots at the Lion, sir,—Bar, sir,—Missis said number nineteen, sir—Alexander Trott, Esq., sir?—Your card at the bar, sir, I think, sir?"

"My name *is* Trott," replied number nineteen, breaking the seal. "You may go, waiter." The waiter pulled down the window-blind, and then pulled it up again—for a regular waiter must do something before he leaves the room—

adjusted the glasses on the sideboard, brushed a place that was *not* dusty, rubbed his hands very hard, walked stealthily to the door, and evaporated.

There was, evidently, something in the contents of the letter, of a nature, if not wholly unexpected, certainly extremely disagreeable. Mr. Alexander Trott laid it down, and took it up again, and walked about the room on particular squares of the carpet, and even attempted, though unsuccessfully, to whistle an air. It wouldn't do. He threw himself into a chair, and read the following epistle aloud :—

"Blue Lion and Stomach-warmer,
Great Winglebury.
Wednesday Morning.

"Sir. Immediately on discovering your intentions, I left our counting house, and followed you. I know the purport of your journey ;—that journey shall never be completed.

"I have no friend here, just now, on whose secresy I can rely. This shall be no obstacle to my revenge. Neither shall Emily Brown be exposed to the mercenary solicitations of a scoundrel, odious in her eyes, and contemptible in everybody else's : nor will I tamely submit to the clandestine attacks of a base umbrella-maker.

"Sir. From Great Winglebury church, a footpath leads through four meadows to a retired spot known to the townspeople as Stiffun's Acre." [Mr. Trott shuddered.] "I shall be waiting there alone, at twenty minutes before six o'clock to-morrow morning. Should I be disappointed in seeing you there, I will do myself the pleasure of calling with a horsewhip.

"HORACE HUNTER.

"PS. There is a gunsmith's in the High-street; and they won't sell gunpowder after dark—you understand me.

"PPS. You had better not order your breakfast in the morning until you have met me. It may be an unnecessary expense."

"Desperate-minded villain! I knew how it would be!" ejaculated the terrified Trott. "I always told father, that once start me on this expedition, and Hunter would pursue me like the Wandering Jew. It's bad enough as it is, to marry with the old people's commands, and without the girl's consent; but what will Emily think of me, if I go down there breathless with running away from this infernal salamander? What *shall* I do? What *can* I do? If I go back to the city, I'm disgraced for ever—lose the girl—and, what's more, lose the money too. Even if I did go on to the Browns' by the coach, Hunter would be after me in a post-chaise; and if I go to this place, this Stiffun's Acre (another shudder), I'm as good as dead. I've seen him hit the man at the Pall-mall shooting-gallery, in the second button-hole of the waistcoat, five times out of every six, and when he didn't hit him there, he hit him in the head." With this consolatory reminiscence Mr. Alexander Trott again ejaculated, "What shall I do?"

Long and weary were his reflections, as, burying his face in his hand, he sat, ruminating on the best course to be pursued. His mental direction-post pointed to London. He thought of the "governor's" anger, and the loss of the fortune which the paternal Brown had promised the paternal Trott his daughter should contribute to the coffers of his son. Then the words "To Brown's" were legibly inscribed on the said direction-post, but Horace Hunter's denunciation rung in his ears;—last of all it bore, in red letters, the words, "To Stiffun's Acre;"

and then Mr. Alexander Trott decided on adopting a plan which he presently matured.

First and foremost, he despatched the under-boots to the Blue Lion and Stomach-warmer, with a gentlemanly note to Mr. Horace Hunter, intimating that he thirsted for his destruction and would do himself the pleasure of slaughtering him next morning, without fail. He then wrote another letter, and requested the attendance of the other boots—for they kept a pair. A modest knock at the room door was heard. "Come in," said Mr. Trott. A man thrust in a red head with one eye in it, and being again desired to "come in," brought in the body and the legs to which the head belonged, and a fur cap which belonged to the head.

"You are the upper-boots, I think?" inquired Mr. Trott.

"Yes, I am the upper-boots," replied a voice from inside a velveteen case, with mother-of-pearl buttons—"that is, I'm the boots as b'longs to the house; the other man's my man, as goes errands and does odd jobs. Top-boots and half-boots, I calls us."

"You're from London?" inquired Mr. Trott.

"Driv a cab once," was the laconic reply.

"Why don't you drive it now?" asked Mr. Trott.

"Over-driv the cab, and driv over a 'ooman," replied the top-boots, with brevity.

"Do you know the mayor's house?" inquired Mr. Trott.

"Rather," replied the boots, significantly, as if he had some good reason to remember it.

"Do you think you could manage to leave a letter there?" interrogated Trott.

"Shouldn't wonder," responded boots.

"But this letter," said Trott, holding a deformed note with a paralytic direction in one hand, and five shillings in the other—"this letter is anonymous."

"A—what?" interrupted the boots.

"Anonymous—he's not to know who it comes from."

"Oh! I see," responded the reg'lar, with a knowing wink, but without evincing the slightest disinclination to undertake the charge—"I see—bit o' Sving, eh?" and his one eye wandered round the room, as if in quest of a dark lantern and phosphorus-box. "But, I say!" he continued, recalling the eye from its search, and bringing it to bear on Mr. Trott. "I say, he's a lawyer, our mayor, and insured in the County. If you've a spite agen him, you'd better not burn his house down—blessed if I don't think it would be the greatest favour you could do him." And he chuckled inwardly.

If Mr. Alexander Trott had been in any other situation, his first act would have been to kick the man down stairs by deputy; or, in other words, to ring the bell, and desire the landlord to take his boots off. He contented himself, however, with doubling the fee and explaining that the letter merely related to a breach of the peace. The top-boots retired, solemnly pledged to secresy; and Mr. Alexander Trott sat down to a fried sole, maintenon cutlet, Madeira, and sundries, with greater composure than he had experienced since the receipt of Horace Hunter's letter of defiance.

The lady who alighted from the London coach had no sooner been installed in number twenty-five, and made some alteration in her travelling-dress, than she indited a note to Joseph Overton, esquire, solicitor, and mayor of Great Wiglebury, requesting his immediate attendance on private business of paramount importance—a summons which that worthy functionary lost no time in obeying; for after sundry openings of his eyes, divers ejaculations of "Bless me!" and other manifestations of surprise, he took his broad-brimmed hat from its accustomed peg in his little front office, and walked briskly down the High-street to the Winglebury Arms; through the hall and up the staircase of which establishment he was ushered by the landlady, and a crowd of officious waiters, to the door of number twenty-five.

"Show the gentleman in," said the stranger lady, in reply to the foremost waiter's announcement. The gentleman was shown in accordingly.

The lady rose from the sofa; the mayor advanced a step from the door; and there they both paused, for a minute or two, looking at one another as if by mutual consent. The mayor saw before him a buxom richly-dressed female of about forty; the lady looked upon a sleek man, about ten years older, in drab shorts and continuations, black coat, neckcloth, and gloves.

"Miss Julia Manners!" exclaimed the mayor at length, "you astonish me."

"That's very unfair of you, Overton," replied Miss Julia, "for I have known you, long enough, not to be surprised at anything you do, and you might extend equal courtesy to me."

"But to run away—actually run away—with a young man!" remonstrated the mayor.

"You wouldn't have me actually run away with an old one, I presume?" was the cool rejoinder.

"And then to ask me—me—of all people in the world—a man of my age and appearance—mayor of the town—to promote such a scheme!" pettishly ejaculated Joseph Overton; throwing himself into an arm-chair, and producing Miss Julia's letter from his pocket, as if to corroborate the assertion that he *had* been asked.

"Now, Overton," replied the lady, "I want your assistance in this matter, and I must have it. In the lifetime of that poor old dear, Mr. Cornberry, who—who—"

"Who was to have married you, and didn't, because he died first; and who left you his property unencumbered with the addition of himself," suggested the mayor.

"Well," replied Miss Julia, reddening slightly, "in the lifetime of the poor old dear, the property had the incumbrance of your management; and all I will say of that, is, that I only wonder *it* didn't die of consumption instead of its master. You helped yourself then:—help me now."

Mr. Joseph Overton was a man of the world, and an attorney; and as certain indistinct recollections of an odd thousand pounds or two, appropriated by mistake, passed across his mind, he hemmed deprecatingly, smiled blandly, remained silent for a few seconds; and finally inquired, "What do you wish me to do?"

"I'll tell you," replied Miss Julia—"I'll tell you in three words. Dear Lord Peter—"

"That's the young man, I suppose—" interrupted the mayor.

"That's the young Nobleman," replied the lady, with a great stress on the last word. "Dear Lord Peter is considerably afraid of the resentment of his family; and we have therefore thought it better to make the match a stolen one. He left town, to avoid suspicion, on a visit to his friend, the Honourable Augustus Flair, whose seat, as you know, is about thirty miles from this, accompanied only by his favourite tiger. We arranged that I should come here alone in the London coach; and that he, leaving his tiger and cab behind him, should come on, and arrive here as soon as possible this afternoon."

"Very well," observed Joseph Overton, "and then he can order the chaise, and you can go on to Gretna Green together, without requiring the presence or interference of a third party, can't you?"

"No," replied Miss Julia. "We have every reason to believe—dear Lord Peter not being considered very prudent or sagacious by his friends, and they having discovered his attachment to me—that, immediately on his absence being observed, pursuit will be made in this direction:—to elude which, and to prevent our being traced, I wish it to be understood in this house, that dear Lord Peter is slightly deranged, though perfectly harmless; and that I am, unknown to him, awaiting his arrival to convey him in a post-chaise to a private asylum—at Berwick, say. If I don't show myself much, I dare say I can manage to pass for his mother."

The thought occurred to the mayor's mind that the lady might show herself a good deal without fear of detection; seeing that she was about double the age of her intended husband. He said nothing, however, and the lady proceeded.

"With the whole of this arrangement dear Lord Peter is acquainted; and all I want you to do, is, to make the delusion more complete by giving it the sanction of your influence in this place, and assigning this as a reason to the people of the house for my taking the young gentleman away. As it would not be consistent with the story that I should see him until after he has entered the chaise, I also wish you to communicate with him, and inform him that it is all going on well."

"Has he arrived?" inquired Overton.

"I don't know," replied the lady.

"Then how am I to know!" inquired the mayor. "Of course he will not give his own name at the bar."

"I begged him, immediately on his arrival, to write you a note," replied Miss Manners; "and to prevent the possibility of our project being discovered through its means, I desired him to write anonymously, and in mysterious terms, to acquaint you with the number of his room."

"Bless me!" exclaimed the mayor, rising from his seat, and searching his pockets—"most extraordinary circumstance—he *has* arrived—mysterious note left at my house in a most mysterious manner, just before yours—didn't know what to make of it before, and certainly shouldn't have attended to it.—Oh! here it is." And Joseph Overton pulled out of an inner coat-pocket the identical letter penned by Alexander Trott. "Is this his lordship's hand?"

"Oh yes," replied Julia; "good, punctual creature! I have not seen it more than once or twice, but I know he writes very badly and very large. These dear, wild young noblemen, you know, Overton—"

"Ay, ay, I see," replied the mayor.—"Horses and dogs, play and wine—grooms, actresses, and cigars—the stable, the green-room, the saloon, and the tavern; and the legislative assembly at last."

"Here's what he says," pursued the mayor; "'Sir,—A young gentleman in number nineteen at the Winglebury Arms, is bent on committing a rash act to-morrow morning at an early hour.' (That's good—he means marrying.) 'If you have any regard for the peace of this town, or the preservation of one—it may be two—human lives'—What the deuce does he mean by that?"

"That he's so anxious for the ceremony, he will expire if it's put off, and that I may possibly do the same," replied the lady with great complacency.

"Oh! I see—not much fear of that;—well—'two human lives, you will cause him to be removed to-night.' (He wants to start at once.) 'Fear not to do this on your responsibility: for to-morrow the absolute necessity of the proceeding will be but too apparent. Remember: number nineteen. The name is Trott. No delay; for life and death depend upon your promptitude.' Passionate language, certainly. Shall I see him?"

"Do," replied Miss Julia; "and entreat him to act his part well. I am half afraid of him. Tell him to be cautious."

"I will," said the mayor.

"Settle all the arrangements."

"I will," said the mayor again.

"And say I think the chaise had better be ordered for one o'clock."

"Very well," said the mayor once more; and, ruminating on the absurdity of the situation in which fate and old acquaintance had placed him, he desired a waiter to herald his approach to the temporary representative of number nineteen.

The announcement, "Gentleman to speak with you, sir," induced Mr. Trott to pause half-way in the glass of port, the contents of which he was in the act of imbibing at the moment; to rise from his chair; and retreat a few paces towards the window, as if to secure a retreat, in the event of the visitor assuming the form and appearance of Horace Hunter. One glance at Joseph Overton, however, quieted his apprehensions. He courteously motioned the stranger to a seat. The waiter, after a little jingling with the decanter and glasses, consented to leave the room; and Joseph Overton, placing the broad-brimmed hat on the chair next him, and bending his body gently forward, opened the business by saying in a very low and cautious tone,

"My lord—"

"Eh?" said Mr. Alexander Trott, in a loud key, with the vacant and mystified stare of a chilly somnambulist.

"Hush—hush!" said the cautious attorney: "to be sure—quite right—no titles here—my name is Overton, sir."

"Overton?"

"Yes: the mayor of this place—you sent me a letter with anonymous information, this afternoon."

"I, sir?" exclaimed Trott with ill-dissembled surprise; for, coward as he was, he would willingly have repudiated the authorship of the letter in question. "I, sir?"

"Yes, you, sir; did you not?" responded Overton, annoyed with what he supposed to be an extreme degree of unnecessary suspicion. "Either this letter is yours, or it is not. If it be, we can converse securely upon the subject at once. If it be not, of course I have no more to say."

"Stay, stay," said Trott, "it *is* mine; I *did* write it. What could I do, sir? I had no friend here."

"To be sure, to be sure," said the mayor, encouragingly, "you could not have managed it better. Well, sir; it will be necessary for you to leave here to-night in a post-chaise and four. And the harder the boys drive, the better. You are not safe from pursuit."

"Bless me!" exclaimed Trott, in an agony of apprehension, "can such things happen in a country like this? Such unrelenting and cold-blooded hostility!" He wiped off the concentrated essence of cowardice that was oozing fast down his forehead, and looked aghast at Joseph Overton.

"It certainly is a very hard case," replied the mayor with a smile, "that, in a free country, people can't marry whom they like, without being hunted down as if they were criminals. However, in the present instance the lady is willing, you know, and that's the main point, after all."

"Lady willing," repeated Trott, mechanically. "How do you know the lady's willing?"

"Come, that's a good one," said the mayor, benevolently tapping Mr. Trott on the arm with his broad-brimmed hat; "I have known her, well, for a long time; and if anybody could entertain the remotest doubt on the subject, I assure you I have none, nor need you have."

"Dear me!" said Mr. Trott, ruminating. "This is *very* extraordinary!"

"Well, Lord Peter," said the mayor, rising.

"Lord Peter?" repeated Mr. Trott.

"Oh—ah, I forgot. Mr. Trott, then—Trott—very good, ha! ha!—Well, sir, the chaise shall be ready at half-past twelve."

"And what is to become of me until then?" inquired Mr. Trott, anxiously. "Wouldn't it save appearances, if I were placed under some restraint?"

"Ah!" replied Overton, "very good thought—capital idea indeed. I'll send somebody up directly. And if you make a little resistance when we put you in the chaise it wouldn't be amiss—look as if you didn't want to be taken away, you know."

"To be sure," said Trott—"to be sure."

"Well, my lord," said Overton, in a low tone, "until then, I wish your lordship a good evening."

"Lord—lordship?" ejaculated Trott again, falling back a step or two, and gazing, in unutterable wonder, on the countenance of the mayor.

"Ha-ha! I see, my lord—practising the madman?—very good indeed—very vacant look—capital, my lord, capital—good evening, Mr.—Trott—ha! ha! ha!"

"That mayor's decidedly drunk," soliloquised Mr. Trott, throwing himself back in his chair, in an attitude of reflection.

"He is a much cleverer fellow than I thought him, that young nobleman—he carries it off uncommonly well," thought Overton, as he went his way to the bar, there to complete his arrangements. This was soon done. Every word of the story was implicitly believed, and the one-eyed boots was immediately instructed to repair to number nineteen, to act as custodian of the person of the supposed lunatic until half-past twelve o'clock. In pursuance of this direction, that somewhat eccentric gentleman armed himself with a walking-stick of gigantic dimensions, and repaired, with his usual equanimity of manner, to Mr. Trott's apartment, which he entered without any ceremony, and mounted guard in, by quietly depositing himself on a chair near the door, where he proceeded to beguile the time by whistling a popular air with great apparent satisfaction.

"What do you want here, you scoundrel?" exclaimed Mr. Alexander Trott, with a proper appearance of indignation at his detention.

The boots beat time with his head, as he looked gently round at Mr. Trott with a smile of pity, and whistled an *adagio* movement.

"Do you attend in this room by Mr. Overton's desire?" inquired Trott, rather astonished at the man's demeanour.

"Keep yourself to yourself, young feller," calmly responded the boots, "and don't say nothin' to nobody." And he whistled again.

"Now, mind!" ejaculated Mr. Trott, anxious to keep up the farce of wishing with great earnestness to fight a duel if they'd let him. "I protest against being kept here. I deny that I have any intention of fighting with anybody. But as it's useless contending with superior numbers, I shall sit quietly down."

"You'd better," observed the placid boots, shaking the large stick expressively.

"Under protest, however," added Alexander Trott, seating himself with indignation in his face, but great content in his heart. "Under protest."

"Oh, certainly!" responded the boots; "anything you please. If you're happy, I'm transported; only don't talk too much—it'll make you worse."

"Make me worse?" exclaimed Trott, in unfeigned astonishment: "the man's drunk!"

"You'd better be quiet, young feller," remarked the boots, going through a threatening piece of pantomime with the stick.

"Or mad!" said Mr. Trott, rather alarmed. "Leave the room, sir, and tell them to send somebody else."

THE GREAT WINGLEBURY DUEL.

"Won't do!" replied the boots.

"Leave the room!" shouted Trott, ringing the bell violently: for he began to be alarmed on a new score.

"Leave that 'ere bell alone, you wretched loo-nattic!" said the boots, suddenly forcing the unfortunate Trott back into his chair, and brandishing the stick aloft. "Be quiet, you miserable object, and don't let everybody know there's a madman in the house."

"He *is* a madman! He *is* a madman!" exclaimed the terrified Mr. Trott, gazing on the one eye of the red-headed boots with a look of abject horror.

"Madman!" replied the boots, "dam'me, I think he *is* a madman with a vengeance! Listen to me, you unfort'nate. Ah! would you?" [a slight tap on the head with the large stick, as Mr. Trott made another move towards the bell-handle] "I caught you there! did I?"

"Spare my life!" exclaimed Trott, raising his hands imploringly.

"I don't want your life," replied the boots, disdainfully, "though I think it 'ud be a charity if somebody took it."

"No, no, it wouldn't," interrupted poor Mr. Trott, hurriedly; "no, no, it wouldn't! I—I—'d rather keep it!"

"O werry well," said the boots: "that's a mere matter of taste—ev'ry one to his liking. Hows'ever, all I've got to say is this here: You sit quietly down in that chair, and I'll sit hoppersite you here, and if you keep quiet and don't stir, I won't damage you; but, if you move hand or foot till half-past twelve o'clock, I shall alter the expression of your countenance so completely, that the next time you look in the glass you'll ask vether you're gone out of town, and ven you're likely to come back again. So sit down."

"I will—I will," responded the victim of mistakes; and down sat Mr. Trott and down sat the boots too, exactly opposite him, with the stick ready fo. immediate action in case of emergency.

Long and dreary were the hours that followed. The bell of Great Winglebury church had just struck ten, and two hours and a half would probably elapse before succour arrived.

For half an hour, the noise occasioned by shutting up the shops in the street beneath, betokened something like life in the town, and rendered Mr. Trott's situation a little less insupportable; but, when even these ceased, and nothing was heard beyond the occasional rattling of a post-chaise as it drove up the yard to change horses, and then drove away again, or the clattering of horses' hoofs in the stables behind, it became almost unbearable. The boots occasionally moved an inch or two, to knock superfluous bits of wax off the candles, which were burning low, but instantaneously resumed his former position; and as he remembered to have heard, somewhere or other, that the human eye had an unfailing effect in controlling mad people, he kept his solitary organ of vision constantly fixed on Mr. Alexander Trott. That unfortunate individual stared at his companion in his turn, until his features grew more and more indistinct—his hair gradually less red—and the room more misty and obscure. Mr. Alexander Trott fell into a sound sleep, from which he was awakened by a rumbling in the street, and a cry of "Chaise-and-four for number twenty-five!" A bustle on the stairs succeeded; the room door was hastily thrown open; and Mr. Joseph Overton entered, followed by four stout waiters, and Mrs. Williamson, the stout landlady of the Winglebury Arms.

"Mr. Overton!" exclaimed Mr. Alexander Trott, jumping up in a frenzy, "Look at this man, sir; consider the situation in which I have been placed for three hours past—the person you sent to guard me, sir, was a madman—a madman—a raging, ravaging, furious madman."

"Bravo!" whispered Overton.

"Poor dear!" said the compassionate Mrs. Williamson, "mad people always thinks other people 's mad."

"Poor dear!" ejaculated Mr. Alexander Trott. "What the devil do you mean by poor dear! Are you the landlady of this house?"

"Yes, yes," replied the stout old lady, "don't exert yourself, there's a dear! Consider your health, now; do."

"Exert myself!" shouted Mr. Alexander Trott, "it's a mercy, ma'am, that I have any breath to exert myself with! I might have been assassinated three hours ago by that one-eyed monster with the oakum head. How dare you have a madman, ma'am—how dare you have a madman, to assault and terrify the visitors to your house?"

"I'll never have another," said Mrs. Williamson, casting a look of reproach at the mayor.

"Capital, capital," whispered Overton again, as he enveloped Mr. Alexander Trott in a thick travelling-cloak.

"Capital, sir!" exclaimed Trott, aloud, "it's horrible. The very recollection makes me shudder. I'd rather fight four duels in three hours, if I survived the first three, than I'd sit for that time face to face with a madman."

"Keep it up, my Lord, as you go down stairs," whispered Overton, "your bill is paid, and your portmanteau in the chaise." And then he added aloud, "Now, waiters, the gentleman's ready."

At this signal, the waiters crowded round Mr. Alexander Trott. One took one arm; another, the other; a third, walked before with a candle; the fourth, behind with another candle; the boots and Mrs. Williamson brought up the rear; and down stairs they went: Mr. Alexander Trott expressing alternately at the very top of his voice either his feigned reluctance to go, or his unfeigned indignation at being shut up with a madman.

Mr. Overton was waiting at the chaise-door, the boys were ready mounted, and a few ostlers and stable nondescripts were standing round to witness the departure of "the mad gentleman." Mr. Alexander Trott's foot was on the step, when he observed (which the dim light had prevented his doing before) a figure seated in the chaise, closely muffled up in a cloak like his own.

"Who's that?" he inquired of Overton, in a whisper.

"Hush, hush," replied the mayor: "the other party of course."

"The other party!" exclaimed Trott, with an effort to retreat.

"Yes, yes; you'll soon find that out, before you go far, I should think—but make a noise, you'll excite suspicion if you whisper to me so much."

"I won't go in this chaise!" shouted Mr. Alexander Trott, all his original fears recurring with tenfold violence. "I shall be assassinated—I shall be—"

"Bravo, bravo," whispered Overton. "I'll push you in."

"But I won't go," exclaimed Mr. Trott. "Help here, help! They're carrying me away against my will. This is a plot to murder me."

"Poor dear!" said Mrs. Williamson again.

"Now, boys, put 'em along," cried the mayor, pushing Trott in and slamming the door. "Off with you, as quick as you can, and stop for nothing till you come to the next stage—all right!"

"Horses are paid, Tom," screamed Mrs. Williamson; and away went the chaise, at the rate of fourteen miles an hour, with Mr. Alexander Trott and Miss Julia Manners carefully shut up in the inside.

Mr. Alexander Trott remained coiled up in one corner of the chaise, and his mysterious companion in the other, for the first two or three miles; Mr. Trott edging more and more into his corner, as he felt his companion gradually edging more and more from hers; and vainly endeavouring in the darkness to catch a glimpse of the furious face of the supposed Horace Hunter.

"We may speak now," said his fellow traveller, at length; "the post-boys can neither see nor hear us."

"That's not Hunter's voice!"—thought Alexander, astonished.

"Dear Lord Peter!" said Miss Julia, most winningly: putting her arm on Mr. Trott's shoulder. "Dear Lord Peter. Not a word?"

"Why, it's a woman!" exclaimed Mr. Trott, in a low tone of excessive wonder.

"Ah! Whose voice is that?" said Julia; "'tis not Lord Peter's."

"No,—it's mine," replied Mr. Trott.

"Yours!" ejaculated Miss Julia Manners; "a strange man! Gracious heaven! How came you here?"

"Whoever you are, you might have known that I came against my will, ma'am," replied Alexander, "for I made noise enough when I got in."

"Do you come from Lord Peter?" inquired Miss Manners.

"Confound Lord Peter," replied Trott pettishly. "I don't know any Lord Peter. I never heard of him before to-night, when I've been Lord Peter'd by one and Lord Peter'd by another, till I verily believe I'm mad, or dreaming—"

"Whither are we going?" inquired the lady tragically.

"How should *I* know, ma'am?" replied Trott with singular coolness; for the events of the evening had completely hardened him.

"Stop! stop!" cried the lady; letting down the front glasses of the chaise.

"Stay, my dear ma'am!" said Mr. Trott, pulling the glasses up again with one hand, and gently squeezing Miss Julia's waist with the other. "There is some mistake here; give me till the end of this stage to explain my share of it. We must go so far; you cannot be set down here alone, at this hour of the night."

The lady consented; the mistake was mutually explained. Mr. Trott was a young man, had highly promising whiskers, an undeniable tailor, and an insinuating address—he wanted nothing but valour, and who wants that with three thousand a-year? The lady had this, and more; she wanted a young husband, and the only course open to Mr. Trott to retrieve his disgrace was a rich wife. So, they came to the conclusion that it would be a pity to have all this trouble and expense for nothing; and that as they were so far on the road already, they had better go to Gretna Green, and marry each other; and they did so. And the very next preceding entry in the Blacksmith's book, was an entry of the marriage of Emily Brown with Horace Hunter. Mr. Hunter took his wife home, and begged pardon, and *was* pardoned; and Mr. Trott took *his* wife home, begged pardon too, and was pardoned also. And Lord Peter, who had been detained beyond his time by drinking champagne and riding a steeple-chase, went back to the Honourable Augustus Flair's, and drank more champagne, and rode another steeple-chase, and was thrown and killed. And Horace Hunter took great credit to himself for practising on the cowardice of Alexander Trott; and all these circumstances were discovered in time, and carefully noted down; and if you ever stop a week at the Winglebury Arms, they will give you just this account of The Great Winglebury Duel.

CHAPTER IX.

MRS. JOSEPH PORTER.

MOST extensive were the preparations at Rose Villa, Clapham Rise, in the occupation of Mr. Gattleton (a stock-broker in especially comfortable circumstances), and great was the anxiety of Mr. Gattleton's interesting family, as the day fixed for the representation of the Private Play which had been "many months in preparation," approached. The whole family was infected with the mania for Private Theatricals; the house, usually so clean and tidy, was, to use Mr. Gattleton's expressive description, "regularly turned out o' windows;" the large dining-room, dismantled of its furniture and ornaments, presented a strange jumble of flats, flies, wings, lamps, bridges, clouds, thunder and lightning, festoons and flowers, daggers and foil, and various other messes in theatrical slang included under the comprehensive name of "properties." The bedrooms were crowded with scenery, the kitchen was occupied by carpenters. Rehearsals took place every other night in the drawing-room, and every sofa in the house was more or less damaged by the perseverance and spirit with which Mr. Sempronius Gattleton, and Miss Lucina, rehearsed the smothering scene in "Othello"—it having been determined that that tragedy should form the first portion of the evening's entertainments.

"When we're a *leetle* more perfect, I think it will go admirably," said Mr. Sempronius, addressing his *corps dramatique*, at the conclusion of the hundred and fiftieth rehearsal. In consideration of his sustaining the trifling inconvenience of bearing all the expenses of the play, Mr. Sempronius had been, in the most handsome manner, unanimously elected stage-manager. "Evans," continued Mr. Gattleton, the younger, addressing a tall, thin, pale young gentleman, with extensive whiskers. "Evans, you play *Roderigo* beautifully."

"Beautifully," echoed the three Miss Gattletons; for Mr. Evans was pronounced by all his lady friends to be "quite a dear." He looked so interesting, and had such lovely whiskers: to say nothing of his talent for writing verses in albums and playing the flute! *Roderigo* simpered and bowed.

"But I think," added the manager, "you are hardly perfect in the—fall—in the fencing-scene, where you are—you understand?"

"It's very difficult," said Mr. Evans, thoughtfully; "I've fallen about, a good deal, in our counting-house lately, for practice, only I find it hurts one so. Being obliged to fall backward you see, it bruises one's head a good deal."

"But you must take care you don't knock a wing down," said Mr. Gattleton, the elder, who had been appointed prompter, and who took as much interest in the play as the youngest of the company. "The stage is very narrow, you know."

"Oh! don't be afraid," said Mr. Evans, with a very self-satisfied air: "I shall fall with my head 'off,' and then I can't do any harm."

"But, egad," said the manager, rubbing his hands, "we shall make a decided hit in 'Masaniello.' Harleigh sings that music admirably."

Everybody echoed the sentiment. Mr. Harleigh smiled, and looked foolish—not an unusual thing with him—hummed "Behold how brightly breaks the morning," and blushed as red as the fisherman's nightcap he was trying on.

"Let's see," resumed the manager, telling the number on his fingers, "we shall have three dancing female peasants, besides *Fenella*, and four fishermen. Then, there's our man Tom; he can have a pair of ducks of mine, and a check shirt of Bob's, and a red nightcap, and he'll do for another—that's five. In the choruses, of course, we can sing at the sides; and in the market-scene we can walk about in cloaks and things. When the revolt takes place, Tom must keep rushing in on one side and out on the other, with a pickaxe, as fast as he can. The effect will be electrical; it will look exactly as if there were an immense number of 'em. And in the eruption scene we must burn the red fire, and upset the tea-trays, and make all sorts of noises—and it's sure to do."

"Sure! sure!" cried all the performers *unâ voce*—and away hurried Mr. Sempronius Gattleton to wash the burnt cork off his face, and superintend the "setting up" of some of the amateur-painted, but never-sufficiently-to-be-admired, scenery.

Mrs. Gattleton was a kind, good-tempered, vulgar soul, exceedingly fond of her husband and children, and entertaining only three dislikes. In the first place, she had a natural antipathy to anybody else's unmarried daughters; in the second, she was in bodily fear of anything in the shape of ridicule; lastly—almost a necessary consequence of this feeling—she regarded, with feelings of the utmost horror, one Mrs. Joseph Porter over the way. However, the good folks of Clapham and its vicinity stood very much in awe of scandal and sarcasm; and thus Mrs. Joseph Porter was courted, and flattered, and caressed, and invited, for much the same reason that induces a poor author, without a farthing in his pocket, to behave with extraordinary civility to a two-penny postman.

"Never mind, ma," said Miss Emma Porter, in colloquy with her respected relative, and trying to look unconcerned; "if they had invited me, you know that neither you nor pa would have allowed me to take part in such an exhibition."

"Just what I should have thought from your high sense of propriety," returned the mother. "I am glad to see, Emma, you know how to designate the proceeding." Miss P., by-the-bye, had only the week before made "an exhibition" of herself for four days, behind a counter at a fancy fair, to all and every of her Majesty's liege subjects who were disposed to pay a shilling each for the privilege of seeing some four dozen girls flirting with strangers, and playing at shop.

"There!" said Mrs. Porter, looking out of window; "there are two rounds of beef and a ham going in—clearly for sandwiches; and Thomas, the pastry-cook, says, there have been twelve dozen tarts ordered, besides blanc-mange and jellies. Upon my word! think of the Miss Gattletons in fancy dresses, too!"

"Oh, it's too ridiculous!" said Miss Porter, hysterically.

"I'll manage to put them a little out of conceit with the business, however," said Mrs. Porter; and out she went on her charitable errand.

"Well, my dear Mrs. Gattleton," said Mrs. Joseph Porter, after they had been closeted for some time, and when, by dint of indefatigable pumping, she had managed to extract all the news about the play, "well, my dear, people may say what they please; indeed we know they will, for some folks are *so* ill-natured. Ah, my dear Miss Lucina, how d'ye do? I was just telling your mamma that I have heard it said, that——"

"What?"

"Mrs. Porter is alluding to the play, my dear," said Mrs. Gattleton; "she was, I am sorry to say, just informing me that——"

"Oh, now pray don't mention it," interrupted Mrs. Porter; "it's most absurd—quite as absurd as young What's-his-name saying he wondered how Miss Caroline, with such a foot and ankle, could have the vanity to play *Fenella.*"

"Highly impertinent, whoever said it," said Mrs. Gattleton, bridling up.

"Certainly, my dear," chimed in the delighted Mrs. Porter; "most undoubtedly! Because, as I said, if Miss Caroline *does* play *Fenella*, it doesn't follow, as a matter of course, that she should think she has a pretty foot;—and then—such puppies as these young men are—he had the impudence to say, that——"

How far the amiable Mrs. Porter might have succeeded in her pleasant purpose, it is impossible to say, had not the entrance of Mr. Thomas Balderstone, Mrs. Gattleton's brother, familiarly called in the family "Uncle Tom," changed the course of conversation, and suggested to her mind an excellent plan of operation on the evening of the play.

Uncle Tom was very rich, and exceedingly fond of his nephews and nieces: as a matter of course, therefore, he was an object of great importance in his own family. He was one of the best-hearted men in existence: always in a good temper, and always talking. It was his boast that he wore top-boots on all occasions, and had never worn a black silk neckerchief; and it was his pride that he remembered all the principal plays of Shakspeare from beginning to end—and so he did. The result of this parrot-like accomplishment was, that he was not only perpetually quoting himself, but that he could never sit by, and hear a misquotation from the "Swan of Avon" without setting the unfortunate delinquent right. He was also something of a wag; never missed an opportunity of saying what he considered a good thing, and invariably laughed until he cried at anything that appeared to him mirth-moving or ridiculous.

"Well, girls!" said Uncle Tom, after the preparatory ceremony of kissing and how-d'ye-do-ing had been gone through—"how d'ye get on? Know your parts, eh?—Lucina, my dear, act ii., scene 1—place, left—cue—'Unknown fate,'—What's next, eh?—Go on—'The Heavens—'"

"Oh, yes," said Miss Lucina, "I recollect—

'The heavens forbid
But that our loves and comforts should increase
Even as our days do grow!'"

"Make a pause here and there," said the old gentleman, who was a great critic. "'But that our loves and comforts should increase'—emphasis on the last syllable, 'crease,'—loud 'even,'—one, two, three, four; then loud again, 'as our days do grow;' emphasis on *days*. That's the way, my dear; trust to your uncle for emphasis, Ah! Sem, my boy, how are you?"

"Very well, thankee, uncle," returned Mr. Sempronius, who had just appeared, looking something like a ringdove, with a small circle round each eye: the result of his constant corking. "Of course we see you on Thursday."

"Of course, of course, my dear boy."

"What a pity it is your nephew didn't think of making you prompter, Mr. Balderstone!" whispered Mrs. Joseph Porter; "you would have been invaluable."

"Well, I flatter myself, I *should* have been tolerably up to the thing," responded Uncle Tom.

"I must bespeak sitting next you on the night," resumed Mrs. Porter; "and then, if our dear young friends here, should be at all wrong, you will be able to enlighten me. I shall be so interested."

"I am sure I shall be most happy to give you any assistance in my power."

"Mind, it's a bargain."

"Certainly."

"I don't know how it is," said Mrs. Gattleton to her daughters, as they were sitting round the fire in the evening, looking over their parts, "but I really very much wish Mrs. Joseph Porter wasn't coming on Thursday. I am sure she's scheming something."

"She can't make *us* ridiculous, however," observed Mr. Sempronius Gattleton, haughtily.

The long-looked-for Thursday arrived in due course, and brought with it, as Mr. Gattleton, senior, philosophically observed, "no disappointments, to speak of." True, it was yet a matter of doubt whether *Cassio* would be enabled to get into the dress which had been sent for him from the masquerade warehouse. It was equally uncertain whether the principal female singer would be sufficiently recovered from the influenza to make her appearance; Mr. Harleigh, the *Masaniello* of the night, was hoarse, and rather unwell, in consequence of the great quantity of lemon and sugar-candy he had eaten to improve his voice; and two flutes and a violoncello had pleaded severe colds. What of that? the audience were all coming. Everybody knew his part: the dresses were covered with tinsel and spangles; the white plumes looked beautiful; Mr. Evans had practised falling until he was bruised from head to foot and quite perfect; *Iago* was sure that, in the stabbing-scene, he should make "a decided hit." A self-taught deaf gentleman, who had kindly offered to bring his flute, would be a most valuable addition to the orchestra; Miss Jenkins's talent for the piano was too well known to be doubted for an instant; Mr. Cape had practised the violin accompaniment with her frequently; and Mr. Brown, who had kindly undertaken, at a few hours' notice, to bring his violoncello, would, no doubt, manage extremely well.

Seven o'clock came, and so did the audience; all the rank and fashion of Clapham and its vicinity was fast filling the theatre. There were the Smiths, the Gubbinses, the Nixons, the Dixons, the Hicksons, people with all sorts of names, two aldermen, a sheriff in perspective, Sir Thomas Glumper (who had been knighted in the last reign for carrying up an address on somebody's escaping from nothing); and last, not least, there were Mrs. Joseph Porter and Uncle Tom, seated in the centre of the third row from the stage; Mrs. P. amusing Uncle Tom with all sorts of stories, and Uncle Tom amusing every one else by laughing most immoderately.

Ting, ting, ting! went the prompter's bell at eight o'clock precisely, and dash went the orchestra into the overture to "The Men of Prometheus." The pianoforte player hammered away with laudable perseverance; and the violoncello, which struck in at intervals, "sounded very well, considering." The unfortunate individual, however, who had undertaken to play the flute accompaniment "at sight," found, from fatal experience, the perfect truth of the old adage, "out of sight, out of mind;" for being very near-sighted, and being placed at a considerable distance from his music-book, all he had an opportunity of doing was to play a bar now and then in the wrong place, and put the other performers out. It is, however, but justice to Mr. Brown to say that he did this to admiration. The overture, in fact, was not unlike a race between the different instruments; the piano came in first by several bars, and the violoncello next, quite distancing the poor flute; for the deaf gentleman *too-too'd* away, quite unconscious that he was at all wrong, until apprised, by the applause of the audience, that the overture was concluded. A considerable bustle and shuffling of feet was then heard upon the stage, accompanied by whispers of "Here's a pretty go!—what's to be done?" &c. The audience applauded again, by way of raising the spirits of the performers; and then Mr. Sempronius desired the prompter, in a very audible voice, to "clear the stage, and ring up."

Ting, ting, ting! went the bell again. Everybody sat down; the curtain shook; rose sufficiently high to display several pair of yellow boots paddling about; and there remained.

Ting, ting, ting! went the bell again. The curtain was violently convulsed, but rose no higher; the audience tittered; Mrs. Porter looked at Uncle Tom; Uncle Tom looked at everybody, rubbing his hands, and laughing with perfect rapture. After as much ringing with the little bell as a muffin-boy would make in going down a tolerably long street, and a vast deal of whispering, hammering, and calling for nails and cord, the curtain at length rose, and discovered Mr. Sempronius Gattleton *solus*, and decked for *Othello*. After three distinct rounds of applause, during which Mr. Sempronius applied his right hand to his left breast, and bowed in the most approved manner, the manager advanced and said:

"Ladies and Gentlemen—I assure you it is with sincere regret, that I regret to be compelled to inform you, that *Iago* who was to have played Mr. Wilson—I beg your pardon, Ladies and Gentlemen, but I am naturally somewhat agitated (applause)—I mean, Mr. Wilson, who was to have played *Iago*, is—that is, has been—or, in other words, Ladies and Gentlemen, the fact is, that I have just received a note, in which I am informed that *Iago* is unavoidably detained at the Post-office this evening. Under these circumstances, I trust—a—a—amateur performance—a—another gentleman undertaken to read the part—request indulgence for a short time—courtesy and kindness of a British audience." Overwhelming applause. Exit Mr. Sempronius Gattleton, and curtain falls.

The audience were, of course, exceedingly good-humoured; the whole business was a joke; and accordingly they waited for an hour with the utmost patience, being enlivened by an interlude of rout-cakes and lemonade. It appeared by Mr. Sempronius's subsequent explanation, that the delay would not have been so great, had it not so happened that when the substitute *Iago* had finished dressing, and just as the play was on the point of commencing, the original *Iago* unexpectedly arrived. The former was therefore compelled to undress, and the latter to dress for his part; which, as he found some difficulty in getting into his clothes, occupied no inconsiderable time. At last, the tragedy began in real earnest. It went off well enough, until the third scene of the first act, in which *Othello* addresses the Senate: the only remarkable circumstance being, that as *Iago* could not get on any of the stage boots, in consequence of his feet being violently swelled with the heat and excitement, he was under the necessity of playing the part in a pair of Wellingtons, which contrasted rather oddly with his richly embroidered pantaloons. When *Othello* started with his address to the Senate (whose dignity was represented by, the *Duke*, a carpenter, two men engaged on the recommendation of the gardener, and a boy), Mrs. Porter found the opportunity she so anxiously sought.

Mr. Sempronius proceeded:

"'Most potent, grave, and reverend signiors,
My very noble and approv'd good masters,
That I have ta'en away this old man's daughter,
It is most true;—rude am I in my speech——'"

"Is that right?" whispered Mrs. Porter to Uncle Tom.

"No."

"Tell him so, then."

"I will. Sem!" called out Uncle Tom, "that's wrong, my boy."

"What's wrong, Uncle?" demanded *Othello*, quite forgetting the dignity of his situation.

"You've left out something. 'True I have married——'"

"Oh, ah!" said Mr. Sempronius, endeavouring to hide his confusion as much and as ineffectually as the audience attempted to conceal their half-suppressed tittering, by coughing with extraordinary violence—

——"'true I have married her;—
The very head and front of my offending
Hath this extent; no more.'

(*Aside*) Why don't you prompt, father?"

"Because I've mislaid my spectacles," said poor Mr. Gattleton, almost dead with the heat and bustle.

"There, now it's 'rude am I,'" said Uncle Tom.

"Yes, I know it is," returned the unfortunate manager, proceeding with his part.

It would be useless and tiresome to quote the number of instances in which Uncle Tom, now completely in his element, and instigated by the mischievous Mrs. Porter, corrected the mistakes of the performers; suffice it to say, that having mounted his hobby, nothing could induce him to dismount; so, during the whole remainder of the play, he performed a kind of running accompaniment, by muttering everybody's part as it was being delivered, in an under tone. The audience were highly amused, Mrs. Porter delighted, the performers embarrassed; Uncle Tom never was better pleased in all his life; and Uncle Tom's nephews and nieces had never, although the declared heirs to his large property, so heartily wished him gathered to his fathers as on that memorable occasion.

Several other minor causes, too, united to damp the ardour of the *dramatis personæ*. None of the performers could walk in their tights, or move their arms in their jackets; the pantaloons were too small, the boots too large, and the swords of all shapes and sizes. Mr. Evans, naturally too tall for the scenery, wore a black velvet hat with immense white plumes, the glory of which was lost in "the flies;" and the only other inconvenience of which was, that when it was off his head he could not put it on, and when it was on he could not take it off. Notwithstanding all his practice, too, he fell with his head and shoulders as neatly through one of the side scenes, as a harlequin would jump through a panel in a Christmas pantomime. The pianoforte player, overpowered by the extreme heat of the room, fainted away at the commencement of the entertainments, leaving the music of "Masaniello" to the flute and violoncello. The orchestra complained that Mr. Harleigh put them out, and Mr. Harleigh declared that the orchestra prevented his singing a note. The fishermen, who were hired for the occasion, revolted to the very life, positively refusing to play without an increased allowance of spirits; and, their demand being complied with, getting drunk in the eruption scene as naturally as possible. The red fire, which was burnt at the conclusion of the second act, not only nearly suffocated the audience, but nearly set the house on fire into the bargain; and, as it was, the remainder of the piece was acted in a thick fog.

In short, the whole affair was, as Mrs. Joseph Porter triumphantly told everybody, "a complete failure." The audience went home at four o'clock in the morning, exhausted with laughter, suffering from severe headaches, and smelling terribly of brimstone and gunpowder. The Messrs. Gattleton, senior and junior, retired to rest, with the vague idea of emigrating to Swan River early in the ensuing week.

Rose Villa has once again resumed its wonted appearance; the dining-room furniture has been replaced; the tables are as nicely polished as formerly; the horsehair chairs are ranged against the wall, as regularly as ever; Venetian blinds have been fitted to every window in the house to intercept the prying gaze of Mrs. Joseph Porter. The subject of theatricals is never mentioned in the Gattleton family, unless, indeed, by Uncle Tom, who cannot refrain from sometimes expressing his surprise and regret at finding that his nephews and nieces appear to have lost the relish they once possessed for the beauties of Shakspeare, and quotations from the works of that immortal bard.

CHAPTER X.

A PASSAGE IN THE LIFE OF MR. WATKINS TOTTLE.

CHAPTER THE FIRST.

MATRIMONY is proverbially a serious undertaking. Like an overweening predilection for brandy-and-water, it is a misfortune into which a man easily falls, and from which he finds it remarkably difficult to extricate himself. It is of no use telling a man who is timorous on these points, that it is but one plunge, and all is over. They say the same thing at the Old Bailey, and the unfortunate victims derive as much comfort from the assurance in the one case as in the other.

Mr. Watkins Tottle was a rather uncommon compound of strong uxorious inclinations, and an unparalleled degree of anti-connubial timidity. He was about fifty years of age; stood four feet six inches and three-quarters, in his socks—for he never stood in stockings at all—plump, clean, and rosy. He looked something like a vignette to one of Richardson's novels, and had a clean-cravatish formality of manner, and kitchen-pokerness of carriage, which Sir Charles Grandison himself might have envied. He lived on an annuity, which was well adapted to the individual who received it, in one respect—it was rather small. He received it in periodical payments on every alternate Monday; but he ran himself out, about a day after the expiration of the first week, as regularly as an eight-day clock; and then, to make the comparison complete, his landlady wound him up, and he went on with a regular tick.

Mr. Watkins Tottle had long lived in a state of single blessedness, as bachelors say, or single cursedness, as spinsters think; but the idea of matrimony had never ceased to haunt him. Wrapt in profound reveries on this never-failing theme, fancy transformed his small parlour in Cecil-street, Strand, into a neat house in the suburbs; the half-hundredweight of coals under the kitchen-stairs suddenly sprang up into three tons of the best Walls-end; his small French bedstead was converted into a regular matrimonial four-poster; and in the empty chair on the opposite side of the fire-place, imagination seated a beautiful young lady, with a very little independence or will of her own, and a very large independence under a will of her father's.

"Who's there?" inquired Mr. Watkins Tottle, as a gentle tap at his room-door disturbed these meditations one evening.

"Tottle, my dear fellow, how *do* you do?" said a short elderly gentleman with a gruffish voice, bursting into the room, and replying to the question by asking another.

"Told you I should drop in some evening," said the short gentleman, as he delivered his hat into Tottle's hand, after a little struggling and dodging.

"Delighted to see you, I'm sure," said Mr. Watkins Tottle, wishing internally that his visitor had "dropped in" to the Thames at the bottom of the street, instead of dropping into his parlour. The fortnight was nearly up, and Watkins was hard up.

"How is Mrs. Gabriel Parsons?" inquired Tottle.

"Quite well, thank you," replied Mr. Gabriel Parsons, for that was the name the short gentleman revelled in. Here there was a pause; the short gentleman looked at the left hob of the fireplace; Mr. Watkins Tottle stared vacancy out of countenance.

"Quite well," repeated the short gentleman, when five minutes had expired. "I may say remarkably well." And he rubbed the palms of his hands as hard as if he were going to strike a light by friction.

"What will you take?" inquired Tottle, with the desperate suddenness of a man who knew that unless the visitor took his leave, he stood very little chance of taking anything else.

"Oh, I don't know—have you any whiskey?"

"Why," replied Tottle, very slowly, for all this was gaining time, "I *had* some capital, and remarkably strong whiskey last week; but it's all gone—and therefore its strength——"

"Is much beyond proof; or, in other words, impossible to be proved," said the short gentleman; and he laughed very heartily, and seemed quite glad the whiskey had been drunk. Mr. Tottle smiled—but it was the smile of despair. When Mr. Gabriel Parsons had done laughing, he delicately insinuated that, in the absence of whiskey, he would not be averse to brandy. And Mr. Watkins Tottle, lighting a flat candle very ostentatiously; and displaying an immense key, which belonged to the street-door, but which, for the sake of appearances, occasionally did duty in an imaginary wine-cellar; left the room to entreat his landlady to charge their glasses, and charge them in the bill. The application was successful; the spirits were speedily called—not from the vasty deep, but the adjacent wine-vaults. The two short gentlemen mixed their grog; and then sat cosily down before the fire—a pair of shorts, airing themselves.

"Tottle," said Mr. Gabriel Parsons, "you know my way—off-hand, open, say what I mean, mean what I say, hate reserve, and can't bear affectation. One, is a bad domino which only hides what good people have about 'em, without making the bad look better; and the other is much about the same thing as pinking a white cotton stocking to make it look like a silk one. Now listen to what I'm going to say."

Here, the little gentleman paused, and took a long pull at his brandy-and-water. Mr. Watkins Tottle took a sip of his, stirred the fire, and assumed an air of profound attention.

"It's of no use humming and ha'ing about the matter," resumed the short gentleman.—"You want to get married."

"Why," replied Mr. Watkins Tottle evasively; for he trembled violently, and felt a sudden tingling throughout his whole frame; "why—I should certainly—at least, I *think* I should like—"

"Won't do," said the short gentleman.—"Plain and free—or there's an end of the matter. Do you want money?"

"You know I do."

"You admire the sex?"

"I do."

"And you'd like to be married?"

"Certainly."

"Then you shall be. There's an end of that." Thus saying, Mr. Gabriel Parsons took a pinch of snuff, and mixed another glass.

"Let me entreat you to be more explanatory," said Tottle. "Really, as the party principally interested, I cannot consent to be disposed of, in this way."

"I'll tell you," replied Mr. Gabriel Parsons, warming with the subject, and the brandy-and-water—"I know a lady—she's stopping with my wife now—who is just the thing for you. Well educated; talks French; plays the piano; knows a good deal about flowers, and shells, and all that sort of thing; and has five hundred a year, with an uncontrolled power of disposing of it, by her last will and testament."

"I'll pay my addresses to her," said Mr. Watkins Tottle. "She isn't *very* young—is she?"

"Not very; just the thing for you. I've said that already."

"What coloured hair has the lady?" inquired Mr. Watkins Tottle.

"Egad, I hardly recollect," replied Gabriel, with coolness. "Perhaps I ought to have observed, at first, she wears a front."

"A what!" ejaculated Tottle.

"One of those things with curls, along here," said Parsons, drawing a straight line across his forehead, just over his eyes, in illustration of his meaning. "I know the front's black; I can't speak quite positively about her own hair; because, unless one walks behind her, and catches a glimpse of it under her bonnet, one seldom sees it; but I should say that it was *rather* lighter than the front—a shade of a greyish tinge, perhaps."

Mr. Watkins Tottle looked as if he had certain misgivings of mind. Mr. Gabriel Parsons perceived it, and thought it would be safe to begin the next attack without delay.

"Now, were you ever in love, Tottle?" he inquired.

Mr. Watkins Tottle blushed up to the eyes, and down to the chin, and exhibited a most extensive combination of colours as he confessed the soft impeachment.

"I suppose you popped the question, more than once when you were a young —I beg your pardon—a younger—man," said Parsons.

"Never in my life!" replied his friend, apparently indignant at being suspected of such an act. "Never! The fact is, that I entertain, as you know, peculiar opinions on these subjects. I am not afraid of ladies, young or old—far from it; but, I think, that in compliance with the custom of the present day, they allow too much freedom of speech and manner to marriageable men. Now, the fact is, that anything like this easy freedom I never could acquire; and as I am always afraid of going too far, I am generally, I dare say, considered formal and cold."

"I shouldn't wonder if you were," replied Parsons, gravely; "I shouldn't wonder. However, you'll be all right in this case; for the strictness and delicacy of this lady's ideas greatly exceed your own. Lord bless you, why when she came to our house, there was an old portrait of some man or other, with two large black staring eyes, hanging up in her bedroom; she positively refused to go to bed there, till it was taken down, considering it decidedly wrong."

"I think so, too," said Mr. Watkins Tottle; "certainly."

"And then, the other night—I never laughed so much in my life"—resumed Mr. Gabriel Parsons; "I had driven home in an easterly wind, and caught a devil of a face-ache. Well; as Fanny—that's Mrs. Parsons, you know—and this friend of hers, and I, and Frank Ross, were playing a rubber, I said, jokingly, that when I went to bed I should wrap my head in Fanny's flannel petticoat. She instantly threw up her cards, and left the room."

"Quite right!" said Mr. Watkins Tottle; "she could not possibly have behaved in a more dignified manner. What did you do?"

"Do?—Frank took dummy; and I won sixpence."

"But, didn't you apologise for hurting her feelings?"

"Devil a bit. Next morning at breakfast, we talked it over. She contended that any reference to a flannel petticoat was improper;—men ought not to be supposed to know that such things were. I pleaded my coverture; being a married man."

"And what did the lady say to that?" inquired Tottle, deeply interested.

"Changed her ground, and said that Frank being a single man, its impropriety was obvious."

"Noble-minded creature!" exclaimed the enraptured Tottle.

"Oh! both Fanny and I said, at once, that she was regularly cut out for you."

A gleam of placid satisfaction shone on the circular face of Mr. Watkins Tottle, as he heard the prophecy.

"There's one thing I can't understand," said Mr. Gabriel Parsons, as he rose to depart; "I cannot, for the life and soul of me imagine, how the deuce you'll ever contrive to come together. The lady would certainly go into convulsions if the subject were mentioned." Mr. Gabriel Parsons sat down again, and laughed until he was weak. Tottle owed him money, so he had a perfect right to laugh at Tottle's expense.

Mr. Watkins Tottle feared, in his own mind, that this was another characteristic which he had in common with this modern Lucretia. He, however, accepted the invitation to dine with the Parsonses on the next day but one, with great firmness; and looked forward to the introduction, when again left alone, with tolerable composure.

The sun that rose on the next day but one, had never beheld a sprucer personage on the outside of the Norwood stage, than Mr. Watkins Tottle; and when the coach drew up before a card-board looking house with disguised chimneys, and a lawn like a large sheet of green letter-paper, he certainly had never lighted to his place of destination a gentleman who felt more uncomfortable.

The coach stopped, and Mr. Watkins Tottle jumped—we beg his pardon—alighted, with great dignity. "All right!" said he, and away went the coach up the hill with that beautiful equanimity of pace for which "short" stages are generally remarkable.

Mr. Watkins Tottle gave a faltering jerk to the handle of the garden-gate bell. He essayed a more energetic tug, and his previous nervousness was not at all diminished by hearing the bell ringing like a fire alarum.

"Is Mr. Parsons at home?" inquired Tottle of the man who opened the gate. He could hardly hear himself speak, for the bell had not yet done tolling.

"Here I am," shouted a voice on the lawn,—and there was Mr. Gabriel Parsons in a flannel jacket, running backwards and forwards, from a wicket to two hats piled on each other, and from the two hats to the wicket, in the most violent manner, while another gentleman with his coat off was getting down the area of the house, after a ball. When the gentleman without the coat had found it—which he did in less than ten minutes—he ran back to the hats, and Gabriel Parsons pulled up. Then, the gentleman without the coat called out "play," very loudly, and bowled. Then Mr. Gabriel Parsons knocked the ball several yards, and took another run. Then, the other gentleman aimed at the wicket, and didn't hit it; and Mr. Gabriel Parsons, having finished running on his own account, laid down the bat and ran after the ball, which went into a neighbouring field. They called this cricket.

"Tottle, will you 'go in?'" inquired Mr. Gabriel Parsons, as he approached him, wiping the perspiration off his face.

Mr. Watkins Tottle declined the offer, the bare idea of accepting which made him even warmer than his friend.

"Then we'll go into the house, as it's past four, and I shall have to wash my hands before dinner," said Mr. Gabriel Parsons. "Here, I hate ceremony, you know! Timson, that's Tottle—Tottle, that's Timson; bred for the church, which I fear will never be bread for him;" and he chuckled at the old joke. Mr. Timson bowed carelessly. Mr. Watkins Tottle bowed stiffly. Mr. Gabriel Parsons led the way to the house. He was a rich sugar-baker, who mistook rudeness for honesty, and abrupt bluntness for an open and candid manner; many besides Gabriel mistake bluntness for sincerity.

Mrs. Gabriel Parsons received the visitors most graciously on the steps, and preceded them to the drawing-room. On the sofa, was seated a lady of very prim appearance, and remarkably inanimate. She was one of those persons at whose age it is impossible to make any reasonable guess; her features might have been remarkably pretty when she was younger, and they might always have presented the same appearance. Her complexion—with a slight trace of powder here and there—was as clear as that of a well-made wax-doll, and her face as expressive. She was handsomely dressed, and was winding up a gold watch.

"Miss Lillerton, my dear, this is our friend Mr. Watkins Tottle; a very old acquaintance I assure you," said Mrs. Parsons, presenting the Strephon of Cecil-street, Strand. The lady rose, and made a deep courtesy; Mr. Watkins Tottle made a bow.

"Splendid, majestic creature!" thought Tottle.

Mr. Timson advanced, and Mr. Watkins Tottle began to hate him. Men generally discover a rival, instinctively, and Mr. Watkins Tottle felt that his hate was deserved.

"May I beg," said the reverend gentleman,—"May I beg to call upon you, Miss Lillerton, for some trifling donation to my soup, coals, and blanket distribution society?"

"Put my name down, for two sovereigns, if you please," responded Miss Lillerton.

"You are truly charitable, madam," said the Reverend Mr. Timson, "and we know that charity will cover a multitude of sins. Let me beg you to understand that I do not say this from the supposition that you have many sins which require palliation; believe me when I say that I never yet met any one who had fewer to atone for, than Miss Lillerton."

Something like a bad imitation of animation lighted up the lady's face, as she acknowledged the compliment. Watkins Tottle incurred the sin of wishing that the ashes of the Reverend Charles Timson were quietly deposited in the church-yard of his curacy, wherever it might be.

"I'll tell you what," interrupted Parsons, who had just appeared with clean hands, and a black coat, "it's my private opinion, Timson, that your 'distribution society' is rather a humbug."

"You are so severe," replied Timson, with a Christian smile: he disliked Parsons, but liked his dinners.

"So positively unjust!" said Miss Lillerton.

"Certainly," observed Tottle. The lady looked up; her eyes met those of Mr. Watkins Tottle. She withdrew them in a sweet confusion, and Watkins Tottle did the same—the confusion was mutual.

"Why," urged Mr. Parsons, pursuing his objections, "what on earth is the use of giving a man coals who has nothing to cook, or giving him blankets when he hasn't a bed, or giving him soup when he requires substantial food?—'like sending them ruffles when wanting a shirt.' Why not give 'em a trifle of money, as I do, when I think they deserve it, and let them purchase what they think best? Why?—because your subscribers wouldn't see their names flourishing in print on the church-door—that's the reason."

"Really, Mr. Parsons, I hope you don't mean to insinuate that I wish to see *my* name in print, on the church-door," interrupted Miss Lillerton.

"I hope not," said Mr. Watkins Tottle, putting in another word, and getting another glance.

"Certainly not," replied Parsons. "I dare say you wouldn't mind seeing it in writing, though, in the church register—eh?"

"Register! What register?" inquired the lady, gravely.

"Why, the register of marriages, to be sure," replied Parsons, chuckling at the sally, and glancing at Tottle. Mr. Watkins Tottle thought he should have fainted.

for shame, and it is quite impossible to imagine what effect the joke would have had upon the lady, if dinner had not been, at that moment, announced. Mr. Watkins Tottle, with an unprecedented effort of gallantry, offered the tip of his little finger; Miss Lillerton accepted it gracefully, with maiden modesty; and they proceeded in due state to the dinner-table, where they were soon deposited side by side. The room was very snug, the dinner very good, and the little party in spirits. The conversation became pretty general, and when Mr. Watkins Tottle had extracted one or two cold observations from his neighbour, and had taken wine with her, he began to acquire confidence rapidly. The cloth was removed; Mrs. Gabriel Parsons drank four glasses of port on the plea of being a nurse just then; and Miss Lillerton took about the same number of sips, on the plea of not wanting any at all. At length, the ladies retired, to the great gratification of Mr. Gabriel Parsons, who had been coughing and frowning at his wife, for half-an-hour previously—signals which Mrs. Parsons never happened to observe, until she had been pressed to take her ordinary quantum, which, to avoid giving trouble, she generally did at once.

"What do you think of her?" inquired Mr. Gabriel Parsons of Mr. Watkins Tottle, in an under tone.

"I dote on her with enthusiasm already!" replied Mr. Watkins Tottle.

"Gentlemen, pray let us drink 'the ladies,'" said the Reverend Mr. Timson.

"The ladies!" said Mr. Watkins Tottle, emptying his glass. In the fulness of his confidence, he felt as if he could make love to a dozen ladies, off hand.

"Ah!" said Mr. Gabriel Parsons, "I remember when I was a young man—fill your glass, Timson."

"I have this moment emptied it."

"Then fill again."

"I will," said Timson, suiting the action to the word.

"I remember," resumed Mr. Gabriel Parsons, "when I was a younger man, with what a strange compound of feelings I used to drink that toast, and how I used to think every woman was an angel."

"Was that before you were married?" mildly inquired Mr. Watkins Tottle.

"Oh! certainly," replied Mr. Gabriel Parsons, "I have never thought so since; and a precious milksop I must have been, ever to have thought so at all. But, you know, I married Fanny under the oddest, and most ridiculous circumstances possible."

"What were they, if one may inquire?" asked Timson, who had heard the story, on an average, twice a week for the last six months. Mr. Watkins Tottle listened attentively, in the hope of picking up some suggestion that might be useful to him in his new undertaking.

"I spent my wedding-night in a back-kitchen chimney," said Parsons, by way of a beginning.

"In a back-kitchen chimney!" ejaculated Watkins Tottle. "How dreadful!"

"Yes, it wasn't very pleasant," replied the small host. "The fact is, Fanny's father and mother liked me well enough as an individual, but had a decided objection to my becoming a husband. You see, I hadn't any money in those days, and they had; and so they wanted Fanny to pick up somebody else. However, we managed to discover the state of each other's affections somehow. I used to meet her, at some mutual friends' parties; at first we danced together, and talked, and flirted, and all that sort of thing; then, I used to like nothing so well as sitting by her side—we didn't talk so much then, but I remember I used to have a great notion of looking at her out of the extreme corner of my left eye—and then I got very miserable and sentimental, and began to write verses, and use Macassar oil. At last I couldn't bear it any longer, and after I had walked up and down the sunny side of Oxford-street in tight boots for a week—and a devilish hot summer it was too—in the hope of meeting her, I sat down and wrote a letter, and begged her to manage to see me clandestinely, for I wanted to hear her decision from her own mouth. I said I had discovered, to my perfect satisfaction, that I couldn't live without her, and that if she didn't have me, I had made up my mind to take prussic acid, or take to drinking, or emigrate, so as to take myself off in some way or other. Well, I borrowed a pound, and bribed the housemaid to give her the note, which she did."

"And what was the reply?" inquired Timson, who had found, before, that to encourage the repetition of old stories is to get a general invitation.

"Oh, the usual one! Fanny expressed herself very miserable; hinted at the possibility of an early grave; said that nothing should induce her to swerve from the duty she owed her parents; implored me to forget her, and find out somebody more deserving, and all that sort of thing. She said she could, on no account, think of meeting me unknown to her pa and ma; and entreated me, as she should be in a particular part of Kensington Gardens at eleven o'clock next morning, not to attempt to meet her there."

"You didn't go, of course?" said Watkins Tottle.

"Didn't I?—Of course I did. There she was, with the identical housemaid in perspective, in order that there might be no interruption. We walked about, for a couple of hours; made ourselves delightfully miserable; and were regularly engaged. Then, we began to 'correspond'—that is to say, we used to exchange about four letters a day; what we used to say in 'em I can't imagine. And I used to have an interview, in the kitchen, or the cellar, or some such place, every evening. Well, things went on in this way for some time; and we got fonder of each other every day. At last, as our love was raised to such a pitch, and as my salary had been raised too, shortly before, we determined on a secret marriage. Fanny arranged to sleep at a friend's, on the previous night; we were to be married early in the morning; and then we were to return to her home and be pathetic. She was to fall at the old gentleman's feet, and bathe his boots with her tears; and I was to hug the old lady and call her 'mother,' and use my pocket handkerchief as much as possible. Married we were, the next morning; two girls—friends of Fanny's—acting as bridesmaids; and a man, who was hired for five shillings and a pint of porter, officiating as father. Now, the old lady unfortunately put off her return from Ramsgate, where she had been paying a visit, until the next morning; and as we placed great reliance on her, we agreed to postpone our confession for four-and-twenty hours. My newly-made wife returned home, and I spent my wedding-day in strolling about Hampstead-heath, and execrating my father-in-law. Of course, I went to comfort my dear little wife at night, as much as I could, with the assurance that our troubles would soon be over. I opened the garden-gate, of which I had a key, and was shown by the servant to our old place of meeting—a back kitchen, with a stone-floor and a dresser: upon which, in the absence of chairs, we used to sit and make love."

"Make love upon a kitchen-dresser!" interrupted Mr. Watkins Tottle, whose ideas of decorum were greatly outraged.

"Ah! On a kitchen-dresser!" replied Parsons. "And let me tell you, old fellow, that, if you were really over head-and-ears in love, and had no other place to make love in, you'd be devilish glad to avail yourself of such an opportunity. However, let me see;—where was I?"

"On the dresser," suggested Timson.

"Oh—ah! Well, here I found poor Fanny, quite disconsolate and uncomfortable. The old boy had been very cross all day, which made her feel still more lonely; and she was quite out of spirits. So, I put a good face on the matter, and laughed it off, and said we should enjoy the pleasures of a matrimonial life more by contrast; and, at length, poor Fanny brightened up a little. I stopped there, till about eleven o'clock, and, just as I was taking my leave for the fourteenth time, the girl came running down the stairs, without her shoes, in a great fright, to tell us that the old villain—Heaven forgive me for calling him so, for he is dead and gone now!—prompted I suppose by the prince of darkness, was coming down, to draw his own beer for supper—a thing he had not done before, for six months, to my certain knowledge; for the cask stood in that very back kitchen. If he discovered me there, explanation would have been out of the question; for he was so outrageously violent, when at all excited, that he never would have listened to me. There was only one thing to be done. The chimney was a very wide one; it had been originally built for an oven; went up perpendicularly for a few feet, and then shot backward and formed a sort of small cavern. My hopes and fortune—the means of our joint existence almost—were at stake. I scrambled in like a squirrel; coiled myself up in this recess; and, as Fanny and the girl replaced the deal chimney-board, I could see the light of the candle which my unconscious father-in-law carried in his hand. I heard him draw the beer; and I never heard beer run so slowly. He was just leaving the kitchen, and I was preparing to descend, when down came the infernal chimney-board with a tremendous crash. He stopped and put down the candle and the jug of beer on the dresser; he was a nervous old fellow, and any unexpected noise annoyed him. He coolly observed that the fireplace was never used, and sending the frightened servant into the next kitchen for a hammer and nails, actually nailed up the board, and locked the door on the outside. So, there was I, on my wedding-night, in the light kerseymere trousers, fancy waistcoat, and blue coat, that I had been married in in the morning, in a back-kitchen chimney, the bottom of which was nailed up, and the top of which had been formerly raised some fifteen feet, to prevent the smoke from annoying the neighbours. And there," added Mr. Gabriel Parsons, as he passed the bottle, "there I remained till half-past seven the next morning, when the housemaid's sweetheart, who was a carpenter, unshelled me. The old dog had nailed me up so securely, that, to this very hour, I firmly believe that no one but a carpenter could ever have got me out."

"And what did Mrs. Parsons's father say, when he found you were married?" inquired Watkins Tottle, who, although he never saw a joke, was not satisfied until he heard a story to the very end.

"Why, the affair of the chimney so tickled his fancy, that he pardoned us off-hand, and allowed us something to live on till he went the way of all flesh. I spent the next night in his second-floor front, much more comfortable than I had spent the preceding one; for, as you will probably guess——"

"Please, sir, missis has made tea," said a middle-aged female servant, bobbing into the room.

"That's the very housemaid that figures in my story," said Mr. Gabriel Parsons. "She went into Fanny's service when we were first married, and has been with us ever since; but I don't think she has felt one atom of respect for me since the morning she saw me released, when she went into violent hysterics, to which she has been subject ever since. Now, shall we join the ladies?"

"If you please," said Mr. Watkins Tottle.

"By all means," added the obsequious Mr. Timson; and the trio made for the drawing-room accordingly.

Tea being concluded, and the toast and cups having been duly handed, and occasionally upset, by Mr. Watkins Tottle, a rubber was proposed. They cut for partners—Mr. and Mrs. Parsons; and Mr. Watkins Tottle and Miss Lillerton. Mr. Timson having conscientious scruples on the subject of card-playing, drank brandy-and-water, and kept up a running spar with Mr. Watkins Tottle. The evening went off well; Mr. Watkins Tottle was in high spirits, having some reason to be gratified with his reception by Miss Lillerton; and before he left, a small party was made up to visit the Beulah Spa on the following Saturday.

"It's all right, I think," said Mr. Gabriel Parsons to Mr. Watkins Tottle as he opened the garden gate for him.

"I hope so," he replied, squeezing his friend's hand.

"You'll be down by the first coach on Saturday," said Mr. Gabriel Parsons.

"Certainly," replied Mr. Watkins Tottle. "Undoubtedly."

But fortune had decreed that Mr. Watkins Tottle should not be down by the first coach on Saturday. His adventures on that day, however, and the success of his wooing, are subjects for another chapter.

CHAPTER THE SECOND.

"THE first coach has not come in yet, has it, Tom?" inquired Mr. Gabriel Parsons, as he very complacently paced up and down the fourteen feet of gravel which bordered the "lawn," on the Saturday morning which had been fixed upon for the Beulah Spa jaunt.

"No, sir; I haven't seen it," replied a gardener in a blue apron, who let himself out to do the ornamental for half-a-crown a day and his "keep."

"Time Tottle was down," said Mr. Gabriel Parsons, ruminating—"Oh, here he is, no doubt," added Gabriel, as a cab drove rapidly up the hill; and he buttoned his dressing-gown, and opened the gate to receive the expected visitor. The cab stopped, and out jumped a man in a coarse Petersham great-coat, whity-brown neckerchief, faded black suit, gamboge-coloured top-boots, and one of those large-crowned hats, formerly seldom met with, but now very generally patronised by gentlemen and costermongers.

"Mr. Parsons?" said the man, looking at the superscription of a note he held in his hand, and addressing Gabriel with an inquiring air.

"*My* name is Parsons," responded the sugar-baker.

"I've brought this here note," replied the individual in the painted tops, in a hoarse whisper: "I've brought this here note from a gen'lm'n as come to our house this mornin'."

"I expected the gentleman at my house," said Parsons, as he broke the seal, which bore the impression of her Majesty's profile as it is seen on a sixpence.

"I've no doubt the gen'lm'n would ha' been here," replied the stranger, "if he hadn't happened to call at our house first; but we never trusts no gen'lm'n furder nor we can see him—no mistake about that there"—added the unknown, with a facetious grin; "beg your pardon, sir, no offence meant, only—once in, and I wish you may—catch the idea, sir?"

Mr. Gabriel Parsons was not remarkable for catching anything suddenly, but a cold. He therefore only bestowed a glance of profound astonishment on his mysterious companion, and proceeded to unfold the note of which he had been the bearer. Once opened and the idea was caught with very little difficulty. Mr. Watkins Tottle had been suddenly arrested for 33*l.* 10*s.* 4*d.*, and dated his communication from a lock-up house in the vicinity of Chancery-lane.

"Unfortunate affair this!" said Parsons, refolding the note.

"Oh! nothin' ven you 're used to it," coolly observed the man in the Petersham.

"Tom!" exclaimed Parsons, after a few minutes' consideration, "just put the horse in, will you?—Tell the gentleman that I shall be there almost as soon as you are," he continued, addressing the sheriff-officer's Mercury.

"Werry well," replied that important functionary; adding, in a confidential manner, "I 'd adwise the gen'lm'n s friends to settle. You see it 's a mere trifle; and, unless the gen'lm'n means to go up afore the court, it 's hardly worth while waiting for detainers you know. Our governor 's wide awake, he is. I 'll never say nothin' agin him, nor no man; but he knows what 's o'clock, he does, uncommon." Having delivered this eloquent, and, to Parsons, particularly intelligible harangue, the meaning of which was eked out by divers nods and winks, the gentleman in the boots reseated himself in the cab, which went rapidly off, and was soon out of sight. Mr. Gabriel Parsons continued to pace up and down the pathway for some minutes, apparently absorbed in deep meditation. The result of his cogitations seemed to be perfectly satisfactory to himself, for he ran briskly into the house; said that business had suddenly summoned him to town; that he had desired the messenger to inform Mr. Watkins Tottle of the fact; and that they would return together to dinner. He then hastily equipped himself for a drive, and mounting his gig, was soon on his way to the establishment of Mr. Solomon Jacobs, situate (as Mr. Watkins Tottle had informed him) in Cursitor-street, Chancery-lane.

When a man is in a violent hurry to get on, and has a specific object in view, the attainment of which depends on the completion of his journey, the difficulties which interpose themselves in his way appear not only to be innumerable, but to have been called into existence especially for the occasion. The remark is by no means a new one, and Mr. Gabriel Parsons had practical and painful experience of its justice in the course of his drive. There are three classes of animated objects which prevent your driving with any degree of comfort or celerity through streets which are but little frequented—they are pigs, children, and old women. On the occasion we are describing, the pigs were luxuriating on cabbage-stalks, and the shuttlecocks fluttered from the little deal battledores, and the children played in the road; and women, with a basket in one hand, and the street-door key in the other, *would* cross just before the horse's head, until Mr. Gabriel Parsons was perfectly savage with vexation, and quite hoarse with hoi-ing and imprecating. Then, when he got into Fleet-street, there was "a stoppage," in which people in vehicles have the satisfaction of remaining stationary for half an hour, and envying the slowest pedestrians; and where policemen rush about, and seize hold of horses' bridles, and back them into shop-windows, by way of clearing the road and preventing confusion. At length Mr. Gabriel Parsons turned into Chancery-lane, and having inquired for, and been directed to Cursitor-street (for it was a locality of which he was quite ignorant), he soon found himself opposite the house of Mr. Solomon Jacobs. Confiding his horse and gig to the care of one of the fourteen boys who had followed him from the other side of Blackfriars-bridge on the chance of his requiring their services, Mr. Gabriel Parsons crossed the road and knocked at an inner door, the upper part of which was of glass, grated like the windows of this inviting mansion with iron bars—painted white to look comfortable.

The knock was answered by a sallow-faced red-haired sulky boy, who, after surveying Mr. Gabriel Parsons through the glass, applied a large key to an immense wooden excrescence, which was in reality a lock, but which, taken in conjunction with the iron nails with which the panels were studded, gave the door the appearance of being subject to warts.

"I want to see Mr. Watkins Tottle," said Parsons.

"It 's the gentleman that come in this morning, Jem," screamed a voice from the top of the kitchen-stairs, which belonged to a dirty woman who had just brought her chin to a level with the passage-floor. "The gentleman 's in the coffee-room."

"Up-stairs, sir," said the boy, just opening the door wide enough to let Parsons in without squeezing him, and double-locking it the moment he had made his way through the aperture—"First floor—door on the left."

Mr. Gabriel Parsons thus instructed, ascended the uncarpeted and ill-lighted staircase, and after giving several subdued taps at the before-mentioned "door on the left," which were rendered inaudible by the hum of voices within the room, and the hissing noise attendant on some frying operations which were carrying on below stairs, turned the handle, and entered the apartment. Being informed that the unfortunate object of his visit had just gone up-stairs to write a letter, he had leisure to sit down and observe the scene before him.

The room—which was a small, confined den—was partitioned off into boxes, like the common-room of some inferior eating-house. The dirty-floor had evidently been as long a stranger to the scrubbing-brush as to carpet or floor-cloth: and the ceiling was completely blackened by the flare of the oil-lamp by which the room was lighted at night. The gray ashes on the edges of the tables, and the cigar ends which were plentifully scattered about the dusty grate, fully accounted for the intolerable smell of tobacco which pervaded the place; and the empty glasses and half-saturated slices of lemon on the tables, together with the porter pots beneath them, bore testimony to the frequent libations in which the individuals who honoured Mr. Solomon Jacobs by a temporary residence in his house indulged. Over the mantel-shelf was a paltry looking-glass, extending about half the width of the chimney-piece; but by way of counterpoise, the ashes were confined by a rusty fender about twice as long as the hearth.

From this cheerful room itself, the attention of Mr. Gabriel Parsons was naturally directed to its inmates. In one of the boxes two men were playing at cribbage with a very dirty pack of cards, some with blue, some with green, and some with red backs—selections from decayed packs. The cribbage board had been long ago formed on the table by some ingenious visitor with the assistance of a pocket-knife and a two-pronged fork, with which the necessary number of holes had been made in the table at proper distances for the reception of the wooden pegs. In another box a stout, hearty-looking man, of about forty, was eating some dinner which his wife—an equally comfortable-looking personage—had brought him in a basket: and in a third, a genteel-looking young man was talking earnestly, and in a low tone, to a young female, whose face was concealed by a thick veil, but whom Mr. Gabriel Parsons immediately set down in his own mind as the debtor's wife. A young fellow of vulgar manners, dressed in the very extreme of the prevailing fashion, was pacing up and down the room, with a lighted cigar in his mouth and his hands in his pockets, ever and anon puffing forth volumes of smoke, and occasionally applying, with much apparent relish, to a pint pot, the contents of which were "chilling" on the hob.

"Fourpence more, by gum!" exclaimed one of the cribbage-players, lighting a pipe, and addressing his adversary at the close of the game; "one 'ud think you'd got luck in a pepper-cruet, and shook it out when you wanted it."

"Well, that a'n't a bad un," replied the other, who was a horse-dealer from Islington.

"No; I'm blessed if it is," interposed the jolly-looking fellow, who, having finished his dinner, was drinking out of the same glass as his wife, in truly conjugal harmony, some hot gin-and-water. The faithful partner of his cares had brought a plentiful supply of the anti-temperance fluid in a large flat stone bottle, which looked like a half-gallon jar that had been successfully tapped for the dropsy. "You're a rum chap, you are, Mr. Walker—will you dip your beak into this, sir?"

"Thank'ee, sir," replied Mr. Walker, leaving his box, and advancing to the other to accept the proffered glass. "Here's your health, sir, and your good 'ooman's here. Gentlemen all—yours, and better luck still. Well, Mr. Willis," continued the facetious prisoner, addressing the young man with the cigar, "you seem rather down to-day—floored, as one may say. What's the matter, sir? Never say die, you know."

"Oh! I'm all right," replied the smoker. "I shall be bailed out to-morrow."

"Shall you, though?" inquired the other. "Damme, I wish I could say the same. I am as regularly over head and ears as the Royal George, and stand about as much chance of being *bailed out*. Ha! ha! ha!"

"Why," said the young man, stopping short, and speaking in a very loud key, "look at me. What d'ye think I've stopped here two days for?"

"'Cause you couldn't get out, I suppose," interrupted Mr. Walker, winking to the company. "Not that you're exactly obliged to stop here, only you can't help it. No compulsion, you know, only you must—eh?"

"A'n't he a rum un?" inquired the delighted individual, who had offered the gin-and-water, of his wife.

"Oh, he just is!" replied the lady, who was quite overcome by these flashes of imagination.

"Why, my case," frowned the victim, throwing the end of his cigar into the fire, and illustrating his argument by knocking the bottom of the pot on the table, at intervals,—"my case is a very singular one. My father's a man of large property, and I am his son."

"That's a very strange circumstance!" interrupted the jocose Mr. Walker, *en passant*.

"— I am his son, and have received a liberal education. I don't owe no man nothing—not the value of a farthing, but I was induced, you see, to put my name to some bills for a friend—bills to a large amount, I may say a very large amount, for which I didn't receive no consideration. What's the consequence?"

"Why, I suppose the bills went out, and you came in. The acceptances weren't taken up, and you were, eh?" inquired Walker.

"To be sure," replied the liberally educated young gentleman. "To be sure; and so here I am, locked up for a matter of twelve hundred pound."

"Why don't you ask your old governor to stump up?" inquired Walker, with a somewhat sceptical air.

"Oh! bless you, he'd never do it," replied the other, in a tone of expostulation —"Never!"

"Well, it is very odd to—be—sure," interposed the owner of the flat bottle, mixing another glass, "but I've been in difficulties, as one may say, now for thirty year. I went to pieces when I was in a milk-walk, thirty year ago; arterwards, when I was a fruiterer, and kept a spring wan; and arter that again in the coal and 'tatur line—but all that time I never see a youngish chap come into a place of this kind, who wasn't going out again directly, and who hadn't been arrested on bills which he'd given a friend and for which he'd received nothing whatsomever —not a fraction."

"Oh! it's always the cry," said Walker. "I can't see the use on it; that's what makes me so wild. Why, I should have a much better opinion of an individual, if he'd say at once in an honourable and gentlemanly manner as he'd done everybody he possible could."

"Ay, to be sure," interposed the horse-dealer, with whose notions of bargain and sale the axiom perfectly coincided, "so should I."

The young gentleman, who had given rise to these observations, was on the point of offering a rather angry reply to these sneers, but the rising of the young man before noticed, and of the female who had been sitting by him, to leave the room, interrupted the conversation. She had been weeping bitterly, and the noxious atmosphere of the room acting upon her excited feelings and delicate frame, rendered the support of her companion necessary as they quitted it together.

There was an air of superiority about them both, and something in their appearance so unusual in such a place, that a respectful silence was observed until the *whirr—r—bang* of the spring door announced that they were out of hearing. It was broken by the wife of the ex-fruiterer.

"Poor creetur!" said she, quenching a sigh in a rivulet of gin-and-water. "She's very young."

"She's a nice-looking 'ooman too," added the horse-dealer.

"What's he in for, Ikey?" inquired Walker, of an individual who was spreading a cloth with numerous blotches of mustard upon it, on one of the tables, and whom Mr. Gabriel Parsons had no difficulty in recognising as the man who had called upon him in the morning.

"Vy," responded the factotum, "it's one of the rummiest rigs you ever heard on. He come in here last Vensday, which by-the-bye he's a going over the water to-night—hows'ever that's neither here nor there. You see I've been a going back'ards and for'ards about his business, and ha' managed to pick up some of his story from the servants and them; and so far as I can make it out, it seems to be summat to this here effect——"

"Cut it short, old fellow," interrupted Walker, who knew from former experience that he of the top-boots was neither very concise nor intelligible in his narratives.

"Let me alone," replied Ikey, "and I'll ha' vound up, and made my lucky in five seconds. This here young gen'lm'n's father—so I'm told, mind ye—and the father o' the young voman, have always been on very bad, out-and-out, rig'lar knock-me-down sort o' terms; but somehow or another, when he was a wisitin' at some gentlefolk's house, as he knowed at college, he came into contract with the young lady. He seed her several times, and then he up and said he'd keep company with her, if so be as she vos agreeable. Vell, she vos as sweet upon him as he vos upon her, and so I s'pose they made it all right; for they got married 'bout six months arterwards, unbeknown, mind ye, to the two fathers—leastways so I'm told. When they heard on it—my eyes, there was such a combustion! Starvation vos the very least that vos to be done to 'em. The young gen'lm'n's father cut him off vith a bob, 'cos he'd cut himself off vith a wife; and the young lady's father he behaved even worser and more unnat'ral, for he not only blow'd her up dreadful, and swore he'd never see her again, but he employed a chap as I knows--and as you knows, Mr. Valker, a precious sight too well—to go about and buy up the bills and them things on which the young husband, thinking his governor 'ud come round agin, had raised the vind just to blow himself on vith for a time; besides vich, he made all the interest he could to set other people agin him. Consequence vos, that he paid as long as he could; but things he never expected to have to meet till he'd had time to turn himself round, come fast upon him, and he vos nabbed. He vos brought here, as I said afore, last Vensday, and I think there's about—ah, half-a-dozen detainers agin him down stairs now. I have been," added Ikey, "in the purfession these fifteen year, and I never met vith such windictiveness afore!"

"Poor creeturs!" exclaimed the coal-dealer's wife once more: again resorting to the same excellent prescription for nipping a sigh in the bud: "Ah! when they've seen as much trouble as I and my old man here have, they'll be as comfortable under it as we are."

"The young lady's a pretty creature," said Walker, "only she's a little too delicate for my taste—there ain't enough of her. As to the young cove, he may be very respectable and what not, but he's too down in the mouth for me—he ain't game."

"Game!" exclaimed Ikey, who had been altering the position of a green-handled knife and fork at least a dozen times, in order that he might remain in the room under the pretext of having something to do. "He's game enough ven there's anything to be fierce about; but who could be game as you call it, Mr. Walker, with a pale young creetur like that, hanging about him?—It's enough to drive any man's heart into his boots to see 'em together—and no mistake at all about it. I never shall forget her first comin' here; he wrote to her on the Thursday to come—I know he did, 'cos I took the letter. Uncommon fidgety he was all day to be sure, and in the evening he goes down into the office, and he says to Jacobs, says he, 'Sir, can I have the loan of a private room for a few minutes this evening, without incurring any additional expense—just to see my wife in?' says he. Jacobs looked as much as to say—'Strike me bountiful if you ain't one of the modest sort!' but as the gen'lm'n who had been in the back parlour had just gone out, and had paid for it for that day, he says—werry grave—'Sir,' says he, 'it's agin our rules to let private rooms to our lodgers on gratis terms, but,' says he, 'for a gentleman, I don't mind breaking through them for once.' So then he turns round to me, and says, 'Ikey, put two mould candles in the back parlour, and charge 'em to this gen'lm'n's account, vich I did. Vell, by-and-by a hackney-coach comes up to the door, and there, sure enough, was the young lady, wrapped up in a hopera-cloak, as it might be, and all alone. I opened the gate that night, so I went up when the coach come, and he vos a waitin' at the parlour-door—and wasn't he a trembling, neither? The poor creetur see him, and could hardly walk to meet him. 'Oh, Harry!' she says, 'that it should have come to this; and all for my sake,' says she, putting her hand upon his shoulder. So he puts his arm round her pretty little waist, and leading her gently a little way into the room, so that he might be able to shut the door, he says, so kind and soft-like—'Why, Kate,' says he——"

"Here's the gentleman you want," said Ikey, abruptly breaking off in his story, and introducing Mr. Gabriel Parsons to the crest-fallen Watkins Tottle, who at that moment entered the room. Watkins advanced with a wooden expression of passive endurance, and accepted the hand which Mr. Gabriel Parsons held out.

"I want to speak to you," said Gabriel, with a look strongly expressive of his dislike of the company.

"This way," replied the imprisoned one, leading the way to the front drawing-room, where rich debtors did the luxurious at the rate of a couple of guineas a day.

"Well, here I am," said Mr. Watkins, as he sat down on the sofa; and placing the palms of his hands on his knees, anxiously glanced at his friend's countenance.

"Yes; and here you're likely to be," said Gabriel, coolly, as he rattled the money in his unmentionable pockets, and looked out of the window.

"What's the amount with the costs?" inquired Parsons, after an awkward pause.

"37*l.* 3*s.* 10*d.*"

"Have you any money?"

"Nine and sixpence halfpenny."

Mr. Gabriel Parsons walked up and down the room for a few seconds, before he could make up his mind to disclose the plan he had formed; he was accustomed to drive hard bargains, but was always most anxions to conceal his avarice. At length he stopped short, and said,—"Tottle, you owe me fifty pounds."

"I do."

"And from all I see, I infer that you are likely to owe it to me."

"I fear I am."

"Though you have every disposition to pay me if you could?"

"Certainly."

"Then," said Mr. Gabriel Parsons, "listen: here's my proposition. You know my way of old. Accept it—yes or no—I will or I wont. I'll pay the debt and costs, and I'll lend you 10*l.* more (which, added to your annuity, will enable you to carry on the war well) if you'll give me your note of hand to pay me one hundred and fifty pounds within six months after you are married to Miss Lillerton."

"My dear——"

"Stop a minute—on one condition; and that is, that you propose to Miss Lillerton at once."

"At once! My dear Parsons, consider."

"It's for you to consider, not me. She knows you well from reputation, though she did not know you personally until lately. Notwithstanding all her maiden modesty, I think she'd be devilish glad to get married out of hand with as little delay as possible. My wife has sounded her on the subject, and she has confessed."

"What—what?" eagerly interrupted the enamoured Watkins.

"Why," replied Parsons, "to say exactly what she has confessed, would be rather difficult, because they only spoke in hints, and so forth; but my wife, who is no bad judge in these cases, declared to me that what she had confessed was as good as to say that she was not insensible of your merits—in fact, that no other man should have her."

Mr. Watkins Tottle rose hastily from his seat, and rang the bell.

"What's that for?" inquired Parsons.

"I want to send the man for the bill stamp," replied Mr. Watkins Tottle.

"Then you've made up your mind?"

"I have,"—and they shook hands most cordially. The note of hand was given—the debt and costs were paid—Ikey was satisfied for his trouble, and the two friends soon found themselves on that side of Mr. Solomon Jacobs's establishment, on which most of his visitors were very happy when they found themselves once again—to wit, the *out*side.

"Now," said Mr. Gabriel Parsons, as they drove to Norwood together—"you shall have an opportunity to make the disclosure to-night, and mind you speak out, Tottle."

"I will—I will!" replied Watkins, valorously.

"How I should like to see you together," ejaculated Mr. Gabriel Parsons.—"What fun!" and he laughed so long and so loudly, that he disconcerted Mr. Watkins Tottle, and frightened the horse.

"There's Fanny and your intended walking about on the lawn," said Gabriel, as they approached the house—"Mind your eye, Tottle."

"Never fear," replied Watkins, resolutely, as he made his way to the spot where the ladies were walking.

"Here's Mr. Tottle, my dear," said Mrs. Parsons, addressing Miss Lillerton. The lady turned quickly round, and acknowledged his courteous salute with the same sort of confusion that Watkins had noticed on their first interview, but with something like a slight expression of disappointment or carelessness.

"Did you see how glad she was to see you?" whispered Parsons to his friend.

"Why I really thought she looked as if she would rather have seen somebody else," replied Tottle.

"Pooh, nonsense!" whispered Parsons again—"it's always the way with the women, young or old. They never show how delighted they are to see those whose presence makes their hearts beat. It's the way with the whole sex, and no man should have lived to your time of life without knowing it. Fanny confessed it to me, when we were first married, over and over again—see what it is to have a wife."

"Certainly," whispered Tottle, whose courage was vanishing fast.

"Well, now, you'd better begin to pave the way," said Parsons, who, having invested some money in the speculation, assumed the office of director.

"Yes, yes, I will—presently," replied Tottle, greatly flurried.

"Say something to her, man," urged Parsons again. "Confound it! pay her a compliment, can't you?"

"No! not till after dinner," replied the bashful Tottle, anxious to postpone the evil moment.

"Well, gentlemen," said Mrs. Parsons, "you are really very polite; you stay away the whole morning, after promising to take us out, and when you do come home, you stand whispering together and take no notice of us."

"We were talking of the *business*, my dear, which detained us this morning," replied Parsons, looking significantly at Tottle.

"Dear me! how very quickly the morning has gone," said Miss Lillerton, referring to the gold watch, which was wound up on state occasions, whether it required it or not.

"*I* think it has passed very slowly," mildly suggested Tottle.

("That's right—bravo!") whispered Parsons.

"Indeed!" said Miss Lillerton, with an air of majestic surprise.

"I can only impute it to my unavoidable absence from your society, madam," said Watkins, "and that of Mrs. Parsons."

During this short dialogue, the ladies had been leading the way to the house.

"What the deuce did you stick Fanny into that last compliment for?" inquired Parsons, as they followed together; "it quite spoilt the effect."

"Oh! it really would have been too broad without," replied Watkins Tottle, "much too broad!"

"He's mad!" Parsons whispered his wife, as they entered the drawing-room, "mad from modesty."

"Dear me!" ejaculated the lady, "I never heard of such a thing."

"You'll find we have quite a family dinner, Mr. Tottle," said Mrs. Parsons, when they sat down to table: "Miss Lillerton is one of us, and, of course, we make no stranger of you."

Mr. Watkins Tottle expressed a hope that the Parsons family never would make a stranger of him; and wished internally that his bashfulness would allow him to feel a little less like a stranger himself.

"Take off the covers, Martha," said Mrs. Parsons, directing the shifting of the scenery with great anxiety. The order was obeyed, and a pair of boiled fowls, with tongue and et ceteras, were displayed at the top, and a fillet of veal at the bottom. On one side of the table two green sauce-tureens, with ladles of the same, were setting to each other in a green dish; and on the other was a curried rabbit, in a brown suit, turned up with lemon.

"Miss Lillerton, my dear," said Mrs. Parsons, "shall I assist you?"

"Thank you, no; I think I'll trouble Mr. Tottle."

Watkins started—trembled—helped the rabbit—and broke a tumbler. The countenance of the lady of the house, which had been all smiles previously, underwent an awful change.

"Extremely sorry," stammered Watkins, assisting himself to currie and parsley and butter, in the extremity of his confusion.

"Not the least consequence," replied Mrs. Parsons, in a tone which implied that it was of the greatest consequence possible,—directing aside the researches of the boy, who was groping under the table for the bits of broken glass.

"I presume," said Miss Lillerton, "that Mr. Tottle is aware of the interest which bachelors usually pay in such cases; a dozen glasses for one is the lowest penalty."

Mr. Gabriel Parsons gave his friend an admonitory tread on the toe. Here was a clear hint that the sooner he ceased to be a bachelor and emancipated himself from such penalties, the better. Mr. Watkins Tottle viewed the observation in the same light, and challenged Mrs. Parsons to take wine, with a degree of presence of mind, which, under all the circumstances, was really extraordinary.

"Miss Lillerton," said Gabriel, "may I have the pleasure?"

"I shall be most happy."

"Tottle, will you assist Miss Lillerton, and pass the decanter. Thank you." (The usual pantomimic ceremony of nodding and sipping gone through)—

"Tottle, were you ever in Suffolk?" inquired the master of the house, who was burning to tell one of his seven stock stories.

"No," responded Watkins, adding, by way of a saving clause, "but I 've been in Devonshire."

"Ah!" replied Gabriel, "it was in Suffolk that a rather singular circumstance happened to me many years ago. Did you ever happen to hear me mention it?"

Mr. Watkins Tottle *had* happened to hear his friend mention it some four hundred times. Of course he expressed great curiosity, and evinced the utmost impatience to hear the story again. Mr. Gabriel Parsons forthwith attempted to proceed, in spite of the interruptions to which, as our readers must frequently have observed, the master of the house is often exposed in such cases. We will attempt to give them an idea of our meaning.

"When I was in Suffolk," said Mr. Gabriel Parsons——

"Take off the fowls first, Martha," said Mrs. Parsons. "I beg your pardon, my dear."

"When I was in Suffolk," resumed Mr. Parsons, with an impatient glance at his wife, who pretended not to observe it, "which is now some years ago, business led me to the town of Bury St. Edmund's. I had to stop at the principal places in my way, and therefore, for the sake of convenience, I travelled in a gig. I left Sudbury one dark night—it was winter time—about nine o'clock: the rain poured in torrents, the wind howled among the trees that skirted the road-side, and I was obliged to proceed at a foot-pace, for I could hardly see my hand before me, it was so dark——"

"John," interrupted Mrs. Parsons, in a low, hollow voice, "don't spill that gravy."

"Fanny," said Parsons impatiently, "I wish you'd defer these domestic reproofs to some more suitable time. Really, my dear, these constant interruptions are very annoying."

"My dear, I didn't interrupt you," said Mrs. Parsons.

"But, my dear, you *did* interrupt me," remonstrated Mr. Parsons.

"How very absurd you are, my love! I must give directions to the servants; I am quite sure that if I sat here and allowed John to spill the gravy over the new carpet, you'd be the first to find fault when you saw the stain to-morrow morning."

"Well," continued Gabriel with a resigned air, as if he knew there was no getting over the point about the carpet, "I was just saying, it was so dark that I could hardly see my hand before me. The road was very lonely, and I assure you, Tottle (this was a device to arrest the wandering attention of that individual, which was distracted by a confidential communication between Mrs. Parsons and Martha, accompanied by the delivery of a large bunch of keys), I assure you, Tottle, I became somehow impressed with a sense of the loneliness of my situation--"

"Pie to your master," interrupted Mrs. Parsons, again directing the servant.

"Now, pray, my dear," remonstrated Parsons once more, very pettishly. Mrs. P. turned up her hands and eyebrows, and appealed in dumb show to Miss Lillerton. "As I turned a corner of the road," resumed Gabriel, "the horse stopped short, and reared tremendously, I pulled up, jumped out, ran to his head, and found a man lying on his back in the middle of the road, with his eyes fixed on the sky. I thought he was dead; but no, he was alive, and there appeared to be nothing the matter with him. He jumped up, and putting his hand to his chest, and fixing upon me the most earnest gaze you can imagine, exclaimed——"

"Pudding here," said Mrs. Parsons.

"Oh! it's no use," exclaimed the host, now rendered desperate. "Here, Tottle; a glass of wine. It's useless to attempt relating anything when Mrs. Parsons is present."

This attack was received in the usual way. Mrs. Parsons talked *to* Miss Lillerton and *at* her better half; expatiated on the impatience of men generally; hinted that her husband was peculiarly vicious in this respect, and wound up by insinuating that she must be one of the best tempers that ever existed, or she never could put up with it. Really what she had to endure sometimes, was more than any one who saw her in every-day life could by possibility suppose.—The story was now a painful subject, and therefore Mr. Parsons declined to enter into any details, and contented himself by stating that the man was a maniac, who had escaped from a neighbouring mad-house.

The cloth was removed; the ladies soon afterwards retired, and Miss Lillerton played the piano in the drawing-room overhead, very loudly, for the edification of the visitor. Mr. Watkins Tottle and Mr. Gabriel Parsons sat chatting comfortably enough, until the conclusion of the second bottle, when the latter, in proposing an adjournment to the drawing-room, informed Watkins that he had concerted a plan with his wife, for leaving him and Miss Lillerton alone, soon after tea.

"I say," said Tottle, as they went up-stairs, "don't you think it would be better if we put if off till—till—to-morrow?"

"Don't *you* think it would have been much better if I had left you in that wretched hole I found you in this morning?" retorted Parsons bluntly.

"Well—well—I only made a suggestion," said poor Watkins Tottle, with a deep sigh.

Tea was soon concluded, and Miss Lillerton, drawing a small work-table on one side of the fire, and placing a little wooden frame upon it, something like a miniature clay-mill without the horse, was soon busily engaged in making a watch-guard with brown silk.

"God bless me!" exclaimed Parsons, starting up with well-feigned surprise, "I 've forgotten those confounded letters. Tottle, I know you 'll excuse me."

If Tottle had been a free agent, he would have allowed no one to leave the room on any pretence, except himself. As it was, however, he was obliged to look cheerful when Parsons quitted the apartment.

He had scarcely left, when Martha put her head into the room, with—"Please, ma'am, you're wanted."

Mrs. Parsons left the room, shut the door carefully after her, and Mr. Watkins Tottle was left alone with Miss Lillerton.

For the first five minutes there was a dead silence.—Mr. Watkins Tottle was thinking how he should begin, and Miss Lillerton appeared to be thinking of nothing. The fire was burning low; Mr. Watkins Tottle stirred it, and put some coals on.

"Hem!" coughed Miss Lillerton; Mr. Watkins Tottle thought the fair creature had spoken. "I beg your pardon," said he.

"Eh?"

"I thought you spoke."

"No."

"Oh!"

"There are some books on the sofa, Mr. Tottle, if you would like to look at them," said Miss Lillerton, after the lapse of another five minutes.

"No, thank you," returned Watkins; and then he added, with a courage which was perfectly astonishing, even to himself, "Madam, that is Miss Lillerton, I wish to speak to you."

"To me!" said Miss Lillerton, letting the silk drop from her hands, and sliding her chair back a few paces.—"Speak—to me!"

"To you, madam—and on the subject of the state of your affections." The lady hastily rose and would have left the room; but Mr. Watkins Tottle gently detained her by the hand, and holding it as far from him as the joint length of their arms would permit, he thus proceeded: "Pray do not misunderstand me, or suppose that I am led to address you, after so short an acquaintance, by any feeling of my own merits—for merits I have none which could give me a claim to your hand. I hope you will acquit me of any presumption when I explain that I have been acquainted through Mrs. Parsons, with the state—that is, that Mrs. Parsons has told me—at least, not Mrs. Parsons, but——" here Watkins began to wander, but Miss Lillerton relieved him.

"Am I to understand, Mr. Tottle, that Mrs. Parsons has acquainted you with my feeling—my affection—I mean my respect, for an individual of the opposite sex?"

"She has."

"Then, what?" inquired Miss Lillerton, averting her face, with a girlish air, "what could induce *you* to seek such an interview as this? What can your object be? How can I promote your happiness, Mr. Tottle?"

Here was the time for a flourish—"By allowing me," replied Watkins, falling bump on his knees, and breaking two brace-buttons and a waistcoat-string, in the act—"By allowing me to be your slave, your servant—in short, by unreservedly making me the confidant of your heart's feelings—may I say for the promotion of your own happiness—may I say, in order that you may become the wife of a kind and affectionate husband?"

"Disinterested creature!" exclaimed Miss Lillerton, hiding her face in a white pocket-handkerchief with an eyelet-hole border.

Mr. Watkins Tottle thought that if the lady knew all, she might possibly alter her opinion on this last point. He raised the tip of her middle finger ceremoniously to his lips, and got off his knees, as gracefully as he could. "My information was correct?" he tremulously inquired, when he was once more on his feet.

"It was." Watkins elevated his hands, and looked up to the ornament in the centre of the ceiling, which had been made for a lamp, by way of expressing his rapture.

"Our situation, Mr. Tottle," resumed the lady, glancing at him through one of the eyelet-holes, "is a most peculiar and delicate one."

"It is," said Mr. Tottle.

"Our acquaintance has been of *so* short duration," said Miss Lillerton.

"Only a week," assented Watkins Tottle.

"Oh! more than that," exclaimed the lady, in a tone of surprise.

"Indeed!" said Tottle.

"More than a month—more than two months!" said Miss Lillerton.

"Rather odd, this," thought Watkins.

"Oh!" he said, recollecting Parsons's assurance that she had known him from report, "I understand. But, my dear madam, pray, consider. The longer this acquaintance has existed, the less reason is there for delay now. Why not at once fix a period for gratifying the hopes of your devoted admirer?"

"It has been represented to me again and again that this is the course I ought to pursue," replied Miss Lillerton, "but pardon my feelings of delicacy, Mr. Tottle—pray excuse this embarrassment—I have peculiar ideas on such subjects, and I am quite sure that I never could summon up fortitude enough to name the day to my future husband."

"Then allow *me* to name it," said Tottle eagerly.

"I should like to fix it myself," replied Miss Lillerton, bashfully, "but I cannot do so without at once resorting to a third party."

"A third party!" thought Watkins Tottle; "who the deuce is that to be, I wonder!"

"Mr. Tottle," continued Miss Lillerton, "you have made me a most disinterested and kind offer—that offer I accept. Will you at once be the bearer of a note from me to—to Mr. Timson?"

"Mr. Timson!" said Watkins.

"After what has passed between us," responded Miss Lillerton, still averting her head, "you must understand whom I mean; Mr. Timson, the—the—clergyman."

"Mr. Timson, the clergyman!" ejaculated Watkins Tottle, in a state of inexpressible beatitude, and positive wonder at his own success. "Angel! Certainly—this moment!"

"I'll prepare it immediately," said Miss Lillerton, making for the door; "the events of this day have flurried me so much, Mr. Tottle, that I shall not leave my room again this evening; I will send you the note by the servant."

"Stay,—stay," cried Watkins Tottle, still keeping a most respectful distance from the lady; "when shall we meet again?"

"Oh! Mr. Tottle," replied Miss Lillerton, coquettishly, "when *we* are married, I can never see you too often, nor thank you too much;" and she left the room.

Mr. Watkins Tottle flung himself into an arm-chair, and indulged in the most delicious reveries of future bliss, in which the idea of "Five hundred pounds per annum, with an uncontrolled power of disposing of it by her last will and testament," was somehow or other the foremost. He had gone through the interview so well, and it had terminated so admirably, that he almost began to wish he had expressly stipulated for the settlement of the annual five hundred on himself.

"May I come in?" said Mr. Gabriel Parsons, peeping in at the door.

"You may," replied Watkins.

"Well, have you done it?" anxiously inquired Gabriel.

"Have I done it!" said Watkins Tottle, "Hush—I'm going to the clergyman"

"No!" said Parsons. "How well you have managed it!"

"Where does Timson live?" inquired Watkins.

"At his uncle's," replied Gabriel, "just round the lane. He's waiting for a living, and has been assisting his uncle here for the last two or three months. But how well you have done it—I didn't think you could have carried it off so!"

Mr. Watkins Tottle was proceeding to demonstrate that the Richardsonian principle was the best on which love could possibly be made, when he was interrupted by the entrance of Martha, with a little pink note folded like a fancy cocked-hat.

"Miss Lillerton's compliments," said Martha, as she delivered it into Tottle's hands, and vanished.

"Do you observe the delicacy?" said Tottle, appealing to Mr. Gabriel Parsons. "*Compliments* not *love*, by the servant, eh?"

Mr. Gabriel Parsons didn't exactly know what reply to make, so he poked the forefinger of his right hand between the third and fourth ribs of Mr. Watkins Tottle.

"Come," said Watkins, when the explosion of mirth, consequent on this practical jest, had subsided, "we'll be off at once—let's lose no time."

"Capital!" echoed Gabriel Parsons; and in five minutes they were at the garden-gate of the villa tenanted by the uncle of Mr. Timson.

"Is Mr. Charles Timson at home?" inquired Mr. Watkins Tottle of Mr. Charles Timson's uncle's man.

"Mr. Charles *is* at home," replied the man, stammering; "but he desired me to say he couldn't be interrupted, sir, by any of the parishioners."

"*I* am not a parishioner," replied Watkins.

"Is Mr. Charles writing a sermon, Tom?" inquired Parsons, thrusting himself forward.

"No, Mr. Parsons, sir; he's not exactly writing a sermon, but he is practising the violoncello in his own bedroom, and gave strict orders not to be disturbed."

"Say I'm here," replied Gabriel, leading the way across the garden; "Mr. Parsons and Mr. Tottle, on private and particular business."

They were shown into the parlour, and the servant departed to deliver his message. The distant groaning of the violoncello ceased; footsteps were heard on the stairs; and Mr. Timson presented himself, and shook hands with Parsons with the utmost cordiality.

"How do you do, sir?" said Watkins Tottle, with great solemnity.

"How do *you* do, sir?" replied Timson, with as much coldness as if it were a matter of perfect indifference to him how he did, as it very likely was.

"I beg to deliver this note to you," said Watkins Tottle, producing the cocked-hat.

"From Miss Lillerton!" said Timson, suddenly changing colour. "Pray sit down."

Mr. Watkins Tottle sat down; and while Timson perused the note, fixed his eyes on an oyster-sauce-coloured portrait of the Archbishop of Canterbury, which hung over the fireplace.

Mr. Timson rose from his seat when he had concluded the note, and looked dubiously at Parsons—"May I ask," he inquired, appealing to Watkins Tottle, "whether our friend here is acquainted with the object of your visit?"

"Our friend is in *my* confidence," replied Watkins, with considerable importance.

"Then, sir," said Timson, seizing both Tottle's hands, "allow me in his presence to thank you most unfeignedly and cordially, for the noble part you have acted in this affair."

"He thinks I recommended him," thought Tottle. "Confound these fellows! they never think of anything but their fees."

"I deeply regret having misunderstood your intentions, my dear sir," continued Timson. "Disinterested and manly, indeed! There are very few men who would have acted as you have done."

MR. WATKINS TOTTLE.

Mr. Watkins Tottle could not help thinking that this last remark was anything but complimentary. He therefore inquired, rather hastily, "When is it to be?"

"On Thursday," replied Timson,—"on Thursday morning at half-past eight."

"Uncommonly early," observed Watkins Tottle, with an air of triumphant self-denial. "I shall hardly be able to get down here by that hour." (This was intended for a joke.)

"Never mind, my dear fellow," replied Timson, all suavity, shaking hands with Tottle again most heartily, "so long as we see you to breakfast, you know—"

"Eh!" said Parsons, with one of the most extraordinary expressions of countenance that ever appeared in a human face.

"What!" ejaculated Watkins Tottle, at the same moment.

"I say that so long as we see you to breakfast," replied Timson, "we will excuse your being absent from the ceremony, though of course your presence at it would give us the utmost pleasure."

Mr. Watkins Tottle staggered against the wall, and fixed his eyes on Timson with appalling perseverance.

"Timson," said Parsons, hurriedly brushing his hat with his left arm, "when you say 'us,' whom do you mean?"

Mr. Timson looked foolish in his turn, when he replied, "Why—Mrs. Timson that will be this day week: Miss Lillerton that is—"

"Now don't stare at that idiot in the corner," angrily exclaimed Parsons, as the extraordinary convulsions of Watkins Tottle's countenance excited the wondering gaze of Timson,—"but have the goodness to tell me in three words the contents of that note."

"This note," replied Timson, "is from Miss Lillerton, to whom I have been for the last five weeks regularly engaged. Her singular scruples and strange feeling on some points have hitherto prevented my bringing the engagement to that termination which I so anxiously desire. She informs me here, that she sounded Mrs. Parsons with the view of making her her confidante and go-between, that Mrs. Parsons informed this elderly gentleman, Mr. Tottle, of the circumstance, and that he, in the most kind and delicate terms, offered to assist us in any way, and even undertook to convey this note, which contains the promise I have long sought in vain—an act of kindness for which I can never be sufficiently grateful."

"Good night, Timson," said Parsons, hurrying off, and carrying the bewildered Tottle with him.

"Won't you stay—and have something?" said Timson.

"No, thank ye," replied Parsons; "I've had quite enough;" and away he went, followed by Watkins Tottle in a state of stupefaction.

Mr. Gabriel Parsons whistled until they had walked some quarter of a mile past his own gate, when he suddenly stopped, and said—

"You are a clever fellow, Tottle, ain't you?"

"I don't know," said the unfortunate Watkins.

"I suppose you'll say this is Fanny's fault, won't you?" inquired Gabriel.

"I don't know anything about it," replied the bewildered Tottle.

"Well," said Parsons, turning on his heel to go home, "the next time you make an offer, you had better speak plainly, and don't throw a chance away. And the next time you're locked up in a spunging-house, just wait there till I come and take you out, there's a good fellow."

How, or at what hour, Mr. Watkins Tottle returned to Cecil-street is unknown. His boots were seen outside his bedroom-door next morning; but we have the authority of his landlady for stating that he neither emerged therefrom nor accepted sustenance for four-and-twenty hours. At the expiration of that period and when a council of war was being held in the kitchen on the propriety of summoning the parochial beadle to break his door open, he rang his bell, and demanded a cup of milk-and-water. The next morning he went through the formalities of eating and drinking as usual, but a week afterwards he was seized with a relapse, while perusing the list of marriages in a morning paper, from which he never perfectly recovered.

A few weeks after the last-named occurrence, the body of a gentleman unknown, was found in the Regent's canal. In the trousers-pockets were four shillings and threepence halfpenny; a matrimonial advertisement from a lady, which appeared to have been cut out of a Sunday paper: a toothpick, and a card-case, which it is confidently believed would have led to the identification of the unfortunate gentleman, but for the circumstance of there being none but blank cards in it. Mr. Watkins Tottle absented himself from his lodgings shortly before. A bill, which has not been taken up, was presented next morning; and a bill, which has not been taken down, was soon afterwards affixed in his parlour-window.

CHAPTER XI.

THE BLOOMSBURY CHRISTENING.

MR. NICODEMUS DUMPS, or, as his acquaintance called him, "long Dumps," was a bachelor, six feet high, and fifty years old: cross, cadaverous, odd, and ill-natured. He was never happy but when he was miserable; and always miserable when he had the best reason to be happy. The only real comfort of his existence was to make everybody about him wretched—then he might be truly said to enjoy life. He was afflicted with a situation in the Bank worth five hundred a-year, and he rented a "first-floor furnished," at Pentonville, which he originally took because it commanded a dismal prospect of an adjacent churchyard. He was familiar with the face of every tombstone, and the burial service seemed to excite his strongest sympathy. His friends said he was surly—he insisted he was nervous; they thought him a lucky dog, but he protested that he was "the most unfortunate man in the world." Cold as he was, and wretched as he declared himself to be, he was not wholly susceptible of attachments. He revered the memory of Hoyle, as he was himself an admirable and imperturbable whist-player, and he chuckled with delight at a fretful and impatient adversary. He adored King Herod for his massacre of the innocents; and if he hated one thing more than another, it was a child. However, he could hardly be said to hate anything in particular, because he disliked everything in general; but perhaps his greatest antipathies were cabs, old women, doors that would not shut, musical amateurs, and omnibus cads. He subscribed to the "Society for the Suppression of Vice" for the pleasure of putting a stop to any harmless amusements; and he contributed largely towards the support of two itinerant methodist parsons, in the amiable hope that if circumstances rendered any people happy in this world, they might perchance be rendered miserable by fears for the next.

Mr. Dumps had a nephew who had been married about a year, and who was somewhat of a favourite with his uncle, because he was an admirable subject to exercise his misery-creating powers upon. Mr. Charles Kitterbell was a small, sharp, spare man, with a very large head, and a broad, good-humoured countenance. He looked like a faded giant, with the head and face partially restored; and he had a cast in his eye which rendered it quite impossible for any one with whom he conversed to know where he was looking. His eyes appeared fixed on the wall, and he was staring you out of countenance; in short, there was no catching his eye, and perhaps it is a merciful dispensation of Providence that such eyes are not catching. In addition to these characteristics, it may be added that Mr Charles Kitterbell was one of the most credulous and matter-of-fact little personages that ever took *to* himself a wife, and *for* himself a house in Great Russell-street, Bedford-square. (Uncle Dumps always dropped the "Bedford-square," and inserted in lieu thereof the dreadful words "Tottenham-court-road.")

"No, but uncle, 'pon my life you must—you must promise to be godfather," said Mr. Kitterbell, as he sat in conversation with his respected relative one morning.

"I cannot, indeed I cannot," returned Dumps.

"Well, but why not? Jemima will think it very unkind. It's very little trouble."

"As to the trouble," rejoined the most unhappy man in existence, "I don't mind that; but my nerves are in that state—I cannot go through the ceremony. You know I don't like going out.—For God's sake, Charles, don't fidget with that stool so; you'll drive me mad." Mr. Kitterbell, quite regardless of his uncle's nerves, had occupied himself for some ten minutes in describing a circle on the floor with one leg of the office-stool on which he was seated, keeping the other three up in the air, and holding fast on by the desk.

"I beg your pardon, uncle," said Kitterbell, quite abashed, suddenly releasing his hold of the desk, and bringing the three wandering legs back to the floor, with a force sufficient to drive them through it.

"But come, don't refuse. If it's a boy, you know, we must have two godfathers."

"*If* it's a boy!" said Dumps; "why can't you say at once whether it *is* a boy or not?"

"I should be very hapyy to tell you, but it's impossible I can undertake to say whether it's a girl or a boy, if the child isn't born yet."

"Not born yet!" echoed Dumps, with a gleam of hope lighting up his lugubrious visage. "Oh, well, it *may* be a girl, and then you won't want me; or if it is a boy, it *may* die before it is christened."

"I hope not," said the father that expected to be, looking very grave.

"I hope not," acquiesced Dumps, evidently pleased with the subject. He was beginning to get happy. "*I* hope not, but distressing cases frequently occur during the first two or three days of a child's life; fits, I am told, are exceedingly common, and alarming convulsions are almost matters of course."

"Lord, uncle!" ejaculated little Kitterbell, gasping for breath.

"Yes; my landlady was confined—let me see—last Tuesday: an uncommonly fine boy. On the Thursday night the nurse was sitting with him upon her knee before the fire, and he was as well as possible. Suddenly he became black in the face, and alarmingly spasmodic. The medical man was instantly sent for, and every remedy was tried, but—"

"How frightful!" interrupted the horror-stricken Kitterbell.

"The child died, of course. However, your child *may* not die; and if it should be a boy, and should *live* to be christened, why I suppose I must be one of the sponsors." Dumps was evidently good-natured on the faith of his anticipations.

"Thank you, uncle," said his agitated nephew, grasping his hand as warmly as if he had done him some essential service. "Perhaps I had better not tell Mrs. K. what you have mentioned."

"Why, if she's low spirited, perhaps you had better not mention the melancholy case to her," returned Dumps, who of course had invented the whole story; "though perhaps it would be but doing your duty as a husband to prepare her for the *worst*."

A day or two afterwards, as Dumps was perusing a morning paper at the chop-house which he regularly frequented, the following paragraph met his eyes:—

Births.—On Saturday, the 18th inst., in Great Russell-street, the lady of Charles Kitterbell, Esq. of a son."

"It *is* a boy!" he exclaimed, dashing down the paper, to the astonishment of the waiters. "It *is* a boy!" But he speedily regained his composure as his eye rested on a paragraph quoting the number of infant deaths from the bills of mortality.

Six weeks passed away, and as no communication had been received from the Kitterbells, Dumps was beginning to flatter himself that the child was dead, when the following note painfully resolved his doubts:—

Great Russell-street,
Monday morning.

"DEAR UNCLE,—You will be delighted to hear that my dear Jemima has left her room, and that your future godson is getting on capitally. He was very thin at first, but he is getting much larger, and nurse says he is filling out every day. He cries a good deal, and is a very singular colour, which made Jemima and me rather uncomfortable; but as nurse says it's natural, and as of course we know nothing about these things yet, we are quite satisfied with what nurse says. We think he will be a sharp child; and nurse says she's sure he will, because he never goes to sleep. You will readily believe that we are all very happy, only we're a little worn out for want of rest, as he keeps us awake all night; but this we must expect, nurse says, for the first six or eight months. He has been vaccinated, but in consequence of the operation being rather awkwardly performed, some small particles of glass were introduced into the arm with the matter. Perhaps this may in some degree account for his being rather fractious; at least, so nurse says. We propose to have him christened at twelve o'clock on Friday, at Saint George's church, in Hart-street, by the name of Frederick Charles William. Pray don't be later than a quarter before twelve. We shall have a very few friends in the evening, when of course we shall see you. I am sorry to say that the dear boy appears rather restless and uneasy to-day: the cause, I fear, is fever.

"Believe me, dear Uncle,
"Yours affectionately,
"CHARLES KITTERBELL.

"P.S.—I open this note to say that we have just discovered the cause of little Frederick's restlessness. It is not fever, as I apprehended, but a small pin, which nurse accidentally stuck in his leg yesterday evening. We have taken it out, and he appears more composed, though he still sobs a good deal."

It is almost unnecessary to say that the perusal of the above interesting statement was no great relief to the mind of the hypochondriacal Dumps. It was impossible to recede, however, and so he put the best face—that is to say, an uncommonly miserable one—upon the matter; and purchased a handsome silver mug for the infant Kitterbell, upon which he ordered the initials "F. C. W. K.," with the customary untrained grape-vine-looking flourishes, and a large full stop, to be engraved forthwith.

Monday was a fine day, Tuesday was delightful, Wednesday was equal to either, and Thursday was finer than ever; four successive fine days in London! Hackney-coachmen became revolutionary, and crossing-sweepers began to doubt the existence of a First Cause. The *Morning Herald* informed its readers that an old woman in Camden Town had been heard to say that the fineness of the season was "unprecedented in the memory of the oldest inhabitant;" and Islington clerks, with large families and small salaries, left off their black gaiters, disdained to carry their once green cotton umbrellas, and walked to town in the conscious pride of white stockings and cleanly brushed Bluchers. Dumps beheld all this with an eye of supreme contempt—his triumph was at hand. He knew that if it had been fine for four weeks instead of four days, it would rain when he went out; he was lugubriously happy in the conviction that Friday would be a wretched day —and so it was. "I knew how it would be," said Dumps, as he turned round opposite the Mansion-house at half-past eleven o'clock on the Friday morning. "I knew how it would be. *I* am concerned, and that's enough;"—and certainly the appearance of the day was sufficient to depress the spirits of a much more buoyant-hearted individual than himself. It had rained, without a moment's cessation, since eight o'clock; everybody that passed up Cheapside, and down Cheapside, looked wet, cold, and dirty. All sorts of forgotten and long-concealed umbrellas had been put into requisition. Cabs whisked about, with the "fare" as carefully boxed up behind two glazed calico curtains as any mysterious picture in any one of Mrs. Radcliffe's castles; omnibus horses smoked like steam-engines; nobody thought of "standing up" under doorways or arches; they were painfully convinced it was a hopeless case; and so everybody went hastily along, jumbling and jostling, and swearing and perspiring, and slipping about, like amateur skaters behind wooden chairs on the Serpentine on a frosty Sunday.

Dumps paused; he could not think of walking, being rather smart for the christening. If he took a cab he was sure to be spilt, and a hackney-coach was too expensive for his economical ideas. An omnibus was waiting at the opposite corner—it was a desperate case—he had never heard of an omnibus upsetting or running away, and if the cad did knock him down, he could "pull him up" in return.

"Now, sir!" cried the young gentleman who officiated as "cad" to the "Lads of the Village," which was the name of the machine just noticed. Dumps crossed.

"This vay, sir!" shouted the driver of the "Hark-away," pulling up his vehicle immediately across the door of the opposition—"This vay, sir—he's full." Dumps hesitated, whereupon the "Lads of the Village" commenced pouring out a torrent of abuse against the "Hark-away;" but the conductor of the "Admiral Napier" settled the contest in a most satisfactory manner, for all parties, by seizing Dumps round the waist, and thrusting him into the middle of his vehicle which had just come up and only wanted the sixteenth inside.

"All right," said the "Admiral," and off the thing thundered, like a fire-engine at full gallop, with the kidnapped customer inside, standing in the position of a half doubled-up bootjack, and falling about with every jerk of the machine, first on the one side, and then on the other, like a "Jack-in-the-green," on May-day, setting to the lady with a brass ladle.

"For Heaven's sake, where am I to sit?" inquired the miserable man of an old gentleman, into whose stomach he had just fallen for the fourth time.

"Anywhere but on my *chest*, sir," replied the old gentleman in a surly tone.

"Perhaps the *box* would suit the gentleman better," suggested a very damp lawyer's clerk, in a pink shirt, and a smirking countenance.

After a great deal of struggling and falling about, Dumps at last managed to squeeze himself into a seat, which in addition to the slight disadvantage of being between a window that would not shut, and a door that must be open, placed him in close contact with a passenger, who had been walking about all the morning without an umbrella, and who looked as if he had spent the day in a full water-butt—only wetter.

"Don't bang the door so," said Dumps to the conductor, as he shut it after letting out four of the passengers; "I am very nervous—it destroys me."

"Did any gen'lm'n say anythink?" replied the cad, thrusting in his head, and trying to look as if he didn't understand the request.

"I told you not to bang the door so!" repeated Dumps, with an expression of countenance like the knave of clubs, in convulsions.

"Oh! vy, it's rather a sing'ler circumstance about this here door, sir, that it von't shut without banging," replied the conductor; and he opened the door very wide, and shut it again with a terrific bang, in proof of the assertion.

"I beg your pardon, sir," said a little prim, wheezing old gentleman, sitting opposite Dumps, "I beg your pardon; but have you ever observed, when you have been in an omnibus on a wet day, that four people out of five always come in with large cotton umbrellas, without a handle at the top, or the brass spike at the bottom?"

"Why, sir," returned Dumps, as he heard the clock strike twelve, "it never struck me before; but now you mention it, I——Hollo! hollo!" shouted the persecuted individual, as the omnibus dashed past Drury-lane, where he had directed to be set down.—"Where is the cad?"

"I think he's on the box, sir," said the young gentleman before noticed in the pink shirt, which looked like a white one ruled with red ink.

"I want to be set down!" said Dumps in a faint voice, overcome by his previous efforts.

"I think these cads want to be *set down*," returned the attorney's clerk, chuckling at his sally.

"Hollo!" cried Dumps again.

"Hollo!" echoed the passengers. The omnibus passed St. Giles's church.

"Hold hard!" said the conductor; "I'm blowed if we ha'n't forgot the gen'lm'n as vas to be set down at Doory-lane.—Now, sir, make haste, if you please," he added, opening the door, and assisting Dumps out with as much coolness as if it was "all right." Dumps's indignation was for once getting the better of his cynical equanimity. "Drury-lane!" he gasped, with the voice of a boy in a cold bath for the first time.

"Doory-lane, sir?—yes, sir,—third turning on the right-hand side, sir."

Dumps's passion was paramount: he clutched his umbrella, and was striding off with the firm determination of not paying the fare. The cad, by a remarkable coincidence, happened to entertain a directly contrary opinion, and Heaven knows how far the altercation would have proceeded, if it had not been most ably and satisfactorily brought to a close by the driver.

"Hollo!" said that respectable person, standing up on the box, and leaning with one hand on the roof of the omnibus. "Hollo, Tom! tell the gentleman if so be as he feels aggrieved, we will take him up to the Edge-er (Edgware) Road for nothing, and set him down at Doory-lane when we comes back. He can't reject that, anyhow."

The argument was irresistible: Dumps paid the disputed sixpence, and in a quarter of an hour was on the staircase of No. 14, Great Russell-street.

Everything indicated that preparations were making for the reception of "a few friends" in the evening. Two dozen extra tumblers, and four ditto wine-glasses —looking anything but transparent, with little bits of straw in them—were on the slab in the passage, just arrived. There was a great smell of nutmeg, port wine, and almonds, on the staircase; the covers were taken off the stair-carpet, and the figure of Venus on the first landing looked as if she were ashamed of the composition-candle in her right hind, which contrasted beautifully with the lamp-blacked drapery of the goddess of love. The female servant (who looked very warm and bustling) ushered Dumps into a front drawing-room, very prettily furnished, with a plentiful sprinkling of little baskets, paper table-mats, china watchmen, pink and gold albums, and rainbow-bound little books on the different tables.

"Ah, uncle!" said Mr. Kitterbell, "how d'ye do? Allow me—Jemima, my dear—my uncle. I think you've seen Jemima before, sir?"

"Have had the *pleasure*," returned big Dumps, his tone and look making it doubtful whether in his life he had ever experienced the sensation.

"I'm sure," said Mrs. Kitterbell, with a languid smile, and a slight cough. "I'm sure—hem—any friend—of Charles's—hem—much less a relation, is——"

"I knew you'd say so, my love," said little Kitterbell, who, while he appeared to be gazing on the opposite houses, was looking at his wife with a most affectionate air: "Bless you!" The last two words were accompanied with a simper, and a squeeze of the hand, which stirred up all Uncle Dumps's bile.

"Jane, tell nurse to bring down baby," said Mrs. Kitterbell, addressing the servant. Mrs. Kitterbell was a tall, thin young lady, with very light hair, and a particularly white face—one of those young women who almost invariably, though one hardly knows why, recal to one's mind the idea of a cold fillet of veal. Out went the servant, and in came the nurse, with a remarkably small parcel in her arms, packed up in a blue mantle trimmed with white fur.—This was the baby.

"Now, uncle," said Mr. Kitterbell, lifting up that part of the mantle which covered the infant's face, with an air of great triumph, "*Who* do you think he's like?"

"He! he! Yes, who?" said Mrs. K., putting her arm through her husband's, and looking up into Dumps's face with an expression of as much interest as she was capable of displaying.

"Good God, how small he is!" cried the amiable uncle, starting back with well-feigned surprise; "*remarkably* small indeed."

"Do you think so?" inquired poor little Kitterbell, rather alarmed. "He's a monster to what he was—ain't he, nurse?"

"He's a dear," said the nurse, squeezing the child, and evading the question—not because she scrupled to disguise the fact, but because she couldn't afford to throw away the chance of Dumps's half-crown.

"Well, but who is he like?" inquired little Kitterbell.

Dumps looked at the little pink heap before him, and only thought at the moment of the best mode of mortifying the youthful parents.

"I really don't know *who* he's like," he answered, very well knowing the reply expected of him.

"Don't you think he's like *me?*" inquired his nephew with a knowing air.

"Oh, *decidedly* not!" returned Dumps, with an emphasis not to be misunderstood "Decidedly not like you.—Oh, certainly not."

"Like Jemima?" asked Kitterbell, faintly.

"Oh, dear no; not in the least. I'm no judge, of course, in such cases; but I really think he's more like one of those little carved representations that one sometimes sees blowing a trumpet on a tombstone!" The nurse stooped down over the child, and with great difficulty prevented an explosion of mirth. Pa and ma looked almost as miserable as their amiable uncle.

"Well!" said the disappointed little father, "you'll be better able to tell what he's like by-and-by. You shall see him this evening with his mantle off."

"Thank you," said Dumps, feeling particularly grateful.

"Now, my love," said Kitterbell to his wife, "it's time we were off. We're to meet the other godfather and the godmother at the church, uncle,—Mr. and Mrs. Wilson from over the way—uncommonly nice people. My love, are you well wrapped up?"

"Yes, dear."

"Are you sure you won't have another shawl?" inquired the anxious husband.

"No, sweet," returned the charming mother, accepting Dumps's proffered arm; and the little party entered the hackney-coach that was to take them to the church; Dumps amusing Mrs. Kitterbell by expatiating largely on the danger of measles, thrush, teeth-cutting, and other interesting diseases to which children are subject.

The ceremony (which occupied about five minutes) passed off without anything particular occurring. The clergyman had to dine some distance from town, and had two churchings, three christenings, and a funeral to perform in something less than an hour. The godfathers and godmother, therefore, promised to renounce the devil and all his works—"and all that sort of thing"—as little Kitterbell said—"in less than no time;" and with the exception of Dumps nearly letting the child fall into the font when he handed it to the clergyman, the whole affair went off in the usual business-like and matter-of-course manner, and Dumps re-entered the Bank-gates at two o'clock with a heavy heart, and the painful conviction that he was regularly booked for an evening party.

Evening came—and so did Dumps's pumps, black silk stockings, and white cravat which he had ordered to be forwarded, per boy, from Pentonville. The depressed godfather dressed himself at a friend's counting-house, from whence, with his spirits fifty degrees below proof, he sallied forth—as the weather had cleared up, and the evening was tolerably fine—to walk to Great Russell-street. Slowly he paced up Cheapside, Newgate-street, down Snow-hill, and up Holborn ditto, looking as grim as the figure-head of a man-of-war, and finding out fresh causes of misery at every step. As he was crossing the corner of Hatton-garden, a man apparently intoxicated, rushed against him, and would have knocked him down, had he not been providentially caught by a very genteel young man, who happened to be close to him at the time. The shock so disarranged Dumps's nerves, as well as his dress, that he could hardly stand. The gentleman took his arm, and in the kindest manner walked with him as far as Furnival's Inn. Dumps, for about the first time in his life, felt grateful and polite; and he and the gentlemanly-looking young man parted with mutual expressions of good will.

"There are at least some well-disposed men in the world," ruminated the misanthropical Dumps, as he proceeded towards his destination.

Rat—tat—ta-ra-ra-ra-ra-rat—knocked a hackney-coachman at Kitterbell's door, in imitation of a gentleman's servant, just as Dumps reached it; and out came an old lady in a large toque, and an old gentleman in a blue coat, and three female copies of the old lady in pink dresses, and shoes to match.

"It's a large party," sighed the unhappy godfather, wiping the perspiration from his forehead, and leaning against the area-railings. It was some time before the miserable man could muster up courage to knock at the door, and when he did, the smart appearance of a neighbouring greengrocer (who had been hired to wait for seven and sixpence, and whose calves alone were worth double the money), the lamp in the passage, and the Venus on the landing, added to the hum of many voices, and the sound of a harp and two violins, painfully convinced him that his surmises were but too well founded.

"How are you?" said little Kitterbell, in a greater bustle than ever, bolting out of the little back parlour with a corkscrew in his hand, and various particles of sawdust, looking like so many inverted commas, on his inexpressibles.

"Good God!" said Dumps, turning into the aforesaid parlour to put his shoes on, which he had brought in his coat-pocket, and still more appalled by the sight of seven fresh-drawn corks, and a corresponding number of decanters. "How many people are there up-stairs?"

"Oh, not above thirty-five. We've had the carpet taken up in the back drawing-room, and the piano and the card-tables are in the front. Jemima thought we'd better have a regular sit-down supper in the front parlour, because of the speechifying, and all that. But, Lord! uncle, what's the matter?" continued the excited little man, as Dumps stood with one shoe on, rummaging his pockets with the most frightful distortion of visage. "What have you lost? Your pocket-book?"

"No," returned Dumps, diving first into one pocket and then into the other, and speaking in a voice like Desdemona with the pillow over her mouth.

"Your card-case? snuff-box? the key of your lodgings?" continued Kitterbell, pouring question on question with the rapidity of lightning.

"No! no!" ejaculated Dumps, still diving eagerly into his empty pocket.

"Not—not—the *mug* you spoke of this morning?"

"Yes, the *mug!*" replied Dumps, sinking into a chair.

"How *could* you have done it?" inquired Kitterbell. "Are you sure you brought it out?"

"Yes! yes! I see it all!" said Dumps, starting up as the idea flashed across his mind; "miserable dog that I am—I was born to suffer. I see it all: it was the gentlemanly-looking young man!"

"Mr. Dumps!" shouted the greengrocer in a stentorian voice, as he ushered the somewhat recovered godfather into the drawing-room half an hour after the above declaration. "Mr. Dumps!"—everybody looked at the door, and in came Dumps, feeling about as much out of place as a salmon might be supposed to be in a gravel-walk.

"Happy to see you again," said Mrs. Kitterbell, quite unconscious of the unfortunate man's confusion and misery; "you must allow me to introduce you to a few of our friends:—my mama, Mr. Dumps—my papa and sisters." Dumps seized the hand of the mother as warmly as if she was his own parent, bowed *to* the young ladies, and *against* a gentleman behind him, and took no notice whatever of the father, who had been bowing incessantly for three minutes and a quarter.

"Uncle," said little Kitterbell, after Dumps had been introduced to a select dozen or two, "you must let me lead you to the other end of the room, to introduce you to my friend Danton. Such a splendid fellow!—I'm sure you'll like him—this way,"—Dumps followed as tractably as a tame bear.

Mr. Danton was a young man of about five-and-twenty, with a considerable stock of impudence, and a very small share of ideas: he was a great favourite, especially with young ladies of from sixteen to twenty-six years of age, both inclusive. He could imitate the French-horn to admiration, sang comic songs most inimitably, and had the most insinuating way of saying impertinent nothings to his doting female admirers. He had acquired, somehow or other, the reputation of being a great wit, and, accordingly, whenever he opened his mouth, everybody who knew him laughed very heartily.

The introduction took place in due form. Mr. Danton bowed, and twirled a lady's handkerchief, which he held in his hand, in a most comic way. Everybody smiled.

"Very warm," said Dumps, feeling it necessary to say something.

"Yes. It was warmer yesterday," returned the brilliant Mr. Danton.—A general laugh.

"I have great pleasure in congratulating you on your first appearance in the character of a father, sir," he continued, addressing Dumps—"godfather, I mean."—The young ladies were convulsed, and the gentleman in ecstasies.

A general hum of admiration interrupted the conversation, and announced the entrance of nurse with the baby. An universal rush of the young ladies immediately took place. (Girls are always *so* fond of babies in company.)

"Oh, you dear!" said one.

"How sweet!" cried another, in a low tone of the most enthusiastic admiration.

"Heavenly!" added a third.

"Oh! what dear little arms!" said a fourth, holding up an arm and fist about the size and shape of the leg of a fowl cleanly picked.

"Did you ever!"—said a little coquette with a large bustle, who looked like a French lithograph, appealing to a gentleman in three waistcoats—"Did you ever!"

"Never, in my life," returned her admirer, pulling up his collar.

"Oh! *do* let me take it, nurse," cried another young lady. "The love!"

"Can it open its eyes, nurse?" inquired another, affecting the utmost innocence. —Suffice it to say, that the single ladies unanimously voted him an angel, and that the married ones, *nem. con.*, agreed that he was decidedly the finest baby they had ever beheld—except their own.

The quadrilles were resumed with great spirit. Mr. Danton was universally admitted to be beyond himself; several young ladies enchanted the company and gained admirers by singing "We met"—"I saw her at the Fancy Fair"—and other equally sentimental and interesting ballads. "The young men,' as Mrs. Kitterbell said, "made themselves very agreeable;" the girls did not lose their opportunity; and the evening promised to go off excellently. Dumps didn't mind it: he had devised a plan for himself—a little bit of fun in his own way—and he was almost happy! He played a rubber and lost every point. Mr. Danton said he could not have lost every point, because he made a point of losing: everybody laughed tremendously. Dumps retorted with a better joke, and nobody smiled, with the exception of the host, who seemed to consider it his duty to laugh till he was black in the face, at everything. There was only one drawback —the musicians did not play with quite as much spirit as could have been wished. The cause, however, was satisfactorily explained; for it appeared, on the testimony of a gentleman who had come up from Gravesend in the afternoon, that they had been engaged on board a steamer all day, and had played almost without cessation all the way to Gravesend, and all the way back again.

The "sit-down supper" was excellent; there were four barley-sugar temples on the table, which would have looked beautiful if they had not melted away when the supper began; and a water-mill, whose only fault was that instead of going round, it ran over the table-cloth. Then there were fowls, and tongue, and trifle, and sweets, and lobster salad, and potted beef—and everything. And little Kitterbell kept calling out for clean plates, and the clean plates did not come: and then the gentlemen who wanted the plates said they didn't mind, they'd take a lady's; and then Mrs. Kitterbell applauded their gallantry, and the greengrocer ran about till he thought his seven and sixpence was very hardly earned; and the young ladies didn't eat much for fear it shouldn't look romantic, and the married ladies eat as much as possible, for fear they shouldn't have enough; and a great deal of wine was drunk, and everybody talked and laughed considerably.

"Hush! hush!" said Mr. Kitterbell, rising and looking very important. "My love (this was addressed to his wife at the other end of the table), take care of Mrs. Maxwell, and your mamma, and the rest of the married ladies; the gentlemen will persuade the young ladies to fill their glasses, I am sure."

"Ladies and gentlemen," said long Dumps, in a very sepulchral voice and rueful accent, rising from his chair like the ghost in Don Juan, "will you have the kindness to charge your glasses? I am desirous of proposing a toast."

A dead silence ensued, and the glasses were filled—everybody looked serious.

"Ladies and gentlemen," slowly continued the ominous Dumps, "I"—(here Mr. Danton imitated two notes from the French-horn, in a very loud key, which electrified the nervous toast-proposer, and convulsed his audience).

"Order! order!" said little Kitterbell, endeavouring to suppress his laughter.

"Order!" said the gentlemen.

"Danton, be quiet," said a particular friend on the opposite side of the table.

"Ladies and gentlemen," resumed Dumps, somewhat recovered, and not much disconcerted, for he was always a pretty good hand at a speech—"In accordance with what is, I believe, the established usage on these occasions, I, as one of the godfathers of Master Frederick Charles William Kitterbell—(here the speaker's voice faltered, for he remembered the mug)—venture to rise to propose a toast. I need hardly say that it is the health and prosperity of that young gentleman, the particular event of whose early life we are here met to celebrate—(applause). Ladies and gentlemen, it is impossible to suppose that our friends here, whose sincere well-wishers we all are, can pass through life without some trials, considerable suffering, severe affliction, and heavy losses!"—Here the arch-traitor paused, and slowly drew forth a long, white pocket-handkerchief—his example was followed by several ladies. "That these trials may be long spared them is my most earnest prayer, my most fervent wish (a distinct sob from the grandmother). I hope and trust, ladies and gentlemen, that the infant whose christening we have this evening met to celebrate, may not be removed from the arms of his parents by premature decay (several cambrics were in requisition): that his young and now *apparently* healthy form, may not be wasted by lingering disease. (Here Dumps cast a sardonic glance around, for a great sensation was manifest among the married ladies.) You, I am sure, will concur with me in wishing that he may live to be a comfort and a blessing to his parents. ('Hear, hear!' and an audible sob from Mr. Kitterbell.) But should he not be what we could wish—should he forget in after times the duty which he owes to them—should they unhappily experience that distracting truth, 'how sharper than a serpent's tooth it is to have a thankless child'"—Here Mrs. Kitterbell, with her handkerchief to her eyes, and accompanied by several ladies, rushed from the room, and went into violent hysterics in the passage, leaving her better half in almost as bad a condition, and a general impression in Dumps's favour; for people like sentiment, after all.

It need hardly be added, that this occurrence quite put a stop to the harmony of the evening. Vinegar, hartshorn, and cold water, were now as much in request as negus, rout-cakes, and *bon-bons* had been a short time before. Mrs. Kitterbell was immediately conveyed to her apartment, the musicians were silenced, flirting ceased, and the company slowly departed. Dumps left the house at the commencement of the bustle, and walked home with a light step, and (for him) a cheerful heart. His landlady, who slept in the next room, has offered to make oath that she heard him laugh, in his peculiar manner, after he had locked his door. The assertion, however, is so improbable, and bears on the face of it such strong evidence of untruth, that it has never obtained credence to this hour.

The family of Mr. Kitterbell has considerably increased since the period to which we have referred; he has now two sons and a daughter; and as he expects, at no distant period, to have another addition to his blooming progeny, he is anxious to secure an eligible godfather for the occasion. He is determined, however, to impose upon him two conditions. He must bind himself, by a solemn obligation, not to make any speech after supper; and it is indispensable that he should be in no way connected with "the most miserable man in the world."

CHAPTER XII.

THE DRUNKARD'S DEATH.

We will be bold to say, that there is scarcely a man in the constant habit of walking, day after day, through any of the crowded thoroughfares of London, who cannot recollect among the people whom he "knows by sight," to use a familiar phrase, some being of abject and wretched appearance whom he remembers to have seen in a very different condition, whom he has observed sinking lower and lower, by almost imperceptible degrees, and the shabbiness and utter destitution of whose appearance, at last, strike forcibly and painfully upon him, as he passes by. Is there any man who has mixed much with society, or whose avocations have caused him to mingle, at one time or other, with a great number of people, who cannot call to mind the time when some shabby, miserable wretch, in rags and filth, who shuffles past him now in all the squalor of disease and poverty, was a respectable tradesman, or clerk, or a man following some thriving pursuit, with good prospects, and decent means?—or cannot any of our readers call to mind from among the list of their *quondam* acquaintance, some fallen and degraded man, who lingers about the pavement in hungry misery—from whom every one turns coldly away, and who preserves himself from sheer starvation, nobody knows how? Alas! such cases are of too frequent occurrence to be rare items in any man's experience; and but too often arise from one cause—drunkenness—that fierce rage for the slow, sure poison, that oversteps every other consideration; that casts aside wife, children, friends, happiness, and station; and hurries its victims madly on to degradation and death.

Some of these men have been impelled, by misfortune and misery, to the vice that has degraded them. The ruin of worldly expectations, the death of those they loved, the sorrow that slowly consumes, but will not break the heart, has driven them wild; and they present the hideous spectacle of madmen, slowly dying by their own hands. But by far the greater part have wilfully, and with open eyes, plunged into the gulf from which the man who once enters it never rises more, but into which he sinks deeper and deeper down, until recovery is hopeless.

Such a man as this once stood by the bedside of his dying wife, while his children knelt around, and mingled low bursts of grief with their innocent prayers. The room was scantily and meanly furnished; and it needed but a glance at the pale form from which the light of life was fast passing away, to know that grief, and want, and anxious care, had been busy at the heart for many a weary year. An elderly woman, with her face bathed in tears, was supporting the head of the dying woman—her daughter—on her arm. But it was not towards her that the wan face turned; it was not her hand that the cold and trembling fingers clasped; they pressed the husband's arm; the eyes so soon to be closed in death rested on his face, and the man shook beneath their gaze. His dress was slovenly and disordered, his face inflamed, his eyes bloodshot and heavy. He had been summoned from some wild debauch to the bed of sorrow and death.

A shaded lamp by the bed-side cast a dim light on the figures around, and left the remainder of the room in thick, deep shadow. The silence of night prevailed without the house, and the stillness of death was in the chamber. A watch hung over the mantel-shelf; its low ticking was the only sound that broke the profound quiet, but it was a solemn one, for well they knew, who heard it, that before it had recorded the passing of another hour, it would beat the knell of a departed spirit.

It is a dreadful thing to wait and watch for the approach of death; to know that hope is gone, and recovery impossible; and to sit and count the dreary hours through long, long nights—such nights as only watchers by the bed of sickness know. It chills the blood to hear the dearest secrets of the heart—the pent-up, hidden secrets of many years—poured forth by the unconscious helpless being before you and to think how little the reserve and cunning of a whole life will avail, when fever and delirium tear off the mask at last. Strange tales have been told in the wanderings of dying men; tales so full of guilt and crime, that those who stood by the sick person's couch have fled in horror and affright, lest they should be scared to madness by what they heard and saw; and many a wretch has died alone, raving of deeds the very name of which has driven the boldest man away.

But no such ravings were to be heard at the bed-side by which the children knelt. Their half-stifled sobs and moanings alone broke the silence of the lonely chamber. And when at last the mother's grasp relaxed, and, turning one look from the children to the father, she vainly strove to speak, and fell backward on the pillow, all was so calm and tranquil that she seemed to sink to sleep. They leant over her; they called upon her name, softly at first, and then in the loud and piercing tones of desperation. But there was no reply. They listened for her breath, but no sound came. They felt for the palpitation of the heart, but no faint throb responded to the touch. That heart was broken, and she was dead!

The husband sunk into a chair by the bed-side, and clasped his hands upon his burning forehead. He gazed from child to child, but when a weeping eye met his, he quailed beneath its look. No word of comfort was whispered in his ear, no look of kindness lighted on his face. All shrunk from and avoided him; and when at last he staggered from the room, no one sought to follow or console the widower.

The time had been when many a friend would have crowded round him in his affliction, and many a heartfelt condolence would have met him in his grief. Where were they now? One by one, friends, relations, the commonest acquaintance even, had fallen off from and deserted the drunkard. His wife alone had clung to him in good and evil, in sickness and poverty; and how had he rewarded her? He had reeled from the tavern to her bed-side in time to see her die.

He rushed from the house, and walked swiftly through the streets. Remorse, fear, shame, all crowded on his mind. Stupefied with drink, and bewildered with the scene he had just witnessed, he re-entered the tavern he had quitted shortly before. Glass succeeded glass. His blood mounted, and his brain whirled round Death! Every one must die, and why not *she*. She was too good for him; her relations had often told him so. Curses on them! Had they not deserted her, and left her to whine away the time at home? Well—she was dead, and happy perhaps. It was better as it was. Another glass—one more! Hurrah! It was a merry life while it lasted; and he would make the most of it.

Time went on; the three children who were left to him, grew up, and were children no longer. The father remained the same—poorer, shabbier, and more dissolute-looking, but the same confirmed and irreclaimable drunkard. The boys had, long ago, run wild in the streets, and left him; the girl alone remained, but she worked hard, and words or blows could always procure him something for the tavern. So he went on in the old course, and a merry life he led.

One night, as early as ten o'clock—for the girl had been sick for many days, and there was, consequently, little to spend at the public-house--he bent his steps homeward, bethinking himself that if he would have her able to earn money, it would be as well to apply to the parish surgeon, or, at all events, to take the trouble of inquiring what ailed her, which he had not yet thought it worth while to do. It was a wet December night; the wind blew piercing cold, and the rain poured heavily down. He begged a few halfpence from a passer-by, and having bought a small loaf (for it was his interest to keep the girl alive, if he could), he shuffled onwards as fast as the wind and rain would let him.

At the back of Fleet-street, and lying between it and the water-side, are several mean and narrow courts, which form a portion of Whitefriars: it was to one of these that he directed his steps.

The alley into which he turned, might, for filth and misery, have competed with the darkest corner of this ancient sanctuary in its dirtiest and most lawless time. The houses, varying from two stories in height to four, were stained with every indescribable hue that long exposure to the weather, damp, and rottenness can impart to tenements composed originally of the roughest and coarsest materials. The windows were patched with paper, and stuffed with the foulest rags; the doors were falling from their hinges; poles with lines on which to dry clothes, projected from every casement, and sounds of quarrelling or drunkenness issued from every room.

The solitary oil lamp in the centre of the court had been blown out, either by the violence of the wind or the act of some inhabitant who had excellent reasons for objecting to his residence being rendered too conspicuous; and the only light which fell upon the broken and uneven pavement, was derived from the miserable candles that here and there twinkled in the rooms of such of the more fortunate residents as could afford to indulge in so expensive a luxury. A gutter ran down the centre of the alley—all the sluggish odours of which had been called forth by the rain; and as the wind whistled through the old houses, the doors and shutters creaked upon their hinges, and the windows shook in their frames, with a violence which every moment seemed to threaten the destruction of the whole place.

The man whom we have followed into this den, walked on in the darkness, sometimes stumbling into the main gutter, and at others into some branch repositories of garbage which had been formed by the rain, until he reached the last house in the court. The door, or rather what was left of it, stood ajar, for he convenience of the numerous lodgers; and he proceeded to grope his way up the old and broken stair, to the attic story.

He was within a step or two of his room door, when it opened, and a girl, whose miserable and emaciated appearance was only to be equalled by that of the candle which she shaded with her hand, peeped anxiously out.

"Is that you, father?" said the girl.

"Who else should it be?" replied the man gruffly. "What are you trembling at? It's little enough that I've had to drink to-day, for there's no drink without money, and no money without work. What the devil's the matter with the girl?"

"I am not well, father—not at all well," said the girl, bursting into tears.

"Ah!" replied the man, in the tone of a person who is compelled to admit a very unpleasant fact, to which he would rather remain blind, if he could. "You must get better somehow, for we must have money. You must go to the parish doctor, and make him give you some medicine. They're paid for it, damn 'em. What are you standing before the door for? Let me come in, can't you?"

"Father," whispered the girl, shutting the door behind her, and placing herself before it, "William has come back."

"Who!" said the man with a start.

"Hush," replied the girl, "William; brother William."

"And what does he want?" said the man, with an effort at composure—"money? meat? drink? He's come to the wrong shop for that, if he does. Give me the candle—give me the candle, fool—I ain't going to hurt him." He snatched the candle from her hand, and walked into the room.

Sitting on an old box, with his head resting on his hand, and his eyes fixed on a wretched cinder fire that was smouldering on the hearth, was a young man of about two-and-twenty, miserably clad in an old coarse jacket and trousers. He started up when his father entered.

"Fasten the door, Mary," said the young man hastily—"Fasten the door. You look as if you didn't know me, father. It's long enough, since you drove me from home; you may well forget me."

"And what do you want here, now?" said the father, seating himself on a stool, on the other side of the fireplace. "What do you want here, now?"

"Shelter," replied the son, "I'm in trouble: that's enough. If I'm caught I shall swing; that's certain. Caught I shall be, unless I stop here; that's *as* certain. And there's an end of it."

"You mean to say, you've been robbing, or murdering, then?" said the father.

"Yes I do," replied the son. "Does it surprise you, father?" He looked steadily in the man's face, but he withdrew his eyes, and bent them on the ground.

"Where's your brothers?" he said, after a long pause.

"Where they'll never trouble you," replied his son: "John's gone to America, and Henry's dead."

"Dead!" said the father, with a shudder, which even he could not repress.

'Dead," replied the young man. "He died in my arm—shot like a dog, by a gamekeeper. He staggered back, I caught him, and his blood trickled down my hands. It poured out from his side like water. He was weak, and it blinded him, but he threw himself down on his knees, on the grass, and prayed to God, that if his mother was in heaven, He would hear her prayers for pardon for her youngest son. 'I was her favourite boy, Will,' he said, 'and I am glad to think, now, that when she was dying, though I was a very young child then, and my little heart was almost bursting, I knelt down at the foot of the bed, and thanked God for having made me so fond of her as to have never once done anything to bring the tears into her eyes. O Will, why was she taken away, and father left?' There's his dying words, father," said the young man; "make the best you can of 'em. You struck him across the face, in a drunken fit, the morning we ran away; and here's the end of it."

The girl wept aloud; and the father, sinking his head upon his knees, rocked himself to and fro.

"If I am taken," said the young man, "I shall be carried back into the country, and hung for that man's murder. They cannot trace me here, without your assistance, father. For aught I know, you may give me up to justice; but unless you do, here I stop, until I can venture to escape abroad."

For two whole days, all three remained in the wretched room, without stirring out. On the third evening, however, the girl was worse than she had been yet, and the few scraps of food they had were gone. It was indispensably necessary that somebody should go out; and as the girl was too weak and ill, the father went, just at nightfall.

He got some medicine for the girl, and a trifle in the way of pecuniary assistance. On his way back, he earned sixpence by holding a horse; and he turned homewards with enough money to supply their most pressing wants for two or three days to come. He had to pass the public-house. He lingered for an instant, walked past it, turned back again, lingered once more, and finally slunk in. Two men whom he had not observed, were on the watch. They were on the point of giving up their search in despair, when his loitering attracted their attention; and when he entered the public-house, they followed him.

"You'll drink with me, master," said one of them, proffering him a glass of liquor.

"And me too," said the other, replenishing the glass as soon as it was drained of its contents.

The man thought of his hungry children, and his son's danger. But they were nothing to the drunkard. He *did* drink; and his reason left him.

"A wet night, Warden," whispered one of the men in his ear, as he at length turned to go away, after spending in liquor one-half of the money on which, perhaps, his daughter's life depended.

"The right sort of night for our friends in hiding, Master Warden," whispered the other.

"Sit down here," said the one who had spoken first, drawing him into a corner. "We have been looking arter the young un. We came to tell him, it's all right now, but we couldn't find him 'cause we hadn't got the precise direction. But that ain't strange, for I don't think he know'd it himself, when he come to London, did he?"

"No, he didn't," replied the father.

The two men exchanged glances.

"There's a vessel down at the docks, to sail at midnight, when it's high water," resumed the first speaker, "and we'll put him on board. His passage is taken in another name, and what's better than that, it's paid for. It's lucky we met you."

"Very," said the second.

"Capital luck," said the first, with a wink to his companion.

"Great," replied the second, with a slight nod of intelligence.

"Another glass here; quick"—said the first speaker. And in five minutes more, the father had unconsciously yielded up his own son into the hangman's hands.

Slowly and heavily the time dragged along, as the brother and sister, in their miserable hiding-place, listened in anxious suspense to the slightest sound. At length, a heavy footstep was heard upon the stair; it approached nearer; it reached the landing; and the father staggered into the room.

The girl saw that he was intoxicated, and advanced with the candle in her hand to meet him; she stopped short, gave a loud scream, and fell senseless on the ground. She had caught sight of the shadow of a man reflected on the floor. They both rushed in, and in another instant the young man was a prisoner, and handcuffed.

"Very quietly done," said one of the men to his companion, "thanks to the old man. Lift up the girl, Tom—come, come, it's no use crying, young woman It's all over now, and can't be helped."

The young man stooped for an instant over the girl, and then turned fiercely round upon his father, who had reeled against the wall, and was gazing on the group with drunken stupidity.

"Listen to me, father," he said, in a tone that made the drunkard's flesh creep. "My brother's blood, and mine, is on your head: I never had kind look, or word, or care, from you, and alive or dead, I never will forgive you. Die when you will, or how, I will be with you. I speak as a dead man now, and I warn you, father, that as surely as you must one day stand before your Maker, so surely shall your children be there, hand in hand, to cry for judgment against you."

He raised his manacled hands in a threatening attitude, fixed his eyes on his shrinking parent, and slowly left the room; and neither father nor sister ever beheld him more, on this side of the grave.

When the dim and misty light of a winter's morning penetrated into the narrow court, and struggled through the begrimed window of the wretched room, Warden awoke from his heavy sleep, and found himself alone. He rose, and looked round him; the old flock mattress on the floor was undisturbed; everything was just as he remembered to have seen it last: and there were no signs of any one, save himself, having occupied the room during the night. He inquired of the other lodgers, and of the neighbours; but his daughter had not been seen or heard of. He rambled through the streets, and scrutinised each wretched face among the crowds that thronged them, with anxious eyes. But his search was fruitless, and he returned to his garret when night came on, desolate and weary.

For many days he occupied himself in the same manner, but no trace of his daughter did he meet with, and no word of her reached his ears. At length he gave up the pursuit as hopeless. He had long thought of the probability of her leaving him, and endeavouring to gain her bread in quiet, elsewhere. She had left him at last to starve alone. He ground his teeth, and cursed her!

He begged his bread from door to door. Every halfpenny he could wring from the pity or credulity of those to whom he addressed himself, was spent in the old way. A year passed over his head; the roof of a jail was the only one that had sheltered him for many months. He slept under archways, and in brickfields—anywhere, where there was some warmth or shelter from the cold and rain. But in the last stage of poverty, disease, and houseless want, he was a drunkard still.

At last, one bitter night, he sunk down on a door-step faint and ill. The premature decay of vice and profligacy had worn him to the bone. His cheeks were hollow and livid; his eyes were sunken, and their sight was dim. His legs trembled beneath his weight, and a cold shiver ran through every limb.

And now the long-forgotten scenes of a misspent life crowded thick and fast upon him. He thought of the time when he had a home—a happy, cheerful home—and of those who peopled it, and flocked about him then, until the forms of his elder children seemed to rise from the grave, and stand about him—so plain, so clear, and so distinct they were that he could touch and feel them. Looks that he had long forgotten were fixed upon him once more; voices long since hushed in death sounded in his ears like the music of village bells. But it was only for an instant. The rain beat heavily upon him; and cold and hunger were gnawing at his heart again.

He rose, and dragged his feeble limbs a few paces further. The street was silent and empty; the few passengers who passed by, at that late hour, hurried quickly on, and his tremulous voice was lost in the violence of the storm. Again that heavy chill struck through his frame, and his blood seemed to stagnate beneath it. He coiled himself up in a projecting doorway, and tried to sleep.

But sleep had fled from his dull and glazed eyes. His mind wandered strangely, but he was awake, and conscious. The well-known shout of drunken mirth sounded in his ear, the glass was at his lips, the board was covered with choice rich food—they were before him: he could see them all, he had but to reach out his hand, and take them—and, though the illusion was reality itself, he knew that he was sitting alone in the deserted street, watching the rain-drops as they pattered on the stones; that death was coming upon him by inches—and that there were none to care for or help him.

Suddenly he started up, in the extremity of terror. He had heard his own voice shouting in the night air, he knew not what, or why. Hark! A groan!—another! His senses were leaving him: half-formed and incoherent words burst from his lips; and his hands sought to tear and lacerate his flesh. He was going mad, and he shrieked for help till his voice failed him.

He raised his head, and looked up the long dismal street. He recollected that outcasts like himself, condemned to wander day and night in those dreadful streets, had sometimes gone distracted with their own loneliness. He remembered to have heard many years before that a homeless wretch had once been found in a solitary corner, sharpening a rusty knife to plunge into his own heart, preferring death to that endless, weary, wandering to and fro. In an instant his resolve was taken, his limbs received new life; he ran quickly from the spot, and paused not for breath until he reached the river-side.

He crept softly down the steep stone stairs that lead from the commencement of Waterloo Bridge, down to the water's level. He crouched into a corner, and held his breath, as the patrol passed. Never did prisoner's heart throb with the hope of liberty and life half so eagerly as did that of the wretched man at the prospect of death. The watch passed close to him, but he remained unobserved; and after waiting till the sound of footsteps had died away in the distance, he cautiously descended, and stood beneath the gloomy arch that forms the landing-place from the river.

The tide was in, and the water flowed at his feet. The rain had ceased, the wind was lulled, and all was, for the moment, still and quiet—so quiet, that the slightest sound on the opposite bank, even the rippling of the water against the barges that were moored there, was distinctly audible to his ear. The stream stole languidly and sluggishly on. Strange and fantastic forms rose to the surface, and beckoned him to approach; dark gleaming eyes peered from the water, and seemed to mock his hesitation, while hollow murmurs from behind, urged him onwards. He retreated a few paces, took a short run, desperate leap, and plunged into the river.

Not five seconds had passed when he rose to the water's surface—but what a change had taken place in that short time, in all his thoughts and feelings! Life—life in any form, poverty, misery, starvation—anything but death. He fought and struggled with the water that closed over his head, and screamed in agonies of terror. The curse of his own son rang in his ears. The shore—but one foot of dry ground—he could almost touch the step. One hand's breadth nearer, and he was saved—but the tide bore him onward, under the dark arches of the bridge, and he sank to the bottom.

Again he rose, and struggled for life. For one instant—for one brief instant—the buildings on the river's banks, the lights on the bridge through which the current had borne him, the black water, and the fast-flying clouds, were distinctly visible—once more he sunk, and once again he rose. Bright flames of fire shot up from earth to heaven, and reeled before his eyes, while the water thundered in his ears, and stunned him with its furious roar.

A week afterwards the body was washed ashore, some miles down the river, a swollen and disfigured mass. Unrecognised and unpitied, it was borne to the grave; and there it has long since mouldered away!

THE END.

HOLIDAY ROMANCE.

IN FOUR PARTS.

PART I.

INTRODUCTORY ROMANCE. FROM THE PEN OF WILLIAM TINKLING, ESQUIRE.*

THIS beginning-part is not made out of anybody's head, you know. It's real. You must believe this beginning-part more than what comes after, else you won't understand how what comes after came to be written. You must believe it all; but you must believe this most, please. I am the editor of it. Bob Redforth (he's my cousin, and shaking the table on purpose) wanted to be the editor of it; but I said he should n't because he could n't. *He* has no idea of being an editor.

Nettie Ashford is my bride. We were married in the right-hand closet in the corner of the dancing-school where first we met, with a ring (a green one) from Wilkingwater's toy-shop. *I* owed for it out of my pocket-money. When the rapturous ceremony was over, we all four went up the lane and let off a cannon (brought loaded in Bob Redforth's waistcoat-pocket) to announce our nuptials. It flew right up when it went off, and turned over. Next day, Lieutenant-Colonel Robin Redforth was united, with similar ceremonies, to Alice Rainbird. This time, the cannon burst with a most terrific explosion, and made a puppy bark.

My peerless bride was, at the period of which we now treat, in captivity at Miss Grimmer's. Drowvey and Grimmer is the partnership, and opinion is divided which is the greatest beast. The lovely bride of the colonel was also immured in the dungeons of the same establishment. A vow was entered into, between the colonel and myself, that we would cut them out on the following Wednesday when walking two and two.

Under the desperate circumstances of the case, the active brain of the colonel, combining with his lawless pursuit (he is a pirate), suggested an attack with fireworks. This, however, from motives of humanity, was abandoned as too expensive.

Lightly armed with a paper-knife buttoned up under his jacket, and waving the dreaded black flag at the end of a cane, the colonel took command of me at two P. M., on the eventful and appointed day. He had drawn out the plan of attack on a piece of paper, which was rolled up round a hoop-stick. He showed it to me. My position and my full-length portrait (but my real ears don't stick out horizontal) was behind a corner lamp-post, with written orders to remain there till I should see Miss Drowvey fall. The Drowvey who was to fall was the one in spectacles, not the one with the large lavender bonnet. At that signal,

* Aged eight.

I was to rush forth, seize my bride, and fight my way to the lane. There a junction would be effected between myself and the colonel; and putting our brides behind us, between ourselves and the palings, we were to conquer or die.

The enemy appeared, — approached. Waving his black flag, the colonel attacked. Confusion ensued. Anxiously I awaited my signal; but my signal came not. So far from falling, the hated Drowvey in spectacles appeared to me to have muffled the colonel's head in his outlawed banner, and to be pitching into him with a parasol. The one in the lavender bonnet also performed prodigies of valor with her fists on his back. Seeing that all was for the moment lost, I fought my desperate way, hand-to-hand, to the lane. Through taking the back road, I was so fortunate as to meet nobody, and arrived there uninterrupted.

It seemed an age ere the colonel joined me. He had been to the jobbing-tailor's to be sewn up in several places, and attributed our defeat to the refusal of the detested Drowvey to fall. Finding her so obstinate, he had said to her "Die recreant!" but had found her no more open to reason on that point than the other.

My blooming bride appeared, accompanied by the colonel's bride, at the dancing-school next day. What? Was her face averted from me? Hah? Even so. With a look of scorn she put into my hand a bit of paper, and took another partner. On the paper was pencilled, "Heavens! Can I write the word? Is my husband a cow?"

In the first bewilderment of my heated brain, I tried to think what slanderer could have traced my family to the ignoble animal mentioned above. Vain were my endeavors. At the end of that dance I whispered the colonel to come into the cloak-room, and I showed him the note.

"There is a syllable wanting," said he, with a gloomy brow.

"Hah! What syllable?" was my inquiry.

"She asks, can she write the word? And no; you see she could n't," said the colonel, pointing out the passage.

"And the word was?" said I.

"Cow — cow — coward," hissed the pirate-colonel in my ear, and gave me back the note.

Feeling that I must forever tread the earth a branded boy, — person, I mean, — or that I must clear up my honor, I demanded to be tried by a court-martial. The colonel admitted my right to be tried. Some difficulty was found in composing the court, on account of the Emperor of France's aunt refusing to let him come out. He was to be the president. Ere yet we had appointed a substitute, he made his escape over the back wall, and stood among us, a free monarch.

The court was held on the grass by the pond. I recognized, in a certain admiral among my judges, my deadliest foe. A cocoanut had given rise to language that I could not brook; but confiding in my innocence, and also in the knowledge that the President of the United States (who sat next him) owed me a knife, I braced myself for the ordeal.

It was a solemn spectacle, that court. Two executioners with pinafores reversed led me in. Under the shade of an umbrella I perceived my bride, supported by the bride of the pirate-colonel. The president, having reproved a little female ensign for tittering, on a matter of life or death, called upon me to plead, "Coward or no coward, guilty or not guilty?" I pleaded in a firm tone, "No coward and not guilty." (The little female ensign being again reproved by the president for misconduct, mutinied, left the court, and threw stones.)

My implacable enemy, the admiral, conducted the case against me. The colonel's bride was called to prove that I had remained behind the corner lamp-post during the engagement. I might have been spared the anguish of my own bride's being also made a witness to the same point, but the admiral knew where to wound me. Be still, my soul, no matter. The colonel was then brought forward with his evidence.

It was for this point that I had saved myself up, as the turning-point of my case. Shaking myself free of my guards, — who had no business to hold me, the stupids, unless I was found guilty, — I asked the colonel what he considered the first duty of a soldier? Ere he could reply, the President of the United States rose and informed the court, that my foe, the admiral, had suggested "Bravery," and that prompting a witness was n't fair. The president of the court immediately ordered the admiral's mouth to be filled with leaves, and tied up with string. I had the satisfaction of seeing the sentence carried into effect before the proceedings went further.

I then took a paper from my trousers-pocket, and asked, "What do you consider, Colonel Redford, the first duty of a soldier? Is it obedience?"

"It is," said the colonel.

"Is that paper — please to look at it — in your hand?"

"It is," said the colonel.

"Is it a military sketch?"

"It is," said the colonel.

"Of an engagement?"

"Quite so," said the colonel.

"Of the late engagement?"

"Of the late engagement."

"Please to describe it, and then hand it to the president of the court."

From that triumphant moment my sufferings and my dangers were at an end. The court rose up and jumped, on discovering that I had strictly obeyed orders. My foe, the admiral, who though muzzled was malignant yet, contrived to suggest that I was dishonored by having quitted the field. But the colonel himself had done as much, and gave his opinion, upon his word and honor as a pirate, that when all was lost the field might be quitted without disgrace. I was going to be found "No coward and not guilty," and my blooming bride was going to be publicly restored to my arms in a procession, when an unlooked-for event disturbed the general rejoicing. This was no other than the Emperor of France's aunt catching hold of his hair. The proceedings abruptly terminated, and the court tumultuously dissolved.

It was when the shades of the next evening but one were beginning to fall, ere yet the silver beams of Luna touched the earth, that four forms might have been descried slowly advancing towards the weeping willow on the borders of the pond, the now deserted scene of the day-before-yesterday's agonies and triumphs. On a nearer approach, and by a practised eye, these might have been identified as the forms of the pirate-colonel with his bride, and of the day-before-yesterday's gallant prisoner with his bride.

On the beauteous faces of the Nymphs dejection sat enthroned. All four reclined under the willow for some minutes without speaking, till at length the bride of the colonel poutingly observed, "It 's of no use pretending any more, and we had better give it up."

"Hah!" exclaimed the pirate. "Pretending?"

"Don't go on like that; you worry me," returned his bride.

The lovely bride of Tinkling echoed the incredible declaration. The two warriors exchanged stony glances.

"If," said the bride of the pirate-colonel, "grown up people WON'T do what they ought to do, and WILL put us out, what comes of our pretending?"

"We only get into scrapes," said the bride of Tinkling.

"You know very well," pursued the colonel's bride, "that Miss Drowvey would n't fall. You complained of it yourself. And you know how disgracefully the court-martial ended. As to our marriage; would my people acknowledge it at home?"

"Or would my people acknowledge ours?" said the bride of Tinkling.

Again the two warriors exchanged stony glances.

"If you knocked at the door and claimed me, after you were told to go away," said the colonel's bride, "you would only have your hair pulled, or your ears, or your nose."

"If you persisted in ringing at the bell and claiming me," said the bride of Tinkling to that gentleman, "you would have things dropped on your head from the window over the handle, or you would be played upon by the garden-engine."

"And at your own homes," resumed the bride of the colonel, "it would be just as bad. You would be sent to bed, or something equally undignified. Again, how would you support us?"

The pirate-colonel replied in a courageous voice, "By rapine!" But his bride retorted, "Suppose the grown-up people would n't be rapined?" "Then," said the colonel, "they should pay the penalty in blood." "But suppose they should object," retorted his bride, "and would n't pay the penalty in blood or anything else?"

A mournful silence ensued.

"Then do you no longer love me, Alice?" asked the colonel.

"Redforth! I am ever thine," returned his bride.

"Then do you no longer love me, Nettie?" asked the present writer.

"Tinkling! I am ever thine," returned my bride.

We all four embraced. Let me not be misunderstood by the giddy. The colonel embraced his own bride, and I embraced mine. But two times two make four.

"Nettie and I," said Alice mournfully, "have been considering our position. The grown-up people are too strong for us. They make us ridiculous. Besides, they have changed the times. William Tinkling's baby brother was christened yesterday. What took place? Was any king present? Answer, William."

I said No, unless disguised as Great-uncle Chopper.

"Any queen?"

There had been no queen that I knew of at our house. There might have been one in the kitchen; but I did n't think so, or the servants would have mentioned it.

"Any fairies?"

None that were visible.

"We had an idea among us, I think," said Alice, with a melancholy smile, "we four, that Miss Grimmer would prove to be the wicked fairy, and would come in at the christening with her crutch-stick, and give the child a bad gift. Was there anything of that sort? Answer, William."

I said that ma had said afterwards (and so she had), that Great-uncle Chopper's gift was a shabby one; but she had n't said a bad one. She had called it shabby, electrotyped, second-hand, and below his income.

"It must be the grown-up people who have changed all this," said Alice. "*We* could n't have changed it, if we had been so inclined, and we never should have been. Or perhaps Miss Grimmer *is* a wicked fairy after all, and won't act up to it because the grown-up people have persuaded her not to. Either way, they would make us ridiculous if we told them what we expected."

"Tyrants!" muttered the pirate-colonel.

"Nay, my Redforth," said Alice, "say not so. Call not names, my Redforth, or they will apply to pa."

"Let 'em!" said the colonel. "I don't care. Who 's he?"

Tinkling here undertook the perilous task of remonstrating with his lawless friend, who consented to withdraw the moody expressions above quoted.

"What remains for us to do?" Alice went on in her mild, wise way. "We must educate, we must pretend in a new manner, we must wait."

The colonel clenched his teeth, — four out in front, and a piece of another, and he had been twice dragged to the door of a dentist-despot, but had escaped from his guards. "How educate? How pretend in a new manner? How wait?"

"Educate the grown-up people," replied Alice. "We part to-night. Yes, Redforth," — for the colonel tucked up his cuffs, — "part to-night! Let us in these next holidays, now going to begin, throw our thoughts into something educational for the grown-up people, hinting to them how things ought to be. Let us veil our meaning under a mask of romance; you, I, and Nettie. William Tinkling being the plainest and quickest writer, shall copy out. Is it agreed?"

The colonel answered sulkily, "I don't mind." He then asked, "How about pretending?"

"We will pretend," said Alice, "that we are children; not that we are those grown-up people who won't help us out as they ought, and who understand us so badly."

The colonel, still much dissatisfied, growled, "How about waiting?"

"We will wait," answered little Alice, taking Nettie's hand in hers, and looking up to the sky, "we will wait — ever constant and true — till the times have got so changed as that everything helps us out, and nothing makes us ridiculous, and the fairies have come back. We will wait — ever constant and true — till we are eighty, ninety, or one hundred. And then the fairies will send *us* children, and we will help them out, poor pretty little creatures, if they pretend ever so much."

"So we will, dear," said Nettie Ashford, taking her round the waist with both arms, and kissing her. "And now if my husband will go and buy some cherries for us, I have got some money."

In the friendliest manner I invited the colonel to go with me; but he so far forgot himself as to acknowledge the invitation by kicking out behind, and then lying down on his stomach on the grass, pulling it up and chewing it. When I came back, however, Alice had nearly brought him out of his vexation, and was soothing him by telling him how soon we should all be ninety.

As we sat under the willow-tree, and ate the cherries (fair, for Alice shared them out), we played at being ninety. Nettie complained that she had a bone in her old back, and it made her hobble; and Alice sang a song in an old woman's way, but it was very pretty, and we were all merry. At least, I don't know about merry exactly, but all comfortable.

There was a most tremendous lot of cherries; and Alice always had with her some neat little bag or box or case, to hold things. In it that night was a tiny wine-glass. So Alice and Nettie said they would make some cherry-wine to drink our love at parting.

Each of us had a glassful, and it was delicious; and each of us drank the toast, "Our love at parting." The colonel drank his wine last; and it got into my head directly that it got into his directly. Anyhow, his eyes rolled immediately after he had turned the glass upside down; and he took me on one side, and proposed in a hoarse whisper, that we should "Cut 'em out still."

"How did he mean?" I asked my lawless friend.

"Cut our brides out," said the colonel, "and then cut our way, without going down a single turning, bang to the Spanish main!"

We might have tried it, though I did n't think it would answer; only we looked round and saw that there was nothing but moonlight under the willow-tree, and that our pretty, pretty wives were gone. We burst out crying. The colonel gave in second, and came to first; but he gave in strong.

We were ashamed of our red eyes, and hung about for half an hour to whiten them. Likewise a piece of chalk round the rims, I doing the colonel's, and he mine, but afterwards found in the bedroom looking-glass not natural, besides inflammation. Our conversation turned on being ninety. The colonel told me he had a pair of boots that wanted soling and heeling; but he thought it hardly worth while to mention it to his father, as he himself should so soon be ninety, when he thought shoes would be more convenient. The colonel also told me, with his hand upon his hip, that he felt himself already getting on in life, and turning rheumatic. And I told him the same. And when they said at our house at supper (they are always bothering about something) that I stooped, I felt so glad!

This is the end of the beginning-part that you were to believe most.

PART II.

ROMANCE. FROM THE PEN OF MISS ALICE RAINBIRD. *

THERE was once a king, and he had a queen; and he was the manliest of his sex, and she was the loveliest of hers. The king was, in his private profession, under government. The queen's father had been a medical man out of town.

They had nineteen children, and were always having more. Seventeen of these children took care of the baby; and Alicia, the eldest, took care of them all. Their ages varied from seven years to seven months.

Let us now resume our story.

One day the king was going to the office, when he stopped at the fishmonger's to buy a pound and a half of salmon not too near the tail, which the queen (who was a careful housekeeper), had requested him to send home. Mr. Pickles, the fishmonger, said, "Certainly, sir, is there any other article? Good morning."

The king went on towards the office in a melancholy mood; for quarter-day was such a long way off, and several of the dear children were growing out of their clothes. He had not proceeded far, when Mr. Pickles's errand-boy came running after him, and said, "Sir, you did n't notice the old lady in our shop."

"What old lady?" inquired the king. "I saw none."

Now, the king had not seen any old lady, because this old lady had been invisible to him, though visible to Mr. Pickles's boy. Probably because he messed and splashed the water about to that degree, and flopped the pairs of soles down in that violent manner, that, if she had not been visible to him, he would have spoilt her clothes.

Just then the old lady came trotting up. She was dressed in shot silk of the richest quality, smelling of dried lavender.

"King Watkins the First, I believe?" said the old lady.

"Watkins," replied the king, "is my name."

* Aged seven.

"Papa, if I am not mistaken, of the beautiful Princess Alicia?" said the old lady.

"And of eighteen other darlings," replied the king.

"Listen. You are going to the office," said the old lady.

It instantly flashed upon the king that she must be a fairy, or how could she know that?

"You are right," said the old lady, answering his thoughts. "I am the good Fairy Grandmarina. Attend! When you return home to dinner, politely invite the Princess Alicia to have some of the salmon you bought just now."

"It may disagree with her," said the king.

The old lady became so very angry at this absurd idea, that the king was quite alarmed, and humbly begged her pardon.

"We hear a great deal too much about this thing disagreeing, and that thing disagreeing," said the old lady, with the greatest contempt it was possible to express. "Don't be greedy. I think you want it all yourself."

The king hung his head under this reproof, and said he would n't talk about things disagreeing any more.

"Be good, then," said the Fairy Grandmarina, "and don't! When the beautiful Princess Alicia consents to partake of the salmon, — as I think she will, — you will find she will leave a fish-bone on her plate. Tell her to dry it, and to rub it, and to polish it till it shines like mother-of-pearl, and to take care of it as a present from me."

"Is that all?" asked the king.

"Don't be impatient, sir," returned the Fairy Grandmarina, scolding him severely. "Don't catch people short, before they have done speaking. Just the way with you grown-uppersons. You are always doing it."

The king again hung his head, and said he would n't do so any more.

"Be good, then," said the Fairy Grandmarina, "and don't! Tell the Princess Alicia, with my love, that the fish-bone is a magic present which can only be used once; but that it will bring her, that once, whatever she wishes for, PROVIDED SHE WISHED FOR IT AT THF RIGHT TIME. That is the message. Take care of it."

The king was beginning, "Might I ask the reason?" when the fairy became absolutely furious.

"*Will* you be good, sir?" she exclaimed, stamping her foot on the ground. "The reason for this, and the reason for that, indeed! You are always wanting the reason. No reason. There! Hoity toity me! I am sick of your grown-up reasons."

The king was extremely frightened by the old lady's flying into such a passion, and said he was very sorry to have offended her, and he would n't ask for reasons any more.

"Be good, then," said the old lady, "and don't!"

With those words, Grandmarina vanished, and the king went on and on, and on, till he came to the office. There he wrote and wrote, and wrote, till it was time to go home again. Then he politely invited the Princess Alicia, as the fairy had directed him, to partake of the salmon. And when she had enjoyed it very much, he saw the fish-bone on her plate, as the fairy had told him he would, and he delivered the fairy's message, and the Princess Alicia took care to dry the bone, and to rub it, and to polish it till it shone like mother-of-pearl.

And so, when the queen was going to get up in the morning, she said, "O, dear me, dear me; my head, my head!" and then she fainted away.

The Princess Alicia, who happened to be looking in at the chamber-door, asking about breakfast, was very much alarmed when she saw her royal mamma in this state, and she rang the bell for Peggy, which was the name of the lord chamberlain. But remembering where the smelling-bottle was, she climbed on a chair and got it; and after that she climbed on another chair by the bedside, and held the smelling-bottle to the queen's nose; and after that she jumped down and got some water; and after that she jumped up again and wetted the queen's forehead; and, in short, when the lord chamberlain came in, that dear old woman said to the little princess, "What a trot you are! I could n't have done it better myself!"

But that was not the worst of the good queen's illness. O no! She was very ill indeed, for a long time. The Princess Alicia kept the seventeen young princes and princesses quiet, and dressed and undressed and danced the baby, and made the kettle boil, and heated the soup, and swept the hearth, and poured out the medicine, and nursed the queen, and did all that ever she could, and was as busy, busy, busy as busy could be; for there were not many servants at that palace for three reasons: because the king was short of money, because a rise in his office never seemed to come, and because quarter-day was so far off that it looked almost as far off and as little as one of the stars.

But on the morning when the queen fainted away, where was the magic fish-bone? Why, there it was in the Princess Alicia's pocket! She had almost taken it out to bring the queen to life again, when she put it back, and looked for the smelling-bottle.

After the queen had come out of her swoon that morning, and was dozing, the Princess Alicia hurried up stairs to tell a most particular secret, to a most particularly confidential friend of hers, who was a duchess. People did suppose her to be a doll, but she was really a duchess, though nobody knew it except the princess.

This most particular secret was the secret about the magic fish-bone, the history of which was well known to the duchess, because the princess told her everything. The princess kneeled down by the bed on which the duchess was lying, full-dressed and wide-awake, and whispered the secret to her. The duchess smiled and nodded. People might have supposed that she never smiled and nodded; but she often did, though nobody knew it except the princess.

Then the Princess Alicia hurried down stairs again, to keep watch in the queen's room. She often kept watch by herself in the queen's room; but every evening, while the illness lasted, she sat there watching with the king. And every evening the king sat looking at her with a cross look, wondering why she never brought out the magic fish-bone. As often as she noticed this, she ran up stairs, whispered the secret to the duchess over again, and said to the duchess besides, "They think we children never have a reason or a meaning!" And the duchess, though the most fashionable duchess that ever was heard of, winked her eye.

"Alicia," said the king, one evening when she wished him good night.

"Yes, papa."

"What is become of the magic fish-bone?"

"In my pocket, papa!"

"I thought you had lost it?"

"O no, papa."

"Or forgotten it?"

"No, indeed, papa."

And so another time the dreadful little snapping pup-dog, next door, made a rush at one of the young princes as he stood on the steps coming home from school, and terrified him out of his wits; and he put his hand through a pane of glass, and bled, bled, bled. When the seventeen other young princes and princesses saw him bleed, bleed, bleed, they were terrified out of their wits too, and screamed themselves black in their seventeen faces all at once. But the Princess Alicia put her hands over all their seventeen mouths, one after another, and persuaded them to be quiet because of the sick queen. And then she put the wounded prince's hand in a basin of fresh cold water, while they stared with their twice seventeen are thirty-four, put down four and carry three, eyes, and then she looked in the hand for bits of glass, and there were fortunately no bits of glass there. And then she said to two chubby-legged princes, who were sturdy though small, "Bring me in the royal rag-bag : I must snip and stitch and cut and contrive." So these two young princes tugged at the royal rag-bag, and lugged it in ; and the Princess Alicia sat down on the floor, with a large pair of scissors and a needle and thread, and snipped and stitched and cut and contrived, and made a bandage, and put it on, and it fitted beautifully ; and so when it was all done, she saw the king her papa looking on by the door.

"Alicia."

"Yes, papa."

"What have you been doing ?"

"Snipping, stitching, cutting, and contriving, papa."

"Where is the magic fish-bone ?"

"In my pocket, papa."

"I thought you had lost it ?"

"O no, papa !"

"Or forgotten it?"

"No, indeed, papa."

After that, she ran up stairs to the duchess, and told her what had passed, and told her the secret over again ; and the duchess shook her flaxen curls, and laughed with her rosy lips.

Well ! and so another time the baby fell under the grate. The seventeen young princes and princesses were used to it ; for they were almost always falling under the grate or down the stairs ; but the baby was not used to it yet, and it gave him a swelled face and a black eye. The way the poor little darling came to tumble was, that he was out of the Princess Alicia's lap just as she was sitting, in a great coarse apron that quite smothered her, in front of the kitchen fire, beginning to peel the turnips for the broth for dinner ; and the way she came to be doing that was, that the king's cook had run away that morning with her own true love, who was a very tall but very tipsy soldier. Then the seventeen young princes and princesses, who cried at everything that happened, cried and roared. But the Princess Alicia (who could n't help crying a little herself) quietly called to them to be still, on account of not throwing back the queen up stairs, who was fast getting well, and said, "Hold your tongues, you wicked little monkeys, every one of you, while I examine baby !" Then she examined baby, and found that he had n't broken anything ; and she held cold iron to his poor dear eye, and smoothed his poor dear face, and he presently fell asleep in her arms. Then she said to the seventeen princes and princesses, "I am afraid to let him down yet, lest he should wake and feel pain ; be good, and you shall all be cooks." They jumped for joy when they heard that, and began making themselves cooks' caps out of old newspapers. So to one she gave the salt-box, and to one she gave the barley, and to one she gave the herbs, and to one she gave the turnips, and to one she gave the carrots, and to one she gave the onions, and to one she gave the spice-box, till they were all cooks, and all running about at work, she sitting in the middle, smothered in the great coarse apron, nursing baby. By and by the broth was done ; and the baby woke up, smiling like an angel, and was trusted to the sedatest princess to hold, while the other princes and princesses were squeezed into a far-off corner to look at the Princess Alicia turning out the saucepanful of broth, for fear (as they were always getting into trouble) they should get splashed and scalded. When the broth came tumbling out, steaming beautifully, and smelling like a nosegay good to eat, they clapped their hands. That made the baby clap his hands; and that, and his looking as if he had a comic toothache, made all the princes and princesses laugh. So the Princess Alicia said, "Laugh and be good; and after dinner we will make him a nest on the floor in a corner, and he shall sit in his nest and see a dance of eighteen cooks." That delighted the young princes and princesses, and they ate up all the broth, and washed up all the plates and dishes, and cleared away, and pushed the table into a corner; and then they in their cooks' caps, and the Princess Alicia in the smothering coarse apron that belonged to the cook that had run away with her own true love that was the very tall but very tipsy soldier, danced a dance of eighteen cooks before the angelic baby, who forgot his swelled face and his black eye, and crowed with joy.

And so then, once more the Princess Alicia saw King Watkins the First, her father, standing in the doorway looking on, and he said, "What have you been doing, Alicia?"

"Cooking and contriving, papa."

"What else have you been doing, Alicia?"

"Keeping the children light-hearted, papa."

"Where is the magic fish-bone, Alicia?"

"In my pocket, papa."

"I thought you had lost it?"

"O no, papa!"

"Or forgotten it?"

"No, indeed, papa."

The king then sighed so heavily, and seemed so low-spirited, and sat down so miserably, leaning his head upon his hand, and his elbow upon the kitchen-table pushed away in the corner, that the seventeen princes and princesses crept softly out of the kitchen, and left him alone with the Princess Alicia and the angelic baby.

"What is the matter, papa?"

"I am dreadfully poor, my child."

"Have you no money at all, papa?"

"None, my child."

"Is there no way of getting any, papa?"

"No way," said the king. "I have tried very hard, and I have tried all ways."

When she heard those last words, the Princess Alicia began to put her hand into the pocket where she kept the magic fish-bone.

"Papa," said she, "when we have tried very hard, and tried all ways, we must have done our very, very best?"

"No doubt, Alicia."

"When we have done our very, very best, papa, and that is not enough, then I think the right time must have come for asking help of others." This was the very secret connected with the magic fish-bone, which she had found out for herself from the good Fairy Grandmarina's words, and which she had so often whispered to her beautiful and fashionable friend, the duchess.

So she took out of her pocket the magic fish-bone that had been dried and rubbed, and polished, till it shone like mother-of-pearl; and she gave it one little kiss, and wished it was quarter-day. And immediately it *was* quarter-day; and the king's quarter's salary came rattling down the chimney, and bounced into the middle of the floor.

But this was not half of what happened, — no, not a quarter; for immediately afterwards the good Fairy Grandmarina came riding in, in a carriage and four (peacocks), with Mr. Pickles's boy up behind, dressed in silver and gold, with a cocked-hat, powdered hair, pink silk stockings, a jewelled cane, and a nosegay. Down jumped Mr. Pickles's boy, with his cocked-hat in his hand, and wonderfully polite (being entirely changed by enchantment), and handed Grandmarina out; and there she stood, in her rich shot-silk smelling of dried lavender, fanning herself with a sparkling fan.

"Alicia, my dear," said this charming old fairy, "how do you do? I hope I see you pretty well? Give me a kiss."

The Princess Alicia embraced her; and then Grandmarina turned to the king, and said rather sharply, "Are you good?"

The king said he hoped so.

"I suppose you know the reason *now*, why my god-daughter here," kissing the princess again, "did not apply to the fish-bone sooner?" said the fairy.

The king made a shy bow.

"Ah! but you did n't *then?*" said the fairy.

The king made a shyer bow.

"Any more reasons to ask for?" said the fairy.

The king said, No, and he was very sorry.

"Be good, then," said the fairy, "and live happy ever afterwards."

Then Grandmarina waved her fan, and the queen came in most splendidly dressed; and the seventeen young princes and princesses, no longer grown out of their clothes, came in, newly fitted out from top to toe, with tucks in everything to admit of its being let out. After that, the fairy tapped the Princess Alicia with her fan; and the smothering coarse apron flew away, and she appeared exquisitely dressed, like a little bride, with a wreath of orange-flowers and a silver veil. After that, the kitchen dresser changed of itself into a wardrobe, made of beautiful woods and gold and looking-glass, which was full of dresses of all sorts, all for her and all exactly fitting her. After that, the angelic baby came in, running alone, with his face and eye not a bit the worse, but much the better. Then Grandmarina begged to be introduced to the duchess; and, when the duchess was brought down, many compliments passed between them.

A little whispering took place between the fairy and the duchess; and then the fairy said out loud, "Yes, I thought she would have told you." Grandmarina then turned to the king and queen, and said, "We are going in search of Prince Certainpersonio. The pleasure of your company is requested at church in half an hour precisely." So she and the Princess Alicia got into the carriage; and Mr. Pickles's boy handed in the duchess, who sat by herself on the opposite seat; and then Mr. Pickles's boy put up the steps and got up behind, and the peacocks flew away with their tails behind.

Prince Certainpersonio was sitting by himself, eating barley-sugar, and waiting to be ninety. When he saw the peacocks, followed by the carriage, coming in at the window, it immediately occurred to him that something uncommon was going to happen.

"Prince," said Grandmarina, "I bring you your bride."

The moment the fairy said those words, Prince Certainpersonio's face left off being sticky, and his jacket and corduroys changed to peach-bloom velvet, and his hair curled, and a cap and feather flew in like a bird and settled on his head. He got into the carriage by the fairy's invitation; and there he renewed his acquaintance with the duchess, whom he had seen before.

In the church were the prince's relations and friends, and the Princess Alicia's relations and friends, and the seventeen princes and princesses, and the baby, and a crowd of the neighbors. The marriage was beautiful beyond expression. The duchess was bridesmaid, and beheld the ceremony from the pulpit, where she was supported by the cushion of the desk.

Grandmarina gave a magnificent wedding-feast afterwards, in which there was everything and more to eat, and everything and more to drink. The wedding-cake was delicately ornamented with white satin ribbons, frosted silver, and white lilies, and was forty-two yards round.

When Grandmarina had drunk her love to the young couple, and Prince Certainpersonio had made a speech, and everybody had cried, Hip, hip, hip, hurrah! Grandmarina announced to the king and queen that in future there would be eight quarter-days in every year, except in leap-year, when there would be ten. She then turned to Certainpersonio and Alicia, and said, "My dears, you will have thirty-five children, and they will all be good and beautiful. Seventeen of your children will be boys, and eighteen will be girls. The hair of the whole of your children will curl naturally. They will never have the measles, and will have recovered from the whooping-cough before being born."

On hearing such good news, everybody cried out, "Hip, hip, hip, hurrah!" again.

"It only remains," said Grandmarina in conclusion, "to make an end of the fish-bone."

So she took it from the hand of the Princess Alicia, and it instantly flew down the throat of the dreadful little snapping pug-dog, next door, and choked him, and he expired in convulsions.

PART III.

ROMANCE. FROM THE PEN OF LIEUTENANT-COLONEL ROBIN REDFORTH.*

THE subject of our present narrative would appear to have devoted himself to the pirate profession at a comparatively early age. We find him in command of a splendid schooner of one hundred guns loaded to the muzzle, ere yet he had had a party in honor of his tenth birthday.

It seems that our hero, considering himself spited by a Latin-grammar master, demanded the satisfaction due from one man of honor to another. Not getting it, he privately withdrew his haughty spirit from such low company, bought a second-hand pocket-pistol, folded up some sandwiches in a paper-bag, made a bottle of Spanish liquorice-water, and entered on a career of valor.

It were tedious to follow Boldheart (for such was his name) through the commencing stages of his story. Suffice it, that we find him bearing the rank of Captain Boldheart, reclining in full uniform on a crimson hearth-rug spread out upon the quarter-deck of his schooner, "The Beauty," in the China Seas. It was a lovely evening; and, as his crew lay grouped about him, he favored them with the following melody:—

O, landsmen are folly!
O, pirates are jolly!
O, diddleum Dolly,
Di!
Chorus.— Heave yo!

The soothing effect of these animated sounds floating over the waters, as the common sailors united their rough voices to take up the rich tones of Boldheart, may be more easily conceived than described.

* Aged nine.

It was under these circumstances that the lookout at the mast-head gave the word, "Whales!"

All was now activity.

"Where away?" cried Captain Boldheart, starting up.

"On the larboard bow, sir," replied the fellow at the mast-head, touching his hat. For such was the height of discipline on board of "The Beauty," that even at that height, he was obliged to mind it, or be shot through the head.

"This adventure belongs to me," said Boldheart. "Boy, my harpoon. Let no man follow"; and, leaping alone into his boat, the captain rowed with admirable dexterity in the direction of the monster.

All was now excitement.

"He nears him!" said an elderly seaman, following the captain through his spy-glass.

"He strikes him!" said another seaman, a mere stripling, but also with a spy-glass.

"He tows him towards us!" said another seaman, a man in the full vigor of life, but also with a spy-glass.

In fact, the captain was seen approaching with the huge bulk following. We will not dwell on the deafening cries of "Boldheart! Boldheart!" with which he was received, when, carelessly leaping on the quarter-deck, he presented his prize to his men. They afterwards made two thousand four hundred and seventeen pound ten and sixpence by it.

Ordering the sails to be braced up, the captain now stood W. N. W. "The Beauty" flew rather than floated over the dark blue waters. Nothing particular occurred for a fortnight, except taking, with considerable slaughter, four Spanish galleons, and a snow from South America, all richly laden. Inaction began to tell upon the spirits of the men. Captain Boldheart called all hands aft, and said, "My lads, I hear there are discontented ones among ye. Let any such stand forth."

After some murmuring, in which the expressions, "Ay, ay, sir!" "Union Jack," "Avast," "Starboard," "Port," "Bowsprit," and similar indications of a mutinous undercurrent, though subdued, were audible, Bill Boozey, captain of the foretop, came out from the rest. His form was that of a giant, but he quailed under the captain's eye.

"What are your wrongs?" said the captain.

"Why, d'ye see, Captain Boldheart," replied the towering mariner, "I've sailed, man and boy, for many a year, but I never yet know'd the milk served out for the ship's company's teas to be so sour as 't is aboard this craft."

At this moment the thrilling cry, "Man overboard!" announced to the astonished crew that Boozey, in stepping back, as the captain (in mere thoughtfulness) laid his hand upon the faithful pocket-pistol which he wore in his belt, had lost his balance, and was struggling with the foaming tide.

All was now stupefaction.

But with Captain Boldheart, to throw off his uniform coat, regardless of the various rich orders with which it was decorated, and to plunge into the sea after the drowning giant, was the work of a moment. Maddening was the excitement when boats were lowered; intense the joy when the captain was seen holding up the drowning man with his teeth; deafening the cheering when both were restored to the main deck of "The Beauty." And, from the instant of his changing his wet clothes for dry ones, Captain Boldheart had no such devoted though humble friend as William Boozey.

Boldheart now pointed to the horizon, and called the attention of his crew to the taper spars of a ship lying snug in harbor under the guns of a fort.

"She shall be ours at sunrise," said he. "Serve out a double allowance of grog, and prepare for action."

All was now preparation.

When morning dawned, after a sleepless night, it was seen that the stranger was crowding on all sail to come out of the harbor and offer battle. As the two ships came nearer to each other, the stranger fired a gun and hoisted Roman colors. Boldheart then perceived her to be the Latin-grammar master's bark. Such indeed she was, and had been tacking about the world in unavailing pursuit, from the time of his first taking to a roving life.

Boldheart now addressed his men, promising to blow them up if he should feel convinced that their reputation required it, and giving orders that the Latin-grammar master should be taken alive. He then dismissed them to their quarters, and the fight began with a broadside from "The Beauty." She then veered around, and poured in another. "The Scorpion" (so was the bark of the Latin-grammar master appropriately called) was not slow to return her fire; and a terrific cannonading ensued, in which the guns of "The Beauty" did tremendous execution.

The Latin-grammar master was seen upon the poop, in the midst of the smoke and fire, encouraging his men. To do him justice, he was no craven, though his white hat, his short gray trousers, and his long snuff-colored surtout reaching to his heels (the self-same coat in which he had spited Boldheart), contrasted most unfavorably with the brilliant uniform of the latter. At this moment, Boldheart, seizing a pike and putting himself at the head of his men, gave the word to board.

A desperate conflict ensued in the hammock-nettings, — or somewhere in about that direction, — until the Latin-grammar master, having all his masts gone, his hull and rigging shot through and through, and seeing Boldheart slashing a path towards him, hauled down his flag himself, gave up his sword to Boldheart, and asked for quarter. Scarce had he been put into the captain's boat, ere "The Scorpion" went down with all on board.

On Captain Boldheart's now assembling his men, a circumstance occurred. He found it necessary with one blow of his cutlass to kill the cook, who, having lost his brother in the late action, was making at the Latin-grammar master in an infuriated state, intent on his destruction with a carving-knife.

Captain Boldheart then turned to the Latin-grammar master, severely reproaching him with his perfidy, and put it to his crew what they considered that a master who spited a boy deserved.

They answered with one voice, "Death."

"It may be so," said the captain; "but it shall never be said that Boldheart stained his hour of triumph with the blood of his enemy. Prepare the cutter."

The cutter was immediately prepared.

"Without taking your life," said the captain, "I must yet forever deprive you of the power of spiting other boys. I shall turn you adrift in this boat. You will find in her two oars, a compass, a bottle of rum, a small cask of water, a piece of pork, a bag of biscuit, and my Latin grammar. Go! and spite the natives, if you can find any."

Deeply conscious of this bitter sarcasm, the unhappy wretch was put into the cutter, and was soon left far behind. He made no effort to row, but was seen lying on his back with his legs up, when last made out by the ship's telescopes.

A stiff breeze now beginning to blow, Captain Boldheart gave orders to keep her S. S. W., easing her a little during the night by falling off a point or two W. by W., or even by W. S., if she complained much. He then retired for the night, having in truth much need of repose. In addition to the fatigues he had undergone, this brave officer had received sixteen wounds in the engagement, but had not mentioned it.

In the morning a white squall came on, and was succeeded by other squalls of various colors. It thundered and lightened heavily for six weeks. Hurricanes then set in for two months. Water-spouts and tornadoes followed. The oldest sailor on board — and he was a very old one — had never seen such weather. "The Beauty" lost all idea where she was, and the carpenter reported six feet two of water in the hold. Everybody fell senseless at the pumps every day.

Provisions now ran very low. Our hero put the crew on short allowance, and put himself on shorter allowance than any man in the ship. But his spirit kept him fat. In this extremity, the gratitude of Boozey, the captain of the foretop, whom our readers may remember, was truly affecting. The loving though lowly William repeatedly requested to be killed, and preserved for the captain's table.

We now approach a change in affairs.

One day during a gleam of sunshine, and when the weather had moderated, the man at the mast-head — too weak now to touch his hat, besides its having been blown away — called out, —

"Savages!"

All was now expectation.

Presently fifteen hundred canoes, each paddled by twenty savages, were seen advancing in excellent order. They were of a light green color (the savages were), and sang, with great energy, the following strain: —

Choo a choo a choo tooth.
Muntch, muntch. Nycey!
Choo a choo a choo tooth.
Muntch, muntch. Nyce!

As the shades of night were by this time closing in, these expressions were supposed to embody this simple people's views of the evening hymn. But it too soon appeared that the song was a translation of "For what we are going to receive," &c.

The chief, imposingly decorated with feathers of lively colors, and having the majestic appearance of a fighting parrot, no sooner understood (he understood English perfectly) that the ship was "The Beauty," Captain Boldheart, than he fell upon his face on the deck, and could not be persuaded to rise until the captain had lifted him up, and told him he would n't hurt him. All the rest of the savages also fell on their faces with marks of terror, and had also to be lifted up one by one. Thus the fame of the great Boldheart had gone before him, even among these children of Nature.

Turtles and oysters were now produced in astonishing numbers; and on these and yams the people made a hearty meal. After dinner the chief told Captain Boldheart that there was better feeding up at the village, and that he would be glad to take him and his officers there. Apprehensive of treachery, Boldheart ordered his boat's crew to attend him completely armed. And well were it for other commanders if their precautions — But let us not anticipate.

When the canoes arrived at the beach, the darkness of the night was illumined by the light of an immense fire. Ordering his boat's crew (with the intrepid though illiterate William at their head) to keep close and be upon their guard, Boldheart bravely went on, arm in arm with the chief.

But how to depict the captain's surprise when he found a ring of savages singing in chorus that barbarous translation of "For what we are going to receive," &c., which has been given above, and dancing hand in hand round the Latin-grammar master, in a hamper with his head shaved, while two savages floured him, before putting him to the fire to be cooked!

Boldheart now took counsel with his officers on the course to be adopted. In the mean time, the miserable captive never ceased begging pardon and imploring to be delivered. On the generous Boldheart's proposal, it was at length resolved that he should not be cooked, but should be allowed to remain raw, on two conditions; namely: —

1. That he should never, under any circumstances, presume to teach any boy anything any more.

2. That, if taken back to England, he should pass his life in travelling to find out boys who wanted their exercises done, and should do their exercises for those boys for nothing, and never say a word about it.

Drawing the sword from its sheath, Boldheart swore him to these conditions on its shining blade. The prisoner wept bitterly, and appeared acutely to feel the errors of his past career.

The captain then ordered his boat's crew to make ready for a volley, and after firing to re-load quickly. "And expect a score or two on ye to go head over heels," murmured William Boozey; "for I 'm a looking at ye." With those words, the derisive though deadly William took a good aim.

"Fire!"

The ringing voice of Boldheart was lost in the report of the guns and the screeching of the savages. Volley after volley awakened the numerous echoes. Hundreds of savages were killed, hundreds wounded, and thousands ran howling into the woods. The Latin-grammar master had a spare nightcap lent him, and a long tail-coat, which he wore hind side before. He presented a ludicrous though pitiable appearance, and serve him right.

We now find Captain Boldheart, with this rescued wretch on board, standing off for other islands. At one of these, not a cannibal island, but a pork and vegetable one, he married (only in fun on his part) the king's daughter. Here he rested some time, receiving from the natives great quantities of precious stones, gold-dust, elephants' teeth, and sandal wood, and getting very rich. This, too, though he almost every day made presents of enormous value to his men.

The ship being at length as full as she could hold of all sorts of valuable things, Boldheart gave orders to weigh the anchor and turn "The Beauty's" head towards England. These orders were obeyed with three cheers; and ere the sun went down full many a hornpipe had been danced on deck by the uncouth though agile William.

We next find Captain Boldheart about three leagues off Madeira, surveying through his spy-glass a stranger of suspicious appearance making sail towards him. On his firing a gun ahead of her to bring her to, she ran up a flag, which he instantly recognized as the flag from the mast in the back-garden at home.

Inferring from this, that his father had put to sea to seek his long-lost son, the captain sent his own boat on board the stranger to inquire if this was so, and, if so, whether his father's intentions were strictly honorable. The boat came back with a present of greens and fresh meat, and reported that the stranger was "The Family," of twelve hundred tons, and had not only the captain's father on board, but also his mother, with the majority of his aunts and uncles, and all his cousins. It was further reported to Boldheart that the whole of these relations had expressed themselves in a becoming manner, and were anxious to embrace him and thank him for the glorious credit he had done them. Boldheart at once invited them to breakfast next morning on board "The Beauty," and gave orders for a brilliant ball that should last all day.

It was in the course of the night that the captain discovered the hopelessness of reclaiming the Latin-grammar master. That thankless traitor was found out, as the two ships lay near each other, communicating with "The Family" by signals, and offering to give up Boldheart. He was hanged at the yard-arm the first thing in the morning, after having it impressively pointed out to him by Boldheart that this was what spiters came to.

The meeting between the captain and his parents was attended with tears. His uncles and aunts would have attended their meeting with tears too, but he was n't going to stand that. His cousins were very much astonished by the size of his ship and the discipline of his men, and were greatly overcome by the splendor of his uniform. He kindly conducted them round the vessel, and pointed out everything worthy of notice. He also fired his hundred guns, and found it amusing to witness their alarm.

The entertainment surpassed everything ever seen on board ship, and lasted from ten in the morning until seven the next morning. Only one disagreeable incident occurred. Captain Boldheart found himself obliged to put his cousin Tom in irons, for being disrespectful. On the boy's promising amendment, however, he was humanely released, after a few hours' close confinement.

Boldheart now took his mother down into the great cabin, and asked after the young lady with whom, it was well known to the world, he was in love. His mother replied that the object of his affections was then at school at Margate, for the benefit of sea-bathing (it was the month of September), but that she feared the young lady's friends were still opposed to the union. Boldheart at once resolved, if necessary, to bombard the town.

Taking the command of his ship with this intention, and putting all but fighting men on board "The Family," with orders to that vessel to keep in company, Boldheart soon anchored in Margate Roads. Here he went ashore well armed, and attended by his boat's crew (at their head the faithful though ferocious William), and demanded to see the mayor, who came out of his office.

"Dost know the name of yon ship, mayor?" asked Boldheart fiercely.

"No," said the mayor, rubbing his eyes, which he could scarce believe when he saw the goodly vessel riding at anchor.

"She is named 'The Beauty,'" said the captain.

"Hah!" exclaimed the mayor with a start. "And you, then, are Captain Boldheart?"

"The same."

A pause ensued. The mayor trembled.

"Now, mayor," said the captain, "choose! Help me to my bride, or be bombarded."

The mayor begged for two hours' grace in which to make inquiries respecting the young lady. Boldheart accorded him but one; and during that one placed William Boozey sentry over him, with a drawn sword, and instructions to accompany him wherever he went, and to run him through the body if he showed a sign of playing false.

At the end of the hour the mayor reappeared more dead than alive, closely waited on by Boozey more alive than dead.

"Captain," said the mayor, "I have ascertained that the young lady is going to bathe. Even now she waits her turn for a machine. The tide is low, though rising. I, in one of our town-boats, shall not be suspected. When she comes forth in her bathing-dress into the shallow water from behind the hood of the machine, my boat shall intercept her and prevent her return. Do you the rest."

"Mayor," returned Captain Boldheart, "thou hast saved thy town."

The captain then signalled his boat to take him off, and, steering her himself, ordered her crew to row towards the bathing-ground, and there to rest upon their oars. All happened as had been arranged. His lovely bride came forth, the mayor glided in behind her, she became confused, and had floated out of her depth, when, with one skilful touch of the rudder and one quivering stroke from the boat's crew, her adoring Boldheart held her in his strong arms. There her shrieks of terror were changed to cries of joy.

Before "The Beauty," could get under way, the hoisting of all the flags in the town and harbor, and the ringing of all the bells, announced to the brave Boldheart that he had nothing to fear. He therefore determined to be married on the spot, and signalled for a clergyman and clerk, who came off promptly in a sailing-boat named "The Skylark." Another great entertainment was then given on board "The Beauty," in the midst of which the mayor was called out by a messenger. He returned with the news that government had sent down to know whether Captain Boldheart, in acknowledgment of the great services he had done his country by being a pirate, would consent to be made a lieutenant-colonel. For himself he would have spurned the worthless boon; but his bride wished it, and he consented.

Only one thing further happened before the good ship "Family" was dismissed, with rich presents to all on board. It is painful to record (but such is human nature in some cousins) that Captain Boldheart's unmannerly Cousin Tom was actually tied up to receive three dozen with a rope's end "for cheekiness and making game," when Captain Boldheart's lady begged for him, and he was spared. "The Beauty" then refitted, and the captain and his bride departed for the Indian Ocean to enjoy themselves forevermore.

PART IV.

ROMANCE. FROM THE PEN OF MISS NETTIE ASHFORD.*

THERE is a country, which I will show you when I get into maps, where the children have everything their own way. It is a most delightful country to live in. The grown-up people are obliged to obey the children, and are never allowed to sit up to supper, except on their birthdays. The children order them to make jam, and jelly, and marmalade, and tarts, and pies, and puddings, and all manner of pastry. If they say they won't, they are put in the corner till they do. They are sometimes allowed to have some; but when they have some, they generally have powders given them afterwards.

One of the inhabitants of this country, a truly sweet young creature of the name of Mrs. Orange, had the misfortune to be sadly plagued by her numerous family. Her parents required a great deal of looking after, and they had connections and companions who were scarcely ever out of mischief. So Mrs. Orange said to herself, "I really cannot be troubled with these torments any longer; I must put them all to school."

Mrs. Orange took off her pinafore, and dressed herself very nicely, and took up her baby, and went out to call upon another lady of the name of Mrs. Lemon, who kept a preparatory establishment. Mrs. Orange stood upon the scraper to pull at the bell, and gave a ring-ting-ting.

Mrs. Lemon's neat little housemaid, pulling up her socks as she came along the passage, answered the ring-ting-ting.

"Good morning," said Mrs. Orange. "Fine day. How do you do? Mrs. Lemon at home?"

"Yes, ma'am."

* Aged half past six.

"Will you say Mrs. Orange and baby?"

"Yes, ma'am. Walk in."

Mrs. Orange's baby was a very fine one, and real wax all over. Mrs. Lemon's baby was leather and bran. However, when Mrs. Lemon came into the drawing-room with her baby in her arms, Mrs. Orange said politely, "Good morning. Fine day. How do you do? And how is little Tootleum-boots?"

"Well, she is but poorly. Cutting her teeth, ma'am," said Mrs. Lemon.

"O, indeed, ma'am!" said Mrs. Orange. "No fits, I hope?"

"No, ma'am."

"How many teeth has she, ma'am?"

"Five, ma'am."

"My Emilia, ma'am, has eight," said Mrs. Orange. "Shall we lay them on the mantel-piece side by side, while we converse?"

"By all means, ma'am," said Mrs. Lemon. "Hem!"

"The first question is, ma'am," said Mrs. Orange, "I don't bore you?"

"Not in the least, ma'am," said Mrs. Lemon. "Far from it, I assure you."

"Then pray *have* you," said Mrs. Orange, "*have* — you any vacancies?"

"Yes, ma'am. How many might you require?"

"Why the truth is, ma'am," said Mrs. Orange, "I have come to the conclusion that my children," — O, I forgot to say that they call the grown-up people children in that country! — "that my children are getting positively too much for me. Let me see. Two parents, two intimate friends of theirs, one godfather, two godmothers, and an aunt. *Have* you as many as eight vacancies?"

"I have just eight, ma'am," said Mrs. Lemon.

"Most fortunate! Terms moderate, I think?"

"Very moderate, ma'am."

"Diet good, I believe?"

"Excellent, ma'am."

"Unlimited?"

"Unlimited."

"Most satisfactory Corporal punishment dispensed with?"

"Why, we do occasionally shake," said Mrs. Lemon, "and we have slapped. But only in extreme cases."

"*Could* I, ma'am," said Mrs. Orange, — "*could* I see the establishment?"

"With the greatest of pleasure, ma'am," said Mrs. Lemon.

Mrs. Lemon took Mrs. Orange into the school-room, where there were a number of pupils. "Stand up, children!" said Mrs. Lemon; and they all stood up.

Mrs. Orange whispered to Mrs. Lemon: "There is a pale, bald child, with red whiskers, in disgrace. Might I ask what he has done?"

"Come here, White," said Mrs. Lemon: "and tell this lady what you have been doing."

"Betting on horses," said White, sulkily.

"Are you sorry for it, you naughty child?" said Mrs. Lemon.

"No," said White. "Sorry to lose, but should n't be sorry to win."

"There 's a vicious boy for you, ma'am," said Mrs. Lemon. "Go along with you, sir. This is Brown, Mrs. Orange. O, a sad case, Brown's! Never knows when he has had enough. Greedy. How is your gout, sir?"

"Bad," said Brown.

"What else can you expect?" said Mrs. Lemon. "Your stomach is the size of two. Go and take exercise directly. Mrs. Black, come here to me. Now, here is a child, Mrs. Orange, ma'am, who is always at play. She can't be kept at home a single day together; always gadding about and spoiling her clothes. Play,

play, play, play, from morning to night, and to morning again. How can she expect to improve?"

"Don't expect to improve," sulked Mrs. Black. "Don't want to."

"There is a specimen of her temper, ma'am," said Mrs. Lemon. "To see her when she is tearing about, neglecting everything else, you would suppose her to be at least good-humored. But bless you, ma'am, she is as pert and flouncing a minx as ever you met with in all your days!"

"You must have a great deal of trouble with them, ma'am," said Mrs. Orange.

"Ah, I have, indeed, ma'am!" said Mrs. Lemon. "What with their tempers, what with their quarrels, what with their never knowing what 's good for them, and what with their always wanting to domineer, deliver me from these unreasonable children!"

"Well, I wish you good morning, ma'am," said Mrs. Orange.

"Well, I wish you good morning, ma'am," said Mrs. Lemon.

So Mrs. Orange took up her baby and went home, and told the family that plagued her so that they were all going to be sent to school. They said they did n't want to go to school; but she packed up their boxes, and packed them off.

"O dear me, dear me! Rest and be thankful!" said Mrs. Orange, throwing herself back in her little arm-chair. "Those troublesome troubles are got rid of, please the pigs!"

Just then another lady, named Mrs. Alicumpaine, came calling at the street-door with a ring-ting-ting.

"My dear Mrs. Alicumpaine," said Mrs. Orange, "how do you do? Pray stay to dinner. We have but a simple joint of sweet-stuff, followed by a plain dish of bread and treacle, but, if you will take us as you find us, it will be *so* kind!"

"Don't mention it," said Mrs. Alicumpaine. "I shall be too glad. But what do you think I have come for, ma'am? Guess, ma'am."

"I really cannot guess, ma'am," said Mrs. Orange.

"Why, I am going to have a small juvenile party to-night," said Mrs. Alicumpaine; "and if you and Mr. Orange and baby would but join us, we should be complete."

"More than charmed, I am sure!" said Mrs. Orange.

"So kind of you!" said Mrs. Alicumpaine. "But I hope the children won't bore you?"

"Dear things! Not at all," said Mrs. Orange. "I dote upon them."

Mr. Orange here came home from the city; and he came, too, with a ring-ting-ting.

"James, love," said Mrs. Orange, "you look tired. What has been doing in the city to-day?"

"Trap, bat, and ball, my dear," said Mr. Orange; "and it knocks a man up."

"That dreadfully anxious city, ma'am," said Mrs. Orange to Mrs. Alicumpaine; "so wearing, is it not?"

"O, so trying!" said Mrs. Alicumpaine. "John has lately been speculating in the peg-top ring; and I often say to him at night, 'John, *is* the result worth the wear and tear?'"

Dinner was ready by this time; so they sat down to dinner; and while Mr. Orange carved the joint of sweet-stuff, he said, "It 's a poor heart that never rejoices. Jane, go down to the cellar, and fetch a bottle of the Upest ginger-beer."

At tea-time, Mr. and Mrs. Orange, and baby, and Mrs. Alicumpaine went off to Mrs. Alicumpaine's house. The children had not come yet; but the ball-room was ready for them, decorated with paper flowers.

"How very sweet!" said Mrs. Orange. "The dear things! How pleased they will be!"

"I don't care for children myself," said Mr. Orange, gaping.

"Not for girls?" said Mrs. Alicumpaine. "Come! you care for girls?"

Mr. Orange shook his head, and gaped again. "Frivolous and vain, ma'am."

"My dear James," cried Mrs. Orange, who had been peeping about, "do look here. Here 's the supper for the darlings, ready laid in the room behind the folding-doors. Here 's their little pickled salmon, I do declare! And here 's their little salad, and their little roast beef and fowls, and their little pastry, and their wee, wee, wee champagne!"

"Yes, I thought it best, ma'am," said Mrs. Alicumpaine, "that they should have their supper by themselves. Our table is in the corner here, where the gentlemen can have their wineglass of negus, and their egg-sandwich, and their quiet game at beggar-my-neighbor, and look on. As for us, ma'am, we shall have quite enough to do to manage the company."

"O, indeed, you may so! Quite enough, ma'am!" said Mrs. Orange.

The company began to come. The first of them was a stout boy, with a white top-knot and spectacles. The housemaid brought him in and said, "Compliments, and at what time was he to be fetched!" Mrs. Alicumpaine said, "Not a moment later than ten. How do you do, sir? Go and sit down." Then a number of other children came; boys by themselves, and girls by themselves, and boys and girls together. They did n't behave at all well. Some of them looked through quizzing-glasses at others, and said, "Who are those? Don't know them." Some of them looked through quizzing-glasses at others, and said, "How do?" Some of them had cups of tea or coffee handed to them by others, and said, "Thanks; much!" A good many boys stood about, and felt their shirt-collars. Four tiresome fat boys *would* stand in the doorway, and talk about the newspapers, till Mrs. Alicumpaine went to them and said, "My dears, I really cannot allow you to prevent people from coming in. I shall be truly sorry to do it; but, if you put yourselves in everybody's way, I must positively send you home." One boy, with a beard and a large white waistcoat, who stood straddling on the hearth-rug warming his coat-tails, *was* sent home. "Highly incorrect, my dear," said Mrs. Alicumpaine, handing him out of the room, "and I cannot permit it."

There was a children's band, — harp, cornet, and piano, — and Mrs. Alicumpaine and Mrs. Orange bustled among the children to persuade them to take partners and dance. But they were so obstinate! For quite a long time they would not be persuaded to take partners and dance, Most of the boys said, "Thanks; much! But not at present." And most of the rest of the boys said, "Thanks; much! But never do."

"O, these children are very wearing!" said Mrs. Alicumpaine to Mrs. Orange.

"Dear things! I dote upon them; but they ARE wearing," said Mrs. Orange to Mrs. Alicumpaine.

At last they did begin in a slow and melancholy way to slide about to the music; though even then they would n't mind what they were told, but would have this partner, and would n't have that partner, and showed temper about it. And they would n't smile, — no, not on any account they would n't; but, when the music stopped, went round and round the room in dismal twos, as if everybody else was dead.

"O, it 's very hard indeed to get these vexing children to be entertained!" said Mrs. Alicumpaine to Mrs. Orange.

"I dote upon the darlings; but it IS hard," said Mrs. Orange to Mrs. Alicumpaine.

They were trying children, that 's the truth. First, they would n't sing when they were asked; and then, when everybody fully believed they would n't, they would. "If you serve us so any more, my love," said Mrs. Alicumpaine to a tall child, with a good deal of white back, in mauve silk trimmed with lace, "it will be my painful privilege to offer you a bed, and to send you to it immediately."

The girls were so ridiculously dressed, too, that they were in rags before supper. How could the boys help treading on their trains? And yet when their trains were trodden on, they often showed temper again, and looked as black, they did! However, they all seemed to be pleased when Mrs. Alicumpaine said, "Supper is ready, children!" And they went crowding and pushing in, as if they had had dry bread for dinner.

"How are the children getting on?" said Mr. Orange to Mrs. Orange, when Mrs. Orange came to look after baby. Mrs. Orange had left baby on a shelf near Mr. Orange while he played at beggar-my-neighbor, and had asked him to keep his eye upon her now and then.

"Most charmingly, my dear!" said Mrs. Orange. "So droll to see their little flirtations and jealousies! Do come and look!"

"Much obliged to you, my dear," said Mr. Orange; "but I don't care about children myself."

So Mrs. Orange, having seen that baby was safe, went back without Mr. Orange to the room where the children were having supper.

"What are they doing now?" said Mrs. Orange to Mrs. Alicumpaine.

"They are making speeches, and playing at Parliament," said Mrs. Alicumpaine to Mrs. Orange.

On hearing this, Mrs. Orange set off once more back again to Mr. Orange, and said, "James dear, do come. The children are playing at Parliament."

"Thank you, my dear," said Mr. Orange, "but I don't care about Parliament myself."

So Mrs. Orange went once again without Mr. Orange to the room where the children were having supper, to see them playing at Parliament. And she found some of the boys crying, "Hear, hear, hear!" while other boys cried, "No, no!" and others "Question!" "Spoke!" and all sorts of nonsense that ever you heard. Then one of those tiresome fat boys who had stopped the doorway told them he was on his legs (as if they could n't see that he was n't on his head, or on his anything else) to explain, and that, with the permission of his honorable friend, if he would allow him to call him so (another tiresome boy bowed), he would proceed to explain. Then he went on for a long time in a sing-song (whatever he meant), did this troublesome fat boy, about that he held in his hand a glass; and about that he had come down to that house that night to discharge what he would call a public duty; and about that, on the present occasion, he would lay his hand (his other hand) upon his heart, and would tell honorable gentlemen that he was about to open the door to general approval. Then he opened the door by saying, "To our hostess!" and everybody else said "To our hostess!" and then there were cheers. Then another tiresome boy started up in sing-song, and then half a dozen noisy and nonsensical boys at once. But at last Mrs. Alicumpaine said, "I cannot have this din. Now, children, you have played at Parliament very nicely; but Parliament gets tiresome after a little while, and it 's time you left off, for you will soon be fetched."

After another dance (with more tearing to rags than before supper), they began to be fetched; and you will be very glad to be told that the tiresome fat boy who had been on his legs was walked off first without any ceremony. When they were all gone, poor Mrs. Alicumpaine dropped upon a sofa, and said to Mrs.

Orange, "These children will be the death of me at last, ma'am, — they will indeed!"

"I quite adore them, ma'am," said Mrs. Orange; "but they DO want variety."

Mr. Orange got his hat, and Mrs. Orange got her bonnet and her baby, and they set out to walk home. They had to pass Mrs. Lemon's preparatory establishment on their way.

"I wonder, James dear," said Mrs. Orange, looking up at the window, "whether the precious children are asleep!"

"I don't care much whether they are or not, myself," said Mr. Orange.

"James, dear!"

"You dote upon them, you know," said Mr. Orange. "That's another thing."

"I do," said Mrs. Orange, rapturously. "O, I DO!"

"I don't," said Mr. Orange.

"But I was thinking, James, love," said Mrs. Orange, pressing his arm, "whether our dear, good, kind Mrs. Lemon would like them to stay the holidays with her."

"If she was paid for it, I daresay she would," said Mr. Orange.

"I adore them, James," said Mrs. Orange; "but SUPPOSE we pay her, then!"

This was what brought that country to such perfection, and made it such a delightful place to live in. The grown-up people (that would be in other countries) soon left off being allowed any holidays after Mr. and Mrs. Orange tried the experiment; and the children (that would be in other countries) kept them at school as long as ever they lived, and made them do whatever they were told.

GEORGE SILVERMAN'S EXPLANATION.

FIRST CHAPTER.

IT happened in this wise, —

But, sitting with my pen in my hand looking at those words again, without descrying any hint in them of the words that should follow, it comes into my mind that they have an abrupt appearance. They may serve, however, if I let them remain, to suggest how very difficult I find it to begin to explain my explanation. An uncouth phrase; and yet I do not see my way to a better.

SECOND CHAPTER.

IT happened in *this* wise, —

But looking at those words, and comparing them with my former opening, I find they are the self-same words repeated. This is the more surprising to me, because I employ them in quite a new connection. For indeed I declare that my intention was to discard the commencement I first had in my thoughts, and to give the preference to another of an entirely different nature, dating my explanation from an anterior period of my life. I will make a third trial, without erasing this second failure, protesting that it is not my design to conceal any of my infirmities, whether they be of head or heart.

THIRD CHAPTER.

NOT as yet directly aiming at how it came to pass, I will come upon it by degrees. The natural manner, after all, for God knows that is how it came upon me.

My parents were in a miserable condition of life, and my infant home was a cellar in Preston. I recollect the sound of father's Lancashire clogs on the street pavement above, as being different in my young hearing from the sound of all other clogs; and I recollect, that, when mother came down the cellar-steps, I used tremblingly to speculate on her feet having a good or an ill tempered look, — on her knees, — on her waist, — until finally her face came into view, and settled the question. From this it will be seen that I was timid, and that the cellar-steps were steep, and that the doorway was very low.

Mother had the gripe and clutch of poverty upon her face, upon her figure, and not least of all upon her voice. Her sharp and high-pitched words were squeezed out of her, as by the compression of bony fingers on a leathern bag; and she had a way of rolling her eyes about and about the cellar, as she scolded, that was gaunt and hungry. Father, with his shoulders rounded, would sit quiet on a three-legged stool, looking at the empty grate, until she would pluck the stool from under him, and bid him go bring some money home. Then he would dismally ascend the steps; and I, holding my ragged shirt and trousers together with a ahnd (my only braces), would feint and dodge from mother's pursuing grasp at my hair.

A worldly little devil was mother's usual name for me. Whether I cried for that I was in the dark, or for that it was cold, or for that I was hungry, or whether I squeezed myself into a warm corner when there was a fire, or ate voraciously when there was food, she would still say, "O you worldly little devil!" And the sting of it was, that I quite well knew myself to be a worldly little devil. Worldly as to wanting to be housed and warmed, worldly as to wanting to be fed, worldly as to the greed with which I inwardly compared how much I got of those good things with how much father and mother got, when, rarely, those good things were going.

Sometimes they both went away seeking work; and then I would be locked up in the cellar for a day or two at a time. I was at my worldliest then. Left alone, I yielded myself up to a worldly yearning for enough of anything (except misery), and for the death of mother's father, who was a machine-maker at Birmingham, and in whose decease, I had heard mother say, she would come into a whole court full of houses "if she had her rights." Worldly little devil, I would stand about, musingly fitting my cold bare feet into cracked bricks and crevices of the damp cellar floor, — walking over my grandfather's body, so to speak, into the court full of houses, and selling them for meat and drink, and clothes to wear.

At last a change came down into our cellar. The universal change came down even as low as that, — so will it mount to any height on which a human creature can perch, — and brought other changes with it.

We had a heap of I don't know what foul litter in the darkest corner, which we called "the bed." For three days mother lay upon it without getting up, and then began at times to laugh. If I had ever heard her laugh before, it had been so seldom that the strange sound frightened me. It frightened father too; and we took it by turns to give her water. Then she began to move her head from side to side, and sing. After that, she getting no better, father fell a-laughing and a-singing; and then there was only I to give them both water, and they both died.

FOURTH CHAPTER.

WHEN I was lifted out of the cellar by two men, of whom one came peeping down alone first, and ran away and brought the other, I could hardly bear the light of the street. I was sitting in the road-way, blinking at it, and at a ring of people collected around me, but not close to me, when, true to my character of worldly little devil, I broke silence by saying, "I am hungry and thirsty!"

"Does he know they are dead?" asked one of another.

"Do you know your father and mother are both dead of fever?" asked a third of me, severely.

"I don't know what it is to be dead. I supposed it meant that, when the cup rattled against their teeth, and the water spilt over them. I am hungry and thirsty." That was all I had to say about it.

The ring of people widened outward from the inner side as I looked around me; and I smelt vinegar, and what I knew to be camphor, thrown in towards where I sat. Presently some one put a great vessel of smoking vinegar on the ground near me; and then they all looked at me in silent horror as I ate and drank of what was brought for me. I knew at the time they had a horror of me, but I could n't help it.

I was still eating and drinking, and a murmur of discussion had begun to arise respecting what was to be done with me next, when I heard a cracked voice somewhere in the ring say, "My name is Hawkyard, Mr. Verity Hawkyard, of West Bromwich." Then the ring split in one place; and a yellow-faced, peak-nosed gentleman, clad all in iron-gray to his gaiters, pressed forward with a policeman and another official of some sort. He came forward close to the vessel of smoking vinegar; from which he sprinkled himself carefully, and me copiously.

"He had a grandfather at Birmingham, this young boy, who is just dead too," said Mr. Hawkyard.

I turned my eyes upon the speaker, and said in a ravening manner, "Where 's his houses?"

"Hah! Horrible worldliness on the edge of the grave," said Mr. Hawkyard, casting more of the vinegar over me, as if to get my devil out of me. "I have undertaken a slight — a ve-ry slight — trust in behalf of this boy; quite a voluntary trust; a matter of mere honor, if not of mere sentiment; still I have taken it upon myself, and it shall be (O yes, it shall be!) discharged."

The bystanders seemed to form an opinion of this gentleman much more favorable than their opinion of me.

"He shall be taught," said Mr. Hawkyard, "(O yes, he shall be taught!) but what is to be done with him for the present? He may be infected. He may disseminate infection." The ring widened considerably. "What is to be done with him?"

He held some talk with the two officials. I could distinguish no word save "Farm-house." There was another sound several times repeated, which was wholly meaningless in my ears then, but which I knew afterwards to be "Hoghton Towers."

"Yes," said Mr. Hawkyard. "I think that sounds promising; I think that sounds hopeful. And he can be put by himself in a ward, for a night or two, you say?"

It seemed to be the police-officer who had said so; for it was he who replied, Yes! It was he, too, who finally took me by the arm, and walked me before him through the streets, into a whitewashed room in a bare building, where I had a chair to sit in, a table to sit at, an iron bedstead and good mattress to lie upon, and a rug and blanket to cover me. Where I had enough to eat, too, and was shown how to clean the tin porringer in which it was conveyed to me, until it was as good as a looking-glass. Here, likewise, I was put in a bath, and had new clothes brought to me; and my old rags were burnt, and I was camphored and vinegared and disinfected in a variety of ways.

When all this was done, — I don't know in how many days or how few, but it matters not, — Mr. Hawkyard stepped in at the door, remaining close to it, and said, "Go and stand against the opposite wall, George Silverman. As far off as you can. That 'll do. How do you feel?"

I told him that I did n't feel cold, and did n't feel hungry, and did n't feel thirsty. That was the whole round of human feelings, as far as I knew, except the pain of being beaten.

"Well," said he, "you are going, George, to a healthy farm-house to be purified. Keep in the air there as much as you can. Live an out-of-door life there, until you are fetched away. You had better not say much — in fact, you had better be very careful not to say anything — about what your parents died of, or they might not like to take you in. Behave well, and I 'll put you to school; O yes! I 'll put you to school, though I am not obligated to do it. I am a servant of the Lord, George; and I have been a good servant to him, I have, these five-and-thirty years. The Lord has had a good servant in me, and he knows it."

What I then supposed him to mean by this, I cannot imagine. As little do I know when I began to comprehend that he was a prominent member of some obscure denomination or congregation, every member of which held forth to the rest when so inclined, and among whom he was called Brother Hawkyard. It was enough for me to know, on that day in the ward, that the farmer's cart was waiting for me at the street corner. I was not slow to get into it; for it was the first ride I ever had in my life.

It made me sleepy, and I slept. First, I stared at Preston streets as long as they lasted; and, meanwhile, I may have had some small dumb wondering within me whereabouts our cellar was; but I doubt it. Such a worldly little devil was I, that I took no thought who would bury father and mother, or where they would be buried, or when. The question whether the eating and drinking by day, and the covering by night, would be as good at the farm-house as at the ward superseded those questions.

The jolting of the cart on a loose stony road awoke me; and I found that we were mounting a steep hill, where the road was a rutty by-road through a field. And so, by fragments of an ancient terrace, and by some rugged out-buildings that had once been fortified, and passing under a ruined gateway we came to the old farm-house in the thick stone wall outside the old quadrangle of Hoghton Towers, which I looked at like a stupid savage, seeing no specialty in, seeing no antiquity in; assuming all farm-houses to resemble it; assigning the decay I noticed to the one potent cause of all ruin that I knew, — poverty; eying the pigeons in their flights, the cattle in their stalls, the ducks in the pond, and the fowls pecking about the yard, with a hungry hope that plenty of them might be killed for dinner while I stayed there; wondering whether the scrubbed dairy vessels, drying in the sunlight, could be goodly porringers out of which the master ate his belly-filling food, and which he polished when he had done, according to my ward experience; shrinkingly doubtful whether the shadows, passing over that airy height on the bright spring day, were not something in the nature of frowns, — sordid, afraid, unadmiring, — a small brute to shudder at.

To that time I had never had the faintest impression of duty. I had had no knowledge whatever that there was anything lovely in this life. When I had occasionally slunk up the cellar-steps into the street, and glared in at shop windows, I had done so with no higher feelings than we may suppose to animate a mangy young dog or wolf-cub. It is equally the fact that I had never been alone, in the sense of holding unselfish converse with myself. I had been solitary often enough, but nothing better.

Such was my condition when I sat down to my dinner that day, in the kitchen of the old farm-house. Such was my condition when I lay on my bed in the old farm-house that night, stretched out opposite the narrow mullioned window, in the cold light of the moon, like a young vampire.

FIFTH CHAPTER.

What do I know now of Hoghton Towers? Very little; for I have been gratefully unwilling to disturb my first impressions. A house, centuries old, on high ground a mile or so removed from the road between Preston and Blackburn, where the first James of England, in his hurry to make money by making baronets, perhaps made some of those remunerative dignitaries. A house, centuries old, deserted and falling to pieces, its woods and gardens long since grass-land or ploughed up, the rivers Ribble and Darwen glancing below it, and a vague haze of smoke, against which not even the supernatural prescience of the first Stuart could foresee a counterblast, hinting at steam-power, powerful in two distances.

What did I know then of Hoghton Towers? When I first peeped in at the gate of the lifeless quadrangle, and started from the mouldering statue becoming visible to me like its guardian ghost; when I stole round by the back of the farm-house, and got in among the ancient rooms, many of them with their floors and ceilings falling, the beams and rafters hanging dangerously down, the plaster dropping as I trod, the oaken panels stripped away, the windows half walled up, half broken; when I discovered a gallery commanding the old kitchen, and looked down between balustrades upon a massive old table and benches, fearing to see I know not what dead-alive creatures come in and seat themselves, and look up with I know not what dreadful eyes, or lack of eyes at me; when all over the house I was awed by gaps and chinks where the sky stared sorrowfully at me, where the birds passed, and the ivy rustled, and the stains of winter weather blotched the rotten floors; when down at the bottom of dark pits of staircase, into which the stairs had sunk, green leaves trembled, butterflies fluttered, and bees hummed in and out through the broken doorways; when encircling the whole ruin were sweet scents, and sights of fresh green growth, and ever-renewing life, that I had never dreamed of, — I say, when I passed into such clouded perception of these things as my dark soul could compass, what did I know then of Hoghton Towers?

I have written that the sky stared sorrowfully at me. Therein have I anticipated the answer. I knew that all these things looked sorrowfully at me; that they seemed to sigh or whisper, not without pity for me, "Alas! poor, worldly little devil!"

There were two or three rats at the bottom of one of the smaller pits of broken staircase when I craned over and looked in. They were scuffling for some prey that was there; and, when they started and hid themselves close together in the dark, I thought of the old life (it had grown old already) in the cellar.

How not to be this worldly little devil? how not to have a repugnance towards myself as I had towards the rats? I hid in a corner of one of the smaller chambers frightened at myself, and crying (it was the first time I had ever cried for any cause not purely physical), and I tried to think about it. One of the farm-ploughs came into my range of view just then; and it seemed to help me as it went on with its two horses up and down the field so peacefully and quietly.

There was a girl of about my own age in the farm-house family, and she sat opposite to me at the narrow table at meal-times. It had come into my mind, at our first dinner, that she might take the fever from me. The thought had not disquieted me then. I had only speculated how she would look under the altered circumstances, and whether she would die. But it came into my mind now, that I might try to prevent her taking the fever by keeping away from her. I knew I should have but scrambling board if I did; so much the less worldly and less devilish the deed would be, I thought.

From that hour I withdrew myself at early morning into secret corners of the ruined house, and remained hidden there until she went to bed. At first, when meals were ready, I used to hear them calling me; and then my resolution weakened. But I strengthened it again, by going farther off into the ruin, and getting out of hearing. I often watched for her at the dim windows; and, when I saw that she was fresh and rosy, felt much happier.

Out of this holding her in my thoughts, to the humanizing of myself, I suppose some childish love arose within me. I felt, in some sort, dignified by the pride of protecting her, — by the pride of making the sacrifice for her. As my heart swelled with that new feeling, it insensibly softened about mother and father. It seemed to have been frozen before, and now to be thawed. The old ruin and all the lovely things that haunted it were not sorrowful for me only, but sorrowful for mother and father as well. Therefore did I cry again, and often too.

The farm-house family conceived me to be of a morose temper, and were very short with me; though they never stinted me in such broken fare as was to be got out of regular hours. One night, when I lifted the kitchen latch at my usual time, Sylvia (that was her pretty name) had but just gone out of the room. Seeing her ascending the opposite stairs, I stood still at the door. She had heard the clink of the latch, and looked round.

"George," she called to me in a pleased voice, "to-morrow is my birthday; and we are to have a fiddler, and there 's a party of boys and girls coming in a cart, and we shall dance. I invite you. Be sociable for once, George."

"I am very sorry, miss," I answered; "but I — but, no; I can't come."

"You are a disagreeable, ill-humored lad," she returned disdainfully; "and I ought not to have asked you. I shall never speak to you again."

As I stood with my eyes fixed on the fire, after she was gone, I felt that the farmer bent his brows upon me.

"Eh, lad!" said he; "Sylvy 's right. You 're as moody and broody a lad as never I set eyes on yet."

I tried to assure him that I meant no harm; but he only said coldly, "Maybe not, maybe not! There! get thy supper, get thy supper; and then thou canst sulk to thy heart's content again."

Ah! if they could have seen me next day, in the ruin, watching for the arrival of the cart full of merry young guests; if they could have seen me at night, gliding out from behind the ghostly statue, listening to the music and the fall of dancing feet, and watching the lighted farm-house windows from the quadrangle when all the ruin was dark; if they could have read my heart, as I crept up to bed by the back way, comforting myself with the reflection, "They will take no hurt from me," — they would not have thought mine a morose or an unsocial nature.

It was in these ways that I began to form a shy disposition; to be of a timidly silent character under misconstruction; to have an inexpressible, perhaps a morbid, dread of ever being sordid or worldly. It was in these ways that my nature came to shape itself to such a mould, even before it was affected by the influences of the studious and retired life of a poor scholar.

SIXTH CHAPTER.

BROTHER HAWKYARD (as he insisted on my calling him) put me to school, and told me to work my way. "You are all right, George," he said. "I have been the best servant the Lord has had in his service for this five-and-thirty year; (O, I have!) and he knows the value of such a servant as I have been to him; (O, yes, he does!) and he 'll prosper your schooling as a part of my reward. That 's what *he* 'll do, George. He 'll do it for me."

From the first I could not like this familiar knowledge of the ways of the sublime, inscrutable Almighty, on Brother Hawkyard's part. As I grew a little wiser, and still a little wiser, I liked it less and less. His manner, too, of confirming himself in a parenthesis, — as if, knowing himself, he doubted his own word, — I found distasteful. I cannot tell how much these dislikes cost me; for I had a dread that they were worldly.

As time went on, I became a Foundation-boy on a good foundation, and I cost Brother Hawkyard nothing. When I had worked my way so far, I worked yet harder, in the hope of ultimately getting a presentation to college and a fellowship. My health has never been strong (some vapor from the Preston cellar cleaves to me, I think); and what with much work and some weakness, I came again to be regarded — that is, by my fellow-students — as unsocial.

All through my time as a foundation-boy, I was within a few miles of Brother Hawkyard's congregation; and whenever I was what we called a leave-boy on a Sunday, I went over there at his desire. Before the knowledge became forced upon me that outside their place of meeting these brothers and sisters were no better than the rest of the human family, but on the whole were, to put the case mildly, as bad as most, in respect of giving short weight in their shops, and not speaking the truth, — I say, before this knowledge became forced upon me, their prolix addresses, their inordinate conceit, their daring ignorance, their investment of the Supreme Ruler of heaven and earth with their own miserable meannesses and littlenesses, greatly shocked me. Still, as their term for the frame of mind that could not perceive them to be in an exalted state of grace was the "worldly" state, I did for a time suffer tortures under my inquiries of myself whether that young worldly-devilish spirit of mine could secretly be lingering at the bottom of my non-appreciation.

Brother Hawkyard was the popular expounder in this assembly, and generally occupied the platform (there was a little platform with a table on it, in lieu of a pulpit) first on a Sunday afternoon. He was by trade a drysalter. Brother Gimblet, an elderly man with a crabbed face, a large dog's-eared shirt-collar, and a spotted blue neckerchief reaching up behind to the crown of his head, was also a drysalter, and an expounder. Brother Gimblet professed the greatest admiration for Brother Hawkyard, but (I had thought more than once) bore him a jealous grudge.

Let whosoever may peruse these lines kindly take the pains here to read twice my solemn pledge, that what I write of the language and customs of the congregation in question I write scrupulously, literally, exactly, from the life and the truth.

On the first Sunday after I had won what I had so long tried for, and when it was certain that I was going up to college, Brother Hawkyard concluded a long exhortation thus: —

"Well, my friends and fellow-sinners, now I told you when I began, that I did n't know a word of what I was going to say to you, (and no, I did not!) but that it was all one to me, because I knew the Lord would put into my mouth the words I wanted."

("That 's it!" from Brother Gimblet.)

"And he did put into my mouth the words I wanted."

("So he did!" from Brother Gimblet.)

"And why?"

("Ah, let 's have that!" from Brother Gimblet.)

'Because I have been his faithful servant for five-and-thirty years, and because he knows it. For five-and-thirty years! And he knows it, mind you! I got those words that I wanted, on account of my wages. I got 'em from the Lord, my fellow-sinners. Down! I said, 'Here's a heap of wages due; let us have something down, on account.' And I got it down, and I paid it over to you; and you won't wrap it up in a napkin, nor yet in a towel, nor yet pocket-ankercher, but you 'll put it out at good interest. Very well. Now, my brothers and sisters and fellow-sinners, I am going to conclude with a question, and I 'll make it so plain (with the help of the Lord, after five-and-thirty years, I should rather hope!) as that the Devil shall not be able to confuse it in your heads, — which he would be overjoyed to do."

("Just his way. Crafty old blackguard!" from Brother Gimblet.)

"And the question is this, Are the angels learned?"

("Not they. Not a bit on it!" from Brother Gimblet, with the greatest confidence.)

"Not they. And where 's the proof? sent ready-made by the hand of the Lord. Why, there 's one among us here now, that has got all the learning that can be crammed into him. *I* got him all the learning that could be crammed into him. His grandfather" (this I had never heard before) "was a brother of ours. He was Brother Parksop. That 's what he was. Parksop; Brother Parksop. His worldly name was Parksop, and he was a brother of this brotherhood. Then was n't he Brother Parksop?"

("Must be. Could n't help hisself!" from Brother Gimblet.)

"Well, he left that one now here present among us to the care of a brother-sinner of his, (and that brother-sinner, mind you, was a sinner of a bigger size in his time than any of you; praise the Lord!) Brother Hawkyard. Me. *I* got him, without fee or reward, — without a morsel of myrrh, or frankincense, nor yet amber, letting alone the honeycomb, — all the learning that could be crammed into him. Has it brought him into our temple, in the spirit? No. Have we had any ignorant brothers and sisters that did n't know round O from crooked S, come in among us meanwhile? Many. Then the angels are *not* learned; then they don't so much as know their alphabet. And now my friends and fellow-sinners, having brought it to that, perhaps some brother present—perhaps you, Brother Gimblet — will pray a bit for us?"

Brother Gimblet undertook the sacred function, after having drawn his sleeve across his mouth, and muttered, "Well! I don't know as I see my way to hitting any of you quite in the right place neither." He said this with a dark smile, and then began to bellow. What we were specially to be preserved from, according to his solicitations, was, despoilment of the orphan, suppression of testamentary intentions on the part of a father or (say) grandfather, appropriation of the orphan's house-property, feigning to give in charity to the wronged one from whom we withheld his due; and that class of sins. He ended with the petition, "Give us peace!" which, speaking for myself, was very much needed after twenty minutes of his bellowing.

Even though I had not seen him when he rose from his knees, steaming with perspiration, glance at Brother Hawkyard, and even though I had not heard Brother Hawkyard's tone of congratulating him on the vigor with which he had roared, I should have detected a malicious application in this prayer. Unformed suspicions to a similar effect had sometimes passed through my mind in my earlier school-days, and had always caused me great distress; for they were worldly in their nature, and wide, very wide, of the spirit that had drawn me from Sylvia. They were sordid suspicions, without a shadow of proof. They were worthy to have originated in the unwholesome cellar. They were not only without proof, but against proof; for was I not myself a living proof of what Brother Hawkyard had done? and without him, how should I ever have seen the sky look sorrowfully down upon that wretched boy at Hoghton Towers?

Although the dread of a relapse into a stage of savage selfishness was less strong upon me as I approached manhood, and could act in an increased degree for myself, yet I was always on my guard against any tendency to such relapse. After getting these suspicions under my feet, I had been troubled by not being able to like Brother Hawkyard's manner, or his professed religion. So it came about, that, as I walked back that Sunday evening, I thought it would be an act of reparation for any such injury my struggling thoughts had unwillingly done him, if I wrote, and placed in his hands, before going to college, a full acknowledgment of his goodness to me, and an ample tribute of thanks. It might serve as an implied vindication of him against any dark scandal from a rival brother and expounder, or from any other quarter.

Accordingly, I wrote the document with much care. I may add with much feeling too; for it affected me as I went on. Having no set studies to pursue, in the brief interval between leaving the Foundation and going to Cambridge, I determined to walk out to his place of business, and give it into his own hands.

It was a winter afternoon, when I tapped at the door of his little counting-house, which was at the farther end of his long, low shop. As I did so (having entered by the back yard, where casks and boxes were taken in, and where there was the inscription, "Private way to the counting-house"), a shopman called to me from the counter that he was engaged.

"Brother Gimblet" (said the shopman, who was one of the brotherhood) "is with him."

I thought this all the better for my purpose, and made bold to tap again. They were talking in a low tone, and money was passing; for I heard it being counted out.

"Who is it?" asked Brother Hawkyard sharply.

"George Silverman," I answered, holding the door open. "May I come in?"

Both brothers seemed so astounded to see me that I felt shyer than usual. But they looked quite cadaverous in the early gaslight, and perhaps that accidental circumstance exaggerated the expression of their faces.

"What is the matter?" asked Brother Hawkyard.

"Ay! what is the matter?" asked Brother Gimblet.

"Nothing at all," I said, diffidently producing my document: "I am only the bearer of a letter from myself."

"From yourself, George?" cried Brother Hawkyard.

"And to you," said I.

"And to me, George?"

He turned paler, and opened it hurriedly; but looking over it, and seeing generally what it was, became less hurried, recovered his color, and said "Praise the Lord!"

"That's it!" cried Brother Gimblet. "Well put! Amen."

Brother Hawkyard then said, in a livelier strain, "You must know, George, that Brother Gimblet and I are going to make our two businesses one. We are going into partnership. We are settling it now. Brother Gimblet is to take one clear half of the profits (O yes! he shall have it; he shall have it to the last far-hing)."

"D. V.!" said Brother Gimblet, with his right fist firmly clinched on his right leg.

"There is no objection," pursued Brother Hawkyard, "to my reading this aloud, George?"

As it was what I expressly desired should be done, after yesterday's prayer, I more than readily begged him to read it aloud. He did so, and Brother Gimblet listened with a crabbed smile.

"It was in a good hour that I came here," he said, wrinkling up his eyes. "It was in a good hour, likewise, that I was moved yesterday to depict for the terror of evil-doers a character the direct opposite of Brother Hawkyard's. But it was the Lord that done it; I felt him at it while I was perspiring."

After that it was proposed, by both of them, that I should attend the congregation once more before my final departure. What my shy reserve would undergo, from being expressly preached at and prayed at, I knew beforehand. But I reflected that it would be for the last time, and that it might add to the weight of my letter. It was well known to the brothers and sisters that there was no place taken for me in *their* paradise; and if I showed this last token of deference to Brother Hawkyard, notoriously in despite of my own sinful inclinations, it might go some little way in aid of my statement that he had been good to me, and that I was grateful to him. Merely stipulating, therefore, that no express endeavor should be made for my conversion, — which would involve the rolling of several brothers and sisters on the floor, declaring that they felt all their sins in a heap on their left side, weighing so many pounds avoirdupois, as I knew from what I had seen of those repulsive mysteries, — I promised.

Since the reading of my letter, Brother Gimblet had been at intervals wiping one eye with an end of his spotted blue neckerchief, and grinning to himself. It was, however, a habit that brother had, to grin in an ugly manner even when expounding. I call to mind a delighted snarl with which he used to detail from the platform the torments reserved for the wicked (meaning all human creation except the brotherhood), as being remarkably hideous.

I left the two to settle their articles of partnership, and count money; and I never saw them again but on the following Sunday. Brother Hawkyard died within two or three years, leaving all he possessed to Brother Gimblet, in virtue of a will dated (as I have been told) that very day.

Now I was so far at rest with myself, when Sunday came, knowing that I had conquered my own mistrust, and righted Brother Hawkyard in the jaundiced vision of a rival, that I went, even to that coarse chapel, in a less sensitive state than usual. How could I foresee that the delicate, perhaps the diseased, corner of my mind, where I winced and shrunk when it was touched, or was even approached, would be handled as the theme of the whole proceedings?

On this occasion it was assigned to Brother Hawkyard to pray, and to Brother Gimblet to preach. The prayer was to open the ceremonies; the discourse was to come next. Brothers Hawkyard and Gimblet were both on the platform; Brother Hawkyard on his knees at the table, unmusically ready to pray; Brother Gimblet sitting against the wall, grinningly ready to preach.

"Let us offer up the sacrifice of prayer, my brothers and sisters and fellow-sinners." Yes! but it was I who was the sacrifice. It was our poor, sinful worldly-minded brother here present who was wrestled for. The now-opening career of this ourunawakened brother might lead to his becoming a minister of what was called "the church." That was what *he* looked to. The church. Not the chapel, Lord. The church. No rectors, no vicars, no archdeacons, no bishops, no archbishops, in the chapel, but, O Lord! many such in the church. Protect our sinful brother from his love of lucre. Cleanse from our unawakened brother's breast his sin of worldly-mindedness. The prayer said infinitely more in words, but nothing more to any intelligible effect.

Then Brother Gimblet came forward, and took (as I knew he would) the text, "My kingdom is not of this world." Ah! but whose was, my fellow-sinners? Whose? Why, our brother's here present was. The only kingdom he had an idea of was of this world. ("That 's it!" from several of the congregation.) What did the woman do when she lost the piece of money? Went and looked for it. What should our brother do when he lost his way? ("Go and look for it," from a sister.) Go and look for it, true. But must he look for it in the right direction, or in the wrong? ("In the right," from a brother.) There spake the prophets! He must look for it in the right direction, or he could n't find it. But he had turned his back upon the right direction, and he would n't find it. Now, my fellow-sinners, to show you the difference betwixt worldly-mindedness and unworldly-mindedness, betwixt kingdoms not of this world and kingdoms *of* this world, here was a letter wrote by even our worldly-minded brother unto Brother Hawkyard. Judge, from hearing of it read, whether Brother Hawkyard was the faithful steward that the Lord had in his mind only t' other day, when, in this very place, he drew you the picter of the unfaithful one; for it was him that done it, not me. Don't doubt that!

Brother Gimblet then groaned and bellowed his way through my composition and subsequently through an hour. The service closed with a hymn, in which the brothers unanimously roared, and the sisters unanimously shrieked at me, That I by wiles of worldly gain was mocked, and they on waters of sweet love were rocked; that I with mammon struggled in the dark, while they were floating in a second ark.

I went out from all this with an aching heart and a weary spirit; not because I was quite so weak as to consider these narrow creatures interpreters of the Divine Majesty and Wisdom; but because I was weak enough to feel as though it were my hard fortune to be misrepresented and misunderstood, when I most tried to subdue any risings of mere worldliness within me, and when I most hoped, that, by dint of trying earnestly, I had succeeded.

SEVENTH CHAPTER.

My timidity and my obscurity occasioned me to live a secluded life at college, and to be little known. No relative ever came to visit me, for I had no relative. No intimate friends broke in upon my studies, for I made no intimate friends. I supported myself on my scholarship, and read much. My college time was otherwise not so very different from my time at Hoghton Towers.

Knowing myself to be unfit for the noisier stir of social existence, but believing myself qualified to do my duty in a moderate, though earnest way, if I could obtain some small preferment in the Church, I applied my mind to the clerical profession. In due sequence I took orders, was ordained, and began to look about me for employment. I must observe that I had taken a good degree, that I had succeeded in winning a good fellowship, and that my means were ample for my retired way of life. By this time I had read with several young men; and the occupation increased my income, while it was highly interesting to me. I once accidentally overheard our greatest don say to my boundless joy, "That he heard it reported of Silverman that his gift of quiet explanation, his patience, his amiable temper, and his conscientiousness made him the best of coaches." May my "gift of quiet explanation" come more seasonably and powerfully to my aid in this present explanation than I think it will!

It may be in a certain degree owing to the situation of my college rooms (in a corner where the daylight was sobered), but it is in a much larger degree referable to the state of my own mind, that I seem to myself, on looking back to this time of my life, to have been always in the peaceful shade. I can see others in the sunlight; I can see our boats' crews and our athletic young men on the glistening water, or speckled with the moving lights of sunlit leaves; but I myself am always in the shadow looking on. Not unsympathetically, — God forbid! — but looking on alone, much as I looked at Sylvia from the shadows of the ruined house, or looked at the red gleam shining through the farmer's windows, and listened to the fall of dancing feet, when all the ruin was dark that night in the quadrangle.

I now come to the reason of my quoting that laudation of myself above given. Without such reason, to repeat it would have been mere boastfulness.

Among those who had read with me was Mr. Fareway, second son of Lady Fareway, widow of Sir Gaston Fareway, baronet. This young gentleman's abilities were much above the average; but he came of a rich family, and was idle and luxurious. He presented himself to me too late, and afterwards came to me too irregularly, to admit of my being of much service to him. In the end, I considered it my duty to dissuade him from going up for an examination which he could never pass; and he left college without a degree. After his departure, Lady Fareway wrote to me, representing the justice of my returning half my fee, as I had been of so little use to her son. Within my knowledge a similar demand had not been made in any other case; and I most freely admit that the justice of it had not occurred to me until it was pointed out. But I at once perceived it, yielded to it, and returned the money.

Mr. Fareway had been gone two years or more, and I had forgotten him, when he one day walked into my rooms as I was sitting at my books.

Said he, after the usual salutations had passed, "Mr. Silverman, my mother is in town here, at the hotel, and wishes me to present you to her."

I was not comfortable with strangers, and I daresay I betrayed that I was a little nervous or unwilling. "For," said he, without my having spoken, "I think the interview may tend to the advancement of your prospects."

It put me to the blush to think that I should be tempted by a worldly reason, and I rose immediately.

Said Mr. Fareway, as we went along, "Are you a good hand at business?"

"I think not," said I.

Said Mr. Fareway then, "My mother is."

"Truly?" said I.

"Yes; my mother is what is usually called a managing woman. Does n't make a bad thing, for instance, even out of the spendthrift habits of my eldest brother abroad. In short, a managing woman. This is in confidence."

He had never spoken to me in confidence, and I was surprised by his doing so. I said I should respect his confidence, of course, and said no more on the delicate subject. We had but a little way to walk, and I was soon in his mother's company. He presented me, shook hands with me, and left us two (as he said) to business.

I saw in my Lady Fareway a handsome, well-preserved lady of somewhat large stature, with a steady glare in her great round dark eyes that embarrassed me.

Said my lady, "I have heard from my son, Mr. Silverman, that you would be glad of some preferment in the Church."

I gave my lady to understand that was so.

"I don't know whether you are aware," my lady proceeded, "that we have a presentation to a living? I say *we* have; but, in point of fact, *I* have."

I gave my lady to understand that I had not been aware of this.

Said my lady, "So it is; indeed, I have two presentations, — one to two hundred a year, one to six. Both livings are in our county, — North Devonshire, — as you probably know. The first is vacant. Would you like it?"

What with my lady's eyes, and what with the suddenness of this proposed gift, I was much confused.

"I am sorry it is not the larger presentation," said my lady, rather coldly; "though I will not, Mr. Silverman, pay you the bad compliment of supposing that *you* are, because that would be mercenary, — and mercenary I am persuaded you are not."

Said I, with my utmost earnestness, "Thank you, Lady Fareway, thank you, thank you! I should be deeply hurt if I thought I bore the character."

"Naturally," said my lady. "Always detestable, but particularly in a clergyman. You have not said whether you will like the living?"

With apologies for my remissness or indistinctness, I assured my lady that I accepted it most readily and gratefully. I added that I hoped she would not estimate my appreciation of the generosity of her choice by my flow of words; for I was not a ready man in that respect when taken by surprise or touched at heart.

"The affair is concluded," said my lady; "concluded. You will find the duties very light, Mr. Silverman. Charming house; charming little garden, orchard, and all that. You will be able to take pupils. By the by! No: I will return to the word afterwards. What was I going to mention, when it put me out?"

My lady stared at me, as if I knew. And I did n't know. And that perplexed me afresh.

Said my lady, after some consideration, "O, of course! How very dull of me! The last incumbent, — least mercenary man I ever saw, — in consideration of the duties being so light and the house so delicious, could n't rest, he said, unless I permitted him to help me with my correspondence, accounts, and various little things of that kind; nothing in themselves, but which it worries a lady to cope with. Would Mr. Silverman also like to — Or shall I —"

I hastened to say that my poor help would be always at her ladyship's service.

"I am absolutely blessed," said my lady, casting up her eyes (and so taking them off of me for one moment), "in having to do with gentlemen who cannot endure an approach to the idea of being mercenary!" She shivered at the word. "And now as to the pupil."

"The?" — I was quite at a loss.

"Mr. Silverman, you have no idea what she is. She is," said my lady, laying her touch upon my coat-sleeve, "I do verily believe, the most extraordinary girl in this world. Already knows more Greek and Latin than Lady Jane Grey. And taught herself! Has not yet, remember, derived a moment's advantage from Mr. Silverman's classical acquirements. To say nothing of mathematics, which she is bent upon becoming versed in, and in which (as I hear from my son and others) Mr. Silverman's reputation is so deservedly high!"

Under my lady's eyes, I must have lost the clew, I felt persuaded; and yet I did not know where I could have dropped it.

"Adelina," said my lady, "is my only daughter. If I did not feel quite convinced that I am not blinded by a mother's partiality; unless I was absolutely sure that when you know her, Mr. Silverman, you will esteem it a high and unusual privilege to direct her studies, — I should introduce a mercenary element into this conversation, and ask you on what terms —"

I entreated my lady to go no further. My lady saw that I was troubled, and did me the honor to comply with my request.

EIGHTH CHAPTER.

EVERYTHING in mental acquisition that her brother might have been, if he would, and everything in all gracious charms and admirable qualities that no one but herself could be, — this was Adelina.

I will not expatiate upon her beauty; I will not expatiate upon her intelligence, her quickness of perception, her powers of memory, her sweet consideration, from the first moment, for the slow-paced tutor who ministered to her wonderful gifts. I was thirty then; I am over sixty now; she is ever present to me in these hours as she was in those, bright and beautiful and young, wise and fanciful and good.

When I discovered that I loved her, how can I say? In the first day? in the first week? in the first month? Impossible to trace. If I be (as I am) unable to represent to myself any previous period of my life as quite separable from her attracting power, how can I answer for this one detail?

Whensoever I made the discovery, it laid a heavy burden on me. And yet, comparing it with the far heavier burden that I afterwards took up, it does not seem to me now to have been very hard to bear. In the knowledge that I did love her, and that I should love her while my life lasted, and that I was ever to hide my secret deep in my own breast, and she was never to find it, there was a kind of sustaining joy or pride or comfort mingled with my pain.

But later on, — say a year later on, — when I made another discovery, then indeed my suffering and my struggle were strong. That other discovery was —

These words will never see the light, if ever, until my heart is dust; until her bright spirit has returned to the regions of which, when imprisoned here, it surely retained some unusual glimpse of remembrance; until all the pulses that ever beat around us shall have long been quiet; until all the fruits of all the tiny victories and defeats achieved in our little breasts shall have withered away. That discovery was, that she loved me.

She may have enhanced my knowledge, and loved me for that; she may have overvalued my discharge of duty to her, and loved me for that; she may have refined upon a playful compassion which she would sometimes show for what she called my want of wisdom, according to the light of the world's dark lantern, and loved me for that; she may — she must — have confused the borrowed light of what I had only learned, with its brightness in its pure, original rays; but she loved me at that time, and she made me know it.

Pride of family and pride of wealth put me as far off from her in my lady's eyes as if I had been some domesticated creature of another kind. But they could not put me farther from her than I put myself when I set my merits against hers. More than that. They could not put me, by millions of fathoms, half so low beneath her as I put myself when in imagination I took advantage of her noble trustfulness, took the fortune that I knew she must possess in her own right, and left her to find herself, in the zenith of her beauty and genius, bound to poor, rusty, plodding me.

No! Worldliness should not enter here, at any cost. If I had tried to keep it out of other ground, how much harder was I bound to try to keep it from this sacred place!

But there was something daring in her broad, generous character, that demanded at so delicate a crisis to be delicately and patiently addressed. After many and many a bitter night (O, I found I could cry for reasons not purely physical, at this pass of my life!) I took my course.

My lady had, in our first interview, unconsciously overstated the accommodation of my pretty house. There was room in it for only one pupil. He was a young gentleman near coming of age, very well connected, but what is called a poor relation. His parents were dead. The charges of his living and reading with me were defrayed by an uncle; and he and I were to do our utmost together for three years towards qualifying him to make his way. At this time he had entered into his second year with me. He was well-looking, clever, energetic, enthusiastic, bold; in the best sense of the term, a thorough young Anglo-Saxon.

I resolved to bring these two together.

NINTH CHAPTER.

SAID I, one night, when I had conquered myself, "Mr. Granville," — Mr. Granville Wharton his name was, — "I doubt if you have ever yet so much as seen Miss Fareway."

"Well, sir," returned he, laughing, "you see her so much yourself, that you hardly give another felow a chance of seeing her."

"I am her tutor, you know," said I.

And there the subject dropped for that time. But I so contrived as that they should come together shortly afterwards. I had previously so contrived as to keep them asunder; for while I loved her, — I mean before I had determined on my sacrifice, — a lurking jealousy of Mr. Granville lay within my unworthy breast

It was quite an ordinary interview in the Fareway Park; but they talked easily together for some time; like takes to like, and they had many points of resemblance. Said Mr. Granville to me, when he and I sat at our supper that night, "Miss Fareway is remarkably beautiful, sir, remarkably engaging. Don't you think so?" "I think so," said I. And I stole a glance at him, and saw that he had reddened and was thoughtful. I remember it most vividly, because the mixed feeling of grave pleasure and acute pain that the slight circumstance caused me was the first of a long, long series of such mixed impressions under which my hair turned slowly gray.

I had not much need to feign to be subdued; but I counterfeited to be older than I was in all respects (Heaven knows! my heart being all too young the while), and feigned to be more of a recluse and bookworm than I had really become, and gradually set up more and more of a fatherly manner towards Adelina. Likewise I made my tuition less imaginative than before; separated myself from my poets and philosophers; was careful to present them in their own light, and me, their lowly servant, in my own shade. Moreover in the matter of apparel I was equally mindful: not that I had ever been dapper that way; but that I was slovenly now.

As I depressed myself with one hand, so did I labor to raise Mr. Granville with the other; directing his attention to such subjects as I too well knew most interested her, and fashioning him (do not deride or misconstrue the expression, unknown reader of this writing; for I have suffered!) into a greater resemblance to myself in my solitary one strong aspect. And gradually, gradually, as I saw him take more and more to these thrown-out lures of mine, then did I come to know better and better that love was drawing him on, and was drawing her from me.

So passed more than another year; every day a year in its number of my mixed impressions of grave pleasure and acute pain; and then these two, being of age and free to act legally for themselves, came before me hand in hand (my hair being now quite white), and entreated me that I would unite them together. "And indeed, dear tutor," said Adelina, "it is but consistent in you that you should do this thing for us, seeing that we should never have spoken together that first time but for you, and that but for you we could never have met so often afterwards." The whole of which was literally true; for I had availed myself of my many business attendances on, and conferences with, my lady, to take Mr. Granville to the house, and leave him in the outer room with Adelina.

I knew that my lady would object to such a marriage for her daughter, or to any marriage that was other than an exchange of her for stipulated lands, goods, and moneys. But looking on the two, and seeing with full eyes that they were both young and beautiful; and knowing that they were alike in the tastes and acquirements that will outlive youth and beauty; and considering that Adelina had a fortune now, in her own keeping; and considering further that Mr. Granville, though for the present poor, was of a good family that had never lived in a cellar in Preston; and believing that their love would endure, neither having any great discrepancy to find out in the other, — I told them of my readiness to do this thing which Adelina asked of her dear tutor, and to send them forth husband and wife, into the shining world with golden gates that awaited them.

It was on a summer morning, that I rose before the sun to compose myself for the crowning of my work with this end; and my dwelling being near to the sea, I walked down to the rocks on the shore, in order that I might behold the sun rise in his majesty.

The tranquillity upon the deep and on the firmament, the orderly withdrawal of the stars, the calm promise of coming day, the rosy suffusion of the sky and waters, the ineffable splendor that then burst forth, attuned my mind afresh after the discords of the night. Methought that all I looked on said to me, and that all I heard in the sea and in the air said to me, "Be comforted, mortal, that thy life is so short. Our preparation for what is to follow has endured, and shall endure, for unimaginable ages."

I married them. I knew that my hand was cold when I placed it on their hands clasped together; but the words with which I had to accompany the action I could say without faltering, and I was at peace.

They being well away from my house and from the place after our simple breakfast, the time was come when I must do what I had pledged myself to them that I would do, — break the intelligence to my lady.

I went up to the house, and found my lady in her ordinary business-room. She happened to have an unusual amount of commissions to intrust to me that day, and she had filled my hands with papers before I could originate a word.

"My lady," I then began, as I stood beside her table.

"Why, what's the matter?" she said quickly, looking up.

"Not much, I would fain hope, after you shall have prepared yourself, and considered a little."

"Prepared myself; and considered a little! You appear to have prepared *your*self but indifferently, any how, Mr. Silverman." This mighty scornfully, as I experienced my usual embarrassment under her stare.

Said I, in self-extenuation once for all, "Lady Fareway, I have but to say for myself that I have tried to do my duty."

"For yourself?" repeated my lady. "Then there are others concerned, I see. Who are they?"

I was about to answer, when she made towards the bell with a dart that stopped me, and said, "Why, where is Adelina?"

"Forbear! be calm, my lady. I married her this morning to Mr. Granville Wharton."

She set her lips, looked more intently at me than ever, raised her right hand, and smote me hard upon the cheek.

"Give me back those papers! give me back those papers!" She tore them out of my hands, and tossed them on her table. Then seating herself defiantly in her great chair, and folding her arms, she stabbed me to the heart with the unlooked-for reproach, "You worldly wretch!"

"Worldly?" I cried. "Worldly?"

"This, if you please," she went on with supreme scorn, pointing me out, as if there were some one there to see, — "this, if you please, is the disinterested scholar, with not a design beyond his books! This, if you please, is the simple creature whom any one could overreach in a bargain! This, if you please, is Mr. Silverman! Not of this world; not he! He has too much simplicity for this world's cunning. He has too much singleness of purpose to be a match for this world's double-dealing. What did he give you for it?"

"For what? And who?"

"How much," she asked, bending forward in her great chair, and insultingly tapping the fingers of her right hand on the palm of her left, — "how much does Mr. Granville Wharton pay you for getting him Adelina's money? What is the amount of your percentage upon Adelina's fortune? What were the terms of the agreement that you proposed to this boy when you, the Rev. George Silverman, licensed to marry, engaged to put him in possession of this girl? You made good terms for yourself, whatever they were. He would stand a poor chance against your keenness."

Bewildered, horrified, stunned by this cruel perversion, I could not speak. But I trust that I looked innocent, being so.

"Listen to me, shrewd hypocrite," said my lady, whose anger increased as she gave it utterance; "attend to my words, you cunning schemer, who have carried this plot through with such a practised double face that I have never suspected you. I had my projects for my daughter; projects for family connection; projects for fortune. You have thwarted them, and overreached me; but I am not one to be thwarted and overreached without retaliation. Do you mean to hold this living another month?"

"Do you deem it possible, Lady Fareway, that I can hold it another hour, under your injurious words?"

"Is it resigned, then?"

"It was mentally resigned, my lady, some minutes ago."

"Don't equivocate, sir. *Is* it resigned?"

"Unconditionally and entirely; and I would that I had never, never come near it!"

"A cordial response from me to *that* wish, Mr. Silverman! But take this with you, sir. If you had not resigned it, I would have had you deprived of it. And though you have resigned it, you will not get quit of me as easily as you think for. I will pursue you with this story. I will make this nefarious conspiracy of yours, for money, known. You have made money by it, but you have at the same time made an enemy by it. *You* will take good care that the money sticks to you; I will take good care that the enemy sticks to you."

Then said I finally, "Lady Fareway, I think my heart is broken. Until I came into this room just now, the possibility of such mean wickedness as you have imputed to me never dawned upon my thoughts. Your suspicions" —

"Suspicions! Pah!" said she, indignantly. "Certainties."

"Your certainties, my lady, as you call them, your suspicions, as I call them, are cruel, unjust, wholly devoid of foundation in fact. I can declare no more; except that I have not acted for my own profit or my own pleasure. I have not in this proceeding considered myself. Once again, I think my heart is broken. If I have unwittingly done any wrong with a righteous motive, that is some penalty to pay."

She received this with another and a more indignant "Pah!" and I made my way out of her room (I think I felt my way out with my hands, although my eyes were open), almost suspecting that my voice had a repulsive sound, and that I was a repulsive object.

There was a great stir made, the bishop was appealed to, I received a severe reprimand, and narrowly escaped suspension. For years a cloud hung over me and my name was tarnished. But my heart did not break, if a broken heart involves death; for I lived through it.

They stood by me, Adelina and her husband, through it all. Those who had known me at college, and even most of those who had only known me there by reputation, stood by me too. Little by little, the belief widened that I was not capable of what was laid to my charge. At length I was presented to a college-living in a sequestered place, and there I now pen my explanation. I pen it at my open window in the summer-time, before me lying, in the churchyard, equal resting-place for sound hearts, wounded hearts, and broken hearts. I pen it for the relief of my own mind, not foreseeing whether or no it will ever have a reader.

www.ingramcontent.com/pod-product-compliance
Lightning Source LLC
LaVergne TN
LVHW021104110826
845150LV00001B/168
9781425565145